Baseball Weekly

1994 Almanac

The All-In-One Baseball Resource

EDITED BY:

Editor / Baseball Weekly, Paul White

Managing Editor / Sports, *USA TODAY,* Gene Policinski

Assistant to Managing Editor / Sports, *USA TODAY,* Robert Barbrow

With contributions from the staffs of Baseball Weekly
and USA TODAY Sports

Managing Editor, Liz Barrett

A Balliett & Fitzgerald Book

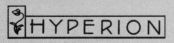

HYPERION

New York

ISBN # 1-56282-795-2

THIRD EDITION
10 9 8 7 6 5 4 3 2 1

Acknowledgments
We are grateful, first of all, for the vision, support, skill and good humor of Susan Bokern, Silvia Molina and Michelle Mattox at Gannett New Business, without whom this book would not have been possible; also many thanks to the support staff at USA TODAY.
We send kudos to everyone at Hyperion, especially publisher Bob Miller, Leslie Wells, Lesley Krauss and Linda Prather. We could never have completed this book without our own hard-working and talented production staff. We truly appreciate the efforts of designer Michael Harvey, computer and graphics consultant Steven Johnson, page artist John Jordan, production assistants Alex Locke and Philip Chin; and especially production editor Duncan Bock and managing editor Lilly Golden.—*Balliett & Fitzgerald*

Major league statistics provided by Elias Sports Bureau.
Minor league statistics provided by Howe SportsData International.
Record book and historical statistics provided by Pete Palmer.
Disabled list information provided by The Baseball Workshop.
Photographs of Major League Baseball are used with the permission of Major League Baseball.

Contents

*L*eading off

▶ **Paul White on the hysterics over history**

▶ **Free agent shopping list**

▶ *and more . . .*

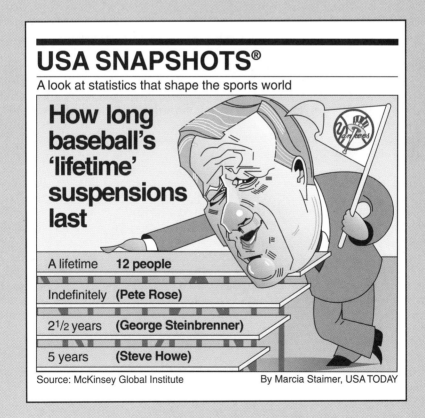

USA SNAPSHOTS®

A look at statistics that shape the sports world

How long baseball's 'lifetime' suspensions last

A lifetime	**12 people**
Indefinitely	**(Pete Rose)**
2½ years	**(George Steinbrenner)**
5 years	**(Steve Howe)**

Source: McKinsey Global Institute   By Marcia Staimer, USA TODAY

Some free advice:
End hysterics over 'history'

So, how much fun was it watching those Phillies in the playoffs and World Series last year? Well, they didn't belong there, you know.

What was it you liked? That everyman feeling? The loading-dock look? The scruff? The scraggle? The sneer at the establishment? Well, they were in the wrong place, you know.

They captured your imagination, didn't they? It's that underdog thing, isn't it? But they didn't belong in the World Series, you know.

The self-proclaimed guardians of baseball said so. It's blasphemy. Impure. They told me so. You see, it's just not right that those interesting, colorful, exciting, refreshing Phillies were in the World Series. The people who know what's good for baseball told me so. (They also told me they are the ones who know what's good for baseball.)

It was Sept. 9, the day realignment and expanded playoffs became reality, that all this nonsense reached a frenzied level. The sanctity of the game has been besmirched, we heard. It'll never be the same. We'll have pretenders in the World Series.

The Phillies in the World Series was bad for baseball?

If so, then watching an aging Willie Mays go for one more ring with the Mets in '73 and darn near pulling it off against the first version of unbeatable Athletics was bad for baseball.

And Kirk Gibson's ninth-inning home run against Dennis Eckersley was bad for baseball. Well, the same theory that says the Phillies didn't belong would have robbed us of that final Say Hey, of the Gibson footage that has a place alongside Carlton Fisk's extra-inning coaxing and Bobby Thomson landing on both feet at home plate.

This season, when eight teams head into the postseason for the first time without the help of a strike, we will have seen the end of a historical system that has been in place since way, way back in 1969. How historical is that?

So, who could not savor those moments? Maybe Whitey Herzog. He's lost two World Series to teams that didn't belong, teams that won their division with fewer victories than the team they met in the playoffs. Like the 1993 Phillies, Gibson's Dodgers and Mays' Mets—the teams that beat Herzog's '85 and '87 Cardinals didn't belong.

We wouldn't have seen the Royals and an umpire or two turn Joaquin Andujar and John Tudor into screaming jelly, or heard screaming of another kind from Hankie-waving Metrodome maniacs.

Look, the new system is fine. We're not talking NBA-style, where we'd play six months just to eliminate the Mets, Padres, Marlins and Rockies.

Some years it will look wonderful, as it would have last year, when those outcast Phillies could have knocked off the mortal-lock Braves PLUS the 103-win Giants. What drama. What fun. What memories.

And some years an 82-win wonder will sidle into the Fall Classic. Like the Mays' Mets team that punched out the 99-victory Reds and took Oakland to seven games.

We've had 25 years for the last so-called sacrilege to sink in—surely you remember how unthinkable, how mercenary it was to split the leagues into two divisions. So, check back in 2018. Just a hunch, but maybe, just maybe, something memorable will have happened in the American League . . . uh, just what are they going to call the new round anyway?

—by Paul White, editor

6

1994's shopping list: Baseball's free agents

National League

►**Atlanta (3):** Sid Bream, 1B; Jay Howell, RHP; Otis Nixon, OF.

►**Chicago:** None.

►**Cincinnati (4):** Jeff Reardon, RHP; Bip Roberts, 2B; Chris Sabo, 3B; Juan Samuel, 2B.

►**Colorado (3):** Daryl Boston, OF; Andres Galarraga, 1B; Bruce Hurst, LHP.

►**Florida (3):** Henry Cotto, OF; Charlie Hough, RHP; Walt Weiss, SS.

►**Houston (3):** Kevin Bass, OF; Mark Portugal, RHP; Jose Uribe, SS.

►**Los Angeles (1):** Jody Reed, 2B.

►**Montreal (2):** Dennis Martinez, RHP; Randy Ready, 2B.

►**New York (4):** Sid Fernandez, LHP; Howard Johnson, 3B; Eddie Murray, 1B; Charlie O'Brien, C.

►**Philadelphia (3):** Larry Andersen, RHP; Jim Eisenreich, OF; Bobby Thigpen, RHP.

►**Pittsburgh (1):** Bob Walk, RHP.

►**St. Louis (3):** Lee Guetterman, LHP; Les Lancaster, RHP; Gerald Perry, 1B.

►**San Diego (1):** Tim Teufel, 2B.

►**San Francisco (4):** Will Clark, 1B; Jim Deshaies, LHP; Scott Sanderson, RHP; Robby Thompson, 2B.

American League

►**Baltimore (7):** Harold Baines, OF; Tim Hulett, 2B; Mike Pagliarulo, 3B; Harold Reynolds, 2B; Lonnie Smith, OF; Rick Sutcliffe, RHP; Fernando Valenzuela, LHP.

►**Boston (6):** Rob Deer, OF; John Dopson, RHP; Steve Lyons, INF; Tony Pena, C; Ernest Riles, 3B; Luis Rivera, SS.

►**California (3):** Rene Gonzales, 3B; Stan Javier, OF; Luis Polonia, OF.

►**Chicago (6):** Tim Belcher, RHP; Ellis Burks, OF; Ivan Calderon, OF; Jose DeLeon, RHP; Bo Jackson, OF; Tim Raines, OF.

►**Cleveland (3):** Bob Ojeda, LHP; Junior Ortiz, C; Jeff Treadway, 2B.

►**Detroit (4):** Storm Davis, RHP; Dan Gladden, OF; Kirk Gibson, OF; David Wells, LHP.

►**Kansas City (5):** Hubie Brooks, OF; Greg Cadaret, LHP; Gary Gaetti, 3B; Mark Gubicza, RHP; Dennis Rasmussen, LHP.

►**Milwaukee (3):** Kevin Seitzer, 3B; Dickie Thon, SS; Robin Yount, OF.

►**Minnesota (1):** Brian Harper, C.

►**New York (5):** Steve Farr, RHP; Dion James, OF; Lee Smith, RHP; Frank Tanana, LHP; Mike Witt, RHP.

►**Oakland (6):** Mike Aldrete, OF; Jerry Browne, 2B; Rich Gossage, RHP; Dave Henderson, OF; Rick Honeycutt, LHP; Edwin Nunez, RHP.

►**Seattle (3):** Tim Leary, RHP; Ted Power, RHP; Dave Valle, C.

►**Texas (5):** Julio Franco, 2B; Craig Lefferts, LHP; Charlie Leibrandt, LHP; Rafael Palmeiro, 1B; Geno Petralli, C.

►**Toronto (5):** Danny Cox, RHP; Mark Eichhorn, RHP; Tony Fernandez, SS; Alfredo Griffin, SS; Rickey Henderson, OF.

1994 team managers

There *were* some pleasant surprises in 1993. Three new skippers were added to baseball's tiny list of minority managers—even though Tony Perez did not last long enough to prove what he could do—and the results were a resounding success. Dusty Baker managed the Giants to a 103-win season, even with a very weak year from Will Clark and an unproven pitching staff. He was voted National League Manager of the Year in his rookie season. Don Baylor took an expansion team, the Colorado Rockies, and lead them to one of the strongest second-half records in baseball, not to mention a fan base that shattered every baseball attendance record in the book. Now, *that is good business.*

Following are major league baseball's team managers for 1994:

Baltimore—John Oates; **Boston**—Butch Hobson; **California**—Buck Rodgers; **Chicago White Sox**—Gene Lamont; **Cleveland**—Mike Hargrove; **Detroit**—Sparky Anderson; **Kansas City**—Hal McRae; **Milwaukee**—Phil Garner; **Minnesota**—Tom Kelly; **New York Yankees**—Buck Showalter; **Oakland**—Tony LaRussa; **Seattle**—Lou Piniella; **Texas**—Kevin Kennedy; **Toronto**—Cito Gaston; **Atlanta**—Bobby Cox; **Chicago Cubs**—Tom Trebelhorn; **Cincinnati**—Dave Johnson; **Colorado**—Don Baylor; **Florida**—Rene Lachemann; **Houston**—Terry Collins; **Los Angeles**—Tom Lasorda; **Montreal**—Felipe Alou; **New York Mets**—Dallas Green; **Philadelphia**—Jim Fregosi; **Pittsburgh**—Jim Leyland; **St. Louis**—Joe Torre; **San Diego**—Jim Riggleman; **San Francisco**—Dusty Baker.

Free agent compensation: How the system works

When Will Clark signed as a free agent with the Texas Rangers, it might seem at first glance that the San Francisco Giants had given up a quality player and received nothing in return.

That is not exactly true, though it might take Giants fans several years to assess the impact of not being able to re-sign Clark. That is because what San Francisco gets back are two draft choices under baseball's compensation system.

Ironically, the compensation system was designed to prevent imbalances, but neither the owners nor the players association is satisfied with it.

Here's how it works: Teams that lose free agents are compensated according to the ranking of the player.

▶Players are divided into five categories (starting pitchers, relief pitchers, catchers, middle infielders/third basemen, and first basemen/outfielders/designated hitters), then are ranked in terms of their performance as it compared to other players at the same position during the past two seasons. The top 30 percent are ranked as "A" players, 31 to 50 percent "B," 51 to 60 percent "C," and the remainder are unranked.

▶Clubs that sign an "A" free agent lose their first-round draft pick the following June (unless they are among the 13 worst teams, in which case they lose their second-round pick). Clubs that lose an "A" agent get the draft pick the signing team lost, plus a "sandwich" pick (an extra selection between the first two rounds).

▶Clubs that lose a "B" player get the signing team's highest available regular pick (the first 13 picks are exempt).

▶Clubs that lose a "C" player get a pick between the first two rounds.

Early Christmas for Texas and Cleveland

It was like kids trying to wait for Christmas morning.

Christmas comes in April for the Cleveland Indians and Texas Rangers this year. That's when they finally get to open those fancy packages they've been waiting for — their new stadiums.

But like any excited kids, the Indians and Rangers just couldn't wait for April.

In fact, they didn't even wait for everybody else's Christmas to unwrap some key free agents.

First baseman Will Clark was Texas' big prize, the first of the free agent season. The ex-San Francisco Giant became the Rangers' replacement for Rafael Palmeiro in a winter for first basemen.

In an otherwise shallow free agent pool, the focus was on the offensive production Clark, Palmeiro, Andres Galarraga and Eddie Murray could add to a lineup.

Galarraga eventually elected to remain with the Colorado Rockies, but Murray was a surprise addition to the Indians on a day that thrust the perennial also-rans into serious contender status in the new American League Central Division.

While Murray was being announced as a first baseman/designated hitter and, most importantly, the power bat to hit behind slugger Albert Belle, an equally important signing was revealed.

The Indians brought aboard veteran pitcher Dennis Martinez to give stability and innings to the club's most glaring weakness — pitching depth.

Despite some noteworthy big-money signings, economy was the winter buzzword. Even the richer teams were becoming more frugal as they anticipated a year with less revenue from national television contracts. Many mid-level free agents were squeezed out of the big-bucks market and even aging big names such as Rickey Henderson found themselves searching for someone willing to gamble a significant pile of cash.

The lack of the traditional major league winter meetings also changed the way the business was done. The mid-December spree for general managers and agents was gone, but they managed to find ways to do their deals.

Among the more noteworthy:

▶ Baltimore signed free agent pitcher Sid Fernandez from the Mets and retained free agent designated hitter Harold Baines.

▶Boston found a leadoff man and center fielder by targeting Otis Nixon, who lost his Atlanta job to Deion Sanders.

▶The Yankees tried to shore up their bullpen by sending pitching prospect Domingo Jean and infielder Andy Stankiewicz to Houston for Xavier Hernandez, with allowed New York to let Lee Smith try free agency.

▶Cincinnati cited economics by not retaining third baseman Chris Sabo and second baseman Bip Roberts but addressed the hole at second by getting Bret Boone, plus pitcher Erik Hanson, from Seattle for pitcher Bobby Ayala and catcher Dan Wilson.

▶Pittsburgh looked for an inexpensive way of adding offense by snaring first baseman Brian Hunter from Atlanta.

▶The Mets got another of Atlanta's expendable players, pitcher Pete Smith, by giving up outfielder Dave Gallagher.

▶Colorado spent some of the money its four million-plus fans provided, grabbing free agents Ellis Burks and Howard Johnson.

▶ Mitch Williams, destined not to return to Philadelphia, found a new home. The Houston Astros acquired him for pitchers Doug Jones and Jeff Juden.

▶Montreal, anticipating an arbitration-induced payroll crunch, sent second baseman Delino DeShields to Los Angeles for pitcher Pedro Martinez.

▶San Francisco, already the favorite in the revised NL West, deepened its pitching staff by signing free agent Mark Portugal from Houston.

—by Paul White

New owners make themselves felt

There's a power shift under way within baseball's ownership ranks.

George Steinbrenner, Ted Turner, Peter O'Malley and Gene Autry remain the most recognizable faces, but in recent years they've had to make room for a formidable group of new faces.

At times these young turks don't show a lot of respect for their elders. They aren't ready to toe the line on players' salaries or follow the traditional ways of selling the game or their team. In many cases, these new owners came in with radical ideas about how to improve their franchise. And they were ready to turn things around in a hurry.

Ex-Safeway executive Peter Magowan stunned his peers by signing Barry Bonds to a six-year, $43.75 million contract shortly after his San Francisco-based ownership group kept the Giants in the Bay Area.

"I've always believed in trusting my own instincts . . ." Magowan says. "I felt once we got Bonds we had a team that would be in contention."

Since 1990, 10 ballclubs have changed hands. These changeovers include:

▶Pizza baron Mike Ilitch buying the Tigers.

▶A Seattle group backed by the Japanese video giant Nintendo, purchasing the Mariners.

▶Entertainment mogul Tom Werner, picking up the Padres.

▶Attorney Peter Angelos and his group, getting the Orioles.

These new owners haven't been silent about where Major League Baseball is headed and what's needed to fix it. To remedy matters, they quickly seized positions of authority throughout the game's infrastructure.

Colorado's Jerry McMorris was named to the executive council soon after the Rockies entered the NL. He has quickly become one of the game's visionaries for international expansion.

Florida's Wayne Huizenga kept the divisional realignment on track. When nobody wanted to move to the new NL Central, he said his Marlins would be happy to, though it made more sense financially to stay in the East. (The Marlins eventually stayed, the Pirates moved).

Even though Werner was dismantling his team back in San Diego, he was at the forefront of the new joint national television deal with ABC and NBC.

Seattle's John Ellis is a proponent of revenue-sharing: "There's no doubt we have some major problems to overcome," he says. "And that's got to be part of the package."

Acting commissioner Bud Selig says the new owners have had an "instantaneous effect" upon MLB.

"People like John Ellis, Drayton McLane, Mike Ilitch — They come from business backgrounds," Selig says. "They have ideas about marketing, how we can better serve the game. But they are fans, too. Their influence has been powerful and good for the game."

The impact of the new owners was illustrated at the divisive meetings last summer in Kohler, Wis.

At one point in the negotiations about revenue-sharing, Ellis and Ilitch joined Player Relations Committee president Richard Ravitch. The trio, bringing a new offer from the small-market clubs, stood in the hallway, outside a banquet room where many of the large-market ballclubs were meeting.

Meanwhile, inside that room, along with such heavyweights as George Steinbrenner, Toronto's Paul Beeston and Texas' George Bush, were McMorris and Huizenga. Whereas once the Rockies and Marlins saw themselves as bit players in baseball's universe, here they were calling the shots with large-market clubs.

If the new owners can reach a consensus, find themselves in the same room, they could change baseball forever.

—by Tim Wendel

Around the
league

▸ Town meeting debates
baseball's big issues

▸ Basics of 1994 realignment

▸ Best of 1993, more . . .

USA SNAPSHOTS®

A look at statistics that shape the sports world

Big split on playoffs

Baseball fans, by region, who favor expanding the
number of major league playoff teams from four to eight:

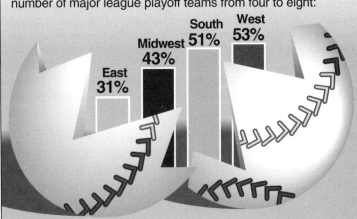

East
31%

Midwest
43%

South 51%

West
53%

Source: Harris poll   By Gary Visgaitis, USA TODAY

Town meeting '93: Insiders and interested observers debate baseball's big issues

The first Baseball Weekly *Town Meeting was held in the B&O Warehouse overlooking Baltimore's Camden Yards on the morning of the 1993 All-Star Game. Here are some highlights of the two-and-a-half hour public session.*

THE PANELISTS

Ken Burns: Producer of *The Civil War*; currently working on a nine-part series on the history of baseball.

Donald Fehr: Executive director of the MLB Players Association.

Bill Giles: President of the Phillies.

Richard Ravitch: Head of the Player Relations Committee and chief labor negotiator for owners/management.

Tom Reich: Players' agent.

Bob Watson: Former player; assistant general manager of the Astros.

Bob Costas: Panel moderator, NBC commentator.

Andrew Zimbalist: Author of *Baseball and Billions*.

ON EXPANDED PLAYOFFS:

▶**Giles:** "It's going to make September much more interesting in many more cities across the country. . . . There's going to be a number of teams . . . who are going to be much more interesting . . . the whole months of September and October will raise the level of excitement and passion about the game much more than in the past."

▶**Reich:** "The second half of the season would have more value if there were an amended playoff system, but I can't see a team not winning their division, getting a chance in the playoffs as a second-place team, then getting a hot weekend and defeating a team that won over a 162-game season. At the same time, I can see six divisions, with a winning team from each and the best record among the rest to create an additional round of playoffs."

▶**Fehr:** "If there is a significant increase in fan interest, the players will take a very hard look at it. The idea of doing everything one can do to retain the integrity of a pennant race or a divisional championship race (with the extended playoff format) is problematic."

ON MARKETING THE GAME:

▶**Fehr:** "Players can't go out and market the game; there has to be a national marketing strategy in which they can take part—they can't go into it on their own. We don't have a Nike or a Reebok spending untold hundreds of millions of dollars a year in advertizing . . . Players also feel that they have been unfairly captured in microcosm by the media. . . . And now people commonly want to write about controversy and problems; they don't want to write about success, so the players have become somewhat skittish. "

▶**Giles:** "I don't think baseball has done a very good job of marketing the game on a national basis. Regionally, folks do an excellent job. But it's going to work better if the players think differently. They have to understand it's not really the owners that pay those salaries . . . it's the fans and the TV and radio sponsors. There's always been this kind of barrier between management and the players—players don't trust management—I think that's very unfortunate."

▶**Burns:** "Baseball is the precise mirror of our national narrative. One thing no one threw out today is why don't we have a third league, or a fourth league. The reason is because we can't deal with it, just like we can't deal with a third political party . . . (baseball) so precisely reflects who we are in this country, it can't help but accrue, like filings to a magnet, all that is good and bad. If we try to be Michael Jordan, we will slam dunk this sport. If we try to do what baseball does best, there won't ever be a problem with its future."

▶**Reich:** "Regardless of what happens with the labor agreement, what happens with the commissioner's office, or lack of it, I would like to emphasize very, very strongly the distinction of success between franchises comes with the difference between good management and stinko management."

ON LOSING YOUNG FANS:

▶**Watson:** "I grew up in inner-city L.A. Yes, there were Little Leagues. But we played in backyards, pickup, in sandlots. You drive around today, how many games are pickup? There's no way: Kids won't play unless they have a uniform on. Kids can't afford a $100 aluminum bat, a glove is $140, shoes are $80. We played with wooden bats, with taped-up balls. . . . That's the problem right now. There's Little Leagues, but kids won't go out and play unless there's a uniform."

▶**Burns:** "If we deny kids the opportunity to watch World Series games because they come on too late at night (to generate greater television revenue), we've squandered an opportunity to reinvigorate a whole generation. But this again is a perfect reflection of the times we're in. When I was a kid, we put baseball cards in the spokes of our bikes with clothespins. Now they put them in acid-free, glassene sleeves and show up in three-piece suits at the card shows."

ON QUALITY OF PLAY:

▶**Zimbalist:** "Common, simple statistics tell us the absolute level of play today is much, much higher than ever before. That's not to say there aren't weak players. There's always going to be a distribution of talent, and there's always going to be players at the bottom of that distribution . . . and fans of that team will always be upset. The difference between the best ballplayers today and the worst ballplayers is much smaller than it's ever been before and it's precisely for that reason that it's a major problem (for

fans)—baseball doesn't have the historical season records challenged anymore. The Babe Ruths of the world faced very few terrific pitchers and large numbers of very weak ones, and players today don't have that luxury. . . . If we got expansion, we'd have more than enough talent."

ON MINORITIES IN THE GAME:

▶**Watson:** "Obviously, baseball has made some strides. I'm sitting here as one of only three minorities (in a high-level front-office position). There is no general manager, no president, there is no ownership. But I think five years ago, you wouldn't have seen me here."

▶**Fehr:** "I don't think baseball did a very good job of indicating what the real attitude of the ownership is. Having said that, and I think this point is absolutely crucial, I don't think this perception problem will go away until you have minority ownership. They have to be part of the club."

ON THE FUTURE:

▶**Watson:** "This game is bigger than everyone in this room. It was a passion for me and it is a way of life. The thing I would like to see is the fan heard more. The fan is No. 1—he is the customer. We need harmony, we need trust. Baseball is a microcosm of us."

▶**Giles:** "You have to kind of do what the networks want you to do. Unless you go to cable—then only 60 percent of the country can see it."

▶**Costas:** "Most fans would say that's a case of the tail wagging the dog."

▶**Burns:** "Baseball is at once supposed to be this vessel in which we contain a heritage—in a sense who we are as Americans—and we want it to remain conservative . . . but it also has to change with the times . . . the game is at once this old, traditional force, and at the same time exactly reflective of the age in which we live."

—by Rick Lawes

15 fab feats:
Oddities you may have missed in '93

John Olerud's chase for .400, Randy Johnson's 308 strikeouts and Mark Whiten's four-homer, 12-RBI game were obvious achievements in '93. But here are 15 little gems you might not have noticed:

▶**15. Oh, Deer:** For the fourth time in seven seasons, outfielder Rob Deer was baseball's strikeout king—169 Ks in 466 at-bats, the all-time worst for players with at least 2,000 at-bats. But when he connects, he's hot—out of 844 career hits, 384 have been for extra bases.

▶**14. Top glove:** Greg Maddux—baseball's winningest pitcher from 1988-93—was also the best fielder on the mound for the fifth year in a row; he broke Grover Cleveland Alexander's mark (1914-17), and tied Bob Lemon's (1948-49, 52-54).

▶**13. Harper's catching up:** Brian Harper tied catchers Smoky Burgess and Manny Sanguillen with four .300-plus seasons. The only catchers with more in the last 40 years were Ted Simmons and Thurman Munson.

▶**12. Fab five:** Frank Thomas became the fifth player in history to hit .300 with 20 home in three consecutive seasons. The others: Babe Ruth, Lou Gehrig, Jimmie Foxx, Ted Williams.

▶**11. Run, don't walk:** Cecil Fielder has played 850 games without a stolen base, second all-time for non-pitchers with at least 700 games this century. First worst: Russ Nixon (906).

▶**10. Who needs a DH?** Pitcher Orel Hershiser hit .356 in 33 games—just four hits shy of .400 and breaking Jack Bentley's NL record (.406 in 1923).

▶**9. Double the pleasure:** Olerud was 37 points short of .400, but he hit 54 doubles, the most since George Kell had 56 in 1950.

▶**8 Canseco speeds up to 750:** Jose Canseco, who played just 46 games in '93 due to an ill-fated attempt at pitching, became the first player since Ted Williams to reach the 750 career RBI mark by his 1,000th game.

▶**7. Murray on his last legs? Not:** Eddie Murray is far from fading away. In '93, he hit a team-high .285, had 27 homers, and drove in 100 runs, the most since 1985. He is the first player in major league history to have at least 75 RBI in each of his first 17 seasons.

▶**6. 16 for 20:** 1993 was Ozzie Smith's 16th consecutive season with 20 or more stolen bases. Since 1900, the only other player to achieve such a streak was Honus Wagner (1900-15).

▶**5. Grand theft:** The NL has a new stolen base king—Chuck Carr. He stole 58 bases for the expansion Marlins to beat out reigning NL king Marquis Grissom. Carr was the first non-Expo or Cardinal to lead the league in stolen bases since Omar Moreno did it for the Pirates in 1979.

▶**4. Passing the Buc:** After three consecutive NL East titles, Pittsburgh fell to fifth place with a team that had a major-league high roster of 21 rookies.

▶**3. Musical pitcher's mound:** Sparky Anderson auditioned a club-record 21 pitchers in '93. Since 1989, the Tigers have suited 55 different pitchers, the equivalent of a different 11-man staff each of five years.

▶**2. First to worst:** The Oakland A's were the worst team in the AL in '93 (68-94), just one season after winning their fourth AL West title in five years. The last team to take such a nosedive was the Philadelphia A's in 1915.

▶**1. Home run derby:** Home runs soared in '93—by 55% in the NL and 16.8% in the AL. The NL hit a record 1,956 (expansion teams had 236) up from 1,262; the AL hit 2,074, up from 1,776. Naturally, ERAs soared too: from 3.50 to 4.04 in the NL, and from 3.94 to 4.32 in the AL.

—*by Scott Kauffman*

Major milestones: 1993's record-setters

Sparky Anderson says his proudest moment was the team effort of his 1987 Tiger club.

by Porter Binks, USA TODAY

Sparky Anderson notches 2,000th win

After 24 seasons at the helm, Sparky Anderson reached the magic mark that only six other major league managers have accomplished: 2,000 wins. Anderson joined Connie Mack (3,776), John McGraw (2,840), Bucky Harris (2,159), Joe McCarthy (2,126), Walter Alston (2,040), and Leo Durocher (2,010).

ANDERSON'S OTHER TRIUMPHS
▶First manager to win a World Series in both leagues.
▶First manager to win 100 or more games in a season with two different teams.
▶NL Manager of the Year ('72, '75) and AL Manager of the Year ('84, '87).
▶No. 7 on list for most World Series games won: 16.

SPARKY'S HIGHS AND LOWS
▶**Best victory:** Fifth and final playoff game in 1972 (Reds vs. Pirates).
▶**Happiest moment:** First game as manager at Crosley Field (1970).
▶**Saddest moment:** The day he left the Tigers (1989) for a sabbatical.
▶**Proudest moment:** The Tigers beating the Blue Jays in the '87 ALCS.

Winfield hits No. 3,000

Dave Winfield collected his 3,000th career hit at the Metrodome on Sept. 16, but during the celebration he recalled that he was originally drafted as a pitcher. Two summers in the collegiate league in Alaska convinced him he was better suited to playing every day.

Winfield played for the Fairbanks Goldpanners, and was acclaimed as a pitcher/outfielder—13-4 with five saves, and .315 with 18 homers. When one home run ball landed on the curling rink beyond the Fairbanks left-field fence, it was apparent his future was at the plate. Twenty-one years later, he became the 19th player in major league history to reach 3,000 hits.

Dave Winfield, the bionic man of baseball, just keeps on going . . . and going . . . and going . . .

by Russell Beeker, USA TODAY

Canseco gets 750 RBI in first 1,000 games

Jose Canseco started the '93 season in Texas with a major milestone—on April 25, he became the first player since Ted Williams to drive in 750 runs in his first 1,000 games. Just a few games later, on May 2, he reached another plateau—his 1,000th hit.

Q & A: Basics of 1994 realignment

Q. How many games would each team play within its division and outside it?

A. That depends upon the division. In the four-team West divisions, there will be 39 games within the division and 123 outside. In the five-team divisions, there will be 52 games within and 110 outside.

Q. Do the players object to making the season longer?

A. Many do. "I can't see playing until Nov. 1," says Rangers' closer Tom Henke. "They're just adding another week to the season without bothering to talk to us about it. I think the playoffs are maybe a good idea, but you have to cut a week off the end of the season." Yet acting commissioner Bud Selig is adamant about the regular season staying at 162 games. This is a major negotiating point between the players and owners.

Q. Will the 1994 schedule change?

A. No. Teams will simply be placed in different divisions.

Q. How will the playoffs work?

A. The new first round will be a best-of-five format; the team with the best record will play the last three games at home. The wild-card team will play the divisional winner with the best record. But if they both come from the same division, the wild-card winner will play the divisional champion with the second-best record in the first round. After that teams from the same division can play each other.

Q. How about the next round?

A. It will be a best-of-seven series to decide the league champion, with the home-field advantage awarded to divisional champions on a rotating basis.

Q. What does this mean for expansion?

A. The move leaves two spots open in both Western divisions. A move to add two more teams is expected by '96.

—*by Tim Wendel*

How '93 would've looked

All four '93 playoff teams would have qualified for postseason play under the realignment scheme for 1994. In addition, Texas and New York would've been in the ALCS; San Francisco and St. Louis in the NLCS. Here's how the '93 standings would have turned out:

▶ **American League East**

Team	W	L	Pct.	GB
Toronto	95	67	.586	—
New York	88	74	.543	7
Baltimore	85	77	.525	10
Detroit	85	77	.525	10
Boston	80	82	.494	15

▶ **American League Central**

Team	W	L	Pct.	GB
Chicago	94	68	.580	—
Kansas City	84	78	.519	10
Cleveland	76	86	.469	18
Minnesota	71	91	.438	23
Milwaukee	69	93	.426	25

▶ **American League West**

Team	W	L	Pct.	GB
Texas	86	76	.531	—
Seattle	82	80	.506	4
California	71	91	.438	15
Oakland	68	94	.420	18

▶ **National League East**

Team	W	L	Pct.	GB
Atlanta	104	58	.642	—
Philadelphia	97	65	.599	7
Montreal	94	68	.580	10
Florida	64	98	.395	40
New York	59	103	.364	45

▶ **National League Central**

Team	W	L	Pct.	GB
St. Louis	87	75	.537	—
Houston	85	77	.525	2
Chicago	84	78	.519	3
Pittsburgh	75	87	.463	12
Cincinnati	73	89	.451	14

▶ **National League West**

Team	W	L	Pct.	GB
San Francisco	103	59	.636	—
Los Angeles	81	81	.500	22
Colorado	67	95	.414	36
San Diego	61	101	.377	42

Around the league: News and highlights

TV deal at a glance

▶**Where the games are:** After the '94 All-Star Game, ABC will be in charge of two Monday night telecasts and three consecutive Saturday night games. NBC will air the last six regular season contests, all on Friday night. No regular-season games are scheduled for network TV before the All-Star Game. The two networks will trade off on the All-Star Game, playoffs and World Series. In postseason play, only the World Series will be seen across the country in its entirety.

▶**Dividing the money:** For the first time, Major League Baseball will receive a percentage of ad sales instead of an up-front rights fee. Baseball will receive 87 1/2% for ad revenue up to $160 million. For ad sales between $160 million and $190 million, baseball and the two networks will each receive 33%. For ad sales above, baseball receives 80% and the networks each 10%. Major League Baseball and the networks are kicking in $10 million each for start-up costs of a new organization in charge of selling commercials and sponsorships.

Orioles go for $173 million

The Baltimore Orioles were sold for a record price at a public auction Aug. 2 in New York. A group led by Baltimore attorney Peter G. Angelos and Cincinnati businessman William O. DeWitt Jr., who started the day as potential rival bidders, agreed to pay $173 million for the team, far surpassing the $125 million paid in '92 for the Seattle Mariners. The team was auctioned after Orioles owner Eli Jacobs filed for bankruptcy protection in April.

By joining with Angelos, DeWitt was able to get closer to his dream of owning a team. His father was owner in the 1940s of the St. Louis Browns—fore-runner of the Orioles—and president of the Cincinnati Reds from 1961–66.

"I was prepared to go as high as I needed within reason, with a premium for keeping the team in Baltimore," said Angelos. "Our intention from the outset was making sure the team had local ownership and that we'd keep the team for Marylanders."

—by Rick Lawes

More grass in the AL

When the Kansas City Royals tear up the artificial turf (in '95) and replace it with grass, the American League will be left with only three teams that play on the fake stuff: Minnesota, Seattle and Toronto, all of which have domes. Six National League teams use turf.

▶**American League:** Baltimore, grass; Boston, grass; California, grass; Chicago, grass; Cleveland, grass; Detroit, grass; Kansas City (grass in '95), turf; Milwaukee, grass; Minnesota, turf; New York, grass; Oakland, grass; Seattle, turf; Texas ,grass; Toronto, turf.

▶**National League:** Atlanta, grass; Chicago, grass; Cincinnati, turf; Colorado, grass; Florida, grass; Houston, turf; Los Angeles, grass; Montreal,turf; New York, grass, Philadelphia, turf; Pittsburgh, turf; St. Louis, turf; San Diego, grass; San Francisco, grass.

Eight for Junior

Ken Griffey Jr.'s eight consecutive games with home runs:
▶1. July 20, Yankee Stadium.
▶2. July 21, Yankee Stadium.
▶3. July 22, Cleveland Stadium.
▶4. July 23, Cleveland Stadium.
▶5. July 24, Cleveland Stadium.
▶6. July 25, Cleveland Stadium.
▶7. July 27, Kingdome; grand slam.
▶8. July 28, Kingdome.

Ryan's, Brett's brilliant careers come to an end

by Anne Ryan, USA Today

In a record 27 seasons Ryan amassed 53 records.

What they say about Ryan

▶**Andre Dawson, 26 Ks vs. Ryan:** "I just liked the matchup because it's strength against strength. He's a power pitcher and I consider myself a fastball hitter. He probably struck me out most of the time on curveballs, or the little balls that he scuffed up and ran down and in at the end. Basically, he'll challenge you; you'll get a pitch to hit."

▶**Jeff Torborg, caught Ryan's first no-hitter:** "As the game kept going he was getting stronger—he was always better conditioned than anyone else."

▶**Art Kusnyer, caught second no-hitter:** "I remember the pitch he made that showed me—he threw a fastball and I went down to block the ball. I put my glove down to the ground and the ball rose up for a strike. That was when I knew they didn't have anybody who was going to touch it."

▶**Sandy Koufax, Ryan's idol:** "He's got good genes, good mechanics—but there's been plenty of pitchers who have had good mechanics that have broken down after a year. There may be someone again like Nolan with that kind of longevity, but I don't think his no-hitters or strikeouts will ever be reached."

▶**Gaylord Perry, beat Ryan in the 1972 Cy Young voting:** "He got to be a better pitcher later. He kept learning his craft . . . but if you could throw it 100 mph like he could, why would you do anything else? . . . He's one of a kind."

The Ryan record book

▶**STRIKEOUTS:**
1. Most Career Strikeouts: 5,714.
2. Most, Season, Major League, AL: 383, California, 1973.
3. Most, Season, AL, right-hander: 383, California, 1973.
4. Most Years, 100 or More, Major League: 24, New York Mets, 1968, 1970-71; California, 1972-79; Houston, 1980-88; Texas, 1989-92.
5. Most Consecutive Years, 100 or More : 23, New York Mets, 1970-71; California, 1972-79; Houston, 1980-88; Texas, 1989-92.
6. Most Years, 200 or More, Major Leagues: 15, California, 1972-79, except 1975; Houston, 1980, 1982, 1985, 1987-88; Texas, 1989-91.
7. Most Years, 200 or More, AL: 10, California, 1972-79, except 1975; Texas, 1989-91.
8. Most Years, 300 or More, Major and American League: 6, California, 1972-74, 1976-77; Texas, 1989.
9. Most, Losing Pitcher, Extra-Inning Game, Major and AL: 19, California, Aug. 20, 1974, 11 innings, lost 1-0.
10. Most Times 15 or More, Game, Major Leagues: 26.
11. Most Times, 15 or More, Game, AL: 23.
12. Most Times, 10 or More, Game, Major Leagues: 215; 67 in NL, 148 in AL.
13. Most Times, 10 or More, Game, AL: 148.
14. Most Times, 10 or More, Game, Season: 23, California, 1973.
15. Three Strikeouts, Inning, on nine pitched balls (tied): N.Y. Mets, April 19, 1968, 3rd inn.; California, July 9, 1972, 2nd inn.
16. Most Consecutive, Game, AL (tied): 8, California, July 9, 1972; California, July 15, 1973.
17. Most, Two Consecutive Games, Major and AL: 32, California, Aug. 7 (13), Aug. 12 (19), 1974, 17 inn.
18. Most, 3 Consecutive Games, Major and AL: 47,California, Aug. 12 (19), Aug. 16 (9), Aug. 20 (19), 1974, 27.1 inn.
19. Oldest Pitcher, 10 or More, Game: 45 yrs., 6 mos., 6 days, Aug. 6, 1992 vs. Oakland.

▶**NO-HIT/LOW-HIT GAMES**
20. Most No-Hitters, Major Leagues: 7, California, 1973 (2), 1974, 1975; Houston, 1981; Texas; 1990, 1991.
21. Most No-Hitters, AL: 6.
22. Most No-Hitters, Season (tied): 2, California, May 15 & July 15, 1973.
23. Oldest Pitcher, No-hitter: 44 yrs., 3 mos., 1 day; May 1, 1991 vs. Toronto.
24. Most Teams, No-Hitter: 3, California (4), Houston, Texas (2).
25. Most Different Decades, No-Hitter: 3, '70's, '80's, '90's.
26. Longest Span Between No-Hitters: 8 yrs., 8 mos., 16 days, Sept. 26, 1981 until June 11, 1990.
27. Most Low-Hit (No-Hit and One-Hit) Games, Season, AL: 3, California, 1973.
28. Most Low-Hit Games, Career, Major League: 19.
29. Most One-Hit Games, Career, Major League: 12.

▶**WALKS**
30. Most Bases on Balls, Major Leagues: 2795.
31. Most Years Leading Majors in Most Bases on Balls: 8, California, 1972-74, 1976-78; Houston, 1980, 1982.
32. Most Years Leading AL in Most Bases on Balls: 6, California, 1972-74, 1976-78.

▶**MISCELLANEOUS**

33. Most Clubs Shut Out (won or tied), Season, Major and American League (tied): 8, California, 1972.
34. Most Years Leading Major Leagues in Wild Pitches: 6.
35. Most Years Leading American League in Wild Pitches: 4
36. Most Wild Pitches, Major Leagues: 274.
37. Most Years Leading American League in Errors, Pitcher: 4.
38. Highest Strikeout Average per Nine Innings, Season: 11.48, Houston, 1987; 270 , 211.2 inn.
39. Highest Strikeout Average per Nine Innings, Career: 9.54.
40. Lowest Hits Allowed Average per Nine Innings, Season: 5.26, California, 1972; 166 hits, 284 inn.
41. Lowest Hits Allowed Avg. per Nine Innings, Career: 6.55.
42. Most Consecutive Starts Without a Relief Appearence: 594, July 30, 1974-Sept. 22, 1993.
43. Most Different Seasons, Major Leagues: 27, New York Mets, 1966, 1968-71; California, 1972-79; Houston, 1980-88; Texas, 1989-93.
44. Most Grand Slams Allowed, Career: 10.

▶**CHAMPIONSHIP SERIES, ALL-STAR GAME**

45. Most Hits Allowed, 5-Game Series, NL: 16, Houston, 1980.
46. Most Strikeouts, Total Series (tied): 46, New York Mets, 1969; California, 1979; Houston, 1980, 1986.
47. Most Strikeouts, Game, Relief Pitcher: 7, New York Mets, Oct. 6, 1969; 7 inn.
48. Most Consecutive Strikeouts, Game (tied): 4, California, Oct. 3, 1979.
49. Most Consecutive Strikeouts, Start of Game (tied): 4, California, Oct. 3, 1979.
50. Highest Fielding Percentage, Pitcher, with Most Chances Accepted, Five-Game Series, NL (tied): 1.000, Houston, 1980, Four Chances Accepted.
51. Most Assists, Pitcher, 5-Game Series, NL (tied): 3, Houston, 1980.
52. Most Chances Accepted, Pitcher, 5-Game Series, NL (tied): 4, Houston, 1980.
53. Oldest Pitcher to Win All-Star Game: 42 yrs., 5 mos., 13 days, July 12, 1989 at California for American League.
Source: Texas Rangers.

by H. Darr Beiser, USA Today

George Brett is proudest of the fact that he played his entire career in a Royals' uniform.

Brett tells why he retired

"I wasn't getting great satisfaction anymore when I did something great or I wasn't getting that down when I did something bad," he said. "I wasn't that happy when we won. I wasn't that sad when we lost. Something was missing.

"About the only thing I can relate it to is riding a roller coaster 162 times, 20 years in a row. Don't you want to go on another ride once in awhile? I want to go on Space Mountain. I'm tired of the Matterhorn Bobsled.

"I think the game just beat me, which it beats everybody in time. It took 26 years to beat Nolan (Ryan). It took 20 years to beat me."

Royals GM Herk Robinson said Brett would have an office next to his on the fifth floor at Kauffman Stadium. He will be a vice president until the year 2000 and will evaluate talent at the major and minor league levels as well as having a say on any Royal trades.

"We are counting on him and want him to be a most viable part of continuing and developing a winning organization," Robinson said. "If he can contribute just a small part of what he contributed throughout his career, we'll be champions forever."

—by Pete Williams

Brett: A Royal for 20 years

After 20 dazzling years, George Brett ended the '93 season by announcing his retirement. He holds every Kansas City career offensive record except stolen bases and was selected to 13 consecutive All-Star Games.

"I've accomplished more in my playing days than I ever thought I would," Brett added. "I played more games, got more hits, hit more home runs, played in more championship series, more All-Star games. I hurt my knee more than I ever thought I would.

"The thing I'm proud of most—and I say this sincerely—is spending my whole career with one team. I always have and will always respect this organization."

Brett had a career .305 average with 3,154 hits in 10,349 at-bats, with 665 doubles, 137 triples, 317 home runs and 201 stolen bases.

1993: Best of the National League

NL Manager of the Year Dusty Baker's Giants won 103 games in his first year at the helm.

1993 Manager of the Year: Dusty Baker

In his first year as a manager, Dusty Baker kept San Francisco in the NL West race until the final innings of the season. The Giants won 103 games and are likely to be major contenders in '94.

THE VOTING

Totals based on a 5-3-1-point basis (5 for a 1st-place vote, 3 for 2nd, 1 for 3rd):

Manager, team	1	2	3	Total
Dusty Baker, S.F.	15	9	3	105
Jim Fregosi, Phi.	11	11	4	92
Felipe Alou, Mtl.	2	2	11	27
Bobby Cox, Atl.	—	6	9	27
Don Baylor, Col.	—	—	1	1

Cy Young winner: Greg Maddux

Atlanta's Greg Maddux (20-10, 2.36 ERA, 267 innings pitched, 197 strikeouts, and eight complete games) became the first pitcher since Sandy Koufax to win back-to-back Cy Young awards (1992-93). Only five have received consecutive awards: Sandy Koufax, L.A., 1965-66; Denny McLain, Det., 1968-69 (tied with Mike Cuellar of Baltimore in 1969); Jim Palmer, Bal., 1975-76; Roger Clemens, Bos., 1986-87; Greg Maddux, Atl., 1992-93.

Bonds wins third MVP

How can you argue with a .336 average, 46 home runs, 123 RBI—stats that in most years would have produced a triple crown—plus 38 doubles, 129 runs, 126 walks, and 29 stolen bases to boot? In winning his third MVP title, Bonds joins the elite company of Mike Schmidt, Roy Campanella and Stan Musial (National League), and Mickey Mantle, Yogi Berra, Joe DiMaggio and Jimmie Foxx (American League).

Voting for the top five candidates (total points only): Barry Bonds, S.F., 372; Lenny Dykstra, Phi., 267; David Justice, Atl., 183; Fred McGriff, Atl., 177; Ron Gant, Atl., 176.

Barry Bonds was among the National League leaders in 10 out of 11 offensive categories.

Dodgers' Piazza is Rookie of the Year

Not only was Mike Piazza unanimously picked as '93 NL Rookie of the Year, he was among league leaders in average (.318), home runs (35), RBI (112), slugging percentage (.561), and total bases (307)—a candidate for MVP. Only five other players have ever been unanimously chosen NL rookie of the year: Frank Robinson, Cin., 1956; Orlando Cepeda, S.F., 1958; Willie McCovey, S.F., 1959; Vince Coleman, St.L., 1985; Benito Santiago, S.D. 1987.

1993: Best of the American League

Lamont named top AL manager

Gene Lamont took his Chicago White Sox all the way to the AL West title and was rewarded for his efforts with the league's highest recognition for a skipper: AL Manager of the Year.

THE VOTING

Totals based on a 5-3-1-point basis (5 for a 1st place vote, 3 for 2nd, 1 for 3rd):

Manager, team	1	2	3	Total
Gene Lamont, Chi	8	9	5	72
Buck Showalter, N.Y.	7	8	4	63
Cito Gaston, Tor.	6	5	4	49
Kevin Kennedy, Tex.	3	3	4	28
Lou Piniella, Sea.	3	2	3	24
Mike Hargrove, Cle.	—	1	5	10
Johnny Oates, Bal. -	—	1	2	5
Butch Hobson, Bos.	—	—	1	1

Gene Lamont's White Sox finished the 1993 season at 94-86, eight games ahead of Texas.

Cy Young winner: McDowell

Jack McDowell led the league in victories (22-10) and shutouts (4), pitched 10 complete games and 256 2/3 innings in leading the White Sox to their AL West title. He received 124 points in the Cy Young voting, followed by Randy Johnson (Sea., 75), Kevin Appier (K.C., 60), Jimmy Key (N.Y., 14), Duane Ward (Tor., 5), Pat Hentgen (Tor., 3), and Juan Guzman (Tor., 1).

Frank Thomas was among the AL's best in walks, runs, on-base percentage and slugging

Frank Thomas is unanimous MVP

Frank Thomas, whom many had considered to be slighted in past MVP voting, was unanimously selected as the AL's top player in '93. Only seven other players have been unanimously selected for MVP honors in the AL, two in the NL: Jose Canseco, Oak., 1988; Mike Schmidt, Phil., 1980; Reggie Jackson, Oak., 1973; Denny McLain, Det., 1968; Orlando Cepeda, St.L., 1967; Frank Robinson, Bal., 1966; Mickey Mantle, N.Y. Yankees, 1956; Al Rosen, Cleve., 1953; Hank Greenberg, Det., 1935.

Angels' Tim Salmon is AL rookie of the year

Tim Salmon looked promising from the start, and he proved his worth with 31 home runs and 95 RBI, a slugging percentage of .536 (including 35 doubles) and 93 runs scored for his California Angels. Like his counterpart in the NL—Mike Piazza—he got all 28 first-place votes for the award. The only other AL players to achieve that were Carlton Fisk, Bos., 1972; Mark McGwire, Oak., 1987; Sandy Alomar, Cleve., 1990.

1993 baseball obituaries (partial listing)

Burgess Whitehead

Burgess "Whitey" Whitehead, a survivor of the St. Louis Cardinals Gashouse Gang of the 1930s, died Nov. 25 in Windsor, N.C. He was 83.

Charlie Gehringer

Hall of Famer, arguably the greatest second baseman of all time, Charlie Gehringer died Jan. 21. He was 89. He spent his entire 19-year major league career with the Detroit Tigers (1924-42).

Merle Anthony

Former American League umpire George Merlyn (Merle) Anthony died Feb. 2. He was 68. Anthony was an AL umpire from 1969 until 1976.

Rip Repulski

Eldin J. "Rip" Replulski, one of the players on the L.A. Dodgers' first world championship team in 1959, died Feb. 10. He was 64.

Bill Dickey

Former New York Yankees catcher and Hall of Famer Bill Dickey died Nov. 12 in Little Rock, Ark. He was 86.

Bob Seeds

Bob Seeds, who played for five major league teams and in one game of the 1936 World Series for the Yankees, died Oct. 28 in Shamrock, Texas. He was 86.

Cliff Young

Cliff Young, 29, was killed Nov. 4 when he lost control of his truck near his hometown of Willis, Texas. The left-hander appeared in 21 games for the Indians last season, posting a 3-3 record with a 4.62 ERA and one save.

Steve Olin

Cleveland Indians' closer Steve Olin died in a boating accident on March 22, along with teammate Tim Crews. He was the first active major leaguer to be killed in an accident since Thurman Munson died in a 1979 plane crash. He was 27.

Tim Crews

Indians' pitcher Tim Crews died along with Steve Olin in the boating accident on March 22. He had spent six years with the Dodgers before signing with the Indians as a free agent in January. He was 31.

Jimmy Crutchfield

Col. Jimmie Crutchfield, a four-time Negro League All-Star outfielder who played primarily for the Newark Eagles and Pittsburgh Crawfords, died March 31. He was 83.

Diego Ruiz

Pitcher Diego Ruiz of the Class A Springfield (Ill.) Cardinals was killed in an automobile accident May 22. He was 22.

Johnny Mize

Hall of Famer Johnny Robert Mize—The Big Cat—died on June 2. He was 80. He hit more than 50 home runs in 1947 and hit three in a game six times, a major league record.

Roy Campanella

Roy Campanella, the Dodgers' Hall of Fame catcher, died June 26, at 71. Campanella was the first black catcher in the major leagues, but his career was cut short by a car accident that left him in a wheelchair since 1958.

Don Drysdale

Hall of Fame pitcher Don Drysdale died July 3 of a heart attack in his Montreal hotel room. He was a broadcaster for his former team, the Los Angeles Dodgers. He was 56.

Ben Chapman

Ben Chapman, the former Yankee outfielder who made history as the first batter in an All-Star Game, died July 7. He was 84.

Ewing Kauffman

Ewing Kauffman, owner of the Kansas City Royals, died Aug. 1. He was 76.

Bob Miller

Bob Miller, a major league pitcher for 17 seasons and the advance scout for the San Francisco Giants, was killed Aug. 6 in a car accident. He was 54.

Cal Koonce

Cal Koonce, a reliever with the 1969 Miracle Mets, died of cancer Oct. 28 in Hope Mills, N.C. He was 52. Koonce, who played for the Chicago Cubs, Mets and Boston between 1962-71, was 6-3 with seven saves for the '69 World Champion Mets.

Granny Hamner

One of the Phillies' "Whiz Kids" in the 1950s, Granny Hamner died Sept. 12, at 66.

Bill Atwood

Bill Atwood, catcher for the Philadelphia Phillies from 1936-40, died Sept. 14 in an automobile accident. He was 81.

NL/AL beat

- ▸ NL East: Worst to first
- ▸ NL West: Last great pennant race
- ▸ AL East: Blue Jays again

- ▸ AL West: Chisox won the west, lost the rest
- ▸ 1993 All-Star Game
- ▸ League leaders

USA SNAPSHOTS®

A look at statistics that shape the sports world

Double-digit All-Stars

How many All-Star teams have scored 10 runs or more in a game?

a. 2
b. 5
c. 9
d. 13

Answer: b. All by the American League, including 1992 13-6 victory.

Source: USA TODAY research   By Bob Laird, USA TODAY

NL East '93: Worst to first for the Phillies

The belief that they could be a contender in '93 hit the Phillies during spring training. They put more of an emphasis on winning, with good reason: They were coming off the third last-place finish in five years. With a little luck and healthy key players, general manager Lee Thomas and manager Jim Fregosi thought the team's new additions—outfielders Pete Incaviglia, Milt Thompson and Jim Eisenreich, and pitchers Danny Jackson and Larry Andersen—would provide a much-needed boost.

That's exactly what happened. They took the lead the first week of the season and never lost it. It shrunk a couple of times—when the Cards and the Expos made runs—but the Phillies held on for their first championship since 1983. Their offense generated 877 runs, the most an NL team had scored since 1962. Lenny Dykstra had an amazing season, scoring 143 runs, and Darren Daulton drove in 100 runs for the second season in a row. Each of the team's five starting pitchers won at least 12 games, and closer Mitch Williams set a team record with 43 saves.

The Expos had trouble early, then pulled within four games in September, but couldn't get closer until the final day, despite a 94-win season.

STANDINGS THROUGH JULY 12, 1993

Team	W	L	Pct.	GB
Philadelphia	57	32	.640	-
St. Louis	51	36	.586	5
Montreal	48	40	.545	8.5
Pittsburgh	42	46	.477	14.5
Chicago	41	45	.477	14.5
Florida	37	50	.425	19
New York	27	60	.310	29

The Cardinals' run came earlier, but their hopes vanished when the Phils swept them in a three-game series at the end of July. Two players picked up in offseason trades—first baseman Gregg Jefferies and right fielder Mark Whiten—proved to be major reasons for the Cards' success; Whiten once hit four homers and drove in 12 runs in a single game against the Reds.

The Cubs never recovered from the loss of free agents Greg Maddux and Andre Dawson, and despite an NL record 53 saves by Randy Myers, never were a factor in the division race. After the season, manager Jim Lefebvre was promptly replaced by Tom Trebelhorn.

The loss of free agents Barry Bonds and Doug Drabek was too much for the Pirates to overcome. Their best remaining player, Andy Van Slyke, was out with a broken collarbone for two months. The biggest problem, though, was pitching: the team ERA was 4.77.

The Marlins proved they could become a factor much sooner than previous expansion teams. They benefitted from the draft of Bryan Harvey, who saved 45 games, and the selection of rookie outfielders Chuck Carr, who led the league with 58 stolen bases, and Jeff Conine, the only player in the league to appear in all 162 games.

The Marlins were saved from the cellar by the ineptness of the Mets, who lost 103 games. During the season-long mess, manager Jeff Torborg and GM Al Harazin were fired—replaced by Dallas Green and Joe McIlvaine. The bad news was endless: Anthony Young's record losing streak reached 27 games; Vince Coleman was placed on leave after allegedly throwing a firecracker at some fans in Los Angeles; and pitcher Bret Saberhagen was involved in a couple of clubhouse disturbances before surgery ended his season.

FINAL STANDINGS

Team	W	L	Pct.	GB
Philadelphia	97	65	.599	-
Montreal	94	68	.580	3
St. Louis	87	75	.537	10
Chicago	84	78	.519	13
Pittsburgh	75	87	.463	22
Florida	64	98	.395	33
New York	59	103	.364	38

—by Rob Rains

NL West '93: The last great pennant race

Not since divisional play began in 1969 had a National League club won 100 games and not won the division title. But the '93 Giants won a club-record 103 games, yet finished one short of the Braves' 104, also a club-mark. They battled until the final day of the season, when the Braves beat the Rockies and the Giants lost to the Dodgers and the race was over.

The Braves had trailed San Francisco by 10 games on July 23, but went 39-11 over their final 50 contests to wipe out that deficit. They built a four-game lead over San Francisco with two weeks to play, winning five of six head-to-head, before the Giants rebounded from a seven-game losing streak to pull back even.

STANDINGS THROUGH JULY 12, 1993

Team	W	L	Pct.	GB
San Francisco	59	30	.663	-
Atlanta	50	39	.562	9
Houston	46	41	.529	12
Los Angeles	46	41	.529	12
Cincinnati	45	45	.500	14.5
Colorado	33	54	.379	25
San Diego	33	56	.371	26

The key to the Braves' stretch run was getting Fred McGriff from San Diego on July 18. They went 51-17 starting with his first game. He hit .310 with 19 homers and 55 RBI in those 68 games.

As expected, the key to the Braves' success was great starting pitching. All four of their starters won at least 15 games and both Greg Maddux and Tom Glavine were 20-game winners. Maddux also led the league in ERA (2.36), innings pitched and complete games. Glavine's 22 wins tied him with the Giants' John Burkett for the most in the league.

Many people didn't even expect the Giants to be in San Francisco in 1993, much less a contender for the division title. A group led by Peter Magowan bought the team and signed free agent Bonds, who had a career year—.336, 46 homers, 123 RBI. The pitching staff was

the big surprise, though: Burkett won 22 games and Bill Swift 21. Closer Rod Beck was one of the league's best relievers, with 48 saves.

Houston finished third, 19 games out, and both manager Art Howe and GM Bill Wood were fired at the end of the year. Mark Portugal went 18-4 with a 2.77 ERA, but the Astros were hurt by poor seasons from free agents Doug Drabek and Greg Swindell, who combined for a 21-31 record.

The Dodgers improved over their last-place finish of 1992, thanks largely to the performance of Rookie of the Year Mike Piazza. The catcher broke nearly every offensive record in the book for rookies, hitting .318 with 35 homers and 112 RBI.

The Reds faded quickly. Manager Tony Perez was fired in May and replaced by Davey Johnson, but the move didn't help. Injuries played a big part in the team's demise; Chris Sabo and Joe Oliver were the only regulars to play more than 101 games.

The Rockies enjoyed a terrific first season, thanks to a record-breaking attendance and the performance of first baseman Andres Galarraga, who hit .370 and became the first player from an expansion team to win a league batting title. He and Charlie Hayes each drove in 98 runs, breaking the RBI record for expansion team players.

The Padres had a dismal season: 101 losses. Economics forced them to make a series of trades, including McGriff, Gary Sheffield, Greg Harris and Bruce Hurst.

FINAL STANDINGS

Team	W	L	Pct.	GB
Atlanta	104	58	.642	-
San Francisco	103	59	.636	1
Houston	85	77	.525	19
Los Angeles	81	81	.500	23
Cincinnati	73	89	.451	31
Colorado	67	95	.414	37
San Diego	61	101	.377	43

—by Rob Rains

AL East '93: The Blue Jays took it all—again

The mix was different—accent on hitting, not pitching—but the Toronto Blue Jays found a way to repeat as champions in the American League East. Paul Molitor replaced Dave Winfield as DH, Dave Stewart filled David Cone's spot in the rotation, and Rickey Henderson was the stretch drive hired gun. Still, the Jays would have been on the sidelines if Pat Hentgen hadn't blossomed into a 19-game winner and John Olerud hadn't won the AL batting title.

Toronto's batting order was one of the most dangerous in the game—so deep that Molitor finished the season batting sixth to protect Olerud. Team RBI leader Joe Carter had another great season, and Devon White and Roberto Alomar just kept getting better.

STANDINGS THROUGH JULY 12, 1993				
Team	W	L	Pct.	GB
Toronto	49	40	.551	-
Detroit	48	40	.545	.5
New York	48	41	.539	1
Baltimore	47	41	.534	1.5
Boston	45	42	.517	3
Cleveland	40	48	.455	8.5
Milwaukee	37	49	.430	10.5

The New York Yankees made huge strides this season and were tied for first place as late as Aug. 29. Jim Abbott provided one of the season's memorable moments by throwing a no-hitter Sept. 4 against Cleveland. Catcher Mike Stanley achieved a personal-best season by hitting .305 with 26 home runs and 84 RBI. But for the Yankees to win in '94, they need more starting pitching and some answers in the bullpen.

The Baltimore Orioles weathered a roller-coaster ride of a season, from a 10-game winning streak to a pair of eight-game losing skeins. Manager Johnny Oates held together a pitching staff that suffered injuries to both ace Mike Mussina and closer Gregg Olson. Catcher Chris Hoiles proved to be one of the unsung stars of the game—he had 29 home runs in 126 games.

Despite Roger Clemens having the worst year of his career, the Boston Red Sox were in contention for much of the season. Veteran Danny Darwin and rookie Aaron Sele picked up the slack, while infielders John Valentin and Tim Naehring proved they could hit in the majors.

The Detroit Tigers got off to a great start in '93—18 games over .500 on June 20. But from there the season unraveled in a hurry, as the Tigers lost 31 of their next 43. They battled back to stay alive until the final week of the season, but they didn't have enough pitching. A late-season slump cost Cecil Fielder a chance to become the first major-leaguer ever to lead the majors in RBI four consecutive seasons. Still, he had a good year with 117 RBI. Tony Phillips reached base 313 times, the most by a Tiger in 30 years and just the 24th AL player ever to top 300.

Manager Mike Hargrove and general manager John Hart held the Cleveland Indians together emotionally after the boating accident that killed relievers Steve Olin and Tim Crews and seriously injured starter Bob Ojeda. The Indians won 76 games, their 1992 total. Albert Belle continued to be one of the dominant hitters in the game—38 homers and a league-high 129 RBI. Carlos Baerga had 21 homers and 114 RBI.

The Milwaukee Brewers never got rolling. Pat Listach, the AL's top rookie in '92, was plagued by injuries that slowed the team's aggressive attack on the basepaths. Greg Vaughn (30 HR, 97 RBI) made the All-Star team. Darryl Hamilton was great in the field and hit .310.

FINAL STANDINGS				
Team	W	L	Pct.	GB
Toronto	95	67	.586	-
New York	88	74	.543	7
Baltimore	85	77	.525	10
Detroit	85	77	.525	10
Boston	80	82	.494	15
Cleveland	76	86	.469	19
Milwaukee	69	93	.426	26

—by Tim Wendel

AL West '93: Chisox won the west, lost the rest

After being the odds-on favorites for several seasons, the Chicago White Sox finally captured the American League West title in '93, only to come up short in the playoffs—again. Losing to the Toronto Blue Jays in the AL Championship Series, the Sox remained winless at home in the postseason since 1959.

Chicago's '93 run was fueled by Frank Thomas' MVP performance and a young pitching staff led by Jack McDowell—Alex Fernandez, Wilson Alvarez and Jason Bere developed so well that veteran pitcher Tim Belcher was in the bullpen for the playoffs.

STANDINGS THROUGH JULY 12, 1993

Team	W	L	Pct.	GB
Chicago	45	41	.523	-
Kansas City	44	42	.512	1
Texas	44	42	.512	1
California	43	43	.500	2
Seattle	44	44	.500	2
Oakland	38	46	.452	6
Minnesota	36	49	.424	8.5

Despite injuries and inconsistent pitching, the Texas Rangers made a strong run at the White Sox. Under first-year manager Kevin Kennedy's direction, they stayed in the hunt until late September—the first time that's happened in 22 years in Arlington.

After an ill-advised pitching stint, Jose Canseco was lost for the season, forcing Juan Gonzalez and Rafael Palmeiro to pick up the offensive slack. Even without Canseco, the Rangers had one of the better attacks in the game, with Gonzalez, Palmeiro and Dean Palmer combining for 116 HRs and 319 RBI.

Manager Hal McRae's Kansas City Royals woke up and climbed into contention, mainly on the strength of their pitching staff—Kevin Appier led the league with a 2.56 ERA, and closer Jeff Montgomery tied for the AL lead in saves with 45.

With Lou Piniella calling the shots the Seattle Mariners were arguably the most improved team in the league, finishing 18 games better than in '92. Ken Griffey (45 home runs and 109 RBI) and Jay Buhner (27-98) had career years, as did Randy Johnson with a league-leading 308 strikeouts—10th best total ever in a single season. From the All-Star break on, Johnson was the dominant pitcher in the AL, finishing with a 19-8 record and 3.24 ERA.

Angels' manager Buck Rodgers had Southern California dreaming when his team stayed in the hunt for the first half of the season. Tim Salmon lived up to his billing as the top rookie in the league and he had plenty of help with Chad Curtis, Damion Easley, Gary DiSarcina and J.T. Snow. Chili Davis, the best everyday designated hitter in the league, also lent a guiding hand.

The two most recent division champs, the Minnesota Twins and Oakland A's, were another story. The Twins, world champions in 1991, saw their pitching staff unravel early on. How fast they can turn it around could ride on such youngsters as shortstop Pat Meares, outfielder David McCarty and pitchers Mike Trombley and Pat Mahomes.

The A's went from first to worst, despite three promising rookies—Brent Gates, Craig Paquette and Troy Neel. If Oakland can find more pitching, it has a nucleus to build from.

FINAL STANDINGS

Team	W	L	Pct.	GB
Chicago	94	68	.580	-
Texas	86	76	.531	8
Kansas City	84	78	.519	10
Seattle	82	80	.506	12
California	71	91	.438	23
Minnesota	71	91	.438	23
Oakland	68	94	.420	26

—by Tim Wendel

Final results for the top vote-getters in the 1993 All-Star balloting:

▸**Catcher:** 1, Darren Daulton, Philadelphia, 2,061,255. 2, Benito Santiago, Florida, 1,227,232. 3, Mike Piazza, Los Angeles, 644,823. 4, Joe Girardi, Colorado, 476,340. 5, Don Slaught, Pittsburgh, 470,113.

▸**First base:** 1, John Kruk, Philadelphia, 1,200,219. 2, Fred McGriff, San Diego, 1,080,347. 3, Will Clark, San Francisco, 992,420. 4, Andres Galarraga, Colorado, 778,562. 5, Jeff Bagwell, Houston, 769,730.

▸**Second base:** 1, Ryne Sandberg, Chicago, 1,770,559. 2, Delino DeShields, Montreal, 1,259,713. 3, Craig Biggio, Houston, 744,885. 4, Bip Roberts, Cincinnati, 522,789. 5, Mark Lemke, Atlanta, 486,548.

▸**Shortstop:** 1, Barry Larkin, Cincinnati, 1,259,939. 2, Ozzie Smith, St. Louis, 1,147,552. 3, Jeff Blauser, Atlanta, 796,981. 4, Jay Bell, Pittsburgh, 529,292. 5, Craig Shipley, San Diego, 454,874.

▸**Third base:** 1, Gary Sheffield, Florida, 1,512,548. 2, Matt Williams, San Francisco, 1,063,392. 3, Terry Pendleton, Atlanta, 910,977. 4, Dave Hollins, Philadelphia, 673,537. 5, Chris Sabo, Cincinnati, 484,707.

▸**Outfield:** 1, Barry Bonds, San Francisco, 3,074,603. 2, Andy Van Slyke, Pittsburgh, 1,125,615. 3, David Justice, Atlanta, 1,056,324. 4, Len Dykstra, Philadelphia, 838,406. 5, Darryl Strawberry, Los Angeles, 816,148. 6, Derek Bell, San Diego, 806,954. 7, Tony Gwynn, San Diego, 757,154. 8, Ron Gant, Atlanta, 694,542. 9, Larry Walker, Montreal, 654,789. 10, Bobby Bonilla, New York, 634,658. 11, Willie McGee, San Francisco, 630,854. 12, Moises Alou, Montreal, 577,854. 13, Alex Cole, Colorado, 531,083. 14, Jeff Conine, Florida, 528,874. 15, Marquis Grissom, Montreal, 521,548.

Randy Johnson, the Mariners' powerful left-hander, was leading the league in strikeouts at the All-Star break.

by H. Darr Beiser, USA TODAY

Powerful AL pitchers ruin NL All-Star hopes—again

Better known as the land of Cecil, Cal, Griffey, Gonzalez and the Big Hurt, the American League struck a blow for its forgotten pitchers at the 64th All-Star Game in Baltimore.

Although the National League took a 2-0 lead in the first inning—the first time the senior circuit has led in All-Star play since the first inning in 1991—the AL pitching staff clamped down on them to gain a 9-3 victory.

"It felt nice to be front and center," said the White Sox's Jack McDowell, the game's winning pitcher. "We're often overshadowed by all the power guys we have in our league. But we have some great pitchers over here. We have to because we face some awesome lineups on a regular basis."

California's Mark Langston, the AL's starting pitcher, got in early trouble when he served up a two-run homer to the Marlins' Gary Sheffield in the first inning. But he then set a trend that the other AL pitchers built upon.

"I knew that if I could hold them right there, we would be all right," Langston said. "I had some great guys following me."

Following Langston to the mound was the Mariners' Randy Johnson—all 6-10 of him. He became the first pitcher to go two perfect innings in All-Star competition since Bret Saberhagen did it for the AL in 1990.

Still, Johnson's perfection had an occasional flaw. With the left-handed-hitting John Kruk at the plate, Johnson uncorked a ball that sailed over Kruk's head, well above catcher Ivan Rodriguez's glove.

"It's a bit humid out there and I think the ball just got away," Johnson said. "But John has the type of personality, I think, that he didn't think anything of it . . ."

Kruk jokingly said he should have turned around and batted right-handed, as the surest way to survive. But with a grim smile, he stayed on the left side, only to strike out for the final out. With the inning over, Kruk bowed, as if to say he gave up. That drew a smile from Johnson.

"If I could get all the batters that intimidated, I would have a lot better record," said Johnson, who came into the game with 10 victories and a league-high 171 strikeouts.

With Johnson doing the job, the AL tied the game on solo home runs by All-Star MVP Kirby Puckett and Roberto Alomar, the first Blue Jay to homer in an All-Star Game (third inning, off Andy Benes).

With the game 2-2, McDowell followed Johnson and continued the AL's dominance on the mound. Puckett drove in his second run of the game as the AL picked up three runs in the fifth inning, giving McDowell a 5-2 lead. Even though the NL got a run back in the top of the sixth inning, the AL added three more in the bottom as its second team (Cecil Fielder, Albert Belle, Carlos Baerga) got into the act.

The second team was also helped by two wild pitches from John Smoltz. The NL soon unraveled on the way to its sixth consecutive All-Star Game loss.

With the mounting lead, AL manager Cito Gaston turned to the Yankees' Jimmy Key for one inning and then he started rolling out his impressive line of closers—the Royals' Jeff Montgomery, the Twins' Rick Aguilera and the Blue Jays' Duane Ward.

Fans fight for bits of history

Mark Pallack didn't bring a glove when he attended the All-Star workout day July 12. But that didn't stop him from making the catch of his life. The 17-year-old from Westminster, Md., snared the Ken Griffey Jr. blast that hit the B&O Warehouse, the first ball ever to kiss the structure that lies beyond the right-field fence at Camden Yards.

"I just looked up and there it was," Pallack said. "It glanced off the wall and I went for it."

Pallack successfully eluded a mob scene that chased every home run ball bounding onto the flagpost area

American League: Top vote-getters

Final results for the top vote-getters in the 1993 All-Star balloting:

▸**Catcher:** 1, Ivan Rodriguez, Texas, 1,380,005. 2, Sandy Alomar, Cleveland, 969,583. 3, Pat Borders, Toronto, 902,570. 4, Mickey Tettleton, Detroit, 693,218. 5, Brian Harper, Minnesota, 670,089.

▸**First base:** 1, John Olerud, Toronto, 1,285,334. 2, Cecil Fielder, Detroit, 946,792. 3, Mark McGwire, Oakland, 853,409. 4, Frank Thomas, Chicago, 727,796. 5, J.T. Snow, California, 559,232.

▸**Second base:** 1, Roberto Alomar, Toronto, 1,852,280. 2, Carlos Baerga, Cleveland, 858,381. 3, Chuck Knoblauch, Minnesota, 729,687. 4, Bill Ripken, Texas, 559,353. 5, Steve Sax, Chicago, 517,692.

▸**Shortstop:** 1, Cal Ripken, Baltimore, 2,077,482. 2, Travis Fryman, Detroit, 848,610. 3, Ozzie Guillen, Chicago, 499,590. 4, Tony Fernandez, Toronto, 495,127. 5, Dick Schofield, Toronto, 434,847.

▸**Third base:** 1, Wade Boggs, New York, 1,523,805. 2, Robin Ventura, Chicago, 920,007. 3, Dean Palmer, Texas, 870,293. 4, Ed Sprague, Toronto, 670,397. 5, Edgar Martinez, Seattle, 524,132.

▸**Outfield:** 1, Ken Griffey, Seattle, 2,696,918. 2, Kirby Puckett, Minnesota, 2,362,551. 3, Joe Carter, Toronto, 1,407,179. 4, Albert Belle, Cleveland, 999,730. 5, Dave Winfield, Minnesota, 973,495. 6, Jose Canseco, Texas, 922,919. 7, Juan Gonzalez, Texas, 899,539. 8, Devon White, Toronto, 847,993. 9, Rickey Henderson, Oakland, 602,429. 10, Kirk Gibson, Detroit, 489,369. 11, Kenny Lofton, Cleveland, 469,922. 12, Shane Mack, Minnesota, 390,828. 13, Andre Dawson, Boston, 390,006. 14, Brady Anderson, Baltimore, 374,509. 15, Rob Deer, Detroit, 371,053.

All-Star Game: NL box score

Nationals 2 0 0 0 0 1 0 0 0 -3
Americans 0 1 1 0 3 3 1 0 x -9

Batter	ab	r	h	bi	lo	bb	so	avg
Grissom,cf	3	0	0	0	2	0	1	.000
Kelly,cf	1	0	0	0	0	0	1	.000
Bonds,lf	3	2	2	0	0	0	0	.667
Bonilla,lf	1	0	1	0	0	0	0	1.000
Sheffield,3b	3	1	2	2	0	0	0	.667
Hollins,3b	1	0	1	0	0	0	0	1.000
Kruk,1b	3	0	0	0	2	0	2	.000
Galarraga,1b	1	0	0	0	2	0	0	.000
Larkin,ss	2	0	0	1	0	0	1	.000
Blauser,ss	1	0	0	0	2	0	1	.000
Grace,dh	3	0	0	0	1	0	0	.000
Jefferies,ph	1	0	0	0	0	0	1	.000
Justice,rf	3	0	1	0	0	0	0	.333
Gwynn,rf	1	0	0	0	0	0	0	.000
Daulton,c	3	0	0	0	0	0	1	.000
Piazza,c	1	0	0	0	0	0	1	.000
Sandberg,2b	1	0	0	0	0	1	0	.000
Bell,2b	1	0	0	0	0	0	0	.000
Totals	**33**	**3**	**7**	**3**	**9**	**1**	**9**	

▶**BATTING**—2B: Bonds (2, off Langston; off Key); Hollins (1, off Aguilera). HR: Sheffield (1, 1st inning off Langston, 1 on, 1 out). RBI, scoring position, less than 2 outs: Sheffield 1-1, Kruk 0-1, Galarraga 0-2, Larkin 1-1. SF: Larkin.
▶**BASERUNNING**—Team LOB: 5.
▶**FIELDING**—E: Blauser (1, ground ball); Justice (1, mishandled base hit). Outfield assist: Kelly (Steinbach at 3B).

Pitcher	ip	h	r	er	bb	so	era
Mulholland	2	1	1	1	2	0	4.50
Benes	2	2	1	1	0	2	4.50
Burkett L	.2	4	3	3	0	1	40.50
Avery	1	1	3	0	1	1	0.00
Smoltz	.1	0	0	0	1	0	0.00
Beck	1	2	1	1	0	1	9.00
Harvey	1	1	0	0	0	2	0.00
Totals	**8**	**11**	**9**	**6**	**4**	**7**	**6.75**

and the Eutaw Street pedestrian mall beyond the right-field scoreboard.

Early on, the big boppers from both leagues served notice that everybody—no matter where they were sitting—had to be heads up. Frank Thomas belted one into the second deck in left field—the first ever to do so. During the Home Run Derby, Ken Griffey, David Justice and Bobby Bonilla created a series of mad fan scrambles out on Eutaw Street between the stands and the warehouse. Justice barely missed being the first to hit the B&O Warehouse, hitting a soda machine 5 feet short of the wall. Stephen Diglas of San Francisco came up with the ball and almost got injured in the process. After he latched onto the ball, he was dogpiled by about 10 fans, all digging for the ball.

"Somebody tried to rip my face off," Diglas said. "I got a finger in the mouth and bit it. Then I started yelling, 'I got it, I got it.' "

Dodgers rookie on cloud nine

One player who couldn't believe he was standing in the NL locker room was Mike Piazza, the first rookie catcher to make the NL team since Gary Carter in 1975, and the first rookie—period—to be selected since Steve Sax in 1982.

"I have no comprehension at all about what I am doing here," Piazza said. "I'm walking on cloud nine. As a young kid I always watched the All-Star Game, and I'm going to go around and ask for autographs later. I'm looking forward to talking with everybody."

While he was talking, former All-Star Steve Garvey came up and asked Piazza for his autograph.

"I'm trying to pick my jaw off the floor," Piazza said.

Johnson on assignment

Seattle Mariners' pitcher Randy Johnson was busy during the workout day. Armed with a zoom lens, he was shooting a photo essay for *Mariners Magazine* and *This Week in Baseball*.

"They're putting me to work," he said.

Big Daddy's bat too big

Maybe you get used to it when your dad is Cecil Fielder, but the quiet kid in the AL clubhouse was living every youngster's dream the day before the All-Star Game. There was Prince Fielder, 9, just hanging out at Frank Thomas' locker having a little chat. Then came a request to pose with Dad at his locker for photos. And some unsolicited advice from Roberto Alomar: "Can you hit?"

(A nod of the head from Prince.)

"Can you hit the long ball like your dad?"

(A solemn shake of his head as if to say nobody can.)

"Can you run quick?"

(Another shake.)

"You better hit the long ball then."

Ruthian ribbies, no stogies

Despite leading the majors in RBI for three years in a row, the Tigers' Fielder dismisses talk that he's the next Babe Ruth.

"I don't chew cigars," Fielder says. "I don't swallow cigars."

At the All-Star break, Fielder had 77 RBI, again tops in the league, and he had played in 86 of Detroit's 88 games.

"I don't run fast enough to pull anything," says Fielder, explaining his longevity. "There have been days where I felt bad. But when I take a day off I feel bad the next day anyway."

Fielder sticks to a basic hitting strategy. "I look for that first pitch to hit," he said. "(The pitchers) usually try to get ahead. So, I'm ready."

Van Slyke loved the park

Even though he couldn't play in the game because of a broken collarbone, Andy Van Slyke showed up anyway. He loved the Orioles' ballpark so much, he said he thought everyone should have one like it.

"If I were commissioner, I would tell every team they had to build a new ballpark like this, except for the Cubs because they've already got it," Van Slyke said. "When you look at this place compared to Three Rivers, you can have seven rivers coming to a point and it wouldn't help our place."

Van Slyke, who was the subject of trade rumors because of the Pirates' financial condition, said he would love to play in Camden Yards someday.

Van Slyke said he liked the way the stadium was constructed, with seats close to the field and real grass instead of artificial turf.

"I like things that grow—grass, children, flowers,

All Star Game: AL box Score

Nationals 2 0 0 0 0 1 0 0 0 -3
Americans 0 1 1 0 3 3 1 0 x -9

Batter	ab	r	h	bi	lo	bb	so	avg
Alomar,2b	3	1	1	1	0	0	0	.333
Baerga,2b	2	1	0	0	0	0	1	.000
Molitor,dh	1	0	0	0	0	1	0	.000
Belle,ph-dh	1	2	1	1	0	1	0	1.000
Thomas,ph-dh	1	0	1	0	0	0	0	1.000
Griffey Jr,cf	3	1	1	1	0	0	1	.333
White,cf	2	1	1	1	1	0	0	.500
Carter,rf	3	0	1	0	2	0	1	.333
Gonzalez,rf	1	0	0	0	1	1	1	.000
Olerud,1b	2	0	0	0	1	0	0	.000
Fielder,1b	1	0	0	0	1	0	0	.000
Puckett,lf	3	1	2	2	0	0	0	.667
Vaughn,lf	1	1	1	0	0	0	0	1.000
Ripken,ss	3	0	0	0	2	0	1	.000
Fryman,ss	1	0	0	0	1	0	0	.000
Boggs,3b	1	0	0	0	0	1	0	.000
Cooper,3b	2	0	0	0	1	0	1	.000
Rodriguez,c	2	1	1	0	0	0	0	.500
Steinbach,c	2	0	1	1	0	0	1	.500
Totals	35	9	11	7	11	4	7	

▶ **BATTING**—2B: White (1, off Avery); Puckett (1, off Burkett); Rodriguez (1, off Burkett); Steinbach (1, off Beck). HR: Alomar (1, 3rd inning off Benes, 0 on, 0 out); Puckett (1, 2nd inning off Mulholland, 0 on, 1 out). 2-out RBI: Steinbach, White, Puckett. RBI, scoring position, less than 2 outs: Alomar 0-1, Belle 1-1, Griffey Jr 1-1, Carter 0-1.

▶ **BASERUNNING**—SB: White (1, 2nd base off Harvey/Piazza). **Team LOB:** 7.

Pitcher	ip	h	r	er	bb	so	era
Langston	2	3	2	2	1	2	9.00
Johnson	2	0	0	0	0	1	0.00
McDowell,W	1	0	0	0	0	0	0.00
Key,H,1	1	2	1	1	0	1	9.00
Montgomery	1	0	0	0	0	1	0.00
Aguilera	1	2	0	0	0	2	0.00
Ward	1	0	0	0	0	2	0.00
Totals	9	7	3	3	1	9	3.00

by Porter Binks, USA Today

MVP Puckett quiets doubters

In a repeat of the '92 award, the All-Star Game's MVP was a member of the last-place team in the American League West at the time. In '92, last-place Seattle's Ken Griffey Jr. was MVP.

Kirby Puckett became the first Minnesota Twins player to win the award. His solo home run in the second inning and RBI double in the fifth delivered the decisive runs in the American League's victory. (Puckett was the first Twin to hit a home run in the All-Star Game since Harmon Killebrew in 1971).

This was Puckett's eighth All-Star Game. He had gone 4-for-16 coming into the game—all singles with no RBI.

"I had no idea I had no extra-base hits," Puckett said. "It took me eight years to do it; I guess it's a relief."

A perennial fan favorite, Puckett was voted to the AL starting lineup despite not having one of his better years. At the break, he was hitting .298, with 11 home runs and 50 RBI.

"A lot of people say I should not be here because my numbers are down," he said, "but I went out and played hard every day. The numbers might not have indicated the way things are going."

things like that," he said. "This park brings back a time of purity and innocence, which the game once had and is trying desperately to hold on to."

And that ain't even peanuts

The All-Star Game menu for fans included:
▸ 23,500 hot dogs or sausages
▸ 3,000 crabcakes
▸ 80,000 ice cubes
▸ 1,000 pounds of popcorn
▸ 1,750 six-inch pizzas
▸ 1,400 pounds of barbecued beef
▸ 3,250 gallons of soft drinks

Between the lines

▸ Catch o' the day: A fifth-inning drive by Texas catcher Ivan Rodriguez hit the fence and wedged in a crease, resulting in a startled left fielder (Barry Bonds) and a ground-rule double. Rodriguez then scored on a single by Albert Belle.

▸ Home Run Derby: It was the first time in All-Star Game history the teams hit home runs in each of the first three innings.

▸ Mr. Versatility: Paul Molitor, the AL's designated hitter, became the second player in All-Star Game history to play five different positions. He has played DH, second base (1988), third base (1985, '91), center field (1985) and first base (1992). Molitor joined Pete Rose (left and right field, first, second and third base in 16 All-Star Games), as the only players to claim that distinction.

▸ Southpaw starters: The game, with Terry Mulholland starting against Mark Langston, marked the first time two left-handed pitchers had started an All-Star game since 1961, when the starters were Whitey Ford and Warren Spahn. It was the sixth matchup of left-handers in the 64 All-Star Games.

—1993 All-Star Game coverage was compiled by Paul White, Tim Wendel, Rob Rains, Rick Lawes, and Pete Williams.

American League leaders final 1993 statistics

Batting

BATTING AVERAGE	G	AB	R	H	AVG
Olerud, Tor	158	551	109	200	.363
Molitor, Tor	160	636	121	211	.332
Alomar, Tor	153	589	109	192	.326
Lofton, Clev	148	569	116	185	.325
Baerga, Clev	154	624	105	200	.321
Thomas, Chi	153	549	106	174	.317
Greenwell, Bos	146	540	77	170	.315
Phillips, Det	151	566	113	177	.313
O'Neill, NY	141	498	71	155	.311
Johnson, Chi	147	540	75	168	.311

HOME RUNS	
Gonzalez, Tex	46
Griffey, Sea	45
Thomas, Chi	41
Belle, Clev	38
Palmeiro, Tex	37
Carter, Tor	33
Palmer, Tex	33
Tettleton, Det	32
Salmon, Cal	31
Tartabull, NY	31

RUNS BATTED IN	
Belle, Clev	129
Thomas, Chi	128
Carter, Tor	121
Gonzalez, Tex	118
Fielder, Det	117
Baerga, Clev	114
Davis, Cal	112
Molitor, Tor	111
Tettleton, Det	110
Griffey, Sea	109

STOLEN BASES	
Lofton, Clev	70
Alomar, Tor	55
Polonia, Cal	55
Henderson, Tor	53
Curtis, Cal	48
Johnson, Chi	35
White, Tor	34
Jose, KC	31
Hulse, Tex	29
Knoblauch, Minn	29

SLUGGING PCT.	
Gonzalez, Tex	.632
Griffey, Sea	.617
Thomas, Chi	.607
Olerud, Tor	.599
Hoiles, Balt	.585
Palmeiro, Tex	.554
Belle, Clev	.552
Salmon, Cal	.536
Vaughn, Bos	.525
Molitor, Tor	.509

RUNS	
Palmeiro, Tex	124
Molitor, Tor	121
Lofton, Clev	116
White, Tor	116
Henderson, Tor	114
Griffey, Sea	113
Phillips, Det	113
Alomar, Tor	109
Olerud, Tor	109
Thomas, Chi	106

HITS	
Molitor, Tor	211
Baerga, Clev	200
Olerud, Tor	200
Alomar, Tor	192
Lofton, Clev	185
Puckett, Minn	184
Fryman, Det	182
Griffey, Sea	180
McRae, KC	177
Phillips, Det	177

WALKS	
Phillips, Det	132
Henderson, Tor	120
Olerud, Tor	114
Thomas, Chi	112
Tettleton, Det	109
Ventura, Chi	105
Buhner, Sea	100
Griffey, Sea	96
Tartabull, NY	92
Fielder, Det	90

DOUBLES	
Olerud, Tor	54
White, Tor	42
Palmeiro, Tex	40
Valentin, Bos	40
Puckett, Minn	39
Greenwell, Bos	38
Griffey, Sea	38
Surhoff, Mil	38
Fryman, Det	37
Molitor, Tor	37

TRIPLES	
Johnson, Chi	14
Cora, Chi	13
Hulse, Tex	10
Fernandez, Tor	9
McRae, KC	9
Anderson, Balt	8
Lofton, Clev	8
Cuyler, Det	7

ON-BASE PCT.	
Olerud, Tor	.473
Phillips, Det	.443
Henderson, Tor	.432
Thomas, Chi	.426
Hoiles, Balt	.416
Griffey, Sea	.408
Alomar, Tor	.408
Lofton, Clev	.408
Molitor, Tor	.402
Vaughn, Bos	.390

TOTAL BASES	
Griffey, Sea	359
Gonzalez, Tex	339
Thomas, Ch	333
Palmeiro, Tex	331
Olerud, Tor	330
Belle, Clev	328
Molitor, Tor	324
Baerga, Clev	303

Pitching

VICTORIES	
McDowell, Chi	22-10
Johnson, Sea	19-8
Hentgen, Tor	19-9
Key, NY	18-6
Appier, KC	18-8
Fernandez, Chi	18-9
Rogers, Tex	16-10
Langston, Cal	16-11
Finley, Cal	16-14
Eldred, Mil	16-16

ERA	
Appier, KC	2.56
Alvarez, Chi	2.95
Key, NY	3.00
Fernandez, Chi	3.13
Viola, Bos	3.14
Finley, Cal	3.15
Langston, Cal	3.20
Johnson, Sea	3.24
Darwin, Bos	3.26
Cone, KC	3.33

GAMES	
Harris, Bos	80
Radinsky, Chi	73
Fossas, Bos	71
Nelson, Sea	71
D. Ward, Tor	71
Frohwirth, Balt	70
Hernandez, Chi	70
Plunk, Clev	70
Montgomery, KC	69
MacDonald, Det	68

SAVES	
Montgomery, KC	45
D. Ward, Tor	45
Henke, Tex	40
Hernandez, Chi	38
Eckersley, Oak	36
Aguilera, Minn	34
Russell, Bos	33
Olson, Balt	29
Farr, NY	25
Henneman, Det	24

INNINGS	
Eldred, Mil	258.0
McDowell, Chi	256.2
Langston, Cal	256.1
Johnson, Sea	255.1
Cone, KC	254.0
Finley, Cal	251.1
Fernandez, Chi	247.1
Appier, KC	238.2
Key, NY	236.2
Brown, Tex	233.0

STRIKEOUTS	
Johnson, Sea	308
Langston, Cal	196
Guzman, Tor	194
Cone, KC	191
Finley, Cal	187
Appier, KC	186
Eldred, Mil	180
Key, NY	173
McDonald, Balt	171
Fernandez, Chi	169

COMP. GAMES	
Finley, Cal	13
Brown, Tex	12
Johnson, Sea	10
McDowell, Chi	10
Eldred, Mil	8
Hanson, Sea	7
Langston, Cal	7
McDonald, Balt	7
Cone, KC	6

SHUTOUTS	
McDowell, Chi	4
Brown, Tex	3
Johnson, Sea	3
Moore, Det	3
Doherty, Det	2
Finley, Cal	2
Key, NY	2
Mussina, Balt	2
Valenzuela, Balt	2

National League leaders final 1993 statistics

Batting

BATTING AVERAGE	G	AB	R	H	AVG
Galarraga, Col	120	470	71	174	.370
Gwynn, SD	122	489	70	175	.358
Jefferies, StL	142	544	89	186	.342
Bonds, SF	159	539	129	181	.336
Grace, Chi	155	594	86	193	.325
Bagwell, Hou	142	535	76	171	.320
Piazza, LA	149	547	81	174	.318
Kruk, Phil	150	535	100	169	.316
Merced, Pitt	137	447	68	140	.313
Thompson, SF	128	494	85	154	.312

HOME RUNS

Bonds, SF	46
Justice, Atl	40
Williams, SF	38
McGriff, Atl	37
Gant, Atl	36
Piazza, LA	35
Bonilla, NY	34
Plantier, SD	34

RUNS BATTED IN

Bonds, SF	123
Justice, Atl	120
Gant, Atl	117
Piazza, LA	112
Williams, SF	110
Daulton, Phil	105
Zeile, StL	103
McGriff, Atl	101
Murray, NY	100
Plantier, SD	100

STOLEN BASES

Carr, Fla	58
Grissom, Mtl	53
Nixon, Atl	47
Jefferies, StL	46
Lewis, SF	46
DeShields, Mtl	43
E. Young, Col	42
Butler, LA	39
Coleman, NY	38
Dykstra, Phil	37

SLUGGING PCT.

Bonds, SF	.677
Galarraga, Col	.602
Williams, SF	.561
Piazza, LA	.561
McGriff, Atl	.549
Bichette, Col	.526
Bonilla, NY	.522
Hayes, Col	.522
Bagwell, Hou	.516
Justice, Atl	.515

RUNS

Dykstra, Phil	143
Bonds, SF	129
Gant, Atl	113
McGriff, Atl	111
Blauser, Atl	110
Williams, SF	105
Grissom, Mtl	104
Hollins, Phil	104
Bell, Pitt	102
Kruk, Phil	100

HITS

Dykstra, Phil	194
Grace, Chi	193
Grissom, Mtl	188
Bell, Pitt	187
Jefferies, StL	186
Blauser, Atl	182
Bonds, SF	181
Butler, LA	181
King, Pitt	180

WALKS

Dykstra, Phil	129
Bonds, SF	126
Daulton, Phil	117
Kruk, Phil	111
Butler, LA	86
Blauser, Atl	85
Hollins, Phil	85
Lankford, StL	81
Walker, Mtl	80
Weiss, Fla	79

DOUBLES

Hayes, Col	45
Dykstra, Phil	44
Bichette, Col	43
Biggio, Hou	41
Gwynn, SD	41
Gilkey, StL	40
Grace, Chi	39
Bonds, SF	38
Bagwell, Hou	37
Zeile, StL	36

TRIPLES

Finley, Hou	13
Butler, LA	10
Bell, Pitt	9
Morandini, Phil	9
Coleman, NY	8
Martin, Pitt	8
E. Young, Col	8

ON-BASE PCT.

Bonds, SF	.458
Kruk, Phil	.430
Dykstra, Phil	.420
Merced, Pitt	.414
Jefferies, StL	.408
Galarraga, Col	.403
Blauser, Atl	.401
Gwynn, SD	.398
Grace, Chi	.393
Daulton, Phil	.392

TOTAL BASES

Bonds, SF	365
Williams, SF	325
Gant, Atl	309
Dykstra, Phil	307
Piazza, LA	307
McGriff, Atl	306
Justice, Atl	301
Hayes, Col	299
Sosa, Chi	290
Biggio, Hou	289

Pitching

VICTORIES

Glavine, Atl	22-6
Burkett, SF	22-7
Swift, SF	21-8
Maddux, Atl	20-10
Portugal, Hou	18-4
Avery, Atl	18-6
Tewksbury, StL	17-10
Greene, Phil	16-4
Schilling, Phil	16-7
Harnisch, Hou	16-9

ERA

Maddux, Atl	2.36
Rijo, Cin	2.48
Portugal, Hou	2.77
Swift, SF	2.82
Avery, Atl	2.94
Harnisch, Hou	2.98
Candiotti, LA	3.12
Glavine, Atl	3.20
Hill, Mtl	3.23
Mulholland, Phil	3.25

GAMES

Jackson, SF	81
Beck, SF	76
West, Phil	76
McMichael, Atl	74
Murphy, StL	73
Myers, Chi	73
Hernandez, Hou	72
D. Jones, Hou	71

SAVES

Myers, Chi	53
Beck, SF	48
Harvey, Fla	45
L. Smith, StL	43
Wetteland, Mtl	43
Mit. Williams, Phil	43
Stanton, Atl	27
D. Jones, Hou	26
Gott, LA	25
Holmes, Col	25

INNINGS

Maddux, Atl	267.0
Rijo, Cin	257.1
Smoltz, Atl	243.2
Glavine, Atl	239.1
Drabek, Hou	237.2
Schilling, Phil	235.1
Swift, SF	232.2
Burkett, SF	231.2
Benes, SD	230.2
Harris, Col	225.1

STRIKEOUTS

Rijo, Cin	227
Smoltz, Atl	208
Maddux, Atl	197
Schilling, Phil	186
Harnisch, Hou	185
Benes, SD	179
Greene, Phil	167
Guzman, Chi	163
Drabek, Hou	157
Swift, SF	157

COMP. GAMES

Maddux, Atl	8
Drabek, Hou	7
Gooden, NY	7
Greene, Phil	7
Mulholland, Phil	7
Schilling, Phil	7

SHUTOUTS

Harnisch, Hou	4
R. Martinez, LA	3

Postseason

▸ **NLCS and ALCS**
game descriptions and
composite box scores

▸ **World Series**
game-by-game wrapups
and box scores

▸ *and more . . .*

USA SNAPSHOTS®

A look at statistics that shape the sports world

Highs, lows of baseball tickets

HIGHEST AVERAGE

TORONTO BLUE JAYS — GAME TIME 7:05 PM — $13.73[1]

NEW YORK YANKEES — GAME TIME 7:05 PM — $13.48

LOWEST AVERAGE

CINCINNATI REDS — $7.95

COLORADO ROCKIES — $7.91

1 – U.S. dollars

Source: Team Marketing Report   By Marty Baumann, USA TODAY

National League Championship Series: Philadelphia Phillies 4, Atlanta Braves 2

by Tim Dillon, USA TODAY

Curt Schilling was named MVP of the NLCS, even though he didn't actually win a decision.

MVP Schilling set up Phillies' NLCS victory

Curt Schilling won the MVP for the NL Championship Series without getting a victory to his credit, but his strong performances in Games 1 and 5 allowed the Phillies to prevail in the end. He gave up just three earned runs and struck out 19 batters in 16 innings.

Even the hockey fans love Schilling in Philly

Curt Schilling's stellar performance apparently earned a place in all Philly sports fans' hearts:

"I went to the Flyers game (during the NLCS) and they gave me a standing ovation. I wasn't ready for that," Schilling said. "I kind of waved, and (the applause) grew louder. Then, I stood up, and they went nuts."

Schilling went nuts too—for hockey—after seeing his first game. He now plans to attend more Flyers games.

—by Rachel Shuster

Game 1: Phils 4, Braves 3

Late-inning substitute Kim Batiste went from goat to hero in the 10th. After throwing a sure out into the outfield, Batiste made up for the error with an RBI single off Greg McMichael in the bottom of the inning. Curt Schilling had a strong start, giving up only two earned runs on seven hits in eight innings, while striking out 10. Pete Incaviglia went 2-for-4 with a home run for the Phillies, while Otis Nixon and Atlanta starter Steve Avery were the only Braves with multi-hit games. **W-Mitch Williams, 1-0. L-McMichael, 0-1.**

Game 2: Braves 14, Phils 3

The Braves bats awakened, as four Atlanta hitters chalked up home runs, led by Fred McGriff's blast in the first inning. The Braves blew the game open in the third inning, scoring six runs—three on Damon Berryhill's home run. Phillies' starter Tommy Greene was uncharacteristically chased after only 2 1/3 innings. McGriff finished the game 3-for-5 with a pair of RBI and two runs scored, while leadoff Nixon went 3-for-4 with two runs and two RBI. Terry Pendleton (3-for-5, three RBI, two runs) and Blauser (2-for-5, one RBI, one run) also homered for Atlanta. **W-Maddux, 1-0. L-Greene, 0-1.**

Game 3: Braves 9, Phils 4

McGriff and Pendleton kept the pressure on, combining to go 4-for-8 with four runs and three RBI. Tom Glavine earned his first career NLCS win, going seven innings, allowing only two earned runs and striking out five. John Kruk led the Phillies offense, hitting a triple and homer off Glavine, driving in three runs. Mariano Duncan, playing second base for the Phillies, hit a pair of triples. McMichael, Atlanta's closer at the end of the regular season, continued to struggle, giving up three hits and a run in one inning of relief. **W-Glavine, 1-0. L-Mulholland, 0-1.**

Game 4: Phils 2, Braves 1

Danny Jackson turned in a strong performance, going 7 2/3 innings and giving up only one run. The Phillies got all the scoring they needed in the fourth inning, when Jackson singled in Milt Thompson, and Kevin Stocker drove in Darren Daulton. McGriff (2-for-4, one run) was the lone bright spot at the plate for the Braves, as Gant (0-for-5) and Pendleton (1-for-4) struggled. John Smoltz pitched well, going 6 1/3 innings (10 strikeouts). **W-Jackson,1-0. L-Smoltz, 0-1. Sv-Mitch Williams (1).**

Game 5: Phils 4, Braves 3

The Phillies won the second extra-inning game of the series when Len Dykstra hit a 10th-inning solo homer off Mark Wohlers, and journeyman Larry Andersen struck out two of three Braves in the bottom of the inning. The Braves were held scoreless through eight innings by Schilling, who picked up nine strikeouts bringing his series total to 19. Atlanta tied the game in the ninth, when pinch-hitter Francisco Cabrera singled in McGriff. Williams finished with his second blown save and his second win of the series. **W-M. Williams, 2-0. L-Wohlers, 0-1. Sv-Andersen (1).**

Game 6: Phils 6, Braves 3

Phillies' starter Tommy Greene rebounded from a poor performance in Game 1, to win the clincher, going seven innings and giving up only three earned runs. The Phillies got plenty of offense—Mickey Morandini hit a two-run triple and Dave Hollins added a two-run home run. The big bats of Ron Gant (.185) and David Justice (.143) remained quiet as both batters went 0-for-4. The Phillies avoided the long-ball threat, walking McGriff three times. Jeff Blauser's two-run shot in the seventh off Greene brought the Braves back into the game, but Phils' reliever David West retired McGriff, Justice and Terry Pendleton in order, before Williams finished for his second save of the series.**W-Greene, 1-1. L-Maddux, 1-1. Sv-Mitch Williams (2).**

—game summaries compiled by Erik B. Arneson

Welcome to Kruk's world

On reliever Mitch Williams' habit of letting runners get on base:
"What can you do now? That's the way he is. I mean, they won't let me bring a gun out there and shoot him if he walks the first guy. . . . At least now I know when he comes in, someone's going to come down to first and I can talk to someone. I just hope the guy who leads off the inning is a nice guy and likes to talk."

On his personal appearance:
"I'd like to get a haircut and shave, but guys like Hollins and Daulton won't let me. They say, 'We'll kill you.' They were saying that I had to stay like this as long as we were in first place."

On the difference between playing on a good team and a bad team:
"When your team's real bad, you can do whatever you want (off the field). Then, all of a sudden you become good and you can't go anywhere. If you stop for a beer on the way home, you're there all night signing autographs. It's more fun off the field when you're bad, but it's a lot more fun on the field when you're good."

NLCS composite box score

▶**Double plays:** Atlanta 1, Philadelphia 2.

▶**Left on base:** Atlanta 47, Philadelphia 52.

▶**Stolen bases:** Morandini, Hollins.

▶**Caught Stealing:** Nixon 2, Gant.

▶**Sacrifices:** Belliard, Nixon 2, Maddux 2, Schilling, Greene 2.

▶**Sacrifice flies:** Justice 2, Stocker, Chamberlain.

▶**Intentional walks:** off Avery 3 (Stocker, Daulton, Chamberlain); off Wohlers (Thompson); off Maddux (Dykstra); off McMichael (Stocker); off Andersen (McGriff).

▶**Hit by pitch:** by Jackson (Olson).

▶**Passed balls:** Daulton 2.

▶**Official scorers:** Bob Kenney, Nick Peters and Paul Newberry.

▶**Times:** Game 1, 3:33; Game 2, 3:14; Game 3, 2:44; Game 4, 3:33; Game 5, 3:21; Game 6, 3:04.

▶**Attendance:** Game 1 at Philadelphia, 62,012; Game 2 at Philadelphia, 62,436; Game 3 at Atlanta, 52,032; Game 4 at Atlanta, 52,032; Game 5 at Atlanta, 52,032; Game 6 at Philadelphia, 63,502.

38

ATLANTA BRAVES BATTING

Player	G	AB	R	H	2B	3B	HR	RBI	SO	BB	Avg.	PO	A	E	Pct.
Bream 1b	1	1	1	1	0	0	0	0	0	0	1.000	1	0	0	1.000
Cabrera ph-c	3	3	0	2	0	0	0	1	1	0	.667	1	0	0	1.000
Avery p	2	4	1	2	1	0	0	0	1	0	.500	0	2	0	1.000
McGriff 1b	6	23	6	10	2	0	1	4	7	4	.435	50	3	0	1.000
Nixon cf	6	23	3	8	2	0	0	4	6	5	.348	13	0	0	1.000
Pendleton 3b	6	26	4	9	1	0	1	5	2	0	.346	7	5	0	1.000
Olson c	2	3	0	1	1	0	0	0	1	0	.333	10	0	0	1.000
Pecota ph	4	3	1	1	0	0	0	0	1	1	.333	0	0	0	—
Blauser ss	6	25	5	7	1	0	2	4	7	4	.280	6	14	0	1.000
Maddux p	2	4	1	1	0	0	0	0	1	0	.250	3	5	1	.889
Berryhill c	6	19	2	4	0	0	1	3	5	1	.211	42	0	0	1.000
Lemke 2b	6	24	2	5	2	0	0	4	6	1	.208	6	19	2	.926
Gant lf	6	27	4	5	3	0	0	3	9	2	.185	10	1	1	.917
Justice rf	6	21	2	3	1	0	0	4	3	3	.143	14	0	1	.933
Glavine p	1	3	0	0	0	0	0	0	0	0	.000	0	3	0	1.000
Sanders ph-cf-pr	5	3	0	0	0	0	0	0	1	0	.000	0	0	0	—
Belliard ph-2b-ss	2	1	1	0	0	0	0	0	1	0	.000	0	0	0	—
Smoltz p	1	1	0	0	0	0	0	0	1	1	.000	0	0	0	—
Tarasco pr-lf-rf	2	1	0	0	0	0	0	0	1	0	.000	0	0	0	—
McMichael p	4	0	0	0	0	0	0	0	0	0	—	0	1	0	1.000
Totals	6	215	33	59	14	0	5	32	54	22	.274	163	53	5	.977

PHILADELPHIA PHILLIES BATTING

Player	G	AB	R	H	2B	3B	HR	RBI	SO	BB	Avg.	PO	A	E	Pct.
Batiste 3b	4	1	0	1	0	0	0	1	0	0	1.000	2	0	2	.500
Chamberlain rf-ph	4	11	1	4	3	0	0	1	3	1	.364	2	2	0	1.000
Dykstra cf	6	25	5	7	1	0	2	2	8	5	.280	13	0	0	1.000
Duncan 2b	3	15	3	4	0	2	0	0	5	0	.267	5	6	1	.917
Daulton c	6	19	2	5	1	0	1	3	3	6	.263	54	3	0	1.000
Jackson p	1	4	0	1	0	0	0	1	3	0	.250	0	0	0	—
Kruk 1b	6	24	4	6	2	1	1	5	5	4	.250	43	2	0	1.000
Morandini 2b-ph	4	16	1	4	0	1	0	2	3	0	.250	8	9	1	.944
Thompson pr-lf-ph	6	13	2	3	1	0	0	0	2	1	.231	3	0	1	.889
Hollins 3b	6	20	2	4	1	0	2	4	4	5	.200	5	4	0	1.000
Stocker ss	6	22	0	4	1	0	0	1	5	2	.182	10	13	1	.958
Incaviglia lf	3	12	2	2	0	0	1	1	3	0	.167	8	0	0	1.000
Eisenreich rf-ph	6	15	0	2	1	0	0	1	2	0	.133	6	0	0	1.000
Schilling p	2	5	0	0	0	0	0	0	2	0	.000	0	0	0	—
Mulholland p	1	2	0	0	0	0	0	0	1	0	.000	0	2	0	1.000
Jordan ph	2	1	0	0	0	0	0	0	0	1	.000	0	0	0	—
Longmire ph	1	1	0	0	0	0	0	0	1	0	.000	0	0	0	—
Pratt c	1	1	0	0	0	0	0	0	1	0	.000	1	0	0	1.000
Greene p	2	0	1	0	0	0	0	0	0	1	.000	0	3	0	1.000
Andersen p	3	0	0	0	0	0	0	0	0	0	—	0	1	0	1.000
Mason p	2	0	0	0	0	0	0	0	0	0	—	0	0	0	—
Rivera p	1	0	0	0	0	0	0	0	0	0	—	0	0	0	—
Thigpen p	2	0	0	0	0	0	0	0	0	0	—	0	0	0	—
West p	3	0	0	0	0	0	0	0	0	0	—	0	1	0	1.000
Williams p	4	0	0	0	0	0	0	0	0	0	—	0	1	1	.500
Totals	6	207	23	47	11	4	7	22	51	26	.227	165	47	7	.968

ATLANTA BRAVES PITCHING

Player	G	CG	IP	H	R	BB	SO	HB	WP	W	L	Sv	Pct.	ER	ERA
Smoltz	1	0	6.1	8	2	5	10	0	0	0	1	0	.000	0	0.00
Stanton	1	0	1	1	0	1	0	0	0	0	0	0	—	0	0.00
Mercker	5	0	5	3	1	2	4	0	0	0	0	0	—	1	1.80
Glavine	1	0	7	6	2	0	5	0	0	1	0	0	1.000	2	2.57
Avery	2	0	13	9	5	6	10	0	2	0	0	0	—	4	2.77
Wohlers	4	0	5.1	2	2	3	10	0	1	0	1	0	.000	2	3.38
Maddux	2	0	12.2	11	8	7	11	0	0	1	1	0	.500	7	4.97
McMichael	4	0	4	7	3	2	1	0	0	0	1	0	.000	3	6.75
Totals	6	0	54.1	47	23	26	51	0	3	2	4	0	.333	19	3.15

PHILADELPHIA PHILLIES PITCHING

Player	G	CG	IP	H	R	BB	SO	HB	WP	W	L	Sv	Pct.	ER	ERA
Mason	2	0	3	1	0	0	2	0	0	0	0	0	—	0	0.00
Jackson	1	0	7.2	9	1	2	6	1	0	1	0	0	1.000	1	1.17
Schilling	2	0	16	11	4	5	19	0	0	0	0	0	—	3	1.67
Williams	4	0	5.1	6	2	2	5	0	0	2	0	2	1.000	1	1.69
Rivera	1	0	2	1	1	1	2	0	0	0	0	0	—	1	4.50
Thigpen	2	0	1.2	1	1	1	2	0	0	0	0	0	—	1	5.40
Mulholland	1	0	5	9	5	1	2	0	0	0	1	0	.000	4	7.20
Greene	2	0	9.1	12	10	7	7	0	0	1	1	0	.500	10	9.64
West	3	0	2.2	5	5	2	5	0	0	0	0	0	—	4	13.50
Andersen	3	0	2.1	4	4	1	3	0	0	0	0	1	—	4	15.43
Totals	6	0	55.0	59	33	22	54	1	0	4	2	3	.667	29	4.75

American League Championship Series: Toronto Blue Jays 4, Chicago White Sox 2

by Anne Ryan, USA TODAY

Dave Stewart, whose playoffs record is now 8-0, was named MVP for the second time in his career.

Stewart seals MVP bid in game six

Dave Stewart sealed his MVP bid in Game 6 of the ALCS, giving up just two runs in the 6-3 victory that clinched the American League pennant for the Blue Jays, just as he had done for the Oakland A's in 1988, '89, and '90.

With a playoffs record of 8-0, he now holds two ALCS MVP awards as well as one for the World Series.

Game 1: Blue Jays 7, White Sox 3

Paul Molitor (4-for-5, HR, 3 RBI) led a 17-hit Toronto barrage that chased Chicago ace Jack McDowell, who gave up an ALCS record 13 hits. Juan Guzman fared better for the Blue Jays, allowing only two earned runs on five hits over six innings. After Tim Raines singled in Ozzie Guillen in the fourth inning to give the White Sox a 3-2 lead, Toronto answered with three runs in the fifth highlighted by John Olerud's two-run double. The Blue Jays pitching staff worked around Frank Thomas all night, walking the White Sox power hitter four times. Thomas set a playoff record, drawing 10 walks in the series. **W-Guzman, 1-0. L-McDowell, 0-1.**

Game 2: Jays 3, Sox 1

The Blue Jays handed the White Sox a second loss at Comiskey Park, as Dave Stewart upped his career playoff record to 7-0, and Molitor set an ALCS record picking up his sixth consecutive hit. Stewart worked out of a bases-loaded, no-out jam in the sixth inning without giving up a run. Chicago used Frank Thomas at DH for the second game in a row, leaving Bo Jackson and George Bell out of the lineup. Alex Fernandez was the hard-luck pitcher for the White Sox—only one earned run over eight innings with five strikeouts—but Dan Pasqua and Joey Cora let mistakes turn into runs. **W-Stewart, 1-0. L-A. Fernandez, 0-1. Sv-D.Ward (1).**

Game 3: Sox 6, Jays 1

Wilson Alvarez picked up a complete-game win, limiting the Blue Jays to a seven-hit, one-run performance. White Sox leadoff man Tim Raines went 4-for-5 with a pair of doubles, while Ellis Burks went 2-for-5 with a run scored and a pair of RBI. Toronto starter Pat Hentgen, a 19-game winner in the regular season, lasted only three innings, giving up six runs on nine hits. Lance Johnson (2-for-5) and Cora (2-for-3) also had multi-hit games for the White Sox, while John Olerud (2-for-4) was the only Blue Jay with more than one hit. **W-Alvarez, 1-0. L-Hentgen, 0-1.**

Game 4: Sox 7, Jays 4

Lance Johnson, a defensive specialist for Chicago, stepped into the offensive spotlight, picking up a career-high four RBI on a triple and a home run, while Tim Belcher relieved White Sox starter Jason Bere and limited the Blue Jays to one run on three hits over 3 2/3 innings. The Blue Jays continued to get little help from leadoff batter Rickey Henderson (0-for-3). **W-Belcher, 1-0. L-Stottlemyre, 0-1. Sv-Hernandez (1).**

Game 5: Jays 5, Sox 3

The Blue Jays again had little trouble with Jack McDowell, who left after 2 1/3 innings. Guzman pitched a gem, giving up only one run on three hits over seven innings. Roberto Alomar went 3-for-3 with three stolen bases for the Jays, while Ellis Burks went 2-for-3 with a home run for the White Sox. Jackson continued to struggle at the plate, going 0-for-4 with two strikeouts. **W-Guzman, 2-0. L-McDowell, 0-2.**

Game 6: Jays 6, Sox 3

Stewart stayed unbeatable in ALCS play, while Devon White's ninth-inning homer off Scott Radinsky began a three-run ninth inning that sealed Chicago's fate. Stewart finished the series with a 2.03 ERA, allowing only three earned runs on eight hits over 13 1/3 innings. With Jackson unable to produce, and George Bell talking his way off the team, Chicago manager Gene Lamont went with Warren Newson, who hit a ninth-inning home run off Toronto closer Duane Ward. Chicago catcher Ron Karkovice, who came in to run for Mike LaValliere in the seventh inning, struck out in the ninth. **W-Stewart, 2-0. L-A. Fernandez, 0-2. Sv-Ward (2).**

—game summaries compiled by
Erik B. Arneson

How the Jays were built

▸**Pitchers:** RH Juan Guzman, trade, from Los Angeles, for IF Mike Sharperson, 1987; RH Dave Stewart, signed as a free agent, 1992; RH Pat Hentgen, fifth-round draft pick, 1986; RH Todd Stottlemyre, first round of secondary draft, 1985; RH Duane Ward, trade, from Atlanta, for Doyle Alexander, July 1986; RH Danny Cox, signed as a free agent, 1993; LH Tony Castillo, signed as minor-league free agent, 1993; LH Al Leiter, trade, from N.Y. Yankees, for Jesse Barfield, 1989; RH Mike Timlin, fifth-round draft choice, 1987; RH Mark Eichorn, trade, from California, for C Greg Myers and OF Rob Ducey, July 1992.

▸**Infielders:** 1B John Olerud, third-round draft choice, 1989; 2B Roberto Alomar, trade, with Joe Carter from San Diego, for IF Tony Fernandez and 1B Fred McGriff, Dec. 1990; SS Tony Fernandez, trade, from N.Y. Mets, for Darrin Jackson, 1993; 3B Ed Sprague, first-round draft choice, 1988; DH Paul Molitor, signed as a free agent, 1992; IF Dick Schofield, signed as a free agent, 1993; IF Alfredo Griffin, signed as a free agent, 1992.

▸**Outfielders:** LF Rickey Henderson, trade, from Oakland, for RHP Steve Karsay, July, 1993; CF Devon White, trade, from California, for Junior Felix and others, 1990; RF Joe Carter, trade, from San Diego, with Roberto Alomar, for Fred McGriff and Tony Fernandez, Dec. 1990; OF Darnell Coles, signed as a free agent, 1992; OF Rob Butler, amateur free agent, 1990; OF Willie Canate, acquired on waivers from Cincinnati, 1993.

▸**Catchers:** Pat Borders, sixth round draft choice, 1982; Randy Knorr, 10th round draft choice, 1986.

TORONTO BLUE JAYS BATTING

Player	G	AB	R	H	2B	3B	HR	RBI	SO	BB	Avg.	PO	A	E	Pct.
White cf	6	27	3	12	1	1	1	2	5	1	.444	15	0	0	1.000
Molitor dh	6	23	7	9	2	1	1	5	3	3	.391	0	0	0	—
Olerud 1b	6	23	5	8	1	0	0	3	1	4	.348	48	9	1	.983
T.Fernandez ss	6	22	1	7	0	0	0	1	4	2	.318	12	8	0	1.000
Alomar 2b	6	24	3	7	1	0	0	4	3	4	.292	14	19	0	1.000
Sprague 3b	6	21	0	6	0	1	0	4	4	2	.286	5	9	0	1.000
Carter rf	6	27	2	7	0	0	0	2	5	1	.259	12	1	0	1.000
Borders c	6	24	1	6	1	0	0	3	6	0	.250	41	4	0	1.000
Henderson lf	6	25	4	3	2	0	0	0	5	4	.120	9	0	1	.900
Castillo p	2	0	0	0	0	0	0	0	0	0	—	0	1	0	1.000
Cox p	2	0	0	0	0	0	0	0	0	0	—	0	1	0	1.000
Eichhorn p	1	0	0	0	0	0	0	0	0	0	—	0	0	0	—
Guzman p	2	0	0	0	0	0	0	0	0	0	—	0	4	0	1.000
Hentgen p	1	0	0	0	0	0	0	0	0	0	—	1	0	0	1.000
Leiter p	2	0	0	0	0	0	0	0	0	0	—	0	0	0	—
Stewart p	2	0	0	0	0	0	0	0	0	0	—	2	0	0	1.000
Stottlemyre p	1	0	0	0	0	0	0	0	0	0	—	0	0	0	—
Timlin p	1	0	0	0	0	0	0	0	0	0	—	1	1	0	1.000
Ward p	4	0	0	0	0	0	0	0	0	0	—	0	0	0	—
Totals	6	216	26	65	8	3	2	24	36	21	.301	162	57	2	.991

CHICAGO WHITE SOX BATTING

Player	G	AB	R	H	2B	3B	HR	RBI	SO	BB	Avg.	PO	A	E	Pct.
Grebeck ph-3b	1	1	0	1	0	0	0	0	0	0	1.000	0	0	0	—
Raines lf	6	27	5	12	3	0	0	1	2	2	.444	12	2	0	1.000
Thomas dh-1b	6	17	2	6	0	0	1	3	5	10	.353	24	3	0	1.000
LaValliere c	2	3	0	1	0	0	0	0	0	1	.333	8	0	0	1.000
Burks rf	6	23	4	7	1	0	1	3	5	3	.304	15	0	0	1.000
Guillen ss	6	22	4	6	1	0	0	2	2	0	.273	12	14	0	1.000
Johnson cf	6	23	2	5	1	1	1	6	1	2	.217	15	0	0	1.000
Ventura 3b-1b	6	20	2	4	0	0	1	5	6	6	.200	9	6	1	.938
Newson ph-dh	2	5	1	1	0	0	1	1	1	0	.200	0	0	0	—
Cora 2b	6	22	1	3	0	0	0	1	6	3	.136	18	19	3	.925
Karkovice c-pr	6	15	0	0	0	0	0	0	7	1	.000	30	2	0	1.000
Jackson dh	3	10	1	0	0	0	0	0	6	3	.000	0	0	0	—
Pasqua 1b	2	6	1	0	0	0	0	0	2	1	.000	13	2	1	.938
Alvarez p	1	0	0	0	0	0	0	0	0	0	—	0	2	0	1.000
Belcher p	1	0	0	0	0	0	0	0	0	0	—	1	1	0	1.000
Bere p	1	0	0	0	0	0	0	0	0	0	—	0	0	0	—
DeLeon p	2	0	0	0	0	0	0	0	0	0	—	0	0	0	—
A.Fernandez p	2	0	0	0	0	0	0	0	0	0	—	2	1	0	1.000
Hernandez p	4	0	0	0	0	0	0	0	0	0	—	0	0	0	—
McCaskill p	3	0	0	0	0	0	0	0	0	0	—	0	2	0	1.000
McDowell p	2	0	0	0	0	0	0	0	0	0	—	0	1	1	.500
Radinsky p	4	0	0	0	0	0	0	0	0	0	—	0	0	1	.000
Totals	6	194	23	46	6	1	5	22	43	32	.237	159	55	7	.968

TORONTO BLUE JAYS PITCHING

Player	G	CG	IP	H	R	BB	SO	HB	WP	W	L	Sv	Pct.	ER	ERA
Cox	2	0	5	3	0	2	5	0	0	0	0	0	—	0	0.00
Castillo	2	0	2	0	0	1	1	0	0	0	0	0	—	0	0.00
Eichhorn	1	0	2	1	0	1	1	0	0	0	0	0	—	0	0.00
Stewart	2	0	13.1	8	3	8	8	1	2	2	0	0	1.000	3	2.03
Guzman	2	0	13	8	4	9	9	1	3	2	0	0	1.000	3	2.08
Leiter	2	0	2.2	4	1	2	2	0	0	0	0	0	—	1	3.38
Timlin	1	0	2.1	3	1	0	2	0	0	0	0	0	—	1	3.86
Ward	4	0	4.2	4	3	3	8	1	0	0	0	2	—	3	5.79
Stottlemyre	1	0	6	6	5	4	4	0	0	0	1	0	.000	5	7.50
Hentgen	1	0	3	9	6	2	3	0	0	0	1	0	.000	6	18.00
Totals	6	0	54.0	46	23	32	43	3	5	4	2	2	.667	22	3.67

CHICAGO WHITE SOX PITCHING

Player	G	CG	IP	H	R	BB	SO	HB	WP	W	L	Sv	Pct.	ER	ERA
Hernandez	4	0	4	4	0	0	1	0	0	0	0	1	—	0	0.00
McCaskill	3	0	3.2	3	0	1	3	0	0	0	0	0	—	0	0.00
Alvarez	1	0	9	7	1	2	6	0	0	1	0	0	1.000	1	1.00
A.Fernandez	2	0	15	15	6	6	10	1	0	0	2	0	.000	3	1.80
DeLeon	2	0	4.2	7	1	1	6	0	0	0	0	0	—	1	1.93
Belcher	1	0	3.2	3	1	3	1	0	1	1	0	0	1.000	1	2.45
Radinsky	4	0	1.2	3	4	1	1	0	0	0	0	0	—	2	10.80
McDowell	2	0	9	18	10	5	5	0	1	0	2	0	.000	10	10.00
Bere	1	0	2.1	5	3	2	3	1	0	0	0	0	—	3	11.57
Totals	6	0	53	65	26	21	36	2	2	2	4	1	.333	21	3.57

ALCS composite box score

▶**Double plays:** Chicago 5, Toronto 7.

▶**Left on base:** Chicago 50, Toronto 56.

▶**Stolen bases:** Guillen, Raines, Johnson, Henderson 2, Borders, Alomar 4.

▶**Caught stealing:** Raines, Burks, White, Henderson.

▶**Sacrifice:** Karkovice 2, Cora 2, Guillen, T. Fernandez.

▶**Sacrifice flies:** Ventura, Sprague.

▶**Intentional walks:** off A. Fernandez (Sprague, T. Fernandez, Molitor), off Guzman (Ventura), off Cox (Thomas, Ventura), off Belcher (Fernandez), off Leiter (Thomas).

▶**Hit by pitch:** by Guzman (Pasqua), by Bere (Olerud), by Ward (Burks), by A. Fernandez (Molitor), by Stewart (Cora).

▶**Balk:** Stottlemyre.

▶**Official scorers:** Bob Rosenberg, Neil MacCarl.

▶**Times:** Game 1, 3:38; Game 2, 3:00; Game 3, 2:56; Game 4, 3:30; Game 5, 3:09; Game 6, 3:31.

▶**Attendance:** Game 1 at Chicago, 46,246; Game 2 at Chicago, 46,101; Game 3 at Toronto, 51,783; Game 4 at Toronto, 51,889; Game 5 at Toronto, 51,375; Game 6 at Chicago, 45,527.

World Series Game 1: Toronto 8, Philadelphia 5

PHILADELPHIA	2	0	1	0	1	0	0	0	1-5
TORONTO	0	2	1	0	1	1	3	0	x-8

BATTING

Philadelphia	ab	r	h	bi	lo	bb	so	avg
Dykstra, cf	4	1	1	0	0	1	0	.250
Duncan, 2b	5	2	3	0	3	0	2	.600
Kruk, 1b	4	2	3	2	3	1	1	.750
Hollins, 3b	4	0	0	0	2	1	1	.000
Daulton, c	4	0	1	1	2	1	2	.250
Eisenreich, rf	5	0	1	1	5	0	2	.200
Jordan, dh	5	0	1	0	3	0	2	.200
Thompson, lf	3	0	0	0	1	0	1	.000
Incaviglia, ph-lf	1	0	0	0	0	0	0	.000
Stocker, ss	3	0	1	0	0	1	0	.333
Totals	**38**	**5**	**11**	**4**	**19**	**5**	**11**	

▶ **BATTING**—3B: Duncan. GDP: Thompson.
▶ **BASERUNNING**—SB: Dykstra; Duncan. Team LOB: 11.
▶ **FIELDING**—E: Thompson. PB: Daulton. DP: 1.

Toronto	ab	r	h	bi	lo	bb	so	avg
Henderson, lf	3	1	1	0	2	1	0	.333
White, cf	4	3	2	2	1	0	0	.500
Alomar, 2b	4	0	1	2	1	0	1	.250
Carter, rf	3	1	1	1	1	0	1	.333
Olerud, 1b	3	2	2	1	0	1	0	.667
Molitor, dh	4	0	1	1	2	0	0	.250
Fernandez, ss	3	0	0	1	0	1	0	.000
Sprague, 3b	4	0	1	0	0	0	2	.250
Borders, c	4	1	1	0	2	0	1	.250
Totals	**32**	**8**	**10**	**8**	**9**	**3**	**5**	

▶ **BATTING**—2B: White; Alomar. HR: White; Olerud. SF: Carter. GDP: White.
▶ **BASERUNNING**—SB: Alomar. CS: Fernandez. Team LOB: 4.
▶ **FIELDING**—E: Alomar; Carter; Sprague. DP: 1.

PITCHING

Philadelphia	ip	h	r	er	bb	so	era
Schilling L,0-1	6.1	8	7	6	2	3	8.53
West	0	2	1	1	0	0	—
Andersen	.2	0	0	0	1	1	0.00
Mason	1	0	0	0	0	1	0.00

Toronto	ip	h	r	er	bb	so	era
Guzman	5	5	4	4	4	6	7.20
Leiter W,1-0	2.2	4	0	0	1	2	0.00
D.Ward S,1	1.1	2	1	0	0	3	0.00

West pitched to 2 batters in 7th.
IBB: Olerud by Andersen; Daulton by Guzman. WP: Guzman. Inherited runners/scored: D.Ward 2/0; West 2/2; Andersen 1/0. Pitches-strikes: Guzman 116-73; Leiter 56-37; D.Ward 30-23; Schilling 99-61; West 12-8; Andersen 7-5; Mason 11-7. Ground balls-fly balls: Guzman 7-3; Leiter 8-1; D.Ward 1-1; Schilling 11-8; Andersen 0-1; Mason 1-1.

▶ **GAME DATA**—T: 3:27. A: 52,011. Indoors.

▶ **UMPIRES**—HP: Phillips. 1B: Runge. 2B: Johnson. 3B: Williams.

▶**Key player:** Toronto center fielder Devon White homered, doubled, reached third on a screw-up in the Phillies' outfield, scored three times, drove in two and loped under a warning-track drive with Joe DiMaggio style.

▶**Key player II:** Toronto's Roberto Alomar showed why he is, as Phillies' coach Larry Bowa noted, "the best second baseman in the game." He made two spectacular plays, robbing Lenny Dykstra of a bloop double and keeping a two-on single by Mariano Duncan in the infield. He also hit a two-run double.

▶**Key pitcher:** Left-handed pitcher Al Leiter came in for Juan Guzman, who had been ineffective, and shut down the Phillies for 2 2/3 critical innings.

▶**Key at-bat:** Phillies' first baseman John Kruk struck out against Leiter in the sixth inning, leaving the bases full in a 4-4 game.

▶**Notable numbers:** Right fielder Jim Eisenreich and left fielder Milt Thompson, the Phillies' left-handed platoon outfielders, will start all World Series games against right-handed pitchers. They were 0-for-7 with three strikeouts and a groundball double play in Game 1.

—*by Rod Beaton*

Game 1: Between the lines

▶**Turf wars:** This was the fourth-ever World Series played entirely on artificial turf. The previous three—1980 (Philadelphia defeated Kansas City 4-2); 1985 (Kansas City defeated St. Louis 4-2); 1987 (Minnesota defeated St. Louis 4-3).

▶**Past Padres:** Eight former members of the San Diego Padres' organization played in the '93 Series—Roberto Alomar, Joe Carter and Tony Fernandez of the Blue Jays, and Larry Andersen, Dave Hollins, John Kruk, Roger Mason and Mitch Williams of the Phillies.

▶**Flawless:** Robby Alomar's eighth-inning error was his first-ever in 24 postseason games.

▶**Strikeout king:** Toronto closer Duane Ward, who fanned three in Game 1, was the all-time postseason strikeout leader among pitchers with a minimum of 15 innings pitched—30 in 21 innings, an average of 12.4 per nine innings.

—*compiled by Scott Kauffman*

World Series Game 2: Philadelphia 6, Toronto 4

▶ **Key lapse:** Toronto starter Dave Stewart walked the first two Phillies he faced in the third inning. Each scored at the front end of a five-run inning.

▶ **Key lapse II:** The Phillies led by two runs with two out in the eighth inning. They conned Roberto Alomar by letting him steal second uncontested—the Jays' second unchallenged steal that inning. Alomar got greedy, went for third, and Mitch Williams was waiting with a spin move that nailed him.

▶ **Waste pitch wasted:** Jim Eisenreich's blow-it-open, three-run homer came on an 0-2 pitch, not wasted quite enough.

▶ **Best defense:** Phillies' center fielder Lenny Dykstra ran into the wall at full speed twice, robbing Devon White and Alomar.

▶ **Best defense, Part II:** Toronto second baseman Alomar—again. He made a standout charge play to nip Kevin Stocker in the second inning, ranged behind the bag to get Ricky Jordan in sixth, and did a quick-release dazzler on Darren Daulton in a two-on threat in the seventh.

▶ **Good fortune:** Kruk and Dave Hollins plopped lazy shallow flies into center field in the middle of the five-run third inning.

▶ **Good riddance:** To Toronto scoreboard imploring fans to "make noise." Philadelphia fans certainly need no such entreaties.

—by Rod Beaton

Game 2: Between the lines

▶ **Stewart scorched:** Dave Stewart may be the best playoff pitcher in history at 8-0, but the World Series is another story. (Who can forget '90?) Game 2 '93 was his worst game ever in 17 postseason starts, dropping his record to 2-4 lifetime in the World Series.

▶ **Streak ends:** Roberto Alomar's postseason high at stealing bases (16-for-16) was wrecked when Mitch Williams nabbed him at third in the eighth.

▶ **Postseason punch:** Len Dykstra's seventh-inning homer was his sixth career postseason leadoff homer, tying him with Davey Lopes and Hank Bauer on top of the all-time list. It was his seventh career postseason homer, tying him with Kirk Gibson, Jose Canseco and Dave Henderson for first among active players.

—compiled by Scott Kauffman

World Series Game 2 box

PHILADELPHIA	0 0 5 0 0 0 1 0 0	-6
TORONTO	0 0 0 2 0 1 0 1 0	-4

BATTING

Philadelphia	ab	r	h	bi	lo	bb	so	avg
Dykstra, cf	4	2	2	1	1	1	0	.375
Duncan, 2b	4	1	1	0	3	1	2	.444
Kruk, 1b	5	1	2	1	3	0	1	.556
Hollins, 3b	4	1	2	1	1	1	2	.250
Batiste, 3b	0	0	0	0	0	0	0	—
Daulton, c	5	0	1	0	1	0	0	.222
Eisenreich, rf	4	1	1	3	4	1	1	.222
Incaviglia, lf	4	0	1	0	1	0	2	.200
Thompson, pr-lf	0	0	0	0	0	0	0	.000
Jordan, dh	4	0	1	0	0	0	0	.222
Stocker, ss	3	0	1	0	2	1	0	.333
Totals	**37**	**6**	**12**	**6**	**16**	**5**	**8**	

▶ **BATTING**—HR: Dykstra; Eisenreich. GDP: Eisenreich.
▶ **BASERUNNING**—CS: Stocker. Team LOB: 9.
▶ **FIELDING**—DP: 1.

Toronto	ab	r	h	bi	lo	bb	so	avg
Henderson, lf	3	0	0	0	1	1	1	.167
White, cf	4	0	1	0	2	0	2	.375
Molitor, dh	3	2	2	0	1	1	0	.429
Carter, rf	4	1	1	2	2	0	1	.286
Olerud, 1b	3	0	0	1	0	0	0	.333
Alomar, 2b	3	1	1	0	0	1	1	.286
Fernandez, ss	3	0	2	1	0	1	0	.333
Sprague, 3b	4	0	0	0	3	0	1	.125
Griffin, pr	0	0	0	0	0	0	0	—
Borders, c	4	0	1	0	1	0	0	.250
Totals	**31**	**4**	**8**	**4**	**10**	**4**	**6**	

▶ **BATTING**—2B: White (2); Molitor; Fernandez. HR: Carter. SF: Olerud. GDP: Borders.
▶ **BASERUNNING**—SB: Molitor; Alomar (2) CS: Henderson; Alomar. Team LOB: 5.
▶ **FIELDING**—DP: 1

PITCHING

Philadelphia	ip	h	r	er	bb	so	era
Mulholland W,1-0	5.2	7	3	3	2	4	4.76
Mason H,1	1.2	1	1	1	0	2	3.38
Williams S,1	1.2	0	0	0	2	0	0.00

Toronto	ip	h	r	er	bb	so	era
Stewart L,0-1	6	6	5	5	4	6	7.50
Castillo	1	3	1	1	0	0	9.00
Eichhorn	0.1	1	0	0	1	0	0.00
Timlin	1.2	2	0	0	0	2	0.00

WP: Stewart. Balks: Stewart. Inherited runners/scored: Timlin 2/0; Mason 1/0; Mit.Williams 1/1. Pitches-strikes: Stewart 122-79; Castillo 21-14; Eichhorn 15-7; Timlin 22-16; Mulholland 105-62; Mason 24-15; Williams 31-15. Ground balls-fly balls: Stewart 7-7; Castillo 2-3; Eichhorn 2-0; Timlin 3-0; Mulholland 6-8; Mason 1-1; Williams 2-1.

▶ **GAME DATA**—T: 3:35. A: 52,062. Indoors.

▶ **UMPIRES**—HP: Runge. 1B: Johnson. 2B: Williams. 3B: McClelland.

World Series Game 3 box

TORONTO	3 0 1	0 0 1	3 0 2-10
PHILADELPHIA	0 0 0	0 0 1	1 0 1-3

Toronto	ab	r	h	bi	lo	bb	so	avg
Henderson, lf	4	2	2	0	0	0	0	.300
White, cf	4	2	1	1	0	1	0	.333
Molitor, 1b	4	3	3	3	0	1	0	.545
Carter, rf	4	1	1	3	0	1	1	.273
Alomar, 2b	5	2	4	2	0	0	0	.500
Fernandez, ss	3	0	2	2	0	1	0	.444
Sprague, 3b	4	0	0	1	4	0	2	.083
Borders, c	4	0	0	0	3	1	0	.167
Hentgen, p	3	0	0	0	1	0	1	.000
Cox, p	1	0	0	0	0	0	0	.000
D.Ward, p	0	0	0	0	0	0	0	—
Totals	36	10	13	10	11	4	4	

▶**BATTING**—2B: Henderson. 3B: White; Molitor; Alomar. HR: Molitor. SF: Sprague, Fernandez, Carter.
▶**BASERUNNING**—SB: Alomar 2 (4). Pickoff: Henderson. Team LOB: 7.
▶**FIELDING**—E: Carter (2). DP: 2.

Philadelphia	ab	r	h	bi	lo	bb	so	avg
Dykstra, cf	5	0	1	0	0	0	1	.308
Duncan, 2b	5	0	2	1	0	0	1	.429
Kruk, 1b	3	1	2	0	0	2	1	.583
Hollins, 3b	3	0	0	0	6	1	1	.182
Daulton, c	3	0	0	4	1	1	1	.167
Eisenreich, rf	4	0	1	1	2	0	0	.231
Incaviglia, lf	3	0	0	0	4	0	2	.125
Thigpen, p	0	0	0	0	0	0	0	—
Morandini, ph	0	0	0	0	0	1	0	—
Andersen, p	0	0	0	0	0	0	0	—
Stocker, ss	4	0	1	0	1	0	2	.300
Jackson, p	1	0	0	0	0	0	1	.000
Chamberlain, ph	1	0	0	0	1	0	0	.000
Rivera, p	0	0	0	0	0	0	0	—
Thompson, lf	2	2	2	1	0	0	0	.400
Totals	34	3	9	3	18	5	10	

▶**BATTING**—2B: Kruk. HR: Thompson. GDP: Hollins, Chamberlain.
▶**BASERUNNING**—Team LOB: 9.

PITCHING							
Toronto	ip	h	r	er	bb	so	era
Hentgen W,1-0	6	5	1	1	3	6	1.50
Cox	2	3	1	1	2	2	4.50
D.Ward	1	1	1	1	0	2	3.86
Philadelphia	ip	h	r	er	bb	so	era
Jackson L,0-1	5	6	4	4	1	1	7.20
Rivera	1.1	4	4	4	2	3	27.00
Thigpen	1.2	0	0	0	1	0	0.00
Andersen	1	3	2	2	0	0	10.80

HBP: Henderson by Thigpen. Inherited runners/scored: Thigpen 2/1. Pitches-strikes: Jackson 89-51; Rivera 50-30; Thigpen 27-15; Andersen 28-18; Hentgen 99-59; Cox 29-17; D.Ward 18-14. Ground balls-fly balls: Jackson 9-7; Thigpen 1-2; Andersen 4-0; Hentgen 8-5; Cox 4-1; D.Ward 1-0.

▶**GAME DATA**—T: 3:16 (plus 1 hour, 12 minute rain delay in 1st). A: 62,689. Temp: 56. Wind: 5 mph, right to left.

▶**UMPIRES**—HP: Johnson. 1B: Williams. 2B: McClelland. 3B: DeMuth.

World Series Game 3: Toronto 10, Philadelphia 3

▶**Key player:** Paul Molitor ruined Philadelphia's hopes with his two-run triple and solo home run.

▶**Cito's savvy:** Toronto manager Cito Gaston ruminated and contemplated ways to keep designated hitter Molitor in the lineup at minimal sacrifice. So he sacrificed batting champ John Olerud. Hard to argue.

▶**Nyah-nyah:** After being caught stealing third in the eighth inning in Game 2—a critical blunder—Roberto Alomar stole second and third in his first baserunning opportunity in Game 3—four steals in the three games. The World Series record is seven.

▶**Best catches:** Phillies' outfielders were forced to work hard again. Left fielder Pete Incaviglia and center fielder Lenny Dykstra (diving grabs) and right fielder Jim Eisenreich (full-tilt catch) came through beautifully, even if it was a losing cause.

▶**Key at-bat:** Dave Hollins grounded sharply into a first-to-second-to-first double play to end a bases-loaded threat in the Phillies' seventh.

—by Rod Beaton

Game 3: Philly fans' boo meter

Philadelphia fans have been known to boo anybody, anytime, anywhere, for any reason—Santa Claus, the Easter Bunny, women, children, players, managers, umpires, even themselves—but during the 10-3 loss, they were uncharacteristically quiet. Here's a look at the Game 3 boo-box score (1 to 10 scale; 10 is loudest):

▶**7.5—Pregame:** Anything in blue and white that moved during introductions.

▶**4.0—Bottom of the third:** First-base umpire Charlie Williams ruled that batter Danny Jackson went around on a third strike.

▶**1.5—Top of the fourth:** Rickey Henderson, just for being Rickey.

▶**2.5—Top of the sixth:** Pat Borders' bat slipped out of his hands and went into stands.

▶**4.0—Top of the seventh:** Rickey again, after he beat a pickoff throw back to second base.

▶**1.5—Bottom of the seventh:** Strike call on John Kruk.

▶**2.5—Top of the eighth:** (Reverse boo) Cheer after Rickey was hit by a pitch.

—by Tom Weir

World Series Game 4:
Toronto 15, Philadelphia 14

▶**Bad relief:** Larry Andersen had set-up Mitch Williams all season, usually with success. This time both faltered badly in Toronto's six-run eruption.

▶**Bad starts:** Tommy Greene of Philadelphia or Stottlemyre of Toronto—each was bottom-line awful, but Stottlemyre gets more debits for all the walks.

▶**Ugliest slide:** Stottlemyre got a walk in his first major-league plate appearance, then ill-advisedly tried to reach third on a two-out single. That stupidity was enhanced by his face-first flop into the cutout that cut his chin. He was out, too.

—by Rod Beaton

What a long, strange game it was

Game 4 was sort of Murphy's Law of the bizarre—anything strange that could happen, did. And in the process, several World Series records were tied or set.

▶**29 runs:** Record for one game by both teams, breaking the record of 22 set in Game 2 of the '36 World Series between the Yankees and Giants.

▶**Nine RBI:** Tony Fernandez set Series record for RBI by a shortstop, breaking Bucky Dent's mark in the '78 Series between the Yankees and the Dodgers.

▶**Four walks in one inning, three in a row:** Both tying records, by Toronto starter Todd Stottlemyre in the first inning. Atlanta's Tom Glavine was the most recent to tie those records, in '91.

▶**Three-run firsts:** Philadelphia's four runs and Toronto's three were the first time in Series history both teams had three or more runs in the first inning.

▶**Four runs:** Lenny Dykstra's four runs tied Series record (most recently done by Oakland's Carney Lansford in '89).

▶**Longest game:** The four-hour, 14-minute game was the longest in Series history, regardless of length, surpassing by one minute a 12-inning game between Oakland and New York in 1973.

▶**Runs by a losing team:** The Phillies' 14 runs beats Game 7 of the 1960 Series, when the Yankees lost 10-9 to the Pirates.

▶**Most runs, four games:** The highest run total for the first four games of a Series (65), besting the previous record of 56 in the '32 Series between the Yankees and the Cubs.

World Series Game 4 box

TORONTO	3 0 4 0 0 2 0 6 0	-15
PHILADELPHIA	4 2 0 1 5 1 1 0 0	-14

BATTING

Toronto	ab	r	h	bi	lo	bb	so	avg
Henderson, lf	5	2	2	2	2	1	1	.333
White, cf	5	2	3	4	1	1	1	.412
Alomar, 2b	6	1	2	1	5	0	1	.444
Carter, rf	6	2	3	0	1	0	0	.353
Olerud, 1b	4	2	1	0	3	2	0	.300
Molitor, 3b	4	2	2	2	1	1	0	.533
Griffin, 3b	0	0	0	0	0	0	0	-
Fernandez, ss	6	2	3	5	1	0	1	.467
Borders, c	4	1	1	1	4	1	0	.188
Stottlemyre, p	0	0	0	0	0	1	0	—
Butler, ph	1	1	0	0	0	0	0	.000
Leiter, p	1	0	1	0	0	0	0	1.000
Castillo, p	1	0	0	0	0	0	1	1.000
Sprague, ph	1	0	0	0	3	0	1	.077
Timlin, p	0	0	0	0	0	0	0	—
Ward, p	0	0	0	0	0	0	0	—
Totals	44	15	18	15	21	7	6	

▶**BATTING**—2B: Henderson (2); White (3); Carter; Leiter; Molitor (2). 3B: White (2).
▶**BASERUNNING**—SB: Henderson; White. Team LOB: 10.

Philadelphia	ab	r	h	bi	lo	bb	so	avg
Dykstra, cf	5	4	3	4	0	1	1	.389
Duncan, 2b	6	1	3	1	1	0	0	.450
Kruk, 1b	5	0	0	0	3	1	2	.412
Hollins, 3b	4	3	2	0	0	2	0	.267
Daulton, c	3	2	1	3	1	1	1	.200
Eisenreich, rf	4	2	1	1	4	1	0	.235
Thompson, lf	5	1	3	5	3	0	0	.500
Stocker, ss	4	0	0	0	2	1	1	.214
Greene, p	1	1	1	0	0	0	0	1.000
Mason, p	1	0	0	0	0	0	0	.000
Jordan, ph	1	0	0	0	1	0	0	.200
West, p	0	0	0	0	0	0	0	—
Chamberlain, p	1	0	0	0	2	0	1	.000
Andersen, p	0	0	0	0	0	0	0	—
Williams, p	0	0	0	0	0	0	0	—
Morandini, ph	1	0	0	0	0	0	1	.000
Thigpen, p	0	0	0	0	0	0	0	—
Totals	41	14	14	14	17	7	7	

▶**BATTING**—2B: Dykstra, Hollins, Thompson. 3B: Thompson. HR: Dykstra 2 (3).
▶**BASERUNNING**—SB: Dykstra (2); Duncan (2). Team LOB: 8.
▶**FIELDING**—Outfield assist: Dykstra.

PITCHING

Toronto	ip	h	r	er	bb	so	era
Stottlemyre	2	3	6	6	4	1	27.00
Leiter	2.2	8	6	6	0	1	10.13
Castillo W,1-0	2.1	3	2	2	3	1	8.10
Timlin H,1	0.2	0	0	0	0	2	0.00
Ward S,2	1.1	0	0	0	0	2	2.45

Philadelphia	ip	h	r	er	bb	so	era
Greene	2.1	7	7	7	4	1	27.00
Mason	2.2	2	0	0	1	2	1.69
West	1	3	2	2	0	0	27.00
Andersen	1.1	2	3	3	1	2	15.00
Williams L,0-1	0.2	3	3	3	1	1	11.57
Thigpen	1	1	0	0	0	0	0.00

▶**GAME DATA**—T: 4:14. A: 62,731. Temp: 62. Wind: 15 mph, in from center.

▶**UMPIRES**—HP: Williams. 1B: McClelland. 2B: DeMuth. 3B: Phillips.

TORONTO	0 0 0	0 0	0 0	0-0
PHILADELPHIA	1 1 0	0 0	0 0	0 x-2

BATTING

Toronto	ab	r	h	bi	lo	bb	so	avg
Henderson, lf	3	0	0	0	0	1	0	.278
White, cf	3	0	0	0	2	1	2	.350
Alomar, 2b	3	0	1	0	4	1	0	.429
Carter, rf	4	0	0	0	2	0	1	.286
Olerud, 1b	4	0	0	0	0	0	1	.214
Molitor, 3b	4	0	1	0	0	0	0	.421
Fernandez, ss	3	0	0	0	2	0	1	.389
Borders, c	3	0	2	0	1	0	0	.263
Canate, pr	0	0	0	0	0	0	0	—
Knorr, c	0	0	0	0	0	0	0	—
Guzman, p	2	0	0	0	1	0	1	.000
Butler, ph	1	0	1	0	0	0	0	.500
Cox, p	0	0	0	0	0	0	0	.000
Totals	**30**	**0**	**5**	**0**	**12**	**3**	**6**	

▸ **BATTING**—GDP: Alomar, Guzman.
▸ **BASERUNNING**—CS: Alomar (2). Team LOB: 6.
▸ **FIELDING**—E: Borders. DP: 1.

Philadelphia	ab	r	h	bi	lo	bb	so	avg
Dykstra, cf	2	1	0	0	1	2	1	.350
Duncan, 2b	4	0	0	0	5	0	1	.375
Kruk, 1b	3	0	1	1	0	1	1	.400
Hollins, 3b	3	0	1	0	0	1	1	.278
Batiste, 3b	0	0	0	0	0	0	0	—
Daulton, c	4	1	1	0	4	0	1	.211
Eisenreich, rf	4	0	0	0	2	0	1	.190
Thompson, lf	3	0	0	0	3	1	1	.385
Stocker, ss	2	0	1	0	1	0	1	.250
Schilling, p	2	0	1	0	1	0	1	.500
Totals	**27**	**2**	**5**	**2**	**16**	**6**	**9**	

▸ **BATTING**—2B: Daulton S: Schilling. GDP: Duncan.
▸ **BASERUNNING**—SB: Dykstra (3). Team LOB: 8.
▸ **FIELDING**—E: Duncan. DP: 3.

PITCHING

Toronto	ip	h	r	er	bb	so	era
Guzman L,0-1	7	5	2	1	4	6	3.75
Cox	1	0	0	0	2	3	3.00

Philadelphia	ip	h	r	er	bb	so	era
Schilling W,1-1	9	5	0	0	3	6	3.52

IBB: Dykstra by Guzman. Pitches-strikes: Schilling 148-100; Guzman 101-59; Cox 24-12. Ground balls-fly balls: Schilling 9-9; Guzman 8-6.

▸ **GAME DATA**—T: 2:53. A: 62,706. Temp: 67. Wind: 14 mph, left to right.

▸ **UMPIRES**—HP: McClelland. 1B: DeMuth. 2B: Phillips. 3B: Runge.

World Series Game 5: Philadephia 2, Toronto 0

▸**Sensational Schilling:** It was a striking perform-ance by Curt Schilling, especially after Toronto scored 15 runs in Game 4. The Phillies needed a complete game—essentially needed a shutout—and got one.

▸**Key inning:** Schilling only allowed the Jays to put two on in one inning twice. But in the eighth, he had runners on the corners, no outs, and the top of the or-der up. He found the resolve—and the stuff—to get a fielder's choice comebacker from Rickey Henderson, strike out Devon White, and get Roberto Alomar on a routine ground-out to second.

▸**Dykstra does it:** The dynamic Lenny Dykstra walked to start the Phillies' first inning, stole second, and advanced to third because second baseman Roberto Alomar shrank from catcher Pat Borders' throw. Dykstra then scored on a ground out.

▸**Best play:** Phillies' first baseman John Kruk rum-bled in to convert Juan Guzman's lame sacrifice bid into a 3-6-4, third-inning double play. The Phillies played superior defense throughout the game. "I went nine because of our defense," Schilling said.

—by Rod Beaton

Judge chaws in her team's honor

The picture was unmistakable. There she was, front page of the *Philadelphia Daily News*, in living color, stuffing a plug of Red Man chewing tobacco in her mouth for the entire city of Philadelphia to see. What was amazing about the photo was not so much that it was a woman chewing tobacco, but that this woman was Lisa Richette, judge of state trial courts.

Richette was passing through downtown when a *Daily News* reporter, doing a story on chewing tobacco, offered her a chaw. By the next day, she was famous. People stopped her on the street to tell her how much better-looking she was in person than in the paper. And if her face wasn't instantly recog-nizable, her outfit certainly turned heads. Bright red from head to toe, including a Phillies cap.

The judge's favorite player is John Kruk. "He exem-plifies the spirit of that team," she said. "Can you be-lieve he never even changed his pants (after he ripped them in the playoffs)?"

—by Bob Velin

World Series Game 6: Toronto 8, Philadelphia 6

The triumphant Toronto Blue Jays rode a cavalcade of convertibles through downtown less than 24 hours after Joe Carter's ninth-inning home run delivered an 8-6 victory that gave Toronto their second consecutive World Series title.

▶**Don't blame it all on the Wild Thing:** The three-run homer came off of—who else—Mitch Williams, who stuck around after the dismal loss to talk to reporters. He made no excuses. After Game 4 he had joked that the key to winning in the Series was to keep him out of the game. But Williams' 43 regular-season saves were a very big part of the reason that the Phillies made it to the World Series at all, as both manager Jim Fregosi and president Bill Giles hastened to point out. "Without Mitch Williams, we wouldn't have been here," Fregosi said after the game. "We would not have won the division without Mitch Williams," agreed Giles.

▶**Stew liked this one best:** Toronto pitcher Dave Stewart, who said 1994 would be his last season, had won World Series titles with the 1981 Los Angeles Dodgers and the 1989 Oakland Athletics before picking up the 1993 trophy with the Toronto Blue Jays. But this one was best, he said. "With the Dodgers . . . I didn't pitch much. And then when I was with Oakland, we had the earthquake (that forced a 12-day delay). This is the first World Series championship I've been able to cut loose."

▶**Souvenir saved:** It took about 75 minutes, but Joe Carter was reunited with the ball he hit for the Series-winning home run. It cleared the fence but didn't make it into the stands. Bullpen coach John Sullivan retrieved it and pushed through a crowd of reporters to give it to Carter.

▶**Bowa bettered:** Mariano Duncan's seventh-inning single, his 10th hit of the Series, broke Phillies' coach Larry Bowa's club-record for most hits in a Series.

▶**Dude did it:** Lenny Dykstra's seventh-inning home run was his fourth of the Series. Only Reggie Jackson has hit more in one series (five in '77). Dykstra, who collected a postseason-record six home runs, tied Lou Gehrig for career postseason homers (10). Only Mickey Mantle, Babe Ruth, Yogi Berra, Duke Snider and Reggie Jackson have more.

—contributing: Scott Kauffman, Hal Bodley, Chuck Johnson, Mel Antonen, Mike Dodd

World Series Game 6 box

PHILADELPHIA	0	0	0	1	0	0	5	0	0-6
TORONTO	3	0	0	1	1	0	0	0	3-8

BATTING

Philadelphia	ab	r	h	bi	lo	bb	so	avg
Dykstra, cf	3	1	1	3	1	2	1	.348
Duncan, dh	5	1	1	0	2	0	1	.345
Kruk, 1b	3	0	0	0	2	2	1	.348
Hollins, 3b	5	1	1	1	4	0	0	.261
Batiste, 3b	0	0	0	0	0	0	0	—
Daulton, c	4	1	1	0	0	1	0	.217
Eisenreich, rf	5	0	2	1	0	0	0	.231
Thompson, lf	3	0	0	0	1	0	0	.313
Incaviglia, ph-lf	0	0	0	1	0	0	0	.125
Stocker, ss	3	1	0	0	2	1	1	.211
Morandini, 2b	4	1	1	0	0	0	1	.200
Totals	35	6	7	6	12	6	5	

▶**BATTING**—2B: Daulton (2). HR: Dykstra (4). SF: Incaviglia.
▶**BASERUNNING**—SB: Dykstra (4); Duncan (3). Team LOB: 9.

Toronto	ab	r	h	bi	lo	bb	so	avg
Henderson, lf	4	1	0	0	2	1	0	.227
White, cf	4	1	0	0	2	1	2	.292
Molitor, dh	5	3	3	2	0	0	0	.500
Carter, rf	4	1	1	4	0	0	0	.280
Olerud, 1b	3	1	1	0	0	1	0	.235
Griffin, pr-3b	0	0	0	0	0	0	0	—
Alomar, 2b	4	1	3	1	0	0	0	.480
Fernandez, ss	3	0	0	0	2	0	1	.333
Sprague, 3b-1b	2	0	0	1	1	1	0	.067
Borders, c	4	0	2	0	4	0	0	.304
Totals	33	8	10	8	11	4	3	

▶**BATTING**—2B: Olerud; Alomar (2). 3B: Molitor (2). HR: Molitor (2); Carter (2). SF: Sprague, Carter.
▶**BASERUNNING**—Team LOB: 7.
▶**FIELDING**—E: Alomar (2); Sprague (2).

PITCHING

Philadelphia	ip	h	r	er	bb	so	era
Mulholland	5	7	5	5	1	1	6.75
Mason	2.1	1	0	0	0	2	1.17
West	0	0	0	0	1	0	27.00
Andersen H,1	0.2	0	0	0	1	0	12.27
Williams L, 0-2 ,	0.2 .1	2	3	3	1	0	20.25

Toronto	ip	h	r	er	bb	so	era
Stewart	6	4	4	4	4	2	6.75
Cox BS,1	0.1	3	2	2	1	1	8.10
Leiter	1.2	0	0	0	1	2	7.71
D.Ward W,1-0	1	0	0	0	0	0	1.93

Stewart pitched to 3 batters in 7th; West pitched to 1 batter in 8th.

HBP: Fernandez by Andersen. Inherited runners/scored: Leiter 3/1; Andersen 1/0. Pitches-strikes: Stewart 120-68; Cox 24-12; Leiter 21-12; D.Ward 7-5; Mulholland 70-42; Mason 27-20; West 5-1; Andersen 27-16; Williams 21-11. Ground balls-fly balls: Stewart 7-9; Cox 2-0; Leiter 1-2; D.Ward 1-2; Mulholland 4-6; Mason 0-4; Andersen 1-1; Williams 0-2.

▶ **GAME DATA**—T: 3:27. A: 52,195. Indoors.

▶ **UMPIRES**—HP: DeMuth. 1B: Phillips. 2B: Runge. 3B: Johnson.

MVP Paul Molitor was much more than a DH

Paul Molitor had a career year for the Blue Jays and capped it off with a World Series MVP award.

by H. Darr Beiser, *USA TODAY*

Paul Molitor, the Blue Jay's 37-year-old designated hitter, found himself on National League soil—where the rules don't allow the DH—for three games of the World Series. He didn't flinch. Instead he played outstandingly at first base for one game and at third in the two others.

He was prepared for the challenge. After all, when he came to Toronto, he had the gigantic task of replacing Dave Winfield, who had become Canada's biggest sports hero when when he drove in the run that clinched the Blue Jays' first World Series title in '92. Molitor responded with the best season of his career—.332 batting average, 22 home runs and 111 runs batted in.

And that was after he left the Milwaukee Brewers because they had asked him to take a pay cut. There's no telling what Brewers' president Bud Selig must have thought when Molitor was named the World Series' Most Valuable Player, going 12-for-24 (.500) with two doubles, two triples, two home runs, eight runs batted in and 10 runs scored.

But Molitor's thoughts were clear: "I'm thankful," he said. "After watching postseason after postseason go by, you want to experience it."

World Series MVPs

1955: Johnny Podres, Brooklyn (NL)
1956: Don Larsen, New York (AL)
1957: Lew Burdette, Milwaukee (NL)
1958: Bob Turley, New York (AL)
1959: Larry Sherry, Los Angeles (NL)
1960: Bobby Richardson, New York (AL)
1961: Whitey Ford, New York (AL)
1962: Ralph Terry, New York (AL)
1963: Sandy Koufax, Los Angeles (NL)
1964: Bob Gibson, St. Louis (NL)
1965: Sandy Koufax, Los Angeles (NL)
1966: Frank Robinson, Baltimore (AL)
1967: Bob Gibson, St. Louis (NL)
1968: Mickey Lolich, Detroit (AL)
1969: Donn Clendenon, New York (NL)
1970: Brooks Robinson, Baltimore (AL)
1971: Roberto Clemente, Pittsburgh (NL)
1972: Gene Tenace, Oakland (AL)
1973: Reggie Jackson, Oakland (AL)
1974: Rollie Fingers, Oakland (AL)
1975: Pete Rose, Cincinnati (NL)
1976: Johnny Bench, Cincinnati (NL)
1977: Reggie Jackson, New York (AL)
1978: Bucky Dent, New York (AL)
1979: Willie Stargell, Pittsburgh (NL)
1980: Mike Schmidt, Philadelphia (NL)
1981: Ron Cey, Pedro Guerrero and Steve Yeager, Los Angeles (NL)
1982: Darrell Porter, St. Louis (NL)
1983: Rick Dempsey, Baltimore (AL)
1984: Alan Trammell, Detroit (AL)
1985: Bret Saberhagen, Kansas City (AL)
1986: Ray Knight, New York (NL)
1987: Frank Viola, Minnesota (AL)
1988: Orel Hershiser, Los Angeles (NL)
1989: Dave Stewart, Oakland (AL)
1990: Jose Rijo, Cincinnati (NL)
1991: Jack Morris, Minnesota (AL)
1992: Pat Borders, Toronto (AL)
1993: Paul Molitor, Toronto (AL)

For the record

- ▸ All-time single-season, league and club records
- ▸ Career records
- ▸ Top fielding marks
- ▸ Active player and individual records
- ▸ All no-hitters
- ▸ Perfect game box scores

USA SNAPSHOTS®

A look at statistics that shape the sports world

Long ball but no Hall

Major league baseball players with the most home runs who are not in the Hall of Fame (eligible players only):

Dave Kingman	442
Frank Howard	382
Orlando Cepeda	379
Tony Perez	379
Norm Cash	377

Source: USA TODAY research   By Julie Stacey, USA TODAY

Active player records

Players listed, active through 1993 season.

Hitters

Games played: Most, career, active players

2856	Robin Yount, 1974-1993
2850	Dave Winfield, 1973-1993
2707	George Brett, 1973-1993
2598	Eddie Murray, 1977-1993
2499	Carlton Fisk, 1969-1993
2431	Andre Dawson, 1976-1993
2349	Ozzie Smith, 1978-1993
2214	Lou Whitaker, 1977-1993
2180	Dale Murphy, 1976-1993
2137	Willie Wilson, 1976-1993

At-bats: Most, career, active players

11008	Robin Yount, 1974-1993
10594	Dave Winfield, 1973-1993
10349	George Brett, 1973-1993
9734	Eddie Murray, 1977-1993
9351	Andre Dawson, 1976-1993
8756	Carlton Fisk, 1969-1993
8632	Ozzie Smith, 1978-1993
8156	Paul Molitor, 1978-1993
7999	Lou Whitaker, 1977-1993
7960	Dale Murphy, 1976-1993

Runs: Most, career, active players

1632	Robin Yount, 1974-1993
1623	Dave Winfield, 1973-1993
1586	Rickey Henderson, 1979-1993
1583	George Brett, 1973-1993
1420	Eddie Murray, 1977-1993
1396	Paul Molitor, 1978-1993
1303	Andre Dawson, 1976-1993
1283	Lou Whitaker, 1977-1993
1276	Carlton Fisk, 1969-1993
1213	Tim Raines, 1979-1993

Hits: Most, career, active players

3154	George Brett, 1973-1993
3142	Robin Yount, 1974-1993
3014	Dave Winfield, 1973-1993
2820	Eddie Murray, 1977-1993
2630	Andre Dawson, 1976-1993
2492	Paul Molitor, 1978-1993
2356	Carlton Fisk, 1969-1993
2267	Wade Boggs, 1982-1993
2265	Ozzie Smith, 1978-1993
2202	Willie Wilson, 1976-1993

Total bases: Most, career, active players

5063	Dave Winfield, 1973-1993
5044	George Brett, 1973-1993
4730	Robin Yount, 1974-1993
4699	Eddie Murray, 1977-1993
4529	Andre Dawson, 1976-1993
3999	Carlton Fisk, 1969-1993
3733	Dale Murphy, 1976-1993
3662	Paul Molitor, 1978-1993
3447	Cal Ripken, 1981-1993
3364	Lou Whitaker, 1977-1993

2B: Most, career, active players

665	George Brett, 1973-1993
583	Robin Yount, 1974-1993
520	Dave Winfield, 1973-1993
490	Eddie Murray, 1977-1993
473	Andre Dawson, 1976-1993
448	Wade Boggs, 1982-1993
442	Paul Molitor, 1978-1993
421	Carlton Fisk, 1969-1993
395	Cal Ripken, 1981-1993
390	Don Mattingly, 1982-1993

3B: Most, career, active players

145	Willie Wilson, 1976-1993
137	George Brett, 1973-1993
126	Robin Yount, 1974-1993
109	Brett Butler, 1981-1993
100	Tim Raines, 1979-1993
95	Andre Dawson, 1976-1993
91	Paul Molitor, 1978-1993
89	Juan Samuel, 1983-1993
86	Andy Van Slyke, 1983-1993
85	Dave Winfield, 1973-1993

HR: Most, career, active players

453	Dave Winfield, 1973-1993
441	Eddie Murray, 1977-1993
412	Andre Dawson, 1976-1993
398	Dale Murphy, 1976-1993
376	Carlton Fisk, 1969-1993
317	George Brett, 1973-1993
317	Lance Parrish, 1977-1993
297	Cal Ripken, 1981-1993
290	Darryl Strawberry, 1983-1993
283	Kent Hrbek, 1981-1993

RBI: Most, career, active players

1786	Dave Winfield, 1973-1993
1662	Eddie Murray, 1977-1993
1595	George Brett, 1973-1993
1492	Andre Dawson, 1976-1993
1406	Robin Yount, 1974-1993
1330	Carlton Fisk, 1969-1993
1266	Dale Murphy, 1976-1993
1144	Harold Baines, 1980-1993
1104	Cal Ripken, 1981-1993
1033	Kent Hrbek, 1981-1993

SB: Most, career, active players

1095	Rickey Henderson, 1979-1993
751	Tim Raines, 1979-1993
667	Willie Wilson, 1976-1993
648	Vince Coleman, 1985-1993
563	Ozzie Smith, 1978-1993
476	Brett Butler, 1981-1993
444	Steve Sax, 1981-1993
434	Paul Molitor, 1978-1993
369	Lonnie Smith, 1978-1993
358	Juan Samuel, 1983-1993

BB: Most, career, active players

1406	Rickey Henderson, 1979-1993
1187	Eddie Murray, 1977-1993
1171	Dave Winfield, 1973-1993
1125	Lou Whitaker, 1977-1993
1096	George Brett, 1973-1993
1078	Wade Boggs, 1982-1993
1003	Tim Raines, 1979-1993
992	Ozzie Smith, 1978-1993
986	Dale Murphy, 1976-1993
966	Robin Yount, 1974-1993

HBP: Most, career, active players

143	Carlton Fisk, 1969-1993
98	Andre Dawson, 1976-1993
91	Lonnie Smith, 1978-1993
69	Joe Carter, 1983-1993
67	Tim Wallach, 1980-1993
63	Juan Samuel, 1983-1993
62	Willie Wilson, 1976-1993
60	Gary Gaetti, 1981-1993
60	Dave Valle, 1984-1993
57	Andres Galarraga, 1985-1993
57	Robby Thompson, 1986-1993

GIDP: Most, career, active players

307	Dave Winfield, 1973-1993
254	Eddie Murray, 1977-1993
235	George Brett, 1973-1993
223	Cal Ripken, 1981-1993
217	Robin Yount, 1974-1993
210	Julio Franco, 1982-1993
209	Dale Murphy, 1976-1993
208	Tony Pena, 1980-1993
204	Carlton Fisk, 1969-1993
199	Harold Baines, 1980-1993

BA: Highest, career, active players

.335	Wade Boggs, 1982-1993
.329	Tony Gwynn, 1982-1993
.320	Frank Thomas, 1990-1993
.319	Kirby Puckett, 1984-1993
.309	Don Mattingly, 1982-1993
.307	Mike Greenwell, 1985-1993
.306	Edgar Martinez, 1987-1993
.306	Paul Molitor, 1978-1993
.305	George Brett, 1973-1993
.304	Mark Grace, 1988-1993

Slug avg: Highest, career, active players

.561	Frank Thomas, 1990-1993
.531	Fred McGriff, 1986-1993
.526	Barry Bonds, 1986-1993
.520	Ken Griffey, 1989-1993
.515	Kevin Mitchell, 1984-1993
.510	Danny Tartabull, 1984-1993
.509	Mark McGwire, 1986-1993
.507	Darryl Strawberry, 1983-1993
.507	Jose Canseco, 1985-1993
.505	Albert Belle, 1989-1993

Extra-base hits: Most, career, active players

1119	George Brett, 1973-1993
1058	Dave Winfield, 1973-1993
980	Andre Dawson, 1976-1993
964	Eddie Murray, 1977-1993
960	Robin Yount, 1974-1993
844	Carlton Fisk, 1969-1993
787	Dale Murphy, 1976-1993
729	Cal Ripken, 1981-1993
715	Paul Molitor, 1978-1993
666	Lou Whitaker, 1977-1993

Pitchers

Games: Most, career, active players

966	Rich Gossage, 1972-1993
869	Jeff Reardon, 1979-1993
850	Lee Smith, 1980-1993
837	Charlie Hough, 1970-1993
807	Nolan Ryan, 1966-1993
804	Dennis Eckersley,1975-1993
714	Jesse Orosco, 1979-1993
698	Bob McClure, 1975-1993
688	Dave Righetti, 1979-1993
670	Larry Andersen, 1975-1993

Complete games: Most, career, active players

222	Nolan Ryan, 1966-1993
174	Jack Morris, 1977-1993
143	Frank Tanana, 1973-1993
112	Fernando Valenzuela, 1980-1993
110	Dennis Martinez, 1976-1993
106	Charlie Hough, 1970-1993
103	Dave Stieb, 1979-1993
100	Dennis Eckersley, 1975-1993
91	Roger Clemens, 1984-1993
83	Bruce Hurst, 1980-1993

Shutouts: Most, career, active players

61	Nolan Ryan, 1966-1993
35	Roger Clemens, 1984-1993
34	Frank Tanana, 1973-1993
31	Fernando Valenzuela, 1980-1993
30	Dave Stieb, 1979-1993
28	Jack Morris, 1977-1993
28	Bob Welch, 1978-1993
24	Orel Hershiser, 1983-1993
23	Dwight Gooden, 1984-1993
23	Bruce Hurst, 1980-1993
23	Dennis Martinez, 1976-1993

Wins: Most, career, active players

324	Nolan Ryan, 1966-1993
244	Jack Morris, 1977-1993
240	Frank Tanana, 1973-1993
211	Charlie Hough, 1970-1993
208	Dennis Martinez, 1976-1993
208	Bob Welch, 1978-1993
183	Dennis Eckersley, 1975-1993
177	John Candelaria, 1975-1993
175	Dave Stieb, 1979-1993
174	Frank Viola, 1982-1993

Losses: Most, career, active players

292	Nolan Ryan, 1966-1993
236	Frank Tanana, 1973-1993
207	Charlie Hough, 1970-1993
180	Jack Morris, 1977-1993
165	Dennis Martinez, 1976-1993
151	Mike Moore, 1982-1993
149	Dennis Eckersley, 1975-1993
145	Frank Viola, 1982-1993
140	Bob Welch, 1978-1993
139	Rick Honeycutt, 1977-1993

HR allowed: Most, career, active players

448	Frank Tanana, 1973-1993
375	Jack Morris, 1977-1993
366	Charlie Hough, 1970-1993
321	Nolan Ryan, 1966-1993
314	Dennis Eckersley, 1975-1993
313	Dennis Martinez, 1976-1993
283	Frank Viola, 1982-1993
266	Scott Sanderson, 1978-1993
258	Bill Gullickson, 1979-1993
257	Bob Welch, 1978-1993

BB: Most career, active players

2795	Nolan Ryan, 1966-1993
1613	Charlie Hough, 1970-1993
1323	Jack Morris, 1977-1993
1255	Frank Tanana, 1973-1993
1049	Rick Sutcliffe, 1976-1993
1027	Mark Langston, 1984-1993
1017	Dave Stieb, 1979-1993
999	Mike Moore, 1982-1993
997	Fernando Valenzuela, 1980-1993
991	Bob Welch, 1978-1993

K: Most, career, active players

5714	Nolan Ryan, 1966-1993
2773	Frank Tanana, 1973-1993
2378	Jack Morris, 1977-1993
2297	Charlie Hough, 1970-1993
2198	Dennis Eckersley, 1975-1993
2033	Roger Clemens, 1984-1993
2001	Mark Langston, 1984-1993
1925	Bob Welch, 1978-1993
1842	Fernando Valenzuela, 1980-1993
1835	Dwight Gooden, 1984-1993

Wild pitches: Most, career, active players

277	Nolan Ryan, 1966-1993
193	Jack Morris, 1977-1993
170	Charlie Hough, 1970-1993
119	Frank Tanana, 1973-1993
117	Mike Moore, 1982-1993
105	Dave Stewart, 1978-1993
103	Fernando Valenzuela, 1980-1993
96	Rick Sutcliffe, 1976-1993
89	Mark Gubicza, 1984-1993
88	Bobby Witt, 1986-1993

Win pct: Highest, career, active players

.655	Dwight Gooden, 1984-1993
.655	Roger Clemens, 1984-1993
.651	Mike Henneman, 1987-1993
.642	John Burkett, 1987-1993
.623	Jack McDowell, 1987-1993
.612	Teddy Higuera, 1985-1993
.608	Kevin Appier, 1989-1993
.606	Jimmy Key, 1984-1993
.598	Bob Welch, 1978-1993
.594	David Cone, 1986-1993

ERA: Lowest, career, active players

2.86	Jesse Orosco, 1979-1993
2.91	Lee Smith, 1980-1993
2.94	Roger Clemens, 1984-1993
2.95	Orel Hershiser, 1983-1993
2.95	Kevin Appier, 1989-1993
2.98	Rich Gossage, 1972-1993
3.00	Mark Eichhorn, 1982-1993
3.04	Dwight Gooden, 1984-1993
3.07	Roger McDowell, 1985-1993
3.10	Larry Andersen, 1975-1993

Innings: Most, career, active players

5386.0	Nolan Ryan, 1966-1993
4188.1	Frank Tanana, 1973-1993
3687.2	Charlie Hough, 1970-1993
3682.2	Jack Morris, 1977-1993
3384.0	Dennis Martinez, 1976-1993
3038.1	Dennis Eckersley, 1975-1993
3023.1	Bob Welch, 1978-1993
2845.0	Dave Stieb, 1979-1993
2760.2	Frank Viola, 1982-1993
2630.0	Rick Sutcliffe, 1976-1993

American League single-season records

Hitters

ACTIVE PLAYERS IN CAPS

At-bats: Most, season, AL

705	WILLIE WILSON, KC-1980
692	Bobby Richardson, NY-1962
691	KIRBY PUCKETT, Min-1985
689	Sandy Alomar, Cal-1971
687	TONY FERNANDEZ, Tor-1986
686	Horace Clarke, NY-1970
680	KIRBY PUCKETT, Min-1986
679	Harvey Kuenn, Det-1953
679	Bobby Richardson, NY-1964
677	DON MATTINGLY, NY-1986
677	Jim Rice, Bos-1978

Runs: Most, season, AL

177	Babe Ruth, NY-1921
167	Lou Gehrig, NY-1936
163	Lou Gehrig, NY-1931
163	Babe Ruth, NY-1928
158	Babe Ruth, NY-1920
158	Babe Ruth, NY-1927
152	Al Simmons, Phi-1930
151	Joe DiMaggio, NY-1937
151	Jimmie Foxx, Phi-1932
151	Babe Ruth, NY-1923

Hits: Most, season, AL

257	George Sisler, StL-1920
253	Al Simmons, Phi-1925
248	Ty Cobb, Det-1911
246	George Sisler, StL-1922
241	Heinie Manush, StL-1928
240	WADE BOGGS, Bos-1985
239	Rod Carew, Min-1977
238	DON MATTINGLY, NY-1986
237	Harry Heilmann, Det-1921
236	Jack Tobin, StL-1921

Total bases: Most, season, AL

457	Babe Ruth, NY-1921
447	Lou Gehrig, NY-1927
438	Jimmie Foxx, Phi-1932
419	Lou Gehrig, NY-1930
418	Joe DiMaggio, NY-1937
417	Babe Ruth, NY-1927
410	Lou Gehrig, NY-1931
409	Lou Gehrig, NY-1934
406	Jim Rice, Bos-1978
405	Hal Trosky, Cle-1936

2B: Most, season, AL

67	Earl Webb, Bos-1931
64	George Burns, Cle-1926
63	Hank Greenberg, Det-1934
60	Charlie Gehringer, Det-1936
59	Tris Speaker, Cle-1923
56	George Kell, Det-1950
55	Gee Walker, Det-1936
54	Hal McRae, KC-1977
54	JOHN OLERUD, Tor-1993
53	DON MATTINGLY, NY-1986
53	Al Simmons, Phi-1926
53	Tris Speaker, Bos-1912

3B: Most, season, AL

26	Sam Crawford, Det-1914
26	Joe Jackson, Cle-1912
25	Sam Crawford, Det-1903
24	Ty Cobb, Det-1911
24	Ty Cobb, Det-1917
23	Ty Cobb, Det-1912
23	Earle Combs, NY-1927
23	Sam Crawford, Det-1913
23	Dale Mitchell, Cle-1949
22	Bill Bradley, Cle-1903
22	Earle Combs, NY-1930
22	Birdie Cree, NY-1911
22	Elmer Flick, Cle-1906
22	Tris Speaker, Bos-1913
22	Snuffy Stirnweiss, NY-1945

HR: Most, season, AL

61	Roger Maris, NY-1961
60	Babe Ruth, NY-1927
59	Babe Ruth, NY-1921
58	Jimmie Foxx, Phi-1932
58	Hank Greenberg, Det-1938
54	Mickey Mantle, NY-1961
54	Babe Ruth, NY-1920
54	Babe Ruth, NY-1928
52	Mickey Mantle, NY-1956
51	CECIL FIELDER, Det-1990

RBI: Most, season, AL

184	Lou Gehrig, NY-1931
183	Hank Greenberg, Det-1937
175	Jimmie Foxx, Bos-1938
175	Lou Gehrig, NY-1927
174	Lou Gehrig, NY-1930
171	Babe Ruth, NY-1921
170	Hank Greenberg, Det-1935
169	Jimmie Foxx, Phi-1932
167	Joe DiMaggio, NY-1937
165	Lou Gehrig, NY-1934
165	Al Simmons, Phi-1930

SB: Most, season, AL

130	RICKEY HENDERSON, Oak-1982
108	RICKEY HENDERSON, Oak-1983
100	RICKEY HENDERSON, Oak-1980
96	Ty Cobb, Det-1915
93	RICKEY HENDERSON, NY-1988
88	Clyde Milan, Was-1912
87	RICKEY HENDERSON, NY-1986
83	Ty Cobb, Det-1911
83	WILLIE WILSON, KC-1979
81	Eddie Collins, Phi-1910

BB: Most, season, AL

170	Babe Ruth, NY-1923
162	Ted Williams, Bos-1947
162	Ted Williams, Bos-1949
156	Ted Williams, Bos-1946
151	Eddie Yost, Was-1956
149	Eddie Joost, Phi-1949
148	Babe Ruth, NY-1920
146	Mickey Mantle, NY-1957
145	Harmon Killebrew, Min-1969
145	Ted Williams, Bos-1941
145	Ted Williams, Bos-1942

K: Most, season, AL

186	ROB DEER, Mil-1987
185	PETE INCAVIGLIA, Tex-1986
182	CECIL FIELDER, Det-1990
179	ROB DEER, Mil-1986
175	JOSE CANSECO, Oak-1986
175	ROB DEER, Det-1991
175	Dave Nicholson, Chi-1963
175	Gorman Thomas, Mil-1979
172	BO JACKSON, KC-1989
172	Jim Presley, Sea-1986

GIDP: Most, season, AL

36	Jim Rice, Bos-1984
35	Jim Rice, Bos-1985
32	Jackie Jensen, Bos-1954
32	CAL RIPKEN, Bal-1985
31	Tony Armas, Bos-1983
31	Bobby Doerr, Bos-1949
31	Jim Rice, Bos-1983
30	Billy Hitchcock, Phi-1950
30	DAVE WINFIELD, NY-1983
30	Carl Yastrzemski, Bos-1964

BA: Highest, season, AL

.426	Nap Lajoie, Phi-1901
.420	George Sisler, StL-1922
.420	Ty Cobb, Det-1911
.409	Ty Cobb, Det-1912
.408	Joe Jackson, Cle-1911
.407	George Sisler, StL-1920
.406	Ted Williams, Bos-1941
.403	Harry Heilmann, Det-1923
.401	Ty Cobb, Det-1922
.398	Harry Heilmann, Det-1927

52

Slug avg: Highest, season, AL

.847	Babe Ruth, NY-1920
.846	Babe Ruth, NY-1921
.772	Babe Ruth, NY-1927
.765	Lou Gehrig, NY-1927
.764	Babe Ruth, NY-1923
.749	Jimmie Foxx, Phi-1932
.739	Babe Ruth, NY-1924
.737	Babe Ruth, NY-1926
.735	Ted Williams, Bos-1941
.732	Babe Ruth, NY-1930

Extra-base hits: Most, season, AL

119	Babe Ruth, NY-1921
117	Lou Gehrig, NY-1927
103	Hank Greenberg, Det-1937
100	Jimmie Foxx, Phi-1932
100	Lou Gehrig, NY-1930
99	Hank Greenberg, Det-1940
99	Babe Ruth, NY-1920
99	Babe Ruth, NY-1923
98	Hank Greenberg, Det-1935
97	Babe Ruth, NY-1927

Pitchers

Games: Most, season, AL

90	Mike Marshall, Min-1979
89	MARK EICHHORN, Tor-1987
88	Wilbur Wood, Chi-1968
85	MITCH WILLIAMS, Tex-1987
84	Dan Quisenberry, KC-1985
83	Ken Sanders, Mil-1971
82	Eddie Fisher, Chi-1965
81	KENNY ROGERS, Tex-1992
81	DUANE WARD, Tor-1991
81	John Wyatt, KC-1964

Complete games: Most, season, AL

48	Jack Chesbro, NY-1904
42	George Mullin, Det-1904
42	Ed Walsh, Chi-1908
41	Cy Young, Bos-1902
40	Cy Young, Bos-1904
39	Bill Dinneen, Bos-1902
39	Joe McGinnity, Bal-1901
39	Rube Waddell, Phi-1904
38	Walter Johnson, Was-1910
38	Jack Powell, NY-1904
38	Cy Young, Bos-1901

Saves: Most, season, AL

57	BOBBY THIGPEN, Chi-1990
51	DENNIS ECKERSLEY, Oak-1992
48	DENNIS ECKERSLEY, Oak-1990
46	BRYAN HARVEY, Cal-1991
46	DAVE RIGHETTI, NY-1986
45	DENNIS ECKERSLEY, Oak-1988
45	JEFF MONTGOMERY, KC-1993
45	Dan Quisenberry, KC-1983
45	DUANE WARD, Tor-1993
44	Dan Quisenberry, KC-1984

Shutouts: Most, season, AL

13	Jack Coombs, Phi-1910
11	Dean Chance, LA-1964
11	Walter Johnson, Was-1913
11	Ed Walsh, Chi-1908
10	Bob Feller, Cle-1946
10	Bob Lemon, Cle-1948
10	Jim Palmer, Bal-1975
10	Ed Walsh, Chi-1906
10	Joe Wood, Bos-1912
10	Cy Young, Bos-1904

Wins: Most, season, AL

41	Jack Chesbro, NY-1904
40	Ed Walsh, Chi-1908
36	Walter Johnson, Was-1913
34	Joe Wood, Bos-1912
33	Walter Johnson, Was-1912
33	Cy Young, Bos-1901
32	Cy Young, Bos-1902
31	Jim Bagby, Cle-1920
31	Jack Coombs, Phi-1910
31	Lefty Grove, Phi-1931
31	Denny McLain, Det-1968

Losses: Most, season, AL

26	Pete Dowling, Mil-Cle-1901
26	Bob Groom, Was-1909
26	Happy Townsend, Was-1904
25	Patsy Flaherty, Chi-1903
25	Fred Glade, StL-1905
25	Walter Johnson, Was-1909
25	Scott Perry, Phi-1920
25	Red Ruffing, Bos-1928
24	Joe Bush, Phi-1916
24	Pat Caraway, Chi-1931
24	Sam Gray, StL-1931
24	Tom Hughes, NY-Was-1904

HR allowed: Most, season, AL

50	Bert Blyleven, Min-1986
46	Bert Blyleven, Min-1987
43	Pedro Ramos, Was-1957
42	Denny McLain, Det-1966
40	Fergie Jenkins, Tex-1979
40	JACK MORRIS, Det-1986
40	Orlando Pena, KC-1964
40	Ralph Terry, NY-1962
39	Catfish Hunter, Oak-1973
39	JACK MORRIS, Det-1987
39	Jim Perry, Min-1971
39	Pedro Ramos, Min-1961

BB: Most season, AL

208	Bob Feller, Cle-1938
204	NOLAN RYAN, Cal-1977
202	NOLAN RYAN, Cal-1974
194	Bob Feller, Cle-1941
192	Bobo Newsom, StL-1938
183	NOLAN RYAN, Cal-1976
181	Bob Turley, Bal-1954
179	Tommy Byrne, NY-1949
177	Bob Turley, NY-1955
171	Bump Hadley, Chi-StL-1932

K: Most, season, AL

383	NOLAN RYAN, Cal-1973
367	NOLAN RYAN, Cal-1974
349	Rube Waddell, Phi-1904
348	Bob Feller, Cle-1946
341	NOLAN RYAN, Cal-1977
329	NOLAN RYAN, Cal-1972
327	NOLAN RYAN, Cal-1976
325	Sam McDowell, Cle-1965
313	Walter Johnson, Was-1910
308	RANDY JOHNSON, Sea-1993
308	Mickey Lolich, Det-1971

Win pct: Highest, season, AL

.938	Johnny Allen, Cle-1937
.893	Ron Guidry, NY-1978
.886	Lefty Grove, Phi-1931
.872	Joe Wood, Bos-1912
.862	Whitey Ford, NY-1961
.862	Bill Donovan, Det-1907
.857	ROGER CLEMENS, Bos-1986
.850	Chief Bender, Phi-1914
.849	Lefty Grove, Phi-1930
.842	Ralph Terry, NY-1961
.842	Schoolboy Rowe, Det-1940
.842	Sandy Consuegra, Chi-1954

ERA: Lowest, season, AL

0.96	Dutch Leonard, Bos-1914
1.14	Walter Johnson, Was-1913
1.16	Addie Joss, Cle-1908
1.26	Cy Young, Bos-1908
1.27	Ed Walsh, Chi-1910
1.27	Walter Johnson, Was-1918
1.30	Jack Coombs, Phi-1910
1.36	Walter Johnson, Was-1910
1.39	Walter Johnson, Was-1912
1.39	Harry Krause, Phi-1909

Innings: Most, season, AL

464.0	Ed Walsh, Chi-1908
454.2	Jack Chesbro, NY-1904
422.1	Ed Walsh, Chi-1907
393.0	Ed Walsh, Chi-1912
390.1	Jack Powell, NY-1904
384.2	Cy Young, Bos-1902
383.0	Rube Waddell, Phi-1904
382.1	George Mullin, Det-1904
382.0	Joe McGinnity, Bal-1901
380.0	Cy Young, Bos-1904

American League club records

Highest Batting Average season, AL

.316	Detroit, 1921
.313	St. Louis, 1922
.309	New York, 1930
.308	St. Louis, 1920
.308	Cleveland, 1921

Lowest Batting Average season, AL

.211 Chicago, 1910
.214 New York, 1968
.217 Texas, 1972
.218 St.Louis, 1910
.221 Chicago, 1909

Highest Slugging Percentage season, AL

.489 New York, 1927
.488 New York, 1930
.483 New York, 1936
.465 Boston, 1977
.464 New York, 1921

Most Runs season, AL

1067 New York, 1931
1065 New York, 1936
1062 New York, 1930
1027 Boston, 1950
1002 New York, 1932

Most Homers season, AL

240 New York, 1961
225 Minnesota, 1963
225 Detroit, 1987
221 Minnesota, 1964
216 Milwaukee, 1982

Most Stolen Bases season, AL

341 Oakland, 1976
288 New York, 1910
287 Washington, 1913
280 Chicago, 1901
280 Detroit, 1909

Most Grounded into Double Plays season, AL

174 Boston, 1990
171 Boston, 1982
171 Boston, 1983
170 Philadelphia, 1950
169 Boston, 1949
169 Boston, 1951
169 Boston, 1989

Highest Fielding Average season, AL

.986 Toronto, 1990
.986 Baltimore, 1989
.986 Minnesota, 1988
.986 Oakland, 1990
.986 Milwaukee, 1992

Most Errors season, AL

410 Detroit, 1901
401 Baltimore, 1901
393 Milwaukee, 1901
385 St. Louis, 1910
382 New York, 1912

Fewest Errors season, AL

84 Minnesota, 1988
86 Toronto, 1990
87 Oakland, 1990
87 Baltimore, 1989
89 Milwaukee, 1992

Most Double Plays season, AL

217 Philadelphia, 1949
214 New York, 1956
208 Philadelphia, 1950
207 Boston, 1949
206 Boston, 1980
206 Toronto, 1980

Lowest Earned Run Average season, AL

1.78 Philadelphia, 1910
1.93 Philadelphia, 1909
1.99 Chicago, 1905
2.02 Cleveland, 1908
2.03 Chicago, 1910

Most Shutouts season, AL

32 Chicago, 1906
28 Los Angeles, 1964
27 Cleveland, 1906
27 Philadelphia, 1907
27 Philadelphia, 1909

Most Homers Allowed season, AL

226 Baltimore, 1987
220 Kansas City, 1964
219 Cleveland, 1987
212 California, 1987
210 Minnesota, 1987

Fewest Homers Allowed season, AL

6 Boston, 1913
7 St. Louis, 1908
8 Philadelphia, 1910
8 Chicago, 1909
8 Detroit, 1907
8 Cleveland, 1907

Most Walks Allowed season, AL

827 Philadelphia, 1915
812 New York, 1949
801 St.Louis, 1951
779 Washington, 1949
770 Cleveland, 1971

National League single-season records

Hitters

ACTIVE PLAYERS IN CAPS

At-bats: Most, season, NL

701 JUAN SAMUEL, Phi-1984
699 Dave Cash, Phi-1975
698 Matty Alou, Pit-1969
696 Woody Jensen, Pit-1936
695 Omar Moreno, Pit-1979
695 Maury Wills, LA-1962
689 Lou Brock, StL-1967
687 Dave Cash, Phi-1974
681 Jo-Jo Moore, NY-1935
681 Lloyd Waner, Pit-1931

Runs: Most, season, NL

192 Billy Hamilton, Phi-1894
166 Billy Hamilton, Phi-1895
165 Willie Keeler, Bal-1894
165 Joe Kelley, Bal-1894
162 Willie Keeler, Bal-1895
160 Jesse Burkett, Cle-1896
160 Hugh Duffy, Bos-1894
159 Hughie Jennings, Bal-1895
158 Chuck Klein, Phi-1930
158 Bobby Lowe, Bos-1894

Hits: Most, season, NL

254 Lefty O'Doul, Phi-1929
254 Bill Terry, NY-1930
250 Rogers Hornsby, StL-1922
250 Chuck Klein, Phi-1930
241 Babe Herman, Bro-1930
240 Jesse Burkett, Cle-1896
239 Willie Keeler, Bal-1897
238 Ed Delahanty, Phi-1899
237 Hugh Duffy, Bos-1894
237 Joe Medwick, StL-1937
237 Paul Waner, Pit-1927

Total bases: Most, season, NL

450 Rogers Hornsby, StL-1922
445 Chuck Klein, Phi-1930
429 Stan Musial, StL-1948
423 Hack Wilson, Chi-1930
420 Chuck Klein, Phi-1932
416 Babe Herman, Bro-1930
409 Rogers Hornsby, Chi-1929
406 Joe Medwick, StL-1937
405 Chuck Klein, Phi-1929
400 Hank Aaron, Mil-1959

2B: Most, season, NL

64 Joe Medwick, StL-1936
62 Paul Waner, Pit-1932
59 Chuck Klein, Phi-1930
57 Billy Herman, Chi-1935
57 Billy Herman, Chi-1936
56 Joe Medwick, StL-1937
55 Ed Delahanty, Phi-1899
53 Stan Musial, StL-1953
53 Paul Waner, Pit-1936
52 Johnny Frederick, Bro-1929
52 Enos Slaughter, StL-1939

3B: Most, season, NL

36 Chief Wilson, Pit-1912
31 Heinie Reitz, Bal-1894
29 Perry Werden, StL-1893
28 Harry Davis, Pit-1897
27 George Davis, NY-1893
27 Jimmy Williams, Pit-1899
26 Kiki Cuyler, Pit-1925
26 John Reilly, Cin-1890
26 George Treadway, Bro-1894
25 Roger Connor, NY-StL-1894
25 Larry Doyle, NY-1911
25 Buck Freeman, Was-1899
25 Tom Long, StL-1915

HR: Most, season, NL

56	Hack Wilson, Chi-1930
54	Ralph Kiner, Pit-1949
52	George Foster, Cin-1977
52	Willie Mays, SF-1965
51	Ralph Kiner, Pit-1947
51	Willie Mays, NY-1955
51	Johnny Mize, NY-1947
49	ANDRE DAWSON, Chi-1987
49	Ted Kluszewski, Cin-1954
49	Willie Mays, SF-1962

RBI: Most, season, NL

190	Hack Wilson, Chi-1930
170	Chuck Klein, Phi-1930
166	Sam Thompson, Det-1887
165	Sam Thompson, Phi-1895
159	Hack Wilson, Chi-1929
154	Joe Medwick, StL-1937
153	Tommy Davis, LA-1962
152	Rogers Hornsby, StL-1922
151	Mel Ott, NY-1929
149	George Foster, Cin-1977
149	Rogers Hornsby, Chi-1929

SB: Most, season, NL

118	Lou Brock, StL-1974
111	Billy Hamilton, Phi-1891
111	John Ward, NY-1887
110	VINCE COLEMAN, StL-1985
109	VINCE COLEMAN, StL-1987
107	VINCE COLEMAN, StL-1986
104	Maury Wills, LA-1962
102	Jim Fogarty, Phi-1887
102	Billy Hamilton, Phi-1890
99	Jim Fogarty, Phi-1889

BB: Most, season, NL

148	Eddie Stanky, Bro-1945
148	Jim Wynn, Hou-1969
147	Jimmy Sheckard, Chi-1911
144	Eddie Stanky, NY-1950
137	Ralph Kiner, Pit-1951
137	Willie McCovey, SF-1970
137	Eddie Stanky, Bro-1946
136	Jack Clark, StL-1987
136	Jack Crooks, StL-1892
132	Jack Clark, SD-1989
132	Joe Morgan, Cin-1975

K: Most, season, NL

189	Bobby Bonds, SF-1970
187	Bobby Bonds, SF-1969
180	Mike Schmidt, Phi-1975
169	ANDRES GALARRAGA, Mon-1990
168	JUAN SAMUEL, Phi-1984
163	Donn Clendenon, Pit-1968
162	JUAN SAMUEL, Phi-1987
161	Dick Allen, Phi-1968
158	ANDRES GALARRAGA, Mon-1989
156	Tommie Agee, NY-1970
156	Dave Kingman, NY-1982

GIDP: Most, season, NL

30	Ernie Lombardi, Cin-1938
29	Ted Simmons, StL-1973
28	Sid Gordon, Bos-1951
27	John Bateman, Mon-1971
27	Carl Furillo, Bro-1956
27	Ron Santo, Chi-1973
27	Ken Singleton, Mon-1973
26	Sid Gordon, NY-1943
26	Cleon Jones, NY-1970
26	Billy Jurges, NY-1939
26	Ernie Lombardi, Cin-1933
26	Willie Montanez, Phi-SF-1975
26	Willie Montanez, SF-Atl-1976
26	Dave Parker, Cin-1985
26	Joe Torre, Mil-1964

BA: Highest, season, NL

.440	Hugh Duffy, Bos-1894
.424	Willie Keeler, Bal-1897
.424	Rogers Hornsby, StL-1924
.410	Ed Delahanty, Phi-1899
.410	Jesse Burkett, Cle-1896
.409	Jesse Burkett, Cle-1895
.407	Ed Delahanty, Phi-1894
.404	Billy Hamilton, Phi-1894
.404	Ed Delahanty, Phi-1895
.403	Rogers Hornsby, StL-1925

Slug avg: Highest, season, NL

.756	Rogers Hornsby, StL-1925
.723	Hack Wilson, Chi-1930
.722	Rogers Hornsby, StL-1922
.702	Stan Musial, StL-1948
.696	Rogers Hornsby, StL-1924
.694	Hugh Duffy, Bos-1894
.687	Chuck Klein, Phi-1930
.679	Rogers Hornsby, Chi-1929
.678	Babe Herman, Bro-1930
.677	BARRY BONDS, SF-1993

Extra-base hits: Most, season, NL

107	Chuck Klein, Phi-1930
103	Chuck Klein, Phi-1932
103	Stan Musial, StL-1948
102	Rogers Hornsby, StL-1922
97	Joe Medwick, StL-1937
97	Hack Wilson, Chi-1930
95	Joe Medwick, StL-1936
94	Babe Herman, Bro-1930
94	Rogers Hornsby, Chi-1929
94	Chuck Klein, Phi-1929

Pitchers

Games: Most, season, NL

106	Mike Marshall, LA-1974
94	Kent Tekulve, Pit-1979
92	Mike Marshall, Mon-1973
91	Kent Tekulve, Pit-1978
90	Wayne Granger, Cin-1969
90	Kent Tekulve, Phi-1987
87	ROB MURPHY, Cin-1987
85	Kent Tekulve, Pit-1982
85	Frank Williams, Cin-1987
84	Ted Abernathy, Chi-1965
84	Enrique Romo, Pit-1979

Complete games: Most, season, NL

75	Will White, Cin-1879
73	Charley Radbourn, Pro-1884
72	Jim Galvin, Buf-1883
72	Jim McCormick, Cle-1880
71	Jim Galvin, Buf-1884
68	John Clarkson, Chi-1885
68	John Clarkson, Bos-1889
67	Bill Hutchison, Chi-1892
66	Jim Devlin, Lou-1876
66	Charley Radbourn, Pro-1883

Saves: Most, season, NL

53	RANDY MYERS, Chi-1993
48	ROD BECK, SF-1993
47	LEE SMITH, StL-1991
45	BRYAN HARVEY, Fla-1993
45	Bruce Sutter, StL-1984
44	MARK DAVIS, SD-1989
43	LEE SMITH, StL-1992
43	LEE SMITH, StL-1993
43	JOHN WETTELAND, Mon-1993
43	MITCH WILLIAMS, Phi-1993

Shutouts: Most, season, NL

16	Pete Alexander, Phi-1916
16	George Bradley, StL-1876
13	Bob Gibson, StL-1968
12	Pete Alexander, Phi-1915
12	Jim Galvin, Buf-1884
11	Tommy Bond, Bos-1879
11	Sandy Koufax, LA-1963
11	Christy Mathewson, NY-1908
11	Charley Radbourn, Pro-1884
10	John Clarkson, Chi-1885
10	Mort Cooper, StL-1942
10	Carl Hubbell, NY-1933
10	Juan Marichal, SF-1965
10	John Tudor, StL-1985

Wins: Most, season, NL

59	Charley Radbourn, Pro-1884
53	John Clarkson, Chi-1885
49	John Clarkson, Bos-1889
48	Charlie Buffinton, Bos-1884
48	Charley Radbourn, Pro-1883
47	Al Spalding, Chi-1876
47	John Ward, Pro-1879
46	Jim Galvin, Buf-1883
46	Jim Galvin, Buf-1884
45	George Bradley, StL-1876
45	Jim McCormick, Cle-1880

Losses: Most, season, NL

48	John Coleman, Phi-1883
42	Will White, Cin-1880
40	George Bradley, Tro-1879
40	Jim McCormick, Cle-1879
37	George Cobb, Bal-1892
36	Bill Hutchison, Chi-1892
36	Stump Weidman, KC-1886
35	Jim Devlin, Lou-1876
35	Red Donahue, StL-1897
35	Jim Galvin, Buf-1880

HR allowed: Most, season, NL

46	Robin Roberts, Phi-1956	
41	Phil Niekro, Atl-1979	
41	Robin Roberts, Phi-1955	
40	Phil Niekro, Atl-1970	
40	Robin Roberts, Phi-1957	
39	Murry Dickson, StL-1948	
38	Lew Burdette, Mil-1959	
38	Warren Hacker, Chi-1955	
38	Don Sutton, LA-1970	
36	TOM BROWNING, Cin-1988	
36	Larry Jansen, NY-1949	
36	Art Mahaffey, Phi-1962	
36	Ed Whitson, SD-1987	

BB: Most season, NL

289	Amos Rusie, NY-1890
267	Amos Rusie, NY-1892
262	Amos Rusie, NY-1891
227	Mark Baldwin, Pit-1891
218	Amos Rusie, NY-1893
213	Cy Seymour, NY-1898
203	John Clarkson, Bos-1889
200	Amos Rusie, NY-1894
199	Bill Hutchison, Chi-1890
194	Mark Baldwin, Pit-1892

K: Most, season, NL

441	Charley Radbourn, Pro-1884
417	Charlie Buffinton, Bos-1884
382	Sandy Koufax, LA-1965
369	Jim Galvin, Buf-1884
345	Mickey Welch, NY-1884
345	Jim Whitney, Bos-1883
341	Amos Rusie, NY-1890
337	Amos Rusie, NY-1891
335	Tim Keefe, NY-1888
323	Lady Baldwin, Det-1886

Win pct: Highest, season, NL

.880	Preacher Roe, Bro-1951
.875	Fred Goldsmith, Chi-1880
.870	DAVID CONE, NY-1988
.864	OREL HERSHISER, LA-1985
.857	DWIGHT GOODEN, NY-1985
.842	Emil Yde, Pit-1924
.842	Tom Hughes, Bos-1916
.838	Bill Hoffer, Bal-1895
.833	King Cole, Chi-1910
.833	Sandy Koufax, LA-1963
.833	Hoyt Wilhelm, NY-1952

ERA: Lowest, season, NL

1.04	Mordecai Brown, Chi-1906
1.12	Bob Gibson, StL-1968
1.14	Christy Mathewson, NY-1909
1.15	Jack Pfiester, Chi-1907
1.17	Carl Lundgren, Chi-1907
1.22	Pete Alexander, Phi-1915
1.23	George Bradley, StL-1876
1.28	Christy Mathewson, NY-1905
1.31	Mordecai Brown, Chi-1909
1.33	Jack Taylor, Chi-1902

Innings: Most, season, NL

680.0	Will White, Cin-1879
678.2	Charley Radbourn, Pro-1884
657.2	Jim McCormick, Cle-1880
656.1	Jim Galvin, Buf-1883
636.1	Jim Galvin, Buf-1884
632.1	Charley Radbourn, Pro-1883
627.0	Bill Hutchison, Chi-1892
623.0	John Clarkson, Chi-1885
622.0	Jim Devlin, Lou-1876
620.0	John Clarkson, Bos-1889

National League club records

Highest Batting Average season, NL

.349	Philadelphia, 1894
.343	Baltimore, 1894
.337	Chicago, 1876
.331	Boston, 1894
.330	Philadelphia, 1895

Lowest Batting Average season, NL

.208	Washington, 1888
.208	Detroit, 1884
.210	Washington, 1886
.213	Brooklyn, 1908
.219	New York, 1963

Highest Slugging Percentage season, NL

.484	Boston, 1894
.483	Baltimore, 1894
.481	Chicago, 1930
.476	Philadelphia, 1894
.474	Brooklyn, 1953

Most Runs season, NL

1220	Boston, 1894
1171	Baltimore, 1894
1143	Philadelphia, 1894
1068	Philadelphia, 1895
1041	Chicago, 1894

Most Homers season, NL

221	New York, 1947
221	Cincinnati, 1956
209	Chicago, 1987
208	Brooklyn, 1953
207	Atlanta, 1966

Most Stolen Bases season, NL

441	Baltimore, 1896
415	New York, 1887
409	Brooklyn, 1892
401	Baltimore, 1897
382	Chicago, 1887

Most Grounded into Double Plays season, NL

166	St.Louis, 1958
157	Chicago, 1938
154	Atlanta, 1985
153	New York, 1939
151	Brooklyn, 1952

Highest Fielding Average season, NL

.985	St. Louis, 1992
.984	Pittsburgh, 1992
.984	Cincinnati, 1977
.984	Cincinnati, 1992
.984	San Francisco, 1993
.984	Cincinnati, 1975

Most Errors season, NL

639	Philadelphia, 1883
607	Pittsburgh, 1890
595	Chicago, 1884
584	Baltimore, 1892
565	New York, 1892

Fewest Errors season, NL

94	St. Louis, 1992
95	Cincinnati, 1977
96	Cincinnati, 1992
100	Cincinnati, 1958
101	Pittsburgh, 1992
101	San Francisco, 1993

Most Double Plays season, NL

215	Pittsburgh, 1966
198	Los Angeles, 1958
197	Atlanta, 1985
195	Pittsburgh, 1963
195	Pittsburgh, 1970

Lowest Earned Run Average season, NL

1.22	St. Louis, 1876
1.61	Providence, 1884
1.64	Providence, 1880
1.67	Hartford, 1876
1.69	Louisville, 1876

Most Shutouts season, NL

32	Chicago, 1907
32	Chicago, 1909
30	Chicago, 1906
30	St. Louis, 1968
29	Chicago, 1908

Most Homers Allowed season, NL

192	New York, 1962
185	St. Louis, 1955
185	Atlanta, 1970
184	Chicago, 1966
181	Colorado, 1993

Fewest Homers Allowed season, NL

5	Cincinnati, 1909
6	Chicago, 1909
8	Philadelphia, 1908
11	Chicago, 1907
12	Pittsburgh, 1909
12	Pittsburgh, 1907
12	Chicago, 1906
12	Pittsburgh, 1905

Most Walks Allowed season, NL

716	Montreal, 1970
715	San Diego, 1974
702	Montreal, 1969
701	St. Louis, 1911
701	Atlanta, 1977

Career records

Hitters

ACTIVE PLAYERS IN CAPS

Games played: Most, career, all-time

3562	Pete Rose, 1963-1986
3308	Carl Yastrzemski, 1961-1983
3298	Hank Aaron, 1954-1976
3035	Ty Cobb, 1905-1928
3026	Stan Musial, 1941-1963
2992	Willie Mays, 1951-1973
2951	Rusty Staub, 1963-1985
2896	Brooks Robinson, 1955-1977
2856	ROBIN YOUNT, 1974-1993
2850	DAVE WINFIELD, 1973-1993
2834	Al Kaline, 1953-1974
2826	Eddie Collins, 1906-1930
2820	Reggie Jackson, 1967-1987
2808	Frank Robinson, 1956-1976
2792	Honus Wagner, 1897-1917
2789	Tris Speaker, 1907-1928
2777	Tony Perez, 1964-1986
2730	Mel Ott, 1926-1947
2707	GEORGE BRETT, 1973-1993
2700	Graig Nettles, 1967-1988

At-bats: Most, career, all-time

14053	Pete Rose, 1963-1986
12364	Hank Aaron, 1954-1976
11988	Carl Yastrzemski, 1961-1983
11434	Ty Cobb, 1905-1928
11008	ROBIN YOUNT, 1974-1993
10972	Stan Musial, 1941-1963
10881	Willie Mays, 1951-1973
10654	Brooks Robinson, 1955-1977
10594	DAVE WINFIELD, 1973-1993
10430	Honus Wagner, 1897-1917
10349	GEORGE BRETT, 1973-1993
10332	Lou Brock, 1961-1979
10274	Cap Anson, 1871-1897
10230	Luis Aparicio, 1956-1973
10195	Tris Speaker, 1907-1928
10116	Al Kaline, 1953-1974
10078	Rabbit Maranville, 1912-1935
10006	Frank Robinson, 1956-1976
9949	Eddie Collins, 1906-1930
9864	Reggie Jackson, 1967-1987

Runs: Most, career, all-time

2246	Ty Cobb, 1905-1928
2174	Hank Aaron, 1954-1976
2174	Babe Ruth, 1914-1935
2165	Pete Rose, 1963-1986
2062	Willie Mays, 1951-1973
1996	Cap Anson, 1871-1897
1949	Stan Musial, 1941-1963
1888	Lou Gehrig, 1923-1939
1882	Tris Speaker, 1907-1928
1859	Mel Ott, 1926-1947
1829	Frank Robinson, 1956-1976
1821	Eddie Collins, 1906-1930
1816	Carl Yastrzemski, 1961-1983

1798	Ted Williams, 1939-1960
1774	Charlie Gehringer, 1924-1942
1751	Jimmie Foxx, 1925-1945
1736	Honus Wagner, 1897-1917
1732	Jim O'Rourke, 1872-1904
1720	Jesse Burkett, 1890-1905
1719	Willie Keeler, 1892-1910

Hits: Most, career, all-time

4256	Pete Rose, 1963-1986
4189	Ty Cobb, 1905-1928
3771	Hank Aaron, 1954-1976
3630	Stan Musial, 1941-1963
3514	Tris Speaker, 1907-1928
3419	Carl Yastrzemski, 1961-1983
3415	Cap Anson, 1871-1897
3415	Honus Wagner, 1897-1917
3312	Eddie Collins, 1906-1930
3283	Willie Mays, 1951-1973
3242	Nap Lajoie, 1896-1916
3154	GEORGE BRETT, 1973-1993
3152	Paul Waner, 1926-1945
3142	ROBIN YOUNT, 1974-1993
3053	Rod Carew, 1967-1985
3023	Lou Brock, 1961-1979
3014	DAVE WINFIELD, 1973-1993
3007	Al Kaline, 1953-1974
3000	Roberto Clemente, 1955-1972
2987	Sam Rice, 1915-1934

Total bases: Most, career, all-time

6856	Hank Aaron, 1954-1976
6134	Stan Musial, 1941-1963
6066	Willie Mays, 1951-1973
5854	Ty Cobb, 1905-1928
5793	Babe Ruth, 1914-1935
5752	Pete Rose, 1963-1986
5539	Carl Yastrzemski, 1961-1983
5373	Frank Robinson, 1956-1976
5101	Tris Speaker, 1907-1928
5063	DAVE WINFIELD, 1973-1993
5060	Lou Gehrig, 1923-1939
5044	GEORGE BRETT, 1973-1993
5041	Mel Ott, 1926-1947
4956	Jimmie Foxx, 1925-1945
4884	Ted Williams, 1939-1960
4862	Honus Wagner, 1897-1917
4852	Al Kaline, 1953-1974
4834	Reggie Jackson, 1967-1987
4730	ROBIN YOUNT, 1974-1993
4712	Rogers Hornsby, 1915-1937

2B: Most, career, all-time

792	Tris Speaker, 1907-1928
746	Pete Rose, 1963-1986
725	Stan Musial, 1941-1963
724	Ty Cobb, 1905-1928
665	GEORGE BRETT, 1973-1993
657	Nap Lajoie, 1896-1916
646	Carl Yastrzemski, 1961-1983
640	Honus Wagner, 1897-1917
624	Hank Aaron, 1954-1976
605	Paul Waner, 1926-1945
583	ROBIN YOUNT, 1974-1993
582	Cap Anson, 1871-1897

574	Charlie Gehringer, 1924-1942
542	Harry Heilmann, 1914-1932
541	Rogers Hornsby, 1915-1937
540	Joe Medwick, 1932-1948
539	Al Simmons, 1924-1944
534	Lou Gehrig, 1923-1939
529	Al Oliver, 1968-1985
528	Frank Robinson, 1956-1976

3B: Most, career, all-time

309	Sam Crawford, 1899-1917
295	Ty Cobb, 1905-1928
252	Honus Wagner, 1897-1917
243	Jake Beckley, 1888-1907
233	Roger Connor, 1880-1897
222	Tris Speaker, 1907-1928
220	Fred Clarke, 1894-1915
205	Dan Brouthers, 1879-1904
194	Joe Kelley, 1891-1908
191	Paul Waner, 1926-1945
188	Bid McPhee, 1882-1899
186	Eddie Collins, 1906-1930
185	Ed Delahanty, 1888-1903
184	Sam Rice, 1915-1934
182	Jesse Burkett, 1890-1905
182	Edd Roush, 1913-1931
181	Ed Konetchy, 1907-1921
178	Buck Ewing, 1880-1897
177	Rabbit Maranville, 1912-1935
177	Stan Musial, 1941-1963

HR: Most, career, all-time

755	Hank Aaron, 1954-1976
714	Babe Ruth, 1914-1935
660	Willie Mays, 1951-1973
586	Frank Robinson, 1956-1976
573	Harmon Killebrew, 1954-1975
563	Reggie Jackson, 1967-1987
548	Mike Schmidt, 1972-1989
536	Mickey Mantle, 1951-1968
534	Jimmie Foxx, 1925-1945
521	Willie McCovey, 1959-1980
521	Ted Williams, 1939-1960
512	Ernie Banks, 1953-1971
512	Eddie Mathews, 1952-1968
511	Mel Ott, 1926-1947
493	Lou Gehrig, 1923-1939
475	Stan Musial, 1941-1963
475	Willie Stargell, 1962-1982
453	DAVE WINFIELD, 1973-1993
452	Carl Yastrzemski, 1961-1983
442	Dave Kingman, 1971-1986

RBI: Most, career, all-time

2297	Hank Aaron, 1954-1976
2213	Babe Ruth, 1914-1935
1995	Lou Gehrig, 1923-1939
1981	Cap Anson, 1871-1897
1951	Stan Musial, 1941-1963
1937	Ty Cobb, 1905-1928
1922	Jimmie Foxx, 1925-1945
1903	Willie Mays, 1951-1973
1860	Mel Ott, 1926-1947
1844	Carl Yastrzemski, 1961-1983
1839	Ted Williams, 1939-1960
1827	Al Simmons, 1924-1944

1812	Frank Robinson, 1956-1976
1786	DAVE WINFIELD, 1973-1993
1732	Honus Wagner, 1897-1917
1702	Reggie Jackson, 1967-1987
1662	EDDIE MURRAY, 1977-1993
1652	Tony Perez, 1964-1986
1636	Ernie Banks, 1953-1971
1609	Goose Goslin, 1921-1938

SB: Most, career, all-time

1095	RICKEY HENDERSON, 1979-1993
938	Lou Brock, 1961-1979
912	Billy Hamilton, 1888-1901
891	Ty Cobb, 1905-1928
751	TIM RAINES, 1979-1993
744	Eddie Collins, 1906-1930
739	Arlie Latham, 1880-1909
738	Max Carey, 1910-1929
722	Honus Wagner, 1897-1917
689	Joe Morgan, 1963-1984
667	WILLIE WILSON, 1976-1993
657	Tom Brown, 1882-1898
649	Bert Campaneris, 1964-1983
648	VINCE COLEMAN, 1985-1993
616	George Davis, 1890-1909
594	Dummy Hoy, 1888-1902
586	Maury Wills, 1959-1972
583	George Vanhaltren, 1887-1903
574	Hugh Duffy, 1888-1906
568	Bid McPhee, 1882-1899

BB: Most, career, all-time

2056	Babe Ruth, 1914-1935
2019	Ted Williams, 1939-1960
1865	Joe Morgan, 1963-1984
1845	Carl Yastrzemski, 1961-1983
1733	Mickey Mantle, 1951-1968
1708	Mel Ott, 1926-1947
1614	Eddie Yost, 1944-1962
1605	Darrell Evans, 1969-1989
1599	Stan Musial, 1941-1963
1566	Pete Rose, 1963-1986
1559	Harmon Killebrew, 1954-1975
1508	Lou Gehrig, 1923-1939
1507	Mike Schmidt, 1972-1989
1499	Eddie Collins, 1906-1930
1464	Willie Mays, 1951-1973
1452	Jimmie Foxx, 1925-1945
1444	Eddie Mathews, 1952-1968
1420	Frank Robinson, 1956-1976
1406	RICKEY HENDERSON, 1979-1993
1402	Hank Aaron, 1954-1976

HBP: Most, career, all-time

287	Hughie Jennings, 1891-1918
272	Tommy Tucker, 1887-1899
267	Don Baylor, 1970-1988
243	Ron Hunt, 1963-1974
229	Dan McGann, 1896-1908
198	Frank Robinson, 1956-1976
192	Minnie Minoso, 1949-1980
180	Jake Beckley, 1888-1907

173	Curt Welch, 1884-1893
165	Kid Elberfeld, 1898-1914
151	Chet Lemon, 1975-1990
150	Fred Clarke, 1894-1915
143	CARLTON FISK, 1969-1993
142	Nellie Fox, 1947-1965
141	Art Fletcher, 1909-1922
139	Bill Dahlen, 1891-1911
135	Frank Chance, 1898-1914
134	Nap Lajoie, 1896-1916
132	John McGraw, 1891-1906
131	Steve Brodie, 1890-1902

K: Most, career, all-time

2597	Reggie Jackson, 1967-1987
1936	Willie Stargell, 1962-1982
1883	Mike Schmidt, 1972-1989
1867	Tony Perez, 1964-1986
1816	Dave Kingman, 1971-1986
1757	Bobby Bonds, 1968-1981
1748	DALE MURPHY, 1976-1993
1730	Lou Brock, 1961-1979
1710	Mickey Mantle, 1951-1968
1699	Harmon Killebrew, 1954-1975
1697	Dwight Evans, 1972-1991
1609	DAVE WINFIELD, 1973-1993
1570	Lee May, 1965-1982
1556	Dick Allen, 1963-1977
1550	Willie McCovey, 1959-1980
1537	Dave Parker, 1973-1991
1532	Frank Robinson, 1956-1976
1526	Willie Mays, 1951-1973
1513	Rick Monday, 1966-1984
1495	Greg Luzinski, 1970-1984

GIDP: Most, career, all-time

328	Hank Aaron, 1954-1976
323	Carl Yastrzemski, 1961-1983
315	Jim Rice, 1974-1989
307	DAVE WINFIELD, 1973-1993
297	Brooks Robinson, 1955-1977
297	Rusty Staub, 1963-1985
287	Ted Simmons, 1968-1988
284	Joe Torre, 1960-1977
277	George Scott, 1966-1979
275	Roberto Clemente, 1955-1972
271	Al Kaline, 1953-1974
270	Frank Robinson, 1956-1976
268	Tony Perez, 1964-1986
266	Dave Concepcion, 1970-1988
261	Ernie Lombardi, 1931-1947
256	Ron Santo, 1960-1974
255	Buddy Bell, 1972-1989
254	EDDIE MURRAY, 1977-1993
254	Al Oliver, 1968-1985
251	Steve Garvey, 1969-1987
251	Willie Mays, 1951-1973

BA: Highest, career, all-time

.366	Ty Cobb, 1905-1928
.359	Rogers Hornsby, 1915-1937
.356	Joe Jackson, 1908-1920
.346	Ed Delahanty, 1888-1903

.345	Tris Speaker, 1907-1928
.344	Ted Williams, 1939-1960
.344	Billy Hamilton, 1888-1901
.342	Dan Brouthers, 1879-1904
.342	Babe Ruth, 1914-1935
.342	Harry Heilmann, 1914-1932
.342	Pete Browning, 1882-1894
.341	Willie Keeler, 1892-1910
.341	Bill Terry, 1923-1936
.340	George Sisler, 1915-1930
.340	Lou Gehrig, 1923-1939
.338	Jesse Burkett, 1890-1905
.338	Nap Lajoie, 1896-1916
.336	Riggs Stephenson, 1921-1934
.335	WADE BOGGS, 1982-1993
.334	Al Simmons, 1924-1944

Slug avg: Highest, career, all-time

.690	Babe Ruth, 1914-1935
.634	Ted Williams, 1939-1960
.632	Lou Gehrig, 1923-1939
.609	Jimmie Foxx, 1925-1945
.605	Hank Greenberg, 1930-1947
.579	Joe DiMaggio, 1936-1951
.577	Rogers Hornsby, 1915-1937
.562	Johnny Mize, 1936-1953
.559	Stan Musial, 1941-1963
.558	Willie Mays, 1951-1973
.557	Mickey Mantle, 1951-1968
.554	Hank Aaron, 1954-1976
.548	Ralph Kiner, 1946-1955
.545	Hack Wilson, 1923-1934
.543	Chuck Klein, 1928-1944
.540	Duke Snider, 1947-1964
.537	Frank Robinson, 1956-1976
.535	Al Simmons, 1924-1944
.534	Dick Allen, 1963-1977
.534	Earl Averill, 1929-1941

Extra-base hits: Most, career, all-time

1477	Hank Aaron, 1954-1976
1377	Stan Musial, 1941-1963
1356	Babe Ruth, 1914-1935
1323	Willie Mays, 1951-1973
1190	Lou Gehrig, 1923-1939
1186	Frank Robinson, 1956-1976
1157	Carl Yastrzemski, 1961-1983
1136	Ty Cobb, 1905-1928
1131	Tris Speaker, 1907-1928
1119	GEORGE BRETT, 1973-1993
1117	Jimmie Foxx, 1925-1945
1117	Ted Williams, 1939-1960
1075	Reggie Jackson, 1967-1987
1071	Mel Ott, 1926-1947
1058	DAVE WINFIELD, 1973-1993
1041	Pete Rose, 1963-1986
1015	Mike Schmidt, 1972-1989
1011	Rogers Hornsby, 1915-1937
1009	Ernie Banks, 1953-1971
995	Al Simmons, 1924-1944

Pitchers

Games: Most, career, all-time

1070	Hoyt Wilhelm, 1952-1972
1050	Kent Tekulve, 1974-1989
987	Lindy McDaniel, 1955-1975
966	RICH GOSSAGE, 1972-1993
944	Rollie Fingers, 1968-1985
931	Gene Garber, 1969-1988
906	Cy Young, 1890-1911
899	Sparky Lyle, 1967-1982
898	Jim Kaat, 1959-1983
874	Don McMahon, 1957-1974
869	JEFF REARDON, 1979-1993
864	Phil Niekro, 1964-1987
850	LEE SMITH, 1980-1993
848	Roy Face, 1953-1969
837	CHARLIE HOUGH, 1970-1993
824	Tug McGraw, 1965-1984
807	NOLAN RYAN, 1966-1993
804	DENNIS ECKERSLEY, 1975-1993
802	Walter Johnson, 1907-1927
777	Gaylord Perry, 1962-1983

Complete games: Most, career, all-time

749	Cy Young, 1890-1911
646	Jim Galvin, 1875-1892
554	Tim Keefe, 1880-1893
531	Walter Johnson, 1907-1927
531	Kid Nichols, 1890-1906
525	Bobby Mathews, 1871-1887
525	Mickey Welch, 1880-1892
489	Charley Radbourn, 1880-1891
485	John Clarkson, 1882-1894
468	Tony Mullane, 1881-1894
466	Jim McCormick, 1878-1887
448	Gus Weyhing, 1887-1901
437	Pete Alexander, 1911-1930
434	Christy Mathewson, 1900-1916
422	Jack Powell, 1897-1912
410	Eddie Plank, 1901-1917
394	Will White, 1877-1886
392	Amos Rusie, 1889-1901
388	Vic Willis, 1898-1910
386	Tommy Bond, 1874-1884

Saves: Most, career, all-time

401	LEE SMITH, 1980-1993
365	JEFF REARDON, 1979-1993
341	Rollie Fingers, 1968-1985
309	RICH GOSSAGE, 1972-1993
300	Bruce Sutter, 1976-1988
275	DENNIS ECKERSLEY, 1975-1993
260	TOM HENKE, 1982-1993
252	DAVE RIGHETTI, 1979-1993
244	Dan Quisenberry, 1979-1990
238	Sparky Lyle, 1967-1982
236	JOHN FRANCO, 1984-1993
227	Hoyt Wilhelm, 1952-1972
218	Gene Garber, 1969-1988

216	Dave Smith, 1980-1992
201	BOBBY THIGPEN, 1986-1993
193	Roy Face, 1953-1969
190	DOUG JONES, 1982-1993
188	Mike Marshall, 1967-1981
186	MITCH WILLIAMS, 1986-1993
184	STEVE BEDROSIAN, 1981-1993
184	RANDY MYERS, 1985-1993
184	Kent Tekulve, 1974-1989
180	Tug McGraw, 1965-1984
179	Ron Perranoski, 1961-1973
172	Lindy McDaniel, 1955-1975

Shutouts: Most, career, all-time

110	Walter Johnson, 1907-1927
90	Pete Alexander, 1911-1930
79	Christy Mathewson, 1900-1916
76	Cy Young, 1890-1911
69	Eddie Plank, 1901-1917
63	Warren Spahn, 1942-1965
61	NOLAN RYAN, 1966-1993
61	Tom Seaver, 1967-1986
60	Bert Blyleven, 1970-1992
58	Don Sutton, 1966-1988
57	Jim Galvin, 1875-1892
57	Ed Walsh, 1904-1917
56	Bob Gibson, 1959-1975
55	Mordecai Brown, 1903-1916
55	Steve Carlton, 1965-1988
53	Jim Palmer, 1965-1984
53	Gaylord Perry, 1962-1983
52	Juan Marichal, 1960-1975
50	Rube Waddell, 1897-1910
50	Vic Willis, 1898-1910

Wins: Most, career, all-time

511	Cy Young, 1890-1911
417	Walter Johnson, 1907-1927
373	Pete Alexander, 1911-1930
373	Christy Mathewson, 1900-1916
364	Jim Galvin, 1875-1892
363	Warren Spahn, 1942-1965
361	Kid Nichols, 1890-1906
342	Tim Keefe, 1880-1893
329	Steve Carlton, 1965-1988
328	John Clarkson, 1882-1894
326	Eddie Plank, 1901-1917
324	NOLAN RYAN, 1966-1993
324	Don Sutton, 1966-1988
318	Phil Niekro, 1964-1987
314	Gaylord Perry, 1962-1983
311	Tom Seaver, 1967-1986
309	Charley Radbourn, 1880-1891
307	Mickey Welch, 1880-1892
300	Lefty Grove, 1925-1941
300	Early Wynn, 1939-1963

Losses: Most, career, all-time

316	Cy Young, 1890-1911
310	Jim Galvin, 1875-1892
292	NOLAN RYAN, 1966-1993
279	Walter Johnson, 1907-1927
274	Phil Niekro, 1964-1987
265	Gaylord Perry, 1962-1983
256	Don Sutton, 1966-1988
254	Jack Powell, 1897-1912
251	Eppa Rixey, 1912-1933
250	Bert Blyleven, 1970-1992
248	Bobby Mathews, 1871-1887
245	Robin Roberts, 1948-1966
245	Warren Spahn, 1942-1965
244	Steve Carlton, 1965-1988
244	Early Wynn, 1939-1963
237	Jim Kaat, 1959-1983
236	FRANK TANANA, 1973-1993
232	Gus Weyhing, 1887-1901
231	Tommy John, 1963-1989
230	Bob Friend, 1951-1966
230	Ted Lyons, 1923-1946

HR allowed: Most, career, all-time

505	Robin Roberts, 1948-1966
484	Fergie Jenkins, 1965-1983
482	Phil Niekro, 1964-1987
472	Don Sutton, 1966-1988
448	FRANK TANANA, 1973-1993
434	Warren Spahn, 1942-1965
430	Bert Blyleven, 1970-1992
414	Steve Carlton, 1965-1988
399	Gaylord Perry, 1962-1983
395	Jim Kaat, 1959-1983
380	Tom Seaver, 1967-1986
375	JACK MORRIS, 1977-1993
374	Catfish Hunter, 1965-1979
372	Jim Bunning, 1955-1971
366	CHARLIE HOUGH, 1970-1993
347	Mickey Lolich, 1963-1979
346	Luis Tiant, 1964-1982
338	Early Wynn, 1939-1963
324	Doyle Alexander, 1971-1989
321	NOLAN RYAN, 1966-1993

BB: Most career, all-time

2795	NOLAN RYAN, 1966-1993
1833	Steve Carlton, 1965-1988
1809	Phil Niekro, 1964-1987
1775	Early Wynn, 1939-1963
1764	Bob Feller, 1936-1956
1732	Bobo Newsom, 1929-1953
1704	Amos Rusie, 1889-1901
1613	CHARLIE HOUGH, 1970-1993
1566	Gus Weyhing, 1887-1901
1541	Red Ruffing, 1924-1947
1442	Bump Hadley, 1926-1941
1434	Warren Spahn, 1942-1965
1431	Earl Whitehill, 1923-1939
1408	Tony Mullane, 1881-1894
1396	Sam Jones, 1914-1935
1390	Tom Seaver, 1967-1986
1379	Gaylord Perry, 1962-1983
1371	Mike Torrez, 1967-1984
1363	Walter Johnson, 1907-1927
1343	Don Sutton, 1966-1988

K: Most, career, all-time

5714	NOLAN RYAN, 1966-1993
4136	Steve Carlton, 1965-1988
3701	Bert Blyleven, 1970-1992
3640	Tom Seaver, 1967-1986
3574	Don Sutton, 1966-1988
3534	Gaylord Perry, 1962-1983
3509	Walter Johnson, 1907-1927
3342	Phil Niekro, 1964-1987
3192	Fergie Jenkins, 1965-1983
3117	Bob Gibson, 1959-1975
2855	Jim Bunning, 1955-1971
2832	Mickey Lolich, 1963-1979
2803	Cy Young, 1890-1911
2773	FRANK TANANA, 1973-1993
2583	Warren Spahn, 1942-1965
2581	Bob Feller, 1936-1956
2556	Jerry Koosman, 1967-1985
2545	Tim Keefe, 1880-1893
2502	Christy Mathewson, 1900-1916
2486	Don Drysdale, 1956-1969

Wild pitches: Most, career, all-time

343	Tony Mullane, 1881-1894
277	NOLAN RYAN, 1966-1993
274	Mickey Welch, 1880-1892
240	Tim Keefe, 1880-1893
240	Gus Weyhing, 1887-1901
226	Phil Niekro, 1964-1987
221	Mark Baldwin, 1887-1893
221	Will White, 1877-1886
220	Jim Galvin, 1875-1892
214	Charley Radbourn, 1880-1891
214	Jim Whitney, 1881-1890
206	Adonis Terry, 1884-1897
203	Matt Kilroy, 1886-1898
193	JACK MORRIS, 1977-1993
187	Tommy John, 1963-1989
185	Bobby Mathews, 1871-1887
183	Steve Carlton, 1965-1988
182	John Clarkson, 1882-1894
179	Toad Ramsey, 1885-1890
178	Hardie Henderson, 1883-1888

Win pct: Highest, career, all-time

.796	Al Spalding, 1871-1878
.717	Spud Chandler, 1937-1947
.690	Dave Foutz, 1884-1896
.690	Whitey Ford, 1950-1967
.688	Bob Caruthers, 1884-1893
.686	Don Gullett, 1970-1978
.680	Lefty Grove, 1925-1941
.671	Joe Wood, 1908-1922
.667	Vic Raschi, 1946-1955
.665	Larry Corcoran, 1880-1887
.665	Christy Mathewson, 1900-1916
.660	Sam Leever, 1898-1910
.657	Sal Maglie, 1945-1958
.656	Dick McBride, 1871-1876
.655	DWIGHT GOODEN, 1984-1993
.655	Sandy Koufax, 1955-1966
.655	ROGER CLEMENS, 1984-1993
.654	Johnny Allen, 1932-1944
.651	Ron Guidry, 1975-1988
.650	Lefty Gomez, 1930-1943

ERA: Lowest, career, all-time

1.82	Ed Walsh, 1904-1917
1.89	Addie Joss, 1902-1910
2.06	Mordecai Brown, 1903-1916
2.10	John Ward, 1878-1894
2.13	Christy Mathewson, 1900-1916
2.14	Al Spalding, 1871-1878
2.16	Rube Waddell, 1897-1910
2.17	Walter Johnson, 1907-1927
2.23	Orval Overall, 1905-1913
2.28	Will White, 1877-1886
2.28	Ed Reulbach, 1905-1917
2.30	Jim Scott, 1909-1917
2.31	Tommy Bond, 1874-1884
2.35	Eddie Plank, 1901-1917
2.35	Larry Corcoran, 1880-1887
2.38	George McQuillan, 1907-1918
2.38	Eddie Cicotte, 1905-1920
2.38	Ed Killian, 1903-1910
2.39	Doc White, 1901-1913
2.42	George Bradley, 1875-1888

Innings: Most, career, all-time

7355.1	Cy Young, 1890-1911
6003.1	Jim Galvin, 1875-1892
5915.0	Walter Johnson, 1907-1927
5404.1	Phil Niekro, 1964-1987
5386.0	NOLAN RYAN, 1966-1993
5350.1	Gaylord Perry, 1962-1983
5282.1	Don Sutton, 1966-1988
5243.2	Warren Spahn, 1942-1965
5217.1	Steve Carlton, 1965-1988
5190.0	Pete Alexander, 1911-1930
5056.1	Kid Nichols, 1890-1906
5047.1	Tim Keefe, 1880-1893
4970.0	Bert Blyleven, 1970-1992
4956.1	Bobby Mathews, 1871-1887
4802.0	Mickey Welch, 1880-1892
4782.2	Tom Seaver, 1967-1986
4780.2	Christy Mathewson, 1900-1916
4710.1	Tommy John, 1963-1989
4688.2	Robin Roberts, 1948-1966
4564.0	Early Wynn, 1939-1963

General club records

Highest percentage for league champion

.832	St. Louis, UA-1884
.798	Chicago, NL-1880
.788	Chicago, NL-1876
.777	Chicago, NL-1885
.763	Chicago, NL-1906

Lowest percentage for league champion

.509	New York, NL-1973
.525	Minnesota, AL-1987
.551	New York, AL-1981
.556	Philadelphia, NL-1983
.556	Oakland, AL-1974

Most Wins

116	Chicago, NL-1906
111	Cleveland, AL-1954
110	Pittsburgh, NL-1909
110	New York, AL-1927
109	New York, AL-1961
109	Baltimore, AL-1969

Fewest Wins

36	Philadelphia, AL-1916
38	Washington, AL-1904
38	Boston, NL-1935
40	New York, NL-1962
42	Washington, AL-1909
42	Philadelphia, NL-1942
42	Pittsburgh, NL-1952

Most league championships

33	New York, AL
21	Brooklyn-Los Angeles, NL
19	New York-San Francisco, NL
16	Chicago, NL
15	St. Louis, NL
15	Philadelphia-Oakland, AL

Individual fielding records

Most Gold Gloves, Pitcher

16	Jim Kaat
9	Bob Gibson
8	Bobby Shantz
5	Phil Niekro
5	Ron Guidry
5	MARK LANGSTON
4	GREG MADDUX
4	Jim Palmer
3	Harvey Haddix
2	Andy Messersmith
2	Mike Norris
2	Rick Reuschel

Most Gold Gloves, Catcher

10	Johnny Bench
7	Bob Boone
6	Jim Sundberg
5	Bill Freehan
4	Del Crandall
4	TONY PENA
3	Sherm Lollar
3	Earl Battey
3	Thurman Munson
3	Gary Carter
3	LANCE PARRISH
3	BENITO SANTIAGO

Most Gold Gloves, First base

11	Keith Hernandez
8	DON MATTINGLY
8	George Scott
7	Vic Power
7	Bill White
6	Wes Parker
4	Steve Garvey
3	Gil Hodges
3	Joe Pepitone
3	EDDIE MURRAY

Most Gold Gloves, Second base

9	RYNE SANDBERG
8	Bill Mazeroski
8	Frank White
5	Bobby Richardson
5	Joe Morgan
4	Bobby Grich
3	ROBERTO ALOMAR
3	Nellie Fox
3	Bobby Knoop
3	Davey Johnson
3	Manny Trillo
3	LOU WHITAKER
3	HAROLD REYNOLDS

Most Gold Gloves, Third base

16	Brooks Robinson
10	Mike Schmidt
6	Buddy Bell
5	Ken Boyer
5	Ron Santo
5	Doug Rader
4	GARY GAETTI
3	Frank Malzone
3	TIM WALLACH
3	TERRY PENDLETON
3	ROBIN VENTURA

Most Gold Gloves, Shortstop

13	OZZIE SMITH
9	Luis Aparicio
8	Mark Belanger
5	Dave Concepcion
4	ALAN TRAMMELL
4	TONY FERNANDEZ
3	Roy McMillan
2	Maury Wills
2	Zoilo Versalles
2	Gene Alley
2	Don Kessinger
2	Larry Bowa
2	CAL RIPKEN

Most Gold Gloves, Outfield

12	Roberto Clemente
12	Willie Mays
10	Al Kaline
8	Paul Blair
8	Garry Maddox
8	Dwight Evans
8	ANDRE DAWSON
7	Curt Flood
7	Carl Yastrzemski
7	DAVE WINFIELD

Fielding Average, Pitcher
(92 chances accepted)

1.000	Kid Nichols, Bos/N-1896
1.000	Frank Owen, Chi/A-1904
1.000	Mordecai Brown, Chi/N-1908
1.000	Pete Alexander, Phi/N-1913
1.000	Walter Johnson, Was/A-1913
1.000	Eppa Rixey, Phi/N-1917
1.000	Walter Johnson, Was/A-1917
1.000	Hal Schumacher, NY/N-1935
1.000	Larry Jackson, Chi/N-1964
1.000	Randy Jones, SD/N-1976
1.000	GREG MADDUX, Chi/N-1990

Fielding Average, Catcher

1.000	Spud Davis, Phi/N-1939
1.000	Buddy Rosar, Phi/A-1946
1.000	Lou Berberet, Was/A-1957
1.000	Pete Daley, Bos/A-1957
1.000	Yogi Berra, NY/A-1958
1.000	Rick Cerone, Bos/A-1988
.999	TOM PAGNOZZI, StL/N-1992
.999	Joe Azcue, Cle/A-1967
.999	Wes Westrum, NY/N-1950
.998	Thurman Munson, NY/A-1971

Fielding Average, First Base

1.000	Steve Garvey, SD/N-1984
.999	Stuffy McInnis, Bos/A-1921
.999	Frank McCormick, Phi/N-1946
.999	Steve Garvey, LA/N-1981
.999	Jim Spencer, Cal-Tex/A-1973
.999	Wes Parker, LA/N-1968
.999	EDDIE MURRAY, Bal/A-1981
.999	HAL MORRIS, Cin/N-1992
.998	Jim Spencer, Chi/A-1976
.998	Jim Spencer, NY-Oak/A-1981

Fielding Average, Second Base

.997	Bobby Grich, Cal/A-1985
.996	JOSE OQUENDO, StL/N-1990
.995	RYNE SANDBERG, Chi/N-1991
.995	Rob Wilfong, Min/A-1980
.995	Bobby Grich, Bal/A-1973
.994	Frank White, KC/A-1988
.994	JOSE OQUENDO, StL/N-1989
.994	Jerry Adair, Bal/A-1964
.994	RYNE SANDBERG, Chi/N-1986
.994	JOSE LIND, KC/A-1993

Fielding Average, Shortstop

.996	CAL RIPKEN, Bal/A-1990
.992	TONY FERNANDEZ, Tor/A-1989
.991	Larry Bowa, Phi/N-1979
.990	Ed Brinkman, Det/A-1972
.990	CAL RIPKEN, Bal/A-1989
.989	SPIKE OWEN, Mon/N-1990
.989	OMAR VIZQUEL, Sea/A-1992
.989	TONY FERNANDEZ, Tor/A-1990
.988	DICK SCHOFIELD, NY/N-1992
.987	OZZIE SMITH, StL/N-1991

Fielding Average, Third Base

.991	STEVE BUECHELE, Tex/A-1991 (counting Pit/N in 1991, Buechele's average was .983)
.989	Don Money, Mil/A-1974
.988	Hank Majeski, Phi/A-1947
.987	Aurelio Rodriguez, Det/A-1978
.984	Willie Kamm, Cle/A-1933
.983	George Kell, Phi-Det/A-1946
.983	Heinie Groh, NY/N-1924
.983	Carney Lansford, Cal/A-1979
.982	George Kell, Det/A-1950
.982	Pinky Whitney, Phi/N-1937

Fielding Average, Outfield

1.000	Danny Litwhiler, Phi/N-1942
1.000	Willard Marshall, Bos/N-1951
1.000	Tony Gonzalez, Phi/N-1962
1.000	Don Demeter, Phi/N-1963
1.000	Rocky Colavito, Cle/A-1965
1.000	Curt Flood, StL/N-1966
1.000	Johnny Callison, Phi/N-1968
1.000	Mickey Stanley, Det/A-1968
1.000	Ken Harrelson, Bos/A-1968
1.000	Ken Berry, Chi/A-1969
1.000	Mickey Stanley, Det/A-1970
1.000	Roy White, NY/A-1971
1.000	Al Kaline, Det/A-1971
1.000	Ken Berry, Cal/A-1972
1.000	Carl Yastrzemski, Bos/A-1977
1.000	Terry Puhl, Hou/N-1979
1.000	Gary Roenicke, Bal/A-1980
1.000	Ken Landreaux, LA/N-1981
1.000	Terry Puhl, Hou/N-1981
1.000	Ken Singleton, Bal/A-1981
1.000	Brian Downing, Cal/A-1982
1.000	John Lowenstein, Bal/A-1982
1.000	Brian Downing, Cal/A-1984
1.000	BRETT BUTLER, LA/N-1991
1.000	DARRYL HAMILTON, Mil/A-1992
1.000	BRETT BUTLER, LA/N-1993
1.000	DARREN LEWIS, SF/N-1993
1.000	TIM RAINES, Chi/A-1993

Fielding Average, Pitcher, active players (60 chances accepted)

1.000	Greg Maddux, Chi/N-1990
1.000	Bob Welch, LA/N-1987
1.000	Tom Glavine, Atl/N-1991
1.000	Jimmy Key, Tor/A-1986
1.000	Jose Rijo, Cin/N-1993
1.000	Bob Tewksbury, StL/N-1993

Fielding Average, Catcher, active players

.999	Tom Pagnozzi, StL/N-1992
.998	Mike LaValliere, Pit/N-1991
.998	Greg Olson, Atl/N-1992
.998	Chris Hoiles, Bal/A-1991
.998	Damon Berryhill, Atl/N-1992
.998	Kirt Manwaring, SF/N-1993

Fielding Average, First Base, active players

.999	Eddie Murray, Bal/A-1981
.999	Hal Morris, Cin/N-1992
.998	Dave Magadan, NY/N-1990
.998	Don Mattingly, NY/A-1993
.998	Mark Grace, Chi/N-1992
.998	Kevin Young, Pit/N-1993

Fielding Average, Second Base, active players

.996	Jose Oquendo, StL/N-1990
.995	Ryne Sandberg, Chi/N-1991
.994	Jose Oquendo, StL/N-1989
.994	Ryne Sandberg, Chi/N-1986
.994	Jose Lind, KC/A-1993
.994	Lou Whitaker, Det/A-1991

Fielding Average, Shortstop, active players

.996	Cal Ripken, Bal/A-1990
.992	Tony Fernandez, Tor/A-1989
.990	Cal Ripken, Bal/A-1989
.989	Spike Owen, Mon/N-1990
.989	Omar Vizquel, Sea/A-1992
.989	Tony Fernandez, Tor/A-1990

Fielding Average, Third Base, active players

.991	Steve Buechele, Tex/A-1991 (counting Pit/N in 1991, Buechele's average was .983)
.977	Gary Gaetti, Min/A-1988
.975	Steve Buechele, Chi/N-1993
.973	Gary Gaetti, Min/A-1987
.973	Gary Gaetti, Min/A-1989

Fielding Average, Outfield, active players

1.000	Brett Butler, LA/N-1991
1.000	Darryl Hamilton, Mil/A-1992
1.000	Brett Butler, LA/N-1993
1.000	Darren Lewis, SF/N-1993
1.000	Tim Raines, Chi/A-1993

Assists, Pitcher

227	Ed Walsh, Chi/A-1907
223	Will White, Cin/A-1882
190	Ed Walsh, Chi/A-1908
178	Harry Howell, StL/A-1905
177	Tony Mullane, Lou/A-1882
174	John Clarkson, Chi/N-1885
172	John Clarkson, Bos/N-1889
166	Jack Chesbro, NY/A-1904
163	George Mullin, Det/A-1904
160	Ed Walsh, Chi/A-1911

Assists, Catcher

238	Bill Rariden, New/F-1915
215	Bill Rariden, Ind/F-1914
214	Pat Moran, Bos/N-1903
212	Oscar Stanage, Det/A-1911
212	Art Wilson, Chi/F-1914
210	Gabby Street, Was/A-1909
204	Frank Snyder, StL/N-1915
203	George Gibson, Pit/N-1910
202	Bill Bergen, Bro/N-1909
202	Claude Berry, Pit/F-1914

Assists, First Base

184	Bill Buckner, Bos/A-1985
180	MARK GRACE, Chi/N-1990
167	MARK GRACE, Chi/N-1991
166	SID BREAM, Pit/N-1986
161	Bill Buckner, Chi/N-1983
159	Bill Buckner, Chi/N-1982
157	Bill Buckner, Bos/A-1986
155	Mickey Vernon, Cle/A-1949
152	Fred Tenney, Bos/N-1905
152	EDDIE MURRAY, Bal/A-1985

Assists, Second Base

641	Frankie Frisch, StL/N-1927
588	Hughie Critz, Cin/N-1926
582	Rogers Hornsby, NY/N-1927
572	Ski Melillo, StL/A-1930
571	RYNE SANDBERG, Chi/N-1983
568	Rabbit Maranville, Pit/N-1924
562	Frank Parkinson, Phi/N-1922
559	Tony Cuccinello, Bos/N-1936
557	Johnny Hodapp, Cle/A-1930
555	Lou Bierbauer, Pit/N-1892

Assists, Shortstop

621	OZZIE SMITH, SD/N-1980
601	Glenn Wright, Pit/N-1924
598	Dave Bancroft, Phi-NY/N-1920
597	Tommy Thevenow, StL/N-1926
595	Ivan DeJesus, Chi/N-1977
583	CAL RIPKEN, Bal/A-1984
581	Whitey Wietelmann, Bos/N-1943
579	Dave Bancroft, NY/N-1922
574	Rabbit Maranville, Bos/N-1914
573	Don Kessinger, Chi/N-1968

Assists, Third Base

412	Graig Nettles, Cle/A-1971
410	Graig Nettles, NY/A-1973
410	Brooks Robinson, Bal/A-1974
405	Harlond Clift, StL/A-1937
405	Brooks Robinson, Bal/A-1967
404	Mike Schmidt, Phi/N-1974
399	Doug DeCinces, Cal/A-1982
396	Clete Boyer, NY/A-1962
396	Mike Schmidt, Phi/N-1977
396	Buddy Bell, Tex/A-1982

Assists, Outfield

50	Orator Shaffer, Chi/N-1879
48	Hugh Nicol, StL/A-1884
45	Hardy Richardson, Buf/N-1881
44	Tommy McCarthy, StL/A-1888
44	Chuck Klein, Phi/N-1930
43	Charlie Duffee, StL/A-1889
43	Jimmy Bannon, Bos/N-1894
42	Jim Fogarty, Phi/N-1889
41	Orator Shaffer, Buf/N-1883
41	Jim Lillie, Buf/N-1884

Assists, Pitcher, active players

64	Fernando Valenzuela, LA/N-1982
64	Greg Maddux, Chi/N-1992
60	Orel Hershiser, LA/N-1988
59	Dennis Martinez, Bal/A-1979
59	Greg Maddux, Atl/N-1993
58	Dave Stieb, Tor/A-1980

Assists, Catcher, active players

100	Tony Pena, Pit/N-1985
100	Benito Santiago, SD/N-1991
99	Tony Pena, Pit/N-1986
99	Mike Piazza, LA/N-1993
95	Tony Pena, Pit/N-1984

Assists, First Base, active players

180	Mark Grace, Chi/N-1990
167	Mark Grace, Chi/N-1991
166	Sid Bream, Pit/N-1986
152	Eddie Murray, Bal/A-1985
147	Eric Karros, LA/N-1993

Assists, Second Base, active players

571	Ryne Sandberg, Chi/N-1983
550	Ryne Sandberg, Chi/N-1984
539	Ryne Sandberg, Chi/N-1992
522	Ryne Sandberg, Chi/N-1988
515	Ryne Sandberg, Chi/N-1991

Assists, Shortstop, active players

621	Ozzie Smith, SD/N-1980
583	Cal Ripken, Bal/A-1984
570	Ozzie Guillen, Chi/A-1988
555	Ozzie Smith, SD/N-1979
549	Ozzie Smith, StL/N-1985

Assists, Third Base, active players

392	Terry Pendleton, StL/N-1989
383	Tim Wallach, Mon/N-1985
373	George Brett, KC/A-1979
372	Robin Ventura, Chi/A-1992
371	Terry Pendleton, StL/N-1986

Assists, Outfield, active players

22	Joe Orsulak, Bal/A-1991
21	Tim Raines, Mon/N-1983
20	Dave Winfield, SD/N-1980
20	Glenn Wilson, Phi/N-1986
19	Brett Butler, Cle/A-1985
19	Kirby Puckett, Min/A-1985
19	Tony Gwynn, SD/N-1986
19	Bernard Gilkey, StL/N-1993
19	Wayne Kirby, Cle/A-1993

Individual records

Hitters

ACTIVE PLAYERS IN CAPS

Most consecutive games played, lifetime

2130	Lou Gehrig, 1925-1939
1897	CAL RIPKEN, 1982-1993
1307	Everett Scott, 1916-1925
1207	Steve Garvey, 1975-1983
1117	Billy Williams, 1963-1970
1103	Joe Sewell, 1922-1930
895	Stan Musial, 1951-1957
829	Eddie Yost, 1949-1955
822	Gus Suhr, 1931-1937
798	Nellie Fox, 1955-1960

Most consecutive games played, lifetime, active players

1897	Cal Ripken, 1982-1993
162	Jeff Conine, 1993

Most consecutive games batted safely, season

56	Joe DiMaggio, NY/AL-1941
44	Willie Keeler, Bal/NL-1897
44	Pete Rose, Cin/NL-1978
42	Bill Dahlen, Chi/NL-1894
41	George Sisler, StL/AL-1922
40	Ty Cobb, Det/AL-1911
39	PAUL MOLITOR, Mil/AL-1987
37	Tommy Holmes, Bos/NL-1945
36	Billy Hamilton, Phi/NL-1894
35	Fred Clarke, Lou/NL-1895
35	Ty Cobb, Det/AL-1917
34	George Sisler, StL/AL-1925
34	George McQuinn, StL/AL-1938
34	Dom DiMaggio, Bos/AL-1949
34	BENITO SANTIAGO, SD/NL-1987
33	Hal Chase, NY/AL-1907
33	George Davis, NY/NL-1893
33	Rogers Hornsby, StL/NL-1922
33	Heinie Manush, Was/AL-1933
31	Ed Delahanty, Phi/NL-1899
31	Nap Lajoie, Cle/AL-1906
31	Sam Rice, Was/AL-1924
31	Willie Davis, LA/NL-1969
31	Rico Carty, Atl/NL-1970
31	Ken Landreaux, Min/AL-1980
30	Elmer Smith, Cin/NL-1898
30	Tris Speaker, Bos/AL-1912
30	Bing Miller, Phi/AL-1929
30	Goose Goslin, Det/AL-1934
30	Stan Musial, StL/NL-1950
30	Ron LeFlore, Det/AL-1976
30	GEORGE BRETT, KC/AL-1980
30	JEROME WALTON, Chi/NL-1989

Most consecutive games batted safely, season, active players

39	Paul Molitor, Mil/AL-1987
34	Benito Santiago, SD/NL-1987
30	George Brett, KC/AL-1980
30	Jerome Walton, Chi/NL-1989
28	Wade Boggs, Bos/AL-1985
26	John Olerud, Tor/AL-1993
25	Tony Gwynn, SD/NL-1983
25	Steve Sax, LA/NL-1986
25	Wade Boggs, Bos/AL-1987
25	Brian Harper, Min/AL-1990
25	Lance Johnson, Chi/AL-1992

Most pinch hits, lifetime

150	Manny Mota, 1962-1982
145	Smoky Burgess, 1949-1967
143	Greg Gross, 1973-1989
123	Jose Morales, 1973-1984
116	Jerry Lynch, 1954-1966
114	Red Lucas, 1923-1938
113	Steve Braun, 1971-1985
108	Terry Crowley, 1969-1983
108	Denny Walling, 1975-1992
107	Gates Brown, 1963-1975
103	Mike Lum, 1967-1981
102	Jim Dwyer, 1973-1990
100	Rusty Staub, 1963-1985

Most pinch hits, lifetime, active players

74	Randy Bush, 1982-1993
72	Gerald Perry, 1983-1993
64	Milt Thompson, 1984-1993
63	Kevin Bass, 1982-1993
58	Gary Varsho, 1988-1993
50	Dwight Smith, 1989-1993
48	Mitch Webster, 1983-1993
47	Mike Aldrete, 1986-1993
43	Ernie Riles, 1985-1993
42	Mackey Sasser, 1987-1993

Most pinch hit home runs, lifetime

20	Cliff Johnson, 1972-1986
18	Jerry Lynch, 1954-1966
16	Gates Brown, 1963-1975
16	Smoky Burgess, 1949-1967
16	Willie McCovey, 1959-1980
14	George Crowe, 1952-1961
12	Joe Adcock, 1950-1966
12	Bob Cerv, 1951-1962
12	Jose Morales, 1973-1984
12	Graig Nettles, 1967-1988
11	Jeff Burroughs, 1970-1985
11	Jay Johnstone, 1966-1985
11	Fred Whitfield, 1962-1970
11	Cy Williams, 1912-1930
10	Jim Dwyer, 1973-1990
10	Mike Lum, 1967-1981
10	Ken McMullen, 1962-1977
10	Don Mincher, 1960-1972
10	Wally Post, 1949-1964
10	Champ Summers, 1974-1984
10	Jerry Turner, 1974-1983
10	Gus Zernial, 1949-1959

Most pinch hit home runs, lifetime, active players

9	Mark Carreon, 1987-1993
9	Candy Maldonado, 1981-1993
7	Tim Teufel, 1983-1993
6	Daryl Boston, 1984-1993
6	Randy Bush, 1982-1993
6	Tommy Gregg, 1987-1993
6	Chris James, 1986-1993
6	Lloyd McClendon, 1987-1993
6	Gerald Perry, 1983-1993
6	Ernie Riles, 1985-1993
5	Sam Horn, 1987-1993
5	Matt Nokes, 1985-1993

Pitchers

Most consecutive scoreless innings, season

59	OREL HERSHISER, LA/NL - August 30 to September 28, 1988 (end of season)
58	Don Drysdale, LA/NL - May 14 to June 8, 1968
55.2	Walter Johnson, Was/AL - April 10 to May 14, 1913
53	Jack Coombs, Phi/AL - September 5 to 25, 1910
47	Bob Gibson, StL/NL - June 2 to 26, 1968
45.1	Carl Hubbell, NY/NL - July 13 to August 1, 1933 (allowed a run charged to starter in a relief appearance on July 19, after 12 scoreless innings, had a 33 inning string afterwards)
45	Cy Young, Bos/AL - April 25 to May 17, 1904
45	Doc White, Chi/AL - September 12 to 30, 1904
45	Sal Maglie, NY/NL - August 16 to September 13, 1950
44	Ed Reulbach, Chi/NL - September 17 to October 3, 1908 (end of season) (added 6 more innings on April 17, 1909 for a total of 50 over 2 years)
43.2	Rube Waddell, Phi/AL - August 22 to September 5, 1905
42	George "Rube" Foster, Bos/AL - May 1 to 26, 1914
41	Jack Chesbro, Pit/NL - June 26 to July 16, 1902
41	Grover Cleveland Alexander, Phi/NL - September 7 to 24, 1911
41	Art Nehf, Bos/NL - September 13 to October 4, 1917
41	Luis Tiant, Cle/AL - April 28 to May 17, 1968
41	GREGG OLSON, Bal/AL had a streak of 41 scoreless innings over two seasons from August 4, 1989 to May 4, 1990, 26 in 1989 and 15 in 1990)

40	Walter Johnson, Was/AL - May 7 to 26, 1918	
40	Gaylord Perry, SF/NL - August 28 to September 10, 1967	
40	Luis Tiant, Bos/AL - August 19 to September 8, 1972	
39.2	Mordecai Brown, Chi/NL - June 8 to July 8, 1908	
39.2	Billy Pierce, Chi/AL - August 3 to 19, 1953	
39	Ed Walsh, Chi/AL - August 10 to 22, 1906	
39	Christy Mathewson, NY/NL - May 3 to 21, 1901	
39	Don Newcombe, Bro/NL - July 25 to August 11, 1956	
39	Ray Culp, Bos/AL - September 7 to 25, 1968	
39	Gaylord Perry, SF/NL - September 1 to 23, 1970	
38.1	Bill Lee, Chi/NL - September 5 to 26, 1938	
38	Jim Galvin, Buf/NL - August 2 to 8, 1884	
38	John Clarkson, Chi/NL - May 18 to 27, 1885	
38	Jim Bagby, Cle/AL - June 30 to July 16, 1917	
38	Ray Herbert, Chi/AL - May 1 to 14, 1963	
37	George Bradley, StL/NL - July 8 to 18, 1876	
37	Cy Young, Bos/AL - June 13 to July 1, 1903	
37	Walter Johnson, Was/AL - June 27 to July 13, 1913	
37	Ed Walsh, Chi/AL - July 31 to August 14, 1910	
37	Joel Horlen, Chi/AL - May 11 to 29, 1968	
37	Mike Torrez, Oak/AL - August 29 to September 15, 1976	

Most strikeouts, game

21	Tom Cheney, Was/AL - September 12, 1962 (16 innings)	
20	ROGER CLEMENS, Bos/AL - April 29, 1986	
19	Charlie Sweeney, Pro/NL - June 7, 1884	
19	Hugh (One Arm) Daily, Chi/UA - July 7, 1884	
19	Luis Tiant, Cle/AL - July 3, 1968 (10 innings)	
19	Steve Carlton, StL/NL - September 15, 1969	
19	Tom Seaver, NY/NL - April 22, 1970	
19	NOLAN RYAN, Cal/AL - June 14, 1974 (12 innings)	
19	NOLAN RYAN, Cal/AL - August 12, 1974	
19	NOLAN RYAN, Cal/AL - August 20, 1974 (11 innings)	
19	NOLAN RYAN, Cal/AL - June 8, 1977 (10 innings)	

19	DAVID CONE, NY/NL - October 6, 1991	
18	Jim Whitney, Bos/NL - June 14, 1884 (15 innings)	
18	Dupee Shaw, Bos/UA - July 19, 1884	
18	Henry Porter, Mil/UA - October 3, 1884	
18	Jack Coombs, Phi/AL - September 1, 1906 (24 innings)	
18	Bob Feller, Cle/AL - October 2, 1938 (1st game)	
18	Warren Spahn, Bos/NL - June 14, 1952 (15 innings)	
18	Sandy Koufax, LA/NL - August 31, 1959	
18	Sandy Koufax, LA/NL - April 24, 1962	
18	Jim Maloney, Cin/NL - June 14, 1965 (11 innings)	
18	Chris Short, Phi/NL - October 2, 1965 (15 innings in an 18 inning game)	
18	Don Wilson, Hou/NL - July 14, 1968	
18	NOLAN RYAN, Cal/AL - September 10, 1976	
18	Ron Guidry, NY/AL - June 17, 1978	
18	BILL GULLICKSON, Mon/NL - September 10, 1980	
18	RAMON MARTINEZ, LA/NL - June 4, 1990	
18	RANDY JOHNSON, Sea/AL - September 27, 1992	

Most bases on balls, game

16	Bill George, NY/NL - May 30, 1887 (1st game)	
16	George Van Haltren, Chi/NL - June 27, 1887	
16	Henry Gruber, Cle/PL - April 19, 1890	
16	Bruno Haas, Phi/AL - June 23, 1915	
16	Tommy Byrne, NY/AL - August 22, 1951 (13 innings)	
15	Carroll Brown, Phi/AL - July 12, 1913	
14	Ed Crane, Was/NL - September 1, 1886	
14	Charlie Hickman, Bos/NL - August 16, 1899 (2nd game)	
14	Henry Mathewson, NY/NL - October 5, 1906	
14	Skipper Friday, Was/AL - June 17, 1923	

No-hit games, nine or more innings (number to left is career total if greater than 1)

Joe Borden, Phi vs Chi NA, 4-0; July 28, 1875.

George Bradley, StL vs Har NL, 2-0; July 15, 1876.

Lee Richmond, Wor vs Cle NL, 1-0; June 12, 1880 (perfect game).

Monte Ward, Pro vs Buf NL, 5-0; June 17, 1880. (perfect game).

Larry Corcoran, Chi vs Bos NL, 6-0; August 19, 1880.

Jim Galvin, Buf at Wor NL, 1-0; August 20, 1880.

Tony Mullane, Lou at Cin AA, 2-0; September 11, 1882.

Guy Hecker, Lou at Pit AA, 3-1; September 19, 1882.

2 Larry Corcoran, Chi vs Wor NL, 5-0; September 20, 1882.

Charley Radbourn, Pro at Cle NL, 8-0; July 25, 1883.

Hugh (One Arm) Daily, Cle at Phi NL; 1-0; September 13, 1883.

Al Atkisson, Phi vs Pit AA, 10-1; May 24, 1884.

Ed Morris, Col at Pit AA, 5-0; May 29, 1884.

Frank Mountain, Col at Was AA, 12-0; June 5, 1884.

3 Larry Corcoran, Chi vs Pro NL, 6-0; June 27, 1884.

2 Jim Galvin, Buf at Det NL, 18-0; August 4, 1884.

Dick Burns, Cin at KC UA, 3-1; August 26, 1884.

Ed Cushman, Mil vs Was UA, 5-0; September 28, 1884.

Sam Kimber, Bro vs Tol AA, 0-0; October 4, 1884 (ten innings, darkness).

John Clarkson, Chi at Pro NL, 4-0; July 27, 1885.

Charlie Ferguson, Phi vs Pro NL, 1-0; August 29, 1885.

2 Al Atkisson, Phi vs NY AA, 3-2; May 1, 1886.

Adonis Terry, Bro vs StL AA, 1-0; July 24, 1886.

Matt Kilroy, Bal at Pit AA, 6-0; October 6, 1886.

2 Adonis Terry, Bro vs Lou AA, 4-0; May 27, 1888.

Henry Porter, KC at Bal AA, 4-0; June 6, 1888.

Ed Seward, Phi vs Cin AA, 12-2; July 26, 1888.

Gus Weyhing, Phi vs KC AA, 4-0; July 31, 1888.

Silver King, Chi vs Bro PL, 0-1; June 21, 1890, (8 innings, lost the game; bottom of 9th not played).

Cannonball Titcomb, Roch vs Syr AA, 7-0; September 15, 1890.

Tom Lovett, Bro vs NY NL, 4-0; June 22, 1891.

Amos Rusie, NY vs Bro NL, 6-0; July 31, 1891.

Ted Breitenstein, StL vs Lou AA, 8-0; October 4, 1891 (1st game, first start in the major leagues).

Jack Stivetts, Bos vs Bro NL, 11-0; August 6, 1892.

Ben Sanders, Lou vs Bal NL, 6-2; August 22, 1892.

Bumpus Jones, Cin vs Pit NL, 7-1; October 15, 1892 (first game in the major leagues).

Bill Hawke, Bal vs Was NL, 5-0; August 16, 1893.

Cy Young, Cle vs Cin NL, 6-0; September 18, 1897 (1st game).

2 Ted Breitenstein, Cin vs Pit NL, 11-0; April 22, 1898.

Jim Hughes, Bal vs Bos NL, 8-0; April 22, 1898.

Red Donahue, Phi vs Bos NL, 5-0; July 8, 1898.

Walter Thornton, Chi vs Bro NL, 2-0; August 21, 1898 (2nd game).

Deacon Phillippe, Lou vs NY NL, 7-0; May 25, 1899.

Noodles Hahn, Cin vs Phi NL, 4-0; July 12, 1900.

Earl Moore, Cle vs Chi AL, 2-4; May 9, 1901 (lost on two hits in the tenth).

Christy Mathewson, NY at StL NL, 5-0; July 15, 1901.

Nixey Callahan, Chi vs Det AL, 3-0; September 20, 1902 (1st game).

Chick Fraser, Phi at Chi NL; 10-0; September 18, 1903 (2nd game).

2 Cy Young, Bos vs Phi AL, 3-0; May 5, 1904 (perfect game).

Bob Wicker, Chi at NY NL, 1-0; June 11, 1904 (won in 12 innings after allowing one hit in the tenth).

Jesse Tannehill, Bos at Chi AL, 6-0; August 17, 1904.

2 Christy Mathewson, NY at Chi NL, 1-0; June 13, 1905.

Weldon Henley, Phi at StL AL, 6-0; July 22, 1905 (1st game).

Frank Smith, Chi at Det AL, 15-0; September 6, 1905 (2nd game).

Bill Dinneen, Bos vs Chi AL, 2-0; September 27, 1905 (1st game).

Johnny Lush, Phi at Bro NL, 6-0; May 1, 1906.

Mal Eason, Bro at StL NL, 2-0; July 20, 1906.

Harry McIntyre, Bro vs Pit NL, 0-1; August 1, 1906 (lost on 4 hits in 13 innings after allowing the first hit in the 11th).

Frank (Jeff) Pfeffer, Bos vs Cin NL, 6-0; May 8, 1907.

Nick Maddox, Pit vs Bro NL, 2-1; September 20, 1907.

3 Cy Young, Bos at NY AL, 8-0; June 30, 1908.

Hooks Wiltse, NY vs Phi NL, 1-0; July 4, 1908 (1st game, ten innings).

Nap Rucker, Bro vs Bos NL, 6-0; September 5, 1908 (2nd game).

Dusty Rhoades, Cle vs Bos AL, 2-1; September 18, 1908.

2 Frank Smith, Chi vs Phi AL, 1-0; September 20, 1908.

Addie Joss, Cle vs Chi AL, 1-0; October 2, 1908 (perfect game).

Red Ames, NY vs Bro NL. 0-3; April 15, 1909 (lost on 7 hits in 13 innings after allowing the first hit in the tenth).

2 Addie Joss, Cle vs Chi AL, 1-0; April 20, 1910.

Chief Bender, Phi vs Cle AL, 4-0; May 12, 1910.

Tom L. Hughes, NY vs Cle AL, 0-5; August 30, 1910 (2nd game) (lost on 7 hits in 11 innings after allowing the first hit in the tenth).

Joe Wood, Bos vs StL AL, 5-0; July 29, 1911 (1st game).

Ed Walsh, Chi vs Bos AL, 5-0; August 27, 1911.

George Mullin, Det vs StL AL, 7-0; July 4, 1912 (2nd game).

Earl Hamilton, StL at Det AL, 5-1; August 30, 1912.

Jeff Tesreau, NY at Phi NL, 3-0; September 6, 1912 (1st game).

Jim Scott, Chi at Was AL, 0-1; May 14, 1914 (lost on 2 hits in the tenth).

Joe Benz, Chi vs Cle AL, 6-1; May 31, 1914.

George Davis, Bos vs Phi NL, 7-0; September 9, 1914 (2nd game).

Ed Lafitte, Bro vs KC FL, 6-2; September 19, 1914.

Rube Marquard, NY vs Bro NL, 2-0; April 15, 1915.

Frank Allen, Pit vs StL FL, 2-0; April 24, 1915.

Claude Hendrix, Chi vs Pit FL, 10-0; May 15, 1915.

Alex Main, KC vs Buf FL, 5-0; August 16, 1915.

Jimmy Lavender, Chi at NY NL, 2-0; August 31, 1915 (1st game).

Dave Davenport, StL vs Chi FL, 3-0; September 7, 1915.

2 Tom L. Hughes, Bos vs Pit NL, 2-0; June 16, 1916.

Rube Foster, Bos vs NY AL, 2-0; June 21, 1916.

Joe Bush, Phi vs Cle AL, 5-0; August 26, 1916.

Hubert (Dutch) Leonard, Bos vs StL AL, 4-0; August 30, 1916.

Eddie Cicotte, Chi at StL AL, 11-0; April 14, 1917.

George Mogridge, NY at Bos AL, 2-1; April 24, 1917.

Fred Toney, Cin at Chi NL, 1-0; May 2, 1917 (ten innings).

Hippo Vaughn, Chi vs Cin NL, 0-1; May 2, 1917. (lost on two hits in the 10th, Toney pitched a no-hitter in this game).

Ernie Koob, StL vs Chi AL, 1-0; May 5, 1917.

Bob Groom, StL vs Chi AL, 3-0; May 6, 1917 (2nd game).

Ernie Shore, Bos vs Was AL, 4-0; June 23, 1917 (1st game, perfect game). (Shore relieved Babe Ruth in the first inning after Ruth had been thrown out of the game for protesting a walk to the first batter. The runner was caught stealing and Shore retired the remaining 26 batters in order).

2 Hubert (Dutch) Leonard, Bos at Det AL, 5-0; June 3, 1918.

Hod Eller, Cin vs StL NL, 6-0; May 11, 1919.

Ray Caldwell, Cle at NY AL, 3-0; September 10, 1919 (1st game).

Walter Johnson, Was at Bos AL, 1-0; July 1, 1920.

Charlie Robertson, Chi at Det AL, 2-0; April 30, 1922 (perfect game).

Jesse Barnes, NY vs Phi NL, 6-0; May 7, 1922.

Sam Jones, NY at Phi AL, 2-0; September 4, 1923.

Howard Ehmke, Bos at Phi AL, 4-0; September 7, 1923.

Jesse Haines, StL vs Bos NL, 5-0; July 17, 1924.

Dazzy Vance, Bro vs Phi NL, 10-1; September 13, 1925 (1st game).

Ted Lyons, Chi at Bos AL, 6-0; August 21, 1926.

Carl Hubbell, NY vs Pit NL, 11-0; May 8, 1929.

Wes Ferrell, Cle vs StL AL, 9-0; April 29, 1931.

Bobby Burke, Was vs Bos AL, 5-0; August 8, 1931.

Bobo Newsom, StL vs Bos AL, 1-2; September 18, 1934 (lost on 1 hit in the tenth).

Paul Dean, StL at Bro NL, 3-0; September 21, 1934 (2nd game).

Vern Kennedy, Chi vs Cle AL, 5-0; August 31, 1935.

Bill Dietrich, Chi vs StL AL, 8-0; June 1, 1937.

Johnny Vander Meer, Cin vs Bos NL, 3-0; June 11, 1938.

2 Johnny Vander Meer, Cin at Bro NL, 6-0; June 15, 1938 (next start after June 11).

Monte Pearson, NY vs Cle AL, 13-0; August 27, 1938 (2nd game).

Bob Feller, Cle at Chi AL, 1-0; April 16, 1940 (opening day).

Tex Carleton, Bro at Cin NL, 3-0; April 30, 1940.

Lon Warneke, StL at Cin NL, 2-0; August 30, 1941.

Jim Tobin, Bos vs Bro NL, 2-0; April 27, 1944.

Clyde Shoun, Cin vs Bos NL, 1-0; May 15, 1944.

Dick Fowler, Phi vs StL AL, 1-0; September 9, 1945 (2nd game).

Ed Head, Bro vs Bos NL, 5-0; April 23, 1946.

2 Bob Feller, Cle at NY AL, 1-0;
   April 30, 1946.
Ewell Blackwell, Cin vs Bos NL, 6-0;
   June 18, 1947.
Don Black, Cle vs Phi AL, 3-0;
   July 10, 1947 (1st game).
Bill McCahan, Phi vs Was AL, 3-0;
   September 3, 1947.
Bob Lemon, Cle at Det AL, 2-0;
   June 30, 1948.
Rex Barney, Bro at NY NL, 2-0;
   September 9, 1948.
Vern Bickford, Bos vs Bro NL, 7-0;
   August 11, 1950.
Cliff Chambers, Pit at Bos NL, 3-0;
   May 6, 1951 (2nd game).
3 Bob Feller, Cle vs Det AL, 2-1; July
   1, 1951 (1st game).
Allie Reynolds, NY at Cle AL, 1-0;
   July 12, 1951.
2 Allie Reynolds, NY vs Bos AL, 8-0;
   September 28, 1951 (1st game).
Virgil Trucks, Det vs Was AL, 1-0;
   May 15, 1952.
Carl Erskine, Bro vs Chi NL, 5-0;
   June 19, 1952.
2 Virgil Trucks, Det at NY AL, 1-0;
   August 25, 1952.
Bobo Holloman, StL vs Phi AL, 6-0;
   May 6, 1953 (first start in the
   major leagues).
Jim Wilson, Mil vs Phi NL, 2-0;
   June 12, 1954.
Sam Jones, Chi vs Pit NL, 4-0;
   May 12, 1955.
2 Carl Erskine, Bro vs NY NL, 3-0;
   May 12, 1956.
Johnny Klippstein (7 innings), Hershell
   Freeman (1 inning) and Joe Black
   (3 innings), Cin at Mil NL, 1-2;
   May 26, 1956 (lost on 3 hits in 11
   innings after allowing the first hit
   in the tenth).
Mel Parnell, Bos vs Chi AL, 4-0;
   July 14, 1956.
Sal Maglie, Bro vs Phi NL, 5-0;
   September 25, 1956.
Don Larsen, NY AL vs Bro NL, 2-0;
   October 8, 1956 (World Series,
   perfect game).
Bob Keegan, Chi vs Was AL, 6-0;
   August 20, 1957 (2nd game).
Jim Bunning, Det at Bos AL, 3-0;
   July 20, 1958 (1st game).
Hoyt Wilhelm, Bal vs NY AL, 1-0;
   September 20, 1958.
Harvey Haddix, Pit at Mil NL, 0-1; May
   26, 1959 (lost on 1 hit in 13 innings
   after pitching 12 perfect innings).
Don Cardwell, Chi vs StL NL, 4-0;
   May 15, 1960 (2nd game).
Lew Burdette, Mil vs Phi NL, 1-0;
   August 18, 1960.
Warren Spahn, Mil vs Phi NL, 4-0;
   September 16, 1960.
2 Warren Spahn, Mil vs SF NL, 1-0;
   April 28, 1961.

Bo Belinsky, LA vs Bal AL, 2-0;
   May 5, 1962.
Earl Wilson, Bos vs LA AL, 2-0;
   June 26, 1962.
Sandy Koufax, LA vs NY NL, 5-0;
   June 30, 1962.
Bill Monbouquette, Bos at Chi AL,
   1-0; August 1, 1962.
Jack Kralick, Min vs KC AL, 1-0;
   August 26, 1962.
2 Sandy Koufax, LA vs SF NL, 8-0;
   May 11, 1963.
Don Nottebart, Hou vs Phi NL, 4-1;
   May 17, 1963.
Juan Marichal, SF vs Hou NL, 1-0;
   June 15, 1963.
Ken T. Johnson, Hou vs Cin NL, 0-1;
   April 23, 1964 (lost the game).
3 Sandy Koufax, LA at Phi NL, 3-0;
   June 4, 1964.
2 Jim Bunning, Phi at NY NL, 6-0;
   June 21, 1964 (1st game, perfect
   game).
Jim Maloney, Cin vs NY NL, 0-1;
   June 14, 1965 (lost on 2 hits in 11
   innings after pitching 10 hitless
   innings).
2 Jim Maloney, Cin at Chi NL, 1-0;
   August 19, 1965 (1st game, 10
   innings).
4 Sandy Koufax, LA vs Chi NL, 1-0;
   September 9, 1965 (perfect
   game).
Dave Morehead, Bos vs Cle AL, 2-0;
   September 16, 1965.
Sonny Siebert, Cle vs Was AL, 2-0;
   June 10, 1966.
Steve D. Barber (8 2/3 innings) and
   Stu Miller (1/3 inning) Bal vs Det
   AL, 1-2; April 30, 1967 (1st game,
   lost the game).
Don Wilson, Hou vs Atl NL, 2-0;
   June 18, 1967.
Dean Chance, Min at Cle AL, 2-1;
   August 25, 1967 (2nd game).
Joe Horlen, Chi vs Det AL, 6-0;
   September 10, 1967 (1st game).
Tom Phoebus, Bal vs Bos AL, 6-0;
   April 27, 1968.
Catfish Hunter, Oak vs Min AL, 4-0;
   May 8, 1968 (perfect game).
George Culver, Cin at Phi NL, 6-1;
   July 29, 1968 (2nd game).
Gaylord Perry, SF vs StL NL, 1-0;
   September 17, 1968.
Ray Washburn, StL at SF NL, 2-0;
   September 18, 1968.
Bill Stoneman, Mon at Phi NL, 7-0;
   April 17, 1969.
3 Jim Maloney, Cin vs Hou NL, 10-0;
   April 30, 1969.
2 Don Wilson, Hou at Cin NL, 4-0;
   May 1, 1969.
Jim Palmer, Bal vs Oak AL, 8-0;
   August 13, 1969.
Ken Holtzman, Chi vs Atl NL, 3-0;
   August 19, 1969.

Bob Moose, Pit at NY NL, 4-0;
   September 20, 1969.
Dock Ellis, Pit at SD NL, 2-0; June 12,
   1970 (1st game).
Clyde Wright, Cal vs Oak AL, 4-0;
   July 3, 1970.
Bill Singer, LA vs Phi NL, 5-0; July 20,
   1970.
Vida Blue, Oak vs Min AL, 6-0;
   September 21, 1970.
2 Ken Holtzman, Chi at Cin NL, 1-0;
   June 3, 1971.
Rick Wise, Phi at Cin NL, 4-0;
   June 23, 1971.
Bob Gibson, StL at Pit NL, 11-0;
   August 14, 1971.
Burt Hooton, Chi vs Phi NL, 4-0;
   April 16, 1972.
Milt Pappas, Chi vs SD NL, 8-0;
   September 2, 1972.
2 Bill Stoneman, Mon vs NY NL, 7-0;
   October 2, 1972 (1st game).
Steve Busby, KC at Det AL, 3-0;
   April 16, 1973.
NOLAN RYAN, Cal at KC AL, 3-0;
   May 15, 1973.
2 NOLAN RYAN, Cal at Det AL, 6-0;
   July 15, 1973.
Jim Bibby, Tex at Oak AL, 6-0;
   July 20, 1973.
Phil Niekro, Atl vs SD NL, 9-0;
   August 5, 1973.
2 Steve Busby, KC at Mil AL, 2-0;
   June 19, 1974.
Dick Bosman, Cle vs Oak AL, 4-0;
   July 19, 1974.
3 NOLAN RYAN, Cal vs Min AL, 4-0;
   September 28, 1974.
4 NOLAN RYAN, Cal vs Bal AL, 1-0;
   June 1, 1975.
Ed Halicki, SF vs NY NL, 6-0;
   August 24, 1975 (2nd game).
Vida Blue (5 innings), Glenn Abbott
   (1 inning), Paul Lindblad
   (1 inning) and Rollie Fingers
   (2 innings), Oak vs Cal AL,
   5-0; September 28, 1975.
Larry Dierker, Hou vs Mon NL, 6-0;
   July 9, 1976.
Blue Moon Odom (5 innings) and
   Francisco Barrios (4 innings), Chi
   at Oak AL, 2-1; July 28, 1976.
JOHN CANDELARIA, Pit vs LA NL,
   2-0; August 9, 1976.
John Montefusco, SF at Atl NL, 9-0;
   September 29, 1976.
Jim Colborn, KC vs Tex AL, 6-0;
   May 14, 1977.
DENNIS ECKERSLEY, Cle vs Cal AL,
   1-0; May 30, 1977.
Bert Blyleven, Tex at Cal AL, 6-0;
   September 22, 1977.
Bob Forsch, StL vs Phi NL, 5-0; April
   16, 1978.
Tom Seaver, Cin vs StL NL, 4-0;
   June 16, 1978.

Ken Forsch, Hou vs AtL NL, 6-0;
April 7, 1979.

Jerry Reuss, LA at SF NL, 8-0;
June 27, 1980.

Charlie Lea, Mon vs SF NL, 4-0;
May 10, 1981 (2nd game).

Len Barker, Cle vs Tor AL, 3-0;
May 15, 1981 (perfect game).

5 NOLAN RYAN, Hou vs LA NL, 5-0;
September 26, 1981.

DAVE RIGHETTI, NY vs Bos AL, 4-0;
July 4, 1983.

2 Bob Forsch, StL vs Mon NL, 3-0;
September 26, 1983.

Mike Warren, Oak vs Chi AL, 3-0;
September 29, 1983.

JACK MORRIS, Det at Chi AL, 4-0;
April 7, 1984.

MIKE WITT, Cal vs Tex AL, 1-0; September 30, 1984 (perfect game).

Joe Cowley, Chi at Cal AL, 7-1;
September 19, 1986.

Mike Scott, Hou vs SF NL, 2-0;
September 25, 1986.

Juan Nieves, Mil at Bal AL, 7-0;
April 15, 1987.

TOM BROWNING, Cin vs LA NL, 1-0;
September 16, 1988 (perfect
game).

MARK LANGSTON (7 innings) and
MIKE WITT (2 innings), Cal vs Sea
AL, 1-0; April 11, 1990.

RANDY JOHNSON, Sea vs Det AL,
2-0; June 2, 1990.

6 NOLAN RYAN, Tex at Oak AL, 5-0;
June 11, 1990.

DAVE STEWART, Oak at Tor AL, 5-0;
June 29, 1990.

FERNANDO VALENZUELA, LA vs
StL NL, 6-0; June 29, 1990.

Andy Hawkins, NY at Chi AL, 0-4;
July 1, 1990 (8 innings, lost the
game; bottom of 9th not played).

TERRY MULHOLLAND, Phi vs SF
NL, 6-0; August 15, 1990.

DAVE STIEB, Tor at Det AL, 3-0;
September 2, 1990.

7 NOLAN RYAN, Tex vs Tor AL, 3-0;
May 1, 1991.

TOMMY GREENE, Phi at Mon NL,
2-0; May 23, 1991.

BOB MILACKI (6 innings), Mike
Flanagan (1 inning), MARK
WILLIAMSON, (1 inning) and
Gregg Olson (1 inning), Bal at
Oak AL, 2-0; July 13, 1991.

MARK GARDNER, Mon at LA NL,
0-1; July 26, 1991 (9 innings, lost
on 2 hits in 10th, relieved by Jeff
Fassero, who allowed 1 more hit).

DENNIS MARTINEZ, Mon at LA NL,
2-0; July 28, 1991 (perfect game).

WILSON ALVAREZ, Chi at Bal AL,
7-0; August 11, 1991.

BRET SABERHAGEN, KC vs Chi AL,
7-0; August 26, 1991.

KENT MERCKER (6 innings), MARK
WOHLERS (2 innings) and
Alejandro Pena (1 inning), Atl at
SD NL, 1-0; September 11, 1991.

MATT YOUNG, Bos at Cle AL, 1-2;
April 12, 1992 (1st game)
(8 innings, lost the game, bottom
of 9th not played).

KEVIN GROSS, LA vs SF NL, 2-0;
August 17, 1992.

CHRIS BOSIO, Sea vs Bos AL, 7-0;
April 22, 1993.

JIM ABBOTT, NY vs Cle AL, 4-0;
September 4, 1993.

DARRYL KILE, Hou vs NY NL, 7-1;
September 8, 1993.

No-hit games, less than nine innings

Larry McKeon, six innings, rain, Ind at
Cin AA, 0-0; May 6, 1884.

Charlie Gagus, eight innings,
darkness, Was vs Wil UA, 12-1;
August 21, 1884.

Charlie Getzien, six innings, rain, Det
vs Phi NL, 1-0; October 1, 1884.

Charlie Sweeney (2 innings) and
Henry Boyle (3 innings), five
innings, rain, StL vs StP UA, 0-1;
October 5,1884.

Dupee Shaw, five innings, agreement,
Pro at Buf NL, 4-0; October 7,
1885 (1st game).

George Van Haltren, six innings, rain,
Chi vs Pit NL, 1-0, June 21,1888.

Ed Crane, seven innings, darkness,
NY vs Was NL, 3-0; September
27, 1888.

Matt Kilroy, seven innings, darkness,
Bal vs StL AA, 0-0; July 29, 1889
(2nd game).

George Nicol, seven innings,
darkness, StL vs Phi AA, 21-2;
September 23, 1890.

Hank Gastright, eight innings,
darkness, Col vs Tol AA, 6-0;
October 12, 1890.

Jack Stivetts, five innings, called so
Boston could catch train to
Cleveland for Temple Cub
playoffs, Bos at Was NL, 6-0;
October 15, 1892 (2nd game).

Elton Chamberlain, seven innings,
darkness, Cin vs Bos NL, 6-0;
September 23, 1893 (2nd game).

Ed Stein, six innings, rain, Bro vs Chi
NL, 6-0; June 2, 1894.

Red Ames, five innings, darkness, NY
at StL NL, 5-0; September 14,
1903 (2nd game, first game in the
major leagues).

Rube Waddell, five innings, rain, Phi
vs StL AL, 2-0; August 15, 1905.

Jake Weimer, seven innings,
agreement, Cin vs Bro NL, 1-0;
August 24, 1906 (2nd game).

Jimmy Dygert (3 innings) and Rube
Waddell (2 innings), five innings,
rain, Phi vs Chi AL, 4-3; August
29, 1906. (Waddell allowed hit
and two runs in 6th, but rain
caused game to revert to 5
innings).

Stoney McGlynn, seven innings,
agreement, StL at Bro NL, 1-1;
September 24, 1906 (2nd game).

Lefty Leifield, six innings, darkness,
Pit at Phi NL, 8-0; September 26,
1906 (2nd game).

Ed Walsh, five innings, rain, Chi vs NY
AL, 8-1; May 26, 1907.

Ed Karger, seven perfect innings,
agreement, StL vs Bos NL, 4-0;
August 11, 1907 (2nd game).

Howie Camnitz, five innings,
agreement, Pit at NY NL, 1-0;
August 23, 1907 (2nd game).

Rube Vickers, five perfect innings,
darkness, Phi at Was AL, 4-0;
October 5, 1907 (2nd game).

Johnny Lush, six innings, rain, StL at
Bro NL, 2-0; August 6, 1908.

King Cole, seven innings, called so
Chicago could catch train, Chi
at StL NL, 4-0; July 31, 1910 (2nd
game).

Jay Cashion, six innings, called so
Cleveland could catch train, Was
vs Cle AL, 2-0; August 20, 1912
(2nd game).

Walter Johnson, seven innings,
rain, Was vs StL AL, 2-0;
August 25, 1924.

Fred Frankhouse, seven and two-
thirds innings, rain, Bro vs Cin NL,
5-0; August 27, 1937.

John Whitehead, six innings, rain, StL
vs Det AL, 4-0; August 5, 1940
(2nd game).

Jim Tobin, five innings, darkness, Bos
vs Phi NL, 7-0; June 22, 1944
(2nd game).

Mike McCormick, five innings, rain,
SF at Phi NL, 3-0; June 12, 1959.
(allowed hit in 6th, but rain
caused game to revert to 5
innings).

Sam Jones, seven innings, rain, SF at
StL NL, 4-0; September 26, 1959.

Dean Chance, five perfect innings,
rain, Min vs Bos AL, 2-0;
August 6, 1967.

David Palmer, five perfect innings,
rain, Mon at StL NL, 4-0; April 21,
1984 (2nd game).

Pascual Perez, five innings, rain, Mon
at Phi NL, 1-0; September 24,
1988.

MELIDO PEREZ, six innings, rain, Chi
at NY AL, 8-0; July 12, 1990.

Lee Richmond, Wor vs Cle NL, 1-0; June 12, 1880

CLEVELAND	ab	r	h	po	a	e
Dunlap,2b	3	0	0	4	2	2
Hankinson,3b	3	0	0	0	0	0
Kennedy,c	3	0	0	9	1	0
Phillips,lb	3	0	0	7	0	0
Shaffer,rf	3	0	0	2	0	0
McCormick,p	3	0	0	0	10	0
Gilligan,cf	3	0	0	1	0	0
Glasscock,ss	3	0	0	0	2	0
Hanlon,lf	3	0	0	1	0	0
Team	27	0	0	24	15	2

WORCESTER	ab	r	h	po	a	e
Wood,lf	4	0	0	0	0	0
Richmond,p	3	0	1	0	6	0
Knight,rf	3	0	0	1	1	0
Irwin,ss	3	0	2	2	3	0
Bennett,c	2	0	0	8	0	0
Whitney,3b	3	0	0	1	2	0
Sullivan,lb	3	0	0	14	0	0
Corey,cf	3	0	0	1	0	0
Creamer,2b	3	0	0	0	4	0
Team	27	1	3	27	16	0

Cleveland	000	000	000	–0	
Worcester	000	010	00x	–1	

Runs batted in - none

Double play - Glasscock, Dunlap and Phillips

	ip	h	r	er	bb	so
McCormick (L)	8	3	1	0	1	7
Richmond (W)	9	0	0	0	0	5

Time - 1:27

Umpire - Bradley

Attendance - 700

John Montgomery Ward, Pro vs Buf NL, 5-0; June 17, 1880 (A.M.)

PROVIDENCE	ab	r	h	po	a	e
Hines,cf	5	0	2	2	0	0
Start,lb	5	1	1	14	0	0
Dorgan,rf	5	0	2	0	0	0
Gross,c	5	0	0	5	1	0
Farrell,2b	4	3	3	0	2	0
Ward,p	4	0	1	2	6	0
Peters,ss	4	0	1	0	6	0
York,lf	4	0	2	3	0	0
Bradley,3b	4	1	1	1	4	0
Team	40	5	13	27	19	0

BUFFALO	ab	r	h	po	a	e
Crowley,rf-c	3	0	0	4	0	2
Richardson,3b	3	0	0	0	1	0
Rowe,c-rf	3	0	0	3	1	0
Walker,lf	3	0	0	3	0	1
Hornung,2b	3	0	0	2	3	0
Mack,ss	3	0	0	3	3	1
Esterbrook,lb	3	0	0	10	0	0
Poorman,cf	3	0	0	2	0	1
Galvin,p	3	0	0	0	5	0
Team	27	0	0	27	13	5

Providence	010	100	111	–5	
Buffalo	000	000	000	–0	

Double - Farrell

Triples - Start, York, Bradley

Runs batted in - Ward, Hines, Dorgan

Passed ball - Crowley

	ip	h	r	er	bb	so
Ward (W)	9	0	0	0	0	6
Galvin (L)	9	13	5	3	0	2

Wild pitches - Galvin 2

Time - 1:40

Umpire - Daniels

Attendance - 2000

Cy Young, Bos vs Phi AL, 3-0; May 5, 1904

PHILADELPHIA	ab	r	h	po	a	e
Hartsel,lf	1	0	0	0	0	0
Hoffman,lf	2	0	0	2	1	0
Pickering,cf	3	0	0	1	0	0
Davis,lb	3	0	0	5	0	1
L.Cross,3b	3	0	0	4	1	0
Seybold,rf	3	0	0	2	0	0
Murphy,2b	3	0	0	1	2	0
M.Cross,ss	3	0	0	2	3	0
Schreck,c	3	0	0	7	0	0
Waddell,p	3	0	0	0	1	0
Team	27	0	0	24	8	1

BOSTON	ab	r	h	po	a	e
Dougherty,lf	4	0	1	1	0	0
Collins,3b	4	0	2	2	0	0
Stahl,cf	4	1	1	3	0	0
Freeman,rf	4	0	1	2	0	0
Parent,ss	4	0	2	1	4	0
LaChance,lb	3	0	1	9	0	0
Ferris,2b	3	1	1	0	3	0
Criger,c	3	1	1	9	0	0
Young,p	3	0	0	0	2	0
Team	32	3	10	27	9	0

Philadelphia	000	000	000	–0	
Boston	000	001	20x	–3	

Doubles - Collins, Criger

Triples - Stahl, Freeman, Ferris

Runs batted in - Freeman, Criger

Sacrifice - LaChance

Double plays - Hoffman and Schreck; L.Cross and Davis

	ip	h	r	er	bb	so
Waddell (L)	8	10	3	2	0	6
Young (W)	9	0	0	0	0	8

Time - 1:30

Umpire - Dwyer

Attendance - 10,267

Addie Joss, Cle vs Chi AL, 1-0; October 2, 1908

CHICAGO	ab	r	h	po	a	e
Hahn,rf	3	0	0	1	0	0
Jones,cf	3	0	0	0	0	0
Isbell,lb	3	0	0	6	1	1
Dougherty,lf	3	0	0	0	0	0
Davis,2b	3	0	0	1	0	0
Parent,ss	3	0	0	0	3	0
Schreck,c	2	0	0	13	1	0
Shaw,c	0	0	0	2	0	0
White,ph	1	0	0	0	0	0
Tannehill,3b	2	0	0	0	0	0

Donohue,ph	1	0	0	0	0	0
Walsh,p	2	0	0	1	3	0
Anderson,ph	1	0	0	0	0	0
Team	27	0	0	24	8	1

CLEVELAND	ab	r	h	po	a	e
Good,rf	4	0	0	1	0	0
Bradley,3b	4	0	0	0	1	0
Hinchman,lf	3	0	0	3	0	0
Lajoie,2b	3	0	1	2	8	1
Stovall,lb	3	0	0	16	0	0
Clarke,c	3	0	0	4	1	0
Birmingham,cf	4	1	2	0	0	0
Perring,ss	2	0	1	1	1	0
Joss,p	3	0	0	0	5	0
Team	29	1	4	27	16	0

Chicago	000	000	000	–0	
Cleveland	001	000	00x	–1	

Runs batted in - none
Stolen bases - Birmingham 2

	ip	h	r	er	bb	so
Walsh (L)	8	4	1	0	1	15
Joss (W)	9	0	0	0	0	3

Wild pitch - Walsh
Time - 1:40
Umpires - Connolly and O'Loughlin
Attendance - 10,598

Ernie Shore, Bos vs Was AL, 4-0; June 23, 1917 (1st game)

WASHINGTON	ab	r	h	po	a	e
Morgan,2b	2	0	0	4	2	0
Foster,3b	3	0	0	1	3	2
Leonard,3b	0	0	0	0	1	0
Milan,cf	3	0	0	1	0	0
Rice,rf	3	0	0	3	0	1
Gharrity,lb	0	0	0	0	0	0
Judge,lb	3	0	0	11	1	0
Jamieson,lf	3	0	0	0	0	0
Shanks,ss	3	0	0	1	2	0
Henry,c	3	0	0	1	0	0
Ayers,p	2	0	0	2	8	0
Menosky,ph	1	0	0	0	0	0
Team	26	0	0	24	17	3

BOSTON	ab	r	h	po	a	e
Hooper,rf	4	0	1	0	0	0
Barry,2b	4	0	0	2	1	0
Hoblitzel,lb	4	0	0	12	2	0
Gardner,3b	4	1	1	2	1	0
Lewis,lf	4	0	3	2	0	0
Walker,cf	3	1	1	4	0	0
Scott,ss	3	0	0	1	5	0
Thomas,c	0	0	0	0	0	0
Agnew,c	3	1	3	2	1	0
Ruth,p	0	0	0	0	0	0
Shore,p	2	1	0	2	6	0
Team	31	4	9	27	16	0

Washington	000	000	000	–0	
Boston	010	000	30x	–4	

Doubles - Walker, Agnew
Runs batted in - Agnew 2, Hooper 2
Sacrifices - Walker, Shore, Scott
Caught stealing - Morgan
Double plays - Ayers, Foster and Judge; Ayers and Judge

	ip	h	r	er	bb	so
Ayers (L)	8	9	4	2	0	0
Ruth	0	0	0	0	1	0
Shore (W)	9	0	0	0	0	2

Time 1:40
Umpires - Owens, McCormick and Dinneen
Attendance - 16,158

Charlie Robertson, Chi at Det AL, 2-0; April 30, 1922

CHICAGO	ab	r	h	po	a	e
Mulligan,ss	4	0	1	0	0	0
McClellan,3b	3	0	1	1	3	0
Collins,2b	3	0	1	4	3	0
Hooper,rf	3	1	0	3	0	0
Mostil,lf	4	1	1	3	0	0
Strunk,cf	3	0	0	0	0	0
Sheely,lb	4	0	2	9	0	0
Schalk,c	4	0	1	7	1	0
Robertson,p	4	0	0	0	1	0
Team	32	2	7	27	8	0

DETROIT	ab	r	h	po	a	e
Blue,lb	3	0	0	11	3	1
Cutshaw,2b	3	0	0	2	3	0
Cobb,cf	3	0	0	1	0	0
Veach,lf	3	0	0	2	0	0
Heilmann,rf	3	0	0	1	0	0
Jones,3b	3	0	0	1	5	0
Rigney,ss	2	0	0	2	1	0
Clark,ph	1	0	0	0	0	0
Manion,c	3	0	0	7	1	0
Pillette,p	2	0	0	0	3	0
Bassler,ph	1	0	0	0	0	0
Team	27	0	0	27	16	1

Chicago	020	000	000	–2	
Detroit	000	000	000	–0	

Doubles - Mulligan, Sheely
Runs batted in - Sheely 2
Sacrifices - McClellan, Collins, Strunk

	ip	h	r	er	bb	so
Robertson (W)	9	0	0	0	0	6
Pillette (L)	9	7	2	2	2	5

Time - 1:55
Umpires - Nallin and Evans
Attendance - 25,000

Don Larsen, NY AL vs Bro NL, 2-0; October 8, 1956 (World Series)

BROOKLYN	ab	r	h	po	a	e
Gilliam,2b	3	0	0	2	0	0
Reese,ss	3	0	0	4	2	0
Snider,cf	3	0	0	1	0	0
Robinson,2b	3	0	0	2	4	0
Hodges,lb	3	0	0	5	1	0
Amoros,lf	3	0	0	3	0	0
Furillo,rf	3	0	0	0	0	0
Campanella,c	3	0	0	7	2	0
Maglie,p	2	0	0	0	1	0
Mitchell,ph	1	0	0	0	0	0
Team	27	0	0	24	10	0

NEW YORK	ab	r	h	po	a	e
Bauer,rf	4	0	1	4	0	0
Collins,lb	4	0	1	7	0	0
Mantle,cf	3	1	1	4	0	0

	ab	r	h	po	a	e
Berra,c	3	0	0	7	0	0
Slaughter,lf	2	0	0	1	0	0
Martin,2b	3	0	1	3	4	0
McDougald,ss	2	0	0	0	2	0
Carey,3b	3	1	1	1	1	0
Larsen,p	2	0	0	0	1	0
Team	26	2	5	27	8	0
Brooklyn	000	000	000	–0		
New York	000	101	00x	–2		

Home run - Mantle

Runs batted in - Mantle, Bauer

Sacrifice - Larsen

Double plays - Reese and Hodges; Hodges, Campanella, Robinson, Campanella and Robinson

	ip	h	r	er	bb	so
Maglie (L)	8	5	2	2	2	5
Larsen (W)	9	0	0	0	0	7

Time - 2:06

Umpires - Pinelli, Soar, Boggess, Napp, Gorman, Runge

Attendance - 64,519

Harvey Haddix, Pit at Mil NL, 0-1;
May 26, 1959 (12 perfect innings, lost on one-hit in the 13th inning)

PITTSBURGH	ab	r	h	po	a	e
Schofield,ss	6	0	3	2	4	0
Virdon,cf	6	0	1	8	0	0
Burgess,c	5	0	0	8	0	0
Nelson,lb	5	0	2	14	0	0
Skinner,lf	5	0	1	4	0	0
Mazeroski,2b	5	0	1	1	1	0
Hoak,3b	5	0	2	0	6	1
Mejias,rf	3	0	1	1	0	0
Stuart,ph	1	0	0	0	0	0
Christopher,rf	1	0	0	0	0	0
Haddix,p	5	0	1	0	2	0
Team	47	0	12	38	13	1

MILWAUKEE	ab	r	h	po	a	e
O'Brien,2b	3	0	0	2	5	0
Rice,ph	1	0	0	0	0	0
Mantilla,2b	1	1	0	1	2	0
Mathews,3b	4	0	0	2	3	0
Aaron,rf	4	0	0	1	0	0
Adcock,lb	5	0	1	17	3	0
Covington,lf	4	0	0	4	0	0
Crandall,c	4	0	0	3	5	0
Pafko,cf	4	0	0	6	0	0
Logan,ss	4	0	0	3	5	0
Burdette,p	4	0	0	1	3	0
Team	38	1	1	39	22	0
Pittsburgh	000	000	000	000	0–0	
Milwaukee	000	000	000	000	1–1	

Double - Adcock

Run batted in - Adcock

Sacrifice - Mathews

Double plays - Adcock, Logan and Adcock; Mathews, O'Brien and Adcock; Adcock and Logan

	ip	h	r	er	bb	so
Haddix (L)	12 2/3	1	1	0	1	8
Burdette (W)	13	12	0	0	0	2

Time - 2:54

Umpires - Smith, Dascoli, Secory and Dixon

Attendance - 19,194

Jim Bunning, Phi at NY NL, 6-0;
June 21, 1964

PHILADELPHIA	ab	r	h	po	a	e
Briggs,cf	4	1	0	2	0	0
Herrnstein,lb	4	0	0	7	0	0
Callison,rf	4	1	2	1	0	0
Allen,3b	3	0	1	0	2	0
Covington,lf	2	0	0	1	0	0
Wine,pr-ss	1	1	0	2	1	0
T.Taylor,2b	3	2	1	0	3	0
Rojas,ss-lf	3	0	1	3	0	0
Triandos,c	4	1	2	11	1	0
Bunning,p	4	0	1	0	0	0
Team	32	6	8	27	7	0

NEW YORK	ab	r	h	po	a	e
Hickman,cf	3	0	0	2	0	0
Hunt,2b	3	0	0	3	2	0
Kranepool,lb	3	0	0	8	1	0
Christopher,rf	3	0	0	4	0	0
Gonder,c	3	0	0	6	2	0
R.Taylor,lf	3	0	0	1	0	0
C.Smith,ss	3	0	0	2	1	0
Samuel,3b	2	0	0	0	1	0
Altman,ph	1	0	0	0	0	0
Stallard,p	1	0	0	0	2	0
Wakefield,p	0	0	0	0	0	0
Kanehl,ph	1	0	0	0	0	0
Sturdivant,p	0	0	0	1	0	0
Stephenson,ph	1	0	0	0	0	0
Team	27	0	0	27	9	0
Philadelphia	110	004	000	– 6		
New York	000	000	000	– 0		

Doubles - Triandos, Bunning

Home run - Callison

Runs batted in - Callison, Allen, Triandos 2, Bunning 2

Sacrifices - Herrnstein, Rojas

	ip	h	r	er	bb	so
Bunning (W)	9	0	0	0	0	10
Stallard (L)	5 2/3	7	6	6	4	3
Wakefield	1/3	0	0	0	0	0
Sturdivant	3	1	0	0	0	3

Wild pitch - Stallard

Time - 2:19

Umpires - Sudol, Pryor, Secory and Burkhart

Attendance - 32,026

Sandy Koufax, LA vs Chi NL, 1-0;
September 9, 1965

CHICAGO	ab	r	h	po	a	e
Young,cf	3	0	0	5	0	0
Beckert,2b	3	0	0	1	1	0
Williams,rf	3	0	0	0	0	0
Santo,3b	3	0	0	1	2	0
Banks,lb	3	0	0	13	0	0
Browne,lf	3	0	0	1	0	0
Krug,c	3	0	0	3	0	1
Kessinger,ss	2	0	0	0	2	0
Amalfitano,ph	1	0	0	0	0	0
Hendley,p	2	0	0	0	5	0
Kuenn,ph	1	0	0	0	0	0
Team	27	0	0	24	10	1

LOS ANGELES	ab	r	h	po	a	e
Wills,ss	3	0	0	0	2	0
Gilliam,3b	3	0	0	0	1	0
W.Davis,cf	3	0	0	2	0	0
Johnson,lf	2	1	1	2	0	0
Fairly,rf	2	0	0	3	0	0
Lefebvre,2b	3	0	0	1	0	0
Tracewski,2b	0	0	0	0	0	0
Parker,lb	3	0	0	4	0	0
Torborg,c	3	0	0	15	0	0
Koufax,p	2	0	0	0	0	0
Team	24	1	1	27	3	0
Chicago	000	000	000	–0		
Los Angeles	000	010	00x	–1		

Double - Johnson
Runs batted in - none
Sacrifice - Fairly
Stolen base - Johnson

	ip	h	r	er	bb	so
Hendley (L)	8	1	1	0	1	3
Koufax (W)	9	0	0	0	0	14

Time - 1:43
Umpires - Vargo, Pelekoudas, Jackowski and Pryor
Attendance - 29,139

Jim "Catfish" Hunter, Oak vs Min AL, 4-0; May 8, 1968

MINNESOTA	ab	r	h	po	a	e
Tovar,3b	3	0	0	1	2	0
Carew,2b	3	0	0	4	1	0
Killebrew,lb	3	0	0	5	0	0
Oliva,rf	3	0	0	3	0	0
Uhlaender,cf	3	0	0	2	0	0
Allison,lf	3	0	0	0	0	0
Hernandez,ss	2	0	0	2	4	0
Roseboro,ph	1	0	0	0	0	0
Look,c	3	0	0	7	2	0
Boswell,p	2	0	0	0	1	1
Perranoski,p	0	0	0	0	0	0
Reese,ph	1	0	0	0	0	0
Team	27	0	0	24	10	1

OAKLAND	ab	r	h	po	a	e
Campaneris,ss	4	0	2	1	3	0
Jackson,rf	4	0	0	3	0	0
Bando,3b	3	0	1	0	2	0
Webster,lb	4	1	2	7	0	0
Donaldson,2b	3	0	1	1	2	0
Pagliaroni,c	3	1	0	11	0	0
Monday,cf	3	2	2	2	0	0
Rudi,lf	3	0	0	2	0	0
Robinson,ph	0	0	0	0	0	0
Cater,ph	0	0	0	0	0	0
Hershberger,lf	0	0	0	0	0	0
Hunter,p	4	0	3	0	0	0
Team	31	4	10	27	7	0
Minnesota	000	000	000 - 0			
Oakland	000	000	13x - 4			

Doubles - Hunter, Monday
Runs batted in - Hunter 3, Cater
Stolen base - Campaneris
Double plays - Boswell, Hernandez and Killebrew; Hernandez, Carew and Killebrew

	ip	h	r	er	bb	so
Boswell (L)	7 2/3	9	4	4	4	6
Perranoski	1/3	1	0	0	1	0
Hunter (W)	9	0	0	0	0	11

Hit by pitch - by Boswell (Donaldson)
Wild pitches - Boswell 2
Time - 2:28
Umpires - Napp, Salerno, Haller and Neudecker
Attendance - 6,298

Len Barker, Cle vs Tor AL, 3-0; May 15, 1981

TORONTO	ab	r	h	po	a	e
Griffin,ss	3	0	0	1	1	1
Moseby,rf	3	0	0	4	0	0
Bell,lf	3	0	0	2	0	0
Mayberry,lb	3	0	0	4	1	1
Upshaw,dh	3	0	0	0	0	0
Garcia,2b	3	0	0	3	2	1
Bosetti,cf	3	0	0	3	0	0
Ainge,3b	2	0	0	1	0	0
Woods,ph	1	0	0	0	0	0
B.Martinez,c	2	0	0	5	1	0
Whitt,ph	1	0	0	0	0	0
Leal,p	0	0	0	1	1	0
Team	27	0	0	24	6	3

CLEVELAND	ab	r	h	po	a	e
Manning,cf	4	1	1	4	0	0
Orta,rf	4	1	3	0	0	0
Hargrove,lb	4	1	1	9	0	0
Thornton,dh	3	0	0	0	0	0
Hassey,c	4	0	1	11	0	0
Harrah,3b	4	0	1	2	0	0
Charbonneau,lf	3	0	0	1	0	0
Kuiper,2b	3	0	0	0	4	0
Veryzer,ss	3	0	0	0	3	0
Barker,p	0	0	0	0	0	0
Team	32	3	7	27	7	0
Toronto	000	000	000 - 0			
Cleveland	200	000	01x - 3			

Home run - Orta
Runs batted in - Thornton, Hassey, Orta
Sacrifice - Thornton

	ip	h	r	er	bb	so
Leal (L)	8	7	3	1	0	5
Barker (W)	9	0	0	0	0	11

Time - 2:09
Umpires - Garcia, Kosc, Denkinger and McKean
Attendance - 7,290

Mike Witt, Cal at Tex AL, 1-0; September 30, 1984

(last game of the season)

CALIFORNIA	ab	r	h	po	a	e
Wilfong,2b	4	0	0	0	8	0
Sconiers,lb	3	0	0	10	1	0
Grich,lb	0	0	0	2	0	0
Lynn,cf-rf	4	0	2	1	0	0
DeCinces,3b	4	1	2	0	1	0
Downing,lf	4	0	0	1	0	0
Thomas,lf	0	0	0	0	0	0
Re.Jackson,dh	4	0	0	0	0	0
M.Brown,rf	3	0	3	2	0	0
Pettis,cf	0	0	0	0	0	0

Boone,c	3	0	0	10	0	0
Schofield,ss	2	0	0	0	3	0
Witt,p	0	0	0	1	0	0
Team	31	1	7	27	13	0

TEXAS	**ab**	**r**	**h**	**po**	**a**	**e**
Rivers,dh	3	0	0	0	0	0
Tolleson,2b	3	0	0	4	5	0
Ward,lf	3	0	0	0	0	0
Parrish,3b	3	0	0	0	3	0
O'Brien,1b	3	0	0	13	0	0
G.Wright,cf	3	0	0	3	0	0
Dunbar,rf	3	0	0	1	0	0
Scott,c	2	0	0	4	3	0
B.Jones,ph	1	0	0	0	0	0
Wilkerson,ss	2	0	0	2	4	0
Foley,ph	1	0	0	0	0	0
Hough,p	0	0	0	0	2	0
Team	27	0	0	27	17	0

California	000	000	100 - 1	
Texas	000	000	000 - 0	

Double - Brown
Triple - Brown
Run batted in - Jackson
Double plays - Parrish, Tolleson and O'Brien; Tolleson, Wilkerson and O'Brien
Passed ball - Scott

	ip	h	r	er	bb	so
Witt (W)	9	0	0	0	0	10
Hough (L)	9	7	1	0	3	3

Wild pitch - Hough
Time - 1:49
Umpires - Kosc, Hendry, Coble and Evans
Attendance - 8,375

Tom Browning, Cin vs LA NL, 1-0; September 16, 1988

LOS ANGELES	**ab**	**r**	**h**	**po**	**a**	**e**
Griffin,ss	3	0	0	0	4	0
Hatcher,lb	3	0	0	10	0	0
Gibson,lf	3	0	0	1	0	0
Gonzalez,lf	0	0	0	0	0	0
Marshall,rf	3	0	0	2	0	0
Shelby,cf	3	0	0	2	0	0
Hamilton,3b	3	0	0	0	1	1
Dempsey,c	3	0	0	7	0	0
Sax,2b	3	0	0	2	2	0
Belcher,p	2	0	0	0	2	0
Woodson,ph	1	0	0	0	0	0
Team	27	0	0	24	9	0

CINCINNATI	**ab**	**r**	**h**	**po**	**a**	**e**
Larkin,ss	3	1	1	0	4	0
Sabo,3b	3	0	1	0	3	0
Daniels,lf	3	0	0	3	0	0
Davis,cf	2	0	0	1	0	0
O'Neill,rf	3	0	0	4	0	0
Esasky,lb	3	0	0	10	1	0
Reed,c	3	0	0	7	0	0
Oester,2b	3	0	1	1	1	0
Browning,p	3	0	0	1	0	0
Team	26	1	3	27	9	0

Los Angeles	000	000	000 - 0	
Cincinnati	000	001	00x - 1	

Double - Larkin
Run batted in - none

	ip	h	r	er	bb	so
Belcher (L)	8	3	1	0	1	7
Browning (W)	9	0	0	0	0	7

Time - 1:51
Umpires - Quick, Hirschbeck, Kibler and Gregg
Attendance - 16,591

Dennis Martinez, Mon at LA NL, 2-0; July 28, 1991

MONTREAL	**ab**	**r**	**h**	**po**	**a**	**e**
DeShields,2b	3	0	1	0	9	0
Grissom,cf	4	0	0	2	0	0
Da.Martinez,rf	4	1	0	0	0	0
Calderon,lf	3	0	0	2	0	0
Wallach,3b	4	0	0	1	1	0
Walker,lb	4	1	1	17	0	0
Hassey,c	3	0	1	5	0	0
Owen,ss	3	0	0	0	2	0
De.Martinez,p	3	0	1	0	2	0
Team	31	2	4	27	14	0

LOS ANGELES	**ab**	**r**	**h**	**po**	**a**	**e**
Butler,cf	3	0	0	1	0	0
Samuel,2b	3	0	0	1	3	0
Murray,lb	3	0	0	8	2	0
Strawberry,rf	3	0	0	4	0	0
Daniels,lf	3	0	0	3	0	0
Harris,3b	3	0	0	0	0	0
Scioscia,c	3	0	0	5	1	0
Griffin,ss	2	0	0	4	4	2
Javier,ph	1	0	0	0	0	0
Morgan,p	2	0	0	1	2	0
Gwynn,ph	1	0	0	0	0	0
Team	27	0	0	26	12	2

Montreal	000	000	200 - 2	
Los Angeles	000	000	000 - 0	

Triple - Walker
Run batted in - Walker
Caught stealing - Hassey

	ip	h	r	er	bb	so
De.Martinez (W)	9	0	0	0	0	5
Morgan (L)	9	4	2	0	1	5

Wild pitch - Morgan
Time - 2:14
Umpires - Poncino, Froemming, DeMuth and Bonin
Attendance - 45,560

*M*ajor

league

report

Philadelphia Phillies

John Kruk batted .316, scored 100 runs and was second in the NL in on-base percentage (.430).

by Eileen Blass, *USA TODAY*

1993 Phillies: Everybody loved the underdogs

Some may call the Braves America's Team, but it was the long-haired, beer-swilling, tobacco-spitting Phillies who were truly a club for Everyman in '93.

The cast of characters—first baseman John Kruk, outfielders Lenny Dykstra and Pete Incaviglia, relief pitcher Mitch "Wild Thing" Williams and catcher Darren Daulton—knocked the Braves out of the NLCS, then took Toronto to six games in one of the most entertaining World Series in years.

The Phils went from worst to first, going from 92 losses in '92 to 97 wins in '93. They scored 877 runs—most in the NL since 1962—and were not shut out until the final week of the season. They got off to a 17-5 start in April, built an 11-game lead in June, then held off charges by the Cardinals and Expos. They held at least a share of first place for an NL record 181 days—every day except one (April 9) all season.

Batting leadoff, Dykstra hit .305 with 44 doubles, 19 HR, 66 RBI and 37 steals. He became just the fifth major leaguer to lead his league in hits (193) and walks (129). He scored 143 runs, the most in the NL since 1932. He played every game until Sept. 29, when the Phils clinched their first division title since 1983.

Kruk, who traded uniform numbers with Williams for a case of beer, hit .316 (14 HR, 85 RBI). Daulton, the heart and soul of the Phils, hit .257 with 24 HR and 105 RBI—just four short of his league-leading total in '92. Third baseman Dave Hollins hit .273 (18 HR, 93 RBI). Shortstop Kevin Stocker hit .324 and stabilized the defense after his July 7 recall.

Role players contributed mightily: Incaviglia hit .274 (101 hits, 24 HR, 89 RBI); Jim Eisenreich hit .318; Milt Thompson hit .262 and saved several victories with wall-banging catches.

The starting rotation was solid: Tommy Greene (16-4, 3.42 ERA); Curt Schilling (16-7, 4.02 ERA); Terry Mulholland (12-9, 3.25 ERA); Danny Jackson (12-11, 3.77 ERA), and Ben Rivera (13-9, 5.09 ERA). It was just the second time in club history five pitchers won more than 10 games apiece. The staff led the league with 24 complete games (Schilling, Greene and Mulholland each had seven).

Schilling was the NLCS MVP, even though he had just two no-decisions to show for his brilliant performances. Then he shut out Toronto in Game 5 of the World Series. Jackson pitched a masterful 2-1 victory against Atlanta in the NLCS.

The Phils didn't have consistency in middle relief, but Williams made things interesting in the closer role with his penchant for getting into—then out of—trouble. During the regular season, he had 43 saves. But he blew two games for Schilling in the NLCS, squandered a 14-9 lead in Game 4 of the Series, then gave up the Series-winning home run to Joe Carter in Game 6.

—by Bill Koenig

1994 Phillies: Preview

Although the Phillies will be in the same division as the Braves, the future looks bright—all the key offensive players are in the fold for '94, and none of the pitchers are eligible for free agency over the winter.

"I think the basic core of this team is going to be here, no question," Dykstra said. "There's always room for improvement. We've got a lot of guys coming into their prime. I see a lot of good things happening. There's no reason why we can't come back next year."

Thomas has to improve the bullpen, though, both in long and middle relief. After the team's immense popularity and success in '93, the Phillies' should have no problem attracting talent.

"Our reputation is better than it has been in the past," Thomas said. "I think some guys are going to want to come here."

—by Bill Koenig

1993 Phillies: Between the lines

▶**April 6:** Reliever Mitch "Wild Thing" Williams had his number changed from 28 to 99, the highest jersey number in major league history. He responded with a save and a vow to try to throw the ball 99 mph every time he came out to the mound.

▶**April 20:** John Kruk got his league-leading fifth homer with two out in the 14th inning to give the Phillies a 4-3 win over San Diego.

▶**April 23:** Curt Schilling shut out the Dodgers on five hits and struck out a career-high nine.

▶**May 9:** Mariano Duncan hit a grand slam in the eighth to beat St. Louis 6-5.

▶**May 10:** Darren Daulton hit a seventh-inning grand slam off Pirate Bob Walk that broke a 1-1 tie and gave the Phillies their fourth win in a row. It was the second game-winning grand slam in as many days for the Phillies, who improved to 23-7, the best 30-game start in club history.

▶**May 12:** John Kruk was 4-for-4 in the Phillies' 4-1 win against the Pirates. *Quote of the day*—Kruk, when Lenny Dykstra ran into the outfield fence: "I think he hit his head. That's good."

▶**May 17:** Kruk raised his average to .382 with his first five-hit game.

▶**May 18:** Tommy Greene tossed his first shutout in two years, fanning 10.

▶**May 24:** Greene lowered his league-low ERA to 1.98 after throwing his third consecutive complete game.

▶**May 29:** Terry Mulholland—injured foot and all—tossed the first major league shutout at Mile High Stadium. It was his first shutout of the season and fourth complete game.

▶**May 30:** Greene raised his record to 7-0, and hit a two-run homer as the Phillies blitzed the Rockies 18-1.

▶**June 5:** Greene's ERA climbed to 1.87 with his fifth complete game.

▶**June 6:** Mariano Duncan was 4-for-5 with a homer, Lenny Dykstra added four hits and Darren Daulton, Jim Eisenreich and Mickey Morandini had three hits apiece.

▶**June 9:** Eisenreich hit his first homer of the year and went 3-for-4 with three RBI as Terry Mulholland tossed his major league-leading sixth complete game and shut out the Astros.

▶**June 12** Danny Jackson threw his first shutout in five years and his first complete game since 1989.

▶**June 14:** Eisenreich's ninth-inning grand slam sealed the victory over the Expos and stretched the Phils' lead over them to 12 1/2 games.

▶**June 28:** Philadelphia's 3-1 loss to St. Louis at soggy Busch Stadium clipped the Phillies' NL East lead to 6 1/2 games. It was the Cardinals' fifth consecutive win and the Phillies' third loss in a row—only their second such streak of the season.

▶**July 1:** Curt Schilling gave up 11 runs, seven earned, taking his third loss in a row. It was the the Phils' fifth defeat in six games.

▶**July 27:** John Kruk tied his career high with five hits.

▶**July 28:** Darren Daulton hit a grand slam and a two-run triple as the Phillies pounded St. Louis 14-6. Lenny Dykstra and Mariano Duncan had three hits each and Dave Hollins drove in three runs.

▶**July 29:** The Phillies completed a three-game sweep of the Cardinals at Veterans Stadium to extend their lead to seven games in the NL East.

▶**July 31:** Pete Incaviglia homered twice in the Phillies' 10-2 win against the Pirates. Danny Jackson threw his second complete game for his ninth win of the season.

▶**August 3:** Incaviglia hit his fourth home run in three games.

▶**August 12:** Five relievers combined for five scoreless innings as the Phillies rallied for a 7-4 win against Montreal.

▶**August 13:** Kim Batiste hit a grand slam with two out in the ninth to account for the only hit off the Mets' hard-luck pitcher, Anthony Young, as the

Phillies rallied for five runs in the ninth to beat the Mets 9-5.

▶**August 18:** John Kruk knocked a pair out of the park, helping the Phillies edge Colorado 7-6.

▶**August 20:** The Phillies called up rookie Kevin Stocker to play shortstop for his glove, not his bat. But his bases-loaded triple in the eighth led the Phils to a 6-4 win against Houston. Two hits brought his average to .365.

▶**August 22:** Lefty Terry Mulholland broke his right hand Aug. 21 when he punched the water cooler after allowing a homer in a 3-2 loss to Houston, but was not expected to miss a start: *Quote of the day*—Mulholland: "It's stupid, but it would have *really* been stupid if I'd hit it with my left hand."

▶**August 24:** Danny Jackson quieted the Rockies' bats, earning his 10th victory of the season. All five Phillies' starters had at least 10 wins, the first time since 1932.

▶**September 1:** Mulholland's seventh complete game of the year was a beauty as he beat the Cubs 4-1. It was the 149th time in a row the Phillies had not been shut out, one short of the modern NL record set by Pittsburgh in 1924-25; the major league record is 308, set by the 1931-33 Yankees.

▶**September 13:** Tommy Greene pitched a complete-game six-hitter, shutting out the Mets 5-0.

▶**September 20:** Curt Schilling fanned a career-high 11 Florida batters during a 7-1 Phillies win.

▶**September 24:** In a matchup of divisional leaders, Tommy Greene tossed three-hit shutout ball for 8 1/3 innings to beat Atlanta 3-0—his fifth win in a row.

▶**October 3:** The Phillies won the NL East by three games, even though they got shut out by the Cardinals, 2-0, on their final day of the season. *League leaders, pitching*—Tommy Greene was eighth in victories (16-4), seventh in strikeouts (167), and tied with teammates Terry Mulholland, Curt Schilling and others for second in complete games (7); Schilling was fourth in strikeouts (186), eighth in victories (16-7), and was sixth in innings pitched (235 1/3);

Mulholland was 10th in ERA (3.25); Dave West was third in games (76); Mitch Williams was tied for fourth in saves (43). *League leaders, batting*—Lenny Dykstra led the league in runs (143), hits (194) and walks (129); was second in doubles (44), third in on-base percentage (.420), tied for fourth in total bases (307), and 10th in stolen bases (37); John Kruk was second in on-base percentage (.430), fourth in walks (111), eighth in batting (.316), and 10th in runs (100); Darren Daulton was third in walks (117) and sixth in RBI (105); Mickey Morandini was tied for third in triples (9); Dave Hollins was tied for sixth in walks (89).

—*by John Hunt, Scott Kauffman, Lisa Winston, Deron Snyder, Matt Young*

Team directory

▶**Owner:** Bill Giles
▶**General Manager:** Lee Thomas
▶**Ballpark:**
Veterans Stadium
Broad Street & Pattison Avenue, Philadelphia, Pa.
215-463-1000
Capacity 62,586
Parking for 10,000 cars; $4.50
Public transportation available
Wheelchair section and ramps, TDD ticket information for hearing impaired (215-463-2998)
▶**Team publications:**
Media guide, yearbook, scorebook
▶**TV, radio broadcast stations:**
WOGL 1210 AM, WPHL Channel 17, Prism Cable
▶**Spring Training:**
Jack Russell Memorial Stadium
Clearwater, Fla.
Capacity 7,350
813-441-8638

PHILADELPHIA PHILLIES 1993 final stats

Batting	BA	SLG	OB	G	AB	R	H	TB	2B	3B	HR	RBI	BB	SO	SB	CS	E
Lindsey	.500	.500	.500	2	2	0	1	1	0	0	0	0	0	1	0	0	0
Amaro	.333	.521	.400	25	48	7	16	25	2	2	1	6	6	5	0	0	1
Stocker	.324	.417	.409	70	259	46	84	108	12	3	2	31	30	43	5	0	14
Eisenreich	.318	.445	.363	153	362	51	115	161	17	4	7	54	26	36	5	0	1
Kruk	.316	.475	.430	150	535	100	169	254	33	5	14	85	111	87	6	2	8
Dykstra	.305	.482	.420	161	637	143	194	307	44	6	19	66	129	64	37	12	10
Jordan	.289	.421	.324	90	159	21	46	67	4	1	5	18	8	32	0	0	2
Pratt	.287	.529	.330	33	87	8	25	46	6	0	5	13	5	19	0	0	2
Duncan	.282	.417	.304	124	496	68	140	207	26	4	11	73	12	88	6	5	21
Batiste	.282	.436	.298	79	156	14	44	68	7	1	5	29	3	29	0	1	10
Chamberlain	.282	.493	.320	96	284	34	80	140	20	2	12	45	17	51	2	1	1
Incaviglia	.274	.530	.318	116	368	60	101	195	16	3	24	89	21	82	1	1	5
Hollins	.273	.442	.372	143	543	104	148	240	30	4	18	93	85	109	2	3	27
Thompson	.262	.350	.341	129	340	42	89	119	14	2	4	44	40	57	9	4	1
Daulton	.257	.482	.392	147	510	90	131	246	35	4	24	105	117	111	5	0	9
Morandini	.247	.355	.309	120	425	57	105	151	19	9	3	33	34	73	13	2	5
Longmire	.231	.231	.231	11	13	1	3	3	0	0	0	1	0	1	0	0	0
Bell	.200	.323	.268	24	65	5	13	21	6	1	0	7	5	12	0	1	9
Millette	.200	.200	.273	10	10	3	2	2	0	0	0	2	1	2	0	0	0
Manto	.056	.056	.105	8	18	0	1	1	0	0	0	0	0	3	0	0	0

Pitching	W-L	ERA	G	GS	CG	GF	Sho	SV	IP	H	R	ER	HR	BB	SO
Fletcher	0-0	0.00	1	0	0	0	0	0	0.1	0	0	0	0	0	0
Pall	1-0	2.55	8	0	0	2	0	0	17.2	15	7	5	1	3	11
Andersen	3-2	2.92	64	0	0	13	0	0	61.2	54	22	20	4	21	67
West	6-4	2.92	76	0	0	27	0	3	86.1	60	37	28	6	51	87
Brink	0-0	3.00	2	0	0	1	0	0	6	3	2	2	1	3	8
Mulholland	12-9	3.25	29	28	7	0	2	0	191	177	80	69	20	40	116
Deleon	3-0	3.26	24	3	0	6	0	0	47	39	25	17	5	27	34
Mit.Williams	3-7	3.34	65	0	0	57	0	43	62	56	30	23	3	44	60
Greene	16-4	3.42	31	30	7	0	2	0	200	175	84	76	12	62	167
Jackson	12-11	3.77	32	32	2	0	1	0	210.1	214	105	88	12	80	120
Schilling	16-7	4.02	34	34	7	0	2	0	235.1	234	114	105	23	57	186
Mason	5-12	4.06	68	0	0	29	0	0	99.2	90	48	45	10	34	71
Rivera	13-9	5.02	30	28	1	1	1	0	163	175	99	91	16	85	123
Mike Williams	1-3	5.29	17	4	0	2	0	0	51	50	32	30	5	22	33

1994 preliminary roster

PITCHERS (19)
Toby Borland
Ricky Bottalico
Brad Brink
Kevin Foster
Tyler Green
Tommy Greene
Danny Jackson
Doug Jones
Jeff Juden
Roger Mason
Terry Mulholland
Donn Pall
Jeff Patterson
Ben Rivera
Curt Schilling
Heathcliff Slocumb
Bob Wells
David West
Mike Williams

CATCHERS (3)
Darren Daulton
Mike Lieberthal
Todd Pratt

INFIELDERS (8)
Kim Batiste
Mariano Duncan
Dave Hollins
Ricky Jordan
John Kruk
Mickey Morandini
Gene Schall
Kevin Stocker

OUTFIELDERS (9)
Wes Chamberlain
Lenny Dykstra
Jim Eisenreich
Phil Geisler
Pete Incaviglia
Jeff Jackson
Tony Longmire
Tom Marsh
Milt Thompson

Games played by position

Player	G	C	1B	2B	3B	SS	OF
Amaro	25	0	0	0	0	0	16
Batiste	79	0	0	0	58	24	0
Bell	24	0	0	0	0	22	0
Chamberlain	96	0	0	0	0	0	76
Daulton	147	146	0	0	0	0	0
Duncan	124	0	0	65	0	59	0
Dykstra	161	0	0	0	0	0	160
Eisenreich	153	0	1	0	0	0	137
Hollins	143	0	0	0	143	0	0
Incaviglia	116	0	0	0	0	0	97
Jordan	90	0	33	0	0	0	0
Kruk	150	0	144	0	0	0	0
Lindsey	2	2	0	0	0	0	0
Longmire	11	0	0	0	0	0	2
Manto	8	0	0	0	6	1	0
Millette	10	0	0	0	3	7	0
Morandini	120	0	0	111	0	0	0
Pratt	33	26	0	0	0	0	0
Stocker	70	0	0	0	0	70	0
Thompson	129	0	0	0	0	0	106

Sick call: 1993 DL Report

Player	Days on the DL
Larry Andersen	19
Wes Chamberlain	18
Jose DeJesus	120
Mariano Duncan	15
Tommy Greene	15
Dave Hollins	17
Todd Pratt	29

Minor League Report

Class AAA: Scranton/Wilkes-Barre finished at 62-80, third in the International League Eastern Division. Victor Rodriguez hit .305 with 12 homers and 64 RBI. Tony Longmire hit .304 with 67 RBI. Jeff Manto had 88 RBI. **Class AA:** Reading finished at 62-77, seventh in the Eastern League. Ricky Bottalico had 20 saves. Steve Bieser hit .312. Jeff Jackson stole 20 bases. Gene Schall hit .326 with 15 homers and 60 RBI. Bob Gaddy had a 2.51 ERA. **Class A:** Clearwater finished at 75-60, winning the first half of the Florida State League West Division and beating St. Lucie in four games to win the league title. Rob Grable hit .313 with 55 RBI. Jon Zuber hit .308 with five homers and 69 RBI. Jason Moler and Phil Geisler each hit 15 homers. . . . Spartanburg finished at 62-80, fifth in the Sally League Northern Division. Luis Brito hit .313. Alan Burke led the league with 96 RBI. **Short-season:** Batavia finished at 37-39, third in the New York-Penn League Stadler Division. Kevin Sefcik hit .299 with 28 RBI. Jeremy Kendall had 31 stolen bases. . . . Martinsville finished at 22-46, last in the Appalachian League Northern Division. Bryan Lundberg was 3-4 with a 2.78 ERA.

Tops in the organization

Batter	Club	Avg	G	AB	R	H	HR	RBI
Brito, Luis	Spt	.313	127	467	56	146	0	33
Zuber, Jon	Clw	.308	129	494	70	152	5	69
Tokheim, David	Rea	.306	106	412	57	126	2	36
Rodriguez, Victor	Swb	.305	118	442	59	135	12	64
Longmire, Tony	Swb	.304	120	447	63	136	6	67

Home Runs			Wins		
Schall, Gene	Swb	19	Tranberg, Mark	Clw	15
Burke, Alan	Clw	18	Brown, Greg	Rea	13
Geisler, Phil	Rea	18	Abbott, Kyle	Swb	12
Moler, Jason	Rea	17	Mitchell, Larry	Clw	10
Manto, Jeff	Swb	17	Trisler, John	Clw	10

RBI			Saves		
Burke, Alan	Clw	99	Bottalico, Ricky	Rea	24
Manto, Jeff	Swb	88	Borland, Toby	Rea	14
Moler, Jason	Rea	83	Mauser, Tim	Swb	10
Schall, Gene	Swb	76	Munoz, J.J.	Clw	9
Geisler, Phil	Rea	76	Several players tied		8

Stolen Bases			Strikeouts		
Murphy, Mike	Spt	33	Mitchell, Larry	Clw	159
Amaro, Ruben	Swb	25	Tranberg, Mark	Clw	142
Evans, Stan	Clw	21	Anderson, Chad	Spt	129
Wills, Shawn	Spt	21	Fletcher, Paul	Swb	116
Edwards, Jay	Clw	21	Goedhart, Darrell	Rea	110

Pitcher	Club	W-L	ERA	IP	H	BB	SO
Tranberg, Mark	Clw	15- 4	2.24	157	132	39	142
Sepeda, Jamie	Clw	9- 9	3.60	160	165	63	97
Gaddy, Bob	Rea	7- 8	3.71	124	118	58	95
Mitchell, Larry	Clw	10-10	3.74	173	163	75	159
Doolan, Blake	Rea	9-10	3.91	168	185	45	95

Philadelphia (1883-1993)

80

Runs: Most, career, all-time

1506	Mike Schmidt, 1972-1989
1367	Ed Delahanty, 1888-1901
1114	Richie Ashburn, 1948-1959
963	Chuck Klein, 1928-1944
924	Sam Thompson, 1889-1898

Hits: Most, career, all-time

2234	Mike Schmidt, 1972-1989
2217	Richie Ashburn, 1948-1959
2213	Ed Delahanty, 1888-1901
1812	Del Ennis, 1946-1956
1798	Larry Bowa, 1970-1981

2B: Most, career, all-time

442	Ed Delahanty, 1888-1901
408	Mike Schmidt, 1972-1989
337	Sherry Magee, 1904-1914
336	Chuck Klein, 1928-1944
310	Del Ennis, 1946-1956

3B: Most, career, all-time

157	Ed Delahanty, 1888-1901
127	Sherry Magee, 1904-1914
106	Sam Thompson, 1889-1898
97	Richie Ashburn, 1948-1959
84	Johnny Callison, 1960-1969

HR: Most, career, all-time

548	Mike Schmidt, 1972-1989
259	Del Ennis, 1946-1956
243	Chuck Klein, 1928-1944
223	Greg Luzinski, 1970-1980
217	Cy Williams, 1918-1930

RBI: Most, career, all-time

1595	Mike Schmidt, 1972-1989
1286	Ed Delahanty, 1888-1901
1124	Del Ennis, 1946-1956
983	Chuck Klein, 1928-1944
957	Sam Thompson, 1889-1898

SB: Most, career, all-time

508	Billy Hamilton, 1890-1895
411	Ed Delahanty, 1888-1901
387	Sherry Magee, 1904-1914
289	Jim Fogarty, 1884-1889
288	Larry Bowa, 1970-1981

BB: Most, career, all-time

1507	Mike Schmidt, 1972-1989
946	Richie Ashburn, 1948-1959
946	Roy Thomas, 1899-1911
693	Willie Jones, 1947-1959
643	Ed Delahanty, 1888-1901

BA: Highest, career, all-time

.361	Billy Hamilton, 1890-1895
.348	Ed Delahanty, 1888-1901
.338	Elmer Flick, 1898-1901
.333	Sam Thompson, 1889-1898
.326	Chuck Klein, 1928-1944

Slug avg: Highest, career, all-time

.553	Chuck Klein, 1928-1944
.530	Dick Allen, 1963-1976
.527	Mike Schmidt, 1972-1989
.510	Dolph Camilli, 1934-1937
.508	Ed Delahanty, 1888-1901

Games started: Most, career, all-time

499	Steve Carlton, 1972-1986
472	Robin Roberts, 1948-1961
301	Chris Short, 1959-1972
280	Pete Alexander, 1911-1930
262	Curt Simmons, 1947-1960

Saves: Most, career, all-time

103	STEVE BEDROSIAN, 1986-1989
102	MITCH WILLIAMS, 1991-1993
94	Tug McGraw, 1975-1984
90	Ron Reed, 1976-1983
65	Turk Farrell, 1956-1969

Shutouts: Most, career, all-time

61	Pete Alexander, 1911-1930
39	Steve Carlton, 1972-1986
35	Robin Roberts, 1948-1961
24	Chris Short, 1959-1972
23	Jim Bunning, 1964-1971

Wins: Most, career, all-time

241	Steve Carlton, 1972-1986
234	Robin Roberts, 1948-1961
190	Pete Alexander, 1911-1930
132	Chris Short, 1959-1972
115	Curt Simmons, 1947-1960

K: Most, career, all-time

3031	Steve Carlton, 1972-1986
1871	Robin Roberts, 1948-1961
1585	Chris Short, 1959-1972
1409	Pete Alexander, 1911-1930
1197	Jim Bunning, 1964-1971

Win pct: Highest, career, all-time

.676	Pete Alexander, 1911-1930
.642	Tom Seaton, 1912-1913
.607	Charlie Ferguson, 1884-1887
.606	Charlie Buffinton, 1887-1889
.603	Red Donahue, 1898-1901

ERA: Lowest, career, all-time

1.79	George McQuillan, 1907-1916
2.18	Pete Alexander, 1911-1930
2.48	Tully Sparks, 1897-1910
2.61	Frank Corridon, 1904-1909
2.63	Earl Moore, 1908-1913

Runs: Most, season

192	Billy Hamilton, 1894
166	Billy Hamilton, 1895
158	Chuck Klein, 1930
152	Chuck Klein, 1932
152	Lefty O'Doul, 1929

Hits: Most, season

254	Lefty O'Doul, 1929
250	Chuck Klein, 1930
238	Ed Delahanty, 1899
226	Chuck Klein, 1932
223	Chuck Klein, 1933

2B: Most, season

59	Chuck Klein, 1930
55	Ed Delahanty, 1899
50	Chuck Klein, 1932
49	Ed Delahanty, 1895
48	Dick Bartell, 1932

3B: Most, season

23	Nap Lajoie, 1897
21	Ed Delahanty, 1892
21	Sam Thompson, 1895
19	JUAN SAMUEL, 1984
19	George Wood, 1887

HR: Most, season

48	Mike Schmidt, 1980
45	Mike Schmidt, 1979
43	Chuck Klein, 1929
41	Cy Williams, 1923
40	Dick Allen, 1966
40	Chuck Klein, 1930
40	Mike Schmidt, 1983

RBI: Most, season

170	Chuck Klein, 1930
165	Sam Thompson, 1895
146	Ed Delahanty, 1893
145	Chuck Klein, 1929
143	Don Hurst, 1932

SB: Most, season

111	Billy Hamilton, 1891
102	Jim Fogarty, 1887
102	Billy Hamilton, 1890
99	Jim Fogarty, 1889
98	Billy Hamilton, 1894
72	JUAN SAMUEL, 1984 (7)

BB: Most, season

129	LENNY DYKSTRA, 1993
128	Mike Schmidt, 1983
126	Billy Hamilton, 1894
125	Richie Ashburn, 1954
121	Von Hayes, 1987

BA: Highest, season

.410	Ed Delahanty, 1899
.407	Ed Delahanty, 1894
.404	Billy Hamilton, 1894
.404	Ed Delahanty, 1895
.398	Lefty O'Doul, 1929

Slug avg: Highest, season

.687	Chuck Klein, 1930
.657	Chuck Klein, 1929
.654	Sam Thompson, 1895
.646	Chuck Klein, 1932
.644	Mike Schmidt, 1981

Games started: Most, season

61	John Coleman, 1883
55	Kid Gleason, 1890
50	Ed Daily, 1885
49	Gus Weyhing, 1892
47	Charlie Ferguson, 1884
45	Pete Alexander, 1916 (8)

Saves: Most, season

43	MITCH WILLIAMS, 1993
40	STEVE BEDROSIAN, 1987
30	MITCH WILLIAMS, 1991
29	STEVE BEDROSIAN, 1986
29	Al Holland, 1984
29	MITCH WILLIAMS, 1992

Shutouts: Most, season

16	Pete Alexander, 1916
12	Pete Alexander, 1915
9	Pete Alexander, 1913
8	Pete Alexander, 1917
8	Steve Carlton, 1972
8	Ben Sanders, 1888

Wins: Most, season

38	Kid Gleason, 1890
33	Pete Alexander, 1916
32	Gus Weyhing, 1892
31	Pete Alexander, 1915
30	Pete Alexander, 1917
30	Charlie Ferguson, 1886

K: Most, season

310	Steve Carlton, 1972
286	Steve Carlton, 1980
286	Steve Carlton, 1982
275	Steve Carlton, 1983
268	Jim Bunning, 1965

Win pct: Highest, season

.800	TOMMY GREENE, 1993
.800	Robin Roberts, 1952
.769	Charlie Ferguson, 1886
.760	Larry Christenson, 1977
.760	John Denny, 1983

ERA: Lowest, season

1.22	Pete Alexander, 1915
1.53	George McQuillan, 1908
1.55	Pete Alexander, 1916
1.83	Lew Richie, 1908
1.83	Pete Alexander, 1917

Most pinch-hit homers, season

5	Gene Freese, 1959
4	Rip Repulski, 1958
4	Del Unser, 1979

Most pinch-hit, homers, career

9	Cy Williams, 1918-1930

Most consecutive games, batting safely

36	Billy Hamilton, 1894
31	Ed Delahanty, 1899
26	Chuck Klein, 1930 (2 streaks)

Most consecutive scoreless innings

41	Grover Cleveland Alexander, 1911

No hit games

Joe Borden, Phi vs Chi NA, 4-0; July 28, 1875.

Charlie Ferguson, Phi vs Pro NL, 1-0; August 29, 1885.

Red Donahue, Phi vs Bos NL, 5-0; July 8, 1898.

Chick Fraser, Phi at Chi NL; 10-0; September 18, 1903 (2nd game).

Johnny Lush, Phi at Bro NL, 6-0; May 1, 1906.

Jim Bunning, Phi at NY NL, 6-0; June 21, 1964 (1st game, perfect game).

Rick Wise, Phi at Cin NL, 4-0; June 23, 1971.

TERRY MULHOLLAND, Phi vs SF NL, 6-0; August 15, 1990.

TOMMY GREENE, Phi at Mon NL, 2-0; May 23, 1991.

ACTIVE PLAYERS in caps.
Leaders from the franchise's current location is included. If not in the top five, leader's rank is listed in parenthesis.

Montreal Expos

Providing both power and speed, Marquis Grissom hit 19 home runs, drove in 95 runs and stole 53 bases..

by Robert Deutsch, *USA TODAY*

1993 Expos: Best home record in baseball

Expos fans may not have had fond memories of postseason glory to keep them warm in the winter, but they can still bask in the glow of the fact that they had the hottest team around in September.

Manager Felipe Alou's team finished at 94-68. While they were three games behind the Phillies, they were only one game behind the team that matters even more to their fans—the Canadian rival Blue Jays.

It was the second-best record in franchise history for the Expos, who led the majors with 55 home wins and 228 stolen bases. They struck out 860 times, the fewest in the NL. They were 52-29 in games decided by one or two runs.

But the season was a story of two pitching rotations—the first-half staff and the second-half staff. Only one member of the original rotation, Dennis Martinez, was there all year. He was 15-9, and won his 100th NL game in his final start to become the seventh player in major league history to win 100 games in each league.

Ken Hill had a 2.62 ERA at the All-Star break, but a groin injury sidelined him for several weeks and he was ineffective when he returned. Chris Nabholz was demoted to Triple-A; he did return and finish strong, but he had a 4.09 ERA. Kent Bottenfield went to the minors, then to the Colorado Rockies. Jimmy Jones was released.

It's hard to imagine what might have been, had left-handers Jeff Fassero and Kirk Rueter been put into the rotation earlier. Fassero thrived in middle relief before he moved into the rotation, then finished 12-5 (2.29 ERA). Rueter rose from Class A in '92 to Montreal in '93 and ensured a spot there in '94 as well by going 8-0 (2.73 ERA).

The club had coveted Montreal native Denis Boucher for years, but the left-hander went through four teams before they got him from San Diego. He went 3-1 with a 1.91 ERA in his September callup.

The bullpen led the league with 61 saves and 30 wins. Closer John Wetteland set a club record with 43 saves.

The outfield—left fielder Moises Alou (85 RBI), center fielder Marquis Grissom (19 homers, 95 RBI, 53 steals) and right fielder Larry Walker (22 homers, 86 RBI, 29 steals)—was the only trio in the NL to all top the 85-RBI plateau. Alou's season ended abruptly in mid-September, though, when he dislocated his ankle and broke his leg.

One of the surprises of the year was infielder Mike Lansing, who made the club only as a backup. When second baseman Delino DeShields got chicken pox the first week of the season, Lansing stepped in and never left the lineup. He played second, short and third, hit .287 and stole 23 bases.

—by Lisa Winston

1994 Expos: Preview

There's good news and bad news for the Expos in 1994. The good news is that president Claude Brochu decided to raise the payroll from $15 million to $20 million. The bad news is that realignment adds the Atlanta Braves to the NL East.

Any off-season plans to move one of the outfielders have been shelved due to Moises Alou's injury. Before he was hurt there was a good chance that either Grissom or Walker would have been trade bait for a starting pitcher.

The emergence of Fassero as an ace, a healthy Ken Hill and newcomer Pedro Martinez would make the promotion of any of the team's near-ready pitching prospects a little less pressure-packed.

Look for Mike Lansing, Wil Cordero and Sean Berry to fill the infield jobs. Prized prospect first baseman Cliff Floyd will need a hot spring to win that job. The Expos may sign a dispensable veteran to allow 21-year-old Floyd to start the year at Triple-A to avoid too much pressure.

—by Lisa Winston

1993 Expos: Between the lines

▶**April 11:** Rookie Mike Lansing—filling in for Delino DeShields (chicken pox)—tied a club record with five hits and hit his second homer of the season.

▶**April 23:** The Expos' young infield showed some pop: Rookie shortstop Wil Cordero had a double, triple and home run; rookie first baseman Greg Colbrunn went 3-for-4 with three RBI; rookie third baseman Mike Lansing went 1-for-3; and the "old man," 24-year-old second baseman Delino DeShields, went 2-for-3.

▶**May 14:** Marquis Grissom posted his second 4-for-5 night in a row—including three doubles—to tie a club record.

▶**May 18:** Called up from Triple-A earlier in the day, Gil Heredia pitched a 1-0 win against red-hot Atlanta.

▶**May 22:** The Expos pulled to within 4 1/2 games of the division leaders with their second consecutive win against the Phillies.

▶**May 23:** Heredia could not get an out in the first inning, allowing five runs before he was relieved. The Expos went on to lose to the Phillies, 14-7. The 14 runs were the most allowed in a game by the Expos in nearly three years. The two teams combined for 17 errors in their four-game series.

▶**May 26:** Ken Hill became the first Montreal starting pitcher ever to open the season 6-0, but he left after seven innings with a strained groin.

▶**June 8:** Marquis Grissom stole three bases in the Expos' 4-2 win against Cincinnati.

▶**June 18:** *Milestone*—Dennis Martinez collected his 200th career win.

▶**June 26:** Relief ace John Wetteland notched his 13th save in a row and ran his scoreless inning streak to 25 by striking out the side in a 4-2 victory against Florida.

▶**June 29:** Moises Alou, Marquis Grissom and Larry Walker hit back-to-back-to-back homers against the Bucs.

▶**July 7:** In an impressive debut, Kirk Rueter limited the Giants—who had 44

hits in their previous three games—to two singles. He allowed a leadoff walk and a single but retired the next 18 batters.

▶**July 9:** Moises Alou went 2-for-4 with two homers and four RBI, and Delino DeShields went 3-for-4 to extend his hitting streak to 12 games.

▶**July 11:** Marquis Grissom's hit scored the go-ahead run in the eighth inning as the Expos won their fifth in a row, beating San Diego 5-4 for a four-game sweep. Dennis Martinez got the final out for his first save since 1980. Moises Alou set a record for most hits that were all homers in consecutive games: six hits, all homers, in four games.

▶**July 20:** DeShields set a club record when he extended his hitting streak to 20 games with a single in his fourth plate appearance of the night. It was the fifth time during the streak that he'd extended it in his fourth at-bat.

▶**July 31:** Pinch-hitter Lou Frazier's single with two out in the ninth inning drove home Marquis Grissom with the winning run as Montreal beat the Marlins 6-5. Frazier hit the first pitch from Matt Turner into left field for his 10th pinch-hit in 30 at-bats.

▶**August 6:** Kirk Rueter raised his ERA—all the way to 1.88—with a complete-game victory as the Expos bashed the Braves 8-2. Rueter also had a two-run single, his first major league hit.

▶**August 7:** Grissom doubled and stole two bases in a 5-3 10-inning victory against the Braves. It was his fourth three-hit effort in five games.

▶**August 13:** Outfielder Lou Frazier became the fourth person in a week to start at first base for the Expos—he followed Oreste Marrero, Randy Ready and Derrick White.

▶**August 19:** Montreal's Jeff Fassero threw his first major league complete game, a six-hit win against the Cubs. Fassero struck out a career-high nine batters to earn the 10-2 win.

August 21: Larry Walker hit his first grand slam on the first swing of the night in the Expos' 6-3 win against the Reds. Sound unlikely? Rookie starter John Roper walked the first three batters on 13 pitches—12 balls and a called strike—and Walker watched two balls and a strike before taking Roper downtown.

August 22: Sean Berry hit two homers—one inside-the-park—and drove in six runs as the Expos beat the Reds 7-2.

August 23: Kirk Rueter came within two outs of his first career shutout in a 1-0 win vs. Chicago. He also started a triple play in the sixth inning, the Expos' first since Sept. 8, 1991, and the eighth in club history.

August 30: Jeff Fassero allowed four hits and struck out a career-high 10 in 7 2/3 innings as Montreal beat Colorado 6-1.

September 3: Unbeaten Rueter led the Expos to their eighth win in a row, 3-0 against Houston. It was the team's longest winning streak since July, 1988.

September 6: A crowd of 40,066 were on hand at Olympic Stadium to see Montreal native Denis Boucher make his Expos debut. It was the second-largest crowd this year at The Big O. Boucher is the first Quebecois pitcher to wear an Expos uniform since Claude Raymond in 1971. Boucher and catcher Joe Siddall, from Windsor, Ontario, formed the first all-Canadian battery in modern baseball history.

September 8: It looked like there might just be a pennant race in the NL East after all. The Expos, behind the pitching of Rueter, climbed to within 6 1/2 games of first place Philadelphia with a 6-1 victory against Colorado. They trailed Philadelphia by 14 1/2 games on Aug. 20, but had won 12 of their last 13, and 15 of 17.

September 12: The streaking Expos beat Cincinnati 3-2, to make it six in a row and 14 of 15.

September 17: Delino DeShields hit a sacrifice fly in the 12th inning to boost the Expos to an 8-7 win against Philadelphia, cutting the Phillies' lead to four games in the NL East.

October 3: The Expos beat the Pirates, 3-1, and finished just three games behind the Phillies, good for second place in the division. *League leaders, pitching*—John Wetteland was tied for fourth in saves (43). *League leaders, batting*— Marquis Grissom was second in stolen bases (53) and tied for seventh in runs (104); Delino DeShields was sixth in stolen bases (43); Larry Walker was ninth in walks (80).

—by John Hunt, Scott Kauffman, Lisa Winston, Deron Snyder, Matt Young

Team directory

Owner: Montreal Baseball Club Inc., Claude R. Brochu (president and general partner)

General Manager: Dan Duquette (vice president), Bill Stoneman (v.p., baseball operations)

Ballpark:
Olympic Stadium
4549 Avenue Pierre-de-Coubertin, Montreal, Que., Canada
514-253-3434
Capacity 46,500
Parking for 4,000 cars; $8
Public transportation available
Wheelchair sections, ramps, extensive food concessions, outfield bleachers

Team publications:
Yearbook, *Expos Magazine*
P.O. Box 500, Station M, Montreal, Que., Canada H1V 3P2

TV, radio broadcast stations:
CIQC 600 AM, C-TV, TSN (English); CKAC 730 AM, FSRC-TV, RDS (French)

Spring Training:
Municipal Stadium
West Palm Beach, Fla.
Capacity 7,500
407-684-6801

MONTREAL EXPOS 1993 final stats

Batting	BA	SLG	OB	G	AB	R	H	TB	2B	3B	HR	RBI	BB	SO	SB	CS	E
Pride	.444	1.111	.444	10	9	3	4	10	1	1	1	5	0	3	1	0	0
Montoyo	.400	.600	.400	4	5	1	2	3	1	0	0	3	0	0	0	0	0
Stairs	.375	.500	.375	6	8	1	3	4	1	0	0	2	1	0	0	0	0
Grissom	.298	.438	.351	157	630	104	188	276	27	2	19	95	52	76	53	10	7
DeShields	.295	.372	.389	123	481	75	142	179	17	7	2	29	72	64	43	10	11
Lansing	.287	.369	.352	141	491	64	141	181	29	1	3	45	46	56	23	5	24
Alou	.286	.483	.340	136	482	70	138	233	29	6	18	85	38	53	17	6	4
Frazier	.286	.349	.340	112	189	27	54	66	7	1	1	16	16	24	17	2	2
Walker	.265	.469	.371	138	490	85	130	230	24	5	22	86	80	76	29	7	6
Berry	.261	.465	.348	122	299	50	78	139	15	2	14	49	41	70	12	2	15
R.White	.260	.411	.321	23	73	9	19	30	3	1	2	15	7	16	1	2	0
Fletcher	.255	.379	.320	133	396	33	101	150	20	1	9	60	34	40	0	0	8
Colbrunn	.255	.392	.282	70	153	15	39	60	9	0	4	23	6	33	4	2	2
Ready	.254	.351	.367	40	134	22	34	47	8	1	1	10	23	8	2	1	8
Cordero	.248	.387	.308	138	475	56	118	184	32	2	10	58	34	60	12	3	36
Vanderwal	.233	.372	.320	106	215	34	50	80	7	4	5	30	27	30	6	3	4
Spehr	.230	.368	.281	53	87	14	20	32	6	0	2	10	6	20	2	0	9
Floyd	.226	.323	.226	10	31	3	7	10	0	0	1	2	0	9	0	0	0
D.White	.224	.408	.269	17	49	6	11	20	3	0	2	4	2	12	2	0	1
Bolick	.211	.329	.298	95	213	25	45	70	13	0	4	24	23	37	1	0	8
Marrero	.210	.333	.326	32	81	10	17	27	5	1	1	4	14	16	1	3	2
Laker	.198	.244	.222	43	86	3	17	21	2	1	0	7	2	16	2	0	2
Wood	.192	.231	.276	13	26	4	5	6	1	0	0	3	3	3	0	0	0
Siddall	.100	.150	.143	19	20	0	2	3	1	0	0	1	1	5	0	0	0
McIntosh	.095	.143	.095	20	21	2	2	3	1	0	0	2	0	7	0	0	0

Pitching	W-L	ERA	G	GS	CG	GF	Sho	SV	IP	H	R	ER	HR	BB	SO
Wetteland	9-3	1.37	70	0	0	58	0	43	85.1	58	17	13	3	28	113
Boucher	3-1	1.91	5	5	0	0	0	0	28.1	24	7	6	1	3	14
Fassero	12-5	2.29	56	15	1	10	0	1	149.2	119	50	38	7	54	140
Rueter	8-0	2.73	14	14	1	0	0	0	85.2	85	33	26	5	18	31
Rojas	5-8	2.95	66	0	0	25	0	10	88.1	80	39	29	6	30	48
Looney	0-0	3.00	3	1	0	1	0	0	6	8	2	2	0	2	7
Scott	7-2	3.01	56	0	0	18	0	1	71.2	69	28	24	4	34	65
Hill	9-7	3.23	28	28	2	0	0	0	183.2	163	84	66	7	74	90
Young	1-0	3.38	4	0	0	2	0	0	5.1	4	2	2	1	0	3
Martinez	15-9	3.85	35	34	2	1	0	1	224.2	211	110	96	27	64	138
Heredia	4-2	3.92	20	9	1	2	0	2	57.1	66	28	25	4	14	40
Nabholz	9-8	4.09	26	21	1	2	0	0	116.2	100	57	53	9	63	74
Shaw	2-7	4.14	55	8	0	13	0	0	95.2	91	47	44	12	32	50
Barnes	2-6	4.41	52	8	0	8	0	3	100	105	53	49	9	48	60
Gardiner	2-3	5.21	24	2	0	3	0	0	38	40	28	22	3	19	21
Risley	0-0	6.00	2	0	0	1	0	0	3	2	3	2	1	2	2
Henry	3-9	6.12	30	16	1	4	0	0	103	135	76	70	15	28	47
Jones	4-1	6.35	12	6	0	3	0	0	39.2	47	34	28	6	9	21
Aldred	1-0	9.00	8	0	0	2	0	0	12	19	14	12	2	10	9
Valdez	0-0	9.00	4	0	0	1	0	0	3	4	4	3	1	1	2
Walton	0-0	9.53	4	0	0	3	0	0	5.2	11	6	6	1	3	0

1994 preliminary roster

PITCHERS (20)
Tavo Alvarez
Ivan Arteaga
Brian Barnes
Miguel Batista
Denis Boucher
Reid Cornelius
Joey Eischen
Jeff Fassero
Gil Heredia
Ken Hill
Brian Looney
Pedro Martinez
Chris Nabholz
Bill Risley
Mel Rojas
Kirk Rueter
Tim Scott
Jeff Shaw
John Wetteland
Gabe White

CATCHERS (3)
Darrin Fletcher
Tim Laker
Tim Spehr

INFIELDERS (7)
Shane Andrews
Sean Berry
Wil Cordero
Cliff Floyd
Mike Hardge
Mike Lansing
Chris Martin

OUTFIELDERS (10)
Moises Alou
Yamil Benitez
Lou Frazier
Marquis Grissom
Glenn Murray
Curtis Pride
John VanderWal
Larry Walker
Rondell White
Tyrone Woods

Games played by position

Player	G	C	1B	2B	3B	SS	OF
Alou	136	0	0	0	0	0	136
Berry	122	0	0	0	96	0	0
Bolick	95	0	51	0	24	0	0
Colbrunn	70	0	61	0	0	0	0
Cordero	138	0	0	0	2	134	0
DeShields	123	0	0	123	0	0	0
Fletcher	133	127	0	0	0	0	0
Floyd	10	0	10	0	0	0	0
Frazier	112	0	8	1	0	0	60
Grissom	157	0	0	0	0	0	157
Laker	43	43	0	0	0	0	0
Lansing	141	0	0	25	81	51	0
Marrero	32	0	32	0	0	0	0
McIntosh	20	5	0	0	0	0	7
Montoyo	4	0	0	3	0	0	0
Pride	10	0	0	0	0	0	2
Ready	40	0	13	28	3	0	0
Siddall	19	15	1	0	0	0	1
Spehr	53	49	0	0	0	0	0
Stairs	6	0	0	0	0	0	1
Vanderwal	106	0	42	0	0	0	38
Walker	138	0	4	0	0	0	132
D. White	17	0	17	0	0	0	0
R. White	23	0	0	0	0	0	21
Wood	13	0	0	0	0	0	8

Sick call: 1993 DL Report

Player	Days on the DL
Scott Aldred	119
Moises Alou	16
Greg Colbrunn*	100
Delino Deshields	30
Ken Hill	21
Jimmy Jones*	34
Chris Nabholz	31
Mel Rojas	15
Larry Walker	15
John Wetteland	18

Two separate terms on Disabled List

Minor League Report

Class AAA: Ottawa finished at 73-69, second in the International League Eastern Division, and fell to Rochester in five games in the playoffs. Scott Bryant hit .283 with 12 homers and 65 RBI. Curtis Pride hit .302 with 29 steals. Denis Boucher was 6-0 with a 2.72 ERA. Bruce Walton had 16 saves. Gil Heredia was 8-4 with a 2.98 ERA. **Class AA:** Harrisburg finished at 93-44, first in the Eastern League, and beat Canton-Akron in five games for the league title. Cliff Floyd was league MVP, hitting .329 with 101 RBI in as many games, 26 homers and 31 stolen bases. Rondell White hit .327 with 12 homers and 52 RBI. Glenn Murray had 26 homers and 96 RBI. Joey Eischen was 14-4 with a 3.62 ERA. Miguel Batista had 13 wins. **Class A:** West Palm Beach finished at 69-67, third in the Florida State League East Division. Rod Henderson was 12-7 with a 2.90 ERA. Billy Wallace was 11-8 with a 3.28 ERA. Mark LaRosa had 19 saves to share the league lead. Burlington finished at 64-71, third in the Midwest League Southern Division. Ivan Arteaga was 6-5 with a 2.83 ERA. Ugueth Urbina was league Pitcher of the Year, going 10-1 with a 1.99 ERA. Isreal Alcantara hit .273 with 18 homers and 73 RBI. Jolbert Cabrera stole 31 bases. **Short-season:** Jamestown finished at 30-46, last in the New York-Penn League Stadler Division. Matt Raleigh had 15 homers. West Palm Beach finished at 27-31, third in the Florida State League Eastern Division. Marc Niethammer led the league with six homers while Randy Culp had five. Roberto Taveras was 2-4 with a 1.48 ERA.

Tops in the organization

Batter	Club	Avg	G	AB	R	H	HR	RBI
White, Rondell	Ott	.343	127	522	100	179	19	84
Pride, Curtis	Ott	.324	119	442	106	143	21	61
Horne, Tyrone	HRb	.315	117	416	65	131	14	66
Floyd, Cliff	Ott	.307	133	505	94	155	28	119
Northrup, Kevin	Wpb	.296	131	459	65	136	6	63

Home Runs			Wins		
Floyd, Cliff	Ott	28	Henderson, Rod	HRb	17
Murray, Glenn	HRb	26	Eischen, Joey	Ott	16
Pride, Curtis	Ott	21	Urbina, Ugueth	HRb	14
White, Rondell	Ott	19	Batista, Miguel	HRb	13
Several players tied		18	Wallace, B.J.	WPb	11

RBI			Saves		
Floyd, Cliff	Ott	119	Larosa, Mark	WPb	19
Murray, Glenn	HRb	96	Walton, Bruce	Ott	16
White, Rondell	Ott	84	Thomas, Mike	HRb	15
Alcantara, Isreal	Bur	73	Brito, Mario	Ott	12
Hmielewski, Chris	Bur	71	Reyes, Alberto	Bur	11

Stolen Bases			Strikeouts		
Pride, Curtis	Ott	50	Looney, Brian	HRb	185
Floyd, Cliff	Ott	33	Urbina, Ugueth	HRb	152
Hardge, Mike	HRb	32	Henderson, Rod	HRb	152
White, Rondell	Ott	31	Eischen, Joey	Ott	139
Cabrera, Jolbert	Bur	31	Wallace, B.J.	WPb	126

Pitcher	Club	W-L	ERA	IP	H	BB	SO
White, Gabe	Ott	9-3	2.44	140	118	34	108
Henderson, Rod	HRb	17-7	2.71	173	130	59	152
Urbina, Ugueth	HRb	14-6	2.78	178	144	68	152
Looney, Brian	HRb	7-8	2.88	163	144	46	185
Pedraza, Rod	Sbr	9-7	3.18	142	145	33	95

Montreal (1969-1993)

Runs: Most, career, all-time

934	TIM RAINES, 1979-1990	
828	ANDRE DAWSON, 1976-1986	
737	TIM WALLACH, 1980-1992	
707	Gary Carter, 1974-1992	
446	Warren Cromartie, 1974-1983	

Hits: Most, career, all-time

1694	TIM WALLACH, 1980-1992
1598	TIM RAINES, 1979-1990
1575	ANDRE DAWSON, 1976-1986
1427	Gary Carter, 1974-1992
1063	Warren Cromartie, 1974-1983

2B: Most, career, all-time

360	TIM WALLACH, 1980-1992
295	ANDRE DAWSON, 1976-1986
274	Gary Carter, 1974-1992
273	TIM RAINES, 1979-1990
222	Warren Cromartie, 1974-1983

3B: Most, career, all-time

81	TIM RAINES, 1979-1990
67	ANDRE DAWSON, 1976-1986
31	TIM WALLACH, 1980-1992
30	Warren Cromartie, 1974-1983
25	DELINO DeSHIELDS, 1990-1993
25	MITCH WEBSTER, 1985-1988

HR: Most, career, all-time

225	ANDRE DAWSON, 1976-1986
220	Gary Carter, 1974-1992
204	TIM WALLACH, 1980-1992
118	Bob Bailey, 1969-1975
106	ANDRES GALARRAGA, 1985-1991

RBI: Most, career, all-time

905	TIM WALLACH, 1980-1992
838	ANDRE DAWSON, 1976-1986
823	Gary Carter, 1974-1992
552	TIM RAINES, 1979-1990
466	Bob Bailey, 1969-1975

SB: Most, career, all-time

634	TIM RAINES, 1979-1990
253	ANDRE DAWSON, 1976-1986
230	MARQUIS GRISSOM, 1989-1993
187	DELINO DeSHIELDS, 1990-1993
139	Rodney Scott, 1976-1982

BB: Most, career, all-time

775	TIM RAINES, 1979-1990
582	Gary Carter, 1974-1992
514	TIM WALLACH, 1980-1992
502	Bob Bailey, 1969-1975
370	Ron Fairly, 1969-1974

BA: Highest, career, all-time

.301	TIM RAINES, 1979-1990
.294	Rusty Staub, 1969-1979
.288	Ellis Valentine, 1975-1981
.280	Warren Cromartie, 1974-1983
.280	ANDRE DAWSON, 1976-1986

Slug avg: Highest, career, all-time

.497	Rusty Staub, 1969-1979
.476	ANDRE DAWSON, 1976-1986
.476	Ellis Valentine, 1975-1981
.462	LARRY WALKER, 1989-1993
.454	Gary Carter, 1974-1992

Games started: Most, career, all-time

393	Steve Rogers, 1973-1985
233	DENNIS MARTINEZ, 1986-1993
193	BRYN SMITH, 1981-1989
192	Steve Renko, 1969-1976
170	BILL GULLICKSON, 1979-1985

Saves: Most, career, all-time

152	JEFF REARDON, 1981-1986
101	Tim Burke, 1985-1991
80	JOHN WETTELAND, 1992-1993
75	Mike Marshall, 1970-1973
52	Woodie Fryman, 1975-1983

Shutouts: Most, career, all-time

37	Steve Rogers, 1973-1985
15	Bill Stoneman, 1969-1973
13	DENNIS MARTINEZ, 1986-1993
8	Woodie Fryman, 1975-1983
8	Charlie Lea, 1980-1987
8	SCOTT SANDERSON, 1978-1983
8	BRYN SMITH, 1981-1989

Wins: Most, career, all-time

158	Steve Rogers, 1973-1985
100	DENNIS MARTINEZ, 1986-1993
81	BRYN SMITH, 1981-1989
72	BILL GULLICKSON, 1979-1985
68	Steve Renko, 1969-1976

K: Most, career, all-time

1621	Steve Rogers, 1973-1985
973	DENNIS MARTINEZ, 1986-1993
838	BRYN SMITH, 1981-1989
831	Bill Stoneman, 1969-1973
810	Steve Renko, 1969-1976

Win pct: Highest, career, all-time

.623	Tim Burke, 1985-1991
.581	DENNIS MARTINEZ, 1986-1993
.573	Charlie Lea, 1980-1987
.556	Mike Torrez, 1971-1974
.544	SCOTT SANDERSON, 1978-1983

ERA: Lowest, career, all-time

3.06	DENNIS MARTINEZ, 1986-1993
3.17	Steve Rogers, 1973-1985
3.28	BRYN SMITH, 1981-1989
3.32	Charlie Lea, 1980-1987
3.33	SCOTT SANDERSON, 1978-1983

Runs: Most, season

133	TIM RAINES, 1983
123	TIM RAINES, 1987
115	TIM RAINES, 1985
107	ANDRE DAWSON, 1982
106	TIM RAINES, 1984

Hits: Most, season

204	Al Oliver, 1982
194	TIM RAINES, 1986
192	TIM RAINES, 1984
189	ANDRE DAWSON, 1983
188	Dave Cash, 1977
188	MARQUIS GRISSOM, 1993

2B: Most, season

46	Warren Cromartie, 1979
43	Al Oliver, 1982
42	Dave Cash, 1977
42	ANDRES GALARRAGA, 1988
42	TIM WALLACH, 1987
42	TIM WALLACH, 1989

3B: Most, season

13	TIM RAINES, 1985
13	Rodney Scott, 1980
13	MITCH WEBSTER, 1986
12	ANDRE DAWSON, 1979
11	Ron LeFlore, 1980

HR: Most, season

32	ANDRE DAWSON, 1983	
31	Gary Carter, 1977	
30	Larry Parrish, 1979	
30	Rusty Staub, 1970	
29	Gary Carter, 1980	
29	Gary Carter, 1982	
29	ANDRES GALARRAGA, 1988	
29	Rusty Staub, 1969	

RBI: Most, season

123	TIM WALLACH, 1987
113	ANDRE DAWSON, 1983
109	Al Oliver, 1982
106	Gary Carter, 1984
103	Ken Singleton, 1973

SB: Most, season

97	Ron LeFlore, 1980
90	TIM RAINES, 1983
78	MARQUIS GRISSOM, 1992
78	TIM RAINES, 1982
76	MARQUIS GRISSOM, 1991

BB: Most, season

123	Ken Singleton, 1973
112	Rusty Staub, 1970
110	Rusty Staub, 1969
100	Bob Bailey, 1974
97	Bob Bailey, 1971
97	TIM RAINES, 1983

BA: Highest, season

.334	TIM RAINES, 1986
.331	Al Oliver, 1982
.330	TIM RAINES, 1987
.320	TIM RAINES, 1985
.311	Rusty Staub, 1971

Slug avg: Highest, season

.553	ANDRE DAWSON, 1981
.551	Larry Parrish, 1979
.540	ANDRES GALARRAGA, 1988
.539	ANDRE DAWSON, 1983
.526	Rusty Staub, 1969
.526	TIM RAINES, 1987

Games started: Most, season

40	Steve Rogers, 1977
39	Bill Stoneman, 1971
38	Steve Rogers, 1974
37	Carl Morton, 1970
37	Steve Renko, 1971
37	Steve Rogers, 1979
37	Steve Rogers, 1980

Saves: Most, season

43	JOHN WETTELAND, 1993
41	JEFF REARDON, 1985
37	JOHN WETTELAND, 1992
35	JEFF REARDON, 1986
31	Mike Marshall, 1973

Shutouts: Most, season

5	DENNIS MARTINEZ, 1991
5	Steve Rogers, 1979
5	Steve Rogers, 1983
5	Bill Stoneman, 1969
4	MARK LANGSTON, 1989
4	Charlie Lea, 1983
4	Carl Morton, 1970
4	Steve Rogers, 1976
4	Steve Rogers, 1977
4	Steve Rogers, 1980
4	Steve Rogers, 1982
4	Bill Stoneman, 1972

Wins: Most, season

20	Ross Grimsley, 1978
19	Steve Rogers, 1982
18	Carl Morton, 1970
18	BRYN SMITH, 1985
17	BILL GULLICKSON, 1983
17	Steve Rogers, 1977
17	Steve Rogers, 1983
17	Bill Stoneman, 1971

K: Most, season

251	Bill Stoneman, 1971
206	Steve Rogers, 1977
202	Floyd Youmans, 1986
185	Bill Stoneman, 1969
179	Steve Rogers, 1982

Win pct: Highest, season

.783	BRYN SMITH, 1985
.704	Steve Rogers, 1982
.696	DENNIS MARTINEZ, 1989
.652	Mike Torrez, 1974
.645	Ross Grimsley, 1978

ERA: Lowest, season

2.39	DENNIS MARTINEZ, 1991
2.39	MARK LANGSTON, 1989
2.40	Steve Rogers, 1982
2.44	Pascual Perez, 1988
2.47	DENNIS MARTINEZ, 1992

Most pinch-hit homers, season

4	Hal Breeden, 1973

Most pinch-hit, homers, career

5	Jose Morales. 1973-1977

Most consecutive games, batting safely

21	DELINO DeSHIELDS, 1993
19	Warren Cromartie, 1979
19	ANDRE DAWSON, 1980

Most consecutive scoreless innings

32	Woodie Fryman, 1975

No hit games

Bill Stoneman, Mon at Phi NL, 7-0; April 17, 1969.

Bill Stoneman, Mon vs NY NL, 7-0; October 2, 1972 (1st game).

Charlie Lea, Mon vs SF NL, 4-0; May 10, 1981 (2nd game).

MARK GARDNER, Mon at LA NL, 0-1; July 26, 1991 (9 innings, lost on 2 hits in 10th, relieved by Jeff Fassero, who allowed 1 more hit).

DENNIS MARTINEZ, Mon at LA NL, 2-0; July 28, 1991 (perfect game).

David Palmer, five perfect innings, rain, Mon at StL NL, 4-0; April 21, 1984 (2nd game).

Pascual Perez, five innings, rain, Mon at Phi NL, 1-0; September 24, 1988.

ACTIVE PLAYERS in caps.

St. Louis Cardinals

by Porter Binks, *USA TODAY*

Outfielder Mark Whiten led the Cardinals with 25 home runs, and was second on the team in RBI (99).

1993 Cardinals: Better wasn't good enough

The St. Louis Cardinals were poised to overtake the Phillies in the NL East as they flew into Philadelphia for a three-game series the last week of July. But after the Cards were swept—outscored 30-17—things got ugly. The freefall did not stop until September and the Cards finished 10 games behind the Phils, in third place. Still, their 87-75 record was a four-game improvement over 1992.

Relief pitching was the biggest culprit in the Cards' collapse. In that Philadelphia series alone, the bullpen gave up 24 hits and 16 runs in 11.1 innings.

Ace Lee Smith was traded to the Yankees Aug. 31, and Todd Burns was released in September. Rob Murphy had a terrible second half and Omar Olivares was downright awful. Mike Perez, Les Lancaster and Paul Kilgus battled injuries.

Fortunately, the Cards' farmhands led five different minor leagues in saves. The bullpen-by-committee approach, so successful in the 1980s, could return next season.

Meanwhile, the Cardinals committed 159 errors, their highest total since 1976. They dropped from first to 10th in the NL in defense. After they made five errors in an 11-9 loss at Chicago in September, first baseman Gregg Jefferies said: "This is enough to give you a headache."

Third baseman Todd Zeile, accused by manager Joe Torre of "lazy feet," nearly offset his 103 RBI with 33 errors. Second baseman Luis Alicea bobbled away too many potential double plays. Even shortstop Ozzie Smith, got in on the act with 19 errors, his second-highest total in 10 years.

A frustrated Torre remarked: "When you don't have people to strike (other) people out, you've got to have people to catch the ball."

On the positive side, offense never was much of a problem. The Cardinals scored 127 more runs last year than in 1992. They hit 118 homers, the most since moving into Busch Memorial Stadium in 1966. Zeile became the Cards' first third baseman with 100 or more RBI (103, 55 more than in '92) since Torre had 134 in 1971, the year he was NL MVP.

Hard hittin' Mark Whiten lived up to his nickname with 25 homers and 99 RBI. He made history on Sept. 7 when he hit four homers and drove in 12 runs—tying two major-league records—at Cincinnati. His 464-foot home run in Pittsburgh was one of the longest all season.

Jefferies finished third in the league with a .342 average. He also had 83 RBI and 46 steals, despite missing a month with back problems. Outfielder Bernard Gilkey hit .305 and scored 99 runs in the leadoff role. Brian Jordan hit .309 and had 10 home runs in 233 at-bats before his season ended with shoulder surgery in September. Ozzie Smith hit .288 and joined Honus Wagner as the only players since 1900 to put together 16 consecutive seasons with 20 or more steals.

On the mound, Bob Tewksbury parlayed excellent control into a team-high 17 victories, the only Cardinal with more than 11 wins. Cuban exile Rene Arocha won only one of his last 11 starts and wound up 11-8.

—by Bill Koenig

1994 Cardinals: Preview

The bullpen and defense must improve for this team to contend in the new NL Central Division next season. Another question is starting pitching. The Cards are still waiting for some of their promising youngsters such as Rene Arocha, Allen Watson and Donovan Osborne to step forward.

One of the biggest questions is who will play second. Geronimo Pena missed a month with a broken foot and was inconsistent in '93. Alicea had lots of injuries and errors. Jose Oquendo, could win back his old job by default.

—by Bill Koenig

1993 Cardinals: Between the lines

▸**April 7:** Geronimo Pena blasted a three-run homer and added a pair of singles and two walks in the Cardinals' 6-2 win against the Giants, giving him a stretch of reaching base nine times in 10 appearances.

▸**April 8:** Closer Lee Smith tied Jeff Reardon's career save record with his 357th as St. Louis beat San Francisco.

▸**May 12:** Luis Alicea's bases-loaded sacrifice fly in the ninth gave the Cardinals a 6-5 win against the Mets, after Mark Whiten's RBI single tied the score in the eighth. Alicea also went 2-for-4 to raise his average to .422.

▸**May 24:** Rheal Cormier retired the only batter he faced—fellow Canadian Larry Walker—to earn his second victory of the year in the Cardinals' 11-inning win in Montreal.

▸**June 3:** Paul Kilgus earned his first major league win in almost four years with four scoreless innings of relief against the Reds, coming on for injured starter Omar Olivares.

▸**June 5:** Erik Pappas extended his hitting streak to 16 games, going 2-for-4 in the Cards' 6-2 loss to the Reds.

▸**June 8:** Pinch-hitter Rod Brewer had a two-run double and Ozzie Smith added a two-run triple in a four-run eighth, and the Cards held off a two-run rally by the Giants to hang on for a 4-3 win. Rene Arocha tossed seven innings of five-hit ball, allowing one run to improve to 5-0. He continued to emerge as the ace of the staff as he lowered his ERA to 2.36.

▸**June 12:** Gregg Jefferies, Ray Lankford and Mark Whiten all went deep in a 13-3 win against the Expos, marking the first time the Cards had three homers in a game since April 9.

▸**June 16:** *Milestone*—Lee Smith recorded his 20th save in his team's 3-2 win against Pittsburgh, marking the 11th year in a row he passed the 20-save plateau, a major league record.

▸**June 17:** Ozzie Smith went 5-for-5 with six RBI in a laugher in sweltering

Chicago; the Cards won 11-10.

▸**June 28:** Philadelphia's 3-1 loss to St. Louis at soggy Busch Stadium clipped the Phillies' NL East lead to 6 1/2 games. It was the Cardinals' fifth consecutive win and the Phillies' third loss in a row—only their second such streak of the season.

▸**June 30:** Mark Whiten made up for a pair of first-inning goofs in right field with a double, a homer and four RBI as the Cards beat Philadelphia 9-3.

▸**July 1:** Brian Jordan's grand slam was the big blow but not the only one as the Cards jumped out to a 14-0 lead and "held on" to beat the Phils, 14-5, sending Philadelphia to its fifth loss in its last six games.

▸**July 6:** The Cards rallied for two runs in the ninth to beat Atlanta 5-4. Gregg Jefferies (homer, three RBI) and Todd Zeile had RBI singles in the inning.

▸**July 15:** Rene Arocha gave up just one run in seven innings for a 4-2 win against Houston.

▸**July 18:** Mark Whiten hit a bases-loaded sacrifice fly in the 11th inning to give the Cardinals a 7-6 win against Houston. Whiten hit a two-run homer earlier in the game.

▸**July 22:** Bob Tewksbury's streak of 55 1/3 innings without a walk was snapped when he put Eric Young on in the seventh inning of a 7-6 loss to Colorado. The NL record for consecutive walkless innings is 68, held by Christy Mathewson (1913) and Randy Jones (1976).

▸**July 23:** Todd Zeile was 2-for-5 with four RBI and Ozzie Smith was 3-for-6 as the Cards beat the Rockies in a 13-11 slugfest.

▸**July 31:** Bernard Gilkey homered and drove in three runs for St. Louis in a 4-3 win against the Mets.

▸**August 5:** St. Louis had 28 baserunners on 19 hits, including 16 singles, and nine walks in a 16-6 demolition of Florida. The Cards batted around in the third and fourth innings, scoring nine runs.

▶ **August 9:** Tom Pagnozzi had three hits, including his sixth home run, and two RBI for the Cards in a 7-3 defeat of Pittsburgh. Rookie Allen Watson gave up only three hits in seven innings of work. He started slowly by allowing a pair of solo homers, to fall behind 2-0, but he gave up just one hit in the final six innings. *Quote of the day*—The unbeaten Watson, about his parents, who were present at the Pittsburgh game but get very nervous when they watch: "My mom's a nervous wreck when I pitch. She can't bear to watch. . . . My dad used to smoke a lot, but he had some heart problems and all he does now is eat (sunflower) seeds. He must have eaten six bags tonight."

▶ **August 10:** Brian Jordan homered twice in the Cardinals' 4-2 win against Pittsburgh. Jordan and Whiten went deep on consecutive pitches from Joel Johnston.

▶ **August 11:** Whiten hit one of the longest homers ever in Three Rivers Stadium. He launched the first pitch he saw from reliever Blas Minor 464 feet into the upper deck in right field. Only 10 balls have been hit into the upper level at the stadium and only three players have reached the top deck in right field: Willie Stargell, Bobby Bonilla and Whiten.

▶ **September 7:** Hard-hittin' Whiten lived up to his nickname in a big way, tying major league records with four homers and 12 RBI.

▶ **September 11:** Bob Tewksbury scattered 10 hits over 7 2/3 innings to earn a 3-1 win against the Giants. Tewksbury held San Francisco to just one run to improve his record after the All-Star break to 8-1.

▶ **October 3:** The Cards beat the Phils, 2-0, but finished 10 games behind them, good for third in the NL East. *League leaders, pitching*—Lee Smith was tied for fourth in saves (43); Bob Tewksbury was seventh in victories (17-10). *League leaders, batting*—Gregg Jefferies was third in batting (.342), tied for fourth in stolen bases (46), fifth in

on-base percentage (.408), and fifth in hits (186); Todd Zeile was seventh in RBI (103) and 10th in doubles (36); Bernard Gilkey was sixth in doubles (40); Ray Lankford was eighth in walks (81).

—by John Hunt, Scott Kauffman, Lisa Winston, Deron Snyder, Matt Young

Team directory

▶ **Owner:** August A. Busch III
▶ **General Manager:** Dal Maxvill
▶ **Ballpark:**
Busch Stadium
250 Stadium Plaza, St. Louis, Mo.
314-421-3060
Capacity 57,001
Parking for over 7,000 cars; $4.50
Public transportation
Wheelchair section, ramps
▶ **Team publications:**
Yearbook, media guide, *The Cardinals Magazine*
314-421-3060
▶ **TV, radio broadcast stations:**
KMOX 1120 AM, KPLR Channel 11
▶ **Spring Training:**
Al Lang Stadium
St. Petersburg, Fla.
Capacity 6,500
813-893-7490

ST. LOUIS CARDINALS 1993 final stats

Batting	BA	SLG	OB	G	AB	R	H	TB	2B	3B	HR	RBI	BB	SO	SB	CS	E
Jefferies	.342	.485	.408	142	544	89	186	264	24	3	16	83	62	32	46	9	9
Perry	.337	.510	.440	96	98	21	33	50	5	0	4	16	18	23	1	1	2
Jordan	.309	.543	.351	67	223	33	69	121	10	6	10	44	12	35	6	6	4
Gilkey	.305	.481	.370	137	557	99	170	268	40	5	16	70	56	66	15	10	8
Royer	.304	.413	.333	24	46	4	14	19	2	0	1	8	2	14	0	1	3
O.Smith	.288	.356	.337	141	545	75	157	194	22	6	1	53	43	18	21	8	19
Brewer	.286	.381	.359	110	147	15	42	56	8	0	2	20	17	26	1	0	3
Alicea	.279	.373	.362	115	362	50	101	135	19	3	3	46	47	54	11	1	11
Zeile	.277	.433	.352	157	571	82	158	247	36	1	17	103	70	76	5	4	33
Pappas	.276	.342	.368	82	228	25	63	78	12	0	1	28	35	35	1	3	6
Jones	.262	.361	.366	29	61	13	16	22	6	0	0	1	9	8	2	2	2
Pagnozzi	.258	.373	.296	92	330	31	85	123	15	1	7	41	19	30	1	0	4
Pena	.256	.406	.330	74	254	34	65	103	19	2	5	30	25	71	13	5	12
Whiten	.253	.423	.323	152	562	81	142	238	13	4	25	99	58	110	15	8	10
Lankford	.238	.346	.366	127	407	64	97	141	17	3	7	45	81	111	14	14	7
Woodson	.208	.234	.215	62	77	4	16	18	2	0	0	2	1	14	0	0	4
Oquendo	.205	.205	.314	46	73	7	15	15	0	0	0	4	12	8	0	0	1
Canseco	.176	.176	.222	6	17	0	3	3	0	0	0	0	1	3	0	0	1
Villanueva	.145	.327	.203	17	55	7	8	18	1	0	3	9	4	17	0	0	0
Cromer	.087	.087	.125	10	23	1	2	2	0	0	0	0	1	6	0	0	3
Ronan	.083	.083	.083	6	12	0	1	1	0	0	0	0	0	5	0	0	0
Maclin	.077	.077	.071	12	13	2	1	1	1	0	0	0	0	5	1	0	0

Pitching	W-L	ERA	G	GS	CG	GF	Sho	SV	IP	H	R	ER	HR	BB	SO
Kilgus	1-0	0.63	22	1	0	7	0	1	28.2	18	2	2	1	8	21
Perez	7-2	2.48	65	0	0	25	0	7	72.2	65	24	20	4	20	58
Guetterman	3-3	2.93	40	0	0	14	0	1	46	41	18	15	1	16	19
Lancaster	4-1	2.93	50	0	0	12	0	0	61.1	56	24	20	5	21	36
Osborne	10-7	3.76	26	26	1	0	0	0	155.2	153	73	65	18	47	83
Arocha	11-8	3.78	32	29	1	0	0	0	188	197	89	79	20	31	96
Tewksbury	17-10	3.83	32	32	2	0	0	0	213.2	258	99	91	15	20	97
Olivares	5-3	4.17	58	9	0	11	0	0	118.2	134	60	55	10	54	63
Cormier	7-6	4.33	38	21	1	4	0	0	145.1	163	80	70	18	27	75
L.Smith	2-4	4.50	55	0	0	48	0	43	50	49	25	25	11	9	49
Watson	6-7	4.60	16	15	0	1	0	0	86	90	53	44	11	28	49
Urbani	1-3	4.65	18	9	0	2	0	0	62	73	44	32	4	26	33
Murphy	5-7	4.87	73	0	0	23	0	1	64.2	73	37	35	8	20	41
Magrane	8-10	4.97	22	20	0	2	0	0	116	127	68	64	15	37	38
Burns	0-4	6.16	24	0	0	5	0	0	30.2	32	21	21	8	9	10
Batchelor	0-0	8.10	9	0	0	2	0	0	10	14	12	9	1	3	4
Dixon	0-0	33.75	4	0	0	0	0	0	2.2	7	10	10	1	5	2
Brewer	0-0	45.00	1	0	0	1	0	0	1	3	5	5	1	2	1

1994 preliminary roster

Pitchers (17)
Rene Arocha
Rich Batchelor
Frank Cimorelli
Rheal Cormier
Paul Creek
Clint Davis
Steve Dixon
Bryan Eversgerd
John Frascatore
Paul Kilgus
Rob Murphy
Omar Olivares
Donovan Osborne
Mike Perez
Bob Tewksbury
Tom Urbani
Allen Watson

Catchers (2)
Tom Pagnozzi
Erik Pappas

Infielders (13)
Luis Alicea
Rod Brewer
Dan Cholowsky
Tripp Cromer
Darrel Deak
Aaron Holbert
Gregg Jefferies
Tim Jones
Jose Oquendo
Geronimo Pena
Stan Royer
Ozzie Smith
Todd Zeile

Outfielders (8)
Terry Bradshaw
Paul Coleman
Bernard Gilkey
Brian Jordan
Ray Lankford
John Mabry
Basil Shabazz
Mark Whiten

Games played by position

Player	G	C	1B	2B	3B	SS	OF
Alicea	115	0	0	96	1	0	4
Brewer	110	0	32	0	0	0	33
Canseco	6	0	0	0	0	0	5
Cromer	10	0	0	0	0	9	0
Gilkey	137	0	3	0	0	0	134
Jefferies	142	0	140	1	0	0	0
Jones	29	0	0	7	0	21	0
Jordan	67	0	0	0	0	0	65
Lankford	127	0	0	0	0	0	121
Maclin	12	0	0	0	0	0	5
Oquendo	46	0	0	16	0	22	0
Pagnozzi	92	92	0	0	0	0	0
Pappas	82	63	2	0	0	0	16
Pena	74	0	0	64	0	0	0
Perry	96	0	15	0	0	0	1
Ronan	6	6	0	0	0	0	0
Royer	24	0	2	0	10	0	0
O. Smith	141	0	0	0	0	134	0
Villanueva	17	17	0	0	0	0	0
Whiten	152	0	0	0	0	0	148
Woodson	62	0	11	0	28	0	0
Zeile	157	0	0	0	153	0	0

Sick call: 1993 DL Report

Player	Days on the DL
Rene Arocha	22
Rheal Cormier	26
Bernard Gilkey	15
Paul Kilgus	69
Les Lancaster	58
Ray Lankford	15
Omar Olivares	16
Jose Oquendo	56
Tom Pagnozzi	40
Geronimo Pena	59
Mike Perez	40

Minor League Report

Class AAA: Louisville finished at 66-76, last in the American Association Eastern Division. Keith Lockhart hit .300 with 13 homers and 68 RBI. Allen Watson was 5-4 with a 2.91 ERA. Steve Dixon had 20 saves. **Class AA:** Arkansas finished at 67-69, second in the Texas League Eastern Division. Darrel Deak hit 19 homers and had 73 RBI. John Mabry had 72 RBI. Doug Creek had 11 wins and 128 strikeouts. John Kelly had 27 saves. **Class A:** St. Petersburg finished at 75-68, third in the Florida State League West Division. Clint Davis shared the league lead with 19 saves while John Corona added 16. Doug Radziewicz won the batting title at .342 with 72 RBI. Aaron Holbert stole 45 bases and Terry Bradshaw stole 43. . . . Springfield finished at 78-58, winning the first half of the Midwest League Southern Division. Joe Biasucci was league MVP, with 26 homers and 86 RBI. Mike Gulan hit 23 homers and Andy Bruce added 21. Darond Stovall had 81 RBI. T.J. Mathews was 12-9 with a 2.71 ERA. Kirk Bullinger led the league with 33 saves. . . . Savannah finished at 94-48, winning both halves of the Sally League Southern Division. Jamie Cochran set a minor league single-season record with 46 saves. Brian Rupp won the batting crown at .320. He had 81 RBI. Aldo Pecorilli hit .305 with 14 homers and 93 RBI. Mike Busby was 12-2 with a 2.44 ERA. Jeff Matranga was 11-3 with a 1.49 ERA. **Short-season:** Glens Falls finished at 36-40, last in the New York-Penn League McNamara Division. Craig Grasser led the league with 19 saves. Jeff Berblinger hit .312. Mike Windham had a 2.65 ERA. . . . Johnson City finished at 37-31, second in the Appalachian League Southern Division. Tom McKinnon had 53 RBI. Aaron Gerteisen had 20 stolen bases. Jeff Battles was 5-4 with a 3.20 ERA. Ron Scott had nine saves while Chris Stewart had seven. Jim Sailors struck out 81. . . . Chandler finished at 31-

22, third in the Arizona League. Dave Madsen had 38 RBI. Travis Welch was 7-1 with a 2.04 ERA. He struck out 67 in 57 innings. Troy Barrick led the league with 12 saves.

Tops in the organization

Batter	Club	Avg	G	AB	R	H	HR	RBI
Radziewicz, Doug	Stp	.342	123	439	66	150	4	72
Rupp, Brian	Sav	.320	122	472	80	151	4	81
Pecorilli, Aldo	Sav	.305	141	515	75	157	14	93
Lockhart, Keith	Lou	.300	132	467	66	140	13	68
Bradshaw, Terry	Stp	.291	125	461	84	134	5	51

Home Runs			Wins		
Biasucci, Joe	Spr	26	Badorek, Mike	Stp	15
Gulan, Mike	Spr	23	Alkire, Jeff	Sav	15
Bruce, Andy	Spr	21	Matranga, Jeff	Sav	13
Stovall, Darond	Spr	20	Several players tied		12
Deak, Darrel	Ark	19			

RBI			Saves		
Pecorilli, Aldo	Sav	93	Cochran, Jamie	Sav	46
Biasucci, Joe	Spr	86	Bullinger, Kirk	Spr	33
Stovall, Darond	Spr	81	Kelly, John	Ark	27
Rupp, Brian	Sav	81	Davis, Clint	Ark	20
Gulan, Mike	Spr	76	Dixon, Steve	Lou	20

Stolen Bases			Strikeouts		
Holbert, Aaron	Stp	45	Alkire, Jeff	Sav	175
Bradshaw, Terry	Stp	43	Carpenter, Brian	Sav	147
Johns, Keith	Spr	40	Mathews, T.J.	Spr	144
Shabazz, Basil	Spr	29	Creek, Doug	Lou	137
Several players tied		22	Barber, Brian	Lou	131

Pitcher	Club	W-L	ERA	IP	H	BB	SO
Matranga, Jeff	Sav	13-3	1.64	131	97	19	111
Martinez, F.	Ark	10-6	1.88	168	133	46	120
Busby, Mike	Sav	12-2	2.44	144	116	31	125
Alkire, Jeff	Sav	15-6	2.46	172	143	68	175
Mathews, T.J.	Spr	12-9	2.71	159	121	29	144

St. Louis (1892-1993)

Runs: Most, career, all-time

1949	Stan Musial, 1941-1963
1427	Lou Brock, 1964-1979
1089	Rogers Hornsby, 1915-1933
1071	Enos Slaughter, 1938-1953
1025	Red Schoendienst, 1945-1963

Hits: Most, career, all-time

3630	Stan Musial, 1941-1963
2713	Lou Brock, 1964-1979
2110	Rogers Hornsby, 1915-1933
2064	Enos Slaughter, 1938-1953
1980	Red Schoendienst, 1945-1963

2B: Most, career, all-time

725	Stan Musial, 1941-1963
434	Lou Brock, 1964-1979
377	Joe Medwick, 1932-1948
367	Rogers Hornsby, 1915-1933
366	Enos Slaughter, 1938-1953

3B: Most, career, all-time

177	Stan Musial, 1941-1963
143	Rogers Hornsby, 1915-1933
135	Enos Slaughter, 1938-1953
121	Lou Brock, 1964-1979
119	Jim Bottomley, 1922-1932

HR: Most, career, all-time

475	Stan Musial, 1941-1963
255	Ken Boyer, 1955-1965
193	Rogers Hornsby, 1915-1933
181	Jim Bottomley, 1922-1932
172	Ted Simmons, 1968-1980

RBI: Most, career, all-time

1951	Stan Musial, 1941-1963
1148	Enos Slaughter, 1938-1953
1105	Jim Bottomley, 1922-1932
1072	Rogers Hornsby, 1915-1933
1001	Ken Boyer, 1955-1965

SB: Most, career, all-time

888	Lou Brock, 1964-1979
549	VINCE COLEMAN, 1985-1990
416	OZZIE SMITH, 1982-1993
274	WILLIE McGEE, 1982-1990
203	Jack Smith, 1915-1926

BB: Most, career, all-time

1599	Stan Musial, 1941-1963
838	Enos Slaughter, 1938-1953
796	OZZIE SMITH, 1982-1993
681	Lou Brock, 1964-1979
660	Rogers Hornsby, 1915-1933

BA: Highest, career, all-time

.359	Rogers Hornsby, 1915-1933
.336	Johnny Mize, 1936-1941
.335	Joe Medwick, 1932-1948
.331	Stan Musial, 1941-1963
.326	Chick Hafey, 1924-1931

Slug avg: Highest, career, all-time

.600	Johnny Mize, 1936-1941
.568	Rogers Hornsby, 1915-1933
.568	Chick Hafey, 1924-1931
.559	Stan Musial, 1941-1963
.545	Joe Medwick, 1932-1948

Games started: Most, career, all-time

482	Bob Gibson, 1959-1975
401	Bob Forsch, 1974-1988
388	Jesse Haines, 1920-1937
319	Bill Doak, 1913-1929
243	Bill Sherdel, 1918-1932

Saves: Most, career, all-time

160	LEE SMITH, 1990-1993
129	TODD WORRELL, 1985-1992
127	Bruce Sutter, 1981-1984
64	Lindy McDaniel, 1955-1962
60	Al Brazle, 1943-1954
60	Joe Hoerner, 1966-1969

Shutouts: Most, career, all-time

56	Bob Gibson, 1959-1975
30	Bill Doak, 1913-1929
28	Mort Cooper, 1938-1945
25	Harry Brecheen, 1940-1952
24	Jesse Haines, 1920-1937

Wins: Most, career, all-time

251	Bob Gibson, 1959-1975
210	Jesse Haines, 1920-1937
163	Bob Forsch, 1974-1988
153	Bill Sherdel, 1918-1932
144	Bill Doak, 1913-1929

K: Most, career, all-time

3117	Bob Gibson, 1959-1975
1095	Dizzy Dean, 1930-1937
1079	Bob Forsch, 1974-1988
979	Jesse Haines, 1920-1937
951	Steve Carlton, 1965-1971

Win pct: Highest, career, all-time

.718	Ted Wilks, 1944-1951
.705	John Tudor, 1985-1990
.677	Mort Cooper, 1938-1945
.667	Al Hrabosky, 1970-1977
.641	Dizzy Dean, 1930-1937

ERA: Lowest, career, all-time

2.52	John Tudor, 1985-1990
2.67	Slim Sallee, 1908-1916
2.67	Jack Taylor, 1904-1906
2.74	Johnny Lush, 1907-1910
2.74	Red Ames, 1915-1919

Runs: Most, season

142	Jesse Burkett, 1901
141	Rogers Hornsby, 1922
135	Stan Musial, 1948
133	Rogers Hornsby, 1925
132	Joe Medwick, 1935

Hits: Most, season

250	Rogers Hornsby, 1922
237	Joe Medwick, 1937
235	Rogers Hornsby, 1921
230	Stan Musial, 1948
230	Joe Torre, 1971

2B: Most, season

64	Joe Medwick, 1936
56	Joe Medwick, 1937
53	Stan Musial, 1953
52	Enos Slaughter, 1939
51	Stan Musial, 1944

3B: Most, season

29	Perry Werden, 1893
25	Tom Long, 1915
20	Jim Bottomley, 1928
20	Duff Cooley, 1895
20	Rogers Hornsby, 1920
20	Stan Musial, 1943
20	Stan Musial, 1946

HR: Most, season

43	Johnny Mize, 1940
42	Rogers Hornsby, 1922
39	Rogers Hornsby, 1925
39	Stan Musial, 1948
36	Stan Musial, 1949

RBI: Most, season

154	Joe Medwick, 1937
152	Rogers Hornsby, 1922
143	Rogers Hornsby, 1925
138	Joe Medwick, 1936
137	Jim Bottomley, 1929
137	Johnny Mize, 1940
137	Joe Torre, 1971

SB: Most, season

118	Lou Brock, 1974
110	VINCE COLEMAN, 1985
109	VINCE COLEMAN, 1987
107	VINCE COLEMAN, 1986
81	VINCE COLEMAN, 1988

BB: Most, season

136	Jack Clark, 1987
136	Jack Crooks, 1892
121	Jack Crooks, 1893
116	Miller Huggins, 1910
107	Stan Musial, 1949

BA: Highest, season

.424	Rogers Hornsby, 1924
.403	Rogers Hornsby, 1925
.401	Rogers Hornsby, 1922
.397	Rogers Hornsby, 1921
.396	Jesse Burkett, 1899

Slug avg: Highest, season

.756	Rogers Hornsby, 1925
.722	Rogers Hornsby, 1922
.702	Stan Musial, 1948
.696	Rogers Hornsby, 1924
.652	Chick Hafey, 1930

Games started: Most, season

50	Ted Breitenstein, 1894
50	Ted Breitenstein, 1895
47	Jack Taylor, 1898
45	Kid Gleason, 1892
45	Kid Gleason, 1893
41	Bob Harmon, 1911 (11)

Saves: Most, season

47	LEE SMITH, 1991
45	Bruce Sutter, 1984
43	LEE SMITH, 1992
43	LEE SMITH, 1993
36	Bruce Sutter, 1982
36	TODD WORRELL, 1986

Shutouts: Most, season

13	Bob Gibson, 1968
10	Mort Cooper, 1942
10	John Tudor, 1985
7	Harry Brecheen, 1948
7	Mort Cooper, 1944
7	Dizzy Dean, 1934
7	Bill Doak, 1914

Wins: Most, season

30	Dizzy Dean, 1934
28	Dizzy Dean, 1935
27	Ted Breitenstein, 1894
26	Cy Young, 1899
24	Dizzy Dean, 1936
24	Jesse Haines, 1927

K: Most, season

274	Bob Gibson, 1970
270	Bob Gibson, 1965
269	Bob Gibson, 1969
268	Bob Gibson, 1968
245	Bob Gibson, 1964

Win pct: Highest, season

.811	Dizzy Dean, 1934
.810	Ted Wilks, 1944
.789	Harry Brecheen, 1945
.778	Johnny Beazley, 1942
.767	Bob Gibson, 1970

ERA: Lowest, season

1.12	Bob Gibson, 1968
1.72	Bill Doak, 1914
1.78	Mort Cooper, 1942
1.90	Max Lanier, 1943
1.93	John Tudor, 1985

Most pinch-hit homers, season

4	George Crowe, 1959
4	George Crowe, 1960
4	Carl Sawatski, 1961

Most pinch-hit, homers, career

| 8 | George Crowe, 1959-1961 |

Most consecutive games, batting safely

| 33 | Rogers Hornsby, 1922 |
| 30 | Stan Musial, 1950 |

Most consecutive scoreless innings

| 47 | Bob Gibson, 1968 |
| 37 | George Bradley, 1876 |

No hit games

George Bradley, StL vs Har NL, 2-0; July 15, 1876.

Jesse Haines, StL vs Bos NL, 5-0; July 17, 1924.

Paul Dean, StL at Bro NL, 3-0; September 21, 1934 (2nd game).

Lon Warneke, StL at Cin NL, 2-0; August 30, 1941.

Ray Washburn, StL at SF NL, 2-0; September 18, 1968.

Bob Gibson, StL at Pit NL, 11-0; August 14, 1971.

Bob Forsch, StL vs Phi NL, 5-0; April 16, 1978.

Bob Forsch, StL vs Mon NL, 3-0; September 26, 1983.

Stoney McGlynn, seven innings, agreement, StL at Bro NL, 1-1; September 24, 1906 (2nd game).

Ed Karger, seven perfect innings, agreement, StL vs Bos NL, 4-0; August 11, 1907 (2nd game).

Johnny Lush, six innings, rain, StL at Bro NL, 2-0; August 6, 1908.

ACTIVE PLAYERS in caps.
Leaders from the franchise's current location is included. If not in the top five, the leader's rank is listed in parentheses.

Chicago Cubs

Joining the 30-30 club, Sammy Sosa led the Cubs with 33 homers (93 RBI), and stole 36 bases.

by Anne Ryan, USA TODAY

1993 Cubs: Another tease down the stretch

Nobody has been spindled, folded or mutilated more over the years than Cubs fans. Still, the Cubs' 18-7 record in September produced their third winning season since 1972 and hopes were raised yet again.

It wasn't enough to save manager Jim Lefebvre's job though, despite having received a ringing endorsement from several players. He was fired three days after the season ended and replaced by Tom Trebelhorn.

Lefebvre was the 10th Cubs manager to come and go in 10 years, following Jim Essian, Joe Altobelli, Don Zimmer, Frank Lucchesi, Gene Michael, John Vukovich, Jim Frey, Charlie Fox and Lee Elia.

"I thought my record spoke for itself," Lefebvre said.

It did, but there was turmoil between Lefebvre and GM Larry Himes brewing beneath the seams. Lefebvre blamed Himes for handing him a mediocre team. Free agents Willie Wilson and Candy Maldonado—finally traded to Cleveland—were no-shows offensively.

The amazing thing is the Cubs improved by six victories (from 78 to 84) minus outfielder Andre Dawson and 1992 Cy Young winner Greg Maddux.

Offensively, Sammy Sosa, Mark Grace, Rick Wilkins, Steve Buechele and Derrick May picked up the slack with big years. Sosa became the Cubs' first 30-30 man. He hit .261 with 33 home runs, 36 stolen bases and 93 RBI. First baseman Grace had a career year, hitting .325 with 14 home runs, a team-high 98 RBI and another stellar season with the glove. His 193 hits trailed only NL-leader Lenny Dykstra (Phillies). Catcher Wilkins hit .303 and amazed everyone around the league with 30 home runs (the most by a Cub catcher since Gabby Hartnett's 37 in 1930) and 73 RBI. Wilkins and Sosa were the first Cub teammates with 30 homers since 1972. Wilkins also threw out 46 percent of opposing runners.

Third baseman Buechele hit .272 (15 HR, 65 RBI); outfielder May hit .295 (10 HR, 77 RBI); second baseman Ryne Sandberg hit .309 despite missing the first month with a broken hand and the last two weeks with a dislocated finger.

The team batting average of .270 was 16 points higher than the previous season. The young outfield—Kevin Roberson, Glenallen Hill and Derrick May—bodes well for the future.

On the mound, the Cubs never did find a replacement for Maddux, although Greg Hibbard, Mike Morgan, Mike Harkey and Jose Guzman each hit double figures in victories. Hibbard, won his last five decisions to finish 15-11, the best record on the staff. Guzman was 12-10, while Harkey was 10-10 with a 5.26 ERA.

Randy Myers set an NL record in the bullpen with 53 saves, breaking Lee Smith's old mark of 47. Jose Bautista, used in various roles, put together a 10-3 season.

"I feel good about what this team has done," Lefebvre said, before leaving, "but I'm disappointed and disheartened that I will not be with them to take them to another level."

—by Bill Koenig

1994 Cubs: Preview

Tom Trebelhorn must settle on a permanent outfield. Glenallen Hill was sensational down the stretch in '93. Karl Rhodes and Eddie Zambrano each hit 30 home runs in the minors.

Another top-flight starter is needed; youngsters Turk Wendell and Steve Trachsel top the list of candidates. Wendell, the licorice-chewing eccentric who brushes his teeth between innings, shut out San Diego for seven innings on the last day of the season. Trachsel gave up four hits in seven innings against the Marlins in his major league debut.

—by Bill Koenig

1993 Cubs: Between the lines

▶**April 6:** Jose Guzman took a perfect game into the eighth inning, and had his no-hit bid broken up with two outs in the ninth on Otis Nixon's single. It would have been the first Cubs' no-hitter since 1972.

▶**April 30:** Ryne Sandberg, sidelined since spring training with a broken left hand, returned to the Cubs' lineup and was 0-for-3 with two walks.

▶**May 7:** Steve Buechele snapped his 13-game hitting streak.

▶**May 9:** Mark Grace hit for the cycle, capping it off with a three-run homer in the ninth. He was the first Cub to do it since Andre Dawson in '87.

▶**May 18:** Frank Castillo earned his first victory in seven games in '93, going eight strong innings for a 4-1 win against St. Louis. He allowed six hits.

▶**May 26:** The Cubs-Giants game was marked by a pair of rare occurrences: The Giants lost, 4-2, for the second time in 10 games and Cubs' second baseman Ryne Sandberg was ejected for the first time since 1981.

▶**May 31:** While Wrigley Field fans watched the scoreboard for updates of Michael Jordan in the other New York-Chicago game, the Mets' scoring outburst went almost unnoticed. In their second-highest scoring game of the season, New York beat the Cubs 9-5.

▶**June 9:** Catcher Rick Wilkins hit two homers in the Cubs' 8-3 win against the Mets, to give him three homers in the last two games and 10 in the last month. Wilkins, whose average was at .122 the last day of April, lifted it to .267. Mark Grace and Ryne Sandberg had three hits each.

▶**June 15:** Coming off a pair of horrendous starts that jeopardized his spot in the Cubs' rotation, Frank Castillo resolidified his slot with 7 1/3 innings of five-hit, shutout ball to beat the Marlins 3-0. He aided his own cause going 2-for-3 with an RBI.

▶**June 17:** Reliever Chuck McElroy collapsed from heat stroke and was treated and released from a nearby hospital.

▶**June 30:** Sammy Sosa posted his fourth two-homer game of the season in a 4-1 win against San Diego.

▶**July 3:** *Milestone*—Ryne Sandberg collected his 2,000th hit. The 50 mph winds at Mile High Stadium must have made him feel right at home.

▶**July 15:** Mike Morgan shut out the Rockies, allowing only one extra-base hit. The 1-0 win was his 10th career shutout, but first of the season. He had been 0-2 with a 10.65 ERA in two previous starts against Colorado.

▶**July 16:** Jose Guzman fanned 11 Rockies' batters in 8 2/3 innings as the Cubs topped Colorado 8-2 at Wrigley Field. Guzman had a 5.22 ERA in five previous starts.

▶**July 17:** Mike Harkey threw eight shutout innings to lead the Cubs to a 5-1 win against Colorado. Harkey gave up three hits and struck out six.

▶**July 18:** Ryne Sandberg had a single and a double in Chicago's eight-run first inning and the Cubs piled up 12 runs in just seven innings. Sandberg collected four hits in the 12-2 rain-shortened win against the Rockies.

▶**July 26:** Jose Vizcaino hit a three-run homer in the bottom of the 11th to give the Cubs a 9-6 win against the Padres. It was his second homer of the year.

▶**July 28:** Rookie outfielder Kevin Roberson's three-run homer highlighted a five-run sixth inning as the Cubs rallied to beat San Diego 8-6. Roberson had 10 hits to his credit, five of which were homers.

▶**August 1:** Sammy Sosa drove in three runs with a single and a home run in the Cubs' 10-4 defeat of Los Angeles. Sosa also stole a base and made two outstanding catches in center field.

▶**August 6:** Sosa had the seventh multi-homer game of his career—and his fifth in '93—as the Cubs downed the Cards 6-4.

▶**August 8:** Greg Hibbard waited three years and 37 at-bats before finally getting his first major league hit, but the Cubs' pitcher's first was worth waiting for—an RBI double to right field in the sixth inning to snap a 1-1 tie and give Chicago a 2-1 win against St. Louis.

▶**August 11:** Florida scored twice in the bottom of the ninth inning to beat the Cubs 12-11. Gary Sheffield singled off Randy Myers to bring home the winning run and give the Marlins the highest single-game run total in their history. Myers had blown saves in each of the last two games.

▶**August 12:** Dwight Smith turned in his first career multi-homer game, hitting two to lead the Cubs to a 5-1 win against the Marlins. His effort backed pitcher Mike Harkey's first complete game in three years, and raised his season total to a career-high 10 homers.

▶**August 14:** Mark Grace singled home Jose Vizcaino with one out in the ninth to lift the Cubs to a 3-2 victory against the Giants. Randy Myers earned the win in relief, despite blowing the save, by allowing San Francisco to tie with two in the top of the ninth. Frank Castillo tossed seven innings of four-hit shutout ball.

▶**August 19:** The Expos scored six unearned runs in the seventh inning. Shortstop Rey Sanchez threw a double-play relay into right field, allowing two runs to score and left fielder Candy Maldonado botched Darrin Fletcher's bases-loaded fly ball, clearing the bases. After the game, Maldonado was dealt to the Cleveland Indians.

▶**August 20:** Ryne Sandberg was 3-for-5 and scored two runs in the Cubs' 6-3 win against the Braves.

▶**August 27:** Derrick May's seventh-inning grand slam off reliever Mike Stanton rallied the Cubs to a 9-7 win against Atlanta.

▶**August 30:** Rick Wilkins hit a two-out, game-winning grand slam in the 11th inning to give Chicago a 10-6 victory against first-place Philadelphia.

▶**September 4:** Shawon Dunston tied the score at 8 with a pinch-hit double—his first hit in 16 months, since coming

off a chronic back injury—as the Cubs rallied for a 9-8 victory against New York. Earlier, Dwight Smith hit a two-run, pinch-hit double for his club-record 47th career pinch-hit.

▶**September 15:** Mike Morgan won for the second time in 11 starts, handing the Giants a 3-1 loss.

▶**October 3:** The Cubs beat the Padres 4-1 and finished in fourth place, 13 games behind the Phillies in the NL East. *League leaders, pitching—* Randy Myers led the league in saves (53); Jose Guzman was eighth in strikeouts (163). *League leaders, batting—* Mark Grace was second in hits (193), fifth overall in batting (.325), seventh in doubles (39), and ninth in on-base percentage (.393); Sammy Sosa was ninth in total bases (290).

—by John Hunt, Scott Kauffman, Lisa Winston, Deron Snyder, Matt Young

Team directory

▶**Owner:** Tribune Company
▶**General Manager:** Larry Himes
▶**Ballpark:**
Wrigley Field
Clark and Addison Streets,
Chicago, Ill.
312-404-2827
Capacity 38,756
Parking for 900; $10 (private lots available)
Public transportation available
Family and wheelchair sections, ramps
▶**Team publications:**
Yearbook, *Vineline, Scorecard Magazine*
312-404-2827
▶**TV, radio broadcast stations:**
WGN 720 AM, WGN Channel 9
▶**Spring Training:**
HoHoKam Park
Mesa, Ariz.
Capacity 8,963
602-644-2149

CHICAGO CUBS 1993 final stats

Batting	BA	SLG	OB	G	AB	R	H	TB	2B	3B	HR	RBI	BB	SO	SB	CS	E
Dunston	.400	.600	.400	7	10	3	4	6	2	0	0	2	0	1	0	0	0
Hill	.345	.770	.387	31	87	14	30	67	7	0	10	22	6	21	1	0	2
Grace	.325	.475	.393	155	594	86	193	282	39	4	14	98	71	32	8	4	5
Sandberg	.309	.412	.359	117	456	67	141	188	20	0	9	45	37	62	9	2	7
Wilkins	.303	.561	.376	136	446	78	135	250	23	1	30	73	50	99	2	1	3
Smith	.300	.494	.355	111	310	51	93	153	17	5	11	35	25	51	8	6	8
May	.295	.422	.336	128	465	62	137	196	25	2	10	77	31	41	10	3	7
Zambrano	.294	.294	.333	8	17	1	5	5	0	0	0	2	1	3	0	0	1
Vizcaino	.287	.358	.340	151	551	74	158	197	19	4	4	54	46	71	12	9	17
Sanchez	.282	.326	.316	105	344	35	97	112	11	2	0	28	15	22	1	1	15
Rhodes	.278	.519	.400	20	54	12	15	28	2	1	3	7	11	9	2	0	1
Buechele	.272	.437	.345	133	460	53	125	201	27	2	15	65	48	87	1	1	8
Sosa	.261	.485	.309	159	598	92	156	290	25	5	33	93	38	135	36	11	9
Wilson	.258	.348	.301	105	221	29	57	77	11	3	1	11	11	40	7	2	1
Jennings	.250	.462	.316	42	52	8	13	24	3	1	2	8	3	10	0	0	0
Lake	.225	.400	.250	44	120	11	27	48	6	0	5	13	4	19	0	0	3
Yelding	.204	.296	.277	69	108	14	22	32	5	1	1	10	11	22	3	2	4
Walbeck	.200	.367	.226	11	30	2	6	11	2	0	1	6	1	6	0	0	0
Roberson	.189	.372	.251	62	180	23	34	67	4	1	9	27	12	48	0	1	3
Maldonado	.186	.286	.260	70	140	8	26	40	5	0	3	15	13	40	0	0	5
Shields	.176	.206	.222	20	34	4	6	7	1	0	0	1	2	10	0	0	0

Pitching	W-L	ERA	G	GS	CG	GF	Sho	SV	IP	H	R	ER	HR	BB	SO
Bautista	10-3	2.82	58	7	1	14	0	2	111.2	105	38	35	11	27	63
Myers	2-4	3.11	73	0	0	69	0	53	75.1	65	26	26	7	26	86
Slocumb	1-0	3.38	10	0	0	4	0	0	10.2	7	5	4	0	4	4
Boskie	5-3	3.43	39	2	0	10	0	0	65.2	63	30	25	7	21	39
Assenmacher	2-1	3.49	46	0	0	15	0	0	38.2	44	15	15	5	13	34
Hibbard	15-11	3.96	31	31	1	0	0	0	191	209	96	84	19	47	82
Morgan	10-15	4.03	32	32	1	0	1	0	207.2	206	100	93	15	74	111
Brennan	2-1	4.20	8	1	0	0	0	0	15	16	8	7	2	8	11
Bullinger	1-0	4.32	15	0	0	6	0	1	16.2	18	9	8	1	9	10
Guzman	12-10	4.34	30	30	2	0	1	0	191	188	98	92	25	74	163
Wendell	1-2	4.37	7	4	0	1	0	0	22.2	24	13	11	0	8	15
Scanlan	4-5	4.54	70	0	0	13	0	0	75.1	79	41	38	6	28	44
McElroy	2-2	4.56	49	0	0	11	0	0	47.1	51	30	24	4	25	31
Trachsel	0-2	4.58	3	3	0	0	0	0	19.2	16	10	10	4	3	14
Plesac	2-1	4.74	57	0	0	12	0	0	62.2	74	37	33	10	21	47
Castillo	5-8	4.84	29	25	2	0	0	0	141.1	162	83	76	20	39	84
Harkey	10-10	5.26	28	28	1	0	0	0	157.1	187	100	92	17	43	67

1994 preliminary roster

PITCHERS (20)
Willie Banks
Jose Bautista
Shawn Boskie
Bill Brennan
Jim Bullinger
Frank Castillo
Lance Dickson
Jose Guzman
Mike Harkey
Greg Hibbard
Jessie Hollins
Blaise Ilsley
Chuck McElroy
Mike Morgan
Randy Myers
Dan Plesac
Bob Scanlan
Steve Trachsel
Randy Vares
Turk Wendell

CATCHERS (1)
Rick Wilkins

INFIELDERS (9)
Steve Buechele
Shawon Dunston
Matt Franco
Mark Grace
Jose Hernandez
Rey Sanchez
Ryne Sandberg
Tommy Shields
Jose Vizcaino

OUTFIELDERS (10)
Doug Glanville
Glenallen Hill
Derrick May
Tuffy Rhodes
Kevin Roberson
Dwight Smith
Sammy Sosa
Ozzie Timmons
Willie Wilson
Eddie Zambrano

Games played by position

Player	G	C	1B	2B	3B	SS	OF
Buechele	133	0	6	0	129	0	0
Dunston	7	0	0	0	0	2	0
Grace	155	0	154	0	0	0	0
Hill	31	0	0	0	0	0	21
Jennings	42	0	10	0	0	0	0
Lake	44	41	0	0	0	0	0
Maldonado	70	0	0	0	0	0	41
May	128	0	0	0	0	0	122
Rhodes	20	0	0	0	0	0	18
Roberson	62	0	0	0	0	0	51
Sanchez	105	0	0	0	0	98	0
Sandberg	117	0	0	115	0	0	0
Shields	20	0	1	7	7	0	1
Smith	111	0	0	0	0	0	89
Sosa	159	0	0	0	0	0	158
Vizcaino	151	0	0	34	44	81	0
Walbeck	11	11	0	0	0	0	0
Wilkins	136	133	0	0	0	0	0
Wilson	105	0	0	0	0	0	82
Yelding	69	0	0	32	7	1	1
Zambrano	8	0	2	0	0	0	4

Sick call: 1993 DL Report

Player	Days on the DL
Steve Buechele	15
Shawon Dunston	149
Mike Harkey*	31
Greg Hibbard	20
Jesse Hollins	182
Mike Morgan	15
Ryne Sandberg	25
Dwight Smith	28

Two separate terms on Disabled List

Minor League Report

Class AAA: Iowa finished at 84-58, winning the American Association Western Division and beating Nashville in seven games for the league title. Tuffy Rhodes hit .318 with 30 homers and 89 RBI. Eddie Zambrano was league MVP, hitting .303 with 32 homers and 115 RBI. Steve Trachsel was 13-6 with a 3.96 ERA. Blaise Ilsley was 12-7 with a 3.94 ERA. Jim Bullinger had 20 saves. **Class AA:** Orlando finished at 71-70, third in the Southern League Eastern Division. Travis Willis had 24 saves. Ozzie Timmons hit .284 with 18 homers and 58 RBI. Corey Kapano stole 17 bases. Jose Hernandez hit .304. Jimmy Williams was 5-5 with a 2.48 ERA. **Class A:** Daytona finished at 57-76, fifth in the Florida State League East Division. Bernie Nunez had 15 homers and 73 RBI. Brant Brown hit .342. Paul Torres hit .278 with 13 homers and 43 RBI. . . . Peoria finished at 59-79, fifth in the Midwest League Southern Division. Robin Jennings hit .308 with 65 RBI. Hector Trinidad was 7-6 with a 2.47 ERA. **Short-season:** Geneva finished at 42-34, second in the New York-Penn League Pinckney Division. Shawn Hill had 12 saves. Joe Biernat hit .286 with 22 stolen bases. Gabe Duross hit .271 with six homers and 41 RBI. . . . Huntington finished at 33-35, third in the Appalachian League Southern Division. Chris Bryant was 5-4 with a 3.18 ERA. Kevin Ellis hit .267 with 13 homers and 48 RBI. Billy Childress was 4-1 with a 2.49 ERA and six saves. . . . St. Lucie finished at 19-40, last in the Gulf Coast League Eastern Division. Gilbert Avalos hit .297 with 14 stolen bases. Bradley Chambers hit .297. Mike Whitfill had a 1.91 ERA.

Tops in the organization

Batter	Club	Avg	G	AB	R	H	HR	RBI
Brown, Brant	Orl	.334	103	377	43	126	7	56
Rhodes, Karl	Iwa	.318	123	490	112	156	30	89
Jennings, Robin	Peo	.308	132	474	65	146	3	65
Franco, Matt	Iwa	.305	130	436	55	133	12	66
Zambrano, Eddie	Iwa	.303	133	469	95	142	32	115

Home Runs			Wins		
Zambrano, Eddie	Iwa	32	Steenstra, Kennie	Orl	14
Rhodes, Karl	Iwa	30	Trachsel, Steve	Iwa	13
Timmons, Ozzie	Orl	18	Ilsley, Blaise	Iwa	12
Several players tied		16	Salles, John	Orl	11
			Several players tied at		10

RBI			Saves		
Zambrano, Eddie	Iwa	115	Willis, Travis	Orl	24
Rhodes, Karl	Iwa	89	Bullinger, Jim	Iwa	20
Valdez, Pedro	Day	85	Daniel, Chuck	Day	12
Grace, Mike	Orl	76	Gavlick, Daryle	Peo	9
Nunez, Bernie	Day	73	Slocumb, Heath	Iwa	7

Stolen Bases			Strikeouts		
Glanville, Doug	Orl	33	Brennan, Bill	Iwa	143
Smith, Greg	Iwa	25	Trachsel, Steve	Iwa	135
Kapano, Corey	Day	20	Telemaco, A.	Peo	133
Petersen, Chris	Day	19	Trinidad, Hector	Orl	131
Several players tied		16	Kerley, Collin	Peo	129

Pitcher	Club	W-L	ERA	IP	H	BB	SO
Williams, Jimmy	Iwa	10-8	2.93	169	158	75	114
Trinidad, Hector	Orl	8-9	3.04	178	176	36	131
Delgado, Tim	Day	7-10	3.05	124	131	37	67
Steenstra, K.	Orl	14-6	3.26	188	176	41	123
Telemaco, A.	Peo	8-11	3.45	144	129	54	133

Chicago (1876-1993)

Runs: Most, career, all-time

1719	Cap Anson, 1876-1897
1409	Jimmy Ryan, 1885-1900
1306	Billy Williams, 1959-1974
1305	Ernie Banks, 1953-1971
1239	Stan Hack, 1932-1947

Hits: Most, career, all-time

2995	Cap Anson, 1876-1897
2583	Ernie Banks, 1953-1971
2510	Billy Williams, 1959-1974
2193	Stan Hack, 1932-1947
2171	Ron Santo, 1960-1973

2B: Most, career, all-time

528	Cap Anson, 1876-1897
407	Ernie Banks, 1953-1971
402	Billy Williams, 1959-1974
391	Gabby Hartnett, 1922-1940
363	Stan Hack, 1932-1947

3B: Most, career, all-time

142	Jimmy Ryan, 1885-1900
124	Cap Anson, 1876-1897
117	Frank Schulte, 1904-1916
106	Bill Dahlen, 1891-1898
99	Phil Cavarretta, 1934-1953

HR: Most, career, all-time

512	Ernie Banks, 1953-1971
392	Billy Williams, 1959-1974
337	Ron Santo, 1960-1973
240	RYNE SANDBERG, 1982-1993
231	Gabby Hartnett, 1922-1940

RBI: Most, career, all-time

1879	Cap Anson, 1876-1897
1636	Ernie Banks, 1953-1971
1353	Billy Williams, 1959-1974
1290	Ron Santo, 1960-1973
1153	Gabby Hartnett, 1922-1940

SB: Most, career, all-time

400	Frank Chance, 1898-1912
399	Bill Lange, 1893-1899
369	Jimmy Ryan, 1885-1900
323	RYNE SANDBERG, 1982-1993
304	Joe Tinker, 1902-1916

BB: Most, career, all-time

1092	Stan Hack, 1932-1947
1071	Ron Santo, 1960-1973
952	Cap Anson, 1876-1897
911	Billy Williams, 1959-1974
794	Phil Cavarretta, 1934-1953

BA: Highest, career, all-time

.336	Riggs Stephenson, 1926-1934
.330	Bill Lange, 1893-1899
.329	Cap Anson, 1876-1897
.325	Kiki Cuyler, 1928-1935
.323	Bill Everett, 1895-1900

Slug avg: Highest, career, all-time

.590	Hack Wilson, 1926-1931
.512	Hank Sauer, 1949-1955
.507	ANDRE DAWSON, 1987-1992
.503	Billy Williams, 1959-1974
.500	Ernie Banks, 1953-1971

Games started: Most, career, all-time

347	Fergie Jenkins, 1966-1983
343	Rick Reuschel, 1972-1984
340	Bill Hutchison, 1889-1895
339	Charlie Root, 1926-1941
296	Bill Lee, 1934-1947

Saves: Most, career, all-time

180	LEE SMITH, 1980-1987
133	Bruce Sutter, 1976-1980
63	Don Elston, 1953-1964
60	Phil Regan, 1968-1972
53	RANDY MYERS, 1993-1993

Shutouts: Most, career, all-time

48	Mordecai Brown, 1904-1916
35	Hippo Vaughn, 1913-1921
31	Ed Reulbach, 1905-1913
29	Fergie Jenkins, 1966-1983
28	Orval Overall, 1906-1913

Wins: Most, career, all-time

201	Charlie Root, 1926-1941
188	Mordecai Brown, 1904-1916
182	Bill Hutchison, 1889-1895
175	Larry Corcoran, 1880-1885
167	Fergie Jenkins, 1966-1983

K: Most, career, all-time

2038	Fergie Jenkins, 1966-1983
1432	Charlie Root, 1926-1941
1367	Rick Reuschel, 1972-1984
1226	Bill Hutchison, 1889-1895
1138	Hippo Vaughn, 1913-1921

Win pct: Highest, career, all-time

.800	Al Spalding, 1876-1878
.773	Jim McCormick, 1885-1886
.706	John Clarkson, 1884-1887
.686	Mordecai Brown, 1904-1916
.677	Ed Reulbach, 1905-1913

ERA: Lowest, career, all-time

1.80	Mordecai Brown, 1904-1916
1.85	Jack Pfiester, 1906-1911
1.91	Orval Overall, 1906-1913
2.14	Jake Weimer, 1903-1905
2.24	Ed Reulbach, 1905-1913

Runs: Most, season

156	Rogers Hornsby, 1929
155	Kiki Cuyler, 1930
155	King Kelly, 1886
152	Woody English, 1930
150	George Gore, 1886

Hits: Most, season

229	Rogers Hornsby, 1929
228	Kiki Cuyler, 1930
227	Billy Herman, 1935
214	Woody English, 1930
212	Frank Demaree, 1936

2B: Most, season

57	Billy Herman, 1935
57	Billy Herman, 1936
50	Kiki Cuyler, 1930
49	Riggs Stephenson, 1932
47	Rogers Hornsby, 1929

3B: Most, season

21	Vic Saier, 1913
21	Frank Schulte, 1911
19	Bill Dahlen, 1892
19	Bill Dahlen, 1896
19	RYNE SANDBERG, 1984

HR: Most, season

56	Hack Wilson, 1930
49	ANDRE DAWSON, 1987
48	Dave Kingman, 1979
47	Ernie Banks, 1958
45	Ernie Banks, 1959

RBI: Most, season

190	Hack Wilson, 1930
159	Hack Wilson, 1929
149	Rogers Hornsby, 1929
147	Cap Anson, 1886
143	Ernie Banks, 1959

SB: Most, season

84	Bill Lange, 1896
76	Walt Wilmot, 1890
74	Walt Wilmot, 1894
73	Bill Lange, 1897
67	Frank Chance, 1903
67	Bill Lange, 1895

BB: Most, season

147	Jimmy Sheckard, 1911
122	Jimmy Sheckard, 1912
116	Richie Ashburn, 1960
113	Cap Anson, 1890
108	Johnny Evers, 1910

BA: Highest, season

.389	Bill Lange, 1895
.388	King Kelly, 1886
.380	Rogers Hornsby, 1929
.372	Heinie Zimmerman, 1912
.371	Cap Anson, 1886

Slug avg: Highest, season

.723	Hack Wilson, 1930
.679	Rogers Hornsby, 1929
.630	Gabby Hartnett, 1930
.618	Hack Wilson, 1929
.614	Ernie Banks, 1958

Games started: Most, season

71	Bill Hutchison, 1892
70	John Clarkson, 1885
66	Bill Hutchison, 1890
60	Larry Corcoran, 1880
60	Al Spalding, 1876
42	Fergie Jenkins, 1969 (18)

Saves: Most, season

53	RANDY MYERS, 1993
37	Bruce Sutter, 1979
36	LEE SMITH, 1987
36	MITCH WILLIAMS, 1989
33	LEE SMITH, 1984
33	LEE SMITH, 1985

Shutouts: Most, season

10	John Clarkson, 1885
9	Pete Alexander, 1919
9	Mordecai Brown, 1906
9	Mordecai Brown, 1908
9	Bill Lee, 1938
9	Orval Overall, 1909

Wins: Most, season

53	John Clarkson, 1885
47	Al Spalding, 1876
44	Bill Hutchison, 1891
43	Larry Corcoran, 1880
42	Bill Hutchison, 1890
29	Mordecai Brown, 1908 (14)

K: Most, season

316	Bill Hutchison, 1892
313	John Clarkson, 1886
308	John Clarkson, 1885
289	Bill Hutchison, 1890
274	Fergie Jenkins, 1970

Win pct: Highest, season

.875	Fred Goldsmith, 1880
.833	King Cole, 1910
.833	Jim McCormick, 1885
.826	Ed Reulbach, 1906
.813	Mordecai Brown, 1906

ERA: Lowest, season

1.04	Mordecai Brown, 1906
1.15	Jack Pfiester, 1907
1.17	Carl Lundgren, 1907
1.31	Mordecai Brown, 1909
1.33	Jack Taylor, 1902

Most pinch-hit homers, season

3	Willie Smith, 1969
3	Thad Bosley, 1985

Most pinch-hit, homers, career

6	Thad Bosley, 1983-1986

Most consecutive games, batting safely

42	Bill Dahlen, 1894
30	JEROME WALTON, 1989

Most consecutive scoreless innings

50	Ed Reulbach, 1908-09
39	Mordecai Brown, 1908
38	Bill Lee, 1938
38	John Clarkson, 1885

No hit games

Larry Corcoran, Chi vs Bos NL, 6-0; August 19, 1880.

Larry Corcoran, Chi vs Wor NL, 5-0; September 20, 1882.

Larry Corcoran, Chi vs Pro NL, 6-0; June 27, 1884.

John Clarkson, Chi at Pro NL, 4-0; July 27, 1885.

Walter Thornton, Chi vs Bro NL, 2-0; August 21, 1898 (2nd game).

Bob Wicker, Chi at NY NL, 1-0; June 11, 1904 (won in 12 innings after allowing one hit in the tenth).

Jimmy Lavender, Chi at NY NL, 2-0; August 31, 1915 (1st game).

Hippo Vaughn, Chi vs Cin NL, 0-1; May 2, 1917. (lost on two hits in the 10th, Toney pitched a no-hitter in this game).

Sam Jones, Chi vs Pit NL, 4-0; May 12, 1955.

Don Cardwell, Chi vs StL NL, 4-0; May 15, 1960 (2nd game).

Ken Holtzman, Chi vs Atl NL, 3-0; August 19, 1969.

Ken Holtzman, Chi at Cin NL, 1-0; June 3, 1971.

Burt Hooton, Chi vs Phi NL, 4-0; April 16, 1972.

Milt Pappas, Chi vs SD NL, 8-0; September 2, 1972.

George Van Haltren, six innings, rain, Chi vs Pit NL, 1-0, June 21,1888.

King Cole, seven innings, called so Chicago could catch train, Chi at StL NL, 4-0; July 31, 1910 (2nd game).

ACTIVE PLAYERS in caps.
Leader from franchise's current location is included. If not in the top five, leader's rank is listed in parenthesis.

Pittsburgh Pirates

by Tim Dillon, USA TODAY

With Bonds gone and Van Slyke injured, Orlando Merced picked up the slack, hitting .313 with 70 RBI.

1993 Pirates: How to play with a skeleton crew

The Pirates began the '93 season as a skeleton version of the team that won three consecutive NL East championships. When veteran center fielder Andy Van Slyke took his first look at a locker room of rookies and low-priced journeymen, he wondered aloud if they should wear name tags.

"Like those ones people wear at conventions that say 'Hi, I'm so-and-so,' " Van Slyke said.

The club had lost 13 of the 25 players on its '92 NLCS roster via a $12 million payroll cut that included trading John Smiley, Jose Lind and Steve Buechele, and letting Barry Bonds, Doug Drabek and much of the bullpen leave via free agency. Then they dealt closer Stan Belinda and the pitching staff was gutted. Two of the three returning starters, Zane Smith (3-7) and Randy Tomlin (4-8), were hurt most of the year, and the third, Bob Walk (13-14), was inconsistent and on the trading block by the end of the season.

Shortly before the '93 season ended, manager Jim Leyland said he'd "be tickled to death" if they finished with 75 victories; they reached that figure on the next-to-last day. It was their worst showing since 1989. But like the '89 team, the new Pirates have some young talent worth developing.

They had as many as 22 rookies in a game at least once in '93, and got solid years out of Carlos Garcia, Al Martin, Steve Cooke, Paul Wagner and Blas Minor. Martin had 18 home runs, most by a Pirate rookie since 1946, and 64 RBI, most by a Pirate rookie since 1969. Minor appeared in 65 games, a club record.

First baseman Kevin Young, who had success as a hitter throughout the minor leagues, was a disappointment offensively with his .237 average and 47 RBI. But he made the transition from third base well and was an asset defensively.

Third baseman Jeff King had a breakthrough season, batting .295 with 98 RBI. Shortstop Jay Bell hit .310 and won a Gold Glove. Knuckleballer Tim Wakefield, who spent two months of the season at Class AA, shut out Chicago and Philadelphia in his last two starts. The Pirates finished the season with a 4.77 team ERA, 13th in the NL and worst for the team since 1954.

Leyland had to count on rookies all year long: "Sometimes you promote people because you have to, not because you want to," he said. "We brought up players all season who weren't ready, and that's going to bite you. We lost four-fifths of our rotation for most of the season when Wakefield went down, and nobody can overcome that."

—by Pete Williams

1994 Pirates: Preview

The Pirates leave the NL East after 25 years to join the new NL Central with Houston, St. Louis, Cincinnati and Chicago.

The nucleus of talented rookies, with a year of seasoning under their belts, could make the Pirates contenders, but it all depends on pitching. General manager Cam Bonifay pledged to use the club's limited financial resources to acquire another starting pitcher. If Tim Wakefield returns to his '92 form, the Pirates' patchwork rotation could be sufficient.

"If we can find a couple of pitchers, who knows?" manager Jim Leyland mused. "I'm not saying we're going to win it, but we could be pretty good."

—by Pete Williams

1993 Pirates: Between the lines

▶**April 6:** The much-touted rookie trio of Al Martin, Kevin Young and Carlos Garcia combined to go 5-for-13, highlighted by Young's four RBI and Martin's double and triple (he had 15 triples at Triple-A Buffalo in 1992).

▶**April 8:** Stan Belinda notched his first save of the year. *Quote of the day*—Belinda: "People can call it a monkey, but I felt like I had a piano on my back all winter long. Maybe a trombone will be next."

▶**April 15:** They took 13 innings to do it, but the Bucs finally beat host San Diego 5-4, for their sixth consecutive victory against the Padres in 1993. *Milestone*—The victory was manager Jim Leyland's 600th, putting him 1,400 behind Sparky Anderson.

▶**April 17:** *Quote of the day*—Bob Walk needed a baseball signed for his nephew, so he told Leyland he only wanted "the stars—Jay Bell, Andy Van Slyke, Tim Wakefield. I thought I'd get yours on it, just to fill out the ball." Leyland replied: "Yeah, that's why I pitch you every fifth day—just to fill out the rotation."

▶**April 24:** The Bucs lost to Houston and dropped below the .500 mark for the first time in more than two years.

▶**April 26:** Lonnie Smith, a Brave for the previous five years, homered on an 0-2 pitch to lead off the 11th inning and give the Bucs a 4-3 victory against his ex-teammates.

▶**April 27:** *Quote of the day*—Jim Leyland, on knuckleballer Tim Wakefield, who had walked 28 batters in three wins: "I was kidding (catcher) Tommy Prince tonight, asking if he knew the middle name of the guy sitting by the backstop. I was sure they were on a first-name basis by the second inning."

▶**May 11:** Dave Otto didn't do much on the mound for the Pirates, allowing four runs on seven hits in five-plus innings, but he tripled and drove in three in an 8-4 win against Philadelphia.

▶**May 25:** Rookie Steve Cooke tossed his first career shutout, beating the Marlins 2-0 and adding all the offense with a two-run double.

▶**June 3:** Blas Minor recorded his first major league save in a 3-1 win against the Giants. He had four of the bullpen's eight wins, and had allowed just two earned runs in his last 10-plus innings.

▶**June 17:** *Milestone*—Bob Walk recorded his 100th career victory with a 6-2 complete game against the Mets.

▶**June 20:** In three games since moving from leadoff to batting third, rookie Al Martin was 5-for-10 with two homers, three RBI and five runs scored and had raised his average 12 points.

▶**June 26:** Rookie Steve Cooke tossed the first complete game victory against the Phillies in '93.

▶**July 6:** Left-hander Jeff Ballard drew rave reviews after ending the team's four-game losing streak. Ballard, called up from Triple-A for a spot start, gave up three runs in 8 2/3 innings. It was his first major league win since 1991.

▶**July 9:** Bob Walk remained unbeaten at home (7-0) and collected his 10th win in the Pirates' 4-1 win against the Reds, the first time in his career he had 10 wins before the All-Star Break. However, he left the game after five innings with a groin injury, the same injury that had caused him to spend three stints on the DL in '92.

▶**July 22:** The Pirates rallied for four ninth-inning runs to defeat the Braves 8-7. Kevin Young's two-out, two-run double off Jay Howell brought home the winning run. Howell, who replaced Mike Stanton after the closer put two men on base, brought his mark to 0-for-3 in save opportunities.

▶**July 23:** After a scoreless contest through eight innings, the Braves exploded for six runs in the top of the ninth and hung on for a 6-2 win. Bucs closer Stan Belinda allowed all six runs, including a three-run homer by Dave Justice. *Quote of the day*—Stan

Belinda: "I stunk tonight. I got spanked. That happens. I was (bad). I had nothing. I lost it. That's all."

▶**July 24:** Seven homers totaled 2,896 feet, highlighted by Pittsburgh rookie Ben Shelton's 454-foot bomb, but the Pirates lost to the Braves 11-6.

▶**July 29:** Reliever Blas Minor retired the first two Montreal batters in the 11th, but walked the last two batters in the lineup before leadoff hitter Delino DeShields singled home the game-winner for the Expos, breaking a 2-2 tie.

▶**August 5:** *Quote of the day*—Jim Leyland about Carlos Garcia's homer in Pittsburgh's 5-2 win against the Cubs: "That may be the hardest hit ball I've seen in my entire life. I was at Comiskey Park once when Dave Winfield hit a ball that smashed into the back of a seat and broke it, but Garcia's might have been hit harder than that."

▶**August 8:** Zane Smith tossed his first complete game in more than a year as the Pirates edged the Mets 3-2. Smith, who recorded 11 groundball outs, had lost four in a row since coming off the DL June 16.

▶**August 10:** *Quote of the day*—Pittsburgh pitcher Joel Johnston, who gave up homers on consecutive pitches, had been bailed out of a jam the inning before when, with runners on first and second, St. Louis' Gregg Jefferies hit into a triple play: "Right then, I thought, 'Geez, things are going my way.'"

▶**August 11:** Lonnie Smith hit two home runs in an 8-6 win against St. Louis.

▶**August 12:** Carlos Garcia was 4-for-6, including a triple in the 11th inning, and scored the winning run as the Pirates pulled out the 5-4 extra-inning win against the Cardinals.

▶**August 15:** Don Slaught's RBI double in the 11th inning backed the Pittsburgh bullpen's effort of five scoreless innings as the Pirates pulled out a 4-3 win against the Marlins. Slaught had driven in the tying or deciding run in four of the Pirates' last five Sunday home games.

▶**September 26:** Tim Wakefield pitched his first shutout of the season to give the Pirates a 1-0 victory against Chicago and a doubleheader sweep.

▶**September 30:** Wakefield threw his second shutout in a row, blanking the Phillies for the first time in '93.

▶**October 3:** The Pirates lost their last game of the season to the Expos, 3-1, and finished fifth in the NL East. *League leaders, batting*—Orlando Merced was fourth in on-base percentage (.414) and ninth in batting (.313); Jay Bell was tied for third in triples (9), was fourth in hits (187), ninth in runs (102); Al Martin was tied for fifth in triples (8).

—by John Hunt, Scott Kauffman, Lisa Winston, Deron Snyder, Matt Young

Team directory

▶**Owner:** Pittsburgh Baseball Associates
▶**General Manager:** Cam Bonifay
▶**Ballpark:**
Three Rivers Stadium
600 Stadium Circle, Pittsburgh, Pa.
412-323-5000
Capacity 47,972
Pay parking lot; $4
Public transportation available
Family and wheelchair sections, ramps, guest relations
▶**Team publications:**
Yearbook, scorecard, and *Info Guide*
▶**TV, radio broadcast stations:**
KDKA 1020 AM, KDKA Channel 2, TCI Cable, KLB Sports Network
▶**Camps and/or clinics:**
Camp Bradenton, 412-323-5089
▶**Spring Training:**
McKechnie Field
Bradenton, Fla.
Capacity 6,562
813-748-4610
Private Instruction Baseball Clinic

PITTSBURGH PIRATES 1993 final stats

Batting	BA	SLG	OB	G	AB	R	H	TB	2B	3B	HR	RBI	BB	SO	SB	CS	E
Merced	.313	.443	.414	137	447	68	140	198	26	4	8	70	77	64	3	3	10
Bell	.310	.437	.392	154	604	102	187	264	32	9	9	51	77	122	16	10	11
Van Slyke	.310	.449	.357	83	323	42	100	145	13	4	8	50	24	40	11	2	1
Slaught	.300	.440	.356	116	377	34	113	166	19	2	10	55	29	56	2	1	4
Goff	.297	.514	.422	14	37	5	11	19	2	0	2	6	8	9	0	0	1
King	.295	.406	.356	158	611	82	180	248	35	3	9	98	59	54	8	6	18
L.Smith	.286	.442	.422	94	199	35	57	88	5	4	6	24	43	42	9	4	2
Tomberlin	.286	.405	.333	27	42	4	12	17	0	1	1	5	2	14	0	0	0
Martin	.281	.481	.338	143	480	85	135	231	26	8	18	64	42	122	16	9	7
Clark	.271	.444	.358	110	277	43	75	123	11	2	11	46	38	58	1	0	6
Garcia	.269	.399	.316	141	546	77	147	218	25	5	12	47	31	67	18	11	11
Foley	.253	.366	.287	86	194	18	49	71	11	1	3	22	11	26	0	0	5
Shelton	.250	.542	.333	15	24	3	6	13	1	0	2	7	3	3	0	0	1
Young	.236	.343	.300	141	449	38	106	154	24	3	6	47	36	82	2	2	3
McClendon	.221	.326	.306	88	181	21	40	59	11	1	2	19	23	17	0	3	3
Pennyfeather	.206	.235	.206	21	34	4	7	8	1	0	0	2	0	6	0	1	0
Bullett	.200	.273	.237	23	55	2	11	15	0	2	0	4	3	15	3	2	0
LaValliere	.200	.200	.200	1	5	0	1	1	0	0	0	0	0	0	0	0	0
Prince	.196	.307	.272	66	179	14	35	55	14	0	2	24	13	38	1	1	5
Wehner	.143	.143	.268	29	35	3	5	5	0	0	0	0	6	10	0	0	0
Wilson	.143	.143	.143	10	14	0	2	2	0	0	0	0	0	9	0	0	1
Aude	.115	.154	.148	13	26	1	3	4	1	0	0	4	1	7	0	0	1
Cummings	.111	.139	.195	13	36	5	4	5	1	0	0	3	4	9	0	0	0
Womack	.083	.083	.185	15	24	5	2	2	0	0	0	0	3	3	2	0	1

Pitching	W-L	ERA	G	GS	CG	GF	Sho	SV	IP	H	R	ER	HR	BB	SO
Dewey	1-2	2.36	21	0	0	17	0	7	26.2	14	8	7	0	10	14
Menendez	2-0	3.00	14	0	0	3	0	0	21	20	8	7	4	4	13
Johnston	2-4	3.38	33	0	0	16	0	2	53.1	38	20	20	7	19	31
Belinda	3-1	3.61	40	0	0	37	0	19	42.1	35	18	17	4	11	30
Toliver	1-0	3.74	12	0	0	3	0	0	21.2	20	10	9	2	8	14
Cooke	10-10	3.89	32	32	3	0	1	0	210.2	207	101	91	22	59	132
Hope	0-2	4.03	7	7	0	0	0	0	38	47	19	17	2	8	8
Minor	8-6	4.10	65	0	0	18	0	2	94.1	94	43	43	8	26	84
Wagner	8-8	4.27	44	17	1	9	1	2	141.1	143	72	67	15	42	114
Z.Smith	3-7	4.55	14	14	1	0	0	0	83	97	43	42	5	22	32
Tomlin	4-8	4.85	18	18	1	0	0	0	98.1	109	57	53	11	15	44
Ballard	4-1	4.86	25	5	0	4	0	0	53.2	70	31	29	3	15	16
Otto	3-4	5.03	28	8	0	7	0	0	68	85	40	38	9	28	30
Miceli	0-0	5.06	9	0	0	1	0	0	5.1	6	3	3	0	3	4
Neagle	3-5	5.31	50	7	0	13	0	1	81.1	82	49	48	10	37	73
Miller	0-0	5.40	3	2	0	1	0	0	10	15	6	6	2	2	2
Wakefield	6-11	5.61	24	20	3	1	2	0	128.1	145	83	80	14	75	59
Walk	13-14	5.68	32	32	3	0	0	0	187	214	121	118	23	70	80
Robertson	0-1	6.00	9	0	0	2	0	0	9	15	6	6	0	4	5
Petkovsek	3-0	6.96	26	0	0	8	0	0	32.1	43	25	25	7	9	14
Candelaria	0-3	8.24	24	0	0	6	0	1	19.2	25	19	18	2	9	17
Shouse	0-0	9.00	6	0	0	1	0	0	4	7	4	4	1	2	3
Moeller	1-0	9.92	10	0	0	3	0	0	16.1	26	20	18	2	7	13

1994 preliminary roster

PITCHERS (17)
Steve Cooke
Mariano DelosSantos
Mark Dewey
John Hope
Joel Johnston
Jeff McCurry
Dan Miceli
Blas Minor
Denny Neagle
Alejandro Pena
Roberto Ramirez
Zane Smith
Randy Tomlin
Paul Wagner
Tim Wakefield
Rick White
Mike Zimmerman

CATCHERS (4)
Angelo Encarnacion
Jerry Goff
Keith Osik
Don Slaught

INFIELDERS (10)
Rich Aude
Jay Bell
Michael Brown
Tom Foley
Carlos Garcia
Brian Hunter
Jeff King
Jose Sandoval
Tony Womack
Kevin Young

OUTFIELDERS (9)
Scott Bullett
Stanton Cameron
Dave Clark
Midre Cummings
Al Martin
Lloyd McClendon
Orlando Merced
William Pennyfeather
Andy Van Slyke

Games played by position

Player	G	C	1B	2B	3B	SS	OF
Aude	13	0	7	0	0	0	1
Bell	154	0	0	0	0	154	0
Bullett	23	0	0	0	0	0	19
Clark	110	0	0	0	0	0	91
Cummings	13	0	0	0	0	0	11
Foley	86	0	12	35	7	6	0
Garcia	141	0	0	140	0	3	0
Goff	14	14	0	0	0	0	0
King	158	0	0	2	156	2	0
LaValliere	1	1	0	0	0	0	0
Martin	143	0	0	0	0	0	136
McClendon	88	0	6	0	0	0	61
Merced	137	0	42	0	0	0	109
Pennyfeather	21	0	0	0	0	0	17
Prince	66	59	0	0	0	0	0
Shelton	15	0	2	0	0	0	6
Slaught	116	105	0	0	0	0	0
L. Smith	94	0	0	0	0	0	60
Tomberlin	27	0	0	0	0	0	7
Van Slyke	83	0	0	0	0	0	78
Wehner	29	0	0	3	3	0	13
Wilson	10	0	0	0	0	0	5
Womack	15	0	0	0	0	6	0
Young	141	0	135	0	6	0	0

Sick call: 1993 DL Report

Player	Days on the DL
John Candelaria	17
Tom Foley	16
Zane Smith	72
Randy Tomlin*	80
Andy VanSlyke	73
Paul Wagner	16

Two separate terms on Disabled List

Minor League Report

Class AAA: Buffalo finished at 70-72, second in the American Association Eastern Division. Russ Morman hit .320 with 22 homers and 77 RBI. Scott Bullett had 28 stolen bases. Roy Smith led the league with 16 wins. Tony Menendez had 24 saves. **Class AA:** Carolina finished at 74-67, second in the Southern League Eastern Division. Rich Aude hit .282 with 18 homers and 73 RBI. Midre Cummings hit .295. Daryl Ratcliff hit .284 and stole 29 bases. Tony Womack batted .304 with 21 stolen bases. Blaine Beatty was 7-3 with a 2.86 ERA. Danny Miceli had 17 saves. **Class A:** Salem finished at 61-79, last in the Carolina League Southern Division. Michael Brown hit .271 with 21 homers and 70 RBI. Ken Bonifay hit .277 with 18 homers and 60 RBI. Jeff Conger stole 24 bases. Tony Womack hit .299 with 28 stolen bases. Jon Farrell hit 20 homers. Jeff McCurry had 22 saves. Augusta finished at 59-82, last in the Sally League Southern Division. Jake Austin hit .294 with seven homers and 54 RBI. Dario Tena stole 39 bases. Jay Cranford led the club with 72 RBI. Dave Doornweerd had a 1.98 ERA. **Short-season:** Welland finished at 34-42, fifth in the New York-Penn League Stadler Division. Jermaine Allensworth hit .308 and stole 18 bases. Louis Collier hit .303. Mitch House had nine homers and 41 RBI. Jamison Nuttle had 10 saves and an 0.65 ERA. He struck out 43 in 27.2 innings. Bradenton finished at 21-38, last in the Gulf Coast League Western Division. Rayon Reid was 4-3 with a 1.74 ERA. Charles Peterson hit .303 and drove in 23 runs. Terrance Staton hit .357. John Ford did not allow a run in six games. Jason Johnson was 1-4 with a 2.33 ERA. Troy Mooney had a 1.75 ERA.

Tops in the organization

Batter	Club	Avg	G	AB	R	H	HR	RBI
Morman, Russ	Buf	.320	119	409	79	131	22	77
Womack, Tony	Car	.301	132	551	82	166	2	41
Aude, Rich	Car	.300	141	486	83	146	22	89
Austin, Jake	Aug	.294	123	449	71	132	7	54
Bullett, Scott	Buf	.287	110	408	62	117	1	30

Home Runs			Wins		
Aude, Rich	Car	22	Smith, Roy	Buf	15
Morman, Russ	Buf	22	Hope, John	Buf	11
Brown, Michael	Sal	21	Klamm, Ted	Aug	10
Farrell, Jon	Sal	20	Delossantos, Mar.	Car	10
Thomas, Keith	Car	19	Several players tied		9

RBI			Saves		
Aude, Rich	Car	89	Menendez, Tony	Buf	24
Morman, Russ	Buf	77	Pisciotta, Marc	Sal	24
Cranford, Jay	Aug	72	Mccurry, Jeff	Car	22
Brown, Michael	Sal	70	Miceli, Dan	Car	17
Goff, Jerry	Buf	69	Toliver, Fred	Buf	13

Stolen Bases			Strikeouts		
Womack, Tony	Car	49	Laplante, Michel	Sal	124
Tena, Dario	Aug	39	Doorneweerd, D.	Aug	117
Ratliff, Daryl	Car	29	Hancock, Lee	Buf	115
Espinosa, Ramon	Sal	28	Delossantos, Mar.	Car	114
Bullett, Scott	Buf	28	Klamm, Ted	Aug	113

Pitcher	Club	W-L	ERA	IP	H	BB	SO
Laplante, Michel	Sal	8-7	3.45	149	160	29	124
Hancock, Lee	Buf	9-9	3.48	166	160	46	115
Loaiza, Steve	Car	8-8	3.49	152	152	42	101
Beatty, Blaine	Buf	9-6	3.58	131	119	43	81
Doorneweerd, D.	Aug	3-13	3.65	148	130	74	117

Pittsburgh (1887-1993)

Runs: Most, career, all-time

1521	Honus Wagner, 1900-1917
1493	Paul Waner, 1926-1940
1416	Roberto Clemente, 1955-1972
1414	Max Carey, 1910-1926
1195	Willie Stargell, 1962-1982

Hits: Most, career, all-time

3000	Roberto Clemente, 1955-1972
2967	Honus Wagner, 1900-1917
2868	Paul Waner, 1926-1940
2416	Max Carey, 1910-1926
2416	Pie Traynor, 1920-1937

2B: Most, career, all-time

558	Paul Waner, 1926-1940
551	Honus Wagner, 1900-1917
440	Roberto Clemente, 1955-1972
423	Willie Stargell, 1962-1982
375	Max Carey, 1910-1926

3B: Most, career, all-time

232	Honus Wagner, 1900-1917
187	Paul Waner, 1926-1940
166	Roberto Clemente, 1955-1972
164	Pie Traynor, 1920-1937
156	Fred Clarke, 1900-1915

HR: Most, career, all-time

475	Willie Stargell, 1962-1982
301	Ralph Kiner, 1946-1953
240	Roberto Clemente, 1955-1972
176	BARRY BONDS, 1986-1992
166	Dave Parker, 1973-1983

RBI: Most, career, all-time

1540	Willie Stargell, 1962-1982
1475	Honus Wagner, 1900-1917
1305	Roberto Clemente, 1955-1972
1273	Pie Traynor, 1920-1937
1177	Paul Waner, 1926-1940

SB: Most, career, all-time

688	Max Carey, 1910-1926
639	Honus Wagner, 1900-1917
412	Omar Moreno, 1975-1982
312	Patsy Donovan, 1892-1899
271	Tommy Leach, 1900-1918

BB: Most, career, all-time

937	Willie Stargell, 1962-1982
918	Max Carey, 1910-1926
909	Paul Waner, 1926-1940
877	Honus Wagner, 1900-1917
795	Ralph Kiner, 1946-1953

BA: Highest, career, all-time

.340	Paul Waner, 1926-1940
.336	Kiki Cuyler, 1921-1927
.328	Honus Wagner, 1900-1917
.327	Matty Alou, 1966-1970
.324	Arky Vaughan, 1932-1941
.324	Elmer Smith, 1892-1901

Slug avg: Highest, career, all-time

.567	Ralph Kiner, 1946-1953
.529	Willie Stargell, 1962-1982
.513	Kiki Cuyler, 1921-1927
.512	Dick Stuart, 1958-1962
.503	BARRY BONDS, 1986-1992

Games started: Most, career, all-time

477	Bob Friend, 1951-1965
371	Wilbur Cooper, 1912-1924
364	Vern Law, 1950-1967
354	Babe Adams, 1907-1926
299	Sam Leever, 1898-1910

Saves: Most, career, all-time

188	Roy Face, 1953-1968
158	Kent Tekulve, 1974-1985
133	Dave Giusti, 1970-1976
61	STAN BELINDA, 1989-1993
59	Al McBean, 1961-1970

Shutouts: Most, career, all-time

44	Babe Adams, 1907-1926
39	Sam Leever, 1898-1910
35	Bob Friend, 1951-1965
33	Wilbur Cooper, 1912-1924
29	Lefty Leifield, 1905-1912

Wins: Most, career, all-time

202	Wilbur Cooper, 1912-1924
194	Babe Adams, 1907-1926
194	Sam Leever, 1898-1910
191	Bob Friend, 1951-1965
168	Deacon Phillippe, 1900-1911

K: Most, career, all-time

1682	Bob Friend, 1951-1965
1652	Bob Veale, 1962-1972
1191	Wilbur Cooper, 1912-1924
1159	JOHN CANDELARIA, 1975-1993
1092	Vern Law, 1950-1967

Win pct: Highest, career, all-time

.683	Nick Maddox, 1907-1910
.667	Jesse Tannehill, 1897-1902
.660	Sam Leever, 1898-1910
.659	Vic Willis, 1906-1909
.656	Emil Yde, 1924-1927

ERA: Lowest, career, all-time

2.08	Vic Willis, 1906-1909
2.38	Lefty Leifield, 1905-1912
2.47	Sam Leever, 1898-1910
2.50	Deacon Phillippe, 1900-1911
2.60	Bob Harmon, 1914-1918

Runs: Most, season

148	Jake Stenzel, 1894
145	Patsy Donovan, 1894
144	Kiki Cuyler, 1925
142	Paul Waner, 1928
140	Max Carey, 1922

Hits: Most, season

237	Paul Waner, 1927
234	Lloyd Waner, 1929
231	Matty Alou, 1969
223	Lloyd Waner, 1927
223	Paul Waner, 1928

2B: Most, season

62	Paul Waner, 1932
53	Paul Waner, 1936
50	Paul Waner, 1928
47	Adam Comorosky, 1930
45	Dave Parker, 1979
45	ANDY VAN SLYKE, 1992
45	Honus Wagner, 1900

3B: Most, season

36	Chief Wilson, 1912
28	Harry Davis, 1897
27	Jimmy Williams, 1899
26	Kiki Cuyler, 1925
23	Adam Comorosky, 1930
23	Elmer Smith, 1893

HR: Most, season

54	Ralph Kiner, 1949
51	Ralph Kiner, 1947
48	Willie Stargell, 1971
47	Ralph Kiner, 1950
44	Willie Stargell, 1973

RBI: Most, season

131	Paul Waner, 1927
127	Ralph Kiner, 1947
127	Ralph Kiner, 1949
126	Honus Wagner, 1901
125	Willie Stargell, 1971

SB: Most, season

96	Omar Moreno, 1980
77	Omar Moreno, 1979
71	Omar Moreno, 1978
71	Billy Sunday, 1888
70	Frank Taveras, 1977

BB: Most, season

137	Ralph Kiner, 1951
127	BARRY BONDS, 1992
122	Ralph Kiner, 1950
119	Elbie Fletcher, 1940
118	Elbie Fletcher, 1941
118	Arky Vaughan, 1936

BA: Highest, season

.385	Arky Vaughan, 1935
.381	Honus Wagner, 1900
.380	Paul Waner, 1927
.374	Jake Stenzel, 1895
.373	Paul Waner, 1936

Slug avg: Highest, season

.658	Ralph Kiner, 1949
.646	Willie Stargell, 1973
.639	Ralph Kiner, 1947
.628	Willie Stargell, 1971
.627	Ralph Kiner, 1951

Games started: Most, season

55	Ed Morris, 1888
53	Mark Baldwin, 1892
50	Mark Baldwin, 1891
50	Jim Galvin, 1888
50	Pink Hawley, 1895
50	Frank Killen, 1896
42	Bob Friend, 1956 (12)

Saves: Most, season

34	JIM GOTT, 1988
31	Kent Tekulve, 1978
31	Kent Tekulve, 1979
30	Dave Giusti, 1971
28	Roy Face, 1962

Shutouts: Most, season

8	Babe Adams, 1920
8	Jack Chesbro, 1902
8	Lefty Leifield, 1906
8	Al Mamaux, 1915
7	Steve Blass, 1968
7	Wilbur Cooper, 1917
7	Sam Leever, 1903
7	Bob Veale, 1965
7	Vic Willis, 1908

Wins: Most, season

36	Frank Killen, 1893
31	Pink Hawley, 1895
30	Frank Killen, 1896
29	Ed Morris, 1888
28	Jack Chesbro, 1902
28	Jim Galvin, 1887

K: Most, season

276	Bob Veale, 1965
250	Bob Veale, 1964
229	Bob Veale, 1966
213	Bob Veale, 1969
199	Larry McWilliams, 1983

Win pct: Highest, season

.842	Emil Yde, 1924
.824	Jack Chesbro, 1902
.806	Howie Camnitz, 1909
.800	JOHN CANDELARIA, 1977
.800	Ed Doheny, 1902
.800	Sam Leever, 1905

ERA: Lowest, season

1.56	Howie Camnitz, 1908
1.62	Howie Camnitz, 1909
1.66	Sam Leever, 1907
1.73	Vic Willis, 1906
1.87	Lefty Leifield, 1906

Most pinch-hit homers, season

3	Ham Hyatt, 1913
3	Al Rubeling, 1944
3	Bob Skinner, 1956
3	Dick Stuart, 1959
3	Gene Freese, 1964
3	Jose Pagan, 1969
3	Willie Stargell, 1982

Most pinch-hit, homers, career

7	Willie Stargell 1962-1982

Most consecutive games, batting safely

27	Jimmy Williams, 1899
26	Danny O'Connell, 1953

Most consecutive scoreless innings

41	Jack Chesbro, 1902
36	Ed Morris, 1888

No hit games

Nick Maddox, Pit vs Bro NL, 2-1; September 20, 1907.

Cliff Chambers, Pit at Bos NL, 3-0; May 6, 1951 (2nd game).

Harvey Haddix, Pit at Mil NL, 0-1; May 26, 1959 (lost on 1 hit in 13 innings after pitching 12 perfect innings).

Bob Moose, Pit at NY NL, 4-0; September 20, 1969.

Dock Ellis, Pit at SD NL, 2-0; June 12, 1970 (1st game).

JOHN CANDELARIA, Pit vs LA NL, 2-0; August 9, 1976.

Lefty Leifield, six innings, darkness, Pit at Phi NL, 8-0; September 26, 1906 (2nd game).

Howie Camnitz, five innings, agreement, Pit at NY NL, 1-0; August 23, 1907 (2nd game).

ACTIVE PLAYERS in caps.
Leader from franchise's current loction is included. If not in the top five, leader's rank is listed in parenthesis.

113

Florida Marlins

Traded from the cost-cutting San Diego Padres, Gary Sheffield hit 20 home runs (tied for Marlins lead).

by H. Darr Beiser, USA TODAY

1993 Marlins: Expansion team with potential

Despite a 64-98 season, 33 games out of first place, the Marlins helped erase the negative connotation attached to "expansion team." Before '93, expansion teams bumbled their way through the season. They were pathetic, a way for the rest of the league to puff up their records or break losing streaks.

But instead of fielding a team of aging has-beens, never-weres and younger never-will-be's, the Marlins front office gave its fans something to build on.

General manager Dave Dombrowski's cast of characters already has a patina of respectability, thanks to at least one young superstar and several other established or emerging players.

Third baseman Gary Sheffield was acquired when the Marlins packaged three promising pitching prospects to San Diego. Florida inked Sheffield to a four-year extension in September.

Bryan Harvey was acquired in the expansion draft when the Angels left the injured closer unprotected. His 45 saves shattered the existing record for saves by a reliever on an expansion team (16), he posted a 1.70 ERA, and he set a major league record by having a hand—via either win or save—in nearly 72 percent of his club's 64 wins.

Center fielder Chuck Carr didn't win the starting center field job on Opening Day—he batted under .200 in spring training—but within a few weeks, he was in the starting lineup and his 58 stolen bases not only led the league but marked the first time, since Pittsburgh's Omar Moreno, in 1979 that the NL's stolen base leader was neither an Expo nor a Cardinal.

Jeff Conine, who split his time between left field and first base, had perhaps the best offensive season of any Marlin, batting .292 with 12 homers and 79 RBI. He became the first expansion player to appear in 162 games, and is now second to Cal Ripken Jr. in consecutive games played. He went 4-for-4 in the first Marlins game.

Not all of the club's acquisitions made them look like geniuses. It seemed like a good public relations coup when they signed free agent Benito Santiago to a $7.2 million dollar contract for two years. He was a four-time all-star for San Diego and it was thought he would appeal to the large Hispanic contingent of fans in Miami. But Santiago hit just .230 and missed the end of the year with injuries. His vaunted defense also tailed off markedly.

Knuckleballer Charlie Hough, 45, earned the team's first win, striking out four in six innings. He also ended with an .032 batting average, becoming just the fourth player this century to fail to hit his age.

—by Lisa Winston

1994 Marlins: Preview

It's unlikely the Marlins will contend for a playoff berth in '94 even with the expanded format. But expansion fans don't look for immediate gratification. They look for an exciting young team to watch grow—all three of the Marlins' full-season farm teams posted winning records in 1993.

Class A High Desert was 85-52, winning the California League championship. Though some of the team stars were veterans, the team was also loaded with prospects. Class A Kane County was 75-62, featuring catcher of the future Charles Johnson, the club's No. 1 pick in 1992, who led the Midwest League in RBI and threw out 50 percent of opposing baserunners.

Don't look for too many new faces in the 1994 Marlins lineup. Big-name signings are unlikely, since they would mean sacrificing more prospects—the future of the team—especially under Dombrowski and Hughes, two of the best in the game in the area of finding and evaluating young talent.

—by Lisa Winston

1993 Marlins: Between the lines

▶**April 16:** Catcher Benito Santiago knew that Charlie Hough's knuckleball would make it difficult to maintain his record streak of 271 games without a passed ball. It took less than an inning: Ken Caminiti swung through a Hough knuckler that evaded Santiago's glove, and the rest is history.

▶**April 20:** Alex Arias hit his first major league home run.

▶**April 21:** Orestes Destrade hit his first home run of the season.

▶**April 26:** *Quote of the day*—The Reds' Bip Roberts on trying to hit a Hough knuckleball: "I've had better success hitting against a Whiffleball."

▶**May 1:** Jeff Conine hit his first major league homer, a grand slam.

▶**May 10:** The Marlins' first complete game turned out to be a defeat. Ryan Bowen went the distance but lost 1-0 to the Mets' Bret Saberhagen.

▶**May 12:** Chuck Carr's first major league home run was a grand slam as the Marlins beat the Expos 10-7.

▶**May 17:** *Quote of the day*—When the Marlins stranded 17 runners, one shy of the NL record, in a 10-3 loss, Phillies' first base host John Kruk said: "It was 'Meet the Marlins' night. Every one of them got on base."

▶**June 4:** Ironman Hough seemed ageless, shutting down San Diego 6-2 and adding his first hit since 1980.

▶**June 6:** Chris Hammond beat San Diego and became the first Florida pitcher to homer as his team completed its first three-game sweep.

▶**June 10:** *Milestone*—Bryan Harvey notched his 17th save in a 4-3 win against Pittsburgh to set a single-season record for saves by a pitcher on an expansion team; it had been set by Enrique Romo of Seattle in 1977.

▶**June 11:** The Marlins posted a club-record 21 hits—four of them coming from Dave Magadan—as they beat Pittsburgh 11-3.

▶**June 13:** The Marlins recorded a four-game sweep of the Pirates with a 5-2 win that gave them sole possession of fourth place in the NL East.

▶**June 16:** Backup catcher Mitch Lyden hit the second major league pitch he saw out of the park, becoming the 67th to homer in his first at-bat.

▶**June 20:** *Milestone*—Charlie Hough became the first pitcher ever to start 400 games and relieve in 400 games. He also became the second player to appear in 400 games in each league; Hoyt Wilhelm was the other.

▶**June 22:** Bryan Harvey stranded both of his inherited runners while notching his 21st save of the year, to continue his perfect record of leaving men on base. The Marlins' closer had inherited 11 runners and left all of them stranded.

▶**June 23:** The crowd of nearly 38,000—packed with a huge Cuban contingent—cheered as Cardinals' pitcher Rene Arocha, a Cuban defector, earned a win and collected his first major league hit.

▶**June 25:** New arrivals Gary Sheffield (acquired from the Padres in a trade) and rookie Darrell Whitmore (making his major league debut) each went 2-for-4 and drove in runs as the Marlins beat the Expos 3-1.

▶**June 26:** Hough got his first RBI since 1980.

▶**July 4:** Rob Natal finally collected the first three hits of his career—snapping an 0-for-18 major league slump and homering off John Smoltz—but the Marlins fell to Atlanta 4-3.

▶**July 17:** Jeff Conine had four hits and drove in three runs as the Marlins beat the Reds 6-3. It was Conine's second four-hit game of the season, the first coming on opening day.

▶**August 6:** Orestes Destrade's tie-breaking homer in the sixth inning was the game-winner as the Marlins edged the Phillies 4-3.

▶**August 8:** Henry Cotto was 2-for-4 with a homer, a double and two RBI as the Marlins eked out a 6-5 win against the Phillies.

▶**August 9:** Cubs' broadcaster Harry Caray got a huge ovation when he led the crowd at Joe Robbie Stadium in a rendition of *Take Me Out to the Ballgame* during the seventh inning stretch, a tradition usually saved for Wrigley Field.

▶**August 11:** Florida scored twice in the bottom of the ninth to beat the Cubs 12-11. It was the highest single-game run total in the Marlins' brief history.

▶**August 14:** Gary Sheffield had two homers, both two-run shots, as the Marlins blasted the Pirates 8-3.

▶**August 15:** Chuck Carr's team-record 15-game hitting streak was snapped in the Marlins' loss to Pittsburgh.

▶**August 20:** Dropped from third to sixth in the batting order to take some pressure off, Jeff Conine responded with a grand slam as the Marlins beat the Giants 5-4. It was his second slam of the season and helped the Marlins become the first team to beat San Francisco starter Bill Swift twice in '93.

▶**August 26:** Pitcher Richie Lewis drove in the winning run with a single in the 13th inning as the Marlins beat Houston 5-4. Manager Rene Lachemann had used all his position players, forcing Lewis to bat. Lewis, who had fanned in one at-bat this season, lined a Doug Jones fastball down the left field line to win the game.

▶**August 27:** Orestes Destrade hit two homers and drove in six runs to pace the Marlins to a 7-4 win against San Francisco.

▶**September 25:** So that's why they call it the senior circuit? Charlie Hough—who allowed two hits and an unearned run in a no-decision for Florida—at age 45 was older than 11 of the 30 players who participated in the Old Timers' Game prior to the Florida-St. Louis contest.

▶**September 30:** One day after signing a $22.45 million, four-year contract, Marlins' third baseman Gary Sheffield made three errors, two of which led to Expos' runs in Florida's 5-3 loss. Sheffield's ninth-inning boot led to Curtis

Pride's game-winning home run. Sheffield was booed loudly at Joe Robbie Stadium.

▶**October 3:** The Mets beat the Marlins, 9-2, in the final game of the season, but the Marlins came out ahead in the NL East—they finished in sixth place, five games up on the last-place Mets. *League leaders, pitching*—Bryan Harvey was third in saves (45). Though he didn't qualify as a league leader in other categories, he finished the season with a sparkling 1.70 ERA in 59 games (54 finished). *League leaders, batting*—Chuck Carr led the league in stolen bases (58).

—by John Hunt, Scott Kauffman, Lisa Winston, Deron Snyder, Matt Younger

Team directory

▶**Owner:** Wayne Huizenga
▶**General Manager:** David Dombrowski
▶**Ballpark:**
Joe Robbie Stadium
2267 N. W. 199th St., Miami Fla.
305-626-7400
Capacity 44,000
Parking available, over 14,000 spaces on site
Public transportation available
Wheelchair section, family section, alcohol-free section, ramps and elevators
▶**TV, radio broadcast stations:**
WBFS Channel 33, Sunshine Network, WQAM 560 AM (English), WCMQ 1210 AM (Spanish)
▶**Spring Training:**
Space Coast Station
Melbourne, Fla.
Capacity 7,500
407-633-9200

FLORIDA MARLINS 1993 final stats

Batting	BA	SLG	OB	G	AB	R	H	TB	2B	3B	HR	RBI	BB	SO	SB	CS	E
Lyden	.300	.600	.300	6	10	2	3	6	0	0	1	1	0	3	0	0	0
Cotto	.296	.415	.312	54	135	15	40	56	7	0	3	14	3	18	11	1	2
Sheffield	.294	.476	.361	140	494	67	145	235	20	5	20	73	47	64	17	5	34
Conine	.292	.403	.351	162	595	75	174	240	24	3	12	79	52	135	2	2	2
Magadan	.286	.392	.400	66	227	22	65	89	12	0	4	29	44	30	0	1	7
Barberie	.277	.371	.344	99	375	45	104	139	16	2	5	33	33	58	2	4	9
Arias	.269	.321	.344	96	249	27	67	80	5	1	2	20	27	18	1	1	6
Carr	.267	.330	.327	142	551	75	147	182	19	2	4	41	49	74	58	22	6
Weiss	.266	.308	.367	158	500	50	133	154	14	2	1	39	79	73	7	3	15
Destrade	.255	.406	.324	153	569	61	145	231	20	3	20	87	58	130	0	2	19
Renteria	.255	.327	.314	103	263	27	67	86	9	2	2	30	21	31	0	2	2
Carrillo	.255	.364	.281	24	55	4	14	20	6	0	0	3	1	7	0	0	0
Felix	.238	.397	.276	57	214	25	51	85	11	1	7	22	10	50	2	1	6
Santiago	.230	.380	.291	139	469	49	108	178	19	6	13	50	37	88	10	7	11
Natal	.214	.291	.273	41	117	3	25	34	4	1	1	6	6	22	1	0	0
Whitmore	.204	.300	.249	76	250	24	51	75	8	2	4	19	10	72	4	2	3
Pose	.195	.244	.233	15	41	0	8	10	2	0	0	3	2	4	0	2	0
Briley	.194	.282	.250	120	170	17	33	48	6	0	3	12	12	42	6	2	1
Fariss	.172	.310	.294	18	29	3	5	9	2	1	0	2	5	13	0	0	0
Polidor	.167	.333	.167	7	6	0	1	2	1	0	0	0	0	2	0	0	0
Berroa	.118	.147	.167	14	34	3	4	5	1	0	0	0	2	7	0	0	2
Everett	.105	.105	.150	11	19	0	2	2	0	0	0	0	1	9	1	0	1
Decker	.000	.000	.158	8	15	0	0	0	0	0	0	1	3	3	0	0	1
McGriff	.000	.000	.125	3	7	0	0	0	0	0	0	0	1	2	0	0	0
Wilson	.000	.000	.000	7	16	0	0	0	0	0	0	0	0	11	0	0	0

Pitching	W-L	ERA	G	GS	CG	GF	Sho	SV	IP	H	R	ER	HR	BB	SO
Harvey	1-5	1.70	59	0	0	54	0	45	69	45	14	13	4	13	73
Carpenter	0-1	2.89	29	0	0	9	0	0	37.1	29	15	12	1	13	26
Turner	4-5	2.91	55	0	0	26	0	0	68	55	23	22	7	26	59
Lewis	6-3	3.26	57	0	0	14	0	0	77.1	68	37	28	7	43	65
Aquino	6-8	3.42	38	13	0	5	0	0	110.2	115	43	42	6	40	67
Rodriguez	2-4	3.79	70	0	0	21	0	3	76	73	38	32	10	33	43
Rapp	4-6	4.02	16	16	1	0	0	0	94	101	49	42	7	39	57
Hough	9-16	4.27	34	34	0	0	0	0	204.1	202	109	97	20	71	126
Bowen	8-12	4.42	27	27	2	0	1	0	156.2	156	83	77	11	87	98
Armstrong	9-17	4.49	36	33	0	2	0	0	196.1	210	105	98	29	78	118
Hammond	11-12	4.66	32	32	1	0	0	0	191	207	106	99	18	66	108
Klink	0-2	5.02	59	0	0	10	0	0	37.2	37	22	21	0	24	22
Weathers	2-3	5.12	14	6	0	2	0	0	45.2	57	26	26	3	13	34
Johnstone	0-2	5.91	7	0	0	3	0	0	10.2	16	8	7	1	7	5
Corsi	0-2	6.64	15	0	0	6	0	0	20.1	28	15	15	1	10	7
Nen	1-0	7.02	15	1	0	2	0	0	33.1	35	28	26	5	20	27
McClure	1-1	7.11	14	0	0	1	0	0	6.1	13	5	5	2	5	6

1994 preliminary roster

PITCHERS (19)
Luis Aquino
Jack Armstrong
Ryan Bowen
Javier Delahoya
Brian Drahman
Chris Hammond
Bryan Harvey
Joe Klink
Richie Lewis
Kurt Miller
Jeff Mutis
Mike Myers
Robb Nen
Pat Rapp
Rich Rodriguez
Matt Turner
David Weathers
Matt Whisenant
Kip Yaughn

CATCHERS (3)
Bob Natal
Greg O'Halloran
Benito Santiago

INFIELDERS (8)
Alex Arias
Bret Barberie
Tim Clark
Greg Colbrunn
Orestes Destrade
Dave Magadan
Ramon Martinez
Rick Renteria

OUTFIELDERS (9)
Chuck Carr
Matias Carrillo
Jeff Conine
Carl Everett
Kerwin Moore
Gary Sheffield
Jesus Tavarez
Darrell Whitmore
Nigel Wilson

Games played by position

Player	G	C	1B	2B	3B	SS	OF
Arias	96	0	0	30	22	18	0
Barberie	99	0	0	97	0	0	0
Berroa	14	0	0	0	0	0	9
Briley	120	0	0	0	0	0	67
Carr	142	0	0	0	0	0	139
Carrillo	24	0	0	0	0	0	16
Conine	162	0	43	0	0	0	147
Cotto	54	0	0	0	0	0	46
Decker	8	5	0	0	0	0	0
Destrade	153	0	152	0	0	0	0
Everett	11	0	0	0	0	0	8
Fariss	18	0	0	0	0	0	8
Felix	57	0	0	0	0	0	52
Lyden	6	2	0	0	0	0	0
Magadan	66	0	2	0	63	0	0
McGriff	3	3	0	0	0	0	0
Natal	41	38	0	0	0	0	0
Polidor	7	0	0	1	1	0	0
Pose	15	0	0	0	0	0	10
Renteria	103	0	0	45	25	0	1
Santiago	139	136	0	0	0	0	1
Sheffield	140	0	0	0	133	0	0
Weiss	158	0	0	0	0	153	0
Whitmore	76	0	0	0	0	0	69
Wilson	7	0	0	0	0	0	3

Sick call: 1993 DL Report

Player	Days on the DL
Luis Aquino	30
Bret Barberie*	68
Chuck Carr	17
Jim Corsi*	115
Steve Decker	139
Bob Natal	21

Two separate terms on Disabled List

Minor League Report

Class AAA: Edmonton finished at 72-69, third in the Pacific Coast League Northern Division. Terry McGriff hit .345 with seven homers and 55 RBI. Dave Weathers was 11-4 with a 3.83 ERA. John Johnstone struck out 126. **Class A:** High Desert finished at 85-52, winning both halves of the California League Southern Division and beating Modesto in five games for the league title. Tim Clark won the batting crown and league MVP, hitting .363 with 17 homers and 126 RBI. John Toale hit 28 homers and 125 RBI. Bryn Kosco hit 27 homers and 121 RBI. Kerwin Moore stole 71 bases to lead the league. . . . Kane County finished at 75-62, fourth in the Midwest League Northern Division. Charles Johnson led the league in RBI with 94. Vic Darensbourg had 16 saves. Reynol Mendoza was 12-5 with a 2.86 ERA and 153 strikeouts. **Short-season:** Elmira finished at 31-43, third in the New York-Penn League Pinckney Division. Bill McMillon hit .304 with six homers and 35 RBI. Rich Seminoff had 11 homers. Ron Brown had 55 RBI. Paul Thornton was 3-5 with a 2.26 ERA. . . . Kissimmee finished at 32-28, second in the Gulf Coast League Northern Division. Maximo Rodriguez hit .326 with 29 RBI. Alex Aranzamendi hit .309 with 31 RBI. Brendan Kingman had 37 RBI. Will Cunnane had 64 strikeouts.

Tops in the organization

Batter	Club	Avg	G	AB	R	H	HR	RBI
Clark, Tim	Hd	.363	128	510	109	185	17	126
Mcgriff, Terry	Edm	.345	105	339	62	117	7	55
Delossantos, Luis	Edm	.311	125	425	49	132	2	66
Kosco, Bryn	Hd	.307	121	450	96	138	27	121
Pedrique, Al	Edm	.305	121	403	54	123	2	42

Home Runs			Wins		
Toale, John	Hd	28	Person, Robert	Hd	12
Kosco, Bryn	Hd	27	Mendoza, Reynol	Knc	12
Johnson, Charles	Knc	19	Weathers, Dave	Edm	11
Wilson, Nigel	Edm	17	Several players tied		9
Clark, Tim	Hd	17	**Saves**		
RBI			Pettit, Doug	Knc	17
Clark, Tim	Hd	126	Darensbourg, Victor	Hd	16
Toale, John	Hd	125	Whitten, Mike	Hd	13
Kosco, Bryn	Hd	121	Turner, Matt	Edm	10
Johnson, Charles	Knc	94	Gleaton, Jerry Don	Edm	7
Pridy, Todd	Knc	75	**Strikeouts**		
Stolen Bases			Mendoza, Reynol	Knc	153
Moore, Kerwin	Hd	71	Carrasco, Hector	Knc	127
Tavarez, Jesus	Hd	47	Johnstone, John	Edm	126
Martinez, Ramon	Hd	46	Petersen, Matthew	Knc	118
Everett, Carl	Edm	36	Weathers, Dave	Edm	117
Wilson, Pookie	Knc	34			

Pitcher	Club	W-L	ERA	IP	H	BB	SO
Mendoza, Reynol	Knc	12-5	2.86	164	129	45	153
Leahy, Pat	Knc	8-11	3.22	140	124	43	106
Weathers, Dave	Edm	11-4	3.83	141	150	47	117
Parisotto, Barry	Hd	6-5	4.03	118	137	34	92
Carrasco, Hector	Knc	6-12	4.11	149	153	76	127

Florida (1993)

Runs: Most, career, all-time

75	CHUCK CARR, 1993	
75	JEFF CONINE, 1993	
61	ORESTES DESTRADE, 1993	
50	WALT WEISS, 1993	
49	BENITO SANTIAGO, 1993	

Hits: Most, career, all-time

174	JEFF CONINE, 1993
147	CHUCK CARR, 1993
145	ORESTES DESTRADE, 1993
133	WALT WEISS, 1993
108	BENITO SANTIAGO, 1993

2B: Most, career, all-time

24	JEFF CONINE, 1993
20	ORESTES DESTRADE, 1993
19	CHUCK CARR, 1993
19	BENITO SANTIAGO, 1993
16	BRET BARBERIE, 1993

3B: Most, career, all-time

6	BENITO SANTIAGO, 1993
3	JEFF CONINE, 1993
3	ORESTES DESTRADE, 1993
3	GARY SHEFFIELD, 1993
2	BRET BARBERIE, 1993
2	CHUCK CARR, 1993
2	RICH RENTERIA, 1993
2	WALT WEISS, 1993
2	DARRELL WHITMORE, 1993

HR: Most, career, all-time

20	ORESTES DESTRADE, 1993
13	BENITO SANTIAGO, 1993
12	JEFF CONINE, 1993
10	GARY SHEFFIELD, 1993
5	BRET BARBERIE, 1993

RBI: Most, career, all-time

87	ORESTES DESTRADE, 1993
79	JEFF CONINE, 1993
50	BENITO SANTIAGO, 1993
41	CHUCK CARR, 1993
39	WALT WEISS, 1993

SB: Most, career, all-time

58	CHUCK CARR, 1993
12	GARY SHEFFIELD, 1993
10	BENITO SANTIAGO, 1993
7	WALT WEISS, 1993
6	GREG BRILEY, 1993

BB: Most, career, all-time

79	WALT WEISS, 1993
58	ORESTES DESTRADE, 1993
52	JEFF CONINE, 1993
49	CHUCK CARR, 1993
37	BENITO SANTIAGO, 1993

BA: Highest, career, all-time

.292	JEFF CONINE, 1993
.267	CHUCK CARR, 1993
.266	WALT WEISS, 1993
.255	ORESTES DESTRADE, 1993
.230	BENITO SANTIAGO, 1993

Slug avg: Highest, career, all-time

.406	ORESTES DESTRADE, 1993
.403	JEFF CONINE, 1993
.380	BENITO SANTIAGO, 1993
.330	CHUCK CARR, 1993
.308	WALT WEISS, 1993

Games started: Most, career, all-time

34	CHARLIE HOUGH, 1993
33	JACK ARMSTRONG, 1993
32	CHRIS HAMMOND, 1993
27	RYAN BOWEN, 1993
16	PAT RAPP, 1993

Saves: Most, career, all-time

45	BRYAN HARVEY, 1993
2	TREVOR HOFFMAN, 1993
1	RICH RODRIGUEZ, 1993

Shutouts: Most, career, all-time

1	RYAN BOWEN, 1993

Wins: Most, career, all-time

11	CHRIS HAMMOND, 1993
9	JACK ARMSTRONG, 1993
9	CHARLIE HOUGH, 1993
8	RYAN BOWEN, 1993
6	LUIS AQUINO, 1993
6	RICHIE LEWIS, 1993

K: Most, career, all-time

126	CHARLIE HOUGH, 1993
118	JACK ARMSTRONG, 1993
108	CHRIS HAMMOND, 1993
98	RYAN BOWEN, 1993
73	BRYAN HARVEY, 1993

Win pct: Highest, career, all-time

.478	CHRIS HAMMOND, 1993

ERA: Lowest, career, all-time

4.27	CHARLIE HOUGH, 1993
4.49	JACK ARMSTRONG, 1993
4.66	CHRIS HAMMOND, 1993

Runs: Most, season

75	CHUCK CARR, 1993
75	JEFF CONINE, 1993
61	ORESTES DESTRADE, 1993
50	WALT WEISS, 1993
49	BENITO SANTIAGO, 1993

Hits: Most, season

174	JEFF CONINE, 1993
147	CHUCK CARR, 1993
145	ORESTES DESTRADE, 1993
133	WALT WEISS, 1993
108	BENITO SANTIAGO, 1993

2B: Most, season

24	JEFF CONINE, 1993
20	ORESTES DESTRADE, 1993
19	CHUCK CARR, 1993
19	BENITO SANTIAGO, 1993
16	BRET BARBERIE, 1993

3B: Most, season

6	BENITO SANTIAGO, 1993
3	JEFF CONINE, 1993
3	ORESTES DESTRADE, 1993
3	GARY SHEFFIELD, 1993
2	BRET BARBERIE, 1993
2	CHUCK CARR, 1993
2	RICH RENTERIA, 1993
2	WALT WEISS, 1993
2	DARRELL WHITMORE, 1993

HR: Most, season

20	ORESTES DESTRADE, 1993
13	BENITO SANTIAGO, 1993
12	JEFF CONINE, 1993
10	GARY SHEFFIELD, 1993
5	BRET BARBERIE, 1993

RBI: Most, season

87	ORESTES DESTRADE, 1993
79	JEFF CONINE, 1993
50	BENITO SANTIAGO, 1993
41	CHUCK CARR, 1993
39	WALT WEISS, 1993

SB: Most, season

58	CHUCK CARR, 1993
12	GARY SHEFFIELD, 1993
10	BENITO SANTIAGO, 1993
7	WALT WEISS, 1993
6	GREG BRILEY, 1993

BB: Most, season

79	WALT WEISS, 1993
58	ORESTES DESTRADE, 1993
52	JEFF CONINE, 1993
49	CHUCK CARR, 1993
37	BENITO SANTIAGO, 1993

BA: Highest, season

.292	JEFF CONINE, 1993
.267	CHUCK CARR, 1993
.266	WALT WEISS, 1993
.255	ORESTES DESTRADE, 1993
.230	BENITO SANTIAGO, 1993

Slug avg: Highest, season

.406	ORESTES DESTRADE, 1993
.403	JEFF CONINE, 1993
.380	BENITO SANTIAGO, 1993
.330	CHUCK CARR, 1993
.308	WALT WEISS, 1993

Games started: Most, season

34	CHARLIE HOUGH, 1993
33	JACK ARMSTRONG, 1993
32	CHRIS HAMMOND, 1993
27	RYAN BOWEN, 1993
16	PAT RAPP, 1993

Saves: Most, season

45	BRYAN HARVEY, 1993
2	TREVOR HOFFMAN, 1993
1	RICH RODRIGUEZ, 1993

Shutouts: Most, season

1	RYAN BOWEN, 1993

Wins: Most, season

11	CHRIS HAMMOND, 1993
9	JACK ARMSTRONG, 1993
9	CHARLIE HOUGH, 1993
8	RYAN BOWEN, 1993
6	LUIS AQUINO, 1993
6	RICHIE LEWIS, 1993

K: Most, season

126	CHARLIE HOUGH, 1993
118	JACK ARMSTRONG, 1993
108	CHRIS HAMMOND, 1993
98	RYAN BOWEN, 1993
73	BRYAN HARVEY, 1993

Win pct: Highest, season

.478	CHRIS HAMMOND, 1993

ERA: Lowest, season

4.27	CHARLIE HOUGH, 1993
4.49	JACK ARMSTRONG, 1993
4.66	CHRIS HAMMOND, 1993

Most pinch-hit homers, season

None

Most pinch-hit homers, career

None

Most consecutive games, batting safely

15	BRET BARBERIE, 1993
15	CHUCK CARR, 1993

Most consecutive scoreless innings

17	RYAN BOWEN, 1993

No hit games

None

New York Mets

by Robert Deutsch, *USA TODAY*

Anthony Young lost 27 consecutive games over the 1992-1993 seasons, a major league record.

1993 Mets: Don't even ask how bad it can get

Last year the New York Mets turned into the New York Mess. Never mind that they were considered a favorite to win the NL East. Never mind that their batting order included Vince Coleman, Tony Fernandez, Howard Johnson, Bobby Bonilla and Eddie Murray, or a rotation featuring Dwight Gooden, Bret Saberhagen, Sid Fernandez, Frank Tanana and Pete Schourek. Or that John Franco, one of the league's best closers, was there to finish it off.

What happened was worse than even their enemies could have imagined: 103 losses and a home in the cellar. Dead last. They had to sweep a three-game set against the Marlins to finish just five games behind the expansion team.

It was tough for everyone involved. Reporters entered a war zone when they went into the Mets' clubhouse. The players used everything from from fists to firecrackers to spewing bleach, and the press had to stay alert just to avoid hurt, harm or danger. Manager Jeff Torborg and GM Al Harazin were both gone by the end of May.

A low point was reached in July when Coleman lit an explosive near a group of fans outside the parking lot at Dodger Stadium, injuring a 2-year-old girl. He'll never be in a Mets uniform again.

One of the few bright spots was Bobby Bonilla, who rebounded from an off season and hit .265, 34 HR (career high) and 87 RBI—despite missing most of September with a shoulder injury. Eddie Murray hit .285 (27 HR, 100 RBI—team-high). Second baseman Jeff Kent had 21 HR and 80 RBI.

There wasn't much good news about pitching. Anthony Young set a major-league record by losing 27 consecutive games (dating back to '92). Saberhagen was a bust again, 7-7 (3.29 ERA). Fernandez missed time with knee surgery and a stiff shoulder. Gooden appeared close to his old self at times, but a tired shoulder led to his shutdown, 12-15 (3.45 ERA). They had hoped Schourek would develop as a fifth starter, but he wasn't up to the task (5-12, 5.96 ERA). And Franco, recovering from elbow surgery, had his worst season yet (10 saves).

Manager Dallas Green had little impact on the club after he took over for Torborg. A noted disciplinarian and no-nonsense manager, he admitted there was only so much he could do with the motley crew he inherited.

Discouraged by the worst season since 1967, fans stayed away. Shea Stadium turned into a ghost town. During the home finale, with 17,567 in paid attendance, co-owner Nelson Doubleday walked through the upper deck and invited fans to move to the field boxes. But the way the Mets played, it was an offer they could easily refuse.

—*by Deron Snyder*

1994 Mets: Preview

After sifting through the wreckage, Dallas Green and GM Joe McIlvaine must begin a massive rebuilding program. McIlvaine believes the Mets can return to the top as quickly as they fell to the bottom. His first order of business will be getting a first baseman to replace Eddie Murray—either Bonilla or a newcomer. The infield's only stable position is second base, where Jeff Kent will return. With Howard Johnson now in a Rockies' uniform, third base is open, as is shortstop. The Mets will likely look outside of their organization.

Catching is another problem, and so is pitching. Todd Hundley is a light hitter and Gooden has seen his best years. Finally, Saberhagen's New York experience has been utterly forgettable, something the Mets will remember as he begins a three-year, $20 million extension this season.

—*by Deron Snyder*

1993 Mets: Between the lines

▶**April 25:** Anthony Young lost his 16th consecutive game (dating back to April 1992) on replacement catcher Charlie O'Brien's throwing error that let the winning run score.

▶**May 7:** Dwight Gooden cut his ERA to 2.13 with his 23rd career shutout.

▶**May 10:** *Milestone*—Eddie Murray moved into 24th place on the all-time RBI list.

▶**May 13:** *Milestone*—Murray moved into a tie for 22nd place on the all-time RBI list (with Harmon Killebrew and Rogers Hornsby).

▶**May 17:** Targeting Torborg, Shea Stadium fans issued their first "Jeff Must Go" chant. *Quote of the day*—Second baseman Jeff Kent on the Mets' miserable record: "It's tough. We're in a serious New York pothole right now."

▶**May 19:** Bobby Bonilla's two-run homer in the 10th beat the Pirates 6-4 in Jeff Torborg's final game as manager; Torborg was replaced by Dallas Green less than 30 minutes later.

▶**May 22:** Gooden turned in a vintage performance on the mound, outhitting every member of the Braves' lineup and blasting his sixth career home run.

▶**June 2:** Gooden struck out six in seven innings, went 2-for-4, and scored a pair of runs in the Mets' 11-3 rout of the Cubs.

▶**June 14:** Frank Tanana scored the first run of his 20-year major-league career, and limited the Braves to one run in seven innings. He struck out eight and walked two in his 237th career victory, tying Waite Hoyt for 48th place on the all-time win list.

▶**June 22:** General manager Al Harazin resigned. Then manager Dallas Green was ejected. Finally, Anthony Young suffered his 23rd loss in a row to tie the major league record.

▶**June 27:** *Milestone*—Anthony Young pitched his 24th consecutive loss, a new major league record for futility.

▶**June 30:** The Mets won two in a row for the first time since April 16-17—a span of 65 games—as they beat the Marlins 7-1. *Quote of the day*—Dallas Green on the Mets first back-to-back wins: "Two-peat. And we got Doc (Gooden) coming. Maybe three tomorrow!"

▶**July 1:** Despite the complete-game loss to the Marlins, the day wasn't a total washout for Mets' starter Dwight Gooden—he hit his second homer of the year and the seventh of his career to pass Tom Seaver for the franchise record for home runs by a pitcher. In fact, Gooden's .279 batting average was the second-highest of all the Mets' starters that day—only reserve outfielder Joe Orsulak's .297 was better.

▶**July 3:** Rookie Jeromy Burnitz had three hits—including a homer—and had four RBI in the Mets' 6-3 win against San Francisco.

▶**July 17:** Frank Tanana no-hit the Giants—until Barry Bonds homered with two out in the seventh inning—and earned the win in a 3-1 Mets victory against the Giants. The 40-year-old Tanana hit Will Clark with a pitch in the first, then retired 18 consecutive batters before serving up Bonds' drive.

▶**July 18:** Dave Gallagher hit a pinch-hit grand slam in the ninth inning of New York's 12-6 win in San Francisco. It was the first career grand slam for Gallagher, who has just 11 home runs in seven seasons. Second baseman Jeff Kent hit a pair of solo homers.

▶**July 21:** *Milestone*—Eddie Murray hit his 427th home run, moving him past Billy Williams into 21st place, second among active players. (Dave Winfield is first.)

▶**July 22:** Murray hit two home runs to lead the Mets to a 10-5 win against the Dodgers. It was the 25th multi-homer game of Murray's career. Meanwhile, Howard Johnson suffered two chip fractures and a tear in his right thumb while sliding into second base and was expected to be out for the season.

▶**July 28:** *At last!* Anthony Young finally snapped his record 27-game losing streak despite allowing an unearned run in the ninth.

▶**July 29:** Geriatric Park II: Senior citzens were charged a dollar for the afternoon game between the Mets and Marlins at Shea Stadium. Appropriately, 45-year-old knuckleballer Charlie Hough outdueled 40-year-old Frank Tanana in a 2-1 Marlins win.

▶**August 5:** Jeromy Burnitz set a Mets' rookie RBI record by hitting a grand slam, doubling, and singling twice.

▶**August 14:** Tim Bogar, a late replacement for Jeff Kent at second base, hit two homers—one inside-the-park—and two doubles to lead the Mets to a 9-5 win against the Phillies. His 12 total bases were one short of the club record.

▶**August 15:** Bogar was back on the bench; he sprained his left hand sliding into home on his inside-the-park home run the night before.

▶**August 16:** Sid Fernandez struck out seven Reds in 7 1/3 innings to earn his first win since April 14. He also singled in the go-ahead run.

▶**August 18:** Frank Tanana hit his first career triple, a bases-loaded shot in a 12-2 rout of Cincinnati.

▶**August 23:** Dwight Gooden was ejected for the first time in his career in New York's 6-2 loss to the Reds. Gooden hit Cincinnati rookie Brian Koelling leading off the third inning and was booted by umpire Gary Darling. Darling felt Gooden's pitch was in retaliation for Reds starter Jose Rijo's plunking of Mets catcher Charlie O'Brien the previous half inning.

▶**August 25:** The New York Mets became the first team to be mathematically eliminated with a 4-1 loss to Cincinnati.

▶**August 26:** *Milestone*—Eddie Murray hit his 20th homer of the season in the Mets' win. It was the 14th time in his 17-year career Murray reached that plateau. The homer was his 434th , good for 21st place all-time.

▶**September 11:** *Quote of the day*— Mets reliever John Franco, booed during his 4-3 loss to the Cubs, his third in a row: "I lost three in a row and I got booed. Anthony Young lost 27 in a row and he got cheered."

▶**October 3:** Pinch-hitting for the first time in '93, Dwight Gooden helped the Mets finish the season with a six-game winning streak. Nevertheless, they finished dead last, 38 games behind the Phillies. *League leaders, pitching—* Dwight Gooden was tied for second in complete games (7). *League leaders, batting—*Bobby Bonilla was tied for seventh in home runs (34) and was seventh in slugging percentage (.522); Eddie Murray was tied for ninth in RBI (100); Vince Coleman was fifth in triples (8) and ninth in stolen bases (38).

—*by John Hunt, Scott Kauffman, Lisa Winston, Deron Snyder, Matt Young*

Team directory

▶**Owners:** Fred Wilpon and Nelson Doubleday
▶**President of Baseball Operations:** Joseph McIlvaine
▶**Ballpark:**
William A. Shea Municipal Stadium
126th Street and Roosevelt Avenue, Flushing, N.Y.
718-507-METS
Capacity 55,601
Parking for 6,000 cars; $5
Public transportation available
Family and wheelchair sections, ramps, elevators
▶**Team publications:**
Inside Pitch, yearbook, scorecard, press guide
919-688-0218
▶**TV, radio broadcast stations:**
WFAN 660 AM, WWOR Channel 9, Sportschannel
▶**Camps and/or clinics:**
Ulti-Met Week, 800-525-METS
▶**Spring Training:**
St. Lucie County Stadium
Port St. Lucie, Fla.
Capacity 7,347
407-871-2121

NEW YORK METS 1993 final stats

Batting	BA	SLG	OB	G	AB	R	H	TB	2B	3B	HR	RBI	BB	SO	SB	CS	E
Murray	.285	.467	.325	154	610	77	174	285	28	1	27	100	40	61	2	2	18
Orsulak	.284	.399	.331	134	409	59	116	163	15	4	8	35	28	25	5	4	5
Coleman	.279	.375	.316	92	373	64	104	140	14	8	2	25	21	58	38	13	3
Gallagher	.274	.443	.338	99	201	34	55	89	12	2	6	28	20	18	1	1	0
Kent	.270	.446	.320	140	496	65	134	221	24	0	21	80	30	88	4	4	22
Bonilla	.265	.522	.352	139	502	81	133	262	21	3	34	87	72	96	3	3	17
Landrum	.263	.316	.263	22	19	2	5	6	1	0	0	1	0	5	0	0	0
McKnight	.256	.323	.311	105	164	19	42	53	3	1	2	13	13	31	0	0	10
O'Brien	.255	.378	.312	67	188	15	48	71	11	0	4	23	14	14	1	1	5
Thompson	.250	.444	.302	80	288	34	72	128	19	2	11	26	19	81	2	7	3
Bogar	.244	.351	.300	78	205	19	50	72	13	0	3	25	14	29	0	1	9
Burnitz	.243	.475	.339	86	263	49	64	125	10	6	13	38	38	66	3	6	4
Johnson	.238	.379	.354	72	235	32	56	89	8	2	7	26	43	43	6	4	11
Hundley	.228	.357	.269	130	417	40	95	149	17	2	11	53	23	62	1	1	8
T.Fernandez	.225	.295	.323	48	173	20	39	51	5	2	1	14	25	19	6	2	6
Walker	.225	.338	.271	115	213	18	48	72	7	1	5	19	14	29	7	0	8
Saunders	.209	.239	.243	28	67	8	14	16	2	0	0	0	3	4	0	0	4
Jackson	.195	.241	.211	31	87	4	17	21	1	0	1	7	2	22	0	0	0
Housie	.188	.250	.235	18	16	2	3	4	1	0	0	1	1	1	0	0	0
Baez	.183	.254	.259	52	126	10	23	32	9	0	0	7	13	17	0	0	6
Huskey	.146	.171	.159	13	41	2	6	7	1	0	0	3	1	13	0	0	3
Navarro	.059	.059	.059	12	17	1	1	1	1	0	0	0	1	4	0	0	0

Pitching	W-L	ERA	G	GS	CG	GF	Sho	SV	IP	H	R	ER	HR	BB	SO
Greer	1-0	0.00	1	0	0	1	0	0	1	0	0	0	0	0	2
Gozzo	0-1	2.57	10	0	0	5	0	1	14	11	5	4	1	5	6
S.Fernandez	5-6	2.93	18	18	1	0	1	0	119.2	82	42	39	17	36	81
Manzanillo	0-0	3.00	6	0	0	2	0	0	12	8	7	4	1	9	11
Saberhagen	7-7	3.29	19	19	4	0	1	0	139.1	131	55	51	11	17	93
Gooden	12-15	3.45	29	29	7	0	2	0	208.2	188	89	80	16	61	149
Maddux	3-8	3.60	58	0	0	31	0	5	75	67	34	30	3	27	57
Jones	2-4	3.65	9	9	0	0	0	0	61.2	61	35	25	6	22	35
Young	1-16	3.77	39	10	1	19	0	3	100.1	103	62	42	8	42	62
Hillman	2-9	3.97	27	22	3	1	1	0	145	173	83	64	12	24	60
Innis	2-3	4.11	67	0	0	30	0	3	76.2	81	39	35	5	38	36
Draper	1-1	4.25	29	1	0	11	0	0	42.1	53	22	20	2	14	16
Tanana	7-15	4.48	29	29	0	0	0	0	183	198	100	91	26	48	104
Telgheder	6-2	4.76	24	7	0	7	0	0	75.2	82	40	40	10	21	35
Gibson	1-1	5.19	8	0	0	1	0	0	8.2	14	6	5	1	2	12
Franco	4-3	5.20	35	0	0	30	0	10	36.1	46	24	21	6	19	29
Schourek	5-12	5.96	41	18	0	6	0	0	128.1	168	90	85	13	45	72
Kaiser	0-0	7.88	9	0	0	3	0	0	8	10	7	7	1	5	9
Weston	0-0	7.94	4	0	0	0	0	0	5.2	11	5	5	0	1	2

1994 preliminary roster

PITCHERS (19)
Juan Castillo
John Franco
Dwight Gooden
Mauro Gozzo
Kenny Greer
Eric Hillman
Jeff Innis
Jason Jacome
Bobby Jones
Mike Maddux
Josias Manzanillo
Bret Saberhagen
Pete Schourek
Pete Smith
Dave Telgheder

Joe Vitko
Pete Walker
Tom Wegmann
Anthony Young

CATCHERS (3)
Brook Fordyce
Todd Hundley
Joe Kmak

INFIELDERS (8)
Tim Bogar
Butch Huskey
Jeff Kent
Aaron Ledesma
Jeff McKnight

Tito Navarro
Quilvio Veras
Alan Zinter

OUTFIELDERS (7)
Bobby Bonilla
Jeromy Burnitz
Vince Coleman
Randy Curtis
Darrin Jackson
Joe Orsulak
Ryan Thompson

Games played by position

Player	G	C	1B	2B	3B	SS	OF
Baez	52	0	0	0	0	52	0
Bogar	78	0	0	6	7	66	0
Bonilla	139	0	6	0	52	0	85
Burnitz	86	0	0	0	0	0	79
Coleman	92	0	0	0	0	0	90
T. Fernandez	48	0	0	0	0	48	0
Gallagher	99	0	9	0	0	0	72
Housie	18	0	0	0	0	0	2
Hundley	130	123	0	0	0	0	0
Huskey	13	0	0	0	13	0	0
Jackson	31	0	0	0	0	0	26
Johnson	72	0	0	0	67	0	0
Kent	140	0	0	127	12	2	0
Landrum	22	0	0	0	0	0	3
McKnight	105	1	10	15	9	29	0
Murray	154	0	154	0	0	0	0
Navarro	12	0	0	0	0	2	0
O'Brien	67	65	0	0	0	0	0
Orsulak	134	0	4	0	0	0	114
Saunders	28	0	0	22	4	1	0
Thompson	80	0	0	0	0	0	76
Walker	115	0	0	24	23	0	15

Sick call: 1993 DL Report

Player	Days on the DL
Tim Bogar	16
Mike Draper	52
Sid Fernandez	89
John Franco*	43
Darrin Jackson	44
Howard Johnson*	94
Jeff Kaiser	20
Darren Reed	157
Bret Saberhagen	62

Two separate terms on Disabled List

Minor League Report

Class AAA: Norfolk finished at 70-71, fourth in the International League Western Division. Eric Bullock stole 45 bases to lead the league. Mauro Gozzo was 8-11 with a 3.45 ERA. Bobby Jones was 12-01 with a 3.63 ERA. **Class AA:** Binghamton finished at 68-71, fifth in the Eastern League. Butch Huskey hit 25 homers and had 98 RBI. Quilvio Veras hit .306 with 51 RBI and 52 stolen bases. Alan Zinter hit 24 homers and had 87 RBI. Denny Harriger won the ERA crown, going 13-10 with a 2.95 ERA. Pete Walker had 19 saves. **Class A:** St. Lucie finished at 78-52, winning the second half of the Florida State League East Division but falling to Clearwater in four games in the league finals. Omar Garcia hit .322 with 76 RBI. Randy Curtis hit .319 and led the league with 52 steals. Edgardo Alfonzo had 86 RBI. Chris Roberts was 13-5 with a 2.75 ERA. . . . Capital City finished at 64-77, sixth in the Sally League Southern Division. Don White hit .304 and stole 43 bases. Erik Hiljus struck out 157. **Short-season:** Pittsfield finished at 40-34, first in the New York-Penn League McNamara Division, but was swept in two games by Niagara Falls in the league finals. Jason Isringhausen led the league with 1-4 strikeouts. Tom Engle fanned 100. . . . Kingsport finished at 30-38, fourth in the Appalachian League Southern Division. Cesar Diaz hit .327 with 11 homers and 37 RBI. Preston Wilson won the league home run title with 16 while Randy warner was right behind him with 15. . . . St. Lucie finished at 39-20, first in the Gulf Coast League Eastern Division, but fell to the Astros in one game in the playoffs. Juan Ramirez hit .304. Yudith Ozario led the league with 39 stolen bases while Tomas Arvelo added 23. Joseph Atwater was 7-1 with an 0.93 ERA. He walked six in 58 innings.

Tops in the organization

Batter	Club	Avg	G	AB	R	H	HR	RBI
Garcia, Omar	Slu	. 322	129	485	73	156	3	76
Curtis, Randy	Slu	.319	126	467	91	149	2	38
Veras, Quilvio	Bng	.306	128	444	87	136	2	51
White, Don	Cap	.304	114	441	86	134	3	41
Alfonzo, Edgardo	Slu	.294	128	494	75	145	11	86

Home Runs		
Huskey, Butch	Bng	25
Zinter, Alan	Bng	24
Springer, Steve	Nor	13
Thompson, Ryan	Nor	12
Several players tied		11

RBI		
Huskey, Butch	Bng	98
Zinter, Alan	Bng	87
Alfonzo, Edgardo	Slu	86
Garcia, Omar	Slu	76
Several players tied		72

Stolen Bases		
Veras, Quilvio	Bng	52
Curtis, Randy	Slu	52
Bullock, Eric	Nor	45
White, Don	Cap	43
Keister, Tripp	Cap	33

Wins		
Jacome, Jason	Bng	14
Roberts, Chris	Slu	13
Harriger, Denny	Bng	13
Several players tied		12

Saves		
Beckerman, Andy	Slu	24
Walker, Pete	Bng	19
Mccready, Jim	Bng	16
Reichenbach, Eric	Cap	12
Vann, Brandy	Nor	11

Strikeouts		
Hiljus, Erik	Cap	157
Pulsipher, Bill	Slu	131
Jones, Bobby	Nor	126
Kroon, Marc	Cap	122
Jacome, Jason	Bng	122

Pitcher	Club	W-L	ERA	IP	H	BB	SO
Pulsipher, Bill	Slu	9- 6	2.19	140	97	51	131
Roberts, Chris	Slu	13- 5	2.75	173	162	36	111
Harriger, Denny	Bng	13-10	2.95	171	174	40	89
Jacome, Jason	Bng	14- 7	3.14	186	191	61	122
Fiegel, Todd	Slu	10- 7	3.39	117	122	42	71

New York (1962-1993)

Runs: Most, career, all-time

662	DARRYL STRAWBERRY, 1983-1990
627	HOWARD JOHNSON, 1985-1993
592	Mookie Wilson, 1980-1989
563	Cleon Jones, 1963-1975
536	Ed Kranepool, 1962-1979

Hits: Most, career, all-time

1418	Ed Kranepool, 1962-1979
1188	Cleon Jones, 1963-1975
1112	Mookie Wilson, 1980-1989
1029	Bud Harrelson, 1965-1977
1025	DARRYL STRAWBERRY, 1983-1990

2B: Most, career, all-time

225	Ed Kranepool, 1962-1979
214	HOWARD JOHNSON, 1985-1993
187	DARRYL STRAWBERRY, 1983-1990
182	Cleon Jones, 1963-1975
170	Mookie Wilson, 1980-1989

3B: Most, career, all-time

62	Mookie Wilson, 1980-1989
45	Bud Harrelson, 1965-1977
33	Cleon Jones, 1963-1975
31	Steve Henderson, 1977-1980
30	DARRYL STRAWBERRY, 1983-1990

HR: Most, career, all-time

252	DARRYL STRAWBERRY, 1983-1990
192	HOWARD JOHNSON, 1985-1993
154	Dave Kingman, 1975-1983
118	Ed Kranepool, 1962-1979
118	KEVIN McREYNOLDS, 1987-1991

RBI: Most, career, all-time

733	DARRYL STRAWBERRY, 1983-1990
629	HOWARD JOHNSON, 1985-1993
614	Ed Kranepool, 1962-1979
521	Cleon Jones, 1963-1975
468	Keith Hernandez, 1983-1989

SB: Most, career, all-time

281	Mookie Wilson, 1980-1989
202	HOWARD JOHNSON, 1985-1993
191	DARRYL STRAWBERRY, 1983-1990
152	Lee Mazzilli, 1976-1989
116	LENNY DYKSTRA, 1985-1989

BB: Most, career, all-time

580	DARRYL STRAWBERRY, 1983-1990
573	Bud Harrelson, 1965-1977
556	HOWARD JOHNSON, 1985-1993
482	Wayne Garrett, 1969-1976
471	Keith Hernandez, 1983-1989

BA: Highest, career, all-time

.297	Keith Hernandez, 1983-1989
.292	DAVE MAGADAN, 1986-1992
.283	WALLY BACKMAN, 1980-1988
.281	Cleon Jones, 1963-1975
.278	LENNY DYKSTRA, 1985-1989

Slug avg: Highest, career, all-time

.520	DARRYL STRAWBERRY, 1983-1990
.463	KEVIN McREYNOLDS, 1987-1991
.459	HOWARD JOHNSON, 1985-1993
.453	Dave Kingman, 1975-1983
.429	Keith Hernandez, 1983-1989

Games started: Most, career, all-time

395	Tom Seaver, 1967-1983
346	Jerry Koosman, 1967-1978
296	DWIGHT GOODEN, 1984-1993
250	SID FERNANDEZ, 1984-1993
241	RON DARLING, 1983-1991

Saves: Most, career, all-time

107	JESSE OROSCO, 1979-1987
88	JOHN FRANCO, 1990-1993
86	Tug McGraw, 1965-1974
84	ROGER McDOWELL, 1985-1989
69	Neil Allen, 1979-1983

Shutouts: Most, career, all-time

44	Tom Seaver, 1967-1983
26	Jerry Koosman, 1967-1978
26	Jon Matlack, 1971-1977
23	DWIGHT GOODEN, 1984-1993
15	DAVID CONE, 1987-1992

Wins: Most, career, all-time

198	Tom Seaver, 1967-1983
154	DWIGHT GOODEN, 1984-1993
140	Jerry Koosman, 1967-1978
99	RON DARLING, 1983-1991
98	SID FERNANDEZ, 1984-1993

K: Most, career, all-time

2541	Tom Seaver, 1967-1983
1835	DWIGHT GOODEN, 1984-1993
1799	Jerry Koosman, 1967-1978
1449	SID FERNANDEZ, 1984-1993
1159	DAVID CONE, 1987-1992

Win pct: Highest, career, all-time

.655	DWIGHT GOODEN, 1984-1993
.625	DAVID CONE, 1987-1992
.615	Tom Seaver, 1967-1983
.586	RON DARLING, 1983-1991
.560	BOB OJEDA, 1986-1990

ERA: Lowest, career, all-time

2.57	Tom Seaver, 1967-1983
3.03	Jon Matlack, 1971-1977
3.04	DWIGHT GOODEN, 1984-1993
3.08	DAVID CONE, 1987-1992
3.09	Jerry Koosman, 1967-1978

Runs: Most, season

108	HOWARD JOHNSON, 1991
108	DARRYL STRAWBERRY, 1987
107	Tommie Agee, 1970
104	HOWARD JOHNSON, 1989
101	DARRYL STRAWBERRY, 1988

Hits: Most, season

191	Felix Millan, 1975
185	Felix Millan, 1973
183	Keith Hernandez, 1985
182	Tommie Agee, 1970
181	Lee Mazzilli, 1979

2B: Most, season

41	HOWARD JOHNSON, 1989
40	GREGG JEFFERIES, 1990
37	LENNY DYKSTRA, 1987
37	HOWARD JOHNSON, 1990
37	Felix Millan, 1975
37	EDDIE MURRAY, 1992
37	Joel Youngblood, 1979

3B: Most, season

10	Mookie Wilson, 1984
9	Steve Henderson, 1978
9	Charlie Neal, 1962
9	Frank Taveras, 1979
9	Mookie Wilson, 1982

HR: Most, season

39	DARRYL STRAWBERRY, 1987
39	DARRYL STRAWBERRY, 1988
38	HOWARD JOHNSON, 1991
37	Dave Kingman, 1976
37	Dave Kingman, 1982
37	DARRYL STRAWBERRY, 1990

RBI: Most, season

117	HOWARD JOHNSON, 1991
108	DARRYL STRAWBERRY, 1990
105	Gary Carter, 1986
105	Rusty Staub, 1975
104	DARRYL STRAWBERRY, 1987

SB: Most, season

58	Mookie Wilson, 1982
54	Mookie Wilson, 1983
46	Mookie Wilson, 1984
42	Frank Taveras, 1979
41	HOWARD JOHNSON, 1989
41	Lee Mazzilli, 1980

BB: Most, season

97	Keith Hernandez, 1984
97	DARRYL STRAWBERRY, 1987
95	Bud Harrelson, 1970
94	Keith Hernandez, 1986
93	Lee Mazzilli, 1979

BA: Highest, season

.340	Cleon Jones, 1969
.328	DAVE MAGADAN, 1990
.319	Cleon Jones, 1971
.311	Keith Hernandez, 1984
.310	Keith Hernandez, 1986

Slug avg: Highest, season

.583	DARRYL STRAWBERRY, 1987
.559	HOWARD JOHNSON, 1989
.545	DARRYL STRAWBERRY, 1988
.535	HOWARD JOHNSON, 1991
.522	BOBBY BONILLA, 1993

Games started: Most, season

36	Jack Fisher, 1965
36	Tom Seaver, 1970
36	Tom Seaver, 1973
36	Tom Seaver, 1975
35	RON DARLING, 1985
35	Gary Gentry, 1969
35	DWIGHT GOODEN, 1985
35	Jerry Koosman, 1973
35	Jerry Koosman, 1974
35	Jon Matlack, 1976
35	Tom Seaver, 1968
35	Tom Seaver, 1969
35	Tom Seaver, 1971
35	Tom Seaver, 1972
35	Craig Swan, 1979
35	FRANK VIOLA, 1990
35	FRANK VIOLA, 1991

Saves: Most, season

33	JOHN FRANCO, 1990
31	JESSE OROSCO, 1984
30	JOHN FRANCO, 1991
27	Tug McGraw, 1972
26	RANDY MYERS, 1988

Shutouts: Most, season

8	DWIGHT GOODEN, 1985
7	Jerry Koosman, 1968
7	Jon Matlack, 1974
6	Jerry Koosman, 1969
6	Jon Matlack, 1976

Wins: Most, season

25	Tom Seaver, 1969
24	DWIGHT GOODEN, 1985
22	Tom Seaver, 1975
21	Jerry Koosman, 1976
21	Tom Seaver, 1972

K: Most, season

289	Tom Seaver, 1971
283	Tom Seaver, 1970
276	DWIGHT GOODEN, 1984
268	DWIGHT GOODEN, 1985
251	Tom Seaver, 1973

Win pct: Highest, season

.870	DAVID CONE, 1988
.857	DWIGHT GOODEN, 1985
.783	BOB OJEDA, 1986
.781	Tom Seaver, 1969
.739	DWIGHT GOODEN, 1986

ERA: Lowest, season

1.53	DWIGHT GOODEN, 1985
1.76	Tom Seaver, 1971
2.08	Tom Seaver, 1973
2.08	Jerry Koosman, 1968
2.20	Tom Seaver, 1968

Most pinch-hit homers, season

4	Danny Heep, 1983
4	MARK CARREON, 1989

Most pinch-hit, homers, career

8	MARK CARREON, 1987-1991

Most consecutive games, batting safely

24	HUBIE BROOKS, 1984
23	Cleon Jones, 1970
23	Mike Vail, 1975

Most consecutive scoreless innings

31	Jerry Koosman, 1973

No hit games

None

ACTIVE PLAYERS in caps.

Atlanta Braves

by Robert Hanashiro, *USA TODAY*

Twenty-game winner Greg Maddux earned a second straight Cy Young award, leading the NL in ERA (2.36).

1993 Braves: The third time wasn't the charm

The Braves won 104 games, overcame a 10-game deficit down the stretch, and took their third consecutive NL West crown—but it was still a disappointing season. The Phillies blew them out of the postseason before they ever got to the World Series.

Indeed, the Braves began the year as the favorite to win it all. With 1992 Cy Young winner Greg Maddux added to a rotation of '91 Cy Young winner Tom Glavine, '92 NLCS MVP John Smoltz and Steve Avery, the Braves looked like a shoo-in.

And in a way, they didn't disappoint—the rotation finished with a 75-33 record for the regular season. The Braves were the first team ever to win three straight NL West titles. Their 104 wins was an all-time franchise record. Three players had MVP-level seasons. David Justice had 40 HR and 120 RBI. Fred McGriff, became the 12th player ever to hit 30 homers in six consecutive seasons. Ron Gant had a career high 36 HR and 117 RBI—of his homers, 18 gave the Braves either the lead or the win.

The acquisition of McGriff, for minor leaguers Donnie Elliott, Vince Moore and Melvin Nieves, helped the Braves make a successful run at the San Francisco Giants, culminating in an NL West division-clinching win against Colorado on the last day of the season.

Glavine and Maddux put together 20-win seasons and Maddux won the ERA (2.36) crown. Avery equalled his career-high victory total of 18 and the Braves were 28-7 in the games he started.

Jeff Blauser had the best-ever all-around season for a shortstop, .305 and 110 runs scored. Rookie closer Greg McMichael put together a string of 15 straight saves and finished the regular season with 19. He appeared in a team-high 74 games and had a 2.06 ERA.

Otis Nixon, despite not taking over the starting center-field role until August, finished third in the league in steals with 47. He is the only Brave this century to steal 40 or more bases in three straight seasons. After a year off, reliever Steve Bedrosian appeared in 49 games with a career-best 1.63 ERA.

All along, the Braves maintained that the season would not be a success unless they won it all. But after the Phillies won the NL pennant, that tune changed.

"I still think we're the better team," Maddux said. "But they beat us, so give them credit."

"People in baseball don't view us as failures," GM John Schuerholz said, "People respect us because they know how tough it is to win a division and win 104 games."

—by Pete Williams

1994 Braves: Preview

The Braves could have a new look for '94, if only because several of their many young prospects are ready to play at the major league level. Shortstop Chipper Jones, first baseman Ryan Klesko, catcher Javier Lopez and outfielder Tony Tarasco could force general manager John Schuerholz into making a trade.

Braves management also is concerned about a rising payroll that could exceed the $55 million mark with Ron Gant, David Justice and Steve Avery leading a large arbitration class.

Greg Maddux, Tom Glavine and John Smoltz—all locked into long-term contracts—should again anchor an imposing Braves rotation, but Atlanta still needs to find a full-time closer. It could still come from the group of Greg McMichael, Mark Wohlers, Mike Stanton and Kent Mercker, but all have faltered at times.

—by Pete Williams

1993 Braves: Between the lines

▶**April 12:** Starter Steve Avery went six innings, giving up three earned runs in the Braves' 5-1 loss to Chicago. The outing raised the Braves' rotation ERA from 0.65 to 0.97. Conversely, Atlanta's bats remained the coldest in the two leagues—.188.

▶**April 30:** The Braves snapped a five-game losing streak. Greg Maddux went 10 innings, striking out eight without walking a batter, but reliever Mike Stanton got the win.

▶**May 17:** Avery beat Montreal as the Braves moved within a half-game of Houston for second place in the NL West.

▶**May 31:** *Milestone*—Greg Maddux won his 100th career game.

▶**June 6:** John Smoltz won for the first time in almost a month, tossing his first shutout of the season.

▶**June 13:** Avery won his seventh game in a row, a personal best, as the Braves beat the Reds 9-2.

▶**June 15:** Tom Glavine snapped a personal three-game losing streak by throwing an amazingly low 79 pitches in his complete game win, as the Braves edged the Mets 2-1.

▶**June 27:** Ron Gant fanned four times against the Astros' Darryl Kile, giving him seven consecutive strikeouts, and 10 in his last three games. The latter tied a major league record.

▶**June 30:** Gant went 3-for-4 with a homer in the Braves' 3-2 win against Colorado.

▶**July 1:** Glavine tossed his second shutout of the year—the 12th of his career—as the Braves blanked the Rockies 4-0.

▶**July 15:** Glavine ran his regular-season career record against Pittsburgh to 12-5, 9-0 at Fulton County Stadium. (He's 0-4, 6.33 ERA against them in the playoffs.)

▶**July 21:** Fred McGriff homered twice to pace Atlanta to a 14-2 demolition of the Cardinals.

▶**July 26:** The Braves hit four homers in a 12-7 romp vs. the Rockies. Deion Sanders hit an inside-the-park homer and Greg Maddux (11-8) won his fourth consecutive game.

▶**July 31:** Maddux earned his 12th win, holding the Astros to two runs in eight innings.

▶**August 8:** Ron Gant hit his 27th homer of the year, a two-run shot, to snap a 1-1 tie and lift the Braves to a 3-2 win against the Expos. It ended a three-game losing streak for Atlanta.

▶**August 11:** Maddux gave up two runs on six hits to earn his 13th win, his third complete-game victory against the Mets in '93.

▶**August 12:** Gant continued his quest for his third 30-30 season, hitting his 28th homer of the year and adding two stolen bases to raise his total in that department to 19.

▶**August 13:** David Justice's 100th career homer led the hit parade of five homers in a 14-0 rout of the Reds.

▶**August 21:** Braves' rookie catcher Javy Lopez hit his first major league homer to help lead Atlanta to a 6-3 win against the Cubs.

▶**August 23:** Steve Avery beat San Francisco for the third time in '93, as Atlanta moved within 6 1/2 games of the first-place Giants in the opener of their NL West showdown.

▶**August 24:** The Braves beat the Giants, 6-4, cutting the Giants' lead in the NL West to 5 1/2 games.

▶**August 25:** Maddux took a no-hitter against the Giants into the sixth inning and the Braves completed a sweep with a 9-1 win, cutting the NL West margin to 4 1/2 games.

▶**August 28:** Avery boosted the Braves to four games out of first in the NL West with a 5-1 win against the Cubs.

▶**August 31:** The Braves beat the Giants—again—to cut their lead in the NL West to just 3 1/2 games.

▶**September 5:** The Braves completed a three-game sweep of the Padres, and moved to just 2 1/2 behind the Giants.

September 11: The Braves moved into first place in the NL West, as they stomped San Diego 13-1.

September 19: Tom Glavine became the first NL pitcher since Ferguson Jenkins (20 years earlier) to post three consecutive 20-win seasons.

September 23: Greg Maddux beat could-have-been Braves' pitcher Dennis Martinez for a 6-3 win against the Expos. (Martinez, vetoed a trade to Atlanta in late August.) It was the Braves' 16th win in 20 games.

September 25: Atlanta beat the Phillies for a franchise-record 99th win.

October 2: Fred McGriff collected his 100th RBI, giving Atlanta three 100-RBI men: McGriff, Gant and Justice. It marked the first time in the NL any team has had three players with 100 RBI since the 1970 Braves.

October 3: The Braves did what no NL team has done this century—sweep a season series from another team—as they went 13-0 against the Rockies with a 5-3 win. It proved to be the NL Western Division clincher as San Francisco was shellacked by Los Angeles 12-1 later in the day. *League leaders, pitching*—Tom Glavine led the NL in victories (22-6), was fourth in innings pitched (239 1/3), and eighth in ERA (3.20); Greg Maddux led the NL in ERA (2.36), complete games (8) and innings pitched (267), was third in strikeouts (197), and fourth in victories (20-10); John Smoltz was second in strikeouts (208) and third in innings pitched (243 2/3); Steve Avery was fifth in ERA (2.94) and sixth in victories (18-6); Mike Stanton was seventh in saves (27); Greg McMichael was fourth in games (74). *League leaders, batting*—David Justice was second in home runs (40), second in RBI (120), and seventh in total bases (301); Fred McGriff was fourth in home runs (37), fourth in runs (111), fifth in slugging percentage (.549), sixth in total bases (306), and eighth in RBI (101); Ron Gant was third in RBI (117), third in runs (113), third in total bases (309), and fifth in home runs (36); Jeff Blauser was fifth in runs (110), sixth in hits (182), tied for sixth in walks (85),

and seventh in on-base percentage (.401); Otis Nixon was third in stolen bases (47).
—by John Hunt, Scott Kauffman, Lisa Winston, Deron Snyder, Matt Young

Team directory

Owner: Ted Turner
General Manager: John Schuerholz
Ballpark:
Atlanta-Fulton County Stadium
521 Capitol Ave., SW, Atlanta, Ga.
404-522-7630
Capacity 52,709
Parking for 3,500 cars; $5
Public transportation available by bus
Family and wheelchair sections, non-alcohol section
Team publications:
Fan Magazine
404-522-7630
TV, radio broadcast stations:
WGST 640 AM, WTBS Channel 17
Camps and/or clinics:
Braves Fantasy Camp (ages 30+),
February, 800-8-BRAVES
Spring Training:
Municipal Stadium
West Palm Beach, Fla.
Capacity 7,200
407-683-6100

ATLANTA BRAVES 1993 final stats

Batting	BA	SLG	OB	G	AB	R	H	TB	2B	3B	HR	RBI	BB	SO	SB	CS	E
Jones	.667	1.000	.750	8	3	2	2	3	1	0	0	0	1	1	0	0	0
Lopez	.375	.750	.412	8	16	1	6	12	1	1	1	2	0	2	0	0	1
Klesko	.353	.765	.450	22	17	3	6	13	1	0	2	5	3	4	0	0	0
Pecota	.323	.387	.344	72	62	17	20	24	2	1	0	5	2	5	1	1	0
Blauser	.305	.436	.401	161	597	110	182	260	29	2	15	73	85	109	16	6	19
McGriff	.291	.549	.375	151	557	111	162	306	29	2	37	101	76	106	5	3	17
Sanders	.276	.452	.321	95	272	42	75	123	18	6	6	28	16	42	19	7	2
Gant	.274	.510	.345	157	606	113	166	309	27	4	36	117	67	117	26	9	11
Pendleton	.272	.408	.311	161	633	81	172	258	33	1	17	84	36	97	5	1	19
Justice	.270	.515	.357	157	585	90	158	301	15	4	40	120	78	90	3	5	5
Nixon	.269	.315	.351	134	461	77	124	145	12	3	1	24	61	63	47	13	3
Bream	.260	.415	.332	117	277	33	72	115	14	1	9	35	31	43	4	2	3
Lemke	.252	.341	.335	151	493	52	124	168	19	2	7	49	65	50	1	2	14
Berryhill	.245	.382	.291	115	335	24	82	128	18	2	8	43	21	64	0	0	6
Cabrera	.241	.422	.308	70	83	8	20	35	3	0	4	11	8	21	0	0	0
Tarasco	.229	.286	.243	24	35	6	8	10	2	0	0	2	0	5	0	1	0
Belliard	.228	.291	.291	91	79	6	18	23	5	0	0	6	4	13	0	0	1
Olson	.225	.309	.304	83	262	23	59	81	10	0	4	24	29	27	1	0	6
Hunter	.138	.200	.153	37	80	4	11	16	3	1	0	8	2	15	0	0	1
Caraballo	--	--	--	6	0	0	0	0	0	0	0	0	0	0	0	0	0

Pitching	W-L	ERA	G	GS	CG	GF	Sho	SV	IP	H	R	ER	HR	BB	SO
Bedrosian	5-2	1.63	49	0	0	12	0	0	49.2	34	11	9	4	14	33
McMichael	2-3	2.06	74	0	0	40	0	19	91.2	68	22	21	3	29	89
Howell	3-3	2.31	54	0	0	22	0	0	58.1	48	16	15	3	16	37
Maddux	20-10	2.36	36	36	8	0	1	0	267	228	85	70	14	52	197
Mercker	3-1	2.86	43	6	0	9	0	0	66	52	24	21	2	36	59
Avery	18-6	2.94	35	35	3	0	1	0	223.1	216	81	73	14	43	125
Glavine	22-6	3.20	36	36	4	0	2	0	239.1	236	91	85	16	90	120
Smoltz	15-11	3.62	35	35	3	0	1	0	243.2	208	104	98	23	100	208
Smith	4-8	4.37	20	14	0	2	0	0	90.2	92	45	44	15	36	53
Wohlers	6-2	4.50	46	0	0	13	0	0	48	37	25	24	2	22	45
Stanton	4-6	4.67	63	0	0	41	0	27	52	51	35	27	4	29	43
Freeman	2-0	6.08	21	0	0	5	0	0	23.2	24	16	16	1	10	25
Borbon	0-0	21.60	3	0	0	0	0	0	1.2	3	4	4	0	3	2

1994 preliminary roster

PITCHERS (16)
Steve Avery
Brian Bark
Steve Bedrosian
Mike Birkbeck
Pedro Borbon
Tom Glavine
Milt Hill
Jerry Koller
Greg Maddux
Greg McMichael
Kent Mercker
Matt Murray
Mike Potts
John Smoltz
Mike Stanton
Mark Wohlers

CATCHERS (5)
Joe Ayrault
Damon Berryhill
Tyler Houston
Javy Lopez
Charlie O'Brien

INFIELDERS (11)
Rafael Belliard
Jeff Blauser
Ramon Caraballo
Tony Graffanino
Chipper Jones
Ryan Klesko
Mark Lemke
Fred McGriff
Jose Oliva
Bill Pecota
Terry Pendleton

OUTFIELDERS (8)
Jarvis Brown
Dave Gallagher
Ron Gant
Troy Hughes
Dave Justice
Mike Kelly
Deion Sanders
Tony Tarasco

Games played by position

Player	G	C	1B	2B	3B	SS	OF
Belliard	91	0	0	24	0	58	0
Berryhill	115	105	0	0	0	0	0
Blauser	161	0	0	0	0	161	0
Bream	117	0	90	0	0	0	0
Cabrera	70	2	12	0	0	0	0
Caraballo	6	0	0	5	0	0	0
Gant	157	0	0	0	0	0	155
Hunter	37	0	29	0	0	0	2
Jones	8	0	0	0	0	3	0
Justice	157	0	0	0	0	0	157
Klesko	22	0	3	0	0	0	2
Lemke	151	0	0	150	0	0	0
Lopez	8	7	0	0	0	0	0
McGriff	151	0	149	0	0	0	0
Nixon	134	0	0	0	0	0	116
Olson	83	81	0	0	0	0	0
Pecota	72	0	0	4	23	0	1
Pendleton	161	0	0	0	161	0	0
Sanders	95	0	0	0	0	0	60
Tarasco	24	0	0	0	0	0	12

Sick call: 1993 DL Report

Player	Days on the DL
Marvin Freeman	64
Brian Hunter	30
Greg Olson	23
Deion Sanders	15
Pete Smith	38

Minor League Report

Class AAA: Richmond finished at 80-62, second in the International League Western Division, and fell to Charlotte in four games in the playoffs. Chipper Jones was league rookie of the year, hitting .325 with 13 homers and 89 RBI. Tony Tarasco hit .330 with 15 homers. Javy Lopez hit .305 with 17 homers and 74 RBI. Mike Birkbeck was 13-8 with a 3.11 ERA and led the league in strikeouts with 136. Bill Taylor led the league in saves with 26. **Class AA:** Greenville finished at 75-67, winning the first half of the Southern League Eastern Division, but fell to Knoxville in the playoffs. Mike Hostetler was 8-5 with a 2.72 ERA and threw a no-hitter against Knoxville in the playoffs. Lee Upshaw was 9-9 with a 3.29 ERA. Don Strange had 18 saves. **Class A:** Durham finished at 69-69, third in the Carolina League Southern Division. Domenic Therrien hit .300. Doug Wollenburg hit .299. Mike Warner stole 29 bases. . . . Macon finished at 74-67, third in the Sally League Southern Division. Kevin Grijak hit .296 with seven homers and 58 RBI. Terrell Wade was 8-2 with a 1.73 ERA and fanned 121 in 83.1 innings. John Knott hit 14 homers. Leo Ramirez had 17 saves. **Short-season:** Danville finished at 38-30, third in the Appalachian League Northern Division. Damon Hollins hit .321 with seven homers and 51 RBI. Andre King hit .309. Esteban Yan was 4-7 with a 3.03 ERA. Matt Byrd had seven saves. . . . Idaho Falls finished at 35-39, third in the Pioneer League Southern Division. Michael Eaglin hit .326 with 35 RBI and stole 28 bases. Tony Stoecklin had eight saves. . . . West Palm Beach finished at 32-26, second in the Gulf Coast League Eastern Division. David Catlett hit .311 with five homers and 33 RBI. Jerrod Miller was 5-2 with a 1.07 ERA. Jason Green struck out 63.

Tops in the organization

Batter	Club	Avg	G	AB	R	H	HR	RBI
Tarasco, Tony	Rmd	.330	93	370	73	122	15	53
Jones, Chipper	Rmd	.325	139	536	97	174	13	89
Lopez, Javy	Rmd	.305	100	380	56	116	17	74
Therrien, Dominic	Dur	.300	117	387	53	116	6	55
Wollenburg, Doug	Dur	.299	113	361	49	108	5	42

Home Runs			Wins		
Klesko, Ryan	Rmd	22	May, Darrell	Dur	15
Oliva, Jose	Rmd	21	Birkbeck, Mike	Rmd	13
Kelly, Mike	Rmd	19	Several players tied		12
Lopez, Javy	Rmd	17			
Several players tied		15			

RBI			Saves		
Jones, Chipper	Rmd	89	Taylor, Billy	Rmd	26
Klesko, Ryan	Rmd	74	Strange, Don	Rmd	19
Lopez, Javy	Rmd	74	Ramirez, Leo	Dur	17
Graffanino, Tony	Dur	69	Clontz, Brad	Dur	12
Oliva, Jose	Rmd	65		Dur	10

Stolen Bases			Strikeouts		
Warner, Mike	Grv	31	Wade, Terrell	Grv	208
Paulino, Nelson	Mac	24	Brock, Chris	Dur	159
Malloy, Marty	Mac	24	May, Darrell	Dur	158
Graffanino, Tony	Dur	24	D'Andrea, Mike	Mac	156
Several players tied		23	Hostetler, Mike	Grv	141

Pitcher	Club	W-L	ERA	IP	H	BB	SO
May, Darrell	Dur	15- 6	2.19	156	125	38	158
Wade, Terrell	Grv	12- 4	2.44	158	115	83	208
Place, Mike	Dur	7- 7	2.54	131	121	32	100
Brock, Chris	Dur	12- 7	2.60	159	124	68	159
Birkbeck, Mike	Rmd	13- 8	3.11	159	143	41	136

Atlanta (1966-1993), incl. Boston (1876-1952) and Milwaukee (1953-1965)

Runs: Most, career, all-time

2107	Hank Aaron, 1954-1974
1452	Eddie Mathews, 1952-1966
1291	Herman Long, 1890-1902
1134	Fred Tenney, 1894-1911
1103	DALE MURPHY, 1976-1990

Hits: Most, career, all-time

3600	Hank Aaron, 1954-1974
2201	Eddie Mathews, 1952-1966
1994	Fred Tenney, 1894-1911
1901	DALE MURPHY, 1976-1990
1900	Herman Long, 1890-1902

2B: Most, career, all-time

600	Hank Aaron, 1954-1974
338	Eddie Mathews, 1952-1966
306	DALE MURPHY, 1976-1990
295	Herman Long, 1890-1902
291	Tommy Holmes, 1942-1951

3B: Most, career, all-time

103	Rabbit Maranville, 1912-1935
96	Hank Aaron, 1954-1974
90	Herman Long, 1890-1902
80	John Morrill, 1876-1888
79	Bill Bruton, 1953-1960

HR: Most, career, all-time

733	Hank Aaron, 1954-1974
493	Eddie Mathews, 1952-1966
371	DALE MURPHY, 1976-1990
239	Joe Adcock, 1953-1962
215	Bob Horner, 1978-1986

RBI: Most, career, all-time

2202	Hank Aaron, 1954-1974
1388	Eddie Mathews, 1952-1966
1143	DALE MURPHY, 1976-1990
964	Herman Long, 1890-1902
927	Hugh Duffy, 1892-1900

SB: Most, career, all-time

431	Herman Long, 1890-1902
331	Hugh Duffy, 1892-1900
274	Billy Hamilton, 1896-1901
260	Bobby Lowe, 1890-1901
260	Fred Tenney, 1894-1911
240	Hank Aaron, 1954-1974 (6)

BB: Most, career, all-time

1376	Eddie Mathews, 1952-1966
1297	Hank Aaron, 1954-1974
912	DALE MURPHY, 1976-1990
750	Fred Tenney, 1894-1911
598	Billy Nash, 1885-1895

BA: Highest, career, all-time

.338	Billy Hamilton, 1896-1901
.332	Hugh Duffy, 1892-1900
.327	Chick Stahl, 1897-1900
.317	Rico Carty, 1963-1972
.317	Ralph Garr, 1968-1975

Slug avg: Highest, career, all-time

.567	Hank Aaron, 1954-1974
.533	Wally Berger, 1930-1937
.517	Eddie Mathews, 1952-1966
.511	Joe Adcock, 1953-1962
.508	Bob Horner, 1978-1986

Games started: Most, career, all-time

635	Warren Spahn, 1942-1964
595	Phil Niekro, 1964-1987
501	Kid Nichols, 1890-1901
330	Lew Burdette, 1951-1963
302	Vic Willis, 1898-1905

Saves: Most, career, all-time

141	Gene Garber, 1978-1987
78	Cecil Upshaw, 1966-1973
57	Rick Camp, 1976-1985
51	MIKE STANTON, 1989-1993
50	Don McMahon, 1957-1962

Shutouts: Most, career, all-time

63	Warren Spahn, 1942-1964
44	Kid Nichols, 1890-1901
43	Phil Niekro, 1964-1987
30	Lew Burdette, 1951-1963
29	Tommy Bond, 1877-1881

Wins: Most, career, all-time

356	Warren Spahn, 1942-1964
329	Kid Nichols, 1890-1901
268	Phil Niekro, 1964-1987
179	Lew Burdette, 1951-1963
151	Vic Willis, 1898-1905

K: Most, career, all-time

2912	Phil Niekro, 1964-1987
2493	Warren Spahn, 1942-1964
1667	Kid Nichols, 1890-1901
1161	Vic Willis, 1898-1905
1157	Jim Whitney, 1881-1885

Win pct: Highest, career, all-time

.679	Fred Klobedanz, 1896-1902
.655	Harry Staley, 1891-1894
.645	John Clarkson, 1888-1892
.643	Kid Nichols, 1890-1901
.631	Tommy Bond, 1877-1881
.590	TOM GLAVINE, 1987-1993 (12)

ERA: Lowest, career, all-time

2.21	Tommy Bond, 1877-1881
2.49	Jim Whitney, 1881-1885
2.52	Art Nehf, 1915-1919
2.62	Dick Rudolph, 1913-1927
2.74	Pat Ragan, 1915-1919
3.20	Phil Niekro, 1964-1987 (16)

Runs: Most, season

160	Hugh Duffy, 1894
158	Bobby Lowe, 1894
152	Billy Hamilton, 1896
152	Billy Hamilton, 1897
149	Herman Long, 1893
131	DALE MURPHY, 1983 (9)

Hits: Most, season

237	Hugh Duffy, 1894
224	Tommy Holmes, 1945
223	Hank Aaron, 1959
219	Ralph Garr, 1971
218	Felipe Alou, 1966

2B: Most, season

51	Hugh Duffy, 1894
47	Tommy Holmes, 1945
46	Hank Aaron, 1959
44	Wally Berger, 1931
44	Lee Maye, 1964
39	TERRY PENDLETON, 1992 (12)

3B: Most, season

20	Dick Johnston, 1887
20	Harry Stovey, 1891
19	Chick Stahl, 1899
18	Dick Johnston, 1888
18	Ray Powell, 1921
17	Ralph Garr, 1974 (6)

HR: Most, season

47	Hank Aaron, 1971
47	Eddie Mathews, 1953
46	Eddie Mathews, 1959
45	Hank Aaron, 1962
44	Hank Aaron, 1957
44	Hank Aaron, 1963
44	Hank Aaron, 1966
44	Hank Aaron, 1969
44	DALE MURPHY, 1987

RBI: Most, season

145	Hugh Duffy, 1894
135	Eddie Mathews, 1953
132	Hank Aaron, 1957
132	Jimmy Collins, 1897
130	Hank Aaron, 1963
130	Wally Berger, 1935
127	Hank Aaron, 1966 (9)

SB: Most, season

84	King Kelly, 1887
83	Billy Hamilton, 1896
72	OTIS NIXON, 1991
68	King Kelly, 1889
66	Billy Hamilton, 1897

BB: Most, season

131	Bob Elliott, 1948
127	Jim Wynn, 1976
126	Darrell Evans, 1974
124	Darrell Evans, 1973
124	Eddie Mathews, 1963

BA: Highest, season

.440	Hugh Duffy, 1894
.387	Rogers Hornsby, 1928
.373	Dan Brouthers, 1889
.369	Billy Hamilton, 1898
.366	Rico Carty, 1970

Slug avg: Highest, season

.694	Hugh Duffy, 1894
.669	Hank Aaron, 1971
.636	Hank Aaron, 1959
.632	Rogers Hornsby, 1928
.627	Eddie Mathews, 1953

Games started: Most, season

72	John Clarkson, 1889
67	Charlie Buffinton, 1884
64	Tommy Bond, 1879
63	Jim Whitney, 1881
59	Tommy Bond, 1878
44	Phil Niekro, 1979 (22)

Saves: Most, season

30	Gene Garber, 1982
27	MIKE STANTON, 1993
27	Cecil Upshaw, 1969
25	Gene Garber, 1979
24	Gene Garber, 1986

Shutouts: Most, season

11	Tommy Bond, 1879
9	Tommy Bond, 1878
8	Charlie Buffinton, 1884
8	John Clarkson, 1889
7	Kid Nichols, 1890
7	Togie Pittinger, 1902
7	Warren Spahn, 1947
7	Warren Spahn, 1951
7	Warren Spahn, 1963
7	Irv Young, 1905
6	Phil Niekro, 1974 (11)

Wins: Most, season

49	John Clarkson, 1889
48	Charlie Buffinton, 1884
43	Tommy Bond, 1879
40	Tommy Bond, 1877
40	Tommy Bond, 1878
23	Phil Niekro, 1969 (*)

K: Most, season

417	Charlie Buffinton, 1884
345	Jim Whitney, 1883
284	John Clarkson, 1889
270	Jim Whitney, 1884
262	Phil Niekro, 1977

Win pct: Highest, season

.842	Tom Hughes, 1916
.810	Phil Niekro, 1982
.788	Fred Klobedanz, 1897
.788	Bill James, 1914
.786	TOM GLAVINE, 1993

ERA: Lowest, season

1.87	Phil Niekro, 1967
1.90	Bill James, 1914
1.96	Tommy Bond, 1879
2.02	Lefty Tyler, 1916
2.06	Tommy Bond, 1878

Most pinch-hit homers, season

5	Butch Nieman, Bos-1945
4	TOMMY GREGG, 1990

Most pinch-hit, homers, career

7	Joe Adcock, Mil-1953-1962
6	TOMMY GREGG, 1988-1992

Most consecutive games, batting safely

37	Tommy Holmes, Bos-1945
31	Rico Carty, 1970

Most consecutive scoreless innings

41	Art Nehf, Bos-1917
29	Phil Niekro, 1974

No hit games

Jack Stivetts, Bos vs Bro NL, 11-0; August 6, 1892.

Frank (Jeff) Pfeffer, Bos vs Cin NL, 6-0; May 8, 1907.

George Davis, Bos vs Phi NL, 7-0; September 9, 1914 (2nd game).

Tom L. Hughes, Bos vs Pit NL, 2-0; June 16, 1916.

Jim Tobin, Bos vs Bro NL, 2-0; April 27, 1944.

Vern Bickford, Bos vs Bro NL, 7-0; August 11, 1950.

Jim Wilson, Mil vs Phi NL, 2-0; June 12, 1954.

Lew Burdette, Mil vs Phi NL, 1-0; August 18, 1960.

Warren Spahn, Mil vs Phi NL, 4-0; September 16, 1960.

Warren Spahn, Mil vs SF NL, 1-0; April 28, 1961.

Phil Niekro, Atl vs SD NL, 9-0; August 5, 1973.

KENT MERCKER (6 innings), MARK WOHLERS (2 innings) and Alejandro Pena (1 inning), Atl at SD NL, 1-0; September 11, 1991.

Jack Stivetts, five innings, called so Boston could catch train to Cleveland for Temple Cub playoffs, Bos at Was NL, 6-0; October 15, 1892 (2nd game).

Jim Tobin, five innings, darkness, Bos vs Phi NL, 7-0; June 22, 1944 (2nd game).

ACTIVE PLAYERS in caps.

Leader from franchise's current location is included. If not in the top five, leader's rank is listed in parenthesis; asterisk (*) indicates player is not in top 25.

137

by H. Darr Beiser, USA TODAY

Barry Bonds won his third MVP award, hitting .336 with a league-leading 46 homers and 123 RBI.

1993 Giants: Thrilling season just a game short

The Giants didn't move down to St. Petersburg, Fla. for the '93 season. But they did move up—in the standings—improving their record by 31 games under first-year manager Dusty Baker.

The Giants were able to stay in San Francisco thanks to a new owner, Peter Magowan, who in turn brought in Baker and the No. 1 prize on the free-agent market, Barry Bonds.

Led by Bonds, who won his third MVP award in four years, the Giants won 103 games and paced their division for most of the season. But they were unable to maintain their near .700 clip, and when they faltered after leading the division from May 10 to Sept. 10, the Braves were right there to move in. The teams stood tied entering the final day of the season, when the Giants were done in by their despised Achilles' heel—the Dodgers—losing the game 12-1 along with the division title.

Baker had maneuvered the Giants through a rash of injuries, aided by strong seasons from John Burkett (22 wins) and Bill Swift (21). Closer Rod Beck set a team record with 48 saves. But left-handers Trevor Wilson and Bud Black each went on the disabled list three times, making only 34 starts combined. Black finished the season on the DL, leaving the rotation depleted come September. Baker had no choice but to use fill-ins Jim Deshaies and rookie Salomon Torres. Torres started strong (3-1) but ended with losses in his final four starts, withering just enough to help cost the Giants the division. Black underwent surgery during the season; Wilson had surgery afterward.

The Giants suffered their share of injuries to hitters as well. Third baseman Matt Williams, second baseman Robby Thompson, first baseman Will Clark and center fielder Darren Lewis all were sidelined for substantial stretches. Baker had his regular lineup for just 29 games. The 23-6 record in those games suggests the Giants might have won even more than 103 games if healthy.

Baker was named NL Manager of the Year for his efforts.

Bonds' performance was a wonder to behold. He had career highs in nearly every offensive category. He hit .336 and tied Texas's Juan Gonzalez for the major-league lead with 46 homers. He also led the league in RBI (123), slugging and on-base percentage, extra-base hits and intentional walks.

Matt Williams thrived with Bonds in the lineup but Clark had a lackluster season. Williams rebounded from his dreadful '92 campaign to set career highs in average (.294) and homers (38). Clark finished at .283, his lowest average since 1988.

Robby Thompson did his part as well: .319, 19 HR, 65 RBI—all career highs.

Magowan provided the magic touch, signing Baker and Bonds, revamping chilly Candlestick and rescheduling more than half of all home games to be played during the day. The fans came: a club-record 2,606,354.

—by Deron Snyder

1994 Giants: Preview

The Thrill may be gone, but if the Giants win 103 games again—without Will Clark—they will certainly win their division, thanks to realignment.

GM Bob Quinn settled his pitching problems by signing former Giant-killer Mark Portugal to round out his rotation, and kept the '93 offense intact by signing Robby Thompson. With Thompson at second, Royce Clayton at short and Williams at third, the question is—obviously—who's on first?

Bonds and Darren Lewis are set in left and center field; right fielder Willie McGee turns 35 on Opening Day, so even though he hit .301 in '93, they'll keep an eye on him—right field could become a weakness.

—by Deron Snyder

1993 Giants: Between the lines

▶**April 12:** After receiving his 1992 NL MVP plaque from his godfather, Willie Mays, Barry Bonds homered in his first at-bat in a Giants' uniform.

▶**April 16:** John Burkett outdueled John Smoltz as the Giants beat the Braves 1-0 and took over first place in the NL West.

▶**April 25:** Bonds hit his fifth homer and eighth double of the season, raising his average to .414.

▶**April 27:** Burkett became baseball's first five-game winner in '93.

▶**May 7:** Bonds raised his average to .432 in the Giants' 11-2 thrashing of the Phillies.

▶**May 29:** Robby Thompson extended his hitting streak to 19 games—best in the majors—as the Giants beat the Braves 6-3. Will Clark snapped a 161-at-bat homerless drought with his second home run of the season.

▶**June 5:** Trevor Wilson came off the DL with a bang—5 1/3 innings of scoreless ball and a home run—in a 3-2 win over Pittsburgh. Matt Williams hit his 17th home run of the season. *Quote of the day*—Pirate Andy Van Slyke on Konishiki, the 576-pound sumo wrestler who threw out the first pitch of the game: "They love him in Japan. He's very big there. Actually, he's big anywhere."

▶**June 12:** Robby Thompson collected five hits in a 5-4 win against the Cubs.

▶**June 17:** Bill Swift took a perfect game into the eighth and had to "settle" for a one-hit victory as the Giants beat the Reds 5-1. *Milestone*—Darren Lewis played his 243rd consecutive errorless game in the outfield to set a major league record for errorless games by an outfielder to start a career.

▶**June 24:** After never having had a multi-home run game in his career, Robby Thompson hit two in a game for the second night in a row.

▶**July 6:** The Giants reached double figures in runs for the third consecutive game, a 13-5 win against Montreal.

▶**July 15:** Bill Swift allowed just one unearned run in seven innings of work to earn his 12th win.

▶**July 16:** Darren Lewis set another record with his 267th consecutive error-less game. He had yet to make an error in his major league career (631 chances).

▶**July 26:** The Giants suffered their worst loss since 1975—a 15-1 beating from their archrivals, the Dodgers.

▶**July 28:** Giant-killer Tom Candiotti led the Dodgers to a 2-1 win against San Francisco, having allowed the NL West leaders just two runs in 24 1/3 innings in '93.

▶**July 30:** Barry Bonds went deep on the first two strikes he saw during a 10-4 win in Colorado. After being intentionally walked in the first inning, he hit the first pitch of the third inning 449 feet. After walking on four pitches in the fifth, he hit a 1-0 pitch for his second homer of the day, 31st of '93.

▶**August 3:** Will Clark hit a three-run homer, a two-run triple and had six RBI—one short of his career-best.

▶**August 10:** Robby Thompson homered, tripled and scored both runs in the Giants' 2-1 win against Cincinnati, raising his average to .323.

▶**August 11:** John Burkett fired a complete-game four hitter to earn his NL-leading 18th win. He had a no-hitter until the sixth and recorded his first shutout of the season.

▶**August 15:** Bonds and Williams each hit two homers (in back-to-back at-bats) as the Giants beat the Cubs 9-7.

▶**August 18:** Bonds had his fifth multi-homer game of the season.

▶**August 24:** The Braves beat the Giants, 6-4, cutting the Giants' lead in the NL West to 5 1/2 games—the smallest it had been since June 8.

▶**August 25:** The Braves completed a sweep of the Giants with a 9-1 win.

▶**August 30:** Todd Benzinger homered from each side of the plate, becoming the second NL player to do so in a game in '93 (Bobby Bonilla had done it twice).

▸**August 31:** The Braves beat the Giants—again—cutting the Giants' lead in the NL West to 3 1/2 games.

▸**September 1:** John Patterson's first swing of 1993 sent the ball out of the park in the top of the ninth to give the Giants a dramatic 3-2 win against Atlanta—a huge victory in the three-game series. Patterson, who had been out all year following offseason shoulder surgery, connected in his pinch-hit appearance against Mark Wohlers, who had not allowed a homer in two years.

▸**September 12:** The Cardinals' win in San Francisco completed a sweep that left the Giants a game behind Atlanta in the NL West.

▸**September 15:** The Giants lost their eighth in a row.

▸**September 20:** Beating Houston put the Giants 2 1/2 games behind Atlanta.

▸**September 23:** With a 7-0 win in Houston, John Burkett became the first Giants' hurler to win 20 games since Mike Krukow in 1986.

▸**September 24:** Robby Thompson was lost for the rest of the regular season with a fractured cheekbone after being hit by a pitch from Trevor Hoffman.

▸**September 25:** Barry Bonds hit two homers in a game for the sixth time in '93; the Giants were 1 1/2 games behind Atlanta.

▸**September 26:** Billy Swift became the Giants' second 20-game winner. The Giants became the first team to have two 20-game winners since Bob Welch and Dave Stewart did it for Oakland in 1990.

▸**September 30:** The Giants climbed back into a first-place tie with Atlanta with a 3-1 win in Los Angeles.

▸**October 2:** The Giants beat the Dodgers and stayed tied atop the NL West with one regular-season game remaining.

▸**October 3:** The Giants lost to the Dodgers, 12-1, and had to settle for second place after winning 103 games. *League leaders, pitching*—Mike Jackson led the league in games (81); John Burkett was second in victories (22-7) and was eighth in innings pitched (231 2/3); Billy Swift was third in victories (21-8),

fourth in ERA (2.82), seventh in innings pitched (232 2/3), and tied for ninth in strikeouts (157); Rod Beck was second in saves (48) and tied for second in games (76). *League leaders, batting*—Barry Bonds led the league in five categories: home runs (46), RBI (123), slugging percentage (.677), on-base percentage (.458) and total bases (365). Bonds was second in runs (129) and walks (126), fourth in batting (.336), tied for seventh in hits (181), and eighth in doubles (38); Matt Williams was second in total bases (325), third in home runs (38), and sixth in runs (105); Robby Thompson was 10th in batting (.312); Darren Lewis was tied for fourth in stolen bases (46).

—by John Hunt, Scott Kauffman, Lisa Winston, Deron Snyder, Matt Young

Team directory

▸**Owner:** Peter Magowan
▸**General Manager:** Bob Quinn
▸**Ballpark:**
Candlestick Park
Jamestown Avenue and Harney Way, San Francisco, Calif.
415-468-3700
Capacity 62,000
Parking for 17,000 cars; $4-$5
Public transportation available
Family and wheelchair sections, ramps, battery charger plug-ins for wheelchairs, designated handicapped pick-up and drop-off sights
▸**Team publications:**
Giants Magazine, Giants Info Guide
415-468-3700, ext. 478
▸**TV, radio broadcast stations:**
KNBR 680 AM, KTVU Channel 2, KIQI (Spanish), SportsChannel
▸**Camps and/or clinics:**
Rob Andrews Baseball, June and July, 510-935-3505
▸**Spring Training:**
Scottsdale Stadium
Scottsdale, Ariz.
Capacity 7,500 (plus 2,500 on outfield grass)
602-990-7972

SAN FRANCISCO GIANTS 1993 final stats

Batting	BA	SLG	OB	G	AB	R	H	TB	2B	3B	HR	RBI	BB	SO	SB	CS	E
Hosey	.500	1.000	.667	3	2	0	1	2	1	0	0	1	1	1	0	0	0
Johnson	.400	.800	.400	4	5	1	2	4	2	0	0	0	0	1	0	0	0
Bonds	.336	.677	.458	159	539	129	181	365	38	4	46	123	126	79	29	12	5
Carreon	.327	.540	.373	78	150	22	49	81	9	1	7	33	13	16	1	0	3
Phillips	.313	.688	.313	11	16	1	5	11	1	1	1	4	0	5	0	0	1
Thompson	.312	.496	.375	128	494	85	154	245	30	2	19	65	45	97	10	4	8
McGee	.301	.389	.353	130	475	53	143	185	28	1	4	46	38	67	10	9	5
Williams	.294	.561	.325	145	579	105	170	325	33	4	38	110	27	80	1	3	12
Benzinger	.288	.452	.332	86	177	25	51	80	7	2	6	26	13	35	0	0	0
Clark	.283	.432	.367	132	491	82	139	212	27	2	14	73	63	68	2	2	14
Clayton	.282	.372	.331	153	549	54	155	204	21	5	6	70	38	91	11	10	27
Manwaring	.275	.350	.345	130	432	48	119	151	15	1	5	49	41	76	1	3	2
Reed	.261	.437	.346	66	119	10	31	52	3	0	6	12	16	22	0	1	0
Lewis	.253	.324	.302	136	522	84	132	169	17	7	2	48	30	40	46	15	0
Scarsone	.252	.398	.278	44	103	16	26	41	9	0	2	15	4	32	0	1	1
Martinez	.241	.361	.317	91	241	28	58	87	12	1	5	27	27	39	6	3	1
Faries	.222	.333	.237	15	36	6	8	12	2	1	0	4	1	4	2	0	1
Benjamin	.199	.329	.264	63	146	22	29	48	7	0	4	16	9	23	0	0	5
Patterson	.188	.375	.188	16	16	1	3	6	0	0	1	2	0	5	0	1	0
Allanson	.167	.208	.200	13	24	3	4	5	1	0	0	2	1	2	0	0	0
Colbert	.162	.297	.225	23	37	2	6	11	2	0	1	5	3	13	0	0	1
Mercedes	.160	.240	.250	18	25	1	4	6	0	1	0	3	1	3	0	1	0
McNamara	.143	.143	.143	4	7	0	1	1	0	0	0	1	0	1	0	0	0
Faneyte	.133	.133	.235	7	15	2	2	2	0	0	0	0	2	4	0	0	0

Pitching	W-L	ERA	G	GS	CG	GF	Sho	SV	IP	H	R	ER	HR	BB	SO
Beck	3-1	2.16	76	0	0	71	0	48	79.1	57	20	19	11	13	86
Rogers	2-2	2.68	64	0	0	24	0	0	80.2	71	28	24	3	28	62
Swift	21-8	2.82	34	34	1	0	1	0	232.2	195	82	73	18	55	157
Jackson	6-6	3.03	81	0	0	17	0	1	77.1	58	28	26	7	24	70
Sanderson	4-2	3.51	11	8	0	1	0	0	48.2	48	20	19	12	7	36
Black	8-2	3.56	16	16	0	0	0	0	93.2	89	44	37	13	33	45
Wilson	7-5	3.60	22	18	1	1	0	0	110	110	45	44	8	40	57
Burkett	22-7	3.65	34	34	2	0	1	0	231.2	224	100	94	18	40	145
Minutelli	0-1	3.77	9	0	0	4	0	0	14.1	7	9	6	2	15	10
Torres	3-5	4.03	8	8	0	0	0	0	44.2	37	21	20	5	27	23
Deshaies	2-2	4.24	5	4	0	1	0	0	17	24	9	8	2	6	5
Burba	10-3	4.25	54	5	0	9	0	0	95.1	95	49	45	14	37	88
Hickerson	7-5	4.26	47	15	0	5	0	0	120.1	137	58	57	14	39	69
Brantley	5-6	4.28	53	12	0	9	0	0	113.2	112	60	54	19	46	76
Brummett	2-3	4.70	8	8	0	0	0	0	46	53	25	24	9	13	20
Righetti	1-1	5.70	51	0	0	15	0	1	47.1	58	31	30	11	17	31

1994 preliminary roster

PITCHERS (18)
Rod Beck
Jeff Brantley
Terry Bross
Dave Burba
John Burkett
Dan Carlson
Chris Hancock
Bryan Hickerson
Mike Jackson
Gino Minutelli
Rich Monteleone
Mark Portugal
Kevin Rogers
Joe Rosselli
Billy Swift
Salomon Torres
Bill VanLandingham
Trevor Wilson

CATCHERS (4)
Eric Christopherson
Marcus Jensen
Kirt Manwaring
Jeff Reed

INFIELDERS (9)
Mike Benjamin
Todd Benzinger
Royce Clayton
Paul Faries
John Patterson
J.R. Phillips
Steve Scarsone
Robby Thompson
Matt Williams

OUTFIELDERS (9)
Barry Bonds
Mark Carreon
Rikkert Faneyte
Steve Hosey
Dax Jones
Darren Lewis
Dave Martinez
Willie McGee
Luis Mercedes

Games played by position

Player	G	C	1B	2B	3B	SS	OF
Allanson	13	8	2	0	0	0	0
Benjamin	63	0	0	23	16	23	0
Benzinger	86	0	40	0	1	0	7
Bonds	159	0	0	0	0	0	157
Carreon	78	0	3	0	0	0	41
Clark	132	0	129	0	0	0	0
Clayton	153	0	0	0	0	153	0
Colbert	23	10	0	2	1	0	0
Faneyte	7	0	0	0	0	0	6
Faries	15	0	0	7	1	4	0
Hosey	3	0	0	0	0	0	1
Johnson	4	0	0	2	1	1	0
Lewis	136	0	0	0	0	0	131
Manwaring	130	130	0	0	0	0	0
Martinez	91	0	0	0	0	0	73
McGee	130	0	0	0	0	0	126
McNamara	4	4	0	0	0	0	0
Mercedes	18	0	0	0	0	0	5
Patterson	16	0	0	0	0	0	0
Phillips	11	0	5	0	0	0	0
Reed	66	37	0	0	0	0	0
Scarsone	44	0	6	20	8	0	0
Thompson	128	0	0	128	0	0	0
Williams	145	0	0	0	144	0	0

Sick call: 1993 DL Report

Player	Days on the DL
Mike Benjamin	29
Bud Black**	103
Will Clark	15
Craig Colbert	79
Mike Jackson	16
Darren Lewis	15
Dave Martinez	35
Willie McGee	19
John Patterson	149
Jeff Reed	34
Steve Scarsone	57
Robby Thompson	17
Matt Williams	16
Trevor Wilson**	75

** Three separate terms on Disabled List

Minor League Report

Class AAA: Phoenix finished at 64-79, fourth in the Pacific Coast League Southern Division. J.R. Phillips led the league with 27 homers and drove in 94 runs. Rob Taylor was 10-8 with a 4.24 ERA. **Class AA:** Shreveport finished at 66-70, winning the second half of the Texas League Eastern Division, but fell to Jackson in the playoffs. Rob Katzaroff hit .300 with 30 RBI. Barry Miller had 82 RBI. Rich Simon had 26 saves. **Class A:** San Jose finished at 79-57, second in the California league Northern Division. Chris Wimmer and Jason McFarlin each stole 49 bases. Wimmer set a league record for fielding percentage. Steve Whitaker was 8-10 with a 3.82 ERA. Doug Vanderweele was 10-6 with a 3.89 ERA. Bill VanLandingham had 14 wins to share the league lead and led the league in strikeouts with 171. . . . Clinton finished at 80-54, winning the second half of the Midwest League Southern Division, but fell to South Bend in four games in the finals. Chad Fonville hit .306 with 44 RBI and 52 stolen bases. Marvin Benard hit .301 with 50 RBI. Jamie Brewington had 13 wins. Jeff Richey had 28 saves. **Short-season:** Everett finished at 42-34, second in the Northwest League North Division. Keith Williams hit .302 with 12 homers and 49 RBI. Bill Mueller hit .300. Brett King stole 26 bases. Kris Franko won the ERA title going 5-0 with a 1.47 ERA. Steve Day led the league in wins with nine. . . . Scottsdale finished at 30-21, second in the Arizona League. Joel Galarza hit .326 with three homers and 26 RBI. Jason Canizaro led the league with 41 RBI. Hiram Ramirez drove in 34. Juan Johnson had 22 stolen bases. Jason Myers won the ERA crown (8-1, 1.69). He struck out 105 in 75 innings, walking just 16. Jorge Vasquez had eight saves.

Tops in the organization

Batter	Club	Avg	G	AB	R	H	HR	RBI
Faneyte, Rikkert	Phx	.312	115	426	71	133	11	71
Fonville, Chad	Cln	.306	120	447	80	137	1	44
Hecht, Steve	Phx	.306	97	337	52	103	5	31
Benard, Marvin	Cln	.301	112	349	84	105	5	50
McFarlin, Jason	Sj	.295	118	454	83	134	7	54

Home Runs			Wins		
Phillips, J.R.	Phx	27	VanLandingham, W.	Phx	14
Hyzdu, Adam	Shr	19	Torres, Salomon	Phx	14
Chimelis, Joel	Phx	19	Brewington, Jamie	Cln	13
Cookson, Brent	Sj	17	Carlson, Dan	Shr	12
Davenport, Adell	Shr	17	Myers, Jeff	Cln	11

RBI			Saves		
Phillips, J.R.	Phx	94	Richey, Jeff	Cln	32
Hosey, Steve	Phx	85	Simon, Rich	Shr	26
Miller, Barry	Shr	82	Minutelli, Gino	Phx	11
Faneyte, Rikkert	Phx	71	Dour, Brian	Sj	10
Davenport, Adell	Shr	70	Layana, Tim	Phx	9

Stolen Bases			Strikeouts		
Murray, Calvin	Phx	55	VanLandingham, W.	Phx	173
McFarlin, Jason	Sj	53	Torres, Salomon	Phx	166
Fonville, Chad	Cln	52	Carlson, Dan	Shr	129
Wimmer, Chris	Sj	49	Brewington, Jamie	Cln	111
Benard, Marvin	Cln	42	Taylor, Rob	Phx	110

Pitcher	Club	W-L	ERA	IP	H	BB	SO
Torres, Salomon	Phx	14-8	3.15	189	172	39	166
Myers, Jeff	Cln	11-8	3.30	131	121	76	107
Whitaker, Steve	Shr	9-10	3.65	136	111	121	106
Vanderweele, Doug	Sj	10-6	3.85	173	188	55	109
Carlson, Dan	Shr	12-10	4.02	170	165	58	129

San Francisco (1958-1993), includes New York (1883-1957)

144

Runs: Most, career, all-time

2011	Willie Mays, 1951-1972	
1859	Mel Ott, 1926-1947	
1313	Mike Tiernan, 1887-1899	
1120	Bill Terry, 1923-1936	
1113	Willie McCovey, 1959-1980	

Hits: Most, career, all-time

3187 Willie Mays, 1951-1972
2876 Mel Ott, 1926-1947
2193 Bill Terry, 1923-1936
1974 Willie McCovey, 1959-1980
1834 Mike Tiernan, 1887-1899

2B: Most, career, all-time

504 Willie Mays, 1951-1972
488 Mel Ott, 1926-1947
373 Bill Terry, 1923-1936
308 Willie McCovey, 1959-1980
291 Travis Jackson, 1922-1936

3B: Most, career, all-time

162 Mike Tiernan, 1887-1899
139 Willie Mays, 1951-1972
131 Roger Connor, 1883-1894
117 Larry Doyle, 1907-1920
112 Bill Terry, 1923-1936

HR: Most, career, all-time

646 Willie Mays, 1951-1972
511 Mel Ott, 1926-1947
469 Willie McCovey, 1959-1980
226 Orlando Cepeda, 1958-1966
189 Bobby Thomson, 1946-1957

RBI: Most, career, all-time

1860 Mel Ott, 1926-1947
1859 Willie Mays, 1951-1972
1388 Willie McCovey, 1959-1980
1078 Bill Terry, 1923-1936
929 Travis Jackson, 1922-1936

SB: Most, career, all-time

428 Mike Tiernan, 1887-1899
354 George Davis, 1893-1903
336 Willie Mays, 1951-1972
334 George Burns, 1911-1921
332 John Ward, 1883-1894

BB: Most, career, all-time

1708 Mel Ott, 1926-1947
1394 Willie Mays, 1951-1972
1168 Willie McCovey, 1959-1980
747 Mike Tiernan, 1887-1899
631 George Burns, 1911-1921

BA: Highest, career, all-time

.341 Bill Terry, 1923-1936
.332 George Davis, 1893-1903
.322 Ross Youngs, 1917-1926
.322 Frankie Frisch, 1919-1926
.321 George Vanhaltren, 1894-1903
.308 Orlando Cepeda, 1958-1966 (12)

Slug avg: Highest, career, all-time

.564 Willie Mays, 1951-1972
.549 Johnny Mize, 1942-1949
.536 KEVIN MITCHELL, 1987-1991
.535 Orlando Cepeda, 1958-1966
.533 Mel Ott, 1926-1947

Games started: Most, career, all-time

550 Christy Mathewson, 1900-1916
446 Juan Marichal, 1960-1973
431 Carl Hubbell, 1928-1943
412 Mickey Welch, 1883-1892
403 Amos Rusie, 1890-1898

Saves: Most, career, all-time

127 Gary Lavelle, 1974-1984
125 Greg Minton, 1975-1987
83 Randy Moffitt, 1972-1981
78 Frank Linzy, 1963-1970
66 ROD BECK, 1991-1993

Shutouts: Most, career, all-time

79 Christy Mathewson, 1900-1916
52 Juan Marichal, 1960-1973
36 Carl Hubbell, 1928-1943
29 Amos Rusie, 1890-1898
28 Mickey Welch, 1883-1892

Wins: Most, career, all-time

372 Christy Mathewson, 1900-1916
253 Carl Hubbell, 1928-1943
238 Juan Marichal, 1960-1973
238 Mickey Welch, 1883-1892
233 Amos Rusie, 1890-1898

K: Most, career, all-time

2499 Christy Mathewson, 1900-1916
2281 Juan Marichal, 1960-1973
1819 Amos Rusie, 1890-1898
1677 Carl Hubbell, 1928-1943
1606 Gaylord Perry, 1962-1971

Win pct: Highest, career, all-time

.693 Sal Maglie, 1945-1955
.680 Tim Keefe, 1885-1891
.664 Christy Mathewson, 1900-1916
.656 Jesse Barnes, 1918-1923
.651 Doc Crandall, 1908-1913
.642 JOHN BURKETT, 1987-1993 (8)

ERA: Lowest, career, all-time

2.12 Christy Mathewson, 1900-1916
2.38 Joe McGinnity, 1902-1908
2.43 Jeff Tesreau, 1912-1918
2.45 Red Ames, 1903-1913
2.48 Hooks Wiltse, 1904-1914
2.82 Gary Lavelle, 1974-1984 (12)

Runs: Most, season

147 Mike Tiernan, 1889
139 Bill Terry, 1930
138 Mel Ott, 1929
137 Johnny Mize, 1947
136 George Vanhaltren, 1896
134 Bobby Bonds, 1970 (6)

Hits: Most, season

254 Bill Terry, 1930
231 Freddy Lindstrom, 1928
231 Freddy Lindstrom, 1930
226 Bill Terry, 1929
225 Bill Terry, 1932
208 Willie Mays, 1958 (13)

2B: Most, season

46 Jack Clark, 1978
43 Willie Mays, 1959
43 Bill Terry, 1931
42 George Kelly, 1921
42 Bill Terry, 1932

3B: Most, season

27 George Davis, 1893
25 Larry Doyle, 1911
22 Roger Connor, 1887
21 Mike Tiernan, 1890
21 Mike Tiernan, 1895
21 George Vanhaltren, 1896
12 Willie Mays, 1960 (*)

HR: Most, season

52	Willie Mays, 1965
51	Willie Mays, 1955
51	Johnny Mize, 1947
49	Willie Mays, 1962
47	Willie Mays, 1964
47	KEVIN MITCHELL, 1989

RBI: Most, season

151	Mel Ott, 1929
142	Orlando Cepeda, 1961
141	Willie Mays, 1962
138	Johnny Mize, 1947
136	George Davis, 1897
136	George Kelly, 1924

SB: Most, season

111	John Ward, 1887
65	George Davis, 1897
62	George Burns, 1914
62	John Ward, 1889
61	Josh Devore, 1911
58	Billy North, 1979 (7)

BB: Most, season

144	Eddie Stanky, 1950
137	Willie McCovey, 1970
127	Eddie Stanky, 1951
126	BARRY BONDS, 1993
121	Willie McCovey, 1969

BA: Highest, season

.401	Bill Terry, 1930
.379	Freddy Lindstrom, 1930
.372	Bill Terry, 1929
.371	Roger Connor, 1885
.369	Mike Tiernan, 1896
.347	Willie Mays, 1958 (22)

Slug avg: Highest, season

.677	BARRY BONDS, 1993
.667	Willie Mays, 1954
.659	Willie Mays, 1955
.656	Willie McCovey, 1969
.645	Willie Mays, 1965

Games started: Most, season

65	Mickey Welch, 1884
64	Tim Keefe, 1886
63	Amos Rusie, 1890
61	Amos Rusie, 1892
59	Mickey Welch, 1886
41	Gaylord Perry, 1970 (*)

Saves: Most, season

48	ROD BECK, 1993
30	Greg Minton, 1982
24	DAVE RIGHETTI, 1991
22	Greg Minton, 1983
21	Frank Linzy, 1965
21	Greg Minton, 1981

Shutouts: Most, season

11	Christy Mathewson, 1908
10	Carl Hubbell, 1933
10	Juan Marichal, 1965
9	Joe McGinnity, 1904
8	Tim Keefe, 1888
8	Juan Marichal, 1969
8	Christy Mathewson, 1902
8	Christy Mathewson, 1905
8	Christy Mathewson, 1907
8	Christy Mathewson, 1909
8	Jeff Tesreau, 1914
8	Jeff Tesreau, 1915

Wins: Most, season

44	Mickey Welch, 1885
42	Tim Keefe, 1886
39	Mickey Welch, 1884
37	Christy Mathewson, 1908
36	Amos Rusie, 1894
26	Juan Marichal, 1968 (25)

K: Most, season

345	Mickey Welch, 1884
341	Amos Rusie, 1890
337	Amos Rusie, 1891
335	Tim Keefe, 1888
297	Tim Keefe, 1886
248	Juan Marichal, 1963 (11)

Win pct: Highest, season

.833	Hoyt Wilhelm, 1952
.818	Sal Maglie, 1950
.814	Joe McGinnity, 1904
.813	Carl Hubbell, 1936
.810	Doc Crandall, 1910
.806	Juan Marichal, 1966 (7)

ERA: Lowest, season

1.14	Christy Mathewson, 1909
1.28	Christy Mathewson, 1905
1.43	Christy Mathewson, 1908
1.44	Fred Anderson, 1917
1.57	Tim Keefe, 1885
1.99	Bobby Bolin, 1968 (16)

Most pinch-hit homers, season

4	Ernie Lombardi, NY-1946
4	Bill Taylor, NY-1955
4	Mike Ivie, 1978
4	CANDY MALDONADO, 1986
4	ERNIE RILES, 1990

Most pinch-hit, homers, career

13	Willie McCovey, 1959-1980

Most consecutive games, batting safely

33	George Davis, NY-1893
26	Jack Clark, 1978

Most consecutive scoreless innings

45	Carl Hubbell, NY-1933
45	Sal Maglie, NY-1950
40	Gaylord Perry, 1967
39	Christy Mathewson, NY-1901
39	Gaylord Perry, 1970

No hit games

Amos Rusie, NY vs Bro NL, 6-0; July 31, 1891.

Christy Mathewson, NY at StL NL, 5-0; July 15, 1901.

Christy Mathewson, NY at Chi NL, 1-0; June 13, 1905.

Hooks Wiltse, NY vs Phi NL, 1-0; July 4, 1908 (1st game, ten innings).

Red Ames, NY vs Bro NL. 0-3; April 15, 1909 (lost on 7 hits in 13 innings after allowing the first hit in the tenth).

Jeff Tesreau, NY at Phi NL, 3-0; September 6, 1912 (1st game).

Rube Marquard, NY vs Bro NL, 2-0; April 15, 1915.

Jesse Barnes, NY vs Phi NL, 6-0; May 7, 1922.

Carl Hubbell, NY vs Pit NL, 11-0; May 8, 1929.

Juan Marichal, SF vs Hou NL, 1-0; June 15, 1963.

Gaylord Perry, SF vs StL NL, 1-0; September 17, 1968.

Ed Halicki, SF vs NY NL, 6-0; August 24, 1975 (2nd game).

John Montefusco, SF at Atl NL, 9-0; September 29, 1976.

Ed Crane, seven innings, darkness, NY vs Was NL, 3-0; September 27, 1888.

Red Ames, five innings, darkness, NY at StL NL, 5-0; September 14, 1903 (2nd game, first game in the major leagues).

Mike McCormick, five innings, rain, SF at Phi NL, 3-0; June 12, 1959. (allowed hit in 6th, but rain caused game to revert to 5 innings).

Sam Jones, seven innings, rain, SF at StL NL, 4-0; September 26, 1959.

ACTIVE PLAYERS in caps.

Leader from franchise's current location is included. If not in the top five, leader's rank is listed in parenthesis; asterisk (*) indicates player is not in top 25.

Houston Astros

by Anne Ryan, USA TODAY

First baseman Jeff Bagwell batted .320 (sixth in the National League) with 20 home runs and 88 RBI.

1993 Astros: Free agent pitchers flopped

After owner Drayton McLane lassoed a pair of premium pitchers—free agents Doug Drabek and Greg Swindell—the Astros had high hopes for 1993. But the native Texans turned out to be a bust, and Houston never challenged for the NL West title. They finished third (85-77), nowhere near the pace of Atlanta and San Francisco. As a result, manager Art Howe was fired after his fifth season, along with GM Bill Wood, who had been with the club since 1976.

Drabek and Swindell's dismal debuts didn't help any. Drabek dropped to rock bottom with a league-low 9-18 record. In one 10-start stretch, he went winless before beating the Mets on Sept. 1.

Swindell finished 12-13 (4.16 ERA) and was particularly bad at home—4.90 ERA (second-worst in the NL) and nine losses (third worst).

On the positive side, Mark Portugal, Pete Harnisch and Darryl Kile turned out to be one of the most effective 1-2-3 punches in the majors. Portugal (18-4, 2.77 ERA) and Harnisch (16-9, 2.98 ERA) were among the NL-leaders in victories and ERA. Harnisch, who finished fifth in strikeouts (185), was particularly effective in the second half, throwing a pair of one-hitters and compiling a league-best 1.16 ERA in September.

But Kile was the team's special story. After barely making the staff in spring training, he was 10-1 at the break, and the Astros' lone representative in the All-Star Game. Two months later, Sept. 8, the 24-year-old tossed the ninth no-hitter in club history. He finished with a 15-8 record (3.51 ERA); the Astros had three 15-game winners for the first time. The staff ERA was 3.49, second to Atlanta's 3.41.

The team also flexed its muscles at the plate, collecting team records in batting average (.267), doubles (288), and home runs (138). Seven players totaled double-digit home runs for the first time in club history.

Two of the top hitters were first baseman Jeff Bagwell and second baseman Craig Biggio. Bagwell was sixth in the NL in hitting (.320) with 20 HR and a team-high 88 RBI. Biggio hit .287 with 21 HR, a club record for home runs by a second baseman. He also was among NL leaders in extra-base hits (67) and doubles (41).

—by Scott Kauffman

1994 Astros: Preview

For Houston, the best news about realignment was saying goodbye to Atlanta and San Francisco—especially now that Mark Portugal is throwing his unhittable stuff for the Giants instead of the Astros.

The future looks much safer in the new Central Division, with St. Louis, Chicago, Pittsburgh and Cincinnati. If the division had been in effect in '93, Houston would have finished second to St. Louis, two games out. Of course, that was when Portugal was pitching in an Astros' uniform. How they'll make up for his loss is uncertain.

One thing is for sure, if the Astros are to get to the top, they're going to have to do it with a tighter pocketbook. According to one report, owner McLane would like to pare the team payroll from $30 million to $26 million—that's a difference of about one top pitcher.

Jeff Bagwell and Pete Harnisch were eligible for arbitration and bound for hefty raises, so it wasn't surprising that Portugal went farther West. Also expendable: center fielder Steve Finley, who had an off year in '93 (.266, 13 triples, 19 SB) due to illness and injury, and third baseman Ken Caminiti.

Whether Houston is a contender depends on two questions: Will Doug Drabek and Greg Swindell return to norm? Will young players like Bagwell, Biggio, Andujar Cedeno and Luis Gonzalez, all coming off career years, continue to improve?

—by Scott Kauffman

1993 Astros: Between the lines

▶**April 10:** After hitting just 10 home runs in all of 1992, outfielder Luis Gonzalez hit three in his last two games. His solo shot helped beat the Mets, 6-3. *Milestone*—The victory, Doug Drabek's first for Houston, was also his 100th career win.

▶**April 16:** Eric Anthony raised his average to .351 with three hits and two RBI. Starter Greg Swindell also had a good day at the plate—he had two hits including a double—in his second win of the season, raising his average to .286.

▶**April 21:** Doug Drabek recorded his third complete game in a row, a six-hit 2-0 shutout of the Cubs. He was the first Houston pitcher to achieve that feat since Joe Niekro's seven in a row in 1982.

▶**April 24:** Eric Anthony's two-run double highlighted a five-run eighth for the Astros as they beat Pittsburgh 8-4. The win gave Houston a share of first place in the NL West.

▶**May 7:** Craig Biggio extended his hitting streak to six games with a 4-for-4 day, including a homer.

▶**May 28:** Ken Caminiti made three errors (giving him seven for the year) in the Astros' 12-inning loss to the Marlins. His first error snapped a 21-inning errorless streak by the Astros.

▶**June 4:** Pitcher Pete Harnisch remained undefeated at home at 5-0 (6-2 overall), tossing a complete-game six-hitter as he beat the Mets 6-2.

▶**June 6:** Scott Servais hit three doubles, the third of which drove in the winning run in the Astros' 5-4 victory against the Mets. It was the third day in a row they rallied from behind to beat New York, and their sixth win in a row against the Mets.

▶**July 3:** Darryl Kile tossed the first shutout of his major league career and helped his cause with his first career homer, as the Astros beat St. Louis, 6-0. Kile ran his scoreless inning streak to 22 1/3.

▶**July 4:** Eddie Taubensee had the first multi-homer game of his career, going deep twice off Cardinal rookie Rene Arocha, as the Astros swept a three-game set from St. Louis 9-4.

▶**July 16:** The Cardinals had scored twice in the eighth inning to move to within one run of the Astros. With the bases loaded, Houston's Jeff Bagwell made a diving stop of Ray Lankford's ground ball and threw to second from his knees to end the threat. The Astros held on to win 7-6.

▶**July 21:** Darryl Kile struck out 10 in 7 2/3 innings to beat the Pirates 5-3. Kile had won his last nine decisions, the longest streak by an Astro since Danny Darwin did it in 1989.

▶**July 23:** Luis Gonzalez extended his hitting streak to 14 games in a 5-1 win against the Cubs. Gonzalez, who had been hitting .500 during the streak, was batting .405 against Chicago for the season.

▶**July 29:** Pete Harnisch fired a four-hitter at the Braves for his second shutout of the year. He shut down an Atlanta lineup that was missing Fred McGriff, who didn't start for the first time since he was acquired 10 days before.

▶**August 3:** Luis Gonzalez tied a club record with three doubles in the Astros' 6-1 victory vs. Los Angeles. Mark Portugal allowed one run on four hits as Houston beat Los Angeles 6-1 at the Astrodome. Portugal, 7-1 at home for the season, was 27-9 at the Astrodome since joining the team in 1989.

▶**August 7:** Eric Anthony, Jeff Bagwell and Ken Caminiti homered to help the Astros to a 6-5 win against the Giants. This gave Houston 96 homers, equalling its 1992 total.

▶**August 14:** Pete Harnisch fanned 12 in a three-hit shutout, as the Astros blanked the Rockies 9-0.

▶**August 15:** Jeff Bagwell pinch-hit in his team's 4-3 loss to the Rockies to keep alive a 280-game streak, second in the majors to Orioles' shortstop Cal

Ripken—who had played more than 1,800 in a row.

▶**August 28:** Chris James stole two bases in the Astros' 7-3 loss to Montreal—they were his first two stolen bases of the year.

▶**September 1:** Doug Drabek snapped a seven-game losing streak and picked up his first victory since July 4, as the Astros edged the Mets 3-2.

▶**September 6:** Luis Gonzalez tied a career best with five RBI as the Astros beat New York 7-2. Gonzalez hit a three-run homer, his career-high 14th, and a two-run double to raise his average to .300. Pete Harnisch won his career-high 13th game in Houston's win.

▶**September 8:** *No-hitter!* Darryl Kile tossed the first no-hitter for Houston since Mike Scott's clinched the NL West title back in 1986, beating the Mets 7-1.

▶**September 11:** Mark Portugal gave up a run on three hits in 8 1/3 innings against the Phillies for his career-high 15th win.

▶**September 12:** Jeff Bagwell was hit by a pitch, breaking his left hand in the Astros' 9-2 win against Philadelphia. Bagwell had played in 304 consecutive games, a franchise record and the second longest current streak in the majors behind Baltimore's Cal Ripken.

▶**September 17:** The only hit of the night off Houston ace Pete Harnisch was a questionable bunt single by San Diego's Jarvis Brown that could have been ruled an error. Nonetheless, Harnisch hung on for his second one-hitter of the season, a 3-0 victory against the Padres.

▶**September 21:** Mark Portugal tied a Houston record with his 10th win in a row, shutting out the Giants.

▶**October 3:** The Astros lost their last game of the year, 7-4 to the Reds but finished the 1993 season with a .525 record, 19 games behind the Braves, for third place in the National League West. *League leaders, pitching*—Pete Harnisch led the NL in shutouts (4), was fifth in strikeouts (185), sixth in ERA (2.98) and 10th in victories (16-9). Mark Portugal was third in ERA (2.77)

and fifth in victories; Doug Drabek was tied for second in complete games (7) and fifth in innings pitched (237 2/3); Xavier Hernandez and Doug Jones were seventh and eighth in games (72 and 71, respectively), and Doug Jones was eighth in saves (26). *League leaders, batting*—Steve Finley led the NL in triples (13); Jeff Bagwell was sixth in batting (.320), ninth in slugging percentage (.516) and ninth in doubles (37); Craig Biggio was tied for fourth in doubles (41) and was tenth in total bases (289).

—by John Hunt, Scott Kauffman, Lisa Winston, Deron Snyder, Matt Young

Team directory

▶**Owner:** Drayton McLane Jr.
▶**General Manager:** Bill Wood
▶**Ballpark:**
Houston Astrodome
8400 Kirby Dr., Houston, Texas
713-799-9500
Capacity 54,223
Parking for 26,000 cars; $4
Public transportation by bus
Wheelchair section and ramps
▶**Team publications:**
Astros Magazine, Astros Media Guide
713-799-9600
▶**TV, radio broadcast stations:**
KPRC 950 AM, KTXH Channel 20, Home Sports Entertainment Cable
▶**Camps and/or clinics:**
Astros Youth Clinics, during the season, 713-799-9877
▶**Spring Training:**
Osceola County Stadium
Kissimmee, Fla.
Capacity 5,130
407-933-5400

HOUSTON ASTROS 1993 final stats

Batting	BA	SLG	OB	G	AB	R	H	TB	2B	3B	HR	RBI	BB	SO	SB	CS	E
Lindeman	.348	.478	.348	9	23	2	8	11	3	0	0	0	0	7	0	0	0
Parker	.333	.400	.375	45	45	11	15	18	3	0	0	4	3	8	1	2	0
Bagwell	.320	.516	.388	142	535	76	171	276	37	4	20	88	62	73	13	4	9
Brumley	.300	.300	.364	8	10	1	3	3	0	0	0	2	1	3	0	1	0
Gonzalez	.300	.457	.361	154	540	82	162	247	34	3	15	72	47	83	20	9	8
Biggio	.287	.474	.373	155	610	98	175	289	41	5	21	64	77	93	15	17	14
Bass	.284	.402	.359	111	229	31	65	92	18	0	3	37	26	31	7	1	1
Cedeno	.283	.412	.346	149	505	69	143	208	24	4	11	56	48	97	9	7	25
Finley	.266	.385	.304	142	545	69	145	210	15	13	8	44	28	65	19	6	4
Caminiti	.262	.390	.321	143	543	75	142	212	31	0	13	75	49	88	8	5	24
Donnels	.257	.391	.327	88	179	18	46	70	14	2	2	24	19	33	2	0	8
James	.256	.488	.333	65	129	19	33	63	10	1	6	19	15	34	2	0	3
Taubensee	.250	.389	.299	94	288	26	72	112	11	1	9	42	21	44	1	0	5
Anthony	.249	.397	.319	145	486	70	121	193	19	4	15	66	49	88	3	5	3
Uribe	.245	.264	.355	45	53	4	13	14	1	0	0	3	8	5	1	0	5
Servais	.244	.415	.313	85	258	24	63	107	11	0	11	32	22	45	0	0	2
Candaele	.240	.331	.298	75	121	18	29	40	8	0	1	7	10	14	2	3	3
Tucker	.192	.231	.250	9	26	1	5	6	1	0	0	3	2	3	0	0	0

Pitching	W-L	ERA	G	GS	CG	GF	Sho	SV	IP	H	R	ER	HR	BB	SO
Reynolds	0-0	0.82	5	1	0	0	0	0	11	11	4	1	0	6	10
Hernandez	4-5	2.61	72	0	0	29	0	9	96.2	75	37	28	6	28	101
Portugal	18-4	2.77	33	33	1	0	1	0	208	194	75	64	10	77	131
Harnisch	16-9	2.98	33	33	5	0	4	0	217.2	171	84	72	20	79	185
Edens	1-1	3.12	38	0	0	20	0	0	49	47	17	17	4	19	21
T.Jones	1-2	3.13	27	0	0	8	0	2	37.1	28	14	13	4	15	25
Osuna	1-1	3.20	44	0	0	6	0	2	25.1	17	10	9	3	13	21
Kile	15-8	3.51	32	26	4	0	2	0	171.2	152	73	67	12	69	141
Drabek	9-18	3.79	34	34	7	0	2	0	237.2	242	108	100	18	60	157
Swindell	12-13	4.16	31	30	1	0	1	0	190.1	215	98	88	24	40	124
D.Jones	4-10	4.54	71	0	0	60	0	26	85.1	102	46	43	7	21	66
Williams	4-4	4.83	42	5	0	12	0	3	82	76	48	44	7	38	56
Juden	0-1	5.40	2	0	0	1	0	0	5	4	3	3	1	4	7
Agosto	0-0	6.00	6	0	0	3	0	0	6	8	4	4	1	0	3
Bell	0-1	6.14	10	0	0	2	0	0	7.1	10	5	5	0	2	2

1994 preliminary roster

PITCHERS (15)
Jim Dougherty
Doug Drabek
Tom Edens
Kevin Gallaher
Pete Harnisch
John Hudek
Domingo Jean
Todd Jones
Darryl Kile
Alvin Morman
Al Osuna
Shane Reynolds
Greg Swindell
Brian Williams
Mitch Williams

CATCHERS (4)
Tony Eusebio
Scott Servais
Eddie Taubensee
Scooter Tucker

INFIELDERS (9)
Jeff Bagwell
Craig Biggio
Ken Caminiti
Andujar Cedeno
Chris Donnels
Orlando Miller
James Mouton
Roberto Petagine
Andy Stankiewicz

OUTFIELDERS (9)
Willie Ansley
Eric Anthony
Braulio Castillo
Steve Finley
Luis Gonzalez
Chris Hatcher
Brian Hunter
Gary Mota
Jimmy White

Games played by position

Player	G	C	1B	2B	3B	SS	OF
Anthony	145	0	0	0	0	0	131
Bagwell	142	0	140	0	0	0	0
Bass	111	0	0	0	0	0	64
Biggio	155	0	0	155	0	0	0
Brumley	8	0	0	0	1	1	1
Caminiti	143	0	0	0	143	0	0
Candaele	75	0	0	19	4	14	17
Cedeno	149	0	0	0	1	149	0
Donnels	88	0	23	1	31	0	0
Finley	142	0	0	0	0	0	140
Gonzalez	154	0	0	0	0	0	149
James	65	0	0	0	0	0	34
Lindeman	9	0	9	0	0	0	0
Parker	45	0	0	1	0	1	16
Servais	85	82	0	0	0	0	0
Taubensee	94	90	0	0	0	0	0
Tucker	9	8	0	0	0	0	0
Uribe	45	0	0	0	0	41	0

Sick call: 1993 DL Report

Player	Days on the DL
Casey Candaele	23
Tom Edens	31
Steve Finley	19
Rob Mallicoat	182
Greg Swindell	20
Brian Williams	15

Minor League Report

Class AAA: Tucson finished at 83-60, winning both halves of the Pacific Coast League Southern Division and beating Portland in six games for the league title. James Mouton was league MVP, hitting .315 with 16 homers, 92 RBI and 40 stolen bases. Jim Lindeman won the batting crown at .362, edging out teammate Mike Brumley's .353. Phil Nevin had 93 RBI. Shane Reynolds was 10-6 with a 3.62 ERA. Jeff Juden had 156 strikeouts. **Class AA:** Jackson finished at 73-62, winning the first half of the Texas League Eastern Division, and swept three games from El Paso for the league title. Roberto Petagine was league MVP and won the batting crown at .334, with 15 homers and 90 RBI. Frank Kellner hit .301. Brian Hunter led the league with 35 steals. James Dougherty led the league with 36 saves. **Class A:** Osceola finished at 56-74, fourth in the Florida State League East Division. Dennis Colon hit .316 with 59 RBI. . . . Quad City finished at 56-74, fourth in the Midwest League Southern Division. Jeff Ball hit .293 with 14 homers and 76 RBI. Chris Holt was 11-10 with a 2.27 ERA and 176 strikeouts. . . . Asheville finished at 51-88, last in the Sally League Northern Division. Sean Fesh had 20 saves. **Short-season:** Auburn finished at 30-44, last in the New York-Penn League Pinckney Division. Noel Rodriguez hit .300 with six homers and 54 RBI. Timothy Kester was 4-6 with a 2.06 ERA. . . . Kissimmee finished at 35-24, first in the Gulf Coast League Northern Division, but fell to the Rangers in two games in the league finals. Ryan Creek had seven wins for a share of the league lead. Edgar Ramos struck out 70. Michael Walter had eight saves.

Tops in the organization

151

Batter	Club	Avg	G	AB	R	H	HR	RBI
Lindeman, Jim	Tcn	.362	101	390	72	141	12	88
Brumley, Mike	Tcn	.353	93	346	65	122	0	47
Petagine, Roberto	Jck	.334	128	437	73	146	15	90
Colon, Dennis	Osc	.316	118	469	51	148	2	59
Mouton, James	Tcn	.315	134	546	126	172	16	92

Home Runs			Wins		
Madsen, Lance	Jck	23	Costello, Fred	Tcn	14
Miller, Orlando	Tcn	16	Bruske, Jim	Tcn	13
Mouton, James	Tcn	16	Several players tied		11
Hatcher, Chris	Jck	15			
Petagine, Roberto	Jck	15			

RBI			Saves		
Nevin, Phil	Tcn	93	Dougherty, James	Jck	36
Mouton, James	Tcn	92	Fesh, Sean	Ash	20
Petagine, Roberto	Jck	90	Ponte, Ed	Qc	17
Miller, Orlando	Tcn	89	Kent, Troy	Jck	15
Lindeman, Jim	Tcn	88	Jones, Todd	Tcn	12

Stolen Bases			Strikeouts		
Ball, Jeff	Qc	40	Holt, Chris	Qc	176
Mouton, James	Tcn	40	Juden, Jeff	Tcn	156
Massarelli, John	Tcn	37	Evans, Jamie	Qc	126
Hunter, Brian	Jck	35	Bruske, Jim	Tcn	125
Roman, Vince	Qc	29	Gallaher, Kevin	Jck	123

Pitcher	Club	W-L	ERA	IP	H	BB	SO
Holt, Chris	Qc	11-10	2.27	186	162	54	176
Bruske, Jim	Tcn	13-7	2.91	164	163	40	125
Costello, Fred	Tcn	14-5	3.32	144	149	46	81
Reynolds, Shane	Tcn	10-6	3.62	139	147	21	106
Gallaher, Kevin	Jck	7-9	3.62	159	146	67	123

Houston (1962-1993)

Runs: Most, career, all-time

890	Cesar Cedeno, 1970-1981
871	Jose Cruz, 1975-1987
829	Jim Wynn, 1963-1973
676	Terry Puhl, 1977-1990
640	Bob Watson, 1966-1979

Hits: Most, career, all-time

1937	Jose Cruz, 1975-1987
1659	Cesar Cedeno, 1970-1981
1448	Bob Watson, 1966-1979
1357	Terry Puhl, 1977-1990
1291	Jim Wynn, 1963-1973

2B: Most, career, all-time

343	Cesar Cedeno, 1970-1981
335	Jose Cruz, 1975-1987
241	Bob Watson, 1966-1979
228	Jim Wynn, 1963-1973
226	Terry Puhl, 1977-1990

3B: Most, career, all-time

80	Jose Cruz, 1975-1987
63	Joe Morgan, 1963-1980
62	Roger Metzger, 1971-1978
56	Terry Puhl, 1977-1990
55	Cesar Cedeno, 1970-1981
55	Craig Reynolds, 1979-1989

152

HR: Most, career, all-time

223	Jim Wynn, 1963-1973
166	GLENN DAVIS, 1984-1990
163	Cesar Cedeno, 1970-1981
139	Bob Watson, 1966-1979
138	Jose Cruz, 1975-1987

RBI: Most, career, all-time

942	Jose Cruz, 1975-1987
782	Bob Watson, 1966-1979
778	Cesar Cedeno, 1970-1981
719	Jim Wynn, 1963-1973
600	Doug Rader, 1967-1975

SB: Most, career, all-time

487	Cesar Cedeno, 1970-1981
288	Jose Cruz, 1975-1987
219	Joe Morgan, 1963-1980
217	Terry Puhl, 1977-1990
191	Enos Cabell, 1975-1985
191	BILL DORAN, 1982-1990

BB: Most, career, all-time

847	Jim Wynn, 1963-1973
730	Jose Cruz, 1975-1987
678	Joe Morgan, 1963-1980
585	BILL DORAN, 1982-1990
534	Cesar Cedeno, 1970-1981

BA: Highest, career, all-time

.297	Bob Watson, 1966-1979
.292	Jose Cruz, 1975-1987
.289	Cesar Cedeno, 1970-1981
.282	Jesus Alou, 1969-1979
.281	Enos Cabell, 1975-1985

Slug avg: Highest, career, all-time

.483	GLENN DAVIS, 1984-1990
.454	Cesar Cedeno, 1970-1981
.445	Jim Wynn, 1963-1973
.444	Bob Watson, 1966-1979
.429	Jose Cruz, 1975-1987

Games started: Most, career, all-time

320	Larry Dierker, 1964-1976
301	Joe Niekro, 1975-1985
282	NOLAN RYAN, 1980-1988
267	Bob Knepper, 1981-1989
259	Mike Scott, 1983-1991

Saves: Most, career, all-time

199	Dave Smith, 1980-1990
76	Fred Gladding, 1968-1973
72	Joe Sambito, 1976-1984
62	DOUG JONES, 1992-1993
50	Ken Forsch, 1970-1980

Shutouts: Most, career, all-time

25	Larry Dierker, 1964-1976
21	Joe Niekro, 1975-1985
21	Mike Scott, 1983-1991
20	Don Wilson, 1966-1974
19	J.R. Richard, 1971-1980

Wins: Most, career, all-time

144	Joe Niekro, 1975-1985
137	Larry Dierker, 1964-1976
110	Mike Scott, 1983-1991
107	J.R. Richard, 1971-1980
106	NOLAN RYAN, 1980-1988

K: Most, career, all-time

1866	NOLAN RYAN, 1980-1988
1493	J.R. Richard, 1971-1980
1487	Larry Dierker, 1964-1976
1318	Mike Scott, 1983-1991
1283	Don Wilson, 1966-1974

Win pct: Highest, career, all-time

.634	MARK PORTUGAL, 1989-1993
.609	Jim Ray, 1965-1973
.601	J.R. Richard, 1971-1980
.576	Mike Scott, 1983-1991
.571	DANNY DARWIN, 1986-1990

ERA: Lowest, career, all-time

2.53	Dave Smith, 1980-1990
3.13	NOLAN RYAN, 1980-1988
3.15	Don Wilson, 1966-1974
3.15	J.R. Richard, 1971-1980
3.18	Ken Forsch, 1970-1980

Runs: Most, season

117	Jim Wynn, 1972
113	Jim Wynn, 1969
103	Cesar Cedeno, 1972
102	Joe Morgan, 1970
102	Jim Wynn, 1967

Hits: Most, season

195	Enos Cabell, 1978
189	Jose Cruz, 1983
187	Jose Cruz, 1984
185	Jose Cruz, 1980
185	Greg Gross, 1974

2B: Most, season

44	Rusty Staub, 1967
41	CRAIG BIGGIO, 1993
40	Cesar Cedeno, 1971
39	Cesar Cedeno, 1972
38	Bob Watson, 1977

3B: Most, season

14	Roger Metzger, 1973
13	Jose Cruz, 1984
13	STEVE FINLEY, 1992
13	STEVE FINLEY, 1993
12	Joe Morgan, 1965

HR: Most, season

37	Jim Wynn, 1967
34	GLENN DAVIS, 1989
33	Jim Wynn, 1969
31	GLENN DAVIS, 1986
30	GLENN DAVIS, 1988

RBI: Most, season

110	Bob Watson, 1977
107	Jim Wynn, 1967
105	Lee May, 1973
102	Cesar Cedeno, 1974
102	Bob Watson, 1976

SB: Most, season

65	GERALD YOUNG, 1988
64	ERIC YELDING, 1990
61	Cesar Cedeno, 1977
58	Cesar Cedeno, 1976
57	Cesar Cedeno, 1974

BB: Most, season

148 Jim Wynn, 1969
110 Joe Morgan, 1969
106 Jim Wynn, 1970
103 Jim Wynn, 1972
102 Joe Morgan, 1970

BA: Highest, season

.333 Rusty Staub, 1967
.324 Bob Watson, 1975
.320 Cesar Cedeno, 1972
.320 Cesar Cedeno, 1973
.320 JEFF BAGWELL, 1993

Slug avg: Highest, season

.537 Cesar Cedeno, 1973
.537 Cesar Cedeno, 1972
.516 JEFF BAGWELL, 1993
.507 Jim Wynn, 1969
.498 Bob Watson, 1977

Games started: Most, season

40 Jerry Reuss, 1973
39 J.R. Richard, 1976
38 Bob Knepper, 1986
38 Joe Niekro, 1979
38 Joe Niekro, 1983
38 Joe Niekro, 1984
38 J.R. Richard, 1979

Saves: Most, season

36 DOUG JONES, 1992
33 Dave Smith, 1986
29 Fred Gladding, 1969
27 Dave Smith, 1985
27 Dave Smith, 1988

Shutouts: Most, season

6 Dave Roberts, 1973
5 Larry Dierker, 1972
5 Bob Knepper, 1981
5 Bob Knepper, 1986
5 Joe Niekro, 1979
5 Joe Niekro, 1982
5 Mike Scott, 1986
5 Mike Scott, 1988

Wins: Most, season

21 Joe Niekro, 1979
20 Larry Dierker, 1969
20 Joe Niekro, 1980
20 J.R. Richard, 1976
20 Mike Scott, 1989

K: Most, season

313 J.R. Richard, 1979
306 Mike Scott, 1986
303 J.R. Richard, 1978
270 NOLAN RYAN, 1987
245 NOLAN RYAN, 1982

Win pct: Highest, season

.818 MARK PORTUGAL, 1993
.692 Mike Scott, 1985
.667 Mike Scott, 1989
.656 Joe Niekro, 1979
.652 DARRYL KILE, 1993
.652 Larry Dierker, 1972

ERA: Lowest, season

2.18 Bob Knepper, 1981
2.21 DANNY DARWIN, 1990
2.22 Mike Cuellar, 1966
2.22 Mike Scott, 1986
2.33 Larry Dierker, 1969

Most pinch-hit homers, season

5 Cliff Johnson, 1974

Most pinch-hit, homers, career

8 Cliff Johnson, 1972-1977

Most consecutive games, batting safely

23 Art Howe, 1981
22 Cesar Cedeno, 1977

Most consecutive scoreless innings

31 J. R. Richard, 1980

No hit games

Don Nottebart, Hou vs Phi NL, 4-1;
    May 17, 1963.
Ken T. Johnson, Hou vs Cin NL, 0-1;
    April 23, 1964 (lost the game).
Don Wilson, Hou vs Atl NL, 2-0;
    June 18, 1967.
Don Wilson, Hou at Cin NL, 4-0;
    May 1, 1969.
Larry Dierker, Hou vs Mon NL, 6-0;
    July 9, 1976.
Ken Forsch, Hou vs Atl NL, 6-0;
    April 7, 1979.
NOLAN RYAN, Hou vs LA NL, 5-0;
    September 26, 1981.
Mike Scott, Hou vs SF NL, 2-0;
    September 25, 1986.
DARRYL KILE, Hou vs NY NL, 7-1;
    September 8, 1993.

ACTIVE PLAYERS in caps.

The second consecutive Dodger to win Rookie of the Year, Mike Piazza led the team with 35 home runs.

by Robert Hanashiro, USA TODAY

1993 Dodgers: Another Rookie of the Year

The Dodgers showed some signs of recovering that old Dodger Blue mystique that is so much a part of the franchise. But there's still a long way to go.

They improved to 81-81 and a fourth-place finish in the NL West, a year after a 63-99 performance and only the second last-place finish in club history, dating back to the days when the team played its games on Flatbush Avenue. But '93 wasn't the kind of year that left the Dodgers satisfied.

"I think we had an identity crisis this year, no doubt about it," said outfielder Brett Butler. "You win 12, you lose eight, you lose four to the Colorado Rockies (in a row and at home)." GM Fred Claire added: "You're never anything but disappointed to be as far out of the race as early as we were."

The brightest spot was behind the plate, where NL Rookie of the Year Mike Piazza hit .318 with 35 homers and 112 RBI. Included in that total was a two-homer, four-RBI outing on the season's final day, when the Dodgers eliminated their hated rival, the San Francisco Giants, from the division race with a 12-1 drubbing.

"We've had a lot of good points," said Tom Lasorda, who is back for an 18th season in '94. "The catcher had a fantastic year, an unbelievable year. I feel very disappointed that we didn't finish higher than we did, but it wasn't because of a lack of effort. It was because of a lack of execution."

A glaring hole was the outfield, where the return of Eric Davis and Darryl Strawberry was such a disaster Davis was dealt to the Detroit Tigers down the stretch. Strawberry was limited to less than 100 at-bats as a result of back surgery in September of '92.

"We did not have the services of a left-handed power hitter (Strawberry) for practically the whole year," Lasorda said. "I think that, if you look at 1991, that's the same guy that hit 30 home runs and drove in 100 runs for us. We didn't have him in '92 and we didn't have him in '93."

Another injury that hurt the Dodgers hopes was second baseman Jody Reed, who suffered a hyperextended left elbow that sidelined him for a month.

"We had a guy (Reed) that I thought was a tremendous asset to our team, and when that Galarraga kicked him (June 15 at Mile High Stadium), we were five games out of first place," Lasorda complained. Actually, they were six games behind, and by the time Reed returned to action, they were 12 games out and falling fast. They never made a run at first place thereafter.

—by Rick Lawes

1994 Dodgers: Preview

This year has to be better for the Dodgers, if for no other reason than realignment. They still must contend with the Giants, but the rest of the division is made up of the Rockies and the Padres—one expansion team and another that looks like one.

Changes are in the offing. GM Fred Claire has made it clear the Dodgers won't again go all year without starting a left-handed pitcher. And their only left-hander in '93 was in the bullpen—young Omar Daal. The first move was to trade a pitcher. Pedro Martinez went to Montreal for second baseman Delino Deshields.

"Something has to be done," Brett Butler said. "You have some unity and you have some division. I guess the key is the front office coming up with the things that need to be done to make it the kind of club that can win with a changed division."

Tommy Lasorda can also hope that stopper Todd Worrell, who signed a three-year contract last offseason, is healthy for the entire year and returns to his '92 form.

—by Rick Lawes

1993 Dodgers: Between the lines

▶**April 6:** Ramon Martinez fanned nine in six innings.

▶**April 7:** Closer Todd Worrell, who had "Tommy John" ligament surgery on his right elbow in 1990, reinjured the elbow and left the game.

▶**April 11:** For the first time in L.A. Dodger history, two brothers pitched in the same game—Ramon Martinez was the starter and younger sibling Pedro relieved in the 3-0 loss to Atlanta.

▶**April 15:** Both Darryl Strawberry and Eric Davis, who played just 31 games together in 1992, were missing in action. With Strawberry batting .129 and Davis .167, Tommy Lasorda chose to rest the un-dynamic duo.

▶**April 20:** Strawberry sat out with a stiff back, reminiscent of the '92 season.

▶**May 5:** Pedro Martinez earned his first career major league win, in relief of his brother, Ramon.

▶**May 9:** *Quote of the day*—Darryl Strawberry, playing after more than a week of chronic back trouble, and Tim Wallach, also plagued by back trouble, homered in consecutive at-bats in the Dodgers' 6-4 win against the Giants. Quipped Wallach: "Bad-back-to-bad-back homers."

▶**May 18:** Eric Davis, who had three extra-base hits in his last 116 at-bats, hit a grand slam and drove in five runs to pace the Dodgers to a 9-1 win against Cincinnati.

▶**May 23:** Ramon Martinez posted his first shutout in almost a year, a three-hitter in a 4-0 win against Colorado. He struck out eight.

▶**May 24:** Sleeping slugger Eric Karros doubled his season home run total in one night, hitting two off San Diego's Greg W. Harris.

▶**May 25:** Lenny Harris' two-out, bases-loaded single in the 10th inning lifted the Dodgers to a 10-9 win against San Diego. It was the team's eighth win in a row, matching the Dodgers' longest winning streak since 1986.

▶**May 26:** Eric Davis and Tim Wallach

had two RBI each as the Dodgers beat San Diego 8-3 to extend their winning streak to nine games, the longest for the Dodgers since they won 10 in a row in 1980. The victory also capped a nine-game home-stand sweep, the first undefeated home stand of more than four games since they moved to L.A. in '58.

▶**May 29:** Ramon Martinez tossed his second complete game in a row to lead the Dodgers to a 6-1 win against Pittsburgh and their 11th win in a row overall, matching the best streak by the team since 1976.

▶**May 30:** The Dodgers' 11-game winning streak ended at the hands of the Pirates. A late business meeting kept Eric Davis out of the starting lineup, but he swiped second and third as a pinch-runner to tie a club record with his 33rd consecutive stolen base—third longest streak in major league history.

▶**June 4:** Ramon Martinez won his third game in a row, the first time he had three consecutive wins since 1990.

▶**June 10:** Reliever Ricky Trlicek was ejected along with Padres third baseman Gary Sheffield during a five-run sixth inning for San Diego. Trlicek hit Sheffield with a pitch and a minor brawl ensued. It might have been the best news for Trlicek's ERA—even with the premature exit, he had allowed seven earned runs in 1 1/3 innings.

▶**June 15:** Mike Piazza was 4-for-5 with two homers and five RBI as the Dodgers clobbered the Rockies 12-4, in a game that featured two brawls and several ejections.

▶**June 20:** Piazza, already a top NL Rookie of the Year candidate, hit a two-run shot into the second deck in center field. His numbers led the Dodgers in average (.345), homers (14) and RBI (46).

▶**July 7:** The game took six hours and 39 players, but Los Angeles and Philadelphia finally concluded play at 1:47 a.m. ET, the Phillies winning 7-6 in 20 innings. The Dodgers used every position player on the roster and were down to their final reliever, Trlicek, when they scored in the 20th. The Phillies had nobody left in the bullpen and only Ruben Amaro and Todd Pratt left on the bench. L.A. scored twice in the ninth to tie the game at 5-5, and went ahead in the 20th. But their celebrating was short-lived, as Lenny Dykstra sliced a bases-loaded double to left.

▶**July 11:** Tom Candiotti became the first pitcher to start two games in the same series since Mike Boddicker did it for Boston against Cleveland in 1988.

▶**July 26:** Each Dodger starter had a hit—Mike Piazza, Eric Davis and Jose Offerman had three RBI apiece—as Los Angeles handed the Giants a 15-1 defeat. It was San Francisco's worst loss since 1975 and Orel Hershiser's 19th career victory over the Giants in 26 decisions. He gave up five hits in pitching his fifth complete game of the year.

▶**July 28:** Giant-killer Tom Candiotti led the Dodgers to a 2-1 win against San Francisco, having allowed the NL West leaders just two runs in 24 1/3 innings in '93.

▶**July 31:** The Dodgers scored five times in the 13th inning to break open a close game at Wrigley Field. Rookie Raul Mondesi's first major league home run capped the scoring in the 7-2 Los Angeles win.

▶**August 14:** Cory Snyder ended a 42-game homerless skid by clouting a pair as the Dodgers ended a seven-game losing streak, 4-3 against the Padres.

▶**August 22:** Ramon Martinez tossed his third shutout and won for the first time in more than a month, beating the Cardinals 3-0. He was 1-4 in his last six starts despite a 2.63 ERA during that span.

▶**September 12:** Pedro Astacio was tagged for only five hits en route to his first shutout of the year, a 1-0 blanking of the Marlins. Astacio had a 1.08 ERA in his last six starts.

▶**September 20:** Third baseman Dave Hansen set a club record with his 18th pinch-hit of the season. Hansen delivered an RBI single as Los Angeles went on to beat Cincinnati 5-2.

▶**October 3:** The Dodgers got sweet revenge against their lifelong rivals, the Giants, by tromping them in a 12-1 laugher that broke the Giants' tie with Atlanta and gave the Braves the NL West title. *League leaders, pitching*—Ramon Martinez was second in shutouts (3); Tom Candiotti was seventh in ERA (3.12). *League leaders, batting*—Brett Butler was second in triples (10) and tied for seventh in hits (181); Mike Piazza was fourth in RBI (112), tied for fourth in total bases (307), sixth in home runs (35), and seventh in batting (.318).

—by John Hunt, Scott Kauffman, Lisa Winston, Deron Snyder, Matt Young

Team directory

▶**Owner:** Peter O'Malley
▶**General Manager:** Fred Claire
▶**Ballpark:**
Dodger Stadium
1000 Elysian Park Ave.,
Los Angeles, Calif.
213-224-1400
Capacity 56,000
Parking for 16,000 cars; $4
Wheelchair section and ramps
▶**Team publications:**
Dodger Magazine, media guide
800-762-1770
▶**TV, radio broadcast stations:**
KABC 790 AM, KWKW 1330 AM
(Spanish), KTLA Channel 5
▶**Camps and/or clinics:**
Twenty clinics per year, 213-224-1435
▶**Spring Training:**
Holman Stadium
Dodgertown
Vero Beach, Fla.
Capacity 7,000
407-878-4337

LOS ANGELES DODGERS 1993 final stats

Batting	BA	SLG	OB	G	AB	R	H	TB	2B	3B	HR	RBI	BB	SO	SB	CS	E
Bournigal	.500	.556	.500	8	18	0	9	10	1	0	0	3	0	2	0	0	0
Hansen	.362	.505	.465	84	105	13	38	53	3	0	4	30	21	13	0	1	3
Piazza	.318	.561	.370	149	547	81	174	307	24	2	35	112	46	86	3	4	11
Butler	.298	.371	.387	156	607	80	181	225	21	10	1	42	86	69	39	19	0
Goodwin	.294	.353	.333	30	17	6	5	6	1	0	0	1	1	4	1	2	0
Mondesi	.291	.488	.322	42	86	13	25	42	3	1	4	10	4	16	4	1	3
Reed	.276	.346	.333	132	445	48	123	154	21	2	2	31	38	40	1	3	5
Offerman	.269	.331	.346	158	590	77	159	195	21	6	1	62	71	75	30	13	37
Snyder	.266	.397	.331	143	516	61	137	205	33	1	11	56	47	147	4	1	9
Sharperson	.256	.367	.299	73	90	13	23	33	4	0	2	10	5	17	2	0	5
Hernandez	.253	.364	.267	50	99	6	25	36	5	0	2	7	2	11	0	0	7
Karros	.247	.409	.287	158	619	74	153	253	27	2	23	80	34	82	0	1	12
Webster	.244	.337	.293	88	172	26	42	58	6	2	2	14	11	24	4	6	4
Ashley	.243	.243	.282	14	37	0	9	9	0	0	0	0	2	11	0	0	0
Harris	.238	.325	.303	107	160	20	38	52	6	1	2	11	15	15	3	1	3
Davis	.234	.391	.308	108	376	57	88	147	17	0	14	53	41	88	33	5	2
Brooks	.222	.667	.222	9	9	2	2	6	1	0	1	1	0	2	0	0	0
Wallach	.222	.342	.271	133	477	42	106	163	19	1	12	62	32	70	0	2	15
Rodriguez	.222	.415	.266	76	176	20	39	73	10	0	8	23	11	39	1	0	1
Strawberry	.140	.310	.267	32	100	12	14	31	2	0	5	12	16	19	1	0	4

Pitching	W-L	ERA	G	GS	CG	GF	Sho	SV	IP	H	R	ER	HR	BB	SO
Ki.Gross	0-0	0.60	10	0	0	0	0	0	15	13	1	1	0	4	12
McDowell	5-3	2.25	54	0	0	19	0	2	68	76	32	17	2	30	27
Gott	4-8	2.32	62	0	0	45	0	25	77.2	71	23	20	6	17	67
P.Martinez	10-5	2.61	65	2	0	20	0	2	107	76	34	31	5	57	119
Candiotti	8-10	3.12	33	32	2	0	0	0	213.2	192	86	74	12	71	155
R.Martinez	10-12	3.44	32	32	4	0	3	0	211.2	202	88	81	15	104	127
Astacio	14-9	3.57	31	31	3	0	2	0	186.1	165	80	74	14	68	122
Hershiser	12-14	3.59	33	33	5	0	1	0	215.2	201	106	86	17	72	141
Trlicek	1-2	4.08	41	0	0	18	0	1	64	59	32	29	3	21	41
Ke.Gross	13-13	4.14	33	32	3	1	0	0	202.1	224	110	93	15	74	150
Wilson	1-0	4.56	25	0	0	4	0	1	25.2	30	13	13	2	14	23
Daal	2-3	5.09	47	0	0	12	0	0	35.1	36	20	20	5	21	19
Nichols	0-1	5.68	4	0	0	2	0	0	6.1	9	5	4	1	2	3
Worrell	1-1	6.05	35	0	0	22	0	5	38.2	46	28	26	6	11	31
DeSilva	0-0	6.75	3	0	0	2	0	0	5.1	6	4	4	0	1	6

1994 preliminary roster

PITCHERS (19)
Pedro Astacio
Tom Candiotti
Nelson Castro
Omar Daal
John DeSilva
Jim Gott
Kevin Gross
Kip Gross
Greg Hansell
Orel Hershiser
Ramon Martinez
Roger McDowell
Jose Parra
Felix Rodriguez
Ricky Trlicek
Ben VanRyn
Todd Williams
Steve Wilson
Todd Worrell

CATCHERS (3)
Jerry Brooks
Carlos Hernandez
Mike Piazza

INFIELDERS (10)
Henry Blanco
Rafael Bournigal
Mike Busch
Delino DeShields
Dave Hansen
Garey Ingram
Eric Karros
Jose Offerman
Eddie Pye
Tim Wallach

OUTFIELDERS (8)
Billy Ashley
Brett Butler
Tom Goodwin
Raul Mondesi
Henry Rodriguez
Cory Snyder
Darryl Strawberry
Mitch Webster

Games played by position

Player	G	C	1B	2B	3B	SS	OF
Ashley	14	0	0	0	0	0	11
Bournigal	8	0	0	4	0	4	0
Brooks	9	0	0	0	0	0	2
Butler	156	0	0	0	0	0	155
Davis	108	0	0	0	0	0	103
Goodwin	30	0	0	0	0	0	12
Hansen	84	0	0	0	18	0	0
Harris	107	0	0	35	17	3	2
Hernandez	50	43	0	0	0	0	0
Karros	158	0	157	0	0	0	0
Mondesi	42	0	0	0	0	0	40
Offerman	158	0	0	0	0	158	0
Piazza	149	146	1	0	0	0	0
Reed	132	0	0	132	0	0	0
Rodriguez	76	0	13	0	0	0	48
Sharperson	73	0	1	17	6	3	1
Snyder	143	0	12	0	23	2	115
Strawberry	32	0	0	0	0	0	29
Wallach	133	0	1	0	130	0	0
Webster	88	0	0	0	0	0	56

Sick call: 1993 DL Report

Player	Days on the DL
Jody Reed	29
Darryl Strawberry*	132
Tim Wallach	22
Todd Worrell*	83

Two separate terms on Disabled List

Minor League Report

Class AAA: Albuquerque finished at 71-72, second in the Pacific Coast League Southern Division. Jerry Brooks hit .344 with 11 homers and 71 RBI. Billy Ashley hit 26 homers and led the league with 100 RBI. Mike Busch had 22 homers. Kip Gross was 13-7. Todd Williams led the league with 21 saves. **Class AA:** San Antonio finished at 58-76, last in the Texas League Western Division. Ben VanRyn was league Pitcher of the Year, going 14-4 and winning the ERA crown at 2.21. He struck out 144 in 134 innings. Roger Cedeno stole 28 bases. Jose Perra was 1-8 but had a 3.15 ERA and walked just 12 in 111 innings. Rick Gorecki was 6-9 with a 3.35 ERA. **Class A:** Bakersfield finished at 42-94, last in the California League Northern Division. Jay Kirkpatrick hit .288 with eight homers and 63 RBI. Karim Garcia hit 19 homers and drove in 54 runs. Jim Martin had 27 stolen bases. . . . Vero Beach finished at 56-77, sixth in the Florida State League East Division. Chris Demetral hit .325 with five homers and 48 RBI. Miguel Cairo hit .315. Ed Lantigua had 79 RBI. Rich Linares won the ERA title in middle relief at 1.81. Dave Pyc was 7-8 with a 2.38 ERA. **Short-season:** Yakima finished at 30-46, last in the Northwest League North Division. Rick Haley had 50 RBI. Chris Latham stole 24 bases. Nathan Bland was 4-6 with a 2.84 ERA. . . . Great Falls finished at 36-34, third in the Pioneer League Northern Division. Daniel Camacho won the ERA crown going 5-2 with a 1.38, striking out 79 in 65 innings. Chris Costello was 4-2 with a 3.21 ERA. Keith Troutman led the league with 16 saves.

Tops in the organization

Batter	Club	Avg	G	AB	R	H	HR	RBI
Brooks, Jerry	Abq	.344	116	421	67	145	11	71
Traxler, Brian	Abq	.333	127	441	81	147	16	83
Pye, Eddie	Abq	.329	101	365	53	120	7	66
Demetral, Chris	Vb	.325	122	437	63	142	5	48
Cairo, Miguel	Vb	.315	90	346	50	109	1	23

Home Runs		Wins		
Ashley, Billy	Abq 26	VanRyn, Ben	Abq	15
Busch, Mike	Abq 22	Gross, Kip	Abq	13
Garcia, Karim	Bak 19	Rodriguez, Felix	Vb	8
Hollandsworth, Todd	San 17	Delahoya, Javier	San	8
Traxler, Brian	Abq 16	Nichols, Rod	Abq	8

RBI		Saves		
Ashley, Billy	Abq 100	Williams, Todd	Abq	21
Traxler, Brian	Abq 83	Henderson, Ryan	San	15
Kirkpatrick, Jay	San 80	Marquez, Isidrio	Abq	14
Lantigua, Ed	Vb 79	Linares, Rich	Vb	13
Brooks, Jerry	Abq 71	Gross, Kip	Abq	13

Stolen Bases		Strikeouts	
Cedeno, Roger	Abq 28	VanRyn, Ben	Abq 153
Martin, Jim	Bak 27	Gorecki, Rick	San 118
Spearman, Vernon	Abq 24	Weaver, Eric	Bak 110
Several players tied	23	Martinez, Jesus	Bak 108
		Delahoya, Javier	San 107

Pitcher	Club	W-L	ERA	IP	H	BB	SO
Pyc, Dave	Vb	7-8	2.38	113	97	47	78
Parra, Jose	San	1-8	3.15	111	103	12	87
Gorecki, Rick	San	6-9	3.35	156	136	62	118
VanRyn, Ben	Abq	15-8	3.52	159	153	55	153
Delahoya, Javier	San	8-10	3.66	125	122	42	107

Los Angeles (1958-1993), includes Brooklyn (1890-1957)

Runs: Most, career, all-time

1338	Pee Wee Reese, 1940-1958
1255	Zack Wheat, 1909-1926
1199	Duke Snider, 1947-1962
1163	Jim Gilliam, 1953-1966
1088	Gil Hodges, 1943-1961

Hits: Most, career, all-time

2804	Zack Wheat, 1909-1926
2170	Pee Wee Reese, 1940-1958
2091	Willie Davis, 1960-1973
1995	Duke Snider, 1947-1962
1968	Steve Garvey, 1969-1982

2B: Most, career, all-time

464	Zack Wheat, 1909-1926
343	Duke Snider, 1947-1962
333	Steve Garvey, 1969-1982
330	Pee Wee Reese, 1940-1958
324	Carl Furillo, 1946-1960

3B: Most, career, all-time

171	Zack Wheat, 1909-1926
110	Willie Davis, 1960-1973
97	Hy Myers, 1909-1922
87	Jake Daubert, 1910-1918
82	John Hummel, 1905-1915
82	Duke Snider, 1947-1962

HR: Most, career, all-time

389	Duke Snider, 1947-1962
361	Gil Hodges, 1943-1961
242	Roy Campanella, 1948-1957
228	Ron Cey, 1971-1982
211	Steve Garvey, 1969-1982

RBI: Most, career, all-time

1271	Duke Snider, 1947-1962
1254	Gil Hodges, 1943-1961
1210	Zack Wheat, 1909-1926
1058	Carl Furillo, 1946-1960
992	Steve Garvey, 1969-1982

SB: Most, career, all-time

490	Maury Wills, 1959-1972
418	Davey Lopes, 1972-1981
335	Willie Davis, 1960-1973
298	Tom Daly, 1890-1901
290	STEVE SAX, 1981-1988

BB: Most, career, all-time

1210	Pee Wee Reese, 1940-1958
1036	Jim Gilliam, 1953-1966
925	Gil Hodges, 1943-1961
893	Duke Snider, 1947-1962
765	Ron Cey, 1971-1982

BA: Highest, career, all-time

.352	Willie Keeler, 1893-1902
.339	Babe Herman, 1926-1945
.337	Jack Fournier, 1923-1926
.317	Zack Wheat, 1909-1926
.315	Babe Phelps, 1935-1941
.315	Manny Mota, 1969-1982 (6)

Slug avg: Highest, career, all-time

.557	Babe Herman, 1926-1945
.553	Duke Snider, 1947-1962
.552	Jack Fournier, 1923-1926
.528	Reggie Smith, 1976-1981
.512	Pedro Guerrero, 1978-1988

Games started: Most, career, all-time

533	Don Sutton, 1966-1988
465	Don Drysdale, 1956-1969
335	Claude Osteen, 1965-1973
332	Brickyard Kennedy, 1892-1901
326	Dazzy Vance, 1922-1935

Saves: Most, career, all-time

125	Jim Brewer, 1964-1975
101	Ron Perranoski, 1961-1972
85	JAY HOWELL, 1988-1992
83	Clem Labine, 1950-1960
64	Tom Niedenfuer, 1981-1987

Shutouts: Most, career, all-time

52	Don Sutton, 1966-1988
49	Don Drysdale, 1956-1969
40	Sandy Koufax, 1955-1966
38	Nap Rucker, 1907-1916
34	Claude Osteen, 1965-1973

Wins: Most, career, all-time

233	Don Sutton, 1966-1988
209	Don Drysdale, 1956-1969
190	Dazzy Vance, 1922-1935
177	Brickyard Kennedy, 1892-1901
165	Sandy Koufax, 1955-1966

K: Most, career, all-time

2696	Don Sutton, 1966-1988
2486	Don Drysdale, 1956-1969
2396	Sandy Koufax, 1955-1966
1918	Dazzy Vance, 1922-1935
1759	FERNANDO VALENZUELA, 1980-1990

Win pct: Highest, career, all-time

.715	Preacher Roe, 1948-1954
.674	Tommy John, 1972-1978
.674	Jim Hughes, 1899-1902
.658	Billy Loes, 1950-1956
.655	Sandy Koufax, 1955-1966

ERA: Lowest, career, all-time

2.31	Jeff Pfeffer, 1913-1921
2.42	Nap Rucker, 1907-1916
2.56	Ron Perranoski, 1961-1972
2.58	Rube Marquard, 1915-1920
2.62	Jim Brewer, 1964-1975

Runs: Most, season

148	Hub Collins, 1890
143	Babe Herman, 1930
140	Mike Griffin, 1895
140	Willie Keeler, 1899
136	Mike Griffin, 1897
130	Maury Wills, 1962 (10)

Hits: Most, season

241	Babe Herman, 1930
230	Tommy Davis, 1962
221	Zack Wheat, 1925
219	Lefty O'Doul, 1932
217	Babe Herman, 1929

2B: Most, season

52	Johnny Frederick, 1929
48	Babe Herman, 1930
47	Wes Parker, 1970
44	Johnny Frederick, 1930
43	Augie Galan, 1944
43	Babe Herman, 1931
43	STEVE SAX, 1986

3B: Most, season

26	George Treadway, 1894
22	Hy Myers, 1920
20	Dan Brouthers, 1892
20	Tommy Corcoran, 1894
19	Jimmy Sheckard, 1901
16	Willie Davis, 1970 (12)

HR: Most, season

43	Duke Snider, 1956
42	Gil Hodges, 1954
42	Duke Snider, 1953
42	Duke Snider, 1955
41	Roy Campanella, 1953
35	MIKE PIAZZA, 1993 (9)

RBI: Most, season

153	Tommy Davis, 1962
142	Roy Campanella, 1953
136	Duke Snider, 1955
130	Jack Fournier, 1925
130	Babe Herman, 1930
130	Gil Hodges, 1954
130	Duke Snider, 1954

SB: Most, season

104	Maury Wills, 1962
94	Maury Wills, 1965
88	John Ward, 1892
85	Hub Collins, 1890
77	Davey Lopes, 1975

BB: Most, season

148	Eddie Stanky, 1945
137	Eddie Stanky, 1946
119	Dolph Camilli, 1938
116	Pee Wee Reese, 1949
114	Augie Galan, 1945
110	Jim Wynn, 1975 (6)

BA: Highest, season

.393	Babe Herman, 1930
.381	Babe Herman, 1929
.379	Willie Keeler, 1899
.375	Zack Wheat, 1924
.368	Lefty O'Doul, 1932
.346	Tommy Davis, 1962 (16)

Slug avg: Highest, season

.678	Babe Herman, 1930
.647	Duke Snider, 1954
.628	Duke Snider, 1955
.627	Duke Snider, 1953
.612	Babe Herman, 1929
.577	Pedro Guerrero, 1985 (14)

Games started: Most, season

44	George Haddock, 1892
44	Brickyard Kennedy, 1893
44	Adonis Terry, 1890
43	Tom Lovett, 1891
42	Don Drysdale, 1963
42	Don Drysdale, 1965
42	Ed Stein, 1892

Saves: Most, season

28	JAY HOWELL, 1989
25	JIM GOTT, 1993
24	Jim Brewer, 1970
24	Jim Hughes, 1954
22	Jim Brewer, 1971
22	CHARLIE HOUGH, 1977

Shutouts: Most, season

11	Sandy Koufax, 1963
9	Don Sutton, 1972
8	TIM BELCHER, 1989
8	Don Drysdale, 1968
8	OREL HERSHISER, 1988
8	Sandy Koufax, 1965
8	FERNANDO VALENZUELA, 1981

Wins: Most, season

30	Tom Lovett, 1890
29	George Haddock, 1892
28	Jim Hughes, 1899
28	Joe McGinnity, 1900
28	Dazzy Vance, 1924
27	Sandy Koufax, 1966 (6)

K: Most, season

382	Sandy Koufax, 1965
317	Sandy Koufax, 1966
306	Sandy Koufax, 1963
269	Sandy Koufax, 1961
262	Dazzy Vance, 1924

Win pct: Highest, season

.880	Preacher Roe, 1951
.864	OREL HERSHISER, 1985
.833	Sandy Koufax, 1963
.824	Jim Hughes, 1899
.824	Dazzy Vance, 1924

ERA: Lowest, season

1.58	Rube Marquard, 1916
1.68	Ned Garvin, 1904
1.73	Sandy Koufax, 1966
1.74	Sandy Koufax, 1964
1.87	Kaiser Wilhelm, 1908

Most pinch-hit homers, season

6	Johnny Frederick, Bro-1932
5	Lee Lacy, 1978

Most pinch-hit, homers, career

8	Johnny Frederick, Bro-1929-1934
8	Lee Lacy, 1972-1978

Most consecutive games, batting safely

31	Willie Davis, 1969
29	Zach Wheat, Bro-1916

Most consecutive scoreless innings

59	OREL HERSHISER, 1988
58	Don Drysdale, 1968
39	Don Newcombe, Bro-1956

No hit games

Tom Lovett, Bro vs NY NL, 4-0; June 22, 1891.

Mal Eason, Bro at StL NL, 2-0; July 20, 1906.

Harry McIntyre, Bro vs Pit NL, 0-1; August 1, 1906 (lost on 4 hits in 13 innings after allowing the first hit in the 11th).

Nap Rucker, Bro vs Bos NL, 6-0; September 5, 1908 (2nd game).

Dazzy Vance, Bro vs Phi NL, 10-1; September 13, 1925 (1st game).

Tex Carleton, Bro at Cin NL, 3-0; April 30, 1940.

Ed Head, Bro vs Bos NL, 5-0; April 23, 1946.

Rex Barney, Bro at NY NL, 2-0; September 9, 1948.

Carl Erskine, Bro vs Chi NL, 5-0; June 19, 1952.

Carl Erskine, Bro vs NY NL, 3-0; May 12, 1956.

Sal Maglie, Bro vs Phi NL, 5-0; September 25, 1956.

Sandy Koufax, LA vs NY NL, 5-0; June 30, 1962.

Sandy Koufax, LA vs SF NL, 8-0; May 11, 1963.

Sandy Koufax, LA at Phi NL, 3-0; June 4, 1964.

Sandy Koufax, LA vs Chi NL, 1-0; September 9, 1965 (perfect game).

Bill Singer, LA vs Phi NL, 5-0; July 20, 1970.

Jerry Reuss, LA at SF NL, 8-0; June 27, 1980.

FERNANDO VALENZUELA, LA vs StL NL, 6-0; June 29, 1990.

KEVIN GROSS, LA vs SF NL, 2-0; August 17, 1992.

Ed Stein, six innings, rain, Bro vs Chi NL, 6-0; June 2, 1894.

Fred Frankhouse, seven and two-thirds innings, rain, Bro vs Cin NL, 5-0; August 27, 1937.

ACTIVE PLAYERS in caps.

Leader from franchise's current location is included. If not in the top five, leader's rank is listed in parentheses; asterisk (*) indicates player is not in top 25.

Cincinnati Reds

by Robert Hanashiro, USA TODAY

Jose Rijo led the National League in strikeouts (227). and was second in ERA (2.48).

1993 Reds: From insults to injuries

In '93, Cincinnati was more like the Red Cross than the Big Red Machine.

After a second-place finish in '92, the Reds appeared to be a legitimate threat to Atlanta's two-year hold on the NL West. Instead, they limped their way to 73-84, their worst record since 1984, and 31 games behind the Braves, their worst deficit since 1949. Compounded by the embarrassment of owner Marge Schott's nine-month suspension and the unpopular firing of manager Tony Perez in May, Cincinnati was one red-faced baseball town.

But rampant injuries caused the most grief. The starting lineup was supposed to be: 1B Hal Morris, 2B Bip Roberts, SS Barry Larkin, 3B Chris Sabo, LF Kevin Mitchell, CF Roberto Kelly, RF Reggie Sanders and C Joe Oliver. By year's end, that lineup was penciled in as a whole only four times (all in June).

Fifteen players were placed on the disabled list a team-record 20 times. The Reds rotated a team-record 51 players into uniform, 28 of whom hadn't played for the team prior to '93. Ten rookie pitchers made 64 starts.

The injuries that really hurt:

▶Morris missed the first two months of the season after hurting his shoulder in a spring training fight. He ended up hitting .317 (seven HR, 49 RBI) in 101 games.

▶Larkin was lost for the season Aug. 5 with a torn ligament in his left thumb. He was hitting .315.

▶Mitchell was bothered by injuries all season, and still hit .341 with 19 HR and 64 RBI in only 93 games. He went on the disabled list for good on Sept. 10.

▶Roberts was lost for the season on Aug. 4 with a thumb injury.

▶LHP John Smiley was lost for the season July 3 for elbow surgery.

▶Tom Browning, senior member of the pitching staff, ended his disappointing season (7-7, 4.74 ERA) Aug. 7 with a fractured left middle finger.

▶Closer Rod Dibble missed 33 games early in the season, then was shelved for the year with shoulder problems in September. It put an end to a dismal season: 1-4, 6.58 ERA.

But the season wasn't all a headache for new manager Davey Johnson, who compiled a 53-65 record after replacing Perez. Jose Rijo was named the club's Outstanding Pitcher for the fourth year in a row. If he'd had any run support, Rijo would have been a Cy Young candidate (14-9, 2.48 ERA). He led the NL in strikeouts (227)—first time for a Reds pitcher since 1947—and was among NL leaders in starts (36) and innings pitched (257.1).

On the offensive side, there was Sabo. He hit .259, had a team-high 33 doubles, 21 HR and 82 RBI. He also led the team in games played (148), despite missing 13 games with a ruptured disc in his lower back.

—by Scott Kauffman

1994 Reds: Preview

With Marge Schott back, don't expect a season like '93 to repeat itself without noise from the czar's office—especially after seeing her $39.8 million payroll, third highest in the NL, produce nothing more than a fifth-place finish.

Despite the miserable '93 campaign, the Reds, if they're healthy, should be as strong a team as you'll find in the new NL Central. Two question marks are whether Bret Boone can replace Bip Roberts and who takes over at third base. Otherwise, the biggest concern is pitching. Unless Tim Pugh (10-15, 5.26 ERA), John Roper (2-5, 5.63 ERA) and Larry Luebbers (2-5, 4.54 ERA) can improve, a healthy John Smiley and Tom Browning won't be enough to put a smile on Schott's face.

—by Scott Kauffman

1993 Reds: Between the lines

▶**April 8:** Bobby Kelly's first NL homer was a grand slam, and Kevin Mitchell was 4-for-6 with a homer and three RBI, but the Reds still lost to the Expos, 14-11.

▶**April 17:** The Reds record dropped to 2-9—their worst start since 1955.

▶**April 20:** Tim Belcher pitched his 14th career shutout (5-0) against the Pirates. Barry Larkin was 3-for-3 when he bruised his left thumb and left the game to get X-rays.

▶**April 21:** Rob Dibble broke his arm making a game-saving tag at home after uncorking a wild pitch. He was expected to be out four to six weeks.

▶**April 22:** Two-thirds of the Reds outfield left the game with injuries. Bobby Kelly and Kevin Mitchell both had hamstring trouble.

▶**April 24:** The Reds got two grand slams in one game for the first time since 1955. Chris Sabo went deep with the bases juiced in the first inning and Joe Oliver followed suit in the seventh.

▶**April 30:** Reggie Sanders was sidelined with a flu bug that had been rampant in the Cincinnati clubhouse, leaving catcher Joe Oliver as the lone Red who had started every game.

▶**May 13:** Kevin Mitchell hit a pair of upper deck homers, including a shot to the red seats in left field at Riverfront Stadium—the first home run hit to that spot in five years. He boosted his average to .378 while helping John Smiley get his first win in a Reds' uniform.

▶**May 14:** Mitchell went 4-for-4 in the 13-5 win against the Rockies. In his last 10 at-bats he had three homers, three doubles and a triple to raise his average to .407.

▶**May 25:** While the Braves played the Reds at Riverfront Stadium, airplanes dragging five different banners criticizing the firing of Reds manager Tony Perez flew overhead.

▶**June 6:** *Quote of the day*—Pitcher Jose Rijo on the Reds' 5-1 loss to St. Louis, which dropped their season mark to 26-30: "We stink. We're worse than our record. . . . But I was as bad as anybody else. I stunk."

▶**June 11:** Mitchell homered in his first at-bat following a three-day hiatus with a sore back, but Rob Dibble blew a ninth-inning lead, then threw part of the clubhouse postgame buffet against the wall. *Quote of the day*—Mitchell, after losing his special-diet dinner: "I asked him how come he couldn't save the cantaloupe; that was my dinner. Can't we all get along?"

▶**June 18:** Prospect John Roper left after 2 2/3 hitless innings with a strained muscle in his side, aggravating an old injury, and was placed on the 15-day DL. *Milestone*—Barry Larkin's 1,000th career hit drove in the winning run in the 10th inning as the Reds beat the Dodgers 4-3.

▶**June 22:** Kevin Mitchell had a homer, triple and two doubles and drove in four runs, while Bobby Kelly was 3-for-6 with a homer and five RBI in the Reds' 16-13 win against Colorado. Chris Jones had his second two-homer game for the Rockies, while Charlie Hayes was 3-for-5 with three stolen bases.

▶**June 25:** Mitchell's three-run homer extended his hitting streak to 19 games, tops in the majors.

▶**June 30:** Randy Milligan hit two homers in a 5-4 win against the Astros.

▶**July 6:** Jacob Brumfield got his fifth consecutive start in center field. Before that, he had played in 54 games and never started more than two in a row.

▶**July 16:** Jose Rijo won for the first time since May 22, shutting out Florida for eight innings.

▶**July 26:** Rijo threw eight innings of four-hit ball to beat the Astros 6-1. He allowed just one unearned run, fanned 10 for his eighth win and drove in a run. His career record against the Astros stood at 12-5.

▶**August 8:** *Quote of the day*—Rookie Johnny Ruffin picked up an 8-5 win over L.A. in his major league debut.

"That was an adrenalin rush right there," Ruffin said. "Walking into the park, all those people knowing I was a big-league player. But then, for some reason, when I got called in to pitch, I wasn't nervous at all. It was like it was my time or something. I just told myself, 'Be poised, you've waited all this time for this.' "

▶**August 9:** First base coach Jose Cardenal was hit on the head by a thrown ball during batting practice, and was totally immobile on the ground for nearly 10 minutes before he began moving his hands and legs. He was taken to a San Francisco hospital and later released with a hairline fracture on the top of his head. Cardenal already has a plate in his head, the result of being hit by a batted ball during a drill in 1990.

▶**August 16:** Barry Larkin had his injured left thumb placed in a cast before the game, ending his season.

▶**August 20:** Shortstop Willie Greene suffered a season-ending dislocated thumb when he collided with third baseman Chris Sabo chasing a foul pop. But at least the Reds won the game; Sabo was 3-for-4 with a homer and Jose Rijo's four strikeouts gave him a career-high 178, tops in the NL in that department.

▶**August 30:** Thomas Howard hit a two-run homer and singled twice as the Reds routed St. Louis, 10-3. Howard, acquired Aug. 20 in a trade with Cleveland, hit his third homer in 10 games. Rijo earned his 12th win. Rijo had not allowed more than two earned runs in any of his 10 starts since the All-Star break for a 1.11 ERA.

▶**September 4:** Rijo's four RBI helped Cincinnati defeat the Phillies 6-5. He also allowed just one run in seven innings, continuing his status as the league's ERA and strikeout leader.

▶**September 23:** The Reds beat Los Angeles 11-2 to snap a 12-game losing streak. It was Cincinnati's longest losing spell since 1945 and only one game short of the major league high of 13, set by the Colorado Rockies. The Reds were outscored 7-28 during the streak.

▶**October 3:** After a season plagued by injury, controversy, and disappoint-ment, the Reds finished on a positive note, beating the Astros 7-4. They finished in fifth place in the NL West, 31 games behind red-hot Atlanta. Stopped short with just 323 at-bats, Kevin Mitchell was batting .341 with 19 homers, a .601 slugging percentage, 110 hits (in 93 games), and a .385 on-base percentage. The percentages would have put him in the league leaders. *League leaders, pitching*—Jose Rijo led the league in strikeouts (227) and was second in both ERA (2.48) and innings pitched (257 1/3).

—by John Hunt, Scott Kauffman, Lisa Winston, Deron Snyder, Matt Young

Team directory

▶**Owner:** Marge Schott and a limited partnership
▶**General Manager:** James G. Bowden
▶**Ballpark:**
Riverfront Stadium
Pete Rose Way, Cincinnati, Ohio
513-421-4510
Capacity 52,952
Parking for 5,022 cars; $3.50-$5
Wheelchair locations, ramps
▶**Team publications:**
Media guide, yearbook/program
513-421-4510
▶**TV, radio broadcast stations:**
WLW 700 AM, WLWT Channel 5,
Sportschannel-Cincinnati
▶**Spring Training:**
Plant City Stadium
Plant City, Fla.
Capacity 6,700
813-752-1878

CINCINNATI REDS 1993 final stats

Batting	BA	SLG	OB	G	AB	R	H	TB	2B	3B	HR	RBI	BB	SO	SB	CS	E
Mitchell	.341	.601	.385	93	323	56	110	194	21	3	19	64	25	48	1	0	7
Kelly	.319	.475	.354	78	320	44	102	152	17	3	9	35	17	43	21	5	1
Morris	.317	.420	.371	101	379	48	120	159	18	0	7	49	34	51	2	2	5
Larkin	.315	.445	.394	100	384	57	121	171	20	3	8	51	51	33	14	1	16
Howard	.277	.461	.331	38	141	22	39	65	8	3	4	13	12	21	5	6	1
Sanders	.274	.444	.343	138	496	90	136	220	16	4	20	83	51	118	27	10	8
Milligan	.274	.406	.394	83	234	30	64	95	11	1	6	29	46	49	0	2	5
Brumfield	.268	.419	.321	103	272	40	73	114	17	3	6	23	21	47	20	8	7
Kessinger	.259	.407	.344	11	27	4	7	11	1	0	1	3	4	4	0	0	2
Sabo	.259	.440	.315	148	552	86	143	243	33	2	21	82	43	105	6	4	11
Dorsett	.254	.413	.288	25	63	7	16	26	4	0	2	12	3	14	0	0	0
Branson	.241	.310	.275	125	381	40	92	118	15	1	3	22	19	73	4	1	11
Roberts	.240	.295	.330	83	292	46	70	86	13	0	1	18	38	46	26	6	6
Oliver	.239	.384	.276	139	482	40	115	185	28	0	14	75	27	91	0	0	7
Espy	.233	.267	.368	40	60	6	14	16	2	0	0	5	14	13	2	2	2
Varsho	.232	.358	.302	77	95	8	22	34	6	0	2	11	9	19	1	0	0
Samuel	.230	.345	.298	103	261	31	60	90	10	4	4	26	23	53	9	7	10
Daugherty	.226	.355	.338	50	62	7	14	22	2	0	2	9	11	15	0	0	1
Costo	.224	.367	.250	31	98	13	22	36	5	0	3	12	4	17	0	0	1
Wilson	.224	.263	.302	36	76	6	17	20	3	0	0	8	9	16	0	0	1
Tubbs	.186	.237	.351	35	59	10	11	14	0	0	1	2	14	10	3	1	1
Gordon	.167	.167	.167	3	6	0	1	1	0	0	0	0	0	2	0	0	0
Gregg	.167	.167	.154	10	12	1	2	2	0	0	0	1	0	0	0	0	0
Greene	.160	.340	.189	15	50	7	8	17	1	1	2	5	2	19	0	0*	1
Hernandez	.083	.083	.120	27	24	3	2	2	0	0	0	1	1	8	1	2	1
Koelling	.067	.067	.125	7	15	2	1	1	0	0	0	0	0	2	0	0	1
Hughes	.000	.000	.000	3	4	0	0	0	0	0	0	0	0	0	0	0	0

Pitching	W-L	ERA	G	GS	CG	GF	Sho	SV	IP	H	R	ER	HR	BB	SO
Foster	2-2	1.75	17	0	0	7	0	0	25.2	23	8	5	1	5	16
Rijo	14-9	2.48	36	36	2	0	1	0	257.1	218	76	71	19	62	227
Spradlin	2-1	3.49	37	0	0	16	0	2	49	44	20	19	4	9	24
Ruffin	2-1	3.58	21	0	0	5	0	2	37.2	36	16	15	4	11	30
Landrum	0-2	3.74	18	0	0	6	0	0	21.2	18	9	9	1	6	14
Henry	0-1	3.86	3	0	0	1	0	0	4.2	6	8	2	0	4	2
Reardon	4-6	4.09	58	0	0	32	0	8	61.2	66	34	28	4	10	35
Service	2-2	4.30	29	0	0	7	0	2	46	44	24	22	6	16	43
Powell	0-3	4.41	9	1	0	1	0	0	16.1	13	8	8	1	6	17
Belcher	9-6	4.47	22	22	4	0	2	0	137	134	72	68	11	47	101
Luebbers	2-5	4.54	14	14	0	0	0	0	77.1	74	49	39	7	38	38
Browning	7-7	4.74	21	20	0	0	0	0	114	159	61	60	15	20	53
Cadaret	2-1	4.96	34	0	0	15	0	1	32.2	40	19	18	3	23	23
Pugh	10-15	5.26	31	27	3	3	1	0	164.1	200	102	96	19	59	94
Ayala	7-10	5.60	43	9	0	8	0	3	98	106	72	61	16	45	65
Smiley	3-9	5.62	18	18	2	0	0	0	105.2	117	69	66	15	31	60
Roper	2-5	5.63	16	15	0	0	0	0	80	92	51	50	10	36	54
Hill	3-0	5.65	19	0	0	2	0	0	28.2	34	18	18	5	9	23
Dibble	1-4	6.48	45	0	0	37	0	19	41.2	34	33	30	8	42	49
Wickander	1-0	6.75	33	0	0	8	0	0	25.1	32	20	19	5	19	20
Bushing	0-0	12.46	6	0	0	2	0	0	4.1	9	7	6	1	4	3
Ruskin	0-0	18.00	4	0	0	0	0	0	1	3	2	2	1	2	0
Anderson	0-0	18.56	3	0	0	0	0	0	5.1	12	11	11	3	3	4

1994 preliminary roster

PITCHERS (20)
Tom Browning
Hector Carrasco
John Courtright
Rob Dibble
Mike Ferry
Steve Foster
Erik Hanson
Brian Holman
Kevin Jarvis
Larry Luebbers
Jeff Pierce
Ross Powell
Tim Pugh
Jose Rijo
John Roper
Johnny Ruffin
Scott Service
John Smiley
Jerry Spradlin
Kevin Wickander

CATCHERS (3)
Darron Cox
Brian Dorsett
Joe Oliver

INFIELDERS (8)
Bret Boone
Jeff Branson
Tim Costo
Jamie Dismuke
Willie Greene
Brian Koelling

Barry Larkin
Hal Morris

OUTFIELDERS (7)
Jacob Brumfield
Steve Gibralter
Keith Gordon
Thomas Howard
Roberto Kelly
Kevin Mitchell
Reggie Sanders

Games played by position

Player	G	C	1B	2B	3B	SS	OF
Branson	125	0	1	45	14	59	0
Brumfield	103	0	0	4	0	0	96
Costo	31	0	2	0	2	0	26
Daugherty	50	0	3	0	0	0	17
Dorsett	25	18	3	0	0	0	0
Espy	40	0	0	0	0	0	18
Gordon	3	0	0	0	0	0	2
Greene	15	0	0	0	5	10	0
Gregg	10	0	0	0	0	0	4
Hernandez	27	0	0	0	0	0	23
Howard	38	0	0	0	0	0	37
Hughes	3	0	0	0	0	0	2
Kelly	78	0	0	0	0	0	77
Kessinger	11	0	0	0	0	11	0
Koelling	7	0	0	3	0	2	0
Larkin	100	0	0	0	0	99	0
Milligan	83	0	61	0	0	0	9
Mitchell	93	0	0	0	0	0	87
Morris	101	0	98	0	0	0	0
Oliver	139	133	12	0	0	0	1
Roberts	83	0	0	64	3	1	11
Sabo	148	0	0	0	148	0	0
Samuel	103	0	6	70	4	0	3
Sanders	138	0	0	0	0	0	137
Tubbs	35	0	0	0	0	0	21
Varsho	77	0	0	0	0	0	22
Wilson	36	35	0	0	0	0	0

Sick call: 1993 DL Report

Player	Days on the DL
Tom Browning	58
Willie Canate#	8
Rob Dibble*	48
Steve Foster*	134
Willie Greene	44
Roberto Kelly	82
Bill Landrum	122
Barry Larkin	60
Kevin Mitchell	15
Hal Morris	63
Bip Roberts*	76
John Roper	30
Chris Sabo	15
John Smiley	93
Kevin Wickander*	35

Two separate terms on Disabled List
 # Willie Canate was on the DL both in Cincinnati and Toronto.

Minor League Report

Class AAA: Indianapolis finished at 66-75, third in the American Association Eastern Division. Tim Costo hit .326 with 11 homers and 57 RBI. Willie Greene hit 22 homers. Mike Anderson was 10-6 with a 3.75 ERA. Scott Ruskin led the league with 28 saves. Ross Powell struck out 133. **Class AA:** Chattanooga finished at 72-69, second in the Southern League Western Division. Jamie Dismuke hit .308 with 20 homers and 91 RBI. Mark Merchant hit .301 with 17 homers and 61 RBI. Mike Ferry led the league in wins at 13-8 with a 3.42 ERA. Chris Hook had 12 wins. Chris Bushing led the league with 29 saves. Jeff Pierce had 22, coming over from Birmingham mid-season. **Class A:** Winston-Salem finished at 72-68, winning the second half of the Carolina League Southern Division. Bubba Smith was league MVP, repeating the honors from 1992, batting .301 with 27 homers and 81 RBI. Tim Belk hit .306 with 14 homers and 65 RBI. Cleveland Ladell hit .284 with 20 homers. Chad Mottola led the league with 91 RBI. Mateo Ozuna stole 32 bases. John Hrusovsky led the league with 25 saves. . . . West Virginia finished at 76-64, second in the Sally League Northern Division. Martin Lister had 32 saves. **Short-season:** Billings finished at 48-25, winning the Pioneer League Northern Division. Chris Sexton hit .333 with 46 RBI. Paul Bako hit .314. Stephen Gann had 51 RBI. Todd Etler was 8-1 with a 2.71 ERA. Jon Hebel was 6-2 with a 3.45 ERA. . . . Princeton finished at 26-42, fourth in the Appalachian League Northern Division. Roger Etheridge was 3-2 with a league-leading 1.49 ERA and 60 strikeouts in 54 innings.

Tops in the organization

Batter	Club	Avg	G	AB	R	H	HR	RBI
Costo, Tim	Ind	.326	106	362	49	118	11	57
Belk, Tim	W-S	.306	134	509	89	156	14	65
Dismuke, Jamie	Cng	.306	136	497	69	152	20	91
Smith, Bubba	W-S	.301	92	342	55	103	27	81
Merchant, Mark	Cng	.298	112	342	58	102	17	61

Home Runs			Wins		
Smith, Bubba	W-S	27	Tuttle, Dave	W-S	15
Greene, Willie	Ind	22	Ferry, Mike	Cng	13
Mottola, Chad	W-S	21	Hook, Chris	Cng	12
Several players tied		20	Several players tied		11

RBI			Saves		
Mottola, Chad	W-S	91	Lister, Martin	Cwv	32
Dismuke, Jamie	Cng	91	Bushing, Chris	Cng	29
Smith, Bubba	W-S	81	Ruskin, Scott	Ind	28
Jones, Motorboat	W-S	79	Hrusovsky, John	W-S	25
Several players tied		74	Pierce, Jeff	Cng	22

Stolen Bases			Strikeouts		
Koelling, Brian	Ind	34	Powell, Ross	Ind	133
Ozuna, Mateo	W-S	32	Tuttle, Dave	W-S	132
Jenkins, Dee	Cwv	27	Steph, Rod	W-S	130
Ladell, Cleveland	W-S	24	Anderson, Mike	Ind	125
Owens, Eric	W-S	21	Stewart, Carl	W-S	125

Pitcher	Club	W-L	ERA	IP	H	BB	SO
Culberson, Calvain	Cng	7- 6	2.74	118	91	43	95
Jarvis, Kevin	Cng	11- 8	3.06	182	159	59	119
Ferry, Mike	Cng	13- 8	3.42	187	176	30	111
Courtright, John	Cng	5-11	3.50	175	179	70	96
Anderson, Mike	Ind	11- 7	3.52	166	160	57	125

Cincinnati (1890-1993)

Runs: Most, career, all-time

1741	Pete Rose, 1963-1986
1091	Johnny Bench, 1967-1983
1043	Frank Robinson, 1956-1965
993	Dave Concepcion, 1970-1988
978	Vada Pinson, 1958-1968

Hits: Most, career, all-time

3358	Pete Rose, 1963-1986
2326	Dave Concepcion, 1970-1988
2048	Johnny Bench, 1967-1983
1934	Tony Perez, 1964-1986
1881	Vada Pinson, 1958-1968

2B: Most, career, all-time

601	Pete Rose, 1963-1986
389	Dave Concepcion, 1970-1988
381	Johnny Bench, 1967-1983
342	Vada Pinson, 1958-1968
339	Tony Perez, 1964-1986

3B: Most, career, all-time

152	Edd Roush, 1916-1931
115	Pete Rose, 1963-1986
112	Bid McPhee, 1890-1899
96	Vada Pinson, 1958-1968
94	Curt Walker, 1924-1930

HR: Most, career, all-time

389	Johnny Bench, 1967-1983
324	Frank Robinson, 1956-1965
287	Tony Perez, 1964-1986
251	Ted Kluszewski, 1947-1957
244	George Foster, 1971-1981

RBI: Most, career, all-time

1376	Johnny Bench, 1967-1983
1192	Tony Perez, 1964-1986
1036	Pete Rose, 1963-1986
1009	Frank Robinson, 1956-1965
950	Dave Concepcion, 1970-1988

SB: Most, career, all-time

406	Joe Morgan, 1972-1979
337	Arlie Latham, 1890-1895
321	Dave Concepcion, 1970-1988
319	Bob Bescher, 1908-1913
316	Bid McPhee, 1890-1899

BB: Most, career, all-time

1210	Pete Rose, 1963-1986
891	Johnny Bench, 1967-1983
881	Joe Morgan, 1972-1979
736	Dave Concepcion, 1970-1988
698	Frank Robinson, 1956-1965

BA: Highest, career, all-time

.332	Cy Seymour, 1902-1906
.331	Edd Roush, 1916-1931
.325	Jake Beckley, 1897-1903
.314	Bubbles Hargrave, 1921-1928
.311	Rube Bressler, 1917-1927

Slug avg: Highest, career, all-time

.554	Frank Robinson, 1956-1965
.514	George Foster, 1971-1981
.512	Ted Kluszewski, 1947-1957
.509	ERIC DAVIS, 1984-1991
.498	Wally Post, 1949-1963

Games started: Most, career, all-time

356	Eppa Rixey, 1921-1933
322	Paul Derringer, 1933-1942
319	Dolf Luque, 1918-1929
296	Bucky Walters, 1938-1948
291	TOM BROWNING, 1984-1993

Saves: Most, career, all-time

148	JOHN FRANCO, 1984-1989
119	Clay Carroll, 1968-1975
88	ROB DIBBLE, 1988-1993
88	Tom Hume, 1977-1987
76	Pedro Borbon, 1970-1979

Shutouts: Most, career, all-time

32	Bucky Walters, 1938-1948
30	Jim Maloney, 1960-1970
29	Johnny Vander Meer, 1937-1949
25	Ken Raffensberger, 1947-1954
24	Paul Derringer, 1933-1942
24	Noodles Hahn, 1899-1905
24	Dolf Luque, 1918-1929

Wins: Most, career, all-time

179	Eppa Rixey, 1921-1933
161	Paul Derringer, 1933-1942
160	Bucky Walters, 1938-1948
154	Dolf Luque, 1918-1929
134	Jim Maloney, 1960-1970

K: Most, career, all-time

1592	Jim Maloney, 1960-1970
1449	Mario Soto, 1977-1988
1289	Joe Nuxhall, 1944-1966
1251	Johnny Vander Meer, 1937-1949
1062	Paul Derringer, 1933-1942

Win pct: Highest, career, all-time

.674	Don Gullett, 1970-1976
.653	Pedro Borbon, 1970-1979
.624	JOSE RIJO, 1988-1993
.623	Jim Maloney, 1960-1970
.623	Clay Carroll, 1968-1975

ERA: Lowest, career, all-time

2.18	Fred Toney, 1915-1918
2.37	Bob Ewing, 1902-1909
2.52	Noodles Hahn, 1899-1905
2.56	JOSE RIJO, 1988-1993
2.62	Hod Eller, 1917-1921

Runs: Most, season

134	Frank Robinson, 1962
131	Vada Pinson, 1959
130	Pete Rose, 1976
129	Arlie Latham, 1894
126	Tommy Harper, 1965

Hits: Most, season

230	Pete Rose, 1973
219	Cy Seymour, 1905
218	Pete Rose, 1969
215	Pete Rose, 1976
210	Pete Rose, 1968
210	Pete Rose, 1975

2B: Most, season

51	Frank Robinson, 1962
51	Pete Rose, 1978
47	Vada Pinson, 1959
47	Pete Rose, 1975
45	George Kelly, 1929
45	Pete Rose, 1974

3B: Most, season

26	John Reilly, 1890
22	Sam Crawford, 1902
22	Jake Daubert, 1922
22	Bid McPhee, 1890
22	Mike Mitchell, 1911

HR: Most, season

52	George Foster, 1977
49	Ted Kluszewski, 1954
47	Ted Kluszewski, 1955
45	Johnny Bench, 1970
40	Johnny Bench, 1972
40	George Foster, 1978
40	Ted Kluszewski, 1953
40	Tony Perez, 1970
40	Wally Post, 1955

RBI: Most, season

149	George Foster,	1977
148	Johnny Bench,	1970
141	Ted Kluszewski,	1954
136	Frank Robinson,	1962
130	Deron Johnson,	1965

SB: Most, season

87	Arlie Latham,	1891
80	Bob Bescher,	1911
80	ERIC DAVIS,	1986
79	Dave Collins,	1980
76	Dusty Miller,	1896

BB: Most, season

132	Joe Morgan,	1975
120	Joe Morgan,	1974
117	Joe Morgan,	1977
115	Joe Morgan,	1972
114	Joe Morgan,	1976

BA: Highest, season

.377	Cy Seymour,	1905
.372	Bug Holliday,	1894
.351	Edd Roush,	1923
.351	Mike Donlin,	1903
.348	Edd Roush,	1924

Slug avg: Highest, season

.642	Ted Kluszewski,	1954
.631	George Foster,	1977
.624	Frank Robinson,	1962
.611	Frank Robinson,	1961
.595	Frank Robinson,	1960

Games started: Most, season

49	Elton Chamberlain,	1892
47	Tony Mullane,	1891
45	Billy Rhines,	1890
43	Billy Rhines,	1891
42	Noodles Hahn,	1901
42	Pete Schneider,	1917
42	Fred Toney,	1917

Saves: Most, season

39	JOHN FRANCO,	1988
37	Clay Carroll,	1972
35	Wayne Granger,	1970
32	JOHN FRANCO,	1987
32	JOHN FRANCO,	1989

Shutouts: Most, season

7	Jack Billingham,	1973
7	Hod Eller,	1919
7	Fred Toney,	1917
6	Ewell Blackwell,	1947
6	Noodles Hahn,	1902
6	Jack Harper,	1904
6	DANNY JACKSON,	1988
6	Dolf Luque,	1923
6	Jim Maloney,	1963
6	Ken Raffensberger,	1952
6	Billy Rhines,	1890
6	Fred Toney,	1915
6	Johnny Vander Meer,	1941
6	Bucky Walters,	1944
6	Jake Weimer,	1906

Wins: Most, season

28	Billy Rhines,	1890
27	Pink Hawley,	1898
27	Dolf Luque,	1923
27	Bucky Walters,	1939
25	Paul Derringer,	1939
25	Eppa Rixey,	1922

K: Most, season

274	Mario Soto,	1982
265	Jim Maloney,	1963
244	Jim Maloney,	1965
242	Mario Soto,	1983
239	Noodles Hahn,	1901

Win pct: Highest, season

.826	Elmer Riddle,	1941
.821	Bob Purkey,	1962
.783	TOM BROWNING,	1988
.781	Paul Derringer,	1939
.771	Dolf Luque,	1923

ERA: Lowest, season

1.58	Fred Toney,	1915
1.73	Bob Ewing,	1907
1.77	Noodles Hahn,	1902
1.82	Dutch Ruether,	1919
1.86	Andy Coakley,	1908

Most pinch-hit homers, season

5	Jerry Lynch,	1961
4	Bob Thurman,	1957

Most pinch-hit, homers, career

13	Jerry Lynch,	1957-1963

Most consecutive games, batting safely

44	Pete Rose,	1978
30	Elmer Smith,	1898

Most consecutive scoreless innings

32	Jim Maloney,	1968-69
27	Tom Seaver,	1977

No hit games

Bumpus Jones, Cin vs Pit NL, 7-1; October 15, 1892 (first game in the major leagues).

Ted Breitenstein, Cin vs Pit NL, 11-0; April 22, 1898.

Noodles Hahn, Cin vs Phi NL, 4-0; July 12, 1900.

Fred Toney, Cin at Chi NL, 1-0; May 2, 1917 (ten innings).

Hod Eller, Cin vs StL NL, 6-0; May 11, 1919.

Johnny Vander Meer, Cin vs Bos NL, 3-0; June 11, 1938.

Johnny Vander Meer, Cin at Bro NL, 6-0; June 15, 1938 (next start after June 11).

Clyde Shoun, Cin vs Bos NL, 1-0; May 15, 1944.

Ewell Blackwell, Cin vs Bos NL, 6-0; June 18, 1947.

Johnny Klippstein (7 innings), Hershell Freeman (1 inning) and Joe Black (3 innings), Cin at Mil NL, 1-2; May 26, 1956 (lost on 3 hits in 11 innings after allowing the first hit in the tenth).

Jim Maloney, Cin vs NY NL, 0-1; June 14, 1965 (lost on 2 hits in 11 innings after pitching 10 hitless innings).

Jim Maloney, Cin at Chi NL, 1-0; August 19, 1965 (1st game, 10 innings).

George Culver, Cin at Phi NL, 6-1; July 29, 1968 (2nd game).

Jim Maloney, Cin vs Hou NL, 10-0; April 30, 1969.

Tom Seaver, Cin vs StL NL, 4-0; June 16, 1978.

TOM BROWNING, Cin vs LA NL, 1-0; September 16, 1988 (perfect game).

Elton Chamberlain, seven innings, darkness, Cin vs Bos NL, 6-0; September 23, 1893 (2nd game).

Jake Weimer, seven innings, agreement, Cin vs Bro NL, 1-0; August 24, 1906 (2nd game).

ACTIVE PLAYERS in caps.

Colorado Rockies

by Dianne Weiss, USA TODAY

Andres Galarraga became the first expansion player ever to lead the league in hitting, with a .370 average.

1993 Rockies: 4.5 million fans came to see 'em

The Rockies rebounded from a 16-40 start to set an NL record for victories by an expansion team. Once they weeded out the dead weight on the pitching staff and learned to use Mile High Stadium to their advantage, they were a respectable club. And manager Don Baylor had them playing hard through the 162nd game. They finished six games ahead of the Padres, and fared three games better than their expansion brethren, the Florida Marlins.

The Rockies established the type of fan base that will allow owner Jerry McMorris to expand the payroll. They drew nearly 4.5 million fans this year, and expect big crowds next year and in 1995, their first season at Coors Field.

Andres Galarraga became a fan favorite and the first player to win a batting title for a first-year club. Dante Bichette and Charlie Hayes put up impressive numbers, and the bullpen—the butt of jokes in April and May—was formidable by the season's end; Darren Holmes, Bruce Ruffin and Steve Reed formed the nucleus.

The team finished 17-9 in September, the best record in one month for an expansion team, and became the first expansion team to sweep a four-game series on the road from an established team (Dodgers, Aug. 9-12).

After losing 13 straight in late July and early August, the Rockies rallied for a 31-18 record before losing the final weekend series in Atlanta. Galarraga and Hayes broke the previous RBI record by an expansion player held by Frank Thomas, who had 94 RBI for the Mets in 1962.

But while there were bright spots, most of the on-field news was bad. Alex Cole, Daryl Boston and Chris Jones all failed to hold down center field, leaving the Rockies to wonder if there is an outfielder alive who can chase down balls in the spacious gaps at Mile High.

The Rockies first-year rotation was in a constant state of flux due to injuries and ineffectiveness. Eventually, the pitching came around, led by ex-Brave Armando Reynoso (12-11, 4.00 ERA). Still, the Rockies' final team ERA of 5.41 was the worst in the majors.

They never found their No. 1 starter to lead the staff. The '93 season was essentially a waste for David Nied, first pick in the expansion draft. He missed more than three months with an elbow injury. The trade that brought Greg Harris and Bruce Hurst from San Diego (for catcher Brad Ausmus) was a dud. Hurst had shoulder problems, and Harris went 1-8 with a 6.50 ERA.

By the end of the year, though, the Rockies were playing nearly as well as anyone. The memory of 10-run losses and 13-game losing streaks had faded. The club's late-season surge was gratifying to Baylor. He said it was a payback to Colorado fans, who turned out in record numbers.

"With the fan support we've had, it would be a disappointment if our guys didn't give 110 percent every time," Baylor said. "I didn't want the season to end. The way we we're playing, I wanted it to go on forever."

—by Pete Williams

1994 Rockies: Preview

With a record-setting fan-base, the Rockies will be under pressure to field a contending team perhaps as early as 1995, when they move into Coors Field.

Owner Jerry McMorris has pledged to put some of the Rockies' huge revenues toward acquiring some pitching help. David Nied is expected to be back at full-force. Elsewhere, the Rockies sent Eric Young to the Arizona instructional league to work on center field play. Jerald Clark closed with a rush, but the club wonders if he's the answer in left field. When GM Bob Gebhard isn't looking to acquire pitching, he'll try to add some left-handed power and infield depth.

—by Pete Williams

1993 Rockies: Between the lines

▶**April 7:** Dante Bichette's seventh-inning home run was the Rockies' first homer and their first-ever run scored.

▶**April 11:** The Expos and Rockies combined for 38 hits at Mile High Stadium, 22 of them off Montreal bats as the visitors prevailed, 19-9.

▶**April 23:** The Rockies met the Marlins for the first time, beating them 5-4. All four RBI came from Junior Felix. Darren Holmes got his first save of the season, lowering his ERA to 24.30.

▶**April 26:** Shortstop Vinny Castilla (3-for-3) became the first Colorado player to triple twice in a game.

▶**May 14:** Jay Gainer gained his share of history when he hit the first major league pitch he saw for a homer, becoming just the 12th player to achieve that feat.

▶**May 9:** The Rockies passed the 1 million mark in attendance in their 17th home game—a major league record.

▶**May 26:** Dante Bichette was 3-for-4 and drove in all the runs in Colorado's 3-2 win against Houston.

▶**June 6:** Rockies' outfielder Chris Jones, signed as a minor league free agent in the offseason, hit two home runs in a losing cause as Colorado fell to the Phillies 11-7.

▶**June 13:** Andres Galarraga hit a two-run homer and drove in three runs, Dante Bichette added four hits, and Bruce Ruffin opened the game with five strikeouts in a row as the Rockies recorded their first-ever series sweep with a 9-1 win against the fading Astros. Bichette set a Colorado team record with seven hits in a row, and had a total of eight within 21 hours.

▶**June 15:** Andres Galarraga celebrated finally getting enough at-bats to qualify for the batting leaders list by going 4-for-5 and raising his average to .435.

▶**June 19:** A day after losing to the Padres 11-1, the Rockies came back to pound San Diego, setting a team record for runs in a 17-3 rout. Alex Cole was 2-for-4 with four RBI, Andres Galarraga went 3-for-5 and Charlie Hayes was 2-for-4 with a homer and three RBI, his third homer in as many games.

▶**June 23:** Shortstop Vinny Castilla hit a pair of homers and tied a club record with five RBI to beat Cincinnati 15-5. Andres Galarraga's single extended his hitting streak to 12 games and was his 1,000th hit.

▶**July 4:** Jeff Parrett was sharp in just his second start in three years, allowing three hits over 6 2/3 innings to lift the Rockies past the Cubs 3-1.

▶**July 9:** The Rockies rallied for three runs in the ninth off Cards ace closer Lee Smith to edge the Cardinals 5-4. The runs came on homers by Chris Jones and Danny Sheaffer. Marcus Moore earned the victory in relief in his major league debut.

▶**July 11:** Steve Reed tossed two perfect innings in the Rockies' 4-1 win against the Cardinals for his first save in the majors. His 43 saves in '92 were a single-season record for the minors.

▶**July 20:** Andres Galarraga hit a 455-foot homer, the longest yet at Joe Robbie Stadium, as the Rockies won the latest tilt of the expansion teams, beating the Marlins 6-3.

▶**July 24:** A crowd of 71,784 fans were on hand to watch their Rockies edge the Cardinals 9-8, at Mile High Stadium, the largest for a night game in NL history.

▶**July 30:** Manager Don Baylor was ejected before the Rockies-Giants game at Mile High Stadium. He argued with umpire Charlie Williams, who crumpled up Baylor's lineup card and threw it to the ground. Williams apparently was upset by Baylor's comments after a game two days earlier in which Williams called a Colorado runner out at the plate. Replays showed that the runner was safe. At one point, Baylor had to be restrained from going after Williams.

▶**August 8:** Mo Sanford pitched seven

innings of one-run ball, fanning five, to boost the Rockies to a 5-2 win against San Diego, snapping their 13-game losing streak.

▶**August 10:** Rookie Roberto Mejia, who fanned five times in the previous game, snapped a 1-for-21 slump by going 4-for-4 in the Rockies' 4-2 win against the Dodgers.

▶**August 12:** Willie Blair pitched his first complete game in 35 starts to lead the Rockies to a 4-1 win against the Dodgers and their first-ever four-game series sweep. The victory extended their winning streak to a club-record five games, and came on the heels of a 13-game losing streak. Jerald Clark drove in two runs.

▶**August 21:** Darren Holmes notched saves in both ends of a doubleheader sweep of the Mets, 4-3 and 8-6.

▶**August 22:** Andres Galarraga had a two-run homer, and red-hot Freddie Benavides' solo shot in the seventh snapped a 3-3 tie to give the Rockies a 4-3 win against the Mets and a three-game series sweep.

▶**August 28:** Armando Reynoso, the Rockies' pitcher, hit his second homer of the year, a three-run shot, to lead Colorado to a 7-5 win against the Mets.

▶**August 30:** The Rockies set a single-season NL attendance record with a total of 3,617,863—breaking the mark set by the 1982 Los Angeles Dodgers (3,608,881)—on their 62nd home date.

▶**September 5:** Freddie Benavides entered the game as a pinch-runner for injured Charlie Hayes, and ended up going 2-for-3 with a triple and three RBI as the Rockies beat Pittsburgh 4-1.

▶**September 13:** The Houston-Colorado game in Colorado was postponed when the Denver area was hit with a late-summer storm that left more than five inches of snow on the playing field at Mile High Stadium. Just 24 hours before game time it had been 92 degrees.

▶**October 3:** The Rockies, one of the NL's hottest second-half teams, lost to the even hotter Braves and gave them the division title as the Giants lost in L.A. Though they finished sixth in the NL West, the Rockies showed a lot of promise and broke every imaginable attendance record in major league baseball. *League leaders, pitching*—Darren Holmes was 10th in saves (25) and Greg W. Harris was 10th in innings pitched (225 1/3). *League leaders, batting*—Andres Galarraga won the NL batting title (.370), was second in slugging percentage (.602), and was sixth in on-base percentage (.403); Dante Bichette was third in doubles (43) and sixth in slugging percentage (.526); Eric Young was seventh in stolen bases (42) tied for fifth in triples (8); Charlie Hayes was eighth in slugging percentage (.522) and total bases (299).

—by John Hunt, Scott Kauffman, Lisa Winston, Deron Snyder, Matt Young

Team directory

▶**Owner:** Jerry McMorris
▶**General Manager:** Bob Gebhard
▶**Ballpark:**
Mile High Stadium
2755 West 17th Ave., Denver, Colo.303-292-0200
Capacity 76,100
Parking 2,022, $4-$5
Public transportation available
Wheelchair section, family section in all price ranges
▶**Team publications:**
Media guide, game program, yearbook
▶**TV, radio broadcast stations:**
KWGN Channel 2, KOA 850 AM
▶**Spring Training:**
Hi Corbett Field
Tucson, Ariz.
Capacity 8,000
602-327-9467

COLORADO ROCKIES 1993 final stats

Batting	BA	SLG	OB	G	AB	R	H	TB	2B	3B	HR	RBI	BB	SO	SB	CS	E
Galarraga	.370	.602	.403	120	470	71	174	283	35	4	22	98	24	73	2	4	11
Bichette	.310	.526	.348	141	538	93	167	283	43	5	21	89	28	99	14	8	9
Hayes	.305	.522	.355	157	573	89	175	299	45	2	25	98	43	82	11	6	20
Liriano	.305	.424	.376	48	151	28	46	64	6	3	2	15	18	22	6	4	6
Girardi	.290	.397	.346	86	310	35	90	123	14	5	3	31	24	41	6	6	6
Benavides	.286	.404	.305	74	213	20	61	86	10	3	3	26	6	27	3	2	13
Clark	.282	.444	.324	140	478	65	135	212	26	6	13	67	20	60	9	6	12
Sheaffer	.278	.384	.299	82	216	26	60	83	9	1	4	32	8	15	2	3	2
Jones	.273	.450	.305	86	209	29	57	94	11	4	6	31	10	48	9	4	2
E.Young	.269	.353	.355	144	490	82	132	173	16	8	3	42	63	41	42	19	18
Boston	.261	.464	.325	124	291	46	76	135	15	1	14	40	26	57	1	6	2
Cole	.256	.305	.339	126	348	50	89	106	9	4	0	24	43	58	30	13	4
Castilla	.255	.404	.283	105	337	36	86	136	9	7	9	30	13	45	2	5	11
Mejia	.231	.402	.275	65	229	31	53	92	14	5	5	20	13	63	4	1	12
Owens	.209	.372	.277	33	86	12	18	32	5	0	3	6	6	30	1	0	7
Tatum	.204	.286	.245	92	98	7	20	28	5	0	1	12	5	27	0	0	2
Castellano	.183	.338	.266	34	71	12	13	24	2	0	3	7	8	16	1	1	4
Wedge	.182	.182	.182	9	11	2	2	2	0	0	0	1	0	4	0	0	0
Gainer	.171	.390	.244	23	41	4	7	16	0	0	3	6	4	12	1	1	1
Murphy	.143	.167	.224	26	42	1	6	7	1	0	0	7	5	15	0	1	0
G.Young	.053	.053	.217	19	19	5	1	1	0	0	0	1	4	1	0	1	2

Pitching	W-L	ERA	G	GS	CG	GF	Sho	SV	IP	H	R	ER	HR	BB	SO
Ruffin	6-5	3.87	59	12	0	8	0	2	139.2	145	71	60	10	69	126
Reynoso	12-11	4.00	30	30	4	0	0	0	189	206	101	84	22	63	117
Holmes	3-3	4.05	62	0	0	51	0	25	66.2	56	31	30	6	20	60
Reed	9-5	4.48	64	0	0	14	0	3	84.1	80	47	42	13	30	51
Munoz	2-1	4.50	21	0	0	7	0	0	18	21	12	9	1	9	16
Harris	11-17	4.59	35	35	4	0	0	0	225.1	239	127	115	33	69	123
Blair	6-10	4.75	46	18	1	5	0	0	146	184	90	77	20	42	84
Wayne	5-3	5.05	65	0	0	21	0	1	62.1	68	40	35	8	26	49
Bottenfield	5-10	5.07	37	25	1	2	0	0	159.2	179	102	90	24	71	63
Nied	5-9	5.17	16	16	1	0	0	0	87	99	53	50	8	42	46
Sanford	1-2	5.30	11	6	0	1	0	0	35.2	37	25	21	4	27	36
Leskanic	1-5	5.37	18	8	0	1	0	0	57	59	40	34	7	27	30
Parrett	3-3	5.38	40	6	0	13	0	1	73.2	78	47	44	6	45	66
Painter	2-2	6.00	10	6	1	2	0	0	39	52	26	26	5	9	16
Fredrickson	0-1	6.21	25	0	0	4	0	0	29	33	25	20	3	17	20
Moore	3-1	6.84	27	0	0	8	0	0	26.1	30	25	20	4	20	13
Shepherd	1-3	6.98	14	1	0	3	0	1	19.1	26	16	15	4	4	7
Grant	0-1	7.46	20	0	0	9	0	1	25.1	34	24	21	4	11	14
Hurst	0-2	7.62	5	5	0	0	0	0	13	15	12	11	1	6	9
Smith	2-4	8.49	11	5	0	2	0	0	29.2	47	29	28	2	11	9
Knudson	0-0	22.24	4	0	0	2	0	0	5.2	16	14	14	4	5	3

1994 preliminary roster

PITCHERS (19)
Willie Blair
Kent Bottenfield
Scott Fredrickson
Marvin Freeman
Greg W. Harris
Ryan Hawblitzel
Darren Holmes
Curtis Leskanic
Marcus Moore
Mike Munoz
David Nied
Lance Painter
Jeff Parrett
Steve Reed
Armando Reynoso
Bruce Ruffin
Mo Sanford
Keith Shepherd
Gary Wayne

CATCHERS (4)
Joe Girardi
Jayhawk Owens
Danny Sheaffer
Eric Wedge

INFIELDERS (9)
Freddie Benavides
Pedro Castellano
Vinny Castilla
Jay Gainer
Andres Galarraga
Charlie Hayes
Nelson Liriano
Roberto Mejia
Jim Tatum

OUTFIELDERS (7)
Dante Bichette
Ellis Burks
Jerald Clark
Howard Johnson
Chris Jones
Darrell Sherman
Eric Young

Games played by position

Player	G	C	1B	2B	3B	SS	OF
Benavides	74	0	1	19	5	48	0
Bichette	141	0	0	0	0	0	137
Boston	124	0	0	0	0	0	79
Castellano	34	0	10	4	13	5	0
Castilla	105	0	0	0	0	104	0
Clark	140	0	37	0	0	0	96
Cole	126	0	0	0	0	0	93
Gainer	23	0	7	0	0	0	0
Galarraga	120	0	119	0	0	0	0
Girardi	86	84	0	0	0	0	0
Hayes	157	0	0	0	154	1	0
Jones	86	0	0	0	0	0	70
Liriano	48	0	0	16	1	35	0
Mejia	65	0	0	65	0	0	0
Murphy	26	0	0	0	0	0	13
Owens	33	32	0	0	0	0	0
Sheaffer	82	65	7	0	1	0	2
Tatum	92	0	12	0	6	0	3
Wedge	9	1	0	0	0	0	0
E. Young	144	0	0	79	0	0	52
G. Young	19	0	0	0	0	0	11

Sick call: 1993 DL Report

Player	Days on the DL
Fred Benavides*	41
Vinny Castilla	15
Andres Galarraga*	44
Joe Girardi	67
Mark Grant*	34
Bruce Hurst*%	42
David Nied	99
Jeff Parrett	67
Kevin Ritz	182
Rudy Seanez	102
Bryn Smith	16
Eric Wedge*	112

* Two separate terms on Disabled List
% Bruce Hurst was on the DL twice with San Diego and twice with Colorado.

Minor League Report

Class AAA: Colorado Springs finished at 66-75, third in the Pacific Coast League Southern Division. Lance Painter was 9-7 with a 4.30 ERA. Edwin Alicea hit .337. Trent Hubbard hit .314 with 33 stolen bases. Roberto Mejia hit 14 homers. Andy Mota batted .344. Jay Gainer hit .294 with 74 RBI. **Class A:** Central Valley finished at 61-75, fourth in the California League Northern Division. Quinton McCracken stole 60 bases. John Burke was 7-8 with a 3.18 ERA. Mike Case hit .276 with 11 homers and 80 RBI. Tom Schmidt hit 19 homers and 62 RBI. Mark Thompson had a 2.20 ERA. **Short-season:** Bend finished at 35-41, last in the Northwest League South Division. Ben Ortman hit .289 with four homers. Nathan Holdren hit 12 homers. Chris Henderson had eight saves. Joel Moore struck out 79. . . . Chandler finished at 21-32, seventh in the Arizona League. Vincente Garcia hit .299. Alger Medina stole 26 bases. Keith Barnes was 5-4 with a 2.67 ERA. Denny McAdams had five saves.

Tops in the organization

Batter	Club	Avg	G	AB	R	H	HR	RBI
Mota, Andy	CSp	.320	172	607	82	194	14	111
Hubbard, Trent	CSp	.314	117	439	83	138	7	56
Turner, Ryan	Cv	.294	112	422	64	124	13	67
McCracken, Quin.	Cv	.292	127	483	94	141	2	58
Counsell, Craig	Cv	.280	131	471	79	132	5	59

Home Runs			Wins		
Schmidt, Tom	Cv	19	Burke, John	CSp	10
Mota, Andy	CSp	14	Acevedo, Juan	Cv	9
Mejia, Roberto	CSp	14	Painter, Lance	CSp	9
Bates, Jason	CSp	13	Several players tied		8
Turner, Ryan	Cv	13			

RBI			Saves		
Mota, Andy	CSp	111	Kotarski, Mike	Cv	11
Case, Mike	Cv	80	Duke, Kyle	Cv	9
Gainer, Jay	CSp	74	Shepherd, Keith	CSp	8
Turner, Ryan	Cv	67	Fredrickson, Scott	CSp	7
Several players tied		62	Reed, Steve	CSp	7

Stolen Bases			Strikeouts		
McCracken, Quinton	Cv	60	Burke, John	CSp	152
Hubbard, Trent	CSp	33	Acevedo, Juan	Cv	107
Rogers, Lamarr	Cv	29	Ridenour, Dana	CSp	105
Case, Mike	Cv	21	Sanford, Mo	CSp	104
Several players tied		14	Thompson, Mark	CSp	94

Pitcher	Club	W-L	ERA	IP	H	BB	SO
Burke, John	CSp	10-10	3.17	168	148	87	152
Painter, Lance	CSp	9- 7	4.30	138	165	44	91
Acevedo, Juan	Cv	9- 8	4.40	119	119	58	107
Bailey, Roger	Cv	4- 7	4.84	112	139	56	84
Ridenour, Dana	CSp	8- 8	5.21	121	156	58	105

Colorado (1993)

Runs: Most, career, all-time

93	DANTE BICHETTE, 1993	
89	CHARLIE HAYES, 1993	
82	ERIC YOUNG, 1993	
71	ANDRES GALARRAGA, 1993	
65	JERALD CLARK, 1993	

Hits: Most, career, all-time

175	CHARLIE HAYES, 1993	
174	ANDRES GALARRAGA, 1993	
167	DANTE BICHETTE, 1993	
135	JERALD CLARK, 1993	
132	ERIC YOUNG, 1993	

2B: Most, career, all-time

45	CHARLIE HAYES, 1993	
43	DANTE BICHETTE, 1993	
35	ANDRES GALARRAGA, 1993	
26	JERALD CLARK, 1993	
16	ERIC YOUNG, 1993	

3B: Most, career, all-time

8	ERIC YOUNG, 1993	
7	VINNY CASTILLA, 1993	
6	JERALD CLARK, 1993	
5	DANTE BICHETTE, 1993	
5	JOE GIRARDI, 1993	

HR: Most, career, all-time

25	CHARLIE HAYES, 1993	
22	ANDRES GALARRAGA, 1993	
21	DANTE BICHETTE, 1993	
14	DARYL BOSTON, 1993	
13	JERALD CLARK, 1993	

RBI: Most, career, all-time

98	ANDRES GALARRAGA, 1993	
98	CHARLIE HAYES, 1993	
89	DANTE BICHETTE, 1993	
67	JERALD CLARK, 1993	
42	ERIC YOUNG, 1993	

SB: Most, career, all-time

42	ERIC YOUNG, 1993	
30	ALEX COLE, 1993	
14	DANTE BICHETTE, 1993	
11	CHARLIE HAYES, 1993	
9	JERALD CLARK, 1993	
9	CHRIS JONES, 1993	

BB: Most, career, all-time

63	ERIC YOUNG, 1993	
43	ALEX COLE, 1993	
43	CHARLIE HAYES, 1993	
28	DANTE BICHETTE, 1993	
26	DARYL BOSTON, 1993	

BA: Highest, career, all-time

.370	ANDRES GALARRAGA, 1993	
.310	DANTE BICHETTE, 1993	
.305	CHARLIE HAYES, 1993	
.282	JERALD CLARK, 1993	
.269	ERIC YOUNG, 1993	

Slug avg: Highest, career, all-time

.602	ANDRES GALARRAGA, 1993	
.526	DANTE BICHETTE, 1993	
.522	CHARLIE HAYES, 1993	
.444	JERALD CLARK, 1993	
.353	ERIC YOUNG, 1993	

Games started: Most, career, all-time

30	ARMANDO REYNOSO, 1993	
18	WILLIE BLAIR, 1993	
16	DAVID NIED, 1993	
15	BUTCH HENRY, 1993	
14	KENT BOTTENFIELD, 1993	

Saves: Most, career, all-time

25	DARREN HOLMES, 1993	
3	STEVE REED, 1993	
2	BRUCE RUFFIN, 1993	
1	ANDY ASHBY, 1993	
1	MARK GRANT, 1993	
1	JEFF PARRETT, 1993	
1	KEITH SHEPHERD, 1993	
1	GARY WAYNE, 1993	

Shutouts: Most, career, all-time

None

Wins: Most, career, all-time

12	ARMANDO REYNOSO, 1993	
9	STEVE REED, 1993	
6	WILLIE BLAIR, 1993	
6	BRUCE RUFFIN, 1993	
5	DAVID NIED, 1993	
5	GARY WAYNE, 1993	

K: Most, career, all-time

126	BRUCE RUFFIN, 1993	
117	ARMANDO REYNOSO, 1993	
84	WILLIE BLAIR, 1993	
66	JEFF PARRETT, 1993	
60	DARREN HOLMES, 1993	

Win pct: Highest, career, all-time

.522	ARMANDO REYNOSO, 1993	

ERA: Lowest, career, all-time

4.00	ARMANDO REYNOSO, 1993	

Runs: Most, season

93	DANTE BICHETTE, 1993	
89	CHARLIE HAYES, 1993	
82	ERIC YOUNG, 1993	
71	ANDRES GALARRAGA, 1993	
65	JERALD CLARK, 1993	

Hits: Most, season

175	CHARLIE HAYES, 1993	
174	ANDRES GALARRAGA, 1993	
167	DANTE BICHETTE, 1993	
135	JERALD CLARK, 1993	
132	ERIC YOUNG, 1993	

2B: Most, season

45	CHARLIE HAYES, 1993	
43	DANTE BICHETTE, 1993	
35	ANDRES GALARRAGA, 1993	
26	JERALD CLARK, 1993	
16	ERIC YOUNG, 1993	

3B: Most, season

8	ERIC YOUNG, 1993	
7	VINNY CASTILLA, 1993	
6	JERALD CLARK, 1993	
5	DANTE BICHETTE, 1993	
5	JOE GIRARDI, 1993	

HR: Most, season

25	CHARLIE HAYES, 1993	
22	ANDRES GALARRAGA, 1993	
21	DANTE BICHETTE, 1993	
14	DARYL BOSTON, 1993	
13	JERALD CLARK, 1993	

RBI: Most, season

98	ANDRES GALARRAGA, 1993	
98	CHARLIE HAYES, 1993	
89	DANTE BICHETTE, 1993	
67	JERALD CLARK, 1993	
42	ERIC YOUNG, 1993	

SB: Most, season

42	ERIC YOUNG, 1993	
30	ALEX COLE, 1993	
14	DANTE BICHETTE, 1993	
11	CHARLIE HAYES, 1993	
9	JERALD CLARK, 1993	
9	CHRIS JONES, 1993	

BB: Most, season

63	ERIC YOUNG, 1993	
43	ALEX COLE, 1993	
43	CHARLIE HAYES, 1993	
28	DANTE BICHETTE, 1993	
26	DARYL BOSTON, 1993	

BA: Highest, season

.370 ANDRES GALARRAGA, 1993
.310 DANTE BICHETTE, 1993
.305 CHARLIE HAYES, 1993
.282 JERALD CLARK, 1993
.269 ERIC YOUNG, 1993

Slug avg: Highest, season

.602 ANDRES GALARRAGA, 1993
.526 DANTE BICHETTE, 1993
.522 CHARLIE HAYES, 1993
.444 JERALD CLARK, 1993
.353 ERIC YOUNG, 1993

Games started: Most, season

30 ARMANDO REYNOSO, 1993
18 WILLIE BLAIR, 1993
16 DAVID NIED, 1993
15 BUTCH HENRY, 1993
14 KENT BOTTENFIELD, 1993

Saves: Most, season

25 DARREN HOLMES, 1993
3 STEVE REED, 1993
2 BRUCE RUFFIN, 1993
1 ANDY ASHBY, 1993
1 JEFF PARRETT, 1993
1 GARY WAYNE, 1993
1 KEITH SHEPHERD, 1993

Shutouts: Most, season

None

Wins: Most, season

12 ARMANDO REYNOSO, 1993
9 STEVE REED, 1993
6 WILLIE BLAIR, 1993
6 BRUCE RUFFIN, 1993
5 DAVID NIED, 1993
5 GARY WAYNE, 1993

K: Most, season

126 BRUCE RUFFIN, 1993
117 ARMANDO REYNOSO, 1993
84 WILLIE BLAIR, 1993
66 JEFF PARRETT, 1993
60 DARREN HOLMES, 1993

Win pct: Highest, season

.522 ARMANDO REYNOSO, 1993

ERA: Lowest, season

4.00 ARMANDO REYNOSO, 1993

Most pinch-hit homers, season

2 JAY GAINER, 1993

Most pinch-hit, homers, career

2 JAY GAINER, 1993

Most consecutive games, batting safely

15 ANDRES GALARRAGA, 1993

Most consecutive scoreless innings

16 BRUCE RUFFIN, 1993

No hit games

None

ACTIVE PLAYERS in caps.

San Diego Padres

by Eileen BLass, USA TODAY

Andy Benes won 15 games, pitched 230 2/3 innings and struck out 179 (sixth in the NL).

1993 Padres: Bargain basement baseball

The big story in San Diego was the personnel purge of the bargain basement Padres, as they slashed their payroll by sending superstars packing in exchange for a variety of prospects.

It almost overshadowed how horribly the team did. Almost, but not quite.

The club's 61-101 record was the worst in the NL West, 43 games behind the Braves—the team's first 100-loss season since '74 and worst-ever finish in terms of games out.

How bad were they? They were victims of one-hitters three times in September alone. They were the first team to lose series to both expansion teams. Fans stayed away in droves, with attendance falling by nearly 350,000.

Among the stars sent packing:

▶Third baseman Gary Sheffield went to Florida June 24 for reliever Trevor Hoffman and minor league pitchers Jose Martinez and Andres Berumen.

▶Pitcher Greg W. Harris went to Colorado July 26 for catcher Brad Ausmus and minor league pitcher Doug Brocail.

▶First baseman Fred McGriff went to Atlanta July 18 for minor league outfielders Melvin Nieves and Vince Moore and pitcher Donnie Elliott.

Not all the club's trades for '93 were to the Padres' disadvantage. At the '92 winter meetings, they got outfielder Phil Plantier from the Red Sox for reliever Jose Melendez. Melendez pitched just 16 innings in an injury-plagued season for Boston. Plantier thrived, tying Dave Winfield's franchise record with 34 homers and driving in 100 runs. Before the season, they sent outfielder Darrin Jackson to Toronto for outfielder Derek Bell. Jackson struggled in Toronto, was traded to the Mets and struggled there as well. Bell became the third player in club history to top the 20-20 mark, joining Winfield and Joe Carter. He hit 21 homers and stole 26 bases.

Until his season came to an early end due to knee problems, Tony Gwynn chased his fifth NL batting title. Though he finished second to Andres Galarraga, his .358 mark was the second-best in Padres history (his own .370 average in 1987 was No.1) and he did collect his 2,000th hit August 6.

Closer Gene Harris led the team with 23 saves while starter Andy Benes was the staff ace, equaling his career high in wins with 15, and striking out 179. Benes and Harris were two of 23 pitchers used by San Diego this year, including eight rookies.

The team finished the 1993 season with 17 rookies on the roster—18 if you count manager Jim Riggleman, whose contract was extended.

—by Lisa Winston

1994 Padres: Preview

If Padres fans can make the mental adjustment from expecting their team to be a contender to watching a work in progress, then 1994 might not be too excruciating.

One player to watch is slugger Dave Staton, who could be the starting first baseman if his shoulder holds up. The top power prospect in the organization before undergoing rotator cuff surgery in September 1992, Staton came back from rehab in July, hit 25 homers in 74 minor league games, and smacked another five in 42 San Diego at-bats in September.

The infield is unsettled, with perhaps the only lock being slick-fielding young Ricky Gutierrez at shortstop.

If Andy Benes is still around, he'll likely be joined in the rotation by such young pitchers as strikeout artist Scott Sanders, Tim Worrell and possibly left-hander Pedro A. Martinez, one of the brightest spots in the bullpen for '94.

The top prospects for a legitimate lead-off hitter—Ray McDavid and Vince Moore—are at least a year away.

—by Lisa Winston

1993 Padres: Between the lines

▶**April 16:** Derek Bell, acquired with a minor leaguer from the Blue Jays in a trade for Darrin Jackson, hit two home runs, both off St. Louis starter Joe Magrane.

▶**May 11:** *Quote of the day*—Hours after Tony Gwynn lined a shot off Reds' pitcher Tim Belcher's right forearm, the stitch marks still showed. Said Belcher: "I look like Popeye. All I need is Olive Oyl and some spinach."

▶**May 17:** Andy Benes blanked the slumping Rockies on three hits, walking two and striking out seven. It was his fourth career shutout, and all six Benes wins this season have followed San Diego losses.

▶**May 29:** Derek Bell ran his hitting streak to 11 games, going 2-for-3 with a two-run homer, in the Padres' 7-4 win against St. Louis. During the span, he was hitting .489 with five homers.

▶**June 16:** Mark Portugal homered off Doug Brocail of San Diego in Houston's 5-4 win against the Padres, marking the third time in a row an opposing pitcher had gone deep off the San Diego rookie.

▶**July 3:** Fred McGriff was 3-for-5 with a homer and four RBI as the Padres beat the Phils 6-4.

▶**July 15:** Tony Gwynn's two-out infield single drove in two runs to break a 2-2 deadlock in the seventh inning of San Diego's 5-2 win against the nose-diving Phillies. Reliever Larry Andersen got Gwynn to punch a hard slider to John Kruk at first base, but Kruk couldn't handle it cleanly. Andersen was late getting to the bag and, after Kruk flipped him the ball, missed the base, allowing Gwynn to reach base and two Padre runs to score.

▶**July 17:** Andy Benes topped All-Star starter Terry Mulholland, allowing two runs on five hits as the Padres beat the slumping Phillies 4-2. Benes, who was on the All-Star team but didn't play, whiffed seven in eight innings. The Padres bunted in three consecutive at-bats during their three-run seventh

inning against Philadelphia. Trailing 2-0 and with Archi Cianfrocco on second, Bob Geren laid down a bunt that third baseman Dave Hollins threw away, allowing Cianfrocco to score and putting Geren on second. Pitcher Benes sacrificed Geren to third and Rickey Gutierrez suicide-squeezed pinch-runner Doug Brocail home to break a 2-2 tie.

▶**July 24:** Phil Clark started at his fifth different position for San Diego in its 11-4 win against Montreal.

▶**July 27:** Tony Gwynn had two doubles in his sixth, career five-hit game— and his third in '93—as the Padres blanked the Cubs 8-0. Gwynn, who has never hit below .300 in his career, raised his season average to .340 and broke the club record for RBI (627) held by Dave Winfield.

▶**July 30:** Phil Plantier's two long balls helped the Padres to an 11-9 win against the Reds. It was the third time Plantier hit two home runs in a game in '93.

▶**August 1:** Andy Benes allowed only an unearned run in seven innings to earn his 12th win, a 3-1 decision against Cincinnati.

▶**August 4:** Four-time NL batting champ Tony Gwynn tied a major—league record with his fourth game of five or more hits this season as the San Diego Padres defeated San Francisco 11-10 in 12 innings. Gwynn tied a major league record set by Willie Keeler of Baltimore in 1897 and matched by Ty Cobb of Detroit in 1922 and Stan Musial of St. Louis in 1948.

▶**August 6:** *Milestones*—Tony Gwynn was 3-for-3 in the first game and 2-for-5 in the nightcap of the Padres' 6-3, 6-2 doubleheader sweep of the Rockies, to collect his 2,000th career hit. With the loss in both ends of the doubleheader, the Rockies' losing streak was extended to a season-high 13 games.

▶**August 9:** Eric Anthony hit a two—run homer and scored the winning run on Luis Gonzalez's safety squeeze bunt in the 10th as Houston beat San

Diego 5-4. A season-low 8,237 fans watched at Jack Murphy Stadium.

▶**August 12:** Archi Cianfrocco was 4-for-5 in the Padres' 5-3 loss to Houston, driving in a run to give him 23 RBI in his last 30 games after driving in just one run in his first 24 games.

▶**August 13:** Derek Bell was 3-for-4 with a homer as the Padres beat Los Angeles 4-1.

▶**August 14:** Tony Gwynn went 4-for-4 with a walk in the Padres' 4-3 loss to Los Angeles to raise his average to .359.

▶**August 24:** Cardinals rookie Allen Watson, who was 4-0 with a 1.36 ERA in his last five starts, couldn't get out of the first inning, helping the host Padres to a club-record 13 runs in that frame in an eventual 17-4 rout.

▶**August 28:** Rookie Scott Sanders allowed one earned run on six hits in 8 1/3 innings as the San Diego Padres collected their fifth win in a row, 5-3 against Pittsburgh. That marked the longest current winning streak in the league. Derek Bell homered while Tim Teufel and Jarvis Brown had two hits each.

▶**August 31:** Derek Bell was 2-for-4 with an RBI in the Padres' 2-1 loss to Florida, but since moving from the outfield to third base, he had a five-game hitting streak and was 8-for-21 (.381) with an RBI in each game and five runs scored.

▶**September 13:** Phil Plantier hit a game-winning, two-run homer in the 11th inning, his 30th HR of the year.

▶**October 3:** The Padres lost to the Cubs, 4-1, to finish off a season marked by what many fans considered a fire sale of the team's most valuable players, and wound up—no big surprise—in the NL West basement with a worse record than either expansion team (61-101). In fact, the only team in the major leagues with a worse record than the Padres was the Mets, whose clubhouse full of highly-paid superstars lost 103 games. League leaders, pitching—Andy Benes was sixth in strikeouts (179) and ninth in innings pitched (230 2/3). League leaders, batting—Tony Gwynn was second in bat-ting (.358), tied for fourth in doubles (41), and eighth in on-base percentage (.398); Phil Plantier was tied for seventh in home runs (34) and tied for ninth in RBI (100).

—by John Hunt, Scott Kauffman, Lisa Winston, Deron Snyder, Matt Young

Team directory

▶**Owner:** San Diego Padres Baseball Partnership
▶**General Manager:** Randy Smith
▶**Ballpark:**
San Diego Jack Murphy Stadium
9449 Friars Rd., San Diego, Calif.
619-283-4494
Capacity 59,254
Parking for 18,751 cars; $4
Public transportation available
Wheelchair sections, ramps, pre-registration for telephone paging, ATM machines
▶**Team publications:**
Padre Magazine
619-283-4494
▶**TV, radio broadcast stations:**
KFMB 760 AM, XEXX AM (Spanish), KUSI Channel 51, Cox Cable
▶**Spring Training:**
Peoria Sports Complex
Peoria, AZ
Capacity 7,000
602-878-4337

SAN DIEGO PADRES 1993 final stats

Batting	BA	SLG	OB	G	AB	R	H	TB	2B	3B	HR	RBI	BB	SO	SB	CS	E
Gwynn	.358	.497	.398	122	489	70	175	243	41	3	7	59	36	19	14	1	5
Clark	.313	.496	.345	102	240	33	75	119	17	0	9	33	8	31	2	0	8
Gardner	.262	.356	.337	140	404	53	106	144	21	7	1	24	45	69	2	6	10
Bell	.262	.417	.303	150	542	73	142	226	19	1	21	72	23	122	26	5	17
Staton	.262	.690	.326	17	42	7	11	29	3	0	5	9	3	12	0	0	0
Bean	.260	.395	.284	88	177	19	46	70	9	0	5	32	6	29	2	4	1
Ausmus	.256	.413	.283	49	160	18	41	66	8	1	5	12	6	28	2	0	8
Gutierrez	.251	.331	.334	133	438	76	110	145	10	5	5	26	50	97	4	3	14
Teufel	.250	.430	.338	96	200	26	50	86	11	2	7	31	27	39	2	2	3
Cianfrocco	.243	.416	.287	96	296	30	72	123	11	2	12	48	17	69	2	0	10
Plantier	.240	.509	.335	138	462	67	111	235	20	1	34	100	61	124	4	5	3
Shipley	.235	.326	.275	105	230	25	54	75	9	0	4	22	10	31	12	3	7
Brown	.233	.331	.335	47	133	21	31	44	9	2	0	8	15	26	3	3	2
Sherman	.222	.238	.315	37	63	8	14	15	1	0	0	2	6	8	2	1	0
Higgins	.221	.254	.294	71	181	17	40	46	4	1	0	13	16	17	0	1	6
Stillwell	.215	.273	.286	57	121	9	26	33	4	0	1	11	11	22	4	3	9
Geren	.214	.317	.278	58	145	8	31	46	6	0	3	6	13	28	0	0	2
Velasquez	.210	.287	.274	79	143	7	30	41	2	0	3	20	13	35	0	0	4
Walters	.202	.266	.255	27	94	6	19	25	3	0	1	10	7	13	0	0	5
Nieves	.191	.319	.255	19	47	4	9	15	0	0	2	3	3	21	0	0	2
Lopez	.116	.140	.114	17	43	1	5	6	1	0	0	1	0	8	0	0	1

Pitching	W-L	ERA	G	GS	CG	GF	Sho	SV	IP	H	R	ER	HR	BB	SO
Martinez	3-1	2.43	32	0	0	9	0	0	37	23	11	10	4	13	32
Ge.Harris	6-6	3.03	59	0	0	48	0	23	59.1	57	27	20	3	37	39
Benes	15-15	3.78	34	34	4	0	2	0	230.2	200	111	97	23	86	179
Whitehurst	4-7	3.83	21	19	0	1	0	0	105.2	109	47	45	11	30	57
Hoffman	4-6	3.90	67	0	0	26	0	5	90	80	43	39	10	39	79
Mauser	0-1	4.00	36	0	0	16	0	0	54	51	28	24	6	24	46
Sanders	3-3	4.13	9	9	0	0	0	0	52.1	54	32	24	4	23	37
Davis	1-5	4.26	60	0	0	13	0	4	69.2	79	37	33	10	44	70
Seminara	3-3	4.47	18	7	0	0	0	0	46.1	53	30	23	5	21	22
Brocail	4-13	4.56	24	24	0	0	0	0	128.1	143	75	65	16	42	70
Hernandez	0-2	4.72	21	0	0	9	0	0	34.1	41	19	18	2	7	26
Worrell	2-7	4.92	21	16	0	1	0	0	100.2	104	63	55	11	43	52
Gomez	1-2	5.12	27	1	0	6	0	0	31.2	35	19	18	2	19	26
Eiland	0-3	5.21	10	9	0	0	0	0	48.1	58	33	28	5	17	14
Taylor	0-5	6.45	36	7	0	9	0	0	68.1	72	53	49	5	49	45
Ettles	1-0	6.50	14	0	0	5	0	0	18	23	16	13	4	4	9
Ashby	3-10	6.80	32	21	0	3	0	1	123	168	100	93	19	56	77

1994 preliminary roster

PITCHERS (19)
Andy Ashby
Robbie Beckett
Andy Benes
Andres Berumen
Doug Bochtler
Doug Brocail
Mark Davis
Donnie Elliott
Bryce Florie
Gene Harris
Trevor Hoffman
Jose Martinez
Pedro A. Martinez
Tim Mauser
Scott Sanders
Frank Seminara
Kerry Taylor
Wally Whitehurst
Tim Worrell

CATCHERS (2)
Brad Ausmus
Brian Johnson

INFIELDERS (9)
Julio Bruno
Archi Cianfrocco
Jeff Gardner
Ricky Gutierrez
Ray Holbert
Luis Lopez
Craig Shipley
Dave Staton
Guillermo Velasquez

OUTFIELDERS (10)
Billy Bean
Derek Bell
Phil Clark
Tony Gwynn
Ray McDavid
Vince Moore
Melvin Nieves
Steve Pegues
Phil Plantier
Tracy Sanders

Games played by position

Player	G	C	1B	2B	3B	SS	OF
Ausmus	49	49	0	0	0	0	0
Bean	88	0	12	0	0	0	54
Bell	150	0	0	0	19	0	125
Brown	47	0	0	0	0	0	43
Cianfrocco	96	0	42	0	64	0	0
Clark	102	11	24	0	5	0	36
Gardner	140	0	0	133	1	1	0
Geren	58	49	1	0	1	0	0
Gutierrez	133	0	0	6	4	117	5
Gwynn	122	0	0	0	0	0	121
Higgins	71	59	3	1	4	0	3
Lopez	17	0	0	15	0	0	0
Nieves	19	0	0	0	0	0	15
Plantier	138	0	0	0	0	0	134
Sherman	37	0	0	0	0	0	26
Shipley	105	0	0	12	37	38	5
Staton	17	0	12	0	0	0	0
Stillwell	57	0	0	0	3	30	0
Teufel	96	0	8	52	9	0	0
Velasquez	79	0	38	0	0	0	6
Walters	27	26	0	0	0	0	0

Sick call: 1993 DL Report

Player	Days on the DL
Pat Gomez	100
Bruce Hurst*%	101
Phil Plantier	15
Mike Scioscia	182
Craig Shipley	17
Kurt Stillwell	22
Wally Whitehurst**	88

*Two separate terms on Disabled List
** Three separate terms on Disabled List
% Bruce Hurst was on the DL twice with San Diego and twice with Colorado.

Minor League Report

Class AAA: Las Vegas finished at 58-85, last in the Pacific Coast League Southern Division. Brian Johnson hit .339 with 10 homers and 71 RBI. Mike Simms hit 24 homers. Mark Ettles had 15 saves. Scott Sanders led the league in strikeouts with 161. **Class AA:** Wichita finished at 68-68, second in the Texas League Western Division, and as a wild-card entry fell to El Paso in the playoffs. Dwayne Hosey had 18 homers. Ray McDavid stole 33 bases, while Ray Holbert had 30 and Billy Hall 29. Bryce Florie was 11-8 with a 3.96 ERA. **Class A:** Rancho Cucamonga finished at 64-72, third in the California League Southern Division. Ira Smith hit .346 with seven homers and 47 RBI. Jason Hardtke hit .319 with 11 homers and 85 RBI. Jeff Huber had 18 saves. Cameron Cairncross struck out 122. . . . Waterloo finished at 54-79, sixth in the Midwest League Southern Division. Homer Bush won the batting title at .322 with five homers and 51 RBI. Todd Schmitt had 25 saves. **Short-season:** Spokane finished at 35-41, third in the Northwest league North Division. Jason Thompson hit .300 with seven homers and 38 RBI. Glenn Dishman was 6-3 with a 2.20 ERA and threw a no-hitter. Chris Prieto led the league with 36 steals. . . . Peoria finished at 23-29, sixth in the Arizona League. Juan Espinal hit .301 with 19 RBI. Devohn Duncan was 3-3 with a 1.96 ERA. Harold Garrett struck out 83 while Matt LaChappa fanned 73.

Tops in the organization

Batter	Club	Avg	G	AB	R	H	HR	RBI
Johnson, Brian	Lvg	.339	115	416	58	141	10	71
Smith, Ira	Wch	.334	105	386	78	129	7	51
Bush, Homer	Wlo	.322	130	472	63	152	5	51
Hardtke, Jason	Rc	.319	130	523	98	167	11	85
Brown, Jarvis	Lvg	.308	100	402	74	124	3	47

Home Runs			Wins		
Staton, Dave	Lvg	25	Grzelaczyk, Ken	Rc	12
Simms, Mike	Lvg	24	Sager, A.J.	Lvg	11
Hosey, Dwayne	Lvg	21	Florie, Bryce	Wch	11
Several players tied		14	Barnes, Jon	Rc	10
			Cairncross, Cam	Rc	10

RBI			Saves		
Hardtke, Jason	Rc	85	Schmitt, Todd	Wlo	25
Drinkwater, Sean	Rc	84	Huber, Jeff	Wch	21
Simms, Mike	Lvg	80	Hoeme, Steve	Wch	19
Hosey, Dwayne	Lvg	73	Ettles, Mark	Lvg	15
Several players tied		71	Several players tied		5

Stolen Bases			Strikeouts		
Bush, Homer	Wlo	39	Sanders, Scott	Lvg	161
Roberts, John	Wlo	33	Florie, Bryce	Wch	133
Mcdavid, Ray	Wch	33	Cairncross, Cam	Rc	122
Smith, Ira	Wch	32	Hernandez, F.	Rc	121
Several players tied		30	Sager, A.J.	Lvg	107

Pitcher	Club	W-L	ERA	IP	H	BB	SO
Sager, A.J.	Lvg	11- 8	3.47	163	160	34	107
Florie, Bryce	Wch	11- 8	3.96	155	128	100	133
Wengert, Bill	Wch	7- 7	4.10	162	167	43	106
Hamilton, Joey	Lvg	8-11	4.12	149	161	60	89
Grzelaczyk, Ken	Rc	12- 7	4.30	165	180	51	100

San Diego (1969-1993)

Runs: Most, career, all-time

912	TONY GWYNN, 1982-1993
599	DAVE WINFIELD, 1973-1980
484	Gene Richards, 1977-1983
442	Nate Colbert, 1969-1974
430	Garry Templeton, 1982-1991

Hits: Most, career, all-time

2039	TONY GWYNN, 1982-1993
1135	Garry Templeton, 1982-1991
1134	DAVE WINFIELD, 1973-1980
994	Gene Richards, 1977-1983
817	Terry Kennedy, 1981-1986

2B: Most, career, all-time

316	TONY GWYNN, 1982-1993
195	Garry Templeton, 1982-1991
179	DAVE WINFIELD, 1973-1980
158	Terry Kennedy, 1981-1986
130	Nate Colbert, 1969-1974

3B: Most, career, all-time

78	TONY GWYNN, 1982-1993
63	Gene Richards, 1977-1983
39	DAVE WINFIELD, 1973-1980
36	Garry Templeton, 1982-1991
29	Cito Gaston, 1969-1974

HR: Most, career, all-time

163	Nate Colbert, 1969-1974
154	DAVE WINFIELD, 1973-1980
85	BENITO SANTIAGO, 1986-1992
84	FRED McGRIFF, 1991-1993
82	Carmelo Martinez, 1984-1989

RBI: Most, career, all-time

650	TONY GWYNN, 1982-1993
626	DAVE WINFIELD, 1973-1980
481	Nate Colbert, 1969-1974
427	Garry Templeton, 1982-1991
424	Terry Kennedy, 1981-1986

SB: Most, career, all-time

263	TONY GWYNN, 1982-1993
242	Gene Richards, 1977-1983
171	Alan Wiggins, 1981-1985
147	OZZIE SMITH, 1978-1981
133	DAVE WINFIELD, 1973-1980

BB: Most, career, all-time

542	TONY GWYNN, 1982-1993
463	DAVE WINFIELD, 1973-1980
423	Gene Tenace, 1977-1980
350	Nate Colbert, 1969-1974
338	Gene Richards, 1977-1983

BA: Highest, career, all-time

.329	TONY GWYNN, 1982-1993
.291	Gene Richards, 1977-1983
.286	Johnny Grubb, 1972-1976
.284	DAVE WINFIELD, 1973-1980
.275	Steve Garvey, 1983-1987

Slug avg: Highest, career, all-time

.468	Nate Colbert, 1969-1974
.464	DAVE WINFIELD, 1973-1980
.438	TONY GWYNN, 1982-1993
.422	Gene Tenace, 1977-1980
.409	Steve Garvey, 1983-1987

**Games started:
Most, career, all-time**

253	Randy Jones, 1973-1980
230	Eric Show, 1981-1990
208	Ed Whitson, 1983-1991
172	Andy Hawkins, 1982-1988
170	Clay Kirby, 1969-1973

Saves: Most, career, all-time

108	Rollie Fingers, 1977-1980
83	RICH GOSSAGE, 1984-1987
78	MARK DAVIS, 1987-1993
64	CRAIG LEFFERTS, 1984-1992
49	Gary Lucas, 1980-1983

Shutouts: Most, career, all-time

18	Randy Jones, 1973-1980
11	Steve Arlin, 1969-1974
11	Eric Show, 1981-1990
10	BRUCE HURST, 1989-1993
7	Andy Hawkins, 1982-1988
7	Clay Kirby, 1969-1973

Wins: Most, career, all-time

100	Eric Show, 1981-1990
92	Randy Jones, 1973-1980
77	Ed Whitson, 1983-1991
60	Andy Hawkins, 1982-1988
59	ANDY BENES, 1989-1993

K: Most, career, all-time

951	Eric Show, 1981-1990
802	Clay Kirby, 1969-1973
767	Ed Whitson, 1983-1991
721	ANDY BENES, 1989-1993
677	Randy Jones, 1973-1980

Win pct: Highest, career, all-time

.591	BRUCE HURST, 1989-1993
.535	Eric Show, 1981-1990
.522	ANDY BENES, 1989-1993
.517	Ed Whitson, 1983-1991
.515	Dave Dravecky, 1982-1987

ERA: Lowest, career, all-time

3.12	Dave Dravecky, 1982-1987
3.27	BRUCE HURST, 1989-1993
3.30	Randy Jones, 1973-1980
3.44	ANDY BENES, 1989-1993
3.59	Eric Show, 1981-1990

Runs: Most, season

119	TONY GWYNN, 1987
107	TONY GWYNN, 1986
106	Alan Wiggins, 1984
104	BIP ROBERTS, 1990
104	DAVE WINFIELD, 1977

Hits: Most, season

218	TONY GWYNN, 1987
213	TONY GWYNN, 1984
211	TONY GWYNN, 1986
203	TONY GWYNN, 1989
197	TONY GWYNN, 1985

2B: Most, season

42	Terry Kennedy, 1982
41	TONY GWYNN, 1993
36	Johnny Grubb, 1975
36	TONY GWYNN, 1987
36	BIP ROBERTS, 1990

3B: Most, season

13	TONY GWYNN, 1987
12	Gene Richards, 1978
12	Gene Richards, 1981
11	Bill Almon, 1977
11	TONY GWYNN, 1991
11	Gene Richards, 1977

HR: Most, season

38	Nate Colbert, 1970
38	Nate Colbert, 1972
35	FRED McGRIFF, 1992
34	PHIL PLANTIER, 1993
34	DAVE WINFIELD, 1979

RBI: Most, season

118	DAVE WINFIELD, 1979
115	JOE CARTER, 1990
111	Nate Colbert, 1972
106	FRED McGRIFF, 1991
104	FRED McGRIFF, 1992

SB: Most, season

70	Alan Wiggins, 1984
66	Alan Wiggins, 1983
61	Gene Richards, 1980
57	OZZIE SMITH, 1980
56	TONY GWYNN, 1987
56	Gene Richards, 1977

BB: Most, season

132	Jack Clark, 1989
125	Gene Tenace, 1977
105	FRED McGRIFF, 1991
105	Gene Tenace, 1979
104	Jack Clark, 1990

BA: Highest, season

.370	TONY GWYNN, 1987
.358	TONY GWYNN, 1993
.352	TONY GWYNN, 1984
.336	TONY GWYNN, 1989
.330	GARY SHEFFIELD, 1992

Slug avg: Highest, season

.580	GARY SHEFFIELD, 1992
.558	DAVE WINFIELD, 1979
.556	FRED McGRIFF, 1992
.543	Cito Gaston, 1970
.511	TONY GWYNN, 1987

Games started: Most, season

40	Randy Jones, 1976
39	Randy Jones, 1979
37	Steve Arlin, 1972
37	Gaylord Perry, 1978
36	Randy Jones, 1975
36	Randy Jones, 1978
36	Clay Kirby, 1971

Saves: Most, season

44	MARK DAVIS, 1989
38	RANDY MYERS, 1992
37	Rollie Fingers, 1978
35	Rollie Fingers, 1977
28	MARK DAVIS, 1988

Shutouts: Most, season

6	Randy Jones, 1975
6	Fred Norman, 1972
5	Randy Jones, 1976
4	Steve Arlin, 1971
4	BRUCE HURST, 1990
4	BRUCE HURST, 1992

Wins: Most, season

22	Randy Jones, 1976
21	Gaylord Perry, 1978
20	Randy Jones, 1975
18	Andy Hawkins, 1985
16	La Marr Hoyt, 1985
16	Tim Lollar, 1982
16	Eric Show, 1988
16	Ed Whitson, 1989

K: Most, season

231	Clay Kirby, 1971
185	Pat Dobson, 1970
179	ANDY BENES, 1993
179	BRUCE HURST, 1989
175	Clay Kirby, 1972

Win pct: Highest, season

.778	Gaylord Perry, 1978
.692	Andy Hawkins, 1985
.667	La Marr Hoyt, 1985
.652	BRUCE HURST, 1991
.640	Tim Lollar, 1982

ERA: Lowest, season

2.10	Dave Roberts, 1971
2.24	Randy Jones, 1975
2.60	Ed Whitson, 1990
2.66	Ed Whitson, 1989
2.69	BRUCE HURST, 1989

Most pinch-hit homers, season

5	Jerry Turner, 1978

Most pinch-hit, homers, career

9	Jerry Turner, 1974-1983

Most consecutive games, batting safely

34	BENITO SANTIAGO, 1987
25	TONY GWYNN, 1983

Most consecutive scoreless innings

30	Randy Jones, 1980

No hit games

None

ACTIVE PLAYERS in caps.

185

Toronto Blue Jays

John Olerud led the league in batting (.363), doubles (54), and on-base percentage (.473).

by Robert Deutsch, *USA TODAY*

1993 Blue Jays: New team, same result

A year after winning the World Series in 1992, the Toronto Blue Jays managed to do what no team had done since the New York Yankees of 1977-78—they repeated as world champions.

Sort of, anyway.

Among the departed who watched on TV while their old uniforms jumped around the field in glee were '92 Series heroes Dave Winfield, David Cone, Jimmy Key, Manuel Lee, Candy Maldonado and Tom Henke. Also gone were David Wells (released), Kelly Gruber (traded) and Derek Bell (traded).

The key free agent re-signing was Joe Carter, who had to decide between returning to the Jays or going to his hometown Kansas City Royals. It was fitting that it should have been Carter who provided the final heroics. A key figure in the Toronto clubhouse as well as at the plate, he had a typical season for him—33 homers, 121 RBI, and nowhere near the acclaim or attention that many of the other hitters in the lineup enjoyed. It was the seventh time in the last eight seasons that he topped the 100-RBI mark (the "off-year" he had 98).

Joining the '93 celebration were free agents Paul Molitor, who hit .500 in the Series and was named MVP, Dave Stewart and Darnell Coles. Tony Fernandez arrived in June via a trade with the Mets, returning to his original organization.

The Jays streaked to their second consecutive trip to the World Series and fourth post-season pass in the last five years riding the wave of a phenomenal lineup, which featured the first trio to finish one-two-three in the batting race this century. John Olerud flirted with .400 for most of the season and locked up the batting title early (.362). Molitor was second (.332) and Alomar (.326) yanked the third spot away from Cleveland's Kenny Lofton with three consecutive three-hit games the final weekend of the year.

Molitor posted 211 hits and scored 121 runs, but also added career highs with 22 homers and 111 RBI—the first time in his career he'd topped the 100-RBI plateau.

The latest addition to the team was left fielder Rickey Henderson, the traditional pennant stretch rent-a-player. Henderson hit just .215 in his 44 games with Toronto (coming off a .327 season with Oakland), but he might have been a case of addition by subtraction—his addition to the team subtracted the possibility of his going to rival Baltimore or New York, where he could have been a factor in the race.

After remaining in a tighter-than-it-should-have-been race for most of the year, the Jays broke the AL East wide open the final month, going 17-4 down the stretch.

—by Lisa Winston

1994 Blue Jays: Preview

If the Jays make it to the 1994 World Series, it may once again be with a new cast of characters. Free agents such as Jack Morris, Rickey Henderson and Tony Fernandez are gone, replaced by home-growns such as Toronto native Rob Butler in left field and fellow Canadian, southpaw Paul Spoljaric, in the rotation. Veteran Dick Schofield may be the anointed Opening Day shortstop, but look for megaprospect Alex Gonzalez to vie for the role. He is among the top prospects in the talent-laden system.

The Jays also have catcher Carlos Delgado not far from ready, coming off a pair of MVP seasons in the minors. He hit 30 homers for Class A Dunedin in '92, only the third 30-homer season in the Florida State League since its inception in 1936, and followed that with a 25 homer, 102-RBI season in '93 to earn Southern League MVP honors.

—by Lisa Winston

1993 Blue Jays: Between the lines

▶ **April 26:** Jack Morris won his first game of the year, allowing four runs in 5 2/3 innings to lower his ERA from 13.24 to 11.76.

▶ **April 29:** John Olerud improved his major league-leading batting average to .455 with a career-high five hits, while Juan Guzman fired his first career shutout.

▶ **May 23:** Pat Hentgen handed the Twins their seventh consecutive loss, giving up just one run in 7 2/3 innings in a 2-1 Toronto victory.

▶ **May 24:** Devon White hit the first pitch he saw over the fence—the 18th time he'd gone deep to start a game. Dave Stewart got his first win of the season after allowing 10 runs in 1 2/3 innings in his previous start.

▶ **June 4:** The Jays won their sixth in a row, putting them in a tie for first place in the AL East with Detroit.

▶ **June 6:** Olerud raised his average to .398 with three hits—two doubles and a home run—but the Jays lost to Oakland, 10-3.

▶ **June 9:** The Jays' loss to the Angels dropped them to one game behind the Tigers in the American League East.

▶ **June 13:** Tony Fernandez, playing in just his second game since returning to the Jays, had a career-high five RBI.

▶ **June 16:** Jack Morris went the distance for a 4-0 shutout against the Twins, his first shutout of the year.

▶ **June 17:** Al Leiter fired a two-hitter at the Red Sox for his first career complete game and shutout.

▶ **June 20:** Toronto beat the Red Sox 3-2 for the Jays' first sweep of Boston since 1988. It was the Jays' sixth consecutive win, but they remained two games behind Detroit in the AL East.

▶ **June 23:** Olerud's 26-game hitting streak came to an end as the Blue Jays fell to the Yankees 4-3 at Skydome.

▶ **June 24:** Hentgen got his 10th win of the year, the second AL pitcher to reach the 10-win plateau.

▶ **June 25:** Milwaukee fans gave Paul Molitor a one-minute standing ovation in his first appearance at County Stadium since leaving to join the Jays.

▶ **June 26:** The Jays beat the Brewers and gained sole possession of first place in the AL East.

▶ **June 27:** Jack Morris took a no-hitter into the seventh inning and held on for his fifth win of the year, a 5-4 decision in Milwaukee.

▶ **June 28:** Roberto Alomar had four hits and scored three times to lead the Blue Jays past Baltimore 7-2. The Jays had won 11 of their last 13 games.

▶ **July 18:** Rookie Willie Canate hit his first major league home run to lift the Jays to a 4-3 win against Kansas City.

▶ **August 1:** Toronto scored twice in the ninth inning to hand Detroit a 2-1 loss, keeping the Jays in first place and dropping the Tigers to the .500 mark.

▶ **August 3:** Newly acquired Rickey Henderson went 1-for-4 with two walks and two runs in his first game for Toronto, as they defeated the Yanks 8-6 for the second consecutive game in this key AL East series.

▶ **August 6:** Toronto beat Milwaukee 11-10 in a wild extra-inning affair at SkyDome. Milwaukee took a 10-8 lead in the top of the 11th but the Blue Jays rallied for three runs in the bottom of the inning. Rickey Henderson drove in a run with a triple and then scored on a wild pitch. Devon White also tripled, and Milwaukee manager Phil Garner walked Roberto Alomar and Joe Carter to load the bases for John Olerud. Olerud lined the first pitch into center field for the game-winner. Of the Blue Jays' last 11 wins, seven had come in their last at-bat.

▶ **August 14:** Pat Hentgen held the Red Sox to an unearned run in seven innings as the Blue Jays beat Boston 5-2.

▶ **August 23:** Joe Carter had a three-homer game for the fifth time in his career, one short of the all-time record set by Hall of Famer Johnny Mize, but the Blue Jays still lost to Cleveland, 9-8.

▶**August 25:** Olerud and Molitor, the top two hitters in the American League, each had four hits and scored a combined seven runs to help the Blue Jays to a 10-7 win against Cleveland.

▶**August 30:** In his first appearance at Oakland Coliseum since being traded by the A's, Rickey Henderson homered and scored two runs to lead Toronto to a 4-2 win, as the Blue Jays moved a half-game ahead of idle New York into first in the AL East.

▶**September 1:** Henderson hit the 63rd leadoff homer of his career, extending his own record.

▶**September 5:** The Angels completed a three-game sweep of the Blue Jays; the loss dropped Toronto into a first-place tie with New York in the AL East.

▶**September 15:** Toronto and Detroit hooked up for the longest nine-inning night game in major league history in Detroit. The 4:12 affair, won by Toronto 14-8, featured 32 hits, 14 walks, 13 pitchers, four errors and 23 left on base.

▶**September 18:** Toronto's 5-1 win against the Twins moved the club's all-time record over the .500 mark (1,341-1,340) for the first time since the first week of its inaugural 1977 season.

▶**September 21:** Todd Stottlemyre pitched a three-hit shutout and struck out a career-high 10, as Toronto beat Boston 5-0 for its ninth consecutive victory, giving the Jays a five-game lead.

▶**September 24:** Juan Guzman fanned seven New York batters in seven innings to win his seventh consecutive decision. The Blue Jays lowered their magic number to three with a 7-3 defeat of the Yankees.

▶**October 3:** The Blue Jays finished with a margin of seven games over the Yankees. *League leaders, pitching—* Pat Hentgen was third in victories (19-9); Duane Ward was tied for the lead in saves (45) and tied for third in games (71); Juan Guzman was third in strikeouts (194). *League leaders, batting—*John Olerud led the league in batting (.363) and on-base percentage (.473) as well as doubles (54), was tied for second in hits (200) and was third in

walks (114), fourth in slugging percentage (.599), and fifth in total bases (330); Paul Molitor led the league in hits (211), was second in batting (.332) and runs (121), seventh in total bases (324), eighth in RBI (111), ninth in on-base percentage (.402), and 10th in slugging percentage (.509); Roberto Alomar was tied for second in stolen bases (55), third in batting (.326), fourth in hits (192), tied for sixth in on-base percentage (.408), andtied for eighth in runs (109); Joe Carter was third in RBI (121), and tied for sixth in home runs (33); Devon White was second in doubles (42), tied for third in runs (116), and seventh in stolen bases (34); Rickey Henderson was second in walks (120), third in on-base percentage (.432), fourth in stolen bases (53), and fifth in runs (114).

—by John Hunt, Scott Kauffman, Lisa Winston, Deron Snyder, Matt Young

Team directory

▶**Owner:** Labatt's Breweries and the Canadian Imperial Bank of Commerce
▶**General Manager:** Pat Gillick
▶**Ballpark:**
Skydome
Toronto, Ontario
416-341-1000
Capacity 51,000
Public transportation available
Family and wheelchair sections, non-alcohol sections, ramps, Playland
▶**Team publications:**
Scorebook Magazine (Buzz Communications), 416-961-3319
▶**TV, radio broadcast stations:**
TSN and Baton Broadcasting, FAN
CBCTV
▶**Spring Training:**
Dunedin Stadium at Grant Field
311 Douglas Ave.
Dunedin, Fla.
Capacity 6,218
813-733-9302

TORONTO BLUE JAYS 1993 final stats

Batting	BA	SLG	OB	G	AB	R	H	TB	2B	3B	HR	RBI	BB	SO	SB	CS	E
Olerud	.363	.599	.473	158	551	109	200	330	54	2	24	107	114	65	0	2	10
Molitor	.332	.509	.402	160	636	121	211	324	37	5	22	111	77	71	22	4	3
Alomar	.326	.492	.408	153	589	109	192	290	35	6	17	93	80	67	55	15	14
Fernandez	.306	.442	.361	94	353	45	108	156	18	9	4	50	31	26	15	8	7
Henderson	.289	.474	.432	134	481	114	139	228	22	2	21	59	120	65	53	8	7
Martinez	.286	.500	.333	8	14	2	4	7	0	0	1	3	1	7	0	0	0
White	.273	.438	.341	146	598	116	163	262	42	6	15	52	57	127	34	4	3
Butler	.271	.354	.375	17	48	8	13	17	4	0	0	2	7	12	2	2	1
Sprague	.260	.386	.310	150	546	50	142	211	31	1	12	73	32	85	1	0	17
Borders	.254	.371	.285	138	488	38	124	181	30	0	9	55	20	66	2	2	13
Carter	.254	.489	.312	155	603	92	153	295	33	5	33	121	47	113	8	3	8
Coles	.253	.371	.319	64	194	26	49	72	9	1	4	26	16	29	1	1	7
Knorr	.248	.436	.309	39	101	11	25	44	3	2	4	20	9	29	0	0	0
Jackson	.216	.347	.250	46	176	15	38	61	8	0	5	19	8	53	0	2	1
Canate	.213	.277	.309	38	47	12	10	13	0	0	1	3	6	15	1	1	0
Griffin	.211	.242	.235	46	95	15	20	23	3	0	0	3	3	13	0	1	4
T.Ward	.192	.311	.287	72	167	20	32	52	4	2	4	28	23	26	3	3	1
Schofield	.191	.236	.294	36	110	11	21	26	1	2	0	5	16	25	3	0	4
Cedeno	.174	.174	.188	15	46	5	8	8	0	0	0	7	1	10	1	0	1
Sojo	.170	.213	.231	19	47	5	8	10	2	0	0	6	4	2	0	0	2
Delgado	.000	.000	.500	2	1	0	0	0	0	0	0	0	1	0	0	0	0
Green	.000	.000	.000	3	6	0	0	0	0	0	0	0	0	1	0	0	0

Pitching	W-L	ERA	G	GS	CG	GF	Sho	SV	IP	H	R	ER	HR	BB	SO
D.Ward	2-3	2.13	71	0	0	70	0	45	71.2	49	17	17	4	25	97
Eichhorn	3-1	2.72	54	0	0	16	0	0	72.2	76	26	22	3	22	47
Cox	7-6	3.12	44	0	0	13	0	2	83.2	73	31	29	8	29	84
Castillo	3-2	3.38	51	0	0	10	0	0	50.2	44	19	19	4	22	28
Hentgen	19-9	3.87	34	32	3	0	0	0	216.1	215	103	93	27	74	122
Guzman	14-3	3.99	33	33	2	0	1	0	221	211	107	98	17	110	194
Flener	0-0	4.05	6	0	0	1	0	0	6.2	7	3	3	0	4	2
Leiter	9-6	4.11	34	12	1	4	1	2	105	93	52	48	8	56	66
Williams	3-1	4.38	30	0	0	9	0	0	37	40	18	18	2	22	24
Stewart	12-8	4.44	26	26	0	0	0	0	162	146	86	80	23	72	96
Timlin	4-2	4.69	54	0	0	27	0	1	55.2	63	32	29	7	27	49
Stottlemyre	11-12	4.84	30	28	1	0	1	0	176.2	204	107	95	11	69	98
Brow	1-1	6.00	6	3	0	1	0	0	18	19	15	12	2	10	7
Morris	7-12	6.19	27	27	4	0	1	0	152.2	189	116	105	18	65	103

1994 preliminary roster

PITCHERS (17)
Scott Brow
Tony Castillo
Danny Cox
Lee Daniels
Huck Flener
Dennis Gray
Juan Guzman
Pat Hentgen
Al Leiter
Paul Menhart
Aaron Small
Paul Spoljaric
Dave Stewart
Todd Stottlemyre
Mike Timlin
Duane Ward
Woody Williams

CATCHERS (4)
Pat Borders
Carlos Delgado
Randy Knorr
Angel Martinez

INFIELDERS (11)
Roberto Alomar
Howard Battle
Tilson Brito
Domingo Cedeno
Darnell Coles
Domingo Martinez
Paul Molitor
John Olerud
Dick Schofield
Ed Sprague
Eddie Zosky

OUTFIELDERS (8)
Brent Bowers
Rob Butler
Willie Canate
Joe Carter
Shawn Green
Rick Holifield
Robert Perez
Devon White

Games played by position

Player	G	C	1B	2B	3B	SS	OF	DH
Alomar	153	0	0	150	0	0	0	0
Borders	138	138	0	0	0	0	0	0
Butler	17	0	0	0	0	0	16	0
Canate	38	0	0	0	0	0	31	1
Carter	155	0	0	0	0	0	151	3
Cedeno	15	0	0	5	0	10	0	0
Coles	64	0	1	0	16	0	44	1
Delgado	2	1	0	0	0	0	0	1
Fernandez	94	0	0	0	0	94	0	0
Green	3	0	0	0	0	0	2	1
Griffin	46	0	0	11	6	20	0	0
Henderson	134	0	0	0	0	0	118	16
Jackson	46	0	0	0	0	0	46	0
Knorr	39	39	0	0	0	0	0	0
Martinez	8	0	7	0	1	0	0	0
Molitor	160	0	23	0	0	0	0	137
Olerud	158	0	137	0	0	0	0	20
Schofield	36	0	0	0	0	36	0	0
Sojo	19	0	0	8	3	8	0	0
Sprague	150	0	0	0	150	0	0	0
T. Ward	72	0	1	0	0	0	65	0
White	146	0	0	0	0	0	145	0

Sick call: 1993 DL Report

Player	Days on the DL
Rob Butler	70
Willie Canate#	32
Alfredo Griffin	25
Al Leiter	15
Jack Morris	19
Dick Schofield	111
Luis Sojo	20
Dave Stewart	38
Todd Stottlemyre	21
Turner Ward	30
Eddie Zosky	128

 # Willie Canate was on the DL both in Cincinnati and Toronto.

Minor League Report

Class AAA: Syracuse finished at 59-82, last in the International League Eastern Division. Robert Perez hit .294 with 12 homers and 64 RBI. Domingo Martinez hit 24 homers. Jesse Cross was 8-6 with a 3.16 ERA and 127 strikeouts. **Class AA:** Knoxville finished at 71-71, winning the second half of the Southern League Eastern Division. Carlos Delgado was league MVP, hitting .303 with a league-high 25 homers and 102 RBI. Tim Hyers hit .306. Alex Gonzalez stole 38 bases while Brent Bowers swiped 36. Huck Flener was 13-6 with a 3.30 ERA. **Class A:** Dunedin finished at 68-64, fifth in the Florida State League West Division. Rick Holifield led the league with 20 homers while Chris Weinke was second with 17. Weinke's 98 RBI led the league. Holifield also stole 30 bases. . . . Hagerstown finished at 74-66, fourth in the Sally League Northern Division. D.J. Boston was league MVP, hitting .315 with 13 homers, 92 RBI and 31 stolen bases. Lonell Roberts stole 54 bases. Jose Silva was 12-5 with a 2.52 ERA and 161 strikeouts in 143 innings. Brad Cornett was 10-8 with a 2.40 ERA and 161 strikeouts. **Short-season:** St. Catharines finished at 49-28, winning the New York-Penn League Stadler Division. Shannon Stewart stole 25 bases. Adam Meinershagen won the ERA title at 8-1 with a 1.88 ERA, striking out 87 in 86 innings. Alonso Beltran was 11-2 with a 2.36 ERA and 101 strikeouts in 99 innings. Edwin Hurtado was 10-2 with a 2.50 ERA. . . . Medicine Hat finished at 39-32, second in the Pioneer League Northern Division. Angel Ramirez hit .352. Freddy Garcia and Lorenzo Delacruz each had 11 homers. Brian Grant was 5-4 with a 2.84 ERA. . . . Dunedin finished at 22-38, last in the Gulf Coast League Northern Division. Aaron Hightower had 37 RBI.

Tops in the organization

Batter	Club	Avg	G	AB	R	H	HR	RBI
Herrera, Jose	Hag	.317	95	388	60	123	5	42
Boston, D.J.	Hag	.315	127	464	76	146	13	92
Hyers, Tim	Knx	.306	140	487	72	149	3	61
Stynes, Chris	Dun	.304	123	496	72	151	7	48
Delgado, Carlos	Knx	.303	140	468	91	142	25	102

Home Runs			Wins		
Delgado, Carlos	Knx	25	Spoljaric, Paul	Syr	15
Martinez, D.	Syr	24	Flener, Huck	Knx	13
Holifield, Rick	Dun	20	Silva, Jose	Hag	12
Weinke, Chris	Dun	17	Dolson, Andy	Hag	10
Several players tied		16	Cornett, Brad	Hag	10

RBI			Saves		
Delgado, Carlos	Knx	102	Small, Aaron	Knx	16
Weinke, Chris	Dun	98	Hall, Darren	Syr	13
Boston, D.J.	Hag	92	Weber, Ben	Dun	12
Martinez, D.	Syr	79	Daniels, Lee	Hag	12
Harmes, Kris	Hag	73	Brown, Daren	Knx	10

Stolen Bases			Strikeouts		
Roberts, Lonell	Hag	54	Spoljaric, Paul	Syr	168
Gonzalez, Alex	Knx	38	Silva, Jose	Hag	161
Herrera, Jose	Hag	36	Cornett, Brad	Hag	161
Bowers, Brent	Knx	36	Dolson, Andy	Hag	143
Boston, D.J.	Hag	31	Cross, Jesse	Syr	127

Pitcher	Club	W-L	ERA	IP	H	BB	SO
Cornett, Brad	Hag	10- 8	2.40	172	164	31	161
Silva, Jose	Hag	12- 5	2.52	143	103	62	161
Cross, Jesse	Syr	8- 6	3.16	151	137	53	127
Flener, Huck	Knx	13- 6	3.30	136	130	39	114
Carrara, G.	Dun	6-11	3.45	141	136	59	108

`Runs: Most, career, all-time

768	Lloyd Moseby, 1980-1989
641	GEORGE BELL, 1981-1990
555	TONY FERNANDEZ, 1983-1993
538	Willie Upshaw, 1978-1987
530	Jesse Barfield, 1981-1989

Hits: Most, career, all-time

1319	Lloyd Moseby, 1980-1989
1294	GEORGE BELL, 1981-1990
1250	TONY FERNANDEZ, 1983-1993
1028	Damaso Garcia, 1980-1986
982	Willie Upshaw, 1978-1987

2B: Most, career, all-time

242	Lloyd Moseby, 1980-1989
237	GEORGE BELL, 1981-1990
210	TONY FERNANDEZ, 1983-1993
204	Rance Mulliniks, 1982-1992
177	Willie Upshaw, 1978-1987

3B: Most, career, all-time

70	TONY FERNANDEZ, 1983-1993
60	Lloyd Moseby, 1980-1989
50	ALFREDO GRIFFIN, 1979--1993
42	Willie Upshaw, 1978-1987
32	GEORGE BELL, 1981-1990

HR: Most, career, all-time

202	GEORGE BELL, 1981-1990
179	Jesse Barfield, 1981-1989
149	Lloyd Moseby, 1980-1989
131	Ernie Whitt, 1977-1989
125	FRED McGRIFF, 1986-1990

RBI: Most, career, all-time

740	GEORGE BELL, 1981-1990
651	Lloyd Moseby, 1980-1989
527	Jesse Barfield, 1981-1989
518	Ernie Whitt, 1977-1989
478	Willie Upshaw, 1978-1987

SB: Most, career, all-time

255	Lloyd Moseby, 1980-1989
194	Damaso Garcia, 1980-1986
157	ROBERTO ALOMAR, 1991-1993
153	TONY FERNANDEZ, 1983-1993
104	DEVON WHITE, 1991-1993

BB: Most, career, all-time

547	Lloyd Moseby, 1980-1989
416	Rance Mulliniks, 1982-1992
403	Ernie Whitt, 1977-1989
390	Willie Upshaw, 1978-1987
352	FRED McGRIFF, 1986-1990

BA: Highest, career, all-time

.297	JOHN OLERUD, 1989-1993
.290	TONY FERNANDEZ, 1983-1993
.288	Damaso Garcia, 1980-1986
.286	GEORGE BELL, 1981-1990
.280	Rance Mulliniks, 1982-1992

Slug avg: Highest, career, all-time

.530	FRED McGRIFF, 1986-1990
.488	JOHN OLERUD, 1989-1993
.486	GEORGE BELL, 1981-1990
.483	Jesse Barfield, 1981-1989
.461	Otto Velez, 1977-1982

Games started: Most, career, all-time

405	DAVE STIEB, 1979-1992
345	Jim Clancy, 1977-1988
250	JIMMY KEY, 1984-1992
156	TODD STOTTLEMYRE, 1988-1993
151	Luis Leal, 1980-1985

Saves: Most, career, all-time

217	TOM HENKE, 1985-1992
121	DUANE WARD, 1986-1993
31	Joey McLaughlin, 1980-1984
30	Roy Lee Jackson, 1981-1984
16	Bill Caudill, 1985-1986

Shutouts: Most, career, all-time

30	DAVE STIEB, 1979-1992
11	Jim Clancy, 1977-1988
10	JIMMY KEY, 1984-1992
4	Jesse Jefferson, 1977-1980
3	Doyle Alexander, 1983-1986
3	Luis Leal, 1980-1985
3	Dave Lemanczyk, 1977-1980
3	TODD STOTTLEMYRE, 1988-1993

Wins: Most, career, all-time

174	DAVE STIEB, 1979-1992
128	Jim Clancy, 1977-1988
116	JIMMY KEY, 1984-1992
62	TODD STOTTLEMYRE, 1988-1993
51	Luis Leal, 1980-1985

K: Most, career, all-time

1631	DAVE STIEB, 1979-1992
1237	Jim Clancy, 1977-1988
944	JIMMY KEY, 1984-1992
668	DUANE WARD, 1986-1993
644	TOM HENKE, 1985-1992

Win pct: Highest, career, all-time

.784	JUAN GUZMAN, 1991-1993
.639	Doyle Alexander, 1983-1986
.589	JIMMY KEY, 1984-1992
.569	DAVE STIEB, 1979-1992
.560	DAVID WELLS, 1987-1992

ERA: Lowest, career, all-time

3.39	DAVE STIEB, 1979-1992
3.42	JIMMY KEY, 1984-1992
3.56	Doyle Alexander, 1983-1986
3.87	John Cerutti, 1985-1990
4.10	Jim Clancy, 1977-1988

Runs: Most, season

121	PAUL MOLITOR, 1993
116	DEVON WHITE, 1993
111	GEORGE BELL, 1987
110	DEVON WHITE, 1991
109	ROBERTO ALOMAR, 1993
109	JOHN OLERUD, 1993

Hits: Most, season

213	TONY FERNANDEZ, 1986
211	PAUL MOLITOR, 1993
200	JOHN OLERUD, 1993
198	GEORGE BELL, 1986
192	ROBERTO ALOMAR, 1993

2B: Most, season

54	JOHN OLERUD, 1993
42	JOE CARTER, 1991
42	DEVON WHITE, 1993
41	ROBERTO ALOMAR, 1991
41	GEORGE BELL, 1989
41	TONY FERNANDEZ, 1988

3B: Most, season

17	TONY FERNANDEZ, 1990
15	Dave Collins, 1984
15	ALFREDO GRIFFIN, 1980
15	Lloyd Moseby, 1984
11	ROBERTO ALOMAR, 1991

HR: Most, season

47	GEORGE BELL, 1987
40	Jesse Barfield, 1986
36	FRED McGRIFF, 1989
35	FRED McGRIFF, 1990
34	JOE CARTER, 1992
34	FRED McGRIFF, 1988

RBI: Most, season

134	GEORGE BELL, 1987
121	JOE CARTER, 1993
119	JOE CARTER, 1992
118	KELLY GRUBER, 1990
111	PAUL MOLITOR, 1993

SB: Most, season

60	Dave Collins, 1984
55	ROBERTO ALOMAR, 1993
54	Damaso Garcia, 1982
53	ROBERTO ALOMAR, 1991
49	ROBERTO ALOMAR, 1992

BB: Most, season

119	FRED McGRIFF, 1989
114	JOHN OLERUD, 1993
94	FRED McGRIFF, 1990
87	ROBERTO ALOMAR, 1992
82	DAVE WINFIELD, 1992

BA: Highest, season

.363	JOHN OLERUD, 1993
.332	PAUL MOLITOR, 1993
.326	ROBERTO ALOMAR, 1993
.322	TONY FERNANDEZ, 1987
.315	Lloyd Moseby, 1983

Slug avg: Highest, season

.605	GEORGE BELL, 1987
.599	JOHN OLERUD, 1993
.559	Jesse Barfield, 1986
.552	FRED McGRIFF, 1988
.536	Jesse Barfield, 1985

Games started: Most, season

40	Jim Clancy, 1982
38	Luis Leal, 1982
38	DAVE STIEB, 1982
37	Jim Clancy, 1987
36	Doyle Alexander, 1985
36	Jim Clancy, 1984
36	JIMMY KEY, 1987
36	DAVE STIEB, 1983
36	DAVE STIEB, 1985

Saves: Most, season

45	DUANE WARD, 1993
34	TOM HENKE, 1987
34	TOM HENKE, 1992
32	TOM HENKE, 1990
27	TOM HENKE, 1986

Shutouts: Most, season

5	DAVE STIEB, 1982
4	DAVE STIEB, 1980
4	DAVE STIEB, 1983
4	DAVE STIEB, 1988
3	Jim Clancy, 1982
3	Jim Clancy, 1986

Wins: Most, season

21	JACK MORRIS, 1992
19	PAT HENTGEN, 1993
18	DAVE STIEB, 1990
17	Doyle Alexander, 1984
17	Doyle Alexander, 1985
17	JIMMY KEY, 1987
17	DAVE STIEB, 1982
17	DAVE STIEB, 1983
17	DAVE STIEB, 1989

K: Most, season

198	DAVE STIEB, 1984
194	JUAN GUZMAN, 1993
187	DAVE STIEB, 1983
180	Jim Clancy, 1987
167	DAVE STIEB, 1985

Win pct: Highest, season

.778	JACK MORRIS, 1992
.762	JUAN GUZMAN, 1992
.750	DAVE STIEB, 1990
.739	Doyle Alexander, 1984
.680	JIMMY KEY, 1987
.680	DAVE STIEB, 1989

ERA: Lowest, season

2.48	DAVE STIEB, 1985
2.64	JUAN GUZMAN, 1992
2.76	JIMMY KEY, 1987
2.83	DAVE STIEB, 1984
2.93	DAVE STIEB, 1990

Most pinch-hit homers, season

2	Al Woods, 1977
2	Otto Velez, 1979
2	Rico Carty, 1979
2	Ernie Whitt, 1982
2	Jeff Burroughs, 1985

Most pinch-hit, homers, career

4	Ernie Whitt, 1977-1989
4	Jesse Barfield, 1981-1989

Most consecutive games, batting safely

26	JOHN OLERUD, 1993
22	GEORGE BELL, 1989
21	Damaso Garcia, 1983
21	Lloyd Moseby, 1983

Most consecutive scoreless innings

31	DAVE STIEB, 1988

No hit games

DAVE STIEB, Tor at Det AL, 3-0;
September 2, 1990.

ACTIVE PLAYERS in caps.

New York Yankees

Mike Stanley's newly-discovered power stroke (26 home runs, 84 RBI) helped keep the Yankees in contention.

by Robert Deutsch, USA TODAY

1993 Yankees: Best year since 1986

Introductions took longer than usual during spring training for the Yankees last season, as several players became acquainted with their new teammates. General manager Gene Michael had been busy signing Jimmy Key, Wade Boggs, Spike Owen and Jim Abbott.

The new faces helped the Yankees to their best finish (second place) since 1986, and their best record (88-74) since '87. Not many had picked the Yankees as contenders, but New York battled with Toronto, Baltimore and Boston through the second half of the season.

Pitching was supposed to be a strong suit, and Jimmy Key delivered on his end (18-6, 3.00 ERA). He was the only Yankee pitcher with more than 15 wins. Jim Abbott and Melido Perez were expected to help provide three solid starters, but neither showed much consistency. Perez and Abbott were a combined 17-28, with ERAs of 5.19 and 4.37 respectively.

Abbott was alternately dazzling and disastrous. He was the former on Sept. 4, when he pitched a no-hitter against Cleveland to move the Yankees within a game of Toronto. Unfortunately, the team collapsed after that, as the Yankees lost 10 of their next 15 games, while the Blue Jays won nine straight.

Compounding the lack of pitching, the Yankees suffered from slumps at the plate. The offense had been one of the league's best during the season, fueled by a revitalized Boggs and Don Mattingly, and a breakout year for catcher Mike Stanley. New York led the league in hits, tied for second in homers, and finished third in RBI. It was the return of the Bronx Bombers.

"I've been on teams that were capable of being this potent," designated hitter Danny Tartabull said. "But I've never been on one that actually did it. We have a lot of guys that people don't know about who are capable of putting up some big numbers."

Not one of those guys came as a bigger surprise than Mike Stanley. A career-platooner, Stanley had averaged .251 with six homers and 24 RBI in six major league seasons. He obliterated those marks (.305-26-84), establishing himself as perhaps the Yankees' MVP.

Manager Buck Showalter finished second in manager of the year voting, massaging the once boisterous and bickering Yankees into a "We Are Family" reincarnation. Utilizing his deep bench, Showalter coaxed productive seasons from Mike Gallego (.283-10-54), Dion James (.332) and Randy Velarde (.301).

Boggs and O'Neill performed at or above expectations. Boggs, reached the .300 mark for the 10th time in his 11-year career (.302). O'Neill recaptured his power (20 HR, 75 RBI) and hit over .300 for the first time (.311).

—by Deron Snyder

1994 Yankees: Preview

Mike Gallego wrested the shortstop job from Spike Owen (who made just one start after Sept. 3), and second baseman Pat Kelly and utility man Randy Velarde were solid, but with Owen signed to a three-year, $7 million contract, movement may be in order.

Don Mattingly and Wade Boggs will return to the corners, and Mike Stanley will attempt to reproduce a career year behind the plate. Bernie Williams and Paul O'Neill patrol the outfield; health will determine whether Danny Tartabull is in right field or a DH.

Jimmy Key can't be expected to do any better than last season. The Yanks will look for significant contributions from their younger pitchers: Mark Hutton and Sterling Hitchcock. Bob Wickman, who won 10 games last season shuttling between the rotation and the bullpen, needs a defined role.

—by Deron Snyder

1993 Yankees: Between the lines

▶**April 8:** Steve Howe, in his first appearance since June 1992, gave up six earned runs without recording an out—he left with an infinite ERA.

▶**April 10:** Jimmy Key threw seven scoreless innings against the White Sox for his second win.

▶**April 12:** Jim Abbott won the home opener. Paul O'Neill was 4-for-4, with a double, a triple and two RBI.

▶**April 14:** Wade Boggs had the 48th four-hit game of his career. Meanwhile, Bob Wickman gave up one earned run in 8 2/3 innings.

▶**April 27:** Jimmy Key pitched his second career one-hitter.

▶**May 1:** Mike Witt, in his second start since returning from elbow surgery, allowed one run in seven innings and got his first win in three seasons.

▶**May 8:** Steve Howe fell down a flight of stairs in the clubhouse at Tiger Stadium and was placed on the 15-day DL. His ERA was a gruesome 19.06.

▶**May 21:** Wade Boggs had four hits in his first game in Boston since being signed by the Yankees in the offseason. Some of the fans at Fenway give him a standing ovation, others responded to his return with Bronx cheers.

▶**May 25:** Wickman improved his record to 5-0 for the season and 11-1 lifetime, the second fastest start by a Yankee next to Whitey Ford (16-1 over his first two seasons, 1950 and 1953).

▶**May 28:** Jimmy Key tossed a three-hitter at the White Sox to record his second shutout of the season.

▶**May 29:** Jim Abbott took a no-hitter into the eighth inning before allowing a single to Chicago's Bo Jackson.

▶**June 8:** Pat Kelly homered, doubled twice and singled home the go-ahead run in the ninth inning. It marked the first four-hit game of his career.

▶**June 10:** Wickman's perfect 7-0 record was the best start by a Yankee since Tommy John went 9-0 in 1979.

▶**June 18:** Jimmy Key threw six shutout innings to earn his eighth win of the

year, a 5-0 defeat of the Twins. His ERA dropped to 2.17.

▶**June 20:** Wickman ran his record to 8-0 with his first career complete game, an 8-0 shutout of the Twins.

▶**June 28:** Jimmy Key got his sixth win in a row, and led the AL with a 2.30 ERA.

▶**June 30:** Jim Abbott allowed just three hits over eight innings as the Yankees shut out the Tigers 7-0. It was the first time the Bombers had shut out the Tigers in 110 games.

▶**July 9:** Key threw a five-hit complete game to run his record to 11-2.

▶**July 18:** Don Mattingly had four hits, including a pair of RBI singles during New York's 10-run seventh inning, as the Yankees clobbered Oakland 13-6. Mike Stanley hit a grand slam.

▶**July 19:** Scott Kamieniecki fanned a career-high eight batters in an 8-2 win over Seattle, his second complete game of the year. The Yanks were tied for first place in the AL East.

▶**July 20:** Stanley hit his second grand slam in three days.

▶**July 22:** Danny Tartabull hit two—out of New York's five—home runs in a 12-1 defeat of the Angels. *Milestone—* Don Mattingly hit his 200th career home run.

▶**July 23:** Mark Hutton, in his major league debut, threw eight innings of three-hit ball to beat California 5-2.

▶**August 3:** Wade Boggs had his 50th career four-hit game in New York's 8-6 loss to Toronto.

▶**August 5:** Jimmy Key struck out John Olerud three times and went the distance for the Yankees in a 5-4 win against the Blue Jays. The Yanks were one game behind Toronto, tied with the Red Sox for second place.

▶**August 8:** Mattingly hit a two-run homer in the 10th inning to give the Yanks an 8-6 victory at the Metrodome. The Yankees were within a game of the Blue Jays in the AL East.

▶**August 13:** Jim Abbott scattered

eight hits in a 4-1 complete game win against the Orioles.

▶**August 23:** Pitcher Scott Radinsky's throwing error in the top of the 10th inning allowed two runs to score as the Yankees defeated the White Sox, 6-5, to climb into a first-place tie with Toronto in the AL East. Bernie Williams extended his hitting streak to a career-high 21 games.

▶**August 24:** Ellis Burks hit a game-winning two-run double in the seventh inning as Chicago defeated New York 4-2, dropping the Yankees a game back of Toronto in the AL East.

▶**September 4:** *No-hitter!* Jim Abbott threw the Yankees' first no-hitter in 10 years, shutting down the Indians for a 4-0 win.

▶**September 5:** Mike Stanley went deep for the 25th time in 1993 in the Yankees' 7-2 win against Cleveland. Stanley entered the season with 24 career home runs.

▶**September 17:** The Yankees pushed across runs with RBI groundouts in the seventh and eighth innings to beat Boston 5-4. The go-ahead run came in when Wade Boggs beat the throw and avoided an inning-ending double play as New York stayed three games behind Toronto.

▶**September 18:** The Yankees took advantage of an unruly fan to score a 4-3 win against the Red Sox. Pinch-hitter Mike Stanley flied out to left field for what should have been the final out of a 3-1 Boston win, but third base umpire Tim Welke revealed that he had called time before the pitch was thrown when a fan ran onto the field near the third base line. Given a second chance, Stanley singled to keep the rally alive. An infield hit and a walk later, Don Mattingly singled in the winning run.

▶**October 1:** Randy Velarde singled home the tying run in the eighth to give the Yankees a 9-6 win against Detroit, clinching second place in the AL East.

▶**October 3:** The Yankees beat Detroit, 2-1, and finished what had been an exciting pennant race in second place in the AL East, seven games behind the Jays. *League leaders, pitching—*

Jimmy Key was third in ERA (3.00), fourth in victories (18-6), tied for fifth in shutouts (2), eighth in strikeouts (173), and ninth in innings pitched (236 2/3). *League leaders, batting—* Paul O'Neill was ninth in batting (.311); Danny Tartabull was ninth in walks (92) and tied for ninth in home runs (31).
—by John Hunt, Scott Kauffman, Lisa Winston, Deron Snyder, Matt Young

Team directory

▶**Owner:** George Steinbrenner
▶**General Manager:** Gene Michael
▶**Ballpark:**Yankee Stadium
East 161st Street and River Avenue, Bronx, New York
718-293-4300
Capacity 57,545
Parking (independently owned); $5
Public transportation available
Family and wheelchair sections, ramps, Senior Citizen Discount ($1 tickets day of game), group discounts, monument park behind right
field with plaques honoring famous Yankees
▶**Team publications:**
Yankees Magazine, media guide, scorecard, yearbook
718-293-4300
▶**TV, radio broadcast stations:**
WABC 770 AM, WPIX Channel 11, MSG Network
▶**Spring Training:**
Fort Lauderdale Stadium
Fort Lauderdale, Florida
Capacity 8,340
305-776-1921

NEW YORK YANKEES 1993 final stats

Batting	BA	SLG	OB	G	AB	R	H	TB	2B	3B	HR	RBI	BB	SO	SB	CS	E
James	.332	.466	.390	115	343	62	114	160	21	2	7	36	31	31	0	0	5
O'Neill	.311	.504	.367	141	498	71	155	251	34	1	20	75	44	69	2	4	2
Leyritz	.309	.525	.410	95	259	43	80	136	14	0	14	53	37	59	0	0	2
Stanley	.305	.534	.389	130	423	70	129	226	17	1	26	84	57	85	1	1	3
Boggs	.302	.363	.378	143	560	83	169	203	26	1	2	59	74	49	0	1	12
Velarde	.301	.469	.360	85	226	28	68	106	13	2	7	24	18	39	2	2	9
Mattingly	.291	.445	.364	134	530	78	154	236	27	2	17	86	61	42	0	0	3
Silvestri	.286	.476	.423	7	21	4	6	10	1	0	1	4	5	3	0	0	3
Gallego	.283	.412	.364	119	403	63	114	166	20	1	10	54	50	65	3	2	13
Kelly	.273	.389	.317	127	406	49	111	158	24	1	7	51	24	68	14	11	14
B.Williams	.268	.400	.333	139	567	67	152	227	31	4	12	68	53	106	9	9	4
Tartabull	.250	.503	.363	138	513	87	128	258	33	2	31	102	92	156	0	0	2
Nokes	.249	.424	.303	76	217	25	54	92	8	0	10	35	16	31	0	0	2
Owen	.234	.311	.294	103	334	41	78	104	16	2	2	20	29	30	3	2	14
Maas	.205	.411	.316	59	151	20	31	62	4	0	9	25	24	32	1	1	2
Humphreys	.171	.371	.250	25	35	6	6	13	2	1	1	6	4	11	2	1	0
Meulens	.170	.340	.279	30	53	8	9	18	1	1	2	5	8	19	0	1	0
G.Williams	.149	.269	.183	42	67	11	10	18	2	3	0	6	1	14	2	0	2
Stankiewicz	.000	.000	.100	16	9	5	0	0	0	0	0	0	1	1	0	0	0

Pitching	W-L	ERA	G	GS	CG	GF	Sho	SV	IP	H	R	ER	HR	BB	SO
Smith	0-0	0.00	8	0	0	8	0	3	8	4	0	0	0	5	11
Key	18-6	3.00	34	34	4	0	2	0	236.2	219	84	79	26	43	173
Gibson	2-0	3.06	20	0	0	9	0	0	35.1	31	15	12	4	9	25
Assenmacher	2-2	3.12	26	0	0	6	0	0	17.1	10	6	6	0	9	11
Tanana	0-2	3.20	3	3	0	0	0	0	19.2	18	10	7	2	7	12
Kamieniecki	10-7	4.08	30	20	2	4	0	1	154.1	163	73	70	17	59	72
Farr	2-2	4.21	49	0	0	37	0	25	47	44	22	22	8	28	39
Abbott	11-14	4.37	32	32	4	0	1	0	214	221	115	104	22	73	95
Jean	1-1	4.46	10	6	0	1	0	0	40.1	37	20	20	7	19	20
Wickman	14-4	4.63	41	19	1	9	1	4	140	156	82	72	13	69	70
Hitchcock	1-2	4.65	6	6	0	0	0	0	31	32	18	16	4	14	26
Monteleone	7-4	4.94	42	0	0	11	0	0	85.2	85	52	47	14	35	50
Howe	3-5	4.97	51	0	0	19	0	4	50.2	58	31	28	7	10	19
Cook	0-1	5.06	4	0	0	3	0	0	5.1	4	3	3	1	7	4
Perez	6-14	5.19	25	25	0	0	0	0	163	173	103	94	22	64	148
Witt	3-2	5.27	9	9	0	0	0	0	41	39	26	24	7	22	30
Munoz	3-3	5.32	38	0	0	12	0	0	45.2	48	27	27	1	26	33
Hutton	1-1	5.73	7	4	0	2	0	0	22	24	17	14	2	17	12
Heaton	1-0	6.00	18	0	0	9	0	0	27	34	19	18	6	11	15
Militello	1-1	6.75	3	2	0	0	0	0	9.1	10	8	7	1	7	5
Johnson	0-2	30.38	2	2	0	0	0	0	2.2	12	10	9	1	2	0

1994 preliminary roster

PITCHERS (14)
Jim Abbott
Paul Assenmacher
Paul Gibson
Xavier Hernandez
Sterling Hitchcock
Steve Howe
Mark Hutton
Scott Kamieniecki
Jimmy Key
Sam Militello
Bobby Munoz
Melido Perez
Mariano Rivera
Bob Wickman

CATCHERS (3)
Jim Leyritz
Matt Nokes
Mike Stanley

INFIELDERS (13)
Wade Boggs
Russ Davis
Robert Eenhoorn
Andy Fox
Mike Gallego
Kevin Jordan
Pat Kelly
Kevin Maas
Don Mattingly
Spike Owen
Tate Seefried
Dave Silvestri

Randy Velarde

OUTFIELDERS (8)
Mike Humphreys
Jalal Leach
Bill Masse
Paul O'Neill
Jason Robertson
Danny Tartabull
Bernie Williams
Gerald Williams

Games played by position

Player	G	C	1B	2B	3B	SS	OF	DH
Boggs	143	0	0	0	134	0	0	8
Gallego	119	0	0	52	27	55	0	1
Humphreys	25	0	0	0	0	0	21	3
James	115	0	1	0	0	0	103	1
Kelly	127	0	0	125	0	0	0	0
Leyritz	95	12	29	0	0	0	28	21
Maas	59	0	17	0	0	0	0	31
Mattingly	134	0	130	0	0	0	0	5
Meulens	30	0	3	0	1	0	24	0
Nokes	76	56	0	0	0	0	0	11
O'Neill	141	0	0	0	0	0	138	2
Owen	103	0	0	0	0	96	0	2
Silvestri	7	0	0	0	3	4	0	0
Stankiewicz	16	0	0	6	4	1	0	1
Stanley	130	122	0	0	0	0	0	2
Tartabull	138	0	0	0	0	0	50	88
Velarde	85	0	0	0	16	26	50	1
B. Williams	139	0	0	0	0	0	139	0
G. Williams	42	0	0	0	0	0	37	1

Sick call: 1993 DL Report

Player	Days on the DL
Jim Abbott	15
Steve Farr	17
Mike Gallego	15
Steve Howe	29
Don Mattingly	27
Matt Nokes	16
Melido Perez	13
Danny Tartabull	21
Randy Velarde	54
Bernie Williams	25
Mike Witt**	144

** Three separate terms on Disabled List

Minor League Report

Class AAA: Columbus finished at 78-61, third in the International League Western Division. Billy Masse hit .316 with 19 homers and 91 RBI. Russ Davis hit 26 homers. Mark Hutton was 10-4 with a 3.18 ERA. Jeff Johnson was 7-6 with a 3.45 ERA while Royal Clayton was 7-6 with a 3.54 ERA. **Class AA:** Albany-Colonie finished at 69-68, fourth in the Eastern League, and lost to Harrisburg in four games in the playoffs. Kevin Jordan had 87 RBI and led the league in total bases. Richard Barnwell hit .298 with 11 homers, 50 RBI and 33 stolen bases. Jason Robertson had 35 steals. Brien Taylor was 13-7 with a 3.48 ERA and 150 strikeouts. Richard Batchelor had 19 saves. **Class A:** Prince William finished at 67-73, third in the Carolina League Northern Division. Carlton Fleming hit .299. Tate Seefried had 21 homers and 89 RBI. Andy Pettitte was 11-9 with a 3.04 ERA. . . . Greensboro finished at 85-58, winning the first half of the Sally League Northern Division, but fell to Savannah in five games in the league finals. Ryan Karp was 13-1 with a 1.81 ERA and 132 strikeouts in 109 innings. Derek Jeter hit .295 with 71 RBI. Kraig Hawkins led the league in steals with 67. Matt Luke and Nick Delvecchio each had 21 homers. Robert Hinds stole 51 bases. **Short-season:** Oneonta finished at 36-39, third in the New York-Penn League McNamara Division. Ruben Rivera had 13 homers. Michael Jerzembeck was 8-4 with a 2.68 ERA. . . . Tampa finished at 30-29, third in the Gulf Coast League Northern Division. Jose Lobaton hit .345 and stole 24 bases. Travion Nelson hit four homers. Mike Gordon was 4-2 with a 1.67 ERA.

Tops in the organization

Batter	Club	Avg	G	AB	R	H	HR	RBI
Turner, Brian	Sbr	.325	109	406	69	132	21	68
Masse, Billy	Col	.316	117	402	81	127	19	91
Fleming, Carlton	Prw	.299	120	442	72	132	0	25
Barnwell, R.	Alb	.298	131	463	98	138	11	50
Jeter, Derek	Gbo	.295	128	515	85	152	5	71

Home Runs			Wins		
Davis, Russ	Col	26	Karp, Ryan	Alb	16
Figga, Mike	Alb	25	Buddie, Mike	Gbo	13
Several players tied		21	Taylor, Brien	Alb	13
RBI			Frazier, Ron	Alb	12
Masse, Billy	Col	91	Pettitte, Andy	Alb	12
Luke, Matt	Gbo	91	**Saves**		
Seefried, Tate	Prw	89	Batchelor, Richard	Col	25
Jordan, Kevin	Alb	87	Ralph, Curtis	Prw	15
Several players tied		83	Coleman, Billy	Gbo	14
Stolen Bases			Croghan, Andy	Prw	11
Hawkins, Kraig	Gbo	67	Munoz, Roberto	Col	10
Hinds, Robert	Gbo	51	**Strikeouts**		
Robertson, J.	Alb	35	Karp, Ryan	Alb	176
Barnwell, R.	Alb	33	Frazier, Ron	Alb	173
Williams, Gerald	Col	29	Taylor, Brien	Alb	150
			Buddie, Mike	Gbo	143
			Pettitte, Andy	Alb	135

Pitcher	Club	W-L	ERA	IP	H	BB	SO
Karp, Ryan	Alb	16-3	2.10	171	121	61	176
Frazier, Ron	Alb	12-6	2.89	181	172	39	173
Pettitte, Andy	Alb	12-9	3.06	165	151	49	135
Hutton, Mark	Col	10-4	3.18	133	98	53	112
Johnson, Jeff	Col	7-6	3.45	115	125	47	59

New York (1903-1993)

Runs: Most, career, all-time

1959	Babe Ruth, 1920-1934
1888	Lou Gehrig, 1923-1939
1677	Mickey Mantle, 1951-1968
1390	Joe DiMaggio, 1936-1951
1186	Earle Combs, 1924-1935

Hits: Most, career, all-time

2721	Lou Gehrig, 1923-1939
2518	Babe Ruth, 1920-1934
2415	Mickey Mantle, 1951-1968
2214	Joe DiMaggio, 1936-1951
2148	Yogi Berra, 1946-1963

2B: Most, career, all-time

534	Lou Gehrig, 1923-1939
424	Babe Ruth, 1920-1934
390	DON MATTINGLY, 1982-1993
389	Joe DiMaggio, 1936-1951
344	Mickey Mantle, 1951-1968

3B: Most, career, all-time

163	Lou Gehrig, 1923-1939
154	Earle Combs, 1924-1935
131	Joe DiMaggio, 1936-1951
121	Wally Pipp, 1915-1925
115	Tony Lazzeri, 1926-1937

HR: Most, career, all-time

659	Babe Ruth, 1920-1934
536	Mickey Mantle, 1951-1968
493	Lou Gehrig, 1923-1939
361	Joe DiMaggio, 1936-1951
358	Yogi Berra, 1946-1963

RBI: Most, career, all-time

1995	Lou Gehrig, 1923-1939
1971	Babe Ruth, 1920-1934
1537	Joe DiMaggio, 1936-1951
1509	Mickey Mantle, 1951-1968
1430	Yogi Berra, 1946-1963

SB: Most, career, all-time

326	RICKEY HENDERSON, 1985-1989
251	Willie Randolph, 1976-1988
248	Hal Chase, 1905-1913
233	Roy White, 1965-1979
184	Ben Chapman, 1930-1936
184	Wid Conroy, 1903-1908

BB: Most, career, all-time

1847	Babe Ruth, 1920-1934
1733	Mickey Mantle, 1951-1968
1508	Lou Gehrig, 1923-1939
1005	Willie Randolph, 1976-1988
934	Roy White, 1965-1979

BA: Highest, career, all-time

.349	Babe Ruth, 1920-1934
.340	Lou Gehrig, 1923-1939
.325	Earle Combs, 1924-1935
.325	Joe DiMaggio, 1936-1951
.313	Bill Dickey, 1928-1946

Slug avg: Highest, career, all-time

.711	Babe Ruth, 1920-1934
.632	Lou Gehrig, 1923-1939
.579	Joe DiMaggio, 1936-1951
.557	Mickey Mantle, 1951-1968
.526	Reggie Jackson, 1977-1981

Games started: Most, career, all-time

438	Whitey Ford, 1950-1967
391	Red Ruffing, 1930-1946
356	Mel Stottlemyre, 1964-1974
323	Ron Guidry, 1975-1988
319	Lefty Gomez, 1930-1942

Saves: Most, career, all-time

224	DAVE RIGHETTI, 1979-1990
151	RICH GOSSAGE, 1978-1989
141	Sparky Lyle, 1972-1978
104	Johnny Murphy, 1932-1946
78	STEVE FARR, 1991-1993

Shutouts: Most, career, all-time

45	Whitey Ford, 1950-1967
40	Red Ruffing, 1930-1946
40	Mel Stottlemyre, 1964-1974
28	Lefty Gomez, 1930-1942
27	Allie Reynolds, 1947-1954

Wins: Most, career, all-time

236	Whitey Ford, 1950-1967
231	Red Ruffing, 1930-1946
189	Lefty Gomez, 1930-1942
170	Ron Guidry, 1975-1988
168	Bob Shawkey, 1915-1927

K: Most, career, all-time

1956	Whitey Ford, 1950-1967
1778	Ron Guidry, 1975-1988
1526	Red Ruffing, 1930-1946
1468	Lefty Gomez, 1930-1942
1257	Mel Stottlemyre, 1964-1974

Win pct: Highest, career, all-time

.725	Johnny Allen, 1932-1935
.717	Spud Chandler, 1937-1947
.706	Vic Raschi, 1946-1953
.700	Monte Pearson, 1936-1940
.690	Whitey Ford, 1950-1967

ERA: Lowest, career, all-time

2.54	Russ Ford, 1909-1913
2.58	Jack Chesbro, 1903-1909
2.72	Al Orth, 1904-1909
2.73	Tiny Bonham, 1940-1946
2.73	George Mogridge, 1915-1920

Runs: Most, season

177	Babe Ruth, 1921
167	Lou Gehrig, 1936
163	Lou Gehrig, 1931
163	Babe Ruth, 1928
158	Babe Ruth, 1920
158	Babe Ruth, 1927

Hits: Most, season

238	DON MATTINGLY, 1986
231	Earle Combs, 1927
220	Lou Gehrig, 1930
218	Lou Gehrig, 1927
215	Joe DiMaggio, 1937

2B: Most, season

53	DON MATTINGLY, 1986
52	Lou Gehrig, 1927
48	DON MATTINGLY, 1985
47	Lou Gehrig, 1926
47	Lou Gehrig, 1928
47	Bob Meusel, 1927

3B: Most, season

23	Earle Combs, 1927
22	Earle Combs, 1930
22	Birdie Cree, 1911
22	Snuffy Stirnweiss, 1945
21	Earle Combs, 1928

HR: Most, season

61	Roger Maris, 1961
60	Babe Ruth, 1927
59	Babe Ruth, 1921
54	Mickey Mantle, 1961
54	Babe Ruth, 1920
54	Babe Ruth, 1928

RBI: Most, season

184	Lou Gehrig, 1931
175	Lou Gehrig, 1927
174	Lou Gehrig, 1930
171	Babe Ruth, 1921
167	Joe DiMaggio, 1937

SB: Most, season

93	RICKEY HENDERSON, 1988
87	RICKEY HENDERSON, 1986
80	RICKEY HENDERSON, 1985
74	Fritz Maisel, 1914
61	Ben Chapman, 1931

BB: Most, season

170	Babe Ruth, 1923
148	Babe Ruth, 1920
146	Mickey Mantle, 1957
144	Babe Ruth, 1921
144	Babe Ruth, 1926

BA: Highest, season

.393	Babe Ruth, 1923
.381	Joe DiMaggio, 1939
.379	Lou Gehrig, 1930
.378	Babe Ruth, 1924
.378	Babe Ruth, 1921

Slug avg: Highest, season

.847	Babe Ruth, 1920
.846	Babe Ruth, 1921
.772	Babe Ruth, 1927
.765	Lou Gehrig, 1927
.764	Babe Ruth, 1923

Games started: Most, season

51	Jack Chesbro, 1904
45	Jack Powell, 1904
42	Jack Chesbro, 1906
39	Pat Dobson, 1974
39	Whitey Ford, 1961
39	Catfish Hunter, 1975
39	Al Orth, 1906
39	Mel Stottlemyre, 1969
39	Ralph Terry, 1962

Saves: Most, season

46	DAVE RIGHETTI, 1986
36	DAVE RIGHETTI, 1990
35	Sparky Lyle, 1972
33	RICH GOSSAGE, 1980
31	DAVE RIGHETTI, 1984
31	DAVE RIGHETTI, 1987

Shutouts: Most, season

9	Ron Guidry, 1978
8	Whitey Ford, 1964
8	Russ Ford, 1910
7	Whitey Ford, 1958
7	Catfish Hunter, 1975
7	Allie Reynolds, 1951
7	Mel Stottlemyre, 1971
7	Mel Stottlemyre, 1972

Wins: Most, season

41	Jack Chesbro, 1904
27	Carl Mays, 1921
27	Al Orth, 1906
26	Joe Bush, 1922
26	Russ Ford, 1910
26	Lefty Gomez, 1934
26	Carl Mays, 1920

K: Most, season

248	Ron Guidry, 1978
239	Jack Chesbro, 1904
218	MELIDO PEREZ, 1992
217	Al Downing, 1964
210	Bob Turley, 1955

Win pct: Highest, season

.893	Ron Guidry, 1978
.862	Whitey Ford, 1961
.842	Ralph Terry, 1961
.839	Lefty Gomez, 1934
.833	Spud Chandler, 1943

ERA: Lowest, season

1.64	Spud Chandler, 1943
1.65	Russ Ford, 1910
1.74	Ron Guidry, 1978
1.82	Jack Chesbro, 1904
1.83	Hippo Vaughn, 1910

Most pinch-hit homers, season

4	Johnny Blanchard, 1961

Most pinch-hit, homers, career

9	Yogi Berra, 1946-1963

Most consecutive games, batting safely

56	Joe DiMaggio, 1941
33	Hal Chase, 1907

Most consecutive scoreless innings

33	Jack Aker, 1969

No hit games

Tom L. Hughes, NY vs Cle AL, 0-5; August 30, 1910 (2nd game) (lost on 7 hits in 11 innings after allowing the first hit in the tenth).

George Mogridge, NY at Bos AL, 2-1; April 24, 1917.

Sam Jones, NY at Phi AL, 2-0; September 4, 1923.

Monte Pearson, NY vs Cle AL, 13-0; August 27, 1938 (2nd game).

Allie Reynolds, NY at Cle AL, 1-0; July 12, 1951.

Allie Reynolds, NY vs Bos AL, 8-0; September 28, 1951 (1st game).

Don Larsen, NY AL vs Bro NL, 2-0; October 8, 1956 (World Series, perfect game).

DAVE RIGHETTI, NY vs Bos AL, 4-0; July 4, 1983.

Andy Hawkins, NY at Chi AL, 0-4; July 1, 1990 (8 innings, lost the game; bottom of 9th not played).

JIM ABBOTT, NY vs Cle AL, 4-0; September 4, 1993.

ACTIVE PLAYERS in caps.

201

Baltimore Orioles

by Russell Beeker, Baseball Weekly

Mike Mussina led the Orioles with 14 wins, although his ERA rose from 2.54 in 1992 to 4.46 last year.

1993 Orioles: They wilted down the stretch

For the second consecutive season, the Orioles remained in the thick of the AL East race through mid-September. And for the second year, they wilted down the stretch against the superior talent and deeper pockets of the Blue Jays.

In retrospect, the O's division hopes may have ended as early as June 6, when a brawl with the Seattle Mariners left their pitching ace, Mike Mussina, at the bottom of a huge pileup. He was never the same. He was dominating the league at the time (8-2, 2.86 ERA), but after the brawl he pitched just 76 innings and finished 14-6 with a 4.46 ERA.

If that wasn't enough, closer Gregg Olson tore a ligament in his elbow and, although he finished with 29 saves, faced just one batter after Aug. 8. Every starting position player except second baseman Harold Reynolds, shortstop Cal Ripken and right fielder Mark McLemore spent time on the DL. Ben McDonald was the only starter to take every turn. He led the rotation with 220.1 innings and a 3.39 ERA.

"We had a chance to win," said Ripken, who extended his consecutive game streak to 1,897—just 233 shy of Lou Gehrig's record. "But we had some injuries that hurt us, and we didn't play well when it counted."

The Orioles got off to a 5-13 start but recovered to spend one day—July 20—alone in first place. They were still only one game out on Sept. 12, then were buried by a 3-10 slide. They finished tied for third place with Detroit with an 85-77 record.

Highlights included catcher Chris Hoiles, who finished with a .310 average, 29 home runs and 82 RBI, despite missing three weeks in August with a strained back muscle. His 82 RBI eclipsed Gus Triandos' club record for a catcher. First baseman David Segui got to play a full season and hit .273. Veteran Harold Baines hit a club-high .313 with 20 home runs and 78 RBI. Rookie Jack Voigt showed great promise with his .296 average. Late-season acquisition Mike Pagliarulo finished at .303. McLemore, a former second baseman, spent most of the year in right and posted career highs in nearly every category. The .267 team batting average was third-highest in club history and seven players finished with 60 or more RBI, led by Ripken's 90.

On the down side, outfielder Mike Devereaux was plagued by a shoulder injury and dropped from 107 to 75 RBI. And first baseman Glenn Davis, who fought off injuries all year, finally was released after three frustrating seasons that culminated in a shouting match with manager John Oates Sept. 8.

McDonald pitched much better than his 13-14 record, allowing three earned runs or less in 28 of 34 starts, and posting six complete games. Jamie Moyer matched his career high with 12 victories. Rick Sutcliffe started the year 8-2, but finished 10-10 with a 5.75 ERA. Fernando Valenzuela, like Moyer a non-roster player in training camp, faded from being AL Pitcher of the Month in July to an 8-10, 4.94 ERA finish.

The O's set a club attendance record of 3,644,965, the seventh-highest figure in major-league history (fourth-best in '94 behind Colorado, Toronto and Atlanta). The club responded with its best home record (48-33) in 10 years.

—by Bill Koenig

1994 Orioles: Preview

The future of the Orioles rests on the more liberal spending habits of their new owners. They helped the offense by signing Rafael Palmeiro and the pitching with Sid Fernandez. Of utmost concern: Gregg Olson's possible elbow surgery that would keep him out for all of 1994, and Jeffrey Hammonds' possible surgery on a herniated disk in his neck that would keep him out 8-10 months.

—by Bill Koenig

1993 Orioles: Between the lines

▸**April 25:** The O's played their sixth consecutive one-run game, a 3-2 loss in Kansas City. They had a major league-best 23-13 record in one-run affairs in '92, but were 2-4 during the '93 streak.

▸**May 2:** Harold Baines reached base for the 12th consecutive time. He had hits in eight consecutive at-bats, two shy of the team record.

▸**May 12:** Danny Darwin blanked the O's 2-0. It was the first time in 10 years they had been shut out twice in a row.

▸**May 26:** Mike Mussina won his sixth game, holding the Yankees to two runs in 8 1/3 innings.

▸**May 27:** Mike Devereaux, fresh off the disabled list, broke up a 3-3 tie in the 10th inning to help the O's take three of four at Yankee Stadium.

▸**May 31:** Mike Mussina allowed one run in a complete-game 3-1 win against the A's. It was the third time in '93 that Mussina stopped O's losing streaks of three or more games.

▸**June 6:** The O's and Mariners hooked up for the longest and bloodiest brawl in years. The fracus started with Bill Haselman charging the mound and ended with seven players and Seattle manager Lou Piniella getting the thumb. Orioles Jeff Tackett and Mark Williamson had facial cuts, and Seattle starter Chris Bosio reinjured his collarbone, which had landed him on the disabled list for 31 days earlier in the year. *Quote of the day*—Mike Mussina: "We don't do any drills in spring training for this kind of stuff."

▸**June 7:** Ben McDonald carried a no-hitter through the fifth inning, but lost it when Oakland's Craig Paquette singled to lead off the sixth.

▸**June 9:** Mark McLemore collected a career-high five hits to lead the Orioles past Oakland 7-4. The five hits—all singles—tied a club record. Twenty-two other Orioles have had five-hit games.

▸**June 10:** Jamie Moyer won at the major league level for the first time since 1990, guiding the Orioles past Boston 2-1.

The 30-year-old went 5 2/3 innings, allowing one run on six hits, to notch his first victory in three years. The win moved the O's ahead of Boston in the AL East.

▸**June 12:** The O's won their 10th in a row—the longest streak in the AL.

▸**June 23:** Rick Sutcliffe went the distance in a 6-2 win against the Tigers. Sutcliffe had won his last six decisions as the O's won 16 of the last 19 games.

▸**June 26:** Chris Hoiles hit two solo homers in a 12-10 Oriole victory over New York. It was the second two-homer effort in five games for Hoiles, who had more than one hit in each of his last six games, including six home runs.

▸**June 30:** Fernando Valenzuela fired a six-hit shutout at the Toronto Blue Jays. It was his 31st career shutout.

▸**July 1:** Chicago's Jack McDowell hooked up with Jamie Moyer for a pitcher's duel at Comiskey Park. The O's manufactured the game's only run. McDowell retired the last 20 Orioles in order. Moyer went eight innings, allowing four singles for his fourth win.

▸**July 6:** Moyer pitched his first complete game since 1990, a four-hitter, as the O's shut out Kansas City 8-0. Moyer won his fifth decision in a row and had thrown 17 consecutive shutout innings.

▸**July 7:** Chris Hoiles hit two home runs for the third time since June 22.

▸**July 9:** Hoiles hit a three-run homer in the Orioles' seven-run sixth inning, and they beat the White Sox 15-6 at Camden Yards.

▸**July 10:** Fernando Valenzuela did not allow a runner past first base and became the first Orioles' starter since Jim Palmer to make three starts without giving up a run. *Milestone*—Cal Ripken got his 2,000th career hit, the 14th active player to reach the plateau.

▸**July 20:** Ben McDonald pitched his first career one-hitter and matched his career-high for strikeouts (9) as the O's shut out Kansas City 7-0, and moved into first in the AL East. It was McDonald's 14th consecutive start allowing three earned runs or less, dating to May 11. The last Oriole to accomplish the feat was Jim Palmer in 1972.

▶**July 23:** Fernando Valenzuela threw a six-hitter in a 5-1 win against Minnesota. In his last five starts Valenzuela had a 4-0 record and a 0.65 ERA.

▶**August 1:** Glenn Davis, recovering from a broken jaw suffered in a bar fight June 7, was knocked unconscious by a foul lined to the Orioles' dugout during a 2-1 loss to the Red Sox. Hit just below the left ear by a ball off the bat of teammate Jeffrey Hammonds, Davis was taken to a nearby hospital and released after tests proved no further damage was done to the jaw.

▶**August 5:** Ben McDonald threw a complete-game eight-hitter as the O's pulled off a four-game sweep against Milwaukee.

▶**August 7:** Cal Ripken had two homers for the first time at Camden Yards and drove in four runs as the Orioles beat Cleveland 8-6. It was the 12th two-homer game of Ripken's career.

▶**August 16:** Seattle roughed up Rick Sutcliffe for eight runs in 3 2/3 innings (the O's seventh consecutive loss) and Baltimore dropped 5 1/2 games behind first-place Toronto.

▶**August 20:** Cal Ripken hit his 20th home run and drove in four runs in the Orioles' win. Ripken has hit 20 or more home runs in 11 of his 12 seasons.

▶**September 1:** Ben McDonald struck out a career-high 10 batters to lead the Orioles to a 5-1 win against California.

▶**September 14:** Fernando Valenzuela got his first win since July 23 and Chris Hoiles continued his torrid hitting with a two-run homer.

▶**September 18:** Mild-mannered manager Johnny Oates threw a tantrum in the seventh inning of Baltimore's 3-0 loss to Milwaukee, kicked dirt on second base umpire Chuck Meriwether, and got his first thumb of the season. As a parting gesture, Oates threw out his hat and jacket in disgust.

▶**October 3:** Baltimore lost it's final game to the Blue Jays, whom they were 10 games behind (third place) in the AL East when all was said and done.

League leaders, pitching—Todd Frohwirth was tied for sixth in games (70); Ben McDonald was ninth in strikeouts (171) and tied for sixth in complete games (7); Greg Olson was eighth in saves (29). *League leaders, batting*— Chris Hoiles was fifth in slugging (.585) and on-base percentage (.416); Brady Anderson was tied for sixth in triples (8).

—*by John Hunt, Scott Kauffman, Lisa Winston, Deron Snyder, Matt Young*

Team directory

▶**Owner:** Peter Angelos
▶**General Manager:** Roland Hemond
▶**Ballpark:**
Oriole Park at Camden Yards
Baltimore, Md., 410-685-9800
Capacity over 48,000
Pay parking for 5,000 cars
Public transportation available
Disability seating, ramps, elevators, sound amplification devices for the hearing impaired, special menu selection board for the speaking impaired
▶**Team publications:**
Orioles Gazette, Orioles Scoreboard, media guide, yearbook
410-685-9800
▶**TV, radio broadcast stations:**
WBAL 1090 AM, Home Team
 Sports Cable
▶**Camps and/or clinics:**
Fantasy Camp (ages 30+), February, 410-685-9800
Cal Ripken Sr. Baseball Camp (ages 8-18), Mount St. Mary's, Emmitsburg, Md., late June and early July, 301-447-5296
Elrod Hendricks Camp, McDonough School, McDonough, Md., July, 410-685-9800
Summer clinics, the Orioles region, during the season, 410-685-9800
▶**Spring Training:**
Al Lang Stadium
St. Petersburg, Fla.
Capacity 6,500
813-893-7490

BALTIMORE ORIOLES 1993 final stats

Batting	BA	SLG	OB	G	AB	R	H	TB	2B	3B	HR	RBI	BB	SO	SB	CS	E
Baines	.313	.510	.390	118	416	64	130	212	22	0	20	78	57	52	0	0	0
Hoiles	.310	.585	.416	126	419	80	130	245	28	0	29	82	69	94	1	1	5
Hammonds	.305	.467	.312	33	105	10	32	49	8	0	3	19	2	16	4	0	2
Pagliarulo	.303	.465	.357	116	370	55	112	172	25	4	9	44	26	49	6	6	8
Hulett	.300	.381	.361	85	260	40	78	99	15	0	2	23	23	56	1	2	8
Voigt	.296	.500	.395	64	152	32	45	76	11	1	6	23	25	33	1	0	1
Mercedes	.292	.375	.414	10	24	1	7	9	2	0	0	0	5	4	1	1	0
McLemore	.284	.368	.353	148	581	81	165	214	27	5	4	72	64	92	21	15	6
Segui	.273	.400	.351	146	450	54	123	180	27	0	10	60	58	53	2	1	5
Obando	.272	.391	.309	31	92	8	25	36	2	0	3	15	4	26	0	0	1
Anderson	.263	.425	.363	142	560	87	147	238	36	8	13	66	82	99	24	12	2
Parent	.259	.519	.293	22	54	7	14	28	2	0	4	12	3	14	0	0	1
Ripken	.257	.420	.329	162	641	87	165	269	26	3	24	90	65	58	1	4	17
Reynolds	.252	.334	.343	145	485	64	122	162	20	4	4	47	66	47	12	11	10
Devereaux	.250	.400	.306	131	527	72	132	211	31	3	14	75	43	99	3	3	4
Buford	.228	.367	.315	53	79	18	18	29	5	0	2	9	9	19	2	2	1
Carey	.213	.234	.288	18	47	1	10	11	1	0	0	3	5	14	0	0	2
Smith	.208	.500	.406	9	24	8	5	12	1	0	2	3	8	10	0	0	0
Gomez	.197	.348	.295	71	244	30	48	85	7	0	10	25	32	60	0	1	10
Davis	.177	.230	.230	30	113	8	20	26	3	0	1	9	7	29	0	1	2
Tackett	.172	.207	.277	39	87	8	15	18	3	0	0	9	13	28	0	0	2
Leonard	.067	.133	.190	10	15	1	1	2	1	0	0	3	3	7	0	0	1
Martinez	.000	.000	.211	8	15	0	0	0	0	0	0	0	4	4	0	0	0
Alexander	--	--	--	3	0	1	0	0	0	0	0	0	0	0	0	0	0

Pitching	W-L	ERA	G	GS	CG	GF	Sho	SV	IP	H	R	ER	HR	BB	SO
Cook	0-0	0.00	2	0	0	0	0	0	3	1	0	0	0	2	3
Tackett	0-0	0.00	1	0	0	1	0	0	1	1	0	0	0	1	0
Olson	0-2	1.60	50	0	0	45	0	29	45	37	9	8	1	18	44
Poole	2-1	2.15	55	0	0	11	0	2	50.1	30	18	12	2	21	29
Mills	5-4	3.23	45	0	0	18	0	4	100.1	80	39	36	14	51	68
McDonald	13-14	3.39	34	34	7	0	1	0	220.1	185	92	83	17	86	171
Moyer	12-9	3.43	25	25	3	0	1	0	152	154	63	58	11	38	90
Frohwirth	6-7	3.83	70	0	0	30	0	3	96.1	91	47	41	7	44	50
Oquist	0-0	3.86	5	0	0	2	0	0	11.2	12	5	5	0	4	8
Mussina	14-6	4.46	25	25	3	0	2	0	167.2	163	84	83	20	44	117
O'Donoghue	0-1	4.58	11	1	0	3	0	0	19.2	22	12	10	4	10	16
Williamson	7-5	4.91	48	1	0	12	0	0	88	106	54	48	5	25	45
Valenzuela	8-10	4.94	32	31	5	0	2	0	178.2	179	104	98	18	79	78
Sutcliffe	10-10	5.75	29	28	3	0	0	0	166	212	112	106	23	74	80
McGehee	0-0	5.94	5	0	0	1	0	0	16.2	18	11	11	5	7	7
Rhodes	5-6	6.51	17	17	0	0	0	0	85.2	91	62	62	16	49	49
Pennington	3-2	6.55	34	0	0	16	0	4	33	34	25	24	7	25	39
Telford	0-0	9.82	3	0	0	2	0	0	7.1	11	8	8	3	1	6

1994 preliminary roster

PITCHERS (19)
Armando Benitez
Mike Cook
Sid Fernandez
Rick Forney
Todd Frohwirth
Rick Krivda
Barry Manuel
Ben McDonald
Kevin McGehee
Alan Mills
Jamie Moyer
Mike Mussina
John O'Donoghue
Gregg Olson
Mike Oquist
Brad Pennington
Jim Poole
Arthur Rhodes
Jeff Williams

CATCHERS (3)
Chris Hoiles
Jeff Tackett
Gregg Zaun

INFIELDERS (7)
Manny Alexander
Paul Carey
Leo Gomez
Tim Hulett
Rafael Palmeiro
Cal Ripken
David Segui

OUTFIELDERS (11)
Brady Anderson
Harold Baines
Damon Buford
Mike Devereaux
Jeffrey Hammonds
Mark McLemore
Sherman Obando
Alex Ochoa
Mark Smith
Jack Voigt
Jim Wawruck

Games played by position

Player	G	C	1B	2B	3B	SS	OF	DH
Alexander	3	0	0	0	0	0	0	1
Anderson	142	0	0	0	0	0	140	2
Baines	118	0	0	0	0	0	0	116
Buford	53	0	0	0	0	0	30	17
Carey	18	0	9	0	0	0	0	5
Davis	30	0	22	0	0	0	0	7
Devereaux	131	0	0	0	0	0	130	0
Gomez	71	0	0	0	70	0	0	1
Hammonds	33	0	0	0	0	0	23	8
Hoiles	126	124	0	0	0	0	0	2
Hulett	85	0	0	4	75	8	0	2
Leonard	10	0	0	0	0	0	4	3
Martinez	8	0	0	0	0	0	5	2
McLemore	148	0	0	25	4	0	124	1
Mercedes	10	0	0	0	0	0	8	2
Obando	31	0	0	0	0	0	8	21
Pagliarulo	116	0	4	0	107	0	0	0
Parent	22	21	0	0	0	0	0	1
Reynolds	145	0	0	141	0	0	0	1
Ripken	162	0	0	0	0	162	0	0
Segui	146	0	144	0	0	0	0	1
Smith	9	0	0	0	0	0	4	5
Tackett	39	38	0	0	0	0	0	0
Voigt	64	0	5	0	3	0	43	9

Sick call: 1993 DL Report

Player	Days on the DL
Brady Anderson	15
Harold Baines	22
Glenn Davis	91
Mike Devereaux	24
Leo Gomez	55
Jeffrey Hammonds	30
Chris Hoiles	21
Mike Mussina	29
Sherman Obando*	45
Gregg Olson	42
Arthur Rhodes	78
Rick Sutcliffe	19

Two separate terms on Disabled List

Minor League Report

Class AAA: Rochester finished 74-67, winning the International League Eastern Division. Paul Carey hit .311 with 12 homers and 50 RBI. Kevin McGehee led the league in ERA at 2.96. Mike Oquist was 9-8 with a 3.50 ERA and 128 strikeouts. **Class AA:** Bowie finished at 72-67, third in the Eastern League. T.R. Lewis hit .304 with five homers and 64 RBI. Stanton Cameron had 21 homers. Rick Krivda was 7-5 with a 3.08 ERA. Terry Farrar was 7-7 with a 3.49 ERA. Rafael Chaves had 20 saves. **Class A:** Frederick finished at 78-62, winning the second half of the Carolina League Northern Division. Alex Ochoa had 90 RBI and 34 stolen bases. Curtis Goodwin led the league with 61 steals. Rick Forney was 14-8 with a 2.78 ERA and 175 strikeouts. Scott Klingenbeck was 13-4 with a 2.98 ERA. Jimmy Haynes was 12-8 with a 3.03 ERA and 174 strikeouts. . . . Albany finished at 71-71, fourth in the Sally League Southern Division. Billy Owens hit .297 with 11 homers and 66 RBI. Eric Chavez had 18 homers. Garrett Stephenson threw a no-hitter, and was 16-7 with a 2.84 ERA. **Short-season:** Bluefield finished at 44-24, tied for first in the Appalachian League Northern Division. Brian Link hit .338 with 14 homers and 60 RBI. Jim Foster batted .326 with 10 homers and 45 RBI. Myles Barnden had 53 RBI. Kimera Bartee (27), Lincoln Martin (26) and Brandon Bridgers (22) ranked top three in the league in steals. Calvin Maduro's nine wins led the league, as did his 83 strikeouts. William Percibal fanned 81. . . . Sarasota finished at 30-28, fourth in the Gulf Coast League Western Division. John Lombardi led the league in ERA at 0.92, going 7-1. Rocco Cafaro was 2-2 with a 1.79 ERA.

Tops in the organization

Batter	Club	Avg	G	AB	R	H	HR	RBI
Carey, Paul	Roc	.311	96	325	63	101	12	50
Lewis, T.R.	Bow	.304	127	480	73	146	5	64
Owens, Billy	Fre	.303	137	518	72	157	11	74
Wawruck, Jim	Bow	.297	128	475	59	141	4	44
Waszgis, B.J.	Aby	.291	117	409	57	119	11	61

Home Runs			Wins		
Cameron, Stanton	Bow	21	Stephenson, Gar.	Aby	16
Coolbaugh, Scott	Roc	18	Forney, Rick	Bow	14
Chavez, Eric	Aby	18	Klingenbeck, Scott	Fre	13
Leonard, Mark	Roc	17	Haynes, Jimmy	Fre	12
Several players tied		14	Dubois, Brian	Roc	12

RBI			Saves		
Ochoa, Alex	Fre	90	Chaves, Rafael	Bow	20
Owens, Billy	Fre	74	Benitez, Armando	Fre	18
Chavez, Eric	Aby	74	Paveloff, Dave	Bow	16
Hinzo, Tommy	Roc	69	Cook, Mike	Roc	13
Several players tied		68	Borowski, Joe	Bow	11

Stolen Bases			Strikeouts		
Goodwin, Curtis	Fre	61	Forney, Rick	Bow	179
Ochoa, Alex	Fre	34	Haynes, Jimmy	Fre	174
Hinzo, Tommy	Roc	29	Sackinsky, Brian	Fre	153
Wawruck, Jim	Bow	28	Stephenson, Gar.	Aby	147
Serra, Jose	Aby	26	Klingenbeck, Scott	Fre	146

Pitcher	Club	W-L	ERA	IP	H	BB	SO
Dedrick, Jim	Roc	9-3	2.54	113	90	32	81
Dubois, Brian	Roc	12-5	2.71	146	141	46	102
Forney, Rick	Bow	14-8	2.72	172	157	65	179
Krivda, Rick	Roc	10-5	2.83	159	134	66	131
Stephenson, Gar.	Aby	16-7	2.84	171	142	44	147

Baltimore (1954-1993), includes St. Louis (1902-1953)

Runs: Most, career, all-time

1232	Brooks Robinson, 1955-1977	
1130	CAL RIPKEN, 1981-1993	
1091	George Sisler, 1915-1927	
1048	EDDIE MURRAY, 1977-1988	
1013	Harlond Clift, 1934-1943	

Hits: Most, career, all-time

2848	Brooks Robinson, 1955-1977	
2295	George Sisler, 1915-1927	
2087	CAL RIPKEN, 1981-1993	
2021	EDDIE MURRAY, 1977-1988	
1574	Boog Powell, 1961-1974	

2B: Most, career, all-time

482	Brooks Robinson, 1955-1977	
395	CAL RIPKEN, 1981-1993	
351	EDDIE MURRAY, 1977-1988	
343	George Sisler, 1915-1927	
294	Harlond Clift, 1934-1943	

3B: Most, career, all-time

145	George Sisler, 1915-1927	
88	Baby Doll Jacobson, 1915-1926	
72	Del Pratt, 1912-1917	
72	Jack Tobin, 1916-1925	
70	Ken Williams, 1918-1927	
68	Brooks Robinson, 1955-1977 (6)	

HR: Most, career, all-time

333	EDDIE MURRAY, 1977-1988	
303	Boog Powell, 1961-1974	
297	CAL RIPKEN, 1981-1993	
268	Brooks Robinson, 1955-1977	
185	Ken Williams, 1918-1927	

RBI: Most, career, all-time

1357	Brooks Robinson, 1955-1977	
1190	EDDIE MURRAY, 1977-1988	
1104	CAL RIPKEN, 1981-1993	
1063	Boog Powell, 1961-1974	
959	George Sisler, 1915-1927	

SB: Most, career, all-time

351	George Sisler, 1915-1927	
252	Al Bumbry, 1972-1984	
247	Burt Shotton, 1909-1917	
192	Jimmy Austin, 1911-1929	
174	Del Pratt, 1912-1917	

BB: Most, career, all-time

986	Harlond Clift, 1934-1943	
889	Boog Powell, 1961-1974	
886	Ken Singleton, 1975-1984	
860	Brooks Robinson, 1955-1977	
857	EDDIE MURRAY, 1977-1988	

BA: Highest, career, all-time

.344	George Sisler, 1915-1927	
.326	Ken Williams, 1918-1927	
.318	Jack Tobin, 1916-1925	
.317	Baby Doll Jacobson, 1915-1926	
.309	Bob Dillinger, 1946-1949	
.301	Bob Boyd, 1956-1960 (8)	

Slug avg: Highest, career, all-time

.558	Ken Williams, 1918-1927	
.543	Frank Robinson, 1966-1971	
.512	Jim Gentile, 1960-1963	
.500	EDDIE MURRAY, 1977-1988	
.486	Bob Nieman, 1951-1959	

Games started: Most, career, all-time

521	Jim Palmer, 1965-1984	
384	Dave McNally, 1962-1974	
328	Mike Flanagan, 1975-1992	
309	Scott McGregor, 1976-1988	
283	Mike Cuellar, 1969-1976	

Saves: Most, career, all-time

160	GREGG OLSON, 1988-1993	
105	Tippy Martinez, 1976-1986	
100	Stu Miller, 1963-1967	
74	Eddie Watt, 1966-1973	
58	Dick Hall, 1961-1971	

Shutouts: Most, career, all-time

53	Jim Palmer, 1965-1984	
33	Dave McNally, 1962-1974	
30	Mike Cuellar, 1969-1976	
27	Jack Powell, 1902-1912	
26	Milt Pappas, 1957-1965	

Wins: Most, career, all-time

268	Jim Palmer, 1965-1984	
181	Dave McNally, 1962-1974	
143	Mike Cuellar, 1969-1976	
141	Mike Flanagan, 1975-1992	
138	Scott McGregor, 1976-1988	

K: Most, career, all-time

2212	Jim Palmer, 1965-1984	
1476	Dave McNally, 1962-1974	
1297	Mike Flanagan, 1975-1992	
1011	Mike Cuellar, 1969-1976	
944	Milt Pappas, 1957-1965	

Win pct: Highest, career, all-time

.638	Jim Palmer, 1965-1984	
.620	Wally Bunker, 1963-1968	
.619	Dick Hall, 1961-1971	
.619	Mike Cuellar, 1969-1976	
.616	Dave McNally, 1962-1974	

ERA: Lowest, career, all-time

2.06	Harry Howell, 1904-1910	
2.52	Fred Glade, 1904-1907	
2.62	Barney Pelty, 1903-1912	
2.63	Jack Powell, 1902-1912	
2.67	Carl Weilman, 1912-1920	
2.86	Jim Palmer, 1965-1984 (6)	

Runs: Most, season

145	Harlond Clift, 1936	
137	George Sisler, 1920	
134	George Sisler, 1922	
132	Jack Tobin, 1921	
128	Ken Williams, 1922	
122	Frank Robinson, 1966 (7)	

Hits: Most, season

257	George Sisler, 1920	
246	George Sisler, 1922	
241	Heinie Manush, 1928	
236	Jack Tobin, 1921	
224	George Sisler, 1925	
211	CAL RIPKEN, 1983 (10)	

2B: Most, season

51	Beau Bell, 1937	
49	George Sisler, 1920	
47	Heinie Manush, 1928	
47	CAL RIPKEN, 1983	
47	Joe Vosmik, 1937	

3B: Most, season

20	Heinie Manush, 1928	
20	George Stone, 1906	
18	George Sisler, 1920	
18	George Sisler, 1921	
18	George Sisler, 1922	
18	Jack Tobin, 1921	
12	Paul Blair, 1967 (24)	

HR: Most, season

49	Frank Robinson, 1966
46	Jim Gentile, 1961
39	Boog Powell, 1964
39	Ken Williams, 1922
37	Boog Powell, 1969

RBI: Most, season

155	Ken Williams, 1922
141	Jim Gentile, 1961
134	Moose Solters, 1936
124	EDDIE MURRAY, 1985
123	Beau Bell, 1936

SB: Most, season

57	Luis Aparicio, 1964
53	BRADY ANDERSON, 1992
51	George Sisler, 1922
46	Armando Marsans, 1916
45	George Sisler, 1918

BB: Most, season

126	Lu Blue, 1929
121	Roy Cullenbine, 1941
118	Harlond Clift, 1938
118	Burt Shotton, 1915
118	Ken Singleton, 1975

BA: Highest, season

.420	George Sisler, 1922
.407	George Sisler, 1920
.378	Heinie Manush, 1928
.371	George Sisler, 1921
.358	George Stone, 1906
.328	Ken Singleton, 1977 (*)

Slug avg: Highest, season

.646	Jim Gentile, 1961
.637	Frank Robinson, 1966
.632	George Sisler, 1920
.627	Ken Williams, 1922
.623	Ken Williams, 1923

Games started: Most, season

40	Mike Cuellar, 1970
40	Mike Flanagan, 1978
40	Dave McNally, 1969
40	Dave McNally, 1970
40	Bobo Newsom, 1938
40	Jim Palmer, 1976

Saves: Most, season

37	GREGG OLSON, 1990
36	GREGG OLSON, 1992
34	Don Aase, 1986
31	GREGG OLSON, 1991
29	GREGG OLSON, 1993

Shutouts: Most, season

10	Jim Palmer, 1975
8	Steve Barber, 1961
7	Milt Pappas, 1964
6	Fred Glade, 1904
6	Harry Howell, 1906
6	Dave McNally, 1972
6	Jim Palmer, 1969
6	Jim Palmer, 1973
6	Jim Palmer, 1976
6	Jim Palmer, 1978

Wins: Most, season

27	Urban Shocker, 1921
25	Steve Stone, 1980
24	Mike Cuellar, 1970
24	Dave McNally, 1970
24	Urban Shocker, 1922

K: Most, season

232	Rube Waddell, 1908
226	Bobo Newsom, 1938
202	Dave McNally, 1968
199	Jim Palmer, 1970
198	Harry Howell, 1905

Win pct: Highest, season

.808	General Crowder, 1928
.808	Dave McNally, 1971
.800	Jim Palmer, 1969
.792	Wally Bunker, 1964
.783	MIKE MUSSINA, 1992

ERA: Lowest, season

1.59	Barney Pelty, 1906
1.77	Jack Powell, 1906
1.89	Harry Howell, 1908
1.89	Rube Waddell, 1908
1.93	Harry Howell, 1907
1.95	Dave McNally, 1968 (7)

Most pinch-hit homers, season

3	Whitey Herzog, 1962
3	Sam Bowens, 1967
3	Pat Kelly, 1979
3	Jim Dwyer, 1986
3	SAM HORN, 1991

Most pinch-hit, homers, career

9	Jim Dwyer, 1980-1988

Most consecutive games, batting safely

41	George Sisler, StL-1922
34	George Sisler, StL-1925
34	George McQuinn, StL-1938
22	EDDIE MURRAY, 1982
22	Doug DeCinces, 1978-1979

Most consecutive scoreless innings

41	GREGG OLSON, 1989-1990
36	Hal Brown, 1961

No hit games

Earl Hamilton, StL at Det AL, 5-1; August 30, 1912.
Ernie Koob, StL vs Chi AL, 1-0; May 5, 1917.
Bob Groom, StL vs Chi AL, 3-0; May 6, 1917 (2nd game).
Bobo Newsom, StL vs Bos AL, 1-2; September 18, 1934 (lost on 1 hit in the tenth).
Bobo Holloman, StL vs Phi AL, 6-0; May 6, 1953 (first start in the major leagues).
Hoyt Wilhelm, Bal vs NY AL, 1-0; September 20, 1958.
Steve D. Barber (8 2/3 innings) and Stu Miller (1/3 inning) Bal vs Det AL, 1-2; April 30, 1967 (1st game, lost the game).
Tom Phoebus, Bal vs Bos AL, 6-0; April 27, 1968.
Jim Palmer, Bal vs Oak AL, 8-0; August 13, 1969.
BOB MILACKI (6 innings), Mike Flanagan (1 inning), MARK WILLIAMSON, (1 inning) and Gregg Olson (1 inning), Bal at Oak AL, 2-0; July 13, 1991.
John Whitehead, 6 innings, rain, StL vs Det AL, 4-0; August 5, 1940 (2nd game).

ACTIVE PLAYERS in caps. Leader from the franchise's current location is included. If not in the top five, leader's rank is listed in parenthesis; asterisk (*) indicates player is not in top 25.

209

Detroit Tigers

by Russell Beeker, Baseball Weekly

Infielder Travis Fryman banged out 22 home runs, 97 RBI and 182 hits (seventh in the AL).

1993 Tigers: Great bats, but pitching fizzled out

Heavy hitting and paltry pitching was the rule in Motown in 1992, and few observers expected any changes in '93. First baseman Cecil Fielder had led the majors in RBI for three consecutive seasons; along with outfielder Rob Deer and catcher Mickey Tettleton, the trio had combined for 99 home runs in '92. Shortstop Travis Fryman and second baseman Lou Whitaker hit 20 and 19 homers, respectively.

Nonetheless, the Tigers weren't expected to improve much beyond their sixth-place finish, because all indications pointed toward their staff being just as ineffective.

Surprise, surprise. At least for a little while. Through June 20, the Tigers had the AL's best record (43-25) and their starters had the fourth-best ERA (3.91). Toronto castoff David Wells emerged as the staff ace with nine victories—only Jack McDowell had more—with John Doherty and Mark Leiter close behind.

A three-city road trip to Baltimore, Boston and New York was the beginning of the end. A 10-game losing streak pushed them down the hill into a 12-31 slide. They made a valiant effort to re-enter the race in early September, but there was just too much ground to cover. The five starters—Wells, Leiter, Doherty, Mike Moore and Bill Gullickson—had combined for 31 wins through June 20; they won only 20 more games combined the rest of the season. Mike Henneman remained a bright spot, though. He tied his career high with 24 saves.

The joy ride was over, but Detroit had fun while it lasted. Perhaps Alan Trammell had the most fun. He and Whitaker had formed baseball's longest-running double-play combination, but Trammell was slated for utility work after appearing in just 29 games last season. When Sparky Anderson sought to shake the Tigers from their tailspin, he moved Fryman to third and returned Trammell to full-time shortstop, who finished with a .329 average, 12 HR and 60 RBI. The move was fine with Fryman,

who hit .300 and had his third consecutive season with 20 homers and 90 RBI—at the tender age of 24.

A late-season slump cost Fielder a chance to be the first player to lead the majors in RBI four consecutive years. He was forced to "settle" for 30 homers and 117 RBI. Tettleton tied his career-high with 32 homers and set a personal mark with 110 RBI.

Tony Phillips was busy playing second base and everywhere in the outfield—as usual—and became the 24th AL player to reach base more than 300 times in a season. He scored 113 of the Tigers' 899 runs—the most by a major-league team since 1953.

The biggest surprise was Chad Kreuter, who took over as regular catcher. A .205 hitter who had appeared in 195 major league games over five years, he passed his career marks (eight homers, 32 RBI) by hitting .286 with 15 homers and 51 RBI.

—by Deron Snyder

1994 Tigers: Preview

The broken record is still playing: Detroit needs pitching. They got free agents in '93, but the team ERA went from 4.60 to 4.65. So it's back to the drawing board. Moore, Krueger, Gullickson and Doherty constitute four-fifths of a legitimate rotation, says one school of thought, but what's missing is a bonafide ace. With all its heavy lumber, Detroit should be willing to trade a hitter for a front-line pitcher.

The Tigers are trying to improve their outfield defensively; an opening could go to rookie Danny Bautista, who impressed the Tigers in 17 games at season's end last year. No worries in the infield: with Fielder, Whitaker, Trammell and Fryman around the horn, the Tigers have one of the most productive infields in baseball.

—by Deron Snyder

1993 Tigers: Between the lines

▶**April 7:** In his major league debut, reliever Greg Gohr served up a three-run homer to the first hitter he faced. He was the third member of the 1993 Tiger bullpen to do so—Mike Munoz and Tom Bolton performed the same dubious feat on Opening Day. Gohr's ERA stood at 135.00.

▶**April 10:** David Wells, released by the Blue Jays during the last week of spring training, gave up only one earned run in five innings, retiring the first 10 batters he faced.

▶**April 15:** *Milestone*—Tiger skipper Sparky Anderson won his 2,000th game, becoming the seventh manager with that many victories. *Quote of the day*—Tony La Russa, the loser in Anderson's milestone victory: "What I saw out there was the best manager in baseball."

▶**April 17:** For the second time in four days, the inhospitable Tigers pounded their visitors for 20 runs. The win brought the Tigers above the .500 mark for the first time since the end of the 1991 season.

▶**April 25:** In a three-game series with the Twins, the Tigers hit 11 homers and averaged 15 runs per game. That almost put them up with the NFL's Detroit Lions, who averaged 17 points per game.

▶**April 30:** David Wells threw seven shutout innings in an 8-0 win over Minnesota, to bring his Tiger record to 4-0.

▶**May 4:** Cecil Fielder ended a 20-game drought with a massive homer, clearing the fence in dead center at Tiger Stadium (440 feet) for the first time.

▶**May 7:** Mickey Tettleton hit home runs from both sides of the plate and drove in the winning run in the 12th inning as the Tigers came back from a 6-0 deficit to defeat the Yankees 7-6.

▶**May 8:** Alan Trammell was 4-for-6 with three RBI and hit his first Tiger Stadium home run since September 1991.

▶**May 9:** *Quote of the day*—After the Tigers dropped a 11-2 decision to New York, Sparky Anderson rationalized the loss: "All baseball is make-believe. If I was in Somalia or Yugoslavia, I'd be worried. But I'm going home, watch a movie, and not give this game another thought."

▶**May 11:** Milt Cuyler had the first four-hit game of his career, and had three-quarters of a cycle by the fourth inning. Needing a homer to become the first Tiger since 1950 to accomplish the feat, he popped out, singled and struck out in his final three at-bats.

▶**May 20:** Milwaukee's Bill Wegman blanked the Tigers for seven innings, but the AL's best offense exploded for six runs in the eighth to down the Brewers 6-2. The Tigers had not been shut out even once in 1993, and no pitcher had kept them scoreless as long as Wegman did. With the win, Detroit completed a three-game sweep of Milwaukee, scoring 19 times without a single homer, even though they led the majors in that category.

▶**June 3:** Mark Leiter, who had been pitching out of the bullpen, tossed the Tigers' first complete game of the year, a 5-3 win against the White Sox, bringing his mark to 4-0 in six starts since moving into the rotation.

▶**June 6:** Cecil Fielder uncorked two three-run homers and added an RBI single to post a career-high seven RBI. It was his 16th two-homer game.

▶**June 17:** Detroit outhomered the Indians at Tiger Stadium to earn a 9-5 win. Travis Fryman and Dan Gladden had two homers each and Rob Deer added one for the Tigers, who held on to their three-game lead in the AL East.

▶**June 18:** Cecil Fielder hit two home runs in a game for the second time in a week, but the Tigers fell to Milwaukee 6-3.

▶**June 30:** The free-falling Tigers lost their ninth in a row, dropping a 7-0 game in New York.

▶**July 1:** The slumping Tigers self-destructed against Texas.

▶**July 2:** Tettleton hit a two-out, two-run home run in the 10th inning to snap Detroit's 10-game winless streak and move them 3 1/2 games behind Toronto.

▶**July 6:** *Milestone*—Sparky Anderson finally moved past Walter Alston into fifth place on baseball's career victory list at 2,041 when the Tigers ended a 10-game road losing streak.

▶**July 18:** John Doherty shut out Texas 2-0 in his first major league complete game.

▶**July 22:** Greg Gagne hit the 10,000th home run in Tiger Stadium during a 12-6 win. Tiger Stadium is the first ballpark to reach the 10,000 mark.

▶**July 28:** Travis Fryman hit for the cycle, but the Tigers fell to the Yankees 12-7. Fryman had the cycle by the sixth inning and is the first Tiger to accomplish the feat since Hoot Evers on Sept. 9, 1950. Fryman's fifth hit of the day, a double, was his 500th career hit.

▶**August 4:** Fryman hit two home runs in a 8-3 win at Cleveland Stadium.

▶**August 6:** Bill Gullickson gave up two first-inning hits but retired 25 of the last 26 batters in a 5-1 win against the Red Sox.

▶**August 8:** Cecil Fielder sent two balls into the upper deck at Tiger Stadium and drove in all of Detroit's runs in a 5-1 win against the Red Sox.

▶**August 10:** Dan Gladden hit a two-out grand slam in the fourth inning of Detroit's 15-1 trounce of the Orioles.

▶**August 11:** Gladden hit a grand slam again, as the Tigers blasted the Orioles 15-5.

▶**August 12:** The Tigers tied a major league record by hitting a grand slam in three consecutive games when Chad Kreuter's sixth-inning pinch-hit homer landed in the left-field stands.

▶**August 18:** Cecil Fielder became the fifth Detroit player with four consecutive 100-RBI seasons.

▶**August 23:** Mike Moore pitched his second one-hit shutout in a month as the Tigers blanked the A's 9-0.

▶**October 3:** The Yankees beat the Tigers, 2-1, and Detroit finished fourth in the AL East—tied with Baltimore—10 games behind the Blue Jays. *League leaders, pitching*—Mike Moore was tied for second in shutouts (3); Mike Henneman was 10th in saves (24); Bob MacDonald was 10th in games (68). *League leaders, batting*—Tony Phillips led the league in walks (132), was second in on-base percentage (.443), tied for sixth in runs (113), and eighth overall in batting (.313); Cecil Fielder was fifth in RBI (117) and 10th in walks (90); Mickey Tettleton was fifth in walks (109), eighth in home runs (32), and ninth in RBI (110); Travis Fryman was seventh in hits (182) and tied for ninth in doubles (37); Milt Cuyler was eighth in triples (7).

—by John Hunt, Scott Kauffman, Lisa Winston, Deron Snyder, Matt Young

Team directory

▶**Owner:** Michael Ilitch
▶**General Manager:** Jerry Walker
▶**Ballpark:**
Tiger Stadium
2121 Trumbull Avenue, Detroit, Mich.
313-962-4000
Capacity 52,416
Pay parking lot (independently owned)
Public transportation available
Wheelchair section, ramps, Group Sales department
▶**Team publications:**
Scorebook/program
▶**TV, radio broadcast stations:**
WJR 760AM, WDIV Channel 4, PASS Cable
▶**Camps and/or clinics:**
Jim Price's Sports Fantasy,
313-353-5643
▶**Spring Training:**
Marchant Stadium
Lakeland, Fla.
Capacity 7,027
813-499-8229

DETROIT TIGERS 1993 final stats

Batting	BA	SLG	OB	G	AB	R	H	TB	2B	3B	HR	RBI	BB	SO	SB	CS	E
Trammell	.329	.496	.388	112	401	72	132	199	25	3	12	60	38	38	12	8	9
Phillips	.313	.398	.443	151	566	113	177	225	27	0	7	57	132	102	16	11	13
Bautista	.311	.410	.317	17	61	6	19	25	3	0	1	9	1	10	3	1	0
Fryman	.300	.486	.379	151	607	98	182	295	37	5	22	97	77	128	9	4	23
Livingstone	.293	.359	.328	98	304	39	89	109	10	2	2	39	19	32	1	3	6
Whitaker	.290	.449	.412	119	383	72	111	172	32	1	9	67	78	46	3	3	11
Kreuter	.286	.484	.371	119	374	59	107	181	23	3	15	51	49	92	2	1	7
Barnes	.281	.381	.318	84	160	24	45	61	8	1	2	27	11	19	5	5	4
Fielder	.267	.464	.368	154	573	80	153	266	23	0	30	117	90	125	0	1	10
Gladden	.267	.433	.312	91	356	52	95	154	16	2	13	56	21	50	8	5	3
Gibson	.261	.432	.337	116	403	62	105	174	18	6	13	62	44	87	15	6	1
E.Davis	.253	.533	.371	23	75	14	19	40	1	1	6	15	14	18	2	2	1
Gomez	.250	.320	.304	46	128	11	32	41	7	1	0	11	9	17	2	2	5
Tettleton	.245	.492	.372	152	522	79	128	257	25	4	32	110	109	139	3	7	6
Rowland	.217	.283	.294	21	46	2	10	13	3	0	0	4	5	16	0	0	1
Thurman	.213	.281	.297	75	89	22	19	25	2	2	0	13	11	30	7	0	3
Cuyler	.213	.313	.276	82	249	46	53	78	11	7	0	19	19	53	13	2	7

Pitching	W-L	ERA	G	GS	CG	GF	Sho	SV	IP	H	R	ER	HR	BB	SO
Henneman	5-3	2.64	63	0	0	50	0	24	71.2	69	28	21	4	32	58
Krueger	6-4	3.40	32	7	0	7	0	0	82	90	43	31	6	30	60
Boever	6-3	3.61	61	0	0	22	0	3	102.1	101	50	41	9	44	63
Gardiner	0-0	3.97	10	0	0	1	0	0	11.1	12	5	5	0	7	4
Wells	11-9	4.19	32	30	0	0	0	0	187	183	93	87	26	42	139
Doherty	14-11	4.44	32	31	3	1	2	0	184.2	205	104	91	19	48	63
Bolton	6-6	4.47	43	8	0	9	0	0	102.2	113	57	51	5	45	66
Leiter	6-6	4.73	27	13	1	4	0	0	106.2	111	61	56	17	44	70
Knudsen	3-2	4.78	30	0	0	7	0	2	37.2	41	22	20	9	16	29
S.Davis	2-8	5.05	43	8	0	12	0	4	98	93	57	55	9	48	73
Moore	13-9	5.22	36	36	4	0	3	0	213.2	227	135	124	35	89	89
MacDonald	3-3	5.35	68	0	0	24	0	3	65.2	67	42	39	8	33	39
Gullickson	13-9	5.37	28	28	2	0	0	0	159.1	186	106	95	28	44	70
Grater	0-0	5.40	6	0	0	1	0	0	5	6	3	3	0	4	4
Bergman	1-4	5.67	9	6	1	1	0	0	39.2	47	29	25	6	23	19
Gohr	0-0	5.96	16	0	0	9	0	0	22.2	26	15	15	1	14	23
Munoz	0-1	6.00	8	0	0	3	0	0	3	4	2	2	1	6	1
Haas	1-2	6.11	20	0	0	5	0	0	28	45	20	19	9	8	17
Groom	0-2	6.14	19	3	0	8	0	0	36.2	48	25	25	4	13	15
Kiely	0-2	7.71	8	0	0	5	0	0	11.2	13	11	10	2	13	5
DeSilva	0-0	9.00	1	0	0	1	0	0	1	2	1	1	0	0	0
Johnson	1-1	12.96	6	0	0	2	0	0	8.1	13	13	12	3	5	7

1994 preliminary roster

PITCHERS (19)
Sean Bergman
Ben Blomdahl
Joe Boever
Tom Bolton
Storm Davis
John Doherty
Mike Gardiner
Greg Gohr
Buddy Groom
Bill Gullickson
Mike Henneman
Kurt Knudsen
Bill Krueger
Mark Leiter
Jose Lima
Felipe Lira
Bob MacDonald
Mike Moore
Shannon Withem

CATCHERS (3)
Chad Kreuter
Rich Rowland
Mickey Tettleton

INFIELDERS (11)
Skeeter Barnes
Rico Brogna
Tony Clark
Brian Dubose
Cecil Fielder
Travis Fryman
Chris Gomez
Scott Livingstone
Tony Phillips
Alan Trammell
Lou Whitaker

OUTFIELDERS (6)
Danny Bautista
Milt Cuyler
Eric Davis
Shawn Hare
Rudy Pemberton
Gary Thurman

Games played by position

Player	G	C	1B	2B	3B	SS	OF	DH
Barnes	84	0	27	10	13	2	18	13
Bautista	17	0	0	0	0	0	16	1
Cuyler	82	0	0	0	0	0	80	0
E. Davis	23	0	0	0	0	0	18	5
Fielder	154	0	119	0	0	0	0	36
Fryman	151	0	0	0	69	81	0	1
Gibson	116	0	0	0	0	0	32	76
Gladden	91	0	0	0	0	0	86	5
Gomez	46	0	0	17	0	29	0	1
Kreuter	119	112	1	0	0	0	0	2
Livingstone	98	0	0	0	62	0	0	32
Phillips	151	0	0	51	1	0	108	4
Rowland	21	17	0	0	0	0	0	3
Tettleton	152	56	59	0	0	0	55	4
Thurman	75	0	0	0	0	0	53	8
Trammell	112	0	0	0	35	63	8	6
Whitaker	119	0	0	110	0	0	0	0

Sick call: 1993 DL Report

Player	Days on the DL
Milt Cuyler	56
Rob Deer	15
John Doherty	15
Dan Gladden	50
Bill Gullickson	35
David Haas	112
Dave Johnson	115
Kurt Knudsen	31
Bill Krueger	49
Mark Leiter	28
Alan Trammell	12
David Wells	19

Minor League Report

Class AAA: Toledo finished at 64-77, last in the International League Western Division. John Cangelosi had 39 stolen bases. John DeSilva shared the league lead with 136 strikeouts. **Class AA:** London finished at 62-75, sixth in the Eastern League. Shannon Penn led the league with 53 stolen bases. Felipe Lira was 10-4 with a 3.38 ERA. Ben Blomdahl was 6-6 with a 3.71 ERA. Jose Lima fanned 138. **Class A:** Lakeland finished at 65-63, winning the second half of the Florida State League East Division, but losing to St. Lucie in three games in the playoffs. Brian Dubose hit .313 with eight homers and 68 RBI. Brian Edmondson was 8-5 with a 2.99 ERA. . . . Fayetteville finished at 75-66, winning the second half of the Sally League Northern Division, but fell to Greensboro in the playoffs. Tim Thomas hit .303. Keith Kimsey hit 19 homers. Matt Evans had 94 RBI. Clint Sodowsky had 14 wins. **Short-season:** Niagara Falls finished at 47-30, second in the New York-Penn League Stadler Division, and swept Pittsfield in two games for the league title. Eric Danapilis won the league batting title at .341. Mike Wiseley hit .321. Glen Barker led the league with 37 steals. Shawn Brown (29) and Wiseley (27) were also in the top five. John Rosengren was 7-3 with a 2.41 ERA. He fanned 91 in 82 innings. Joshua Neese was 12-3 with a 2.54 ERA. Gabriel Sollecito had 14 saves. . . . Bristol finished at 28-39, last in the Appalachian League Southern Division. Sean Wooten won the league batting crown with a .350. He had eight homers. Frank Catalanotto hit .307. William Hunt had eight saves.

Tops in the organization

Batter	Club	Avg	G	AB	R	H	HR	RBI
Dubose, Brian	Lak	.313	122	448	74	140	8	68
Higginson, Bob	Lon	.304	124	447	67	136	7	60
Cangelosi, John	Tol	.292	113	439	73	128	6	42
Thomas, Tim	Fay	.287	119	428	85	123	4	50
Bautista, Danny	Lon	.285	117	424	55	121	6	48

Home Runs			Wins		
Rowland, Rich	Tol	21	Sodowsky, Clint	Fay	14
Hare, Shawn	Tol	20	Maxcy, Brian	Fay	12
Kimsey, Keith	Fay	19	Lira, Felipe	Tol	11
Evans, Matt	Fay	17	Withem, Shannon	Lak	10
Pemberton, Rudy	Lon	15	Fraser, Willie	Tol	10

RBI			Saves		
Evans, Matt	Fay	94	Schwarber, Tom	Lon	16
Kimsey, Keith	Fay	85	Grimm, John	Lak	13
Rendina, Mike	Lon	77	Stidham, Phillip	Lon	11
Hare, Shawn	Tol	76	Maxcy, Brian	Fay	9
Dubose, Brian	Lak	68	Several players tied		8

Stolen Bases			Strikeouts		
Penn, Shannon	Lon	53	Lira, Felipe	Tol	145
Cangelosi, John	Tol	39	Lima, Jose	Lon	138
Williams, Ted	Lon	32	Desilva, John	Tol	136
Rojas, Roberto	Fay	30	Thompson, Justin	Lon	118
Several players tied		28	Miller, Trever	Fay	116

Pitcher	Club	W-L	ERA	IP	H	BB	SO
Maxcy, Brian	Fay	12-4	2.93	114	111	42	101
Mysel, David	Lak	9-7	3.10	142	128	44	92
Cedeno, Blas	Fay	6-6	3.15	149	145	55	103
Withem, Shannon	Lak	10-2	3.42	113	108	24	62
Edmondson, Brian	Lon	8-9	3.54	137	145	56	81

Detroit (1901-1993)

Runs: Most, career, all-time

2088	Ty Cobb, 1905-1926	
1774	Charlie Gehringer, 1924-1942	
1622	Al Kaline, 1953-1974	
1283	LOU WHITAKER, 1977-1993	
1242	Donie Bush, 1908-1921	

Hits: Most, career, all-time

3900	Ty Cobb, 1905-1926
3007	Al Kaline, 1953-1974
2839	Charlie Gehringer, 1924-1942
2499	Harry Heilmann, 1914-1929
2466	Sam Crawford, 1903-1917

2B: Most, career, all-time

665	Ty Cobb, 1905-1926
574	Charlie Gehringer, 1924-1942
498	Al Kaline, 1953-1974
497	Harry Heilmann, 1914-1929
402	Sam Crawford, 1903-1917

3B: Most, career, all-time

284	Ty Cobb, 1905-1926
249	Sam Crawford, 1903-1917
146	Charlie Gehringer, 1924-1942
145	Harry Heilmann, 1914-1929
136	Bobby Veach, 1912-1923

HR: Most, career, all-time

399	Al Kaline, 1953-1974
373	Norm Cash, 1960-1974
306	Hank Greenberg, 1930-1946
262	Willie Horton, 1963-1977
239	Rudy York, 1934-1945

RBI: Most, career, all-time

1804	Ty Cobb, 1905-1926
1583	Al Kaline, 1953-1974
1442	Harry Heilmann, 1914-1929
1427	Charlie Gehringer, 1924-1942
1264	Sam Crawford, 1903-1917

SB: Most, career, all-time

864	Ty Cobb, 1905-1926
400	Donie Bush, 1908-1921
317	Sam Crawford, 1903-1917
294	Ron LeFlore, 1974-1979
224	ALAN TRAMMELL, 1977-1993

BB: Most, career, all-time

1277	Al Kaline, 1953-1974
1186	Charlie Gehringer, 1924-1942
1148	Ty Cobb, 1905-1926
1125	Donie Bush, 1908-1921
1125	LOU WHITAKER, 1977-1993

BA: Highest, career, all-time

.368	Ty Cobb, 1905-1926
.342	Harry Heilmann, 1914-1929
.337	Bob Fothergill, 1922-1930
.325	George Kell, 1946-1952
.321	Heinie Manush, 1923-1927

Slug avg: Highest, career, all-time

.616	Hank Greenberg, 1930-1946
.518	Harry Heilmann, 1914-1929
.516	Ty Cobb, 1905-1926
.506	CECIL FIELDER, 1990-1993
.503	Rudy York, 1934-1945

Games started: Most, career, all-time

459	Mickey Lolich, 1963-1975
408	JACK MORRIS, 1977-1990
395	George Mullin, 1902-1913
388	Hooks Dauss, 1912-1926
373	Hal Newhouser, 1939-1953

Saves: Most, career, all-time

128	MIKE HENNEMAN, 1987-1993
125	John Hiller, 1965-1980
120	Willie Hernandez, 1984-1989
85	Aurelio Lopez, 1979-1985
55	Terry Fox, 1961-1966

Shutouts: Most, career, all-time

39	Mickey Lolich, 1963-1975
34	George Mullin, 1902-1913
33	Tommy Bridges, 1930-1946
33	Hal Newhouser, 1939-1953
29	Bill Donovan, 1903-1918

Wins: Most, career, all-time

222	Hooks Dauss, 1912-1926
209	George Mullin, 1902-1913
207	Mickey Lolich, 1963-1975
200	Hal Newhouser, 1939-1953
198	JACK MORRIS, 1977-1990

K: Most, career, all-time

2679	Mickey Lolich, 1963-1975
1980	JACK MORRIS, 1977-1990
1770	Hal Newhouser, 1939-1953
1674	Tommy Bridges, 1930-1946
1406	Jim Bunning, 1955-1963

Win pct: Highest, career, all-time

.654	Denny McLain, 1963-1970
.651	MIKE HENNEMAN, 1987-1993
.639	Aurelio Lopez, 1979-1985
.629	Schoolboy Rowe, 1933-1942
.616	Harry Coveleski, 1914-1918

ERA: Lowest, career, all-time

2.34	Harry Coveleski, 1914-1918
2.38	Ed Killian, 1904-1910
2.42	Ed Summers, 1908-1912
2.49	Bill Donovan, 1903-1918
2.61	Ed Siever, 1901-1908

Runs: Most, season

147	Ty Cobb, 1911
144	Ty Cobb, 1915
144	Charlie Gehringer, 1930
144	Charlie Gehringer, 1936
144	Hank Greenberg, 1938

Hits: Most, season

248	Ty Cobb, 1911
237	Harry Heilmann, 1921
227	Charlie Gehringer, 1936
226	Ty Cobb, 1912
225	Ty Cobb, 1917
225	Harry Heilmann, 1925

2B: Most, season

63	Hank Greenberg, 1934
60	Charlie Gehringer, 1936
56	George Kell, 1950
55	Gee Walker, 1936
50	Charlie Gehringer, 1934
50	Hank Greenberg, 1940
50	Harry Heilmann, 1927

3B: Most, season

26	Sam Crawford, 1914
25	Sam Crawford, 1903
24	Ty Cobb, 1911
24	Ty Cobb, 1917
23	Ty Cobb, 1912
23	Sam Crawford, 1913

HR: Most, season

58	Hank Greenberg, 1938
51	CECIL FIELDER, 1990
45	Rocky Colavito, 1961
44	CECIL FIELDER, 1991
44	Hank Greenberg, 1946

RBI: Most, season

183	Hank Greenberg, 1937
170	Hank Greenberg, 1935
150	Hank Greenberg, 1940
146	Hank Greenberg, 1938
140	Rocky Colavito, 1961

SB: Most, season

96	Ty Cobb, 1915
83	Ty Cobb, 1911
78	Ron LeFlore, 1979
76	Ty Cobb, 1909
68	Ty Cobb, 1916
68	Ron LeFlore, 1978

BB: Most, season

137	Roy Cullenbine, 1947
135	Eddie Yost, 1959
132	TONY PHILLIPS, 1993
125	Eddie Yost, 1960
124	Norm Cash, 1961

BA: Highest, season

.420	Ty Cobb, 1911
.409	Ty Cobb, 1912
.403	Harry Heilmann, 1923
.401	Ty Cobb, 1922
.398	Harry Heilmann, 1927

Slug avg: Highest, season

.683	Hank Greenberg, 1938
.670	Hank Greenberg, 1940
.668	Hank Greenberg, 1937
.662	Norm Cash, 1961
.632	Harry Heilmann, 1923

Games started: Most, season

45	Mickey Lolich, 1971
44	George Mullin, 1904
42	Mickey Lolich, 1973
42	George Mullin, 1907
41	Joe Coleman, 1974
41	Mickey Lolich, 1972
41	Mickey Lolich, 1974
41	Denny McLain, 1968
41	Denny McLain, 1969
41	George Mullin, 1905

Saves: Most, season

38	John Hiller, 1973
32	Willie Hernandez, 1984
31	Willie Hernandez, 1985
27	Tom Timmermann, 1970
24	MIKE HENNEMAN, 1992
24	MIKE HENNEMAN, 1993
24	Willie Hernandez, 1986

Shutouts: Most, season

9	Denny McLain, 1969
8	Ed Killian, 1905
8	Hal Newhouser, 1945
7	Billy Hoeft, 1955
7	George Mullin, 1904
7	Dizzy Trout, 1944

Wins: Most, season

31	Denny McLain, 1968
29	George Mullin, 1909
29	Hal Newhouser, 1944
27	Dizzy Trout, 1944
26	Hal Newhouser, 1946

K: Most, season

308	Mickey Lolich, 1971
280	Denny McLain, 1968
275	Hal Newhouser, 1946
271	Mickey Lolich, 1969
250	Mickey Lolich, 1972

Win pct: Highest, season

.862	Bill Donovan, 1907
.842	Schoolboy Rowe, 1940
.838	Denny McLain, 1968
.808	Bobo Newsom, 1940
.784	George Mullin, 1909

ERA: Lowest, season

1.64	Ed Summers, 1908
1.71	Ed Killian, 1909
1.78	Ed Killian, 1907
1.81	Hal Newhouser, 1945
1.91	Ed Siever, 1902

Most pinch-hit homers, season

3	Gus Zernial, 1958
3	Norm Cash, 1960
3	Vic Wertz, 1962
3	Gates Brown, 1968
3	Ben Oglivie, 1976
3	John Grubb, 1984
3	Larry Herndon, 1986

Most pinch-hit, homers, career

16	Gates Brown, 1963-1975

Most consecutive games, batting safely

40	Ty Cobb, 1911
35	Ty Cobb, 1917
30	Goose Goslin, 1934
30	Ron LeFlore, 1976

Most consecutive scoreless innings

33	Harry Coveleskie, 1914

No hit games

George Mullin, Det vs StL AL, 7-0; July 4, 1912 (2nd game).
Virgil Trucks, Det vs Was AL, 1-0; May 15, 1952.
Virgil Trucks, Det at NY AL, 1-0; August 25, 1952.
Jim Bunning, Det at Bos AL, 3-0; July 20, 1958 (1st game).
JACK MORRIS, Det at Chi AL, 4-0; April 7, 1984.

ACTIVE PLAYERS in caps.

Boston Red Sox

by Rick Wiley, USA TODAY

Right-hander Danny Darwin led the Red Sox with 15 wins and a 3.26 ERA (ninth in the AL).

1993 Red Sox: Another roller-coaster season

The Red Sox tortured their fans once again in '93. They stayed in the AL East race into September and despite a late-season slump improved by seven games over '92. But they lost their final six games and finished a game under .500, 15 behind Toronto.

"This club played their hearts out every day," said manager Butch Hobson. "To me, that's as important as winning 100 games."

As they entered the offseason, surgery was the team's operative word. Frank Viola and Joe Hesketh both had elbow surgery before the end of the year, while Mike Greenwell (left knee) and Billy Hatcher (right elbow, left ankle) had postseason surgery.

Clemens and Viola, the Red Sox's reputed one-two punch entering the season, both had their campaigns cut short because of elbow injuries. The pair, making around $9 million between them, each won 11 games. Before '93, Viola had never missed a start, but a right ankle sprain on May 3rd started a series of events that hurt his elbow, too. Clemens ended his season with an elbow injury in September. He finished at 11-14 with a 4.46 ERA, after coming into the season with a 152-72 lifetime record and 2.80 career ERA.

There were many bright spots in the Red Sox's roller-coaster year. Mo Vaughn beat out Carlos Quintana for the first base job in spring training and became the team's only true power threat, with 29 homers and 101 RBIs. Vaughn was inspired all season by an 11-year-old cancer patient, Jason Leader. In April, Vaughn delivered on a promise to hit a home run for Leader. In October, the youngster—now in remission—came to Fenway and met his favorite player. Vaughn was honored as Man of the Year by the BoSox Club, the Sox's booster group.

Scott Cooper was a solid replacement for Wade Boggs at third and earned a spot on the All-Star team. Shortstop John Valentin hit a surprising .278 with a team-high 40 doubles. Greenwell returned from elbow surgery to regain his left-field slot and hit .315. Outfielder Jeff McNeely hit .297 in 21 games with a .409 on-base percentage.

The most pleasant surprise was rookie Aaron Sele, who went 7-2 with a 2.74 ERA after being called up in late June. Ken Ryan also went 7-2 and could be the Sox closer of the future.

The Red Sox were hoping to go last-to-first, and for much of the season were in a position to do so. Boston started strong, slumped in June, then rebounded in July to contend for the AL East lead. By mid-August, they had the best home record in the AL and were to play 31 of their last 50 games at Fenway Park. The Red Sox, who have not won a World Series since 1918, had many fans believing they would finally win another Fall Classic. But once again, BoSox fans were let down as their team lost 33 of the last 50 games, including 23 of the 31 at home.

—by Pete Williams

1994 Red Sox: Preview

The Red Sox enter '94 with many questions. Will Clemens and Viola rebound from injuries and ineffectiveness? Hobson believes Clemens will.

"He'll come back and win the Cy Young Award," he said.

But other questions abound. How effective will Andre Dawson be? Can Jeff Russell continue to be a reliable closer? Where will the next catcher come from? Will anyone provide some speed?

Boston needs several young players to contribute. In addition to Jeff McNeely, Tim Naehring hit around .400 the last month of '93 and is projected as the starting second baseman for '94.

"We have the makings of a good ball club," said Hobson, "but we need to add some links."

—by Pete Williams

1993 Red Sox: Between the lines

▶**April 10:** Roger Clemens won for only the second time in four seasons at Arlington Stadium.

▶**April 15:** The Sox swept their second series of the season with a 4-3 victory against Cleveland in 13 innings.

▶**April 17:** Joe Hesketh tossed eight shutout innings at the White Sox in a 5-1 win at Fenway Park.

▶**April 14:** Frank Viola lowered his ERA to 0.75 with a complete-game shutout over the White Sox at Fenway.

▶**April 19:** John Dopson, who had not won in his last 16 starts, shut out the White Sox 6-0 on three hits. Mo Vaughn had two doubles and a single to raise his average to .442. The Red Sox were off to their best start (10-3) since 1952.

▶**May 1:** Roger Clemens struck out every California starter except Gary DiSarcina and Luis Polonia to record his seventh consecutive win against the Angels at Fenway. The Rocket was still firing 93 mph fastballs in the eighth inning, despite tendinitis in his elbow.

▶**May 3:** Frank Viola injured his right ankle covering first base and left the game in the fifth inning.

▶**May 11:** Clemens recorded his 35th career shutout and whiffed a season-high baker's dozen at Camden Yards.

▶**May 23:** Mo Vaughn had the first two-homer game of his career.

▶**May 28:** Clemens broke out of what he called a "mini-slump" by holding the Rangers to two hits in a 4-1 Red Sox victory at Fenway. He struck out 11 in eight innings.

▶**May 30:** John Valentin doubled home the winning run with one out in the 12th inning to give the Red Sox a series sweep of the Rangers. Both teams ran out of bench players in the last inning—Billy Hatcher played second base for the first time in his career and Rangers' reliever Jeff Bronkey was forced to bat.

▶**June 13:** Clemens' nine Ks in eight innings ended Baltimore's 10-game winning streak and Boston's seven-game losing streak.

▶**June 18:** Roger Clemens was placed on the disabled list with a groin injury.

▶**June 23:** Rookie Aaron Sele, who replaced Clemens in Boston's rotation, won in his major league debut. Sele, considered the top prospect in the Red Sox system, struck out eight in seven innings and beat Minnesota 3-1.

▶**July 6:** Mike Greenwell went 2-for-3 with a home run to extend his hitting streak to 16 games (four homers and 15 RBI). The Red Sox, however, lost to California 3-2.

▶**July 7:** The Angels entered the ninth inning trailing Boston by two runs, but Jeff Russell gave up hits to four of the five batters he faced—without recording an out—and California won 7-4. It was Russell's second blown save in three games after 18 successful chances this season—21 in a row dating to August 1992.

▶**July 8:** Mo Vaughn hit a grand slam and drove in a career-high five runs. Billy Hatcher homered, drove in four runs and scored three times.

▶**July 16:** Clemens made a successful return to the mound, going six strong innings against Seattle for his eighth win.

▶**July 21:** Clemens won his second start since coming off the DL, downing the Angels 4-1. He went eight innings and retired 22 of the last 25 batters.

▶**July 22:** Pitcher Danny Darwin didn't like Rickey Henderson's slow-motion home run trot; as Henderson approached the plate after his second homer of the game, he turned toward Darwin, who took a few steps toward the Oakland outfielder. Both benches cleared but no punches were thrown.

▶**July 25:** Mo Vaughn hit a grand slam and a pair of doubles in Boston's 8-1 defeat of Oakland.

▶**July 29:** Billy Hatcher homered and drove in three runs as the Red Sox beat Milwaukee 7-3. It was the 32nd multi-hit game for Hatcher, tops among Boston hitters.

▶**July 30:** Andre Dawson clubbed a home run and a double to drive in five runs in an 8-7 Red Sox win in Baltimore. Dawson's home run, a three-run shot in the first, was his 407th, tying him with Duke Snider for 24th on the career list.

▶**August 5:** Frank Viola won in the Metrodome for the first time since the Twins traded him to the Mets in 1989 after he won the '88 Cy Young Award.

▶**August 6:** Clemens gave up three home runs in a game for only the third time in his career as Boston lost to Detroit 5-1 at Tiger Stadium.

▶**August 11:** *Milestone*—Clemens recorded his 2,000th career strikeout. He is Boston's all-time strikeout leader. Cy Young is second with 1,341.

▶**August 18:** Danny Darwin threw 8 1/3 innings of no-hit ball before Dan Pasqua tripled off the green monster. Darwin settled for his third career one-hitter and his first shutout since August 1987.

▶**August 22:** Former Detroit outfielder Rob Deer had a successful debut with his new team—Boston—homering and making a diving catch in the 3-2 loss to Cleveland. Rookie Aaron Sele allowed three hits in seven innings of shutout ball, but didn't get the decision. Sele, who made his major league debut in June, had not allowed more than three earned runs in any of his 11 starts.

▶**August 28:** Sele no-hit the Royals for six innings but wound up with a no-decision. The Red Sox won in 11 innings.

▶**September 5:** Clemens was tagged for his first career grand slam in Boston's 5-2 loss to Kansas City. The culprit? Gary Gaetti, who has a career average of just .183 against the Rocket.

▶**September 12:** Nate Minchey got the win in his major league debut. He went the distance, gave up one run and 10 hits, walked none and struck out five.

▶**October 3:** The Sox finished in a disappointing fifth place, 15 games behind the Blue Jays in the AL East. *League leaders, pitching*—Greg Harris led the league in games (80), with Tony Fossas tied for third (71); In ERA, Frank Viola was fifth and Danny Darwin was ninth (3.14 and 3.26, respectively); Jeff Russell was seventh in saves (33). *League leaders, batting*—Mike Greenwell was seventh in batting (.315) and tied for sixth in doubles (38); John Valentin was tied for third in doubles (40); Mo Vaughn was ninth in slugging (.525) and 10th in on-base percentage (.390).

—by John Hunt, Scott Kauffman, Lisa Winston, Deron Snyder, Matt Young

Team directory

▶**Owners:** JRY Corporation and Haywood Sullivan
▶**General Manager:** Lou Gorman
▶**Ballpark:**
Fenway Park
4 Yawkey Way, Boston, Mass.
617-267-9440
Capacity 33,925
Public transportation available
Family, wheelchair, and vision-impaired sections, ramps, sound amplification and TDD ticket information for hearing impaired
▶**Team publications:**
Media guide, official scorebook, yearbook
617-267-9440
▶**TV, radio broadcast stations:**
WRKO 680 AM, WSBK Channel 38, New England Sports Network Cable TV
▶**Spring Training:**
City of Palms Park
Ft. Myers, Fla.
Capacity 6,850
813-334-4700

BOSTON RED SOX 1993 final stats

Batting	BA	SLG	OB	G	AB	R	H	TB	2B	3B	HR	RBI	BB	SO	SB	CS	E
Naehring	.331	.433	.377	39	127	14	42	55	10	0	1	17	10	26	1	0	2
Greenwell	.315	.480	.379	146	540	77	170	259	38	6	13	72	54	46	5	4	2
McNeely	.297	.378	.409	21	37	10	11	14	1	1	0	1	7	9	6	0	2
Vaughn	.297	.525	.390	152	539	86	160	283	34	1	29	101	79	130	4	3	16
Hatcher	.287	.400	.336	136	508	71	146	203	24	3	9	57	28	46	14	7	2
Fletcher	.285	.402	.341	121	480	81	137	193	31	5	5	45	37	35	16	3	11
Cooper	.279	.397	.355	156	526	67	147	209	29	3	9	63	58	81	5	2	24
Valentin	.278	.447	.346	144	468	50	130	209	40	3	11	66	49	77	3	4	20
Dawson	.273	.425	.313	121	461	44	126	196	29	1	13	67	17	49	2	1	0
Ortiz	.250	.250	.250	9	12	0	3	3	0	0	0	1	0	2	0	0	0
Quintana	.244	.271	.317	101	303	31	74	82	5	0	1	19	31	52	1	0	3
Zupcic	.241	.360	.308	141	286	40	69	103	24	2	2	26	27	54	5	2	4
Melvin	.222	.313	.251	77	176	13	39	55	7	0	3	23	7	44	0	0	2
Deer	.210	.386	.303	128	466	66	98	180	17	1	21	55	58	169	5	2	8
Richardson	.208	.292	.240	15	24	3	5	7	2	0	0	2	1	3	0	0	0
Rivera	.208	.308	.273	62	130	13	27	40	8	1	1	7	11	36	1	2	6
Riles	.189	.350	.292	94	143	15	27	50	8	0	5	20	20	40	1	3	0
Pena	.181	.257	.246	126	304	20	55	78	11	0	4	19	25	46	1	3	4
Lyons	.130	.174	.200	28	23	4	3	4	1	0	0	0	2	5	1	2	0
Flaherty	.120	.200	.214	13	25	3	3	5	2	0	0	2	2	6	0	0	0
Blosser	.071	.107	.133	17	28	1	2	3	1	0	0	1	2	7	1	0	0
Byrd	--	--	--	2	0	0	0	0	0	0	0	0	0	0	0	0	0

Pitching	W-L	ERA	G	GS	CG	GF	Sho	SV	IP	H	R	ER	HR	BB	SO
Melendez	2-1	2.25	9	0	0	5	0	0	16	10	4	4	2	5	14
Russell	1-4	2.70	51	0	0	48	0	33	46.2	39	16	14	1	14	45
Sele	7-2	2.74	18	18	0	0	0	0	111.2	100	42	34	5	48	93
Viola	11-8	3.14	29	29	2	0	1	0	183.2	180	76	64	12	72	91
Darwin	15-11	3.26	34	34	2	0	1	0	229.1	196	93	83	31	49	130
Bailey	0-1	3.45	11	0	0	5	0	0	15.2	12	7	6	0	12	11
Bankhead	2-1	3.50	40	0	0	4	0	0	64.1	59	28	25	7	29	47
Minchey	1-2	3.55	5	5	1	0	0	0	33	35	16	13	5	8	18
Ryan	7-2	3.60	47	0	0	26	0	1	50	43	23	20	2	29	49
Harris	6-7	3.77	80	0	0	24	0	8	112.1	95	55	47	7	60	103
Quantrill	6-12	3.91	49	14	1	8	1	1	138	151	73	60	13	44	66
Clemens	11-14	4.46	29	29	2	0	1	0	191.2	175	99	95	17	67	160
Dopson	7-11	4.97	34	28	1	3	1	0	155.2	170	93	86	16	59	89
Hesketh	3-4	5.06	28	5	0	8	0	1	53.1	62	35	30	4	29	34
Fossas	1-1	5.18	71	0	0	19	0	0	40	38	28	23	4	15	39
Taylor	0-1	8.18	16	0	0	3	0	0	11	14	10	10	1	12	8

1994 preliminary roster

PITCHERS (21)
Cory Bailey
Scott Bankhead
Joe Caruso
Joe Ciccarella
Roger Clemens
Brian Conroy
Danny Darwin
Gar Finnvold
Tony Fossas
Greg A. Harris
Rob Henkel
Joe Hesketh
Jose Melendez
Nate Minchey
Paul Quantrill
Jeff Russell
Ken Ryan
Aaron Sele

Scott Taylor
Tim Vanegmond
Frank Viola

CATCHERS (3)
John Flaherty
Scott Hatteberg
Bob Melvin

INFIELDERS (7)
Scott Cooper
Scott Fletcher
Tim Naehring
Luis Ortiz
Carlos Quintana
John Valentin
Mo Vaughn

OUTFIELDERS (7)
Greg Blosser
Andre Dawson
Mike Greenwell
Billy Hatcher
Jose Malave
Jeff McNeely
Bob Zupcic

Games played by position

Player	G	C	1B	2B	3B	SS	OF	DH
Blosser	17	0	0	0	0	0	9	1
Byrd	2	0	0	0	0	0	0	1
Cooper	156	0	2	0	154	1	0	0
Dawson	121	0	0	0	0	0	20	97
Deer	128	0	0	0	0	0	122	6
Flaherty	13	13	0	0	0	0	0	0
Fletcher	121	0	0	116	1	2	0	1
Greenwell	146	0	0	0	0	0	134	10
Hatcher	136	0	0	2	0	0	130	0
Lyons	28	1	1	9	1	0	10	1
McNeely	21	0	0	0	0	0	13	3
Melvin	77	76	1	0	0	0	0	0
Naehring	39	0	0	15	9	4	0	10
Ortiz	9	0	0	0	5	0	0	3
Pena	126	125	0	0	0	0	0	1
Quintana	101	0	53	0	0	0	51	0
Richardson	15	0	0	8	1	5	0	2
Riles	94	0	1	20	11	0	0	15
Rivera	62	0	0	27	2	27	0	7
Valentin	144	0	0	0	0	144	0	0
Vaughn	152	0	131	0	0	0	0	19
Zupcic	141	0	0	0	0	0	122	5

Sick call: 1993 DL Report

Player	Days on the DL
Ivan Calderon	19
Roger Clemens	27
Andre Dawson	19
Scott Fletcher	15
Mike Greenwell	15
Joe Hesketh	45
Jose Melendez*	147
Bob Melvin	15
Tim Naehring	88
Jeff Richardson*	127
Luis Rivera*	42
Jeff Russell	30
John Valentin	15

Two separate terms on Disabled List

Minor League Report

Class AAA: Pawtucket finished at 60-82, fourth in the International League Eastern Division. Luis Ortiz hit .294 with 18 homers and 81 RBI. Greg Blosser hit 23 homers. Jeff McNeely stole 40 bases. Cory Bailey set a franchise record with 20 saves. **Class AA:** New Britain finished at 51-88, last in the Eastern League. Frank Rodriguez was 7-11 with a 3.74 ERA and 161 strikeouts, second in the league. Tim Vanegmond led the loop in strikeouts with 163. Tim Smith was 7-13 with a 3.79 ERA. **Class A:** Lynchburg finished at 65-74, last in the Carolina League Northern Division. Felix Colon won the batting title with a .320 mark, hitting 16 homers and 58 RBI. Robert Juday hit .297. Doug Hecker had 73 RBI. Joel Bennett's 221 strikeouts led the minors. . . . Fort Lauderdale finished at 46-85, last in the Florida State League East Division. Derek Vinyard stole 26 bases. Brian Bright hit .301. Ryan McGuire hit .321. **Short-season:** Utica finished at 37-38, second in the New York-Penn League McNamara Division. T.J. O'Donnell hit .329. Daniel Collier hit 15 homers and drove in 48 runs. Eric Cormier had 93 strikeouts. . . . Fort Myers finished at 32-28, third in the Gulf Coast League Western Division. Gavin Jackson hit .313. Simon Pinango was 0-4 but had a 1.73 ERA and struck out 57 in 52 innings. Jeff Suppan struck out 64.

Tops in the organization

Batter	Club	Avg	G	AB	R	H	HR	RBI
Thoutsis, Paul	Paw	.305	124	429	47	131	4	48
Juday, Robert	Lyn	.297	114	354	67	105	4	32
Ortiz, Luis	Paw	.294	102	402	45	118	18	81
Chick, Bruce	Nbr	.279	123	434	41	121	6	40
Rodriguez, Steve	Lyn	.274	120	493	78	135	3	42

Home Runs			Wins		
Blosser, Greg	Paw	23	Bakkum, Scott	Lyn	12
Hecker, Doug	Lyn	21	Hoy, Peter	Nbr	9
Ortiz, Luis	Paw	18	Several players tied		8
Colon, Felix	Lyn	16			
Several players tied		15			

RBI			Saves		
Ortiz, Luis	Paw	81	Bailey, Cory	Paw	20
Hecker, Doug	Lyn	73	Ciccarella, Joe	Nbr	15
Blosser, Greg	Paw	66	Gakeler, Dan	Paw	9
Eierman, John	Lyn	62	Ryan, Ken	Paw	8
Several players tied		58	Mintz, Steve	Nbr	7

Stolen Bases			Strikeouts		
Mcneely, Jeff	Paw	40	Bennett, Joel	Lyn	221
Vinyard, Derek	Ftl	26	Vanegmond, Tim	Nbr	163
Rodriguez, Steve	Lyn	20	Rodriguez, Frank	Nbr	151
Durkin, Marty	Ftl	15	Glaze, Gettys	Lyn	137
Dimare, Gino	Ftl	12	Finnvold, Gar	Paw	123

Pitcher	Club	W-L	ERA	IP	H	BB	SO
Nies, Joel	Ftl	5-9	3.55	127	123	31	85
Hansen, Brent	Nbr	6-17	3.72	196	193	67	115
Rodriguez, Frank	Nbr	7-11	3.74	171	147	78	151
Bakkum, Scott	Lyn	12-11	3.77	170	201	31	98
Finnvold, Gar	Paw	5-9	3.77	136	128	51	123

Boston (1901-1993)

Runs: Most, career, all-time

1816	Carl Yastrzemski, 1961-1983
1798	Ted Williams, 1939-1960
1435	Dwight Evans, 1972-1990
1249	Jim Rice, 1974-1989
1094	Bobby Doerr, 1937-1951

Hits: Most, career, all-time

3419	Carl Yastrzemski, 1961-1983
2654	Ted Williams, 1939-1960
2452	Jim Rice, 1974-1989
2373	Dwight Evans, 1972-1990
2098	WADE BOGGS, 1982-1992

2B: Most, career, all-time

646	Carl Yastrzemski, 1961-1983
525	Ted Williams, 1939-1960
474	Dwight Evans, 1972-1990
422	WADE BOGGS, 1982-1992
381	Bobby Doerr, 1937-1951

3B: Most, career, all-time

130	Harry Hooper, 1909-1920
106	Tris Speaker, 1907-1915
90	Buck Freeman, 1901-1907
89	Bobby Doerr, 1937-1951
87	Larry Gardner, 1908-1917

HR: Most, career, all-time

521	Ted Williams, 1939-1960
452	Carl Yastrzemski, 1961-1983
382	Jim Rice, 1974-1989
379	Dwight Evans, 1972-1990
223	Bobby Doerr, 1937-1951

RBI: Most, career, all-time

1844	Carl Yastrzemski, 1961-1983
1839	Ted Williams, 1939-1960
1451	Jim Rice, 1974-1989
1346	Dwight Evans, 1972-1990
1247	Bobby Doerr, 1937-1951

SB: Most, career, all-time

300	Harry Hooper, 1909-1920
267	Tris Speaker, 1907-1915
168	Carl Yastrzemski, 1961-1983
141	Heinie Wagner, 1906-1918
134	Larry Gardner, 1908-1917

BB: Most, career, all-time

2019	Ted Williams, 1939-1960
1845	Carl Yastrzemski, 1961-1983
1337	Dwight Evans, 1972-1990
1004	WADE BOGGS, 1982-1992
826	Harry Hooper, 1909-1920

BA: Highest, career, all-time

.344	Ted Williams, 1939-1960
.338	WADE BOGGS, 1982-1992
.337	Tris Speaker, 1907-1915
.320	Pete Runnels, 1958-1962
.320	Jimmie Foxx, 1936-1942

Slug avg: Highest, career, all-time

.634	Ted Williams, 1939-1960
.605	Jimmie Foxx, 1936-1942
.520	Fred Lynn, 1974-1980
.502	Jim Rice, 1974-1989
.492	Vern Stephens, 1948-1952

Games started: Most, career, all-time

301	ROGER CLEMENS, 1984-1993
297	Cy Young, 1901-1908
238	Luis Tiant, 1971-1978
232	Mel Parnell, 1947-1956
228	Bill Monbouquette, 1958 1965

Saves: Most, career, all-time

132	Bob Stanley, 1977-1989
104	Dick Radatz, 1962-1966
91	Ellis Kinder, 1948-1955
88	JEFF REARDON, 1990-1992
69	Sparky Lyle, 1967-1971

Shutouts: Most, career, all-time

38	Cy Young, 1901-1908
35	ROGER CLEMENS, 1984-1993
28	Joe Wood, 1908-1915
26	Luis Tiant, 1971-1978
25	Dutch Leonard, 1913-1918

Wins: Most, career, all-time

192	Cy Young, 1901-1908
163	ROGER CLEMENS, 1984-1993
123	Mel Parnell, 1947-1956
122	Luis Tiant, 1971-1978
116	Joe Wood, 1908-1915

K: Most, career, all-time

2033	ROGER CLEMENS, 1984-1993
1341	Cy Young, 1901-1908
1075	Luis Tiant, 1971-1978
1043	BRUCE HURST, 1980-1988
986	Joe Wood, 1908-1915

Win pct: Highest, career, all-time

.695	Roger Moret, 1970-1975
.684	Dave Ferriss, 1945-1950
.674	Joe Wood, 1908-1915
.659	Babe Ruth, 1914-1919
.655	ROGER CLEMENS, 1984-1993

ERA: Lowest, career, all-time

1.99	Joe Wood, 1908-1915
2.00	Cy Young, 1901-1908
2.12	Ernie Shore, 1914-1917
2.13	Dutch Leonard, 1913-1918
2.19	Babe Ruth, 1914-1919

Runs: Most, season

150	Ted Williams, 1949
142	Ted Williams, 1946
141	Ted Williams, 1942
139	Jimmie Foxx, 1938
136	Tris Speaker, 1912

Hits: Most, season

240	WADE BOGGS, 1985
222	Tris Speaker, 1912
214	WADE BOGGS, 1988
213	Jim Rice, 1978
210	WADE BOGGS, 1983

2B: Most, season

67	Earl Webb, 1931
53	Tris Speaker, 1912
51	WADE BOGGS, 1989
51	Joe Cronin, 1938
47	WADE BOGGS, 1986
47	George Burns, 1923
47	Fred Lynn, 1975

3B: Most, season

22	Tris Speaker, 1913
20	Buck Freeman, 1903
19	Buck Freeman, 1902
19	Buck Freeman, 1904
19	Larry Gardner, 1914
19	Chick Stahl, 1904

HR: Most, season

50	Jimmie Foxx, 1938
46	Jim Rice, 1978
44	Carl Yastrzemski, 1967
43	Tony Armas, 1984
43	Ted Williams, 1949

RBI: Most, season

175	Jimmie Foxx, 1938
159	Vern Stephens, 1949
159	Ted Williams, 1949
145	Ted Williams, 1939
144	Walt Dropo, 1950
144	Vern Stephens, 1950

224

SB: Most, season

54	Tommy Harper, 1973	
52	Tris Speaker, 1912	
46	Tris Speaker, 1913	
42	Tris Speaker, 1914	
40	Harry Hooper, 1910	
40	Billy Werber, 1934	

BB: Most, season

162	Ted Williams, 1947
162	Ted Williams, 1949
156	Ted Williams, 1946
145	Ted Williams, 1941
145	Ted Williams, 1942

BA: Highest, season

.406	Ted Williams, 1941
.388	Ted Williams, 1957
.383	Tris Speaker, 1912
.369	Ted Williams, 1948
.368	WADE BOGGS, 1985

Slug avg: Highest, season

.735	Ted Williams, 1941
.731	Ted Williams, 1957
.704	Jimmie Foxx, 1938
.694	Jimmie Foxx, 1939
.667	Ted Williams, 1946

Games started: Most, season

43	Cy Young, 1902
42	Bill Dinneen, 1902
41	Babe Ruth, 1916
41	Cy Young, 1901
41	Cy Young, 1904

Saves: Most, season

40	JEFF REARDON, 1991
33	JEFF RUSSELL, 1993
33	Bob Stanley, 1983
31	Bill Campbell, 1977
29	Dick Radatz, 1964
29	LEE SMITH, 1988

Shutouts: Most, season

10	Joe Wood, 1912
10	Cy Young, 1904
9	Babe Ruth, 1916
8	ROGER CLEMENS, 1988
8	Carl Mays, 1918

Wins: Most, season

34	Joe Wood, 1912
33	Cy Young, 1901
32	Cy Young, 1902
28	Cy Young, 1903
26	Cy Young, 1904

K: Most, season

291	ROGER CLEMENS, 1988
258	Joe Wood, 1912
256	ROGER CLEMENS, 1987
246	Jim Lonborg, 1967
241	ROGER CLEMENS, 1991

Win pct: Highest, season

.872	Joe Wood, 1912
.857	ROGER CLEMENS, 1986
.806	Dave Ferriss, 1946
.793	Ellis Kinder, 1949
.792	Dutch Leonard, 1914

ERA: Lowest, season

0.96	Dutch Leonard, 1914
1.26	Cy Young, 1908
1.49	Joe Wood, 1915
1.62	Ray Collins, 1910
1.62	Cy Young, 1901

Most pinch-hit homers, season

5	Joe Cronin, 1943
4	Del Wilber, 1953

Most pinch-hit, homers, career

7	Ted Williams, 1939-1960

Most consecutive games, batting safely

34	Dom DiMaggio, 1949
30	Tris Speaker, 1912

Most consecutive scoreless innings

45	Cy Young, 1904
42	Rube Foster, 1914
40	Luis Tiant, 1972
39	Ray Culp, 1968
37	Cy Young, 1903

No hit games

Cy Young, Bos vs Phi AL, 3-0; May 5, 1904 (perfect game).

Jesse Tannehill, Bos at Chi AL, 6-0; August 17, 1904.

Bill Dinneen, Bos vs Chi AL, 2-0; September 27, 1905 (1st game).

Cy Young, Bos at NY AL, 8-0; June 30, 1908.

Joe Wood, Bos vs StL AL, 5-0; July 29, 1911 (1st game).

Rube Foster, Bos vs NY AL, 2-0; June 21, 1916.

Hubert (Dutch) Leonard, Bos vs StL AL, 4-0; August 30, 1916.

Ernie Shore, Bos vs Was AL, 4-0; June 23, 1917 (1st game, perfect game). (Shore relieved Babe Ruth in the first inning after Ruth had been throw out of the game for protesting a walk to the first batter. The runner was caught stealing and Shore retired the remaining 26 batters in order).

Hubert (Dutch) Leonard, Bos at Det AL, 5-0; June 3, 1918.

Howard Ehmke, Bos at Phi AL, 4-0; September 7, 1923.

Mel Parnell, Bos vs Chi AL, 4-0; July 14, 1956.

Earl Wilson, Bos vs LA AL, 2-0; June 26, 1962.

Bill Monbouquette, Bos at Chi AL, 1-0; August 1, 1962.

Dave Morehead, Bos vs Cle AL, 2-0; September 16, 1965.

MATT YOUNG, Bos at Cle AL, 1-2; April 12, 1992 (1st game) (8 innings, lost the game, bottom of 9th not played).

ACTIVE PLAYERS in caps.

Leader from the franchise's current location is included. If not in the top five, leader's rank is listed in paranthesis; asterisk (*) indicates player is not in top 25.

Albert Belle knocked in a league-leading 129 runs, hit 38 home runs, and stole 23 bases.

by H. Darr Beiser, *USA TODAY*

1993 Indians: Character pulled them through

Cleveland will never forget 1993. The March 22 boating accident that killed relief pitchers Steve Olin and Tim Crews and seriously injured starter Bob Ojeda left the team in a daze from which it never quite emerged. But the Indians managed to win 76 games—matching their '92 total—with a patchwork pitching staff and a bullpen torn apart by the emotional fallout of the crash on Little Lake Nellie.

"We have reason to be proud," manager Mike Hargrove said. "Everyone said the wheels were going to fall off this club, and they didn't."

Indeed, there were bright spots. Albert Belle, Carlos Baerga and Kenny Lofton—all of whom are signed to long-term deals—enjoyed banner years. Belle hit 38 homers and led the majors with 129 RBI. Baerga, who missed all but one game of the final week due to an ankle infection, had his second straight season with at least 200 hits, 20 home runs and 100 RBI. Lofton hit .325—fourth in the AL—and led the majors with a team-record 70 stolen bases.

At age 29, Wayne Kirby contributed a fine rookie season with 60 RBI and 17 steals. First baseman Paul Sorrento had 18 homers and 65 RBI.

It wasn't easy. They played much of the season without their No. 1 starter Charles Nagy and catcher Sandy Alomar, Jr. Pitching was a huge problem—they used 26 pitchers, one short of the major league record. Jose Mesa became the ace of the staff at 10-12 (4.92 ERA.) A horde of relievers—led by Eric Plunk, Derek Lilliquist, Jerry DiPoto and Jeremy Hernandez—shared Olin's old role as the closer.

Hargrove, who was nicknamed the "Human Rain Delay" for fidgeting at the plate, took a calculated, easy approach to his team, allowing players to deal with grief on their own terms and offering an ear when needed. At the same time, he managed to guide the team to a respectable showing despite being further depleted by injuries.

"He did a great job dealing with everything and helping us deal with it," said Kirby, who spent a decade in the minors before finally getting a full-time shot at the majors in '93. "Getting people through adversity is what being a leader is all about."

"Given our circumstances from spring training on," said Hargrove, "what made me so proud was the character I saw on this club day in and day out."

After playing baseball at Cleveland Stadium for 61 years, the Indians said goodbye on Oct. 3—They will move into a new ballpark at the Gateway complex next season. (Their final three-game series at the Stadium drew 216,349 fans, a major league record.) Then the ground crew, dressed in tuxedoes, dug up home plate, scheduled to be placed in the new Gateway ballpark.

"I got tears in my eyes when they dug up the plate," said Baerga. "This stadium made me an All-Star. This stadium is where I got my two 200-hit seasons and where I hit home runs from both sides of the plates in one inning. It's special. I'll never forget it."

—by Pete Williams

1994 Indians: Preview

The Indians used free agency to become an instant contender, adding pitcher Dennis Martinez and slugger Eddie Murray. Charles Nagy's return will help, too. Jerry DiPoto, who throws a nasty sinker, seems most likely to win the closer job next season. Out-fielder Manny Ramirez, one of the top power prospects in the minors in 1993, will compete for a spot in spring training.

"We're all looking at next season with a sense of relief," Hargrove said. "I don't think I've ever looked forward to a season as a manager or a player as much as I'm looking forward to next year."

—by Pete Williams

1993 Indians: Between the lines

▶**April 8:** Carlos Baerga became the first major leaguer to homer from both sides of the plate in a single inning. Batting right-handed in the seventh, he hit a Steve Howe fastball into the seats for a two-run homer. Then with two outs, batting left-handed, he took a Steve Farr pitch deep for his second homer. Eddie Murray and Mickey Mantle homered from both sides of the plate in a game 10 times, but neither managed the feat in the same inning.

▶**April 18:** Albert Belle and Paul Sorrento both extended their hitting streaks with two-run homers in the Indians' 6-5 win against Toronto. Belle's streak was a career-high 11 games and Sorrento's stood at 10.

▶**May 3:** Belle hit a solo homer in the seventh and a three-run blast in the eighth to assume the major-league lead with 10 long shots.

▶**May 13:** Belle charged the mound in the eighth inning of the Indians' 7-3 loss to Kansas City after being plunked by a Hipolito Pichardo pitch. Belle felt Pichardo was throwing at him because he had taken out Royals' shortstop Greg Gagne with an aggressive slide in the third inning. The benches cleared and Belle was ejected from the game.

▶**May 17:** Orioles' castoff Jose Mesa blanked his former team on three hits through eight innings of a 2-0 Indian win at Camden Yards. Belle's first-inning homer into the Orioles' bullpen provided all the offense.

▶**May 20:** Pitcher Dennis Cook recorded a scorebook rarity—he caught a runner stealing, pitcher unassisted. Orioles' right fielder Mark McLemore was on second base, and made a break for third. Cook, who had not started his motion toward the plate, stepped off, freezing McLemore. The pitcher then ran at the runner, and tagged him out.

▶**May 24:** Rookie Tommy Kramer threw a one-hitter in his second major league start and gained his first win.

▶**June 1:** The Indians feasted on Yankee pitching, racking up 16 hits. The absence of a single is the only thing that kept Carlos Baerga from hitting for the cycle. Albert Belle whacked a pair of home runs to maintain his position as major league leader.

▶**June 8:** Baerga extended his current hitting streak to 12 games in a 5-4 victory against Boston.

▶**June 11:** Baerga homered and drove in four runs to lead the Indians to an 8-3 win against Texas, extending his streak to a career-high 14 games.

▶**June 12:** Matt Young broke a two-year losing streak, striking out eight in 4 2/3 innings of relief work during a 10-9 defeat of the Rangers.

▶**June 27:** Reggie Jefferson's solo home run with one out in the ninth gave Cleveland a 3-2 win against the Royals. The Indians moved into sixth place in the AL East and left the cellar to Milwaukee.

▶**June 29:** Kenny Lofton hit his first career grand slam during a six-run fourth inning. He also tripled in the first inning.

▶**July 2:** Wayne Kirby drove home four runs with a three-run homer and an RBI single to aid the Indians in a 10-8 win against California. Meanwhile, Kenny Lofton robbed Tim Salmon of a home run by pulling it back into the park. It was a repeat of Lofton's 1992 heroics that robbed Salmon of what would have been his first major league homer.

▶**July 17:** Jeff Mutis, making his sixth major league start, shut out the Angels on four hits and recorded his first complete game in the 3-0 win.

▶**July 23:** Baerga had four hits in a 9-4 win against Seattle. He also stole home.

▶**July 25:** Albert Belle hit his 27th and 28th home runs in a 11-9 win against Seattle.

▶**August 3:** Wayne Kirby homered and tripled for three RBI in Cleveland's 9-4 victory against Detroit.

August 7: Sandy Alomar had a triple and a home run, driving in three runs in his first game since early May. Bob Ojeda made his first appearance since the boating accident that took the lives of teammates Steve Olin and Tim Crews in spring training. Ojeda entered the game in Baltimore to a long standing ovation.

August 8: With two Tribe runners in scoring position in the first inning of Baltimore's win, Mark McLemore robbed Albert Belle of a three-run homer, pulling a shot to right-center field back into the park. But McLemore stumbled after hitting the wall and Harold Reynolds hesitated with the relay throw, and both runners scored, giving Belle a rare two-run sacrifice fly.

September 3: Rookie Manny Ramirez hit two home runs and thought he had another as the Indians beat New York 7-3. Ramirez hit a ground-rule double for his first major league hit in the second inning but thought the ball had reached the seats on the fly. Ramirez, who was appearing in his second major league game, went into his home run trot and was heading for third base before realizing his mistake. He later homered in the sixth and eighth innings.

September 19: Sam Horn went deep twice in just his second major league game this year. He hadn't homered since July 1, 1992.

September 22: Kenny Lofton returned to the lineup after missing six games because of a strained hamstring and promptly went 2-for-4 with his league-leading 64th stolen base.

September 24: Albert Belle hit two home runs in the Indians' 11-8 loss to Milwaukee. Despite not homering in nearly a month, Belle's 36 long balls were the most for a Tribe player since Rocky Colavito hit 42 in 1959. Belle's 122 RBI were the most since Larry Doby knocked in 126 in 1954.

October 1: *Milestone*—Carlos Baerga got his 200th hit of the season. It was his second consecutive season with a .300 average, 200 hits, 20 homers and 100 RBI. Rogers Hornsby is the only other second baseman ever to reach those numbers.

October 3: The White Sox beat Cleveland, 4-0, and the Indians finished in sixth place, 19 games behind the Blue Jays in the AL East. *League leaders, pitching*— Eric Plunk was tied for sixth in games (70). *League leaders, batting*—Kenny Lofton led the league in stolen bases (70), was tied for third in runs (116), was fourth in batting (.325), fifth in hits (185), tied for sixth in triples (8), and eighth in on-base percentage (.408); Albert Belle led the league in RBI (129), was fourth in home runs (38), sixth in total bases (328), and seventh in slugging percentage (.552); Carlos Baerga was tied for second in hits (200), fifth in batting (.321), sixth in RBI (114), and eighth in total bases (303).

—by John Hunt, Scott Kauffman, Lisa Winston, Deron Snyder, Matt Young

Team directory

Owner: Richard E. Jacobs
General Manager: John Hart
Ballpark:
Indians Park
2401 Ontario Ave., Cleveland, Ohio
216-420-4200
Capacity 42,400
Downtown parking available; public transportation; handicapped seating; extremely accessible with escalators, elevators and ramps; all 38 bathrooms have diaper-changing areas; two unisex bathrooms for physically challenged and kids
Team publications:
Game Face Magazine, Tribe Talk
216-861-1200
TV, radio broadcast stations:
WKNR 1220 AM, WUAB Channel 43, SportsChannel Ohio
Camps and/or clinics:
Cleveland Indians Baseball Heaven (fantasy camp), January, 800-75-TRIBE
Spring Training:
Chain O' Lakes Park
Winter Haven, Fla.
Capacity 4,520
813-293-3900

CLEVELAND INDIANS 1993 final stats

Batting	BA	SLG	OB	G	AB	R	H	TB	2B	3B	HR	RBI	BB	SO	SB	CS	E
Horn	.455	.848	.472	12	33	8	15	28	1	0	4	8	1	5	0	0	0
Milligan	.426	.574	.557	19	47	7	20	27	7	0	0	7	14	4	0	0	0
Lofton	.325	.408	.408	148	569	116	185	232	28	8	1	42	81	83	70	14	9
Baerga	.321	.486	.355	154	624	105	200	303	28	6	21	114	34	68	15	4	17
Treadway	.303	.403	.347	97	221	25	67	89	14	1	2	27	14	21	1	1	10
Belle	.290	.552	.370	159	594	93	172	328	36	3	38	129	76	96	23	12	5
Espinoza	.278	.380	.298	129	263	34	73	100	15	0	4	27	8	36	2	2	12
Alomar	.270	.395	.318	64	215	24	58	85	7	1	6	32	11	28	3	1	6
Kirby	.269	.371	.323	131	458	71	123	170	19	5	6	60	37	58	17	5	5
Thome	.266	.474	.385	47	154	28	41	73	11	0	7	22	29	36	2	1	6
Fermin	.263	.317	.303	140	480	48	126	152	16	2	2	45	24	14	4	5	23
Sorrento	.257	.434	.340	148	463	75	119	201	26	1	18	65	58	121	3	1	6
Lewis	.250	.346	.250	14	52	6	13	18	2	0	1	5	0	7	3	0	2
Jefferson	.249	.372	.310	113	366	35	91	136	11	2	10	34	28	78	1	3	3
Maldonado	.247	.457	.333	28	81	11	20	37	2	0	5	20	11	18	0	1	1
Martinez	.244	.340	.295	80	262	26	64	89	10	0	5	31	20	29	1	1	9
Howard	.236	.326	.278	74	178	26	42	58	7	0	3	23	12	42	5	1	2
Hill	.224	.374	.268	66	174	19	39	65	7	2	5	25	11	50	7	3	4
Ortiz	.221	.273	.267	95	249	19	55	68	13	0	0	20	11	26	1	0	5
Parrish	.200	.400	.333	10	20	2	4	8	1	0	1	2	4	5	1	0	3
Levis	.175	.206	.197	31	63	7	11	13	2	0	0	4	2	10	0	0	1
Ramirez	.170	.302	.200	22	53	5	9	16	1	0	2	5	2	8	0	0	0

Pitching	W-L	ERA	G	GS	CG	GF	Sho	SV	IP	H	R	ER	HR	BB	SO
Milacki	1-1	3.38	5	2	0	0	0	0	16	19	8	6	3	11	7
Mlicki	0-0	3.38	3	3	0	0	0	0	13.1	11	6	5	2	6	7
Wertz	2-3	3.62	34	0	0	7	0	0	59.2	54	28	24	5	32	53
Christopher	0-0	3.86	9	0	0	3	0	0	11.2	14	6	5	3	2	8
Kramer	7-3	4.02	39	16	1	6	0	0	121	126	60	54	19	59	71
Wickander	0-0	4.15	11	0	0	1	0	0	8.2	15	7	4	3	3	3
Clark	7-5	4.28	26	15	1	1	0	0	109.1	119	55	52	18	25	57
Slocumb	3-1	4.28	20	0	0	5	0	0	27.1	28	14	13	3	16	18
Ojeda	2-1	4.40	9	7	0	0	0	0	43	48	22	21	5	21	27
C.Young	3-3	4.62	21	7	0	3	0	1	60.1	74	35	31	9	18	31
Mesa	10-12	4.92	34	33	3	0	0	0	208.2	232	122	114	21	62	118
M.Young	1-6	5.21	22	8	0	2	0	0	74.1	75	45	43	8	57	65
Grimsley	3-4	5.31	10	6	0	1	0	0	42.1	52	26	25	3	20	27
Cook	5-5	5.67	25	6	0	2	0	0	54	62	36	34	9	16	34
Mutis	3-6	5.78	17	13	1	1	1	0	81	93	56	52	14	33	29
Bielecki	4-5	5.90	13	13	0	0	0	0	68.2	90	47	45	8	23	38
Lopez	3-1	5.98	9	9	0	0	0	0	49.2	49	34	33	7	32	25
Nagy	2-6	6.29	9	9	1	0	0	0	48.2	66	38	34	6	13	30
Abbott	0-1	6.38	5	5	0	0	0	0	18.1	19	15	13	5	11	7
Tavarez	2-2	6.57	8	7	0	0	0	0	37	53	29	27	7	13	19

1994 preliminary roster

PITCHERS (20)
Shawn Bryant
John Carter
Mark Clark
Carlos Crawford
Jerry DiPoto
Alan Embree
Jason Grimsley
Jeremy Hernandez
Tommy Kramer
Derek Lilliquist
Kevin Logsdon
Albie Lopez
Dennis Martinez
Greg McCarthy
Jose Mesa
Dave Mlicki
Charles Nagy
Eric Plunk
Julian Tavarez
Bill Wertz

CATCHERS (2)
Sandy Alomar
Jesse Levis

INFIELDERS (10)
Carlos Baerga
David Bell
Alvaro Espinoza
Felix Fermin
Reggie Jefferson
Mark Lewis
Eddie Murray
Herbert Perry
Paul Sorrento
Jim Thome

OUTFIELDERS (8)
Ruben Amaro
Albert Belle
Wayne Kirby
Kenny Lofton
Candy Maldonado
Manny Ramirez
Omar Ramirez
Ken Ramos

Games played by position

Player	G	C	1B	2B	3B	SS	OF	DH
Alomar	64	64	0	0	0	0	0	0
Baerga	154	0	0	150	0	0	0	4
Belle	159	0	0	0	0	0	150	9
Espinoza	129	0	0	2	99	35	0	0
Fermin	140	0	0	0	0	140	0	0
Hill	66	0	0	0	0	0	39	18
Horn	12	0	0	0	0	0	0	11
Howard	74	0	0	0	0	0	47	7
Jefferson	113	0	15	0	0	0	0	88
Kirby	131	0	0	0	0	0	123	5
Levis	31	29	0	0	0	0	0	0
Lewis	14	0	0	0	0	13	0	0
Lofton	148	0	0	0	0	0	146	0
Maldonado	28	0	0	0	0	0	26	2
Martinez	80	0	22	0	35	0	0	19
Milligan	19	0	18	0	0	0	0	1
Ortiz	95	95	0	0	0	0	0	0
Parrish	10	10	0	0	0	0	0	0
Ramirez	22	0	0	0	0	0	1	21
Sorrento	148	0	144	0	0	0	3	1
Thome	47	0	0	0	47	0	0	0
Treadway	97	0	0	19	42	0	0	4

Sick call: 1993 DL Report

Player	Days on the DL
Sandy Alomar	98
Mark Clark	54
Alan Embree*	182
Tommy Kramer	18
Dave Mlicki	121
Charles Nagy	138
Bob Ojeda	124
Ted Power*	55
Scott Scudder	43
Joel Skinner	182
Cliff Young	70

Two separate terms on Disabled List

Minor League Report

Class AAA: Charlotte finished at 86-55, winning the International League Western Division. Jim Thome won the batting crown at .332, hitting 25 homers and driving in 102 runs. Sam Horn hit 38 homers to lead the minors and drove in 96 runs. Jason Grimsley was 6-6 with a 3.39 ERA. Chad Ogea had 13 wins. Mike Christopher had 22 saves. **Class AA:** Canton-Akron finished at 75-62, second in the Eastern League. Manny Ramirez won the batting title at .340, hitting 17 homers and driving in 79 runs in just over a half-season. Brian Giles hit .327. Omar Ramirez batted .314. Miguel Flores stole 36 bases. Shawn Bryant was 10-5 with a 3.72 ERA. Calvin Jones led the league in saves with 22. **Class A:** Kinston finished at 71-67, winning the first half of the Carolina League Southern Division. Marc Marini hit .300. Pat Maxwell hit .293. Jason Fronio was 7-9 but led the league in ERA at 2.41, allowing 95 hits in 138 innings while striking out 147. Julian Tavarez was 11-5 with a 2.42 ERA in a half-season. Ian Doyle had 23 saves. . . . Columbus finished at 86-56, second in the Sally League Southern Division. Derek Hacopian hit .315 with 24 homers and 82 RBI. J.J. Thobe won the league ERA title, (11-2, 1.91). John Carter won 17 games, with a 2.79 ERA. Jose Cabrera had a 2.67 ERA and Charles York was 10-7 with a league-best 182 strikeouts. Cesar Perez had 35 saves. **Short-season:** Watertown finished at 44-32, winning the New York-Penn League Pinckney Division. Greg Thomas hit .307 with nine homers and 63 RBI, best in the league. Casey Whitten was 6-3 with a 2.42 ERA. Roland DeLaMaza was 10-3 with a 2.52 ERA. Christopher Plumlee had 15 saves. . . . Burlington finished at 44-24, tied for first in the Appalachian League Northern Division. Eric White hit .321 with 45 RBI. Alex Ramirez had 58 RBI. Jason Mackey was 6-0 with a 2.15 ERA. Johnny Martinez was 6-1 with a 2.22 ERA. Cesar Ramos led the league with 14 saves.

Tops in the organization

231

Batter	Club	Avg	G	AB	R	H	HR	RBI
Ramirez, Manny	Chr	.333	129	489	105	163	31	115
Thome, Jim	Chr	.332	115	410	85	136	25	102
Giles, Brian	Can	.327	123	425	64	139	8	64
Hacopian, Derek	Clm	.315	131	454	81	143	24	82
Ramirez, Omar	Can	.314	125	516	116	162	7	53

Home Runs			Wins		
Horn, Sam	Chr	38	Carter, John	Clm	17
Ramirez, Manny	Chr	31	Tavarez, Julian	Can	13
Thome, Jim	Chr	25	Ogea, Chad	Chr	13
Hacopian, Derek	Clm	24	Thobe, J.J	Kin	12
Allred, Beau	Chr	20	Williams, Matt	Kin	12

RBI			Saves		
Ramirez, Manny	Chr	115	Perez, Cesar	Clm	35
Thome, Jim	Chr	102	Doyle, Ian	Kin	23
Horn, Sam	Chr	96	Christopher, Mike	Chr	22
Hacopian, Derek	Clm	82	Jones, Calvin	Can	22
Lopez, Luis	Chr	78	Dipoto, Jerry	Chr	12

Stolen Bases			Strikeouts		
Bryant, Pat	Clm	43	York, Charles	Clm	182
Claudio, Patricio	Clm	40	Fronio, Jason	Kin	147
Flores, Miguel	Can	36	Ogea, Chad	Chr	135
White, Andre	Clm	29	Williams, Matt	Kin	134
Cotton, John	Kin	28	Carter, John	Clm	134

Pitcher	Club	W-L	ERA	IP	H	BB	SO
Thobe, J.J	Kin	12-4	2.09	155	131	34	117
Tavarez, Julian	Can	13-6	2.22	138	116	29	118
Fronio, Jason	Kin	7-9	2.41	138	95	66	147
Cabrera, Jose	Clm	11-6	2.67	155	122	53	105
York, Charles	Clm	10-7	2.79	158	127	78	182

Cleveland (1901-1993)

Runs: Most, career, all-time

1154	Earl Averill, 1929-1939	
1079	Tris Speaker, 1916-1926	
942	Charlie Jamieson, 1919-1932	
865	Nap Lajoie, 1902-1914	
857	Joe Sewell, 1920-1930	

Hits: Most, career, all-time

2046	Nap Lajoie, 1902-1914
1965	Tris Speaker, 1916-1926
1903	Earl Averill, 1929-1939
1800	Joe Sewell, 1920-1930
1753	Charlie Jamieson, 1919-1932

2B: Most, career, all-time

486	Tris Speaker, 1916-1926
424	Nap Lajoie, 1902-1914
377	Earl Averill, 1929-1939
375	Joe Sewell, 1920-1930
367	Lou Boudreau, 1938-1950

3B: Most, career, all-time

121	Earl Averill, 1929-1939
108	Tris Speaker, 1916-1926
106	Elmer Flick, 1902-1910
89	Joe Jackson, 1910-1915
83	Jeff Heath, 1936-1945

HR: Most, career, all-time

226	Earl Averill, 1929-1939
216	Hal Trosky, 1933-1941
215	Larry Doby, 1947-1958
214	Andy Thornton, 1977-1987
192	Al Rosen, 1947-1956

RBI: Most, career, all-time

1084	Earl Averill, 1929-1939
919	Nap Lajoie, 1902-1914
911	Hal Trosky, 1933-1941
884	Tris Speaker, 1916-1926
869	Joe Sewell, 1920-1930

SB: Most, career, all-time

254	Terry Turner, 1904-1918
240	Nap Lajoie, 1902-1914
233	Ray Chapman, 1912-1920
207	Elmer Flick, 1902-1910
165	Harry Bay, 1902-1908

BB: Most, career, all-time

857	Tris Speaker, 1916-1926
766	Lou Boudreau, 1938-1950
725	Earl Averill, 1929-1939
712	Jack Graney, 1908-1922
703	Larry Doby, 1947-1958

BA: Highest, career, all-time

.375	Joe Jackson, 1910-1915
.354	Tris Speaker, 1916-1926
.339	Nap Lajoie, 1902-1914
.327	George Burns, 1920-1928
.323	Ed Morgan, 1928-1933

Slug avg: Highest, career, all-time

.551	Hal Trosky, 1933-1941
.542	Joe Jackson, 1910-1915
.542	Earl Averill, 1929-1939
.520	Tris Speaker, 1916-1926
.506	Jeff Heath, 1936-1945

Games started: Most, career, all-time

484	Bob Feller, 1936-1956
433	Mel Harder, 1928-1947
350	Bob Lemon, 1941-1958
320	Willis Hudlin, 1926-1940
305	Stan Coveleski, 1916-1924

Saves: Most, career, all-time

128	DOUG JONES, 1986-1991
53	Ray Narleski, 1954-1958
48	Steve Olin, 1989-1992
46	Jim Kern, 1974-1986
46	Sid Monge, 1977-1981

Shutouts: Most, career, all-time

45	Addie Joss, 1902-1910
44	Bob Feller, 1936-1956
31	Stan Coveleski, 1916-1924
31	Bob Lemon, 1941-1958
27	Mike Garcia, 1948-1959

Wins: Most, career, all-time

266	Bob Feller, 1936-1956
223	Mel Harder, 1928-1947
207	Bob Lemon, 1941-1958
172	Stan Coveleski, 1916-1924
164	Early Wynn, 1949-1963

K: Most, career, all-time

2581	Bob Feller, 1936-1956
2159	Sam McDowell, 1961-1971
1277	Bob Lemon, 1941-1958
1277	Early Wynn, 1949-1963
1160	Mel Harder, 1928-1947

Win pct: Highest, career, all-time

.667	Vean Gregg, 1911-1914
.663	Johnny Allen, 1936-1940
.630	Cal McLish, 1956-1959
.623	Addie Joss, 1902-1910
.622	Wes Ferrell, 1927-1933

ERA: Lowest, career, all-time

1.89	Addie Joss, 1902-1910
2.31	Vean Gregg, 1911-1914
2.39	Bob Rhoads, 1903-1909
2.45	Bill Bernhard, 1902-1907
2.50	Otto Hess, 1902-1908

Runs: Most, season

140	Earl Averill, 1931
137	Tris Speaker, 1920
136	Earl Averill, 1936
133	Tris Speaker, 1923
130	Charlie Jamieson, 1923

Hits: Most, season

233	Joe Jackson, 1911
232	Earl Averill, 1936
227	Nap Lajoie, 1910
226	Joe Jackson, 1912
225	Johnny Hodapp, 1930

2B: Most, season

64	George Burns, 1926
59	Tris Speaker, 1923
52	Tris Speaker, 1921
52	Tris Speaker, 1926
51	George Burns, 1927
51	Johnny Hodapp, 1930
51	Nap Lajoie, 1910

3B: Most, season

26	Joe Jackson, 1912
23	Dale Mitchell, 1949
22	Bill Bradley, 1903
22	Elmer Flick, 1906
20	Jeff Heath, 1941
20	Joe Vosmik, 1935

HR: Most, season

43	Al Rosen, 1953
42	Rocky Colavito, 1959
42	Hal Trosky, 1936
41	Rocky Colavito, 1958
38	ALBERT BELLE, 1993

RBI: Most, season

162	Hal Trosky, 1936
145	Al Rosen, 1953
143	Earl Averill, 1931
142	Hal Trosky, 1934
136	Ed Morgan, 1930

SB: Most, season

70	KENNY LOFTON, 1993
66	KENNY LOFTON, 1992
61	Miguel Dilone, 1980
52	BRETT BUTLER, 1984
52	Ray Chapman, 1917

BB: Most, season

111	Mike Hargrove, 1980
109	Andy Thornton, 1982
106	Les Fleming, 1942
105	Jack Graney, 1919
102	Jack Graney, 1916

BA: Highest, season

.408	Joe Jackson, 1911
.395	Joe Jackson, 1912
.389	Tris Speaker, 1925
.388	Tris Speaker, 1920
.386	Tris Speaker, 1916

Slug avg: Highest, season

.644	Hal Trosky, 1936
.627	Earl Averill, 1936
.620	Rocky Colavito, 1958
.613	Al Rosen, 1953
.610	Tris Speaker, 1923

Games started: Most, season

44	George Uhle, 1923
42	Bob Feller, 1946
41	Gaylord Perry, 1973
40	Stan Coveleski, 1921
40	Bob Feller, 1941
40	Gaylord Perry, 1972
40	Dick Tidrow, 1973
40	George Uhle, 1922

Saves: Most, season

43	DOUG JONES, 1990
37	DOUG JONES, 1988
32	DOUG JONES, 1989
29	Steve Olin, 1992
23	Ernie Camacho, 1984

Shutouts: Most, season

10	Bob Feller, 1946
10	Bob Lemon, 1948
9	Stan Coveleski, 1917
9	Addie Joss, 1906
9	Addie Joss, 1908
9	Luis Tiant, 1968

Wins: Most, season

31	Jim Bagby, 1920
27	Bob Feller, 1940
27	Addie Joss, 1907
27	George Uhle, 1926
26	Bob Feller, 1946
26	George Uhle, 1923

K: Most, season

348	Bob Feller, 1946
325	Sam McDowell, 1965
304	Sam McDowell, 1970
283	Sam McDowell, 1968
279	Sam McDowell, 1969

Win pct: Highest, season

.938	Johnny Allen, 1937
.773	Bill Bernhard, 1902
.767	Vean Gregg, 1911
.767	Bob Lemon, 1954
.741	Gene Bearden, 1948

ERA: Lowest, season

1.16	Addie Joss, 1908
1.59	Addie Joss, 1904
1.60	Luis Tiant, 1968
1.71	Addie Joss, 1909
1.72	Addie Joss, 1906

Most pinch-hit homers, season

3	Gene Green, 1962
3	Fred Whitfield, 1965
3	Ted Ulaender, 1970
3	Ron Kittle, 1987

Most pinch-hit, homers, career

8	Fred Whitfield, 1963-1967

Most consecutive games, batting safely

31	Nap Lajoie, 1906
29	Bill Bradley, 1902

Most consecutive scoreless innings

41	Luis Tiant, 1968
38	Jim Bagby, 1917

No hit games

Earl Moore, Cle vs Chi AL, 2-4; May 9, 1901 (lost on two hits in the tenth).

Dusty Rhoades, Cle vs Bos AL, 2-1; September 18, 1908.

Addie Joss, Cle vs Chi AL, 1-0; October 2, 1908 (perfect game).

Addie Joss, Cle vs Chi AL, 1-0; April 20, 1910.

Ray Caldwell, Cle at NY AL, 3-0; September 10, 1919 (1st game).

Wes Ferrell, Cle vs StL AL, 9-0; April 29, 1931.

Bob Feller, Cle at Chi AL, 1-0; April 16, 1940 (opening day).

Bob Feller, Cle at NY AL, 1-0; April 30, 1946.

Don Black, Cle vs Phi AL, 3-0; July 10, 1947 (1st game).

Bob Lemon, Cle at Det AL, 2-0; June 30, 1948.

Bob Feller, Cle vs Det AL, 2-1; July 1, 1951 (1st game).

Sonny Siebert, Cle vs Was AL, 2-0; June 10, 1966.

Dick Bosman, Cle vs Oak AL, 4-0; July 19, 1974.

DENNIS ECKERSLEY, Cle vs Cal AL, 1-0; May 30, 1977.

Len Barker, Cle vs Tor AL, 3-0; May 15, 1981 (perfect game).

ACTIVE PLAYERS in caps.

by Neil Seiler, *USA TODAY*

Outfielder Darryl Hamilton hit .310, stole 21 bases and scored 74 runs in 135 games.

1993 Brewers: From 92 wins to 93 losses

A year after flirting with Toronto for the AL East championship—four games behind the Blue Jays with a 92-70 record—the Brewers dropped to rock bottom: last place with a 69-93 record. It was only the sixth time in major league history a team went from 90 wins to 90 losses in one year.

Losing two of their top veteran players via free agency didn't help. Chris Bosio, who won 67 games for Milwaukee from 1986-92, ended up in Seattle, where he pitched a no-hitter. Paul Molitor, (.320, 89 runs, 12 HR, 89 RBI in '92) left after management asked him to take a pay cut and won a World Series with Toronto.

The Brewers brought in some veteran free agents, but they couldn't replace the void left by Bosio and Molitor. Tom Brunansky hit .183 in 80 games, and Kevin Reimer (13 homers and 60 RBI) had no homers and eight RBI after the All-Star break. Mike Boddicker was acquired from Kansas City early in the season, but retired months later with an unimpressive 3-5 record (5.67 ERA).

Added to the loss of Bosio and Molitor was disappointing pitching. Jaime Navarro, a 17-game winner in '92, went 11-12 (5.33 ERA). Ricky Bones showed signs of improvement, but still finished at 11-11 (4.86 ERA). Veteran Bill Wegman, 28-21 the previous two seasons, was on his way to 20 losses before injuries and a bad stomach sidelined him. He finished at 4-14 (4.48 ERA).

The bullpen wasn't much better. Closer Doug Henry blew seven of the team's 22 saves, and was eventually replaced by 36-year-old Jesse Orosco, who pitched well down the stretch, finishing with eight saves (3.18 ERA). Even Cal Eldred, slumped. He dropped from 11-1 (1.45 ERA) in '92 to 16-16 (4.01 ERA) and 32 home runs allowed, three shy of the club record. On the bright side, he became the first-ever Brewer to lead the league in innings pitched (258), and one of only four pitch-ers in major-league history to get 20 career victories in just 30 career appearances.

Meanwhile, left fielder Greg Vaughn was his steady self, hitting .267 with team-highs in home runs (30) and RBI (97). He was the Brewers' lone repre-sentative in the All-Star Game, falling just short of 100 RBI when he played with a sore shoulder the final two weeks. Darryl Hamilton had another productive season (.310, nine HR, 48 RBI, 21 SB), but Robin Yount, who was bothered by a knee injury, probably had his worst season in 14 years (.258, eight HR, 51 RBI). Shortstop Pat Listach was also bothered by injuries all season and saw his average drop from .290 to .244, and his stolen bases from 54 to 17.

Otherwise, the infield looked good. In his first full season, first baseman John Jaha hit .264 and was second on the team in HR (19), and third in RBI (70) and stolen bases (13).

—by Scott Kauffman

1994 Brewers: Preview

The biggest challenge for the Brewers in '94 will be winning with untested young players, and with no real help from the free agent market.

"We simply don't have the money to compete with the large-market clubs for many of these ballplayers," said Brew-ers president Bud Selig. But they've found a future starting pitcher in Angel Miranda, a 24-year-old lefty (4-5 with a 3.30 ERA in 17 starts) and reacquired third baseman Kevin Seitzer from Oak-land (.269, 11 HR, 57 RBI), which made B.J. Surhoff enticing trade bait. Other top prospects: outfielder Matt Mieske and infielder Jose Valentin, acquired from San Diego in the Gary Sheffield trade, and outfielders Alex Diaz and Troy O'Leary.

—by Scott Kauffman

1993 Brewers: Between the lines

▶**April 12:** Due to parasitic contamination of the city's water supply, water fountains and soda machines were shut down at Milwaukee County Stadium for the home opener. Appropriately, however, the beer supply continued to flow.

▶**April 14:** Jaime Navarro lowered his ERA to 0.75 after a seven-inning, one-run effort against California. But the Brewers' bullpen—which had given up six Angels' runs in the ninth inning in the previous two games—allowed 11 in the final two frames after Navarro was lifted. Reliever Graeme Lloyd and catcher Dave Nilsson formed the first Australian battery in major league history.

▶**April 18:** Cal Eldred pitched eight scoreless innings in the Brewers' 8-0 win against Oakland.

▶**April 23:** Eldred gave up a one-out double to Rafael Palmeiro but retired the next 23 batters in order in the Brewers' 3-0 win against the Rangers. He recorded nine strikeouts in the first five innings. Garner was booed when he lifted Eldred in the ninth. Jesse Orosco got the save.

▶**April 27:** Pat Listach hit four singles in as many at-bats and also stole a base in the Brewers' 3-2 win against Minnesota. It was the third four-hit game of Listach's career.

▶**May 20:** Bill Wegman blanked the Tigers for seven innings, but the AL's best offense exploded for six runs in the eighth to down the Brewers 6-2. The Tigers had not been shut out in 1993, and no pitcher had kept them scoreless as long as Wegman did.

▶**May 26:** Jaime Navarro allowed 10 hits but only one run—unearned—in eight innings as the Brewers downed Toronto 8-1.

▶**May 27:** Robin Yount had four hits, including career home run No. 245, and scored three times in a 9-3 victory against the Blue Jays. Yount went 3-for-3 the previous day and had raised his average 56 points—from .224 to .280—

in two games.

▶**May 28:** Eldred faced just two batters over the minimum in his four-hit 5-1 win against the Royals. He struck out eight in his first complete game of the year to give the Brewers their third win in a row.

▶**June 1:** Navarro pitched his first shutout of the season. He struck out five and walked none.

▶**June 12:** Eldred threw a six-hitter for his eighth win as the Brew Crew beat the Yankees 9-1. Eldred, who lost his shutout with one out in the ninth, won for the 14th time in 16 decisions in Milwaukee.

▶**July 7:** *Milestone*—Robin Yount's eighth-inning single moved him into 12th place on the career hit list (3,082).

▶**July 8:** Bill Spiers led Milwaukee to a 15-3 demolition of the Twins. Spiers had three hits and drove in five runs for the last-place Brewers. B.J. Surhoff and Greg Vaughn had four hits each; Surhoff drove in four runs.

▶**July 10:** Minnesota scored twice in the top of the ninth to take a 4-3 lead against the Brewers, but Milwaukee rallied for a pair of runs in the bottom of the inning for the win. Bill Spiers drove in the tying run with a one-out triple. After Darryl Hamilton and Robin Yount were walked intentionally, Greg Vaughn singled home the game-winner.

▶**July 23:** Greg Vaughn hit a two-run home run in the ninth inning to give the Brewers a 3-2 win in Chicago. Scott Radinsky walked Darryl Hamilton to lead off the ninth and was replaced by Roberto Hernandez, who served up Vaughn's 20th homer. The White Sox threatened in the bottom half of the ninth, but with two men on, pinch-hitter Dan Pasqua hit into a game-ending double play.

▶**July 26:** Tom Brunansky hit a two-out, two-run home run in the bottom of the ninth to give the Brewers a 3-2 come-from-behind win against the Red Sox. Brunansky, batting just .175, homered off Jeff Russell to end Boston's 10-game win streak.

▶ **August 7:** Rookie Angel Miranda earned his first major league win, shutting down the Blue Jays. Miranda fanned a career-high 10 batters to become the first left-handed starter to win for the Brewers since Dan Plesac on April 24, 1992.

▶ **August 10:** Dickie Thon's pinch-hit single drove in the winning run in the 10th inning as the Brewers topped Cleveland 5-4. The Indians scored a run in the top of the inning to take the lead, but Sandy Alomar's error allowed Pat Listach to score the tying run from third base. After Derek Lilliquist intentionally walked Greg Vaughn to load the bases, Thon stroked a single to center.

▶ **August 13:** Detroit was held to two runs in 18 innings as the Brewers swept a doubleheader, 6-1 and 7-1. Angel Miranda and Ricky Bones pitched complete games, giving up six hits each. The Tigers had scored 47 runs in their previous three games.

▶ **August 19:** Graeme Lloyd threw a wild pitch in the 12th inning, allowing Luis Polonia to score the winning run in a 5-4 Angels' victory. Lloyd uncorked his wild pitch on a 2-2 count to Tim Salmon, who hit a home run earlier in the game.

▶ **August 20:** Cal Eldred went 10 innings, striking out nine Angels in a 7-2 win. It was the longest outing of the year for Eldred, 13-12.

▶ **August 24:** Jesse Orosco, who struck out in the 11th inning of the second game of Milwaukee's doubleheader sweep of Oakland, was the first Brewer pitcher to bat since Rick Waits on July 11, 1985 against Oakland. Matt Maysey, who pitched the 13th for the victory, also singled, becoming the first Brewers pitcher to get a hit since Ed Rodriguez tripled on Sept. 3, 1973.

▶ **August 26:** Angel Miranda threw eight shutout innings against Oakland before leaving with a stiff neck. Miranda gave up three hits, walked two and struck out eight to give the Brewers a 5-3 win and their first ever four-game sweep of the Athletics.

▶ **August 30:** Eldred went the distance, allowing a run on four hits in Milwaukee's 2-1 win against Kansas City. He improved his record to 15-12 with the seven-strikeout performance.

▶ **September 17:** Eldred blanked the Orioles on three hits for his second career shutout. Eldred outdueled Ben McDonald, who also threw a three-hitter, for a 2-0 win.

▶ **October 3:** The Brewers finished on a positive note, winning their final game of the season against Boston, 6-3, even if they did finish in the AL East cellar, 26 games behind the Blue Jays. *League leaders, pitching*—Cal Eldred led the league in innings pitched (258), was fifth in complete games (8), seventh in strikeouts (180), and 10th in victories (16-16). *League leaders, batting*—B.J. Surhoff was tied for sixth in doubles (38).

—by John Hunt, Scott Kauffman, Lisa Winston, Deron Snyder, Matt Young

Team directory

▶ **Owner:** Allan H. (Bud) Selig
▶ **General Manager:** Sal Bando
▶ **Ballpark:**
Milwaukee County Stadium
201 South 46th St., Milwaukee, Wis.
414-933-4114
Capacity 53,192
Pay parking lot; $5 (11,000 spaces)
Public transportation available
Family and wheelchair sections, ramps,
Designated Driver Program including
free taxi transportation for single ticket
holders participating in the DDP
▶ **Team publications:**
Media guide, *Lead Off*
▶ **TV, radio broadcast stations:**
WTMJ 620 AM, WVTV-TV
▶ **Camps and/or clinics:**
Gatorade Youth Camp, during the
season, 414-933-4114
Fantasy Camp, January, 414-933-4114
▶ **Spring Training:**
Compadre Stadium
Chandler, Ariz.,
Capacity 5,000
602-895-1200

MILWAUKEE BREWERS 1993 final stats

Batting	BA	SLG	OB	G	AB	R	H	TB	2B	3B	HR	RBI	BB	SO	SB	CS	E
Diaz	.319	.348	.319	32	69	9	22	24	2	0	0	1	0	12	5	3	1
Hamilton	.310	.406	.367	135	520	74	161	211	21	1	9	48	45	62	21	13	3
O'Leary	.293	.366	.370	19	41	3	12	15	3	0	0	3	5	9	0	0	0
Suero	.286	.286	.333	15	14	0	4	4	0	0	0	0	1	3	0	1	1
Surhoff	.274	.391	.318	148	552	66	151	216	38	3	7	79	36	47	12	9	18
Thon	.269	.331	.324	85	245	23	66	81	10	1	1	33	22	39	6	5	7
Seitzer	.269	.396	.338	120	417	45	112	165	16	2	11	57	44	48	7	7	12
Vaughn	.267	.482	.369	154	569	97	152	274	28	2	30	97	89	118	10	7	6
Jaha	.264	.416	.337	153	515	78	136	214	21	0	19	70	51	109	13	9	10
Yount	.258	.379	.326	127	454	62	117	172	25	3	8	51	44	93	9	2	1
Nilsson	.257	.375	.336	100	296	35	76	111	10	2	7	40	37	36	3	6	9
Reimer	.249	.394	.303	125	437	53	109	172	22	1	13	60	30	72	5	4	3
Valentin	.245	.396	.344	19	53	10	13	21	1	2	1	7	7	16	1	0	6
Listach	.244	.317	.319	98	356	50	87	113	15	1	3	30	37	70	18	9	10
Mieske	.241	.397	.290	23	58	9	14	23	0	0	3	7	4	14	0	2	3
Spiers	.238	.303	.302	113	340	43	81	103	8	4	2	36	29	51	9	8	13
Bell	.234	.322	.321	91	286	42	67	92	6	2	5	29	36	64	6	6	12
Kmak	.218	.264	.317	51	110	9	24	29	5	0	0	7	14	13	6	2	0
Doran	.217	.283	.284	28	60	7	13	17	4	0	0	6	6	3	1	0	2
Lampkin	.198	.321	.280	73	162	22	32	52	8	0	4	25	20	26	7	3	6
Brunansky	.183	.321	.265	80	224	20	41	72	7	3	6	29	25	59	3	4	2
McIntosh	--	--	--	1	0	0	0	0	0	0	0	0	0	0	0	0	0

Pitching	W-L	ERA	G	GS	CG	GF	Sho	SV	IP	H	R	ER	HR	BB	SO
Kiefer	0-0	0.00	6	0	0	4	0	1	9.1	3	0	0	0	5	7
Seitzer	0-0	0.00	1	0	0	1	0	0	0.1	0	0	0	0	0	1
Lloyd	3-4	2.83	55	0	0	12	0	0	63.2	64	24	20	5	13	31
Orosco	3-5	3.18	57	0	0	27	0	8	56.2	47	25	20	2	17	67
Miranda	4-5	3.30	22	17	2	0	0	0	120	100	53	44	12	52	88
Fetters	3-3	3.34	45	0	0	14	0	0	59.1	59	29	22	4	22	23
Ignasiak	1-1	3.65	27	0	0	4	0	0	37	32	17	15	2	21	28
Austin	1-2	3.82	31	0	0	8	0	0	33	28	15	14	3	13	15
Eldred	16-16	4.01	36	36	8	0	1	0	258	232	120	115	32	91	180
Wegman	4-14	4.48	20	18	5	0	0	0	120.2	135	70	60	13	34	50
Novoa	0-3	4.50	15	7	2	0	0	0	56	58	32	28	7	22	17
Maldonado	2-2	4.58	29	0	0	9	0	1	37.1	40	20	19	2	17	18
Bones	11-11	4.86	32	31	3	1	0	0	203.2	222	122	110	28	63	63
Navarro	11-12	5.33	35	34	5	0	1	0	214.1	254	135	127	21	73	114
Henry	4-4	5.56	54	0	0	41	0	17	55	67	37	34	7	25	38
Boddicker	3-5	5.67	10	10	1	0	0	0	54	77	35	34	6	15	24
Maysey	1-2	5.73	23	0	0	12	0	1	22	28	14	14	4	13	10
Higuera	1-3	7.20	8	8	0	0	0	0	30	43	24	24	4	16	27
Manzanillo	1-1	9.53	10	1	0	4	0	1	17	22	20	18	1	10	10

1994 preliminary roster

PITCHERS (20)
Ricky Bones
Marshall Boze
Byron Browne
Cal Eldred
Mike Fetters
Francisco Gamez
Doug Henry
Ted Higuera
Tyrone Hill
Mike Ignasiak
Mark Kiefer
Graeme Lloyd
Jamie McAndrew
Angel Miranda
Jaime Navarro
Rafael Novoa
Jesse Orosco
Charlie Rogers
Scott Taylor
Bill Wegman

CATCHERS (4)
Tom Lampkin
Mike Matheny
Dave Nilsson
Mike Stefanski

INFIELDERS (7)
Juan Bell
Jeff Cirillo
John Jaha
Pat Listach
Bill Spiers
B.J. Surhoff
Jose Valentin

OUTFIELDERS (9)
Alex Diaz
Darryl Hamilton
Matt Mieske
Troy O'Leary
Kevin Reimer
Duane Singleton
Greg Vaughn
Derek Wachter
Turner Ward

Games played by position

Player	G	C	1B	2B	3B	SS	OF	DH
Bell	91	0	0	47	0	40	3	2
Brunansky	80	0	0	0	0	0	71	6
Diaz	32	0	0	0	0	0	28	1
Doran	28	0	4	17	0	0	0	0
Hamilton	135	0	0	0	0	0	129	1
Jaha	153	0	150	1	1	0	0	0
Kmak	51	50	0	0	0	0	0	0
Lampkin	73	60	0	0	0	0	3	1
Listach	98	0	0	0	0	95	6	0
McIntosh	1	1	0	0	0	0	0	0
Mieske	23	0	0	0	0	0	22	0
Nilsson	100	91	4	0	0	0	0	4
O'Leary	19	0	0	0	0	0	19	0
Reimer	125	0	0	0	0	0	37	83
Seitzer	120	0	31	3	79	1	4	6
Spiers	113	0	0	104	0	4	7	1
Suero	15	0	0	8	1	0	0	0
Surhoff	148	3	8	0	121	0	24	1
Thon	85	0	0	22	25	28	0	14
Valentin	19	0	0	0	0	19	0	0
Vaughn	154	0	0	0	0	0	94	58
Yount	127	0	7	0	0	0	114	6

Sick call: 1993 DL Report

Player	Days on the DL
James Austin	15
Mike Boddicker@	39
Tom Brunansky	60
Alex Diaz	119
Bill Doran*	45
Darryl Hamilton	15
Teddy Higuera	131
Pat Listach	46
Graeme Lloyd	15
Angel Miranda	57
Dave Nilsson*	44
Rafael Novoa	15
Dickie Thon	16
Bill Wegman	69
Robin Yount	17

*Two separate terms on Disabled List
@ Mike Boddicker was on the DL both in Kansas City and in Milwaukee.

Minor League Report

Class AAA: New Orleans finished at 79-63, second in the American Association Western Division. Edgar Caceres hit .317. Larry Sheets had 98 RBI. John Finn stole 27 bases. Steve Sparks was 9-13 with a 3.84 ERA. Jamie McAndrew was 11-6 with a 3.94 ERA. **Class AA:** El Paso finished at 76-59, winning both halves of the Texas League Western Division, but was swept by Jackson in three games in the league finals. Bo Dodson hit .312 with nine homers and 59 RBI. Ed Smith hit .294 with 69 RBI. Scott Karl was 13-8 with a 2.45 ERA. Charlie Rogers had 23 saves. **Class A:** Stockton finished at 79-57, winning the second half of the California League Northern Division but losing to Modesto in the first round of the playoffs. Kevin Riggs hit .347. Mike Stefanski hit .322 with 10 homers and 57 RBI. Derek Wachter had 22 homers and 108 RBI. Sid Roberson led the league in ERA at 2.60. Bubba Hardwick had 14 saves. . . . Beloit finished at 60-74, last in the Midwest League Northern Division. Dan Perez hit .300 with 10 homers and 59 RBI. Scott Talanoa had 25 homers in an injury-shortened season. Scott Richardson stole 50 bases. **Short-season:** Helena finished at 41-30, winning the Pioneer League Southern Division, but fell to Billings in three games in the league finals. Chris McInnes hit .312. Hayland Hardy (that's his real name) had 13 homers and 52 RBI. Greg Martinez and McInnes each stole 30 bases, while Ruben Cephas had 26. Fabian Salmon was 8-3 with a 2.64 ERA. . . . Chandler finished at 26-26, fifth in the Arizona League. Franklin Garcia hit .311 and led the league in stolen bases with 36. Cecilio Sanchez hit .302. Derrick Cantrell stole 30 bases while Wilson Soto had 20 steals. Tano Tijerina was 6-1 with a 2.94 ERA.

Tops in the organization

Batter	Club	Avg	G	AB	R	H	HR	RBI
Riggs, Kevin	Stk	.347	108	377	84	131	3	45
Stefanski, M.	Stk	.322	97	345	58	111	10	57
Cirillo, Jeff	No	.319	125	464	84	148	12	73
Caceres, Edgar	No	.317	114	420	73	133	5	45
Dodson, Bo	Elp	.312	101	330	58	103	9	59

Home Runs			Wins		
Talanoa, Scott	Blt	25	Boze, Marshall	Elp	17
Wachter, Derek	Stk	22	Karl, Scott	Elp	13
Sheets, Larry	No	18	Roberson, Sid	Stk	12
Hughes, Bobby	Blt	17	Several players tied		11
Several players tied		15			

RBI			Saves		
Wachter, Derek	Stk	108	Rogers, Charlie	Elp	23
Sheets, Larry	No	98	Kyslinger, Dan	Blt	15
Glenn, Leon	Stk	76	Hardwick, Bill	Stk	14
Cirillo, Jeff	No	73	Archer, Kurt	Elp	11
Fairman, Andy	Stk	70	Wishnevski, Rob	No	10

Stolen Bases			Strikeouts		
Richardson, Scott	Blt	50	Blair, Donnie	Stk	130
Diggs, Tony	Stk	38	Taylor, Scott	No	123
Samples, Todd	Stk	36	Jones, Robert	Blt	115
Glenn, Leon	Stk	35	Browne, Byron	Stk	110
Finn, John	No	27	Sparks, Steve	No	104

Pitcher	Club	W-L	ERA	IP	H	BB	SO
Karl, Scott	Elp	13-8	2.45	180	172	35	95
Roberson, Sid	Stk	12-8	2.60	166	157	34	87
Boze, Marshall	Elp	17-5	2.68	175	160	73	102
Taylor, Scott	No	11-7	3.24	167	153	52	123
Novoa, Rafael	No	10-5	3.42	113	105	38	74

Milwaukee (1970-1993), incl. Seattle (1969)

Runs: Most, career, all-time

1632	ROBIN YOUNT, 1974-1993
1275	PAUL MOLITOR, 1978-1992
821	Cecil Cooper, 1977-1987
726	Jim Gantner, 1976-1992
596	Don Money, 1973-1983

Hits: Most, career, all-time

3142	ROBIN YOUNT, 1974-1993
2281	PAUL MOLITOR, 1978-1992
1815	Cecil Cooper, 1977-1987
1696	Jim Gantner, 1976-1992
1168	Don Money, 1973-1983

2B: Most, career, all-time

583	ROBIN YOUNT, 1974-1993
405	PAUL MOLITOR, 1978-1992
345	Cecil Cooper, 1977-1987
262	Jim Gantner, 1976-1992
215	Don Money, 1973-1983

3B: Most, career, all-time

126	ROBIN YOUNT, 1974-1993
86	PAUL MOLITOR, 1978-1992
42	Charlie Moore, 1973-1986
38	Jim Gantner, 1976-1992
33	Cecil Cooper, 1977-1987

HR: Most, career, all-time

251	ROBIN YOUNT, 1974-1993
208	Gorman Thomas, 1973-1986
201	Cecil Cooper, 1977-1987
176	Ben Oglivie, 1978-1986
160	PAUL MOLITOR, 1978-1992

RBI: Most, career, all-time

1406	ROBIN YOUNT, 1974-1993
944	Cecil Cooper, 1977-1987
790	PAUL MOLITOR, 1978-1992
685	Ben Oglivie, 1978-1986
605	Gorman Thomas, 1973-1986

SB: Most, career, all-time

412	PAUL MOLITOR, 1978-1992
271	ROBIN YOUNT, 1974-1993
137	Jim Gantner, 1976-1992
136	Tommy Harper, 1969-1971
108	MIKE FELDER, 1985-1990

BB: Most, career, all-time

966	ROBIN YOUNT, 1974-1993
755	PAUL MOLITOR, 1978-1992
501	Gorman Thomas, 1973-1986
440	Don Money, 1973-1983
432	Ben Oglivie, 1978-1986

BA: Highest, career, all-time

.303	PAUL MOLITOR, 1978-1992
.302	Cecil Cooper, 1977-1987
.297	DARRYL HAMILTON, 1988-1993
.285	ROBIN YOUNT, 1974-1993
.283	George Scott, 1972-1976

Slug avg: Highest, career, all-time

.470	Cecil Cooper, 1977-1987
.461	Gorman Thomas, 1973-1986
.461	Ben Oglivie, 1978-1986
.456	George Scott, 1972-1976
.452	Sixto Lezcano, 1974-1980

Games started: Most, career, all-time

268	Jim Slaton, 1971-1983
231	Moose Haas, 1976-1985
217	Mike Caldwell, 1977-1984
193	TEDDY HIGUERA, 1985-1993
193	BILL WEGMAN, 1985-1993

Saves: Most, career, all-time

133	DAN PLESAC, 1986-1992
97	Rollie Fingers, 1981-1985
61	DOUG HENRY, 1991-1993
61	Ken Sanders, 1970-1972
44	Bill Castro, 1974-1980

Shutouts: Most, career, all-time

19	Jim Slaton, 1971-1983
18	Mike Caldwell, 1977-1984
12	TEDDY HIGUERA, 1985-1993
10	Bill Travers, 1974-1980
8	CHRIS BOSIO, 1986-1992
8	Moose Haas, 1976-1985

Wins: Most, career, all-time

117	Jim Slaton, 1971-1983
102	Mike Caldwell, 1977-1984
93	TEDDY HIGUERA, 1985-1993
91	Moose Haas, 1976-1985
68	BILL WEGMAN, 1985-1993

K: Most, career, all-time

1046	TEDDY HIGUERA, 1985-1993
929	Jim Slaton, 1971-1983
800	Moose Haas, 1976-1985
749	CHRIS BOSIO, 1986-1992
587	BILL WEGMAN, 1985-1993

Win pct: Highest, career, all-time

.612	TEDDY HIGUERA, 1985-1993
.606	Pete Vuckovich, 1981-1986
.560	Mike Caldwell, 1977-1984
.537	JAIME NAVARRO, 1989-1993
.535	Moose Haas, 1976-1985

ERA: Lowest, career, all-time

3.46	TEDDY HIGUERA, 1985-1993
3.65	Jim Colborn, 1972-1976
3.72	Lary Sorensen, 1977-1980
3.74	Mike Caldwell, 1977-1984
3.76	CHRIS BOSIO, 1986-1992

Runs: Most, season

136	PAUL MOLITOR, 1982
133	PAUL MOLITOR, 1991
129	ROBIN YOUNT, 1982
121	ROBIN YOUNT, 1980
115	PAUL MOLITOR, 1988

Hits: Most, season

219	Cecil Cooper, 1980
216	PAUL MOLITOR, 1991
210	ROBIN YOUNT, 1982
205	Cecil Cooper, 1982
203	Cecil Cooper, 1983

2B: Most, season

49	ROBIN YOUNT, 1980
46	ROBIN YOUNT, 1982
44	Cecil Cooper, 1979
42	ROBIN YOUNT, 1983
41	PAUL MOLITOR, 1987

3B: Most, season

16	PAUL MOLITOR, 1979
13	PAUL MOLITOR, 1991
12	ROBIN YOUNT, 1982
11	ROBIN YOUNT, 1988
10	ROBIN YOUNT, 1980
10	ROBIN YOUNT, 1983

HR: Most, season

45	Gorman Thomas, 1979
41	Ben Oglivie, 1980
39	Gorman Thomas, 1982
38	Gorman Thomas, 1980
36	George Scott, 1975

RBI: Most, season

126	Cecil Cooper, 1983
123	Gorman Thomas, 1979
122	Cecil Cooper, 1980
121	Cecil Cooper, 1982
118	Ben Oglivie, 1980

SB: Most, season

73	Tommy Harper, 1969
54	PAT LISTACH, 1992
45	PAUL MOLITOR, 1987
41	DARRYL HAMILTON, 1992
41	PAUL MOLITOR, 1982
41	PAUL MOLITOR, 1983
41	PAUL MOLITOR, 1988

BB: Most, season

98	Gorman Thomas, 1979
95	Tommy Harper, 1969
89	Darrell Porter, 1975
89	GREG VAUGHN, 1993
87	John Briggs, 1973

BA: Highest, season

.353	PAUL MOLITOR, 1987
.352	Cecil Cooper, 1980
.331	ROBIN YOUNT, 1982
.327	Willie Randolph, 1991
.325	PAUL MOLITOR, 1991

Slug avg: Highest, season

.578	ROBIN YOUNT, 1982
.573	Sixto Lezcano, 1979
.566	PAUL MOLITOR, 1987
.563	Ben Oglivie, 1980
.539	Cecil Cooper, 1980
.539	Gorman Thomas, 1979

Games started: Most, season

38	Jim Slaton, 1973
38	Jim Slaton, 1976
36	Jim Colborn, 1973
36	CAL ELDRED, 1993
36	Marty Pattin, 1971
36	Lary Sorensen, 1978

Saves: Most, season

33	DAN PLESAC, 1989
31	Ken Sanders, 1971
30	DAN PLESAC, 1988
29	Rollie Fingers, 1982
29	DOUG HENRY, 1992

Shutouts: Most, season

6	Mike Caldwell, 1978
5	Marty Pattin, 1971
4	Mike Caldwell, 1979
4	Jim Colborn, 1973
4	TEDDY HIGUERA, 1986
4	Bill Parsons, 1971

Wins: Most, season

22	Mike Caldwell, 1978
20	Jim Colborn, 1973
20	TEDDY HIGUERA, 1986
18	TEDDY HIGUERA, 1987
18	Lary Sorensen, 1978
18	Pete Vuckovich, 1982

K: Most, season

240	TEDDY HIGUERA, 1987
207	TEDDY HIGUERA, 1986
192	TEDDY HIGUERA, 1988
180	CAL ELDRED, 1993
173	CHRIS BOSIO, 1989

Win pct: Highest, season

.750	Pete Vuckovich, 1982
.727	Mike Caldwell, 1979
.727	CHRIS BOSIO, 1992
.710	Mike Caldwell, 1978
.682	BILL WEGMAN, 1991

ERA: Lowest, season

2.36	Mike Caldwell, 1978
2.45	TEDDY HIGUERA, 1988
2.79	TEDDY HIGUERA, 1986
2.81	Bill Travers, 1976
2.83	Jim Lonborg, 1972

Most pinch-hit homers, season

2	Max Alvis, 1970
2	Andy Kosco, 1971
2	Bob Hansen, 1974
2	Bobby Darwin, 1975
2	Ken McMullen, 1977

Most pinch-hit, homers, career

2	Mike Hegan, Sea-1969, 1970-1977
2	Max Alvis, 1970
2	Andy Kosco, 1971
2	Bob Hansen, 1974-1976
2	Bobby Darwin, 1975-1976
2	Ken McMullen, 1977

Most consecutive games, batting safely

39	PAUL MOLITOR, 1987
24	Dave May, 1973

Most consecutive scoreless innings

32	TED HIGUERA, 1987

No hit games

Juan Nieves, Mil at Bal AL, 7-0; April 15, 1987.

ACTIVE PLAYERS in caps.

Cy Young Award winner Jack McDowell led the American League in wins (22) and shutouts (four).

by Porter Binks, *USA TODAY*

1993 White Sox: Thomas couldn't do it alone

Throughout the '93 season, the White Sox were an enigma—a team loaded with talent that couldn't put away the division, a winning team that failed to capture the hearts of its hometown.

Yet despite the unsettled mood—which started when Carlton Fisk was summarily dismissed after setting his all-time catching record, through a couple of beanball wars including Nolan Ryan's six-noogie punchout of Robin Ventura, and finally all the playoff turmoil—the ChiSox are looking forward to putting those lessons to good use.

"You've got to seize the moment when you're there. We fell behind 2-0 and it was a little too much," first baseman Frank Thomas said. "We'll be back next season and we'll be ready to take a step up to the next level."

The Sox battled back in the ALCS, losing the series 4-2 to the World Champion Blue Jays. But they lost all three games at Comiskey Park, including the first two of the series—yet still fought back to a tie after winning the first two at SkyDome.

"It was a learning experience for us. You deal with it, and it's over with. I don't want to talk about how difficult it was—it's over," Thomas said.

Thomas was the White Sox leader—physically and spiritually. He was the AL MVP, hitting .317 with 41 HR, 128 RBI and 112 walks. How much he was feared by the Blue Jays—and how seriously the rest of the lineup let manager Gene Lamont down—was obvious by the 10 walks Toronto pitchers issued Thomas during the series.

Shortstop Ozzie Guillen was the comeback player of the year. Bo Jackson's return was amazing, but Guillen's infield presence, calming influence on the young pitchers and .280 bat brought the AL West flag to the South Side.

Robin Ventura hit .262 with 22 homers, while Ellis Burks had a resurgence, hitting .275 with 17 homers and six steals. But the DH spot was a black hole. Jackson hit .232 in 85 games, and while he hit 16 homers and some in clutch situations, his option wasn't picked up by the Sox. George Bell managed just a .217 average and 13 homers, and after popping off in the ALCS, he was released by Scheuler on the first day of Chicago's offseason.

The rotation, the youngest in championship series history, featured a Cy Young winner—27-year-old Jack McDowell—and three other pitchers under 25: Alex Fernandez (24), Wilson Alvarez (23) and Jason Bere (22). They were so strong that hired gun Tim Belcher spent the ALCS in the bullpen.

McDowell went 22-10 (3.37 ERA, 10 complete games, 158 strikeouts, 256 2/3 innings pitched, 34 games). Also, Roberto Hernandez developed into one of the top closers in the league—38 saves in 70 appearances—in his first full year in the role.

—by Rick Lawes

1994 White Sox: Preview

The White Sox could look drastically different in '94. GM Ron Schueler wanted a left-handed power-hitter to back up Frank Thomas and was willing to go to the free-agent market to acquire one. But Schueler will have to prune more of the White Sox payroll if he's to get it down to the $32 million Jerry Reinsdorf wants to see. It isn't so discouraging when Schueler looks at his new division (AL Central): short-armed Cleveland and worse-off Milwaukee came from the East and Kansas City and Minnesota finished in the dust in '93.

Ellis Burks' defection to Colorado left a hole to one side of center fielder Lance Johnson. Tim Raines is likely to return in left.

—by Rick Lawes

1993 White Sox: Between the lines

▶**April 9:** Bo Jackson got a standing ovation after he hit the first home run by a player with an artificial hip in major league history.

▶**April 10:** Tim Raines underwent surgery after tearing ligaments in his right thumb while sliding into second base the day before. He was expected to be absent from the White Sox lineup for six weeks.

▶**April 23:** *Milestone*—George Bell played in his 1,500th game. The event took place in Toronto, Bell's stomping grounds from 1981 to 1990.

▶**April 30:** Frank Thomas hit an RBI double and his second career grand slam as the White Sox demolished Toronto 10-2. Thomas had knocked in 15 runs in the last five games.

▶**May 14:** Jack McDowell shut out the Rangers to become the majors' first seven-game winner, despite his less than spectacular 4.42 ERA.

▶**June 2:** Ron Karkovice hit two homers, including a grand slam, and Joey Cora hit his first major league homer.

▶**June 15:** Wilson Alvarez faced just 28 batters and didn't allow a baserunner past first base. His 11 strikeouts were a career high.

▶**June 16:** McDowell shut down the A's 4-0 and became the first pitcher to reach 10 wins in 1993.

▶**June 20:** George Bell hit a first-inning grand slam and added a solo shot in the eighth to lead the White Sox to a 11-6 win against the Angels.

▶**July 11:** Frank Thomas hit a three-run homer in the first inning, then went deep again with one man aboard in the seventh as the White Sox stomped the Orioles 11-5. The five-RBI performance was a career high.

▶**July 16:** Ron Karkovice laid down a perfect suicide squeeze to bring home Lance Johnson with the winning run in the ninth inning of Chicago's 4-3 win in Milwaukee. Johnson tripled to lead off the inning before Karkovice's bunt slipped under the glove of charging

third baseman B.J. Surhoff.

▶**July 17:** McDowell won his 14th.

▶**July 22:** McDowell became the first major leaguer to win 15.

▶**July 30:** The White Sox came back from a two-run deficit to beat Seattle 6-4 in 10 innings. Frank Thomas tied the game at 4-4 with a bases-loaded single in the ninth. Lance Johnson hit his league-leading 11th triple in the 10th to drive in the go-ahead run and scored on a suicide squeeze.

▶**August 1:** McDowell shut out the Mariners 2-0 on two hits for win No. 17, best in the majors. The shutout was his third of the season and the seventh of his career. It was also his fifth win in a row, his third such streak in '93.

▶**August 4:** Robin Ventura charged Texas pitcher Nolan Ryan after the 46-year-old plunked him in the third inning. Ryan walked down the front of the mound, got Ventura in a headlock and delivered six blows to the third baseman's head and face before other players could reach the mound and end the mismatch.

▶**August 7:** McDowell gave up four runs in the first three innings, but settled down to win No. 18, still tops in the major leagues.

▶**August 9:** Frank Thomas hit a tie-breaking home run (his 29th) in the seventh inning to lead the White Sox to a 5-4 win against Oakland.

▶**August 10:** Tim Belcher earned his first American League win, holding Oakland to just two hits in a 4-0 White Sox victory.

▶**August 13:** Frank Thomas hit a two-run homer (No. 30) in a three-run eighth inning as the White Sox rallied to beat the Royals 5-4.

▶**August 14:** Alex Fernandez held the Royals to two hits in a 4-1 White Sox win. Fernandez gave up a first-inning single and a solo homer to Brent Mayne in the second, then retired 22 consecutive batters before walking Brian McRae with two outs in the ninth. Scott

Radinsky got the final out to preserve the win.

▶**August 18:** McDowell became baseball's first 19-game winner as Steve Sax's sixth-inning tie-breaking, broken-bat hit gave the White Sox a 3-2 victory against Boston. The game didn't finish until 1:25 a.m. because of a three-hour, two-minute rain delay at the start.

▶**August 20:** Alex Fernandez threw eight innings of five-hit ball in a 4-2 win against the Twins. It was his 15th win.

▶**August 22:** McDowell became the major leagues' first 20-game winner in Chicago's 1-0 victory against the Twins.

▶**August 30:** Fernandez threw seven innings of three-hit ball, giving the White Sox a 4-1 win against the Twins. Fernandez gave up only an unearned run, doubling his '92 victory total.

▶**September 1:** McDowell won No. 21, still leading the majors, as the White Sox beat New York 5-3. Meanwhile, Frank Thomas broke the White Sox's single-season record for home runs, hitting his 38th.

▶**September 11:** Wilson Alvarez threw eight innings of three-hit ball as the White Sox shut down Detroit 3-1. It was Alvarez's fourth win in a row since returning from a stint in the minor leagues. Meanwhile, Frank Thomas was approaching the White Sox record for RBI in a season. He drove in No. 122 and 123 to move into third place past Shoeless Joe Jackson, who amassed 121 in 1920.

▶**September 17:** Alvarez shut out the A's for eight innings to earn his 13th win. He fanned six in the 8-0 victory.

▶**September 20:** Rookie Jason Bere won his fifth consecutive start.

▶**September 23:** No big surprise—McDowell won his 22nd game.

▶**October 3:** The Sox beat Cleveland, 4-0, and finished the season on top of the AL West, with a 94-68 record, eight games ahead of second-place Texas. *League leaders, pitching*—Jack McDowell led the league in victories (22-10) and shutouts (4), was second in innings pitched (256 2/3), and tied for third in complete games (10); Wilson Alvarez was second in ERA (2.95); Scott Radinsky was second in games (73); Alex Fernandez was fourth in ERA (3.13), sixth in victories (18-9), and seventh in innings pitched (247 1/3); Roberto Hernandez was fourth in saves (38) and seventh in games (70). *League leaders, batting*—Frank Thomas was second in RBI (128), third in home runs (41), third in slugging percentage (.607), third in total bases (333), fourth in on-base percentage (.426), fourth in walks (112), sixth in batting (.317), and 10th in runs (106); Lance Johnson led the league in triples (14), was sixth in stolen bases (35), and tenth in batting (.311); Joey Cora was second in triples (13); Robin Ventura was sixth in walks (105).

—by John Hunt, Scott Kauffman, Lisa Winston, Deron Snyder, Matt Young

Team directory

▶**Owner:** Jerry Reinsdorf (chairman), Eddie Einhorn (vice-chairman), and a board of directors

▶**General Manager:** Ron Schueler

▶**Ballpark:**
Comiskey Park
333 West 35th St., Chicago, Ill.
312-924-1000
Capacity 44,321
Parking for 7,000 vehicles, $8; Public transportation available Kids Corner (with photo booth and uniforms for imitation baseball cards), elevators and seating for the handicapped, escalators, ramps, cash station, Hall of Fame

▶**Team publications:**
Program, yearbook, media guide, calendar, team photos, and player photos 312-451-5300

▶**TV, radio broadcast stations:**
WMAQ 670 AM, WGN TV-9, Sports Channel Chicago

▶**Camps and/or clinics:**
Dream Week, Winter 800-888-4376

▶**Spring Training:**
Ed Smith Stadium
Sarasota, Fla.
Capacity 7,500
813-953-3388

CHICAGO WHITE SOX 1993 final stats

Batting	BA	SLG	OB	G	AB	R	H	TB	2B	3B	HR	RBI	BB	SO	SB	CS	E
Martin	.357	.357	.400	8	14	3	5	5	0	0	0	2	1	1	0	0	1
Thomas	.317	.607	.426	153	549	106	174	333	36	0	41	128	112	54	4	2	15
Johnson	.311	.396	.354	147	540	75	168	214	18	14	0	47	36	33	35	7	9
Raines	.306	.480	.401	115	415	75	127	199	16	4	16	54	64	35	21	7	0
Newson	.300	.450	.429	26	40	9	12	18	0	0	2	6	9	12	0	0	0
Guillen	.280	.374	.292	134	457	44	128	171	23	4	4	50	10	41	5	4	16
Burks	.275	.441	.352	146	499	75	137	220	24	4	17	74	60	97	6	9	6
Cora	.268	.349	.351	153	579	95	155	202	15	13	2	51	67	63	20	8	19
Ventura	.262	.433	.379	157	554	85	145	240	27	1	22	94	105	82	1	6	14
LaValliere	.258	.278	.282	37	97	6	25	27	2	0	0	8	4	14	0	1	0
Sax	.235	.303	.283	57	119	20	28	36	5	0	1	8	8	6	7	3	0
Jackson	.232	.433	.289	85	284	32	66	123	9	0	16	45	23	106	0	2	1
Karkovice	.228	.424	.287	128	403	60	92	171	17	1	20	54	29	126	2	2	5
Grebeck	.226	.268	.319	72	190	25	43	51	5	0	1	12	26	26	1	2	5
Bell	.217	.363	.243	102	410	36	89	149	17	2	13	64	13	49	1	1	0
Calderon	.209	.280	.274	82	239	26	50	67	10	2	1	22	21	33	4	2	0
Pasqua	.205	.358	.302	78	176	22	36	63	10	1	5	20	26	51	2	2	3
Denson	.200	.200	.200	4	5	0	1	1	0	0	0	0	0	2	0	0	1
Fisk	.189	.245	.228	25	53	2	10	13	0	0	1	4	2	11	0	1	0
Huff	.182	.295	.321	43	44	4	8	13	2	0	1	6	9	15	1	0	0
Wrona	.125	.125	.125	4	8	0	1	1	0	0	0	1	0	4	0	0	0
Merullo	.050	.050	.050	8	20	1	1	1	0	0	0	0	0	1	0	0	0
Lindsey	.000	.000	.000	2	1	0	0	0	0	0	0	0	0	0	0	0	0

Pitching	W-L	ERA	G	GS	CG	GF	Sho	SV	IP	H	R	ER	HR	BB	SO
Drahman	0-0	0.00	5	0	0	4	0	1	5.1	7	0	0	0	2	3
Howard	1-0	0.00	3	0	0	0	0	0	2.1	2	0	0	0	3	1
DeLeon	0-0	1.74	11	0	0	1	0	0	10.1	5	2	2	2	3	6
Hernandez	3-4	2.29	70	0	0	67	0	38	78.2	66	21	20	6	20	71
Leach	0-0	2.81	14	0	0	8	0	1	16	15	5	5	0	2	3
Alvarez	15-8	2.95	31	31	1	0	1	0	207.2	168	78	68	14	122	155
Fernandez	18-9	3.13	34	34	3	0	1	0	247.1	221	95	86	27	67	169
Pall	2-3	3.22	39	0	0	9	0	1	58.2	62	25	21	5	11	29
McDowell	22-10	3.37	34	34	10	0	4	0	256.2	261	104	96	20	69	158
Bere	12-5	3.47	24	24	1	0	0	0	142.2	109	60	55	12	81	129
Schwarz	2-2	3.71	41	0	0	10	0	0	51	35	21	21	1	38	41
Radinsky	8-2	4.28	73	0	0	24	0	4	54.2	61	33	26	3	19	44
Belcher	3-5	4.40	12	11	1	0	1	0	71.2	64	36	35	8	27	34
Cary	1-0	5.23	16	0	0	4	0	0	20.2	22	12	12	1	11	10
McCaskill	4-8	5.23	30	14	0	6	0	2	113.2	144	71	66	12	36	65
Thigpen	0-0	5.71	25	0	0	11	0	1	34.2	51	25	22	5	12	19
Stieb	1-3	6.04	4	4	0	0	0	0	22.1	27	17	15	1	14	11
Bolton	2-6	7.44	9	8	0	0	0	0	42.1	55	40	35	4	16	17
Ruffcorn	0-2	8.10	3	2	0	1	0	0	10	9	11	9	2	10	2
Jones	0-1	8.59	6	0	0	1	0	0	7.1	14	8	7	2	3	7

1994 preliminary roster

PITCHERS (17)
Wilson Alvarez
Luis Andujar
James Baldwin
Jason Bere
Brian Bohringer
Rodney Bolton
Robert Ellis
Alex Fernandez
Roberto Hernandez
Chris Howard
Kirk McCaskill
Jack McDowell
Scott Radinsky
Scott Ruffcorn
Steve Schrenk
Jeff Schwarz
Larry Thomas

CATCHERS (4)
Ron Karkovice
Mike Lavalliere
Doug Lindsey
Matt Merullo

INFIELDERS (12)
Esteban Beltre
Ron Coomer
Joey Cora
Glenn DiSarcina
Ray Durham
Craig Grebeck
Ozzie Guillen
Paco Martin
Steve Sax
Frank Thomas
Robin Ventura
Brandon Wilson

OUTFIELDERS (5)
Drew Denson
Mike Huff
Lance Johnson
Warren Newson
Dan Pasqua

Games played by position

Player	G	C	1B	2B	3B	SS	OF	DH
Bell	102	0	0	0	0	0	0	102
Burks	146	0	0	0	0	0	146	0
Calderon	82	0	0	0	0	0	47	25
Cora	153	0	0	151	3	0	0	0
Denson	4	0	3	0	0	0	0	0
Fisk	25	25	0	0	0	0	0	0
Grebeck	72	0	0	16	14	46	0	0
Guillen	134	0	0	0	0	133	0	0
Huff	43	0	0	0	0	0	43	0
Jackson	85	0	0	0	0	0	47	36
Johnson	147	0	0	0	0	0	146	0
Karkovice	128	127	0	0	0	0	0	0
LaValliere	37	37	0	0	0	0	0	0
Lindsey	2	2	0	0	0	0	0	0
Martin	8	0	0	5	0	0	0	1
Merullo	8	0	0	0	0	0	0	6
Newson	26	0	0	0	0	0	5	10
Pasqua	78	0	32	0	0	0	37	6
Raines	115	0	0	0	0	0	112	0
Sax	57	0	0	1	0	0	32	21
Thomas	153	0	150	0	0	0	0	4
Ventura	157	0	4	0	155	0	0	0
Wrona	4	4	0	0	0	0	0	0

Sick call: 1993 DL Report

Player	Days on the DL
George Bell	41
Chuck Cary*	127
Mike Dunne	107
Ron Karkovice	16
Terry Leach*	133
Kirk McCaskill	15
Tim Raines	42
Jeff Schwarz	15
Dave Stieb	23

* Two separate terms on Disabled List

Minor League Report

Class AAA: Nashville finished at 80-61, winning the American Association Eastern Division but falling to Iowa in seven games in the league championship. Matt Merullo won the batting title at .332. Paco Martin hit .309 and stole 31 bases. Drew Denson hit 24 homers and drove in 103 runs. Rodney Bolton was 10-1 and won the ERA title at 2.88. Frank Campos was 7-5 with a 3.55 ERA. Brian Drahman had 20 saves. **Class AA:** Birmingham finished at 78-64, winning the second half of the Southern League Western Division, and beat Knoxville in four games for the league title. Jerry Wolak hit .305 with nine homers and 64 RBI. Brandon Wilson (43) and Ray Durham (39) were 1-2 in steals in the league. James Baldwin won the ERA title (8-5, 2.25). Scott Ruffcorn was 9-4 with a 2.73 ERA, striking out a league-best 141 in 135 innings. **Class A:** Sarasota finished at 77-57, second in the Florida State League West Division. Brian Boehringer was 10-4 with a 2.80 ERA. Alan Levine led the league in strikeouts with 129. Kevin Coughlin hit .312. Doug Brady stole 26 bases. Steve Gajkowski had 15 saves. Barry Johnson was 5-0 with an 0.70 ERA in 17 games. . . . South Bend finished at 77-59, winning the Midwest League Northern Division, and beat Clinton in four games in the league finals. Essex Burton led the minor leagues with 74 steals. Carmine Cappuccio hit .306. Jimmy Hurst had 79 RBI. Michael Call had 15 wins. . . . Hickory finished at 52-88, last in the Sally League Northern Division. Eric Richardson stole 42 bases. Juan Thomas had 12 homers. Chris Mader hit .270. Ricky Bennett was 8-7 with a 3.29 ERA. **Short-season:** Sarasota finished at 32-27, second in the Gulf Coast League Western Division. The club led the league in ERA at 2.59 despite not having any of its hurlers in the league's top 10.

Tops in the organization

Batter	Club	Avg	G	AB	R	H	HR	RBI
Merullo, Matt	Nvl	.332	103	352	50	117	12	65
Coomer, Ron	Nvl	.319	128	473	78	151	26	101
Saenz, Olmedo	Bir	.317	95	344	46	109	6	63
Coughlin, Kevin	Nvl	.313	114	422	53	132	2	35
Martin, Norberto	Nvl	.309	137	580	87	179	9	74

Home Runs			Wins		
Coomer, Ron	Nvl	26	Call, Michael	Sbn	15
Denson, Drew	Nvl	24	Johnston, Sean	Sar	14
Cron, Chris	Nvl	22	Pierson, Jason	Sbn	13
Hurst, Jimmy	Sbn	20	Ellis, Robert	Bir	13
Cepicky, Scott	Bir	19	Baldwin, James	Nvl	13

RBI			Saves		
Denson, Drew	Nvl	103	Drahman, Brian	Nvl	20
Coomer, Ron	Nvl	101	Watkins, Jason	Sbn	16
Fryman, Troy	Sar	87	Gajkowski, Steve	Bir	15
Hurst, Jimmy	Sbn	79	Worrell, Steve	Sbn	10
Martin, Norberto	Nvl	74	Several players tied		8

Stolen Bases			Strikeouts		
Burton, Essex	Sbn	74	Bertotti, Mike	Sbn	185
Wilson, Brandon	Bir	43	Ruffcorn, Scott	Nvl	185
Richardson, Eric	Hck	42	Baldwin, James	Nvl	168
Durham, Ray	Bir	39	Ellis, Robert	Bir	156
Martin, Norberto	Nvl	31	Several players tied		129

Pitcher	Club	W-L	ERA	IP	H	BB	SO
Andujar, Luis	Bir	11-6	1.93	126	98	46	124
Baldwin, James	Nvl	13-9	2.38	189	137	79	168
Ruffcorn, Scott	Nvl	11-6	2.75	180	138	60	185
Ellis, Robert	Bir	13-11	2.77	185	149	52	156
Bolton, Rodney	Nvl	10-1	2.88	116	108	37	75

247

Chicago (1901-1993)

Runs: Most, career, all-time

1319	Luke Appling, 1930-1950
1187	Nellie Fox, 1950-1963
1065	Eddie Collins, 1915-1926
893	Minnie Minoso, 1951-1980
791	Luis Aparicio, 1956-1970

Hits: Most, career, all-time

2749	Luke Appling, 1930-1950
2470	Nellie Fox, 1950-1963
2007	Eddie Collins, 1915-1926
1576	Luis Aparicio, 1956-1970
1523	Minnie Minoso, 1951-1980

2B: Most, career, all-time

440	Luke Appling, 1930-1950
335	Nellie Fox, 1950-1963
267	HAROLD BAINES, 1980-1989
266	Eddie Collins, 1915-1926
260	Minnie Minoso, 1951-1980

3B: Most, career, all-time

104	Shano Collins, 1910-1920
104	Nellie Fox, 1950-1963
102	Luke Appling, 1930-1950
102	Eddie Collins, 1915-1926
82	Johnny Mostil, 1918-1929

248

HR: Most, career, all-time

214	CARLTON FISK, 1981-1993
186	HAROLD BAINES, 1980-1989
154	Bill Melton, 1968-1975
140	Ron Kittle, 1982-1991
135	Minnie Minoso, 1951-1980

RBI: Most, career, all-time

1116	Luke Appling, 1930-1950
819	HAROLD BAINES, 1980-1989
808	Minnie Minoso, 1951-1980
804	Eddie Collins, 1915-1926
762	CARLTON FISK, 1981-1993

SB: Most, career, all-time

368	Eddie Collins, 1915-1926
318	Luis Aparicio, 1956-1970
250	Frank Isbell, 1901-1909
206	Fielder Jones, 1901-1908
192	Shano Collins, 1910-1920

BB: Most, career, all-time

1302	Luke Appling, 1930-1950
965	Eddie Collins, 1915-1926
658	Nellie Fox, 1950-1963
658	Minnie Minoso, 1951-1980
638	Ray Schalk, 1912-1928

BA: Highest, career, all-time

.340	Joe Jackson, 1915-1920
.331	Eddie Collins, 1915-1926
.320	FRANK THOMAS, 1990-1993
.317	Zeke Bonura, 1934-1937
.315	Bibb Falk, 1920-1928

Slug avg: Highest, career, all-time

.561	FRANK THOMAS, 1990-1993
.518	Zeke Bonura, 1934-1937
.499	Joe Jackson, 1915-1920
.470	Ron Kittle, 1982-1991
.468	Minnie Minoso, 1951-1980

Games started: Most, career, all-time

484	Ted Lyons, 1923-1946
483	Red Faber, 1914-1933
390	Billy Pierce, 1949-1961
312	Ed Walsh, 1904-1916
301	Doc White, 1903-1913

Saves: Most, career, all-time

201	BOBBY THIGPEN, 1986-1993
98	Hoyt Wilhelm, 1963-1968
75	Terry Forster, 1971-1976
57	Wilbur Wood, 1967-1978
56	Bob James, 1985-1987

Shutouts: Most, career, all-time

57	Ed Walsh, 1904-1916
42	Doc White, 1903-1913
35	Billy Pierce, 1949-1961
29	Red Faber, 1914-1933
28	Eddie Cicotte, 1912-1920

Wins: Most, career, all-time

260	Ted Lyons, 1923-1946
254	Red Faber, 1914-1933
195	Ed Walsh, 1904-1916
186	Billy Pierce, 1949-1961
163	Wilbur Wood, 1967-1978

K: Most, career, all-time

1796	Billy Pierce, 1949-1961
1732	Ed Walsh, 1904-1916
1471	Red Faber, 1914-1933
1332	Wilbur Wood, 1967-1978
1098	Gary Peters, 1959-1969

Win pct: Highest, career, all-time

.648	Lefty Williams, 1916-1920
.644	Virgil Trucks, 1953-1955
.623	JACK McDOWELL, 1987-1993
.616	Jim Kaat, 1973-1975
.615	Juan Pizarro, 1961-1966

ERA: Lowest, career, all-time

1.81	Ed Walsh, 1904-1916
2.18	Frank Smith, 1904-1910
2.25	Eddie Cicotte, 1912-1920
2.30	Jim Scott, 1909-1917
2.30	Doc White, 1903-1913

Runs: Most, season

135	Johnny Mostil, 1925
120	Zeke Bonura, 1936
120	Fielder Jones, 1901
120	Johnny Mostil, 1926
120	Rip Radcliff, 1936

Hits: Most, season

224	Eddie Collins, 1920
218	Joe Jackson, 1920
208	Buck Weaver, 1920
207	Rip Radcliff, 1936
204	Luke Appling, 1936

2B: Most, season

46	FRANK THOMAS, 1992
45	Floyd Robinson, 1962
44	IVAN CALDERON, 1990
44	Chet Lemon, 1979
43	Bibb Falk, 1926
43	Earl Sheely, 1925

3B: Most, season

21	Joe Jackson, 1916
20	Joe Jackson, 1920
18	Jack Fournier, 1915
18	Harry Lord, 1911
18	Minnie Minoso, 1954
18	Carl Reynolds, 1930

HR: Most, season

41	FRANK THOMAS, 1993
37	Dick Allen, 1972
37	CARLTON FISK, 1985
35	Ron Kittle, 1983
33	Bill Melton, 1970
33	Bill Melton, 1971

RBI: Most, season

138	Zeke Bonura, 1936
128	Luke Appling, 1936
128	FRANK THOMAS, 1993
121	Joe Jackson, 1920
119	Al Simmons, 1933

SB: Most, season

77	Rudy Law, 1983
56	Luis Aparicio, 1959
56	Wally Moses, 1943
53	Luis Aparicio, 1961
53	Eddie Collins, 1917

BB: Most, season

138	FRANK THOMAS, 1991	
127	Lu Blue, 1931	
122	Luke Appling, 1935	
122	FRANK THOMAS, 1992	
121	Luke Appling, 1949	

BA: Highest, season

.388	Luke Appling, 1936
.382	Joe Jackson, 1920
.372	Eddie Collins, 1920
.360	Eddie Collins, 1923
.359	Carl Reynolds, 1930

Slug avg: Highest, season

.607	FRANK THOMAS, 1993
.603	Dick Allen, 1972
.589	Joe Jackson, 1920
.584	Carl Reynolds, 1930
.573	Zeke Bonura, 1937

Games started: Most, season

49	Ed Walsh, 1908
49	Wilbur Wood, 1972
48	Wilbur Wood, 1973
46	Ed Walsh, 1907
43	Wilbur Wood, 1975

Saves: Most, season

57	BOBBY THIGPEN, 1990
38	ROBERTO HERNANDEZ, 1993
34	BOBBY THIGPEN, 1988
34	BOBBY THIGPEN, 1989
32	Bob James, 1985

Shutouts: Most, season

11	Ed Walsh, 1908
10	Ed Walsh, 1906
8	Reb Russell, 1913
8	Ed Walsh, 1909
8	Wilbur Wood, 1972

Wins: Most, season

40	Ed Walsh, 1908
29	Eddie Cicotte, 1919
28	Eddie Cicotte, 1917
27	Ed Walsh, 1911
27	Ed Walsh, 1912
27	Doc White, 1907

K: Most, season

269	Ed Walsh, 1908
258	Ed Walsh, 1910
255	Ed Walsh, 1911
254	Ed Walsh, 1912
215	Gary Peters, 1967

Win pct: Highest, season

.842	Sandy Consuegra, 1954
.806	Eddie Cicotte, 1919
.774	Clark Griffith, 1901
.759	Richard Dotson, 1983
.750	Reb Russell, 1917
.750	Bob Shaw, 1959
.750	Monty Stratton, 1937
.750	Doc White, 1906

ERA: Lowest, season

1.27	Ed Walsh, 1910
1.41	Ed Walsh, 1909
1.42	Ed Walsh, 1908
1.52	Doc White, 1906
1.53	Eddie Cicotte, 1917

Most pinch-hit homers, season

3	Ron Northey, 1956
3	John Romano, 1959
3	Oscar Gamble, 1977

Most pinch-hit, homers, career

7	Jerry Hairston, 1973-1989

Most consecutive games, batting safely

27	Luke Appling, 1936
26	Guy Curtwright, 1943
25	LANCE JOHNSON, 1992

Most consecutive scoreless innings

45	Doc White, 1904
39	Billy Pierce, 1953
39	Ed Walsh, 1906
38	Ray Herbert, 1963
37	Ed Walsh, 1910
37	Joel Horlen, 1968

No hit games

Nixey Callahan, Chi vs Det AL, 3-0; September 20, 1902 (1st game).

Frank Smith, Chi at Det AL, 15-0; September 6, 1905 (2nd game).

Frank Smith, Chi vs Phi AL, 1-0; September 20, 1908.

Ed Walsh, Chi vs Bos AL, 5-0; August 27, 1911.

Jim Scott, Chi at Was AL, 0-1; May 14, 1914 (lost on 2 hits in the tenth).

Joe Benz, Chi vs Cle AL, 6-1; May 31, 1914.

Eddie Cicotte, Chi at StL AL, 11-0; April 14, 1917.

Charlie Robertson, Chi at Det AL, 2-0; April 30, 1922 (perfect game).

Ted Lyons, Chi at Bos AL, 6-0; August 21, 1926.

Vern Kennedy, Chi vs Cle AL, 5-0; August 31, 1935.

Bill Dietrich, Chi vs StL AL, 8-0; June 1, 1937.

Bob Keegan, Chi vs Was AL, 6-0; August 20, 1957 (2nd game).

Joe Horlen, Chi vs Det AL, 6-0; September 10, 1967 (1st game).

Joe Cowley, Chi at Cal AL, 7-1; September 19, 1986.

WILSON ALVAREZ, Chi at Bal AL, 7-0; August 11, 1991.

Ed Walsh, five innings, rain, Chi vs NY AL, 8-1; May 26, 1907.

MELIDO PEREZ, six innings, rain, Chi at NY AL, 8-0; July 12, 1990.

ACTIVE PLAYERS in caps.

Texas Rangers

Tom Henke saved 40 games (third in the AL) and struck out 79 batters in 74 1/3 innings.

by Robert Deutsch, *USA TODAY*

1993 Rangers: They stayed in it until the end

At times, the Texas Rangers training room had more players in it than the clubhouse. Yet despite an unbelievable spate of injuries, the Rangers stayed in contention for their first divisional title until fading in late September, settling for a second-place finish behind the Chicago White Sox.

First-year manager Kevin Kennedy often had to throw out a makeshift line-up, always with a depleted rotation and a patchwork bullpen, but still managed to guide the team to an 86-76 record, the best in seven years for the Rangers.

"I really believe we have the talent here to win," Kennedy said. "I said that last fall. I think we proved that, but we do have to push it over the edge, got to find a way to minimize injuries."

The list of injured Kennedy had to deal with reads like a Who's Who on the Rangers roster—Nolan Ryan, Jose Canseco, Julio Franco, Manuel Lee, Charlie Leibrandt. Now add to that Butch Davis, Billy Ripken, Mario Diaz, David Hulse, Jeff Huson, Gary Redus and Craig Lefferts—all expected to make major contributions.

"I've never been on a team with so much hurt and so much heart," said Texas closer Tom Henke, who joined the Rangers as a free agent over the winter after leading the Toronto Blue Jays to their first World Series title.

Kennedy perhaps unwittingly caused the biggest injury of the season, when he called on Canseco to pitch the ninth inning in a loss to Boston June 24. The slugger, acquired from the A's in a trading-deadline deal in 1992, was left with a season-ending torn elbow ligament and a year of rehabilitation.

Yet the offense was even better after Canseco's departure.

Juan Gonzalez (46 homers), Rafael Palmeiro (37) and Dean Palmer (33) combined for 116 home runs, an AL record. The three all had career highs in homers and provided Texas with 90 or more RBI from three players for the first time in club history.

Gonzalez won consecutive AL home run crowns for the first time since Boston's Jim Rice in 1977-78, after hitting 43 in 1992. But he missed 22 games with a bad back as the Rangers made their desperate chase of the White Sox down the stretch.

"If he ever stays healthy for 160, 162 games, he'd hit 50 home runs easily," Kennedy said.

Gonzalez hit .310 with 33 doubles, 105 runs and 118 RBI. Palmeiro, heading into free agency, hit .295 with a team-record 124 runs, 40 doubles and 105 RBI, and added a team-record 113-game errorless streak at first base. Palmer had 96 RBI.

On the mound, Kenny Rogers had a 16-12 season after winning 21 in '92. Roger Pavlik chipped in with a 12-6 record, while Henke's 40 saves were a career-high and a Rangers' club record. But they couldn't make up for disappointing seasons by Ryan (5-5), Leibrandt (9-10) and Lefferts (3-9).

—by Rick Lawes

1994 Rangers: Preview

As the Rangers move into their ballpark right next door to Arlington Stadium, Juan Gonzalez is the type of player who could lead the franchise to its first playoff appearance, given new enthusiasm around the team and an advantageous spot in the reformed AL West. The biggest change is in high-priced first basemen, with Will Clark taking over. Jose Canseco's $5 million salary would be hard to trade and he might have to be used only at DH if his arm hasn't healed enough to play the outfield.

Finally Kennedy says rebuilding the team's pitching is a key, specifically the rotation and middle relief.

—by Rick Lawes

1993 Rangers: Between the lines

▶**April 9:** Nolan Ryan beat Boston 3-1 in the home opener, the beginning of Ryan's final season and the last home opener ever in Arlington Stadium.

▶**April 11:** Kevin Brown came off the disabled list and beat the Red Sox 4-1.

▶**April 17:** Brown pitched a complete-game shutout of the Yankees. He was 2-0 with a 0.54 ERA.

▶**April 18:** Jose Canseco homered, doubled and drove in four runs.

▶**April 24:** Canseco went 3-for-4 with four RBI—a two-run double and a two-run homer.

▶**April 25:** *Milestone*—Canseco became the first player since Ted Williams to drive in 750 runs in his first 1,000 games.

▶**May 1:** Canseco was 3-for-4 with a double and a triple.

▶**May 2:** *Milestone*—Canseco got his 1,000th hit.

▶**May 21:** Juan Gonzalez hit a two-run homer in the ninth inning to tie the score at four, then blasted another two-run shot with two outs in the 10th to give the Rangers a 6-4 win against California. The pair of homers gave Gonzalez 14, tying him with Cleveland's Albert Belle for the AL lead.

▶**May 26:** Canseco found new and exciting ways to play the outfield in the Rangers' 7-6 loss to the Indians. When Cleveland's Carlos Martinez hit a fly ball to the warning track in right, Canseco raced back and appeared to have the ball measured when he peeked at the approaching wall. The ball glanced off Canseco's glove, bounced off his head and over the fence for a home run.

▶**May 29:** Canseco took the mound to work the eighth inning of Texas' 15-1 loss to the Red Sox. He walked the bases loaded before allowing two run-scoring singles.

▶**June 4:** Brown beat the Yankees for the eighth consecutive time.

▶**June 17:** Juan Gonzalez paced an 18-hit attack as the Rangers clobbered the Angels 18-2. Gonzalez had a three-run double in the second inning and hit his second career grand slam in the fifth. His eight RBI was the highest single-game total in the AL since Eddie Murray drove in nine runs Aug. 6, 1985.

▶**July 8:** Kenny Rogers threw a complete-game five-hitter, striking out 10 Toronto batters in a 6-1 Texas win.

▶**July 9:** Rafael Palmeiro drove in all four Texas runs in a 4-2 win against the Blue Jays. He hit a two-run homer and a two-run single.

▶**July 10:** Dean Palmer drove in five runs—three on a homer—as Texas beat the sliding Blue Jays 10-7.

▶**July 16:** Juan Gonzalez had a pair of two-run homers in a 9-6 win against Detroit, becoming the 11th youngest player to hit 100 home runs.

▶**July 19:** In his first start since May 7, Nolan Ryan pitched 5 2/3 innings, allowing two runs on three hits, as Texas defeated Milwaukee 5-3. Ryan got a standing ovation from the sellout crowd as he took the mound in the first inning and another as he left in the sixth.

▶**July 26:** Juan Gonzalez had solo homers in both ends of the Rangers' doubleheader against Kansas City and took over the AL lead with 29.

▶**July 28:** Rafael Palmeiro had a pair of home runs—his 22nd and 23rd—in a 10-3 win in Kansas City. Meanwhile, Ivan Rodriguez had four base hits to tie a club record with eight consecutive hits. The major league record is 12 by Michael Higgins and Walt Dropo.

▶**July 30:** Nolan Ryan was greeted warmly by the crowd but rudely by the A's in Oakland. He allowed four runs in six innings in his last appearance in the Coliseum. Ryan tipped his cap to the crowd, which gave him a standing ovation when he was lifted in the seventh. Ryan was winless against the A's in six starts since his June 11, 1990, no-hitter in Oakland.

▶**July 31:** Palmeiro had three hits, including a two-run homer, and drove in three runs in an 8-2 win in Oakland.

▶**August 1:** Palmeiro hit two homers in a 9-5 loss to the A's. It was his fourth two-homer game of the year.

▶**August 4:** Robin Ventura charged Texas Pitcher Nolan Ryan after the 46-year-old plunked him in the third inning. Ryan walked down the front of the mound, got Ventura in a headlock and delivered six blows to the third baseman's head and face before other players could reach the mound and end the mismatch.

▶**August 10:** Julio Franco hit a grand slam in a 6-3 win against the Angels.

▶**August 15:** A crowd of 60,727 came out to Cleveland Stadium—also in its last season—to say goodbye to Nolan Ryan, who pitched seven innings of two-hit ball to run his record to 5-3.

▶**August 18:** Juan Gonzalez tied Barry Bonds for the majors' lead in homers (36).

▶**August 21:** Ryan left the Rangers game in Baltimore after three innings. He had pulled a muscle in the left side of his rib cage fielding a ground ball.

▶**August 22:** Butch Davis hit the first inside-the-park home run in Camden Yards in the Rangers' 11-4 win, but he paid a price for it—his helmet flew off as he headed for the plate and Harold Reynolds' relay throw hit him in the back of the head.

▶**August 28:** Gonzalez hit three home runs in a 11-1 rout of the Orioles.

▶**September 12:** Ryan returned to action and left to another standing ovation after throwing 102 pitches—the fastest at 96 mph.

▶**September 17:** Ryan made his final appearance at Anaheim Stadium, giving up an unearned run in seven innings of a 2-1 loss to the Angels. He got a standing ovation when he walked to the bullpen to warm up, then gave the fans two curtain calls after he left the game in the eighth inning.

▶**September 22:** Ryan stepped off the mound for the final time in Seattle's Kingdome, where he threw only 28 pitches and failed to retire a batter before leaving the game with a torn ligament in his right elbow.

▶**October 3:** Texas lost to Kansas City, 4-1, but finished second in the AL West. ***League leaders, pitching***—Tom Henke was third in saves (40); Kenny Rogers was seventh in victories (16-10); Kevin Brown was second in complete games (12), tied for second in shutouts (3), and 10th in innings pitched (233). ***League leaders, batting***—Juan Gonzalez led the league in home runs (46) and slugging percentage (.632), was second in total bases (339), and fourth in RBI (118); Rafael Palmiero led the league in runs (124), was tied for third in doubles (40), fourth in total bases (331), fifth in home runs (37), and sixth in slugging percentage (.554); David Hulse was third in triples (10) and tied for ninth in stolen bases (29); Dean Palmer was tied for sixth in home runs (33).

—*by John Hunt, Scott Kauffman, Lisa Winston, Deron Snyder, Matt Young*

Team directory

▶**Owner:** George W. Bush and Edward W. Rose

▶**General Manager:** Thomas A. Grieve

▶**Ballpark:**
The Ballpark in Arlington
1000 Ballpark Way, Arlington, Tex.
817-273-5222
Capacity 48,100; Parking capacity and price TBA; Public transportation status TBA; Approximately 480 wheelchair seats with additional hadicapped seating; restrooms with diaper-changing areas; ramps, escalators and elevators to serve all areas

▶**Team publications:**
On Deck Newsletter, yearbook, *Program Magazine*
817-273-5222

▶**TV, radio broadcast stations:**
WBAP-AM 820, KTVT-TV 11, Home Sports Entertainment

▶**Camps and/or clinics:**
Texas Ranger Coaches Clinic, June,
817-273-5222

▶**Spring Training:**
Charlotte County Stadium
Port Charlotte, Fla.
Capacity 6,026
813-625-9500

TEXAS RANGERS 1993 final stats

Batting	BA	SLG	OB	G	AB	R	H	TB	2B	3B	HR	RBI	BB	SO	SB	CS	E
Balboni	.600	.600	.600	2	5	0	3	3	0	0	0	0	0	2	0	0	0
James	.355	.677	.412	8	31	5	11	21	1	0	3	7	3	6	0	0	0
Shave	.319	.362	.306	17	47	3	15	17	2	0	0	7	0	8	1	3	3
Gonzalez	.310	.632	.368	140	536	105	166	339	33	1	46	118	37	99	4	1	4
Palmeiro	.295	.554	.371	160	597	124	176	331	40	2	37	105	73	85	22	3	5
Hulse	.290	.369	.333	114	407	71	118	150	9	10	1	29	26	57	29	9	3
Franco	.289	.438	.360	144	532	85	154	233	31	3	14	84	62	95	9	3	0
Redus	.288	.459	.351	77	222	28	64	102	12	4	6	31	23	35	4	4	3
Ducey	.282	.494	.351	27	85	15	24	42	6	3	2	9	10	17	2	3	0
Diaz	.273	.361	.297	71	205	24	56	74	10	1	2	24	8	13	1	0	3
Rodriguez	.273	.412	.315	137	473	56	129	195	28	4	10	66	29	70	8	7	8
Peltier	.269	.344	.352	65	160	23	43	55	7	1	1	17	20	27	0	4	4
Strange	.256	.360	.318	145	484	58	124	174	29	0	7	60	43	69	6	4	13
Canseco	.255	.455	.308	60	231	30	59	105	14	1	10	46	16	62	6	6	3
Davis	.245	.415	.273	62	159	24	39	66	10	4	3	20	5	28	3	1	4
Palmer	.245	.503	.321	148	519	88	127	261	31	2	33	96	53	154	11	10	29
Petralli	.241	.301	.348	59	133	16	32	40	5	0	1	13	22	17	2	0	2
Russell	.227	.409	.292	18	22	1	5	9	1	0	1	3	2	10	0	0	0
Lee	.220	.259	.300	73	205	31	45	53	3	1	1	12	22	39	2	4	10
Dascenzo	.199	.288	.239	76	146	20	29	42	5	1	2	10	8	22	2	0	1
Harris	.197	.263	.253	40	76	10	15	20	2	0	1	8	5	18	0	1	3
Ripken	.189	.220	.270	50	132	12	25	29	4	0	0	11	11	19	0	2	2
Huson	.133	.200	.133	23	45	3	6	9	1	1	0	2	0	10	0	0	6
Gil	.123	.123	.194	22	57	3	7	7	0	0	0	2	5	22	1	2	5

Pitching	W-L	ERA	G	GS	CG	GF	Sho	SV	IP	H	R	ER	HR	BB	SO
Henke	5-5	2.91	66	0	0	60	0	40	74.1	55	25	24	7	27	79
Nelson	0-5	3.12	52	0	0	22	0	5	60.2	60	28	21	3	24	35
Pavlik	12-6	3.41	26	26	2	0	0	0	166.1	151	67	63	18	80	131
Brown	15-12	3.59	34	34	12	0	3	0	233	228	105	93	14	74	142
Bronkey	1-1	4.00	21	0	0	6	0	1	36	39	20	16	4	11	18
Rogers	16-10	4.10	35	33	5	0	0	0	208.1	210	108	95	18	71	140
Carpenter	4-1	4.22	27	0	0	8	0	1	32	35	15	15	4	12	27
Whiteside	2-1	4.32	60	0	0	10	0	1	73	78	37	35	7	23	39
Leibrandt	9-10	4.55	26	26	1	0	0	0	150.1	169	84	76	15	45	89
Burns	0-4	4.57	25	5	0	8	0	0	65	63	36	33	6	32	35
Bohanon	4-4	4.76	36	8	0	4	0	0	92.2	107	54	49	8	46	45
Patterson	2-4	4.78	52	0	0	29	0	1	52.2	59	28	28	8	11	46
Ryan	5-5	4.88	13	13	0	0	0	0	66.1	54	47	36	5	40	46
Schooler	3-0	5.55	17	0	0	0	0	0	24.1	30	17	15	3	10	16
Dreyer	3-3	5.71	10	6	0	1	0	0	41	48	26	26	7	20	23
Reed	1-0	5.87	3	0	0	0	0	0	7.2	12	5	5	1	2	5
Lefferts	3-9	6.05	52	8	0	9	0	0	83.1	102	57	56	17	28	58
Nen	1-1	6.35	9	3	0	3	0	0	22.2	28	17	16	1	26	12

1994 preliminary roster

PITCHERS (16)
Jeff Bronkey
Kevin Brown
Duff Brumley
Terry Burrows
Cris Carpenter
Steve Dreyer
Hector Fajardo
Tom Henke
Rick Honeycutt
James Hurst
Darren Oliver
Roger Pavlik
Kenny Rogers
Julio Santana
Dan Smith

Matt Whiteside

CATCHERS (1)
Ivan Rodriguez

INFIELDERS (11)
Will Clark
Jeff Frye
Benji Gil
Rusty Greer
Jeff Huson
Manuel Lee
Dean Palmer
Gary Redus
Jon Shave
Doug Strange

Desi Wilson

OUTFIELDERS (8)
Jose Canseco
Rob Ducey
Juan Gonzalez
Donald Harris
David Hulse
Chris James
Terrell Lowery
Dan Peltier

Games played by position

Player	G	C	1B	2B	3B	SS	OF	DH
Balboni	2	0	0	0	0	0	0	2
Canseco	60	0	0	0	0	0	49	9
Dascenzo	76	0	0	0	0	0	68	2
Davis	62	0	0	0	0	0	44	11
Diaz	71	0	1	0	12	57	0	0
Ducey	27	0	0	0	0	0	26	0
Franco	144	0	0	0	0	0	0	140
Gil	22	0	0	0	0	22	0	0
Gonzalez	140	0	0	0	0	0	129	10
Harris	40	0	0	0	0	0	38	3
Hulse	114	0	0	0	0	0	112	2
Huson	23	0	0	5	2	12	0	2
James	8	0	0	0	0	0	7	0
Lee	73	0	0	0	0	72	0	1
Palmeiro	160	0	160	0	0	0	0	0
Palmer	148	0	0	0	148	1	0	0
Peltier	65	0	5	0	0	0	55	0
Petralli	59	39	0	1	1	0	0	2
Redus	77	0	5	1	0	0	61	1
Ripken	50	0	0	34	1	18	0	0
Rodriguez	137	134	0	0	0	0	0	1
Russell	18	11	1	0	1	0	1	0
Shave	17	0	0	8	0	9	0	0
Strange	145	0	0	135	9	1	0	0

Sick call: 1993 DL Report

Player	Days on the DL
Brian Bohanon	21
Kevin Brown	6
Jose Canseco	102
Butch Davis	15
Hector Fajardo	148
Jeff Frye	182
David Hulse	18
Jeff Huson**	122
Manuel Lee*	80
Craig Lefferts	15
Charlie Leibrandt*	36
Barry Manuel	76
Rob Maurer	182
Robb Nen	35
Geno Petralli	39
Gary Redus	17
Bill Ripken*	87
Nolan Ryan**	115
Dan Smith*	76

* Two separate terms on Disabled List
** Three separate terms on Disabled List

Minor League Report

Class AAA: Oklahoma City finished at 52-90, last in the American Association Western Division. Rob Ducey hit .303 with 17 homers and 56 RBI. Steve Balboni hit 36 homers and drove in 108 runs. Rick Reed was 12-7 with a 3.32 ERA. **Class AA:** Tulsa finished at 66-69, third in the Texas League Eastern Division. Cris Colon hit .300 with 11 homers and 47 RBI. Trey McCoy led the league with 29 homers and 95 RBI. Duff Brumley was 7-7 with a 2.93 ERA and 121 strikeouts in 111 innings. Rick Helling was 12-8 with a 3.60 ERA and 188 strikeouts to lead the league. **Class A:** Charlotte finished at 84-49, winning the second half of the Florida State League West Division but falling to Clearwater in three games in the playoffs. Richard Aurilia hit .309 with five homers and 56 RBI. Todd Guggiana and Mike Edwards each had 79 RBI. Desi Wilson stole 29 bases. John Dettmer was 16-3 with a 2.15 ERA and won 12 in a row down the stretch. Dave Geeve was 11-8 with a 2.85 ERA. Lance Schuermann had 16 saves. . . . Charleston, S.C. finished at 65-77, fifth in the Sally League Southern Division. Kerry Lacy had 36 saves. Scott Malone hit .289 with 12 homers, 71 RBI and 20 steals. Guillermo Mercedes had 41 stolen bases. Scott Eyre was 11-7 with a 3.45 ERA and 154 strikeouts. **Short-season:** Erie finished at 36-40, fourth in the New York-Penn League Stadler Division. Wes Shook hit .321 with a league-best 17 homers and 52 RBI. Jeffrey Davis had 13 saves. Pete Hartmann struck out 98. . . . Charlotte finished at 40-20, winning the Gulf Coast League Western Division and sweeping the Astros in two games for the league title. Larry Ephan won the batting crown at .350 and led the league in RBI with 39. Mike Bell hit .317 with three homers and 34 RBI. Ed Diaz hit .305. Leland Macon stole 29 bases while Andreaus Lewis swiped 24. Julio Santana had seven saves.

Tops in the organization

Batter	Club	Avg	G	AB	R	H	HR	RBI
Aurilia, Richard	Chl	.309	122	440	80	136	5	56
Wilson, Desi	Chl	.305	131	511	83	156	3	70
Ducey, Rob	Okc	.303	105	389	68	118	17	56
Colon, Cris	Tul	.300	124	490	63	147	11	47
McCoy, Trey	Okc	.290	133	448	78	130	32	106

Home Runs			Wins		
Balboni, Steve	Okc	36	Dettmer, John	Chl	16
Mccoy, Trey	Okc	32	Helling, Ricky	Okc	13
Gil, Benji	Tul	17	Reed, Rick	Okc	12
Ducey, Rob	Okc	17	Several players tied		11
Greer, Rusty	Okc	16	**Saves**		

RBI			Saves		
			Lacy, Kerry	Chl	38
Balboni, Steve	Okc	108	Moody, Ritchie	Tul	16
McCoy, Trey	Okc	106	Schuermann, L.	Chl	16
Guggiana, Todd	Chl	79	Heredia, Wilson	Chl	15
Edwards, Mike	Chl	79	Bronkey, Jeff	Okc	14
Malone, Scott	CSc	71	**Strikeouts**		

Stolen Bases			Strikeouts		
			Helling, Ricky	Okc	205
Mercedes, G.	CSc	41	Eyre, Scott	CSc	154
Wilson, Desi	Chl	29	Martinez, Ramiro	CSc	129
Frias, Hanley	CSc	27	Dettmer, John	Chl	128
Lowery, Terrell	Tul	24	Brumley, Duff	Tul	121
Several players tied		20			

Pitcher	Club	W-L	ERA	IP	H	BB	SO
Dettmer, John	Chl	16-3	2.15	163	132	33	128
Geeve, Dave	Chl	11-8	2.85	133	141	19	80
Manning, David	CSc	6-7	3.03	116	112	39	83
Dreyer, Steve	Okc	6-8	3.19	138	134	39	86
Reed, Rick	Okc	12-7	3.32	163	159	16	79

Texas (1972-1993), includes Washington (1961-1971)

Runs: Most, career, all-time

631	Toby Harrah, 1969-1986	
571	RUBEN SIERRA, 1986-1992	
544	Frank Howard, 1965-1972	
482	Jim Sundberg, 1974-1989	
471	Buddy Bell, 1979-1989	
471	RAFAEL PALMEIRO, 1989-1993	

Hits: Most, career, all-time

1180	Jim Sundberg, 1974-1989
1174	Toby Harrah, 1969-1986
1141	Frank Howard, 1965-1972
1132	RUBEN SIERRA, 1986-1992
1060	Buddy Bell, 1979-1989

2B: Most, career, all-time

226	RUBEN SIERRA, 1986-1992
200	Jim Sundberg, 1974-1989
197	Buddy Bell, 1979-1989
187	Toby Harrah, 1969-1986
174	RAFAEL PALMEIRO, 1989-1993

3B: Most, career, all-time

43	RUBEN SIERRA, 1986-1992
30	Chuck Hinton, 1961-1964
27	Ed Brinkman, 1961-1975
27	Jim Sundberg, 1974-1989
24	Ed Stroud, 1967-1970

HR: Most, career, all-time

246	Frank Howard, 1965-1972
153	RUBEN SIERRA, 1986-1992
149	Larry Parrish, 1982-1988
124	Toby Harrah, 1969-1986
124	PETE INCAVIGLIA, 1986-1990

RBI: Most, career, all-time

701	Frank Howard, 1965-1972
656	RUBEN SIERRA, 1986-1992
568	Toby Harrah, 1969-1986
522	Larry Parrish, 1982-1988
499	Buddy Bell, 1979-1989

SB: Most, career, all-time

161	Bump Wills, 1977-1981
153	Toby Harrah, 1969-1986
144	Dave Nelson, 1970-1975
115	Oddibe McDowell, 1985-1988
98	JULIO FRANCO, 1989-1993

BB: Most, career, all-time

708	Toby Harrah, 1969-1986
575	Frank Howard, 1965-1972
544	Jim Sundberg, 1974-1989
435	Mike Hargrove, 1974-1978
404	PETE O'BRIEN, 1982-1988

BA: Highest, career, all-time

.319	Al Oliver, 1978-1981
.307	JULIO FRANCO, 1989-1993
.303	Mickey Rivers, 1979-1984
.296	RAFAEL PALMEIRO, 1989-1993
.293	Mike Hargrove, 1974-1978

Slug avg: Highest, career, all-time

.503	Frank Howard, 1965-1972
.474	RAFAEL PALMEIRO, 1989-1993
.471	RUBEN SIERRA, 1986-1992
.466	Al Oliver, 1978-1981
.459	PETE INCAVIGLIA, 1986-1990

Games started: Most, career, all-time

313	CHARLIE HOUGH, 1980-1990
190	Fergie Jenkins, 1974-1981
182	BOBBY WITT, 1986-1992
161	KEVIN BROWN, 1986-1993
155	Dick Bosman, 1966-1973

Saves: Most, career, all-time

111	JEFF RUSSELL, 1985-1992
83	Ron Kline, 1963-1966
64	Darold Knowles, 1967-1977
43	TOM HENKE, 1982-1993
37	Jim Kern, 1979-1981

Shutouts: Most, career, all-time

17	Fergie Jenkins, 1974-1981
12	Gaylord Perry, 1975-1980
11	CHARLIE HOUGH, 1980-1990
9	Dick Bosman, 1966-1973
8	Jim Bibby, 1973-1984

Wins: Most, career, all-time

139	CHARLIE HOUGH, 1980-1990
93	Fergie Jenkins, 1974-1981
71	KEVIN BROWN, 1986-1993
68	BOBBY WITT, 1986-1992
66	JOSE GUZMAN, 1985-1992

K: Most, career, all-time

1452	CHARLIE HOUGH, 1980-1990
1051	BOBBY WITT, 1986-1992
939	NOLAN RYAN, 1989-1993
895	Fergie Jenkins, 1974-1981
715	JOSE GUZMAN, 1985-1992

Win pct: Highest, career, all-time

.567	NOLAN RYAN, 1989-1993
.564	Fergie Jenkins, 1974-1981
.563	KEVIN BROWN, 1986-1993
.538	KENNY ROGERS, 1989-1993
.538	Doc Medich, 1978-1982

ERA: Lowest, career, all-time

3.26	Gaylord Perry, 1975-1980
3.35	Dick Bosman, 1966-1973
3.41	Jon Matlack, 1978-1983
3.43	NOLAN RYAN, 1989-1993
3.51	Joe Coleman, 1965-1970

Runs: Most, season

124	RAFAEL PALMEIRO, 1993
115	RAFAEL PALMEIRO, 1991
111	Frank Howard, 1969
110	RUBEN SIERRA, 1991
108	JULIO FRANCO, 1991

Hits: Most, season

210	Mickey Rivers, 1980
209	Al Oliver, 1980
203	RAFAEL PALMEIRO, 1991
203	RUBEN SIERRA, 1991
201	JULIO FRANCO, 1991

2B: Most, season

49	RAFAEL PALMEIRO, 1991
44	RUBEN SIERRA, 1991
43	Al Oliver, 1980
42	Buddy Bell, 1979
42	Larry Parrish, 1984

3B: Most, season

14	RUBEN SIERRA, 1989
12	Chuck Hinton, 1963
10	DAVID HULSE, 1993
10	RUBEN SIERRA, 1986
10	Ed Stroud, 1968

HR: Most, season

48	Frank Howard, 1969
46	JUAN GONZALEZ, 1993
44	Frank Howard, 1968
44	Frank Howard, 1970
43	JUAN GONZALEZ, 1992

RBI: Most, season

126	Frank Howard, 1970
119	RUBEN SIERRA, 1989
118	Jeff Burroughs, 1974
118	JUAN GONZALEZ, 1993
117	Al Oliver, 1980

SB: Most, season

52	Bump Wills, 1978
51	Dave Nelson, 1972
45	CECIL ESPY, 1989
44	Bill Sample, 1983
43	Dave Nelson, 1973

BB: Most, season

132	Frank Howard, 1970
113	Toby Harrah, 1985
109	Toby Harrah, 1977
107	Mike Hargrove, 1978
103	Mike Hargrove, 1977

BA: Highest, season

.341	JULIO FRANCO, 1991
.333	Mickey Rivers, 1980
.329	Buddy Bell, 1980
.324	Al Oliver, 1978
.323	Al Oliver, 1979

Slug avg: Highest, season

.632	JUAN GONZALEZ, 1993
.574	Frank Howard, 1969
.554	RAFAEL PALMEIRO, 1993
.552	Frank Howard, 1968
.546	Frank Howard, 1970

Games started: Most, season

41	Jim Bibby, 1974
41	Fergie Jenkins, 1974
40	CHARLIE HOUGH, 1987
37	Fergie Jenkins, 1975
37	Fergie Jenkins, 1979

Saves: Most, season

40	TOM HENKE, 1993
38	JEFF RUSSELL, 1989
30	JEFF RUSSELL, 1991
29	Jim Kern, 1979
29	Ron Kline, 1965

Shutouts: Most, season

6	Bert Blyleven, 1976
6	Fergie Jenkins, 1974
5	Jim Bibby, 1974
5	Bert Blyleven, 1977
4	Joe Coleman, 1969
4	Fergie Jenkins, 1975
4	Fergie Jenkins, 1978
4	Camilo Pascual, 1968
4	Gaylord Perry, 1975
4	Gaylord Perry, 1977

Wins: Most, season

25	Fergie Jenkins, 1974
21	KEVIN BROWN, 1992
19	Jim Bibby, 1974
18	CHARLIE HOUGH, 1987
18	Fergie Jenkins, 1978

K: Most, season

301	NOLAN RYAN, 1989
232	NOLAN RYAN, 1990
225	Fergie Jenkins, 1974
223	CHARLIE HOUGH, 1987
221	BOBBY WITT, 1990

Win pct: Highest, season

.692	Fergie Jenkins, 1978
.676	Fergie Jenkins, 1974
.656	KEVIN BROWN, 1992
.630	CHARLIE HOUGH, 1986
.630	BOBBY WITT, 1990

ERA: Lowest, season

2.19	Dick Bosman, 1969
2.27	Jon Matlack, 1978
2.40	Dick Donovan, 1961
2.42	RICK HONEYCUTT, 1983
2.60	Pete Richert, 1965

Most pinch-hit homers, season

3	Don Lock, Was-1966
3	Brant Alyea, Was-1969
3	Rick Reichardt, Was-1970
3	Tom McCraw, Was-1971
3	Darrell Porter, 1987

Most pinch-hit, homers, career

6	Brant Alyea, Was-1965-1969
6	GENO PETRALLI, 1985-1992

Most consecutive games, batting safely

24	Mickey Rivers, 1980
22	Jim Sundberg, 1978

Most consecutive scoreless innings

36	CHARLIE HOUGH, 1983

No hit games

Jim Bibby, Tex at Oak AL, 6-0; July 20, 1973.

Bert Blyleven, Tex at Cal AL, 6-0; September 22, 1977.

NOLAN RYAN, Tex at Oak AL, 5-0; June 11, 1990.

NOLAN RYAN, Tex vs Tor AL, 3-0; May 1, 1991.

ACTIVE PLAYERS in caps. Leaders in the franchise's current location is included. If not in the top five, leader's rank is listed in parenthesis; asterisk (*) indicates player is not in top 25.

Kansas City Royals

Jeff Montgomery saved 45 games (tied for the league-lead), finishing 63 of the 69 games he entered.

by Russell Beeker, *Baseball Weekly*

1993 Royals: Pitching, defense wasn't enough

The Royals were on the path to oblivion when manager Hal McRae threw a temper-tantrum in a postgame press conference and sparked his team out of its doldrums. But he couldn't step up to the plate and lend his legendary hitting exploits to the Royals' offense. They finished third in the AL West with an 84-78 record, a figure that seemed a long way away when McRae started throwing around phones and tape recorders.

Despite good pitching and defense—things that are supposed to win pennants—the Royals were never in contention for the division title.

"If the guys can only score some runs . . ." was McRae's mantra during the season. The Royals scored 675 runs all season, an average of 4.2 per game—more than a run under league average. The top run producer was 40-year-old George Brett, who retired at the end of the season to join the team's front office.

The heart of the offense was supposed to come from a trio of former Mets, obtained for two-time Cy Young winner Bret Saberhagen before '92 season. Kevin McReynolds was supposed to be the power in the lineup—a 25-homer, 85-RBI man in the Big Apple—but he had just 42 RBI in '93 and the Royals headed into the offseason looking to deal him. Keith Miller was touted as a utility man who could play 150 games at about five different positions—but he's been hurt both seasons in Kansas City, managing just 108 at-bats in '93. And Gregg Jefferies was sent across the state to the Cardinals for switch-hitter Felix Jose before the '93 season. Jose developed a mysterious shoulder malady that prevented him from batting from the right side—his best side. That meant McRae had to pinch-hit for his cleanup hitter when the other team brought in a left-hander to face Jose. Eventually McRae moved Jose up in the order, then Jose committed base-running gaffes that seemed to have McRae running out of patience as the season wound down.

The defense and pitching, though, were the strong suits. Shortstop Greg Gagne and second baseman Jose "Chico" Lind were amazing in the middle infield. (Gagne was a free agent and Lind was stolen from the Bucs in their fire sale.) Add center fielder Brian McRae, and the Royals defensive strength up the middle is among the best in the game.

McRae also had his best season offensively, hitting better than .300 most of the year before falling off to .282 at season's end. But he also played a full season and might have simply worn out after 682 at-bats.

On the mound, Kevin Appier won 18 games after missing the final month of '92 with a sore shoulder. Until losing two of his last three starts, he was a candidate for the AL Cy Young award; still, he led the league with a 2.56 ERA. Along with David Cone, Appier gave the Royals a solid top two starters.

There wasn't much help in the bullpen, beyond closer Jeff Montgomery. McRae searched all year for what he called his "bridge" to Montgomery, who tied Dan Quisenberry's club record with 45 saves.

—by Rick Lawes

1994 Royals: Preview

The biggest problem is the need for a big bat in the middle of the lineup. Yet GM Herk Robinson and a five-person board of directors are faced with trying cut a $40 million payroll while suffering a major loss in television revenue—they are already operating in one of the smallest TV markets in the game.

Bob Hamelin, who has shown a big bat in the minors, has a chance to be the thumper, especially with the DH void created by George Brett's retirement. The other most likely new, full-time face in the lineup is third baseman Phil Hiatt, with great promise and a taste of the majors from '93.

—by Rick Lawes

1993 Royals: Between the lines

▶**April 9:** *Milestone*—George Brett passed Al Kaline for 16th place on the all-time career hit list.

▶**April 10:** On the 20th anniversary of the opening of Royals' Stadium, Kansas City remained the last major league team without a win.

▶**May 11:** The Royals had three consecutive pinch-hits during a two—run seventh inning at Cleveland. Kevin McReynolds (single), Hubie Brooks (single) and Mike McFarlane (RBI double) delivered the 7-6 victory.

▶**May 13:** *Milestone*—Brett, two days shy of his 40th birthday, had an RBI single and his 300th career home run as the Royals beat the Indians 7-3. He became only the sixth player with 3,000 hits and 300 home runs, joining Hank Aaron, Al Kaline, Willie Mays, Stan Musial and Carl Yastrzemski.

▶**May 20:** David Cone couldn't shake the hard-luck label. After nine starts, he had an enviable 2.70 ERA, but his record stood at 1-5. He shut out Oakland for seven innings—fanning eight batters—and departed with a 1-0 lead, but the Royals' bullpen allowed the A's to scratch out a run in the eighth inning, killing any chance Cone had for his second win of the season. The Royals had scored a grand total of 19 runs in Cone's nine starts.

▶**May 21:** Rookie Phil Hiatt ended Randy Johnson's 20-inning scoreless streak with a two-run homer that proved to be the difference in Kansas City's 2-1 win over Seattle.

▶**May 27:** Kansas City crawled into the AL West race. They took a three-game set from the White Sox, and won eight of 10 games, putting them squarely in fourth place, one game behind Chicago and California, who shared the lead.

▶**June 1:** The Royals played in their league-high 24th one-run game, and upped their league-best record in the category to 16-8. Not coincidentally, reliever Jeff Montgomery picked up his league-leading 17th save.

▶**June 2:** The Royals pulled into a tie for first place with the Angels as they beat the Red Sox 7-2.

▶**June 3:** KC beat the Brewers to take sole possession of first place in the AL West—the first time since June 8, 1987.

▶**June 23:** California's Kelly Gruber homered and drove in four runs as the Angels beat Kansas City 8-7 to drop the Royals out of first place.

▶**June 24:** Home plate umpire Gary Cederstrom lost track of the count to Kevin McReynolds in the fifth inning of Kansas City's 7-1 win against the Angels. McReynolds took strike two and was promptly called out by Cederstrom. The Angels left the field and the Royals began to warm up before McReynolds and manager Hal McRae pointed out the mistake. Cederstrom then watched in embarrassment as McReynolds grounded out to truly end the inning.

▶**July 9:** Chris Haney was tagged for seven of Detroit's eight first-inning runs at Ewing Kauffman Stadium. His ERA for the game was 162.00.

▶**July 11:** Brian McRae had four hits, including a two-run homer, in Kansas City's 6-2 win against Detroit. He extended his hitting streak to 14 games, entering the All-Star break at .316.

▶**July 17:** McRae hit a game-winning, inside-the-park home run against the Blue Jays.

▶**July 23:** Wally Joyner hit two home runs—including his fourth career grand slam—to help the Royals beat Detroit 7-6. He hit a solo shot to lead off the fourth inning and went deep with the bases loaded in the seventh. His six RBI tied a career high.

▶**July 24:** Brett celebrated the 10th anniversary of his infamous pine tar homer by going deep twice in a 6-3 defeat of Detroit. This time, both homers counted.

▶**July 26:** Brett had the 56th four-hit game of his career as Kansas City beat Texas 12-3 in the first game of a double-header.

▶**July 30:** David Cone shut out the Indians on five hits. It was his first shutout of the year; in fact, Kansas City had been shut out on one hit in each of Cone's last two starts.

▶**August 3:** After hitting a two-run homer in the fifth inning of a 3-2 loss to California, Brian McRae left the game with tightness in his left hamstring. He was listed as day-to-day.

▶**August 9:** Jeff Montgomery notched his 35th save.

▶**August 19:** Cone tossed seven shutout innings, fanning a season-high 11 Twins in a 4-2 win.

▶**August 29:** *Milestone*—Brett stole second base, making him only the third player—along with Willie Mays and Hank Aaron—to amass 3,000 hits, 300 homers, and 200 stolen bases.

▶**September 18:** Kevin Appier threw a three-hitter to gain a 1-0 win in Seattle, and ran his scoreless streak to 28 1/3 innings, lowering his AL-leading ERA from 2.73 to 2.62. It was his seventh career shutout.

▶**September 20:** Cone pitched his fifth complete game of the season, allowing only two first-inning runs, but it wasn't good enough as Oakland's Todd Van Poppel outdueled him for a 2-1 victory. It was Cone's first loss since Aug. 14—a span of seven starts—and the ninth time in his 32 starts that Kansas City batters failed to score more than two runs.

▶**September 26:** George Brett spent the final days of his remarkable career just as he had spent all the the rest—hitting the ball and winning games for his team. One day after announcing that '93 would be his final season, Brett hit a solo home run in the 10th inning to beat California 9-8. He had already hit a three-run homer in the fourth and doubled in a run in the first.

▶**October 3:** Kansas City finished their season by beating the second-place Texas Rangers, 4-1, leaving the Royals in third place in the AL West, 10 games behind the White Sox. *League leaders, pitching*—Kevin Appier led the league in ERA (2.56), was fifth in victories (18-8), seventh in strikeouts (180), and

eighth in innnings pitched (238 2/3); Jeff Montgomery was tied for the league lead in saves (45) and was ninth in games (69); David Cone was fourth in strikeouts (191), fifth in innings pitched (254) and tenth in ERA (3.33). *League leaders, batting*—Felix Jose was eighth in stolen bases (30); Brian McRae was tied for fourth in triples (9) and tied for ninth in hits (177).

—by John Hunt, Scott Kauffman, Lisa Winston, Deron Snyder, Matt Young

Team directory

▶**Owner:** David Glass/Kauffman family
▶**General Manager:** Herk Robinson
▶**Ballpark:**
Ewing Kauffman Stadium
1 Royal Way, Kansas City, Mo.
816-921-2200
Capacity 40,625
Pay parking lot; $5
Public transportation available
Wheelchair section and ramps, handicapped accessible
▶**Team publications:**
Yearbook, scorecard, media guide
▶**TV, radio broadcast stations:**
WDAF 610 AM, KSMO Channel 4
▶**Spring Training:**
Baseball City Stadium
Baseball City, Fla.
Capacity 7,000 (1,000 on grass)
813-424-7211

KANSAS CITY ROYALS 1993 final stats

Batting	BA	SLG	OB	G	AB	R	H	TB	2B	3B	HR	RBI	BB	SO	SB	CS	E
Howard	.333	.417	.370	15	24	5	8	10	0	1	0	2	2	5	1	0	3
Gwynn	.300	.387	.354	103	287	36	86	111	14	4	1	25	24	34	0	1	1
Joyner	.292	.467	.375	141	497	83	145	232	36	3	15	65	66	67	5	9	7
Brooks	.286	.375	.331	75	168	14	48	63	12	0	1	24	11	27	0	1	2
McRae	.282	.413	.325	153	627	78	177	259	28	9	12	69	37	105	23	14	7
Gagne	.280	.406	.319	159	540	66	151	219	32	3	10	57	33	93	10	12	10
Macfarlane	.273	.497	.360	117	388	55	106	193	27	0	20	67	40	83	2	5	11
Koslofski	.269	.385	.387	15	26	4	7	10	0	0	1	2	4	5	0	1	0
Brett	.266	.434	.312	145	560	69	149	243	31	3	19	75	39	67	7	5	0
Wilson	.265	.347	.357	21	49	6	13	17	1	0	1	3	7	6	1	1	1
Pulliam	.258	.387	.292	27	62	7	16	24	5	0	1	6	2	14	0	0	1
Mayne	.254	.337	.317	71	205	22	52	69	9	1	2	22	18	31	3	2	2
Jose	.253	.349	.303	149	499	64	126	174	24	3	6	43	36	95	31	13	7
Lind	.248	.288	.271	136	431	33	107	124	13	2	0	37	13	36	3	2	4
McReynolds	.245	.425	.316	110	351	44	86	149	22	4	11	42	37	56	2	2	2
Gaetti	.245	.438	.300	102	331	40	81	145	20	1	14	50	21	87	1	3	7
Hamelin	.224	.408	.309	16	49	2	11	20	3	0	2	5	6	15	0	0	2
Rossy	.221	.337	.302	46	86	10	19	29	4	0	2	12	9	11	0	0	1
Hiatt	.218	.366	.285	81	238	30	52	87	12	1	7	36	16	82	6	3	16
Miller	.167	.194	.229	37	108	9	18	21	3	0	0	3	8	19	3	1	6
Wilkerson	.143	.143	.172	12	28	1	4	4	0	0	0	0	1	6	2	0	0
Santovenia	.125	.125	.222	4	8	0	1	1	0	0	0	0	1	2	0	0	0
Shumpert	.100	.100	.250	8	10	0	1	1`	0	0	0	0	2	2	1	0	0

Pitching	W-L	ERA	G	GS	CG	GF	Sho	SV	IP	H	R	ER	HR	BB	SO
Montgomery	7-5	2.27	69	0	0	63	0	45	87.1	65	22	22	3	23	66
Appier	18-8	2.56	34	34	5	0	1	0	238.2	183	74	68	8	81	186
Cadaret	1-1	2.93	13	0	0	3	0	0	15.1	14	5	5	0	7	2
Cone	11-14	3.33	34	34	6	0	1	0	254	205	102	94	20	114	191
Brewer	2-2	3.46	46	0	0	14	0	0	39	31	16	15	6	20	28
Gordon	12-6	3.58	48	14	2	18	0	1	155.2	125	65	62	11	77	143
Pichardo	7-8	4.04	30	25	2	2	0	0	165	183	85	74	10	53	70
Magnante	1-2	4.08	7	6	0	0	0	0	35.1	37	16	16	3	11	16
Habyan	2-1	4.15	48	0	0	23	0	1	56.1	59	27	26	6	20	39
Belinda	1-1	4.28	23	0	0	7	0	0	27.1	30	13	13	2	6	25
Gubicza	5-8	4.66	49	6	0	12	0	2	104.1	128	61	54	2	43	80
Meacham	2-2	5.57	15	0	0	11	0	0	21	31	15	13	2	5	13
Sampen	2-2	5.89	18	0	0	3	0	0	18.1	25	12	12	1	9	9
Haney	9-9	6.02	23	23	1	0	1	0	124	141	87	83	13	53	65
Gardner	4-6	6.19	17	16	0	0	0	0	91.2	92	65	63	17	36	54
DiPino	1-1	6.89	11	0	0	5	0	0	15.2	21	12	12	2	6	5
Rasmussen	1-2	7.45	9	4	0	3	0	0	29	40	25	24	4	14	12

1994 preliminary roster

PITCHERS (15)
Kevin Appier
Stan Belinda
Billy Brewer
Enrique Burgos
David Cone
Mark Gardner
Tom Gordon
Jeff Granger
John Habyan
Chris Haney
Doug Harris
Mike Magnante
Rusty Meacham
Jeff Montgomery
Hipolito Pichardo

CATCHERS (4)
Lance Jennings
Mike Macfarlane
Brent Mayne
Chad Strickland

INFIELDERS (13)
Gary Caraballo
Greg Gagne
Shane Halter
Bob Hamelin
Phil Hiatt
David Howard
Wally Joyner
Jose Lind
Keith Miller
Joe Randa
Terry Shumpert

Joe Vitiello
Craig Wilson

OUTFIELDERS (7)
Darren Burton
Chris Gwynn
Felix Jose
Kevin Koslofski
Brian McRae
Kevin McReynolds
Les Norman

Games played by position

Player	G	C	1B	2B	3B	SS	OF	DH
Brett	145	0	0	0	0	0	0	140
Brooks	75	0	3	0	0	0	40	9
Gaetti	102	0	24	0	79	0	0	6
Gagne	159	0	0	0	0	159	0	0
Gwynn	103	0	1	0	0	0	83	5
Hamelin	16	0	15	0	0	0	0	0
Hiatt	81	0	0	0	70	0	0	9
Howard	15	0	0	7	2	3	1	0
Jose	149	0	0	0	0	0	144	1
Joyner	141	0	140	0	0	0	0	0
Koslofski	15	0	0	0	0	0	13	1
Lind	136	0	0	136	0	0	0	0
Macfarlane	117	114	0	0	0	0	0	0
Mayne	71	68	0	0	0	0	0	1
McRae	153	0	0	0	0	0	153	0
McReynolds	110	0	0	0	0	0	104	1
Miller	37	0	0	3	21	0	4	6
Pulliam	27	0	0	0	0	0	26	0
Rossy	46	0	0	24	16	11	0	0
Santovenia	4	4	0	0	0	0	0	0
Shumpert	8	0	0	8	0	0	0	0
Wilkerson	12	0	0	10	0	4	0	0
Wilson	21	0	0	1	15	0	1	0

Sick call: 1993 DL Report

Player	Days on the DL
Mike Boddicker@	21
Frank Dipino	31
Mark Gardner	51
David Howard*	92
Kevin McReynolds	23
Rusty Meacham*	171
Keith Miller*	94
Hipolito Pichardo	18
Dennis Rasmussen*	60
Rico Rossy	15
Curtis Wilkerson	140

Two separate terms on Disabled List
@ Mike Boddicker was on the DL both in Kansas City and in Milwaukee.

Minor League Report

Class AAA: Omaha finished at 70-72, third in the American Association Western Division. Terry Shumpert hit .300 with 14 homers and 59 RBI and led the league with 36 steals. Jose Mota had 27 steals. Bob Hamelin hit 24 homers. Keith Brown had 13 wins. **Class AA:** Memphis finished at 63-77, last in the Southern League Western Division. Adam Casillas hit .304. Joe Randa hit .295 with 11 homers and 72 RBI. Les Norman had 81 RBI. Mike Fyhrie was 11-4 with a 3.56 ERA. **Class A:** Wilmington finished at 74-65, winning the first half of the Carolina League Northern Division, but fell to Winston-Salem in four games of the league finals. Darren Burton had 30 stolen bases. Jon Lieber was 9-3 with a 2.67 ERA. He walked just nine in 115 innings. Brian Harrison had 13 wins. Jeff Smith had 24 saves. . . . Rockford finished at 78-54, third in the Midwest League Northern Division, but fell to South Bend in the playoffs. Johnny Damon had 59 stolen bases. Steve Murphy hit .292. Rod Myers had 49 stolen bases. Chris Sheehan was 9-5 with a 2.85 ERA. **Short-season:** Eugene finished at 40-36, second in the Northwest League South Division. Braxton Hickman hit .299 with five homers and 30 RBI. Jeremy Carr stole 30 bases. Luke Oglesby stole 26 bases. Kris Ralston was 7-3 with a 2.74 ERA. . . . Fort Myers finished at 29-30, fifth in the Gulf Coast League Western Division. Carlos Mendez hit .313 with four homers and 27 RBI. Glendon Rusch was 4-2 with a 1.60 ERA. Kevin Hodges was 7-2 with a 2.03 ERA.

Tops in the organization

Batter	Club	Avg	G	AB	R	H	HR	RBI
Casillas, Adam	Mem	.304	126	450	53	137	4	50
Shumpert, Terry	Oma	.300	111	413	70	124	14	59
Randa, Joe	Mem	.295	131	505	74	149	11	72
Murphy, Steve	Rkf	.292	110	349	56	102	2	49
Tucker, Mike	Mem	.292	133	483	80	141	15	79

Home Runs			Wins		
Hamelin, Bob	Oma	29	Fyhrie, Mike	Mem	14
Walker, Hugh	Wil	21	Harrison, Brian	Wil	13
Rohrmeier, Dan	Oma	17	Brown, Keith	Oma	13
Norman, Les	Mem	17	Gross, John	Wil	11
McGinnis, Russ	Oma	16	Bunch, Melvin	Wil	11

RBI			Saves		
Hamelin, Bob	Oma	84	Smith, Jeff	Wil	24
Norman, Les	Mem	81	Dorlarque, Aaron	Rkf	16
Tucker, Mike	Mem	79	Eddy, Chris	Wil	14
Randa, Joe	Mem	72	Burgos, Enrique	Oma	9
Walker, Hugh	Wil	71	Sampen, Bill	Oma	8

Stolen Bases			Strikeouts		
Damon, Johnny	Rkf	59	Toth, Robert	Wil	129
Myers, Rod	Rkf	49	Bunch, Melvin	Wil	125
Shumpert, Terry	Oma	36	Evans, Bart	Rkf	120
Burton, Darren	Wil	30	Bovee, Mike	Rkf	111
Murphy, Steve	Rkf	29	Myers, Rodney	Mem	107

Pitcher	Club	W-L	ERA	IP	H	BB	SO
Bunch, Melvin	Wil	11- 7	2.21	151	131	32	125
Lieber, Jon	Wil	9- 3	2.67	115	125	9	89
Sheehan, Chris	Rkf	9- 5	2.85	117	97	22	99
Toth, Robert	Wil	8- 7	2.91	152	129	40	129
Harrison, Brian	Wil	13- 6	3.28	173	168	38	98

263

Kansas City (1969-1993)

Runs: Most, career, all-time

1583	GEORGE BRETT, 1973-1993	
1074	Amos Otis, 1970-1983	
1060	WILLIE WILSON, 1976-1990	
912	Frank White, 1973-1990	
873	Hal McRae, 1973-1987	

Hits: Most, career, all-time

3154	GEORGE BRETT, 1973-1993
2006	Frank White, 1973-1990
1977	Amos Otis, 1970-1983
1968	WILLIE WILSON, 1976-1990
1924	Hal McRae, 1973-1987

2B: Most, career, all-time

665	GEORGE BRETT, 1973-1993
449	Hal McRae, 1973-1987
407	Frank White, 1973-1990
365	Amos Otis, 1970-1983
241	WILLIE WILSON, 1976-1990

3B: Most, career, all-time

137	GEORGE BRETT, 1973-1993
133	WILLIE WILSON, 1976-1990
65	Amos Otis, 1970-1983
63	Hal McRae, 1973-1987
58	Frank White, 1973-1990

264

HR: Most, career, all-time

317	GEORGE BRETT, 1973-1993
193	Amos Otis, 1970-1983
169	Hal McRae, 1973-1987
160	Frank White, 1973-1990
143	John Mayberry, 1972-1977

RBI: Most, career, all-time

1595	GEORGE BRETT, 1973-1993
1012	Hal McRae, 1973-1987
992	Amos Otis, 1970-1983
886	Frank White, 1973-1990
552	John Mayberry, 1972-1977

SB: Most, career, all-time

612	WILLIE WILSON, 1976-1990
340	Amos Otis, 1970-1983
336	Freddie Patek, 1971-1979
201	GEORGE BRETT, 1973-1993
178	Frank White, 1973-1990

BB: Most, career, all-time

1096	GEORGE BRETT, 1973-1993
739	Amos Otis, 1970-1983
616	Hal McRae, 1973-1987
561	John Mayberry, 1972-1977
413	Freddie Patek, 1971-1979

BA: Highest, career, all-time

.305	GEORGE BRETT, 1973-1993
.294	KEVIN SEITZER, 1986-1991
.293	Hal McRae, 1973-1987
.290	DANNY TARTABULL, 1987-1991
.289	WILLIE WILSON, 1976-1990

Slug avg: Highest, career, all-time

.518	DANNY TARTABULL, 1987-1991
.487	GEORGE BRETT, 1973-1993
.480	BO JACKSON, 1986-1990
.469	Willie Aikens, 1980-1983
.459	STEVE BALBONI, 1984-1988

Games started: Most, career, all-time

392	Paul Splittorff, 1970-1984
302	Dennis Leonard, 1974-1986
253	MARK GUBICZA, 1984-1993
226	BRET SABERHAGEN, 1984-1991
219	Larry Gura, 1976-1985

Saves: Most, career, all-time

238	Dan Quisenberry, 1979-1988
160	JEFF MONTGOMERY, 1988-1993
58	Doug Bird, 1973-1978
49	STEVE FARR, 1985-1990
40	Ted Abernathy, 1970-1972

Shutouts: Most, career, all-time

23	Dennis Leonard, 1974-1986
17	Paul Splittorff, 1970-1984
14	Larry Gura, 1976-1985
14	BRET SABERHAGEN, 1984-1991
13	MARK GUBICZA, 1984-1993

Wins: Most, career, all-time

166	Paul Splittorff, 1970-1984
144	Dennis Leonard, 1974-1986
111	Larry Gura, 1976-1985
110	BRET SABERHAGEN, 1984-1991
109	MARK GUBICZA, 1984-1993

K: Most, career, all-time

1323	Dennis Leonard, 1974-1986
1171	MARK GUBICZA, 1984-1993
1093	BRET SABERHAGEN, 1984-1991
1057	Paul Splittorff, 1970-1984
754	TOM GORDON, 1988-1993

Win pct: Highest, career, all-time

.608	KEVIN APPIER, 1989-1993
.593	Al Fitzmorris, 1969-1976
.587	Larry Gura, 1976-1985
.585	BRET SABERHAGEN, 1984-1991
.576	Doug Bird, 1973-1978

ERA: Lowest, career, all-time

2.55	Dan Quisenberry, 1979-1988
2.95	KEVIN APPIER, 1989-1993
3.21	BRET SABERHAGEN, 1984-1991
3.46	Al Fitzmorris, 1969-1976
3.48	Marty Pattin, 1974-1980

Runs: Most, season

133	WILLIE WILSON, 1980
119	GEORGE BRETT, 1979
113	WILLIE WILSON, 1979
108	GEORGE BRETT, 1985
105	GEORGE BRETT, 1977
105	KEVIN SEITZER, 1987

Hits: Most, season

230	WILLIE WILSON, 1980
215	GEORGE BRETT, 1976
212	GEORGE BRETT, 1979
207	KEVIN SEITZER, 1987
195	GEORGE BRETT, 1975

2B: Most, season

54	Hal McRae, 1977
46	Hal McRae, 1982
45	GEORGE BRETT, 1978
45	GEORGE BRETT, 1990
45	Frank White, 1982

3B: Most, season

21	WILLIE WILSON, 1985
20	GEORGE BRETT, 1979
15	WILLIE WILSON, 1980
15	WILLIE WILSON, 1982
15	WILLIE WILSON, 1987

HR: Most, season

36	STEVE BALBONI, 1985
34	John Mayberry, 1975
34	DANNY TARTABULL, 1987
32	BO JACKSON, 1989
31	DANNY TARTABULL, 1991

RBI: Most, season

133	Hal McRae, 1982
118	GEORGE BRETT, 1980
112	GEORGE BRETT, 1985
112	Al Cowens, 1977
112	Darrell Porter, 1979

SB: Most, season

83	WILLIE WILSON, 1979	
79	WILLIE WILSON, 1980	
59	WILLIE WILSON, 1983	
59	WILLIE WILSON, 1987	
53	Freddie Patek, 1977	

BB: Most, season

122	John Mayberry, 1973
121	Darrell Porter, 1979
119	John Mayberry, 1975
103	GEORGE BRETT, 1985
103	Paul Schaal, 1971

BA: Highest, season

.390	GEORGE BRETT, 1980
.335	GEORGE BRETT, 1985
.333	GEORGE BRETT, 1976
.332	Hal McRae, 1976
.332	WILLIE WILSON, 1982

Slug avg: Highest, season

.664	GEORGE BRETT, 1980
.593	DANNY TARTABULL, 1991
.585	GEORGE BRETT, 1985
.563	GEORGE BRETT, 1979
.563	GEORGE BRETT, 1983

Games started: Most, season

40	Dennis Leonard, 1978
38	Steve Busby, 1974
38	Dennis Leonard, 1980
38	Paul Splittorff, 1973
38	Paul Splittorff, 1978

Saves: Most, season

45	JEFF MONTGOMERY, 1993
45	Dan Quisenberry, 1983
44	Dan Quisenberry, 1984
39	JEFF MONTGOMERY, 1992
37	Dan Quisenberry, 1985

Shutouts: Most, season

6	Roger Nelson, 1972
5	Dennis Leonard, 1977
5	Dennis Leonard, 1979
4	Bill Butler, 1969
4	Dick Drago, 1971
4	Al Fitzmorris, 1974
4	MARK GUBICZA, 1988
4	Larry Gura, 1980
4	Dennis Leonard, 1978
4	BRET SABERHAGEN, 1987
4	BRET SABERHAGEN, 1989

Wins: Most, season

23	BRET SABERHAGEN, 1989
22	Steve Busby, 1974
21	Dennis Leonard, 1978
20	MARK GUBICZA, 1988
20	Dennis Leonard, 1977
20	Dennis Leonard, 1980
20	BRET SABERHAGEN, 1985
20	Paul Splittorff, 1973

K: Most, season

244	Dennis Leonard, 1977
206	Bob Johnson, 1970
198	Steve Busby, 1974
193	BRET SABERHAGEN, 1989
191	DAVID CONE, 1993

Win pct: Highest, season

.800	Larry Gura, 1978
.793	BRET SABERHAGEN, 1989
.769	BRET SABERHAGEN, 1985
.727	Paul Splittorff, 1977
.714	MARK GUBICZA, 1988

ERA: Lowest, season

2.08	Roger Nelson, 1972
2.16	BRET SABERHAGEN, 1989
2.46	KEVIN APPIER, 1992
2.56	KEVIN APPIER, 1993
2.69	CHARLIE LEIBRANDT, 1985

Most pinch-hit homers, season

2	Hal McRae, 1986
2	Carmelo Martinez, 1991

Most pinch-hit, homers, career

2	Chuck Harrison, 1969-1971
2	Bob Oliver, 1969-1972
2	Amos Otis, 1970-1983
2	Hal McRae, 1973-1987
2	STEVE BALBONI, 1984-1988
2	JIM EISENREICH, 1987-1991
2	Carmelo Martinez, 1991

Most consecutive games, batting safely

30	GEORGE BRETT, 1980
22	BRIAN McRAE, 1991

Most consecutive scoreless innings

31	BRET SABERHAGEN, 1989

No hit games

Steve Busby, KC at Det AL, 3-0; April 16, 1973.

Steve Busby, KC at Mil AL, 2-0; June 19, 1974.

Jim Colborn, KC vs Tex AL, 6-0; May 14, 1977.

BRET SABERHAGEN, KC vs Chi AL, 7-0; August 26, 1991.

ACTIVE PLAYERS in caps.

Seattle Mariners

Left hander Randy Johnson led the majors in strikeouts (308) and won 19 games (second in the AL).

by Russell Becker, Baseball Weekly

1993 Mariners: Johnson and Griffey shone

Randy Johnson and Ken Griffey Jr. single-handedly carried the Seattle Mariners to a near team-record number of wins. The 82 wins were one victory shy of the 83 they had under Jim Lefebvre in 1991, best in the 17-year history of the franchise.

The two received considerable backing in the AL Cy Young and MVP balloting and most people know them only by reputation, because Seattle is still somewhat of a baseball wasteland on national television with its late starts.

Johnson equaled Mark Langston's club record of 19 victories set in 1987, and struck out 308 batters—a whopping 116 more than his nearest pursuer, Toronto's Juan Guzman.

In Griffey, the Mariners have a three-time Gold Glove center fielder who had a team-record 45 home runs, a career-best 109 RBI and a .309 batting average. Griffey, 24 in November, tied a major-league record in 1993 by hitting home runs in eight consecutive games.

Manager Lou Piniella was willing to trade Johnson just before the trading deadline in August. The Mariners came close to swapping their ace pitcher to Toronto and the Yankees. Now, he would like to see the Japanese-controlled ownership group try to sign both superstars.

The Mariners have said they're going to lose about $15 million this season. And next season, clubs are expected to have $8 million less in national television money.

The team has also said they're going to have to trim their player payroll of $32 million this season. They haven't said by how much.

Privately, Piniella has said he can get the job done with a budget of $28 million or $27 million next season. If it's lower than that, it will be a lot tougher to field a competitive team.

This year, injuries cost the services of third baseman Edgar Martinez, the 1992 AL batting champion, and first baseman Tino Martinez, as well as pitchers Dave Fleming, Chris Bosio and Norm Charlton. Piniella had to work with players named Mike Blowers, Brian Turang, Greg Litton and Ted Power.

"Let's hope the numbers are right so we can get all our people re-signed and at the same time fill in a couple of our holes," he said. "We hope to improve our ball club a little bit over the winter."

Still, the injuries, the losing tradition in Seattle and the financial difficulties couldn't put out the fire inside Piniella.

"Looking at it, I think it's been very positive," he said. "I think it's gone very well."

—by Rick Lawes

1994 Mariners: Preview

Lou Piniella performed a near miracle in 1993, guiding the Seattle Mariners to just the second winning season in franchise history. But given the team's financial status, a bigger miracle could be keeping the team there in 1994—paying Ken Griffey and Randy Johnson what they're now worth.

Griffey signed a four-year, $24 million contract before the '93 season—a real bargain. Johnson, 30, wants a four-year contract to stay in Seattle. It probably will take $20 million to sign him to an extension—and he has a lot of leverage because he can become a free agent after the '94 season.

The question is, can the Mariners afford not to give Johnson whatever he wants? He is, after all, the top strikeout pitcher in the majors, a 6-foot-10 left-hander who dominates AL hitters like Nolan Ryan did in the 1970s and Roger Clemens did in the 1980s. If they can't sign him, they may have to face him.

—by Rick Lawes

1993 Mariners: Between the lines

▶**April 21:** Randy Johnson pitched his sixth career shutout and struck out eight for a league-high total of 37 Ks.

▶**April 22:** *No-hitter!* Chris Bosio tossed 1993's first no-hitter, a 7-0 gem against the Red Sox in the Kingdome. After he walked the first two batters, he did not allow another Boston batter to reach base. It was the Mariners' second no-hitter; the first was Randy Johnson's in 1990.

▶**April 27:** Bosio broke his collarbone in a collision and was expected to be sidelined for up to two months.

▶**May 3:** Erik Hanson extended his scoreless streak to 22 1/3 innings.

▶**May 8:** Hanson gave up a run, but came away with a 7-2 win against the Twins. He retired 19 of the last 21 batters he faced, and was 5-0 in 1993 after leading the majors with 17 losses in 1992.

▶**May 16:** Johnson carried a perfect game into the eighth inning, then walked Oakland's Kevin Seitzer with one out. The no-hitter was still on until the ninth, when Lance Blankenship slapped a single to right. Johnson had 14 strikeouts in the shutout.

▶**May 17:** Mike Blowers tied a major league record, hitting a grand slam for the second consecutive game. It was the 14th time a player had managed back-to-back slams.

▶**May 23:** *Milestone*—Skipper Lou Piniella got his 500th win, a 10-7 triumph at Royals Stadium. His lifetime record, including the Yankees and Reds, stood at 500-447.

▶**June 5:** Ken Griffey Jr. had four hits, including a ninth-inning homer, and drove in all three Mariner runs in a 5-3 loss to Baltimore.

▶**June 6:** The Orioles and Mariners had the longest and bloodiest brawl in years during the seventh inning of the M's 5-2 loss at Camden Yards. The fracus started with Bill Haselman charging the mound and ended with seven players and Lou Piniella getting the

thumb. Orioles Jeff Tackett and Mark Williamson had facial cuts, while Mariner starter Chris Bosio reinjured his collarbone.

▶**June 9:** Randy Johnson fanned 11 batters in eight innings and the Mariners beat Milwaukee 6-1. It was Johnson's seventh win.

▶**June 12:** Dave Fleming, returning to form, threw a three-hit shutout against California for his first win of the year. He threw only 93 pitches and faced 28 batters, one more than the minimum, in the 2-0 win.

▶**June 20:** Ken Griffey Jr. hit a pair of two-run homers in a 13-2 win against Texas. It was the third time in 1993 and the eighth time in his career that Griffey had hit multiple homers.

▶**June 23:** Jay Buhner became the first player to hit for the cycle in Mariners' history during Seattle's 8-7 defeat of Oakland. Buhner hit a grand slam in the first inning, doubled in the third and singled in the fifth before hitting a three-bagger in the 14th to complete the cycle. He also scored the winning run of the game.

▶**June 28:** Dave Fleming allowed just one run on five hits to beat the Twins 4-1. It was his third consecutive win.

▶**June 30:** Randy Johnson earned his 10th win with another 10-strikeout game. He had fanned 10 or more batters in five consecutive starts.

▶**July 1:** Erik Hanson threw a complete-game eight-hitter to break his six-game losing streak.

▶**July 2:** Jay Buhner had four hits, including his 16th home run, and drove in four runs but Seattle fell short, 9-8, against the Red Sox.

▶**July 21:** Buhner collected five hits in a 10-3 win at Yankee Stadium.

▶**July 24:** Griffey homered in his fifth consecutive game, tying a team record set by Richie Zisk in 1981.

▶**July 25:** Griffey's fifth-inning home run broke the Mariners' record and left him just two short of the ML record held by Dale Long and Don Mattingly.

▶**July 27:** Griffey homered in his seventh consecutive game—the fifth grand slam and 116th home run of the 23-year-old's career.

▶**July 28:** Griffey hit his eighth home run in as many games, tying the record held by Long and Mattingly.

▶**July 29:** Seattle sold a club-record 30,220 game-day tickets, but Griffey failed to homer, settling for the tie.

▶**August 3:** Randy Johnson increased his league-leading strikeout total to 199.

▶**August 8:** Griffey finally made an error—his AL record for consecutive chances without an error ended at 573. His last error had been back in 1992.

▶**August 10:** Griffey broke Seattle's single-season home run mark with his 33rd four-bagger of the year.

▶**August 14:** Johnson struck out 10 Angels in eight innings and picked up a 7-2 win, bringing his record to 12-8.

▶**August 20:** Johnson recorded his seventh complete game of the year and raised his strikeout total to 226.

▶**August 26:** Griffey hit two home runs for the second consecutive game, giving him 10 such games in his career, five in '93, most in the majors.

▶**September 22:** Johnson pitched a three-hitter for his career-high seventh consecutive win and third shutout of '93. He also fanned 10 or more for the 13th time in 1993.

▶**September 26:** *Milestone*—Johnson became the 12th pitcher to strike out 300 batters in a season. He raised his season total to 301, becoming the first pitcher to top 300 since Nolan Ryan fanned 301 in 1989.

▶**October 1:** Johnson tied a Seattle record with his 19th win, and struck out seven to bring his total to 308, 10th best in AL history.

▶**October 3:** Seattle lost to Minnesota 7-2, but finished fourth in the AL West.
League leaders, pitching— Randy Johnson led the league (and the majors) in strikeouts (308), was second in victories (19-8), tied for third in complete games (10), tied for second in shutouts (3), fourth in innings pitched (255 1/3), and seventh in ERA (3.20). *League*

leaders, batting— Ken Griffey Jr. led the league in total bases (359), was second in homers (45) and slugging percentage (.617), tied for sixth in runs (113), on-base percentage (.408) and doubles (38), eighth in walks (96), and tenth in RBI (109); Jay Buhner was seventh in walks (100).
—*by John Hunt, Scott Kauffman, Lisa Winston, Deron Snyder, Matt Young*

Team directory

▶**Owner:** Baseball Club of Seattle
▶**General Manager:** Woody Woodward
▶**Ballpark:**
The Kingdome
201 South King St., Seattle, Wash.
206-628-3555
Capacity 58,879
Public transportation available
Parking for 4,000 vehicles;
Family and wheelchair sections,
birthday package, anniversary
package
▶**Team publications:**
Mariners Magazine, scorecard, media guide
206-628-3555
▶**TV, radio broadcast stations:**
KIRO-AM 710, KSTW-TV Channel 11
▶**Spring Training:**
Peoria Sports Complex
Peoria, Ariz.
Capacity 7,000
602-784-4444

SEATTLE MARINERS 1993 final stats

Batting	BA	SLG	OB	G	AB	R	H	TB	2B	3B	HR	RBI	BB	SO	SB	CS	E
Griffey	.309	.617	.408	156	582	113	180	359	38	3	45	109	96	91	17	9	3
Litton	.299	.448	.366	72	174	25	52	78	17	0	3	25	18	30	0	1	0
Amaral	.290	.367	.348	110	373	53	108	137	24	1	1	44	33	54	19	11	10
Blowers	.280	.475	.357	127	379	55	106	180	23	3	15	57	44	98	1	5	15
Buhner	.272	.476	.379	158	563	91	153	268	28	3	27	98	100	144	2	5	6
T.Martinez	.265	.456	.343	109	408	48	108	186	25	1	17	60	45	56	0	3	3
Magadan	.259	.320	.356	71	228	27	59	73	11	0	1	21	36	33	2	0	5
Valle	.258	.395	.354	135	423	48	109	167	19	0	13	63	48	56	1	0	5
O'Brien	.257	.390	.335	72	210	30	54	82	7	0	7	27	26	21	0	0	1
Haselman	.255	.423	.316	58	137	21	35	58	8	0	5	16	12	19	2	1	2
Vizquel	.255	.298	.319	158	560	68	143	167	14	2	2	31	50	71	12	14	15
Boone	.251	.443	.301	76	271	31	68	120	12	2	12	38	17	52	2	3	3
Turang	.250	.343	.340	40	140	22	35	48	11	1	0	7	17	20	6	2	1
E.Martinez	.237	.378	.366	42	135	20	32	51	7	0	4	13	28	19	0	0	2
Newfield	.227	.318	.257	22	66	5	15	21	3	0	1	7	2	8	0	1	0
Vina	.222	.267	.327	24	45	5	10	12	2	0	0	2	4	3	6	0	0
Sasser	.218	.309	.274	83	188	18	41	58	10	2	1	21	15	30	1	0	3
Felder	.211	.269	.262	109	342	31	72	92	7	5	1	20	22	34	15	9	2
Howitt	.211	.355	.250	32	76	6	16	27	3	1	2	8	4	18	0	0	0
Cotto	.190	.257	.213	54	105	10	20	27	1	0	2	7	2	22	5	4	1
Pirkl	.174	.304	.174	7	23	1	4	7	0	0	1	4	0	4	0	0	0
Tinsley	.158	.368	.238	11	19	2	3	7	1	0	1	2	2	9	0	0	1
Backman	.138	.138	.167	10	29	2	4	4	0	0	0	0	1	8	0	0	3
Sheets	.118	.176	.250	11	17	0	2	3	1	0	0	1	2	1	0	0	0
Howard	.000	.000	.000	4	1	0	0	0	0	0	0	0	0	0	0	0	0

Pitching	W-L	ERA	G	GS	CG	GF	Sho	SV	IP	H	R	ER	HR	BB	SO
Ontiveros	0-2	1.00	14	0	0	8	0	0	18	18	3	2	0	6	13
Charlton	1-3	2.34	34	0	0	29	0	18	34.2	22	12	9	4	17	48
Salkeld	0-0	2.51	3	2	0	0	0	0	14.1	13	4	4	0	4	13
Ayrault	1-1	3.20	14	0	0	6	0	0	19.2	18	8	7	1	6	7
Johnson	19-8	3.24	35	34	10	1	3	1	255.1	185	97	92	22	99	308
Shinall	0-0	3.38	1	0	0	0	0	0	2.2	4	1	1	1	2	0
Bosio	9-9	3.45	29	24	3	2	1	1	164.1	138	75	63	14	59	119
Hanson	11-12	3.47	31	30	7	0	0	0	215	215	91	83	17	60	163
Holman	1-3	3.72	19	0	0	9	0	3	36.1	27	17	15	1	16	17
Powell	0-0	4.15	33	2	0	7	0	0	47.2	42	22	22	7	24	32
Nelson	5-3	4.35	71	0	0	13	0	1	60	57	30	29	5	34	61
Fleming	12-5	4.36	26	26	1	0	1	0	167.1	189	84	81	15	67	75
DeLucia	3-6	4.64	30	1	0	11	0	0	42.2	46	24	22	5	23	48
Leary	11-9	5.05	33	27	0	6	0	0	169.1	202	104	95	21	58	68
Converse	1-3	5.31	4	4	0	0	0	0	20.1	23	12	12	0	14	10
Power	2-4	5.36	45	0	0	24	0	13	45.1	57	28	27	3	17	27
Cummings	0-6	6.02	10	8	1	0	0	0	46.1	59	34	31	6	16	19
King	0-1	6.17	13	0	0	3	0	0	11.2	9	8	8	3	4	8
Plantenberg	0-0	6.52	20	0	0	4	0	1	9.2	11	7	7	0	12	3
Henry	2-1	6.67	31	1	0	15	0	2	54	56	40	40	6	35	35
Swan	3-3	9.15	23	0	0	6	0	0	19.2	25	20	20	2	18	10
Hampton	1-3	9.53	13	3	0	2	0	1	17	28	20	18	3	17	8

1994 preliminary roster

PITCHERS (19)
Bobby Ayala
Chris Bosio
Travis Buckley
Craig Clayton
Jim Converse
John Cummings
Jeff Darwin
Rich DeLucia
Dave Fleming
Mike Hampton
Reggie Harris
Brad Holman
Randy Johnson
Kevin King
Jeff Nelson
Erik Plantenberg
Ted Power
Roger Salkeld
David Wainhouse

CATCHERS (4)
Bill Haselman
Chris Howard
Mackey Sasser
Dan Wilson

INFIELDERS (11)
Rich Amaral
Mike Blowers
Greg Litton
Anthony Manahan
Edgar Martinez
Tino Martinez
Marc Newfield
Greg Pirkl
Alex Rodriguez
Ruben Santana
Omar Vizquel

OUTFIELDERS (5)
Jay Buhner
Mike Felder
Ken Griffey
Lee Tinsley
Brian Turang

Games played by position

Player	G	C	1B	2B	3B	SS	OF	DH
Amaral	110	0	3	77	19	14	0	9
Backman	10	0	0	1	9	0	0	0
Blowers	127	1	1	0	117	0	2	3
Boone	76	0	0	74	0	0	0	1
Buhner	158	0	0	0	0	0	148	10
Cotto	54	0	0	0	0	0	34	15
Felder	109	0	0	0	2	0	95	6
Griffey	156	0	1	0	0	0	139	19
Haselman	58	49	0	0	0	0	2	4
Howard	4	4	0	0	0	0	0	0
Howitt	32	0	0	0	0	0	29	2
Litton	72	0	13	17	7	5	22	12
Magadan	71	0	41	0	27	0	0	2
T. Martinez	109	0	103	0	0	0	0	6
E. Martinez	42	0	0	0	16	0	0	24
Newfield	22	0	0	0	0	0	5	15
O'Brien	72	0	9	0	0	0	1	52
Pirkl	7	0	5	0	0	0	0	2
Sasser	83	4	1	0	0	0	37	19
Sheets	11	0	0	0	0	0	1	5
Tinsley	11	0	0	0	0	0	6	2
Turang	40	0	0	1	2	0	38	1
Valle	135	135	0	0	0	0	0	0
Vina	24	0	0	16	0	4	0	2
Vizquel	158	0	0	0	0	155	0	2

Sick call: 1993 DL Report

Player	Days on the DL
Rich Amaral	15
Wally Backman	16
Chris Bosio*	48
Norm Charlton*	72
Rich Delucia	24
Mike Felder	20
Dave Fleming	48
Dwayne Henry	30
Brad Holman	19
Brian Holman	182
Tino Martinez	55
Edgar Martinez**	126
Mackey Sasser	16
Russ Swan	42
Kerry Woodson	182

* Two separate terms on Disabled List
** Three separate terms on Disabled List

Minor League Report

Class AAA: Calgary finished at 68-72, fourth in the Pacific Coast League Northern Division. Brian Turang hit .324 with eight homers and 54 RBI. Greg Pirkl had 94 RBI. Mike Walker was 13-8 with a 4.03 ERA. **Class AA:** Jacksonville finished at 59-81, last in the Southern League Eastern Division. Ruben Santana hit .301 with 21 homers and 84 RBI. Marc Newfield hit 19 homers. **Class A:** Riverside finished at 76-61, second in the California League Southern Division. Arquimedez Pozo hit .342 with 13 homers and 83 RBI. Greg Shockey hit .311 with 63 RBI. Jim Gutierrez was 12-9 with a 3.78 ERA. Tony Phillips had 15 saves. . . . Appleton finished at 62-73, sixth in the Midwest League Northern Division. Jackie Nickell was 7-7 with a 3.06 ERA and 151 strikeouts in 150 innings. Robert Worley had 22 saves. **Short-season:** Bellingham finished at 44-32, first in the Northwest League North Division, but was swept in two games by Boise in the league finals. Brian Doughty was 5-4 with a 2.49 ERA. Bob Wolcott was 8-4 with a 2.64 ERA. Ryan Franklin was 5-3 with a 2.92 ERA. Matt Mantei led the league with 12 saves. . . . Peoria finished at 17-35, last in the Arizona League. Jason Cook hit .319 with 24 RBI. Santo Deleon hit .311. Chris Green had six saves.

Tops in the organization

Batter	Club	Avg	G	AB	R	H	HR	RBI
Pozo, A.	Riv	.342	127	515	98	176	13	83
Turang, Brian	CGy	.324	110	423	83	137	8	54
Clayton, Craig	Jax	.313	119	450	60	141	2	55
Shockey, Greg	Riv	.311	95	354	61	110	6	63
Pirkl, Greg	CGy	.308	115	445	67	137	21	94

Home Runs			Wins		
Howitt, Dann	CGy	21	Davis, Tim	Riv	13
Pirkl, Greg	CGy	21	Walker, Mike	CGy	13
Santana, Ruben	Jax	21	Gutierrez, Jim	Riv	12
Newfield, Marc	Jax	19	Lowe, Derek	Riv	12
Koehler, Jim	App	19	Adam, Dave	Riv	12

RBI			Saves		
Pirkl, Greg	CGy	94	Worley, Robert	App	22
Santana, Ruben	Jax	84	Phillips, Tony	Jax	20
Pozo, A.	Riv	83	Davis, Tim	Riv	9
Howitt, Dann	CGy	77	Borski, Jeff	Riv	8
Holley, Bobby	Jax	75	Darwin, Jeff	Jax	7

Stolen Bases			Strikeouts		
Maynard, Tow	Riv	37	Nickell, Jackie	App	151
Tinsley, Lee	CGy	34	Villone, Ron	Jax	148
Turang, Brian	CGy	24	Davis, Tim	Riv	145
Gipson, Charles	App	21	Sanchez, Jose	App	133
Bryant, Craig	Riv	20	Walker, Mike	CGy	131

Pitcher	Club	W-L	ERA	IP	H	BB	SO
Nickell, Jackie	App	7- 7	3.06	150	135	41	151
Cummings, J.	CGy	5- 6	3.73	111	119	30	77
Gutierrez, Jim	Riv	12- 9	3.78	171	182	53	84
Walker, Mike	CGy	13- 8	4.03	170	197	47	131
Adam, Dave	Riv	12- 8	4.05	169	180	51	98

Seattle (1977-1993)

Runs: Most, career, all-time

563	Alvin Davis, 1984-1991
543	HAROLD REYNOLDS, 1983-1992
424	KEN GRIFFEY, 1989-1993
402	Julio Cruz, 1977-1983
351	Jim Presley, 1984-1989

Hits: Most, career, all-time

1163 Alvin Davis, 1984-1991
1063 HAROLD REYNOLDS, 1983-1992
832 KEN GRIFFEY, 1989-1993
736 Jim Presley, 1984-1989
697 Bruce Bochte, 1978-1982

2B: Most, career, all-time

212 Alvin Davis, 1984-1991
200 HAROLD REYNOLDS, 1983-1992
170 KEN GRIFFEY, 1989-1993
147 Jim Presley, 1984-1989
134 Bruce Bochte, 1978-1982

3B: Most, career, all-time

48 HAROLD REYNOLDS, 1983-1992
26 Phil Bradley, 1983-1987
23 SPIKE OWEN, 1983-1986
20 Ruppert Jones, 1977-1979
19 Dan Meyer, 1977-1981

HR: Most, career, all-time

160 Alvin Davis, 1984-1991
132 KEN GRIFFEY, 1989-1993
115 Jim Presley, 1984-1989
105 JAY BUHNER, 1988-1993
105 Ken Phelps, 1983-1988

RBI: Most, career, all-time

667 Alvin Davis, 1984-1991
453 KEN GRIFFEY, 1989-1993
418 Jim Presley, 1984-1989
345 JAY BUHNER, 1988-1993
329 Bruce Bochte, 1978-1982

SB: Most, career, all-time

290 Julio Cruz, 1977-1983
228 HAROLD REYNOLDS, 1983-1992
107 Phil Bradley, 1983-1987
102 HENRY COTTO, 1988-1993
77 KEN GRIFFEY, 1989-1993

BB: Most, career, all-time

672 Alvin Davis, 1984-1991
391 HAROLD REYNOLDS, 1983-1992
330 Julio Cruz, 1977-1983
318 KEN GRIFFEY, 1989-1993
317 Ken Phelps, 1983-1988

BA: Highest, career, all-time

.306 EDGAR MARTINEZ, 1987-1993
.303 KEN GRIFFEY, 1989-1993
.301 Phil Bradley, 1983-1987
.290 Bruce Bochte, 1978-1982
.281 Alvin Davis, 1984-1991

Slug avg: Highest, career, all-time

.521 Ken Phelps, 1983-1988
.520 KEN GRIFFEY, 1989-1993
.466 JAY BUHNER, 1988-1993
.456 EDGAR MARTINEZ, 1987-1993
.453 Alvin Davis, 1984-1991

Games started: Most, career, all-time

217 MIKE MOORE, 1982-1988
173 MARK LANGSTON, 1984-1989
153 RANDY JOHNSON, 1989-1993
147 Jim Beattie, 1980-1986
146 Glenn Abbott, 1977-1983

Saves: Most, career, all-time

98 MIKE SCHOOLER, 1988-1992
52 Bill Caudill, 1982-1983
36 Shane Rawley, 1978-1981
35 EDWIN NUNEZ, 1982-1988
28 MIKE JACKSON, 1988-1991

Shutouts: Most, career, all-time

9 MARK LANGSTON, 1984-1989
9 MIKE MOORE, 1982-1988
8 RANDY JOHNSON, 1989-1993
7 Floyd Bannister, 1979-1982
6 Jim Beattie, 1980-1986

Wins: Most, career, all-time

74 MARK LANGSTON, 1984-1989
66 MIKE MOORE, 1982-1988
65 RANDY JOHNSON, 1989-1993
56 ERIK HANSON, 1988-1993
45 MATT YOUNG, 1983-1990

K: Most, career, all-time

1078 MARK LANGSTON, 1984-1989
1075 RANDY JOHNSON, 1989-1993
937 MIKE MOORE, 1982-1988
740 ERIK HANSON, 1988-1993
597 MATT YOUNG, 1983-1990

Win pct: Highest, career, all-time

.556 RANDY JOHNSON, 1989-1993
.525 MARK LANGSTON, 1984-1989
.509 ERIK HANSON, 1988-1993
.444 Floyd Bannister, 1979-1982
.415 Glenn Abbott, 1977-1983

ERA: Lowest, career, all-time

3.69 ERIK HANSON, 1988-1993
3.73 RANDY JOHNSON, 1989-1993
3.75 Floyd Bannister, 1979-1982
4.01 MARK LANGSTON, 1984-1989
4.04 BILL SWIFT, 1985-1991

Runs: Most, season

113 KEN GRIFFEY, 1993
109 Ruppert Jones, 1979
101 Phil Bradley, 1987
100 Phil Bradley, 1985
100 EDGAR MARTINEZ, 1992
100 HAROLD REYNOLDS, 1990

Hits: Most, season

192 Phil Bradley, 1985
184 HAROLD REYNOLDS, 1989
181 EDGAR MARTINEZ, 1992
180 KEN GRIFFEY, 1993
180 Willie Horton, 1979
180 Jack Perconte, 1984

2B: Most, season

46 EDGAR MARTINEZ, 1992
42 KEN GRIFFEY, 1991
39 Al Cowens, 1982
39 KEN GRIFFEY, 1992
38 Bruce Bochte, 1979
38 Phil Bradley, 1987
38 KEN GRIFFEY, 1993

3B: Most, season

11	HAROLD REYNOLDS, 1988
10	Phil Bradley, 1987
9	Ruppert Jones, 1979
9	HAROLD REYNOLDS, 1989
8	Phil Bradley, 1985
8	Al Cowens, 1982
8	Ruppert Jones, 1977
8	SPIKE OWEN, 1984
8	HAROLD REYNOLDS, 1987

HR: Most, season

45	KEN GRIFFEY, 1993
32	Gorman Thomas, 1985
29	Alvin Davis, 1987
29	Willie Horton, 1979
28	Jim Presley, 1985

RBI: Most, season

116	Alvin Davis, 1984
109	KEN GRIFFEY, 1993
107	Jim Presley, 1986
106	Willie Horton, 1979
103	KEN GRIFFEY, 1992

SB: Most, season

60	HAROLD REYNOLDS, 1987
59	Julio Cruz, 1978
49	Julio Cruz, 1979
46	Julio Cruz, 1982
45	Julio Cruz, 1980

BB: Most, season

101	Alvin Davis, 1989
100	JAY BUHNER, 1993
97	Alvin Davis, 1984
96	KEN GRIFFEY, 1993
95	Alvin Davis, 1988

BA: Highest, season

.343	EDGAR MARTINEZ, 1992
.327	KEN GRIFFEY, 1991
.326	Tom Paciorek, 1981
.316	Bruce Bochte, 1979
.310	Phil Bradley, 1986

Slug avg: Highest, season

.617	KEN GRIFFEY, 1993
.544	EDGAR MARTINEZ, 1992
.535	KEN GRIFFEY, 1992
.527	KEN GRIFFEY, 1991
.516	Alvin Davis, 1987

Games started: Most, season

37	MIKE MOORE, 1986
36	MARK LANGSTON, 1986
35	Floyd Bannister, 1982
35	MARK LANGSTON, 1987
35	MARK LANGSTON, 1988
35	MATT YOUNG, 1985

Saves: Most, season

33	MIKE SCHOOLER, 1989
26	Bill Caudill, 1982
26	Bill Caudill, 1983
17	BILL SWIFT, 1991
16	EDWIN NUNEZ, 1985
16	Enrique Romo, 1977

Shutouts: Most, season

4	DAVE FLEMING, 1992
3	Floyd Bannister, 1982
3	Brian Holman, 1991
3	RANDY JOHNSON, 1993
3	MARK LANGSTON, 1987
3	MARK LANGSTON, 1988
3	MIKE MOORE, 1988

Wins: Most, season

19	RANDY JOHNSON, 1993
19	MARK LANGSTON, 1987
18	ERIK HANSON, 1990
17	DAVE FLEMING, 1992
17	MARK LANGSTON, 1984
17	MIKE MOORE, 1985

K: Most, season

308	RANDY JOHNSON, 1993
262	MARK LANGSTON, 1987
245	MARK LANGSTON, 1986
241	RANDY JOHNSON, 1992
235	MARK LANGSTON, 1988

Win pct: Highest, season

.704	RANDY JOHNSON, 1993
.667	ERIK HANSON, 1990
.630	DAVE FLEMING, 1992
.630	MARK LANGSTON, 1984
.630	MIKE MOORE, 1985

ERA: Lowest, season

3.24	ERIK HANSON, 1990
3.24	RANDY JOHNSON, 1993
3.27	MATT YOUNG, 1983
3.34	SCOTT BANKHEAD, 1989
3.34	MARK LANGSTON, 1988

Most pinch-hit homers, season

2	Leon Roberts, 1978
2	Gary Gray, 1981
2	Ken Phelps, 1986
2	GREG BRILEY, 1992

Most pinch-hit, homers, career

4	Ken Phelps, 1983-1988

Most consecutive games, batting safely

21	Dan Meyer, 1979
21	Richie Zisk, 1982

Most consecutive scoreless innings

34	MARK LANGSTON, 1988

No hit games

RANDY JOHNSON, Sea vs Det AL, 2-0; June 2, 1990.
CHRIS BOSIO, Sea vs Bos AL, 7-0; April 22, 1993.

ACTIVE PLAYERS in caps.

California Angels

AL Rookie of the Year Tim Salmon hit 31 homers (tied for ninth in the league) and drove in 95 runs.

by Russell Beeker, Baseball Weekly

1993 Angels: The Kiddie Korps looked great

When they redesigned the Angels' logo, they should have put Mickey Mouse ears on the caps—the average age of the team in '93 was nearly young enough to qualify them for half-price admission to Disneyland.

That wasn't all bad, though. In fact, the team's youth could be considered one of its big advantages. They were exuberant. Even long after the team had been eliminated from the pennant race, they had fun in pre-game drills. Why, manager Buck Rodgers' boys gave you the idea that, hey, being a baseball player can be fun!

The club finished at 71-91, tied for fifth place. But they were the hottest team around in April, jumping out to a 13-5 start, and were playing .500 ball as late as the All-Star break.

The Angels headed into the second half just two games out of first before injuries and inexperience finally took their inevitable toll. They lost 11 of the first 12 games after the break and were never again a factor in the race.

The Angels crowned their first Rookie of the Year, as right fielder Tim Salmon led the club in homers with 31. He hit .283 and had 95 RBI. His season came to an abrupt end in mid-August when he broke his ring finger, but fittingly, in his final at-bat he hit a grand slam.

Center fielder Chad Curtis led the team with a .285 average and stole 48 bases, proving that his fine rookie campaign was no fluke.

The club didn't get to see much of its double play combo—second baseman Damion Easley and shortstop Gary DiSarcina—but they liked what they saw. Easley was troubled with chronic shinsplints, but hit .313 in limited playing time before finally hanging up his spikes. DiSarcina was smooth afield but broke his finger in August.

First baseman J.T. Snow was the plum player acquired from the Yankees in exchange for fan favorite Jim Abbott. He got off to a hot start, hitting over .400, but slumped and by mid-July was in Triple-A Vancouver to try to regain his swing and his confidence. It worked. He was recalled in late August, and won the last AL Player of the Week award. He wound up with 16 homers, 57 RBI, and outstanding defense.

Meanwhile, Chili Davis' 27 homers set a club record in that category for a DH, breaking Frank Robinson's mark of 26. Davis also led the club with 112 RBI.

Mark Langston (16-11, 3.20 ERA) and Chuck Finley (16-14, 3.15 ERA) led the starting staff. No other starter collected more than four wins. The bullpen was the team's lowlight. Injured closer Bryan Harvey was left unprotected in the expansion draft—perhaps the worst move made by an existing club—and the Marlins were thrilled to draft a proven closer who insisted his arm was fine. He finished with a 1.70 ERA and 45 saves—four more than the entire Angels bullpen combined.

—by Lisa Winston

1994 Angels: Preview

If the club's pitching gets it together, the young, talented lineup could make the newly-aligned AL West very interesting. Joining the infield fray should be third baseman Eduardo Perez—son of Tony—and second baseman Damion Easley should be back full-time. Look for improved production at catcher if rookie Chris Turner is given the job—he hit over .280 in September.

Chuck Finley and Mark Langston will be joined by left-hander Joe Magrane, and any of a number of rookies from Phil Leftwich and Hilly Hathaway to southpaw Brian Anderson. For the Angels to contend, a closer must emerge from '93's core of effective middlemen.

—by Lisa Winston

1993 Angels: Between the lines

▶**April 6:** J.T. Snow, acquired from the Yankees in the Jim Abbott deal, began his career in California with a bang: 2-for-4 with a solo home run.

▶**April 11:** Left-hander Mark Langston left after just three innings of work against Detroit with a strained muscle in his rib cage.

▶**April 25:** Scott Sanderson outdueled Roger Clemens as the Angels used two solo home runs to win their sixth consecutive game. Torey Lovullo and rookie Tim Salmon blasted solo shots off Clemens, who suffered his first loss of 1993. The Angels' 12-4 record was their best start since 1979, when they won the AL West title.

▶**May 14:** Langston struck out 12 Kansas City batters in nine innings but wound up with a no-decision as the Royals won 2-1 in 10.

▶**May 17:** *Milestone*—Chili Davis hit his 200th career home run. He has hit 20 or more home runs in five different seasons.

▶**May 23:** Salmon, the 1992 Minor League Player of the Year, drove in a career-high four runs to lead the Angels past Texas 6-2. He hit a single, double and his seventh homer of '93.

▶**May 25:** Chuck Finley beat Seattle 6-3, marking his seventh consecutive win against the Mariners (10-3 lifetime). Luis Polonia hit his first home run since an inside-the-parker 840 at-bats ago, in the seventh off Tim Leary.

▶**May 27:** Scott Sanderson—continuing to haunt teams that passed him up during the offseason—blanked the Mariners, who toyed with the idea of signing him during the winter. Seattle managed just five hits; no Mariner baserunner made it past second base. The shutout (5-0) was the 14th of Sanderson's career. It tied him with Chicago's Jack McDowell for the league lead (seven wins).

▶**May 30:** The Angels beat Baltimore 7-5 for a three-game sweep, their first since the Carter administration.

▶**June 2:** The Angels' 7-6 loss to the Blue Jays was interrupted by 18 minutes of fisticuffs that began with a hit batter and ended with hundreds of blue and red souvenir baseballs littering the field at Anaheim Stadium. Chad Curtis was plunked by Toronto starter Pat Hentgen and scored on Tim Salmon's home run down the left field line. After Salmon's homer, fans began showering the field with their "ball night" mementos. Several fights broke out near the Toronto dugout before police restored order.

▶**June 6:** Five pitchers took the mound for the Angels in their 11-4 loss to Detroit, but the only one to pitch a 1-2-3 inning was an infielder—Rene Gonzales—who hadn't pitched since American Legion days.

▶**June 9:** Langston went 7 2/3 innings without allowing an earned run in his win over the Blue Jays. He struck out seven and ran his record to 7-1.

▶**June 17:** Chili Davis had been given the day off, but Angels' manager Buck Rodgers called upon the designated hitter to pitch the final two innings in California's 18-2 loss. The only batter to reach base against Davis was Jose Canseco, who also had tried his hand at pitching in an earlier game. Canseco was hit by a pitch.

▶**June 18:** California beat the White Sox 9-8 on Davis' two-run ninth-inning homer, the first time the Angels overcame a ninth-inning deficit in '93.

▶**June 26:** Finley threw a three-hit shutout for his sixth win in his last seven starts, a 4-0 defeat of the Twins. It was his second shutout of the year, eighth of his career.

▶**July 8:** The Yankees' Jimmy Key outdueled Mark Langston as the Angels lost 3-2. Key threw a five-hit complete game; Langston struggled, allowing 12 hits but only three runs.

▶**July 11:** Torey Lovullo singled with the bases loaded in the bottom of the 14th inning to give the Angels a 3-2 win against the Yankees. The nearly five-hour game moved the Angels to a .500 mark at the break.

▸**July 15:** *Quote of the day*—Buck Rodgers after his team's 7-3, five-error loss to the Indians: "We couldn't catch a cold tonight. It's like we had used anti-leather repellant."

▸**July 31:** Rookie Eduardo Perez hit a two-run homer with one out in the ninth to give the Angels a 4-3 win against Minnesota. Perez hit safely in each of his first five major league games after being called up to replace J.T. Snow. Chuck Finley went the distance for the Angels.

▸**August 5:** Chili Davis doubled and homered against the Royals, driving in four runs in a 5-4 win, to give him 82 RBI for the season.

▸**August 13:** Erik Hanson topped Chuck Finley in a pitcher's duel at the Kingdome. Hanson gave up a run on four hits; Finley gave up eight hits and recorded his eighth complete game but gave up the game-winning hit in the eighth inning. The Angels lost 2-1.

▸**August 15:** Greg Myers drove in a career-high four RBI on three singles as the Angels clobbered the Mariners.

▸**August 18:** Tim Salmon hit two home runs against Detroit, bringing his total to 27, two better than the Angels' rookie record set by Ken Hunt in 1961.

▸**August 25:** Mark Langston took a no-hitter into the seventh and ended up with a 2-1, one-hit win at Camden Yards. It was his 13th win of the year.

▸**September 4:** Joe Magrane won for the first time in the AL, holding the Blue Jays to two runs over seven innings of a 4-2 win. Three of Toronto's five hits off Magrane failed to leave the infield .

▸**September 5:** Phil Leftwich threw a six-hitter to lead the Angels to a 5-1 win and a three-game sweep of the Blue Jays.

▸**September 15:** Chili Davis hit a pair of three-run homers to help the Angels to a 15-2 rout of Seattle. His six RBI put him over the 100 mark for the first time in his 12-year career. Unfortunately, during the same game, Tim Salmon broke the ring finger on his left hand, putting an end to his outstanding rookie year. Salmon finished his season with a .283 average, 31 home runs and 95 RBI.

▸**October 3:** The Angels beat the A's, 5-3, and finished fifth, 23 games out of first place. *League leaders, pitching*— Chuck Finley led the league in complete games (13), was fifth in strikeouts (187), sixth in ERA (3.15), tied for fifth in shutouts (2), sixth in innings pitched (251 1/3), and ninth in victories (16-14); Mark Langston was second in strikeouts (196), third in innings pitched (256 1/3), and eighth in victories (16-11) and tied for sixth in complete games (7). *League leaders, batting*— Luis Polonia was third and Chad Curtis was fifth in stolen bases (55 and 48, respectively); Chili Davis was seventh in RBI (112); Tim Salmon was eighth in slugging percentage (.536) and tied for ninth in home runs (31).

—by John Hunt, Scott Kauffman, Lisa Winston, Deron Snyder, Matt Young

Team directory

▸**Owner:** Gene Autry
▸**General Manager:** Whitey Herzog
▸**Ballpark:**
Anaheim Stadium
2000 Gene Autry Way, Anaheim, Calif., 714-937-6700
Capacity 64,593
Parking for 15,000 vehicles; $5
Public transportation available
Family and wheelchair sections, elevators, ramps, picnic section
▸**Team publications:**
Halo Magazine, media guide, yearbook
714-937-6700, ext. 7281
▸**TV, radio broadcast stations:**
KMPC 710AM, KORG (Spanish), KTLA Channel 5, SportsChannel
▸**Camps and/or clinics:**
MCI/Angels Clinic, dates TBA, 714-937-6700
▸**Spring Training:**
Diablo Stadium,
Tempe, Ariz.
Capacity 7,285 (9,785 includes lawn)
602-438-4300

CALIFORNIA ANGELS 1993 final stats

Batting	BA	SLG	OB	G	AB	R	H	TB	2B	3B	HR	RBI	BB	SO	SB	CS	E
L.Gonzales	.500	.500	.667	2	2	0	1	1	0	0	0	1	1	0	0	0	0
Easley	.313	.413	.392	73	230	33	72	95	13	2	2	22	28	35	6	6	6
Javier	.291	.405	.362	92	237	33	69	96	10	4	3	28	27	33	12	2	4
Curtis	.285	.369	.361	152	583	94	166	215	25	3	6	59	70	89	48	24	9
Salmon	.283	.536	.382	142	515	93	146	276	35	1	31	95	82	135	5	6	7
Turner	.280	.387	.360	25	75	9	21	29	5	0	1	13	9	16	1	1	1
Gruber	.277	.462	.309	18	65	10	18	30	3	0	3	9	2	11	0	0	4
Polonia	.271	.326	.328	152	576	75	156	188	17	6	1	32	48	53	55	24	5
Correia	.266	.305	.319	64	128	12	34	39	5	0	0	9	6	20	2	4	3
Stillwell	.262	.361	.299	22	61	2	16	22	2	2	0	3	4	11	2	0	5
Myers	.255	.362	.298	108	290	27	74	105	10	0	7	40	17	47	3	3	6
R.Gonzales	.251	.319	.346	118	335	34	84	107	17	0	2	31	49	45	5	5	12
Lovullo	.251	.354	.318	116	367	42	92	130	20	0	6	30	36	49	7	6	11
Perez	.250	.372	.292	52	180	16	45	67	6	2	4	30	9	39	5	4	5
Edmonds	.246	.344	.270	18	61	5	15	21	4	1	0	4	2	16	0	2	1
Davis	.243	.440	.327	153	573	74	139	252	32	0	27	112	71	135	4	1	0
Snow	.241	.408	.328	129	419	60	101	171	18	2	16	57	55	88	3	0	6
DiSarcina	.238	.313	.273	126	416	44	99	130	20	1	3	45	15	38	5	7	14
Tingley	.200	.278	.277	58	90	7	18	25	7	0	0	12	9	22	1	2	1
Orton	.189	.274	.252	37	95	5	18	26	5	0	1	4	7	24	1	2	4
Van Burkleo	.152	.333	.282	12	33	2	5	11	3	0	1	1	6	9	1	0	0
Walewander	.125	.125	.429	12	8	2	1	1	0	0	0	3	5	1	1	1	0
Walton	.000	.000	.333	5	2	2	0	0	0	0	0	0	1	2	1	0	0

Pitching	W-L	ERA	G	GS	CG	GF	Sho	SV	IP	H	R	ER	HR	BB	SO
Butcher	1-0	2.86	23	0	0	11	0	8	28.1	21	12	9	2	15	24
Grahe	4-1	2.86	45	0	0	32	0	11	56.2	54	22	18	5	25	31
Frey	2-3	2.98	55	0	0	28	0	13	48.1	41	20	16	1	26	22
Finley	16-14	3.15	35	35	13	0	2	0	251.1	243	108	88	22	82	187
Langston	16-11	3.20	35	35	7	0	0	0	256.1	220	100	91	22	85	196
Leftwich	4-6	3.79	12	12	1	0	0	0	80.2	81	35	34	5	27	31
Magrane	3-2	3.94	8	8	0	0	0	0	48	48	27	21	4	21	24
Anderson	0-0	3.97	4	1	0	3	0	0	11.1	11	5	5	1	2	4
Lewis	1-2	4.22	15	4	0	2	0	0	32	37	16	15	3	12	10
Sanderson	7-11	4.46	21	21	4	0	1	0	135.1	153	77	67	15	27	66
Patterson	1-1	4.58	46	0	0	9	0	1	59	54	30	30	7	35	36
Hathaway	4-3	5.02	11	11	0	0	0	0	57.1	71	35	32	6	26	11
Scott	1-2	5.85	16	0	0	2	0	0	20	19	13	13	1	11	13
Crim	2-2	5.87	11	0	0	3	0	0	15.1	17	11	10	2	5	10
Valera	3-6	6.62	19	5	0	8	0	4	53	77	44	39	8	15	28
Springer	1-6	7.20	14	9	1	3	0	0	60	73	48	48	11	32	31
Farrell	3-12	7.35	21	17	0	1	0	0	90.2	110	74	74	22	44	45
Linton	2-1	7.36	23	1	0	6	0	0	36.2	46	30	30	8	23	23
Nielsen	0-0	8.03	10	0	0	3	0	0	12.1	18	13	11	1	4	8
Swingle	0-1	8.38	9	0	0	2	0	0	9.2	15	9	9	2	6	6
Holzemer	0-3	8.87	5	4	0	1	0	0	23.1	34	24	23	2	13	10

1994 preliminary roster

PITCHERS (22)
Brian Anderson
Mike Butcher
John Farrell
Chuck Finley
Steve Frey
Bob Gamez
Joe Grahe
Hilly Hathaway
Mark Holzemer
Pete Janicki
Mark Langston
Phil Leftwich
Scott Lewis
Joe Magrane
Jose Musset

Troy Percival
Kyle Sebach
Russ Springer
Paul Swingle
Julio Valera
Julian Vasquez
Ron Watson

CATCHERS (3)
Mark Dalesandro
Greg Myers
Chris Turner

INFIELDERS (7)
Mike Brumley
Rod Correia
Gary DiSarcina
Damion Easley
Torey Lovullo
Eduardo Perez
J.T. Snow

OUTFIELDERS (7)
Garret Anderson
Chad Curtis
Chili Davis
Jim Edmonds
Kevin Flora
Tim Salmon
Mark Sweeney

Games played by position

Player	G	C	1B	2B	3B	SS	OF	DH
Correia	64	0	0	11	3	40	0	6
Curtis	152	0	0	3	0	0	151	0
Davis	153	0	0	0	0	0	0	150
DiSarcina	126	0	0	0	0	126	0	0
Easley	73	0	0	54	14	0	0	1
Edmonds	18	0	0	0	0	0	17	0
L. Gonzales	2	2	0	0	0	0	0	0
R. Gonzales	118	0	31	4	79	5	0	0
Gruber	18	0	0	0	17	0	1	1
Javier	92	0	12	2	0	0	64	1
Lovullo	116	0	1	91	14	9	2	1
Myers	108	97	0	0	0	0	0	2
Orton	37	35	0	0	0	0	1	0
Perez	52	0	0	0	45	0	0	3
Polonia	152	0	0	0	0	0	141	4
Salmon	142	0	0	0	0	0	140	1
Snow	129	0	129	0	0	0	0	0
Stillwell	22	0	0	18	0	7	0	0
Tingley	58	58	0	0	0	0	0	0
Turner	25	25	0	0	0	0	0	0
Van Burkleo	12	0	12	0	0	0	0	0
Walewander	12	0	0	2	0	6	0	3
Walton	5	0	0	0	0	0	1	4

Sick call: 1993 DL Report

Player	Days on the DL
Mike Butcher	71
Gary Disarcina	38
Damion Easley*	83
Joe Grahe	40
Kelly Gruber*	152
Hilly Hathaway	24
Scott Lewis	19
John Orton*	84
Russ Springer	63
Julio Valera	102

Two separate terms on Disabled List

Minor League Report

Class AAA: Vancouver finished at 72-68, second in the Pacific Coast League Northern Division. Garret Anderson hit .293 with 71 RBI. Reggie Williams led the league with 50 steals. Jim Walewander had 36 steals. Darryl Scott had 15 saves. **Class AA:** Midland finished at 67-68, third in the Texas League Western Division. P.J. Forbes batted .319 with 15 homers and 64 RBI. Chris Pritchett hit .308. Orlando Palmeiro batted .305. John Fritz was 9-5 with a 3.61 ERA. Jose Musset had 21 saves. **Class A:** Palm Springs finished at 61-75, last in the California League Southern Division. Marquis Riley stole 69 bases. Korey Keling was 8-8 with a 3.29 ERA and 131 strikeouts. Mark Ratekin was 7-7 with a 3.89 ERA. Keith Morrison led the league in wins with 14. John Pricher led the league in saves with 26. . . . Cedar Rapids finished at 54-80, last in the Midwest League Southern Division. Kyle Sebach was 6-9 with a 3.04 ERA. Clifton Garrett hit .323. Morisse Daniels had 25 stolen bases. Mike Wolff had 17 homers and 72 RBI. Tony Chavez had 16 saves. Dave Marcon was 10-5 with a 2.96 ERA. **Short-season:** Boise finished at 41-35, first in the Northwest League South Division, and swept Bellingham two games for the league title. Mark Simmons won the batting title at .304. Jamie Burke hit .301. Aaron Iatarola hit .289 with seven homers and 39 RBI. Todd Greene won the home run crown with 15 and led the league in RBI with 71. David Kennedy drove in 49 runs. Bryan Harris was 8-3 with a 1.89 ERA and a league-best 96 strikeouts. Brooks Drysdale had 11 saves. . . . Mesa finished at 28-23, fourth in the Arizona League. Juan Henderson hit .323. Jason Herrick hit .301 with 36 RBI. Jose Aguirre was 5-5 with a 2.75 ERA. Matt Perisho won seven games.

Tops in the organization

Batter	Club	Avg	G	AB	R	H	HR	RBI
Sweeney, Mark	Mdl	.356	117	433	82	154	12	79
Forbes, P.J.	Van	.317	131	514	91	163	15	67
Edmonds, Jim	Van	.315	95	356	59	112	9	74
Boykin, Tyrone	Mdl	.311	112	418	77	130	5	57
Jackson, John	Van	.309	125	444	71	137	5	54

Home Runs			Wins		
Kipila, Jeff	Mdl	17	Morrison, Keith	Psp	14
Wolff, Mike	Cr	17	Fritz, John	Van	12
Forbes, P.J.	Van	15	Bennett, Erik	Van	11
Sweeney, Mark	Mdl	12	Marcon, David	Psp	10
Perez, Eddie	Van	12	Ratekin, Mark	Mdl	10

RBI			Saves		
Raven, Luis	Psp	82	Pricher, John	Psp	26
Sweeney, Mark	Mdl	79	Musset, Jose	Mdl	21
Dalesandro, Mark	Van	76	Chavez, Tony	Mdl	17
Edmonds, Jim	Van	74	Scott, Darryl	Van	15
Wolff, Mike	Cr	72	Lewis, Scott	Van	9

Stolen Bases			Strikeouts		
Riley, Marquis	Psp	69	Sebach, Kyle	Cr	138
Williams, Reggie	Van	50	Keling, Korey	Psp	131
Walewander, Jim	Van	36	Butler, Mike	Psp	123
Daniels, Morisse	Cr	25	Holdridge, David	Mdl	123
Jackson, John	Van	24	Hingle, Larry	Cr	115

Pitcher	Club	W-L	ERA	IP	H	BB	SO
Sebach, Kyle	Cr	6-9	3.04	154	138	70	138
Keling, Korey	Psp	8-8	3.29	159	152	62	131
Fritz, John	Van	12-6	3.72	172	177	60	114
Ratekin, Mark	Mdl	10-8	4.08	188	201	57	90
Morrison, Keith	Psp	14-6	4.14	176	200	55	107

279

California (1965-1993), includes Los Angeles (1961-1964)

Runs: Most, career, all-time

889	Brian Downing, 1978-1990
691	Jim Fregosi, 1961-1971
601	Bobby Grich, 1977-1986
481	Don Baylor, 1977-1982
474	Rod Carew, 1979-1985

Hits: Most, career, all-time

1588	Brian Downing, 1978-1990
1408	Jim Fregosi, 1961-1971
1103	Bobby Grich, 1977-1986
968	Rod Carew, 1979-1985
925	WALLY JOYNER, 1986-1991

2B: Most, career, all-time

282	Brian Downing, 1978-1990
219	Jim Fregosi, 1961-1971
183	Bobby Grich, 1977-1986
170	WALLY JOYNER, 1986-1991
149	Doug DeCinces, 1982-1987

3B: Most, career, all-time

70	Jim Fregosi, 1961-1971
32	Mickey Rivers, 1970-1975
27	LUIS POLONIA, 1990-1993
27	DICK SCHOFIELD, 1983-1992
25	Bobby Knoop, 1964-1969

HR: Most, career, all-time

222	Brian Downing, 1978-1990
154	Bobby Grich, 1977-1986
141	Don Baylor, 1977-1982
130	Doug DeCinces, 1982-1987
123	Reggie Jackson, 1982-1986

RBI: Most, career, all-time

846	Brian Downing, 1978-1990
557	Bobby Grich, 1977-1986
546	Jim Fregosi, 1961-1971
523	Don Baylor, 1977-1982
518	WALLY JOYNER, 1986-1991

SB: Most, career, all-time

186	Gary Pettis, 1982-1987
174	LUIS POLONIA, 1990-1993
139	Sandy Alomar, 1969-1974
126	Mickey Rivers, 1970-1975
123	DEVON WHITE, 1985-1990

BB: Most, career, all-time

866	Brian Downing, 1978-1990
630	Bobby Grich, 1977-1986
558	Jim Fregosi, 1961-1971
405	Rod Carew, 1979-1985
369	Albie Pearson, 1961-1966

BA: Highest, career, all-time

.314	Rod Carew, 1979-1985
.294	LUIS POLONIA, 1990-1993
.293	Juan Beniquez, 1981-1985
.288	WALLY JOYNER, 1986-1991
.275	Albie Pearson, 1961-1966

Slug avg: Highest, career, all-time

.463	Doug DeCinces, 1982-1987
.455	WALLY JOYNER, 1986-1991
.448	Don Baylor, 1977-1982
.441	Brian Downing, 1978-1990
.440	Reggie Jackson, 1982-1986

Games started: Most, career, all-time

288	NOLAN RYAN, 1972-1979
272	MIKE WITT, 1981-1990
218	FRANK TANANA, 1973-1980
195	CHUCK FINLEY, 1986-1993
189	KIRK McCASKILL, 1985-1991
189	Clyde Wright, 1966-1973

Saves: Most, career, all-time

126	BRYAN HARVEY, 1987-1992
65	Dave LaRoche, 1970-1980
61	Donnie Moore, 1985-1988
58	Bob Lee, 1964-1966
43	Minnie Rojas, 1966-1968

Shutouts: Most, career, all-time

40	NOLAN RYAN, 1972-1979
24	FRANK TANANA, 1973-1980
21	Dean Chance, 1961-1966
14	George Brunet, 1964-1969
13	Geoff Zahn, 1981-1985

Wins: Most, career, all-time

138	NOLAN RYAN, 1972-1979
109	MIKE WITT, 1981-1990
102	FRANK TANANA, 1973-1980
89	CHUCK FINLEY, 1986-1993
87	Clyde Wright, 1966-1973

K: Most, career, all-time

2416	NOLAN RYAN, 1972-1979
1283	MIKE WITT, 1981-1990
1233	FRANK TANANA, 1973-1980
1026	CHUCK FINLEY, 1986-1993
857	Dean Chance, 1961-1966

Win pct: Highest, career, all-time

.567	FRANK TANANA, 1973-1980
.557	Andy Messersmith, 1968-1972
.553	Geoff Zahn, 1981-1985
.539	CHUCK FINLEY, 1986-1993
.537	MARK LANGSTON, 1990-1993

ERA: Lowest, career, all-time

2.78	Andy Messersmith, 1968-1972
2.83	Dean Chance, 1961-1966
3.07	NOLAN RYAN, 1972-1979
3.08	FRANK TANANA, 1973-1980
3.13	George Brunet, 1964-1969

Runs: Most, season

120	Don Baylor, 1979
115	Albie Pearson, 1962
114	Carney Lansford, 1979
110	Brian Downing, 1987
109	Brian Downing, 1982

Hits: Most, season

202	Alex Johnson, 1970
188	Carney Lansford, 1979
186	Don Baylor, 1979
186	Billy Moran, 1962
184	Johnny Ray, 1988

2B: Most, season

42	Doug DeCinces, 1982
42	Johnny Ray, 1988
38	Fred Lynn, 1982
37	Brian Downing, 1982
35	TIM SALMON, 1993

3B: Most, season

13	Jim Fregosi, 1968
13	Mickey Rivers, 1975
13	DEVON WHITE, 1989
12	Jim Fregosi, 1963
11	Bobby Knoop, 1966
11	Mickey Rivers, 1974

HR: Most, season

39	Reggie Jackson, 1982
37	Bobby Bonds, 1977
37	Leon Wagner, 1962
36	Don Baylor, 1979
34	Don Baylor, 1978
34	WALLY JOYNER, 1987

280

RBI: Most, season

139	Don Baylor, 1979	
117	WALLY JOYNER, 1987	
115	Bobby Bonds, 1977	
112	CHILI DAVIS, 1993	
107	Leon Wagner, 1962	

SB: Most, season

70	Mickey Rivers, 1975
56	Gary Pettis, 1985
55	LUIS POLONIA, 1993
51	LUIS POLONIA, 1992
50	Gary Pettis, 1986

BB: Most, season

106	Brian Downing, 1987
96	Albie Pearson, 1961
95	Albie Pearson, 1962
93	Jim Fregosi, 1969
92	Reggie Jackson, 1986
92	Albie Pearson, 1963

BA: Highest, season

.339	Rod Carew, 1983
.331	Rod Carew, 1980
.329	Alex Johnson, 1970
.326	Brian Downing, 1979
.319	Rod Carew, 1982

Slug avg: Highest, season

.548	Doug DeCinces, 1982
.543	Bobby Grich, 1981
.537	Bobby Grich, 1979
.536	TIM SALMON, 1993
.532	Reggie Jackson, 1982

Games started: Most, season

41	NOLAN RYAN, 1974
40	Bill Singer, 1973
39	NOLAN RYAN, 1972
39	NOLAN RYAN, 1973
39	NOLAN RYAN, 1976
39	Clyde Wright, 1970

Saves: Most, season

46	BRYAN HARVEY, 1991
31	Donnie Moore, 1985
27	Minnie Rojas, 1967
25	BRYAN HARVEY, 1989
25	BRYAN HARVEY, 1990
25	Dave LaRoche, 1978

Shutouts: Most, season

11	Dean Chance, 1964
9	NOLAN RYAN, 1972
7	NOLAN RYAN, 1976
7	FRANK TANANA, 1977
6	Jim McGlothlin, 1967

Wins: Most, season

22	NOLAN RYAN, 1974
22	Clyde Wright, 1970
21	NOLAN RYAN, 1973
20	Dean Chance, 1964
20	Andy Messersmith, 1971
20	Bill Singer, 1973

K: Most, season

383	NOLAN RYAN, 1973
367	NOLAN RYAN, 1974
341	NOLAN RYAN, 1977
329	NOLAN RYAN, 1972
327	NOLAN RYAN, 1976

Win pct: Highest, season

.773	Bert Blyleven, 1989
.704	MARK LANGSTON, 1991
.692	Geoff Zahn, 1982
.690	Dean Chance, 1964
.667	CHUCK FINLEY, 1990
.667	CHUCK FINLEY, 1991

ERA: Lowest, season

1.65	Dean Chance, 1964
2.28	NOLAN RYAN, 1972
2.40	CHUCK FINLEY, 1990
2.43	FRANK TANANA, 1976
2.52	Andy Messersmith, 1969

Most pinch-hit homers, season

3	Joe Adcock, 1966
3	George Hendrick, 1987

Most pinch-hit, homers, career

4	Ruppert Jones, 1985-1987
4	George Hendrick, 1985-1988

Most consecutive games, batting safely

25	Rod Carew, 1982
22	Sandy Alomar, 1970

Most consecutive scoreless innings

36	Jim McGlothlin, 1967

No hit games

Bo Belinsky, LA vs Bal AL, 2-0;
May 5, 1962.
Clyde Wright, Cal vs Oak AL, 4-0;
July 3, 1970.
NOLAN RYAN, Cal at KC AL, 3-0;
May 15, 1973.
NOLAN RYAN, Cal at Det AL, 6-0;
July 15, 1973.
NOLAN RYAN, Cal vs Min AL, 4-0;
September 28, 1974.
NOLAN RYAN, Cal vs Bal AL, 1-0;
June 1, 1975.
MIKE WITT, Cal at Tex AL, 1-0;
September 30, 1984 (perfect
game).
MARK LANGSTON (7 innings) and
MIKE WITT (2 innings), Cal vs
Sea AL, 1-0; April 11, 1990.

ACTIVE PLAYERS in caps.

Leader from the franchise's current location is included. If not in the top five, leader's rank is listed in parenthesis; asterisk (*) indicates player is not in top 25.

281

Minnesota Twins

by Russell Beeker, *Baseball Weekly*

Kirby Puckett, one of the Twins' most popular players, was voted the 1993 All-Star MVP.

1993 Twins: Their stars—and their record—fell

Kerplunk! After winning the '91 World Championship and posting 90 victories in '92, the Minnesota Twins came back to earth with a thud. They were 71-91, tied for fifth, 23 games out—their worst showing in the Andy MacPhail-Tom Kelly era. One of three teams to go from 90 wins to 90 losses last season, the Twins had only to look to the stars to find the reason for their descent:

▶First baseman Kent Hrbek hit a career-low .242. He finished with a respectable 83 RBI, but 32 of them came in the Twins' last 39 games—long after their hopes were over. Backup David McCarty, the Twins' hottest prospect, hit just .214 his rookie season.

▶Outfielder Kirby Puckett had a year coveted by most players—.296, 22 HR, 89 RBI. But it was a letdown for Puckett, who had a .321 lifetime average and was coming off a 110-RBI season.

▶Designated hitter Dave Winfield attracted attention with his 3,000th hit on Sept. 16, but overall the returning hometown hero finished with just 76 RBI—his fewest in a non-strike season since 1976. He hit .220 with runners in scoring position and struck out 106 times. At one point, he went 32 games without a home run.

▶Right-hander Scott Erickson narrowly avoided becoming the majors' first 20-game loser since 1980. He was saved by a couple of no-decisions in his final two starts of the season, finishing 8-19 (5.19 ERA). Opponents hit .305 against him. He anchored a pitching staff that gave up 10 or more runs at least 20 times.

▶Right-hander Kevin Tapani, coming off two consecutive 16-win years, went 12-15 (4.43 ERA). In his 16 starts after the All-Star break, however, he was 9-4 (3.12 ERA). He developed a cut fastball and was more aggressive.

▶Neither Chuck Knoblauch nor Shane Mack was a solid leadoff batter. Mack continued to battle shoulder problems all year.

The season was not without its high points, though. Catcher Brian Harper hit above .300 with runners in scoring position. He also was the first catcher since Thurman Munson (1976-78) to hit .300 for three consecutive seasons and had a career-high 73 RBI. With 34 saves, Rick Aguilera stood out in an overworked bullpen.

—by Bill Koenig

1994 Twins: Preview

The Twins need pitching and hitting from the left side, but with so many players getting old, and with the Twins strapped by the "small-market syndrome" that prevents a free-agent spending spree, the immediate future is not bright. Much depends on the ability of some veterans to bounce back. Dave Winfield, 42, who led the Blue Jays to a World Series championship in '92 and slipped last season made it clear he isn't thinking about retirement. Kent Hrbek is 33, injury-prone and has talked about retiring after '94. Puckett turns 32 in March and the Twins already have moved him from center to right field.

Minnesota has to hope that young players such as David McCarty and Pedro Munoz will develop quickly to help the Twins contend next season in the new, five-team AL Central.

On the mound, there is no way Scott Erickson can lose 19 games again. Kevin Tapani had a hot second half, and the Twins are building for the future with Greg Brummett, Mike Trombley and 1993 Southern League Pitcher of the Year Oscar Munoz.

—by Bill Koenig

1993 Twins: Between the lines

▶**April 6:** Dave Winfield, the Twins' new 41-year-old bionic man, hit a two-run homer in his Minnesota debut.

▶**April 7:** Winfield's three-run double off Scott Radinsky gave him six RBI after just two games in a Minnesota uniform.

▶**April 21:** Kent Hrbek hit his eighth career grand slam.

▶**April 29:** The Twins suffered their seventh consecutive loss in a blowout at Camden Yards. The last time they had such a streak was 1987, the year they won their first World Series title.

▶**May 1:** The Twins ended an eight-game skid by beating the Tigers 5-3. Shane Mack had a double and three RBI.

▶**May 26:** The Twins beat the A's 12-11 in a game that featured five lead changes and three blown saves. Kirby Puckett singled in two runs in the top of the ninth inning to give the Twins a 12-10 lead. George Tsamis allowed a run in the bottom of the inning but finally ended the four-hour affair by inducing a pop-up from Ruben Sierra.

▶**May 30:** Chuck Knoblauch had the sixth four-hit game of his career.

▶**June 13:** Shane Mack homered twice—for four RBI—but the Twins lost to Oakland, 7-6.

▶**June 25:** Kirby Puckett homered and drove in four runs in Minnesota's 8-5 victory over the Angels. It snapped a nine-game losing streak for the Twins, who had already suffered through three losing streaks of eight or more games in 1993. No other major league team had lost more than seven in a row.

▶**June 27:** Jim Deshaies threw eight innings of four-hit ball as the Twins sank California 2-0. Of Deshaies' nine wins in 1993, seven had come in the Metrodome. Closer Rick Aguilera set down the side in order to gain his 21st save. In a span of nine games, he retired 27 consecutive batters, the equivalent of a perfect game.

▶**July 9:** Dave Winfield had four hits, including a home run, and drove in three runs for the Twins as they beat the Brewers 10-6.

▶**July 15:** *Milestone*—Dave Winfield passed Frank Robinson on the all-time hits list with No. 2,944. His double was the 505th of his 20-year career, tying him with Tony Perez for 27th place.

▶**August 1:** *Milestone*—Dave Winfield hit his 450th home run, but had to barter to get the ball. Winfield, who is 35 hits short of 3,000 hits, traded an autographed bat and ball, wristbands and several autographed cards for the memento. Winfield is one of only five players to gather 450 homers and at least 2,950 hits.

▶**August 3:** Willie Banks worked out of jams in five consecutive innings to give Minnesota a 6-1 victory against Boston. It was the 1987, first-round draft pick's third consecutive victory since a mid-July demotion to the bullpen. He allowed seven hits, walked one and struck out five in seven innings.

▶**August 6:** Dave Winfield was robbed of two RBI during Minnesota's 4-3 win against the Yankees. Winfield hit a line drive between second and third that hit Kirby Puckett, who was heading to third base. Puckett was called out, and the inning ended. Winfield got credit for a hit, his 2,971st.

▶**August 7:** Kirby Puckett singled up the middle, bringing home Pat Meares in the ninth as the Twins beat the Yankees 6-5. Puckett fouled off four Steve Farr pitches before lining a two-out delivery to center for the game-winner.

▶**August 12:** Kirby Puckett doubled and homered twice as the Twins downed Toronto 9-2.

▶**August 13:** Kent Hrbek hit two homers as Minnesota beat the A's 5-2. Hrbek hit a three-run shot in the first inning that glanced off the glove of left fielder Scott Lydy. Hrbek also hit a two-run shot in the third to record his 15th two-homer game. His five RBI matched a career high.

▶**August 14:** Mike Pagliarulo's sacrifice fly broke a 12th-inning tie and Jeff Reboulet's three-run double broke the game open as the Twins beat Oakland 5-1 in the first game of a doubleheader. In the second game, Shane Mack singled, doubled and hit a three-run homer, good for four RBI, as the Twins handed the A's a 6-2 defeat.

▶**August 15:** Kirby Puckett was 5-for-5, with a pair of two-run home runs to lead the Twins to a 12-5 rout in Oakland. It was Puckett's second two-homer game in four days and the 10th of his career. Bernardo Brito, a 29-year-old rookie, also hit two homers for the Twins. Brito hit his homers, both two-run shots, in the second and third innings.

▶**August 19:** Kirby Puckett was hitting .458 with four homers and seven RBI in his last six games, but struck out four times against David Cone in the Twins' 4-2 loss to Kansas City.

▶**August 21:** Twins' starter Willie Banks gave up four runs in three innings of a 9-4 loss to the White Sox, yet cut his ERA against them from 54.00 to 27.00. In his only other appearance against the Chisox, he was tagged for 10 earned runs in 1 2/3 innings.

▶**September 22:** Pedro Munoz knocked in all five of Minnesota's runs with a pair of homers, to give the Twins a 5-4 victory against the Yankees, who fell to 8-11 this month.

▶**October 3:** Minnesota beat Seattle, 7-2, to finish off the disappointing 1993 season in sixth place (tied with the California Angels), 23 games behind first-place Chicago. *League leaders, pitching*—Rick Aguilera finished sixth in saves (34). *League leaders, batting*—Kirby Puckett was fifth in doubles (39) and sixth in hits (184); Chuck Knoblauch was tied for ninth in stolen bases (29).

—by John Hunt, Scott Kauffman, Lisa Winston, Deron Snyder, Matt Young

Team directory

▶**Owner:** Carl R. Pohlad
▶**General Manager:** Andy MacPhail
▶**Ballpark:**
Hubert H. Humphrey Metrodome
501 Chicago Avenue South,
Minneapolis, Minn.
612-375-1366
Capacity 56,000
Public transportation available
Family and wheelchair sections, elevators
▶**Team publications:**
Twins Magazine
612-375-7458
▶**TV, radio broadcast stations:**
WCCO 830 AM, WCCO-TV Channel 4
▶**Camps and/or clinics:**
Twins Clinics, weekends throughout the summer, 612-375-7498
▶**Spring Training:**
Lee County Sports Complex
Fort Myers, Fla.
Capacity 7,500
813-768-4200

MINNESOTA TWINS 1993 final stats

Batting	BA	SLG	OB	G	AB	R	H	TB	2B	3B	HR	RBI	BB	SO	SB	CS	E
Hale	.333	.425	.408	69	186	25	62	79	6	1	3	27	18	17	2	1	4
Harper	.304	.425	.347	147	530	52	161	225	26	1	12	73	29	29	1	3	10
Puckett	.296	.474	.349	156	622	89	184	295	39	3	22	89	47	93	8	6	2
Becker	.286	.571	.583	3	7	3	2	4	2	0	0	0	5	4	1	1	1
Knoblauch	.277	.346	.354	153	602	82	167	208	27	4	2	41	65	44	29	11	9
Mack	.276	.412	.335	128	503	66	139	207	30	4	10	61	41	76	15	5	5
Winfield	.271	.442	.325	143	547	72	148	242	27	2	21	76	45	106	2	3	0
Larkin	.264	.347	.357	56	144	17	38	50	7	1	1	19	21	16	0	1	2
Reboulet	.258	.304	.356	109	240	33	62	73	8	0	1	15	35	37	5	5	6
Meares	.251	.309	.266	111	346	33	87	107	14	3	0	33	7	52	4	5	19
Bruett	.250	.350	.318	17	20	2	5	7	2	0	0	1	1	4	0	0	2
Hrbek	.242	.467	.357	123	392	60	95	183	11	1	25	83	71	57	4	2	5
Brito	.241	.500	.255	27	54	8	13	27	2	0	4	9	1	20	0	0	0
Munoz	.233	.393	.294	104	326	34	76	128	11	1	13	38	25	97	1	2	3
Jorgensen	.224	.289	.270	59	152	15	34	44	7	0	1	12	10	21	1	0	3
McCarty	.214	.286	.257	98	350	36	75	100	15	2	2	21	19	80	2	6	8
Parks	.200	.200	.238	7	20	3	4	4	0	0	0	1	1	2	0	0	1
Webster	.198	.245	.274	49	106	14	21	26	2	0	1	8	11	8	1	0	0
Stahoviak	.193	.263	.233	20	57	1	11	15	4	0	0	1	3	22	0	2	4
Leius	.167	.167	.227	10	18	4	3	3	0	0	0	2	2	4	0	0	2
Maksudian	.167	.250	.353	5	12	2	2	3	1	0	0	2	4	2	0	0	0
Bush	.156	.200	.269	35	45	1	7	9	2	0	0	3	7	13	0	0	0
Lee	.152	.182	.176	15	33	3	5	6	1	0	0	4	1	4	0	0	0
Hocking	.139	.167	.262	15	36	7	5	6	1	0	0	0	6	8	1	0	1

Pitching	W-L	ERA	G	GS	CG	GF	Sho	SV	IP	H	R	ER	HR	BB	SO
Garces	0-0	0.00	3	0	0	1	0	0	4	4	2	0	0	2	3
Casian	5-3	3.02	54	0	0	8	0	1	56.2	59	23	19	1	14	31
Willis	3-0	3.10	53	0	0	21	0	5	58	56	23	20	2	17	44
Aguilera	4-3	3.11	65	0	0	61	0	34	72.1	60	25	25	9	14	59
Hartley	1-2	4.00	53	0	0	21	0	1	81	86	38	36	4	36	57
Banks	11-12	4.04	31	30	0	1	0	0	171.1	186	91	77	17	78	138
Deshaies	11-13	4.41	27	27	1	0	0	0	167.1	159	85	82	24	51	80
Tapani	12-15	4.43	36	35	3	0	1	0	225.2	243	123	111	21	57	150
Guthrie	2-1	4.71	22	0	0	2	0	0	21	20	11	11	2	16	15
Trombley	6-6	4.88	44	10	0	8	0	2	114.1	131	72	62	15	41	85
Erickson	8-19	5.19	34	34	1	0	0	0	218.2	266	138	126	17	71	116
Brummett	2-1	5.74	5	5	0	0	0	0	26.2	29	17	17	3	15	10
Guardado	3-8	6.18	19	16	0	2	0	0	94.2	123	68	65	13	36	46
Tsamis	1-2	6.19	41	0	0	18	0	1	68.1	86	51	47	9	27	30
Mahomes	1-5	7.71	12	5	0	4	0	0	37.1	47	34	32	8	16	23
Merriman	1-1	9.67	19	0	0	10	0	0	27	36	29	29	3	23	14

1994 preliminary roster

Pitchers (17)
Rick Aguilera
Greg Brummett
Ron Caridad
Larry Casian
Jose Correa
Scott Erickson
Eddie Guardado
Mark Guthrie
Pat Mahomes
Brett Merriman
Oscar Munoz
Carlos Pulido
Todd Ritchie
Dave Stevens
Kevin Tapani
Mike Trombley
Carl Willis

Catchers (4)
Mike Durant
Derek Parks
Matt Walbeck
Lenny Webster

Infielders (10)
Steve Dunn
Chip Hale
Denny Hocking
Kent Hrbek
Chuck Knoblauch
Scott Leius
Pat Meares
Jeff Reboulet
Gary Scott
Scott Stahoviak

Outfielders (8)
Rich Becker
J.T. Bruett
Marty Cordova
Shane Mack
David McCarty
Pedro Munoz
Kirby Puckett
Dave Winfield

Games played by position

Player	G	C	1B	2B	3B	SS	OF	DH
Becker	3	0	0	0	0	0	3	0
Brito	27	0	0	0	0	0	10	7
Bruett	17	0	0	0	0	0	13	0
Bush	35	0	4	0	0	0	1	5
Hale	69	0	1	21	19	1	0	19
Harper	147	134	0	0	0	0	0	7
Hocking	15	0	0	1	0	12	0	0
Hrbek	123	0	115	0	0	0	0	2
Jorgensen	59	0	9	0	45	6	0	0
Knoblauch	153	0	0	148	0	6	1	0
Larkin	56	0	18	0	2	0	28	3
Lee	15	0	0	0	0	0	13	0
Leius	10	0	0	0	0	9	0	0
Mack	128	0	0	0	0	0	128	0
Maksudian	5	0	4	0	1	0	0	0
McCarty	98	0	36	0	0	0	67	2
Meares	111	0	0	0	0	111	0	0
Munoz	104	0	0	0	0	0	102	0
Parks	7	7	0	0	0	0	0	0
Puckett	156	0	0	0	0	0	139	17
Reboulet	109	0	0	11	35	62	3	1
Stahoviak	20	0	0	0	19	0	0	0
Webster	49	45	0	0	0	0	0	1
Winfield	143	0	5	0	0	0	31	105

Sick call: 1993 DL Report

Player	Days on the DL
Rich Becker	21
Larry Casian	44
Scott Erickson	13
Mark Guthrie	128
Kent Hrbek	15
Gene Larkin**	99
Scott Leius	165
Shane Mack	15
Mike Maksudian	13
Pedro Munoz	25
Carl Willis	39

** Three separate terms on Disabled List

Minor League Report

Class AAA: Portland finished at 87-56, winning both halves of the Pacific Coast League Northern Division, but fell to Tucson in six games in the league finals. Bernardo Brito hit .339 with 20 homers and 72 RBI. Jeff Carter hit .325. Pat Howell stole 36 bases. Pat Mahomes won the league ERA crown, (11-4, 3.03). Brett Merriman had 15 saves. Tom Drees had 15 wins. **Class AA:** Nashville finished at 72-70, winning the first half of the Southern League Western Division, but fell to Birmingham in the playoffs. Marty Cordova had 19 homers. David Rivera stole 35 bases. Oscar Munoz was 11-4 with a 3.08 ERA and struck out 139 in 132 innings. **Class A:** Fort Myers finished at 55-79, last in the Florida State League West Division. Brent Brede hit .330. Chad Roper had eight homers and 62 RBI. Ted Corbin stole 22 bases. . . . Fort Wayne finished at 68-67, fifth in the Midwest League Northern Division. LaTroy Hawkins was 15-5 with a league-best 2.06 ERA and also led the loop with 179 strikeouts in 157 innings. Gustavo Gandarillas had 25 saves. Ken Tirpack hit .294 with nine homers and 70 RBI. Anthony Byrd hit .292 with 16 homers and 79 RBI. **Short-season:** Elizabethton finished at 37-30, first in the Appalachian League Southern Division, but was swept in two games by Burlington in the league finals. Danny Venezia hit .310 and stole 21 bases. Shawn Miller was 5-0 with a 2.63 ERA. Javier DeJesus was 9-0 with a 2.99 ERA and 79 strikeouts. Troy Carrasco struck out 75. . . . Fort Myers finished at 23-36, sixth in the Gulf Coast League Western Division. Robert DeBrino led the league with 11 saves. Jason Tatar led the league with 73 strikeouts. The team's .216 average was next to last in the league.

Tops in the organization

Batter	Club	Avg	G	AB	R	H	HR	RBI
Carter, Jeff	Por	.325	101	381	73	124	0	48
Bruett, J.T.	Por	.322	90	320	70	103	2	40
Lee, Derek	Por	.315	106	381	79	120	10	80
Parks, Derek	Por	.311	107	363	63	113	17	71
Tirpack, Ken	Ftw	.294	127	473	71	139	9	70

Home Runs			Wins		
Brito, Bernardo	Por	20	Hawkins, LaTroy	Ftw	15
Cordova, Marty	Nsh	19	Drees, Tom	Por	15
Parks, Derek	Por	17	Fultz, Aaron	Ftw	14
Byrd, Anthony	Ftw	16	Munoz, Oscar	Por	13
Becker, Rich	Nsh	15	Mahomes, Pat	Por	11

RBI			Saves		
Lee, Derek	Por	80	Gandarillas, G.	Ftw	25
Byrd, Anthony	Ftw	79	Merriman, Brett	Por	15
Cordova, Marty	Nsh	77	Johnson, Greg	Nsh	14
Brito, Bernardo	Por	72	Chapin, Darrin	Por	14
Parks, Derek	Por	71	Garcia, Luis	Ftm	10

Stolen Bases			Strikeouts		
Howell, Pat	Por	36	Hawkins, LaTroy	Ftw	179
Rivera, David	Nsh	35	Munoz, Oscar	Por	168
Becker, Rich	Nsh	29	Fultz, Aaron	Ftw	147
Byrd, Anthony	Ftw	24	Serafini, Dan	Ftw	147
Several players tied		23	Radke, Brad	Nsh	145

Pitcher	Club	W-L	ERA	IP	H	BB	SO
Hawkins, LaTroy	Ftw	15-5	2.06	157	110	41	179
Mahomes, Pat	Por	11-4	3.03	116	89	54	94
Munoz, Oscar	Por	13-6	3.31	163	152	68	168
Caridad, Ron	Ftw	6-8	3.51	144	138	91	124
Fultz, Aaron	Ftw	14-8	3.55	152	142	64	147

Minnesota (1961-1993), includes Wash. (1901-1960)

Runs: Most, career, all-time

1466	Sam Rice, 1915-1933
1258	Harmon Killebrew, 1954-1974
1154	Joe Judge, 1915-1932
1037	Buddy Myer, 1925-1941
1004	Clyde Milan, 1907-1922

Hits: Most, career, all-time

2889	Sam Rice, 1915-1933
2291	Joe Judge, 1915-1932
2100	Clyde Milan, 1907-1922
2085	Rod Carew, 1967-1978
2024	Harmon Killebrew, 1954-1974

2B: Most, career, all-time

479	Sam Rice, 1915-1933
421	Joe Judge, 1915-1932
391	Mickey Vernon, 1939-1955
343	KIRBY PUCKETT, 1984-1993
329	Tony Oliva, 1962-1976

3B: Most, career, all-time

183	Sam Rice, 1915-1933
157	Joe Judge, 1915-1932
125	Goose Goslin, 1921-1938
113	Buddy Myer, 1925-1941
108	Mickey Vernon, 1939-1955
90	Rod Carew, 1967-1978 (8)

HR: Most, career, all-time

559	Harmon Killebrew, 1954-1974
283	KENT HRBEK, 1981-1993
256	Bob Allison, 1958-1970
220	Tony Oliva, 1962-1976
201	GARY GAETTI, 1981-1990

RBI: Most, career, all-time

1540	Harmon Killebrew, 1954-1974
1045	Sam Rice, 1915-1933
1033	KENT HRBEK, 1981-1993
1026	Mickey Vernon, 1939-1955
1001	Joe Judge, 1915-1932

SB: Most, career, all-time

495	Clyde Milan, 1907-1922
346	Sam Rice, 1915-1933
321	George Case, 1937-1947
271	Rod Carew, 1967-1978
210	Joe Judge, 1915-1932

BB: Most, career, all-time

1505	Harmon Killebrew, 1954-1974
1274	Eddie Yost, 1944-1958
943	Joe Judge, 1915-1932
864	Buddy Myer, 1925-1941
801	KENT HRBEK, 1981-1993

BA: Highest, career, all-time

.334	Rod Carew, 1967-1978
.328	Heinie Manush, 1930-1935
.323	Sam Rice, 1915-1933
.323	Goose Goslin, 1921-1938
.319	KIRBY PUCKETT, 1984-1993

Slug avg: Highest, career, all-time

.514	Harmon Killebrew, 1954-1974
.502	Goose Goslin, 1921-1938
.500	Roy Sievers, 1954-1959
.483	KENT HRBEK, 1981-1993
.481	Jimmie Hall, 1963-1966

Games started: Most, career, all-time

666	Walter Johnson, 1907-1927
433	Jim Kaat, 1959-1973
345	Bert Blyleven, 1970-1988
331	Camilo Pascual, 1954-1966
259	FRANK VIOLA, 1982-1989

Saves: Most, career, all-time

149	RICK AGUILERA, 1989-1993
108	Ron Davis, 1982-1986
104	JEFF REARDON, 1987-1989
96	Firpo Marberry, 1923-1936
88	Al Worthington, 1964-1969

Shutouts: Most, career, all-time

110	Walter Johnson, 1907-1927
31	Camilo Pascual, 1954-1966
29	Bert Blyleven, 1970-1988
23	Jim Kaat, 1959-1973
23	Dutch Leonard, 1938-1946

Wins: Most, career, all-time

417	Walter Johnson, 1907-1927
190	Jim Kaat, 1959-1973
149	Bert Blyleven, 1970-1988
145	Camilo Pascual, 1954-1966
128	Jim Perry, 1963-1972

K: Most, career, all-time

3509	Walter Johnson, 1907-1927
2035	Bert Blyleven, 1970-1988
1885	Camilo Pascual, 1954-1966
1851	Jim Kaat, 1959-1973
1214	FRANK VIOLA, 1982-1989

Win pct: Highest, career, all-time

.622	Firpo Marberry, 1923-1936
.602	Sam Jones, 1928-1931
.599	Walter Johnson, 1907-1927
.598	Earl Whitehill, 1933-1936
.588	Mudcat Grant, 1964-1967

ERA: Lowest, career, all-time

2.17	Walter Johnson, 1907-1927
2.64	Doc Ayers, 1913-1919
2.75	Harry Harper, 1913-1919
2.76	Charlie Smith, 1906-1909
2.83	Bert Gallia, 1912-1917
3.15	Jim Perry, 1963-1972 (10)

Runs: Most, season

128	Rod Carew, 1977
127	Joe Cronin, 1930
126	Zoilo Versalles, 1965
122	Buddy Lewis, 1938
121	Heinie Manush, 1932
121	Sam Rice, 1930

Hits: Most, season

239	Rod Carew, 1977
234	KIRBY PUCKETT, 1988
227	Sam Rice, 1925
223	KIRBY PUCKETT, 1986
221	Heinie Manush, 1933

2B: Most, season

51	Mickey Vernon, 1946
50	Stan Spence, 1946
45	Joe Cronin, 1933
45	KIRBY PUCKETT, 1989
45	Zoilo Versalles, 1965

3B: Most, season

20	Goose Goslin, 1925
19	Joe Cassidy, 1904
19	Cecil Travis, 1941
18	Joe Cronin, 1932
18	Goose Goslin, 1923
18	Sam Rice, 1923
18	Howie Shanks, 1921
18	John Stone, 1935
16	Rod Carew, 1977 (11)

HR: Most, season

49	Harmon Killebrew, 1964
49	Harmon Killebrew, 1969
48	Harmon Killebrew, 1962
46	Harmon Killebrew, 1961
45	Harmon Killebrew, 1963

RBI: Most, season

140	Harmon Killebrew, 1969
129	Goose Goslin, 1924
126	Joe Cronin, 1930
126	Joe Cronin, 1931
126	Harmon Killebrew, 1962

SB: Most, season

88	Clyde Milan, 1912
75	Clyde Milan, 1913
63	Sam Rice, 1920
62	Danny Moeller, 1913
61	George Case, 1943
49	Rod Carew, 1976 (8)

BB: Most, season

151	Eddie Yost, 1956
145	Harmon Killebrew, 1969
141	Eddie Yost, 1950
131	Harmon Killebrew, 1967
131	Eddie Yost, 1954

BA: Highest, season

.388	Rod Carew, 1977
.379	Goose Goslin, 1928
.376	Ed Delahanty, 1902
.364	Rod Carew, 1974
.359	Rod Carew, 1975

Slug avg: Highest, season

.614	Goose Goslin, 1928
.606	Harmon Killebrew, 1961
.590	Ed Delahanty, 1902
.584	Harmon Killebrew, 1969
.579	Roy Sievers, 1957

Games started: Most, season

42	Walter Johnson, 1910
42	Jim Kaat, 1965
41	Jim Kaat, 1966
40	Bert Blyleven, 1973
40	Bob Groom, 1912
40	Walter Johnson, 1914
40	Jim Perry, 1970

Saves: Most, season

42	RICK AGUILERA, 1991
42	JEFF REARDON, 1988
41	RICK AGUILERA, 1992
34	RICK AGUILERA, 1993
34	Ron Perranoski, 1970

Shutouts: Most, season

11	Walter Johnson, 1913
9	Bert Blyleven, 1973
9	Walter Johnson, 1914
9	Bob Porterfield, 1953
8	Walter Johnson, 1910
8	Walter Johnson, 1917
8	Walter Johnson, 1918
8	Camilo Pascual, 1961

Wins: Most, season

36	Walter Johnson, 1913
33	Walter Johnson, 1912
28	Walter Johnson, 1914
27	Walter Johnson, 1915
26	General Crowder, 1932
25	Jim Kaat, 1966 (6)

K: Most, season

313	Walter Johnson, 1910
303	Walter Johnson, 1912
258	Bert Blyleven, 1973
249	Bert Blyleven, 1974
243	Walter Johnson, 1913

Win pct: Highest, season

.837	Walter Johnson, 1913
.800	Stan Coveleski, 1925
.800	Firpo Marberry, 1931
.774	FRANK VIOLA, 1988
.773	Bill Campbell, 1976

ERA: Lowest, season

1.14	Walter Johnson, 1913
1.27	Walter Johnson, 1918
1.36	Walter Johnson, 1910
1.39	Walter Johnson, 1912
1.49	Walter Johnson, 1919
2.49	Dave Goltz, 1978 (*)

Most pinch-hit homers, season

4	Don Mincher, 1964

Most pinch-hit, homers, career

8	Bob Allison, 1961-1970 (none with Was-1958-1960)

Most consecutive games, batting safely

33	Heine Manush, Was-1933
31	Sam Rice, Was-1924
31	Ken Landreaux, 1980

Most consecutive scoreless innings

55	Walter Johnson, Was-1913
40	Walter Johnson, Was-1918
37	Walter Johnson, Was-1913

No hit games

Walter Johnson, Was at Bos AL, 1-0; July 1, 1920.

Bobby Burke, Was vs Bos AL, 5-0; August 8, 1931.

Jack Kralick, Min vs KC AL, 1-0; August 26, 1962.

Dean Chance, Min at Cle AL, 2-1; August 25, 1967 (2nd game).

Jay Cashion, six innings, called so Cleveland could catch train, Was vs Cle AL, 2-0; August 20, 1912 (2nd game).

Walter Johnson, seven innings, rain, Was vs StL AL, 2-0; August 25, 1924.

Dean Chance, five perfect innings, rain, Min vs Bos AL, 2-0; August 6, 1967.

ACTIVE PLAYERS in caps. Leader from the franchise's current location is included. If not in the top five, leader's rank is listed in parenthesis; asterisk (*) indicates player is not in top 25.

289

Oakland Athletics

by H. Darr Beiser, USA TODAY

Troy Neel emerged as a new bat in the A's lineup, hitting .290 with 19 home runs in 123 games.

1993 Athletics: A dismal fall to the cellar

At least the Oakland A's fall from first to worst wasn't unprecedented—their forebears, the Philadelphia Athletics won the league title in 1914 and finished in last place the next season.

The Oakland A's, who won four AL West titles in five years, turned in the league's worst record in '93: 68-94, even after they won 16 of their final 27.

When the A's lost the 1992 ALCS to Toronto, everyone knew it was over. With 15 free agents on the roster and ownership dedicated to tightening the budget, it was common knowledge that a lot of faces would be in other places come the following year. Jose Canseco had been traded before the playoffs began, Carney Lansford retired afterward, Walt Weiss was lost in the expansion draft, and Mike Moore, Harold Baines and Willie Wilson departed as free agents.

When Mark McGwire suffered a heel injury that sidelined him in May, Oakland was down and out. Looking for offensive leadership, the team turned to Ruben Sierra, acquired in the Canseco deal. Although he led the team with 101 RBI and 22 homers, his average was a woeful .233. Dennis Eckersley, a year after winning both the AL MVP and Cy Young award, struggled from the outset and never righted himself. He saved just 36 of 46 opportunites (.783), and had a 4.16 ERA, his worst in seven seasons as Oakland's closer.

He spoke for the entire team after the final game: "We've been waiting for this day since August. For me personally, it's a relief to have it end. It's a relief from all of the pain of the season."

Pain abounded on the Athletics. In addition to McGwire's heel, Dave Henderson suffered his second consecutive injury-plagued season, Lance Blankenship missed most of the final two months and catcher Terry Steinbach missed the final six weeks.

Performance was the problem on the mound. Four of five veteran pitchers—Bob Welch, Ron Darling, Storm Davis and Shawn Hillegas—struggled. Davis was released; Hillegas was demoted. Bobby Witt was the team's best pitcher (14-13, 4.21 ERA).

There was a silver lining to this cloud of despair, though: the emergence of several young players. Rookie pitchers Mike Mohler, Todd Van Poppel, Miguel Jimenez and Steve Karsay (the latter acquired in the Rickey Henderson trade) provide a glimmer of hope for '94. Offensively, second baseman Brent Gates, designated hitter Troy Neel and third baseman Craig Paquette had productive seasons. Gates was the biggest surprise, hitting .290 with 69 RBI while committing just 14 errors. Neel ended with a .290 average and 19 homers. Paquette showed steady defense and hit 12 homers.

Winning almost 60% of their games in the final month, though, the A's gave manager Tony LaRussa hope. "We had a chance to really disappear but we had a winning September," he said.

—*by Deron Snyder*

1994 Athletics: Preview

The A's will be built around youngsters, but first baseman Mark McGwire remains the main man in Oakland—his full return from heel surgery is vital to the team' success.

Dave Henderson and Lance Blankenship were slated to play centerfield last season, but both suffered injuries and neither may be the answer in '94. Aside from Ruben Sierra in right, the outfield positions are far from settled. Chances are good for another no-name or free agent to be roaming the outfield.

With veteran Ron Darling or Bobby Witt to anchor the staff, Karsay and Van Poppel should be able to hold down two of the five spots in the rotation.

Terry Steinbach returns, coming off a career-high .285 average in '93.

—*by Deron Snyder*

1993 Athletics: Between the lines

▶**April 11:** *Milestone*—Rickey Henderson hit his 200th career home run.

▶**April 17:** It was early in the year, but the handwriting was already on the wall: The A's dipped below .500 for the first time since Sept. 29, 1987.

▶**April 21:** More bad news: Dennis Eckersley blew his third consecutive save. He had never before blown even two in a row.

▶**May 2:** Third baseman Kevin Seitzer volunteered to take the mound when pitcher Kelly Downs was ejected in the eighth inning following a yelling match with Cleveland DH Carlos Martinez, who charged the mound. Glenallen Hill replaced Martinez and took a called third strike from Seitzer, who hadn't pitched since his senior year in high school.

▶**May 3:** Mark McGwire blasted a pair of two-run homers—the 25th multi-homer game of his career. Meanwhile Rickey Henderson crashed into the outfield wall and had to leave the game with a sore left shoulder.

▶**May 6:** McGwire had his second two-homer game in four days (multi-homer game No. 26).

▶**May 12:** Eckersley blew his fourth save of the season, more than all of 1992, and upped his ERA to 4.97.

▶**May 21:** Things were still looking good for Rickey Henderson—he hit a three-run homer in the eighth inning, drove in two more runs in the ninth with a triple, and then scored the winning run as the A's came back from a six-run deficit to top the White Sox 12-11 at Comiskey Park.

▶**May 26:** The Twins beat the A's 12-11 in a game that featured five lead changes and three blown saves, including Eckersley's fifth of the year.

▶**June 16:** Rickey Henderson truly became the world's all-time stolen base leader when his 1,066th swipe surpassed the record of Yutaka Fukumoto, who played in Japan from 1970-88.

Fukumoto was at the game, and Henderson presented him with the base.

▶**June 23:** Rickey Henderson broke his own record—again—by homering to start Oakland's 8-7 loss to the Mariners. It was his fourth leadoff homer of the season and 59th of his career. Bobby Bonds is second on the all-time list with 35.

▶**July 5:** Henderson led off both games of a doubleheader against the Indians with homers. He was only the second player in history to achieve the feat. The other was Harry Hooper, who did it in 1913 for the Red Sox. *Quote of the day*—Henderson, on his historic feat: "It's a great feeling in that sense, but for me, the biggest thing is getting our team a run and getting us in the ballgame."

▶**July 8:** Troy Neel drove in seven of Oakland's nine runs, but the A's fell to the Red Sox 11-9.

▶**July 9:** Neel homered twice for the second consecutive game, giving him four home runs in five plate appearances.

▶**July 15:** Ruben Sierra hit a three-run homer and matched his career high with five RBI in Oakland's 8-3 win against the slumping Yankees.

▶**July 21:** Scott Hemond hit his first major league home run and drove in five runs as the A's beat Cleveland 7-2.

▶**July 25:** Bob Welch threw 69 pitches, ending manager Tony La Russa's rather unsuccessful—and unpopular—experiment with a 50-pitch limit. The A's had gone 1-6 under the new arrangement, in which pitchers were held to about 50 pitches and expected to work every three days.

▶**July 29:** Bob Welch threw seven shutout innings in a 2-1 win against the Angels, running his career record against California to 13-2.

▶**July 31:** In a move that shocked some fans as much as the Canseco trade of '92, Rickey Henderson was shipped off to the Blue Jays. In the thick of their pennant drive, the Jays gave up their top pitching prospect, Steve Karsay, for Henderson, who would become a free agent at the end of the season. In his last game in an A's uniform, Henderson went 1-for-3 with two stolen bases and scored Oakland's only runs in an 8-2 loss to Texas. Oakland fans gave him a standing ovation as he walked to the dugout after grounding out in his last at-bat, but Henderson did not acknowledge the gesture.

▶**August 14:** Bobby Witt threw nine innings of five-hit ball but wound up with a no-decision as the Twins beat the A's 5-1 in 12 innings.

▶**August 16:** Rookie Todd Van Poppel allowed two hits in 6 2/3 innings to win his fourth consecutive start as Oakland beat Milwaukee 4-1. Van Poppel struck out one and walked five in the longest outing of his big-league career. He was 4-0 with a 2.41 ERA in his last four starts after going 0-3 with a 7.47 ERA in his first four outings.

▶**August 18:** Steve Karsay, acquired in the Rickey Henderson trade, won his major league debut as the A's defeated Milwaukee 6-3. Karsay (2.84 ERA) had never pitched above Double-A.

▶**August 20:** It was a rematch of the protagonists in one of baseball's most famous moments, but the result was slightly different. Dennis Eckersley faced Kirk Gibson for the first time since Gibson tagged him for the game-winning homer in Game One of the 1988 World Series. Gibson again came to the plate in the ninth with men on base, but could manage only an RBI single. Eckersley later struck out Tony Phillips to save the 7-6 Oakland win.

▶**September 3:** Mark McGwire returned to the lineup after missing 100 games with torn tissue in his left foot. He grounded out with the bases loaded in a fifth-inning, pinch-hit appearence, but got a standing ovation from the Oakland crowd anyway.

▶**September 20:** Todd Van Poppel pitched into the seventh inning for the first time in 13 career major league starts in a 2-1 win over Kansas City.

▶**September 22:** Ron Darling threw eight shutout innings but failed to win for the first time since Aug. 18—he was the victim of Dennis Eckersley's 10th blown save of '93.

▶**September 23:** Bobby Witt fanned 11 Kansas City batters in eight innings as the A's slipped past the Royals 2-1.

▶**October 1:** Dave Henderson hit his first grand slam in 11 years to lead the A's to a 7-2 win against California. He reached the 20-homer plateau for the fourth time in six seasons.

▶**October 3:** The first-to-worst A's ended up in the cellar, 26 games out. *League leaders, pitching—*Dennis Eckersley was fifth in saves (36).

—by John Hunt, Scott Kauffman, Lisa Winston, Deron Snyder, Matt Young

Team directory

▶**Owner:** Walter A. Haas, Jr.
▶**General Manager:** Sandy Alderson
▶**Ballpark:**
Oakland Coliseum
Nimitz Freeway & Hegenberger Road,
Oakland, Calif.
510-568-5600
Capacity 48,800
Public transportation available
Wheelchair sections and ramps,
picnic areas
▶**Team publications:**
A's Magazine, media guide
510-638-4900, ext. 386
▶**TV, radio broadcast stations:**
KNEW 910 AM, KRON Channel 4,
SportsChannel
▶**Spring Training:**
Phoenix Municipal Stadium
Phoenix, Ariz.
Capacity 8,500
602-392-0074

OAKLAND ATHLETICS 1993 final stats

Batting	BA	SLG	OB	G	AB	R	H	TB	2B	3B	HR	RBI	BB	SO	SB	CS	E
McGwire	.333	.726	.467	27	84	16	28	61	6	0	9	24	21	19	0	1	0
Neel	.290	.473	.367	123	427	59	124	202	21	0	19	63	49	101	3	5	5
Gates	.290	.391	.357	139	535	64	155	209	29	2	7	69	56	75	7	3	14
Steinbach	.285	.416	.333	104	389	47	111	162	19	1	10	43	25	65	3	3	7
Aldrete	.267	.443	.353	95	255	40	68	113	13	1	10	33	34	45	1	1	2
Hemond	.256	.414	.353	91	215	31	55	89	16	0	6	26	32	55	14	5	4
Browne	.250	.323	.306	76	260	27	65	84	13	0	2	19	22	17	4	0	6
Bordick	.249	.311	.332	159	546	60	136	170	21	2	3	48	60	58	10	10	13
Brosius	.249	.390	.296	70	213	26	53	83	10	1	6	25	14	37	6	0	2
Abbott	.246	.410	.281	20	61	11	15	25	1	0	3	9	3	20	2	0	2
Sierra	.233	.390	.288	158	630	77	147	246	23	5	22	101	52	97	25	5	7
Helfand	.231	.231	.231	8	13	1	3	3	0	0	0	1	0	1	0	0	0
Lydy	.225	.333	.288	41	102	11	23	34	5	0	2	7	8	39	2	0	3
D.Henderson	.220	.427	.275	107	382	37	84	163	19	0	20	53	32	113	0	3	2.
Paquette	.219	.382	.245	105	393	35	86	150	20	4	12	46	14	108	4	2	13
Mercedes	.213	.255	.260	20	47	5	10	12	2	0	0	3	2	15	1	1	1
Armas	.194	.355	.242	15	31	7	6	11	2	0	1	1	1	12	1	0	0
Blankenship	.190	.254	.363	94	252	43	48	64	8	1	2	23	67	64	13	5	5
Sveum	.177	.304	.316	30	79	12	14	24	2	1	2	6	16	21	0	0	3
Fox	.143	.214	.172	29	56	5	8	12	1	0	1	5	2	7	0	2	0

Pitching	W-L	ERA	G	GS	CG	GF	Sho	SV	IP	H	R	ER	HR	BB	SO
Smithberg	1-2	2.75	13	0	0	9	0	3	19.2	13	7	6	2	7	4
Honeycutt	1-4	2.81	52	0	0	7	0	1	41.2	30	18	13	2	20	21
Nunez	3-6	3.81	56	0	0	16	0	1	75.2	89	36	32	2	29	58
Jimenez	1-0	4.00	5	4	0	0	0	0	27	27	12	12	5	16	13
Karsay	3-3	4.04	8	8	0	0	0	0	49	49	23	22	4	16	33
Eckersley	2-4	4.16	64	0	0	52	0	36	67	67	32	31	7	13	80
Witt	14-13	4.21	35	33	5	0	1	0	220	226	112	103	16	91	131
Young	1-1	4.30	3	3	0	0	0	0	14.2	14	7	7	5	6	4
Gossage	4-5	4.53	39	0	0	12	0	1	47.2	49	24	24	6	26	40
Van Poppel	6-6	5.04	16	16	0	0	0	0	84	76	50	47	10	62	47
Darling	5-9	5.16	31	29	3	1	0	0	178	198	107	102	22	72	95
Slusarski	0-0	5.19	2	1	0	0	0	0	8.2	9	5	5	1	11	1
Welch	9-11	5.29	30	28	0	0	0	0	166.2	208	102	98	25	56	63
Horsman	2-0	5.40	40	0	0	5	0	0	25	25	15	15	2	15	17
Mohler	1-6	5.60	42	9	0	4	0	0	64.1	57	45	40	10	44	42
Downs	5-10	5.64	42	12	0	12	0	0	119.2	135	80	75	14	60	66
Hillegas	3-6	6.97	18	11	0	4	0	0	60.2	78	48	47	8	33	29
Campbell	0-0	7.31	11	0	0	4	0	0	16	20	13	13	1	11	9
Briscoe	1-0	8.03	17	0	0	6	0	0	24.2	26	25	22	2	26	24

1994 preliminary roster

PITCHERS (15)
Mark Acre
Scott Baker
John Briscoe
Ron Darling
Kelly Downs
Dennis Eckersley
Vince Horsman
Miguel Jimenez
Steve Karsay
Curtis Shaw
Roger Smithberg
Tanyon Sturtze
Todd Van Poppel
Bob Welch
Bobby Witt

CATCHERS (6)
Eric Helfand
Scott Hemond
Henry Mercedes
Izzy Molina
Terry Steinbach
George Williams

INFIELDERS (9)
Kurt Abbott
Mike Aldrete
Marcos Armas
Mike Bordick
Fausto Cruz
Brent Gates
Mark McGwire
Troy Neel
Craig Paquette

OUTFIELDERS (6)
Lance Blankenship
Scott Brosius
Jose Herrera
Scott Lydy
Ruben Sierra
Ernie Young

Games played by position

Player	G	C	1B	2B	3B	SS	OF	DH
Abbott	20	0	0	2	0	6	13	0
Aldrete	95	0	59	0	0	0	20	6
Armas	15	0	12	0	0	0	1	2
Blankenship	94	0	6	19	0	2	66	5
Bordick	159	0	0	1	0	159	0	0
Brosius	70	0	11	0	10	6	46	2
Browne	76	0	2	3	13	0	56	0
Fox	29	0	0	0	0	0	26	2
Gates	139	0	0	139	0	0	0	0
Helfand	8	5	0	0	0	0	0	0
Hemond	91	75	1	1	0	0	6	3
D. Henderson	107	0	0	0	0	0	76	28
Lydy	41	0	0	0	0	0	38	2
McGwire	27	0	25	0	0	0	0	0
Mercedes	20	18	0	0	0	0	0	1
Neel	123	0	34	0	0	0	0	85
Paquette	105	0	0	0	104	0	1	1
Sierra	158	0	0	0	0	0	133	25
Steinbach	104	86	15	0	0	0	0	6
Sveum	30	0	14	4	7	1	1	2

Sick call: 1993 DL Report

Player	Days on the DL
Lance Blankenship	49
Jerry Browne	90
Rich Gossage	26
Dave Henderson	24
Rick Honeycutt	39
Mark McGwire	112
Todd Revenig	182
Terry Steinbach	49
Bob Welch	16
Curt Young*	110

Two separate terms on Disabled List

Minor League Report

Class AAA: Tacoma finished at 69-74, last in the Pacific Coast League Northern Division. Kurt Abbott hit .319 with 12 homers, 79 RBI and 19 steals. Mike Aldrete hit .320. Marcos Armas batted .290 with 15 homers and 89 RBI. Eric Fox hit .312. Kevin Campbell had 12 saves. **Class AA:** Huntsville finished at 71-70, fourth in the Southern League Western Division. Jim Bowie won the batting crown at .333 with 14 homers and 101 RBI. George Williams hit .295 with 14 homers and 77 RBI. Curtis Shaw had 132 strikeouts despite losing 13 in a row. **Class A:** Modesto finished at 72-64, winning the first half of the California League Northern Division but falling to High Desert in five games in the league finals. Joel Wolfe hit .350. Ernie Young had 23 homers. Scott Shockey had 87 RBI. Russ Brock was 12-4 with a 3.81 ERA. Rob Pierce had 14 saves. . . . Madison finished at 77-68, first overall in the Midwest League Northern Division, but did not go to the playoffs. Cliff Foster was 10-8 with a 3.14 ERA. Mark Acre had 21 saves. **Short-season:** Southern Oregon finished at 37-39, third in the Northwest League South Division. Geoff Loomis had 50 RBI. Tim Kubinski was 5-5 with a 2.83 ERA. Christian Michalak was 7-3 with a 2.85 ERA. . . . Scottsdale finished at 31-19, first in the Arizona League. John Jones won the league batting crown at .341. He had five homers and 39 RBI. Leon Hamburg and Fred Soriano each had five homers as well. Trent Montgomery was 4-3 with a 3.12 ERA. Brian Domenico was 4-1 with a 3.17 ERA. Gustavo Gil had seven wins. Francis Mojica had five saves.

Tops in the organization

Batter	Club	Avg	G	AB	R	H	HR	RBI
Wolfe, Joel	Hvl	.334	123	434	74	145	9	74
Bowie, Jim	Hvl	.333	138	501	77	167	14	101
Martinez, M.	Tac	.320	129	518	97	166	12	58
Abbott, Kurt	Tac	.319	133	480	75	153	12	79
Garrison, W.	Tac	.303	138	544	91	165	7	73

Home Runs			Wins		
Young, Ernie	Hvl	28	Osteen, Gavin	Tac	14
Shockey, Scott	Mod	21	Brock, Russ	Mod	12
Gubanich, C.	Mad	19	Jimenez, Miguel	Tac	12
Armas, Marcos	Tac	15	Wojciechowski, S.	Hvl	12
Several players tied		14	Several players tied		10

RBI			Saves		
Bowie, Jim	Hvl	101	Acre, Mark	Hvl	30
Shockey, Scott	Mod	99	Briscoe, John	Tac	22
Armas, Marcos	Tac	89	Pierce, Rob	Mod	14
Young, Ernie	Hvl	86	Campbell, Kevin	Tac	12
Abbott, Kurt	Tac	79	Ingram, Todd	Mod	9

Stolen Bases			Strikeouts		
Young, Ernie	Hvl	31	Foster, Cliff	Mad	146
Martinez, M.	Tac	30	Jimenez, Miguel	Tac	139
Francisco, David	Mad	27	Shaw, Curtis	Hvl	132
Wolfe, Joel	Hvl	24	Karsay, Steve	Hvl	122
Frazier, Terance	Mod	22	Brock, Russ	Mod	121

Pitcher	Club	W-L	ERA	IP	H	BB	SO
Foster, Cliff	Mad	10-8	3.14	140	106	92	146
Jimenez, Miguel	Tac	12-9	3.42	145	124	88	139
Karsay, Steve	Hvl	8-4	3.58	118	111	35	122
Wojciechowski, S.	Hvl	12-8	3.79	152	155	66	104
Osteen, Gavin	Tac	14-10	3.81	154	145	56	92

Oakland (1968-1993), incl. Philadelphia (1901-1952) and Kansas City (1953-1967)

Runs: Most, career, all-time

1036	RICKEY HENDERSON, 1979-1993
997	Bob Johnson, 1933-1942
983	Bert Campaneris, 1964-1976
975	Jimmie Foxx, 1925-1935
969	Al Simmons, 1924-1944

Hits: Most, career, all-time

1882	Bert Campaneris, 1964-1976
1827	Al Simmons, 1924-1944
1705	Jimmy Dykes, 1918-1932
1617	Bob Johnson, 1933-1942
1500	Harry Davis, 1901-1917

2B: Most, career, all-time

365	Jimmy Dykes, 1918-1932
348	Al Simmons, 1924-1944
321	Harry Davis, 1901-1917
307	Bob Johnson, 1933-1942
292	Bing Miller, 1922-1934
270	Bert Campaneris, 1964-1976 (8)

3B: Most, career, all-time

102	Danny Murphy, 1902-1913
98	Al Simmons, 1924-1944
88	Frank Baker, 1908-1914
84	Eddie Collins, 1906-1930
82	Harry Davis, 1901-1917
70	Bert Campaneris, 1964-1976 (12)

HR: Most, career, all-time

302	Jimmie Foxx, 1925-1935
269	Reggie Jackson, 1967-1987
252	Bob Johnson, 1933-1942
231	JOSE CANSECO, 1985-1992
229	MARK McGWIRE, 1986-1993

RBI: Most, career, all-time

1178	Al Simmons, 1924-1944
1075	Jimmie Foxx, 1925-1935
1040	Bob Johnson, 1933-1942
796	Sal Bando, 1966-1976
776	Reggie Jackson, 1967-1987

SB: Most, career, all-time

747	RICKEY HENDERSON, 1979-1993
566	Bert Campaneris, 1964-1976
376	Eddie Collins, 1906-1930
232	Billy North, 1973-1978
223	Harry Davis, 1901-1917

BB: Most, career, all-time

1043	Max Bishop, 1924-1933
965	RICKEY HENDERSON, 1979-1993
853	Bob Johnson, 1933-1942
820	Elmer Valo, 1940-1956
792	Sal Bando, 1966-1976

BA: Highest, career, all-time

.356	Al Simmons, 1924-1944
.339	Jimmie Foxx, 1925-1935
.336	Eddie Collins, 1906-1930
.321	Mickey Cochrane, 1925-1933
.321	Frank Baker, 1908-1914
.294	RICKEY HENDERSON, 1979-1993 (17)

Slug avg: Highest, career, all-time

.640	Jimmie Foxx, 1925-1935
.584	Al Simmons, 1924-1944
.520	Bob Johnson, 1933-1942
.512	JOSE CANSECO, 1985-1992
.509	MARK McGWIRE, 1986-1993

Games started: Most, career, all-time

458	Eddie Plank, 1901-1914
340	Catfish Hunter, 1965-1974
288	Chief Bender, 1903-1914
267	Lefty Grove, 1925-1933
267	Rube Walberg, 1923-1933

Saves: Most, career, all-time

272	DENNIS ECKERSLEY, 1987-1993
136	Rollie Fingers, 1968-1976
73	John Wyatt, 1961-1969
61	JAY HOWELL, 1985-1987
58	Jack Aker, 1964-1968

Shutouts: Most, career, all-time

59	Eddie Plank, 1901-1914
37	Rube Waddell, 1902-1907
36	Chief Bender, 1903-1914
31	Catfish Hunter, 1965-1974
28	Vida Blue, 1969-1977
28	Jack Coombs, 1906-1914

Wins: Most, career, all-time

284	Eddie Plank, 1901-1914
195	Lefty Grove, 1925-1933
193	Chief Bender, 1903-1914
171	Eddie Rommel, 1920-1932
161	Catfish Hunter, 1965-1974

K: Most, career, all-time

1985	Eddie Plank, 1901-1914
1576	Rube Waddell, 1902-1907
1536	Chief Bender, 1903-1914
1523	Lefty Grove, 1925-1933
1520	Catfish Hunter, 1965-1974

Win pct: Highest, career, all-time

.712	Lefty Grove, 1925-1933
.654	Chief Bender, 1903-1914
.637	Eddie Plank, 1901-1914
.633	BOB WELCH, 1988-1993
.632	Jack Coombs, 1906-1914

ERA: Lowest, career, all-time

1.97	Rube Waddell, 1902-1907
2.15	Cy Morgan, 1909-1912
2.32	Chief Bender, 1903-1914
2.39	Eddie Plank, 1901-1914
2.60	Jack Coombs, 1906-1914
2.91	Rollie Fingers, 1968-1976 (8)

Runs: Most, season

152	Al Simmons, 1930
151	Jimmie Foxx, 1932
145	Nap Lajoie, 1901
144	Al Simmons, 1932
137	Eddie Collins, 1912
123	Reggie Jackson, 1969 (10)

Hits: Most, season

253	Al Simmons, 1925
232	Nap Lajoie, 1901
216	Al Simmons, 1932
214	Doc Cramer, 1935
213	Jimmie Foxx, 1932
187	JOSE CANSECO, 1968 (*)

2B: Most, season

53	Al Simmons, 1926
48	Nap Lajoie, 1901
48	Wally Moses, 1937
47	Harry Davis, 1905
47	Eric McNair, 1932
39	Reggie Jackson, 1975 (22)

3B: Most, season

21	Frank Baker, 1912
19	Frank Baker, 1909
18	Danny Murphy, 1910
17	Danny Murphy, 1904
16	Bing Miller, 1929
16	Al Simmons, 1930
16	Amos Strunk, 1915
12	Bert Campaneris, 1965 (*)
12	Phil Garner, 1976 (*)

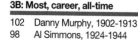

HR: Most, season

58	Jimmie Foxx, 1932	
49	MARK McGWIRE, 1987	
48	Jimmie Foxx, 1933	
47	Reggie Jackson, 1969	
44	JOSE CANSECO, 1991	
44	Jimmie Foxx, 1934	

RBI: Most, season

169	Jimmie Foxx, 1932
165	Al Simmons, 1930
163	Jimmie Foxx, 1933
157	Al Simmons, 1929
156	Jimmie Foxx, 1930
124	JOSE CANSECO, 1988 (13)

SB: Most, season

130	RICKEY HENDERSON, 1982
108	RICKEY HENDERSON, 1983
100	RICKEY HENDERSON, 1980
81	Eddie Collins, 1910
75	Billy North, 1976

BB: Most, season

149	Eddie Joost, 1949
136	Ferris Fain, 1949
133	Ferris Fain, 1950
128	Max Bishop, 1929
128	Max Bishop, 1930
118	Sal Bando, 1970 (10)

BA: Highest, season

.426	Nap Lajoie, 1901
.390	Al Simmons, 1931
.387	Al Simmons, 1925
.381	Al Simmons, 1930
.365	Eddie Collins, 1911
.328	RICKEY HENDERSON, 1990 (*)

Slug avg: Highest, season

.749	Jimmie Foxx, 1932
.708	Al Simmons, 1930
.703	Jimmie Foxx, 1933
.653	Jimmie Foxx, 1934
.643	Nap Lajoie, 1901
.618	MARK McGWIRE, 1987 (11)

Games started: Most, season

46	Rube Waddell, 1904
43	Eddie Plank, 1904
41	Catfish Hunter, 1974
41	Eddie Plank, 1905
40	Vida Blue, 1974
40	George Caster, 1938
40	Jack Coombs, 1911
40	Chuck Dobson, 1970
40	Ken Holtzman, 1973
40	Catfish Hunter, 1970
40	Eddie Plank, 1903
40	Eddie Plank, 1907

Saves: Most, season

51	DENNIS ECKERSLEY, 1992
48	DENNIS ECKERSLEY, 1990
45	DENNIS ECKERSLEY, 1988
43	DENNIS ECKERSLEY, 1991
36	Bill Caudill, 1984
36	DENNIS ECKERSLEY, 1993

Shutouts: Most, season

13	Jack Coombs, 1910
8	Vida Blue, 1971
8	Joe Bush, 1916
8	Eddie Plank, 1907
8	Rube Waddell, 1904
8	Rube Waddell, 1906

Wins: Most, season

31	Jack Coombs, 1910
31	Lefty Grove, 1931
28	Jack Coombs, 1911
28	Lefty Grove, 1930
27	Eddie Rommel, 1922
27	Rube Waddell, 1905
27	BOB WELCH, 1990

K: Most, season

349	Rube Waddell, 1904
302	Rube Waddell, 1903
301	Vida Blue, 1971
287	Rube Waddell, 1905
232	Rube Waddell, 1907

Win pct: Highest, season

.886	Lefty Grove, 1931
.850	Chief Bender, 1914
.849	Lefty Grove, 1930
.821	Chief Bender, 1910
.818	BOB WELCH, 1990

ERA: Lowest, season

1.30	Jack Coombs, 1910
1.39	Harry Krause, 1909
1.48	Rube Waddell, 1905
1.55	Cy Morgan, 1910
1.58	Chief Bender, 1910
1.82	Vida Blue, 1971 (10)

Most pinch-hit homers, season

4	Jeff Burroughs, 1982

Most pinch-hit, homers, career

5	Jeff Burroughs, 1982-1984

Most consecutive games, batting safely

30	Bing Miller, Phi-1929
29	Billy Lamar, Phi-1925
24	Carney Lansford, 1984

Most consecutive scoreless innings

53	Jack Coombs, Phi-1910
43	Rube Waddell, Phi-1905
37	Mike Torrez, 1976

No hit games

Weldon Henley, Phi at StL AL, 6-0; July 22, 1905 (1st game).

Chief Bender, Phi vs Cle AL, 4-0; May 12, 1910.

Joe Bush, Phi vs Cle AL, 5-0; August 26, 1916.

Dick Fowler, Phi vs StL AL, 1-0; September 9, 1945 (2nd game).

Bill McCahan, Phi vs Was AL, 3-0; September 3, 1947.

Catfish Hunter, Oak vs Min AL, 4-0; May 8, 1968 (perfect game).

Vida Blue, Oak vs Min AL, 6-0; September 21, 1970.

Vida Blue (5 innings), Glenn Abbott (1 inning), Paul Lindblad (1 inning) and Rollie Fingers (2 innings), Oak vs Cal AL, 5-0; September 28, 1975.

Blue Moon Odom (5 innings) and Francisco Barrios (4 innings), Chi at Oak AL, 2-1; July 28, 1976.

Mike Warren, Oak vs Chi AL, 3-0; September 29, 1983.

DAVE STEWART, Oak at Tor AL, 5-0; June 29, 1990.

Rube Waddell, five innings, rain, Phi vs StL AL, 2-0; August 15, 1905.

Jimmy Dygert (3 innings) and Rube Waddell (2 innings), five innings, rain, Phi vs Chi AL, 4-3; August 29, 1906. (Waddell allowed hit and two runs in 6th, but rain caused game to revert to 5 innings).

Rube Vickers, five perfect innings, darkness, Phi at Was AL, 4-0; October 5, 1907 (2nd game).

ACTIVE PLAYERS in caps.
Leaders from the franchise's in their current location is included. If not in the top five, leader's rank is listed in parenthesis; asterisk (*) indicates player is not in top 25.

297

Resource directory

Major League Baseball

▶**MLB Headquarters**
350 Park Avenue
New York, NY 10022
212-339-7800

▶**MLB Office of the Commissioner**
350 Park Avenue
New York, NY 10022
212-339-7800

▶**American League**
350 Park Avenue
New York, NY 10022
212-339-7600

▶**National League**
350 Park Avenue
New York, NY 10022
212-339-7700

▶**MLB Players Association**
12 East 49 Street, 24th flr.
New York, NY 10017
212-826-0808

Amateur Baseball Organizations

▶**All American Amateur Baseball Association**
340 Walker Drive
Zanesville, OH 43701
614-453-7349

▶**American Amateur Baseball Congress**
118-19 Redfield Plaza
P.O. Box 467
Marshall, MI 49068
616-781-2002

▶**International Baseball Association**
201 S. Capitol Ave., Ste. 490
Indianapolis, IN 46225
317-237-5757

▶**National Baseball Congress**
P.O. Box 1420
Wichita, KS 67201
316-267-3372

▶**United States Baseball Federation**
2160 Greenwood Ave.
Trenton, NJ 08609
609-586-2381

Youth Leagues

▶**American Legion Baseball National Headquarters**
700 North Pennsylvania
Indianapolis, IN 46204
317-630-1200

▶**Babe Ruth Baseball**
1770 Brunswick Pike
Lawrenceville, NJ 08648
609-695-1434

▶**Little League Baseball, Inc.**
P.O. Box 3485
Williamsport, PA 17701
717-326-1921

▶**Pony Baseball, Inc.**
P.O. Box 225
Washington, PA 15301
412-225-1060

Senior Leagues

▶**Men's Senior Baseball League**
8 Sutton Terrace
Jericho, NY 11753
516-931-2615

Collegiate Baseball Organizations

▶**National Collegiate Athletic Association**
6201 College Boulevard
Overland Park, KS 66211
913-339-1906

▶**National Association of Intercollegiate Athletics**
Baseball Administrator
6120 South Yale Ave.
Suite 1450
Tulsa, Okla. 74136
918-494-8828

▶**National Junior College Athletic Association**
Baseball Tournament Director
P.O. Box 7305
Colorado Springs, CO 80933
719-590-9788

High School Baseball Organizations

▶**National Federation of State High School Associations**
Editor of Baseball Rules Book
11724 NW Plaza Circle
P.O. Box 20626
Kansas City, MO 64195
816-464-5400

Museums, Halls of Fame, etc.

▶**Babe Ruth Birthplace/Baltimore Orioles Museum**
216 Emory Street
Baltimore, MD 21230
410-727-1539

▶**Baseball Hall of Fame**
25 Main Street
Cooperstown, NY 13326
607-547-9988

▶**Peter J. McGovern Little League Baseball Museum**
Route 15
South Williamsport, PA 17701
717-326-3607

▶**USA Baseball**
4880 Navy Road
Millington, TN 38053
901-872-3311

Collectors Shows

▶**Madison Square Garden Baseball Card & Sports Collectors Show**
Madison Square Garden
4 Pennsylvania Plaza
New York, NY 10001
212-465-6000

League forecasts

▶ A team-by-team look at 1994 realignment

▶ East, West and Central Divisions

▶ Prophecies *and more . . .*

USA SNAPSHOTS®

A look at statistics that shape the sports world

Mile-high pitching problem

How the team earned-run average of the Colorado Rockies compares to the worst ERAs of previous expansion teams:

1993 Colorado Rockies
5.49

1962 N.Y. Mets
5.04

1969 Seattle Pilots
4.35

1969 Montreal Expos
4.33

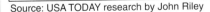

Source: USA TODAY research by John Riley   By Julie Stacey, USA TODAY

Baseball 1994: Surprise! Realignment may make it a lot more fun to follow the game

They call it realignment, but for fans it means regrouping.

Baseball 1994 style is going to sneak up on people and it probably will be giving people little surprises well into the season.

It's just natural for Cleveland fans to wake up in the morning, check out the Indians score from last night, then see how the Yankees did, and the Blue Jays, and the Red Sox.

It could be a warm day in June before it finally sinks in that what really matters is how the Royals did, and the Twins, and the White Sox.

In some cases, it could be a satisfying revelation. Think of all those Giants' and Dodgers' fans who won't care what the Braves did—unless it was beat up on the Giants or Dodgers.

Yes, this realignment thing is going to take some getting used to. The schedule is the same one we had in 1993, so it won't be so obviously noticeable that the Pirates vs. the Phillies doesn't matter so much any more, but the Cardinals vs. the Astros suddenly does.

But this new look shouldn't be judged on what team is in what division, where the power seems to lie (that Atlanta-Philadelphia-Montreal triple play in the NL East doesn't look bad, does it?), or where it doesn't (could the Giants really win the NL West by 22 games?).

Those things are just cyclical. Not so long ago, teams would have begged to have the Braves placed in their division or would have turned maps sideways and inside-out to try to prove Oakland belongs in somebody else's division—anybody else's.

But look at it this way: The intra-division rivalries will be more focused. The new ones will kindle quickly and the remaining ones will become more intense if for no other reason than fans and teams will have only three or four other teams to focus on when it really counts.

And we all know that what really counts is a pennant race, or the hope that builds through the winter in anticipation of our favorite team getting into a pennant race. Now, we throw in this entirely new race . . . the run for the wild-card spot.

As un-baseball as that might sound, even the most cynical among us is going to toss sentiment aside and feel more than a little twinge of excitement when our team is 12 games off the division lead on Labor Day, but only a game-and-a-half out of the wild card spot.

Will this brave new world work? Well, don't ask in April or May, when the season is slowly building and you're still grumbling about how you can't get used to who's in what division.

Ask instead in September. Are you excited? What scores are you looking for? And why? Does it seem just a little less like football season where you live?

How interested are you in what's left of the baseball season? After all, that's what this is all about. Interest and having fun.

And if this bold gamble by the lords of baseball to create more interest (and more money, of course) has us excited in September, then it works.

Stay tuned.

—by Paul White, editor

NL 1994: A peek into the crystal ball

Atlanta Braves

Convinced they have baseball's best team on paper, the Braves will lobby for a strike and wait for the season's computer simulations.

Chicago Cubs

Mike Harkey will get hurt and the Cubs will not make the playoffs. How's that for going out on a limb?

Cincinnati Reds

In her quieter, more patient way, owner Marge Schott will keep manager Davey Johnson and GM Jim Bowden around until June, when they'll begin selling peanuts on Pete Rose Way.

Colorado Rockies

David Nied will post an ERA under 4.00 in Mile High ERA Stadium and earn heavy Cy Young consideration.

Florida Marlins

Ticket prices for seats along the first base line in Joe Robbie Stadium will be cut in half if Gary Sheffield plays third base.

Houston Astros

The Astros will win the NL Central title. They will have finally ditched their '70s-style uniforms. Coincidence? Don't think so.

Los Angeles Dodgers

Strangely enough, the Dodgers will not have the 1994 NL Rookie of the Year—unless they trade for Cliff Floyd, that is.

Montreal Expos

Expos' baserunners will wear shin-guards, costing them stolen bases but eliminating the possiblility of another Moises Alou-like shin-snapping.

New York Mets

Shea Stadium will replace its giant apple with a huge lemon in honor of Vince Coleman.

Philadelphia Phillies

The Philadelphia police force, still fuming over Mitch Williams' World Series performance, will crack down on jaywalkers.

Pittsburgh Pirates

Jim Leyland will be immediately inducted into the Hall of Fame after coaxing a winning season out of this sparsely talented team.

St. Louis Cardinals

Rich Batchelor will have to wear a batting helmet at all times to protect himself against angry fantasy players who owned Lee Smith.

San Diego Padres

Added expense of Oxy-10 in the locker room will force the Padres to sell their last remaining veteran.

San Francisco Giants

Barry Bonds will win the triple crown and get rid of postseason goat horns in one year.

—*by John Hunt*

AL 1994: A peek into the crystal ball

Baltimore Orioles

Having resurrected the careers of Fernando Valenzuela and Jamie Moyer, the Orioles will coax Jim Palmer out of retirement for another "brief" comeback.

Boston Red Sox

Rid for the first time of Matt Young's salary (signed in 1990), Boston will hold the most enthusiastic celebration seen since the Tea Party.

California Angels

Adopting an old baseball saying for their erratic second-year first baseman, the Angels' motto will be "Curtis, Lovullo and pray for Snow."

Chicago White Sox

No White Sox players, not even Steve Sax, will complain about playing time.

Cleveland Indians

In an amazing story only Hollywood could have scripted, Charlie Sheen actually will join the Indians' bullpen.

Detroit Tigers

Motown needs mo' pitching—mo' than Mike Moore—but will once again sing the mo' pitching blues.

Kansas City Royals

David Cone will become the first pitcher in history to lead the major leagues in ERA and finish without a single victory.

Milwaukee Brewers

Legendary Robin Yount will go from Milwaukee's Best to Old Milwaukee—enough to give anybody a headache.

Minnesota Twins

Twins' plodding prospects David McCarty and Willie Banks will once again prove that youth is wasted on the young.

New York Yankees

In brainstorming Steinbrenner's effort to boost attendance in the Bronx, the Yankees will hold a new promotion: flak jacket night.

Oakland Athletics

After going from first-to-worst in '93, Oakland will see its reliever Dennis Eckersley go from god-to-dog.

Seattle Mariners

Manager Lou Piniella will forever lose his nickname "Sweet Lou" if Edgar Martinez has another case of Coleman Hamstring.

Texas Rangers

In honor of their new ballpark—the Ballpark—the Rangers will wear plain white uniforms and change their name to the Ballclub.

Toronto Blue Jays

Trying to win their third in a row, the Blue Jays will once again open their deep pocketbook and sign guaranteed three-peater Michael Jordan.

—*by John Hunt*

National League '94: Who'll come out ahead?

Realignment is coming a year too late to help the San Francisco Giants, but general manager Bob Quinn still believes it is a good idea.

"As much of a purist as I am, and I've been in the game my entire adult life, I think it's going to be a format the fans are going to welcome," Quinn said.

Who will benefit and who will be hurt by realignment? An early line:

Eastern Division

▶**Winner: Atlanta**
The Braves will move from the West to the East in the new division alignment in 1994, and that is bad news for every other team in the division.

Especially considering their playoff loss to the Phillies, the Braves are going to have added incentive for wanting to win. They have the money to spend and the baseball people who know how to spend it, and that combination has been lethal the past couple of winters.

Even without acquiring any new players over the winter the Braves returning players were enough to make them the division favorite. Cy Young winner Greg Maddux anchors the best starting rotation in the league, and having Fred McGriff in the lineup for an entire season figures to make the offense even better.

If any of their veterans falter, the Braves also have the best crop of minor leaguers of the NL's 14 teams ready to take over, led by catcher Javier Lopez, shortstop Chipper Jones and first baseman Ryan Klesko.

▶**Losers: Philadelphia, Montreal, New York**
The Phillies just spent 10 years trying to get back to the playoffs, and now they find themselves in the same division with the Braves.

"We're going to see if we can move to the West," joked Phillies GM Lee Thomas. "But I think what we will probably have is the best division in baseball."

Thomas acknowledges that having the Braves in their division, even though there is no difference in how many games will be played against each opponent, changed the offseason plans for the Phillies.

He said the team likely will have to spend more money and be more interested in signing free agents than it would otherwise in an attempt to keep pace with Atlanta. Adding help in the bullpen is a must.

Otherwise, the Phillies have to hope that their luck in staying healthy repeats itself in 1994. Their key core players—Lenny Dykstra, John Kruk, Darren Daulton and Dave Hollins—all remained in the lineup virtually all season, and the result was obvious in the team's performance. Pitcher Curt Schilling showed in the playoffs and World Series that he is ready to step up and be a true No. 1 starter.

The Expos, even though they didn't win the division, also will feel the effects of the Braves' move. They have enough good young players they might have been able to trade one of their stars and keep their payroll down and still be a contending team.

Now, they probably will be forced to hang onto their current players and suffer the economic consequences unless they don't want to have any chance of making the playoffs.

They have perhaps the division's best outfield, if Moises Alou is recovered from the broken leg he suffered in September. Larry Walker and Marquis Grissom both won Gold Gloves, and the Expos' only big question mark is finding a replacement for No. 1 starter Dennis Martinez.

The Braves' move also hurts the Mets, who already were looking at a long uphill climb back to respectability, much less playoff contention. That hike will now be more difficult.

They entered the off-season with only one untouchable player, pitcher Dwight Gooden, but needed help in far too many areas to make the leap up to contender status. Outfielders Ryan Thompson and Jeromy Burnitz showed in the second half of last year they should be able to make a contribution, but a lot of holes remain.

▶No effect: Florida

From a competition standpoint, the Marlins naturally would have preferred the Braves to be in another division. But their best chance of developing a rivalry is with the Braves, so from that point of view they like being in the same division.

The Marlins will spend their winter trying to make the moves they would have made anyway to improve their club—including adding a power hitter. Their attempt to get an outfielder may have ended with the decision to move Gary Sheffield from third base to the outfield, enabling them to reacquire Dave Magadan from the Mariners.

Central Division

▶Winners: Houston, St. Louis, Pittsburgh

Of the three divisions, this should have the most balance. That will help teams that are watching their budgets, like Houston and St. Louis, and those deep into rebuilding, like Pittsburgh.

Former Astros' manager Art Howe likes his ex-team's chances in what as of now shapes up to be the most balanced of the three divisions.

"This is one heck of a good team, one that's not very far from winning the thing," Howe said. "I really feel this team is ready to go."

The Astros' chances might be determined by budget restrictions. If they are forced to trade off a star or two, like Steve Finley and Ken Caminiti, they will have a harder time winning. Being

in a division with four teams that are almost on an equal financial basis should help.

New manager Terry Collins was an aggresive manager in the minor leagues and figures to be the same with the Astros. The question will be how much talent he has to work with when spring training begins.

The Cardinals, if realignment had gone into effect a year earlier, would have won the Central Division in 1993 and qualified for the playoffs.

Finding someone to become a No. 1 starter is crucial, even if that means using the trade route rather than waiting for one of their younger pitchers to assert himself.

They also have to hope center fielder Ray Lankford bounces back from a disappointing 1993 and that Todd Zeile and Gregg Jefferies can play as well again as they did a year ago.

The Pirates, the team that agreed to switch with Atlanta and move from the East to the Central to avoid a major fight, are in a much better division for their continued rebuilding program. They won't have to compete with the big-money teams and might find their road back to the postseason much shorter, especially if they can upgrade pitching as well.

The team will again be built around center fielder Andy Van Slyke, who hopes he can avoid the injury problems of 1993, and shortstop Jay Bell, who beat out 13-time winner Ozzie Smith for the Gold Glove to establish himself as one of the best shortstops in the league.

▶No effect: Chicago, Cincinnati

The Cubs were determined to be very quiet on the free agent market, and Cincinnati can't afford to increase its payroll; if anything they will be looking to make cuts.

New Cubs' manager Tom Trebelhorn will not offer much of a departure from the style of Jim Lefebvre, with the keys to his success the same as the reasons for Lefebvre's failure in 1993—still looking for a replacement for the departed Maddux and Andre Dawson.

If the Reds are healthier they will be a better team but without major changes neither Chicago or Cincinnati is likely to be pennant contender, no matter what division they are in, in 1994.

Their first significant trade of the winter, acquiring starter Erik Hanson and second baseman Bret Boone, should help. Neither Dan Wilson or Bobby Ayala figured in the team's plans for 1994.

Western Division

▶**Winners: San Francisco, Colorado**

Quinn downplays the talk that the Giants' 103 wins in 1993 automatically makes them the favorite in this Atlanta-less division.

"It's totally premature to say that," Quinn said.

The Giants made a necessary move by re-signing second baseman Robby Thompson, but face a big hole at first base because of Will Clark's free agency.

Quinn also hopes the starting pitching will continue to improve. Bill Swift and John Burkett were the '93 keys and rookie Salomon Torres showed promise at the end of the season. The team's success in 1993 improved the financial picture, going from a projected loss of $10 million to a slight profit.

Quinn thinks the Rockies could benefit from the new division setup as much as any other team. It is a desirable location to play and live, they have a good offensive lineup and will have money to spend on pitchers.

"If they can get some pitching I think they can be a hell of a sleeper," Quinn said.

The Rockies avoided a potential big hole when first baseman Andres Galarraga elected free agency then signed. The Rockies also could benefit from the Western Division being the four-team division in the current set up.

▶**Losers: San Diego**

The switch to a three-division format will not help the Padres. They are looking beyond 1994 for their success and that's good, because it appears their fans will be in for another long year.

Starting pitcher Andy Benes is the one remaining star and the one very trade-able commodity to help accelerate the rebuilding with the best, young, cheapest players available. The franchise player is still outfielder Tony Gywnn, but a move might also be in the works for him, to first base, to try to help his sore knees.

The play of outfielder Phil Plantier was a pleasant surprise in 1993, but the Padres will need many more surprises to become a factor in the division in 1994.

▶**No effect: Los Angeles**

The Dodgers could move up in a hurry if they were willing to patch some of their holes with free agents, but GM Fred Claire is committed to youth. It looks as if the players coming up now will have a hard time matching the Rookie of the Year performances of Eric Karros and Mike Piazza.

Their big unknown is Darryl Strawberry. Predicting what he will do in 1994 is almost impossible. The one apparent certainty is that he will move to left field, with the thinking being it is an easier position to play and might keep him in the lineup more.

Strawberry also could be helped by the addition of new hitting coach Reggie Smith, who appears to be a very positive role model for Strawberry.

—by Rob Rains

American League '94: Winners and losers

One of the sweet ironies of the recent realignment is that the team that protested the loudest and longest about it—the Texas Rangers—could be the biggest winner when the new three-division format, with a wild-card team, takes effect next season.

George W. Bush, the Ranger's general partner, might be a fine politican. Besides eyeing the Texas statehouse, Bush stood by his principles on realignment. He didn't allow potential benefits for his constituency to sway him from the belief that this move was bad for baseball. Of course, Bush's impassioned stand didn't have a chance against the carpetbaggers that run this game.

Still, under this new format, if Bush's Rangers can put together a season equal to last year, they'll be in the playoffs in '94. The Chicago White Sox have moved to the AL Central Division and all Texas has to do is beat out Seattle, California and Oakland to make the big dance for the first time in club history.

Besides the Rangers, there are other winners in the American League, as well as several losers, in the wake of realignment:

Eastern Division

▶Winner: Toronto

The defending world champions will be the favorites again in '94, no matter how much executive vice president Pat Gillick remakes this team in the offseason. In any case, the core of the team is there, with Joe Carter, Roberto Alomar, Paul Molitor and Devon White back for another year. Sure they could use more pitching, but so could anybody and that nucleus is second to none.

The Blue Jays also won't have to concern themselves with competition from Cleveland's improving Indians. Instead they can focus on their long-time rivals, the Boston Red Sox and New York Yankees.

The Red Sox have to find more speed and defense, plus more young prospects. After pitcher Aaron Sele and Mo Vaughn, this ballclub gets old in a hurry.

The Yankees, led by Don Mattingly, will be knocking on the door again. This team has a great offense. Like the rest of the division, they need more pitching. But beware. Owner George Steinbrenner, a.k.a. "The Boss," was quiet for most of the '93 season. If this team gets off to a slow start, he'll explode and he may lose Buck Showalter, one of the best young managers in the game, in the process.

The bottom-line here is that if the Blue Jays can mirror those teams' free-agent moves, the divisional title will rest in Toronto another year.

▶Loser: Detroit

Tigers owner Mike Ilitch insisted on staying in the East. Indeed that's where his team's traditional matchups are. But come August, when the Tigers don't have the pitching to stay in the hunt, Motown fans will be wondering why their ballclub didn't take the plunge and join the new AL Central. They would have stood more of a chance with a change of scenery.

Ilitch is doing his best, though, keeping the core of his team together. While other teams have been skinflints, he's spread the wealth, re-signing Travis Fryman, Alan Trammell and Eric Davis.

▶No effect: Baltimore, Boston and New York

It's still difficult to get used to the Red Sox as a pitching-dominated team. And that's after the worst season of Roger Clemens' career. Assuming any kind of return to form by the Rocket, Boston will again have the best starting staff in the division.

But to parlay that into pennant contention, Butch Hobson must continue to create offense with the aggressive style he used in '93 to begin winning over his team and its fans.

The Yankees' dilemma is nearly the opposite. The emergence of Mike Stanley and Bernie Williams plus the veteran presence of Wade Boggs, Don Mattingly, Paul O'Neill and Danny Tartabull ensures runs.

New Yorkers have to hope more is forthcoming from Jim Abbott and a couple of stars emerge from the club's collection of vaunted young arms.

In Baltimore, Mike Mussina and Ben McDonald need to be dominant starters while Gregg Olson returns to form in the bullpen.

Central Division

▶**Winners: Chicago, Cleveland and Minnesota**

The White Sox, like the Blue Jays, find that the pack trying to catch them has thinned a bit. With their young pitching staff and superstar Frank Thomas, they remain the team to beat even if they are in the Central instead of the West.

The White Sox have made Thomas happy with a $29 million, four-year contract extension. With basketball's Michael Jordan retired, the "Big Hurt" is arguably the best-known active sports player in the Windy City.

When the Tigers' Ilitch wouldn't budge from the East, Cleveland owner Richard Jacobs agreed to move to the new Central. Dennis Martinez bolsters a shaky pitching staff. Meanwhile, their everyday lineup is potentially the best—power-wise—in the central division. With Albert Belle ('93 AL RBI leader), Carlos Baerga, Wayne Kirby, Eddie Murray and Kenny Lofton, this ballclub can beat up just about any opposing pitcher.

The Twins have a rare ability to bounce back from dismal seasons. If their pitching rotation can pull itself together, Minnesota can hang with Chicago on that score, especially if the White Sox's pitching drops off. And if Kirby Puckett and David McCarty can

turn it around in '93, who knows? Twins manager Tom Kelly might have another miracle season on his hands. At least the division is more conducive to another rapid rise to the top.

▶**Loser: Milwaukee**

With or without Robin Yount, the Brewers don't have the bats to compete in this division. When the White Sox visit County Stadium, Chicago fans already outnumber the hometown cheeseheads. That embarrassment will become more pronounced now that they are divisional rivals.

▶**No effect: Kansas City**

Someone, maybe Bob Hamelin, must step into George Brett's offensive shoes in Kansas City and a healthy, productive Felix Jose is a must. But the Kevin Appier-David Cone combination means the pitching is always more than adequate, especially with closer Jeff Montgomery at the other end.

The greatest unknown in the Royals' future is how ownership will spend after the death of Ewing Kauffman. It's unlikely Kansas City will continue to be a small-market team acting like a large-market one.

Western Division

▶**Winners: Texas, Seattle, California and Oakland**

That's right, the whole division has gotten a new lease on life by crawling out from behind the White Sox's long shadow. While Bush did his best to derail this new deal, his general manager couldn't wait for the ink to dry.

"I wish it was retroactive," said Tom Grieve.

With Will Clark replacing Rafael Palmeiro, Juan Gonzalez eager to call the franchise his own, plus a new ballpark ready for '94, their future looks bright.

Pitchers Kenny Rogers and Roger Pavlik became front-line starters last season, the ballclub responded to new manager Kevin Kennedy and Dean

Palmer had his best season power-wise.

Right behind the Rangers are the Mariners. They were the most improved team in the AL last season and with manager Lou Piniella settling in for his second season as manager, Seattle could find itself with pennant fever in late September for the first time in club history.

Mariners' superstar Ken Griffey could be better next year with a healthy Edgar Martinez ('92 AL batting champion) in the lineup for the entire season. The key to the Mariners' season will be the bullpen and whether or not they trade Cy Young candidate Randy Johnson for more pitching.

Last season the Mariners finally found some bench help. Mike Blowers, a spring training invitee, took over for Martinez. Meanwhile Jay Buhner became the first Mariner to hit for cycle.

The Angels and the A's are rebuilding. But with only three teams to beat to reach the postseason promised land, their timetables have been moved up a year or so.

The Angels, especially with Whitey Herzog having full power to call the personnel shots, could make the leap to first place in a hurry. Manager Buck Rodgers is great at handling young players, and in the old, more competitive, AL West, the Angels were in contention past the All-Star break.

After a year in the big leagues, kids like Tim Salmon and J.T. Snow are only going to get better. The supporting cast of Chad Curtis, Damion Easley and Gary DiSarcina should improve too. The only question is if Herzog can find more pitching. Sound familiar?

The Angels believe veteran left-hander Joe Magrane, and youngsters Hilly Hathaway and Phil Leftwich will be part of that solution.

A's manager Tony La Russa has more work to do. But, like the Twins' Kelly, he can turn around a team in a hurry. The A's showed their spirit coming down the stretch last year when they temporarily derailed the Blue Jays' bid for another AL East title.

Bobby Witt will be back to anchor the starting rotation. He could be complemented by Mike Mohler, Todd Van Poppel, Steve Karsay or Miguel Jimenez—four rookie pitchers.

The rookie lift was limited to the pitching staff as second baseman Brent Gates, designated hitter Troy Neel and Craig Paquette won starting jobs.

La Russa, like many baseball purists, isn't too crazy about this new setup. He opposes wild-card teams and would rather see more divisions, with only the divisional champions reaching postseason play. But here, as in Texas, Oakland could be in the playoffs sooner than expected in the brave new world of realignment.

—by Tim Wendel

by H. Darr Beiser, USA TODAY

With hitters like Carlos Baerga (above, .321, 21 HR, 114 RBI), Albert Belle, Wayne Kirby and Kenny Lofton, Cleveland's Tribe may find itself on top of the new AL Central Division.

Final player statistics

American League

National League

Statistics are provided by the Elias Sports Bureau.

Stats key for pitchers
T–Throws right or left; W–Wins; L–Losses; ERA–Earned run average; G–Games; GS–Games started; CG– Complete games; SHO–Shutouts; GF–Games finished in relief; SV–Saves; IP–Innings pitched; H–Hits; R–Runs; ER–Earned runs; HR–Home runs; BB–Bases on balls; SO–Strikeouts; WP–Wild pitches; BK–Balks; BA–Batting average against; HB–Hit batters; PCT–Winning percentage; IBB–Intentional bases on balls.

Stats key for fielding
E–Errors; PO–Put outs; A–Assists; DP–Double plays; PCT–Fielding percentage.

Stats key for batters
B–Bats right, left, or both; BA or AVG–Batting average; G–Games; AB–At-bats; R–Runs; H–Hits; TB–Total Bases; 2B–Doubles; 3B–Triples; HR–Home runs; RBI–Runs batted in; SH–Sacrifice hits; SF–Sacrifice flies; BB–Bases on balls; SO–Strikeouts; SB–Stolen bases; CS–Caught stealing; GIDP–Grounded into double play; SLG–Slugging percentage; OBA or OB–On base average; LOB–Runners left on base by a team.

Players are listed alphabetically by position, within each league. Each player is listed at the position where he played the most games in 1993; all statistics are for the complete season.

American League starting pitchers

Name/Team	T	W	L	ERA	G	GS	CG	SHO	GF	SV	IP	H	R	ER	HR	BB	SO	WP	BK	BA
Abbott, Jim, NY-A	L	11	14	4.37	32	32	4	1	0	0	214.0	221	115	104	22	73	95	9	0	.271
Abbott, Paul, Cle.	R	0	1	6.38	5	5	0	0	0	0	18.1	19	15	13	5	11	7	1	0	.260
Alvarez, Wilson, ChiA	L	15	8	2.95	31	31	1	1	0	0	207.2	168	78	68	14	122	155	2	1	.230
Appier, Kevin, K.C.	R	18	8	2.56	34	34	5	1	0	0	238.2	183	74	68	8	81	186	5	0	.212
Banks, Willie, Min.	R	11	12	4.04	31	30	0	0	1	0	171.1	186	91	77	17	78	138	9	5	.280
Belcher, Tim, ChiA	R	3	5	4.40	12	11	1	1	0	0	71.2	64	36	35	8	27	34	0	0	.242
Bere, Jason, ChiA	R	12	5	3.47	24	24	1	0	0	0	142.2	109	60	55	12	81	129	8	0	.210
Bergman, Sean, Det.	R	1	4	5.67	9	6	1	0	1	0	39.2	47	29	25	6	23	19	3	1	.294
Bielecki, Mike, Cle.	R	4	5	5.90	13	13	0	0	0	0	68.2	90	47	45	8	23	38	1	0	.310
Boddicker, Mike, Mil.	R	3	5	5.67	10	10	1	0	0	0	54.0	77	35	34	6	15	24	0	0	.338
Bolton, Rodney, ChiA	R	2	6	7.44	9	8	0	0	0	0	42.1	55	40	35	4	16	17	4	0	.314
Bones, Ricky, Mil.	R	11	11	4.86	32	31	3	0	1	0	203.2	222	122	110	28	63	63	6	1	.277
Bosio, Chris, Sea.	R	9	9	3.45	29	24	3	1	2	1	164.1	138	75	63	14	59	119	5	0	.229
Brown, J. Kevin, Tex.	R	15	12	3.59	34	34	12	3	0	0	233.0	228	105	93	14	74	142	8	1	.252
Brummett, Greg, Min.	R	2	1	5.74	5	5	0	0	0	0	26.2	29	17	17	3	15	10	0	0	.299
Clark, Mark, Cle.	R	7	5	4.28	26	15	1	0	1	0	109.1	119	55	52	18	25	57	1	0	.279
Clemens, Roger, Bos.	R	11	14	4.46	29	29	2	1	0	0	191.2	175	99	95	17	67	160	3	1	.244
Cone, David, K.C.	R	11	14	3.33	34	34	6	1	0	0	254.0	205	102	94	20	114	191	14	2	.223
Converse, Jim, Sea.	R	1	3	5.31	4	4	0	0	0	0	20.1	23	12	12	0	14	10	0	0	.295
Cummings, John, Sea.	L	0	6	6.02	10	8	1	0	0	0	46.1	59	34	31	6	16	19	1	1	.316
Darling, Ron, Oak.	R	5	9	5.16	31	29	3	0	1	0	178.0	198	107	102	22	72	95	3	1	.281
Darwin, Danny, Bos.	R	15	11	3.26	34	34	2	1	0	0	229.1	196	93	83	31	49	130	5	1	.230
Deshaies, Jim, Min.	L	11	13	4.41	27	27	1	0	0	0	167.1	159	85	82	24	51	80	0	4	.254
Doherty, John, Det.	R	14	11	4.44	32	31	3	2	1	0	184.2	205	104	91	19	48	63	4	1	.286
Dopson, John, Bos.	R	7	11	4.97	34	28	1	1	3	0	155.2	170	93	86	16	59	89	1	3	.281
Dreyer, Steve, Tex.	R	3	3	5.71	10	6	0	0	1	0	41.0	48	26	26	7	20	23	0	0	.291
Eldred, Cal, Mil.	R	16	16	4.01	36	36	8	1	0	0	258.0	232	120	115	32	91	180	2	0	.239
Erickson, Scott, Min.	R	8	19	5.19	34	34	1	0	0	0	218.2	266	138	126	17	71	116	5	0	.305
Farrell, John E., Cal.	R	3	12	7.35	21	17	0	0	1	0	90.2	110	74	74	22	44	45	3	0	.301
Fernandez, Alex, ChiA	R	18	9	3.13	34	34	3	1	0	0	247.1	221	95	86	27	67	169	8	0	.240
Finley, Chuck, Cal.	L	16	14	3.15	35	35	13	2	0	0	251.1	243	108	88	22	82	187	8	1	.253
Fleming, Dave, Sea.	L	12	5	4.36	26	26	1	1	0	0	167.1	189	84	81	15	67	75	2	0	.290
Gardner, Mark, K.C.	R	4	6	6.19	17	16	0	0	0	0	91.2	92	65	63	17	36	54	2	0	.272
Grimsley, Jason, Cle.	R	3	4	5.31	10	6	0	0	1	0	42.1	52	26	25	3	20	27	2	0	.302
Guardado, Eddie, Min.	L	3	8	6.18	19	16	0	0	2	0	94.2	123	68	65	13	36	46	0	0	.319
Gullickson, Bill, Det.	R	13	9	5.37	28	28	2	0	0	0	159.1	186	106	95	28	44	70	2	0	.291
Guzman, Juan, Tor.	R	14	3	3.99	33	33	2	1	0	0	221.0	211	107	98	17	110	194	26	1	.252
Haney, Chris, K.C.	L	9	9	6.02	23	23	1	1	0	0	124.0	141	87	83	13	53	65	6	1	.286
Hanson, Erik, Sea.	R	11	12	3.47	31	30	7	0	0	0	215.0	215	91	83	17	60	163	8	0	.263
Hathaway, Hilly, Cal.	L	4	3	5.02	11	11	0	0	0	0	57.1	71	35	32	6	26	11	5	1	.326
Hentgen, Pat, Tor.	R	19	9	3.87	34	32	3	0	0	0	216.1	215	103	93	27	74	122	11	1	.258
Higuera, Ted, Mil.	L	1	3	7.20	8	8	0	0	0	0	30.0	43	24	24	4	16	27	0	3	.333
Hillegas, Shawn, Oak.	R	3	6	6.97	18	11	0	0	4	0	60.2	78	48	47	8	33	29	1	0	.317
Hitchcock, Sterling, NY-A	L	1	2	4.65	6	6	0	0	0	0	31.0	32	18	16	4	14	26	3	2	.271
Holzemer, Mark, Cal.	L	0	3	8.87	5	4	0	0	1	0	23.1	34	24	23	2	13	10	1	0	.340
Hutton, Mark, NY-A	R	1	1	5.73	7	4	0	0	2	0	22.0	24	17	14	2	17	12	0	0	.293
Jean, Domingo, NY-A	R	1	1	4.46	10	6	0	0	1	0	40.1	37	20	20	7	19	20	1	0	.237
Jimenez, Miguel, Oak.	R	1	0	4.00	5	4	0	0	0	0	27.0	27	12	12	5	16	13	0	0	.262
Johnson, Jeff, NY-A	L	0	2	30.38	2	2	0	0	0	0	2.2	12	10	9	1	2	0	0	0	.600
Johnson, Randy D., Sea.	L	19	8	3.24	35	34	10	3	1	1	255.1	185	97	92	22	99	308	8	2	.203
Kamieniecki, Scott, NY-A	R	10	7	4.08	30	20	2	0	4	1	154.1	163	73	70	17	59	72	2	0	.277
Karsay, Steve, Oak.	R	3	3	4.04	8	8	0	0	0	0	49.0	49	23	22	4	16	33	1	0	.258
Key, Jimmy, NY-A	L	18	6	3.00	34	34	4	2	0	0	236.2	219	84	79	26	43	173	3	0	.246
Langston, Mark, Cal.	L	16	11	3.20	35	35	7	0	0	0	256.1	220	100	91	22	85	196	10	2	.234
Leary, Tim, Sea.	R	11	9	5.05	33	27	0	0	6	0	169.1	202	104	95	21	58	68	6	2	.300
Leftwich, Phil, Cal.	R	4	6	3.79	12	12	1	0	0	0	80.2	81	35	34	5	27	31	1	0	.262
Leibrandt, Charlie, Tex.	L	9	10	4.55	26	26	1	0	0	0	150.1	169	84	76	15	45	89	5	2	.284
Lopez, Albie, Cle.	R	3	1	5.98	9	9	0	0	0	0	49.2	49	34	33	7	32	25	0	0	.262
Magnante, Mike, K.C.	L	1	2	4.08	7	6	0	0	0	0	35.1	37	16	16	3	11	16	1	0	.282
Magrane, Joe, Cal.	L	3	2	3.94	8	8	0	0	0	0	48.0	48	27	21	4	21	24	4	0	.265
McDonald, Ben, Bal.	R	13	14	3.39	34	34	7	1	0	0	220.1	185	92	83	17	86	171	7	1	.228
McDowell, Jack, ChiA	R	22	10	3.37	34	34	10	4	0	0	256.2	261	104	96	20	69	158	8	1	.266
Mesa, Jose, Cle.	R	10	12	4.92	34	33	3	0	0	0	208.2	232	122	114	21	62	118	8	2	.286
Militello, Sam, NY-A	R	1	1	6.75	3	2	0	0	0	0	9.1	10	8	7	1	7	5	0	0	.270
Minchey, Nate, Bos.	R	1	2	3.55	5	5	0	0	0	0	33.0	35	16	13	5	8	18	2	0	.265
Miranda, Angel, Mil.	L	4	5	3.30	22	17	2	0	0	0	120.0	100	53	44	12	52	88	4	2	.226
Mlicki, Dave, Cle.	R	0	0	3.38	3	3	0	0	0	0	13.1	11	6	5	2	6	7	2	0	.220
Moore, Mike, Det.	R	13	9	5.22	36	36	4	3	0	0	213.2	227	135	124	35	89	89	9	0	.271
Morris, Jack, Tor.	R	7	12	6.19	27	27	4	1	0	0	152.2	189	116	105	18	65	103	14	1	.302
Moyer, Jamie, Bal.	L	12	9	3.43	25	25	3	1	0	0	152.0	154	63	58	11	38	90	1	1	.265

American League starting pitchers

Name/Team	T	W	L	ERA	G	GS	CG	SHO	GF	SV	IP	H	R	ER	HR	BB	SO	WP	BK	BA
Mussina, Mike, Bal.	R	14	6	4.46	25	25	3	2	0	0	167.2	163	84	83	20	44	117	5	0	.256
Mutis, Jeff, Cle.	L	3	6	5.78	17	13	1	1	1	0	81.0	93	56	52	14	33	29	1	0	.289
Nagy, Charles, Cle.	R	2	6	6.29	9	9	1	0	0	0	48.2	66	38	34	6	13	30	2	0	.322
Navarro, Jaime, Mil.	R	11	12	5.33	35	34	5	1	0	0	214.1	254	135	127	21	73	114	11	0	.300
Ojeda, Bob, Cle.	L	2	1	4.40	9	7	0	0	0	0	43.0	48	22	21	5	21	27	3	0	.289
Pavlik, Roger, Tex.	R	12	6	3.41	26	26	2	0	0	0	166.1	151	67	63	18	80	131	6	0	.245
Perez, Melido, NY-A	R	6	14	5.19	25	25	0	0	0	0	163.0	173	103	94	22	64	148	3	1	.267
Pichardo, Hipolito, K.C.	R	7	8	4.04	30	25	2	0	2	0	165.0	183	85	74	10	53	70	5	3	.282
Rhodes, Arthur, Bal.	L	5	6	6.51	17	17	0	0	0	0	85.2	91	62	62	16	49	49	2	0	.274
Rogers, Kenny, Tex.	L	16	10	4.10	35	33	5	0	0	0	208.1	210	108	95	18	71	140	6	5	.263
Ruffcorn, Scott, ChiA	R	0	2	8.10	3	2	0	0	1	0	10.0	9	11	9	2	10	2	1	0	.265
Ryan, Nolan, Tex.	R	5	5	4.88	13	13	0	0	0	0	66.1	54	47	36	5	40	46	3	0	.220
Salkeld, Roger, Sea.	R	0	0	2.51	3	2	0	0	0	0	14.1	13	4	4	0	4	13	0	0	.232
Sanderson, Scott, Cal.	R	7	11	4.46	21	21	4	1	0	0	135.1	153	77	67	15	27	66	1	2	.289
Sele, Aaron, Bos.	R	7	2	2.74	18	18	0	0	0	0	111.2	100	42	34	5	48	93	5	0	.237
Springer, Russ, Cal.	R	1	6	7.20	14	9	1	0	3	0	60.0	73	48	48	11	32	31	6	0	.303
Stewart, Dave, Tor.	R	12	8	4.44	26	26	0	0	0	0	162.0	146	86	80	23	72	96	4	1	.242
Stieb, Dave, ChiA	R	1	3	6.04	4	4	0	0	0	0	22.1	27	17	15	1	14	11	0	0	.300
Stottlemyre, Todd, Tor.	R	11	12	4.84	30	28	1	1	0	0	176.2	204	107	95	11	69	98	7	1	.292
Sutcliffe, Rick, Bal.	R	10	10	5.75	29	28	3	0	0	0	166.0	212	112	106	23	74	80	1	0	.314
Tanana, Frank, NY-A	L	0	2	3.20	3	3	0	0	0	0	19.2	18	10	7	2	7	12	0	0	.222
Tapani, Kevin, Min.	R	12	15	4.43	36	35	3	1	0	0	225.2	243	123	111	21	57	150	4	0	.272
Tavarez, Julian, Cle.	R	2	2	6.57	8	7	0	0	0	0	37.0	53	29	27	7	13	19	3	1	.340
Valenzuela, Fernando, Bal.	L	8	10	4.94	32	31	5	2	0	0	178.2	179	104	98	18	79	78	8	0	.266
Van Poppel, Todd, Oak.	R	6	6	5.04	16	16	0	0	0	0	84.0	76	50	47	10	62	47	3	0	.243
Viola, Frank, Bos.	L	11	8	3.14	29	29	2	1	0	0	183.2	180	76	64	12	72	91	5	0	.259
Wegman, Bill, Mil.	R	4	14	4.48	20	18	5	0	0	0	120.2	135	70	60	13	34	50	0	0	.291
Welch, Bob, Oak.	R	9	11	5.29	30	28	0	0	0	0	166.2	208	102	98	25	56	63	1	0	.310
Wells, David, Det.	L	11	9	4.19	32	30	0	0	0	0	187.0	183	93	87	26	42	139	13	0	.254
Witt, Bobby, Oak.	R	14	13	4.21	35	33	5	1	0	0	220.0	226	112	103	16	91	131	8	1	.269
Witt, Mike, NY-A	R	3	2	5.27	9	9	0	0	0	0	41.0	39	26	24	7	22	30	1	0	.248
Young, Curt, Oak.	L	1	1	4.30	3	3	0	0	0	0	14.2	14	7	7	5	6	4	0	0	.241

American League relief pitchers

Name/Team	T	W	L	ERA	G	GS	CG	SHO	GF	SV	IP	H	R	ER	HR	BB	SO	WP	BK	BA
Aguilera, Rick, Min.	R	4	3	3.11	65	0	0	0	61	34	72.1	60	25	25	9	14	59	1	0	.223
Anderson, Brian, Cal.	L	0	0	3.97	4	1	0	0	3	0	11.1	11	5	5	1	2	4	0	0	.256
Assenmacher, Paul, NY-A	L	2	2	3.12	26	0	0	0	6	0	17.1	10	6	6	0	9	11	0	0	.175
Austin, James, Mil.	R	1	2	3.82	31	0	0	0	8	0	33.0	28	15	14	3	13	15	4	0	.230
Ayrault, Bob, Sea.	R	1	1	3.20	14	0	0	0	6	0	19.2	18	8	7	1	6	7	0	0	.254
Bailey, Cory, Bos.	R	0	1	3.45	11	0	0	0	5	0	15.2	12	7	6	0	12	11	2	1	.231
Bankhead, Scott, Bos.	R	2	1	3.50	40	0	0	0	4	0	64.1	59	28	25	7	29	47	1	0	.250
Belinda, Stan, K.C.	R	1	1	4.28	23	0	0	0	7	0	27.1	30	13	13	2	6	25	2	0	.280
Boever, Joe, Oak.-Det.	R	6	3	3.61	61	0	0	0	22	3	102.1	101	50	41	9	44	63	1	0	.260
Bohanon, Brian, Tex.	L	4	4	4.76	36	8	0	0	4	0	92.2	107	54	49	8	46	45	10	0	.296
Bolton, Tom, Det.	L	6	6	4.47	43	8	0	0	9	0	102.2	113	57	51	5	45	66	5	1	.282
Brewer, Billy, K.C.	L	2	2	3.46	46	0	0	0	14	0	39.0	31	16	15	6	20	28	2	1	.230
Briscoe, John, Oak.	R	1	0	8.03	17	0	0	0	6	0	24.2	26	25	22	2	26	24	5	0	.277
Bronkey, Jeff, Tex.	R	1	1	4.00	21	0	0	0	6	1	36.0	39	20	16	4	11	18	2	0	.285
Brow, Scott, Tor.	R	1	1	6.00	6	3	0	0	1	0	18.0	19	15	12	2	10	7	0	0	.275
Burgos, Enrique, K.C.	L	0	1	9.00	5	0	0	0	3	0	5.0	5	5	5	0	6	6	3	0	.238
Burns, Todd, Tex.	R	0	4	4.57	25	5	0	0	8	0	65.0	63	36	33	6	32	35	3	2	.253
Butcher, Mike, Cal.	R	1	0	2.86	23	0	0	0	11	8	28.1	21	12	9	2	15	24	0	0	.204
Cadaret, Greg, K.C.	L	1	1	2.93	13	0	0	0	3	0	15.1	14	5	5	0	7	2	0	0	.264
Campbell, Kevin, Oak.	R	0	0	7.31	11	0	0	0	4	0	16.0	20	13	13	1	11	9	0	0	.313
Carpenter, Cris, Tex.	R	4	1	4.22	27	0	0	0	8	1	32.0	35	15	15	4	12	27	2	0	.289
Cary, Chuck, ChiA	L	1	0	5.23	16	0	0	0	4	0	20.2	22	12	12	1	11	10	4	0	.286
Casian, Larry, Min.	L	5	3	3.02	54	0	0	0	8	1	56.2	59	23	19	1	14	31	2	0	.268
Castillo, Tony J., Tor.	L	3	2	3.38	51	0	0	0	10	0	50.2	44	19	19	4	22	28	1	0	.242
Charlton, Norm, Sea.	L	1	3	2.34	34	0	0	0	29	18	34.2	22	12	9	4	17	48	6	0	.179
Christopher, Mike, Cle.	R	0	0	3.86	9	0	0	0	3	0	11.2	14	6	5	3	2	8	0	0	.286
Cook, Andy, NY-A	R	0	1	5.06	4	0	0	0	3	0	5.1	4	3	3	1	7	4	2	0	.200
Cook, Dennis, Cle.	L	5	5	5.67	25	6	0	0	2	0	54.0	62	36	34	9	16	34	0	1	.295
Cook, Mike, Bal.	R	0	0	0.00	2	0	0	0	0	0	3.0	1	0	0	0	2	3	1	0	.091
Cox, Danny, Tor.	R	7	6	3.12	44	0	0	0	13	2	83.2	73	31	29	8	29	84	5	0	.230
Crim, Chuck, Cal.	R	2	2	5.87	11	0	0	0	3	0	15.1	17	11	10	2	5	10	0	0	.298
Davis, Storm, Oak.-Det.	R	2	8	5.05	43	8	0	0	12	4	98.0	93	57	55	9	48	73	3	0	.250
Dayley, Ken, Tor.	L	0	0	0.00	2	0	0	0	0	0	0.2	1	2	0	0	4	2	0	0	.333

American League relief pitchers

Name/Team	T	W	L	ERA	G	GS	CG	SHO	GF	SV	IP	H	R	ER	HR	BB	SO	WP	BK	BA
DeLeon, Jose, ChiA	R	0	0	1.74	11	0	0	0	1	0	10.1	5	2	2	2	3	6	0	0	.152
DeLucia, Rich, Sea.	R	3	6	4.64	30	1	0	0	11	0	42.2	46	24	22	5	23	48	4	0	.272
DeSilva, John, Det.	R	0	0	9.00	1	0	0	0	1	0	1.0	2	1	1	0	0	0	0	0	.667
DiPino, Frank, K.C.	L	1	1	6.89	11	0	0	0	5	0	15.2	21	12	12	2	6	5	0	0	.328
DiPoto, Jerry, Cle.	R	4	4	2.40	46	0	0	0	26	11	56.1	57	21	15	0	30	41	0	0	.270
Downs, Kelly, Oak.	R	5	10	5.64	42	12	0	0	12	0	119.2	135	80	75	14	60	66	4	1	.287
Drahman, Brian, ChiA	R	0	0	0.00	5	0	0	0	4	1	5.1	7	0	0	0	2	3	0	0	.333
Eckersley, Dennis, Oak.	R	2	4	4.16	64	0	0	0	52	36	67.0	67	32	31	7	13	80	0	0	.261
Eichhorn, Mark, Tor.	R	3	1	2.72	54	0	0	0	16	0	72.2	76	26	22	3	22	47	2	0	.272
Fajardo, Hector, Tex.	R	0	0	0.00	1	0	0	0	1	0	0.2	0	0	0	0	0	1	0	0	.000
Farr, Steve, NY-A	R	2	2	4.21	49	0	0	0	37	25	47.0	44	22	22	8	28	39	2	0	.253
Fetters, Mike, Mil.	R	3	3	3.34	45	0	0	0	14	0	59.1	59	29	22	4	22	23	0	0	.278
Flener, Huck, Tor.	L	0	0	4.05	6	0	0	0	1	0	6.2	7	3	3	0	4	2	1	0	.269
Fossas, Tony, Bos.	L	1	1	5.18	71	0	0	0	19	0	40.0	38	28	23	4	15	39	1	1	.242
Frey, Steve, Cal.	L	2	3	2.98	55	0	0	0	28	13	48.1	41	20	16	1	26	22	3	0	.230
Frohwirth, Todd, Bal.	R	6	7	3.83	70	0	0	0	30	3	96.1	91	47	41	7	44	50	1	0	.256
Garces, Rich, Min.	R	0	0	0.00	3	0	0	0	1	0	4.0	4	2	0	0	2	3	0	0	.250
Gardiner, Mike, Det.	R	0	0	3.97	10	0	0	0	1	0	11.1	12	5	5	0	7	4	2	0	.279
Gibson, Paul, NY-A	L	2	0	3.06	20	0	0	0	9	0	35.1	31	15	12	4	9	25	0	0	.238
Gohr, Greg, Det.	R	0	0	5.96	16	0	0	0	9	0	22.2	26	15	15	1	14	12	0	0	.289
Gordon, Tom, K.C.	R	12	6	3.58	48	14	2	0	18	1	155.2	125	65	62	11	77	143	17	0	.223
Gossage, Goose, Oak.	R	4	5	4.53	39	0	0	0	12	1	47.2	49	24	24	6	26	40	4	0	.266
Grahe, Joe, Cal.	R	4	1	2.86	45	0	0	0	32	11	56.2	54	22	18	5	25	31	3	0	.251
Granger, Jeff, K.C.	L	0	0	27.00	1	0	0	0	0	0	1.0	3	3	3	0	2	1	0	0	.500
Grater, Mark, Det.	R	0	0	5.40	6	0	0	0	1	0	5.0	6	3	3	0	4	4	1	0	.286
Groom, Buddy, Det.	L	0	2	6.14	19	3	0	0	8	0	36.2	48	25	25	4	13	15	2	1	.322
Gubicza, Mark, K.C.	R	5	8	4.66	49	6	0	0	12	2	104.1	128	61	54	2	43	80	12	0	.307
Guthrie, Mark, Min.	L	2	1	4.71	22	0	0	0	2	0	21.0	20	11	11	2	16	15	1	3	.267
Haas, David, Det.	R	1	2	6.11	20	0	0	0	5	0	28.0	45	20	19	9	8	17	0	0	.375
Habyan, John, NY-A-K.C.	R	2	1	4.15	48	0	0	0	23	1	56.1	59	27	26	6	20	39	0	2	.272
Hampton, Mike, Sea.	L	1	3	9.53	13	0	0	0	2	1	17.0	28	20	18	3	17	8	1	1	.368
Harris, Greg A., Bos.	R	6	7	3.77	80	0	0	0	24	8	112.1	95	55	47	7	60	103	8	1	.232
Hartley, Mike, Min.	R	1	2	4.00	53	0	0	0	21	1	81.0	86	38	36	4	36	57	8	0	.281
Heaton, Neal, NY-A	L	1	0	6.00	18	0	0	0	9	0	27.0	34	19	18	6	11	15	2	0	.301
Henke, Tom, Tex.	R	5	5	2.91	66	0	0	0	60	40	74.1	55	25	24	7	27	79	3	0	.205
Henneman, Mike, Det.	R	5	3	2.64	63	0	0	0	50	24	71.2	69	28	21	4	32	58	4	0	.251
Henry, Doug, Mil.	R	4	4	5.56	54	0	0	0	41	17	55.0	67	37	34	7	25	38	4	0	.300
Henry, Dwayne, Sea.	R	2	1	6.67	31	1	0	0	15	2	54.0	56	40	40	6	35	35	7	0	.273
Hernandez, Jeremy, Cle.	R	6	5	3.14	49	0	0	0	22	8	77.1	75	33	27	12	27	44	2	0	.261
Hernandez, Roberto, ChiA	R	3	4	2.29	70	0	0	0	67	38	78.2	66	21	20	6	20	71	2	0	.228
Hesketh, Joe, Bos.	L	3	4	5.06	28	5	0	0	8	1	53.1	62	35	30	4	29	34	4	2	.294
Holman, Brad, Sea.	R	1	3	3.72	19	0	0	0	9	3	36.1	27	17	15	1	16	17	2	0	.208
Honeycutt, Rick, Oak.	L	1	4	2.81	52	0	0	0	7	1	41.2	30	18	13	2	20	21	0	0	.211
Horsman, Vince, Oak.	L	2	0	5.40	40	0	0	0	5	0	25.0	25	15	15	2	15	17	1	0	.255
Howard, Chris, ChiA	L	1	0	0.00	3	0	0	0	0	0	2.1	2	0	0	0	3	1	0	0	.286
Howe, Steve, NY-A	L	3	5	4.97	51	0	0	0	19	4	50.2	58	31	28	7	10	19	0	0	.297
Ignasiak, Mike, Mil.	R	1	1	3.65	27	0	0	0	4	0	37.0	32	17	15	2	21	28	0	0	.241
Johnson, Dave W., Det.	R	1	1	12.96	6	0	0	0	2	0	8.1	13	13	12	3	5	7	1	0	.342
Jones, Barry, ChiA	R	0	1	8.59	6	0	0	0	1	0	7.1	14	8	7	2	3	7	0	0	.412
Kiefer, Mark, Mil.	R	0	0	0.00	6	0	0	0	4	1	9.1	3	0	0	0	5	7	0	0	.097
Kiely, John, Det.	R	0	2	7.71	8	0	0	0	5	0	11.2	13	11	10	2	13	5	2	0	.295
King, Kevin, Sea.	L	0	1	6.17	13	0	0	0	3	0	11.2	9	8	8	3	4	8	0	0	.231
Knudsen, Kurt, Det.	R	3	2	4.78	30	0	0	0	7	2	37.2	41	22	20	9	16	29	2	0	.281
Kramer, Tom, Cle.	R	7	3	4.02	39	16	1	0	6	0	121.0	126	60	54	19	59	71	1	0	.269
Krueger, Bill, Det.	L	6	4	3.40	32	7	0	0	7	0	82.0	90	43	31	6	30	60	8	0	.285
Leach, Terry, ChiA	R	0	0	2.81	14	0	0	0	8	1	16.0	15	5	5	0	2	3	0	0	.250
Lefferts, Craig, Tex.	L	3	9	6.05	52	8	0	0	9	0	83.1	102	57	56	17	28	58	0	1	.304
Leiter, Al, Tor.	L	9	6	4.11	34	12	1	1	4	2	105.0	93	52	48	8	56	66	2	2	.240
Leiter, Mark, Det.	R	6	6	4.73	27	13	1	0	4	0	106.2	111	61	56	17	44	70	5	0	.267
Lewis, Scott, Cal.	R	1	2	4.22	15	4	0	0	2	0	32.0	37	16	15	3	12	10	1	0	.311
Lilliquist, Derek, Cle.	L	4	4	2.25	56	2	0	0	28	10	64.0	64	20	16	5	19	40	1	0	.264
Linton, Doug, Tor.-Cal.	R	2	1	7.36	23	1	0	0	6	0	36.2	46	30	30	8	23	23	2	0	.305
Lloyd, Graeme, Mil.	L	3	4	2.83	55	0	0	0	12	0	63.2	64	24	20	5	13	31	4	0	.256
MacDonald, Bob, Det.	L	3	3	5.35	68	0	0	0	24	3	65.2	67	42	39	8	33	39	3	1	.268
Mahomes, Pat, Min.	R	1	5	7.71	12	5	0	0	4	0	37.1	47	34	32	8	16	23	3	0	.309
Maldonado, Carlos, Min.	R	2	2	4.58	29	0	0	0	9	1	37.1	40	20	19	2	17	18	1	0	.282
Manzanillo, Josias, Mil.	R	1	1	9.53	10	1	0	0	4	1	17.0	22	20	18	1	10	10	1	0	.314
Maysey, Matt, Mil.	R	1	2	5.73	23	0	0	0	12	1	22.0	28	14	14	4	13	10	4	0	.322
McCaskill, Kirk, ChiA	R	4	8	5.23	30	14	0	0	6	2	113.2	144	71	66	12	36	65	6	0	.313
McGehee, Kevin, Bal.	R	0	0	5.94	5	0	0	0	1	0	16.2	18	11	11	5	7	7	1	0	.281

American League relief pitchers

Name/Team	T	W	L	ERA	G	GS	CG	SHO	GF	SV	IP	H	R	ER	HR	BB	SO	WP	BK	BA
Meacham, Rusty, K.C.	R	2	2	5.57	15	0	0	0	11	0	21.0	31	15	13	2	5	13	0	0	.326
Melendez, Jose, Bos.	R	2	1	2.25	9	0	0	0	5	0	16.0	10	4	4	2	5	14	0	0	.179
Merriman, Brett, Min.	R	1	1	9.67	19	0	0	0	10	0	27.0	36	29	29	3	23	14	1	0	.343
Milacki, Bob, Cle.	R	1	1	3.38	5	2	0	0	0	0	16.0	19	8	6	3	11	7	0	0	.302
Mills, Alan, Bal.	R	5	4	3.23	45	0	0	0	18	4	100.1	80	39	36	14	51	68	3	0	.225
Mohler, Mike, Oak.	L	1	6	5.60	42	9	0	0	4	0	64.1	57	45	40	10	44	42	0	1	.241
Monteleone, Rich, NY-A	R	7	4	4.94	42	0	0	0	11	0	85.2	85	52	47	14	35	50	1	0	.262
Montgomery, Jeff, K.C.	R	7	5	2.27	69	0	0	0	63	45	87.1	65	22	22	3	23	66	3	0	.206
Munoz, Bobby, NY-A	R	3	3	5.32	38	0	0	0	12	0	45.2	48	27	27	1	26	33	2	0	.270
Munoz, Mike, Det.	L	0	1	6.00	8	0	0	0	3	0	3.0	4	2	2	1	6	1	0	0	.308
Nelson, Gene, Cal.-Tex.	R	0	5	3.12	52	0	0	0	22	5	60.2	60	28	21	3	24	35	2	0	.259
Nelson, Jeff, Sea.	R	5	3	4.35	71	0	0	0	13	1	60.0	57	30	29	5	34	61	2	0	.258
Nen, Robb, Tex.	R	1	1	6.35	9	3	0	0	3	0	22.2	28	17	16	1	26	12	2	1	.326
Nielsen, Jerry, Cal.	L	0	0	8.03	10	0	0	0	3	0	12.1	18	13	11	1	4	8	0	1	.340
Novoa, Rafael, Mil.	L	0	3	4.50	15	7	2	0	0	0	56.0	58	32	28	7	22	17	1	0	.267
Nunez, Edwin, Oak.	R	3	6	3.81	56	0	0	0	16	1	75.2	89	36	32	2	29	58	4	2	.298
O'Donoghue, John P., Bal.	L	0	1	4.58	11	1	0	0	3	0	19.2	22	12	10	4	10	16	0	0	.278
Oliver, Darren, Tex.	L	0	0	2.70	2	0	0	0	0	0	3.1	2	1	1	1	1	4	0	0	.154
Olson, Gregg, Bal.	R	0	2	1.60	50	0	0	0	45	29	45.0	37	9	8	1	18	44	5	0	.223
Ontiveros, Steve, Sea.	R	0	2	1.00	14	0	0	0	8	0	18.0	18	3	2	0	6	13	1	0	.277
Oquist, Mike, Bal.	R	0	0	3.86	5	0	0	0	2	0	11.2	12	5	5	0	4	8	0	0	.261
Orosco, Jesse, Mil.	L	3	5	3.18	57	0	0	0	27	8	56.2	47	25	20	2	17	67	3	1	.224
Pall, Donn, ChiA	R	2	3	3.22	39	0	0	0	9	1	58.2	62	25	21	5	11	29	3	0	.268
Patterson, Bob, Tex.	L	2	4	4.78	52	0	0	0	29	1	52.2	59	28	28	8	11	46	0	0	.282
Patterson, Ken, Cal.	L	1	1	4.58	46	0	0	0	9	1	59.0	54	30	30	7	35	36	2	0	.249
Pennington, Brad, Bal.	L	3	2	6.55	34	0	0	0	16	4	33.0	34	25	24	7	25	39	3	0	.266
Plantenberg, Erik, Sea.	L	0	0	6.52	20	0	0	0	4	1	9.2	11	7	7	0	12	3	1	0	.282
Plunk, Eric, Cle.	R	4	5	2.79	70	0	0	0	40	15	71.0	61	29	22	5	30	77	6	0	.226
Poole, Jim Ri., Bal.	L	2	1	2.15	55	0	0	0	11	2	50.1	30	18	12	2	21	29	0	0	.175
Powell, Dennis, Sea.	L	0	0	4.15	33	2	0	0	7	0	47.2	42	22	22	7	24	32	2	0	.255
Power, Ted, Cle.-Sea.	R	2	4	5.36	45	0	0	0	24	13	45.1	57	28	27	3	17	27	2	0	.310
Quantrill, Paul, Bos.	R	6	12	3.91	49	14	1	1	8	1	138.0	151	73	60	13	44	66	0	1	.279
Radinsky, Scott, ChiA	L	8	2	4.28	73	0	0	0	24	4	54.2	61	33	26	3	19	44	0	4	.268
Rasmussen, Dennis, K.C.	L	1	2	7.45	9	4	0	0	3	0	29.0	40	25	24	4	14	12	2	0	.328
Reed, Rick, K.C.-Tex.	R	1	0	5.87	3	0	0	0	0	0	7.2	12	5	5	1	2	5	0	0	.375
Russell, Jeff, Bos.	R	1	4	2.70	51	0	0	0	48	33	46.2	39	16	14	1	14	45	2	0	.231
Ryan, Ken, Bos.	R	7	2	3.60	47	0	0	0	26	1	50.0	43	23	20	2	29	49	3	0	.235
Sampen, Bill, K.C.	R	2	2	5.89	18	0	0	0	3	0	18.1	25	12	12	1	9	9	2	0	.338
Schooler, Mike, Tex.	R	3	0	5.55	17	0	0	0	9	0	24.1	30	17	15	3	10	16	1	0	.303
Schwarz, Jeff, ChiA	R	2	2	3.71	41	0	0	0	10	0	51.0	35	21	21	1	38	41	5	1	.201
Scott, Darryl, Cal.	R	1	2	5.85	16	0	0	0	2	0	20.0	19	13	13	1	11	13	2	0	.250
Scudder, Scott, Cle.	R	0	1	9.00	2	1	0	0	1	0	4.0	5	4	4	0	4	1	0	0	.333
Shinall, Zak, Sea.	R	0	0	3.38	1	0	0	0	0	0	2.2	4	1	1	1	2	0	0	0	.333
Slocumb, Heathcliff, Cle.	R	3	1	4.28	20	0	0	0	5	0	27.1	28	14	13	3	16	18	0	0	.272
Slusarski, Joe, Oak.	R	0	0	5.19	2	1	0	0	0	0	8.2	9	5	5	1	11	1	0	0	.300
Smith, Lee, NY-A	R	0	0	0.00	8	0	0	0	8	3	8.0	4	0	0	0	5	11	0	0	.148
Smithberg, Roger, Oak.	R	1	2	2.75	13	0	0	0	9	3	19.2	13	7	6	2	7	4	1	0	.197
Swan, Russ, Sea.	L	3	3	9.15	23	0	0	0	6	0	19.2	25	20	20	2	18	10	0	0	.316
Swingle, Paul, Cal.	R	0	1	8.38	9	0	0	0	2	0	9.2	15	9	9	2	6	6	0	0	.357
Taylor, Scott, Bos.	L	0	1	8.18	16	0	0	0	3	0	11.0	14	10	10	1	12	8	0	0	.311
Telford, Anthony, Bal.	R	0	0	9.82	3	0	0	0	2	0	7.1	11	8	8	3	1	6	1	0	.344
Thigpen, Bobby, ChiA	R	0	0	5.71	25	0	0	0	11	1	34.2	51	25	22	5	12	19	0	0	.349
Timlin, Mike, Tor.	R	4	2	4.69	54	0	0	0	27	1	55.2	63	32	29	7	27	49	1	0	.284
Trombley, Mike, Min.	R	6	6	4.88	44	10	0	0	8	2	114.1	131	72	62	15	41	85	5	0	.290
Tsamis, George, Min.	L	1	2	6.19	41	0	0	0	18	1	68.1	86	51	47	9	27	30	1	1	.317
Valera, Julio, Cal.	R	3	6	6.62	19	5	0	0	8	4	53.0	77	44	39	8	15	28	2	0	.344
Wainhouse, Dave, Sea.	R	0	0	27.00	3	0	0	0	0	0	2.1	7	7	7	1	5	2	0	0	.500
Ward, Duane, Tor.	R	2	3	2.13	71	0	0	0	70	45	71.2	49	17	17	4	25	97	7	0	.193
Wertz, Bill, Cle.	R	2	3	3.62	34	0	0	0	9	0	59.2	54	28	24	5	32	53	0	0	.238
Whiteside, Matt, Tex.	R	2	1	4.32	60	0	0	0	10	1	73.0	78	37	35	7	23	39	0	2	.281
Wickander, Kevin, Cle.	L	0	0	4.15	11	0	0	0	1	0	8.2	15	7	4	3	3	3	1	0	.366
Wickman, Bob, NY-A	R	14	4	4.63	41	19	1	1	9	4	140.0	156	82	72	13	69	70	2	0	.284
Williams, Woody, Tor.	R	3	1	4.38	30	0	0	0	9	0	37.0	40	18	18	2	22	24	2	1	.274
Williamson, Mark, Bal.	R	7	5	4.91	48	1	0	0	12	0	88.0	106	54	48	5	25	45	2	0	.304
Willis, Carl, Min.	R	3	0	3.10	53	0	0	0	21	5	58.0	56	23	20	2	17	44	3	0	.259
Young, Cliff, Cle.	L	3	3	4.62	21	7	0	0	3	1	60.1	74	35	31	9	18	31	0	0	.298
Young, Matt, Cle.	L	1	6	5.21	22	8	0	0	2	0	74.1	75	45	43	8	57	65	5	1	.266

American League catchers

Name/Team	B	BA	G	AB	R	H	TB	2B	3B	HR	RBI	SH	SF	£B	SO	SB	CS	GIDP	SLG	OBA
Alomar, Sandy Jr., Cle.	R	.270	64	215	24	58	85	7	1	6	32	1	4	11	28	3	1	3	.395	.318
Borders, Pat, Tor.	R	.254	138	488	38	124	181	30	0	9	55	7	3	20	66	2	2	18	.371	.285
Delgado, Carlos, Tor.	L	.000	2	1	0	0	0	0	0	0	0	0	0	1	0	0	0	0	.000	.500
Fisk, Carlton, ChiA	R	.189	25	53	2	10	13	0	0	1	4	1	1	2	11	0	1	0	.245	.228
Flaherty, John, Bos.	R	.120	13	25	3	3	5	2	0	0	2	1	0	2	6	0	0	0	.200	.214
Gonzales, Larry, Cal.	R	.500	2	2	0	1	1	0	0	0	1	0	0	1	0	0	0	0	.500	.667
Harper, Brian, Min.	R	.304	147	530	52	161	225	26	1	12	73	0	5	29	29	1	3	15	.425	.347
Haselman, Bill, Sea.	R	.255	58	137	21	35	58	8	0	5	16	2	2	12	19	2	1	5	.423	.316
Helfand, Eric, Oak.	L	.231	8	13	.1	3	3	0	0	0	1	0	0	1	0	0	0	0	.231	.231
Hemond, Scott, Oak.	R	.256	91	215	31	55	89	16	0	6	26	6	1	32	55	14	5	2	.414	.353
Hoiles, Chris, Bal.	R	.310	126	419	80	130	245	28	0	29	82	3	3	69	94	1	1	10	.585	.416
Howard, Chris H., Sea.	R	.000	4	1	0	0	0	0	0	0	0	0	0	0	0	0	0	0	.000	.000
Karkovice, Ron, ChiA	R	.228	128	403	60	92	171	17	1	20	54	11	4	29	126	2	2	12	.424	.287
Kmak, Joe, Mil.	R	.218	51	110	9	24	29	5	0	0	7	1	0	14	13	6	2	2	.264	.317
Knorr, Randy, Tor.	R	.248	39	101	11	25	44	3	2	4	20	2	0	9	29	0	0	2	.436	.309
Kreuter, Chad, Det.	B	.286	119	374	59	107	181	23	3	15	51	2	3	49	92	2	1	5	.484	.371
LaValliere, Mike, ChiA	L	.258	37	97	6	25	27	2	0	0	8	7	2	4	14	0	1	1	.278	.282
Lampkin, Tom, Mil.	L	.198	73	162	22	32	52	8	0	4	25	2	4	20	26	7	3	2	.321	.280
Levis, Jesse, Cle.	L	.175	31	63	7	11	13	2	0	0	4	1	1	2	10	0	0	0	.206	.197
Lindsey, Doug, ChiA	R	.000	2	1	0	0	0	0	0	0	0	0	0	0	0	0	0	0	.000	.000
Macfarlane, Mike, K.C.	R	.273	117	388	55	106	193	27	0	20	67	1	6	40	83	2	5	8	.497	.360
Mayne, Brent, K.C.	L	.254	71	205	22	52	69	9	1	2	22	3	0	18	31	3	2	6	.337	.317
Melvin, Bob, Bos.	R	.222	77	176	13	39	55	7	0	3	23	3	3	7	44	0	0	2	.313	.251
Mercedes, Henry, Oak.	R	.213	20	47	5	10	12	2	0	0	3	0	0	2	15	1	1	0	.255	.260
Myers, Greg, Cal.	L	.255	108	290	27	74	105	10	0	7	40	3	3	17	47	3	3	8	.362	.298
Nilsson, Dave, Mil.	L	.257	100	296	35	76	111	10	2	7	40	4	3	37	36	3	6	10	.375	.336
Nokes, Matt, NY-A	L	.249	76	217	25	54	92	8	0	10	35	0	3	16	31	0	0	4	.424	.303
Ortiz, Junior, Cle.	R	.221	95	249	19	55	68	13	0	0	20	4	1	11	26	1	0	10	.273	.267
Orton, John, Cal.	R	.189	37	95	5	18	26	5	0	1	4	2	0	7	24	1	2	1	.274	.252
Parent, Mark, Bal.	R	.259	22	54	7	14	28	2	0	4	12	3	1	3	14	0	0	1	.519	.293
Parks, Derek, Min.	R	.200	7	20	3	4	4	0	0	0	1	0	0	1	2	0	0	0	.200	.238
Parrish, Lance, Cle.	R	.200	10	20	2	4	8	1	0	1	2	0	0	4	5	1	0	2	.400	.333
Pena, Tony, Bos.	R	.181	126	304	20	55	78	11	0	4	19	13	3	25	46	1	3	12	.257	.246
Petralli, Geno, Tex.	B	.241	59	133	16	32	40	5	0	1	13	1	0	22	17	2	0	5	.301	.348
Rodriguez, Ivan, Tex.	R	.273	137	473	56	129	195	28	4	10	66	5	8	29	70	8	7	16	.412	.315
Rowland, Rich, Det.	R	.217	21	46	2	10	13	3	0	0	4	1	0	5	16	0	0	1	.283	.294
Russell, John W., Tex.	R	.227	18	22	1	5	9	1	0	1	3	0	0	2	10	0	0	0	.409	.292
Santovenia, Nelson, K.C.	R	.125	4	8	0	1	1	0	0	0	0	0	0	1	2	0	0	0	.125	.222
Stanley, Mike, NY-A	R	.305	130	423	70	129	226	17	1	26	84	0	6	57	85	1	1	10	.534	.389
Steinbach, Terry, Oak.	R	.285	104	389	47	111	162	19	1	10	43	0	1	25	65	3	3	13	.416	.333
Tackett, Jeff, Bal.	R	.172	39	87	8	15	18	3	0	0	9	2	1	13	28	0	0	5	.207	.277
Tingley, Ron, Cal.	R	.200	58	90	7	18	25	7	0	0	12	3	1	9	22	1	2	4	.278	.277
Turner, Chris, Cal.	R	.280	25	75	9	21	29	5	0	1	13	0	1	9	16	1	1	1	.387	.360
Valle, Dave, Sea.	R	.258	135	423	48	109	167	19	0	13	63	8	4	48	56	1	0	18	.395	.354
Webster, Lenny, Min.	R	.198	49	106	14	21	26	2	0	1	8	0	0	11	8	1	0	1	.245	.274
Wrona, Rick, ChiA	R	.125	4	8	0	1	1	0	0	0	1	0	0	0	4	0	0	0	.125	.125

American League first basemen

Name/Team	B	BA	G	AB	R	H	TB	2B	3B	HR	RBI	SH	SF	BB	SO	SB	CS	GIDP	SLG	OBA
Aldrete, Mike, Oak.	L	.267	95	255	40	68	113	13	1	10	33	3	0	34	45	1	1	7	.443	.353
Armas, Marcos, Oak.	R	.194	15	31	7	6	11	2	0	1	1	0	0	1	12	1	0	0	.355	.242
Barnes, Skeeter, Det.	R	.281	84	160	24	45	61	8	1	2	27	4	5	11	19	5	5	2	.381	.318
Carey, Paul, Bal.	L	.213	18	47	1	10	11	1	0	0	3	0	0	5	14	0	0	4	.234	.288
Davis, Glenn, Bal.	R	.177	30	113	8	20	26	3	0	1	9	1	1	7	29	0	1	2	.230	.230
Denson, Drew, ChiA	B	.200	4	5	0	1	1	0	0	0	0	0	0	0	2	0	0	0	.200	.200
Fielder, Cecil, Det.	R	.267	154	573	80	153	266	23	0	30	117	0	5	90	125	0	1	22	.464	.368
Hamelin, Bob, K.C.	L	.224	16	49	2	11	20	3	0	2	5	0	0	6	15	0	0	2	.408	.309
Hrbek, Kent, Min.	L	.242	123	392	60	95	183	11	1	25	83	3	4	71	57	4	2	12	.467	.357
Jaha, John, Mil.	R	.264	153	515	78	136	214	21	0	19	70	4	4	51	109	13	9	6	.416	.337
Joyner, Wally, K.C.	L	.292	141	497	83	145	232	36	3	15	65	2	5	66	67	5	9	6	.467	.375
Leyritz, Jim, NY-A	R	.309	95	259	43	80	136	14	0	14	53	0	1	37	59	0	0	12	.525	.410
Magadan, Dave, Sea.	L	.259	71	228	27	59	73	11	0	1	21	2	3	36	33	2	0	9	.320	.356
Maksudian, Mike, Min.	L	.167	5	12	2	2	3	1	0	0	2	0	1	4	2	0	0	2	.250	.353
Martinez, Domingo, Tor.	R	.286	8	14	2	4	7	0	0	1	3	0	0	1	7	0	0	0	.500	.333
Martinez, Tino, Sea.	L	.265	109	408	48	108	186	25	1	17	60	3	3	45	56	0	3	7	.456	.343
Mattingly, Don, NY-A	L	.291	134	530	78	154	236	27	2	17	86	0	3	61	42	0	0	20	.445	.364
McGwire, Mark, Oak.	R	.333	27	84	16	28	61	6	0	9	24	0	1	21	19	0	1	0	.726	.467
Milligan, Randy, Cle.	R	.426	19	47	7	20	27	7	0	0	7	0	0	14	4	0	0	0	.574	.557

American League first basemen

Name/Team	B	BA	G	AB	R	H	TB	2B	3B	HR	RBI	SH	SF	BB	SO	SB	CS	GIDP	SLG	OBA
Olerud, John, Tor.	L	.363	158	551	109	200	330	54	2	24	107	0	7	114	65	0	2	12	.599	.473
Palmeiro, Rafael, Tex.	L	.295	160	597	124	176	331	40	2	37	105	2	9	73	85	22	3	8	.554	.371
Pasqua, Dan, ChiA	L	.205	78	176	22	36	63	10	1	5	20	1	3	26	51	2	2	3	.358	.302
Pirkl, Greg, Sea.	R	.174	7	23	1	4	7	0	0	1	4	0	0	0	4	0	0	2	.304	.174
Quintana, Carlos, Bos.	R	.244	101	303	31	74	82	5	0	1	19	5	2	31	52	1	0	13	.271	.317
Segui, David, Bal.	B	.273	146	450	54	123	180	27	0	10	60	3	8	58	53	2	1	18	.400	.351
Snow, J.T., Cal.	B	.241	129	419	60	101	171	18	2	16	57	7	6	55	88	3	0	10	.408	.328
Sorrento, Paul, Cle.	L	.257	148	463	75	119	201	26	1	18	65	0	4	58	121	3	1	10	.434	.340
Sveum, Dale, Oak.	B	.177	30	79	12	14	24	2	1	2	6	1	0	16	21	0	0	2	.304	.316
Tettleton, Mickey, Det.	B	.245	152	522	79	128	257	25	4	32	110	0	6	109	139	3	7	5	.492	.372
Thomas, Frank E., ChiA	R	.317	153	549	106	174	333	36	0	41	128	0	13	112	54	4	2	10	.607	.426
Van Burkleo, Ty, Cal.	L	.152	12	33	2	5	11	3	0	1	1	0	0	6	9	1	0	0	.333	.282
Vaughn, Mo, Bos.	L	.297	152	539	86	160	283	34	1	29	101	0	7	79	130	4	3	14	.525	.390

American League second basemen

Name/Team	B	BA	G	AB	R	H	TB	2B	3B	HR	RBI	SH	SF	BB	SO	SB	CS	GIDP	SLG	OBA
Alomar, Roberto, Tor.	B	.326	153	589	109	192	290	35	6	17	93	4	5	80	67	55	15	13	.492	.408
Amaral, Rich, Sea.	R	.290	110	373	53	108	137	24	1	1	44	7	5	33	54	19	11	5	.367	.348
Baerga, Carlos, Cle.	B	.321	154	624	105	200	303	28	6	21	114	3	13	34	68	15	4	17	.486	.355
Bell, Juan, Mil.	B	.234	91	286	42	67	92	6	2	5	29	3	1	36	64	6	6	4	.322	.321
Boone, Bret, Sea.	R	.251	76	271	31	68	120	12	2	12	38	6	4	17	52	2	3	6	.443	.301
Cora, Joey, ChiA	B	.268	153	579	95	155	202	15	13	2	51	19	4	67	63	20	8	14	.349	.351
Doran, Bill D., Mil.	B	.217	28	60	7	13	17	4	0	0	6	0	1	6	3	1	0	3	.283	.284
Easley, Damion, Cal.	R	.313	73	230	33	72	95	13	2	2	22	1	2	28	35	6	6	5	.413	.392
Fletcher, Scott, Bos.	R	.285	121	480	81	137	193	31	5	5	45	6	3	37	35	16	3	12	.402	.341
Gates, Brent, Oak.	B	.290	139	535	64	155	209	29	2	7	69	6	8	56	75	7	3	17	.391	.357
Hale, Chip, Min.	L	.333	69	186	25	62	79	6	1	3	27	2	1	18	17	2	1	3	.425	.408
Howard, David, K.C.	B	.333	15	24	5	8	10	0	1	0	2	2	1	2	5	1	0	0	.417	.370
Kelly, Pat, NY-A	R	.273	127	406	49	111	158	24	1	7	51	10	6	24	68	14	11	9	.389	.317
Knoblauch, Chuck, Min.	R	.277	153	602	82	167	208	27	4	2	41	4	5	65	44	29	11	11	.346	.354
Lind, Jose, K.C.	R	.248	136	431	33	107	124	13	2	0	37	13	5	13	36	3	2	7	.288	.271
Lovullo, Torey, Cal.	B	.251	116	367	42	92	130	20	0	6	30	3	2	36	49	7	6	8	.354	.318
Lyons, Steve, Bos.	L	.130	28	23	4	3	4	1	0	0	0	0	0	2	5	1	2	0	.174	.200
Martin, Norberto, ChiA	R	.357	8	14	3	5	5	0	0	0	2	0	0	1	1	0	0	0	.357	.400
Naehring, Tim, Bos.	R	.331	39	127	14	42	55	10	0	1	17	3	1	10	26	1	0	3	.433	.377
Reynolds, Harold, Bal.	B	.252	145	485	64	122	162	20	4	4	47	10	5	66	47	12	11	4	.334	.343
Richardson, Jeff, Bos.	R	.208	15	24	3	5	7	2	0	0	2	2	0	1	3	0	0	0	.292	.240
Riles, Ernest, Bos.	L	.189	94	143	15	27	50	8	0	5	20	2	3	20	40	1	3	3	.350	.292
Ripken, Billy, Tex.	R	.189	50	132	12	25	29	4	0	0	11	5	1	11	19	0	2	6	.220	.270
Rivera, Luis, Bos.	R	.208	62	130	13	27	40	8	1	1	7	2	1	11	36	1	2	2	.308	.273
Rossy, Rico, K.C.	R	.221	46	86	10	19	29	4	0	2	12	1	0	9	11	0	0	2	.337	.302
Shumpert, Terry, K.C.	R	.100	8	10	0	1	1	0	0	0	0	0	0	2	2	1	0	0	.100	.250
Sojo, Luis, Tor.	R	.170	19	47	5	8	10	2	0	0	6	2	1	4	2	0	0	3	.213	.231
Spiers, Bill, Mil.	B	.238	113	340	43	81	103	8	4	2	36	9	4	29	51	9	8	11	.303	.302
Stankiewicz, Andy, NY-A	R	.000	16	9	5	0	0	0	0	0	0	0	0	1	1	0	0	0	.000	.100
Stillwell, Kurt, Cal.	B	.262	22	61	2	16	22	2	2	0	3	1	2	4	11	2	0	2	.361	.299
Strange, Doug, Tex.	B	.256	145	484	58	124	174	29	0	7	60	8	4	43	69	6	4	12	.360	.318
Suero, William, Mil.	R	.286	15	14	0	4	4	0	0	0	0	0	0	1	3	0	1	1	.286	.333
Vina, Fernando, Sea.	L	.222	24	45	5	10	12	2	0	0	2	1	0	4	3	6	0	0	.267	.327
Whitaker, Lou, Det.	L	.290	119	383	72	111	172	32	1	9	67	7	4	78	46	3	3	5	.449	.412
Wilkerson, Curtis, K.C.	B	.143	12	28	1	4	4	0	0	0	0	0	0	1	6	2	0	1	.143	.172

American League third basemen

Name/Team	B	BA	G	AB	R	H	TB	2B	3B	HR	RBI	SH	SF	BB	SO	SB	CS	GIDP	SLG	OBA
Backman, Wally, Sea.	B	.138	10	29	2	4	4	0	0	0	0	1	0	1	8	0	0	0	.138	.167
Blowers, Mike, Sea.	R	.280	127	379	55	106	180	23	3	15	57	3	1	44	98	1	5	12	.475	.357
Boggs, Wade, NY-A	L	.302	143	560	83	169	203	26	1	2	59	1	9	74	49	0	1	10	.363	.378
Cooper, Scott, Bos.	L	.279	156	526	67	147	209	29	3	9	63	4	3	58	81	5	2	8	.397	.355
Espinoza, Alvaro, Cle.	R	.278	129	263	34	73	100	15	0	4	27	8	3	8	36	2	2	7	.380	.298
Gaetti, Gary, Cal.-K.C.	R	.245	102	331	40	81	145	20	1	14	50	2	7	21	87	1	3	5	.438	.300
Gomez, Leo, Bal.	R	.197	71	244	30	48	85	7	0	10	25	3	2	32	60	0	1	2	.348	.295
Gonzales, Rene, Cal.	R	.251	118	335	34	84	107	17	0	2	31	2	2	49	45	5	5	12	.319	.346
Gruber, Kelly, Cal.	R	.277	18	65	10	18	30	3	0	3	9	2	0	2	11	0	0	2	.462	.309
Hiatt, Phil, K.C.	R	.218	81	238	30	52	87	12	1	7	36	0	2	16	82	6	3	8	.366	.285
Hulett, Tim, Bal.	R	.300	85	260	40	78	99	15	0	2	23	1	2	23	56	1	2	5	.381	.361
Jorgensen, Terry, Min.	R	.224	59	152	15	34	44	7	0	1	12	0	1	10	21	1	0	7	.289	.270

American League third basemen

Name/Team	B	BA	G	AB	R	H	TB	2B	3B	HR	RBI	SH	SF	BB	SO	SB	CS	GIDP	SLG	OBA
Livingstone, Scott, Det.	L	.293	98	304	39	89	109	10	2	2	39	1	6	19	32	1	3	4	.359	.328
Martinez, Carlos, Cle.	R	.244	80	262	26	64	89	10	0	5	31	0	3	20	29	1	1	5	.340	.295
Miller, Keith A., K.C.	R	.167	37	108	9	18	21	3	0	0	3	0	1	8	19	3	1	3	.194	.229
Ortiz, Luis, Bos.	R	.250	9	12	0	3	3	0	0	0	1	0	0	0	2	0	0	0	.250	.250
Pagliarulo, Mike, Min.-Bal.	L	.303	116	370	55	112	172	25	4	9	44	2	1	26	49	6	6	7	.465	.357
Palmer, Dean, Tex.	R	.245	148	519	88	127	261	31	2	33	96	0	5	53	154	11	10	5	.503	.321
Paquette, Craig, Oak.	R	.219	105	393	35	86	150	20	4	12	46	1	1	14	108	4	2	7	.382	.245
Perez, Eduardo, Cal.	R	.250	52	180	16	45	67	6	2	4	30	0	1	9	39	5	4	4	.372	.292
Seitzer, Kevin, Oak.-Mil.	R	.269	120	417	45	112	165	16	2	11	57	3	5	44	48	7	7	14	.396	.338
Sprague, Ed Jr., Tor.	R	.260	150	546	50	142	211	31	1	12	73	2	6	32	85	1	0	23	.386	.310
Stahoviak, Scott, Min.	L	.193	20	57	1	11	15	4	0	0	1	0	0	3	22	0	2	2	.263	.233
Surhoff, B.J., Mil.	L	.274	148	552	66	151	216	38	3	7	79	4	5	36	47	12	9	9	.391	.318
Thome, Jim, Cle.	L	.266	47	154	28	41	73	11	0	7	22	0	5	29	36	2	1	3	.474	.385
Treadway, Jeff, Cle.	L	.303	97	221	25	67	89	14	1	2	27	1	2	14	21	1	1	6	.403	.347
Ventura, Robin, ChiA	L	.262	157	554	85	145	240	27	1	22	94	1	6	105	82	1	6	18	.433	.379
Wilson, Craig, K.C.	R	.265	21	49	6	13	17	1	0	1	3	1	0	7	6	1	1	0	.347	.357

American League shortstops

Name/Team	B	BA	G	AB	R	H	TB	2B	3B	HR	RBI	SH	SF	BB	SO	SB	CS	GIDP	SLG	OBA
Bordick, Mike, Oak.	R	.249	159	546	60	136	170	21	2	3	48	10	6	60	58	10	10	9	.311	.332
Cedeno, Domingo, Tor.	B	.174	15	46	5	8	8	0	0	0	7	2	1	1	10	1	0	2	.174	.188
Correia, Rod, Cal.	R	.266	64	128	12	34	39	5	0	0	9	5	0	6	20	2	4	1	.305	.319
DiSarcina, Gary, Cal.	R	.238	126	416	44	99	130	20	1	3	45	5	3	15	38	5	7	13	.313	.273
Diaz, Mario, Tex.	R	.273	71	205	24	56	74	10	1	2	24	7	5	8	13	1	0	6	.361	.297
Fermin, Felix, Cle.	R	.262	140	480	48	126	152	16	2	2	45	5	1	24	14	4	5	12	.317	.303
Fernandez, Tony, Tor.	B	.306	94	353	45	108	156	18	9	4	50	5	1	31	26	15	8	13	.442	.361
Fryman, Travis, Det.	R	.300	151	607	98	182	295	37	5	22	97	1	6	77	128	9	4	8	.486	.379
Gagne, Greg, K.C.	R	.280	159	540	66	151	219	32	3	10	57	4	4	33	93	10	12	7	.406	.319
Gallego, Mike, NY-A	R	.283	119	403	63	114	166	20	1	10	54	3	5	50	65	3	2	16	.412	.364
Gil, Benji, Tex.	R	.123	22	57	3	7	7	0	0	0	2	4	0	5	22	1	2	0	.123	.194
Gomez, Chris, Det.	R	.250	46	128	11	32	41	7	1	0	11	3	0	9	17	2	2	2	.320	.304
Grebeck, Craig, ChiA	R	.226	72	190	25	43	51	5	0	1	12	7	0	26	26	1	2	9	.268	.319
Griffin, Alfredo, Tor.	B	.211	46	95	15	20	23	3	0	0	3	4	0	3	13	0	0	3	.242	.235
Guillen, Ozzie, ChiA	L	.280	134	457	44	128	171	23	4	4	50	13	6	10	41	5	4	6	.374	.292
Hocking, Denny, Min.	B	.139	15	36	7	5	6	1	0	0	0	0	0	6	8	1	0	1	.167	.262
Huson, Jeff, Tex.	L	.133	23	45	3	6	9	1	1	0	2	1	0	10	10	0	0	2	.200	.133
Lee, Manuel, Tex.	R	.220	73	205	31	45	53	3	1	1	12	9	1	22	39	2	4	2	.259	.300
Leius, Scott, Min.	R	.167	10	18	4	3	3	0	0	0	2	0	2	2	4	0	0	1	.167	.227
Lewis, Mark, Cle.	R	.250	14	52	6	13	18	2	0	1	5	1	0	0	7	3	0	1	.346	.250
Listach, Pat, Mil.	B	.244	98	356	50	87	113	15	1	3	30	5	2	37	70	18	9	7	.317	.319
Meares, Pat, Min.	R	.251	111	346	33	87	107	14	3	0	33	4	3	7	52	4	5	11	.309	.266
Owen, Spike, NY-A	B	.234	103	334	41	78	104	16	2	2	20	3	1	29	30	3	2	6	.311	.294
Reboulet, Jeff, Min.	R	.258	109	240	33	62	73	8	0	1	15	5	1	35	37	5	5	6	.304	.356
Ripken, Cal, Bal.	R	.257	162	641	87	165	269	26	3	24	90	0	6	65	58	1	4	17	.420	.329
Schofield, Dick C., Tor.	R	.191	36	110	11	21	26	1	2	0	5	2	0	16	25	3	0	1	.236	.294
Shave, Jon, Tex.	R	.319	17	47	3	15	17	2	0	0	7	3	2	0	8	1	3	0	.362	.306
Silvestri, Dave, NY-A	R	.286	7	21	4	6	10	1	0	1	4	0	0	5	3	0	0	1	.476	.423
Thon, Dickie, Mil.	R	.269	85	245	23	66	81	10	1	1	33	3	5	22	39	6	5	4	.331	.324
Trammell, Alan, Det.	R	.329	112	401	72	132	199	25	3	12	60	4	2	38	38	12	8	7	.496	.388
Valentin, John, Bos.	R	.278	144	468	50	130	209	40	3	11	66	16	4	49	77	3	4	9	.447	.346
Valentin, Jose, Mil.	B	.245	19	53	10	13	21	1	2	1	7	2	0	7	16	1	0	1	.396	.344
Vizquel, Omar, Sea.	B	.255	158	560	68	143	167	14	2	2	31	13	3	50	71	12	14	7	.298	.319
Walewander, Jim, Cal.	B	.125	12	8	2	1	1	0	0	0	3	0	1	5	1	1	1	0	.125	.429

American League outfielders

Name/Team	B	BA	G	AB	R	H	TB	2B	3B	HR	RBI	SH	SF	BB	SO	SB	CS	GIDP	SLG	OBA
Abbott, Kurt, Oak.	R	.246	20	61	11	15	25	1	0	3	9	3	0	3	20	2	0	3	.410	.281
Anderson, Brady, Bal.	L	.262	142	560	87	147	238	36	8	13	66	6	6	82	99	24	12	4	.425	.363
Bautista, Danny, Det.	R	.311	17	61	6	19	25	3	0	1	9	0	1	10	3	1	1	0	.410	.317
Becker, Rich, Min.	B	.286	3	7	3	2	4	2	0	0	0	0	0	5	4	1	1	0	.571	.583
Belle, Albert, Cle.	R	.290	159	594	93	172	328	36	3	38	129	1	14	76	96	23	12	18	.552	.370
Blankenship, Lance, Oak.	R	.190	94	252	43	48	64	8	1	2	23	6	1	67	64	13	5	9	.254	.363
Blosser, Greg, Bos.	L	.071	17	28	1	2	3	1	0	0	1	0	0	2	7	1	0	0	.107	.133
Brito, Bernardo, Min.	R	.241	27	54	8	13	27	2	0	4	9	0	0	1	20	0	0	1	.500	.255
Brooks, Hubie, K.C.	R	.286	75	168	14	48	63	12	0	1	24	0	1	11	27	0	1	5	.375	.331
Brosius, Scott, Oak.	R	.249	70	213	26	53	83	10	1	6	25	3	2	14	37	6	0	6	.390	.296

American League outfielders

Name/Team	B	BA	G	AB	R	H	TB	2B	3B	HR	RBI	SH	SF	BB	SO	SB	CS	GIDP	SLG	OBA
Browne, Jerry, Oak.	B	.250	76	260	27	65	84	13	0	2	19	2	2	22	17	4	0	9	.323	.306
Bruett, J.T., Min.	L	.250	17	20	2	5	7	2	0	0	1	0	0	1	4	0	0	1	.350	.318
Brunansky, Tom, Mil.	R	.183	80	224	20	41	72	7	3	6	29	2	0	25	59	3	4	5	.321	.265
Buford, Damon, Bal.	R	.228	53	79	18	18	29	5	0	2	9	1	0	9	19	2	2	1	.367	.315
Buhner, Jay, Sea.	R	.272	158	563	91	153	268	28	3	27	98	2	8	100	144	2	5	12	.476	.379
Burks, Ellis, ChiA	R	.275	146	499	75	137	220	24	4	17	74	3	8	60	97	6	9	11	.441	.352
Butler, Rob, Tor.	L	.271	17	48	8	13	17	4	0	0	2	0	0	7	12	2	2	0	.354	.375
Calderon, Ivan, Bos.-ChiA	R	.209	82	239	26	50	67	10	2	1	22	2	2	21	33	4	2	12	.280	.274
Canate, William, Tor.	R	.213	38	47	12	10	13	0	0	1	3	2	1	6	15	1	1	2	.277	.309
Canseco, Jose, Tex.	R	.255	60	231	30	59	105	14	1	10	46	0	3	16	62	6	6	6	.455	.308
Carter, Joe, Tor.	R	.254	155	603	92	153	295	33	5	33	121	0	10	47	113	8	3	10	.489	.312
Coles, Darnell, Tor.	R	.253	64	194	26	49	72	9	1	4	26	1	2	16	29	1	1	3	.371	.319
Cotto, Henry, Sea.	R	.190	54	105	10	20	27	1	0	2	7	1	0	2	22	5	4	0	.257	.213
Curtis, Chad, Cal.	R	.285	152	583	94	166	215	25	3	6	59	7	7	70	89	48	24	16	.369	.361
Cuyler, Milt, Det.	B	.213	82	249	46	53	78	11	7	0	19	4	1	19	53	13	2	2	.313	.276
Dascenzo, Doug, Tex.	B	.199	76	146	20	29	42	5	1	2	10	3	1	8	22	2	0	1	.288	.239
Davis, Butch, Tex.	R	.245	62	159	24	39	66	10	4	3	20	5	0	5	28	3	1	0	.415	.273
Davis, Eric, Det.	R	.253	23	75	14	19	40	1	1	6	15	0	0	14	18	2	2	4	.533	.371
Deer, Rob, Det.-Bos.	R	.210	128	466	66	98	180	17	1	21	55	0	3	58	169	5	2	6	.386	.303
Devereaux, Mike, Bal.	R	.250	131	527	72	132	211	31	3	14	75	2	4	43	99	3	3	13	.400	.306
Diaz, Alex, Mil.	B	.319	32	69	9	22	24	2	0	0	1	3	0	0	12	5	3	3	.348	.319
Ducey, Rob, Tex.	L	.282	27	85	15	24	42	6	3	2	9	2	2	10	17	2	3	1	.494	.351
Edmonds, Jim, Cal.	L	.246	18	61	5	15	21	4	1	0	4	0	0	2	16	0	2	1	.344	.270
Felder, Mike, Sea.	B	.211	109	342	31	72	92	7	5	1	20	7	1	22	34	15	9	2	.269	.262
Fox, Eric, Oak.	B	.143	29	56	5	8	12	1	0	1	5	3	0	2	7	0	2	0	.214	.172
Gladden, Dan, Det.	R	.267	91	356	52	95	154	16	2	13	56	4	2	21	50	8	5	14	.433	.312
Gonzalez, Juan, Tex.	R	.310	140	536	105	166	339	33	1	46	118	0	1	37	99	4	1	12	.632	.368
Green, Shawn, Tor.	L	.000	3	6	0	0	0	0	0	0	0	0	0	0	1	0	0	0	.000	.000
Greenwell, Mike, Bos.	L	.315	146	540	77	170	259	38	6	13	72	2	5	54	46	5	4	17	.480	.379
Griffey, Ken Jr., Sea.	L	.309	156	582	113	180	359	38	3	45	109	0	7	96	91	17	9	14	.617	.408
Gwynn, Chris, K.C.	L	.300	103	287	36	86	111	14	4	1	25	2	2	24	34	0	1	7	.387	.354
Hamilton, Darryl, Mil.	L	.310	135	520	74	161	211	21	1	9	48	4	1	45	62	21	13	9	.406	.367
Hammonds, Jeffrey, Bal.	R	.305	33	105	10	32	49	8	0	3	19	1	2	2	16	4	0	3	.467	.312
Harris, Donald, Tex.	R	.197	40	76	10	15	20	2	0	1	8	3	1	5	18	0	1	0	.263	.253
Hatcher, Billy, Bos.	R	.287	136	508	71	146	203	24	3	9	57	11	4	28	46	14	7	14	.400	.336
Henderson, Dave, Oak.	R	.220	107	382	37	84	163	19	0	20	53	0	8	32	113	0	3	1	.427	.275
Henderson, Rickey, Oak.-Tor.	R	.289	134	481	114	139	228	22	2	21	59	1	4	120	65	53	8	9	.474	.432
Hill, Glenallen, Cle.	R	.224	66	174	19	39	65	7	2	5	25	1	4	11	50	7	3	3	.374	.268
Howard, Thomas, Cle.	B	.236	74	178	26	42	58	7	0	3	23	0	4	12	42	5	1	5	.326	.278
Howitt, Dann, Sea.	L	.211	32	76	6	16	27	3	1	2	8	0	0	4	18	0	0	0	.355	.250
Huff, Mike, ChiA	R	.182	43	44	4	8	13	2	0	1	6	1	2	9	15	1	0	0	.295	.321
Hulse, David, Tex.	L	.290	114	407	71	118	150	9	10	1	29	5	2	26	57	29	9	9	.369	.333
Humphreys, Mike, NY-A	R	.171	25	35	6	6	13	2	1	1	6	0	1	4	11	2	1	0	.371	.250
Jackson, Darrin, Tor.	R	.216	46	176	15	38	61	8	0	5	19	5	0	8	53	0	2	9	.347	.250
James, Chris, Tex.	R	.355	8	31	5	11	21	1	0	3	7	0	0	3	6	0	0	0	.677	.412
James, Dion, NY-A	L	.332	115	343	62	114	160	21	2	7	36	1	1	31	31	0	0	5	.466	.390
Javier, Stan, Cal.	B	.291	92	237	33	69	96	10	4	3	28	1	3	27	33	12	2	7	.405	.362
Johnson, Lance, ChiA	L	.311	147	540	75	168	214	18	14	0	47	3	0	36	33	35	7	10	.396	.354
Jose, Felix, K.C.	B	.253	149	499	64	126	174	24	3	6	43	1	2	36	95	31	13	5	.349	.303
Kirby, Wayne, Cle.	L	.269	131	458	71	123	170	19	5	6	60	7	6	37	58	17	5	8	.371	.323
Koslofski, Kevin, K.C.	L	.269	15	26	4	7	10	0	0	1	2	1	0	4	5	0	1	1	.385	.387
Larkin, Gene, Min.	B	.264	56	144	17	38	50	7	1	1	19	2	4	21	16	0	1	5	.347	.357
Lee, Derek, Min.	B	.152	15	33	3	5	6	1	0	0	4	0	0	1	4	0	0	0	.182	.176
Leonard, Mark, Bal.	L	.067	10	15	1	1	2	1	0	0	3	0	3	3	7	0	0	0	.133	.190
Litton, Greg, Sea.	R	.299	72	174	25	52	78	17	0	3	25	5	1	18	30	0	1	6	.448	.366
Lofton, Kenny, Cle.	L	.325	148	569	116	185	232	28	8	1	42	2	4	81	83	70	14	8	.408	.408
Lydy, Scott, Oak.	R	.225	41	102	11	23	34	5	0	2	7	0	0	8	39	2	0	1	.333	.288
Mack, Shane, Min.	R	.276	128	503	66	139	207	30	4	10	61	3	2	41	76	15	5	13	.412	.335
Maldonado, Candy, Cle.	R	.247	28	81	11	20	37	2	0	5	20	1	1	11	18	0	1	2	.457	.333
Martinez, Chito, Bal.	L	.000	8	15	0	0	0	0	0	0	0	0	0	4	4	0	0	0	.000	.211
McCarty, David, Min.	R	.214	98	350	36	75	100	15	2	2	21	1	0	19	80	2	6	13	.286	.257
McLemore, Mark, Bal.	B	.284	148	581	81	165	214	27	5	4	72	11	6	64	92	21	15	21	.368	.353
McNeely, Jeff, Bos.	R	.297	21	37	10	11	14	1	1	0	1	0	0	7	9	6	0	0	.378	.409
McRae, Brian, K.C.	B	.282	153	627	78	177	259	28	9	12	69	14	3	37	105	23	14	8	.413	.325
McReynolds, Kevin, K.C.	R	.245	110	351	44	86	149	22	4	11	42	1	5	37	56	2	2	8	.425	.316
Mercedes, Luis, Bal.	R	.292	10	24	1	7	9	2	0	0	1	0	1	0	5	4	1	1	.375	.414
Meulens, Hensley, NY-A	R	.170	30	53	8	9	18	1	1	2	5	0	0	8	19	0	1	2	.340	.279
Mieske, Matt, Mil.	R	.241	23	58	9	14	23	0	0	3	7	1	0	4	14	0	2	2	.397	.290
Munoz, Pedro, Min.	R	.233	104	326	34	76	128	11	1	13	38	0	0	25	97	1	2	7	.393	.294
O'Leary, Troy, Mil.	L	.293	19	41	3	12	15	3	0	0	3	3	0	5	9	0	0	1	.366	.370

American League outfielders

Name/Team	B	BA	G	AB	R	H	TB	2B	3B	HR	RBI	SH	SF	BB	SO	SB	CS	GIDP	SLG	OBA
O'Neill, Paul, NY-A	L	.311	141	498	71	155	251	34	1	20	75	0	3	44	69	2	4	13	.504	.367
Peltier, Dan, Tex.	L	.269	65	160	23	43	55	7	1	1	17	1	1	20	27	0	4	3	.344	.352
Phillips, Tony, Det.	B	.313	151	566	113	177	225	27	0	7	57	1	4	132	102	16	11	11	.398	.443
Polonia, Luis, Cal.	L	.271	152	576	75	156	188	17	6	1	32	8	3	48	53	55	24	7	.326	.328
Puckett, Kirby, Min.	R	.296	156	622	89	184	295	39	3	22	89	1	5	47	93	8	6	15	.474	.349
Pulliam, Harvey, K.C.	R	.258	27	62	7	16	24	5	0	1	6	0	0	2	14	0	0	3	.387	.292
Raines, Tim, ChiA	B	.306	115	415	75	127	199	16	4	16	54	2	2	64	35	21	7	7	.480	.401
Redus, Gary, Tex.	R	.288	77	222	28	64	102	12	4	6	31	0	3	23	35	4	4	3	.459	.351
Salmon, Tim, Cal.	R	.283	142	515	93	146	276	35	1	31	95	0	8	82	135	5	6	6	.536	.382
Sasser, Mackey, Sea.	L	.218	83	188	18	41	58	10	2	1	21	0	4	15	30	1	0	7	.309	.274
Sax, Steve, ChiA	R	.235	57	119	20	28	36	5	0	1	8	2	0	8	6	7	3	1	.303	.283
Sierra, Ruben, Oak.	B	.233	158	630	77	147	246	23	5	22	101	0	10	52	97	25	5	17	.390	.288
Thurman, Gary, Det.	R	.213	75	89	22	19	25	2	2	0	13	1	1	11	30	7	0	2	.281	.297
Tinsley, Lee, Sea.	B	.158	11	19	2	3	7	1	0	1	2	0	0	2	9	0	0	1	.368	.238
Turang, Brian, Sea.	R	.250	40	140	22	35	48	11	1	0	7	1	0	17	20	6	2	3	.343	.340
Vaughn, Greg, Mil.	R	.267	154	569	97	152	274	28	2	30	97	0	4	89	118	10	7	6	.482	.369
Velarde, Randy, NY-A	R	.301	85	226	28	68	106	13	2	7	24	3	2	18	39	2	2	12	.469	.360
Voigt, Jack, Bal.	R	.296	64	152	32	45	76	11	1	6	23	0	0	25	33	1	0	3	.500	.395
Ward, Turner, Tor.	B	.192	72	167	20	32	52	4	2	4	28	3	4	23	26	3	3	7	.311	.287
White, Devon, Tor.	R	.273	146	598	116	163	262	42	6	15	52	3	3	57	127	34	4	3	.438	.341
Williams, Bernie, NY-A	B	.268	139	567	67	152	227	31	4	12	68	1	3	53	106	9	9	17	.400	.333
Williams, Gerald, NY-A	R	.149	42	67	11	10	18	2	3	0	6	0	1	1	14	2	0	2	.269	.183
Yount, Robin, Mil.	R	.258	127	454	62	117	172	25	3	8	51	5	6	44	93	9	2	12	.379	.326
Zupcic, Bob, Bos.	R	.241	141	286	40	69	103	24	2	2	26	8	3	27	54	5	2	7	.360	.308

American League designated hitters

Name/Team	B	BA	G	AB	R	H	TB	2B	3B	HR	RBI	SH	SF	BB	SO	SB	CS	GIDP	SLG	OBA
Baines, Harold, Bal.	L	.313	118	416	64	130	212	22	0	20	78	1	6	57	52	0	0	14	.510	.390
Balboni, Steve, Tex.	R	.600	2	5	0	3	3	0	0	0	0	0	0	0	2	0	0	0	.600	.600
Bell, George A., ChiA	R	.217	102	410	36	89	149	17	2	13	64	0	9	13	49	1	1	14	.363	.243
Brett, George, K.C.	L	.266	145	560	69	149	243	31	3	19	75	0	10	39	67	7	5	20	.434	.312
Bush, Randy, Min.	L	.156	35	45	1	7	9	2	0	0	3	0	0	7	13	0	0	3	.200	.269
Davis, Chili, Cal.	B	.243	153	573	74	139	252	32	0	27	112	0	0	71	135	4	1	18	.440	.327
Dawson, Andre, Bos.	R	.273	121	461	44	126	196	29	1	13	67	0	7	17	49	2	1	18	.425	.313
Franco, Julio, Tex.	R	.289	144	532	85	154	233	31	3	14	84	5	7	62	95	9	3	16	.438	.360
Gibson, Kirk, Det.	L	.261	116	403	62	105	174	18	6	13	62	0	3	44	87	15	6	2	.432	.337
Horn, Sam, Cle.	L	.455	12	33	8	15	28	1	0	4	8	0	1	1	5	0	0	1	.848	.472
Jackson, Bo, ChiA	R	.232	85	284	32	66	123	9	0	16	45	0	1	23	106	0	2	5	.433	.289
Jefferson, Reggie, Cle.	B	.249	113	366	35	91	136	11	2	10	34	3	1	28	78	1	3	7	.372	.310
Maas, Kevin, NY-A	L	.205	59	151	20	31	62	4	0	9	25	0	1	24	32	1	1	2	.411	.316
Martinez, Edgar, Sea.	R	.237	42	135	20	32	51	7	0	4	13	1	1	28	19	0	0	4	.378	.366
Merullo, Matt, ChiA	L	.050	8	20	1	1	1	0	0	0	0	1	0	1	0	0	1	.050	.050
Molitor, Paul, Tor.	R	.332	160	636	121	211	324	37	5	22	111	1	8	57	71	22	4	13	.509	.402
Neel, Troy, Oak.	L	.290	123	427	59	124	202	21	0	19	63	0	2	49	101	3	5	7	.473	.367
Newfield, Marc, Sea.	R	.227	22	66	5	15	21	3	0	1	7	0	1	2	8	0	1	2	.318	.257
Newson, Warren, ChiA	L	.300	26	40	9	12	18	0	0	2	6	0	0	9	12	0	0	2	.450	.429
O'Brien, Pete M., Sea.	L	.257	72	210	30	54	82	7	0	7	27	0	3	26	21	0	0	8	.390	.335
Obando, Sherman, Bal.	R	.272	31	92	8	25	36	2	0	3	15	0	0	4	26	0	0	1	.391	.309
Ramirez, Manny, Cle.	R	.170	22	53	5	9	16	1	0	2	5	0	0	2	8	0	0	3	.302	.200
Reimer, Kevin, Mil.	L	.249	125	437	53	109	172	22	1	13	60	1	4	30	72	5	4	12	.394	.303
Sheets, Larry, Sea.	L	.118	11	17	0	2	3	1	0	0	1	0	0	2	1	0	0	2	.176	.250
Smith, Lonnie, Bal.	R	.208	9	24	8	5	12	1	0	2	3	0	0	8	10	0	0	0	.500	.406
Tartabull, Danny, NY-A	R	.250	138	513	87	128	258	33	2	31	102	0	4	92	156	0	0	8	.503	.363
Walton, Jerome, Cal.	R	.000	5	2	2	0	0	0	0	0	0	0	0	1	2	1	0	0	.000	.333
Winfield, Dave, Min.	R	.271	143	547	72	148	242	27	2	21	76	0	2	45	106	2	3	15	.442	.325

American League pitchers (batting)

Name/Team	B	BA	G	AB	R	H	TB	2B	3B	HR	RBI	SH	SF	BB	SO	SB	CS	GIDP	SLG	OBA
Bronkey, Jeff, Tex.	R	.000	21	1	0	0	0	0	0	0	0	0	0	0	0	0	0	0	.000	.000
Maysey, Matt, Mil.	R	1.000	23	1	0	1	1	0	0	0	0	0	0	0	0	0	0	0	1.000	1.000
Olson, Gregg, Bal.	R	.000	50	1	0	0	0	0	0	0	0	0	0	0	1	0	0	0	.000	.000
Orosco, Jesse, Mil.	R	.000	57	1	0	0	0	0	0	0	0	0	0	0	1	0	0	0	.000	.000

National League starting pitchers

Name/Team	T	W	L	ERA	G	GS	CG	SHO	GF	SV	IP	H	R	ER	HR	BB	SO	WP	BK	BA
Armstrong, Jack, Fla.	R	9	17	4.49	36	33	0	0	2	0	196.1	210	105	98	29	78	118	7	2	.271
Arocha, Rene, St.L	R	11	8	3.78	32	29	1	0	0	0	188.0	197	89	79	20	31	96	3	1	.271
Ashby, Andy, Col.-S.D.	R	3	10	6.80	32	21	0	0	3	0	123.0	168	100	93	19	56	77	6	3	.333
Astacio, Pedro, L.A.	R	14	9	3.57	31	31	3	2	0	0	186.1	165	80	74	14	68	122	8	9	.239
Avery, Steve, Atl.	L	18	6	2.94	35	35	3	1	0	0	223.1	216	81	73	14	43	125	3	1	.261
Belcher, Tim, Cin.	R	9	6	4.47	22	22	4	2	0	0	137.0	134	72	68	11	47	101	6	0	.254
Benes, Andy, S.D.	R	15	15	3.78	34	34	4	2	0	0	230.2	200	111	97	23	86	179	14	2	.232
Black, Bud, S.F.	L	8	2	3.56	16	16	0	0	0	0	93.2	89	44	37	13	33	45	0	4	.256
Bottenfield, Kent, Mon.-Col.R		5	10	5.07	37	25	1	0	2	0	159.2	179	102	90	24	71	63	4	1	.294
Boucher, Denis, Mon.	L	3	1	1.91	5	5	0	0	0	0	28.1	24	7	6	1	3	14	0	2	.229
Bowen, Ryan, Fla.	R	8	12	4.42	27	27	2	1	0	0	156.2	156	83	77	11	87	98	10	4	.263
Brocail, Doug, S.D.	R	4	13	4.56	24	24	0	0	0	0	128.1	143	75	65	16	42	70	4	1	.283
Browning, Tom, Cin.	L	7	7	4.74	21	20	0	0	0	0	114.0	159	61	60	15	20	53	1	1	.333
Brummett, Greg, S.F.	R	2	3	4.70	8	8	0	0	0	0	46.0	53	25	24	9	13	20	2	2	.296
Burkett, John, S.F.	R	22	7	3.65	34	34	2	1	0	0	231.2	224	100	94	18	40	145	1	2	.255
Candiotti, Tom, L.A.	R	8	10	3.12	33	32	2	0	0	0	213.2	192	86	74	12	71	155	6	0	.241
Castillo, Frank, ChiN	R	5	8	4.84	29	25	2	0	0	0	141.1	162	83	76	20	39	84	5	3	.293
Cooke, Steve, Pit.	L	10	10	3.89	32	32	3	1	0	0	210.2	207	101	91	22	59	132	3	3	.258
Cormier, Rheal, St.L	L	7	6	4.33	38	21	1	0	4	0	145.1	163	80	70	18	27	75	6	0	.284
Deshaies, Jim, S.F.	L	2	2	4.24	5	4	0	0	1	0	17.0	24	9	8	2	6	5	1	0	.348
Drabek, Doug, Hou.	R	9	18	3.79	34	34	7	2	0	0	237.2	242	108	100	18	60	157	12	0	.267
Eiland, Dave, S.D.	R	0	3	5.21	10	9	0	0	0	0	48.1	58	33	28	5	17	14	1	0	.297
Fernandez, Sid, NY-N	L	5	6	2.93	18	18	1	1	0	0	119.2	82	42	39	17	36	81	2	0	.192
Glavine, Tom, Atl.	L	22	6	3.20	36	36	4	2	0	0	239.1	236	91	85	16	90	120	4	0	.259
Gooden, Dwight, NY-N	R	12	15	3.45	29	29	7	2	0	0	208.2	188	89	80	16	61	149	5	2	.242
Green, Tyler, Phi.	R	0	0	7.36	3	2	0	0	1	0	7.1	16	9	6	1	5	7	2	0	.444
Greene, Tommy, Phi.	R	16	4	3.42	31	30	7	2	0	0	200.0	175	84	76	12	62	167	15	0	.233
Gross, Kevin, L.A.	R	13	13	4.14	33	32	3	0	1	0	202.1	224	110	93	15	74	150	2	5	.282
Guzman, Jose, ChiN	R	12	10	4.34	30	30	2	1	0	0	191.0	188	98	92	25	74	163	6	5	.258
Hammond, Chris, Fla.	L	11	12	4.66	32	32	1	0	0	0	191.0	207	106	99	18	66	108	10	5	.277
Harkey, Mike, ChiN	R	10	10	5.26	28	28	1	0	0	0	157.1	187	100	92	17	43	67	1	3	.305
Harnisch, Pete, Hou.	R	16	9	2.98	33	33	5	4	0	0	217.2	171	84	72	20	79	185	3	1	.214
Harris, Greg W., S.D.-Col.	R	11	17	4.59	35	35	4	0	0	0	225.1	239	127	115	33	69	123	6	6	.271
Henry, Butch, Col.-Mon.	L	3	9	6.12	30	16	1	0	4	0	103.0	135	76	70	15	28	47	1	0	.317
Hershiser, Orel, L.A.	R	12	14	3.59	33	33	5	1	0	0	215.2	201	106	86	17	72	141	7	0	.246
Hibbard, Greg, ChiN	L	15	11	3.96	31	31	1	0	0	0	191.0	209	96	84	19	47	82	1	2	.286
Hill, Ken, Mon.	R	9	7	3.23	28	28	2	0	0	0	183.2	163	84	66	7	74	90	6	2	.238
Hillman, Eric, NY-N	L	2	9	3.97	27	22	3	1	1	0	145.0	173	83	64	12	24	60	0	1	.299
Hope, John, Pit.	R	0	2	4.03	7	7	0	0	0	0	38.0	47	19	17	2	8	8	1	0	.313
Hough, Charlie, Fla.	R	9	16	4.27	34	34	0	0	0	0	204.1	202	109	97	20	71	126	11	4	.259
Hurst, Bruce, S.D.-Col.	L	0	2	7.62	5	5	0	0	0	0	13.0	15	12	11	1	6	9	1	1	.283
Jackson, Danny, Phi.	L	12	11	3.77	32	32	2	1	0	0	210.1	214	105	88	12	80	120	4	0	.263
Jones, Bobby J., NY-N	R	2	4	3.65	9	9	0	0	0	0	61.2	61	35	25	6	22	35	1	0	.262
Kile, Darryl, Hou.	R	15	8	3.51	32	26	4	2	0	0	171.2	152	73	67	12	69	141	9	3	.239
Luebbers, Larry, Cin.	R	2	5	4.54	14	14	0	0	0	0	77.1	74	49	39	7	38	38	4	0	.261
Maddux, Greg, Atl.	R	20	10	2.36	36	36	8	1	0	0	267.0	228	85	70	14	52	197	5	1	.232
Magrane, Joe, St.L	L	8	10	4.97	22	20	0	0	2	0	116.0	127	68	64	15	37	38	4	0	.286
Martinez, Dennis, Mon.	R	15	9	3.85	35	34	2	0	1	1	224.2	211	110	96	27	64	138	2	4	.246
Martinez, Ramon, L.A.	R	10	12	3.44	32	32	4	3	0	0	211.2	202	88	81	15	104	127	2	2	.255
Miller, Paul, Pit.	R	0	0	5.40	3	2	0	0	1	0	10.0	15	6	6	2	2	2	1	0	.349
Morgan, Mike, ChiN	R	10	15	4.03	32	32	1	1	0	0	207.2	206	100	93	15	74	111	8	2	.262
Mulholland, Terry, Phi.	L	12	9	3.25	29	28	7	2	0	0	191.0	177	80	69	20	40	116	5	0	.241
Nabholz, Chris, Mon.	L	9	8	4.09	26	21	1	0	2	0	116.2	100	57	53	9	63	74	7	0	.236
Nied, David, Col.	R	5	9	5.17	16	16	1	0	0	0	87.0	99	53	50	8	42	46	1	1	.296
Osborne, Donovan, St.L	L	10	7	3.76	26	26	1	0	0	0	155.2	153	73	65	18	47	83	4	0	.257
Painter, Lance, Col.	L	2	2	6.00	10	6	1	0	2	0	39.0	52	26	26	5	9	16	2	0	.333
Portugal, Mark, Hou.	R	18	4	2.77	33	33	1	1	0	0	208.0	194	75	64	10	77	131	9	2	.248
Pugh, Tim, Cin.	R	10	15	5.26	31	27	3	1	3	0	164.1	200	102	96	19	59	94	3	2	.303
Rapp, Pat, Fla.	R	4	6	4.02	16	16	1	0	0	0	94.0	101	49	42	7	39	57	6	0	.281
Reynoso, Armando, Col.	R	12	11	4.00	30	30	4	0	0	0	189.0	206	101	84	22	63	117	7	6	.277
Rijo, Jose, Cin.	R	14	9	2.48	36	36	2	1	0	0	257.1	218	76	71	19	62	227	0	1	.230
Rivera, Ben, Phi.	R	13	9	5.02	30	28	1	1	0	0	163.0	175	99	91	16	85	123	13	0	.273
Roper, John, Cin.	R	2	5	5.63	16	15	0	0	0	0	80.0	92	51	50	10	36	54	5	1	.295
Rueter, Kirk, Mon.	L	8	0	2.73	14	14	1	0	0	0	85.2	85	33	26	5	18	31	0	0	.264
Saberhagen, Bret, NY-N	R	7	7	3.29	19	19	4	1	0	0	139.1	131	55	51	11	17	93	2	2	.250
Sanders, Scott, S.D.	R	3	3	4.13	9	9	0	0	0	0	52.1	54	32	24	4	23	37	0	1	.265
Sanderson, Scott, S.F.	R	4	2	3.51	11	8	0	0	1	0	48.2	48	20	19	12	7	36	0	3	.255
Sanford, Mo, Col.	R	1	2	5.30	11	6	0	0	0	0	35.2	37	25	21	4	27	36	2	1	.278
Schilling, Curt, Phi.	R	16	7	4.02	34	34	7	2	0	0	235.1	234	114	105	23	57	186	9	3	.259
Smiley, John, Cin.	L	3	9	5.62	18	18	2	0	0	0	105.2	117	69	66	15	31	60	2	1	.286

National League starting pitchers

Name/Team	T	W	L	ERA	G	GS	CG	SHO	GF	SV	IP	H	R	ER	HR	BB	SO	WP	BK	BA
Smith, Pete J., Atl.	R	4	8	4.37	20	14	0	0	2	0	90.2	92	45	44	15	36	53	1	1	.270
Smith, Zane, Pit.	L	3	7	4.55	14	14	1	0	0	0	83.0	97	43	42	5	22	32	2	0	.298
Smoltz, John, Atl.	R	15	11	3.62	35	35	3	1	0	0	243.2	208	104	98	23	100	208	13	1	.230
Swift, Bill C., S.F.	R	21	8	2.82	34	34	1	1	0	0	232.2	195	82	73	18	55	157	4	0	.226
Swindell, Greg, Hou.	L	12	13	4.16	31	30	1	1	0	0	190.1	215	98	88	24	40	124	2	2	.283
Tanana, Frank, NY-N	L	7	15	4.48	29	29	0	0	0	0	183.0	198	100	91	26	48	104	7	2	.278
Tewksbury, Bob, St.L	R	17	10	3.83	32	32	2	0	0	0	213.2	258	99	91	15	20	97	2	0	.301
Tomlin, Randy, Pit.	L	4	8	4.85	18	18	1	0	0	0	98.1	109	57	53	11	15	44	4	2	.291
Torres, Salomon, S.F.	R	3	5	4.03	8	8	0	0	0	0	44.2	37	21	20	5	27	23	3	1	.231
Trachsel, Steve, ChiN	R	0	2	4.58	3	3	0	0	0	0	19.2	16	10	10	4	3	14	1	0	.219
Wakefield, Tim, Pit.	R	6	11	5.61	24	20	3	2	1	0	128.1	145	83	80	14	75	59	6	0	.291
Walk, Bob, Pit.	R	13	14	5.68	32	32	3	0	0	0	187.0	214	121	118	23	70	80	2	3	.294
Watson, Allen, St.L	L	6	7	4.60	16	15	0	0	1	0	86.0	90	53	44	11	28	49	2	1	.271
Wendell, Turk, ChiN	R	1	2	4.37	7	4	0	0	1	0	22.2	24	13	11	0	8	15	1	1	.273
Whitehurst, Wally, S.D.	R	4	7	3.83	21	19	0	0	1	0	105.2	109	47	45	11	30	57	5	1	.276
Wilson, Trevor, S.F.	L	7	5	3.60	22	18	1	0	1	0	110.0	110	45	44	8	40	57	0	0	.275
Worrell, Tim, S.D.	R	2	7	4.92	21	16	0	0	1	0	100.2	104	63	55	11	43	52	3	0	.269

National League relief pitchers

Name/Team	T	W	L	ERA	G	GS	CG	SHO	GF	SV	IP	H	R	ER	HR	BB	SO	WP	BK	BA
Agosto, Juan, Hou.	L	0	0	6.00	6	0	0	0	3	0	6.0	8	4	4	1	0	3	0	1	.308
Aldred, Scott, Col.-Mon.	L	1	0	9.00	8	0	0	0	2	0	12.0	19	14	12	2	10	9	2	0	.365
Andersen, Larry E., Phi.	R	3	2	2.92	64	0	0	0	13	0	61.2	54	22	20	4	21	67	2	1	.233
Anderson, Mike J., Cin.	R	0	0	18.56	3	0	0	0	0	0	5.1	12	11	11	3	3	4	0	0	.444
Aquino, Luis, Fla.	R	6	8	3.42	38	13	0	0	5	0	110.2	115	43	42	6	40	67	4	0	.276
Assenmacher, Paul, ChiN	L	2	1	3.49	46	0	0	0	16	0	38.2	44	15	15	5	13	34	0	0	.288
Ayala, Bobby, Cin.	R	7	10	5.60	43	9	0	0	8	3	98.0	106	72	61	16	45	65	5	0	.274
Ayrault, Bob, Phi.	R	2	0	9.58	10	0	0	0	3	0	10.1	18	11	11	1	10	8	1	0	.375
Ballard, Jeff, Pit.	L	4	1	4.86	25	5	0	0	4	0	53.2	70	31	29	3	15	16	2	0	.332
Barnes, Brian, Mon.	L	2	6	4.41	52	8	0	0	8	3	100.0	105	53	49	9	48	60	5	1	.274
Batchelor, Rich, St.L	R	0	0	8.10	9	0	0	0	2	0	10.0	14	12	9	1	3	4	0	0	.359
Bautista, Jose, ChiN	R	10	3	2.82	58	7	1	0	14	2	111.2	105	38	35	11	27	63	4	1	.250
Beck, Rod, S.F.	R	3	1	2.16	76	0	0	0	71	48	79.1	57	20	19	11	13	86	4	0	.201
Bedrosian, Steve, Atl.	R	5	2	1.63	49	0	0	0	12	0	49.2	34	11	9	4	14	33	5	1	.194
Belinda, Stan, Pit.	R	3	1	3.61	40	0	0	0	37	19	42.1	35	18	17	4	11	30	0	0	.224
Bell, Eric, Hou.	L	0	1	6.14	10	0	0	0	2	0	7.1	10	5	5	0	2	2	0	0	.313
Blair, Willie, Col.	R	6	10	4.75	46	18	1	0	5	0	146.0	184	90	77	20	42	84	6	1	.306
Borbon, Pedro Jr., Atl.	L	0	0	21.60	3	0	0	0	1	0	1.2	3	4	4	0	3	2	0	0	.429
Boskie, Shawn, ChiN	R	5	3	3.43	39	2	0	0	10	0	65.2	63	30	25	7	21	39	5	0	.258
Brantley, Jeff, S.F.	R	5	6	4.28	53	12	0	0	9	0	113.2	112	60	54	19	46	76	3	4	.259
Brennan, Bill, ChiN	R	2	1	4.20	8	1	0	0	0	0	15.0	16	8	7	2	8	11	0	0	.291
Brink, Brad, Phi.	R	0	0	3.00	2	0	0	0	1	0	6.0	3	2	2	1	3	8	1	0	.143
Bross, Terry, S.F.	R	0	0	9.00	2	0	0	0	1	0	2.0	3	2	2	1	1	1	0	0	.333
Bullinger, Jim, ChiN	R	1	0	4.32	15	0	0	0	6	1	16.2	18	9	8	1	9	10	0	0	.277
Burba, Dave, S.F.	R	10	3	4.25	54	5	0	0	9	0	95.1	95	49	45	14	37	88	4	0	.265
Burns, Todd, St.L	R	0	4	6.16	24	0	0	0	5	0	30.2	32	21	21	8	9	10	0	1	.274
Bushing, Chris, Cin.	R	0	0	12.46	6	0	0	0	2	0	4.1	9	7	6	1	4	3	2	0	.450
Cadaret, Greg, Cin.	L	2	1	4.96	34	0	0	0	15	1	32.2	40	19	18	3	23	23	2	0	.305
Candelaria, John, Pit.	L	0	3	8.24	24	0	0	0	6	1	19.2	25	19	18	2	9	17	1	0	.313
Carpenter, Cris, Fla.	R	0	1	2.89	29	0	0	0	9	0	37.1	29	15	12	1	13	26	5	0	.212
Corsi, Jim, Fla.	R	0	2	6.64	15	0	0	0	6	0	20.1	28	15	15	1	10	7	0	0	.337
Daal, Omar, L.A.	L	2	3	5.09	47	0	0	0	12	0	35.1	36	20	20	5	21	19	1	2	.277
Davis, Mark W., Phi.-S.D.	L	1	5	4.26	60	0	0	0	13	4	69.2	79	37	33	10	44	70	2	1	.285
DeLeon, Jose, Phi.	R	3	0	3.26	24	3	0	0	6	0	47.0	39	25	17	5	27	34	5	0	.231
DeSilva, John, L.A.	R	0	0	6.75	3	0	0	0	2	0	5.1	6	4	4	0	1	6	0	0	.273
Dewey, Mark, Pit.	R	1	2	2.36	21	0	0	0	17	7	26.2	14	8	7	0	10	14	0	0	.157
Dibble, Rob, Cin.	R	1	4	6.48	45	0	0	0	37	19	41.2	34	33	30	8	42	49	4	0	.225
Dixon, Steve, St.L	L	0	0	33.75	4	0	0	0	0	0	2.2	7	10	10	1	5	2	0	0	.538
Draper, Mike, NY-N	R	1	1	4.25	29	1	0	0	11	0	42.1	53	22	20	2	14	16	0	1	.327
Edens, Tom, Hou.	R	1	1	3.12	38	0	0	0	20	0	49.0	47	17	17	4	19	21	3	0	.263
Ettles, Mark, S.D.	R	1	0	6.50	14	0	0	0	5	0	18.0	23	16	13	4	4	9	3	0	.307
Fassero, Jeff, Mon.	L	12	5	2.29	56	15	1	0	10	1	149.2	119	50	38	7	54	140	5	0	.216
Fletcher, Paul, Phi.	R	0	0	0.00	1	0	0	0	0	0	0.1	0	0	0	0	0	0	1	0	.000
Foster, Kevin, Phi.	R	0	1	14.85	2	1	0	0	0	0	6.2	13	11	11	3	7	6	2	0	.394
Foster, Steve, Cin.	R	2	2	1.75	17	0	0	0	7	0	25.2	23	8	5	1	5	16	0	0	.235
Franco, John, NY-N	L	4	3	5.20	35	0	0	0	30	10	36.1	46	24	21	6	19	29	5	0	.313
Fredrickson, Scott, Col.	R	0	1	6.21	25	0	0	0	4	0	29.0	33	25	20	3	17	20	4	1	.287
Freeman, Marvin, Atl.	R	2	0	6.08	21	0	0	0	5	0	23.2	24	16	16	1	10	25	3	0	.261

National League relief pitchers

Name/Team	T	W	L	ERA	G	GS	CG	SHO	GF	SV	IP	H	R	ER	HR	BB	SO	WP	BK	BA
Gardiner, Mike, Mon.	R	2	3	5.21	24	2	0	0	3	0	38.0	40	28	22	3	19	21	0	0	.268
Gibson, Paul, NY-N	L	1	1	5.19	8	0	0	0	1	0	8.2	14	6	5	1	2	12	1	0	.350
Gomez, Pat, S.D.	L	1	2	5.12	27	1	0	0	6	0	31.2	35	19	18	2	19	26	2	0	.294
Gott, Jim, L.A.	R	4	8	2.32	62	0	0	0	45	25	77.2	71	23	20	6	17	67	5	0	.248
Gozzo, Mauro, NY-N	R	0	1	2.57	10	0	0	0	5	1	14.0	11	5	4	1	5	6	0	0	.212
Grant, Mark, Hou.-Col.	R	0	1	7.46	20	0	0	0	9	1	25.1	34	24	21	4	11	14	2	0	.337
Greer, Kenny, NY-N	R	1	0	0.00	1	0	0	0	1	0	1.0	0	0	0	0	0	2	0	0	.000
Gross, Kip, L.A.	R	0	0	0.60	10	0	0	0	0	0	15.0	13	1	1	0	4	12	0	0	.236
Guetterman, Lee, St.L	L	3	3	2.93	40	0	0	0	14	1	46.0	41	18	15	1	16	19	1	0	.240
Harris, Gene, S.D.	R	6	6	3.03	59	0	0	0	48	23	59.1	57	27	20	3	37	39	7	0	.256
Harvey, Bryan, Fla.	R	1	5	1.70	59	0	0	0	54	45	69.0	45	14	13	4	13	73	0	1	.186
Henry, Dwayne, Cin.	R	0	1	3.86	3	0	0	0	1	0	4.2	6	8	2	0	4	2	1	0	.273
Heredia, Gil, Mon.	R	4	2	3.92	20	9	1	0	2	2	57.1	66	28	25	4	14	40	0	0	.293
Hernandez, Jeremy, S.D.	R	0	2	4.72	21	0	0	0	9	0	34.1	41	19	18	2	7	26	0	2	.301
Hernandez, Xavier, Hou.	R	4	5	2.61	72	0	0	0	29	9	96.2	75	37	28	6	28	101	6	0	.212
Hickerson, Bryan, S.F.	L	7	5	4.26	47	15	0	0	5	0	120.1	137	58	57	14	39	69	4	0	.291
Hill, Milt, Cin.	R	3	0	5.65	19	0	0	0	2	0	28.2	34	18	18	5	9	23	1	0	.301
Hoffman, Trevor, Fla.-S.D.	R	4	6	3.90	67	0	0	0	26	5	90.0	80	43	39	10	39	79	5	0	.234
Holmes, Darren, Col.	R	3	3	4.05	62	0	0	0	51	25	66.2	56	31	30	6	20	60	2	1	.222
Howell, Jay, Atl.	R	3	3	2.31	54	0	0	0	22	0	58.1	48	16	15	3	16	37	0	2	.229
Innis, Jeff, NY-N	R	2	3	4.11	67	0	0	0	30	3	76.2	81	39	35	5	38	36	3	1	.278
Jackson, Mike R., S.F.	R	6	6	3.03	81	0	0	0	17	1	77.1	58	28	26	7	24	70	2	2	.204
Johnston, Joel, Pit.	R	2	4	3.38	33	0	0	0	16	2	53.1	38	20	20	7	19	31	1	0	.203
Johnstone, John, Fla.	R	0	2	5.91	7	0	0	0	3	0	10.2	16	8	7	1	7	5	1	0	.340
Jones, Doug, Hou.	R	4	10	4.54	71	0	0	0	60	26	85.1	102	46	43	7	21	66	3	0	.298
Jones, Jimmy, Mon.	R	4	1	6.35	12	6	0	0	3	0	39.2	47	34	28	6	9	21	1	1	.285
Jones, Todd, Hou.	R	1	2	3.13	27	0	0	0	8	2	37.1	28	14	13	4	15	25	1	1	.214
Juden, Jeff, Hou.	R	0	1	5.40	2	0	0	0	1	0	5.0	4	3	3	1	4	7	0	0	.222
Kaiser, Jeff, Cin.-NY-N	L	0	0	7.88	9	0	0	0	3	0	8.0	10	7	7	1	5	9	0	0	.323
Kilgus, Paul, St.L	L	1	0	0.63	22	1	0	0	7	1	28.2	18	2	2	1	8	21	0	0	.180
Klink, Joe, Fla.	L	0	2	5.02	59	0	0	0	10	0	37.2	37	22	21	0	24	22	1	2	.266
Knudson, Mark, Col.	R	0	0	22.24	4	0	0	0	2	0	5.2	16	14	14	4	5	3	2	0	.471
Lancaster, Les, St.L	R	4	1	2.93	50	0	0	0	12	0	61.1	56	24	20	5	21	36	5	0	.242
Landrum, Bill, Cin.	R	0	2	3.74	18	0	0	0	6	0	21.2	18	9	9	1	6	14	0	0	.231
Layana, Tim, S.F.	R	0	0	22.50	1	0	0	0	0	0	2.0	7	5	5	1	1	1	0	0	.538
Leskanic, Curt, Col.	R	1	5	5.37	18	8	0	0	1	0	57.0	59	40	34	7	27	30	8	2	.266
Lewis, Richie, Fla.	R	6	3	3.26	57	0	0	0	14	0	77.1	68	37	28	7	43	65	9	1	.239
Looney, Brian, Mon.	L	0	0	3.00	3	1	0	0	1	0	6.0	8	2	2	0	2	7	0	1	.308
Maddux, Mike, NY-N	R	3	8	3.60	58	0	0	0	31	5	75.0	67	34	30	3	27	57	4	1	.243
Manzanillo, Josias, NY-N	R	0	0	3.00	6	0	0	0	2	0	12.0	8	7	4	1	9	11	0	0	.186
Martinez, Pedro A., S.D.	L	3	1	2.43	32	0	0	0	9	0	37.0	23	11	10	4	13	32	0	0	.172
Martinez, Pedro J., L.A.	R	10	5	2.61	65	2	0	0	20	2	107.0	76	34	31	5	57	119	3	1	.201
Mason, Roger, S.D.-Phi.	R	5	12	4.06	68	0	0	0	29	0	99.2	90	48	45	10	34	71	2	3	.244
Mauser, Tim, Phi.-S.D.	R	0	1	4.00	36	0	0	0	16	0	54.0	51	28	24	6	24	46	2	0	.245
McClure, Bob, Fla.	L	1	1	7.11	14	0	0	0	1	0	6.1	13	5	5	2	5	6	0	0	.419
McDowell, Roger, L.A.	R	5	3	2.25	54	0	0	0	19	2	68.0	76	32	17	2	30	27	5	0	.288
McElroy, Chuck, ChiN	L	2	2	4.56	49	0	0	0	11	0	47.1	51	30	24	4	25	31	3	0	.280
McMichael, Greg, Atl.	R	2	3	2.06	74	0	0	0	40	19	91.2	68	22	21	3	29	89	6	1	.206
Menendez, Tony, Pit.	R	2	0	3.00	14	0	0	0	3	0	21.0	20	8	7	4	4	13	0	0	.256
Mercker, Kent, Atl.	L	3	1	2.86	43	6	0	0	9	0	66.0	52	24	21	2	36	59	5	1	.214
Miceli, Danny, Pit.	R	0	0	5.06	9	0	0	0	1	0	5.1	6	3	3	0	3	4	0	1	.273
Minor, Blas, Pit.	R	8	6	4.10	65	0	0	0	18	2	94.1	94	43	43	8	26	84	5	0	.263
Minutelli, Gino, S.F.	L	0	1	3.77	9	0	0	0	4	0	14.1	7	9	6	2	15	10	1	0	.152
Moeller, Dennis, Pit.	L	1	0	9.92	10	0	0	0	3	0	16.1	26	20	18	2	7	13	1	2	.356
Moore, Marcus, Col.	R	3	1	6.84	27	0	0	0	8	0	26.1	30	25	20	4	20	13	4	0	.291
Munoz, Mike, Col.	L	2	1	4.50	21	0	0	0	7	0	18.0	21	12	9	1	9	16	2	0	.309
Murphy, Rob, St.L	L	5	7	4.87	73	0	0	0	23	1	64.2	73	37	35	8	20	41	5	0	.290
Myers, Randy, ChiN	L	2	4	3.11	73	0	0	0	69	53	75.1	65	26	26	7	26	86	3	0	.230
Neagle, Denny, Pit.	L	3	5	5.31	50	7	0	0	13	1	81.1	82	49	48	10	37	73	5	0	.258
Nen, Robb, Fla.	R	1	0	7.02	15	1	0	0	2	0	33.1	35	28	26	5	20	27	4	0	.255
Nichols, Rod, L.A.	R	0	1	5.68	4	0	0	0	2	0	6.1	9	5	4	1	2	3	0	0	.360
Olivares, Omar, St.L	R	5	3	4.17	58	9	0	0	11	1	118.2	134	60	55	10	54	63	4	3	.288
Osuna, Al, Hou.	L	1	1	3.20	44	0	0	0	6	2	25.1	17	10	9	3	13	21	3	0	.200
Otto, Dave, Pit.	L	3	4	5.03	28	8	0	0	7	0	68.0	85	40	38	9	28	30	4	0	.317
Pall, Donn, Phi.	R	1	0	2.55	8	0	0	0	2	0	17.2	15	7	5	1	3	11	0	1	.231
Parrett, Jeff, Col.	R	3	3	5.38	40	0	0	0	13	1	73.2	78	47	44	6	45	66	11	1	.274
Perez, Mike, St.L	R	7	2	2.48	65	0	0	0	25	7	72.2	65	24	20	4	20	58	2	0	.244
Petkovsek, Mark, Pit.	R	3	0	6.96	26	0	0	0	8	0	32.1	43	25	25	7	9	14	4	0	.328
Plesac, Dan, ChiN	L	2	1	4.74	57	0	0	0	12	0	62.2	74	37	33	10	21	47	5	2	.298
Powell, Ross, Cin.	L	0	3	4.41	9	1	0	0	1	0	16.1	13	8	8	1	6	17	0	0	.224

National League relief pitchers

Name/Team	T	W	L	ERA	G	GS	CG	SHO	GF	SV	IP	H	R	ER	HR	BB	SO	WP	BK	BA
Reardon, Jeff, Cin.	R	4	6	4.09	58	0	0	0	32	8	61.2	66	34	28	4	10	35	2	0	.270
Reed, Steve, Col.	R	9	5	4.48	64	0	0	0	14	3	84.1	80	47	42	13	30	51	1	0	.259
Reynolds, Shane, Hou.	R	0	0	0.82	5	1	0	0	0	0	11.0	11	4	1	0	6	10	0	0	.256
Righetti, Dave, S.F.	L	1	1	5.70	51	0	0	0	15	1	47.1	58	31	30	11	17	31	1	0	.305
Risley, Bill, Mon.	R	0	0	6.00	2	0	0	0	1	0	3.0	2	3	2	1	2	2	0	0	.200
Robertson, Rich, Pit.	L	0	1	6.00	9	0	0	0	2	0	9.0	15	6	6	0	4	5	0	0	.385
Rodriguez, Rich, S.D.-Fla.	L	2	4	3.79	70	0	0	0	21	3	76.0	73	38	32	10	33	43	3	0	.251
Rogers, Kevin, S.F.	L	2	2	2.68	64	0	0	0	24	0	80.2	71	28	24	3	28	62	3	0	.236
Rojas, Mel, Mon.	R	5	8	2.95	66	0	0	0	25	10	88.1	80	39	29	6	30	48	5	0	.242
Ruffin, Bruce, Col.	L	6	5	3.87	59	12	0	0	8	2	139.2	145	71	60	10	69	126	8	0	.269
Ruffin, Johnny, Cin.	R	2	1	3.58	21	0	0	0	5	2	37.2	36	16	15	4	11	30	2	0	.247
Ruskin, Scott, Cin.	L	0	0	18.00	4	0	0	0	0	0	1.0	3	2	2	1	2	0	0	0	.500
Scanlan, Bob, ChiN	R	4	5	4.54	70	0	0	0	13	0	75.1	79	41	38	6	28	44	0	2	.278
Schourek, Pete, NY-N	L	5	12	5.96	41	18	0	0	6	0	128.1	168	90	85	13	45	72	1	2	.319
Scott, Tim, S.D.-Mon.	R	7	2	3.01	56	0	0	0	18	1	71.2	69	28	24	4	34	65	2	1	.253
Seanez, Rudy, S.D.	R	0	0	13.50	3	0	0	0	3	0	3.1	8	6	5	1	2	1	0	0	.471
Seminara, Frank, S.D.	R	3	3	4.47	18	7	0	0	0	0	46.1	53	30	23	5	21	22	1	0	.294
Service, Scott, Col.-Cin.	R	2	2	4.30	29	0	0	0	7	2	46.0	44	24	22	6	16	43	0	0	.254
Shaw, Jeff, Mon.	R	2	7	4.14	55	8	0	0	13	0	95.2	91	44	44	12	32	50	2	0	.254
Shepherd, Keith, Col.	R	1	3	6.98	14	1	0	0	3	1	19.1	26	16	15	4	4	7	1	0	.333
Shouse, Brian, Pit.	L	0	0	9.00	6	0	0	0	1	0	4.0	7	4	4	1	2	3	1	0	.368
Slocumb, Heathcliff, ChiN	R	1	0	3.38	10	0	0	0	4	0	10.2	7	5	4	0	4	4	0	0	.189
Smith, Bryn, Col.	R	2	4	8.49	11	5	0	0	2	0	29.2	47	29	28	2	11	9	1	0	.362
Smith, Lee, St.L	R	2	4	4.50	55	0	0	0	48	43	50.0	49	25	25	11	9	49	1	0	.251
Spradlin, Jerry, Cin.	R	2	1	3.49	37	0	0	0	16	2	49.0	44	20	19	4	9	24	3	1	.249
Stanton, Mike, Atl.	L	4	6	4.67	63	0	0	0	41	27	52.0	51	35	27	4	29	43	1	0	.255
Taylor, Kerry, S.D.	R	0	5	6.45	36	7	0	0	9	0	68.1	72	53	49	5	49	45	4	0	.277
Telgheder, Dave, NY-N	R	6	2	4.76	24	7	0	0	7	0	75.2	82	40	40	10	21	35	1	0	.276
Thigpen, Bobby, Phi.	R	3	1	6.05	17	0	0	0	5	0	19.1	23	13	13	2	9	10	0	1	.307
Toliver, Freddie, Pit.	R	1	0	3.74	12	0	0	0	3	0	21.2	20	10	9	2	8	14	0	0	.267
Trlicek, Rick, L.A.	R	1	2	4.08	41	0	0	0	18	1	64.0	59	32	29	3	21	41	4	1	.244
Turner, Matt, Fla.	R	4	5	2.91	55	0	0	0	26	0	68.0	55	23	22	7	26	59	6	1	.227
Urbani, Tom, St.L	L	1	3	4.65	18	9	0	0	2	0	62.0	73	44	32	4	26	33	1	1	.296
Valdez, Sergio, Mon.	R	0	0	9.00	4	0	0	0	1	0	3.0	4	4	3	1	1	2	0	0	.308
Wagner, Paul, Pit.	R	8	8	4.27	44	17	1	1	9	2	141.1	143	72	67	15	42	114	12	0	.263
Walton, Bruce, Mon.	R	0	0	9.53	4	0	0	0	3	0	5.2	11	6	6	1	3	0	0	0	.407
Wayne, Gary, Col.	L	5	3	5.05	65	0	0	0	21	1	62.1	68	40	35	8	26	49	9	1	.276
Weathers, Dave, Fla.	R	2	3	5.12	14	6	0	0	2	0	45.2	57	26	26	3	13	34	6	0	.306
West, David, Phi.	L	6	4	2.92	76	0	0	0	27	3	86.1	60	37	28	6	51	87	3	0	.194
Weston, Mickey, NY-N	R	0	0	7.94	4	0	0	0	0	0	5.2	11	5	5	0	1	2	0	0	.393
Wetteland, John, Mon.	R	9	3	1.37	70	0	0	0	58	43	85.1	58	17	13	8	28	113	7	0	.188
Wickander, Kevin, Cin.	L	1	0	6.75	33	0	0	0	8	0	25.1	32	20	19	5	19	20	4	1	.308
Williams, Brian, Hou.	R	4	4	4.83	42	5	0	0	12	3	82.0	76	48	44	7	38	56	9	2	.248
Williams, Mike, Phi.	R	1	3	5.29	17	4	0	0	2	0	51.0	50	32	30	5	22	33	2	0	.253
Williams, Mitch, Phi.	L	3	7	3.34	65	0	0	0	57	43	62.0	56	30	23	4	44	60	6	0	.245
Wilson, Steve, L.A.	L	1	0	4.56	25	0	0	0	4	1	25.2	30	13	13	2	14	23	3	0	.288
Wohlers, Mark, Atl.	R	6	2	4.50	46	0	0	0	13	0	48.0	37	25	24	2	22	45	0	0	.218
Worrell, Todd, L.A.	R	1	1	6.05	35	0	0	0	22	5	38.2	46	28	26	6	11	31	1	0	.313
Young, Anthony, NY-N	R	1	16	3.77	39	10	1	0	19	3	100.1	103	62	42	8	42	62	0	2	.265
Young, Pete, Mon.	R	1	0	3.38	4	0	0	0	2	0	5.1	4	2	2	1	0	3	0	0	.211

National League catchers

Name/Team	B	BA	G	AB	R	H	TB	2B	3B	HR	RBI	SH	SF	BB	SO	SB	CS	GIDP	SLG	OBA
Allanson, Andy, S.F.	R	.167	13	24	3	4	5	1	0	0	2	1	0	1	2	0	0	1	.208	.200
Ausmus, Brad, S.D.	R	.256	49	160	18	41	66	8	1	5	12	0	0	6	28	2	0	2	.413	.283
Berryhill, Damon, Atl.	B	.245	115	335	24	82	128	18	2	8	43	2	3	21	64	0	0	7	.382	.291
Colbert, Craig, S.F.	R	.162	23	37	2	6	11	2	0	1	5	0	0	3	13	0	0	0	.297	.225
Daulton, Darren, Phi.	L	.257	147	510	90	131	246	35	4	24	105	0	8	117	111	5	0	2	.482	.392
Decker, Steve, Fla.	R	.000	8	15	0	0	0	0	0	0	0	1	0	3	3	0	0	2	.000	.158
Dorsett, Brian, Cin.	R	.254	25	63	7	16	26	4	0	2	12	0	0	3	14	0	0	1	.413	.288
Fletcher, Darrin, Mon.	L	.255	133	396	33	101	150	20	1	9	60	5	4	34	40	0	0	7	.379	.320
Geren, Bob, S.D.	R	.214	58	145	8	31	46	6	0	3	6	4	0	13	28	0	0	4	.317	.278
Girardi, Joe, Col.	R	.290	86	310	35	90	123	14	5	3	31	12	1	24	41	6	6	9	.397	.346
Goff, Jerry, Pit.	L	.297	14	37	5	11	19	2	0	2	6	1	0	8	9	0	0	0	.514	.422
Hernandez, Carlos, L.A.	R	.253	50	99	6	25	36	5	0	2	7	1	0	2	11	0	0	0	.364	.267
Higgins, Kevin, S.D.	L	.221	71	181	17	40	46	4	1	0	13	1	1	16	17	0	1	7	.254	.294
Hundley, Todd, NY-N	B	.228	130	417	40	95	149	17	2	11	53	2	4	23	62	1	1	10	.357	.269
LaValliere, Mike, Pit.	L	.200	1	5	0	1	1	0	0	0	0	0	0	0	0	0	0	0	.200	.200

National League catchers

Name/Team	B	BA	G	AB	R	H	TB	2B	3B	HR	RBI	SH	SF	BB	SO	SB	CS	GIDP	SLG	OBA
Lake, Steve, ChiN	R	.225	44	120	11	27	48	6	0	5	13	2	0	4	19	0	0	8	.400	.250
Laker, Tim, Mon.	R	.198	43	86	3	17	21	2	1	0	7	3	1	2	16	2	0	2	.244	.222
Lindsey, Doug, Phi.	R	.500	2	2	0	1	1	0	0	0	0	0	0	0	1	0	0	0	.500	.500
Lopez, Javier, Atl.	R	.375	8	16	1	6	12	1	1	1	2	0	0	0	2	0	0	0	.750	.412
Lyden, Mitch, Fla.	R	.300	6	10	2	3	6	0	0	1	1	0	0	0	3	0	0	0	.600	.300
Manwaring, Kirt, S.F.	R	.275	130	432	48	119	151	15	1	5	49	5	2	41	76	1	3	14	.350	.345
McGriff, Terry, Fla.	R	.000	3	7	0	0	0	0	0	0	0	0	0	1	2	0	0	0	.000	.125
McNamara, Jim, S.F.	L	.143	4	7	0	1	1	0	0	0	1	0	0	0	1	0	0	0	.143	.143
Natal, Bob, Fla.	R	.214	41	117	3	25	34	4	1	1	6	3	1	6	22	1	0	6	.291	.273
O'Brien, Charlie, NY-N	R	.255	67	188	15	48	71	11	0	4	23	3	1	14	14	1	1	4	.378	.312
Oliver, Joe, Cin.	R	.239	139	482	40	115	185	28	0	14	75	2	9	27	91	0	0	13	.384	.276
Olson, Greg, Atl.	R	.225	83	262	23	59	81	10	0	4	24	2	1	29	27	1	0	11	.309	.304
Owens, Jayhawk, Col.	R	.209	33	86	12	18	32	5	0	3	6	0	0	6	30	1	0	1	.372	.277
Pagnozzi, Tom, St.L	R	.258	92	330	31	85	123	15	1	7	41	0	5	19	30	1	0	7	.373	.296
Pappas, Erik, St.L	R	.276	82	228	25	63	78	12	0	1	28	0	3	35	35	1	3	7	.342	.368
Piazza, Mike, L.A.	R	.318	149	547	81	174	307	24	2	35	112	0	6	46	86	3	4	10	.561	.370
Pratt, Todd, Phi.	R	.287	33	87	8	25	46	6	0	5	13	1	1	5	19	0	0	2	.529	.330
Prince, Tom, Pit.	R	.196	66	179	14	35	55	14	0	2	24	2	3	13	38	1	1	5	.307	.272
Reed, Jeff, S.F.	L	.261	66	119	10	31	52	3	0	6	12	0	1	16	22	0	1	2	.437	.346
Ronan, Marc, St.L	L	.083	6	12	0	1	1	0	0	0	0	0	0	0	5	0	0	0	.083	.083
Santiago, Benito, Fla.	R	.230	139	469	49	108	178	19	6	13	50	0	4	37	88	10	7	9	.380	.291
Servais, Scott, Hou.	R	.244	85	258	24	63	107	11	0	11	32	3	3	22	45	0	0	6	.415	.313
Sheaffer, Danny, Col.	R	.278	82	216	26	60	83	9	1	4	32	2	6	8	15	2	3	9	.384	.299
Siddall, Joe, Mon.	L	.100	19	20	0	2	3	1	0	0	1	0	0	1	5	0	0	0	.150	.143
Slaught, Don, Pit.	R	.300	116	377	34	113	166	19	2	10	55	4	4	29	56	2	1	13	.440	.356
Spehr, Tim, Mon.	R	.230	53	87	14	20	32	6	0	2	10	3	2	6	20	2	0	0	.368	.281
Taubensee, Eddie, Hou.	L	.250	94	288	26	72	112	11	1	9	42	1	2	21	44	1	0	8	.389	.299
Tucker, Scooter, Hou.	R	.192	9	26	1	5	6	1	0	0	3	0	0	2	3	0	0	0	.231	.250
Villanueva, Hector, St.L	R	.145	17	55	7	8	18	1	0	3	9	0	0	4	17	0	0	3	.327	.203
Walbeck, Matt, ChiN	B	.200	11	30	2	6	11	2	0	1	6	0	0	1	6	0	0	0	.367	.226
Walters, Dan, S.D.	R	.202	27	94	6	19	25	3	0	1	10	0	1	7	13	0	0	2	.266	.255
Wedge, Eric, Col.	R	.182	9	11	2	2	2	0	0	0	1	0	0	0	4	0	0	0	.182	.182
Wilkins, Rick, ChiN	L	.303	136	446	78	135	250	23	1	30	73	0	1	50	99	2	1	6	.561	.376
Wilson, Dan, Cin.	R	.224	36	76	6	17	20	3	0	0	8	2	1	9	16	0	0	2	.263	.302

National League first basemen

Name/Team	B	BA	G	AB	R	H	TB	2B	3B	HR	RBI	SH	SF	BB	SO	SB	CS	GIDP	SLG	OBA
Aude, Rich, Pit.	R	.115	13	26	1	3	4	1	0	0	4	0	0	1	7	0	0	0	.154	.148
Bagwell, Jeff, Hou.	R	.320	142	535	76	171	276	37	4	20	88	0	9	62	73	13	4	20	.516	.388
Benzinger, Todd, S.F.	B	.288	86	177	25	51	80	7	2	6	26	1	3	13	35	0	0	2	.452	.332
Bolick, Frank, Mon.	B	.211	95	213	25	45	70	13	0	4	24	0	2	23	37	1	0	4	.329	.298
Bream, Sid, Atl.	L	.260	117	277	33	72	115	14	1	9	35	1	2	31	43	4	2	6	.415	.332
Brewer, Rod, St.L	L	.286	110	147	15	42	56	8	0	2	20	2	2	17	26	1	0	5	.381	.359
Cabrera, Francisco, Atl.	R	.241	70	83	8	20	35	3	0	4	11	0	0	8	21	0	0	2	.422	.308
Clark, Phil, S.D.	R	.313	102	240	33	75	119	17	0	9	33	1	2	8	31	2	0	2	.496	.345
Clark, Will, S.F.	L	.283	132	491	82	139	212	27	2	14	73	1	6	63	68	2	2	10	.432	.367
Colbrunn, Greg, Mon.	B	.255	70	153	15	39	60	9	0	4	23	1	3	6	33	4	2	1	.392	.282
Destrade, Orestes, Fla.	B	.255	153	569	61	145	231	20	3	20	87	1	6	58	130	0	2	17	.406	.324
Floyd, Cliff, Mon.	L	.226	10	31	3	7	10	0	0	1	2	0	0	0	9	0	0	0	.323	.226
Gainer, Jay, Col.	L	.171	23	41	4	7	16	0	0	3	6	0	0	4	12	1	1	0	.390	.244
Galarraga, Andres, Col.	R	.370	120	470	71	174	283	35	4	22	98	0	6	24	73	2	4	9	.602	.403
Grace, Mark, ChiN	L	.325	155	594	86	193	282	39	4	14	98	1	9	71	32	8	4	25	.475	.393
Hunter, Brian, Atl.	R	.138	37	80	4	11	16	3	1	0	8	0	3	2	15	0	0	1	.200	.153
Jefferies, Gregg, St.L	B	.342	142	544	89	186	264	24	3	16	83	0	4	62	32	46	9	15	.485	.408
Jennings, Doug, ChiN	L	.250	42	52	8	13	24	3	1	2	8	0	0	3	10	0	0	0	.462	.316
Jordan, Ricky, Phi.	R	.289	90	159	21	46	67	4	1	5	18	0	2	8	32	0	0	2	.421	.324
Karros, Eric, L.A.	R	.247	158	619	74	153	253	27	2	23	80	0	3	34	82	0	1	17	.409	.287
Klesko, Ryan, Atl.	L	.353	22	17	3	6	13	1	0	2	5	0	0	3	4	0	0	0	.765	.450
Kruk, John, Phi.	L	.316	150	535	100	169	254	33	5	14	85	0	5	111	87	6	2	11	.475	.430
Lindeman, Jim, Hou.	R	.348	9	23	2	8	11	3	0	0	0	0	0	0	7	0	0	0	.478	.348
Marrero, Oreste, Mon.	L	.210	32	81	10	17	27	5	1	1	4	0	0	14	16	1	3	0	.333	.326
McGriff, Fred, S.D.-Atl.	L	.291	151	557	111	162	306	29	2	37	101	0	5	76	106	5	3	14	.549	.375
Milligan, Randy, Cin.	R	.274	83	234	30	64	95	11	1	6	29	0	1	46	49	0	2	3	.406	.394
Morris, Hal, Cin.	L	.317	101	379	48	120	159	18	0	7	49	0	6	34	51	2	2	5	.420	.371
Murray, Eddie, NY-N	B	.285	154	610	77	174	285	28	1	27	100	0	9	40	61	2	2	24	.467	.325
Perry, Gerald, St.L	L	.337	96	98	21	33	50	5	0	4	16	0	0	18	23	1	1	4	.510	.440
Phillips, J.R., S.F.	L	.313	11	16	1	5	11	1	1	1	4	0	0	0	5	0	0	0	.688	.313
Staton, Dave, S.D.	R	.262	17	42	7	11	29	3	0	5	9	0	0	3	12	0	0	2	.690	.326

National League first basemen

Name/Team	B	BA	G	AB	R	H	TB	2B	3B	HR	RBI	SH	SF	BB	SO	SB	CS	GIDP	SLG	OBA
Tatum, Jim, Col.	R	.204	92	98	7	20	28	5	0	1	12	0	2	5	27	0	0	0	.286	.245
Vanderwal, John, Mon.	L	.233	106	215	34	50	80	7	4	5	30	0	1	27	30	6	3	4	.372	.320
Velasquez, Guillermo, S.D.	L	.210	79	143	7	30	41	2	0	3	20	0	1	13	35	0	0	3	.287	.274
White, Derrick, Mon.	R	.224	17	49	6	11	20	3	0	2	4	0	0	2	12	2	0	1	.408	.269
Young, Kevin, Pit.	R	.236	141	449	38	106	154	24	3	6	47	5	9	36	82	2	2	10	.343	.300

National League second basemen

Name/Team	B	BA	G	AB	R	H	TB	2B	3B	HR	RBI	SH	SF	BB	SO	SB	CS	GIDP	SLG	OBA
Alicea, Luis, St.L	B	.279	115	362	50	101	135	19	3	3	46	1	7	47	54	11	1	9	.373	.362
Arias, Alex, Fla.	R	.269	96	249	27	67	80	5	1	2	20	1	3	27	18	1	1	5	.321	.344
Barberie, Bret, Fla.	B	.277	99	375	45	104	139	16	2	5	33	5	3	33	58	2	4	7	.371	.344
Benjamin, Mike, S.F.	R	.199	63	146	22	29	48	7	0	4	16	6	0	9	23	0	0	3	.329	.264
Biggio, Craig, Hou.	R	.287	155	610	98	175	289	41	5	21	64	4	5	77	93	15	17	10	.474	.373
Bournigal, Rafael, L.A.	R	.500	8	18	0	9	10	1	0	0	3	0	0	0	2	0	0	0	.556	.500
Candaele, Casey, Hou.	B	.240	75	121	18	29	40	8	0	1	7	0	0	10	14	2	3	0	.331	.298
DeShields, Delino, Mon.	L	.295	123	481	75	142	179	17	7	2	29	4	2	72	64	43	10	6	.372	.389
Duncan, Mariano, Phi.	R	.282	124	496	68	140	207	26	4	11	73	4	2	12	88	6	5	13	.417	.304
Faries, Paul, S.F.	R	.222	15	36	6	8	12	2	1	0	4	1	1	4	2	0	1	.333	.237
Foley, Tom, Pit.	L	.253	86	194	18	49	71	11	1	3	22	2	4	11	26	0	0	4	.366	.287
Garcia, Carlos, Pit.	R	.269	141	546	77	147	218	25	5	12	47	6	5	31	67	18	11	9	.399	.316
Gardner, Jeff, S.D.	L	.262	140	404	53	106	144	21	7	1	24	1	1	45	69	2	6	3	.356	.337
Harris, Lenny, L.A.	L	.238	107	160	20	38	52	6	1	2	11	1	0	15	15	3	1	4	.325	.303
Johnson, Erik, S.F.	R	.400	4	5	1	2	4	2	0	0	0	0	0	0	1	0	0	0	.800	.400
Kent, Jeff, NY-N	R	.270	140	496	65	134	221	24	0	21	80	6	4	30	88	4	4	11	.446	.320
Koelling, Brian, Cin.	R	.067	7	15	2	1	1	0	0	0	0	0	0	0	2	0	0	0	.067	.125
Lemke, Mark, Atl.	B	.252	151	493	52	124	168	19	2	7	49	5	6	65	50	1	2	21	.341	.335
Lopez, Luis M., S.D.	B	.116	17	43	1	5	6	1	0	0	1	0	1	0	8	0	0	0	.140	.114
Mejia, Roberto, Col.	R	.231	65	229	31	53	92	14	5	5	20	4	1	13	63	4	1	2	.402	.275
Montoyo, Charlie, Mon.	R	.400	4	5	1	2	3	1	0	0	3	0	0	0	0	0	0	0	.600	.400
Morandini, Mickey, Phi.	L	.247	120	425	57	105	151	19	9	3	33	4	2	34	73	13	2	7	.355	.309
Patterson, John, S.F.	B	.188	16	16	1	3	6	0	0	1	2	0	0	0	5	0	1	0	.375	.188
Pena, Geronimo, St.L	B	.256	74	254	34	65	103	19	2	5	30	4	2	25	71	13	5	3	.406	.330
Polidor, Gus, Fla.	R	.167	7	6	0	1	2	1	0	0	0	0	0	0	2	0	0	0	.333	.167
Ready, Randy, Mon.	R	.254	40	134	22	34	47	8	1	1	10	1	0	23	8	2	1	4	.351	.367
Reed, Jody, L.A.	R	.276	132	445	48	123	154	21	2	2	31	17	3	38	40	1	3	16	.346	.333
Renteria, Rich, Fla.	R	.255	103	263	27	67	86	9	2	2	30	3	1	21	31	0	2	8	.327	.314
Roberts, Bip, Cin.	B	.240	83	292	46	70	86	13	0	1	18	0	3	38	46	26	6	2	.295	.330
Samuel, Juan, Cin.	R	.230	103	261	31	60	90	10	4	4	26	0	2	23	53	9	7	2	.345	.298
Sandberg, Ryne, ChiN	R	.309	117	456	67	141	188	20	0	9	45	2	6	37	62	9	2	12	.412	.359
Saunders, Doug, NY-N	R	.209	28	67	8	14	16	2	0	0	3	0	3	4	0	0	2	.239	.243
Scarsone, Steve, S.F.	R	.252	44	103	16	26	41	9	0	2	15	4	1	4	32	0	1	0	.398	.278
Sharperson, Mike, L.A.	R	.256	73	90	13	23	33	4	0	2	10	0	1	5	17	2	0	2	.367	.299
Shields, Tommy, ChiN	R	.176	20	34	4	6	7	1	0	0	1	0	0	2	10	0	0	1	.206	.222
Teufel, Tim, S.D.	R	.250	96	200	26	50	86	11	2	7	31	3	1	27	39	2	2	9	.430	.338
Thompson, Robby, S.F.	R	.312	128	494	85	154	245	30	2	19	65	9	4	45	97	10	4	7	.496	.375
Walker, Chico, NY-N	B	.225	115	213	18	48	72	7	1	5	19	0	2	14	29	7	0	3	.338	.271
Yelding, Eric, ChiN	R	.204	69	108	14	22	32	5	1	1	10	4	0	11	22	3	2	3	.296	.277
Young, Eric, Col.	R	.269	144	490	82	132	173	16	8	3	42	4	4	63	41	42	19	9	.353	.355

National League third basemen

Name/Team	B	BA	G	AB	R	H	TB	2B	3B	HR	RBI	SH	SF	BB	SO	SB	CS	GIDP	SLG	OBA
Batiste, Kim, Phi.	R	.282	79	156	14	44	68	7	1	5	29	0	1	3	29	0	1	3	.436	.298
Berry, Sean, Mon.	R	.261	122	299	50	78	139	15	2	14	49	3	6	41	70	12	2	4	.465	.348
Brumley, A. Mike, Hou.	B	.300	8	10	1	3	3	0	0	0	2	0	0	1	3	0	1	0	.300	.364
Buechele, Steve, ChiN	R	.272	133	460	53	125	201	27	2	15	65	4	3	48	87	1	1	12	.437	.345
Caminiti, Ken, Hou.	B	.262	143	543	75	142	212	31	0	13	75	1	3	49	88	8	5	15	.390	.321
Castellano, Pedro, Col.	R	.183	34	71	12	13	24	2	0	3	7	0	0	8	16	1	1	1	.338	.266
Cianfrocco, Archi, Mon.-S.D.	R	.243	96	296	30	72	123	11	2	12	48	2	5	17	69	2	0	9	.416	.287
Donnels, Chris, Hou.	L	.257	88	179	18	46	70	14	2	2	24	0	1	19	33	2	0	6	.391	.327
Hansen, Dave, L.A.	L	.362	84	105	13	38	53	3	0	4	30	0	1	21	13	0	1	0	.505	.465
Hayes, Charlie, Col.	R	.305	157	573	89	175	299	45	2	25	98	1	8	43	82	11	6	25	.522	.355
Hollins, David, Phi.	B	.273	143	543	104	148	240	30	4	18	93	0	7	85	109	2	3	15	.442	.372
Huskey, Butch, NY-N	R	.146	13	41	2	6	7	1	0	0	3	0	2	1	13	0	0	0	.171	.159
Johnson, Howard, NY-N	B	.238	72	235	32	56	89	8	2	7	26	0	2	43	43	6	4	3	.379	.354
King, Jeff, Pit.	R	.295	158	611	82	180	248	35	3	9	98	1	8	59	54	8	6	17	.406	.356
Lansing, Mike, Mon.	R	.287	141	491	64	141	181	29	1	3	45	10	3	46	56	23	5	16	.369	.352

National League third basemen

Name/Team	B	BA	G	AB	R	H	TB	2B	3B	HR	RBI	SH	SF	BB	SO	SB	CS	GIDP	SLG	OBA
Magadan, Dave, Fla.	L	.286	66	227	22	65	89	12	0	4	29	0	3	44	30	0	1	3	.392	.400
Manto, Jeff, Phi.	R	.056	8	18	0	1	1	0	0	0	0	0	0	0	3	0	0	0	.056	.105
Pecota, Bill, Atl.	R	.323	72	62	17	20	24	2	1	0	5	1	0	2	5	1	1	0	.387	.344
Pendleton, Terry, Atl.	B	.272	161	633	81	172	258	33	1	17	84	3	7	36	97	5	1	18	.408	.311
Royer, Stan, St.L	R	.304	24	46	4	14	19	2	0	1	8	0	0	2	14	0	1	2	.413	.333
Sabo, Chris, Cin.	R	.259	148	552	86	143	243	33	2	21	82	2	8	43	105	6	4	10	.440	.315
Sheffield, Gary, S.D.-Fla.	R	.294	140	494	67	145	235	20	5	20	73	0	7	47	64	17	5	11	.476	.361
Wallach, Tim, L.A.	R	.222	133	477	42	106	163	19	1	12	62	1	9	32	70	0	2	10	.342	.271
Williams, Matt D., S.F.	R	.294	145	579	105	170	325	33	4	38	110	0	9	27	80	1	3	12	.561	.325
Woodson, Tracy, St.L	R	.208	62	77	4	16	18	2	0	0	2	0	1	1	14	0	0	1	.234	.215
Zeile, Todd, St.L	R	.277	157	571	82	158	247	36	1	17	103	0	6	70	76	5	4	15	.433	.352

National League shortstops

Name/Team	B	BA	G	AB	R	H	TB	2B	3B	HR	RBI	SH	SF	BB	SO	SB	CS	GIDP	SLG	OBA
Baez, Kevin, NY-N	R	.183	52	126	10	23	32	9	0	0	7	4	0	13	17	0	0	1	.254	.259
Bell, Jay, Pit.	R	.310	154	604	102	187	264	32	9	9	51	13	1	77	122	16	10	16	.437	.392
Bell, Juan, Phi.	B	.200	24	65	5	13	21	6	1	0	7	2	0	5	12	0	1	0	.323	.268
Belliard, Rafael, Atl.	R	.228	91	79	6	18	23	5	0	0	6	3	0	4	13	0	0	1	.291	.291
Benavides, Freddie, Col.	R	.286	74	213	20	61	86	10	3	3	26	3	1	6	27	3	2	4	.404	.305
Blauser, Jeff, Atl.	R	.305	161	597	110	182	260	29	2	15	73	5	7	85	109	16	6	13	.436	.401
Bogar, Tim, NY-N	R	.244	78	205	19	50	72	13	0	3	25	1	1	14	29	0	1	2	.351	.300
Branson, Jeff, Cin.	L	.241	125	381	40	92	118	15	1	3	22	8	4	19	73	4	1	4	.310	.275
Castilla, Vinny, Col.	R	.255	105	337	36	86	136	9	7	9	30	0	5	13	45	2	5	10	.404	.283
Cedeno, Andujar, Hou.	R	.283	149	505	69	143	208	24	4	11	56	4	5	48	97	9	7	17	.412	.346
Clayton, Royce, S.F.	R	.282	153	549	54	155	204	21	5	6	70	8	7	38	91	11	10	16	.372	.331
Cordero, Wil, Mon.	R	.248	138	475	56	118	184	32	2	10	58	4	1	34	60	12	3	12	.387	.308
Cromer, Tripp, St.L	R	.087	10	23	1	2	2	0	0	0	0	0	0	1	6	0	0	0	.087	.125
Dunston, Shawon, ChiN	R	.400	7	10	3	4	6	2	0	0	2	0	0	0	1	0	0	0	.600	.400
Fernandez, Tony, NY-N	B	.225	48	173	20	39	51	5	2	1	14	3	2	25	19	6	2	3	.295	.323
Greene, Willie, Cin.	L	.160	15	50	7	8	17	1	1	2	5	0	1	2	19	0	0	1	.340	.189
Gutierrez, Ricky, S.D.	R	.251	133	438	76	110	145	10	5	5	26	1	1	50	97	4	3	7	.331	.334
Jones, Chipper, Atl.	B	.667	8	3	2	2	3	1	0	0	0	0	0	1	1	0	0	0	1.000	.750
Jones, W. Tim, St.L	L	.262	29	61	13	16	22	6	0	0	1	2	0	9	8	2	2	0	.361	.366
Kessinger, Keith, Cin.	B	.259	11	27	4	7	11	1	0	1	3	0	1	4	4	0	0	1	.407	.344
Larkin, Barry, Cin.	R	.315	100	384	57	121	171	20	3	8	51	1	3	51	33	14	1	13	.445	.394
Liriano, Nelson, Col.	B	.305	48	151	28	46	64	6	3	2	15	5	1	18	22	6	4	6	.424	.376
McKnight, Jeff, NY-N	B	.256	105	164	19	42	53	3	1	2	13	3	2	13	31	0	0	3	.323	.311
Millette, Joe, Phi.	R	.200	10	10	3	2	2	0	0	0	2	3	0	1	2	0	0	1	.200	.273
Navarro, Tito, NY-N	B	.059	12	17	1	1	1	0	0	0	1	1	0	0	4	0	0	1	.059	.059
Offerman, Jose, L.A.	B	.269	158	590	77	159	195	21	6	1	62	25	8	71	75	30	13	12	.331	.346
Oquendo, Jose, St.L	B	.205	46	73	7	15	15	0	0	0	4	3	1	12	8	0	0	5	.205	.314
Sanchez, Rey, ChiN	R	.282	105	344	35	97	112	11	2	0	28	9	2	15	22	1	1	8	.326	.316
Shipley, Craig, S.D.	R	.235	105	230	25	54	75	9	0	4	22	1	1	10	31	12	3	3	.326	.275
Smith, Ozzie, St.L	B	.288	141	545	75	157	194	22	6	1	53	7	7	43	18	21	8	11	.356	.337
Stillwell, Kurt, S.D.	B	.215	57	121	9	26	33	4	0	1	11	2	0	11	22	4	3	2	.273	.286
Stocker, Kevin, Phi.	B	.324	70	259	46	84	108	12	3	2	31	4	1	30	43	5	0	8	.417	.409
Uribe, Jose, Hou.	B	.245	45	53	4	13	14	1	0	0	3	4	0	8	5	1	0	1	.264	.355
Vizcaino, Jose, ChiN	B	.287	151	551	74	158	197	19	4	4	54	8	9	46	71	12	9	9	.358	.340
Weiss, Walt, Fla.	B	.266	158	500	50	133	154	14	2	1	39	5	4	79	73	7	3	5	.308	.367
Womack, Tony, Pit.	L	.083	15	24	5	2	2	0	0	0	0	1	0	3	3	2	0	0	.083	.185

National League outfielders

Name/Team	B	BA	G	AB	R	H	TB	2B	3B	HR	RBI	SH	SF	BB	SO	SB	CS	GIDP	SLG	OBA
Alou, Moises, Mon.	R	.286	136	482	70	138	233	29	6	18	85	3	7	38	53	17	6	9	.483	.340
Amaro, Ruben Jr., Phi.	B	.333	25	48	7	16	25	2	2	1	6	3	1	6	5	0	0	1	.521	.400
Anthony, Eric, Hou.	L	.249	145	486	70	121	193	19	4	15	66	0	2	49	88	3	5	9	.397	.319
Ashley, Billy, L.A.	R	.243	14	37	0	9	9	0	0	0	0	0	0	2	11	0	0	0	.243	.282
Bass, Kevin, Hou.	B	.284	111	229	31	65	92	18	0	3	37	2	0	26	31	7	1	4	.402	.359
Bean, Billy, S.D.	L	.260	88	177	19	46	70	9	0	5	32	2	5	6	29	2	4	4	.395	.284
Bell, Derek, S.D.	R	.262	150	542	73	142	226	19	1	21	72	0	8	23	122	26	5	7	.417	.303
Berroa, Geronimo, Fla.	R	.118	14	34	3	4	5	1	0	0	0	0	0	2	7	0	0	2	.147	.167
Bichette, Dante, Col.	R	.310	141	538	93	167	283	43	5	21	89	0	8	28	99	14	8	7	.526	.348
Bonds, Barry, S.F.	L	.336	159	539	129	181	365	38	4	46	123	0	7	126	79	29	12	11	.677	.458
Bonilla, Bobby, NY-N	B	.265	139	502	81	133	262	21	3	34	87	0	8	72	96	3	3	12	.522	.352
Boston, Daryl, Col.	L	.261	124	291	46	76	135	15	1	14	40	0	1	26	57	1	6	5	.464	.325
Briley, Greg, Fla.	L	.194	120	170	17	33	48	6	0	3	12	1	1	12	42	6	2	5	.282	.250

National League outfielders

Name/Team	B	BA	G	AB	R	H	TB	2B	3B	HR	RBI	SH	SF	BB	SO	SB	CS	GIDP	SLG	OBA
Brooks, Jerry, L.A.	R	.222	9	9	2	2	6	1	0	1	1	0	0	0	2	0	0	0	.667	.222
Brown, Jarvis, S.D.	R	.233	47	133	21	31	44	9	2	0	8	2	1	15	26	3	3	4	.331	.335
Brumfield, Jacob, Cin.	R	.268	103	272	40	73	114	17	3	6	23	3	2	21	47	20	8	1	.419	.321
Bullett, Scott, Pit.	L	.200	23	55	2	11	15	0	2	0	4	0	1	3	15	3	2	1	.273	.237
Burnitz, Jeromy, NY-N	L	.243	86	263	49	64	125	10	6	13	38	2	2	38	66	3	6	2	.475	.339
Butler, Brett, L.A.	L	.298	156	607	80	181	225	21	10	1	42	14	4	86	69	39	19	6	.371	.387
Canseco, Ozzie, St.L	R	.176	6	17	0	3	3	0	0	0	0	0	0	1	3	0	0	0	.176	.222
Carr, Chuck, Fla.	B	.267	142	551	75	147	182	19	2	4	41	7	4	49	74	58	22	6	.330	.327
Carreon, Mark, S.F.	R	.327	78	150	22	49	81	9	1	7	33	0	5	13	16	1	0	8	.540	.373
Carrillo, Matias, Fla.	L	.255	24	55	4	14	20	6	0	0	3	1	0	1	7	0	0	5	.364	.281
Chamberlain, Wes, Phi.	R	.282	96	284	34	80	140	20	2	12	45	0	4	17	51	2	1	8	.493	.320
Clark, Dave, Pit.	L	.271	110	277	43	75	123	11	2	11	46	0	2	38	58	1	0	10	.444	.358
Clark, Jerald, Col.	R	.282	140	478	65	135	212	26	6	13	67	3	1	20	60	9	6	12	.444	.324
Cole, Alex, Col.	L	.256	126	348	50	89	106	9	4	0	24	4	2	43	58	30	13	6	.305	.339
Coleman, Vince, NY-N	B	.279	92	373	64	104	140	14	8	2	25	3	2	21	58	38	13	2	.375	.316
Conine, Jeff, Fla.	R	.292	162	595	75	174	240	24	3	12	79	0	6	52	135	2	2	14	.403	.351
Costo, Tim, Cin.	R	.224	31	98	13	22	36	5	0	3	12	0	2	4	17	0	0	1	.367	.250
Cotto, Henry, Fla.	R	.296	54	135	15	40	56	7	0	3	14	1	2	3	18	11	1	3	.415	.312
Cummings, Midre, Pit.	L	.111	13	36	5	4	5	1	0	0	3	0	1	4	9	0	0	1	.139	.195
Daugherty, Jack, Hou.-Cin.	B	.226	50	62	7	14	22	2	0	2	9	0	1	11	15	0	0	0	.355	.338
Davis, Eric, L.A.	R	.234	108	376	57	88	147	17	0	14	53	0	4	41	88	33	5	8	.391	.308
Dykstra, Len, Phi.	L	.305	161	637	143	194	307	44	6	19	66	0	5	129	64	37	12	8	.482	.420
Eisenreich, Jim, Phi.	L	.318	153	362	51	115	161	17	4	7	54	3	2	26	36	5	0	6	.445	.363
Espy, Cecil, Cin.	B	.233	40	60	6	14	16	2	0	0	5	0	2	14	13	2	2	2	.267	.368
Everett, Carl, Fla.	B	.105	11	19	0	2	2	0	0	0	0	0	0	1	9	1	0	0	.105	.150
Faneyte, Rikkert, S.F.	R	.133	7	15	2	2	2	0	0	0	0	0	0	2	4	0	0	0	.133	.235
Fariss, Monty, Fla.	R	.172	18	29	3	5	9	2	1	0	2	0	0	5	13	0	0	2	.310	.294
Felix, Junior, Fla.	B	.238	57	214	25	51	85	11	1	7	22	0	0	10	50	2	1	6	.397	.276
Finley, Steve, Hou.	L	.266	142	545	69	145	210	15	13	8	44	6	3	28	65	19	6	8	.385	.304
Frazier, Lou, Mon.	B	.286	112	189	27	54	66	7	1	1	16	5	1	16	24	17	2	3	.349	.340
Gallagher, Dave, NY-N	R	.274	99	201	34	55	89	12	2	6	28	7	1	20	18	1	1	7	.443	.338
Gant, Ron, Atl.	R	.274	157	606	113	166	309	27	4	36	117	0	7	67	117	26	9	14	.510	.345
Gilkey, Bernard, St.L	R	.305	137	557	99	170	268	40	5	16	70	0	5	56	66	15	10	16	.481	.370
Gonzalez, Luis, Hou.	L	.300	154	540	82	162	247	34	3	15	72	3	10	47	83	20	9	9	.457	.361
Goodwin, Tom, L.A.	L	.294	30	17	6	5	6	1	0	0	1	0	0	1	4	1	2	1	.353	.333
Gordon, Keith, Cin.	R	.167	3	6	0	1	1	0	0	0	0	0	0	0	2	0	0	0	.167	.167
Gregg, Tommy, Cin.	L	.167	10	12	1	2	2	0	0	0	1	0	1	0	0	0	0	0	.167	.154
Grissom, Marquis, Mon.	R	.298	157	630	104	188	276	27	2	19	95	0	8	52	76	53	10	9	.438	.351
Gwynn, Tony, S.D.	L	.358	122	489	70	175	243	41	3	7	59	1	7	36	19	14	1	18	.497	.398
Hernandez, Cesar, Cin.	R	.083	27	24	3	2	2	0	0	0	1	1	0	1	8	1	2	0	.083	.120
Hill, Glenallen, ChiN	R	.345	31	87	14	30	67	7	0	10	22	0	0	6	21	1	0	1	.770	.387
Hosey, Steve, S.F.	R	.500	3	2	0	1	2	1	0	0	1	0	0	1	1	0	0	0	1.000	.667
Housie, Wayne, NY-N	B	.188	18	16	2	3	4	1	0	0	1	0	0	1	1	0	0	0	.250	.235
Howard, Thomas, Cin.	B	.277	38	141	22	39	65	8	3	4	13	0	1	12	21	5	6	4	.461	.331
Hughes, Keith, Cin.	L	.000	3	4	0	0	0	0	0	0	0	0	0	0	0	0	0	0	.000	.000
Incaviglia, Pete, Phi.	R	.274	116	368	60	101	195	16	3	24	89	0	7	21	82	1	1	9	.530	.318
Jackson, Darrin, NY-N	R	.195	31	87	4	17	21	1	0	1	7	1	1	2	22	0	0	0	.241	.211
James, Chris, Hou.	R	.256	65	129	19	33	63	10	1	6	19	1	2	15	34	2	0	2	.488	.333
Jones, Chris, Col.	R	.273	86	209	29	57	94	11	4	6	31	5	1	10	48	9	4	6	.450	.305
Jordan, Brian, St.L	R	.309	67	223	33	69	121	10	6	10	44	0	3	12	35	6	6	6	.543	.351
Justice, David, Atl.	L	.270	157	585	90	158	301	15	4	40	120	0	4	78	90	3	5	9	.515	.357
Kelly, Bobby, Cin.	R	.319	78	320	44	102	152	17	3	9	35	0	3	17	43	21	5	10	.475	.354
Landrum, Ced, NY-N	L	.263	22	19	2	5	6	1	0	0	1	1	0	0	5	0	0	0	.316	.263
Lankford, Ray, St.L	R	.238	127	407	64	97	141	17	3	7	45	1	3	81	111	14	14	5	.346	.366
Lewis, Darren, S.F.	R	.253	136	522	84	132	169	17	7	2	48	12	1	30	40	46	15	4	.324	.302
Longmire, Tony, Phi.	L	.231	11	13	1	3	3	0	0	0	1	0	0	0	1	0	0	0	.231	.231
Maclin, Lonnie, St.L	L	.077	12	13	2	1	1	0	0	0	1	0	1	0	5	1	0	0	.077	.077
Maldonado, Candy, ChiN	R	.186	70	140	8	26	40	5	0	3	15	0	0	13	40	0	0	3	.286	.260
Martin, Al, Pit.	L	.281	143	480	85	135	231	26	8	18	64	2	3	42	122	16	9	5	.481	.338
Martinez, Dave, S.F.	L	.241	91	241	28	58	87	12	1	5	27	0	0	27	39	6	3	5	.361	.317
May, Derrick, ChiN	L	.295	128	465	62	137	196	25	2	10	77	0	6	31	41	10	3	15	.422	.336
McClendon, Lloyd, Pit.	R	.221	88	181	21	40	59	11	1	2	19	1	2	23	17	0	3	4	.326	.306
McGee, Willie, S.F.	B	.301	130	475	53	143	185	28	1	4	46	3	2	38	67	10	9	12	.389	.353
McIntosh, Tim, Mon.	R	.095	20	21	2	2	3	1	0	0	2	0	0	0	7	0	0	0	.143	.095
Merced, Orlando, Pit.	L	.313	137	447	68	140	198	26	4	8	70	0	2	77	64	3	3	9	.443	.414
Mercedes, Luis, S.F.	R	.160	18	25	1	4	6	0	1	0	3	1	0	1	3	0	1	0	.240	.250
Mitchell, Kevin, Cin.	R	.341	93	323	56	110	194	21	3	19	64	0	4	25	48	1	0	14	.601	.385
Mondesi, Raul, L.A.	R	.291	42	86	13	25	42	3	1	4	10	1	0	4	16	4	1	1	.488	.322
Murphy, Dale, Col.	R	.143	26	42	1	6	7	1	0	0	7	0	2	5	15	0	0	5	.167	.224
Nieves, Melvin, S.D.	B	.191	19	47	4	9	15	0	0	2	3	0	0	3	21	0	0	0	.319	.255

National League outfielders

Name/Team	B	BA	G	AB	R	H	TB	2B	3B	HR	RBI	SH	SF	BB	SO	SB	CS	GIDP	SLG	OBA
Nixon, Otis, Atl.	B	.269	134	461	77	124	145	12	3	1	24	5	5	61	63	47	13	10	.315	.351
Orsulak, Joe, NY-N	L	.284	134	409	59	116	163	15	4	8	35	0	2	28	25	5	4	6	.399	.331
Parker, Rick, Hou.	R	.333	45	45	11	15	18	3	0	0	4	1	0	3	8	1	2	2	.400	.375
Pennyfeather, William, Pit.	R	.206	21	34	4	7	8	1	0	0	2	0	0	0	6	0	1	1	.235	.206
Plantier, Phil, S.D.	L	.240	138	462	67	111	235	20	1	34	100	1	5	61	124	4	5	4	.509	.335
Pose, Scott, Fla.	L	.195	15	41	0	8	10	2	0	0	3	0	0	2	4	0	2	0	.244	.233
Pride, Curtis, Mon.	L	.444	10	9	3	4	10	1	1	1	5	0	0	0	3	1	0	0	1.111	.444
Rhodes, Karl, Hou.-ChiN	L	.278	20	54	12	15	28	2	1	3	7	0	0	11	9	2	0	0	.519	.400
Roberson, Kevin, ChiN	B	.189	62	180	23	34	67	4	1	9	27	0	0	12	48	0	1	2	.372	.251
Rodriguez, Henry, L.A.	L	.222	76	176	20	39	73	10	0	8	23	0	1	11	39	1	0	1	.415	.266
Sanders, Deion, Atl.	L	.276	95	272	42	75	123	18	6	6	28	1	2	16	42	19	7	3	.452	.321
Sanders, Reggie, Cin.	R	.274	138	496	90	136	220	16	4	20	83	3	8	51	118	27	10	10	.444	.343
Shelton, Ben, Pit.	L	.250	15	24	3	6	13	1	0	2	7	0	0	3	3	0	0	2	.542	.333
Sherman, Darrell, S.D.	L	.222	37	63	8	14	15	1	0	0	2	1	1	6	8	2	1	0	.238	.315
Smith, Dwight, ChiN	L	.300	111	310	51	93	153	17	5	11	35	1	3	25	51	8	6	3	.494	.355
Smith, Lonnie, Pit.	R	.286	94	199	35	57	88	5	4	6	24	3	2	43	42	9	4	3	.442	.422
Snyder, Cory, L.A.	R	.266	143	516	61	137	205	33	1	11	56	2	1	47	147	4	1	8	.397	.331
Sosa, Sammy, ChiN	R	.261	159	598	92	156	290	25	5	33	93	0	1	38	135	36	11	14	.485	.309
Stairs, Matt, Mon.	L	.375	6	8	1	3	4	1	0	0	2	0	0	0	1	0	0	1	.500	.375
Strawberry, Darryl, L.A.	L	.140	32	100	12	14	31	2	0	5	12	0	2	16	19	1	0	1	.310	.267
Tarasco, Tony, Atl.	L	.229	24	35	6	8	10	2	0	0	2	0	1	0	5	0	1	1	.286	.243
Thompson, Milt, Phi.	L	.262	129	340	42	89	119	14	2	4	44	3	2	40	57	9	4	8	.350	.341
Thompson, Ryan, NY-N	R	.250	80	288	34	72	128	19	2	11	26	5	1	19	81	2	7	5	.444	.302
Tomberlin, Andy, Pit.	L	.286	27	42	4	12	17	0	1	1	5	0	0	2	14	0	0	0	.405	.333
Tubbs, Greg, Cin.	R	.186	35	59	10	11	14	0	0	1	2	0	0	14	10	3	1	0	.237	.351
Van Slyke, Andy, Pit.	L	.310	83	323	42	100	145	13	4	8	50	0	4	24	40	11	2	13	.449	.357
Varsho, Gary, Cin.	L	.232	77	95	8	22	34	6	0	2	11	3	1	9	19	1	0	1	.358	.302
Walker, Larry, Mon.	L	.265	138	490	85	130	230	24	5	22	86	0	6	80	76	29	7	8	.469	.371
Webster, Mitch, L.A.	B	.244	88	172	26	42	58	6	2	2	14	4	3	11	24	4	6	3	.337	.293
Wehner, John, Pit.	R	.143	29	35	3	5	5	0	0	0	0	2	0	6	10	0	0	0	.143	.268
White, Rondell, Mon.	R	.260	23	73	9	19	30	3	1	2	15	2	1	7	16	1	2	2	.411	.321
Whiten, Mark, St.L	B	.253	152	562	81	142	238	13	4	25	99	0	4	58	110	15	8	11	.423	.323
Whitmore, Darrell, Fla.	L	.204	76	250	24	51	75	8	2	4	19	2	0	10	72	4	2	8	.300	.249
Wilson, Glenn, Pit.	R	.143	10	14	0	2	2	0	0	0	0	1	0	0	9	0	0	0	.143	.143
Wilson, Nigel, Fla.	L	.000	7	16	0	0	0	0	0	0	0	0	0	0	11	0	0	0	.000	.000
Wilson, Willie, ChiN	B	.258	105	221	29	57	77	11	3	1	11	1	1	11	40	7	2	2	.348	.301
Wood, Ted, Mon.	L	.192	13	26	4	5	6	1	0	0	3	3	0	3	3	0	0	0	.231	.276
Young, Gerald, Col.	R	.053	19	19	5	1	1	0	0	0	1	0	0	4	1	0	1	2	.053	.217
Zambrano, Eddie, ChiN	R	.294	8	17	1	5	5	0	0	0	2	0	0	1	3	0	0	1	.294	.333

National League starting pitchers (batting)

Name/Team	B	BA	G	AB	R	H	TB	2B	3B	HR	RBI	SH	SF	BB	SO	SB	CS	GIDP	SLG	OBA
Armstrong, Jack, Fla.	R	.152	36	66	3	10	11	1	0	0	3	4	0	0	29	0	0	2	.167	.152
Arocha, Rene, St.L	R	.103	32	58	3	6	7	1	0	0	3	7	0	2	24	0	0	0	.121	.133
Ashby, Andy, Col.-S.D.	R	.139	32	36	3	5	6	1	0	0	1	2	0	2	9	0	0	0	.167	.184
Astacio, Pedro, L.A.	R	.161	31	62	4	10	10	0	0	0	2	7	0	0	26	0	1	0	.161	.161
Avery, Steve, Atl.	L	.160	35	75	4	12	16	4	0	0	5	8	0	2	19	0	0	1	.213	.182
Belcher, Tim, Cin.	R	.200	22	50	2	10	11	1	0	0	7	3	0	0	15	0	1	0	.220	.216
Benes, Andy, S.D.	R	.125	34	72	5	9	15	3	0	1	4	14	0	1	33	0	0	0	.208	.149
Black, Bud, S.F.	L	.243	16	37	2	9	9	0	0	0	3	3	0	2	8	0	0	1	.243	.282
Bottenfield, Kent, Mon.-Col.	B	.220	37	50	2	11	11	0	0	0	3	3	0	1	15	1	0	0	.220	.260
Boucher, Denis, Mon.	R	.167	5	6	0	1	2	1	0	0	0	2	0	0	3	0	0	0	.333	.167
Bowen, Ryan, Fla.	R	.118	27	51	3	6	9	1	1	0	3	3	0	1	15	0	0	0	.176	.135
Brocail, Doug, S.D.	L	.182	30	33	4	6	6	0	0	0	0	11	0	0	8	2	0	2	.182	.182
Browning, Tom, Cin.	L	.216	21	37	4	8	12	1	0	1	4	4	1	2	6	0	0	0	.324	.250
Brummett, Greg, S.F.	R	.000	8	15	0	0	0	0	0	0	0	2	0	1	5	0	0	0	.000	.063
Burkett, John, S.F.	R	.118	34	76	7	9	9	0	0	0	4	12	0	5	31	0	0	4	.118	.173
Candiotti, Tom, L.A.	R	.133	33	60	1	8	10	2	0	0	2	9	0	1	13	0	0	2	.167	.148
Castillo, Frank, ChiN	R	.163	29	43	1	7	7	0	0	0	3	8	0	1	3	0	0	2	.163	.182
Cooke, Steve, Pit.	R	.155	32	71	4	11	13	2	0	0	5	6	1	0	17	0	0	4	.183	.164
Cormier, Rheal, St.L	L	.234	38	47	5	11	13	2	0	0	4	6	0	0	11	0	0	1	.277	.234
Deshaies, Jim, S.F.	L	.000	5	5	0	0	0	0	0	0	0	1	0	0	3	0	0	0	.000	.000
Drabek, Doug, Hou.	R	.085	34	71	2	6	11	2	0	1	3	9	0	2	22	0	0	3	.155	.110
Eiland, Dave, S.D.	R	.083	10	12	1	1	1	0	0	0	0	3	0	0	4	0	0	0	.083	.083
Fernandez, Sid, NY-N	L	.094	18	32	2	3	3	0	0	0	0	8	0	2	13	0	0	2	.094	.147
Glavine, Tom, Atl.	L	.173	36	81	3	14	15	1	0	0	3	11	0	4	27	0	0	1	.185	.212
Gooden, Dwight, NY-N	R	.200	30	70	5	14	26	2	2	2	9	6	0	0	11	0	0	1	.371	.200
Green, Tyler, Phi.	R	.000	3	2	0	0	0	0	0	0	0	1	0	0	2	0	0	0	.000	.000

National League starting pitchers (batting)

Name/Team	B	BA	G	AB	R	H	TB	2B	3B	HR	RBI	SH	SF	BB	SO	SB	CS	GIDP	SLG	OBA
Greene, Tommy, Phi.	R	.222	32	72	9	16	24	2	0	2	10	6	1	5	20	0	0	1	.333	.269
Gross, Kevin, L.A.	R	.203	33	64	6	13	18	2	0	1	7	8	0	5	32	0	0	1	.281	.271
Guzman, Jose, ChiN	R	.111	30	63	1	7	7	0	0	0	2	9	0	1	15	0	0	1	.111	.125
Hammond, Chris, Fla.	L	.190	33	63	10	12	20	0	1	2	4	5	0	9	26	0	0	0	.317	.292
Harkey, Mike, ChiN	R	.093	28	54	0	5	6	1	0	0	0	5	0	1	18	0	0	0	.111	.109
Harnisch, Pete, Hou.	R	.104	33	67	6	7	9	2	0	0	2	10	0	2	19	0	0	3	.134	.143
Harris, Greg W., S.D.-Col.	R	.137	35	73	2	10	13	3	0	0	4	5	2	5	25	0	0	0	.178	.188
Henry, Butch, Col.-Mon.	L	.083	30	24	1	2	2	0	0	0	2	3	1	1	3	0	0	1	.083	.115
Hershiser, Orel, L.A.	R	.356	34	73	11	26	30	4	0	0	6	8	0	2	5	0	1	1	.411	.373
Hibbard, Greg, ChiN	L	.092	32	65	4	6	7	1	0	0	3	3	0	2	17	0	0	1	.108	.119
Hill, Ken, Mon.	R	.115	29	52	4	6	8	2	0	0	3	14	0	4	15	0	0	0	.154	.179
Hillman, Eric, NY-N	L	.159	27	44	2	7	8	1	0	0	0	6	0	0	14	0	0	0	.182	.178
Hope, John, Pit.	R	.077	7	13	0	1	1	0	0	0	0	0	0	0	7	0	0	0	.077	.077
Hough, Charlie, Fla.	R	.032	34	63	1	2	2	0	0	0	1	4	0	2	20	0	0	4	.032	.076
Hurst, Bruce, S.D.-Col.	L	.000	5	1	0	0	0	0	0	0	0	0	1	0	0	1	0	0	.000	.000
Jackson, Danny, Phi.	R	.077	32	65	3	5	7	2	0	0	2	12	0	3	37	0	0	0	.108	.130
Jones, Bobby J., NY-N	R	.050	9	20	0	1	1	0	0	0	0	2	0	0	7	0	0	0	.050	.050
Kile, Darryl, Hou.	R	.094	32	53	5	5	9	1	0	1	1	8	0	3	20	0	0	0	.170	.143
Luebbers, Larry, Cin.	R	.250	14	24	1	6	7	1	0	0	0	1	0	0	8	0	0	0	.292	.280
Maddux, Greg, Atl.	R	.165	36	91	5	15	16	1	0	0	4	10	0	1	32	0	0	0	.176	.174
Magrane, Joe, St.L	R	.114	22	35	2	4	5	1	0	0	1	4	0	1	20	0	0	0	.143	.139
Martinez, Dennis, Mon.	R	.159	36	69	1	11	13	2	0	0	4	9	2	2	17	0	0	1	.188	.178
Martinez, Ramon, L.A.	L	.129	32	70	2	9	10	1	0	0	2	7	1	0	23	0	0	1	.143	.127
Miller, Paul, Pit.	R	.000	3	2	0	0	0	0	0	0	0	0	0	0	0	0	0	0	.000	.000
Morgan, Mike, ChiN	R	.061	32	66	1	4	6	2	0	0	1	5	0	2	22	0	0	1	.091	.088
Mulholland, Terry, Phi.	R	.065	29	62	3	4	4	0	0	0	0	8	0	1	27	0	0	0	.065	.079
Nabholz, Chris, Mon.	L	.128	26	39	1	5	5	0	0	0	1	3	0	1	9	0	0	0	.128	.150
Nied, David, Col.	R	.174	16	23	3	4	4	0	0	0	2	3	0	3	8	0	0	0	.174	.269
Osborne, Donovan, St.L	L	.204	29	49	4	10	11	1	0	0	3	7	0	3	13	0	0	0	.224	.250
Painter, Lance, Col.	L	.300	10	10	2	3	5	0	1	0	1	3	0	1	5	0	0	0	.500	.364
Portugal, Mark, Hou.	R	.231	33	65	4	15	18	0	0	1	8	10	2	3	13	0	0	2	.277	.257
Pugh, Tim, Cin.	R	.222	31	54	2	12	13	1	0	0	1	7	0	0	20	0	0	0	.241	.236
Rapp, Pat, Fla.	R	.194	16	31	3	6	7	1	0	0	2	2	0	1	11	0	0	0	.226	.219
Reynoso, Armando, Col.	R	.127	31	63	4	8	14	0	0	2	4	6	0	3	20	0	0	0	.222	.167
Rijo, Jose, Cin.	R	.268	36	82	5	22	29	4	0	1	8	12	0	3	18	0	0	2	.354	.294
Rivera, Ben, Phi.	R	.098	30	51	3	5	5	0	0	0	0	13	0	3	24	0	0	0	.098	.148
Roper, John, Cin.	R	.179	16	28	1	5	5	0	0	0	2	1	0	0	11	0	0	1	.179	.179
Rueter, Kirk, Mon.	L	.077	14	26	0	2	2	0	0	0	3	8	0	3	10	0	0	0	.077	.172
Saberhagen, Bret, NY-N	R	.111	19	45	2	5	6	1	0	0	0	8	0	5	10	0	0	1	.133	.200
Sanders, Scott, S.D.	R	.063	9	16	0	1	1	0	0	0	1	4	0	0	6	0	0	0	.063	.063
Sanderson, Scott, S.F.	R	.000	11	14	1	0	0	0	0	0	0	1	0	1	11	0	0	0	.000	.067
Sanford, Mo, Col.	R	.000	11	8	0	0	0	0	0	0	0	1	0	1	4	0	0	0	.000	.111
Schilling, Curt, Phi.	R	.147	34	75	3	11	12	1	0	0	2	13	0	2	19	0	0	0	.160	.169
Smiley, John, Cin.	L	.250	18	32	2	8	9	1	0	0	5	5	1	1	10	0	0	0	.281	.265
Smith, Pete J., Atl.	R	.222	20	27	2	6	7	1	0	0	5	3	1	1	11	0	0	0	.259	.241
Smith, Zane, Pit.	L	.080	14	25	0	2	2	0	0	0	0	4	0	0	6	0	0	0	.080	.080
Smoltz, John, Atl.	R	.183	35	71	2	13	14	1	0	0	4	11	0	9	24	1	1	2	.197	.275
Swift, Bill C., S.F.	R	.262	34	80	12	21	22	1	0	0	4	10	1	5	19	0	0	3	.275	.30
Swindell, Greg, Hou.	R	.183	31	60	3	11	12	1	0	0	4	10	0	0	16	0	0	0	.200	.183
Tanana, Frank, NY-N	L	.155	29	58	3	9	12	1	1	0	5	3	0	2	11	0	1	0	.207	.183
Tewksbury, Bob, St.L	R	.203	33	69	4	14	15	1	0	0	5	7	0	4	27	0	0	1	.217	.247
Tomlin, Randy, Pit.	L	.182	18	33	3	6	6	0	0	0	1	2	0	1	4	0	0	1	.182	.206
Torres, Salomon, S.F.	R	.231	8	13	0	3	3	0	0	0	0	3	0	0	4	0	0	1	.231	.231
Trachsel, Steve, ChiN	R	.167	3	6	1	1	1	0	0	0	0	0	0	1	2	0	0	0	.167	.286
Wakefield, Tim, Pit.	R	.163	24	43	3	7	12	2	0	1	3	4	0	0	11	0	0	0	.279	.163
Walk, Bob, Pit.	R	.121	32	58	2	7	8	1	0	0	2	7	0	0	15	0	0	0	.138	.136
Watson, Allen, St.L	L	.231	16	26	0	6	9	3	0	0	2	1	0	1	2	0	0	1	.346	.259
Wendell, Turk, ChiN	B	.143	7	7	0	1	1	0	0	0	0	0	0	0	3	0	0	0	.143	.143
Whitehurst, Wally, S.D.	R	.083	21	24	1	2	2	0	0	0	0	10	0	0	11	0	0	1	.083	.083
Wilson, Trevor, S.F.	L	.138	22	29	2	4	7	0	0	1	2	8	0	1	10	1	0	2	.241	.194
Worrell, Tim, S.D.	R	.032	21	31	1	1	2	1	0	0	1	2	0	0	15	0	0	0	.065	.032

*M*inor league report

▶ **Attendance marks broken** ▶ **Final AAA & AA player stats**

▶ **1993 minor league wrapups** ▶ **Class of '93: Top prospects**

USA SNAPSHOTS®

A look at statistics that shape the sports world

Fulfilling rookie promise

Major league baseball players who played the most and fewest seasons after being named Rookie of the Year:

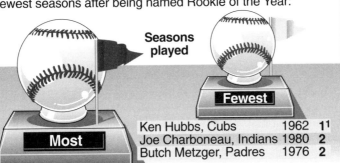

Seasons played

Fewest

Ken Hubbs, Cubs	1962	1[1]
Joe Charboneau, Indians	1980	2
Butch Metzger, Padres	1976	2

Most

Pete Rose, Reds	1963	23
Willie Mays, Giants	1951	22

1— Died in plane crash

Source: USA TODAY research   By Suzy Parker, USA TODAY

Minor leagues 1993: They packed 'em in

In the ninth consecutive year of attendance growth, National Association teams drew 30 million fans—the highest total since 1950; a 10% gain over 1992; and sixth highest total ever.

Overall average of 3,316 per minor league game was an all-time high. The Buffalo Bisons again led the charge with 1,058,620—their sixth consecutive million-plus season. Eight leagues set records: International, Eastern, Southern, California, Carolina, South Atlantic, Northwest, and Appalachian. The IL, buoyed by the addition of Ottawa and Charlotte, set a record for any league with 4.6 million fans. Ottawa broke the league's 47-year-old record with 663,926 fans as baseball returned to the Canadian capital for the first time since 1954. Some 103 individual teams reported increases over the '92 season, including all eight clubs in the Class A Carolina League.

▶*Movers and shakers:* The Rancho Cucamonga Quakes registered a 7.5 on the Richter scale, drawing a league record 331,005 fans. Their $7 million playpen is known as the Epicenter. The void they left in their old home was quickly filled by the San Bernardino Spurs (formerly of Salinas). . . . The Reno franchise moved to Riverside for the '93 season. . . . The Hickory Crawdads drew 283,727 to lead the Class A South Atlantic League after moving up the road from Gastonia, N.C. . . . Daytona Beach (Cubs) returned to the Florida State League after a five-year absence when owner Jordan Kobritz purchased the Baseball City franchise and moved it to the East Coast. . . . Denver's old Triple-A team is now the New Orleans Zephyrs. . . . The Wilmington Blue Rocks, playing less than 25 miles from Veterans Stadium in Philadelphia drew 332,132 fans as baseball returned to Delaware for the first time in 41 years. . . . The Fort Wayne Wizards got a four-minute standing ovation on Opening Night,

then drew 318,506 fans. . . . Other new stadiums opened in Norfolk, Va., and Albany, Ga.

▶*Right at home:* The Orioles' Double-A farm team was forced to play the 1993 season at Memorial Stadium in Baltimore when its stadium in Bowie, Md., was not completed (nor, for that matter, even started) in time. Mike Flanagan, who threw the last major league pitch at Memorial Stadium in 1991, threw out the first ball on Opening Night. It was the first time since 1915 that a minor league team played an entire season in the same city as its parent club.

▶*Nashville network:* For the first time in 21 years, there were two minor league teams in one city. Nashville, Tenn., hosted both the Triple-A Sounds (White Sox) and the Double-A Xpress (Twins). Xpress owner George Shinn was unable to find a home for his team, the former Charlotte franchise that was dislodged when the city got a Triple-A expansion team. Sounds owner Larry Schmittou offered to take on the extra team on a one-year temporary basis. The gamble paid off. Both Nashville clubs made their playoffs and the Sounds drew 438,745 fans while the Xpress drew 178,737.

▶*Independence Day:* 1993 marked the debut of two independent leagues, the Northern League (St. Paul, Duluth and Rochester, Minn.; Sioux City, Iowa; Sioux Falls, S.D., and Thunder Bay, Ontario) and the Frontier League (Portsmouth, Lancaster, Zanesville and Chillicothe, Ohio; Wayne and Parkersburg, W.Va., and Ashland and Paintsville-Pikeville, Ky.). The Northern League drew a short-season record 651,452, but the Frontier League's Wayne and Ashland franchises folded in July, Paintsville-Pikeville manager Roy Cutright and his coaches quit in August, the league office was moved and its president was fired (also in August).

▶**High-water mark:** The Quad City River Bandits in Davenport were most severely hit by the flooding of the Mississippi River, which left O'Donnell Stadium submerged. Damage and lost revenue was estimated at more than $1 million. Meanwhile, the Iowa Cubs of were on a 15-day road trip when water from the Raccoon River covered Sec Taylor Stadium.

▶**Expansion teams:** Double-A Eastern League expansion franchises were awarded to New Haven, Conn., and Portland, Maine. The New Haven Ravens will be affiliated with the Colorado Rockies, while the Portland Sea Dogs will be a Florida Marlins farm club. Both begin play this season.

▶**Feats of note:** Modesto A's catcher **Izzy Molina** hit for the cycle with eight RBI April 24 in a 22-1 rout of Stockton. The Omaha Royals hit four consecutive home runs—by **Karl Rhodes, Terry Shumpert, Russ McGinnis** and **Bob Hamelin**—with two out in the eighth inning against Oklahoma City pitcher **Gerald Alexander** on May 7. They were hit in a span of 13 pitches. After an out was recorded, the 89ers' **Benny Distefano** led off the visitors' ninth with a home run. The Royals won 11-4. The Las Vegas Stars had a club-record eight consecutive hits in the third inning against Calgary in a PCL game May 12. Batters: **Jarvis Brown, Billy Bean, Chris Jelic, Steve Pegues, Mike Simms, Brian Johnson, Kevin Higgins** and **Luis Lopez.** The league record is nine. Despite the onslaught, the Stars lost 13-9. The Cannons got revenge by scoring 52 runs on 75 hits in three games at Las Vegas June 27-29. The Cannons won 23-12, 18-3 and 11-1. Phoenix Firebirds pitcher **Dan Rambo** set a PCL record May 29 with four wild pitches in one inning against Albuquerque. Memphis infielder **Jeff Garber** went 5-for-6 with a Southern League record eight RBI in a 25-5 rout of Nashville on Aug. 1. The Chicks set league records for runs and hits (32) in one game. The Stockton Ports set California League records with 29 hits and 56 at-bats in a 25-7 romp against Rancho Cucamonga, also on Aug. 1.

Savannah Cardinals' reliever **Jamie Cochran** set a minor league record with 46 saves. Four Reading Phillies' pitchers—**Ricky Bottalico, Craig Holman, Greg Brown,** and **Toby Borland**—combined to no-hit New Britain 2-0 in the Eastern League Sept. 4. It was the fourth consecutive EL no-hitter that involved those two teams.

▶**News and notes:** The National Association and the major leagues held separate winter meetings. The minors met in December in Atlanta, but the major league general managers got together in November and the owners, in January. . . . Minor league clubs got a one-year extension of the deadline to upgrade facilities to meet minimum standards set by Major League Baseball. The deadline now is April 1, 1995. . . . The Major League Scouting Bureau, formed in 1975, laid off 23 scouts in January when their contracts expired. The reason: cost-cutting. . . . Some 30 members of the U.S. House of Representatives formed the Congressional Minor League Baseball Caucus, a bi-partisan group founded by Rep. Sherwood Boehlert, R-New York, to look after minor league interests in areas that have teams.

▶**Sad farewells:** Springfield Cardinals' pitcher **Diego Ruiz** was killed and catching prospect **Eddie Williams** was injured in a car crash May 22. Ruiz, 22, died of chest injuries when a car driven by Williams struck a cement pole. Meanwhile, fans in Durham, N.C., said farewell to historical Durham Athletic Park in 1993. The stadium was built in 1939 and gained notoriety in Kevin Costner's hit film, *Bull Durham.* The Class A Carolina League team is now moving into a new $11 million stadium and will open the 1994 season there. To mark the final year at the DAP, three old-timers reunions were staged. Alas, the last scheduled game on Sept. 4—sold out for weeks—was rained out.

—*by Bill Koenig*

Class AAA WRAPUPS

American Association

The Iowa Cubs won their first American Association championship since joining the league in 1969, beating Nashville (White Sox) in the playoffs. Outfielder **Karl Rhodes**, obtained in a trade from Omaha, hit a home run in the 11th inning to win Game Seven, 3-2. Iowa outfielder **Eddie Zambrano** (.303, 32 HR, 115 RBI) was league MVP. Oklahoma City DH **Steve Balboni** won his second consecutive homer crown with 36; Nashville catcher **Matt Merullo** (.332) was batting champ. The Sounds' **Rod Bolton** (10-1) led in ERA (2.88); Iowa's **Bill Brennan** led in strikeouts (143). **Rick Renick** of Nashville was Manager of the Year.

FINAL STANDINGS
Eastern Division

Nashville	80-61	.567	—
Buffalo	70-72	.493	10.5
Indianapolis	66-75	.468	14
Louisville	66-76	.465	14

Western Division

Iowa	84-58	.592	—
New Orleans	79-63	.556	5
Omaha	70-72	.493	14.5
Okla. City	52-90	.366	32

Playoffs
Iowa 4, Nashville 3

Switch-hitter
* Left-handed
(Players in major leagues are listed with last minor league team.)

332

Final AAA Player Stats

American Association

Buffalo Bisons (Pirates) AAA

BATTING	Avg.	AB	R	H	2B	3B	HR	RBI	SB
Aude, Rich, 1B	.375	64	17	24	9	0	4	16	0
Beasley, Tony, 2B	.189	95	9	18	3	0	0	8	1
*Bell, Mike, 1B	.155	97	12	15	4	1	4	13	0
*Bullett, Scott, Of	.287	408	62	117	13	6	1	30	28
Cooper, Gary, 3B	.269	349	66	94	27	2	16	63	2
*Cummings, Midre, Of	.276	232	36	64	12	1	9	21	5
Edge, Tim, C	.000	2	0	0	0	0	0	0	0
Encarnacion, Angelo, C	.333	9	1	3	0	0	0	2	0
*Goff, Jerry, C	.251	362	52	91	27	3	14	69	1
Green, Tom, Of	.346	26	3	9	2	0	0	9	0
*Leiper, Tim, Of	.327	208	21	68	15	5	2	33	1
Marx, Tim, C	.143	14	0	2	1	0	0	0	0
Morman, Russ, 1B	.320	409	79	131	34	2	22	77	0
Munoz, Omer, 2B	.217	129	7	28	4	1	2	16	0
Pennyfeather, William, Of	.249	457	54	114	18	3	14	41	10
#Rohde, Dave, Ss	.244	464	64	113	22	2	11	48	4
#Romero, Mandy, C	.228	136	11	31	6	1	2	14	1
Sandoval, Jose, Ss	.230	209	23	48	7	2	5	21	1
Schreiber, Bruce, 3B	.200	40	0	8	1	0	0	2	0
Shelton, Ben, 1B	.277	173	25	48	8	1	5	22	0
*Tomberlin, Andy, Of	.285	221	41	63	11	6	12	45	3
Wehner, John, 3B	.252	330	61	83	22	2	7	34	17
Wilson, Glenn, Dh	.279	201	32	56	14	1	12	43	0

PITCHING	W	L	ERA	G	SV	IP	H	BB	SO
Backlund, Brett	0	4	10.55	5	0	21.1	30	14	10
*Ballard, Jeff	6	1	2.29	12	0	74.2	79	17	40
*Beatty, Blaine	2	3	5.50	20	1	36.0	51	8	14
Cecena, Jose	0	1	4.91	6	0	7.1	12	8	7
*Dalton, Mike	3	1	4.11	25	2	35.0	37	12	16
Dewey, Mark	2	0	1.23	22	6	29.1	21	5	17
*Hancock, Lee	2	6	4.91	11	0	66.0	73	14	30
Hope, John	2	1	6.33	4	0	21.1	30	2	6
Hunter, Bobby	0	1	9.64	11	0	14.0	18	10	8
Irvine, Daryl	1	3	4.30	37	0	46.0	41	26	19
Johnston, Joel	1	3	7.76	26	1	31.1	30	25	26
McMurtry, Craig	6	4	3.44	30	1	96.2	102	38	63
Menendez, Tony	4	5	2.42	54	24	63.1	50	21	48
Miller, Paul	3	1	4.47	10	0	52.1	57	14	25
*Moeller, Dennis	3	4	4.34	24	0	76.2	85	21	38
*Neagle, Denny	0	0	.00	3	0	3.1	3	2	6
Petkovsek, Mark	3	4	4.33	14	0	70.2	74	16	27
*Robertson, Rich	9	8	4.28	23	0	132.1	141	52	71
*Shouse, Brian	1	0	3.83	48	2	51.2	54	17	25
Smith, Roy	15	11	4.13	28	0	167.2	178	38	87
Toliver, Fred	1	3	3.65	13	1	12.1	13	9	11
*Tomberlin, Andy	0	0	.00	2	0	2.0	0	3	1
White, Rick	0	3	3.54	7	0	28.0	25	8	16
Zimmerman, Mike	3	1	4.08	33	1	46.1	45	28	32

Indianapolis Indians (Reds) AAA

BATTING	Avg.	AB	R	H	2B	3B	HR	RBI	SB
Afenir, Troy, C	.240	254	29	61	14	2	8	35	2
Anderson, Kent, Ss	.238	273	34	65	13	0	3	22	3
Brumfield, Jacob, Of	.325	126	23	41	14	1	4	19	11
Canate, William, Ph	.000	5	0	0	0	0	0	0	0
*Carter, Steve, Of	.264	212	21	56	13	0	3	22	5
Costo, Tim, 1B	.326	362	49	118	30	2	11	57	3
*Dauphin, Phil, Of	.240	75	5	18	4	1	1	4	2
Dorsett, Brian, C	.299	278	38	83	27	0	18	57	2
#Espy, Cecil, Of	.229	83	10	19	3	0	0	7	2
Green, Gary, Ss	.188	218	15	41	7	0	2	14	1
*Greene, Willie, 3B	.267	341	62	91	19	0	22	58	2

BATTING	Avg.	AB	R	H	2B	3B	HR	RBI	SB
*Gregg, Tommy, 1B	.318	198	34	63	12	5	7	30	3
Hernandez, Cesar, Of	.257	272	30	70	12	4	5	22	5
*Hughes, Keith, Of	.286	283	55	81	28	4	13	42	5
#Kessinger, Keith, Ss	.283	120	17	34	9	0	2	15	0
Koelling, Brian, 2B	.222	9	1	2	0	0	0	0	0
Kremblas, Frank, Ss	.243	341	38	83	15	4	8	46	7
Lofton, Rod, 3B	.667	3	0	2	0	0	0	2	0
#Merchant, Mark, Of	.167	6	2	1	1	0	0	0	0
*Morris, Hal, 1B	.462	13	4	6	0	1	1	5	0
Noboa, Junior, 2B	.283	180	27	51	11	1	0	14	0
Scott, Gary, 2B	.211	284	39	60	12	1	3	18	2
#Shines, Razor, 1B	.276	192	24	53	13	0	5	35	1
Tubbs, Greg, Of	.305	334	59	102	21	4	10	45	15
*Varsho, Gary, Of	.289	121	19	35	8	1	3	18	1
Wilson, Dan, C	.262	191	18	50	11	1	1	17	1
#Young, Gerald, Of	.301	103	15	31	10	0	1	6	7

PITCHING	W	L	ERA	G	SV	IP	H	BB	SO
Anderson, Mike	10	6	3.75	23	0	151.0	150	56	111
Ayala, Bobby	0	2	5.67	5	0	27.0	36	12	19
Bennett, Chris	0	0	4.85	3	0	13.0	21	1	10
Culberson, Calvain	1	0	.69	2	0	13.0	9	7	9
*Grott, Matt	7	5	3.59	33	1	100.1	88	40	73
Hill, Milt	3	5	4.08	20	2	53.0	53	17	45
Kennedy, Bo	3	7	4.96	39	1	118.0	135	47	79
Luebbers, Larry	4	7	4.16	15	0	84.1	81	47	51
*Lynch, Dave	9	4	3.21	59	1	84.0	73	48	76
Moore, Brad	0	1	5.86	21	0	43.0	46	22	22
*Newman, Alan	1	3	8.55	8	0	20.0	24	27	15
*Powell, Ross	10	10	4.11	28	0	179.2	159	71	133
Robinson, Scott	2	5	6.42	9	0	47.2	55	24	29
Roper, John	3	5	4.45	12	0	54.2	56	30	42
Ruffin, Johnny	4	5	3.11	32	2	66.2	51	18	75
*Ruskin, Scott	1	5	5.14	49	28	56.0	60	22	41
*Sauveur, Rich	2	0	1.82	5	0	34.2	41	7	21
Service, Scott	4	2	4.45	21	2	30.1	25	17	28
Spradlin, Jerry	3	2	3.49	34	1	56.2	58	12	46
Tracy, Jim	4	9	5.24	27	0	77.1	85	32	36
*Wickander, Kevin	0	0	.00	1	0	3.0	2	1	2

Iowa Cubs (Cubs) AAA

BATTING	Avg.	AB	R	H	2B	3B	HR	RBI	SB
Chance, Tony, Of	.282	294	50	83	23	0	16	46	5
*Franco, Matt, 1B	.291	199	24	58	17	4	5	29	4
Gomez, Rudy, 3B	.150	20	0	3	0	0	0	0	0
*Grayum, Richie, Pr	.143	7	0	1	0	0	0	0	0
Hernandez, Jose, Ss	.250	24	3	6	1	0	0	3	0
*Jennings, Doug, 1B	.294	228	38	67	20	1	7	37	3
*Jensen, John, Of	.177	62	5	11	3	0	2	8	2
*Lewis, Dan, Dh	.197	122	10	24	7	0	3	13	0
Lonigro, Greg, Ss	.254	114	14	29	5	0	3	10	2
Mercado, Orlando, C	.357	28	4	10	2	0	1	5	0
Pedre, George, C	.211	232	27	49	12	1	7	21	2
Ramsey, Fernando, Of	.270	545	76	147	30	7	5	42	13
*Rhodes, Karl, Of	.318	490	112	156	43	3	30	89	16
*Roberson, Kevin, Of	.304	263	48	80	20	1	16	50	3
Shields, Tommy, Ss	.287	314	48	90	16	1	9	48	10
#Smith, Greg, 2B	.282	500	82	141	27	1	9	54	25
Wade, Scott, Of	.170	147	14	25	8	0	3	15	9
#Walbeck, Matt, C	.281	331	31	93	18	2	6	43	1
Worthington, Craig, 3B	.273	469	63	128	23	0	13	66	1
Zambrano, Eddie, Of	.303	469	95	142	29	2	32	115	10

PITCHING	W	L	ERA	G	SV	IP	H	BB	SO
Boskie, Shawn	6	1	4.27	11	0	71.2	70	21	35
Brennan, Bill	10	7	4.42	28	0	179.0	180	64	143
Bullinger, Jim	4	6	3.42	49	20	73.2	64	43	74
*Corbett, Sherm	0	1	3.77	8	0	14.1	11	4	9
Czajkowski, Jim	7	5	3.84	42	0	70.1	64	32	43
*Dickson, Lance	0	1	10.38	2	0	4.1	6	1	3
Dyer, Mike	1	0	4.81	14	0	24.1	18	20	18
Hartsock, Jeff	0	4	6.32	9	0	47.0	68	20	17
*Ilsley, Blaise	12	7	3.94	48	4	134.2	147	32	78
*Johnson, Earnie	1	1	3.21	9	1	14.0	12	4	11
*McElroy, Chuck	0	1	4.60	9	2	15.2	19	9	13

Class AAA WRAPUPS

International League

The Charlotte Knights beat Rochester to win the Governors' Cup (3-2) and led the charge as the Cleveland Indians' clubs posted a .579 record (best in baseball) and put all six farm clubs into the playoffs. Third baseman **Jim Thome** was voted MVP and led the league in batting (.332) and RBI (102). His teammate, **Sam Horn**, hit 38 home runs, most in the minors since 1987. **Mike Quade** (Ottawa) was the IL Manager of the Year. **Kevin McGehee** (Rochester) won the ERA title (2.96), but **Aaron Sele** of Pawtucket was voted Pitcher of the Year, even though he spent half the season in Boston. Richmond's **Mike Birkbeck** and Toledo's **John De Silva** tied for the strikeout lead (136), one more than Charlotte's **Chad Ogea**.

FINAL STANDINGS
Eastern Division

Rochester	74-67	.525	—
Ottawa	73-69	.514	1.5
Scrntn-WB	62-80	.437	12.5
Pawtucket	60-82	.423	14.5
Syracuse	59-82	.418	15

Western Division

Charlotte	86-55	.610	—
Richmond	80-62	.563	6.5
Columbus	78-61	.561	7
Norfolk	70-71	.496	16
Toledo	64-77	.454	22

Playoffs
First round: Charlotte 3, Richmond 1;
Rochester 3, Ottawa 2
Finals: Charlotte 3, Rochester 2

Class AAA WRAPUPS

Pacific Coast League

The Tucson Toros clinched their second PCL crown in three years. This was the first time since the league went to a split season (1979) that both division winners—Tucson in the South and Portland in the North—won both halves. The Toros won the championship series in six games. Tucson second baseman **James Mouton** was MVP. He hit .413 in August as the Toros put together a record 15-game winning streak. Teammates **Jim Lindeman** (.362) and **Mike Brumley** (.353) were 1-2 in the batting race. **J.R. Phillips** of Phoenix led in homers (27); Albuquerque outfielder **Billy Ashley** led in RBI (100). **Pat Mahomes** of Portland was the top pitcher (3.03 ERA); **Scott Sanders** of Las Vegas led in strikeouts (161). Portland's **Scott Ullger** was Manager of the Year.

FINAL STANDINGS

Northern Division

z-Portland	87-56	.608	—
Vancouver	72-68	.514	13.5
Edmonton	72-69	.511	14
Calgary	68-72	.486	17.5
Tacoma	69-74	.483	18

Southern Division

z-Tucson	83-60	.580	—
Albuquerque	71-72	.497	12
Colo Spgs	66-75	.468	16
Phoenix	64-79	.448	19
Las Vegas	58-85	.406	25

z-won both halves

Playoffs

Tucson 4, Portland 2

PITCHING	W	L	ERA	G	SV	IP	H	BB	SO
Slocumb, Heath	1	0	1.50	10	7	12.0	7	8	10
Steenstra, Kennie	1	0	6.75	1	0	6.2	9	4	6
Stevens, Dave	4	0	4.19	24	4	34.1	24	14	29
Swartzbaugh, Dave	4	6	5.30	26	1	86.2	90	44	69
Trachsel, Steve	13	6	3.96	27	0	170.2	170	45	135
*Vosberg, Ed	5	1	3.57	52	3	63.0	67	22	64
Walker, Mike	1	1	2.70	12	0	23.1	22	9	11
Wallace, Derek	0	0	11.25	1	0	4.0	8	1	2
Wendell, Turk	10	8	4.60	25	0	148.2	148	47	110
*Williams, Jimmy	5	3	3.46	17	0	78.0	74	37	49

Louisville Redbirds (Cardinals) AAA

BATTING	Avg.	AB	R	H	2B	3B	HR	RBI	SB
Canseco, Ozzie, Of	.240	154	20	37	6	1	13	33	1
Cromer, Tripp, Ss	.275	309	39	85	8	4	11	33	1
Dozier, D.J., Of	.230	139	24	32	10	1	6	15	0
*Ellis, Paul, C	.200	125	12	25	6	0	0	8	0
Figueroa, Bien, Ss	.239	272	44	65	17	1	0	15	1
*Fulton, Ed, C	.211	147	13	31	5	0	3	18	0
*Jones, Tim, 2B	.289	408	72	118	22	10	5	46	13
Jordan, Brian, Of	.375	144	24	54	13	2	5	35	9
*Lockhart, Keith, 3B	.300	467	66	140	24	3	13	68	3
Lyons, Barry, 1B	.269	401	36	108	19	0	18	65	0
*Mabry, John, Ph	.143	7	0	1	0	0	0	1	0
*Maclin, Lonnie, Of	.277	220	29	61	10	3	4	18	4
*Morris, John, Of	.239	71	13	17	5	0	2	9	1
Pagnozzi, Tom, C	.279	43	5	12	3	0	1	1	0
Pappas, Erik, C	.338	71	19	24	6	1	4	13	0
Patterson, Dave, 1B	.278	180	26	6	1	4	13	0	
.#Pena, Geronimo, 2B	.174	23	4	4	1	0	0	0	1
*Prager, Howard, 1B	.263	209	27	55	17	0	4	28	0
Royer, Stan, 3B	.280	368	46	103	19	0	16	54	2
Savinon, Odalis, Of	.203	59	10	12	1	1	0	2	0
*Snider, Van, Of	.265	423	54	112	29	4	14	56	3
*Thomas, Skeets, Of	.276	377	30	104	15	1	9	40	1
Villanueva, Hector, C	.242	124	13	30	9	0	5	20	0

PITCHING	W	L	ERA	G	SV	IP	H	BB	SO
Anderson, Paul	3	5	4.89	11	0	70.0	74	14	32
Arnsberg, Brad	0	2	5.31	29	0	40.2	47	27	19
Barber, Brian	0	1	4.76	1	0	5.2	4	4	5
Buckels, Gary	4	2	5.42	40	1	88.0	116	25	64
Cimorelli, Frank	2	1	2.93	27	2	43.0	34	25	24
Compres, Fidel	3	5	6.91	21	0	27.1	41	19	18
*Creek, Doug	0	0	3.21	2	0	14.0	10	9	9
*Dixon, Steve	5	7	4.92	57	20	67.2	57	33	61
Fulton, Ed	0	0	.00	2	0	3.0	1	1	3
*Guetterman, Lee	2	1	2.94	25	2	33.2	35	12	20
*Kilgus, Paul	7	1	2.65	9	0	68.0	59	19	54
*Knox, Kerry	1	4	4.50	7	0	44.0	48	10	24
Meier, Kevin	8	6	5.80	27	0	135.0	156	44	98
*Milchin, Mike	3	7	3.95	32	0	111.2	108	43	72
Ozuna, Gab	0	4	2.93	35	4	40.0	32	18	41
Sebra, Bob	9	12	4.90	27	0	145.0	173	52	83
*Urbani, Tom	9	5	2.47	18	1	94.2	86	23	65
*Watson, Allen	5	4	2.91	17	0	120.2	101	31	86
Wiseman, Dennis	7	9	5.06	33	1	112.0	144	23	39

Nashville Sounds (White Sox) AAA

BATTING	Avg.	AB	R	H	2B	3B	HR	RBI	SB
Alvarez, Clemente, C	.207	29	1	6	0	0	0	2	0
Beltre, Esteban, Ss	.292	489	67	143	24	4	8	52	18
#Brady, Doug, 2B	.000	3	0	0	0	0	0	0	0
*Cepicky, Scott, Of	.212	137	22	29	3	1	12	27	0
Coomer, Ron, 3B	.313	211	34	66	19	0	13	51	1
*Coughlin, Kevin, Of	.571	7	0	4	1	0	0	3	0
Cron, Chris, 1B	.257	460	69	118	27	0	22	68	2
Denson, Drew, Dh	.281	513	82	144	36	0	24	103	0
Gilbert, Shawn, 3B	.227	278	28	63	17	2	0	17	6
Hall, Joe, Of	.290	424	66	123	33	5	10	58	10
Huff, Mike, Of	.294	344	65	101	12	6	8	32	18
*Jeter, Shawn, Of	.208	149	14	31	2	2	2	22	6
Komminsk, Brad, Of	.266	383	55	102	18	2	11	49	7

BATTING	Avg.	AB	R	H	2B	3B	HR	RBI	SB
#Martin, Norberto, 2B	.309	580	87	179	21	6	9	74	31
*Merullo, Matt, C	.332	352	50	117	30	1	12	65	0
*Newson, Warren, Of	.341	176	40	60	8	2	4	21	5
#Raines, Tim, Of	.455	11	3	5	1	0	0	2	2
*Tedder, Scott, Of	.288	111	24	32	5	0	3	15	2
Wrona, Rick, C	.212	184	24	39	13	0	3	22	0

PITCHING	W	L	ERA	G	SV	IP	H	BB	SO
*Alvarez, Wilson	0	1	2.84	1	0	6.1	7	2	8
Baldwin, James	5	4	2.61	10	0	69.0	43	36	61
*Barfield, John	3	1	4.11	14	1	35.0	36	11	15
Bere, Jason	5	1	2.37	8	0	49.1	36	25	52
Bolton, Rodney	10	1	2.88	18	1	115.2	108	37	75
Campos, Frank	7	5	3.55	19	0	116.2	104	58	86
Carter, Jeff	2	4	6.99	11	0	37.1	43	17	21
*Cary, Chuck	0	1	9.00	1	0	2.0	4	2	1
*Dabney, Fred	2	5	4.86	51	3	63.0	65	21	44
Drahman, Brian	9	4	2.91	54	20	55.2	59	19	49
Garcia, Ramon	4	1	4.01	7	0	42.2	45	11	25
*Howard, Chris	4	3	3.38	43	3	66.2	55	16	53
Jones, Barry	0	0	2.60	7	2	17.1	16	2	19
Keyser, Brian	9	5	4.66	30	1	121.2	142	27	44
Leach, Terry	0	0	3.18	5	1	5.2	4	0	4
Merigliano, Frank	0	1	6.48	7	0	8.1	7	6	10
Mongiello, Michael	6	4	4.25	39	7	91.0	88	41	73
Ruffcorn, Scott	2	2	2.80	7	0	45.0	30	8	44
Schrenk, Steve	6	8	3.90	21	0	122.1	117	47	78
Schwarz, Jeff	0	0	2.45	7	0	11.0	1	12	8
*Thomas, Larry	4	6	5.99	18	0	100.2	114	32	67

New Orleans Zephyrs (Brewers) AAA

BATTING	Avg.	AB	R	H	2B	3B	HR	RBI	SB
*Barbara, Don, 1B	.294	255	34	75	10	1	4	38	1
Byington, John, 3B	.280	436	58	122	33	2	11	63	3
#Caceres, Edgar, 2B	.317	420	73	133	20	2	5	45	7
Carter, Mike, Of	.276	369	49	102	18	5	3	31	20
Cirillo, Jeff, 3B	.293	215	31	63	13	2	3	32	2
Davis, Mark, Of	.174	23	4	4	1	1	1	2	0
#Diaz, Alex, Of	.291	55	8	16	2	0	0	5	7
#Diggs, Tony, Of	.259	27	4	7	3	0	0	1	4
Finn, John, 2B	.281	335	47	94	13	2	1	37	27
Fitzgerald, Mike, C	.259	297	35	77	21	0	7	35	3
#Housie, Wayne, Of	.274	113	22	31	6	1	0	7	6
Kappesser, Bob, C	.091	11	0	1	1	0	0	2	0
Kmak, Joe, C	.303	76	9	23	3	2	1	13	1
*Kremers, Jimmy, C	.265	155	29	41	10	0	9	26	0
*Lampkin, Tom, C	.325	80	18	26	5	0	2	10	5
*Lukachyk, Rob, Of	.167	24	5	4	1	0	2	6	0
Mieske, Matt, Of	.260	219	36	57	14	2	8	22	6
*Nilsson, Dave, C	.344	61	9	21	6	0	1	9	0
*O'Leary, Troy, Of	.273	388	65	106	32	1	7	59	6
Riesgo, Nikco, Of	.291	79	9	23	5	3	1	12	0
*Sheets, Larry, Dh	.280	457	60	128	28	1	18	98	3
Suero, William, 2B	.226	124	14	28	4	1	1	13	8
#Valentin, Jose, Ss	.247	389	56	96	22	5	9	53	9
Williams, Eddie, 3B	.259	27	2	7	0	1	1	4	0
#Yacopino, Ed, Of	.203	69	7	14	3	1	0	0	0

PITCHING	W	L	ERA	G	SV	IP	H	BB	SO
Austin, Jim	1	2	5.06	8	0	16.0	17	7	7
Cole, Victor	1	5	8.91	12	0	32.1	44	31	19
Farmer, Howard	4	3	5.73	20	0	75.1	93	24	55
*Farrell, Mike	9	9	4.86	26	0	152.0	164	32	63
*Higuera, Ted	0	1	9.00	3	0	8.0	11	7	7
Hunter, Jim	5	2	4.19	39	1	68.2	82	25	35
Ignasiak, Mike	6	0	1.09	35	9	57.2	26	20	61
Johnson, Dane	0	0	2.40	13	6	15.0	11	4	10
Kiefer, Mark	3	2	5.08	5	0	28.1	28	17	23
*Kiser, Garland	5	4	5.40	50	1	66.2	69	24	42
Maldonado, Carlos	1	0	.47	12	7	19.1	13	7	14
Maysey, Matt	0	3	4.13	29	2	52.1	48	14	40
McAndrew, Jamie	11	6	3.94	27	0	166.2	172	45	97
*Miranda, Angel	0	1	3.44	9	0	18.1	11	10	24
*Nolte, Eric	0	0	6.35	7	0	5.2	7	2	3
*Novoa, Rafael	10	5	3.42	20	0	113.0	105	38	74

CLASS AA WRAPUPS

Texas League

The Jackson Generals took charge in the Texas League. They raced to a 41-27 record in the first half, survived the loss of three starting pitchers to promotions and beat Shreveport and El Paso in the playoffs. Pitcher **Kevin Gallaher**, a late-season addition from Single-A, won two playoff games to help Jackson win its first title since 1985. The General's **Roberto Petagine** was MVP, only the second player from the Eastern Division (first since 1972) to win the batting title (.334). Tulsa designated hitter **Trey McCoy** led the league in home runs (29) and RBI (95). San Antonio's **Ben VanRyn** (14-4, 2.21) was Pitcher of the Year, but Tulsa's **Rick Helling** led with 188 strikeouts. **Jim Dougherty** of Jackson set a league record with 36 saves. The Generals' **Sal Butera** was Manager of the Year.

FINAL STANDINGS:
Eastern Division

x-Jackson	73-62	.541	—
Arkansas	67-69	.493	6.5
Tulsa	66-69	.489	7
y-Shreveport	66-70	.485	7.5

Western Division

z-El Paso	76-59	.563	—
w-Wichita	68-68	.500	8.5
Midland	67-68	.496	9
Sn Antnio	58-76	.433	17.5

x-Won first half; y-Won second half; z-Won both halves; w-Wild card

Playoffs

First round: Jackson 3, Shreveport 1; El Paso 3, Wichita 1
Finals: Jackson 3, El Paso 0

Class AA
WRAPUPS

Southern League

After finishing the first half one game under .500, the Birmingham Barons went 43-28, won the second half, then beat Nashville and Knoxville to win the playoffs and league championship. Knoxville's **Carlos Delgado** was MVP, hitting .303 and leading the league in home runs (25) and RBI (102). **Jim Bowie** of Huntsville won the batting title (.333); Birmingham's **James Baldwin** led in ERA (2.25) while his teammate **Scott Ruffcorn** led in strikeouts (141). Greenville's **Mike Hostetler** tossed a no-hitter against Knoxville in the playoffs. **Terry Francona** of Birmingham was Manager of the Year.

FINAL STANDINGS
Eastern Division

x-Greenville	75-67	.528	—
Carolina	74-67	.525	0.5
Orlando	71-70	.504	3.5
y-Knoxville	71-71	.500	4
Jacksonville	59-81	.421	15

Western Division

y-Birmingham	78-64	.549	—
Chattanooga	72-69	.511	5.5
x-Nashville	72-70	.507	6
Huntsville	71-70	.504	6.5
Memphis	63-77	.450	14

x-Won first half; y-Won second half

Playoffs
First round: Birmingham 3, Nashville 0; Knoxville 3, Greenville 2
Finals: Birmingham 3, Knoxville 1

PITCHING	W	L	ERA	G	SV	IP	H	BB	SO
Rightnowar, Ron	0	0	10.38	4	0	8.2	19	2	8
Sparks, Steve	9	13	3.84	29	0	180.1	174	80	104
*Tabaka, Jeff	6	6	3.24	53	1	58.1	50	30	63
Taylor, Scott	5	1	2.31	12	0	62.1	48	21	47
Wishnevski, Rob	5	3	4.09	52	10	70.1	68	17	72

Oklahoma City 89ers (Rangers) AAA

BATTING	Avg.	AB	R	H	2B	3B	HR	RBI	SB
Balboni, Steve, Dh	.244	471	67	115	22	0	36	108	0
Berger, Mike, Dh	.286	14	2	4	0	0	0	1	0
#Dascenzo, Doug, Of	.248	157	21	39	8	2	1	13	6
Davis, Doug, C	.207	241	34	50	10	2	4	21	2
Diaz, Mario, 3B	.328	177	24	58	12	2	3	20	3
*Distefano, Benny, Of	.222	414	51	92	17	5	6	34	2
*Ducey, Rob, Of	.303	389	68	118	17	10	17	56	17
*Greer, Rusty, Of	.222	27	6	6	2	0	1	4	0
Hanlon, Larry, Ss	.223	376	45	84	16	0	4	37	5
Harris, Donald, Of	.253	367	48	93	13	9	6	40	4
*Huson, Jeff, 3B	.289	76	11	22	5	0	1	10	1
Jackson, Chuck, 3B	.316	316	51	100	24	4	6	43	0
Kennedy, Darryl, C	.063	16	2	1	0	0	0	0	0
*Magallanes, Ever, 2B	.310	116	16	36	6	1	0	18	0
McCoy, Trey, Dh	.250	28	6	7	1	1	3	11	0
#Miller, Keith, 1B	.285	316	37	90	19	0	5	45	2
*Morris, Rod, Of	.212	33	4	7	2	0	0	1	0
Morrow, Timmie, Of	.259	27	2	7	2	0	0	5	0
*Peltier, Dan, 1B	.321	187	28	60	15	4	5	33	2
#Petralli, Geno, Dh	.200	20	2	4	1	0	1	1	0
Sable, Luke, 3B	.207	295	42	61	11	0	0	17	3
Shave, Jon, 2B	.263	399	58	105	17	3	4	41	4
Stephens, Ray, C	.228	333	29	76	15	2	7	49	0

PITCHING	W	L	ERA	G	SV	IP	H	BB	SO
Acker, Jim	0	1	8.31	6	0	4.1	7	4	2
Alberro, Jose	0	0	6.88	12	0	17.0	25	11	14
Alexander, Gerald	1	2	9.25	10	0	24.1	40	9	13
*Anderson, Allan	2	8	5.32	19	1	115.0	137	37	52
*Bohanon, Brian	0	1	6.43	2	0	7.0	7	3	7
Bronkey, Jeff	2	2	2.65	29	14	37.1	29	7	19
Brown, Rob	5	8	6.09	30	1	99.0	134	41	60
*Burrows, Terry	7	15	6.39	27	0	138.0	171	76	74
Dreyer, Steve	4	6	3.03	16	0	107.0	108	31	59
Eiland, Dave	3	1	4.29	7	0	35.2	39	9	15
Fireovid, Steve	1	1	7.59	7	0	21.1	35	4	14
Helling, Ricky	1	1	1.64	2	0	11.0	5	3	17
*Hurst, James	4	6	4.53	16	0	91.1	106	29	60
*Lee, Mark	5	3	4.34	52	4	101.2	112	43	65
Lefferts, Craig	0	1	7.50	1	0	6.0	9	2	1
Leon, Danilo	2	2	5.52	13	0	31.0	28	26	33
Manuel, Barry	2	2	7.99	21	2	23.2	29	16	19
Nen, Robb	0	2	6.67	6	0	28.1	45	18	12
Oliveras, Francisco	4	8	5.68	44	2	123.2	146	52	77
Pavlik, Roger	3	2	1.70	6	0	37.0	26	14	32
Perez, David	1	0	12.27	2	0	7.1	8	4	3
Reed, Rick	12	7	3.32	24	0	162.1	159	16	79
Sable, Luke	0	0	.00	2	0	3.0	0	2	1
Sadecki, Steve	0	3	7.08	12	0	20.1	22	15	13
Schooler, Mike	1	3	5.91	28	5	45.2	59	11	31
*Shaw, Cedric	2	6	7.91	28	0	52.1	78	36	28
*Smith, Dan	1	2	4.70	3	0	15.1	16	5	12
Whiteside, Matt	2	1	5.56	8	1	11.1	17	8	10

Omaha Royals (Royals) AAA

BATTING	Avg.	AB	R	H	2B	3B	HR	RBI	SB
Abner, Shawn, Of	.248	133	14	33	6	2	2	16	2
Diaz, Kiki, Ss	.273	154	21	42	5	2	0	14	0
*Hamelin, Bob, 1B	.259	479	77	124	19	3	29	84	8
Hiatt, Phil, 3B	.235	51	8	12	2	0	3	10	0
#Howard, Dave, Ss	.255	157	15	40	8	2	0	18	3
*Kingery, Mike, Of	.263	399	61	105	19	5	10	41	9
Knapp, Mike, C	.290	200	22	58	7	0	2	19	2
*Koslofski, Kevin, Of	.276	395	58	109	22	5	7	45	15
*Long, Kevin, Of	.255	51	7	13	2	0	0	4	3

BATTING	Avg.	AB	R	H	2B	3B	HR	RBI	SB
McGinnis, Russ, 3B	.291	275	53	80	20	2	16	54	1
Miller, Keith, 3B	.292	24	2	7	1	1	0	2	1
#Mota, Jose, Ss	.282	330	46	93	11	2	3	35	27
Ortiz, Javier, Of	.250	8	0	2	0	0	0	2	0
Pulliam, Harvey, Of	.264	208	28	55	10	0	5	26	1
Rohrmeier, Dan, Dh	.248	432	51	107	23	3	17	70	2
Rossy, Rico, Ss	.298	131	25	39	10	1	5	21	3
Santovenia, Nelson, C	.237	274	33	65	13	0	11	42	0
Shumpert, Terry, 2B	.300	413	70	124	29	1	14	59	36
*Stephenson, Phil, Of	.306	72	12	22	7	1	4	8	0
Vindivich, Paul, Ph	.000	2	0	0	0	0	0	0	0
Wilson, Craig, 3B	.278	234	26	65	13	1	3	28	7

PITCHING	W	L	ERA	G	SV	IP	H	BB	SO
Ahern, Brian	1	2	5.68	6	0	19.0	18	13	16
Boddicker, Mike	0	2	4.60	3	0	15.2	18	4	12
Brown, Keith	13	8	4.84	26	0	148.2	166	36	98
*Burgos, Enrique	2	4	3.16	48	9	62.2	36	37	91
*Campbell, Jim	3	5	5.04	27	0	55.1	72	17	33
Clark, Dera	4	4	4.37	51	5	82.1	86	30	53
Curry, Steve	6	7	4.88	33	0	145.2	141	56	91
*DiPino, Frank	1	2	2.78	15	1	22.2	21	4	9
Gardner, Mark	4	2	2.79	8	0	48.1	34	19	41
*Haney, Chris	6	1	2.27	8	0	47.2	43	14	32
Knapp, Mike	0	0	13.50	1	0	2.0	6	0	0
*Magnante, Mike	2	6	3.67	33	2	105.1	97	29	74
Meacham, Rusty	0	0	4.82	7	0	9.1	10	1	10
*Pierce, Eddie	0	2	5.45	12	0	34.2	40	13	20
*Rasmussen, Dennis	7	8	5.03	17	0	105.2	124	27	59
Roesler, Mike	1	1	6.16	4	0	19.0	21	10	6
Sampen, Bill	1	2	3.41	33	8	37.0	37	13	34
Sanchez, Alex	2	8	8.12	16	0	51.0	62	28	31
Shifflett, Steve	3	3	4.98	43	5	56.0	78	15	31
Stieb, Dave	3	4	6.09	10	0	54.2	71	14	21

International League

Charlotte Knights (Indians) AAA

BATTING	Avg.	AB	R	H	2B	3B	HR	RBI	SB
*Allred, Beau, Of	.245	347	59	85	13	3	20	61	4
Alomar, Sandy, Dh	.364	44	8	16	5	0	1	8	0
*Canale, George, 1B	.216	208	32	45	8	0	6	27	1
Cockrell, Alan, Of	.276	275	31	76	12	2	8	39	0
Davidson, Mark, Of	.281	263	39	74	12	2	9	36	1
*Horn, Sam, Dh	.269	402	62	108	17	1	38	96	1
*Kirby, Wayne, Of	.289	76	10	22	6	2	3	7	4
Kunkel, Jeff, 1B	.281	430	65	121	34	3	11	46	12
*Levis, Jesse, C	.248	129	10	32	6	1	2	20	0
Lewis, Mark, Ss	.284	507	93	144	30	4	17	67	9
Lopez, Luis, 1B	.314	242	36	76	15	0	12	37	0
Martinez, Carlos, 1B	.367	79	17	29	7	1	3	12	2
Marzano, John, C	.111	9	0	1	0	0	0	0	0
Mercado, Orlando, C	.143	21	0	3	0	0	0	0	0
Mota, Carlos, C	.200	25	4	5	1	0	0	1	1
Nixon, Donell, Pr	.333	24	8	8	0	0	0	1	3
Ramirez, Manny, Of	.317	145	38	46	12	0	14	36	1
*Ramos, Ken, Of	.292	480	77	140	16	11	3	41	12
Schaefer, Jeff, 2B	.279	448	53	125	20	3	7	43	5
Stinnett, Kelly, C	.274	288	42	79	10	3	6	33	0
*Thome, Jim, 3B	.332	410	85	136	21	4	25	102	1

PITCHING	W	L	ERA	G	Sv	IP	H	BB	SO
Abbott, Paul	0	1	6.63	4	0	19.0	25	7	12
*Anderson, Allan	0	0	9.64	7	0	14.0	30	4	5
August, Don	3	1	5.48	14	0	44.1	57	10	24
Byrd, Paul	7	4	3.89	14	0	81.0	80	30	54
*Charland, Colin	1	0	6.75	6	0	14.2	20	5	16
Christopher, Mike	3	6	3.22	50	22	50.1	51	6	36
Clark, Mark	1	0	2.08	2	0	13.0	9	2	12
*Cook, Dennis	3	2	5.06	12	0	42.2	46	6	40
*Curtis, Mike	2	1	5.23	7	0	10.1	10	3	10

Class AA WRAPUPS

Eastern League

The Harrisburg Senators won 94 games, leading the league by 19. Down two games to none in the play-offs, they roared back to win three consecutive games in Canton-Akron and claim the title. The league had two of the best prospects in baseball: **Manny Ramirez** (.340) of Canton won the batting title, and Harrisburg's **Cliff Floyd** led in homers (26) and RBI (101) and was MVP. Both spent most of August in Triple-A. Harrisburg's **Glenn Murray** also hit 26 home runs. London's **Shannon Penn** nosed out Binghamton's **Quilvio Veras** 53-52 for the stolen base crown. Binghamton's **Denny Harriger** had a 2.95 ERA, while New Britain's **Tim Vanegmond** led with 163 strikeouts. **Jim Tracy** of Harrisburg was Manager of the Year.

FINAL STANDINGS

Harrisburg	94-44	.681	—
Canton-Akron	75-63	.543	19
Bowie	72-68	.514	23
Albany	70-68	.507	24
Binghamton	68-72	.486	27
London	63-75	.457	31
Reading	62-78	.443	33
New Britain	52-88	.371	43

Playoffs

First round: Harrisburg 3, Albany 1
Canton-Akron 3, Bowie 1
Finals: Harrisbrg 3, Canton-Akron 2

Switch-hitter
* Left-handed
(Players in major leagues are listed with last minor league team.)

Class A WRAPUPS

California League

The Florida Marlins' role in the expansion draft didn't create much of a stir in Adelanto, Calif., but soon afterward, an agreement was signed with the High Desert Mavericks—and players such as **Kerwin Moore**, **Jesus Tavarez** and **Robert Person** helped the Mavs win their second California League title in three years. Mav **Tim Clark** (.363-17-126) was MVP, leading the league in batting and RBI. He also topped the minor leagues with 185 hits. Clark and teammates **John Toale** (125) and **Bryn Kosco** (121) finished 1-2-3 in the minors in RBI. Moore had 71 steals. **Arquimedez Pozo** (Riverside) had 44 doubles. **Sid Roberson** (12-8, 2.60) of Stockton was Pitcher of the Year, breaking San Jose's six-year stranglehold on the award. However, the Giants' **Bill Vanlandingham** led in strikeouts (171).

FINAL STANDINGS

Northern Division

y-Stockton	79-57	.581	—
San Jose	79-57	.581	—
x-Modesto	72-64	.529	7
Central Valley	61-75	.449	18
Bakersfield	42-94	.309	37

Southern Division

z-Hi Dsert	85-52	.620	—
Riverside	76-61	.555	9
Rcho Cuca	64-72	.471	20.5
Sn Brndno	62-74	.456	22.5
Palm Springs	61-75	.449	23.5

x-Won first half; y-Won second half; z-Won both halves

Playoffs

First round: High Desert 3, Riverside, 1; Modesto 3, Stockton, 1
Finals: High Desert 3, Modesto 2

PITCHING	W	L	ERA	G	SV	IP	H	BB	SO
DiPoto, Jerry	6	3	1.93	34	12	46.2	34	13	44
Eiland, Dave	1	3	5.30	8	0	35.2	42	12	13
Grimsley, Jason	6	6	3.39	28	0	135.1	138	49	102
Lopez, Albie	1	0	2.25	3	0	12.0	8	2	7
McCarthy, Tom	6	5	4.11	45	2	105.0	104	26	61
Milacki, Bob	4	3	3.39	21	4	71.2	59	19	46
*Mutis, Jeff	6	0	2.62	12	0	75.2	64	25	59
Ogea, Chad	13	8	3.81	29	0	181.2	169	54	135
Robinson, Nap	4	6	5.81	20	0	52.2	62	26	43
Scudder, Scott	7	7	5.03	23	0	136.0	148	52	64
Slocumb, Heath	3	2	3.56	23	1	30.1	25	11	25
Solano, Julio	0	0	7.50	3	0	6.0	7	3	5
*Wells, Terry	0	0	4.26	6	0	6.1	9	6	5
Wertz, Bill	7	2	1.95	28	0	50.2	42	14	47
*Young, Cliff	3	1	2.15	5	0	37.2	30	2	21

Columbus Clippers (Yankees) AAA

BATTING	Avg.	AB	R	H	2B	3B	HR	RBI	SB
*Carpenter, Bubba, Of	.266	199	29	53	9	0	5	17	2
Davis, Russ, 3B	.255	424	63	108	24	1	26	83	1
#Dejardin, Bobby, 2B	.275	360	45	99	17	7	5	37	10
*Gedman, Rich, C	.262	275	30	72	15	0	12	35	0
Hernandez, Kiki, C	.241	54	8	13	4	0	1	8	0
Humphreys, Mike, Of	.288	330	59	95	16	2	6	42	18
Knoblauh, Jay, Of	.187	171	23	32	13	0	4	21	1
Livesey, Jeff, C	.247	89	9	22	5	0	2	8	0
*Maas, Kevin, 1B	.279	104	14	29	6	0	4	18	0
Masse, Billy, Of	.316	402	81	127	35	3	19	91	17
Meulens, Hensley, Of	.204	279	39	57	14	0	14	45	6
Ramos, John, Dh	.259	158	17	41	7	0	1	18	1
#Rodriguez, Carlos, Ss	.253	154	25	39	9	1	1	11	2
*Sanchez, Gordon, C	.173	75	12	13	2	2	0	6	0
Silvestri, Dave, Ss	.269	428	76	115	26	4	20	65	6
Sparks, Don, 1B	.284	475	63	135	33	7	11	72	0
Stankiewicz, Andy, 2B	.242	331	45	80	12	5	0	32	12
*Viera, John, Of	.500	6	2	3	1	0	0	1	0
Williams, Gerald, Of	.283	336	53	95	19	6	8	38	29

PITCHING	W	L	ERA	G	SV	IP	H	BB	SO
Batchelor, Richard	1	1	2.76	15	6	16.1	14	8	17
Clayton, Royal	7	6	3.54	47	8	117.0	119	31	66
Cook, Andy	6	7	6.54	21	0	118.1	149	49	47
Dejardin, Bobby	0	0	.00	3	0	5.0	3	0	1
Delarosa, Francisco	1	1	6.45	31	1	44.2	45	31	31
*Gibson, Paul	2	1	.64	17	8	28.0	14	6	36
Gogolewski, Doug	5	3	4.38	28	3	51.1	63	14	32
Greer, Ken	9	4	4.42	46	6	79.1	78	36	50
*Hines, Rich	2	5	4.02	43	4	56.0	50	34	40
*Hitchcock, Sterling	3	5	4.81	16	0	76.2	80	28	85
*Howe, Steve	0	1	10.13	2	0	2.2	6	1	1
Hutton, Mark	10	4	3.18	21	0	133.0	98	53	112
Jean, Domingo	2	2	2.82	7	0	44.2	40	13	39
*Johnson, Jeff	7	6	3.45	19	0	114.2	125	47	59
Kamieniecki, Scott	1	0	1.50	1	0	6.0	5	0	4
Militello, Sam	1	3	5.73	7	0	33.0	36	20	39
Munoz, Roberto	3	1	1.44	22	10	31.1	24	8	16
*Ojala, Kirt	8	9	5.50	31	0	126.0	145	71	83
Popplewell, Tom	0	0	4.50	1	0	2.0	2	1	2
*Quirico, Rafael	2	0	7.36	5	0	11.0	12	7	16
*Seiler, Keith	0	0	13.50	1	0	2.0	2	2	1
Stanford, Don	5	3	5.04	36	0	103.2	119	56	44
Taylor, Wade	3	1	4.45	7	0	30.1	31	11	16
Witt, Mike	1	0	1.98	3	0	13.2	11	5	11

Norfolk Tides (Mets) AAA

BATTING	Avg.	AB	R	H	2B	3B	HR	RBI	SB
#Allison, Tom, 2B	.235	34	9	8	0	0	0	3	0
Baez, Kevin, Ss	.258	209	23	54	11	1	2	21	0
Bilardello, Dann, C	.241	145	13	35	6	1	3	15	1
*Bullock, Eric, Of	.254	437	65	111	26	8	4	48	45
*Burnitz, Jeromy, Of	.227	255	33	58	15	3	8	44	10
Dellicarri, Joe, Ss	.077	13	0	1	0	0	0	1	1
Fordyce, Brook, C	.259	409	33	106	21	2	2	41	2

BATTING	Avg.	AB	R	H	2B	3B	HR	RBI	SB
#Housie, Wayne, Of	.209	67	5	14	0	0	1	5	7
*Howard, Tim, Of	.264	197	18	52	7	2	3	16	2
Hunter, Bert, Of	.170	53	7	9	2	0	0	1	2
*Landrum, Ced, Of	.291	275	39	80	13	5	5	29	16
Martinez, Luis, Ss	.248	202	18	50	3	1	4	22	0
#Navarro, Tito, Dh	.282	273	35	77	11	1	0	16	19
*Robinson, Dwight, 3B	.143	7	0	1	0	0	0	0	0
*Sandy, Tim, Of	.250	16	1	4	1	0	0	1	0
Saunders, Doug, 2B	.247	356	37	88	12	6	2	24	6
Springer, Steve, 3B	.267	484	52	129	22	4	13	69	5
Thompson, Ryan, Of	.259	224	39	58	11	2	12	34	6
*Twardoski, Mike, 1B	.281	427	66	120	15	2	9	38	9
*Vina, Fernando, Ss	.230	287	24	66	6	4	4	27	16
Wade, Scott, Of	.190	79	10	15	3	1	6	13	0
*Winningham, Herm, Of	.254	338	46	86	10	4	7	33	15

PITCHING	W	L	ERA	G	SV	IP	H	BB	SO
Bilardello, Dann	0	0	.00	2	0	2.0	0	1	0
Filer, Tom	2	10	3.79	22	0	123.1	132	34	65
Gozzo, Mauro	8	11	3.45	28	0	190.1	208	49	97
*Gunderson, Eric	3	2	3.71	6	0	34.0	41	9	26
*Hillman, Eric	6	2	2.21	10	0	61.0	52	12	27
Jones, Bobby	12	10	3.63	24	0	166.0	149	32	126
*Kaiser, Jeff	1	1	5.64	21	9	22.1	23	6	23
*Langbehn, Greg	2	2	5.43	49	2	69.2	76	34	58
Lazorko, Jack	0	0	3.38	2	0	2.2	4	1	2
Manzanillo, Josias	1	5	3.11	14	0	84.0	82	25	79
*Marshall, Randy	0	2	19.64	4	0	7.1	19	4	3
Plummer, Dale	7	3	5.16	47	4	75.0	93	26	47
*Smith, Ottis	0	2	6.38	5	0	18.1	22	10	11
Telgheder, Dave	7	3	2.95	13	1	76.1	81	19	52
Vann, Brandy	4	4	3.22	53	11	64.1	53	33	52
Wegmann, Tom	5	3	3.23	44	2	86.1	68	34	99
Weston, Mickey	10	9	4.24	21	0	127.1	149	18	41
Young, Anthony	1	1	1.13	3	0	16.0	14	5	8

Ottawa Lynx (Expos) AAA

BATTING	Avg.	AB	R	H	2B	3B	HR	RBI	SB
Barker, Tim, Ss	.228	167	25	38	5	1	2	14	5
#Bolick, Frank, 3B	.125	8	0	1	0	0	0	0	0
Bryant, Scott, Of	.283	364	48	103	19	1	12	65	1
*Castaldo, Vince, 3B	.241	241	22	58	9	1	2	45	0
Cianfrocco, Archi, Of	.298	188	21	56	14	2	4	27	4
Colbrunn, Greg, 1B	.273	22	4	6	1	0	0	8	1
*Floyd, Cliff, 1B	.240	125	12	30	2	2	2	18	2
Garner, Kevin, Dh	.273	99	15	27	9	0	7	28	0
Haney, Todd, 2B	.291	506	69	147	30	4	3	46	11
Hansen, Terrel, Of	.230	352	45	81	19	0	10	39	1
*Hirtensteiner, Rick, Of	.214	14	1	3	0	0	0	0	1
Hymel, Gary, C	.000	3	0	0	0	0	0	0	0
*Kremers, Jimmy, C	.200	15	1	3	0	0	1	2	0
Laker, Tim, C	.230	204	26	47	10	0	4	23	3
*Mack, Quinn, Of	.095	21	1	2	0	0	0	0	0
McIntosh, Tim, Of	.292	106	15	31	7	1	6	21	1
Montoyo, Charlie, 3B	.279	319	43	89	18	2	1	43	0
*Pride, Curtis, Of	.302	262	55	79	11	4	6	22	29
#Santangelo, F.P., Of	.274	453	86	124	21	2	4	45	18
*Siddall, Joe, C	.213	136	14	29	6	0	1	16	2
Spehr, Tim, C	.199	141	15	28	6	1	4	13	2
Stairs, Matt, Of	.280	125	18	35	4	2	3	20	4
Vargas, Hector, 3B	.183	93	10	17	3	1	0	6	3
White, Derrick, 1B	.281	249	32	70	15	1	4	29	10
White, Rondell, Of	.380	150	28	57	8	2	7	32	10
*Wood, Ted, Of	.255	231	39	59	11	4	1	21	12

PITCHING	W	L	ERA	G	SV	IP	H	BB	SO
Alvarez, Tavo	7	10	4.22	25	0	140.2	163	55	77
*Boucher, Denis	6	0	2.72	11	0	43.0	36	11	22
Brantley, Cliff	2	8	6.50	13	0	54.0	81	37	37
Brito, Mario	2	0	1.32	23	2	34.0	25	17	29
*Eischen, Joey	2	2	3.54	6	0	40.2	34	15	29
Farmer, Howard	0	1	11.25	2	0	4.0	7	0	1
*Fortugno, Tim	2	1	3.60	28	1	40.0	28	31	42
*Henry, Butch	3	1	3.73	5	0	31.1	34	1	25
Heredia, Gil	8	4	2.98	16	0	102.2	97	26	66

Class A WRAPUPS

Carolina League

The Winston-Salem Spirits won their first league title since 1986. Spirits' pitchers lowered their ERA from a regular-season 4.27 to 2.61 in the playoffs as they beat Kinston and Wilmington. Winston-Salem DH **Bubba Smith** (.301-27-81) became the first player in the league to win a second MVP award. Teammate **Chad Mottola** led the league with 91 RBI, while **Felix Colon** (.320) of Lynchburg won the batting title. **Julian Tavarez** (11-5, 2.42) was Pitcher of the Year, but teammate **Jason Fronio** (2.41) had the lowest ERA. **Joel Bennett** (Lynchburg) led the entire minors with 221 strikeouts. **Pete Mackanin** of Frederick and **Dave Keller** of Kinston were voted co-Managers of the Year, the second tie in league history.

FINAL STANDINGS
Northern Division

y-Frederick	78-62	.557	—
x-Wilmington	74-65	.532	3.5
Prnc Willm	67-73	.479	11
Lynchburg	65-74	.468	12.5

Southern Division

x-Kinston	71-67	.514	—
y-Wstn-Slm	72-68	.514	—
Durham	69-69	.500	2
Salem	61-79	.439	11

x-Won first half; y-Won second half.

Playoffs
First round: Wilmington 2, Frederick 0;
Winston-Salem 2, Kinston 1
Finals: Winston-Salem 3, Wilmington 1

Class A WRAPUPS

Midwest League

On the same day that Notre Dame upset Michigan, South Bend beat Clinton for the league championship. The Sox had a couple of stars in **Carmine Cappuccio** (.305) and **Essex Burton** (74 steals), but the MVP was **Joe Biasucci** of Springfield, who led the league in home runs (26) and was second in RBI (35). Waterloo's **Homer Bush** won the batting title (.322); **Charles Johnson** of Kane County led with 94 RBI; Fort Wayne's **LaTroy Hawkins** was 15-5 and led in ERA (2.06) and strikeouts (179); **Kirk Bullinger** of Springfield had 33 saves. **Johnny Damon** of Rockford was voted top prospect. Veteran Clinton skipper **Jack Mull**, who won his 1,000th game in '93, was Manager of the Year.

FINAL STANDINGS

Northern Division

x-Rockford	78-54	.591	—
Madison	77-58	.570	2.5
y-So Bend	77-59	.566	3
Kane County	75-62	.547	5.5
Ft Wayne	68-67	.504	11.5
Appleton	62-73	.459	17.5
Beloit	60-74	.448	19

Southern Division

y-Clinton	80-54	.597	—
x-Springfield	78-58	.574	3
Burlington	64-71	.474	16
Quad City	56-74	.431	22
Peoria	59-79	.428	23
Waterloo	54-79	.406	25
Cedr Rpds	54-79	.403	26

x-Won first half; y-Won second half

Playoffs

First round: South Bend 2, Rockford 0; Clinton 2, Springfield 0
Finals: South Bend 3, Clinton 1

PITCHING	W	L	ERA	G	SV	IP	H	BB	SO
Hill, Ken	0	0	.00	1	0	4.0	1	1	0
Hurst, Jonathan	1	5	6.63	8	0	36.2	44	17	28
Jones, Jimmy	1	0	1.20	3	0	15.0	10	5	12
Mathile, Mike	9	9	4.17	31	1	140.1	147	41	56
*Nabholz, Chris	1	1	4.39	5	0	26.2	24	7	20
*Perez, Yorkis	0	1	3.60	20	0	20.0	14	7	17
Picota, Len	0	1	7.36	8	5	7.1	12	5	3
Risley, Bill	2	4	2.69	41	1	63.2	51	34	74
*Rosario, Dave	1	1	3.58	22	0	27.2	22	21	28
*Rueter, Kirk	4	2	2.70	7	0	43.1	46	3	27
Shaw, Jeff	0	0	.00	2	0	4.0	5	2	1
*Simons, Doug	7	7	4.75	34	0	115.2	134	16	75
Valdez, Sergio	5	3	3.12	30	1	83.2	77	22	53
Walton, Bruce	4	4	1.05	40	16	42.2	32	8	40
*White, Gabe	2	1	3.12	6	0	40.1	38	6	28
Young, Pete	4	5	3.72	48	1	72.2	63	33	46

Pawtucket Red Sox (Red Sox) AAA

BATTING	Avg.	AB	R	H	2B	3B	HR	RBI	SB
*Blosser, Greg, Of	.228	478	66	109	22	2	23	66	3
Byrd, Jim, Ss	.177	378	33	67	12	4	3	26	10
Chick, Bruce, Of	.305	82	8	25	6	0	2	12	0
Crowley, Jim, 2B	.171	35	2	6	0	0	0	2	0
Flaherty, John, C	.271	365	29	99	22	0	6	35	0
Garcia, Cheo, 2B	.260	373	48	97	16	3	4	32	3
*Hatteberg, Scott, C	.189	53	6	10	0	0	1	2	0
*Lyons, Steve, Of	.213	197	24	42	6	0	4	18	3
*Malzone, John, 3B	.237	207	14	49	7	0	2	15	2
Martin, Jeff, C	.211	19	5	4	1	0	1	2	1
Mcneely, Jeff, Of	.261	498	65	130	14	3	2	35	40
Milstien, Dave, 1B	.252	258	28	65	8	3	1	18	1
Naehring, Tim, 3B	.307	202	38	62	9	1	7	36	0
Ortiz, Luis, 3B	.294	402	45	118	28	1	18	81	1
Richardson, Jeff, Ss	.321	28	2	9	1	0	0	1	0
*Riles, Ernie, Ss	.278	18	4	5	0	0	2	6	0
Rodriguez, Ruben, C	.320	97	12	31	5	0	1	10	1
*Ross, Sean, Of	.225	80	14	18	2	0	2	5	4
*Sparks, Greg, 1B	.172	198	7	34	6	0	4	21	0
*Stubbs, Franklin, 1B	.237	334	47	79	18	1	15	58	3
#Tatum, Willie, 1B	.083	24	5	2	1	1	0	2	0
*Thoutsis, Paul, Of	.319	216	30	69	10	1	4	27	1
Valentin, John, Ss	.333	9	3	3	0	0	1	1	0

PITCHING	W	L	ERA	G	SV	IP	H	BB	SO
Bailey, Cory	4	5	2.88	52	20	65.2	48	31	59
Caruso, Joe	5	10	5.44	36	0	122.1	138	68	65
*Ciccarella, Joe	0	1	5.60	12	0	17.2	27	12	8
Clemens, Roger	0	0	.00	1	0	3.2	1	4	8
Conroy, Brian	5	7	5.86	19	0	106.0	126	40	64
Finnvold, Gar	5	9	3.77	24	0	136.0	128	51	123
*Florence, Don	7	8	3.36	57	2	59.0	56	18	46
Gakeler, Dan	0	1	7.50	6	0	12.0	21	9	8
Livernois, Derek	2	6	5.72	27	0	85.0	89	37	69
Lyons, Steve	0	0	9.00	2	0	2.0	3	2	4
Melendez, Jose	2	3	5.40	19	2	35.0	37	7	31
Milstien, Dave	0	0	15.19	5	0	5.1	9	4	4
Minchey, Nate	7	14	4.02	29	0	194.2	182	50	113
Plympton, Jeff	2	1	4.44	30	1	50.2	54	15	48
*Riley, Ed	4	4	5.01	14	0	70.0	90	23	44
Ryan, Ken	0	2	2.49	18	8	25.1	18	17	22
Sele, Aaron	8	2	2.19	14	0	94.1	74	23	87
*Shea, John	2	2	7.00	12	0	36.0	51	19	20
*Taylor, Scott	7	7	4.04	47	1	122.2	132	48	88

Richmond Braves (Braves) AAA

BATTING	Avg.	AB	R	H	2B	3B	HR	RBI	SB
#Caraballo, Ramon, 2B	.272	470	73	128	25	9	3	41	20
*Houston, Tyler, C	.139	36	4	5	1	1	1	3	0
Hunter, Brian, 1B	.242	99	16	24	7	0	6	26	4
*Jones, Barry, Of	.167	30	1	5	0	0	0	4	0
#Jones, Chipper, Ss	.325	536	97	174	31	12	13	89	23
*Jones, Ron, Dh	.291	203	25	59	9	0	10	41	0
Kelly, Mike, Of	.243	424	63	103	13	1	19	58	11

BATTING	Avg.	AB	R	H	2B	3B	HR	RBI	SB
Klesko, Ryan, 1B	.274	343	59	94	14	2	22	74	4
*Kowitz, Brian, Of	.267	45	10	12	1	3	0	8	1
Lopez, Javy, C	.305	380	56	116	23	2	17	74	1
Mitchell, Keith, Of	.232	353	59	82	23	1	4	44	9
Moore, Bobby, Of	.667	3	2	2	0	0	0	0	1
Mordecai, Bobby, 2B	.268	205	29	55	8	1	2	14	10
#Nieves, Melvin, Of	.278	273	38	76	10	3	10	36	4
Oliva, Jose, 3B	.235	412	63	97	20	6	21	65	1
*Rodriguez, Boi, 1B	.267	236	34	63	13	1	10	22	4
*Tarasco, Tony, Of	.330	370	73	122	15	7	15	53	19
*Willard, Jerry, C	.319	317	37	101	21	0	8	44	0

PITCHING	W	L	ERA	G	SV	IP	H	BB	SO
*Bark, Brian	12	9	3.67	29	0	162.0	153	72	110
Birkbeck, Mike	13	8	3.11	27	0	159.1	143	41	136
*Borbon, Pedro	5	5	4.23	52	1	76.2	71	42	95
Burlingame, Dennis	2	0	4.91	6	0	14.2	12	14	5
Elliott, Donnie	8	5	4.72	18	0	103.0	108	39	99
Freeman, Marvin	0	0	2.25	2	0	4.0	4	1	5
Holman, Shawn	12	7	4.18	37	0	155.0	174	46	101
Hostetler, Mike	1	3	5.06	9	0	48.0	50	18	36
*Johnson, Judd	4	2	2.65	49	0	85.0	85	22	55
*Lovelace, Vance	0	0	5.00	5	0	9.0	10	6	7
Loynd, Mike	8	5	3.85	18	0	107.2	98	34	85
*Polley, Dale	1	0	3.93	10	0	18.1	21	11	14
Reyes, Carlos	1	0	3.77	18	1	28.2	30	11	30
Strange, Don	1	2	3.88	34	1	46.1	45	19	34
Taylor, Billy	2	4	1.98	59	26	68.1	56	26	81
Wohlers, Mark	1	3	1.84	25	4	29.1	21	11	39
*Woodall, Brad	5	3	4.21	10	0	57.2	59	16	45

Rochester Red Wings (Orioles) AAA

BATTING	Avg.	AB	R	H	2B	3B	HR	RBI	SB
Alexander, Manny, Ss	.244	471	55	115	23	8	6	51	19
*Alstead, Jason, Of	.178	45	8	8	1	0	0	4	2
Buford, Damon, Of	.284	116	24	33	6	1	1	4	10
Campbell, Darrin, C	.183	115	21	21	9	1	1	11	0
Carey, Paul, 1B	.311	325	63	101	20	4	12	50	0
Coolbaugh, Scott, 3B	.245	421	52	103	26	4	18	67	0
Davis, Glenn, 1B	.250	24	2	6	1	1	0	3	0
Dickerson, Bobby, Ss	.250	88	12	22	3	1	3	18	0
*Dostal, Bruce, Of	.294	310	46	91	12	5	3	30	14
Gomez, Leo, 3B	.200	15	3	3	1	0	0	1	0
Hammonds, Jeffrey, Of	.311	151	25	47	9	1	5	23	6
#Hinzo, Tommy, 2B	.271	560	83	152	25	5	6	69	29
Holland, Tim, Ss	.107	28	4	3	2	0	0	0	0
*Leonard, Mark, Of	.276	330	57	91	23	1	17	58	0
*Martinez, Chito, Of	.262	145	14	38	11	0	5	23	0
Palacios, Rey, C	.000	1	0	0	0	0	0	0	0
Parent, Mark, C	.247	332	47	82	15	0	14	56	0
Ready, Randy, 3B	.289	305	48	88	17	3	9	46	4
Smith, Mark, Of	.280	485	69	136	27	1	12	68	4
Tackett, Jeff, C	.320	25	1	8	2	0	0	2	0
Voigt, Jack, Of	.361	61	16	22	6	1	3	11	0
Wearing, Melvin, Dh	.235	379	52	89	14	2	14	61	5
#Yacopino, Ed, Of	.149	47	6	7	1	0	0	5	0
#Zaun, Gregg, C	.256	78	10	20	4	2	1	11	0

PITCHING	W	L	ERA	G	SV	IP	H	BB	SO
Bielecki, Mike	5	3	5.03	9	0	48.1	56	16	31
*Clements, Pat	0	0	5.91	8	1	10.2	14	8	8
Cook, Mike	6	7	3.10	57	13	81.1	77	48	74
Dedrick, Jim	1	0	2.57	1	0	7.0	6	0	3
*DuBois, Brian	0	2	9.00	3	0	13.0	20	4	10
*Krivda, Rick	3	0	1.89	5	0	33.1	20	16	23
Manuel, Barry	1	1	3.66	9	0	19.2	14	7	11
McGehee, Kevin	7	6	2.96	20	0	133.2	124	37	92
*Moyer, Jamie	6	0	1.67	8	0	54.0	42	13	41
*O'Donoghue, John	7	4	3.88	22	0	127.2	122	41	111
Oquist, Mike	9	8	3.50	28	0	149.1	144	41	128
*Pennington, Brad	1	2	3.45	17	8	15.2	12	13	19
*Rhodes, Arthur	1	1	4.05	6	0	26.2	26	15	33
Ricci, Chuck	0	0	5.63	4	0	8.0	11	3	6
Satre, Jason	4	5	5.85	15	0	80.0	87	45	42
Schulze, Don	8	5	4.10	39	7	96.2	111	24	65

Class A WRAPUPS

New York-Penn League

Niagara Falls stole 195 bases and ran off with its first championship since 1982. Not that the standings weren't close. In fact, the Rapids made the playoffs as a wild card team and beat Pittsfield 1-0 on a 10th-inning squeeze bunt to win the title. Oneonta's **Ruben Rivera**, who hit 13 home runs, was named MVP. St. Catharine's **Alonso Beltran** (11-2, 2.36) was voted best prospect. Erie's **Wes Shook** was Rookie of the Year. **Eric Danapilis** of Niagara Falls won the batting title (.341), Shook led in home runs (17) and **Greg Thomas** of Watertown was tops with 63 RBI. **Glen Barker** had a league-high 37 steals. St. Catharine's **Adam Meinershagen** (8-1) won the ERA title (1.88); **Jason Isringhausen** of Pittsfield was strikeout king (104).

FINAL STANDINGS
McNamara Division

Pittsfield	40-34	.541	—
Utica	37-38	.493	3.5
Oneonta	36-39	.480	4.5
Glens Falls	36-40	.474	5

Pinckney Division

Watertown	44-32	.579	—
Geneva	42-34	.553	2
Elmira	31-43	.419	12
Auburn	30-44	.405	13

Stadler Division

St. Catherine	49-28	.636	—
Niagara Falls	47-30	.610	2
Batavia	37-39	.487	11.5
Erie	36-40	.474	12.5
Welland	34-42	.447	14.5
Jamestown	30-46	.395	18.5

Playoffs
First round: Niagara Falls 1, St. Cath 0; Pittsfield 1, Watertown 0
Finals: Niagara Falls 2, Pittsfield 0

Class A WRAPUPS

Northwest League

It was the **Todd Greene** Show. The Boise Hawks' outfielder was named MVP and then hit two home runs in the playoff clincher, a 15-4 dethroning of the defending champs—the Bellingham Mariners. He hit .270 and led the league with 15 home runs and 71 RBI. Teammate **Mark Simmons** won the batting title at .304, two points higher than Everett's **Keith Williams**. Spokane's **Chris Prieto** led with 36 steals. The Giants' **Kris Franko** (5-0) had the best ERA (1.47); Boise's **Bryan Harris** (8-3, 1.89) had a league-high 96 strikeouts. Spokane's **Glenn Dishman** retired 26 consecutive batters in July before an error by **Jason Thompson** cost him a perfect game. **Dick Scott** of Southern Oregon was Manager of the Year.

FINAL STANDINGS

North Division

Bellingham	44-32	.579	—
Everett	42-34	.553	2
Spokane	35-41	.461	9
Yakima	30-46	.395	14

South Division

Boise	41-35	.539	—
Eugene	40-36	.526	1
So Oregon	37-39	.487	4
Bend	35-41	.461	6

Playoffs

Boise 2, Bellingham 0

Switch-hitter
* Left-handed
(Players in major leagues are listed with last minor league team.)

PITCHING	Avg.	AB	R	H	2B	3B	HR	RBI	SB
*Searcy, Steve	2	1	6.00	16	1	15.0	19	15	12
Stephan, Todd	3	7	5.10	29	1	95.1	98	35	71
Telford, Anthony	7	7	4.27	38	2	90.2	98	33	66
*Valenzuela, Fernando	0	1	10.80	1	0	3.1	6	3	1
Williams, Jeff	2	5	5.76	33	1	86.0	95	47	59
Wood, Brian	1	2	2.70	30	3	53.1	47	32	59

Scranton/WB Red Barons (Phillies) AAA

BATTING	Avg.	AB	R	H	2B	3B	HR	RBI	SB
#Amaro, Ruben, Of	.291	412	76	120	30	5	9	37	25
#Bieser, Steve, Of	.253	83	3	21	4	0	0	4	3
*Brady, Pat, Of	.228	189	28	43	10	4	8	26	1
*Fernandez, Jose, Ph	.188	32	2	6	1	0	0	1	0
Hyde, Mickey, Of	.167	6	1	1	0	0	0	0	0
Legg, Greg, 2B	.280	225	27	63	13	3	0	25	2
Lieberthal, Mike, C	.262	382	35	100	17	0	7	40	2
Lindsey, Doug, C	.174	121	9	21	4	1	2	7	0
*Longmire, Tony, Of	.304	447	63	136	36	4	6	67	12
Manto, Jeff, 3B	.289	388	62	112	30	1	17	88	4
Marsh, Tom, Of	.286	315	45	90	16	8	12	57	10
Millette, Joe, Ss	.224	343	27	77	15	2	1	24	5
Pratt, Todd, C	.222	9	1	2	1	0	0	1	0
Rodriguez, Victor, 3B	.305	442	59	135	24	3	12	64	2
#Ryan, Sean, 1B	.221	208	14	46	9	0	1	16	0
Schall, Gene, 1B	.237	139	16	33	6	1	4	16	4
#Stocker, Kevin, Ss	.233	313	54	73	14	1	3	17	17
*Taylor, Sam, Of	.241	191	24	46	7	1	6	25	4
#Waller, Casey, 3B	.176	170	19	30	7	1	1	13	2
Williams, Cary, Of	.216	232	27	50	15	2	0	14	3

PITCHING	W	L	ERA	G	SV	IP	H	BB	SO
*Abbott, Kyle	12	10	3.95	27	0	173.0	163	62	109
Allen, Ronnie	0	2	5.18	5	0	24.1	30	8	12
Ayrault, Bob	0	1	1.23	5	0	7.1	8	3	9
Borland, Toby	2	4	5.76	26	1	29.2	31	20	26
Brink, Brad	7	7	4.22	18	0	106.2	104	27	89
*Carter, Andy	7	7	4.54	30	1	109.0	104	35	68
*Combs, Pat	0	9	4.84	15	0	83.2	97	27	60
Fletcher, Paul	4	12	5.66	34	0	140.0	146	60	116
Foster, Kevin	1	1	3.93	17	0	71.0	63	29	59
*Gaddy, Bob	1	4	5.59	23	0	48.1	54	29	40
Green, Tyler	6	10	3.95	28	0	118.1	102	43	87
*Hall, Drew	2	2	2.76	61	7	65.1	55	23	62
Mauser, Tim	2	0	.87	19	10	20.2	10	5	25
Parris, Steve	0	0	12.71	3	0	5.2	9	3	4
Patterson, Jeff	7	5	2.69	62	8	93.2	79	42	68
Wells, Bob	1	1	2.79	11	0	19.1	19	5	8
Williams, Mike	9	2	2.87	14	0	97.1	93	16	53

Syracuse Chiefs (Blue Jays) AAA

BATTING	Avg.	AB	R	H	2B	3B	HR	RBI	SB
*Butler, Rob, Of	.284	208	30	59	11	2	1	14	7
Canate, William, Of	.250	24	3	6	0	0	2	5	0
#Cedeno, Domingo, Ss	.272	382	58	104	16	10	2	28	15
Delarosa, Juan, Of	.227	198	17	45	10	2	4	15	4
*Giannelli, Ray, 2B	.253	411	51	104	18	4	11	42	1
Henderson, Derek, Ss	.370	27	2	10	1	0	0	3	0
Martinez, Domingo, 1B	.273	465	50	127	24	2	24	79	4
Montalvo, Rob, 2B	.214	234	25	50	6	1	0	16	1
Monzon, Jose, C	.239	197	14	47	7	0	3	21	0
*O'Halloran, Greg, C	.267	322	32	86	14	3	3	35	2
Perez, Robert, Of	.294	524	67	154	26	10	12	64	13
Quinlan, Tom, 3B	.236	461	63	109	20	5	16	53	6
#Scott, Shawn, Of	.210	290	30	61	9	1	0	18	7
Sojo, Luis, 2B	.218	142	17	31	7	2	1	12	2
*Stevens, Lee, 1B	.264	401	61	106	30	1	14	66	2
Yan, Julian, Dh	.266	278	30	74	9	5	7	36	3
Zosky, Eddie, Ss	.215	93	9	20	5	0	0	8	0

PITCHING	W	L	ERA	G	SV	IP	H	BB	SO
*Adkins, Steve	0	0	4.91	5	0	3.2	4	3	0
Akerfelds, Darrel	3	4	4.36	40	0	64.0	68	30	34
*Bailes, Scott	0	1	2.21	19	2	20.1	19	3	22

PITCHING	W	L	ERA	G	SV	IP	H	BB	SO
Blohm, Pete	2	6	5.44	30	0	102.2	122	52	57
Brow, Scott	6	8	4.38	20	0	121.1	119	37	64
Brown, Tim	5	13	4.47	28	0	151.0	159	35	87
*Castillo, Tony	0	0	.00	1	0	6.0	4	0	2
Cross, Jesse	8	6	3.16	29	0	151.0	137	53	127
Duey, Kyle	2	1	4.05	11	1	20.0	19	7	13
Hall, Darren	6	7	5.33	60	13	79.1	75	31	68
Linton, Doug	2	6	5.32	13	2	47.1	48	14	42
Menhart, Paul	9	10	3.64	25	0	151.0	143	67	108
Ohlms, Mark	3	6	7.05	47	5	60.0	85	42	37
*Spoljaric, Paul	8	7	5.29	18	0	95.1	97	52	88
St.Claire, Randy	1	2	2.93	20	0	30.2	34	6	16
Terrell, Walt	0	1	5.30	8	0	35.2	41	11	20
*Ward, Anthony	1	2	3.70	35	1	41.1	37	25	45
Williams, Woody	1	1	2.20	12	3	16.1	15	5	16
Yan, Julian	0	0	18.00	2	0	2.0	4	0	1
*Young, Matt	5	1	2.37	10	0	49.1	33	19	55

Toledo Mud Hens (Tigers) AAA

BATTING	Avg.	AB	R	H	2B	3B	HR	RBI	SB
*Brogna, Rico, 1B	.273	483	55	132	30	3	11	59	7
#Cangelosi, John, Of	.292	439	73	128	23	4	6	42	39
*Cruz, Ivan, Dh	.226	402	44	91	18	4	13	50	1
#Givens, Jim, Ss	.257	148	18	38	4	2	0	13	6
Gladden, Dan, Of	.393	28	6	11	1	0	1	7	1
Gomez, Chris, Ss	.245	277	29	68	12	2	0	20	6
*Hare, Shawn, Of	.264	470	81	124	29	3	20	76	8
Hurst, Jody, Of	.250	200	26	50	6	2	6	27	15
Ingram, Riccardo, Of	.270	415	41	112	20	4	13	62	9
Paredes, Johnny, 2B	.257	471	70	121	19	4	2	41	21
*Pevey, Marty, C	.274	175	11	48	8	1	2	18	3
#Reimink, Bob, 3B	.197	193	18	38	7	0	1	10	4
#Robertson, Rod, 3B	.235	409	54	96	13	2	12	48	15
Rowland, Rich, C	.268	325	58	87	24	2	21	59	1
Sellers, Rick, C	.283	46	6	13	4	1	2	7	0
#Williams, Ted, Of	.247	194	21	48	7	3	1	16	22

PITCHING	W	L	ERA	G	SV	IP	H	BB	SO
Bergman, Sean	8	9	4.38	19	0	117.0	124	53	91
Blomdahl, Ben	3	4	4.88	11	0	62.2	67	19	27
Carlyle, Kenny	2	10	6.42	15	0	75.2	88	36	43
*Corbett, Sherm	0	0	4.76	5	0	5.2	6	2	6
DeSilva, John	7	10	3.69	25	0	161.0	145	60	136
Fraser, Willie	10	7	4.69	53	8	71.0	79	24	63
Gardiner, Mike	1	2	2.70	9	1	30.0	23	11	35
Gohr, Greg	3	10	5.80	18	0	107.0	127	38	77
Gomez, Henrique	1	1	6.61	6	0	16.1	21	4	15
*Gonzales, Frank	6	3	3.95	29	0	109.1	116	37	71
Grater, Mark	1	2	8.13	28	4	31.0	42	12	31
*Groom, Buddy	9	3	2.74	16	0	102.0	98	30	78
Gullickson, Bill	1	0	9.00	1	0	6.0	8	0	4
Haas, David	0	0	18.69	2	0	4.1	8	6	2
Hudek, John	1	3	5.82	16	0	38.2	44	22	32
Johnson, Dave	1	0	.00	9	0	17.1	6	5	8
Kiely, John	3	4	3.88	37	4	58.0	65	25	48
Knudsen, Kurt	2	2	3.78	23	6	33.1	24	11	39
*Krueger, Bill	1	0	1.59	3	0	11.1	11	3	8
Lira, Felipe	1	2	4.60	5	0	31.1	32	11	23
Lumley, Mike	0	2	6.57	6	0	12.1	13	8	7
Rightnowar, Ron	2	2	3.55	22	1	58.1	57	19	32
*Ritchie, Wally	1	0	4.76	62	4	45.1	44	15	29
Warren, Brian	2	2	3.44	24	0	36.2	40	11	26

Pacific Coast League

Albuquerque Dukes (Dodgers) AAA

BATTING	Avg.	AB	R	H	2B	3B	HR	RBI	SB
Ashley, Billy, Of	.297	482	88	143	31	4	26	100	6
Barron, Tony, Of	.290	259	42	75	22	1	8	36	6

Class A WRAPUPS

South Atlantic League

The Savannah Cardinals won their first championship since 1960 and won a league-record 94 victories. Savannah's **Brian Rupp** won the batting title (.320) while **Jamie Cochran** set a minor league record with 46 saves. Hagerstown's **D.J. Boston** was MVP (.315-13-92). Greensboro's **Ryan Karp** (14-1 before a July promotion) was Most Outstanding Pitcher. The Hornets' **Derek Jeter** was named best prospect. Columbus's **Derek Hacopian** led the league with 24 home runs, while Spartanburg's **Alan Burke** had 96 RBI. Greensboro's **Kraig Hawkins** led with 67 stolen bases. **J.J. Thobe** of Columbus was 11-2 with a league-best 1.91 ERA, and teammate **Charles York** led in strikeouts (182).

FINAL STANDINGS
Northern Division

x-Greensboro	85-56	.603	—
W Virginia	76-64	.543	8.5
y-Fayetteville	75-66	.532	10
Hagerstown	74-66	.529	10.5
Spartanburg	62-80	.437	23.5
Hickory	52-88	.371	32.5
Asheville	51-88	.367	33

Southern Division

z-Savannah	94-48	.662	—
Columbus	86-56	.606	8
Macon	74-67	.525	19.5
Albany	71-71	.500	23
Chrlstn,SC	65-77	.458	29
Capital City	64-77	.454	29.5
Augusta	59-82	.418	34.5

x-Won first half; y-Won second half; z-Won both halves
Playoffs
First round: Greensboro 2, Fayetteville 1
Finals: Savannah 3, Greensboro 2

Class A WRAPUPS

Florida State League

Clearwater's Phillies won their first title since joining the Florida State League nine years ago. They beat Port Charlotte and St. Lucie in the playoffs. **Randy Curtis** (.319, 52 stolen bases) of St. Lucie was MVP; St. Petersburg's **Doug Radziewicz** (.342) won the batting title; **Rick Holifield** of Dunedin led in home runs (20) while teammate **Chris Weinke** led in RBI (98). **Rich Linares** of Vero Beach had a league-high 181 strikeouts, as one of the league's many outstanding pitching prospects, who included **John Dettmer** of Port Charlotte (16-3, 2.15 ERA, 128 SO) and **Alan Levine** of Sarasota (127 SO). Other hot pitchers included **Rod Henderson** and **Billy Wallace** of West Palm Beach, **Chris Roberts** of St. Lucie and **Brian Boehringer** of Sarasota.

FINAL STANDINGS
East Division
y-St. Lucie	78-52	.600	—
x-Lakeland	65-63	.509	12
W Plm Bch	69-67	.507	12
Osceola	56-74	.431	22
Daytona	57-76	.429	22.5
Vero Bch	56-77	.421	23.5
Ft Lauderdale	46-85	.351	32.5

West Division
y-Charlotte	84-49	.632	—
Sarasota	77-77	.575	7.5
St. Pete	75-58	.564	9
x-Clearwater	75-60	.556	10
Dunedin	68-64	.515	15.5
Fort Myers	55-79	.410	29.5

x-Won first half; y-Won second half

Playoffs
First round: Clearwtr 2, Charlotte 1; St. Lucie 2, Lakeland 1
Finals: Clearwater 3, St. Lucie 1

BATTING	Avg.	AB	R	H	2B	3B	HR	RBI	SB
Bournigal, Rafael, Ss	.277	465	75	129	25	0	4	55	3
Brooks, Jerry, C	.344	421	67	145	28	4	11	71	3
Busch, Mike, 3B	.283	431	87	122	32	4	22	70	1
#Cedeno, Roger, Of	.222	18	1	4	1	1	0	4	0
*Goodwin, Tom, Of	.260	289	48	75	5	5	1	28	21
Howard, Matt, 2B	.154	26	3	4	0	1	0	4	1
Maurer, Ron, Ss	.293	116	19	34	7	0	3	14	1
Mondesi, Raul, Of	.280	425	65	119	22	7	12	65	13
#Munoz, Jose, 2B	.288	438	66	126	21	5	1	54	6
Ortiz, Hector, C	.182	44	0	8	1	1	0	3	0
Parrish, Lance, C	.273	33	4	9	2	0	0	1	0
Pye, Eddie, 2B	.329	365	53	120	21	7	7	66	5
*Rodriguez, Henry, 1B	.296	179	26	53	13	5	4	30	1
*Spearman, Vernon, Of	.254	185	31	47	6	5	0	15	11
*Strawberry, Darryl, Of	.316	19	3	6	2	0	1	2	1
*Traxler, Brian, 1B	.333	441	81	147	36	3	16	83	0
Wakamatsu, Don, C	.337	181	30	61	11	1	7	31	0

PITCHING	W	L	ERA	G	SV	IP	H	BB	SO
Ayrault, Bob	2	2	7.11	14	1	19.0	29	9	16
Bustillos, Albert	2	1	4.45	20	2	30.1	37	13	17
*Daal, Omar	1	1	3.38	6	2	5.1	5	3	2
*Dayley, Ken	0	0	12.19	9	0	10.1	14	12	9
Gross, Kip	13	7	4.05	59	13	124.1	115	41	96
Hansell, Greg	5	10	6.93	26	0	101.1	131	60	60
Hurst, Jonathan	7	2	4.15	18	0	86.2	101	29	62
James, Mike	1	0	7.47	16	2	31.1	38	19	32
Kutzler, Jerry	5	6	5.58	35	1	100.0	124	31	50
Marquez, Isidrio	1	0	1.50	9	2	12.0	7	3	10
*Martinez, Fili	0	2	4.32	4	0	8.1	11	1	2
Martinez, Pedro	0	0	3.00	1	0	3.0	1	1	4
*Mimbs, Mark	0	1	10.13	19	1	18.2	20	16	12
Nichols, Rod	8	5	4.30	21	0	127.2	132	50	79
*Nolte, Eric	3	5	6.34	33	1	71.0	101	30	63
Perschke, Greg	7	4	6.36	33	0	104.2	146	24	63
Springer, Dennis	3	8	5.99	35	0	130.2	173	39	69
*Traxler, Brian	1	0	11.57	2	0	2.1	3	2	1
Treadwell, Jody	5	4	4.70	39	0	105.1	119	52	102
*VanRyn, Ben	1	4	10.73	6	0	24.1	35	17	9
*Vierra, Joey	0	4	4.91	29	1	33.0	38	18	24
Williams, Todd	5	5	4.99	65	21	70.1	87	31	56
*Wilson, Steve	0	3	4.38	13	0	51.1	57	14	44
Worrell, Todd	1	0	1.04	7	0	8.2	7	2	13

Calgary Cannons (Mariners) AAA

BATTING	Avg.	AB	R	H	2B	3B	HR	RBI	SB
Boone, Bret, 2B	.332	274	48	91	18	3	8	56	3
Deak, Brian, C	.247	235	43	58	12	0	11	41	5
Furtado, Tim, Of	.188	16	1	3	1	0	0	1	0
Holley, Bobby, Of	.263	38	8	10	2	2	2	9	1
Howard, Chris, C	.320	331	40	106	23	0	6	55	1
*Howitt, Dann, Of	.279	333	57	93	20	1	21	77	7
*Jeter, Shawn, Of	.156	32	3	5	2	0	0	3	3
Litton, Greg, 3B	.318	170	35	54	16	3	6	27	3
*Mack, Quinn, Of	.308	325	48	100	25	1	6	39	9
Manahan, Anthony, 3B	.302	451	70	136	31	4	3	62	19
Martinez, Carmelo, Dh	.255	149	21	38	5	0	4	18	4
Maynard, Tow, Of	.143	21	7	3	0	0	0	0	4
Pirkl, Greg, 1B	.308	445	67	137	24	1	21	94	3
#Quinones, Luis, 3B	.257	175	21	45	13	3	3	25	0
Smith, Jack, Ss	.286	458	61	131	30	3	8	57	5
#Sveum, Dale, Dh	.313	163	41	51	12	1	8	32	2
#Tinsley, Lee, Of	.302	450	95	136	25	18	10	63	34
Turang, Brian, Of	.324	423	83	137	20	11	8	54	24
*Turner, Shane, 3B	.303	323	46	98	22	1	0	38	6
*Waggoner, Aubrey, Of	.263	38	9	10	2	1	2	4	3
Wilson, Jim, 1B	.254	63	10	16	3	0	1	9	0
#Young, Gerald, Of	.298	104	19	31	8	2	1	10	7

PITCHING	W	L	ERA	G	SV	IP	H	BB	SO
*Barton, Shawn	3	1	3.56	51	4	60.2	64	27	29
*Brundage, Dave	0	1	2.25	4	0	8.0	8	4	4
*Carman, Don	1	0	3.55	6	0	12.2	12	2	6
Converse, Jim	7	8	5.40	23	0	121.2	144	64	78
*Cummings, John	3	4	4.13	11	0	65.1	69	21	42

PITCHING	W	L	ERA	G	SV	IP	H	BB	SO
*Czarkowski, Mark	1	4	7.61	9	0	36.2	62	11	11
DeLucia, Rich	1	5	5.73	8	1	44.0	45	20	38
Grater, Mark	0	1	7.71	9	0	11.2	19	6	4
*Gunderson, Eric	0	1	18.90	5	0	6.2	14	8	3
Harris, Reggie	8	6	5.20	17	0	88.1	74	61	75
Holman, Brad	8	4	4.74	21	0	98.2	109	42	54
Kent, Troy	0	1	11.45	9	0	11.0	21	8	10
McCullers, Lance	4	5	5.67	33	1	87.1	106	40	42
Nelson, Jeff	1	0	1.17	5	0	7.2	6	2	6
Parkins, Rob	0	0	10.13	3	0	2.2	6	0	3
Picota, Len	1	2	6.14	22	5	29.1	32	16	10
*Powell, Dennis	3	2	3.60	12	1	40.0	37	19	30
*Remlinger, Mike	4	3	5.53	19	0	84.2	100	52	51
Shinall, Zak	2	1	5.01	33	5	46.2	55	18	25
St.Claire, Randy	4	6	6.79	27	3	51.2	70	13	45
*Swan, Russ	2	1	8.44	9	0	10.2	14	8	7
Wainhouse, David	0	1	4.02	13	5	15.2	10	7	7
Walker, Mike	13	8	4.03	28	0	169.2	197	47	131
Wapnick, Steve	1	5	4.96	32	2	61.2	74	24	26

Colo. Springs Sky Sox (Rockies) AAA

BATTING	Avg.	AB	R	H	2B	3B	HR	RBI	SB
#Alicea, Ed, Of	.337	205	44	69	8	4	1	23	3
Ausmus, Brad, C	.270	241	31	65	10	4	2	33	10
#Bates, Jason, Ss	.267	449	76	120	21	2	13	62	9
Benavides, Freddie, Ss	.438	16	3	7	1	0	0	2	0
*Canale, George, 1B	.287	115	15	33	9	1	5	15	2
Case, Mike, Ph	.333	3	0	1	0	0	0	0	0
Castellano, Pedro, 3B	.313	304	61	95	21	2	12	60	3
Cole, Stu, 3B	.281	324	54	91	22	3	5	35	10
*Gainer, Jay, 1B	.294	293	51	86	11	3	10	74	4
Girardi, Joe, C	.484	31	6	15	1	1	1	6	1
Hubbard, Trent, Of	.314	439	83	138	24	8	7	56	33
Jones, Chris, Of	.280	168	41	47	5	5	12	40	8
#Liriano, Nelson, 2B	.358	293	48	105	23	6	6	46	9
List, Paul, Of	.300	50	9	15	7	1	0	5	0
Mejia, Roberto, 2B	.299	291	51	87	15	2	14	48	12
Mota, Andy, Of	.301	345	46	104	29	4	7	61	8
Olander, Jim, Of	.300	200	43	60.	16	3	6	25	4
Owens, J., C	.310	174	24	54	11	3	6	43	5
Reyes, Gilberto, C	.236	174	22	41	6	2	9	29	1
Ricker, Troy, Of	.045	22	0	1	0	0	0	1	2
*Ross, Sean, Of	.303	119	15	36	13	3	1	14	3
Strittmatter, Mark, C	.200	10	1	2	1	0	0	2	0
Tatum, Jimmy, 3B	.222	45	5	10	2	0	2	7	0
Ward, Kevin, Of	.233	73	12	17	2	2	3	13	1
Wedge, Eric, 1B	.267	90	17	24	6	0	3	13	0

PITCHING	W	L	ERA	G	SV	IP	H	BB	SO
Allen, Steve	6	4	4.10	37	2	63.2	73	28	32
Ashby, Andy	4	2	4.10	7	0	41.2	45	12	35
Buckley, Travis	1	2	6.00	6	0	9.0	12	7	5
Burke, John	3	2	3.14	8	0	48.2	44	23	38
Fredrickson, Scott	1	3	5.47	23	7	26.1	25	19	20
Hawblitzel, Ryan	8	13	6.15	29	0	165.1	221	49	90
Holmes, Darren	1	0	.00	3	0	8.2	1	1	9
*Hurst, Bruce	1	2	7.78	4	0	19.2	30	4	15
Knudson, Mark	3	1	2.25	5	0	28.0	30	8	15
Leskanic, Curt	4	3	4.47	9	0	44.1	39	26	38
*Marshall, Randy	1	0	3.86	11	1	21.0	35	6	12
Metzinger, Bill	1	0	10.07	12	0	19.2	25	19	21
Moore, Marcus	1	5	4.47	30	4	44.1	54	29	38
*Munoz, Mike	1	2	1.67	40	3	37.2	46	9	30
Nied, David	0	2	9.00	3	0	15.0	24	6	11
*Painter, Lance	9	7	4.30	23	0	138.0	165	44	91
Reed, Steve	0	0	.00	11	7	12.1	8	3	10
Reynoso, Armando	2	1	3.22	4	0	22.1	19	8	22
Ridenour, Dana	8	8	5.21	39	0	121.0	156	58	105
Sanford, Mo	3	6	5.23	20	0	105.0	103	57	104
Shepherd, Keith	3	6	6.78	37	8	67.2	90	44	57
Thompson, Mark	3	0	2.70	4	0	33.1	31	11	22
*Wells, Terry	2	3	6.67	16	1	27.0	33	25	22
Zavaras, Clint	0	0	2.25	6	0	8.0	5	11	9

Rookie League WRAPUPS

Appalachian League

Two new Indians prospects named Ramirez—Alex and Richard—helped Burlington win its first league title since 1987. The Tribe swept Elizabethton in the playoffs. **Alex Ramirez** sent Game Two into extra innings with a ninth-inning RBI single, then **Richard Ramirez** doubled home the winner in the 12th. Bluefield's **Brian Link** (.338, 14 HR, 60 RBI) was Player of the Year; Bristol's **Sean Wooten** won the batting title (.350). Link led in RBI; King-sport's **Preston Wilson** (16) and **Randy Warner** (15) finished 1-2 in homers. Princeton's **Roger Etheridge** (3-2, 1.49) won the ERA crown, but Bristol's **Jason Mackey** (6-0), and Elizabethton's **Javier DeJesus** (9-0) and **Shawn Miller** (5-0) were unbeaten. **Calvin Maduro** of Bluefield had a league-high 83 strikeouts. **Joe Cunningham** of Johnson City was Manager of the Year.

FINAL STANDINGS

Northern Division

Burlington	44-24	.647	—
Bluefield	44-24	.647	—
Danville	38-30	.559	6
Princeton	26-42	.382	18
Martinsville	22-46	.324	22

Southern Division

Elizabethton	37-30	.552	—
Johnson City	37-31	.544	0.5
Huntington	33-35	.485	4.5
Kingsport	30-38	.441	7.5
Bristol	28-39	.418	9

Playoffs
Burlington 2, Elizabethton 0

Rookie League WRAPUPS

Arizona League

The Athletics beat out the Giants and Cardinals by one and a half games to win the Arizona League, which does not have postseason playoffs. The A's **John Jones** won the batting title with a .341 average. He also tied teammates **Leon Hamburg** and **Fred Soriano** for the home run lead with five, and drove in 39 runs, two behind league leader **Jason Canizaro** (Giants). The Brewers' **Franklin Garcia** stole a league-high 36 bases. **Jason Myers** of the Giants had a fabulous year on the mound, posting a 8-1 record with a league-low 1.69 ERA. He also led the league with 105 strikeouts.

FINAL STANDINGS

Athletics	31-19	.620	—
Giants	30-21	.588	1.5
Cardinals	31-22	.585	1.5
Angels	28-23	.549	3.5
Brewers	26-26	.500	6
Padres	23-29	.442	9
Rockies	21-32	.396	11.5
Mariners	17-35	.327	15

Edmonton Trappers (Marlins) AAA

BATTING	Avg.	AB	R	H	2B	3B	HR	RBI	SB
#Barberie, Bret, 2B	.421	19	3	8	2	0	1	8	0
Berroa, Geronimo, Of	.327	327	64	107	33	4	16	68	1
Capra, Nick, 3B	.278	389	71	108	19	4	7	44	20
Delossantos, Luis, 1B	.311	425	49	132	25	2	2	66	0
#Everett, Carl, Of	.309	136	28	42	13	4	6	16	12
Fariss, Monty, Of	.256	254	32	65	11	4	6	37	1
#Felix, Junior, Of	.355	31	7	11	2	0	0	5	0
Jackson, Chuck, 3B	.279	129	23	36	4	3	5	11	0
Lyden, Mitch, C	.306	160	34	49	15	1	8	31	1
McGriff, Terry, C	.345	339	62	117	29	2	7	55	2
Natal, Bob, C	.318	66	16	21	6	1	3	16	0
Pedrique, Al, Ss	.305	403	54	123	14	1	2	42	5
Polidor, Gus, Ss	.285	249	26	71	16	2	3	40	1
*Pose, Scott, Of	.284	398	61	113	8	6	0	27	19
Renteria, Ed, 2B	.265	68	6	18	0	0	1	8	0
#Santana, Andres, 2B	.228	171	20	39	3	1	0	11	5
Small, Jeff, 2B	.271	328	29	89	19	6	2	39	3
#Snyder, Randy, C	.266	94	12	25	6	0	1	10	0
*Whitmore, Darrell, Of	.355	273	52	97	24	2	9	62	11
*Wilson, Nigel, Of	.292	370	66	108	26	7	17	68	8

PITCHING	W	L	ERA	G	SV	IP	H	BB	SO
*Adamson, Joel	1	2	6.92	5	0	26.0	39	13	7
Anderson, Scott	5	4	3.53	44	4	66.1	74	15	52
Darwin, Jeff	2	2	8.51	25	2	30.2	50	10	22
*Gleaton, Jerry Don	3	1	3.99	46	7	65.1	73	26	46
*Jeffcoat, Mike	4	3	4.14	33	3	54.1	58	6	32
Johnstone, John	4	15	5.18	30	4	144.1	167	59	126
Kramer, Randy	5	4	5.52	46	5	62.0	76	24	44
Lemon, Don	3	3	5.21	21	0	74.1	89	20	52
*McGraw, Tom	2	0	5.59	5	0	9.2	12	4	8
Miller, Kurt	3	3	4.50	9	0	48.0	42	34	19
*Myers, Mike	7	14	5.18	27	0	161.2	195	52	112
Newlin, Jim	0	0	13.50	4	0	6.0	11	4	3
Rapp, Pat	8	3	3.43	17	0	107.2	89	34	93
*Scheid, Rich	5	7	5.07	38	0	110.0	130	38	84
Snyder, Randy	0	0	22.50	2	0	2.0	7	1	2
Turner, Matt	0	0	.66	12	10	13.2	9	2	15
*Walter, Gene	2	0	7.88	6	0	8.0	13	3	4
Weathers, Dave	11	4	3.83	22	0	141.0	150	47	117
Yaughn, Kip	1	0	.00	1	0	5.0	6	1	2

Las Vegas Stars (Padres) AAA

BATTING	Avg.	AB	R	H	2B	3B	HR	RBI	SB
Basso, Mike, C	.253	91	12	23	6	0	4	17	1
*Bean, Billy, Of	.353	167	31	59	11	2	7	40	3
#Bethea, Steve, 2B	.180	61	7	11	2	0	0	2	0
Brown, Jarvis, Of	.308	402	74	124	27	9	3	47	22
Dozier, D.J., Of	.270	122	25	33	10	3	2	13	6
*Gonzalez, Paul, 3B	.240	267	36	64	11	4	7	34	3
Gutierrez, Ricky, 2B	.417	24	4	10	4	0	0	4	4
*Higgins, Kevin, 3B	.359	142	22	51	8	0	1	22	1
#Hosey, Dwayne, Of	.264	110	21	29	4	4	3	12	7
Jelic, Chris, 3B	.208	130	16	27	4	2	2	14	2
Johnson, Brian, C	.339	416	58	141	35	6	10	71	0
#Lopez, Luis, Ss	.305	491	52	150	36	6	6	58	8
#Martinez, Pablo, Ss	.231	251	24	58	4	1	2	20	8
#Nieves, Melvin, Of	.308	159	31	49	10	1	7	24	2
Pegues, Steve, Of	.352	270	52	95	20	5	9	50	12
*Sherman, Darrell, Of	.265	272	52	72	8	2	0	11	20
Simms, Mike, 1B	.268	414	74	111	25	2	24	80	1
Staton, Dave, 1B	.270	37	8	10	0	0	7	11	0
Vatcher, Jim, Of	.317	293	36	93	17	2	7	45	3
*Velasquez, Guillermo, 1B	.333	129	23	43	6	1	5	24	0
Walters, Dan, C	.287	223	26	64	14	0	5	39	1
Witkowski, Mat, 2B	.283	286	49	81	6	3	1	35	10

PITCHING	W	L	ERA	G	Sv	IP	H	BB	SO
Bochtler, Doug	1	9	6.18	19	0	90.1	123	37	68
*Boucher, Denis	4	7	6.43	24	1	70.0	101	27	46
Brocail, Doug	4	2	3.68	10	1	51.1	51	14	32
*Brown, Jeff	0	0	9.00	1	0	5.0	9	0	4

Switch-hitter
* Left-handed
(Players in major leagues are listed with last minor league team.)

PITCHING	W	L	ERA	G	SV	IP	H	BB	SO
Campbell, Mike	2	1	5.40	21	1	31.2	39	9	24
Compres, Fidel	1	1	5.54	24	4	26.0	33	10	7
Davis, Rick	1	8	7.14	34	3	51.2	94	20	27
Elliott, Donnie	2	5	6.37	8	0	41.0	48	24	44
Ettles, Mark	3	6	4.71	47	15	49.2	58	22	29
Garrelts, Scott	0	0	21.00	1	0	3.0	10	2	1
Hamilton, Joey	3	2	4.40	8	0	47.0	49	22	33
*Linskey, Mike	4	5	4.68	30	1	107.2	130	46	77
Martinez, Jose	8	7	6.01	27	0	115.1	148	39	45
*Martinez, Pedro	3	5	4.72	15	0	87.2	94	40	65
*Pena, Jim	1	2	6.10	39	1	51.2	69	16	31
Sager, A.J.	6	5	3.70	21	1	90.0	91	18	58
Sanders, Scott	5	10	4.96	24	0	152.1	170	62	161
Seanez, Rudy	0	1	6.75	17	0	22.2	27	12	19
Seminara, Frank	8	5	5.43	21	1	114.1	136	52	99
Strong, Joe	1	3	5.67	21	0	27.0	37	10	18
Vatcher, Jim	0	0	9.00	2	0	3.0	7	0	3
Worrell, Tim	5	6	5.48	15	0	87.0	102	26	89
Young, Ray	1	2	6.10	14	2	20.2	29	8	20

Phoenix Firebirds (Giants) AAA

BATTING	Avg.	AB	R	H	2B	3B	HR	RBI	SB
Allanson, Andy, C	.354	161	31	57	15	2	6	23	7
Bellinger, Clay, 3B	.256	407	50	104	20	3	6	49	7
Brantley, Mickey, Of	.364	247	45	90	23	6	8	49	2
Calcagno, Danny, C	.206	34	4	7	1	0	0	2	1
Chimelis, Joel, 3B	.309	262	40	81	14	3	13	46	4
Colbert, Craig, C	.222	45	5	10	2	1	1	7	0
Davenport, Adell, 3B	.300	40	5	12	1	0	2	8	0
#Duncan, Andres, Ss	.500	4	1	2	0	0	0	0	0
Faneyte, Rikkert, Of	.312	426	71	133	23	2	11	71	15
Faries, Paul, Ss	.303	327	56	99	14	5	2	32	18
Fernandez, Danny, C	.263	118	17	31	3	1	0	7	1
*Hecht, Steve, 2B	.314	169	27	53	8	1	2	20	9
*Heffernan, Bert, C	.286	49	7	14	1	1	0	6	2
Hosey, Steve, Of	.292	455	70	133	40	4	16	85	16
Johnson, Erik, Ss	.248	363	33	90	8	5	0	33	3
#Johnson, Juan, Ss	.000	4	0	0	0	0	0	0	0
Katzaroff, Rob, Of	.154	26	2	4	0	0	0	3	0
*Martinez, Dave, Of	.467	15	4	7	0	0	0	2	1
*McNamara, Jim, C	.196	158	10	31	5	0	1	23	1
Mercedes, Luis, Of	.291	244	28	71	5	3	0	15	14
Murray, Calvin, Of	.316	19	4	6	1	1	0	0	1
Peters, Reed, Of	.300	240	43	72	16	4	5	31	8
*Phillips, J.R., 1B	.263	506	80	133	35	2	27	94	7
Scarsone, Steve, 2B	.257	70	13	18	1	2	3	9	2
*Smiley, Reuben, Of	.300	313	58	94	16	7	7	37	24

PITCHING	W	L	ERA	G	SV	IP	H	BB	SO
Bross, Terry	4	4	3.97	54	5	79.1	76	37	69
*Brown, Kevin	6	10	4.94	23	0	120.1	134	60	75
Brummett, Greg	7	7	3.62	18	0	107.0	114	27	84
Carlson, Dan	5	6	6.56	13	0	70.0	79	32	48
Carter, Larry	3	1	2.88	7	0	34.1	28	15	31
Fisher, Brian	3	4	8.08	14	0	49.0	75	15	25
Hanselman, Carl	2	6	5.98	21	0	87.1	115	35	45
Hartsock, Jeff	2	5	5.53	12	0	55.1	83	20	35
Layana, Tim	3	2	4.81	55	9	67.1	80	24	55
McGehee, Kevin	0	3	4.91	4	0	22.0	28	8	16
*Minutelli, Gino	2	2	4.02	49	11	53.2	55	26	57
Myers, Jimmy	2	5	3.68	31	0	58.2	69	22	20
*Peltzer, Kurt	2	0	6.75	12	2	16.0	16	7	16
Peters, Reed	0	0	18.00	1	0	2.0	4	2	2
Rambo, Dan	1	3	7.14	18	0	51.2	77	33	31
Taylor, Rob	10	8	4.24	49	2	144.1	166	49	110
Torres, Salomon	7	4	3.50	14	0	105.1	105	27	99
Van Landingham, William	0	1	6.43	1	0	7.0	8	0	2
Wassenaar, Rob	2	4	6.56	34	2	70.0	117	24	50

Portland Beavers (Twins) AAA

BATTING	Avg.	AB	R	H	2B	3B	HR	RBI	SB
Brito, Bernardo, Dh	.339	319	64	108	18	3	20	72	0
*Bruett, J.T., Of	.322	320	70	103	17	6	2	40	12

Rookie League WRAPUPS

Pioneer League

The Billings Mustangs were the only repeat champions in the minor leagues, taking their second consecutive Pioneer League title. The Mustangs beat Helena two games to one in the playoffs. Billings also won back-to-back titles in 1972-73. **Todd Takayoshi** of the independent Pocatello Posse won the batting title (.358). The Posse was a last-minute addition when the Salt Lake Trappers were forced to move because of the demolition of Derks Field. Pocatello also had the RBI leader in **Will Fitzpatrick** (58), while **Willie Brown** of Lethbridge won the home run crown (16). **Derek Vaughn** of Pocatello had a league-high 40 stolen bases. **Daniel Camacho** of Great Falls (5-2, 1.38) won the ERA title by more than a run, while **Gene Caruso** of Pocatello was the runaway strikeout leader with 163 in 111 innings.

FINAL STANDINGS
Northern Division

Billings	48-25	.658	—
Medcn Hat	39-32	.549	8
Great Falls	36-34	.514	10.5
Lethbridge	27-44	.380	20

Southern Division

Helena	41-30	.577	—
Pocatello	36-37	.493	6
Idaho Falls	35-39	.473	7.5
Butte	26-47	.356	16

Playoffs
Billings 2, Helena 1

Switch-hitter
* Left-handed
(Players in major leagues are listed with last minor league team.)

347

Rookie League WRAPUPS

Gulf Coast League

The Rangers were the toast of the coast. Manager Chino Cadahia's team posted a 40-20 record, then beat the Astros in two playoff games to win the league championship. The club featured the Texas Rangers' top seven 1993 draft picks; **Larry Ephan** hit .350 and won the batting title. **Marc Niethammer** of the Expos hit six home runs to lead that category, while Ephan had a league-high 39 RBI. **Yudith Ozario** of the Mets had 39 stolen bases. **John Lombardi** of the Orioles (7-1, 0.92) nosed out **Joe Atwater** of the Mets (7-1, 0.93) for the ERA title. The pitching-rich league had nine hurlers with ERAs under 2.00. **Jason Tatar** of the Twins had 73 strikeouts, and Astro **Edgar Ramos** had 70.

FINAL STANDINGS
Eastern Division

Mets	39-20	.661	—
Braves	32-26	.552	6.5
Expos	27-31	.466	11.5
Cubs	19-40	.322	20

Northern Division

Astros	35-24	.593	—
Marlins	32-28	.533	3.5
Yankees	30-29	.508	5
Blue Jays	22-38	.367	13.5

Western Division

Rangers	40-20	.667	—
White Sox	32-27	.542	7.5
Red Sox	32-28	.533	8
Orioles	30-28	.517	9
Royals	29-30	.492	10.5
Twins	23-36	.390	16.5
Pirates	21-38	.356	18.5

Playoffs

First round: Astros 1, Mets 0
Finals: Rangers 2, Astros 0

BATTING	Avg.	AB	R	H	2B	3B	HR	RBI	SB
#Carter, Jeff, 2B	.325	381	73	124	21	7	0	48	17
Grifol, Pedro, C	.330	94	14	31	4	2	2	17	0
*Grotewold, Jeff, C	.252	151	27	38	6	3	6	30	2
*Hale, Chip, 2B	.280	211	37	59	15	3	1	24	2
#Howell, Pat, Of	.209	369	57	77	11	3	2	29	36
Jorgensen, Terry, 3B	.307	238	37	73	18	2	4	44	1
*Landrum, Ced, Of	.000	4	0	0	0	0	0	0	1
*Lee, Derek, Of	.315	381	79	120	30	7	10	80	16
*Maksudian, Mike, 1B	.314	264	57	83	16	7	10	49	5
*Masteller, Dan, 1B	.322	211	35	68	13	4	7	47	3
McCarty, Dave, Of	.385	143	42	55	11	0	8	31	5
Meares, Pat, Ss	.296	54	6	16	5	0	0	3	0
*Ortiz, Ray, Of	.283	357	42	101	18	2	5	53	2
Parks, Derek, C	.311	363	63	113	23	1	17	71	0
Russo, Paul, 3B	.281	288	43	81	24	2	10	47	0
Schunk, Jerry, Ss	.270	397	53	107	28	1	2	47	5
Scott, Gary, 3B	.291	189	26	55	8	4	1	28	3
Wade, Scott, Of	.324	37	6	12	3	1	0	4	0

PITCHING	W	L	ERA	G	SV	IP	H	BB	SO
*Casian, Larry	1	0	.00	7	2	7.2	9	2	2
Chapin, Darrin	5	2	4.31	47	14	56.1	58	24	43
*Drees, Tom	15	10	6.22	31	0	153.1	183	62	83
Garces, Rich	1	3	8.33	35	0	54.0	70	64	48
Henry, Jon	6	5	5.70	26	1	94.2	122	30	62
*Lapoint, Dave	6	4	6.09	13	0	75.1	99	29	40
Mahomes, Pat	11	4	3.03	17	0	115.2	89	54	94
Merriman, Brett	5	0	3.00	39	15	48.0	46	18	29
Munoz, Oscar	2	2	4.31	5	0	31.1	29	17	29
Neidlinger, Jim	9	8	5.19	29	0	157.2	175	54	112
Ontiveros, Steve	7	6	2.87	20	0	103.1	90	20	73
*Ortiz, Ray	0	0	18.00	1	0	2.0	6	2	2
*Pulido, Carlos	10	6	4.19	33	0	146.0	169	45	79
*Sims, Mark	3	1	3.41	50	3	66.0	69	36	32
Stevens, Matt	5	3	1.98	53	2	81.2	75	35	60
*Tsamis, George	1	8	8.36	3	0	14.0	27	5	10
Willis, Carl	0	0	2.25	2	0	4.0	6	1	2

Tacoma Tigers (Athletics) AAA

BATTING	Avg.	AB	R	H	2B	3B	HR	RBI	SB
Abbott, Kurt, Ss	.319	480	75	153	36	11	12	79	19
*Aldrete, Mike, Of	.320	122	20	39	11	2	7	21	2
Armas, Marcos, 1B	.290	434	69	126	27	8	15	89	4
Batista, Tony, Ss	.167	12	1	2	1	0	0	1	0
Beard, Garrett, 3B	.143	49	3	7	4	0	0	2	1
Borrelli, Dean, C	.243	210	29	51	7	2	1	19	1
Brosius, Scott, 3B	.297	209	38	62	13	2	8	41	8
#Browne, Jerry, 3B	.240	25	3	6	0	0	0	2	1
Buccheri, Jim, Of	.276	293	45	81	9	3	2	40	12
Cruz, Fausto, 3B	.243	74	13	18	2	1	0	6	3
#Dattola, Kevin, Of	.193	57	6	11	1	0	0	2	1
#Fox, Eric, Of	.312	317	49	99	14	5	11	52	18
Garrison, Webster, 2B	.303	544	91	165	29	5	7	73	17
#Gates, Brent, 2B	.341	44	7	15	7	0	1	4	2
Gomez, Fabio, Of	.282	252	28	71	10	1	2	29	5
Henderson, Dave, Of	.182	11	1	2	1	0	0	2	0
*Killeen, Tim, Dh	.444	9	4	4	0	0	0	0	0
Lydy, Scott, Of	.293	341	70	100	22	6	9	41	10
Martinez, Manuel, Of	.305	59	9	18	2	0	1	6	2
Mercedes, Henry, C	.238	256	37	61	13	1	4	32	1
Morales, Willie, C	.000	3	0	0	0	0	0	0	0
*Neel, Troy, Dh	.360	50	11	18	4	0	1	9	2
Paquette, Craig, 3B	.268	183	29	49	8	0	8	29	3
#Pettis, Gary, Of	.237	76	16	18	4	0	0	6	5
Robbins, Doug, Dh	.226	164	23	37	9	1	3	18	1
*Shockey, Scott, 1B	.254	71	2	18	5	0	1	12	1
Soriano, Fred, Ss	.167	6	3	1	1	0	0	3	0
*Witmeyer, Ron, Of	.254	452	52	115	22	4	3	52	7

PITCHING	W	L	ERA	G	SV	IP	H	BB	SO
*Allison, Dana	3	3	4.48	23	0	62.1	75	19	30
Arnsberg, Brad	3	2	7.48	21	1	27.2	31	21	12
Briscoe, John	1	1	2.92	9	6	12.1	13	9	16
Campbell, Kevin	3	5	2.75	40	12	55.2	42	19	46
Chitren, Steve	1	0	3.00	14	1	24.0	21	14	27

PITCHING	W	L	ERA	G	SV	IP	H	BB	SO
*Guzman, Johnny	2	7	7.32	20	0	87.1	130	44	50
Hillegas, Shawn	2	3	5.48	9	0	47.2	62	13	29
*Horsman, Vince	1	2	4.28	26	3	33.2	37	9	23
Jimenez, Miguel	2	3	4.78	8	0	37.2	32	24	34
*Osteen, Gavin	7	7	5.08	16	0	83.1	89	31	46
Patrick, Bronswell	3	8	7.05	35	1	104.2	156	42	56
Peek, Tim	9	6	3.95	60	5	86.2	103	28	63
Phoenix, Steve	0	2	6.97	11	0	31.0	42	27	21
*Raczka, Mike	2	1	5.37	55	0	60.1	65	30	40
Shikles, Larry	7	7	4.49	38	2	148.1	179	34	68
Slusarski, Joe	7	5	4.76	24	0	113.1	133	40	61
Smith, Tim	3	0	7.15	6	0	22.2	31	11	16
Smithberg, Roger	3	3	1.78	28	4	50.2	50	11	25
Van Poppel, Todd	4	8	5.83	16	0	78.2	67	54	71
*Young, Curt	6	1	1.93	10	0	65.1	53	16	31

Tucson Toros (Astros) AAA

BATTING	Avg.	AB	R	H	2B	3B	HR	RBI	SB
Ansley, Willie, Of	.262	382	71	100	20	7	5	61	22
#Barrett, Tom, 3B	.279	204	31	57	3	5	1	19	5
#Brumley, Mike, Of	.353	346	65	122	25	8	0	47	24
#Candaele, Casey, Of	.296	27	4	8	1	0	0	4	1
*Carter, Steve, Of	.247	146	26	36	7	0	1	17	6
Castillo, Braulio, Of	.363	212	40	77	20	4	2	37	9
#Daugherty, Jack, 1B	.390	141	23	55	9	2	2	29	1
Eusebio, Tony, C	.324	281	39	91	20	1	1	43	1
Lindeman, Jim, 1B	.362	390	72	141	28	7	12	88	5
Massarelli, John, Dh	.281	423	66	119	28	4	2	42	37
Mikulik, Joe, Of	.301	296	48	89	24	2	4	45	9
Miller, Orlando, Ss	.304	471	86	143	29	16	16	89	2
Montgomery, Ray, Of	.340	50	9	17	3	1	2	6	1
Mouton, James, 2B	.315	546	126	172	42	12	16	92	40
Nevin, Phil, 3B	.286	448	67	128	21	3	10	93	8
Parker, Rick, Of	.308	120	28	37	9	3	2	12	6
Trafton, Todd, 1B	.250	20	3	5	1	1	0	2	0
Tucker, Scooter, C	.274	318	54	87	20	2	1	37	1

PITCHING	W	L	ERA	G	SV	IP	H	BB	SO
*Agosto, Juan	7	3	5.29	51	3	51.0	66	29	33
Barrett, Tom	1	0	.00	3	0	4.0	3	1	1
*Bell, Eric	4	6	4.05	22	0	106.2	131	39	53
Bruske, Jim	4	2	3.78	12	1	66.2	77	18	42
Capel, Mike	0	4	7.16	25	3	32.2	46	11	33
Costello, Fred	6	2	3.69	14	0	83.0	92	33	36
Dixon, Eddie	4	3	4.15	50	0	80.1	92	22	41
Edens, Tom	1	0	6.14	5	0	7.1	9	3	6
*Hartgraves, Dean	1	6	6.37	23	0	77.2	90	40	42
Hudek, John	3	1	3.79	13	0	19.0	17	11	18
Huisman, Rick	4	4	6.04	16	0	76.0	84	46	63
*Hurta, Bob	2	1	6.00	8	1	12.0	11	13	10
Jones, Todd	4	2	4.44	41	12	48.2	49	31	45
Juden, Jeff	11	6	4.63	27	0	169.0	174	76	156
Mathews, Terry	5	0	3.55	16	2	33.0	40	11	34
*Osuna, Al	3	1	4.50	13	1	30.0	26	17	38
Reynolds, Shane	10	6	3.62	25	1	139.1	147	21	106
Robinson, Jeff	1	0	5.06	13	1	21.1	22	9	15
Veres, Dave	6	10	4.90	43	5	130.1	156	32	122
Wall, Donnie	6	4	3.83	25	0	131.2	147	35	89
Walton, Bruce	2	0	1.80	13	7	15.0	12	3	14
Williams, Brian	1	0	.00	2	0	3.0	1	0	3
*Windes, Rodney	1	3	9.00	13	0	12.0	20	6	10

Vancouver Canadians (Angels) AAA

BATTING	Avg.	AB	R	H	2B	3B	HR	RBI	SB
*Anderson, Garret, Of	.293	467	57	137	34	4	4	71	3
Correia, Rod, Ss	.271	207	43	56	10	4	4	28	11
Dalesandro, Mark, 3B	.299	107	16	32	8	1	2	15	1
#Davis, Kevin, 2B	.271	210	24	57	8	3	2	25	3
#Dodge, Thomas, C	.235	17	3	4	1	0	0	4	3
*Edmonds, Jim, Of	.315	356	59	112	28	4	9	74	6
*Fabregas, Jorge, C	.231	13	1	3	1	0	0	1	0
Flora, Kevin, Dh	.330	94	17	31	2	0	1	12	6
Forbes, P.J., 2B	.250	16	1	4	2	0	0	3	0

Class AAA Directory

American Association

Buffalo Bisons (Pirates)
Pilot Field (capacity 20,900)
Indianapolis Indians (Reds)
Bush Stadium (12,934)
Iowa Cubs (Cubs)
Sec Taylor Stadium (10,500)
Louisville Redbirds (Cardinals)
Cardinal Stadium (33,500)
Nashville Sounds (White Sox)
Herschel Greer Stadium (17,000)
New Orleans Zephyrs (Brewers)
Privateer Park (5,116)
Oklahoma City 89ers (Rangers)
All-Sports Stadium (15,000)
Omaha Royals (Royals)
Rosenblatt Stadium (19,500)

Switch-hitter
* Left-handed
(Players in major leagues are listed with last minor league team.)

349

MINOR LEAGUE REPORT

Class AAA Directory

International League

Charlotte Knights (Indians)
Knights Castle (10,917)
Columbus Clippers (Yankees)
Harold Cooper Stadium (15,000)
Norfolk Tides (Mets)
Harbor Park (12,000)
Ottawa Lynx (Expos)
Rec Complex (10,000)
Pawtucket Red Sox (Red Sox)
McCoy Stadium (6,010)
Richmond Braves (Braves)
The Diamond (12,500)
Rochester Red Wings (Orioles)
Silver Stadium (12,503)
Scranton/Wilkes-Barre Red Barons (Phillies)
Lackawanna County Stadium (10,800)
Syracuse Chiefs (Blue Jays)
MacArthur Stadium (8,316)
Toledo Mud Hens (Tigers)
Ned Skeldon Stadium (10,025)

Richmond Braves (Braves)

BATTING	Avg.	AB	R	H	2B	3B	HR	RBI	SB
Gonzales, Larry, C	.261	264	30	69	9	0	2	27	5
Gruber, Kelly, Dh	.458	24	4	11	1	0	1	5	0
*Hill, Orsino, Of	.222	36	4	8	3	1	1	4	0
*Jackson, John, Of	.289	201	28	58	9	4	2	20	12
Kipila, Jeff, Dh	.313	99	18	31	7	0	5	21	2
Martinez, Ray, Ss	.252	357	54	90	24	2	3	35	5
Perez, Eddie, 3B	.306	363	66	111	23	6	12	70	21
#Snow, J.T., 1B	.340	94	19	32	9	1	5	24	0
Tejero, Fausto, C	.153	59	2	9	0	0	0	2	1
Turner, Chris, C	.276	283	50	78	12	1	4	57	6
*Van Burkleo, Ty, 1B	.274	361	47	99	19	2	6	56	7
#Walewander, Jim, 2B	.305	351	77	107	12	1	1	43	36
Walton, Jerome, Of	.313	176	34	55	11	1	2	20	5
#Williams, Reggie, Of	.274	481	92	132	17	6	2	53	50

PITCHING	W	L	ERA	G	SV	IP	H	BB	SO
*Anderson, Brian	0	1	12.38	2	0	8.0	13	6	2
Bennett, Erik	6	6	6.05	18	1	80.1	101	21	51
Burcham, Tim	0	2	11.30	13	1	14.1	29	8	11
Butcher, Mike	2	3	4.44	14	3	24.1	21	12	12
*Charland, Colin	3	2	3.86	6	0	32.2	37	17	27
Edenfield, Ken	0	0	.00	2	0	3.2	1	1	5
Egloff, Bruce	0	0	3.50	12	1	18.0	20	3	9
Farrell, John	4	5	3.99	12	0	85.2	83	28	71
Fritz, John	3	1	4.07	8	0	42.0	52	18	29
*Gamez, Bob	1	0	4.73	9	0	13.1	11	9	15
Grahe, Joe	1	1	4.50	4	0	6.0	4	2	5
Grant, Mark	1	0	.87	5	0	10.1	5	6	11
*Green, Otis	2	8	5.61	25	0	109.0	109	53	97
*Hathaway, Hilly	7	0	4.09	12	0	70.1	60	27	44
*Holzemer, Mark	9	6	4.82	24	0	145.2	158	70	80
Leftwich, Phillip	7	7	4.64	20	0	126.0	138	45	102
Lewis, Scott	3	1	1.37	24	9	39.1	31	9	38
*Nielsen, Jerry	2	5	4.20	33	0	55.2	70	20	45
Peck, Steve	5	3	4.85	31	0	72.1	91	29	47
Percival, Troy	0	1	6.27	18	4	18.2	24	13	19
Pico, Jeff	3	1	4.21	18	0	25.2	29	20	16
Scott, Darryl	7	1	2.09	46	15	51.2	35	19	57
Springer, Russ	5	4	4.27	11	0	59.0	58	33	40
Swingle, Paul	2	9	6.92	37	1	67.2	85	32	61
Zappelli, Mark	0	1	3.91	17	1	25.1	31	5	13

Final AA Player Stats

Eastern League

Albany-Colonie Yankees (Yankees) AA

BATTING	Avg.	AB	R	H	2B	3B	HR	RBI	SB
Barnwell, Richard, Dh	.298	463	98	138	24	7	11	50	33
*Carpenter, Bubba, Of	.321	53	8	17	4	0	2	14	2
*DeBerry, Joe, 1B	.256	446	58	114	19	7	12	63	3
Eenhoorn, Robert, Ss	.280	314	48	88	24	3	6	46	3
#Erickson, Greg, 3B	.100	10	2	1	0	0	0	0	0
Figga, Mike, C	.227	22	3	5	0	0	0	2	1
*Flannelly, Tim, 3B	.272	184	21	50	9	2	2	18	5
*Fox, Andy, 3B	.275	236	44	65	16	1	3	24	12
#Hankins, Mike, 3B	.223	175	16	39	2	0	0	12	2
Jordan, Kevin, 2B	.283	513	87	145	33	4	16	87	8
*Leach, Jalal, Of	.282	457	64	129	19	9	14	79	15
*Leshnock, Donnie, C	.000	3	0	0	0	0	0	0	0
Livesey, Jeff, C	.154	104	6	16	4	0	0	6	0
Mouton, Lyle, Of	.255	491	74	125	22	3	16	76	18
#Oster, Paul, 1B	.208	106	11	22	7	1	0	8	1
Pineda, Jose, C	.150	107	12	16	2	0	2	12	0
#Posada, Jorge, C	.280	25	3	7	0	0	0	0	0
*Robertson, Jason, Of	.228	483	65	110	30	4	6	41	35
*Rodriguez, Carlos, Ss	.368	152	16	56	14	1	0	30	2
*Sanchez, Gordon, C	.215	195	23	42	11	0	1	21	3
Velarde, Randy, Ss	.235	17	2	4	0	0	1	2	0

Switch-hitter
* Left-handed
(Players in major leagues are listed with last minor league team.)

PITCHING	W	L	ERA	G	SV	IP	H	BB	SO
Barnwell, Richard	0	0	.00	1	0	2.0	2	0	2
Batchelor, Richard	1	3	.89	36	19	40.1	27	12	40
Carper, Mark	7	10	4.52	25	0	155.1	148	70	98
*Dunbar, Matt	1	0	2.66	15	0	23.2	23	6	18
Faw, Brian	9	5	5.23	45	4	86.0	95	36	52
Frazier, Ron	4	3	3.84	12	0	79.2	93	16	65
*Garagozzo, Keith	4	6	4.48	17	0	86.1	88	24	71
Gogolewski, Doug	4	1	2.21	13	1	20.1	20	4	10
*Haller, Jim	2	2	3.99	41	0	67.2	66	29	53
*Hines, Richard	0	1	2.08	14	0	26.0	17	11	27
Hodges, Darren	10	10	4.72	30	0	152.2	161	61	96
Jean, Domingo	5	3	2.51	11	0	61.0	42	33	41
*Karp, Ryan	0	0	4.15	3	0	13.0	13	9	10
*Ojala, Kirt	1	0	.00	1	0	6.1	5	2	6
*Pettitte, Andy	1	0	3.60	1	0	5.0	5	2	6
Polak, Rich	3	4	4.55	21	5	27.2	34	10	16
Popplewell, Tom	1	3	5.88	34	1	64.1	60	48	59
Prybylinski, Bruce	0	0	1.93	2	0	4.2	4	1	1
*Quirico, Rafael	4	10	3.52	36	7	94.2	92	33	79
*Taylor, Brien	13	7	3.48	27	0	163.0	127	102	150
Witt, Mike	0	0	.00	1	0	2.0	2	0	2

Binghamton Mets (Mets) AA

BATTING	Avg.	AB	R	H	2B	3B	HR	RBI	SB
#Allison, Tom, Ss	.200	130	16	26	7	2	0	5	5
#Butterfield, Chris, Of	.211	237	32	50	10	5	9	37	0
*Davis, Jay, Of	.279	409	52	114	15	4	1	35	5
Dellicarri, Joe, Ss	.250	252	37	63	15	1	1	19	2
*Dziadkowiec, Andy, C	.210	176	19	37	12	1	1	18	0
Gonzalez, Javier, C	.230	257	30	59	7	0	10	36	0
*Howard, Tim, Of	.300	100	13	30	6	1	2	15	2
Hunter, Bert, Of	.224	308	38	69	10	3	5	30	9
Huskey, Butch, 3B	.251	526	72	132	23	1	25	98	11
*Jacobs, Frank, 1B	.269	346	50	93	17	3	9	46	2
Ledesma, Aaron, Dh	.267	206	23	55	12	0	5	22	2
#Lowery, David, Ph	.050	20	0	1	0	1	0	0	0
#Otero, Ricky, Of	.264	503	63	133	21	10	2	54	29
*Sandy, Tim, Of	.242	157	29	38	8	2	5	26	0
#Veras, Quilvio, 2B	.306	444	87	136	19	7	2	51	52
#Zinter, Alan, 1B	.262	432	68	113	24	4	24	87	1

PITCHING	W	L	ERA	G	SV	IP	H	BB	SO
Castillo, Juan	7	11	4.56	26	0	165.2	167	55	118
Dorn, Chris	2	1	5.44	23	0	41.1	48	17	22
*Douma, Todd	0	3	6.90	15	0	30.0	46	16	23
*Fernandez, Sid	0	1	1.80	2	0	10.0	6	3	11
*Gunderson, Eric	2	1	5.24	20	1	22.1	20	14	26
Guzik, Robbie	1	1	8.06	15	0	22.1	36	7	12
Harriger, Denny	13	10	2.95	35	1	170.2	174	40	89
*Jacome, Jason	8	4	3.21	14	0	87.0	85	38	56
Knackert, Brent	1	3	5.56	15	0	43.2	59	13	27
Long, Steve	12	8	3.96	38	1	156.2	165	58	70
*Marshall, Randy	0	3	8.49	7	0	35.0	61	8	21
Mccready, Jim	1	1	3.44	14	0	18.1	18	4	12
Miller, Pat	0	0	9.00	2	0	2.0	3	1	2
Reich, Andy	0	4	3.34	24	4	35.0	38	9	16
Roa, Joe	12	7	3.87	32	0	167.1	190	24	73
Rogers, Bryan	5	4	2.34	62	8	84.2	80	25	42
Silcox, Rusty	0	1	6.97	3	0	10.1	10	9	8
Walker, Pete	4	9	3.44	45	19	99.1	89	46	89

Bowie Baysox (Orioles) AA

BATTING	Avg.	AB	R	H	2B	3B	HR	RBI	SB
Alfonzo, Ed, 3B	.264	459	45	121	22	3	5	49	14
*Alstead, Jason, Of	.298	124	25	37	4	3	2	13	12
*Baines, Harold, Dh	.000	6	0	0	0	0	0	0	0
Cameron, Stanton, Of	.276	384	65	106	27	1	21	64	6
Davis, Glenn, 1B	.333	6	2	2	1	0	1	1	0
Devarez, Cesar, C	.224	174	14	39	7	1	0	17	5
Devereaux, Mike, Of	.286	7	1	2	1	0	0	2	0
Ferretti, Sam, 3B	.238	164	24	39	6	0	4	18	2
Hammonds, Jeffrey, Of	.283	92	13	26	3	0	3	10	4
Holland, Tim, Ss	.249	449	49	112	17	5	9	53	9

Class AAA Directory

Pacific Coast League

Albuquerque Dukes (Dodgers)
Albuquerque Sports Stadium (10,510)
Calgary Cannons (Mariners)
Foothills Stadium (7,500)
Colorado Springs Sky Sox (Rockies)
Sky Sox Stadium (6,130)
Edmonton Trappers (Marlins)
John Ducey Park (6,200)
Las Vegas Stars (Padres)
Cashman Field (9,370)
Phoenix Firebirds (Giants)
Scottsdale Stadium (10,000)
Salt Lake Buzz (Twins)
Franklin Quest Field (15,000)
Tacoma Tigers (A's)
Cheney Stadium (8,002)
Tucson Toros (Astros)
Hi Corbett Field (9,500)
Vancouver Canadians (Angels)
Nat Bailey Stadium (6,500)

Switch-hitter
* Left-handed
(Players in major leagues are listed with last minor league team.)

Class AA Directory

Eastern League

Albany-Colonie Yankees (Yankees)
Heritage Park (5,600)
Binghamton Mets (Mets)
Municipal Stadium (6,064)
Bowie Baysox (Orioles)
Prince Georges County Stadium (10,000)
Canton-Akron Indians (Indians)
Thurman Munson Stadium (5,765)
Harrisburg Senators (Expos)
RiverSide Stadium (5,600)
New Britain Red Sox (Red Sox)
Beehive Field (4,700)
New Haven Ravens (Rockies)
Yale Field (6,200)
Portland Sea Dogs (Mariners)
Hadlock Field (6,000)
Reading Phillies (Phillies)
Municipal Stadium (7,500)
Trenton Thunder (Tigers)
Waterfront Park (6,200)

BATTING	Avg.	AB	R	H	2B	3B	HR	RBI	SB
Lewis, T.R., Dh	.304	480	73	146	26	2	5	64	22
*Martinez, Chito, Dh	.077	13	5	1	0	0	0	0	0
Millares, Jose, 2B	.280	50	6	14	1	2	0	5	1
*Miller, Brent, 1B	.257	404	35	104	13	0	11	66	6
Obando, Sherman, Of	.241	58	8	14	2	0	3	12	1
Ortiz, Bo, Of	.200	30	1	6	0	1	0	3	0
Ramirez, Danny, 2B	.065	31	3	2	0	0	0	0	0
#Roso, Jimmy, C	.231	117	12	27	5	0	0	9	2
*Tyler, Brad, 2B	.236	437	85	103	24	17	10	44	24
Washington, Kyle, Of	.252	389	50	98	23	4	7	33	16
*Wawruck, Jim, Of	.297	475	59	141	21	5	4	44	28
#Zaun, Gregg, C	.306	258	25	79	10	0	3	38	4

PITCHING	W	L	ERA	G	SV	IP	H	BB	SO
Borowski, Joe	3	0	.00	9	0	17.2	11	11	17
Chaves, Rafael	2	5	3.94	45	20	48.0	56	16	39
Dedrick, Jim	8	3	2.54	38	3	106.1	84	32	78
*DuBois, Brian	6	1	2.52	13	0	75.0	71	29	37
*Farrar, Terry	7	7	3.49	24	0	116.0	114	40	85
Forney, Rick	0	0	1.29	1	0	7.0	1	1	4
*Krivda, Rick	7	5	3.08	22	0	125.2	114	50	108
Mercedes, Jose	6	8	4.78	26	0	147.0	170	65	75
Mussina, Mike	1	0	2.25	2	0	8.0	5	1	10
Paveloff, Dave	5	4	1.73	32	1	57.1	50	19	31
Ricci, Chuck	7	4	3.20	34	5	81.2	72	20	83
Ryan, Kevin	3	10	5.30	16	0	88.1	106	34	40
Satre, Jason	7	3	3.11	13	0	84.0	68	20	65
Schullstrom, Erik	5	10	4.27	24	1	109.2	119	45	97
Smith, Daryl	0	0	2.45	3	0	22.0	14	11	23
Smith, Mark	0	1	8.22	5	0	7.2	11	1	4
Taylor, Tom	4	7	5.62	40	4	89.2	90	47	69
*Valenzuela, Fernando	0	0	1.50	1	0	6.0	4	0	4
Wood, Brian	1	0	3.38	8	1	13.1	13	8	15
Zaun, Gregg	0	0	.00	1	0	2.1	1	0	0

Canton-Akron Indians (Indians) AA

BATTING	Avg.	AB	R	H	2B	3B	HR	RBI	SB
Bell, David, 3B	.292	483	69	141	20	2	9	60	3
Flores, Miguel, 2B	.292	435	73	127	20	5	3	54	36
*Giles, Brian, Of	.327	425	64	139	17	6	8	64	18
*Harvey, Raymond, 1B	.244	41	5	10	1	0	0	4	0
Hernandez, Jose, Ss	.200	150	19	30	6	0	2	17	9
Lennon, Pat, Of	.257	152	24	39	7	1	4	23	4
Lopez, Luis, 1B	.277	231	30	64	16	0	2	41	0
Martindale, Ryan, C	.219	310	44	68	19	1	10	39	1
Mota, Carlos, C	.286	84	12	24	1	0	0	10	2
Odor, Rouglas, Ss	.209	263	39	55	9	2	3	18	10
#Peguero, Julio, Of	.226	177	19	40	6	5	0	14	5
Perry, Herbert, 1B	.269	327	52	88	21	1	9	55	7
Ramirez, Manny, Of	.340	344	67	117	32	0	17	79	2
Ramirez, Omar, Of	.314	516	116	162	24	6	7	53	24
*Sanders, Tracy, Of	.213	136	20	29	6	2	5	20	4
Sarbaugh, Mike, 1B	.249	277	29	69	13	5	6	31	3
Skinner, Joel, C	.239	46	6	11	3	0	2	5	0
*Sparks, Greg, 1B	.231	117	11	27	9	0	4	23	0
Sued, Nick, C	.254	63	5	16	2	0	1	6	0
Vargas, Hector, Ss	.222	90	9	20	2	0	1	8	3

PITCHING	W	L	ERA	G	SV	IP	H	BB	SO
Abbott, Paul	4	5	4.06	13	0	75.1	72	28	86
Alexander, Gerald	1	0	6.00	6	1	9.0	8	7	6
Allen, Chad	0	1	5.16	18	1	22.2	34	12	10
*Bryant, Shawn	10	5	3.72	27	0	172.0	179	61	111
Byrd, Paul	0	0	3.60	2	0	10.0	7	3	8
*Charland, Colin	2	2	7.43	5	0	23.0	33	8	18
Dyer, Mike	7	4	5.55	17	0	94.0	90	55	75
*Embree, Alan	0	0	3.38	1	0	5.1	3	3	4
Garcia, Apolinar	8	4	3.89	42	3	111.0	103	37	110
*Gardella, Mike	2	1	4.37	21	4	22.2	26	22	14
Hernandez, Fernando	0	1	11.74	2	0	7.2	14	5	8
Jones, Calvin	5	5	3.30	43	22	62.2	40	26	73
Lopez, Albie	9	4	3.11	16	0	110.0	79	47	80
*McCarthy, Greg	2	3	4.72	33	6	34.1	28	37	39
Mlicki, Dave	2	1	.39	6	0	23.0	15	8	21
Nagy, Charles	0	0	1.13	2	0	8.0	8	2	4

Switch-hitter
* Left-handed
(Players in major leagues are listed with last minor league team.)

PITCHING	W	L	ERA	G	SV	IP	H	BB	SO
Power, Ted	0	0	4.67	7	0	17.1	22	8	16
*Rivera, Roberto	0	1	5.02	8	0	14.1	22	3	6
Robinson, Nap	3	2	4.56	9	0	47.1	49	18	26
*Romanoli, Paul	1	2	4.54	30	0	39.2	37	21	38
Sarbaugh, Mike	0	0	.00	3	0	3.0	2	2	0
Shuey, Paul	4	8	7.30	27	0	61.2	76	36	41
Soper, Mike	1	3	5.63	8	4	8.0	8	4	11
Stone, Eric	3	0	3.05	13	0	20.2	17	17	15
Tavarez, Julian	2	1	.95	3	0	19.0	14	1	11
*Trice, Wally	3	2	5.61	19	1	51.1	65	24	30
Turek, Joe	1	0	2.25	3	0	16.0	11	7	7
Valdez, Rafael	1	0	.00	5	1	11.1	7	2	12
Veres, Randy	1	5	4.89	13	0	57.0	59	19	49
Wilkins, Mike	3	3	3.89	11	0	44.0	44	13	37

Harrisburg Senators (Expos) AA

BATTING	Avg.	AB	R	H	2B	3B	HR	RBI	SB
Andrews, Shane, 3B	.260	442	77	115	29	2	18	70	10
Barker, Tim, Ss	.308	185	40	57	10	1	4	16	7
Bradbury, Miah, C	.313	32	4	10	5	0	1	6	0
Daniel, Mike, 1B	.333	6	1	2	0	1	0	1	0
Fitzpatrick, Rob, C	.226	341	44	77	10	1	11	46	6
*Floyd, Cliff, 1B	.329	380	82	125	17	4	26	101	31
#Fulton, Greg, C	.000	4	0	0	0	0	0	0	0
*Griffin, Mark, Of	.151	53	5	8	2	0	0	6	5
Hardge, Mike, 2B	.244	386	70	94	15	10	6	35	27
*Horne, Tyrone, Of	.359	128	22	46	8	1	4	22	3
*Krause, Ron, 2B	.288	59	12	17	5	1	1	8	2
*Marrero, Oreste, 1B	.333	255	39	85	18	1	10	49	3
Martin, Chris, Ss	.294	395	68	116	23	1	7	54	16
Murray, Glenn, Of	.253	475	82	120	21	4	26	96	16
*Pride, Curtis, Of	.356	180	51	64	6	3	15	39	21
#Rice, Lance, C	.235	136	12	32	10	0	1	20	0
Rundels, Matt, Of	.342	117	27	40	5	0	6	17	8
Simons, Mitch, Dh	.234	77	5	18	1	1	0	5	2
Tovar, Edgar, Ss	.262	42	5	11	0	0	0	3	0
White, Derrick, 1B	.228	79	14	18	1	0	2	12	2
White, Rondell, Of	.328	372	72	122	16	10	12	52	21
*Wilstead, Randy, 1B	.259	108	10	28	7	0	4	15	1
Woods, Tyrone, Of	.252	318	50	80	15	1	16	59	4

PITCHING	W	L	ERA	G	SV	IP	H	BB	SO
Ausanio, Joe	2	0	1.21	19	6	22.1	16	4	30
Batista, Miguel	13	5	4.34	26	0	141.0	139	86	91
Brito, Mario	4	3	2.68	36	10	50.1	41	11	51
Corbin, Archie	5	3	3.68	42	4	73.1	43	59	91
Cornelius, Reid	10	7	4.17	27	0	157.2	146	82	119
*Dehart, Rick	2	4	7.68	12	0	34.0	45	19	18
Diaz, Rafael	5	4	3.56	31	0	91.0	86	31	62
*Eischen, Joey	14	4	3.62	20	0	119.1	122	60	110
Haynes, Heath	8	0	2.59	57	5	66.0	46	19	78
Henderson, Rod	5	0	1.82	5	0	29.2	20	15	25
*Looney, Brian	3	2	2.38	8	0	56.2	36	17	76
*Perez, Yorkis	4	2	3.45	34	3	44.1	49	20	58
*Puig, Benny	0	1	2.45	14	1	18.1	16	7	10
*Rueter, Kirk	5	0	1.36	9	0	59.2	47	7	36
*Thomas, Mike	2	2	4.73	25	6	32.1	34	19	40
Urbina, Ugueth	4	5	3.99	11	0	70.0	66	32	45
*White, Gabe	7	2	2.16	16	0	100.0	80	28	80
*Winston, Darrin	1	0	4.63	24	1	44.2	53	19	36

London Tigers (Tigers) AA

BATTING	Avg.	AB	R	H	2B	3B	HR	RBI	SB
Alder, Jimmy, 3B	.193	119	8	23	7	1	0	7	2
Bautista, Danny, Of	.285	424	55	121	21	1	6	48	28
*Cornelius, Brian, Of	.262	229	21	60	11	0	4	24	1
Decillis, Dean, Dh	.293	208	28	61	13	0	5	26	1
#Givens, Jim, Ss	.263	262	24	69	8	3	3	28	17
Gonzalez, Pete, C	.156	64	5	10	3	0	0	6	0
*Higginson, Bob, Of	.308	224	25	69	15	4	4	35	3
Mendenhall, Kirk, Ss	.204	275	41	56	5	1	1	18	21
Milne, Darren, Dh	.050	20	2	1	0	0	0	1	0
Pemberton, Rudy, Of	.276	471	70	130	22	4	15	67	14

Class AA Directory

Southern League

Birmingham Barons (White Sox)
Hoover Met (10,000)
Carolina Mudcats (Pirates)
Five County Stadium (6,000)
Chattanooga Lookouts (Reds)
Engel Stadium (7,500)
Greenville Braves (Braves)
Municipal Stadium (7,027)
Huntsville Stars (A's)
Joe W. Davis Stadium (10,200)
Jacksonville Suns (Mariners)
Wolfson Park (8,200)
Knoxville Smokies (Blue Jays)
Bill Meyer Stadium (6,412)
Memphis Chicks (Royals)
Tim McCarver Stadium (10,000)
Nashville Xpress (Twins)
Herschel Greer Stadium (17,000)
Orlando Cubs (Cubs)
Tinker Field (6,000)

Switch-hitter
* Left-handed
(Players in major leagues are listed with last minor league team.)

Class AA Directory

Texas League

Arkansas Travelers (Cardinals)
Ray Winder Field (6,083)

El Paso Diablos (Brewers)
Cohen Stadium (10,000)

Jackson Generals (Astros)
Smith-Wills Stadium (5,200)

Midland Angels (Angels)
Angels Stadium (4,000)

San Antonio Missions (Dodgers)
Municipal Stadium (6,500)

Shreveport Captains (Giants)
Fairgrounds Field (6,200)

Tulsa Drillers (Rangers)
Drillers Stadium (10,500)

Wichita Wranglers (Padres)
Lawrence-Dumont Stadium (7,488)

Pitching

Blomdahl, Ben 6 6 3.71 17 0 119.0 108 42 72

BATTING	Avg.	AB	R	H	2B	3B	HR	RBI	SB
#Penn, Shannon, 2B	.260	493	78	128	13	6	0	36	53
Perona, Joe, C	.269	349	34	94	17	2	5	29	2
#Pratte, Evan, 3B	.238	408	44	97	24	2	3	46	5
*Rendina, Mike, 1B	.282	475	59	134	30	1	10	77	8
Saltzgaber, Brian, Of	.212	241	28	51	9	1	2	17	13
Sellers, Rick, C	.264	239	31	63	11	0	6	31	5
#Williams, Ted, Of	.240	125	17	30	8	0	0	9	10

PITCHING	W	L	ERA	G	SV	IP	H	BB	SO
Blomdahl, Ben	6	6	3.71	17	0	119.0	108	42	72
Braley, Jeff	1	2	4.73	9	2	13.1	19	6	6
Carlyle, Ken	4	6	3.69	12	0	78.0	72	35	50
Edmondson, Brian	0	4	6.26	5	0	23.0	30	13	17
Garcia, Mike	1	0	5.56	6	0	11.1	12	6	12
Gomez, Henrique	4	3	3.53	29	1	71.1	56	27	67
Greene, Rick	2	2	6.52	23	0	29.0	31	20	19
*Guilfoyle, Mike	1	2	3.73	49	3	41.0	43	16	35
*Henry, Jim	1	3	5.28	33	0	30.2	33	28	25
*Kelley, Rich	0	0	9.00	7	0	5.0	7	5	3
Lima, Jose	8	13	4.07	27	0	177.0	160	59	138
Lira, Felipe	10	4	3.38	22	0	152.0	157	39	122
Lumley, Mike	4	2	4.57	26	0	41.1	32	20	26
Pfaff, Jason	6	9	5.73	23	0	132.0	176	45	62
Schwarber, Tom	5	2	5.03	48	16	53.2	54	28	58
Stidham, Phillip	2	2	2.38	33	2	34.0	40	19	39
*Thompson, Justin	3	6	4.09	14	0	83.2	96	37	72
Undorf, Bob	0	1	3.58	19	1	32.2	37	6	15
Warren, Brian	3	3	5.83	22	5	29.1	36	9	21
Wolf, Steven	2	5	4.99	14	0	61.1	56	45	55

New Britain Red Sox (Red Sox) AA

BATTING	Avg.	AB	R	H	2B	3B	HR	RBI	SB
Beams, Mike, Of	.236	263	26	62	16	1	5	36	3
*Bethea, Scott, Ss	.228	395	47	90	13	1	0	30	3
Brown, Bryan, Of	.230	113	13	26	5	1	3	17	0
Carroll, Kevin, C	.149	168	9	25	6	0	0	6	1
Chick, Bruce, Of	.259	193	20	50	8	1	3	14	2
Crowley, Jim, 2B	.241	369	49	89	19	1	11	51	3
Delgado, Alex, C	.184	87	10	16	2	0	1	9	2
Dixon, Colin, 3B	.210	214	11	45	10	0	3	22	1
*Friedman, Jason, 1B	.248	294	22	73	15	1	1	24	2
*Hatteberg, Scott, C	.278	227	35	63	10	2	7	28	1
*Mahay, Ron, Of	.120	25	2	3	0	0	1	2	1
Moore, Boo, Of	.209	301	35	63	8	1	11	32	7
Morrison, Jim, Of	.221	249	30	55	10	1	4	25	11
*Norris, Bill, 3B	.259	398	43	103	17	4	3	36	4
*Rappoli, Paul, Of	.213	356	49	76	16	5	3	26	6
Rodriguez, Tony, Ss	.228	355	37	81	16	4	0	31	8
#Tatum, Willie, 1B	.276	152	25	42	7	0	1	21	4
*Thoutsis, Paul, Of	.291	213	17	62	12	2	0	21	0
*Wallin, Les, Dh	.231	195	22	45	10	0	3	23	1

PITCHING	W	L	ERA	G	SV	IP	H	BB	SO
Carter, Glenn	5	4	3.14	12	0	80.1	67	35	55
*Ciccarella, Joe	0	4	4.22	30	15	32.0	31	23	34
Dzafic, Zack	2	7	4.04	45	2	64.2	86	17	31
*Fischer, Tom	0	2	12.46	16	0	17.1	36	15	12
Hansen, Brent	2	11	4.92	15	0	93.1	99	30	56
Hoy, Peter	9	4	3.84	51	0	79.2	86	41	37
Mintz, Steve	2	4	2.08	43	7	69.1	52	30	51
Mitchell, John	1	1	1.04	8	1	17.1	15	2	8
*Mosley, Tony	0	0	6.17	15	0	11.2	12	9	11
Painter, Gary	3	6	4.06	14	0	77.2	76	29	57
*Riley, Ed	4	6	3.55	14	0	83.2	85	29	50
Rodriguez, Frank	7	11	3.74	28	0	170.2	147	78	151
*Shea, John	4	2	3.65	48	1	56.2	48	22	62
Smith, Tim	7	13	3.79	28	0	180.1	192	44	81
Uhrhan, Kevin	0	1	11.57	9	0	9.1	14	6	3
Vanegmond, Tim	6	12	3.97	29	0	190.1	182	44	163

Reading Phillies (Phillies) AA

BATTING	Avg.	AB	R	H	2B	3B	HR	RBI	SB
#Bieser, Steve, C	.312	170	21	53	6	3	1	19	9

Switch-hitter
* Left-handed
(Players in major leagues are listed with last minor league team.)

BATTING	Avg.	AB	R	H	2B	3B	HR	RBI	SB
*Brady, Pat, Of	.236	140	23	33	8	0	5	14	1
Colombino, Carlo, 3B	.228	325	31	74	8	1	2	22	4
Escobar, John, 2B	.193	202	15	39	4	0	3	17	0
*Fernandez, Jose, C	.248	129	8	32	5	0	3	18	0
*Geisler, Phil, Of	.270	178	25	48	14	1	3	14	4
Grable, Rob, 3B	.233	120	10	28	4	1	1	10	2
Hyde, Mickey, Of	.285	277	32	79	6	2	5	30	3
Jackson, Jeff, Of	.238	374	45	89	14	3	9	51	20
#Kimberlin, Keith, Ss	.264	504	56	133	13	3	2	29	19
Lewis, Mica, 2B	.189	243	29	46	12	2	0	16	13
*Lockett, Ron, 1B	.242	368	53	89	18	5	11	53	12
Moler, Jason, C	.283	138	15	39	11	0	2	19	1
Nuneviller, Thomas, Of	.230	226	24	52	11	0	2	32	3
#Rosado, Ed, C	.171	76	6	13	3	0	0	0	0
*Rusk, Troy, Dh	.243	144	14	35	6	1	6	26	0
Schall, Gene, 1B	.326	285	51	93	12	4	15	60	2
*Taylor, Sam, Of	.277	173	31	48	12	0	5	27	9
*Tokheim, David, Of	.292	257	30	75	11	6	2	25	9
#Waller, Casey, 2B	.260	169	25	44	8	4	2	18	1

PITCHING	W	L	ERA	G	SV	IP	H	BB	SO
Allen, Ron	4	5	4.45	15	0	85.0	82	35	63
Borland, Toby	2	2	2.52	44	13	53.2	38	20	74
Bottalico, Ricky	3	3	2.25	49	20	72.0	63	26	65
Brown, Greg	5	6	5.72	18	0	94.1	119	29	42
*Carter, Andy	1	1	2.82	4	0	22.1	15	12	16
Doolan, Blake	7	8	5.09	27	0	109.2	135	36	61
*Farmer, Mike	5	10	5.03	22	0	102.0	125	34	64
*Gaddy, Bob	6	4	2.51	22	0	75.1	64	29	55
Goedhart, Darrell	9	12	5.20	27	0	152.1	160	54	110
Goergen, Todd	2	1	3.06	3	0	17.2	14	4	10
Hassinger, Brad	0	0	9.00	1	0	2.0	4	0	0
Hill, Eric	2	3	4.59	21	0	68.2	72	30	37
Holman, Craig	8	13	4.14	24	0	139.0	134	43	86
*Marchok, Chris	2	5	5.59	40	0	77.1	82	19	50
Sullivan, Mike	0	3	3.38	31	4	45.1	42	13	29
*Wiegandt, Scott	6	2	3.56	56	0	73.1	75	44	60

Southern League

Birmingham Barons (White Sox) AA

BATTING	Avg.	AB	R	H	2B	3B	HR	RBI	SB
Alvarez, Clemente, C	.225	111	8	25	4	0	1	8	0
Belcher, Kevin, Of	.222	360	38	80	13	2	13	50	11
Cairo, Sergio, 2B	.228	189	20	43	2	0	2	13	6
*Cepicky, Scott, Dh	.242	236	30	57	12	1	7	35	4
Coleman, Ken, 2B	.233	129	11	30	3	0	0	14	2
Coomer, Ron, 3B	.324	262	44	85	18	0	13	50	1
*Disarcina, Glenn, Ss	.400	5	1	2	0	0	0	1	1
#Durham, Ray, 2B	.271	528	83	143	22	10	3	37	39
Hood, Randy, Of	.250	20	6	5	3	1	0	2	0
Manning, Henry, C	.179	106	7	19	3	1	2	9	0
Miranda, Geovany, 2B	.094	32	2	3	0	0	0	0	0
#Nunez, Rogelio, C	.214	257	22	55	10	3	0	21	2
*Pledger, Kinnis, Of	.242	393	70	95	10	6	14	56	19
*Robertson, Mike, 1B	.270	511	73	138	31	3	11	73	10
Saenz, Olmedo, 3B	.347	173	30	60	17	2	6	29	2
Strange, Keith, C	.235	17	1	4	0	0	0	3	0
*Tedder, Scott, Of	.254	118	20	30	5	0	1	12	1
Walker, Dennis, 3B	.214	126	10	27	4	2	2	16	2
Wilson, Brandon, Ss	.270	500	76	135	19	5	2	48	43
Wolak, Jerry, Of	.305	525	78	160	35	4	9	64	16

PITCHING	W	L	ERA	G	SV	IP	H	BB	SO
*Adkins, Steve	1	4	4.14	26	2	50.0	46	20	40
Andujar, Luis	5	0	1.82	6	0	39.2	31	18	48
Baldwin, James	8	5	2.25	17	0	120.0	94	43	107
*Barfield, John	5	2	3.86	13	1	42.0	57	5	18
Boehringer, Brian	2	1	3.54	7	0	40.2	41	14	29
Campos, Frank	2	4	3.25	9	0	55.1	49	26	41
Carter, Jeff	2	1	1.02	13	8	17.2	9	6	21

Class A Directory (full season)

California League

Bakersfield Dodgers (Dodgers)
Sam Lynn Ballpark (3,200)
Central Valley Rockies (Rockies)
Recreation Park (2,000)
High Desert Mavericks (TBA)
Maverick Stadium (3,500)
Lake Elsinore Storm (Angels)
Lake Elsinore Diamond (6,000)
Modesto A's (A's)
Thurman Field (2,500)
Rancho Cucamonga Quakes (Padres)
R.C. Sports Complex (4,600)
Riverside Pilots (Mariners)
Sports Center (3,500)
San Bernardino Spirit (Independent)
Fiscalini Field (3,500)
San Jose Giants (Giants)
Municipal Stadium (4,500)
Stockton Ports (Brewers)
Billy Hebert Field (3,500)

355

Switch-hitter
* Left-handed
(Players in major leagues are listed with last minor league team.)

Class A Directory
(full season)

Carolina League

Durham Bulls (Braves)
Durham Athletic Park
(5,000)

Frederick Keys (Orioles)
Harry Grove Stadium
(5,200)

Kinston Indians (Indians)
Grainger Stadium (4,100)

Lynchburg Red Sox (Red Sox)
City Stadium (4,200)

Prince William Cannons (White Sox)
County Stadium (6,000)

Salem Buccaneers (Pirates)
Municipal Field (5,000)

Wilmington Blue Rocks (Royals)
Legends Stadium (5,500)

Winston-Salem Spirits (Reds)
Ernie Shore Field (6,280)

PITCHING	W	L	ERA	G	SV	IP	H	BB	SO
Ellis, Robert	6	3	3.10	12	0	81.1	68	21	77
Gajkowski, Steve	0	0	.00	1	0	2.1	0	0	2
Gardner, John	2	5	5.50	26	1	75.1	70	43	46
*Gordon, Tony	3	2	2.58	37	1	45.1	32	35	49
Johnson, Barry	2	0	3.32	13	1	21.2	27	6	16
Keyser, Brian	0	2	5.73	2	0	11.0	15	5	8
Leach, Terry	0	0	4.15	4	1	4.1	4	2	5
*Locklear, Dean	2	0	6.14	9	0	22.0	29	11	20
Manon, Ramon	10	7	3.63	25	0	131.1	134	65	88
Mongiello, Mike	0	1	1.54	7	1	11.2	5	4	9
Olsen, Steve	10	9	4.75	25	0	142.0	156	52	92
Perigny, Don	3	4	4.22	48	3	70.1	69	15	57
Ruffcorn, Scott	9	4	2.73	20	0	135.0	108	52	141
Ruffin, Johnny	0	4	2.82	11	2	22.1	16	9	23
Schrenk, Steve	5	1	1.17	8	0	61.2	31	7	51
*Thomas, Larry	0	1	5.14	1	0	7.0	9	1	5

Carolina Mudcats (Pirates) AA

BATTING	Avg.	AB	R	H	2B	3B	HR	RBI	SB
Aude, Rich, 1B	.289	422	66	122	25	3	18	73	8
Banister, Jeff, Ph	.333	15	2	5	1	0	0	4	0
Beasley, Tony, 2B	.202	252	39	51	7	3	4	13	11
*Cummings, Midre, Of	.295	237	33	70	17	2	6	26	5
De los Santos, Al, Of	.223	148	17	33	5	3	0	10	4
Edge, Tim, C	.219	160	12	35	8	0	3	16	1
Green, Tom, Of	.238	311	42	74	14	4	5	48	4
*Johnson, Mark, 1B	.233	399	48	93	18	4	14	52	6
Krevokuch, Jim, 3B	.253	395	58	100	15	3	4	30	4
*Leiper, Tim, 3B	.258	132	11	34	4	0	1	11	0
Neff, Marty, Of	.222	63	2	14	3	0	0	5	0
Ortiz, Javier, Of	.339	109	17	37	10	1	5	24	1
Osik, Keith, C	.280	371	47	104	21	2	10	47	0
Polcovich, Kevin, 2B	.273	11	5	3	0	0	0	1	0
Purdy, Alan, 2B	.268	56	9	15	3	1	0	9	0
Ratliff, Daryl, Of	.284	454	59	129	15	4	0	47	29
Rodriguez, Roman, 2B	.182	11	0	2	0	0	0	0	0
Schreiber, Bruce, Ss	.260	296	42	77	11	3	2	28	1
Sondrini, Joe, 2B	.222	185	21	41	8	0	0	13	2
Thomas, Keith, Of	.238	336	40	80	9	2	15	52	12
*Van Slyke, Andy, Of	.000	4	0	0	0	0	0	1	0
*Womack, Tony, Ss	.304	247	41	75	7	2	0	23	21

PITCHING	W	L	ERA	G	SV	IP	H	BB	SO
Backlund, Brett	7	5	4.58	20	0	106.0	115	28	94
*Beatty, Blaine	7	3	2.85	18	0	94.2	68	35	67
Cecena, Jose	3	3	2.20	14	0	16.1	10	6	21
*Christiansen, Jason	0	0	.00	2	0	2.2	3	1	2
Cole, Victor	0	4	5.93	27	8	41.0	39	31	35
Delossantos, Mariano	1	2	4.73	8	0	40.0	49	15	34
Garza, Alejandro	4	3	3.69	35	1	68.1	63	24	45
*Hancock, Lee	7	3	2.53	25	0	99.2	87	32	85
Harrah, Doug	1	4	9.47	6	0	25.2	40	9	17
Hope, John	9	4	4.37	21	0	111.1	123	29	66
Hunter, Bobby	5	3	1.01	46	7	71.0	54	35	53
Jones, Dan	0	5	4.82	11	1	52.1	63	21	34
*Leiper, Dave	2	1	1.48	8	0	30.1	26	5	16
Lieber, Jon	6	3	5.07	10	0	55.0	71	16	45
Loaiza, Steve	2	1	3.77	7	0	43.0	39	12	40
McCurry, Jeff	2	1	2.79	23	0	29.0	24	14	14
Miceli, Dan	6	6	4.69	53	17	71.0	65	43	87
Miller, Paul	2	2	2.82	6	0	38.1	31	12	33
Parkinson, Eric	0	0	2.08	2	0	4.1	4	1	2
Piatt, Doug	0	1	10.06	14	0	17.0	29	7	11
*Smith, Zane	1	2	3.05	4	0	20.2	20	5	13
Tafoya, Dennis	5	4	3.09	49	0	81.2	87	21	55
Toliver, Fred	2	2	3.15	33	12	40.0	32	24	48
*Tomlin, Randy	1	0	.75	2	0	12.0	7	1	9
Wakefield, Tim	3	5	6.99	9	0	56.2	68	22	36
White, Rick	4	3	3.50	12	0	69.1	59	12	52
Zimmerman, Mike	2	3	3.60	33	9	45.0	40	21	30

 # Switch-hitter
* Left-handed
(Players in major leagues are listed with last minor league team.)

Chattanooga Lookouts (Reds) AA

BATTING	Avg.	AB	R	H	2B	3B	HR	RBI	SB
#Arias, Amador, 2B	.215	65	6	14	1	1	0	2	1
Beauchamp, Kash, Of	.400	60	16	24	6	1	5	15	1
Buckley, Troy, C	.256	43	4	11	1	0	1	4	0
Cox, Darron, C	.217	300	35	65	9	5	3	26	7
*Dismuke, Jamie, 1B	.306	497	69	152	22	1	20	91	4
Fuller, Jon, C	.270	148	22	40	8	1	3	17	3
*Garner, Kevin, Dh	.151	53	6	8	1	0	2	5	2
Gibralter, Steve, Of	.237	477	65	113	25	3	11	47	7
Gill, Chris, Ss	.000	2	0	0	0	0	0	0	0
*Gillum, K.C., Of	.245	216	31	53	9	1	6	24	3
Gordon, Keith, Of	.291	419	69	122	26	3	14	59	13
Hammond, Greg, C	.281	32	3	9	3	0	0	5	0
Houk, Tom, 3B	.237	278	36	66	6	4	2	29	6
Jenkins, Bernie, Of	.252	290	31	73	9	1	3	26	18
Jones, Motorboat, Of	.225	89	10	20	4	0	1	10	3
#Kessinger, Keith, Ss	.311	161	24	50	9	0	3	28	0
Koelling, Brian, 2B	.277	430	64	119	17	6	4	47	34
Lane, Brian, 3B	.264	425	60	112	29	4	10	57	1
Lofton, Rod, Ss	.111	27	1	3	0	0	0	2	2
#Merchant, Mark, Dh	.301	336	56	101	16	0	17	61	3
Reese, Pokey, Ss	.212	345	35	73	17	4	3	37	8
Spann, Tookie, Ph	.071	14	0	1	0	0	0	0	0

PITCHING	W	L	ERA	G	SV	IP	H	BB	SO
Anderson, Mike	1	1	1.20	2	0	15.0	10	1	14
*Burgos, John	2	2	3.56	31	1	48.0	33	14	35
Bushing, Chris	6	1	2.31	61	29	70.0	50	23	84
*Courtright, John	5	11	3.50	27	0	175.0	179	70	96
Culberson, Calvain	6	6	2.99	37	1	105.1	82	36	86
Ferry, Mike	13	8	3.42	28	0	186.2	176	30	111
Garcia, Victor	0	2	5.85	15	0	20.0	24	11	14
*Holcomb, Scott	0	2	13.50	6	0	4.0	5	5	3
Hook, Chris	12	8	3.62	28	0	166.2	163	66	122
Jarvis, Kevin	3	1	1.69	7	0	37.1	26	11	18
Kennedy, Bo	1	1	6.75	2	0	9.1	12	5	10
*Kilgo, Rusty	11	7	2.80	53	6	80.1	92	31	61
*Lynch, David	0	0	.00	3	1	2.1	0	0	3
Pierce, Jeff	3	4	2.60	46	22	69.1	51	16	67
Ray, Johnny	3	7	6.82	30	0	62.0	79	28	46
Robinson, Scott	6	5	3.54	20	0	112.0	114	40	58
Shaw, Kevin	0	1	3.82	25	1	37.2	50	9	14
Stewart, Carl	3	4	5.03	10	0	53.2	57	24	47
Tatar, Kevin	0	1	1.93	4	0	14.0	9	5	7

Greenville Braves (Braves) AA

BATTING	Avg.	AB	R	H	2B	3B	HR	RBI	SB
#Alicea, Ed, 2B	.065	31	5	2	0	0	0	2	1
*Bradley, Scott, C	.333	57	6	19	2	0	1	11	0
Gillis, Tim, 1B	.251	451	58	113	22	3	14	62	1
*Giovanola, Ed, 3B	.281	384	70	108	21	5	5	43	6
#Heath, Lee, Of	.243	432	47	105	15	6	6	36	16
*Houston, Tyler, C	.279	262	27	73	14	1	5	33	5
Hughes, Troy, Of	.266	383	49	102	20	4	14	59	7
Kelly, Pat, 2B	.255	212	23	54	10	1	0	17	2
*Kowitz, Brian, Of	.278	450	63	125	20	5	5	48	13
*O'Connor, Kevin, Of	.189	355	63	67	15	2	7	30	18
#Olmeda, Jose, 2B	.279	451	61	126	33	2	9	51	15
Perez, Eddie, 1B	.333	84	15	28	6	0	6	17	1
Ripplemeyer, Brad, C	.191	277	25	53	14	0	4	27	0
Roa, Hector, Ss	.246	447	50	110	28	4	6	58	6
*Sanchez, Ozzie, Of	.220	100	8	22	3	0	4	13	2
*Swann, Pedro, Of	.306	157	19	48	9	2	3	21	2
*Warner, Mike, Of	.350	20	4	7	0	2	0	3	2

PITCHING	W	L	ERA	G	SV	IP	H	BB	SO
*Boltz, Brian	1	2	3.23	9	0	39.0	33	17	22
Burlingame, Dennis	4	4	5.00	15	0	66.2	76	37	35
Hassinger, Brad	3	1	1.57	12	0	23.0	19	8	11
Hostetler, Mike	8	5	2.72	19	0	135.2	122	36	105
Lomon, Kevin	3	4	3.86	13	0	79.1	76	31	68
*Lovelace, Vance	2	0	1.65	11	0	16.1	10	12	21
*Polley, Dale	8	1	4.12	42	2	59.0	44	21	66

Class A Directory (full season)

Florida State League

Brevard Marlins (Marlins)
Space Coast Stadium (7,200)

Charlotte Rangers (Rangers)
Charlotte County Stadium (6,026)

Clearwater Phillies (Phillies)
Jack Russell Stadium (7,385)

Daytona Cubs (Cubs)
Jackie Robinson Ballpark (4,900)

Dunedin Blue Jays (Blue Jays)
Grant Field (6,218)

Fort Lauderdale Red Sox (Red Sox)
Fort Lauderdale Stadium (8,300)

Fort Myers Miracle (Twins)
Lee County Complex (7,500)

Lakeland Tigers (Tigers)
Joker Marchant Stadium (7,000)

Osceola Astros (Astros)
Osceola County Stadium (5,100)

St. Lucie Mets (Mets)
Sports Complex (7,400)

St. Petersburg Cardinals (Cardinals)
Al Lang Stadium (7,004)

Tampa Yankees (Yankees)
McEwen Field (3,000)

Vero Beach Dodgers (Dodgers)
Holman Stadium (6,500)

West Palm Beach Expos (Expos)
Municipal Stadium (4,400)

Class A Directory
(full season)

Midwest League

Appleton Foxes (Mariners)
Goodland Field (4,300)
Beloit Brewers (Brewers)
Pohlman Field (3,500)
Burlington Bees (Expos)
Community Field (3,500)
Cedar Rapids Kernels (Angels)
Veterans Memorial Ballpark (6,000)
Clinton LumberKings (Giants)
Riverview Stadium (3,400)
Fort Wayne Wizards (Twins)
Memorial Stadium (6,000)
Kane County Cougars (Marlins)
Elfstrom Stadium (4,800)
Peoria Chiefs (Cubs)
Pete Vonachen Stadium (6,200)
Quad City River Bandits (Astros)
John O'Donnell Stadium (5,500)
Rockford Royals (Royals)
Marinelli Field (4,300)
South Bend White Sox (White Sox)
Coveleski Stadium (5,000)
Springfield Cardinals (Cardinals)
Lanphier Park (5,000)
Waterloo Diamonds (Padres)
Municipal Stadium (5,500)
West Michigan Whitecaps (A's)
Old Kent Park (5,500)

PITCHING	W	L	ERA	G	SV	IP	H	BB	SO
*Potts, Mike	7	6	3.88	25	0	141.2	131	86	116
Reyes, Carlos	8	1	2.06	33	2	70.0	64	24	57
Ritter, Darren	4	6	6.06	35	3	65.1	81	26	49
*Schutz, Carl	2	1	5.06	22	3	21.1	17	22	19
Sparma, Blase	5	12	4.85	28	0	150.1	170	68	97
Strange, Don	1	1	3.65	27	18	24.2	27	9	27
*Upshaw, Lee	9	9	3.29	34	2	120.1	109	56	99
Vasquez, Marcos	4	5	4.61	43	3	82.0	96	37	61
*Wade, Terrell	2	1	3.21	8	0	42.0	32	29	40
Williams, Dave	2	4	4.15	45	3	56.1	51	27	35
Woodall, Brad	2	4	3.38	8	0	53.1	43	24	38

Huntsville Stars (Athletics) AA

BATTING	Avg.	AB	R	H	2B	3B	HR	RBI	SB
Beard, Garrett, 3B	.262	61	8	16	3	1	0	6	1
*Bowie, Jim, 1B	.333	501	77	167	33	1	14	101	8
Brito, Jorge, Dh	.278	36	6	10	3	0	4	11	0
Cruz, Fausto, Ss	.335	251	45	84	15	2	3	31	2
#Dattola, Kevin, Of	.253	296	43	75	17	1	10	32	12
#Gates, Brent, 2B	.333	45	7	15	4	0	1	11	0
Gomez, Fabio, 3B	.259	220	26	57	10	1	7	33	5
Hart, Chris, Of	.256	301	39	77	7	3	6	42	12
*Helfand, Eric, C	.228	302	38	69	15	2	10	48	1
Johnson, Herman, Dh	.333	3	0	1	0	0	0	0	1
#Kuehl, John, Dh	.240	379	49	91	28	2	11	67	3
#Mashore, Damon, Of	.233	253	35	59	7	2	3	20	18
Matos, Francisco, 2B	.275	461	69	127	12	3	1	32	16
*Neill, Mike, Of	.246	179	30	44	8	0	1	15	3
Simmons, Enoch, Of	.229	140	24	32	7	0	3	20	5
*Waggoner, Jim, 2B	.140	129	12	18	3	0	1	8	2
#Williams, George, C	.295	434	80	128	26	2	14	77	6
Wolfe, Joel, Of	.299	134	20	40	6	0	3	18	6
Wood, Jason, Ss	.230	370	44	85	21	2	3	36	2
Young, Ernie, Of	.208	120	26	25	5	0	5	15	8

PITCHING	W	L	ERA	G	SV	IP	H	BB	SO
Acre, Mark	1	1	2.42	19	10	22.1	22	3	21
*Allison, Dana	2	3	1.80	19	0	40.0	40	4	18
*Baker, Scott	10	4	4.14	25	0	130.1	141	84	97
*Bowie, Jim	0	0	4.00	8	0	9.0	9	4	4
Briscoe, John	4	0	3.03	30	16	38.2	28	16	62
Chitren, Steve	2	1	5.17	32	1	55.2	53	35	39
Connolly, Craig	1	1	5.59	20	1	37.0	37	12	29
Dattola, Kevin	0	0	.00	2	0	2.0	0	0	1
Garland, Chaon	3	3	7.26	23	0	48.1	58	35	37
Jimenez, Miguel	10	6	2.94	20	0	107.0	92	64	105
*Johns, Doug	7	5	2.97	40	1	91.0	82	31	56
Karsay, Steve	8	4	3.58	21	0	118.0	111	35	122
Latter, Dave	0	0	15.00	6	0	9.0	19	7	5
*Osteen, Gavin	7	3	2.30	11	0	70.1	56	25	46
Phoenix, Steve	2	2	1.40	11	1	19.1	13	5	15
*Shaw, Curtis	6	16	4.93	28	0	151.2	141	89	132
Smith, Tim	1	3	3.35	9	0	43.0	46	18	31
Smithberg, Roger	4	2	2.21	27	0	36.2	34	16	36
Strebeck, Rick	2	2	5.18	23	0	48.2	54	22	29
Sturtze, Tanyon	5	12	4.78	28	0	165.2	169	85	112
*Wojciechowski, Steve	4	6	5.32	13	0	67.2	91	30	52

Jacksonville Suns (Mariners) AA

BATTING	Avg.	AB	R	H	2B	3B	HR	RBI	SB
Adams, Tommy, Of	.276	232	19	64	12	2	4	20	4
Beeler, Pete, C	.207	58	6	12	3	0	1	6	1
*Bragg, Darren, Of	.264	451	74	119	26	3	11	46	19
Campanis, Jim, C	.245	212	16	52	7	0	3	22	0
Clayton, Craig, 3B	.298	215	23	64	8	2	1	23	10
*Cornelius, Brian, Of	.286	168	28	48	11	0	3	17	5
Diaz, Eddy, Of	.251	259	36	65	16	0	6	26	6
Holley, Bobby, 1B	.247	388	59	96	22	1	13	66	7
Jackson, Kenny, Of	.000	10	1	0	0	0	0	1	0
Kounas, Tony, C	.278	158	22	44	14	0	4	22	2
*Marquez, Jesus, Of	.313	32	7	10	0	0	2	5	3
Martinez, Edgar, Dh	.357	14	2	5	0	0	1	3	0
Maynard, Tow, Of	.215	195	21	42	5	1	2	8	17

BATTING	Avg.	AB	R	H	2B	3B	HR	RBI	SB
Morales, Jorge, C	.282	170	15	48	9	0	3	25	9
Nava, Lipso, 3B	.254	397	52	101	20	0	7	41	5
Newfield, Marc, 1B	.307	336	48	103	18	0	19	51	1
#Relaford, Desi, Ss	.244	472	49	115	16	4	8	47	16
Santana, Ruben, 2B	.301	499	79	150	21	2	21	84	13
Scruggs, Tony, Of	.241	224	26	54	11	1	7	38	5
Smith, Bubba, 1B	.219	137	12	30	8	0	6	21	0
*Waggoner, Aubrey, Of	.245	102	29	25	8	2	3	7	7

PITCHING	W	L	ERA	G	SV	IP	H	BB	SO
Bicknell, Greg	6	6	4.31	24	1	94.0	96	28	45
Buckley, Travis	2	4	5.75	12	0	56.1	64	22	44
Clayton, Craig	0	0	.00	3	0	4.0	3	1	1
Coffman, Kevin	1	7	5.40	10	0	50.0	33	47	45
*Cummings, John	2	2	3.15	7	0	45.2	50	9	35
*Czarkowski, Mark	0	3	4.19	25	1	58.0	68	16	26
Darwin, Jeff	3	5	2.97	27	7	36.1	29	17	39
*Fleming, Dave	0	2	4.41	4	0	16.1	16	7	10
Foster, Kevin	4	4	3.97	12	0	65.2	53	29	72
Glinatsis, George	5	2	6.75	9	0	34.2	39	15	25
*Hampton, Mike	6	4	3.71	15	0	87.1	71	33	84
Harris, Reggie	1	4	4.78	9	0	37.2	33	22	30
Kent, Troy	0	0	5.21	14	1	19.0	26	5	17
*King, Kevin	2	0	3.14	16	1	28.2	25	7	13
Knackert, Brent	0	1	2.57	4	1	14.0	6	4	10
Parris, Steve	0	1	5.93	7	0	13.2	15	6	5
Perkins, Paul	2	4	5.40	36	1	60.0	69	23	34
Phillips, Tony	1	3	1.72	27	5	31.1	34	5	26
Picota, Len	0	4	4.87	11	0	20.1	26	12	7
*Plantenberg, Erik	2	1	2.01	34	1	44.2	38	14	49
*Remlinger, Mike	1	3	6.58	7	0	39.2	40	19	23
Russell, Lagrande	4	9	552	17	0	89.2	115	32	52
Salkeld, Roger	4	3	3.27	14	0	77.0	71	29	56
Schanz, Scott	7	4	2.56	49	1	102.0	77	51	81
*Villone, Ron	3	4	4.38	11	0	63.2	49	41	66
Weber, Weston	2	1	1.69	17	1	26.2	25	7	12

Knoxville Smokies (Blue Jays) AA

BATTING	Avg.	AB	R	H	2B	3B	HR	RBI	SB
Adriana, Sharnol, 2B	.215	177	19	38	3	1	0	18	9
Battle, Howard, 3B	.278	521	66	145	21	5	7	70	12
*Bowers, Brent, Of	.248	577	63	143	23	4	5	43	36
*Butler, Rich, Of	.095	21	3	2	0	1	0	0	0
Canate, William, Of	.270	37	8	10	2	0	1	4	2
*Delgado, Carlos, C	.303	468	91	142	28	0	25	102	10
Gonzalez, Alex, Ss	.289	561	93	162	29	7	16	69	38
*Green, Shawn, Of	.283	360	40	102	14	2	4	34	4
Henderson, Derek, Dh	.241	29	4	7	0	0	0	1	1
*Hodge, Tim, Dh	.242	289	21	70	18	0	1	31	5
*Hyers, Tim, 1B	.306	487	72	149	26	3	3	61	12
Lis, Joe, 2B	.290	448	66	130	29	3	8	64	6
Morland, Michael, C	.232	112	7	26	4	1	0	15	1
Reams, Ron, Of	.227	299	39	68	14	1	6	33	16
Rosario, Gabriel, 2B	.500	4	0	2	0	0	0	0	0
Sheppard, Don, Of	.281	249	32	70	11	1	2	27	5
#Ward, Turner, Of	.261	23	6	6	2	0	0	2	3

PITCHING	W	L	ERA	G	SV	IP	H	BB	SO
Adriana, Sharnol	0	0	13.50	1	0	2.0	5	1	0
*Baptist, Travis	1	3	4.09	7	0	33.0	37	7	24
Brow, Scott	1	2	3.32	3	0	19.0	13	9	12
Brown, Daren	4	5	5.00	46	10	72.0	72	32	67
Crabtree, Tim	9	14	4.08	27	0	158.2	178	59	67
*Cromwell, Nate	0	1	11.00	6	0	9.0	15	10	11
Duey, Kyle	2	3	6.88	37	0	68.0	92	27	40
*Flener, Huck	13	6	3.30	38	4	136.1	130	39	114
Ganote, Joe	8	6	4.15	33	1	138.2	149	52	87
Grove, Scott	0	2	7.16	10	0	16.1	18	9	10
Heble, Kurt	0	1	3.72	6	0	9.2	12	4	13
*Jordan, Ricardo	1	4	2.45	25	2	36.2	33	18	35
Kizziah, Daren	3	0	2.83	27	0	54.0	47	18	33
*Montoya, Al	1	0	5.14	5	0	7.0	8	3	9
Newlin, Jim	1	3	7.21	21	0	43.2	63	16	30
Ohlms, Mark	1	0	2.70	7	1	6.2	6	3	4
Phillips, Randy	2	2	6.12	5	0	25.0	32	12	12

Class A Directory
(full season)

South Atlantic League

Albany Polecats (Orioles)
Paul Eames Complex (4,200)

Asheville Tourists (Rockies)
McCormick Field (4,000)

Augusta GreenJackets (Pirates)
Heaton Stadium (4,000)

Capital City Bombers (Mets)
Capital City Stadium (6,100)

Charleston (S.C.) RiverDogs (Rangers)
College Park (4,300)

Charleston (W. Va.) Wheelers (Reds)
Watt Powell Park (6,000)

Columbus Redstixx (Indians)
Golden Park (5,500)

Fayetteville Generals (Tigers)
J.P. Riddle Stadium (3,200)

Greensboro Bats (Yankees)
War Memorial Stadium (7,500)

Hagerstown Suns (Blue Jays)
Municipal Stadium (4,500)

Hickory Crawdads (White Sox)
L.P. Frans Stadium (4,500)

Macon Braves (Braves)
Luther Williams Field (3,500)

Savannah Cardinals (Cardinals)
Grayson Stadium (8,000)

Spartanburg Phillies (Phillies)
Duncan Park (3,900)

Batting leaders across all leagues

(Only includes full-season leagues. Through games of Sept. 6, 1993.)

BATTING AVERAGE

(Minimum 350 TPA)

Player	Club	Lg.	Avg.
*Clark, Tim	HD	CAL	.363
T*Sweeney, M.	MDL	TEX	.356
*Riggs, Kevin	STK	CAL	.347
T White, R.	OTT	INT	.343
Pozo, A.	RIV	CAL	.342
*Radziewicz, D.	STP	FSL	.342
T Wolfe, Joel	HVL	SOU	.334
T*Brown, Brant	ORL	SOU	.334
*Petagine, R.	JCK	TEX	.334
T Smith, I.	WCH	TEX	.334
T Ramirez, M.	CHR	INT	.333
*Bowie, Jim	HVL	SOU	.333
*Merullo, Matt	NVL	AMAS	.332
*Thome, Jim	CHR	INT	.332
*Tarasco, Tony	RMD	INT	.330

HOME RUNS

Player	Club	Lg.	HR
*Horn, Sam	HR	INT	38
Balboni, Steve	KC	AMAS	36
T Smith, Bubba	W-S	CARO	33
T McCoy, Trey	OKC	AMAS	32
Zambrano, E.	IW	AMAS	32
T Ramirez, M.	CHR	INT	31
T Rhodes, Karl	IWA	AMAS	30
*Hamelin, Bob	OMA	AMAS	29
T Young, Ernie	HVL	SOU	28
*Toale, John	HD	CAL	28
T*Floyd, Cliff	OTT	INT	28
*Kosco, Byrn	HD	CAL	27
SEVERAL TIED AT			26

RBI

Player	Club	Lg.	RBI
*Clark, Tim	HD	CAL	126
*Toale, John	HD	CAL	125
*Kosco, Bryn	HD	CAL	121
T*Floyd, Cliff	OTT	INT	119
T Ramirez, M.	CHR	INT	115
Zambrano, E.	IWA	AMAS	115
Balboni, Steve	OKC	AMAS	108
Wachter, Derek	STK	CAL	108
T McCoy, Trey	OKC	AMAS	106
T Smith, Bubba	W-S	CARO	105
Denson, Drew	NVL	AMAS	103
*Thome, Jim	CHR	INT	102

 # Switch-hitter

* Left-handed

T Player has been with more than one team, listed with last team.

(Players in major leagues are listed with last minor league team.)

PITCHING	W	L	ERA	G	SV	IP	H	BB	SO
Renko, Steve	1	3	3.63	12	0	34.2	38	8	30
Rogers, Jimmy	7	7	4.04	19	0	100.1	107	33	80
Small, Aaron	4	4	3.39	48	0	93.0	99	40	44
*Spoljaric, Paul	4	1	2.28	7	0	43.1	30	22	51
Ward, Anthony	1	1	1.71	11	3	21.0	17	10	23

Memphis Chicks (Royals) AA

BATTING	Avg.	AB	R	H	2B	3B	HR	RBI	SB
*Casillas, Adam, Of	.304	450	53	137	33	6	4	50	3
Cole, Butch, Of	.257	292	33	75	16	0	2	36	5
Colvard, Benny, Dh	.236	182	20	43	10	0	4	25	0
*Dempsey, John, C	.250	4	0	1	0	0	0	0	0
Diaz, Carlos, C	.215	163	13	35	3	0	3	25	1
Diaz, Kiki, Ss	.282	78	12	22	2	0	0	5	1
Garber, Jeff, 2B	.281	253	40	71	13	0	12	32	1
Guerrero, Mike, Ss	.265	68	7	18	6	0	0	4	0
Halter, Shane, Ss	.258	306	50	79	7	0	4	20	4
Jaster, Scott, Of	.251	183	24	46	11	1	6	24	6
Jennings, Lance, C	.205	327	27	67	11	0	4	33	0
*Johnson, Mark, Of	.197	213	24	42	4	3	5	22	6
*Long, Kevin, Of	.272	301	47	82	14	6	1	20	7
#May, Lee, Of	.205	39	3	8	0	0	0	3	2
Mota, Domingo, 2B	.214	196	22	42	7	3	1	16	10
Norman, Les, Of	.291	484	78	141	32	5	17	81	11
Randa, Joe, 3B	.295	505	74	149	31	5	11	72	8
*Tucker, Mike, Ss	.279	244	38	68	7	4	9	35	12
Vitiello, Joe, 1B	.288	413	62	119	25	2	15	66	2

PITCHING	W	L	ERA	G	SV	IP	H	BB	SO
Ahern, Brian	4	9	5.34	18	0	97.2	113	46	63
Bevil, Brian	3	3	4.36	6	0	33.0	36	14	26
Bittiger, Jeff	1	0	1.59	2	0	11.1	6	3	11
*Campbell, Jim	1	1	5.82	11	0	21.2	23	10	11
*Casillas, Adam	0	1	9.00	3	0	3.0	7	0	1
Chrisman, Jim	0	0	4.66	8	0	19.1	20	5	15
Fyhrie, Mike	11	4	3.56	22	0	131.1	143	59	59
*Givens, Brian	1	3	4.58	14	2	35.1	37	11	29
Harris, Doug	3	6	4.67	22	0	86.2	99	13	38
Karchner, Matt	3	2	4.20	6	0	30.0	34	4	14
Landress, Roger	3	4	3.14	26	2	51.2	55	15	25
*Limbach, Chris	3	4	2.73	42	6	92.1	85	22	82
*Mason, Mike	1	0	.00	1	0	2.0	0	1	0
*Morton, Kevin	3	6	4.81	20	1	73.0	88	29	59
Myers, Rodney	3	6	5.62	12	0	65.2	73	32	42
Perez, Vladimir	1	0	3.00	18	3	42.0	37	11	35
Peters, Doug	1	2	5.87	6	0	23.0	32	10	14
*Pierce, Ed	6	5	3.74	37	1	67.1	65	34	53
*Richards, Dave	0	1	3.68	7	1	22.0	12	12	24
Roesler, Mike	2	1	2.38	3	0	22.2	11	4	16
Sanchez, Alex	1	4	4.37	15	0	70.0	64	35	47
Ventura, Jose	2	5	3.94	20	0	82.1	88	45	61
Wagner, Hector	2	4	4.50	10	0	36.0	38	4	19

Nashville Xpress (Twins) AA

BATTING	Avg.	AB	R	H	2B	3B	HR	RBI	SB
#Becker, Rich, Of	.287	516	93	148	25	7	15	66	29
#Corbin, Ted, Ss	.333	15	2	5	1	0	0	1	0
Cordova, Marty, Of	.250	508	83	127	30	5	19	77	10
Delanuez, Rex, Of	.236	352	71	83	20	3	8	43	23
*Dunn, Steve, 1B	.262	366	48	96	20	2	14	60	1
Durant, Mike, C	.243	437	58	106	23	1	8	57	17
Grifol, Pedro, C	.203	197	22	40	13	0	5	29	0
#Hocking, Denny, Ss	.267	409	54	109	9	4	8	50	15
*Masteller, Dan, 1B	.273	121	19	33	3	0	3	16	2
*McDonald, Mike, Of	.257	268	28	69	12	1	7	31	1
Miller, Damian, C	.231	13	0	3	0	0	0	0	0
#Mota, Willie, 1B	.234	201	16	47	10	2	2	26	1
Raabe, Brian, 2B	.286	524	80	150	23	2	6	52	18
Rivera, David, 2B	.237	325	41	77	7	2	3	33	35
*Stahoviak, Scott, 3B	.272	331	40	90	25	1	12	56	10

PITCHING	W	L	ERA	G	SV	IP	H	BB	SO
Barcelo, Marc	1	0	3.86	2	0	9.1	9	5	5

PITCHING	W	L	ERA	G	SV	IP	H	BB	SO
Best, Jayson	1	0	11.81	3	1	5.1	11	4	7
Delanuez, Rex	0	0	9.00	3	0	3.0	7	0	3
Gavaghan, Sean	4	0	.49	20	1	36.2	21	12	30
*Guardado, Eddie	4	0	1.24	10	0	65.1	53	10	57
Henry, Jon	4	2	2.74	6	0	42.2	41	7	20
Johnson, Greg	3	1	2.80	31	13	35.1	30	10	54
*Klonoski, Jason	4	6	3.16	56	3	77.0	69	34	56
*Konieczki, Dominic	2	6	6.66	42	4	48.2	65	16	39
*Mansur, Jeff	10	8	4.25	33	0	158.2	180	38	89
McCreary, Bob	3	8	5.31	38	1	78.0	111	20	42
Misuraca, Mike	6	6	3.82	25	0	113.0	103	40	80
Munoz, Oscar	11	4	3.08	20	0	131.2	123	51	139
*Newman, Alan	1	6	6.03	14	0	65.2	75	40	35
Radke, Brad	2	6	4.62	13	0	76.0	81	16	76
Ritchie, Todd	3	2	3.66	12	0	46.2	46	15	41
Robinson, Bob	2	4	5.16	35	3	45.1	64	15	26
Schullstrom, Erik	1	0	4.85	4	0	13.0	16	6	11
Watkins, Scott	0	1	5.94	13	0	16.2	19	7	17
Wissler, Bill	10	10	3.95	29	0	175.1	169	48	115

Orlando Cubs (Cubs) AA

BATTING	Avg.	AB	R	H	2B	3B	HR	RBI	SB
*Brown, Adam, C	.500	6	0	3	1	0	0	1	0
*Brown, Brant, 1B	.315	111	17	35	11	3	4	23	2
Busby, Wayne, Ss	.203	74	8	15	5	0	0	4	1
Crockett, Russ, 2B	.204	98	15	20	4	0	0	3	1
*Dauphin, Phil, Of	.264	299	53	79	16	2	11	35	7
Davisson, Sean, 2B	.000	1	1	0	0	0	0	0	0
*Ebright, Chris, 1B	.283	318	49	90	21	1	10	56	2
Erdman, Brad, C	.181	171	12	31	5	0	1	17	2
*Franco, Matt, 1B	.316	237	31	75	20	1	7	37	3
Glanville, Doug, Of	.264	296	42	78	14	4	9	40	15
Gomez, Rudy, 2B	.329	140	26	46	8	0	1	17	5
Grace, Mike, 3B	.271	425	65	115	29	3	13	76	2
*Grayum, Richie, Of	.295	234	45	69	13	1	10	33	1
Hernandez, Jose, Ss	.304	263	42	80	8	3	8	33	8
*Jensen, John, Of	.266	192	27	51	10	2	6	34	4
Johnson, Jack, C	.232	82	9	19	6	0	0	5	0
Kapano, Corey, Of	.255	263	44	67	12	1	8	35	17
Kieschnick, Brooks, Of	.341	91	12	31	8	0	2	10	1
Lewis, Mica, Of	.244	86	14	21	3	0	1	10	3
Lonigro, Greg, Ss	.273	216	20	59	12	0	4	22	4
Magallanes, Willie, Of	.176	17	1	3	0	0	0	0	1
Mann, Kelly, C	.244	82	11	20	3	1	1	7	0
#McDonnell, Shawn, C	.213	47	2	10	2	0	0	8	0
Raasch, Glen, C	.214	14	0	3	0	0	0	1	0
Robinson, Jim, C	.231	52	3	12	2	0	0	1	1
Sandberg, Ryne, 2B	.222	9	0	2	0	0	0	1	0
Timmons, Ozzie, Of	.284	359	65	102	22	2	18	58	5
Torres, Paul, Of	.255	55	10	14	4	0	3	10	3
#Vice, Darryl, 2B	.273	220	36	60	5	2	3	24	6
Viera, Jose, 3B	.091	11	0	1	0	0	0	1	0
White, Billy, 2B	.242	120	14	29	11	1	2	14	1
Zambrano, Roberto, 3B	.135	37	4	5	1	0	0	1	0

PITCHING	W	L	ERA	G	SV	IP	H	BB	SO
*Corbett, Sherm	2	1	3.16	5	0	25.2	32	9	16
Czajkowski, Jim	1	2	2.84	10	1	19.0	15	3	16
Delgado, Tim	1	3	5.90	9	0	39.2	53	9	23
*Dickson, Lance	2	3	3.83	9	0	49.1	37	17	46
*Ebright, Chris	0	0	.00	3	0	4.0	4	0	0
Galvez, Balvino	0	1	8.44	3	0	10.2	16	3	9
Harkey, Mike	0	0	1.69	1	0	5.1	4	2	5
Hartsock, Jeff	3	4	3.47	8	0	49.1	43	17	24
Johnson, Chris	0	1	2.96	15	1	27.1	31	15	14
*Johnson, Earnie	6	5	5.94	53	2	66.2	84	31	58
Melvin, Bill	0	1	3.88	36	1	65.0	57	40	60
Morones, Geno	2	2	4.88	4	0	24.0	29	9	14
Salles, John	11	9	4.38	33	1	176.2	203	50	115
Steenstra, Kennie	8	3	3.59	14	0	100.1	103	25	60
Stevens, Dave	6	1	4.22	11	0	70.1	69	35	49
Strauss, Julio	0	2	3.54	15	0	28.0	22	15	21
Swartzbaugh, Dave	1	3	4.23	10	0	66.0	52	18	59
Taylor, Aaron	5	4	4.85	28	0	55.2	73	15	37
Trinidad, Hector	1	3	6.57	4	0	24.2	34	7	13

(Cont'd from previous page.)

STOLEN BASES

Player	Club	Lg.	SB
#Burton, Essex	SBN	MID	74
#Moore, K.	HD	CAL	71
Riley, Marquis	PSP	CAL	69
#Hawkins, K.	GBO	SAL	67
*Goodwin, C.	FRE	CARO	61

HITS

Player	Club	Lg.	Hits
*Clark, Tim	HD	CAL	185
#Martin, N.	NVL	AMAS	179
T White, R.	OTT	INT	179
Pozo, A.	RIV	CAL	176
#Jones, C.	RMD	INT	174
#Hardtke, J.	RC	CAL	38

DOUBLES

Player	Club	Lg.	2B
T Ramirez, M.	CHR	INT	44
Pozo, A.	RIV	CAL	44
T Rhodes, Karl	IWA	AMAS	43
*Clark, Tim	HD	CAL	42
Chavez, Eric	ABY	SAL	38
#Hardtke, J.	RC	CAL	38
*Pridy, Todd	KNC	MID	38

TRIPLES

Player	Club	Lg.	3B
*Tyler, Brad	BOW	EAST	17
*Abreu, Bob	OSC	FSL	17
*Damon, J.	RKF	MID	13
*Holifield, Rick	DUN	FSL	12
Henry, S.	HAG	SAL	12
#Jones, C.	RMD	INT	12
*White, Jimmy	OSC	FSL	12
T White, R.	OTT	INT	12
*Curtis, Randy	SLU	FSL	12
Battle, Allen	ARK	TEX	12

EXTRA BASE HITS

Player	Club	Lg.	EBH
T Rhodes, Karl	IWA	AMAS	76
T Ramirez, M.	CHR	INT	75
*Clark, Tim	HD	CAL	69
T McCoy, Trey	OKC	AMAS	64
*Luke, Matt	GBO	SAL	63
T Coomer, Ron	NVL	AMAS	63
Pozo, A.	RIV	CAL	63
Zambrano, E.	IWA	AMAS	63

Switch-hitter
* Left-handed
T Player has been with more than one team, listed with last team.
(Players in major leagues are listed with last minor league team.)

(Cont'd from previous page.)

SLUGGING PERCENTAGE

Player	Club	Lg.	Slg.
T Ramirez, M.	CHR	INT	.613
T Rhodes, Karl	IWA	AMAS	.602
*Horn, Sam	CHR	INT	.600
*Thome, Jim	CHR	INT	.585
T McCoy, Trey	OKC	AMAS	.585
*Clark, Tim	HD	CAL	.584

ON-BASE PERCENTAGE

Player	Club	Lg.	OBP
*Riggs, Kevin	STK	CAL	.482
T*Sweeney, M.	MDL	TEX	.447
*Petagine, R.	JCK	TEX	.447
*Thome, Jim	CHR	INT	.441
Malinoski, C.	HD	CAL	.439
T*Keister, Tripp	CAP	SAL	.439

TOTAL PLATE APP.S/SO RATIO

Player	Club	Lg.	Ratio
*Casillas, A.	MEM	SOU	28.89
Hajek, Dave	JCK	TEX	25.36
Gomez, Mike	CLW	FSL	23.22
#Fleming, C.	PRW	CARO	23.00
Raabe, Brian	NSH	SOU	21.57

SWITCH-HITTERS

Player	Club	Lg.	Avg.
#Jones, C.	RMD	INT	.325
#Hardtke, J.	RC	CAL	.319
#Caceres, E.	NO	AMAS	.317
#Brito, Luis	SPT	SAL	.313
T#Rodriguez, C.	ALB	EAST	.310

Switch-hitter
* Left-handed
T Player has been with more than one team, listed with last team.
(Players in major leagues are listed with last minor league team.)

PITCHING	W	L	ERA	G	SV	IP	H	BB	SO
Walker, Mike	2	3	7.31	16	1	28.1	42	9	21
Wallace, Derek	5	7	5.03	15	0	96.2	105	28	69
*Williams, Jimmy	5	5	2.48	15	0	90.2	84	38	65
Willis, Travis	8	6	2.84	61	24	82.1	91	22	56

Texas League

Arkansas Travelers (Cardinals) AA

BATTING	Avg.	AB	R	H	2B	3B	HR	RBI	SB
#Aversa, Joe, 3B	.181	199	23	36	4	2	0	5	3
Battle, Allen, Of	.274	390	71	107	24	12	3	40	20
Cholowsky, Dan, 3B	.217	212	31	46	10	2	3	16	10
Coleman, Paul, Of	.244	401	44	98	24	3	7	30	8
#Deak, Darrel, 2B	.242	414	63	100	22	1	19	73	4
*Ellis, Paul, C	.333	78	5	26	3	0	1	11	0
Fanning, Steve, 3B	.213	249	28	53	14	0	3	20	5
Faulkner, Craig, 1B	.237	299	34	71	18	0	15	55	1
*Lewis, Anthony, Of	.264	326	48	86	28	2	13	50	3
*Mabry, John, Of	.290	528	68	153	32	2	16	72	7
Pimentel, Wander, Ss	.204	49	3	10	0	0	0	5	0
*Prager, Howard, 1B	.316	158	31	50	8	1	7	21	4
*Ronan, Marc, C	.214	281	33	60	16	1	7	34	1
Savinon, Odalis, Of	.200	20	3	4	1	0	0	1	0
#Shireman, Jeff, Ss	.285	333	32	95	20	0	2	32	3
Tahan, Kevin, C	.154	65	5	10	1	1	1	5	1
#Young, Dmitri, 1B	.247	166	13	41	11	2	3	21	4

PITCHING	W	L	ERA	G	SV	IP	H	BB	SO
Anderson, Paul	6	9	3.76	17	0	107.2	102	24	81
Barber, Brian	9	8	4.02	24	0	143.1	154	56	126
*Beltran, Rigo	5	5	3.25	18	0	88.2	74	38	82
Cimorelli, Frank	1	1	2.54	37	1	56.2	44	23	36
*Creek, Doug	11	10	4.02	25	0	147.2	142	48	128
Davis, Clint	2	0	1.95	28	1	37.0	22	10	37
*Eversgerd, Bryan	4	4	2.18	62	0	66.0	60	19	68
Faccio, Luis	0	3	8.37	8	0	23.2	33	7	20
Fanning, Steve	1	0	1.80	3	0	5.0	4	1	0
Johnson, Steve	2	2	4.33	11	0	27.0	30	7	18
Kelly, John	2	4	3.55	51	27	58.1	53	12	40
*Knox, Kerry	4	4	2.78	22	0	81.0	78	14	61
Martinez, Francisco	0	1	6.43	2	0	7.0	8	1	3
Montgomery, Steve	3	3	3.94	6	0	32.0	34	12	19
Perez, Mike	0	0	7.36	4	0	3.2	7	0	4
Santos, Gerald	3	6	2.63	57	3	82.0	80	41	65
Shackle, Rick	4	1	4.57	10	0	41.1	48	12	19
*Simmons, Scott	6	3	2.70	13	0	76.2	68	18	35

El Paso Diablos (Brewers) AA

BATTING	Avg.	AB	R	H	2B	3B	HR	RBI	SB
*Basse, Mike, Of	.267	386	65	103	14	5	1	36	26
Campillo, Rob, C	.000	11	0	0	0	0	0	0	0
Carter, Mike, Of	.370	73	16	27	4	1	2	16	6
*Castleberry, Kevin, 2B	.300	327	46	98	9	5	2	49	13
Cirillo, Jeff, 2B	.341	249	53	85	16	2	9	41	2
#Cole, Mark, 2B	.313	16	3	5	1	0	0	1	1
Couture, Mike, Of	.000	4	0	0	0	0	0	0	0
#Diggs, Tony, Of	.143	63	5	9	1	0	1	3	3
*Dodson, Bo, 1B	.312	330	58	103	27	4	9	59	1
#Doran, Bill, 2B	.364	11	3	4	1	0	0	0	0
*Gill, Steve, Of	.246	329	50	81	18	4	5	43	14
Kappesser, Bob, C	.249	173	25	43	9	1	2	23	7
*Lewis, Al, 3B	.258	380	53	98	22	5	4	48	4
Lofton, Rodney, 2B	.265	200	39	53	8	5	2	21	16
*Lukachyk, Rob, Of	.265	362	58	96	24	7	9	63	8
#Matheny, Mike, C	.254	339	39	86	21	2	2	28	1
*Nilsson, Dave, C	.471	17	5	8	1	0	1	7	1
Riesgo, Nikco, Dh	.280	93	15	26	6	1	7	21	2
*Singleton, Duane, Of	.230	456	52	105	21	6	2	61	23
Smith, Ed, 1B	.294	419	64	123	23	6	8	69	13
Weger, Wes, Ss	.291	471	69	137	24	5	5	53	9

PITCHING	W	L	ERA	G	SV	IP	H	BB	SO
Archer, Kurt	9	8	4.90	54	11	104.2	129	38	50
Boze, Marshall	10	3	2.71	13	0	86.1	78	32	48
Carter, Glenn	3	5	5.12	18	0	63.1	65	22	47
Correa, Ramser	1	0	5.06	5	0	10.2	15	7	5
Dell, Tim	4	2	5.13	48	1	105.1	151	32	56
Farmer, Howard	2	1	3.33	4	0	24.1	14	10	16
*Felix, Nick	2	1	4.32	42	4	66.2	61	32	69
Gamez, Francisco	2	8	5.40	15	0	68.1	92	25	26
*Gill, Steve	0	0	.00	4	0	5.0	1	4	2
*Hancock, Brian	1	0	7.04	10	0	30.2	40	30	15
Hunter, Jim	3	1	2.45	14	1	22.0	20	6	10
Johnson, Dane	2	2	3.91	15	1	25.1	23	10	26
Kappesser, Bob	0	0	.00	2	0	3.0	2	1	1
*Karl, Scott	13	8	2.45	27	0	180.0	172	35	95
Kiefer, Mark	3	4	4.01	11	0	51.2	48	19	44
Kloek, Kevin	9	6	4.11	23	0	135.2	148	53	97
Lewis, Al	0	0	1.59	2	0	5.2	3	0	2
Pitcher, Scott	2	0	8.24	13	1	19.2	32	10	12
*Richards, Dave	2	2	3.80	35	1	64.0	66	26	54
*Rogers, Charlie	4	3	1.74	48	23	72.1	50	23	55
Taylor, Scott	6	6	3.80	17	0	104.1	105	31	76

Jackson Generals (Astros) AA

BATTING	Avg.	AB	R	H	2B	3B	HR	RBI	SB
Gilmore, Tony, C	.172	145	14	25	4	0	2	7	1
Groppuso, Mike, 3B	.241	370	41	89	18	0	10	49	3
Hajek, Dave, 2B	.292	332	50	97	20	2	5	27	6
Hatcher, Chris, Of	.259	367	45	95	15	3	15	64	5
Hunter, Brian, Of	.294	523	84	154	22	5	10	52	35
#Kellner, Frank, Ss	.301	355	51	107	27	2	4	36	11
Madsen, Lance, Of	.221	353	58	78	19	1	23	65	2
Makarewicz, Scott, C	.246	285	31	70	14	1	7	35	1
Montgomery, Ray, Of	.281	338	50	95	16	3	10	59	12
Mota, Gary, Of	.144	90	7	13	2	0	3	8	1
Nevers, Tom, Ss	.272	184	21	50	8	2	1	10	7
*Petagine, Roberto, 1B	.334	437	73	146	36	2	15	90	6
Scott, Kevin, C	.284	109	11	31	4	0	1	13	2
*Thompson, Fletcher, 2B	.294	316	64	93	15	2	4	29	23

PITCHING	W	L	ERA	G	SV	IP	H	BB	SO
Anderson, Tom	2	5	6.05	8	0	38.2	47	20	27
Bruske, Jim	9	5	2.31	15	0	97.1	86	22	83
Costello, Fred	8	3	2.82	12	0	60.2	57	13	45
Dougherty, James	2	2	1.87	52	36	53.0	39	21	55
Gallaher, Kevin	0	2	2.63	4	0	24.0	14	10	30
Gonzales, Ben	2	2	5.12	41	0	65.0	90	15	36
Hajek, Dave	0	0	27.00	2	0	2.0	4	1	2
*Hill, Chris	6	4	3.86	58	2	105.0	90	53	93
*Hurta, Bob	7	9	4.42	36	2	93.2	101	38	72
Kent, Troy	1	0	2.45	2	0	3.2	2	1	1
Ketchen, Doug	7	12	4.11	27	0	159.2	160	50	104
Mathews, Terry	6	5	3.67	17	0	103.0	116	29	74
*Morman, Alvin	8	2	2.96	19	0	97.1	77	28	101
Small, Mark	7	2	3.19	51	0	84.2	71	41	64
White, Chris	3	5	7.35	16	1	60.0	80	25	44
*Windes, Rodney	5	4	2.93	41	2	95.1	84	22	84

Midland Angels (Angels) AA

BATTING	Avg.	AB	R	H	2B	3B	HR	RBI	SB
Boykin, Tyrone, Of	.280	132	29	37	3	3	2	17	1
Brakebill, Mark, 3B	.230	222	21	51	9	1	5	32	0
#Claus, Todd, 3B	.188	32	7	6	1	1	0	3	1
*Cohick, Emmitt, Of	.270	356	59	96	18	5	11	53	6
Dalesandro, Mark, 3B	.294	235	33	69	9	0	2	36	1
#Davis, Kevin, Ss	.276	156	29	43	5	1	7	28	6
*Fabregas, Jorge, C	.289	409	63	118	26	3	6	56	1
Forbes, P.J., 2B	.319	498	90	159	23	2	15	64	6
*Garrett, Clifton, Of	.359	39	3	14	2	0	0	5	2
Grebeck, Brian, Ss	.294	405	65	119	20	4	5	54	6
*Jackson, John, Of	.325	243	43	79	18	2	3	34	12
Kipila, Jeff, Dh	.232	203	32	47	7	1	12	47	0
#Munoz, Orlando, 3B	.263	118	24	31	8	1	0	10	0
*Palmeiro, Orlando, Of	.305	535	85	163	19	5	0	64	18

Batting leaders by position

CATCHER

Player	Club	Lg. Avg.
*Merullo, Matt	NVL	AMAS .332
Lopez, Javy	RMD	INT .305
*Delgado, C.	KNX	SOU .303
T#Zaun, Gregg	ROC	INT .295
*Fabregas, J.	MDL	TEX .289

FIRST BASE

Player	Club	Lg.Avg.
T*Brown, Brant	ORL	SOU .334
*Petagine, R.	JCK	TEX .334
*Bowie, Jim	HVL	SOU .333
*Turner, Brian	SBR	CAL .325
Garcia, Omar	SLU	FSL .322
Morman, Russ	BUF	AMAS .320

SECOND BASE

Player	Club	Lg. Avg.
*Riggs, Kevin	STK	CAL .347
Pozo, A.	RIV	CAL .342
*Demetral, C.	VB	FSL .325
Bush, Homer	WLO	MID .322
Forbes, P.J.	MDL	TEX .319

THIRD BASE

Player	Club	Lg. Avg.
*Thome, Jim	CHR	INT .332
T Cirillo, Jeff	NO	AMAS.319
T Coomer, R.	NVL	AMAS.319
T Saenz, O.	BIR	SOU .317
T Clayton, C.	JAX	SOU .313
Stynes, Chris	DUN	FSL .304

SHORTSTOP

Player	Club	Lg. Avg.
#Jones, C.	RMD	INT .325
#Brito, Luis	SPT	SAL .313
T#Rodriguez, C.	ALB	EAST .310
Aurilia, Richard	CHL	FSL .309
#Fonville, Chad	CLN	MID.306

OUTFIELD

Player	Club	Lg. Avg.
*Clark, Tim	HD	CAL .363
T*Sweeney, M.	MDL	TEX .356
T White, R.	OTT	INT .343
T Wolfe, Joel	HVL	SOU .334
T Ramirez, M.	CHR	INT .333

Switch-hitter

* Left-handed

T Player has been with more than one team, listed with last team.

(Players in major leagues are listed with last minor league team.)

Pitching leaders across all leagues

ERA
(Minimum 112 IP)

Player	Club	Lg.	ERA
T Matranga, J.	SAV	SAL	1.64
T Martinez, F.	ARK	TEX	1.88
T Andujar, L.	BIR	SOU	1.93
Hawkins, L.T.	FTW	MID	2.06
T Thobe, J.J	KIN	CARO	2.09
T*Karp, Ryan	ALB	EAST	2.10
Dettmer, John	CHL	FSL	2.15
T Brumley, Duff	TUL	TEX	2.16
T*May, Darrell	DUR	CARO	2.19
T*Pulsipher, Bill	SLU	FSL	2.19
T Bunch, M.	WIL	CARO	2.21
*VanRyn, Ben	SAN	TEX	2.21

WINS

Player	Club	Lg.	Wins
T Boze, M.	ELP	TEX	17
T Henderson, R.	HRB	EAST	17
Carter, John	CLM	SAL	17
Stephenson, G.	ABY	SAL	16
T*Karp, Ryan	ALB	EAST	16
T*Eischen, Joey	OTT	INT	16
Dettmer, John	CHL	FSL	16
SEVERAL TIED AT			15

COMPLETE GAMES

Player	Club	Lg.	CG
T Ellis, Robert	BIR	SOU	10
Holt, Chris	QC	MID	10
*Jarvis, Matt	ABY	SAL	8
T Ratekin, Mark	MDL	TEX	8
Henkel, Rob	LYN	CARO	7
Sparks, Steve	NO	AMAS	7
Minchey, Nate	PAW	INT	7
T Urbina, U.	HRB	EAST	7

SHUTOUTS

Player	Club	Lg.	Sho
Bakkum, Scott	LYN	CARO	4
Brooks, Wes	FTL	FSL	3
T Ellis, Robert	BIR	SOU	3
T Ruffcorn, S.	NVL	AMAS	3
T Myers, R.	MEM	SOU	3
Hawkins, L.T.	FTW	MID	3
T Steenstra, K.	ORL	SOU	3
Holt, Chris	QC	MID	3
Harriger, Denny	BNG	EAST	3
Jones, Bobby	NOR	INT	3
*Adamson, Joel	HD	CAL	3

Switch-hitter
* Left-handed
T Player has been with more than one team, listed with last team.
(Players in major leagues are listed with last minor league team.)

BATTING	Avg.	AB	R	H	2B	3B	HR	RBI	SB
*Pritchett, Chris, 1B	.308	464	61	143	30	6	2	66	3
Raven, Luis, Of	.257	167	21	43	12	1	2	30	4
*Rumsey, Dan, Of	.059	51	3	3	1	0	0	1	0
*Sweeney, Mark, Of	.356	188	41	67	13	2	9	32	1
Tejero, Fausto, C	.130	69	3	9	1	1	1	7	0
Wasinger, Mark, Dh	.214	117	17	25	4	0	2	17	0

PITCHING	W	L	ERA	G	SV	IP	H	BB	SO
*Anderson, Brian	0	1	3.38	2	0	10.2	16	0	9
Bennett, Erik	5	4	6.49	11	0	69.1	87	17	33
*Charland, Colin	6	2	5.01	10	0	59.1	66	17	54
Chavez, Tony	0	0	4.15	5	1	8.2	11	4	9
Edenfield, Ken	5	8	4.61	48	4	93.2	93	35	84
Fritz, John	9	5	3.61	20	0	129.2	125	42	85
*Gamez, Bob	5	2	3.26	44	0	60.2	68	18	50
Gledhill, Chance	6	11	5.41	28	0	141.1	169	41	66
Heredia, Julian	5	3	3.12	46	0	89.1	77	19	89
Holdridge, David	8	10	6.08	27	0	151.0	202	55	123
Lewis, Scott	1	0	1.50	1	0	6.0	6	0	2
Musset, Jose	2	6	5.49	59	21	62.1	59	32	59
*Perez, Beban	0	1	19.64	3	0	3.2	8	2	1
Purdy, Shawn	2	2	5.06	5	0	32.0	38	9	18
Ratekin, Mark	3	1	4.67	7	0	44.1	50	11	24
*Stroud, Derek	1	1	4.61	13	0	13.2	16	9	13
Watson, Ron	2	1	3.88	36	3	46.1	39	43	41
Williams, Shad	7	10	4.71	27	0	175.2	192	65	91

San Antonio Missions (Dodgers) AA

BATTING	Avg.	AB	R	H	2B	3B	HR	RBI	SB
Abbe, Chris, C	.205	254	32	52	7	1	13	36	0
Alvarez, Jorge, 2B	.271	251	26	68	24	0	4	34	9
Blanco, Henry, 3B	.195	374	33	73	19	1	10	42	3
Castro, Juan, Ss	.276	424	55	117	23	8	7	41	12
#Cedeno, Roger, Of	.288	465	70	134	13	8	4	30	28
*Collier, Anthony, Of	.207	193	21	40	8	0	4	15	2
*Doffek, Scott, 2B	.259	85	5	22	7	0	0	8	1
Elster, Kevin, Ss	.282	39	5	11	2	1	0	7	0
*Hollandsworth, Todd, Of	.251	474	57	119	24	9	17	63	23
Howard, Matt, 2B	.287	122	12	35	5	1	0	5	4
Huckaby, Ken, C	.220	82	4	18	1	0	0	5	0
Ingram, Garey, 2B	.269	305	43	82	14	5	6	33	19
*Kirkpatrick, Jay, 1B	.320	97	17	31	6	1	6	17	0
Kliafas, Stephen, Ss	.143	14	2	2	0	0	0	0	0
Lott, Billy, Of	.254	418	49	106	17	2	15	49	5
Magnusson, Brett, Ph	.111	9	1	1	1	0	0	0	0
Maurer, Ron, 3B	.189	37	6	7	1	0	1	4	0
*Melendez, Dan, 3B	.241	158	25	38	11	0	7	30	0
Ortiz, Hector, C	.214	131	6	28	5	0	1	6	0
#Proctor, Murph, 1B	.252	294	38	74	10	0	5	42	1
*Spearman, Vernon, Of	.259	162	22	42	4	2	0	13	13

PITCHING	W	L	ERA	G	SV	IP	H	BB	SO
Bene, Bill	5	6	4.84	46	1	70.2	50	53	82
*Brosnan, Jason	0	2	4.43	3	0	20.1	21	7	10
Castro, Nelson	2	1	4.94	5	0	27.1	35	4	15
Correa, Edwin	0	2	8.00	2	0	9.0	17	8	8
Daspit, Jimmy	3	8	4.43	15	0	81.1	92	33	58
Delahoya, Javier	8	10	3.66	21	0	125.1	122	42	107
Gorecki, Rick	6	9	3.35	26	0	156.0	136	62	118
Henderson, Ryan	0	0	2.52	23	5	25.0	19	16	22
Jones, Kiki	0	1	4.50	3	0	14.0	14	8	7
Kutzler, Jerry	1	0	1.59	2	0	5.2	3	0	3
Marquez, Isidrio	1	4	2.84	30	12	31.2	34	8	25
McFarlin, Terry	4	7	2.83	52	4	95.1	87	37	77
*Mimbs, Mark	3	3	1.60	49	10	67.2	49	18	77
Parra, Jose	1	8	3.15	17	0	111.1	103	12	87
Piotrowicz, Brian	0	0	4.66	6	0	19.1	31	7	12
Snedeker, Sean	4	5	4.35	12	0	70.1	92	17	36
Thomas, Royal	4	6	3.94	47	2	109.2	116	44	52
Valdez, Ismael	1	0	1.38	3	0	13.0	12	0	11
*VanRyn, Ben	14	4	2.21	21	0	134.1	118	38	144
*Vierra, Joey	1	0	5.40	9	1	11.2	14	4	6

Shreveport Captains (Giants) AA

BATTING	Avg.	AB	R	H	2B	3B	HR	RBI	SB
Bellomo, Kevin, Of	.083	12	0	1	0	0	0	1	0
Calcagno, Dan, C	.500	4	1	2	0	0	0	0	0
Cavanagh, Mike, C	.571	7	3	4	1	0	1	3	0
Chimelis, Joel, 2B	.202	114	10	23	5	0	6	18	3
Christopherson, Eric, C	.152	46	5	7	2	0	0	2	1
Davenport, Adell, 3B	.262	370	43	97	21	0	15	62	4
#Davis, Matt, Ss	.270	423	44	114	25	0	4	42	3
Decillis, Dean, Ss	.200	5	0	1	0	0	0	1	0
#Duncan, Andres, Ss	.147	75	4	11	2	1	1	9	2
Fernandez, Dan, C	.188	128	12	24	5	1	1	13	1
Florez, Tim, 2B	.255	318	33	81	17	2	1	26	3
*Hecht, Steve, 2B	.298	168	25	50	8	6	3	11	5
*Heffernan, Bert, C	.235	98	8	23	2	0	0	7	1
Hyzdu, Adam, Of	.202	302	30	61	17	0	6	25	0
Jones, Dax, Of	.284	436	59	124	19	5	4	36	13
Kasper, Kevin, 3B	.215	121	13	26	5	0	0	11	4
Katzaroff, Robbie, Of	.300	406	52	122	22	4	0	30	15
*McFarlin, Jason, Of	.186	59	12	11	2	1	0	1	4
*Miller, Barry, 1B	.288	452	59	130	30	2	13	82	5
Miller, Roger, C	.247	194	19	48	10	0	2	12	0
Murray, Calvin, Of	.188	138	15	26	6	0	0	6	12
Ward, Ricky, 3B	.256	90	8	23	8	0	0	5	0
*Weber, Pete, Of	.194	278	33	54	14	0	6	27	7

PITCHING	W	L	ERA	G	SV	IP	H	BB	SO
Ard, Johnny	0	0	.00	3	0	5.0	1	4	0
Carlson, Dan	7	4	2.24	15	0	100.1	86	26	81
*Gardella, Mike	0	0	1.04	5	1	8.2	4	3	11
Griffiths, Brian	5	11	4.85	24	0	133.2	152	68	83
*Hancock, Chris	8	8	4.06	23	0	124.0	126	52	93
Hanselman, Carl	1	5	2.91	15	2	55.2	54	13	36
Hyde, Rich	1	1	7.78	6	0	19.2	33	2	14
Jones, Stacy	4	1	3.58	24	1	50.1	53	19	28
Kasper, Kevin	0	0	30.86	1	0	2.1	9	3	0
Masters, Dave	0	2	1.07	14	2	25.1	21	15	25
Myers, Jim	2	2	2.01	29	1	49.1	50	19	23
*Peltzer, Kurt	4	3	3.19	30	1	42.1	33	9	28
Pote, Lou	8	7	4.07	19	0	108.1	111	45	81
Rambo, Dan	7	5	3.18	15	0	102.0	98	27	61
*Rosselli, Joe	0	1	3.13	4	0	23.0	22	7	19
Simon, Rich	2	7	4.33	52	26	54.0	56	24	38
Smith, Shad	6	3	3.76	24	0	95.2	95	37	65
Torres, Salomon	7	4	2.70	12	0	83.1	67	12	67
Vanderweele, Doug	0	0	.00	1	0	2.0	0	0	3
*Whitaker, Steve	1	0	1.08	4	0	8.1	5	7	12
*Yockey, Mark	3	6	2.13	48	4	71.2	60	20	60

Tulsa Drillers (Rangers) AA

BATTING	Avg.	AB	R	H	2B	3B	HR	RBI	SB
Castellanos, Miguel, 3B	.169	142	10	24	4	1	1	13	1
Castillo, Ben, Of	.228	272	34	62	12	1	5	14	6
Clinton, Jim, 3B	.083	12	0	1	0	0	0	2	0
#Colon, Cris, 3B	.300	490	63	147	27	3	11	47	6
*Epley, Daren, Of	.151	53	4	8	0	0	1	2	0
Gil, Benji, Ss	.275	342	45	94	9	1	17	59	20
*Greer, Rusty, 1B	.291	474	76	138	25	6	15	59	10
List, Paul, Of	.200	125	8	25	3	1	0	6	2
Lowery, Terrell, Of	.240	258	29	62	5	1	3	14	10
Luce, Roger, C	.193	321	35	62	14	2	8	29	2
*Magallanes, Ever, 2B	.326	184	20	60	12	2	1	14	0
McCoy, Trey, Dh	.293	420	72	123	27	3	29	95	3
*McDowell, Oddibe, Of	.342	114	26	39	7	1	8	31	3
Morrow, Timmie, Of	.246	390	46	96	25	2	9	45	11
Rolls, David, C	.240	221	23	53	9	0	5	23	1
Simonson, Bob, Of	.237	118	11	28	4	0	4	14	3
Turco, Frank, 2B	.267	423	45	113	13	2	8	39	13

PITCHING	W	L	ERA	G	SV	IP	H	BB	SO
Alberro, Jose	0	0	.95	17	5	19.0	11	8	24
Arner, Mike	1	0	4.53	27	0	57.2	58	14	37
Brumley, Duff	7	7	2.93	18	0	110.2	87	35	121
Dreyer, Steve	2	2	3.73	5	0	31.1	26	8	27

Pitching leaders across all leagues

(Cont'd from previous page.)

SAVES

Player	Club	Lg.	Sv
Cochran, J.	SAV	SAL	46
T Lacy, Kerry	CHL	FSL	38
Dougherty, J.	JCK	TEX	36
T Perez, Cesar	CLM	SAL	35
Bullinger, Kirk	SPR	MID	33

GAMES

Player	Club	Lg.	G
T Borland, T.	REA	EAST	70
T Zimmerman, M.	BUF	AMAS	66
*Fesh, Sean	ASH	SAL	65
T*Dunbar, Matt	ALB	EAST	64
T McCurry, Jeff	CAR	SOU	64
T Cimorelli, F.	LOU	AMAS	64
T*Johnson, E.	ORL	SOU	62
T Lynch, Dave	IND	AMAS	62
T Lacy, Kerry	CHL	FSL	62
*Ritchie, Wally	TOL	INT	62
Rogers, Bryan	BNG	EAST	62
Patterson, Jeff	SWB	INT	62
T Bottalico, R.	REA	EAST	62
*Eversgerd, B.	ARK	TEX	62

INNINGS PITCHED

Pitcher	Club	Lg.	IP
T Hansen, B.	NBR	EAST	196.0
Minchey, Nate	PAW	INT	194.2
Anderson, C.	SPT	SAL	191.1
Vanegmond, T.	NBR	EAST	190.1
Gozzo, Mauro	NOR	INT	190.1
T Baldwin, J.	NVL	AMAS	189.0
T Helling, Ricky	OKC	AMAS	188.1
T Steenstra, K.	ORL	SOU	188.1

STRIKE OUTS

Pitcher	Club	Lg .	SO
Bennett, Joel	LYN	CARO	221
T*Wade, Terrell	GRV	SOU	208
T Helling, Ricky	OKC	AMAS	205
T Brumley, Duff	TUL	TEX	188
T*Bertotti, Mike	SBN	MID	185
T Ruffcorn, S.	NVL	AMAS	185
T*Looney, B.	HRB	EAST	185

Switch-hitter
* Left-handed
T Player has been with more than one team, listed with last team.
(Players in major leagues are listed with last minor league team.)

Starting pitchers

(Minimum 10 starts.)

SO/9 IP RATIO

Pitcher	Club	Lg.	Ratio
T*Davis, Tim	RIV	CAL	12.05
T*Wade, Terrell	GRV	SOU	11.82
Bennett, Joel	LYN	CARO	10.99
Evans, Bart	RKF	MID	10.91
*York, Charles	CLM	SAL	10.37

AVERAGE AGAINST

Pitcher	Club	Lg.	Avg.
Hennis, Randall	OSC	FSL	.176
T*Davis, Tim	RIV	CAL	.179
Thompson, M.	CV	CAL	.183
Coffman, Kevin	JAX	SOU	.185
*Hill, Tyrone	STK	CAL	.185
T Brumley, Duff	TUL	TEX	.189

Relief pitchers

(Minimum 50 games.)

SO/9 IP RATIO

Pitcher	Club	Lg.	Ratio
T Benitez, A.	FRE	CARO	15.04
Bullinger, Kirk	SPR	MID	12.62
*Eggert, David	BUR	MID	12.38
Schmitt, Todd	WLO	MID	11.66
T Richey, Jeff	CLN	MID	11.62
T Davis, Clint	ARK	TEX	11.22

AVERAGE AGAINST

Pitcher	Club	Lg.	Avg.
T Perez, Cesar	CLM	SAL	.138
Bullinger, Kirk	SPR	MID	.144
T Benitez, A.	FRE	CARO	.165
Maberry, Louis	CWV	SAL	.169
T Richey, Jeff	CLN	MID	.184

366

PITCHING	W	L	ERA	G	SV	IP	H	BB	SO
Gies, Chris	1	5	5.02	26	1	66.1	67	24	28
Goetz, Barry	2	3	6.55	38	1	56.1	70	44	57
Helling, Rick	12	8	3.60	26	0	177.1	150	46	188
*Hurst, James	2	3	3.26	11	1	49.2	41	12	44
Miller, Kurt	6	8	5.06	18	0	96.0	102	45	68
*Moody, Ritchie	3	2	2.18	46	16	66.0	58	34	60
*Oliver, Darren	7	5	1.96	46	6	73.1	51	41	77
Perez, David	9	10	4.02	33	2	125.1	119	34	111
Reed, Bobby	5	7	4.26	15	0	76.0	88	22	35
*Romero, Brian	5	6	3.91	21	0	94.1	98	34	72
Rowley, Steve	8	7	6.04	20	0	92.1	103	33	63
Sadecki, Steve	0	1	3.94	9	1	16.0	16	4	12

Wichita Wranglers (Padres) AA

BATTING	Avg.	AB	R	H	2B	3B	HR	RBI	SB
Abercrombie, John, 1B	.254	181	21	46	7	0	7	31	6
#Bethea, Steve, 3B	.265	49	2	13	0	0	0	1	0
Bish, Brent, 2B	.266	64	12	17	2	1	0	6	2
Bruno, Julio, 3B	.285	246	34	70	17	1	3	24	3
#Gash, Darius, Of	.269	271	34	73	9	4	5	37	15
#Gieseke, Mark, 1B	.244	41	5	10	3	0	0	4	0
*Gonzalez, Paul, 3B	.270	215	36	58	7	3	7	33	5
*Hall, Billy, 2B	.270	486	80	131	27	7	4	46	29
#Harris, Vince, Of	.274	350	55	96	13	2	0	36	27
Henderson, Lee, C	.176	74	7	13	0	0	0	3	1
Holbert, Ray, Ss	.260	388	56	101	13	5	5	48	30
#Hosey, Dwayne, Of	.291	326	52	95	19	2	18	61	13
Lopez, Pedro, C	.204	142	12	29	7	0	4	14	3
#Martinez, Pablo, Ss	.277	130	19	36	5	1	2	14	8
*McDavid, Ray, Of	.270	441	65	119	18	5	11	55	33
*Pugh, Scott, 1B	.316	79	15	25	1	0	4	11	0
*Sanders, Tracy, Of	.323	266	44	86	13	4	13	47	6
Smith, Ira, Of	.231	39	7	9	0	1	0	4	0
Spann, Tookie, 1B	.274	281	30	77	17	1	8	42	6
Staton, Dave, Dh	.417	12	2	5	3	0	0	2	0
Thurston, Jerrey, C	.244	197	22	48	10	0	2	22	2

PITCHING	W	L	ERA	G	SV	IP	H	BB	SO
Berumen, Andres	3	1	5.74	7	0	26.2	35	11	17
*Bryand, Renay	3	5	2.41	52	2	71.0	67	32	63
Clark, Terry	3	0	2.43	19	0	29.2	27	7	30
*Cromwell, Nate	3	5	4.13	21	0	89.1	90	38	86
Florie, Bryce	11	8	3.96	27	0	154.2	128	100	133
Freitas, Mike	0	2	10.57	8	0	7.2	13	2	4
Hamilton, Joey	4	9	3.97	15	0	90.2	101	36	50
Heinkel, Don	2	5	5.47	33	0	49.1	59	6	41
Hoeme, Steve	2	3	2.42	44	19	48.1	41	16	47
*Huber, Jeff	3	1	3.26	15	3	19.1	16	9	18
Kellogg, Geoff	7	11	5.37	22	0	124.0	137	45	71
Leskanic, Curt	3	2	3.45	7	0	44.1	37	17	42
Lifgren, Kelly	5	3	5.35	37	2	74.0	88	28	45
Paskievitch, Tom	1	2	7.00	7	0	9.0	11	8	5
*Pena, Jim	2	0	1.69	10	0	16.0	10	2	12
Sager, A.J.	5	3	3.19	11	0	73.1	69	16	49
Strong, Joe	1	0	6.75	4	0	14.2	13	11	13
Wengert, Bill	7	7	4.10	28	0	162.1	167	43	106
Whitehurst, Wally	1	0	1.27	4	0	21.1	11	5	14

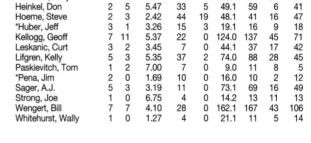

Switch-hitter
* Left-handed
T Player has been with more than one team, listed with last team.
(Players in major leagues are listed with last minor league team.)

Class of '93: The minors' hottest prospects

During the season, *Baseball Weekly* examined the minors' hottest prospects; here are some names to look for in '94, beginning at the very top.

PLAYER OF THE YEAR

At 6-4 and 220 pounds, **Cornelius Clifford Floyd Jr.**, Expos' first baseman/outfielder, is heads above other prospects, and *Baseball Weekly*'s Minor League Player of the Year for 1993. In 101 games for the Senators, Floyd hit .329 with 26 HR, 101 RBI and 31 stolen bases—Eastern League MVP. He was in the league's top three in six offensive categories. At the end of the season, he joined the parent club as a non-roster player, and replaced left-fielder Moises Alou when he broke his leg. Then he made his first start at first base, went 2-for-4, and two nights later hit a two-run homer. Manager Felipe Alou said Floyd was ready to be his starting first baseman.

PITCHERS

▶**RHP Jose Silva, (Blue Jays):** "He probably has the best fastball in the (South Atlantic) league," Hagerstown manager Jim Nettles said.

▶**RHP Brien Taylor (Yankees):** No one doubts his potential—he throws in the mid-90s and has reached 97.

▶**LHP Rick Krivda (Orioles):** Not overpowering, but has a big curveball and a penchant for winning. Entered '93 at 24-7 lifetime with a 2.71 ERA.

▶**RHP John Dettmer (Rangers):** 16-3 with a 2.17 ERA at Port Charlotte. Good movement on his pitches and a good curve. Knows how to work the plate.

▶**RHP LaTroy Hawkins (Twins):** Won 13 consecutive decisions and allowed just five earned runs in August (39 IP). Eighty-eight-mph fastball, slider, curve and change.

▶**RHP James Baldwin (White Sox):** Won the Southern League ERA crown. Pitches inside well; throws a good curve and fastball.

▶**RHP Ugueth Urbina (Expos):** 10-1 with a 1.99 ERA at Burlington. Ninety-five-mph fastball.

▶**LHP Hiawatha Terrell Wade (Braves):** Throws in the 90s; also has a slider and change. His 203 strikeouts were second in all the minors.

▶**RHP Mike Busby (Cardinals):** 6-4, 210-pounds; 12-2 with a 2.44 ERA.

CATCHERS

▶**Carlos Delgado (Blue Jays):** Led Southern League with 25 HR, 102 RBI and 102 walks. Had 28 doubles and a .524 slugging percentage.

▶**Charles Johnson (Marlins):** Hit .275 (29 doubles, club-record 19 HR, 94 RBI). Midwest League All-Star. Made just 12 errors; threw out 47.6% of runners trying to steal.

▶**Jason Moler (Phillies):** Hit .289 in 97 games (17 doubles, 15 HR, 64 RBI). Drew 46 walks, struck out 40 times.

▶**Jason Kendall (Pirates):** Hit .276 at Augusta (17 doubles, 40 RBI) in 102 games. Voted best defensive catcher in the Sally League—at only 19 years old.

▶**Mike Matheny (Brewers):** Hit .256 (21 doubles, two HR, 28 RBI) in 107 games, with just nine errors. Led the Texas League, gunning down 54.3% of enemy runners.

▶**Aldo Pecorilli (Cardinals):** Hit .305 (30 doubles, seven triples, 14 HR, club-record 93 RBI). All-Star DH.

▶**Marcus Jensen (Giants):** Most respected arm in the Midwest League: gunned down 45% of runners. Switch-hitter; hit .262 (24 doubles, 11 HR, 56 RBI).

▶**Tony Eusebio (Astros):** Hit .324 (43 RBI). "He's got the strongest arm in the Pacific Coast League," said manager Rick Sweet.

▶**Jorge Fabregas (Angels):** Threw out 51% of runners. All-Star catcher; hit .289 (26 doubles, six HR, 56 RBI).

INFIELDERS

▸ **2B Chris Wimmer (Giants):** Set a league record for second basemen with .9917 fielding percentage. Hit .264 (21 doubles, 3 HR, 53 RBI, 49 steals).

▸ **1B Roberto Petagine (Astros):** Hit .334; won Texas League batting title. Had 15 HR, 90 RBI. League MVP. Also led league with 36 doubles, 84 walks, .442 on-base percentage.

▸ **2B James Mouton (Astros):** MVP in the Pacific Coast League. Hit .315 (42 doubles, 12 triples, 16 HR, 92 RBI, 40 steals). Led the PCL in at-bats (546), runs (126) hits (172), doubles (42) and extra-base hits (70).

▸ **SS Chipper Jones (Braves):** Hit .325 (31 doubles, 12 triples, 13 HR, 89 RBI). International League Rookie of the Year.

▸ **2B Quilvio Veras (Mets):** Hit .306 with a club-record 52 steals at Class AA Binghamton.

▸ **2B Michael Tucker (Royals):** Hit .305 in 61 games (6 HR, 44 RBI, 12 steals) in Class A, promoted to Double-A, finished at .279 in 72 games (9 HR, 35 RBI, 12 steals).

▸ **1B D.J. Boston (Blue Jays):** MVP in South Atlantic League. Hit .315 (35 doubles, 4 triples, 13 HR, 92 RBI).

▸ **SS Alex Gonzalez (Blue Jays):** Played in all 142 games in '93. Hit .289 (29 doubles, 7 triples, 16 HR, 69 RBI, 91 runs scored).

▸ **SS Derek Jeter (Yankees):** Hit .295 (14 doubles, 11 triples, 5 HR, 71 RBI). South Atlantic League's Most Outstanding Prospect.

▸ **1B Rich Aude (Pirates):** Hit .289 (18 HR, 73 RBI) at Double-A, then .375 (four HR, 16 RBI) at Triple-A. September call-up to Pittsburgh.

OUTFIELDERS

▸ **Brian Hunter (Astros):** Led the Texas League with 35 steals, hit .294 (22 doubles, 10 HR, 52 RBI), and was on the All-Star Team.

▸ **Chad Mottola (Reds):** Led the league in RBI (91), hit .280 (21 HR, 25 doubles).

▸ **Vince Moore (Padres):** Was hitting .292 (14 HR, 23 RBI) when he was part of Atlanta's trade for Fred McGriff. Since then, he hit .258 (six HR, 23 RBI) in 39 games. Switch-hitter.

▸ **Rondell White (Expos):** Hit .327 (12 HR, 52 RBI) at Harrisburg, then was promoted to Ottawa and hit .393 (seven HR, 28 RBI) in 28 games. Promoted to Montreal in August.

▸ **Carl Everett (Marlins):** Switch-hitter. Voted best defensive outfielder in the California League. Promoted to PCL and finished at .309 (13 doubles, four triples, six HR, 16 RBI, 12 steals) in 35 games.

▸ **Garret Anderson (Angels):** Hit .293 (34 doubles, 71 RBI), but needs to be more selective at the plate: 31 walks and 95 strikeouts.

▸ **Manny Ramirez (Indians):** Hit two HR in his second major league game—at hometown Yankee Stadium. Hit .340 (17 HR, 79 RBI) in 89 games in Double-A, then .317 (14 HR, 36 RBI) in 40 games in Triple-A. Had a .706 slugging percentage; won league batting title.

▸ **Johnny Damon (Royals):** Hit .290 (25 doubles, 13 triples, 5 HR, 50 RBI) and tied Delino DeShields' record with 59 steals. His 148 hits broke the old club mark of 134 set by Tyrone Horne. Voted the top prospect, and most exciting player in the Midwest League.

▸ **Curis Goodwin and Alex Ochoa (Orioles):** Go for the package deal. Goodwin hit .277 (60 steals, 95 runs scored) and was MVP of the Carolina League All-Star Game. Ochoa hit .276 (13 HR, 90 RBI, 34 steals).

▸ **Shawn Green (Blue Jays):** Hit .283 in 99 games (14 doubles, four HR, 34 RBI).

Youth leagues

- ▸ Little League
- ▸ American Legion
- ▸ Babe Ruth Baseball
- ▸ PONY League
- ▸ Championship coverage
- ▸ Plus: How to find a team

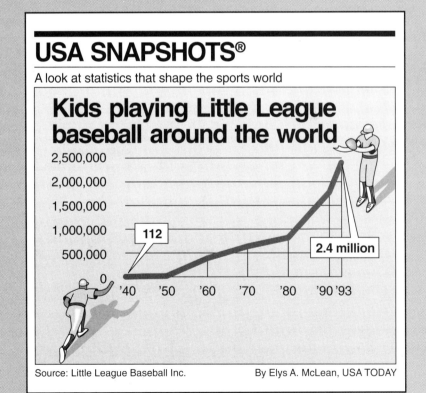

USA SNAPSHOTS®

A look at statistics that shape the sports world

Kids playing Little League baseball around the world

112

2.4 million

Source: Little League Baseball Inc.   By Elys A. McLean, USA TODAY

Long Beach wins series—on the field, not after the fact

▶**Aug. 23:** Bedford, N.H. 1, Richmond, Va. 0; Long Beach, Calif. 8, Hamilton, Ohio 0; David Chiriqui, Panama 6, N. Vancouver, B.C., Canada 0; Kaiserslautern, Germany 7, Garapan City, Saipan 3.

▶**Aug. 24:** Long Beach, Calif. 12, Richmond, Va. 8; Bedford, N.H. 1, Hamilton, Ohio 0; David Chiriqui, Panama 4, Garapan City, Saipan 1; N. Vancouver, B.C., Canada 8, Kaiserslautern, Germany 1.

▶**Aug. 25:** Long Beach, Calif. 21, Bedford, N.H. 1; Hamilton, Ohio 1, Richmond, Va. 0; Garapan City, Saipan 4, N. Vancouver, B.C., Canada 3; Kaiserslautern, Germany 5, David Chiriqui, Panama 1.

▶**Aug. 26:** (USA Championship) Long Beach, Calif. 11, Bedford, N.H. 0; (International Championship) David Chiriqui, Panama 5, Kaiserslautern, Germany 0.

▶**Aug. 28:** (World Championship) Long Beach, Calif. 3, David Chiriqui, Panama 2.

For the record books, Long Beach became the first U.S. team to repeat as champions—a feat performed twice before, by Monterrey, Mexico, in 1957-58 and by Seoul, South Korea, in 1984-85. But Long Beach's second win came only after it was awarded the 1992 championship, when the 1992 champion from Zamboanga City, the Philippines, was disqualified for using overage players.

"It's just a great feeling to leave the ballpark knowing we won on the field with all of our kids out there," said Long Beach manager Larry Lewis.

Long Beach's big gun was Sean Burroughs, son of Jeff Burroughs—American League MVP in 1974 with the Texas Rangers. Trying to hit his fastball—clocked at 74 mph—at the Little League distance of 46 feet was comparable to an adult trying to hit a 97-mph fastball at 60 feet, 6 inches. In the 8-0 series opener against Hamilton, Ohio, he struck out 16 in a no-hitter. In the next game, he hit a mammoth homer to straight-away center in a 12-8 win against Tuckahoe L.L. from Richmond, Va. Then, against Bedford, N.H., he went 3-for-5 with one RBI in a 21-1 win.

In the final, Panama's Alex Beitia matched Long Beach's Brady Werner pitch for pitch. Heading into the bottom of the sixth inning, the score was tied at 2. But three singles and a botched sacrifice attempt left the bases loaded with one out. After Panama reliever Abel Navarro got a strikeout, pinch-hitter Jeremy Hess ripped a fastball to the right-center field fence, and Long Beach had finally won on the field.

—by Rick Lawes

More scandals haunt series

Memories of last year's Philippine team being stripped of its title for recruiting players from all over the island and using players older than 12—came back to haunt the '93 series. After the Dominican Republic won the Latin American region, the Panamanian team filed a protest. When the Dominican team was found to have broken the rules, the Panamanian team replaced it and advanced to the championship game. Meanwhile, on the other side of the world, Taiwan was winning the Far East title for the 19th time in the last 25 years. But a new rule limiting the size of school districts housing leagues, aimed primarily at foreigners, caught the Taiwanese—and Japan, Korea and China. In their place came the ballclub from Garapan City, Saipan, capital of the Commonwealth of Northern Mariana Islands, a group of four small islands in the middle of the Pacific Ocean northeast of the Philippines.

The Saipanese youngsters had managed just a 4-4 record in the Far East regional, a fifth-place finish. But they were in Williamsport because "we just were able to verify that Saipan was in conformity and decided as a tournament committee to invite them," said Joe Losch, international tournament director.

—by Rick Lawes

How to find a team

The best known of all youth baseball associations, Little League was founded in 1939 in Williamsport, Pa., site of its annual World Series for 11- and 12-year-olds. It encompasses at least 46 countries and 2.5 million youngsters, with four age groups in baseball and three in girls' softball. To find a local team, contact the regional headquarters listed below:

▶**National Headquarters:** P.O. Box 3485, Williamsport, PA 17701; (717) 326-1921.

▶**Western Region:** 6707 Little League Dr., San Bernardino, CA 92407; (714) 887-6444.

▶**Central Region:** 4360 N. Mitthoeffer Rd., Indianapolis, IN 46236; (317) 897-6127.

▶**Southern Region:** P.O. Box 13366, St. Petersburg, FL 33733; (813) 344-2661.

▶**Eastern Region:** Same as national headquarters.

▶**Texas State:** 1612 University-Parks Dr., Waco, TX 76706; (817) 756-1816.

RBI series is a big winner

An excited Alex Martinez sat in the dugout at Busch Stadium in St. Louis, beads of perspiration glistening from his forehead from the hot morning sun. The 15-year-old from Los Angeles had just pitched three innings in the RBI World Series.

"This is one of the most exciting things I could imagine," Martinez said as he watched his club play Cleveland in an opening-round game of the Series. "It's fun playing on a major league field. I can't believe I'm sitting here."

Martinez was one of 400 youths, ages 13-17, participating in the inaugural RBI World Series. Twenty-one teams from 12 cities played in the two-division tournament.

Roundup of champions

Winners of other divisions of Little League:

▶**Big League World Series (ages 16-18):** Taiwan 7, Broward County, Fla. 0.

▶**Senior League World Series (ages 13-15):** La Vega, Dominican Republic , Taiwan

▶**Junior League World Series (age 13):** Cayey, Puerto Rico 9, Reynoso, Mexico 1.

Little League: Quick facts

Here is a nutshell look at Little League:

▶**Founded:** 1939

▶**Ages:** 11-18

▶**Divisions:** Little League (11-12); Junior League (13); Senior League (13-15); Big League (16-18).

▶**Total Active players:** 2.5 million.

▶**Countries:** USA; 45 foreign.

▶**Palomino (ages 17-18):** Houston 11, Honolulu 1.

▶**Colt (ages 15-16):** Fountain Valley, Calif. 11, Maui, Hawaii 0.

▶**Pony (ages 13-14):** Joliet, Ill. 4, Bayamon, Puerto Rico 2.

▶**Bronco (ages 11-12):** Bayamon, Puerto Rico 9, Joliet, Ill. 6.

Reviving Baseball in Inner-Cities (RBI) is a community-based program that combines education and baseball. The World Series, sponsored by Major League Baseball and the Sporting Goods Manufacturers Association, featured teams from Atlanta, Boston, Cleveland, Kansas City, Los Angeles, St. Louis, Miami, Newark (N.J.), New York, Richmond (Va.), Philadelphia, and San Juan, P.R.

The league is the brainchild of John Young, a former professional baseball player now a scout for the Florida Marlins. In 1988, while driving along the streets of South Central Los Angeles where he had grown up, he realized something was wrong. It was a summer day, the sun was out, the temperature was in the upper-80s, and school was out. But most of the baseball fields in the city parks stood empty.

"The kids just weren't getting the chance to play," he said, ". . . Programs for their age groups simply didn't exist or were poorly organized in the inner-city." Plans are now under way to make the RBI World Series an annual fixture. The '94 event is scheduled to be held at Anaheim Stadium.

—by Myron Holtzman

PONY wins all-star tourney

Coming as it did three weeks after the major league draft, the first National Amateur All-Star tournament was unlikely to produce many surprise diamonds in the rough. But Richard Petru might have opened some eyes. The '93 graduate from Westbury (Texas) High School went 11-for-13 overall, leading PONY Baseball to the championship with a 4-2 final win against Dixie Baseball.

The tournament pitted all-stars from five organizations—PONY, Dixie, Babe Ruth, the American Amateur Baseball Congress (Connie Mack) and the National Amateur Baseball Federation. Players were from the organizations' 16- to 18-year-old groups or primarily graduating high school seniors.

Of the 99 players in Battle Creek, Mich.—site of the tournament—27 had been drafted and 17 were either still in high school or already attending college.

But 19 other teenagers originally selected for the tournament already had signed professional contracts by the start of the tourney and could not play.

"We hope to get a waiver next year from (Major League Baseball)," said Ron Berryman, president of Amateur All-Star Baseball, the event's organizers.

—by Rick Lawes

Bayside Yankees win NABF's Junior Olympic Super Series

The Bayside (N.Y.) Yankees, winners of the National Amateur Baseball Federation's Junior Division, rolled through the round-robin undefeated then squeaked out a 1-0 win against Meridian, Miss. to take the Junior Olympic Super Series in Beaumont, Texas. Bayside won all five of its round-robin games, including a 10-0 win against Meridian, the Dixie Baseball representative as champion of its Pre-Majors division.

James Rowson's single in the bottom of the seventh in a 3-2 win against AABC participant Glendale, Calif., moved the Yankees into the final. He hit in the final a first-inning homer for all the runs Jeff Tyler needed. Tyler allowed just three hits and struck out 10, outdueling Jamie Brown, who gave up four hits and struck out nine. A national championship sponsored by USA Baseball, the super series matches winners of the organizations' 15-16 age group.

American Legion: The original

Oldest of all the youth leagues, American Legion was founded in 1925 for players 17 and under. It now includes players up to age 19 and has been a springboard for many young players. Major league scouts are a common sight at the national playoffs, staged since 1926. Headquartered in Indianapolis, the league hosts over 760,000 registered players.

Rapid City, S.D. Post 22 won the 1993 American Legion World Series in Roseburg, Ore. with a 7-4 win against Green Valley Post 8 (Las Vegas, Nev.). Rapid City pounded its way to the title, scoring 57 runs in its five games.

Babe Ruth: Always a big hit

Started in Hamilton Township, N.J. in 1951, Babe Ruth baseball was organized for players age 13 to 15. An older division (16-18) was started in 1968, with a separate division for 13-year-olds formed in 1974. More than 600,000 youngsters play Babe Ruth baseball including the Bambino League, which incorporates Rookie League (ages 7-9). Rookie League uses pitching machines, softer balls, and 12 players on the field.

Championship scores: NABF

▶**Major (unlimited):** Long Island, N.Y. 14, Bridgeport, Conn. 6.

▶**College (22 and under):** Cincinnati 14, Macomb, Mich. 3.

▶**High School:** Apopka, Fla. 5, Dr. Phillips H.S. (Orlando, Fla.) 2.

▶**Senior (17-18):** Marietta, Ga. 7, Bayside, N.Y. 6.

▶**Junior (15-16):** Bayside, N.Y. 7, Dearborn Heights, Mich. 5.

▶**Sophomore (13-14):** Baltimore 6, W. Bloomfield, Mich. 0.

▶**Freshman (11-12):** Joliet, Ill. 7, Dayton, Ohio 2.

1993 American Legion World Series scores

▶**Aug. 27:** Rockland County, N.Y. 13, Norman, Okla. 12; Las Vegas, Nev. 6, New Bedford, Mass. 4; Rapid City, S.D. 15, Osseo, Minn. 2; Fairfield, Calif. 12, Miami, Fla. 11.

▶**Aug. 28:** Norman, Okla. 10, Osseo, Minn. 7; Miami, Fla. 9, New Bedford, Mass. 5; Rapid City, S.D. 14, Rockland County, N.Y. 5; Las Vegas, Nev. 1, Fairfield, Calif. 0.

▶**Aug. 29:** Rockland County, N.Y. 6, Miami, Fla. 5; Norman, Okla. 5, Fairfield, Calif. 3; Rapid City, S.D. 16, Las Vegas, Nev. 0.

▶**Aug. 30:** Las Vegas, Nev. 12, Rockland County, N.Y. 0; Norman, Okla 11, Rapid City, S.D. 5.

▶**Aug. 31:** Las Vegas, Nev. 16, Norman, Okla. 4; Rapid City, S.D. 7; Las Vegas, Nev. 4.

▶**Championship scores:** American Legion Rapid City Post 22 (S.D.) 7, Green Valley Post 8 (Las Vegas) 4.

Championship scores: Babe Ruth

▶**Age 16-18:** San Gabriel, Mich. 15, Lincoln Park, Mich. 2.

▶**Age 13-15:** Carolina, Puerto Rico 6, Sarasota, Fla. 0.

▶**Age 13:** Taylorsville, Utah 4, Lexington, Ky. 2.

▶**Bambino (11-12):** Connersville, Ind. 11, Willamette, Ore. 6.

Championship scores: AABC

▶**Stan Musial (unlimited):** San Juan, Puerto Rico 12, Chicago 9.

▶**Connie Mack (17-18):** Cincinnati Midland 8, Dallas Mustangs 2.

▶**Mickey Mantle (15-16):** Glendale, Calif. 1, Cincinnati Midland 0.

▶**Sandy Koufax (13-14):** Pico Rivera, Calif. 11, Dallas Texas Tornado 5.

▶**Pee Wee Reese (11-12):** Cardiff, Calif. 13, Kansas City 11.

Championship scores: Dixie

▶**Majors (17-18):** Lufkin, Texas 9, Goodlettsville, Tenn. 6.

▶**Pre-Majors (15-16):** Meridian, Miss. 11, Columbus County, N.C. 6.

▶**Boys (13-14):** Bossier City, La. 8, Lexington, S.C. 0.

▶**Youth (11-12):** Columbus County, N.C. 8, Glencoe, Ala. 6.

Something for everybody

▶**PONY League:** Founded in 1951 in Washington, Pa. to fill the gap between Little League and high school players, PONY (Protect Our Nation's Youth) baseball uses 80-foot baselines (20 feet longer than Little League, but 10 feet shorter than high schoolers and up).

▶**Dixie Baseball:** Initially called Little Boys Baseball, Dixie was founded in 1955 as an alternative to Little League in South Carolina. It spread through the South and took the Dixie name in 1962 and now has more members than any youth organization except Little League and Babe Ruth.

▶**Junior Olympic Super Series:** A national championship, it matches winners (from the USA) of amateur organizations ages 15 and 16.

▶**National Amateur Baseball Federation:** Begun in 1914, the NABF is the oldest amateur baseball organization in the USA. Started to organize sandlot baseball, the first players were high school age and older. The NABF holds competitions in six age groups.

▶**American Amateur Baseball Congress:** Started primarily as a "senior" league, the AABC now includes a division for players 18 and under (since 1954) and has six divisions. The AABC world series—called the Stan Musial World Series—was first held in Battle Creek, Mich.

How to find a team

To find a team in your area, contact one of the headquarters listed below:

▶**Babe Ruth:** International Headquarters, 1771 Brunswick Ave., P.O. Box 5000, Trenton, NJ 08638; (609) 695-1434.

▶**PONY:** National Headquarters, P.O. Box 225, Washington, PA 15301-0225.

▶**Dixie Baseball:** P.O. Box 222, Lookout Mountain, TN 37350; (615) 821-6811.

▶**National Amateur Baseball Federation:** P.O. Box 705, Bowie, MD 20718; (301) 262-5005.

▶**American Amateur Baseball Congress:** National Headquarters, 118-19 Redfield Plaza, P.O. Box 467, Marshall, MI 49068; (616) 781-2002.

High school & college baseball

▸ 1993 Super 25 high schools   ▸ 1993 College World Series

▸ All-USA high school players   ▸ 1994 college preview

USA SNAPSHOTS®

A look at statistics that shape the sports world

Pro baseball scores with kids

Percentage of children who say they have attended a pro sports event:

62% Baseball
27% Basketball
27% Football
15% Hockey

Source: Child Research Services in-person survey of 600 children for *Sports Illustrated for Kids*

By Marcy E. Mullins, USA TODAY

1993 USA TODAY Super 25: Final high school rankings

▶**1. Fresno, Calif., Bullard (26-3-1)**
Central Section Division I champion for record-tying fifth time. The top hitter was Tony Sciola, with a .432 batting average, five home runs and 28 RBI. The top pitcher was John Phillips, with a 14-0 record, 2.46 ERA, 120 strikeouts and 23 walks in 97⅓ innings.

▶**2. Phoenix, Ariz., Greenway (32-2)**
Class 4A state champion for second time. The top hitter was Jeff Strasser, with a .447 batting average, 44 RBI, 14 doubles and six home runs. The top pitcher was also Strasser, with a 12-0 record and 1.18 ERA.

▶**3. Wilmington, N.C. New Hanover (26-1)**
Class 4A state champion second time. The top hitter was Trot Nixon, with a .517 batting average, 47 runs, 12 home runs and a state-record 56 RBI. The top pitcher was also Nixon, with a 12-0 record, 0.12 ERA, 142 strikeouts and 31 walks in 80 innings.

▶**4. Edison, N.J. (27-2)**
Group IV state champion for fourth time. The top hitter was Pete Rusinko, with a .432 batting average, 13 doubles and 25 RBI. The top pitcher was Brian Appleman, with a 14-0 record, 0.33 ERA, and a school-record 138 strikeouts in 84 innings.

▶**5. Anaheim, Calif., Esperanza (25-5)**
Southern Section Division I champion for second time. The top hitter was Jason Murrietta, with a .524 batting average, 28 runs and 25 RBI. The top pitcher was Marcus Jones, with a 12-2 record and 1.42 ERA.

▶**6. Sarasota, Fla. (28-6)**
Class 4A state champion for third time. The top hitter was Jason Franklin, with a .400 batting average, 34 runs and 19-for-20 stolen bases. The top pitcher was Matt Drews, with a 10-2 record, 1.25 ERA, 125

strikeouts and 29 walks in 88 innings.

▶**7. Arlington, Texas, Martin (34-5)**
Class 5A state champion first time. The top hitter was Dan Sims, with a .387 batting average, 42 runs and 23 RBI. The top pitcher was Matt Blank, with a 13-2 record and 1.20 ERA.

▶**8. Cincinnati, Ohio, Moeller (27-4)**
Division I state champion third time. The top hitter was Mike Bell, with a .400 batting average, 39 runs, 28 RBI, 11 doubles and five home runs. The top pitcher was Mark Drexler, with a 9-1 record and 1.78 ERA.

▶**9. Virginia Beach, Va., First Colonial (28-0)**
Group 3A state champion first time. The top hitter was Nathan Thomas, with a .569 batting average, 32 walks, 26 RBI and seven home runs. The top pitcher was Jason Mann, with a 14-0 record, 1.60 ERA and 102 strikeouts in 70 innings.

▶**10. Atlanta, Ga., Marist (30-3)**
Class 3A state champion fifth time. The top hitter was Brian Walsh, with a .408 batting average and 23 RBI. The top pitcher was Mark Watson, with a 13-1 record, 0.80 ERA, 128 strikeouts and 19 walks in 80 innings.

▶**11. Simi Valley, Calif. (27-4)**
Southern Section Division I runner-up; champion in Upper Deck Classic. The top hitter was Britten Pond, with a .523 batting average, 47 RBI and a school-record 51 runs. The top pitcher was Bill Scheffels, with an 11-2 record and 1.16 ERA.

▶**12. Mauldin, S.C. (31-2)**
Class 4A state champion first time. The top hitter was Dave Delgado, with a .421 batting average, 35 runs and 23 steals. The top pitcher was Clark Maxwell, with a 14-1 record, 0.65 ERA, 187 strikeouts and 28 walks in 102 innings.

▶**13. Gambrills, Md.,**
 Arundel (21-1)
Class 4A state champion sixth time. The top hitter was Tim Giles, with a .571 batting average, 40 RBI and six home runs. The top pitcher was Brandon Agamennone, with an 8-0 record, 0.71 ERA and four saves.

▶**14. Lake Wales, Fla. (28-8)**
Class 3A state champion first time. The top hitter was Johnathan Rockness, with a .477 batting average and 44 RBI. The top pitcher was Tony Elrod, with an 11-0 record and 1.58 ERA.

▶**15. Elizabethtown, Pa. (23-3)**
Class 3A state champion first time. The top hitter was John Frantz, with a .430 batting average and 21 RBI. The top pitcher was Greg Garber, with a 13-1 record and 1.51 ERA.

▶**16. Evansville, Ind.,**
 Memorial (36-2)
Won third state title with 1-0 victory against Huntington North. John Sartore (11-0) pitched a two-hitter, with John Ambrose getting the final four outs for a save. Ambrose (12-1) pitched a two-hitter with no walks to beat Richmond 7-0 in semifinals.

▶**17. Woodland Hills, Calif.,**
 El Camino Real (24-2)
Los Angeles Class 4A city champion, first time. The top hitter was Daniel Cey, with a .448 batting average, 38 runs, six home runs and a school-record 46 RBI. The top pitcher was Randy Wolf, with an 11-1 record, 1.05 ERA and two no-hitters, including a perfect game.

▶**18. Melbourne, Fla.,**
 Air Academy (26-7)
Class 4A state champion first time. The top hitter was John Mussenden, with a .422 batting average, 14 doubles and 22 RBI. The top pitcher was Alexis Ortiz, with a 9-2 record and 2.00 ERA.

▶**19. Cheshire, Conn. (24-0)**
Class LL state champion second consecutive time. The top hitter was Jeff Sutherland, with a .522 batting average, a school-record 35 RBI and a record-tying six home runs. The top pitcher was Dennis Hogan, with an 11-0 record and 1.59 ERA.

▶**20. Oak Grove, Miss. (31-1)**
Class 4A state champion fifth time. The top hitter was Rusty Thomas, with a .538 batting average, eight home runs and 46 RBI. The top pitcher was Cal Logan, with a 9-0 record and 0.66 ERA.

▶**21. Redmond, Wash. (23-3)**
Class 3A state champion second time. The top hitter was Jeff D'Amico, with a .417 batting average, 32 RBI and five home runs. The top pitcher was Jesse Travis, with a 9-0 record and 2.39 ERA.

▶**22. Montgomery, Ala.,**
 Jeff Davis (32-3)
Class 6A state champion second time. The top hitter was Brian Perry, with a .455 batting average, 30 runs and 19 RBI. The top pitcher was Thomas Dovell, with an 11-0 record, 0.99 ERA and three saves.

▶**23. Kansas City, Miss.,**
 Oak Park (22-0)
Class 4A state champion fifth time. The top hitter was Pete Forster, with a .475 batting average, 28 RBI and four home runs. The top pitcher was Craig Burroughs, with a 10-0 record and 2.58 ERA.

▶**24. Edmond, Okla. (33-7)**
Class 5A state champion second consecutive year. The top hitter was Jeramie Simpson, with a .371 batting average, 47 runs and 34 RBI. The top pitcher was Steve Foral, with an 11-0 record and 1.55 ERA.

▶**25. Elmhurst, Ill., York (32-8)**
Class 2A state champion second time. The top hitter was David Sloan, with a .367 batting average, 40 RBI and nine home runs. The top pitcher was Jeff Doll, with an 8-1 record and 2.42 ERA.

▶**Honorable Mention:**
Evans, Georgia, (26-5); Henderson, Nevada, Green Valley (29-2); Murray, Utah, Taylorsville (26-2); Nashville, Tennessee, Montgomery Bell (27-6); San Mateo, California, Serra (25-8); Shenandoah Junction West Virginia, Jefferson (34-4); Thiells, New York, North Rockland (23-4-1); Vista, California, (29-6).

—Ranked for USA TODAY *by consulting high school editor Dave Krider*

1993 USA TODAY
All-USA high school team

1993 Player of the Year
▶**ALEX RODRIGUEZ, SS**
Miami Westminster
Ht: 6-3 **Wt:** 195
Class: Senior
Bats: R **Throws:** R
BA: .505 **Runs:** 56
HR: 9 **RBI:** 36
First round No. 1 draft pick by the Seattle Mariners.

▶**John Roskos, C**
Albuquerque, N.M., Cibola
Ht: 5-11 **Wt:** 190
Class: Senior
Bats: R **Throws:** R
BA: .613 **Runs:** 39
HR: 15 **RBI:** 42
Drafted by the Florida Marlins.

▶**Derrick Lee, 1B**
Sacramento, Calif., El Camino
Ht: 6-5 **Wt:** 205
Class: Senior
Bats: R **Throws:** R
BA: .459 **Runs:** 45
HR: 10 **RBI:** 47
Drafted by the San Diego Padres.

▶**Anthony Medrano, SS**
Long Beach, Calif., Jordan
Ht: 5-11 **Wt:** 165
Class: Senior
Bats: R **Throws:** R
BA: .351 **Runs:** 17
HR: 2 **RBI:** 20
Drafted by the Toronto Blue Jays.

▶**Michael Torti, SS**
Carrollton, Tex., Newman Smith
Ht: 5-11 **Wt:** 180
Class: Senior
Bats: R **Throws:** R
BA: .535 **Runs:** 45
HR: 6 **RBI:** 42
Drafted by the Minnesota Twins.

▶**Christopher Trot Nixon, RF**
Wilmington, N. C., New Hanover
Ht: 6-2 **Wt:** 198
Class: Senior
Bats: L **Throws:** L
BA: .517 **Runs:** 47
HR: 12 **RBI:** 56
Drafted by the Boston Red Sox.

▶**Charles Peterson, CF**
Laurens, S.C.
Ht: 6-4 **Wt:** 207
Class: Senior
Bats: R **Throws:** R
BA: .429 **Runs:** 26
HR: 6 **RBI:** 26
Drafted by the Pittsburgh Pirates.

▶**Torii Hunter, CF**
Pine Bluff, Ark.
Ht: 6-1 **Wt:** 195
Class: Senior
Bats: B **Throws:** R
BA: .436 **Runs:** 30
HR: 6 **RBI:** 30
Drafted by the Minnesota Twins.

▶**Kirk Presley, P**
Tupelo, Miss.
Ht: 6-3 **Wt:** 195
Class: Senior
Bats: R **Throws:** R
W-L: 15-0 **ERA:** 0.58
Innings: 97
Strikeouts: 161 **Walks:** 15
Drafted by the New York Mets.

▶**Troy Carrasco, P**
Tampa, Fla., Jesuit
Ht: 5-11 **Wt:** 180
Class: Senior
Bats: L **Throws:** L
W-L: 15-1 **ERA:** 0.56
Innings: 94
Strikeouts: 186 **Walks:** 31
Drafted by the Minnesota Twins.

Alex Rodriguez:
He runs, he hits,
he's tops on the list

by Tom DiPace

Alex Rodriguez says he's still learning. Never mind that the senior shortstop was pro baseball's No. 1 draft pick in 1993, averaged .419 during his three-year varsity career and helped Miami Westminster to the USA TODAY national championship as a junior.

"It is so competitive every day. You have to prove yourself over and over," said Rodriguez, who batted .505 in '93 and reached base 89 times in 125 plate appearances for a school-record .712 on-base percentage.

Through his natural ability and tireless work ethic, Rodriguez proved the natural choice for USA TODAY national high school player of the year.

He scored 135 runs, drove in 70, walked 58 times and hit 26 doubles, seven triples and 17 home runs in his high school career. He had a .577 on-base percentage and made 24 errors.

If speed is a key to professional stardom, Rodriguez is a top candidate: he runs a 6.5 60-yard dash and gets to first base in 4.0 seconds. He stole 90 bases in 94 tries his last three seasons.

"I've always been fast, but I'm stronger now," Rodriguez said. "I've worked with weights and jumped rope to strengthen my legs and have lengthened my stride. My arm is strong, but I have worked on a quick release. . . . Instinct and fielding are the things that have come easiest."

Coach Rich Hofman used Rodriguez as his leadoff batter, and at one time during the '93 season, Rodriguez got on base 21 consecutive times.

"When he got on base, we were successful," Hofman said. "When he didn't, we struggled. He's an awesome weapon offensively and defensively through his speed. He has that rare ingredient of power and speed. A single for Alex has potential to be a triple."

Shortstop Alex Rodriguez has what it takes to be a star: speed, power and tireless devotion.

Hofman says Rodriguez is probably the greatest high school player to come out of south Florida. "He's received more attention than any high school baseball player I've ever been around," said Hofman of Rodriguez, who was born in New York, started playing baseball at age 7 in the Dominican Republic and a year later moved to Miami.

"He's brought unbelievable recognition to the school. He's not only a great player but a great young man. Even though he's very popular now, that legend will grow."

Rodriguez credits his best friend's father, Juan Arteaga for his development as a player. "He was like my second father," says Rodriguez of Arteaga, who died two years ago. "I still play in his honor."

—by Dave Krider

1993 USA TODAY/*Baseball Weekly* Top 25 coaches' poll

▶**1. Louisiana State (53-17)** Poll points: 825 (33 No. 1 votes). College World Series champions (4-1); 8-0 victory over Wichita State in final. South Regional champions; won SEC Western Division.

▶**2. Wichita State (58-17)** Poll points: 782. College World Series runner-up (3-1); undefeated in Bracket Two. Atlantic Regional champions; won Missouri Valley Conference.

▶**3. Long Beach State (46-19)** Poll points: 734. Third place in College World Series. East Regional champions; won Big West Conference.

▶**4. Texas A&M (53-11)** Poll points: 710. Tied for fifth in College World Series. Central I Regional champions; won Southwest Conference.

▶**5. Oklahoma State (45-17)** Poll points: 697. Fourth, College World Series (2-2). Midwest Regional champions; won Big Eight.

▶**6. Texas (52-16)** Poll points: 672. Tied for fifth, College World Series. Central II Regional champions; second in Southwest Conference.

▶**7. Arizona State (46-20)** Poll points: 647. Tied for seventh, College World Series. West Regional champions; won Pac-10 South.

▶**8. Kansas (45-18)** Poll points: 568. Tied for seventh, College World Series. Mideast Regional champions; second in Big Eight.

▶**9. Georgia Tech (47-13)** Poll points: 477. Third, Atlantic Regional; won Atlantic Coast Conference regular season title.

▶**10. Arizona (35-26)** Poll points: 427. Second, Midwest Regional; second, Pac-10 South.

▶**11. North Carolina State (49-17)** Poll points: 374. Third, Midwest Regional; second, Atlantic Coast Conference tournament.

▶**12. Fresno State (41-22)** Poll points: 355. Second, Mideast Regional; won Western Athletic Conference championship.

▶**13. Florida State (46-19)** Poll points: 343. Third, East Regional; third, Atlantic Coast Conference.

▶**14. Pepperdine (41-17)** Poll points: 339. Fourth, West Regional; won West Coast Conference.

▶**15. Cal St.-Fullerton (35-19)** Poll points: 321. Third, Central II Regional; second, Big West Conference.

▶**16. Clemson (45-20)** Poll points: 310. Third, Mideast Regional; won Atlantic Coast Conference tournament.

▶**17. Notre Dame (46-16)** Poll points: 279. Second, East Regional; won Midwestern Collegiate Conference.

▶**18. Ohio State (44-19)** Poll points: 264. Second, Atlantic Regional; won Big Ten regular season title.

▶**19. Tennessee (45-20)** Poll points: 207. Tied for third, Mideast Regional; won SEC Eastern Division tournament.

▶**20. Southern Cal (35-29)** Poll points: 203. Second, Central II Regional; fourth, Pac-10 South.

▶**21. Mississippi State (41-21)** Poll points: 166. Tied for fifth, East Regional; second, SEC Western Division tournament.

▶**22. UCLA (37-23)** Poll points: 160. Third, Central I Regional; second, Pac-10 South.

▶**23. North Carolina (43-20)** Poll points: 142. Second, Central II Regional; fourth, Atlantic Coast Conference.

▶**24. Baylor (41-19)** Poll points: 135. Tied for fourth, South Regional; won Southwest Conference tournament.

▶**25. South Carolina (41-18)** Poll points: 84. Tied for fourth, Atlantic Regional; won SEC Eastern Division regular season title.

The Baseball Weekly/American Baseball Coaches Association poll is voted on by 33 Division I head coaches, representing all areas of the USA. Records are final.

1994 college preview: The top contenders

The cry for '94 could be "Stop the Tigers!" Still, some new powers on the rise and some old, familiar faces in Omaha are primed to make sure the title won't be handed to the Bayou Bengals. Here's a look at the top contenders for the 1994 season.

▶**Louisiana State:** All-American second baseman Todd Walker (.398, 19 HR, 90 RBI), a potential first-round pick in the June draft, leads the Tigers' charge. Brett Laxton (11-1, 1.88) had a sparkling freshman season, pitching the Tigers' 8-0 championship win, and shortstop Russ Johnson (.353, 7 HR, 56 RBI) joined him on the U.S. national team last summer.

▶**Texas A&M:** The Aggies have a wealth of returnees led by shortstop Robert Harris (.326, 11 HR, 52 RBI) and third baseman Lee Fedora (.326, 8 HR, 45 RBI), but coach Mark Johnson will have to make up for the loss of two of his top three starters.

▶**Georgia Tech:** Shortstop Nomar Garciaparra leads a large group of returnees, including centerfielder Jay Payton (.353, 13 HR, 59 RBI) and Brad Rigby (12-1, 2.58 ERA).

▶**Miami:** Replacing coaching legend Ron Fraser after 30 years, Brad Kelley faces a large number of losses, but is counting on the maturing of right-hander Kenny Henderson (the fifth pick overall out of high school in 1991) to head the pitching staff. A strong recruiting class, including USA TODAY All-USA third baseman Michael Torti, will keep the 'Canes in contention.

▶**Wichita State:** The Shockers won't have pitcher/DH Darren Dreifort, after he was selected second overall in the draft, but the return of Joel Bradberry (from injury) and Shane Dennis and Shane Bryan (from bad years) will help ease his loss. Third baseman Casey Blake (.376) led the offense in his freshman season.

▶**Texas:** Cliff Gustafson will have to overcome the loss of two-time Dick

Howser Trophy winner, all-world Brooks Kieschnick (.376, 19 HR, 80 RBI; 15-3, 3.09 ERA) and first baseman Braxton Hickman (.393, 9 HR, 74 RBI). But Coach Gus always seems to find the horses somewhere.

▶**Florida State:** The strength of the '94 Seminoles will be pitching. Two stalwarts return: U.S. national team member junior Paul Wilson (11-4, 1.73 ERA) and sophomore Jonathan Johnson (9-1, 1.65).

▶**Southern California:** Led by shortstop Gabe Alvarez, the Men of Troy could finally make the return trip to Omaha. Alvarez hit .333 as a freshman and was the only freshman named all-Pac-10. But the pitching staff was racked by the loss of senior Dan Hubbs (17 saves).

▶**Tennessee:** Volunteers' coach Rod Delmonico had a veteran team in 1993, but the return of all-everything Todd Helton will help. Helton, a third-round pick out of high school, spurned the San Diego Padres to play football and baseball. On the diamond, he hit .356 with 11 homers and 65 RBI while posting a 6-2, 3.38 ERA and capped his season with a berth on the U.S. national team.

▶**North Carolina State:** First baseman Andy Barkett (.337, 7 HR, 45 RBI), outfielder Pat Clougherty (.377, 20 HR, 78 RBI) and pitcher Terry Harvey (10-2, 3.07 ERA) return after playing on the U.S. national team. Harvey turned down the pros after being drafted to return for his junior year and play quarterback for the Wolfpack football team.

—by Rick Lawes

381

1993 College World Series wrapup

LSU's long journey ended with shutout

They've been talking dynasty in Baton Rouge after Louisiana State's College World Series championship for two big reasons: second baseman Todd Walker and pitcher Brett Laxton, who helped LSU bury Wichita State 8-0 in the final, return to the Tigers in '94.

Walker, named the series' MVP, fell just short in his bid to become the Southeastern Conference's first triple crown winner in nine years. He finished his sophomore season with a .394 average, 22 homers and 102 RBI.

Laxton set a CWS championship single-game record with 16 strikeouts against the Shockers to finish his freshman season 12-1. He also threw a three-hitter, the first since Penn State's Cal Emery defeated California 1-0 in 1957. It was the first complete-game shutout in the championship game since 1961 when Southern Cal's Jim Withers shut out Oklahoma State 1-0.

Walker's performance was indicative of the Tigers' 1993 comeback season. He started 1-for-11, but the one hit was a grand slam that capped a six-run comeback in LSU's 13-8 win against Texas A&M.

In fact, the entire CWS might be aptly renamed the "Comeback World Series." Ten of the 14 games in the series were come-from-behind wins, with seven decided from the seventh inning on. Six were one-run games.

—by Rick Lawes

1994 CWS scores

▶**June 4:** Texas A&M 5, Kansas 1; LSU 7, Long Beach State 1.
▶**June 5:** Wichita State 4, Arizona State 3 (11 inn.); Texas 6, Oklahoma State 5.
▶**June 6:** Long Beach State 6, Kansas 1; LSU 13, Texas A&M 8. Kansas eliminated.
▶**June 7:** Oklahoma State 5, Arizona State 4; Wichita State 7, Texas 6. Arizona State eliminated.
▶**June 8:** Long Beach State 6, Texas A&M 2; Oklahoma State 7, Texas 6. Texas, Texas A&M eliminated.
▶**June 9:** Long Beach State 10, LSU 8.
▶**June 10:** Wichita State 10, Oklahoma State 4. Oklahoma State eliminated.
▶**June 11:** LSU 6, Long Beach State 5. Long Beach State eliminated.
▶**June 12:** LSU 8, Wichita State 0. (Championship game)

Second baseman Todd Walker—Most Outstanding Player—helped carry LSU to the title.

Fantasy report

- ▶ Roto vs. real life baseball
- ▶ Fantasy leagues: Gambling or just clean fun?
- ▶ How-to's of Roto-lingo
- ▶ Oddball awards

USA SNAPSHOTS®

A look at statistics that shape the sports world

Griffey in good company

Ken Griffey Jr. is the 13th player to hit 40 home runs in a season before age 24. Most successful home run hitters who attained that feat:

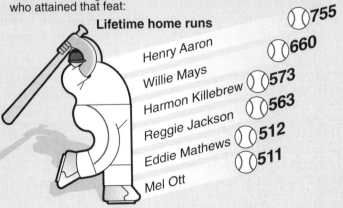

Lifetime home runs

Player	Home runs
Henry Aaron	755
Willie Mays	660
Harmon Killebrew	573
Reggie Jackson	563
Eddie Mathews	512
Mel Ott	511

Source: USA TODAY research by John Riley   By Marty Baumann, USA TODAY

Study links success in Roto to real life

Just how closely Rotisserie baseball approximates the real thing is debatable, but not crucial to the enjoyment of the game. Yet it's interesting to compare how real teams' actual, yearly standings and how the same teams fare by Rotisserie calculations. Are they close? Why exactly does a team of good Roto players not win on the field? Or vice versa?

F.X. Flynn, a member of the original Rotisserie League, did a study on the correlation between each year's actual Major League standings and Rotisserie-generated standings since 1982. He found a surprisingly strong correlation between Rotisserie success and real-life success—much stronger than other allegedly "more accurate" games like 5x5 or Front-Office Baseball.

In addition to satisfying the egos of Rotisserie players, Flynn's study points out the failures of big league teams from big markets. Mets fans couldn't understand how their team couldn't make the World Series in 1987 and 1988. Mets fans in Rotisserie leagues had even more difficulty trying to explain how a team loaded with power, speed (Strawberry and HoJo both had 30-30 seasons in '87) and pitching could fail. Those Mets fans can commiserate with Cubs fans (1984, '89), Yankees fans (1986), White Sox fans (1983) and Blue Jays fans (1987). Do we see a pattern developing here?

Of teams who won the "Roto pennant" but not the real pennant since 1983, only Toronto did not come from one of the three major-market cities. And Toronto is certainly under a media magnifying glass similar to New York, Chicago and Los Angeles—even if it is in a Canadian kind of way.

"If you look for a common denominator to these big-market failures," Flynn explains, "you have to begin with the high-intensity media coverage these teams attract. How many of us could do our work well in such an atmosphere?"

For the past three years, Roto-pennant winners matched perfectly with real-life ones. When small-market teams throw up a winner, Flynn points out, it seems they're actually capable of accomplishing the task at hand.

"Ballplayers have great skills we don't have, but they aren't necessarily better equipped to deal with the kind of attention the *New York Post* gives them.

"Steinbrenner and his ilk of owner, and the tabloids and their ilk of reporter might just be strangling the goose that lays the golden egg," said Flynn.

—by John Hunt

Big market blues

Here's how Rotisserie-generated standings have compared with actual Major League Baseball pennants since 1982:

Year	Actual	Roto-pennant
1993	Toronto	Toronto
	Philadelphia	San Francisco
1992	Toronto	Toronto
	Atlanta	Atlanta
1991	Minnesota	Minnesota
	Atlanta	Atlanta
1990	Oakland	Oakland
	Cincinnati	Cincinnati
1989	Oakland	Oakland
	San Francisco	Chicago
1988	Oakland	Oakland
	Los Angeles	N.Y. Mets
1987	Minnesota	Toronto
	St. Louis	N.Y. Mets
1986	Boston	N.Y. Yankees
	N.Y. Mets	N.Y. Mets
1985	Kansas City	N.Y. Mets
	St. Louis	St. Louis
1984	Detroit	Detroit
	San Diego	Chicago
1983	Baltimore	Chicago
	Philadelphia	Los Angeles

Source: F.X. Flynn

The Ron Gant Award is given to the Rotisserie owner who pulls off the best steal of the draft. Gant had a 30-30 season for the Braves in 1990 after going undrafted in many fantasy leagues.

Oddball awards add zest to competition

The thrill of competition, the quest for monetary prize, the fear of drafting a total loser—all of these things are part of every fantasy league. What separates a league from the crowd is the manner in which it celebrates its winners and losers. Here are some real-life examples:

The **Tequila League** of Orange County, Calif., presents two unusual awards: the Beheaded Bart Simpson Trophy and the Gary Gaetti Pig Award. The former—awarded to the worst team in the league—was once an anatomically correct statue, but the first recipient punched it and knocked its block off. The latter is bestowed in memory of the selection of Gaetti in the first round of the 1990 draft (he went on to hit a hellish .229 for the Twins).

The Simpson family is also big with the **Montgomery Burns Liver Spots League** of Hartford, Conn., which presents its champion with a toilet seat bearing the likeness of Homer Simp-

son's less-than-philanthropic boss, Monty Burns. Treasurer Doug Quat explains: "(Burns) is ruthless, conceited, shifty, egomaniacal and single-minded to a fault—perfect traits for a fantasy league owner."

The unfortunate owner who finishes last in the **Hard Knox Rotisserie League** of Knoxville, Tenn., must begin the next year's auction with an a cappella version of the Star Spangled Banner.

The **Dutch Masters League** of Illinois features the Nick Esasky Award, given to the owner whose team finishes with the worst batting average. The trophy is an oversized whiffle ball. The Bo Nose Picks Award goes to the team having the best supplemental draft. That owner gets a package of Kleenex and much admiration from fellow owners. Finally, they present the Harry Award—for announcer Harry Caray—to the owner who exhibits "masochistic tendencies" by carrying the most Cubs.

One league in Tampa has a unique local rule. The owners pick from the entire league except from the Florida Marlins. They're still bitter over Miami getting an expansion franchise while the Suncoast Dome sits empty in St. Petersburg.

Bill Taylor, an avid Orioles fan in an Arkansas league, each year claims he will back off on outrageous bids for Cal Ripken. And each year, he can't resist. When Draft Day rolls around, the other owners bid Ripken up to a salary approaching his real-life contract; with Ripken and his fat salary once again on his roster, Bill always asks: "Would you have gone a dollar more?"

The UGH League of Johnson City, N.Y., awards the Ron Gant Award to the best steal of the draft. UGH owners agree there will never be another Ron Gant, who had a 30/30 season in 1990 for Atlanta after going undrafted in many fantasy leagues. Owner Steve Shimer says in some ways the Gant Award is the most coveted—almost as highly as winning the league—because it means the Gant winner is "smarter than the other guy."

The Shoeless Joe Baseball League of Portland, Maine, has an outing every year to Fenway Park—their Mecca—where any league dispute is resolved by posing the question: "What would Shoeless Joe Jackson have done in this situation?"

The Accountants, Brokers & Other Scum League presents the Laborer Award (for pitching destruction) and the Doggie Brown Award (for offensive futility). Rick "The Laborer" Mahler, who had some truly ugly years in Atlanta, inspired the former. The Doggie Brown Award is named after Chris Brown, that third baseman who was supposed to be a Roto G-O-D but was actually a D-O-G. The league's motto: "Reveling in the misery of others." Come on, be honest, isn't that what fantasy baseball is all about?

—by John Hunt

'Moral virtue' lost in agency's pursuit

Fantasy baseball owners Dave Sjogren and Peter Hull have gambled and lost. Or have they?

The two employees of the U.S. Department of Treasury's Office of Thrift Supervision (the agency responsible for policing savings and loans) were recently given 14-day, unpaid suspensions.

The crime? Operating and participating in fantasy sports—that hobby you and I and about 4 million other people enjoy.

The suspensions culminated a massive, seven-month witch hunt, er, investigation, that resulted in the suspensions and possibly damaging black marks on the records of Sjogren and Hull, who have a combined 19 years of exemplary service.

"If the consequences weren't so draconian, it would be laughable," said attorney Charles T. Smith II.

Now don't go burning your stat sheets and erasing your E-mail just yet—Sjogren and Hull were not found guilty of civil or criminal statutes prohibiting gambling; rather, they were in violation of a federal regulation that prohibits gambling on government property.

But if you work for Uncle Sam, then by all means, panic.

Thrift officials had no comment, other than to say that it was a personnel matter.

Sjogren's supervisor, Thomas Loeffler, could not be reached. It was Loeffler who issued the notice of suspension.

And it was Loeffler who admittedly asked Sjogren to co-own a fantasy basketball team two years ago—but not on federal property.

Sjogren's suspension didn't go into effect immediately because his office had a particularly heavy workload that week.

In the nation's capital, more heads were shaking as Sjogren, Hull and

Smith told their story than hands shaking in an election year.

For Sjogren, with a wife and kids to support, the humor of the situation quickly wore off.

Hull already had made some tee times and was eager to take advantage of the time off.

Smith knew there were plenty of lawyers who didn't share his pie-in-the-sky approach to justice, but didn't realize something this bizarre could happen. He was embarrassed for his profession.

"It's an agency with two or three lawyers too many," Smith said. "And they're trying to justify their existence."

The agency did make one shrewd move, however, reducing the suspension from 30 days to 14. Any suspension of more than 14 days is subject to review by the Merit Systems Protection Board.

Would the board toss this case aside? Impossible to say, but it would give Smith a chance to present his case to an independent party, perhaps an ear of reason.

As it is, his next step will be a quick exercise in futility: filing a grievance with the OTS.

When that's done, the case will be heard by a randomly chosen arbiter, where Smith's chances will be better.

Smith & Co. are still waiting to see the reams of documentation collected in the investigation.

The OTS offered to sell Sjogren the information for $1,000, then lowered the price tag to around $500. Sjogren then applied for a waiver of the fee, which is still pending.

The major questions here are:

Why is the government spending so much time, effort and money to punish small-time (their league has a modest $30 entrance fee) fantasy baseball players?

Is this really gambling?

The answer to the first question is unclear. But Smith, whose legal fees already are approaching $10,000, is very confident he will win the case.

If so, he said, "They will owe me a lot of money."

The second question concerns all 4 million of us who spend so much of our time in an activity that borders on illegality.

Is it gambling? Common sense says no, but what do the courts say?

While nobody has been convicted of gambling for playing fantasy sports, it is illegal by the letter of the law in most states.

Some states are rewriting their gambling laws to allow fantasy sports.

Many of those states are legislating in such a way to guard against those few who play "bookie" and make money on the hobby.

Mike Gelbwasser plays in a Rotisserie league and has researched its legality. He noted that Aristotle proposed an ethical guideline called the Golden Mean, in which "moral virtue is appropriate location between two extremes."

For example, social drinking would be the "golden mean" between alcoholism and prohibition. And, similarly, fantasy sports would constitute a "golden mean" between professional gambling and prohibiting gambling outright.

Unfortunately most of today's gambling laws are written in such a way to exclude the "golden mean," written in a way that's Greek to me and 4 million others.

—by John Hunt

Linguistic twists of Rotisserie fate

"How's your team doing?"

"Well, I got Hanson for a billyripken, but my staff has had some wellsly outings, and I've been hurt badly by McCartyism."

If this doesn't make sense, you're not keeping up with the latest Roto lingo. Here are some terms that might not be in Webster's, but could become part of fantasy baseball lexicology:

▶**Billyripken:** An auction bid for a player of one dollar that goes unchallenged. The term was submitted by the Bill Buckner League ("because fielding doesn't count").

▶**Wellsly:** An adjective used to describe a pitcher who gets a slow hook from the manager despite surrendering an ERA-destroying and ratio-blowing number of runs. The term is in memory of Cito Gaston doing nothing as Brewers circled the bases around hapless David Wells, who gave up 11 runs, four walks and 13 hits in 4 ⅓ innings.

▶**McCartyism:** A phenomenon that occurs when a player tears up the minor leagues but never gets that call-up. It is inspired by Minnesota's vow not to call up phenom David McCarty unless he could play every day. By the time Shane Mack went on the DL and the Twins finally saw fit to give McCarty a call, he was batting .398 with six homers and 27 RBI in 31 games for Triple-A Portland.

▶**Upside-down smiley:** If you expect big things from a pitcher but the only big thing he delivers is a double-digit ERA, you have an upside-down smiley. The opposite—a smiley—is an accolade given in honor of John Smiley's performance in the 1991 NLCS. Oddly enough, the upside-down smiley applied to its own namesake for the first two months of 1993.

—*by John Hunt*

McCartyism is named after Dave McCarty, who tore up the minor leagues (.398, 6 HR, 27 RBI in Triple-A) but never got a chance to play for the Twins until Shane Mack went on the DL.

*C*ollectibles

- ▶ Negro League memorabilia
- ▶ Baseball fights Leukemia
- ▶ Dog lovers' baseball cards
- ▶ Collectors con man gets caught
- ▶ and more . . .

USA SNAPSHOTS®

A look at statistics that shape the sports world

Can Orioles continue to soar?

The record $173 million paid for the Baltimore Orioles might change its status as major league sports' most profitable franchise.

Source: *Financial World* magazine (for seasons ending in 1992)

Net income (millions)

$34.2	$34.0	$25.7	$13.6
Baltimore Orioles	Detroit Pistons	Detroit Red Wings	Pittsburgh Steelers
MLB	**NBA**	**NHL**	**NFL**

By Marty Baumann, USA TODAY

Frank Thomas, who lost a sister to leukemia when he was 10, joined the fight against the disease.

Frank Thomas cards help fight leukemia

Chicago White Sox slugger Frank Thomas has gone to bat for the Leukemia Society of America. He and card manufacturer Leaf Inc. will offer a new, numbered Leaf card available only through the mail for a $20 donation to the Frank Thomas Charitable Foundation, of which the main benefactor is the Leukemia Society of America.

"This is a very special card to me and definitely something that hits home," Thomas said. "When I was 10 years old, I lost a sister (Pamela) to leukemia. All my life I have said that when the right time came, I would get involved to help the (Leukemia) Society. And now I'm at that point in my career."

Thomas became the first-ever spokesman for Leaf, and joked that he had ulterior motives for signing with the company, which produces such candy products as Milk Duds, Jolly Rancher and Whoppers.

"I like their candy bars," he said.

Only 50,000 charity cards were produced, and each is individually numbered. Robert Bangamon, a student at Chicago Arts and Science High School who was in remission from leukemia, was presented with card No. 1.

"It's exciting, scary," he said. "To think that someone (Thomas) is putting out all of this effort to help the Leukemia Society is nice. At least in my lifetime I've never heard of anyone doing that."

The borderless card features the Leaf logo on the front, a photo of Thomas at bat and "Frank" in big gold letters. The front is UV-coated, so forget about getting it signed. A signature, even with a Sharpie pen, will not stick; it bubbles. The card back, however, is ideal for autographs.

This is Thomas' second special, numbered card. In 1992, the Donruss Elite Series printed 10,000 Thomas cards; they now sell for $250 apiece.

For information or to order the charity card, send $20 check or money order to: Frank Thomas Charitable Foundation, P.O. Box 125, Morgantown, Pa., 19543.

—by Ross Forman, a freelance writer based in Northbrook, Ill.

Ten players join Carter, Thomas to raise money

Gary Carter, the former National League catcher who works as a broadcaster for the Florida Marlins, first came up with the idea of asking fans to make a donation to the Leukemia Society in exchange for one of his signed baseball cards prior to the 1985 baseball season. An avid collector himself, Carter has raised more than $2.5 million for the society in memory of his mother, who died from leukemia in 1966.

Other players who have signed on to the charitable cause are Mark Grace, Pete Harnisch, Jay Howell, Ted Power, Todd Worrell, Sid Fernandez, Dave Hollins, Tim Teufel, Chris Bosio and Todd Stottlemyre. The cards are sold for $10 except Carter's, which goes for $25. All cards are available through the New York-based Leukemia Society at 1-800-955-4LSA.

Milk Bone offers collectors something new to chew on

If you don't have a dog, you might have a hard time collecting a new set of baseball cards, unless you don't mind eating a lot of dog biscuits.

Milk Bone, the nation's top-selling dog biscuit, has produced a 20-card set featuring pictures of major leaguers and their dogs. The cards come two to a box and feature information on the card backs about the players and their dogs.

On Rafael Palmeiro's card, for instance, it is revealed that the Rangers' first baseman named his cocker spaniels Kirby and Wrigley after Kirby Puckett and Wrigley Field. Six-year-old Wrigley weighs 35 pounds; Kirby, four, weighs

26. Their owner's age and weight also are listed.

Actually, collectors without dogs won't get shut out. A complete set of 20 cards can be ordered by filling out a mail-order form on the panel of each specially marked box. For every set of cards ordered, 50 cents will be donated to the American Society for the Prevention of Cruelty of Animals.

Expansion logos produce revenue

They might not win a National League pennant for awhile, but already the Florida Marlins and Colorado Rockies have positioned themselves as championship contenders in licensed products sales.

Before the 1993 season even started, both teams had surged into baseball's top five in sales, according to Major League Baseball Properties, the game's licensing arm. Although the rankings include sales of everything with a team logo—from clothing to bed linens to trash cans—a significant percentage of sales comes from sports memorabilia.

Collectors have been snatching up anything with an expansion team logo, fueling an investment craze normally reserved for hot rookie players. During the Rockies' first game (at New York) and their home opener, collectors hoarded game programs. At Mile High Stadium, the magazines were packaged in shrink-wrapped groups of 10. Many collectors bought an entire packet to preserve the programs in mint condition. More than 300,000 programs were printed for the first homestand. The U.S. post office set up booths at the stadium, offering to stamp each program with a "first day" seal for 29 cents. Even Kent Bottenfield, the Expos pitcher who was bombed by the Rockies April 9, had a 10-pack at his locker after the game.

Fans entering the stadium had their tickets inspected, but left intact, and were given a plastic cover to store their collectibles. Each player was given a commemorative bottle of wine.

"People here can't get enough of the Rockies," said John Brennan, owner of Superfan, a chain of 11 sports apparel and memorabilia stores in Colorado. "Denver has waited for baseball here for such a long time. Fans want to prove baseball was right for giving them a team."

That has translated into strong sales for both teams, although that does not necessarily mean the new clubs keep most of the windfalls. When a licensed team product sells at a retail outlet, the royalties go into a pool from which revenues are distributed equally to all 28 teams. Of course, the teams act as retailers themselves by marketing products through stadium stores.

According to MLB Properties, more than a million Marlins hats had been sold by the second week of the inaugural season. Though caps ranked as the top selling product for both new teams, climate also played a part in determining popular items—the second-best-selling product for the Marlins is T-shirts, jackets for the Rockies.

Of course, any first milestone piece of memorabilia is particularly valuable. San Francisco Giants fan Tony Leon caught the first home run hit by a Marlins player, but gave it back. He caught the ball in the sixth inning at Candlestick Park on April 12 and held on to it for about 30 seconds—enduring a shower of ice and peanuts from all directions—before he gave in to the crowd and threw it back onto the field. Giants' center fielder Darren Lewis retrieved it and threw it to Marlins first base coach Vada Pinson, who tossed it into the dugout.

By surrendering the baseball, Leon cost himself a travel package valued at more than $1,000. The Marlins were prepared to trade airfare to Miami, accommodations and tickets to a Marlins' series.

—*by Pete Williams*

Interest up for Negro League memorabilia

The baseball memorabilia industry, like the sport itself, has been slow to recognize the accomplishments of players who starred in the Negro Leagues. But there's growing evidence, at least among baseball collectors, that Negro League memorabilia is gaining a foothold.

The Negro League Baseball Museum in Kansas City, which runs the licensing program of the Negro Leagues, has seen a spurt of licensees in the last couple of years.

"As people have become more aware of the Negro Leagues, we've seen a lot of excitement over our products, particularly apparel," said Tom Busch, the museum's general counsel who handles Negro League licensing.

Eye-catching logos and catchy team names have made Negro League apparel popular, although the marketing strategy has not always been by design. Thousands of Cuban X Giants hats were sold last year to fans who thought they were buying the "X" caps made popular by the Spike Lee film *Malcolm X*.

The Negro League Museum has researched and done the artwork for 27 teams. In addition to the Cuban X Giants, other best-selling teams include the Kansas City Monarchs, New York Black Yankees, Homestead Grays, Pittsburgh Crawfords, Chicago American Giants and Birmingham Black Barons. As the Negro Leagues ended, the logos became public domain, except for the Monarchs, whose owner, Tom Rasberry, has maintained the trademark and sits on the board of directors of the Negro League Museum. Even though the museum cannot require companies to obtain a license, collectors should look for its seal to guarantee that the product has remained true to the colors and logos of the teams.

—*by Pete Williams*

Fraud case reflects industry's problems

Family and friends knew him by his real name—Randy Marshall. As a cartoonist and artist, he was known as Hal King. But to everyone else, he was Geoff Wayne, a young Cincinnati memorabilia dealer who brokered some of the most treasured collectibles in the sports memorabilia industry.

He sold vintage flannel jerseys, rare autographs and one-of-a-kind pieces. He swapped goods with some of the industry's major players. His clients included collectors with deep pockets. Much of his memorabilia was authentic, backed up by the testimonials of some of the industry's most respected dealers.

But as it turns out, many of the collectibles sold by Marshall, 31, were as phony as the name Geoff Wayne. On May 24, 1993, Marshall pleaded guilty in Ohio to federal mail and wire fraud charges resulting from the manufacturing and selling of bogus sports memorabilia. The FBI, acting on a tip from a collector who thought Marshall had offered him false memorabilia, conducted a lengthy investigation that involved U.S. attorneys in Minnesota and Ohio, two major auction houses and collectors and dealers nationwide. When the investigation was over, the Bureau had uncovered a trail of fraudulent memorabilia that could continue to trickle out for years. Marshall cooperated fully with the FBI.

That someone would commit such acts in an industry plagued by card counterfeits and autograph forgeries should come as little surprise. But the professional touch and attention given to every fraudulent detail made Marshall a particularly dangerous dealer.

"He's a knowledgeable guy," said Jerome Zuckerman of Sports Heroes Inc., an Oradell, N.J., memorabilia firm. "The tricky thing was that he'd mix in legitimate items with fake ones."

Marshall's counterfeit memorabilia, experts say, looked far more authentic than the usual forgeries and fabricated collectibles. Using a special process to artifically age fabric, he made counterfeit baseball jerseys of Babe Ruth, Mickey Mantle, Pete Rose and others. The jerseys looked so real that law officials refuse to give specifics of the aging process so as not to inspire other fakes.

"Not only was he a very good forger, but his letters (of authenticity) looked very old," said Terry Lehman, an assistant district attorney who worked on the case. "He duplicated the letterheads for the Brooklyn Dodgers, got the same model typewriter from that era and, using organic substances and microwaves, made the paper look aged."

Typically, no action is taken on false merchandise. Since the authenticity of a piece of memorabilia never can be definitively proven, many dealers avoid speaking out for fear of a slander suit. No dealer ever confronted Marshall.

Many collectors wonder what effect the case will have on an industry plagued by unscrupulous practices.

"There really aren't a lot of these guys," said Richard Russek, a New York dealer. "But one Randy Marshall can ruin the hobby for the people who have good intentions."

—by Pete Williams

Grissom gets mitts on his stolen glove

Montreal outfielder Marquis Grissom's glove, which he'd used for four years, was stolen along with the rest of his equipment en route to the All-Star Game in Baltimore. Two weeks later, a fan approached him in front of the team's Pittsburgh hotel and requested an autograph—on the very same glove. Grissom took the glove from the fan and arranged a swap. Unfortunately for the fan, who had paid $185 for it at a New York card show, all he received when he returned two days later to pick up his replacement glove was a meeting with Cliff O'Hara, the security representative for Major League Baseball in Pittsburgh. The glove was custom-made for Grissom by Rawlings in black leather with distinctive yellow stitching in the pocket. It was the only glove Grissom has used in his four-year major league career. The glove was packed with other equipment for Grissom's All-Star debut. When he arrived in Baltimore, his three suitcases were there but the glove was missing from an equipment bag. The Expos had alerted Major League Baseball's security force. The team believes the equipment bag was stolen during a plane stop at LaGuardia Airport. The other items haven't turned up, but Grissom doesn't care. The fan told Grissom his jersey was on sale for $580 at the same show. "I don't know what surprised me more—that somebody would steal this or that it would be worth so much," Grissom said.

Murphy card prices below a Hall mark

When Dale Murphy announced his retirement last May, the debate began on whether his injury-shortened career would earn him a spot in the Hall of Fame. If the price of baseball cards is any indication, he might not make it.

Card collectors have a solid track record of predicting Hall of Famers. In 1993, many observers felt Steve Garvey, Phil Niekro or Tony Perez would be elected to the Hall with Reggie Jackson. But while the price of Jackson's cards soared in the year leading up to the voting, the cards of Garvey, Perez and Niekro sold only modestly. Collectors began to abandon Murphy cards several years ago. His 1977 Topps rookie card, once sold for $60, dropped to under $20.

"The price indicates that most people see him as borderline," said Rick Klein, a price analyst for Beckett Baseball Card Monthly. "His career didn't have

that finishing kick that would have made him an automatic."

Murphy has good credentials: five Gold Gloves, seven All-Star appearances, two MVP awards, 398 home runs, 2,111 hits and membership in the 30-30 club. From 1982 to 1987, no one was better. He was a favorite among teammates, fans and the media, but his career declined before the card business turned into a multibillion-dollar industry.

In the past couple of years, however, collectors have begun to hoard cards of George Brett, Robin Yount and Dave Winfield as they piled up Hall of Fame credentials. It wouldn't be surprising to see a similar phenomenon in the late '90s as collectors examine Murphy's career more as a whole and less for its unfortunate ending.

Hall of Famer?

How Murphy's rookie card compares to his contemporaries:

George Brett (1975 #228)	$140-225
Andre Dawson (1977 #473)	$50-75
Dennis Eckersley (1976 #98)	$45-70
Rickey Henderson (1980 #482)	$70-100
Dale Murphy (1977 #476)	$15-30
Eddie Murray (1978 #36)	$50-75
Cal Ripken (1982 #21)	$50-75
Ryne Sandberg (1983 #83)	$35-60
Ozzie Smith (1979 #116)	$45-75
Dave Winfield (1974 #456)	$120-180
Robin Yount (1975 #223)	$140-225

Source: Beckett Baseball Card Monthly, *June 1993 issue. All listed are Topps.*

Nostalgia

▶ **Remembering Mr. October**

▶ **The rule that saved baseball**

▶ **Campanella: A true champion**

USA SNAPSHOTS®

A look at statistics that shape the sports world

Who's the lightest hitter?

The major league record for home runs in a season is 240 by the 1961 New York Yankees. Who hit the fewest?

A. 1908 Chicago White Sox

B. 1926 Boston Red Sox

C. 1939 St. Louis Browns

D. 1962 New York Mets

Answer: A. The White Sox hit 3 homers in 1908

Source: USA TODAY research

By Julie Stacey, USA TODAY

REG-GIE! REG-GIE! The night Jackson rocked the 1977 World Series

This was not the first time on center stage for Reginald Martinez Jackson. He had left his mark on October games previously, most notably four years earlier when he won the 1973 World Series MVP—to accompany the regular season version he would also win.

No, Jackson was well-accustomed to the glare of prime time as the Yankees prepared for Game Six of the 1977 World Series against the Dodgers. He thrived on the attention.

"If I played in New York," he once said, "they would name a candy bar for me." They did, but it wasn't as sweet as the champagne the Yankees would drink on that Tuesday night—Oct. 18, 1977—after winning their first World Series in 15 years. It was a night that would forever define Jackson as Mr. October, as he pulled off one of the greatest feats in the history of sports, joining Babe Ruth as the only player to clear the fences three times in a World Series game.

Several of Jackson's teammates say everything appeared normal as game time drew near.

"You didn't really have to pump Reggie up," says former outfielder Paul Blair. "That was just Reggie. He liked the thrill of being in those moments like the World Series. Other types of guys you had to settle down. But basically, it was really just business as usual before the game."

But third-string catcher Fran Healy, currently a Mets' broadcaster, disagrees. Something was different: batting practice. "I can't remember a ball he hit that didn't go over the fence. It was the most incredible batting practice I've ever seen."

"I felt light, quick, strong," Jackson says. "I had spring. I had adrenaline. I had zoom. The balls were springing off the bat. It was barrel to baseball. Snap! . . . There were a million people on the field that day, a lot of media. It really got my adrenaline going. I took maybe 50 swings and I'd say 35 balls went out into the seats."

When the Dodgers took a 2-0 lead in the first, it looked for a moment as if the wild celebration of 56,407 fans would have to be postponed for at least one night. It even appeared Jackson might eventually be fitted for goat horns, rather than the hero's halo.

Jackson seemed overly cautious as he fielded a Steve Garvey drive to the right-field corner. Perhaps Ron Cey wouldn't have scored the second run if Jackson had played the carom more aggressively. New York manager Billy Martin had a little chat with Jackson once the Dodgers were retired and the Yankees returned to the dugout.

Subsequent greetings upon Jackson's returns to the dugout took on a drastically different tone.

The deficit remained 2-0 when Jackson led off the second inning. It was time for a home run—but not Jackson's. Chris Chambliss' blast to right-center tied the score after Jackson walked. The free pass kept Jackson's home run streak intact. He had homered off Don Sutton in his final at-bat of Game Five, giving him dingers in back-to-back games and raising his Series average to .333.

With the score tied at 2-2, Jackson stepped to the plate in the fourth inning. The first offering from right-hander Burt Hooton was a fastball, low and away.

"Thurman was on first," Jackson recalls. "So I knew he was going to pitch to me this time. . . . I thought, 'Just give me a ball to hit.' I backed off the plate and leaned forward, hoping (Steve) Yeager wouldn't see that I had backed off. When Hooton let go of the ball, I leaned back again and—smack! It was gone." Jackson sent a slow arch into the right-field seats, around the 353-foot mark.

Right-hander Elias Sosa had replaced Hooton when Jackson came to bat in the fifth inning, with Randolph on first.

"I got up to the plate," remembers Jackson, "stood back and leaned over, again hoping Yeager wouldn't notice. I thought, 'Please God, let him throw a strike.' I hit that one better than the first. I hit it on top . . . a kind of hook. As I was running down the first base line, I was saying, 'Stay up! Stay up!' Well it made it! I saw it go over. I was rolling around the bases thinking, 'Maybe I got a trophy out of this or something! I can't believe it!' "

Next victim: Charlie Hough. Hough said he had one thought as Jackson strode to the plate in the eighth inning: "Don't walk him."

Jackson's solo homer off Hough—again, on the first pitch—was the most majestic of the trio, a towering blast to dead center.

"I'm a knuckleball hitter," says Jackson. "So when Hough threw the knuckleball, it was like room service. I crushed it." Accounts on the following day estimated that the ball traveled 450 to 500 feet.

Jackson remembers, "As I was running around the bases, I felt a foot above the ground. When I got back, everybody was cheering. My teammates were hugging me. Billy Martin was hugging me!

"I went into the dugout and the crowd was cheering for a curtain call. So I went out there and waved and the first thing I said was, 'Hi Mom!' "

The 8-4 win clinched the Series for the Yankees. In his final nine at-bats, Jackson scored seven runs and had six hits and seven RBI. Five of the six hits were home runs.

Three pitches, three swings, and three homers in Game Six. Add one for his last swing of Game Five. He ended the Series with a .450 average (9-for-20) and a bushel of records.

—by Deron Snyder and
Marlene Lozada

Reggie Jackson tips his cap to the Yankee crowd after hitting back-to-back-to-back home runs in the 1977 World Series.

Mound moves back, averages go up

For those who believe baseball is on the verge of a fatal breakdown, a look back at the birth of the sport's modern era might spark a little optimism. The rule change that saved the National League from its predicted collapse was a hundred years old in 1993, but some of the issues are still being argued today.

The league was deep in debt at the start of the 1893 season, having bought out its rival, the American Association the previous year, but its financial difficulties were symptomatic of deeper problems: declining attendance and dwindling public enthusiasm for the game. (Sound familiar?) People went to the park to see freewheeling displays of hitting, fielding and baserunning. Instead, they got low-scoring pitching duels often won by the team with the best bunters.

Team owners needed to rekindle popular interest in the sport; the rules committee recommended that the pitcher be moved 8 feet back—from a box 55-1/2 feet from home plate to a 12-by-4-inch rubber slab 63-1/2 feet from home plate. Team representatives angrily debated for hours before agreeing to replace the box with the rubber, 60-1/2 feet from home. Although no one realized it at the time, the modern game of baseball had taken shape.

Players and managers responded to the new rules with approval, although opinions varied as to their exact effect. Harry Wright, manager of the Phillies,

When the pitcher's mound moved back in 1893, Cy Young's ERA ballooned from 1.93 to 3.36— but he still racked up a 34-16 record.

said the additional 5 feet might actually be a boon to some of his pitchers: "Those who have been practicing at the increased distance say that they are able to get much better curves than under the old rules."

The batter did benefit in at least one respect: He gained an extra split second to gauge whether an inside pitch was about to break across the plate or drill him in the ribs. Wright conceded that the extra margin of safety would help "timid" hitters.

For the most part, younger pitchers with the stronger arms fared best under the new rules. Three-year veteran Cy Young of the Cleveland Spiders saw his 1892 league-leading ERA of 1.93 balloon to 3.36 in 1893, but he still hurled 42 complete games on his way to a 34-16 record.

The 1893 season ended with Boston snagging a third consecutive championship. In that sense, the new rules hadn't changed a thing—the Bean-eaters captured the title with a familiar combination of strong pitching and a scrappy style of play that made frequent use of the bunt (to the immense disgust of sportswriters, who considered bunting an "effeminate" art).

But when the stats for the season were added up, hitters had posted a solid .280 batting average (up from .237) and team run production had jumped from 5.1 to 6.6 runs per game. The numbers at the gate also told a significant story: attendance had surged, giving the National League enough cash to pay off its debt, while all 12 teams registered a profit, thanks to their revenue-sharing plan.

"The new pitching rule . . . restored to the game much of that action, life, snap and sparkle which in olden times, before the ultra-scientific mania seized the rule-makers, made it the king of sports," enthused the *Sporting Life* in its season wrap-up.

—*by Jeff Seiken, a freelance writer based in Pittsburgh, Pa.*

Campanella was a true champion— on and off the field

Roy Campanella, the Dodger organization's own personal profile in courage, died of a heart attack last June at his home in Woodland Hills, Calif. He was 71.

"To me, he was the greatest Dodger of them all," said Los Angeles Dodgers president Peter O'Malley.

Campanella was at the height of his career, having just won the third of his three Most Valuable Player Awards (in a span of five seasons), when Don Drysdale, another Dodger Hall of Famer who died last year, joined the Brooklyn roster in 1956.

"When I first got there, I remember it was always 'Son' or 'Kid,'" said Drysdale, who was a Los Angeles announcer at the time of Campanella's death. "I remember going up to him and Carl Furillo in right field during spring training and saying to both of them, 'What do I have to do to pitch in the major leagues? What's it going to take?'

"He just said, 'Son, you don't have to do any more than you're doing right now. Just keep throwing the ball the way you're throwing it and ol' Campy will take care of you.' "

Drysdale also recalled hearing the news of Campanella's accident while serving in the Army reserve with Sandy Koufax (yet another future Dodger Hall of Famer) at Fort Dix, N.J. The accident happened in 1958 just months before the Dodgers played their first game in Los Angeles.

Campanella was driving to his Long Island home one night when his car skidded and overturned. A spinal injury left him a quadriplegic. Hard work in therapy enabled him to regain use of his arms and some use of his hands.

"There's no telling what he would have done (if his career hadn't been cut short)," Drysdale mused.

Campanella was the first black catcher in the major leagues. He came to the Brooklyn Dodgers in 1948, joining Jackie Robinson, who a year earlier had broken baseball's color barrier. In his first game, Campanella hit a home run, a double and two singles. The Dodgers won five pennants with him behind the plate—and beat the rival Yankees in the 1955 World Series.

After the accident cut short his playing career, Campanella served the Dodgers as an instructor each spring, watching a procession of catchers try to follow in his footsteps.

"He took (Mike) Scioscia and made him an All-Star," manager Tommy Lasorda said of Campanella's work with the former Dodger catcher.

In 1969, Campanella became the second black player elected to the Hall of Fame—after Robinson.

—by Bill Plunkett, who reports for the Palm Springs *(Calif.)* Desert Sun

Campy's company

Roy Campanella was one of only eight players to win the MVP award three times:

Player	Years
Yogi Berra	1951, 54, 55
Roy Campanella	1951, 53, 55
Joe DiMaggio	1939, 41, 47
Jimmie Foxx	1932, 33, 38
Mickey Mantle	1956, 57, 62
Stan Musial	1943, 46, 48
Mike Schmidt	1980, 81, 86
Barry Bonds	1990, 92, 93